Shown below and on the inside back cover are several "classics" of social psychology. These events, which appear in chronological order, were selected on the basis of a survey completed by several hundred social psychologists. Only items published prior to 1970 are included, since we feel that a minimum of twenty years must elapse before a specific contribution can be described as an established classic in our field.

Influential Research on the Measurement of Attitudes

1928

L.L. Thurstone published an important paper in which he expounded the view that attitudes can be measured scientifically, and offered specific methods for doing so.

The Nature and Impact of Social Norms

1936

Muzafir Sherif published an account of research illustrating the important role of social norms (and social influence) in perception.

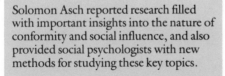

Conformity and Group Pressure

1951

Solomon Asch reported research filled with important insights into the nature of conformity and social influence, and also provided social psychologists with new methods for studying these key topics.

Communication and Persuasion

1953

Carl Hovland, Irving Janis, and Harold Kelley presented a highly influential framework for understanding the nature of persuasion and attitude change.

Instructor's Edition
SOCIAL PSYCHOLOGY
Understanding Human Interaction

SIXTH EDITION

Robert A. Baron
Rensselaer Polytechnic Institute

Donn Byrne
University at Albany/State University of New York

Instructor's Section Prepared by

Bem P. Allen
Western Illinois University

Gene F. Smith
Western Illinois University

Allyn and Bacon
Boston London Toronto Sydney Tokyo Singapore

INSTRUCTOR'S SECTION

INSTRUCTOR'S SECTION

Series Editor: Susan Badger
Series Editorial Assistant: Dana Lamothe
Production Administrator: Susan McIntyre
Cover Administrator: Linda K. Dickinson
Composition Buyer: Linda Cox
Manufacturing Buyer: Megan Cochran
Text Designers: Anne Marie Fleming/Karen Mason

Copyright © 1991, 1987, 1984, 1981, 1977, 1974 by Allyn and Bacon
A Division of Simon & Schuster, Inc.
160 Gould Street
Needham Heights, MA 02194

Printed in the United States of America

10 9 8 7 6 5 4 3 2 1   95 94 93 92 91 90

ISBN 0–205–12603–0

Instructor's Edition
CONTENTS

■ *Instructor's Section*

■ *Student Text Section*

INSTRUCTOR'S SECTION

Twenty Years of Listening: Thoughts on Becoming a "Classic"

An Introduction to:
SOCIAL PSYCHOLOGY
Sixth Edition
by Robert A. Baron and Donn Byrne

The world was a very different place when, in 1971, we began work on the first edition of *Social Psychology: Understanding Human Interaction.* Consider: gasoline was selling for under forty cents a gallon, Richard Nixon was in the White House, the conflict in Vietnam raged; and no one had yet heard of Watergate, space shuttles, the Greenhouse Effect, Mikhail Gorbachev, or AIDS. In many ways it seems like another age; and social psychology, too was very different from what it is today. The "cognitive revolution," which has altered our field in crucial ways, was just then stirring. And many lines of research described in this new edition were as yet unknown — or were mere intellectual glimmers in the minds of their future creators.

Despite all this change, our book has kept pace and remained immensely popular. Indeed, almost 1,000,000 students have learned about social psychology from this text (or from its briefer companion, *Exploring Social Psychology*) during the past two decades. Needless to say, we are deeply gratified by this widespread, continuing acceptance. As we move into a third decade of writing *Social Psychology*, though, it seems appropriate to ask what it is about our text that has made it such a long-time favorite — a book which is frequently described as a publishing "classic." The answer, at least from our point of view, seems clear: as suggested by the title of this Preface, we **listen**, and listen hard! In other words, we do our very best to obtain the advice and feedback of our colleagues and students, and then make concerted efforts to incorporate this feedback into our text.

The result of trying to be "good listeners," we believe, is a text that truly represents input from hundreds of talented, helpful persons. In our view, it is this commitment to listening that accounts for the fact that you are now reading the 6th edition, and that writing *Social Psychology* has become a career-long project for both of us.

Now, permit us to summarize what this process of **hard listening** told us this time around, and how we have altered the text to take account of **your** input and suggestions. Please note that the changes below were based, in large measure, on the results of a survey to which **more than five hundred social psychologists** kindly responded. It is the combined views of these colleagues (perhaps including your own) that are reflected in the following pages.

Updated for the 90's this new edition is characterized by a wealth of new material on a wide variety of topics.

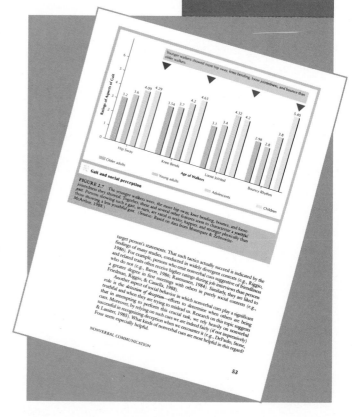

Up-to-date Content

The sixth edition represents a major shift in content — perhaps the largest overall change in this respect in several editions. Among the most important of these changes are the following:

Inclusion of Three New Chapters

A new chapter on intimate relationships (Chapter 7, Close Relationships). This chapter describes how relationships form, develop, and then, sometimes, dissolve, and also considers important aspects of love and sexuality.

A new chapter on applications of social psychology in work settings (Chapter 15, Social Psychology in Work Settings: Applications of Its Principles, Methods, and Findings). This chapter describes the many ways in which principles and findings of social psychology contribute to our understanding of important aspects of behavior in work settings.

A new chapter dealing with several important forms of interpersonal behavior ranging from *helping* others on the one hand, to *conflict* with them on the other (Chapter 9, Cooperation, Competition, and Conflict). Much of the material in this chapter is new, and the discussion of interpersonal conflict is entirely new to this edition.

Coverage of Literally Dozens of New Topics

Within chapters, too, a tremendous amount of new material has been inserted. Here is a partial listing of some of the new topics covered:

Chapter 1:
Theories — Their Potential Dangers in Research • The Multicultural Perspective in Social Psychology

Chapter 2:
The Face-in-the-Crowd Phenomenon • Gait as a Nonverbal Cue • Context Effects in Attribution • Gender Differences in the Self-Serving Bias

Chapter 3:
Automatic Priming • Counterfactual Thinking and Mental Simulation • Framing and Anchoring • Implicit Theories of Stability and Change • Vascular Theory of Emotion • Greatly Expanded Coverage of Affect-Cognition Links • The Self, Self Schemas, Possible Selves • The Self-Reference Effect

Chapter 4:
Attitude Change and Age • Cognitive Perspective on Persuasion • Mood and Persuasion • Dissonance and Responsibility for Negative Outcomes • Leading Questions and Attitude Change

Chapter 5:
Recategorization and the Reduction of Prejudice • In-Group Differentiation and Out-Group Homogeneity • Stereotypes and Biased Processing of Social

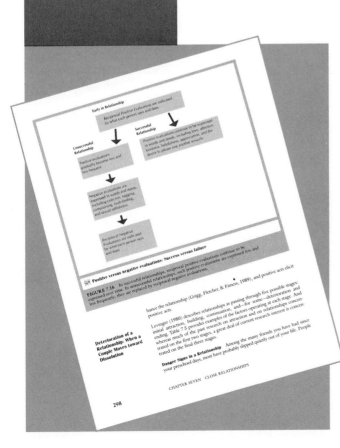

A new chapter on close relationships will capture student interest with material on how intimate human relationships evolve.

An entirely new Chapter 15, *Applications of Social Psychology in Work Settings,* covers the latest topics such as perceived fairness, and attributions.

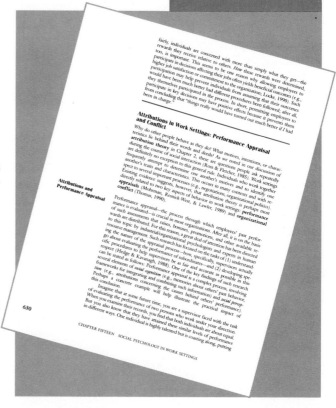

New Themes: Gender and a Multicultural Perspective

In response to feedback from our colleagues, we have also expanded our coverage of two themes within the text: **gender** and **cross-cultural comparisons**. The emphasis on gender is suggested by the addition of special sections dealing with this topic in virtually all chapters. A few examples:

Gender Differences in the Self-Serving Bias (Chapter 2)
Women's Implicit Theories About Menstrual Symptoms (Chapter 3)
Gender Stereotypes and Sexism (Chapter 5)
Gender Differences in Effects of Height (Chapter 6)
Gender Differences in Preferences About Partner's Age (Chapter 7)
Gender Differences in Responding to Sexual Intimacy (Chapter 7)
Gender Differences in Conformity (Chapter 8)
Gender Differences in Aggression (Chapter 10)
Gender Differences in Leadership (Chapter 11)
Gender Differences in Personal Space (Chapter 13)

A cross-cultural or multicultural perspective has been incorporated into the text through discussion of this topic in several chapters, and through the inclusion of special sections, *Social Psychology: A Multicultural Perspective*, throughout the text. These sections include:

Friendship and Dating in the U.S. and Hong Kong (Chapter 1)
Self-Concepts in Japan and the U.S. (Chapter 3)
Interracial Contact in South Africa (Chapter 5)
Response to Childlike Voices in the U.S. and Korea (Chapter 6)
Jealousy in the U.S., Hungary, Yugoslavia, Ireland, the Soviet Union,
   The Netherlands, and Mexico (Chapter 7)
Resisting Authority on Behalf of Freedom (Chapter 8)
Aggression by Type As and Type Bs in the U.S. and India (Chapter 10)
Coping with Free Riders in the U.S. and Japan (Chapter 11)
Adapting to Population Density Among British, Southern Europeans, and Asians (Chapter 13)
Husbands in the Delivery Room in Israel and Canada (Chapter 14)
Attitudes About Product Quality in the U.S. and Japan (Chapter 15)

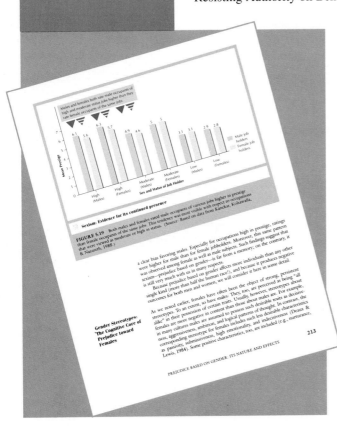

High-Interest Special Features

We have also made numerous changes in instructional aids and special features in order to make the book more useful and appealing to students. These include:

Special Sections

Four distinct types are included. Three types have been retained from the 5th edition because feedback from colleagues indicated that they were viewed as both effective and useful:

FOCUS ON RESEARCH:
   CLASSIC CONTRIBUTIONS

We should note, though, that in terms of content, virtually all special sections themselves are new to this edition.

A fourth type of section, SOCIAL PSYCHOLOGY: A MULTICULTURAL PERSPECTIVE, is entirely new to this edition, and reflects the major cross-cultural themes described above.

Please note: all four types of special sections occur at logical points within chapters and do **not** interrupt the flow of text material in any manner. On the contrary, all are introduced in the text, and are integrated into the materials and topics that precede them.

Expanded Summary and Review

Each chapter now concludes with an expanded *Summary and Review* section. These are more complete and detailed than in previous editions, and are divided into discrete sections corresponding to the major segments of the chapter. We have found them to be very helpful to students who want to review the materials covered, and to form a useful schema, or cognitive framework, for each chapter.

Full-Color Illustrations

All illustrations in the text are now printed in full color. This greatly enhances their visual appeal, and makes all graphs and charts much more effective from the standpoint of conveying important information.

Together, these changes enhance the appeal of the text to students, and make the book more accessible and easier to use.

Outstanding Supplement Package

All good texts should be supported by a complete package of ancillary materials. We believe that ours are outstanding, and will make the teaching process both more enjoyable and more effective. Major components available to users of *Social Psychology* include the following:

Instructor's Edition with bound-in Instructor's Manual

This new teaching aid offers an Instructor's section with learning objectives, suggestions for class discussion, activities and exercises, plus annotated lists of videos and readings, bound together with the text for added convenience. Transparency Masters are also available.

Study Guide

Written by Bem Allen and Gene Smith, the Study Guide gives students practice with short answer, definition, matching, multiple-choice, and completion type questions. Self-tests are accompanied by answers cross-referenced to the appropriate discussion in the text. A list of suggested readings is also included.

A new section, *Social Psychology: A Multicultural Perspective*, gives students an up-close look at today's most interesting cross-cultural issues.

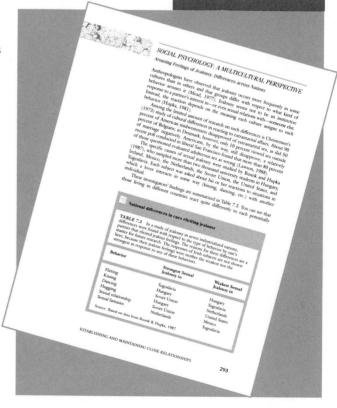

Video Library

New video segments featuring Bob Baron and noted social psychologist Margaret Clark, use a special dramatization technique to illustrate material from the text. Each segment is approximately 30 minutes. All are available to adopters of *Social Psychology, Sixth Edition.*

Testbank

Written by Bem Allen and Gene Smith, the Testbank provides you with 1500 multiple-choice questions cross-referenced to the textbook. All questions are categorized by type and difficulty.

Computerized Testbank

Allyn & Bacon Test Manager with Grade Manager provides you with a convenient way to produce tailor-made tests with your IBM computer.
Resource Navigator for the Macintosh allows instructors to incorporate graphic images in a computer-generated test.

Call-in and FAX Testing Services

Our call-in testing center will run your exams for you and send you finished tests, ready for duplication, within 48 hours of placing your request. For the last-minute time crunch when you need to prepare an exam quickly and don't want to bother with a computer, this service will generate your exam on the same day your request is called in and FAX you the "hard copy" for duplication.

Custom-Published Ancillaries

We know it's important for you to have class materials that suit your specific needs. For large adoptions, Allyn & Bacon can provide professionally produced publications to meet individual classroom needs. Course syllabi; special exercises; selected readings; custom workbooks, lab manuals, or study guides; lecture notes; or other original classroom material are all possibilities.

For more information, contact your Allyn & Bacon sales representative.

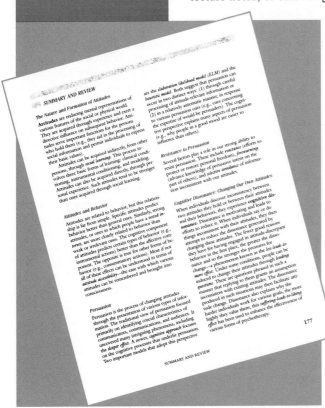

More complete and detailed summary and review sections at the end of each chapter offer students an excellent study aid keyed to major segments of the chapter.

A Concluding Comment, and a Look to the Future

This preface has focused, appropriately, on past efforts — steps we have taken to improve our text. Looking back, we can state, once again, that we have spared no effort to enrich and enhance the book in many different ways. We fully realize, though, that in a crucial sense, this task is never done: even as we complete work on this edition, we are thinking about and planning the next one. For this reason, we fervently invite your comments, your advice, and your recommendations. We don't claim that our egos can't be bruised by such feedback — on the contrary, they certainly can! But if there's something you feel can be improved, **we want to know about it!**

So, please give us a call or send us your feedback in any format you wish. Doing so definitely won't be wasted effort because as we said at the start (and as those who know us personally can affirm), we **really will listen.**

I N S T R U C T O R ' S   S E C T I O N

Acknowledgments

Writing is a solitary task, best performed alone. Converting authors' words into a finished book, though, requires the efforts and assistance of many persons. In preparing this text, we have been aided by a large number of dedicated, talented people. We can't possibly thank all of them here, but we do wish to express our appreciation to those whose help has been most valuable.

First, our sincere thanks to the colleagues listed below who read and commented on various portions of the manuscript: Dr. David Meissner, Alfred University; Professor Galen Bodenhausen, Michigan State University; Dr. Marjorie Krebs, Gannon University; Professor Adrian Rapp, North Harris County College; Professor Lynda Dodgen, North Harris County College; Professor Blair Johnson, Syracuse University; Dr. Robert D. Johnson, Arkansas State University; Professor Rosina Chia, East Carolina University; Professor Jack Dovidio, Colgate University; Professor Wade Harrison, Northern Arizona University; and Dr. B. Tara Rao, Ferris State University. Thanks also to the following colleagues who reviewed the previous edition: Robert S. Baron, University of Iowa; Russell Clark, III, Florida State University; Herbert Fink, SUNY–Brockport; Jeffrey Fisher, University of Connecticut; Robert Gifford, University of Victoria; Daniel Gilbert, University of Texas–Austin; Steven Prentice-Dunn, University of Alabama; and Daniel Wegner, Trinity University. In addition, of course, we are indebted to the more than five hundred colleagues who kindly completed our preliminary survey; to a large degree, data from that survey guided major changes in the book: Charles Ackerson, Dowling College; Frederic Agatstein, Rhode Island College; Robin Akert, Wellesley College; Charles Alexander, Rock Valley College; Sheldon Alexander, Wayne State University; Bem Allen, Western Illinois University; Rhianon Allen, Long Island University; Richard Archer, Southwest Texas State University; Charles Bahn, John Jay College of Criminal Justice; Bruce Bainum, Pacific Union College; R. Baumeister, Case Western Reserve University; Gordon Bear, Ramapo College; Percy Black, Pace University; Thomas Blass, University of Maryland; J.R. Bloomingdale, Washington College; Jeanine Bloyd, Spoon River College; Susan Boland, Drury College; George Boeree, Shippensburg University; Arthur Bohart, California State University; N. Branscombe, University of Kansas; John Braun, University of Bridgeport; Steven Breckler, Johns Hopkins University; June Breninger, Columbia Christian College; Robert Bringle, Indiana University–Purdue University; John Bruni, Jr., Western Kentucky University; Janet Weigel Bruno, Black Hawk College; Robert Buckhout, Brooklyn College; Albert Bugaj, University of Wisconsin–Richland; Shelly Chaiken, New York University; William Chambers, Shorter College; Jerome Chertkoff, Indiana University at Bloomington; Paul Cherulnik, Southeast Missouri State University; Shirley Chrisman, Saint Leo College; Emily Claspell, Chaminade University of Honolulu; Edward Clemmer, Emerson College; Winona Cochran, Bloomsburg University; Ronald Cohen, Bennington College; Alfred Cohn, Hofstra University; Steven G. Cole, Texas Christian University; James Collins, Corpus Christi State University; W.D. Crano, Texas A & M University; Carol Creedon, Reed College; David Cressler, Portland State University; Salvatore Cullari, Lebanon Valley College; James Dabbs, Georgia State University; Kenneth DeBono, Union College; Darlene DeFour, CUNY Hunter College; Linda DeRosier, Rocky Mountain College; David Dodd, Eastern Illinois University; William Dragan, Cornell College; Karen Duffy, SUNY–Geneseo; Thomas Eckle, Modesto Junior College; S. Ellyson, Youngstown State University; James Emshoff, Georgia State University; Robert O. Engbretson, Southern Illinois University; Charles Evans, LaGrange College; Ronald Evans, Washburn University of Topeka; Ann Ewing, Mesa Community College; Lorraine Fahey, Stevens Institute of Technology; Chris Falvey, Grand Valley State University; Michael Flaherty, Eckerd College; Bill Fleming, Nazareth College; John Fleming, University of Minnesota; Linda Foley, University of North Florida; Earl Folse, Nicholls State University; Becky Francis, West Virginia State College; Robin Franck, Southwestern College; Lyle Frank, Blackfeet Community College; Arthur Frankel, Salve Regina College; Stephen Franzoi, Marquette University; Marcia Freer, Doane College; William Rick Fry, Youngstown State University; Solomon Fulero, Sinclair College; Eleanor Gaer, Glassboro State College; Russell Geen, University of Missouri; Florence Geis, University of Delaware; Edward Gelb, Keystone Junior College; Keith Gerritz, Wilmington College; L.W. Giesbrecht-Bettoli,

Tennessee Tech University; Eugene Gilden, Linfield College; Richard Gillies, Cosumnes River College; Rod Gillis, University of Miami; D. Glascoe, University of Utah; Jeffrey Goldstein, Temple University; Randall Gould, Cuesta College; Edith Greene, University of Colorado; Larry Gregory, New Mexico State University; A.F. Gromoll, Millikin University; Michael Haggerty, Mallinckrodt College; Amy Halberstadt, Vassar College; Lily Halstead, Barb College; Richard Halverson, Luther College; Gordon Hammerie, Adrian College; W. Bruce Haslam, Weber State College; George Hearn, Los Angeles College; Robert Heper, Community College of Rhode Island; Rex Hieser, University of Wisconsin–Marinette; Spencer Hildahl, Wells College; Larry Hjelle, SUNY–Brockport; Bert Hodges, Gordon College; George Holden, University of Texas–Austin; Robert Holt, George Mason University; E. Hough, Rutgers University; Teri Hudson, Diablo Valley College; Karen Huffman, Palomar College; Jay Hull, Dartmouth College; Eugene Indebaum, SUNY–Farmingdale; Jacquelyne Jackson, St. Mary's College; Thomas Jackson, Fort Hays State University; Norine Jalbert, Western Connecticut State University; Anthony Johnson, LaGrange College; David Johnson, John Brown University; Jerry Johnson, University of Hawaii–Hilo; Robert Johnson, Arkansas State University; Ruth Ann Johnson, Augustana College; Donn Kaiser, Southwest Missouri State University; Kathy Kalab, Western Kentucky University; Sheldon Kalick, University of Massachusetts–Boston; George Kent, Bridgewater College; Mo Kian, Edinboro University; Andrew Kinney, Mohawk Valley Community College; Richard Klein, Adelphi University; Linda Kline, Murray State University; Gregory Kolden, Colby College; Marjorie Krebs, Gannon University; Ken Kressel, Rutgers University; Neil Kressel, William Patterson College; Kathleen L'Armand, Widener University; Jan LeFrancois, Converse College; Christopher Leone, University of North Florida; L.W. Littig, Howard University; Rolando Diaz Loving, National University of Mexico; Kevin MacDonald, California State University–Long Beach; Margaret Madden, Franklin Pierce College; Santiago Madril, Cochise College; John Mahoney, Virginia Commonwealth University; Richard Mamolen, Edmonds Community College; Grace Martin, Armstrong State College; James May, North Adams State College; L.K. McBride, Willamette University; Lynn McCutcheon, Northern Virginia Community College; Peter McDonald, North Georgia College; Robert McKelvain, Harding University; Ralph McKenna, Hendrix College; Charles McMullen, Tompkins Cortland Community College; Gregory Meissen, Wichita State University; Richard Miller, Navarro College; Robert Miller, Palomar College; Rowland Miller, Sam Houston State University; Barbara Moburg, Skagit Valley College; M. Moore, Webster University; Brian Mullen, Syracuse University; Linda Nelson, California Polytechnic–San Luis Obispo; Steve Nida, Franklin University; John O'Connor, Western Kentucky University; Paul Olczak, SUNY–Geneseo; Timothy Osberg, Niagara University; Don Osborn, Bellarmine College; Chris O'Sullivan, University of Kentucky; Robert Pellegrini, San Jose State University; James Phillips, Oklahoma State University; Jack Powell, University of Hartford; Anthony Pratkanis, University of California–Santa Cruz; Perry Prestholdt, Louisiana State University; Wendall Pribyl, Muscatine Community College; Melvyn Price, Oklahoma City University; Dick Proctor, Andrews University; Thomas Radecki, Siena Heights College; Robert Radlow, San Diego State University; Donald Rajecki, Indiana University–Purdue; Susan Ratwik, Lake Superior State College; Robert Reenes, Augusta College; Harry Reis, University of Rochester; D.R. Richardson, University of North Carolina; Marc Riess, Middlebury College; Stephanie Riger, Lake Forest College; Janet Riggs, Gettysburg College; Ron Rogers, University of Alabama; Joan Rollins, Rhode Island College; Barry Ruback, Georgia State University; Karen Salley, Southern Oregon State College; Jeffrey Sanders, Towson State University; Nicholas Santilli, John Carroll University; Michael Scheier, Carnegie Mellon University; Constance Schick, Bloomsburg University; Pat Schoenrade, University of Kansas; Janet Schofield, University of Pittsburgh; Gregory Schmutte, American International College; John Scileppi, Marist College; Robert Seaton, College of Du Page; Charles Seidel, Mansfield University; Susan Shapiro, Mount Marty College; Eugene Sheehan, University of Northern Colorado; Mary Sheridan, Hawaii Pacific College; Linda Silka, University of Lowell; Eleanor Smith, University at Albany; Gene Smith, Western Illinois University; Vicki Smith, Northwestern University; Anthony Sorem, College of St. Benedict; Shirlynn Spacapan, Harvey Mudd College; Charles Stangor, University of Maryland; Frank Stanicek, South Suburban College; Walter Stephan, New Mexico State University; Lloyd Stires, Indiana University of Pennsylvania; Ellen Sullins, Bard College; Harold Takooshian, Fordham University; Jerome Tobacyk, Louisiana Tech University; Stephen Thayer, CCNY; Vaida Thompson, University of North Carolina; Joe Trimble, Western Washington University; Vernon Tyler, Western Washington University; William Wallace, University of Montevallo; Ann Weber, University of North Carolina–Asheville; Carolyn Wells, Texas Southern University; C.K. Whalen, University of California–Irvine; Debbie White, Collin County Community College; Lawrence White, Beloit College; Michael White, Ball State University; Edmond Willis, Central College; David Wilson, Culver-Stockton College; Midge Wilson, DePaul University; Wayne Winborne, New York University; L.A. Witt, Western Illinois University; Guy Wylie, Western Nebraska Community College; Jan Yettl, USCS–Spartanburg; and William Zachry, University of Tennessee.

Second, we want to thank Susan Badger, our editor

ACKNOWLEDGMENTS IS–xiii

at Allyn and Bacon. Her expertise, energy, and élan (!) were major assets in virtually every step of the process; working with her has truly been a pleasure.

Third, our sincere thanks to our Project Manager, Susan McIntyre, who oversaw innumerable, crucial aspects of production. We were fortunate indeed to have her—and her considerable talent—as an important part of the team.

Fourth, our thanks to several other people who contributed to various aspects of the production process: to Nancy Benjamin for adeptly handling myriad details in the day-to-day process of production, to Laurel Anderson for yet another job of outstanding photo research, to Melinda Grosser for a very attractive design, and to Linda Dickinson for a very striking cover.

Fifth, our thanks to the following colleagues for providing reprints and preprints of their work (Bram Buunk, Bill Fisher, Phil Rushton), and to several others for their aid in a variety of ways too numerous to mention (Barbara Becker, Warren Chiu, Linda Pearson, Lisa Schulte, Ruth Van Wangenen). Last but certainly not least, our sincere appreciation to George Smeaton for his assistance with respect to several aspects of Chapter 9.

Sixth, we want to take this opportunity to thank those colleagues who, over the years, have provided us with reprints and preprints of their work. By doing so, they have helped keep this text on the very *cutting edge* of social psychology. We look forward to their continued help in this respect in the future.

Finally, we wish to thank Bem P. Allen and Gene F. Smith for their outstanding work on the Instructor's Section, and for their help in preparing the Test Bank and Study Guide.

To all these truly outstanding people, and to many others, too, our warm personal regards.

Introduction to the Instructor's Section

We are proud once again to present the ancillaries for Baron and Byrne's *Social Psychology*. The sixth edition of *Social Psychology* maintains the excellence and innovation that have traditionally made Baron and Byrne's text a winner.

In this new Instructor's Edition we have coordinated the Instructor's Section and the student Study Guide to be used as a paired pedagogical unit. For example, instructions on the conduct of exercises are included in the Instructor's Section and materials students need to participate in exercises are provided in the Study Guide. Also new is the emphasis on critical thinking.

To help instructors encourage students' enthusiasm for social psychology, we have developed a new and expanded film and video list that emphasizes easily acquired, interesting audiovisual supplements to the text. Included are new video segments related to each chapter featuring discussion on chapter material by text author Robert A. Baron and noted social psychologist Margaret Clark, using some effective dramatizations. All of these segments, each about twenty minutes long, will be available to you through your Allyn and Bacon sales representative.

In tune with the focus on critical thinking, the Study Guide includes a new section entitled "How Come?" It contains sixty teaser questions to begin class sessions. One reason for these interrogatives is to switch students' attention from the class they just attended—or whatever else occupied their minds before your session—to the subject matter you will cover. The most important reason for the "How Come?" questions, however, is to promote critical thinking. Each question is simple, straightforward, and based on reality as students perceive it. There are no right or wrong answers; in fact, the whole point is to stimulate students to develop alternative answers, to find alternative ways to look at everyday social situations. This will start students thinking critically for the remainder of the class period.

Each chapter in the Instructor's Section begins with an outline containing all chapter headings.

As has always been the case, learning objectives are included to guide you and the students (the same objectives are provided in the Study Guide).

The new "Topics for Discussion" found in each chapter are designed to be user friendly. More detail is provided than ever before. You are given extensive background information that will help you lead the discussion. Also, suggestions are made concerning how to start the discussion and how to avoid sensitive, but perhaps irrelevant, issues. Finally, you are told what to expect, the potential value of the discussion, and how to conclude it.

The exercises found in the Instructor's Section are designed to be both easy and interesting to use. We have underscored measures that have appeared in reports of research or were previously used effectively by psychology professionals. In tune with the coordination of the Instructor's Section and Study Guide, these measures are also found in the Study Guide so that there is no need for you to copy and distribute materials that students will use in exercises. (If you do not assign the Study Guide, you will be provided with a copy so that you can reproduce measures.) This Instructor's Section is all that you need to conduct each exercise. In almost every case you will need little or no preparation before class to comfortably conduct the entire exercise during class. Expected results will graphically make important points for students and provide them with enjoyable in-class experiences. You are told what to do, what to expect, and how to guide students to meaningful conclusions. Suggested analyses are easy and quick to do.

Essay questions in this edition center on provoking thought rather than just reproducing information contained in the text. Students are often asked to apply what they have learned from their readings.

As always, "Sources for Lecture" is a compilation of current articles from popular and often nonpsychological sources that will allow you to spice up your in-class presentations.

The transparencies section of the text is refined and improved. Once again, you are provided with materials for the overhead projector that will make in-class presentations easier and more meaningful.

The multiple choice test-item file is provided separately. This time, items focus more on inspiring students to think and reason, rather than to regurgitate what they have just studied. We believe that these items will convince you that multiple choice tests can promote critical thinking and make testing a learning experience, instead of just an occasion for evaluation.

Just as Baron and Byrne's *Social Psychology* is even better than before, we believe our ancillaries are the most productive associated with any social psychology text. We expect that use of them will make life in class more interesting for both you and your students.

BEM ALLEN
GENE SMITH

Instructor's Section Contents

INSTRUCTOR'S SECTION

1

The Field of Social Psychology

How We Think About and Interact with Others

Chapter Outline: Getting the Overall Picture

I. Social Psychology: A Working Definition
  A. Social Psychology Is Scientific in Nature
  B. Social Psychology Focuses on the Behavior of Individuals
  C. Social Psychology Seeks to Understand the Causes of Social Behavior and Thought
    1. The Actions and Characteristics of Others
    2. Cognitive Processes
    3. Ecological Variables: Impact of the Physical Environment
    4. Cultural and Biological Factors
    5. Social Psychology: Summing Up

II. Social Psychology: A Capsule Memoir
  A. The Early Years: Social Psychology Gets Started
  B. Social Psychology's Youth: The 1940s, 1950s, and 1960s
  C. The 1970s and 1980s: A Maturing Field
    1. Growing Influence of a Cognitive Perspective
    2. Growing Emphasis on Application: Exporting Social Knowledge
      a. Perceived Fairness in Work Settings: Why (Sometimes) Bigger Offices Yield Higher Output
  D. The 1990s and Beyond: A Look at the Future
    1. Cognition and Application: The Adventure Continues

    2. The Internationalization of Social Psychology: Adoption of a Multicultural Perspective
      a. Friendship and Dating in the United States and Hong Kong: Differences and Similarities
    3. Social Psychology As an Importer As Well As an Exporter of Knowledge

III. Answering Questions About Social Behavior and Social Thought: Research Methods in Social Psychology
  A. The Experimental Method: Knowledge Through Intervention
    1. Experimentation: Its Basic Nature
    2. Successful Experimentation: Two Basic Requirements
  B. The Correlational Method: Knowledge Through Systematic Observation
  C. The Role of Theory in Social Psychology: Major Benefits and a Few Potential Dangers
    1. Theories: Some Potential Dangers
  D. The Quest for Knowledge and the Rights of Individuals: Seeking a Reasonable Balance

IV. Using This Book: A Displaced Preface

Learning Objectives

1. Why isn't informal common knowledge a particularly valid source of information about social behavior?
2. Summarize the working definition of social psychology, focusing on the three key aspects of the definition.
3. Describe the five major categories of factors that influence social reactions.
4. Compare the approaches of the early social psychology texts by McDougall and by Allport.
5. Note the contributions of Sherif and Lewin in the 1930s. Summarize trends of the 1940s, 1950s, and 1960s.
6. What two larger-scale trends began in the 1970s and continue to expand?
7. How did being moved to a new office of a new size affect work output in the Greenberg (1988) study?
8. What three trends does the text predict for the future?
9. Compare friendship and dating patterns in the United States and Hong Kong.
10. Discuss the study dealing with the effects of X-rated videos, and note the advantages of varying two independent variables in the same experiment.
11. Cite examples that describe why random assigning of subjects to groups and avoiding confounding are essential to experimentation.
12. What two general reasons often make it impossible to use the experimental approach?
13. Outline the procedures followed in a correlational study, and indicate advantages of the correlational strategy.
14. Give examples that illustrate the major disadvantage of the correlational approach.
15. Describe the role of theory in social psychological research, and describe the process by which theories are tested.
16. Describe how theory testing can be distorted by confirmation bias, and indicate safeguards that decrease the likelihood of confirmation bias.
17. Why do social psychologists often use deception methodology?
18. What potential problems exist when a researcher uses deception?
19. Describe the informed consent and debriefing safeguards.

Topics for Discussion

1. Middlemist, Knowles, and Matter (1976) conducted a naturalistic field study to determine the degree to which invasion of one's personal space arouses stress. Male users of a college restroom were observed through a periscope to determine whether onset of urination and amount of time taken to complete urination would be affected by the presence of a nearby confederate. Is this an invasion of the subjects' privacy? Ask your students whether they believe this is a legitimate psychological study. (The Middlemist, Knowles, and Matter study is in the *Journal of Personality and Social Psychology, 33,* 541–546.) A later issue of *JPSP (35,* 120–124) has a couple of brief articles debating the ethics of the study.

2. Have one of the more verbal students in class engage in role playing. Give the student a complete description of an experiment, and have him or her tell the class how he or she would behave in the experiment, or you might have the entire class write down how they'd behave. The ideal experiment to choose is one in which the role player will behave differently from actual subjects. Possibilities include Milgram's obedience paradigm, the bystander studies, or West, Gunn, and Chernicky's "Watergate Study."

Consider, for example, a role-playing replication of the Milgram obedience study. Describe in detail the teacher's situation, and then ask the students to imagine themselves in the learner's position. Ask the students whether they would obey the experimenter's commands and ultimately deliver 450 volts. Also ask them to estimate the proportion of people in the general population that would deliver 450 volts. If you ask the above questions before your students have been exposed to the results of Milgram's research, you will find that very few expect that they would deliver 450 volts. Furthermore, the students will greatly underestimate the proportion of the population that would fully obey.

After demonstrating that students' predictions are inaccurate, discuss reasons why intuition is unable to predict behavior. Among the reasons that role playing underestimates the level of obedience are the following: (a) People don't know where their focus of attention would lie in the actual situation. Although they imagine that the victim would grab their attention, in fact, in the actual situation the experimenter may be the focus. (b) People are unable to recreate the physiological components of their reaction. (c) People can't imagine the degree to which the flow of events traps them into obedience.

You might conclude the discussion by emphasizing the necessity for empirical research using involved subjects. The two methods, role playing and involved subjects, exhibit different behavior, and a psychology that relied on subjects' introspective reports of behavior would often be in error.

3. To introduce students to the idea of experimenter bias, a discussion of the role played by the examiner giving a lie detector test might be helpful. The polygraph is, of course, a sensitive physiological recording device that measures the emotional arousal of a suspect by recording changes in galvanic skin potential. The basic assumption is that a guilty person will become emotionally aroused whenever he or she tells a lie in response to an incriminating question. However, it is probable that even innocent people become emotionally aroused when being questioned, and their arousal may well be greatest to "incriminating" questions. The person being questioned knows he or she is a suspect; thus, when the examiner asks a question such as, "Where were you the night your neighbor died?" an emotional response might well be elicited, irrespective of guilt.

To correct for the above problem, the examiner often determines a set of facts about the crime that only a guilty suspect would know. This relevant information is then presented to the suspect embedded in other equally plausible facts. Presumably, a guilty person would respond more strongly than an innocent person to the special meaning of the significant facts.

Even with the procedure described above, however, there is still a potential problem. The polygraph examiner and others present during the test are usually aware of the critical pieces of information. These people have usually formed a hypothesis about the guilt or innocence of the particular suspect, and they are in a position to influence the suspect's responses. Discuss with students ways in which subtle and inadvertent cues given by the examiner might influence the suspect. Is the examiner in an analogous position to the psychological experimenter? What might be done to prevent the kind of influence discussed above from happening?

4. Former Senator William Proxmire of Wisconsin has argued that some aspects of social behavior are best left unstudied. One topic that he has placed in that category has been research on the nature of love. He has criticized the work of Ellen Berscheid and Elaine Hatfield (formerly Walster), saying, "Americans want to leave some things in life a mystery, and right at the top of things we don't want to know is why a man falls in love with a woman and vice versa." Is the question of how people fall in love and how long-term relationships develop worthy of psychological study? Do the students agree with Senator Proxmire that some topics should be placed out of bounds?

5. Does the requirement of obtaining informed consent from research subjects have any effect on their behavior in an experiment? A couple of research studies have suggested that the use of informed consent forms can change subjects' behavior in significant ways. Gardner (1978) argued that the forms change behavior in environmental stressor research. Gardner's article is in the *Journal of Personality and Social Psychology* (*36*, 628–634). Second, Dill and colleagues (1982) have argued that human subjects regulations are a source of methodological artifact. Their study appears in *Personality and Social Psychology Bulletin 8*, 417–425).

Classroom Exercises/Demonstrations

1. Art Lyons of Moravian College suggests a demonstration to be used on the first day of the term by faculty members teaching two sections of social psychology. Lyons suggests that the faculty member vary his or her style of dress in the two different sections and gather the students' first impressions of their professor. For example, Lyons reports in *Teaching of Psychology* (*8*(3), 173–174) that he wears a coat and tie in one section and removes them in another section. Lyons has the students rate him on several trait dimensions using a semantic differential format. He reports that discussing the results provides an excellent opportunity for active class participation and sets the stage for dealing with both methodological and conceptual issues later in the course. A discussion of the uses Lyons makes of this demonstration is found in his *Teaching of Psychology* article. Possible dimensions to be used in the ratings are as follows:

attractive	—|—|—|—|—	unattractive
intelligent	—|—|—|—|—	unintelligent
openminded	—|—|—|—|—	closeminded
conservative	—|—|—|—|—	liberal
talkative	—|—|—|—|—	quiet
emotional	—|—|—|—|—	unemotional
self-confident	—|—|—|—|—	lacks self-confidence

2. Chapter 1 begins by discussing the wisdom contained in everyday, commonsense knowledge. The present exercise is designed to show students that, despite the intuitive appeal of commonsense ideas, they should be careful in wholeheartedly accepting them. The exercise asks students to provide their friends with information that certain commonsense notions are true. Each student in the class should provide one friend with information stating that research has supported the idea that similar people like each other, and another friend with information that opposites attract. The friends should be asked to indicate in a sentence or two why they think the statement is true, and then they should rate the degree to which the notion is true. A sheet for your students to use in doing this exercise is found in Chapter 1 of the Study Guide. Have the students bring their friends' ratings to class so that you can test whether both of these conflicting statements are rated to be true.

3. Have students watch newspapers or magazines for reports of research. They might watch for stories that draw erroneous conclusions about cause and effect. Or they might watch for reports that they understand better because they're taking social psychology. Encourage them to be alert for these materials, and encourage them to bring relevant articles to class.

4. Quiz the students regarding their own reaction to various field studies in social psychology. This exercise repeats the procedure of the Wilson and Donnerstein (1976) study (published in the *American Psychologist, 31*(11), 765–773). Wilson and Donnerstein read brief descriptions of actual experiments, and asked subjects to rate each experiment for its ethics, its appropriateness, its legality, and so forth. The descriptions of the experiments from Wilson

and Donnerstein are presented in Chapter 1 of your students' Study Guide. Have your students answer some or all of the following questions about each of the experiments. For each question, the students should answer "yes," "no," or "not sure."

1. If you discovered that you had been a subject in this experiment, would you feel that you had been harassed or annoyed?
2. If you discovered that you had been a subject in this experiment, would you feel that your privacy had been invaded?
3. Do you feel that such an experiment is unethical or immoral?
4. Would you mind being a subject in such an experiment?
5. Do you feel that psychologists should be doing such an experiment?
6. Is doing such an experiment justified by its contribution to our scientific knowledge of behavior?
7. Does such an experiment lower your trust in social scientists and their work?
8. Do you feel that the psychologist's actions in this experiment are against the law?

Film Notes: A Picture Is Sometimes Worth a Thousand Words

The Case of ESP, 1985, color videocassette, 57 mins. Time-Life Video, 100 Eisenhower Drive, P.O. Box 644, Paramus, NJ 07653. This "NOVA" program explores recent research into extrasensory perception and claims for and against paranormal phenomena. Can serve to introduce discussions of research ethics, values, and methodology.

Inferential Statistics: Hypothesis Testing—Rats, Robots, and Roller Skates, 33877, 1975, color, 28 mins. Pennsylvania State University, Audiovisual Services, Special Services Building, University Park, PA 16802 (814-865-6314). Uses humorous sketches to explain hypothesis testing, one of the most important applications of inferential statistics. Illustrates the need for a control group and for random assignment of subjects to groups, the necessity of statistics as a way to overcome population variability, the formulation of a statistical hypothesis and the possible errors of decision that can be made, and the way in which hypotheses about the mean are tested. Produced by Robert Johnson.

Invitation to Social Psychology, 32074, 1975, color, 25 mins. Pennsylvania State University, Audiovisual Services, Special Services Building, University Park, PA 16802 (814-865-6314). Introduction to social psychology with emphasis on three questions: What is the subject

matter of social psychology? What are its methods of investigation? What are some of its findings? Examples include interpersonal events in a cafeteria, reactions of bystanders on a city street, Milgram's obedience study, and Zimbardo's prison simulation. From the *Social Psychology* series. Stanley Milgram.

Methodology: The Psychologist and the Experiment, 32000, 1975, color, 30 mins. Pennsylvania State University, Audiovisual Services, Special Services Building, University Park, PA 16802 (814-865-6314). Documents research methodology used in Stanley Schachter's "fear and affiliation" experiment in social psychology and Austin Riesen's physiological experiment on visual motor coordination. Discusses independent and dependent variables, control groups, random assignment to conditions, and use of statistics in research. From the *Psychology Today* series. A CRM production.

Social Psychology, videotape, (Cost to buy: $59), 30 mins. CRM Films, 2233 Faraday Ave., Carlsbad, CA 92008 (800-421-0833). This tape introduces the subject matter and methods of social psychology by tracing attempts to desegregate an urban school.

Social Psychology Laboratory, 33167, 1975, color, 24 mins. Pennsylvania State University, Audiovisual Services, Special Services Building, University Park, PA 16802 (814-865-6314). Introduces three experiments in social psychology to demonstrate some of the standard features of experimental methodology. Shows such experimental procedures as the briefing and debriefing sessions, as well as aspects of establishing the environmental setting such as design of the laboratory, standard seating arrangements, and the type of apparatus which is commonly used to monitor the progress of the experiment. Experiments explore the stability of three-person groups, nonverbal communication, and interaction in problem solving. Produced for the British Open University. V. Lockwood.

Understanding Research, Number 2 in this 1990 videotape series, 30 mins. The Annenbørg Project, Holt, Rinehart & Winston, 1990, contact Lee Sutherlin, Marketing Manager (817-334-7632). This tape covers basic research techniques used in both the laboratory and in the field.

▧ *Transparencies*

1.1 *Correlation versus Causation*
1.2 *Testing a Hypothesis with Correlation Method*
1.3 *Testing a Hypothesis Experimentally*

1.4 *Confounding of Variables*
1.5 *Correlation versus Causation*

▧ *Critical Thinking/Essay Questions*

1. Provide a definition of social psychology and describe the essential features of the field of social psychology.
2. Summarize the basic steps that are followed when one conducts an experiment. Include in your answer a discussion of the independent and dependent variables, random assignment of subjects to groups, and the necessity of avoiding confounding.
3. Compare laboratory and field settings for conducting research in social psychology, and describe the advantages and disadvantages of each setting.

4. Compare the experimental and correlational techniques for conducting social psychological studies. What are the advantages and disadvantages of each technique?
5. Describe the role of theory in social psychological research. What is the role of theory in explaining behavior and in predicting behavior?

▧ *Sources for Lecture*

Berkowitz, L. (1971). Sex and violence—We can't have it both ways. *Psychology Today,* December, pp. 14–23. Is this a case where social scientists' values, as well as the general public's values, interfere with our ability to interpret the information found in research? Research results on both violence and pornography were similar, yet different policy decisions were advocated.

Campbell, D., & Tavris, C. (1975). The experimenting society: To find programs that work, government must measure its failures. *Psychology Today,* September, pp. 46–56. Campbell advocates using experimental methods to determine which social programs work and which ones don't.

Cornell, J. (1984). Science vs. the paranormal. *Psychology Today,* March, pp. 28–34. Why do so many people continue to believe in the paranormal despite disconfirmations? The Committee for the Scientific Investigation of the Paranormal is reviewed.

Hogan, R., & Schroeder, D. (1981). Seven biases in psychology. *Psychology Today,* July, pp. 8–10, 12, 14. Biases in psychology textbooks are reviewed. What kinds of values are being presented to students in this way?

Rubenstein, C. (1982). Psychology's fruit flies. *Psychology Today,* July, pp. 83–84. Do the college students used in so many of our experiments behave and think like other adults? This article argues that the answer may be no.

Rubin, Z. (1983). Taking deception for granted. *Psychology Today,* March, pp. 74–75. This critical overview notes that the use of deception remains at a high level among social psychologists, and it argues that the use of deception retards progress.

Update: Current Articles from Professional Sources

Anderson, C. A., & Sechler, E. S. (1986). Effects of explanation and counterexplanation on the development and use of social theories. *Journal of Personality and Social Psychology, 50,* 24–34. When subjects explained how or why two variables might be related, it increased their use of and belief in the explained relationship. A counterexplanation task eliminated this bias. Might scientists be affected by these processes?

Hedges, L. V. (1987). How hard is hard science, how soft is soft science? The empirical cumulativeness of research. *American Psychologist, 42,* 443–455. Are research results in the behavioral sciences less replicable than results in the physical sciences? Although many say yes, the article questions this assumption. Methods for examining the consistency of research results are presented and examined.

Horvat, J. (1986). Detection of suspiciousness as a function of pleas for honesty. *Journal of Personality and Social Psychology, 50,* 921–924. This experiment reports results that indicate that properly designed postexperimental techniques can accurately measure suspiciousness in deception experiments. Truly suspicious subjects will be found whereas naive subjects will be kept from falsely reporting suspiciousness.

2

Social Perception

Understanding Others—and Ourselves

Chapter Outline: Getting the Overall Picture

Learning Objectives

1. List examples of how temporary factors such as moods affect behavior, and indicate how nonverbal cues help us interpret these temporary factors.
2. Summarize evidence supporting the idea that facial expressions are universal.
3. Describe the relationship between facial muscle activity and subjective emotional experience.
4. How are survival value and the face-in-the-crowd phenomenon related to the fact that facial expressions are universal?
5. Compare the impact on us of high levels of eye contact with staring.
6. Describe the roles played by body movements, emblems, and gait in our judgments about others.
7. Describe how nonverbal cues serve as self-presentation tactics.
8. List the four nonverbal cues that help us to detect deception, and indicate whether training improves our ability to detect deception.
9. Summarize Jones and Davis's theory of correspondent inference, indicating the role played by choice, noncommon effects, and social desirability in shaping our judgments about others.
10. Describe how consensus, consistency, and distinctiveness help us to decide whether someone's actions are internally or externally caused.
11. Why is it that we often fail to do the careful attributional analysis suggested by Kelley's theory?
12. Describe how consensus and distinctiveness information can be overshadowed by the context in which behavior takes place.
13. Provide examples that clearly illustrate the discounting and augmenting principles.
14. Compare Asch's interpretation of primacy effects with the cognitive miser hypothesis.
15. Describe the fundamental attribution error.
16. Describe the actor-observer effect, and indicate how one's perspective affects it.
17. Describe self-serving bias and its implications.
18. Compare the attributions of men and women with regard to their sexual experiences.
19. How do attributions about the negative behaviors of one's spouse differ in distressed and nondistressed marriages?
20. How can attribution theory be used to help reduce interpersonal conflict?
21. Describe how "attribution therapy" has been used to help people adjust to college and work, and also to handle depression.
22. Summarize the basic ideas of Schachter's theory of emotion, and indicate how we can be induced to misattribute arousal to external factors.
23. According to Allen's self-perception theory, how do we come to know our inner feelings and views?
24. Describe the overjustification effect and the circumstances under which it occurs.
25. Describe self-handicapping and the circumstances under which it occurs.

Topics for Discussion

1. How does one's name affect interpersonal judgments? You might ask the class to imagine a person named David, and then to list five traits that David possesses. Next, ask the class to imagine a person named Winthrop and have them list his traits. Do the two lists differ? Why?

Another way to approach this question is to ask the class whether they have ever felt that the names they were given implied a certain set of attributes. You might particularly seek responses from those with popular names or those with unusual names to see if they ever felt dissatisfied with their first names and why. Do we form impressions of people based in part on their names?

2. How does one's choice of clothing affect the ratings received from others? Assuming that clothing does influence the personality attributed to a person, is this a case of biased judgment? Or is it simply rational processing of available information?

3. Have students look for applications of attributional principles in advertising. For example, the person trying to get us to buy a product may be presented as a person who doesn't generally like the type of product. He may declare that he "doesn't like bran cereals," for instance. But we then see that the particular brand he tries is so extraordinarily good that it wins him over. In attributional terms, the response to the particular brand is high in distinctiveness.

Another example might be the communicator who tries to convince us that the majority of people prefers his brand. This time the attributional strategy is one of high consensus. Many examples of attributional strategies exist. Alert your students to be thinking in attributional terms when they see advertisements, and have them report relevant examples to the class.

4. Discuss the basis for judging celebrities, political candidates, and the like. Do the same rules apply to interpersonal perception in a face-to-face encounter and in our

judgment of people we know only in the media? Would it be an advantage for a political candidate to be familiar with the social perception research? It might be interesting to design an advertising campaign, based on this research, to create a favorable impression of a candidate. Or, analyze the ads employed by a candidate to determine whether the principles presented Chapter 2 are being followed.

5. Paul Ekman has thoroughly investigated the use of gestures, voice qualities, and facial expressions as cues to whether a person is telling the truth. There is much evidence that there are some concealment cues that are obvious to most people, and other cues that can only be detected by trained observers. For example, there are muscles located mainly in the forehead that momentarily express our sincere emotions, and that can be detected by a keen observer who knows what to look for. In total, Ekman's behavioral checklist contains twenty-two separate clues for detecting deceit.

An interesting question is the degree to which historical figures have fallen victim to deception from others. Ekman has analyzed several historical cases of deception, including the willingness of British Prime Minister Neville Chamberlain to believe Hitler in 1938 when he said Germany's intentions were nonaggressive. Should a U.S. president be given lie detection training before going off to a summit with the Soviets? (Ekman's work is summarized in a recent book, *Telling Lies,* published by W.W. Norton. Included in the book is the list of twenty-two clues for detecting deceit.)

Classroom Exercises/Demonstrations

1. This exercise asks students to read a story in which six characters appear. The story is presented in Chapter 2 of your students' Study Guide. The subjects are instructed to rank the characters in descending order according to how responsible each is perceived to be for the woman's death. (It is possible to read or tell the story to the class, but the exercise works better if each person has his or her own copy.)

The class will tend to split evenly, with about half the class ranking the wife as most responsible and about half ranking the highwayman first. A few people will also choose other characters. A quite lively discussion can develop, in which each group supports its own choice and challenges the others. As course instructor, you should remain neutral in the debate. Rather than telling them what you believe the correct answer is, challenge them to reach their own conclusions. (The idea and materials for this exercise were provided by Jeanine Bloyd of Spoon River Junior College, Canton, Illinois.)

2. It is relatively easy to demonstrate in class the difference in causal attributions made by actors and observers. An interesting way to demonstrate the effect is based on the experimental procedure devised by Nisbett and colleagues (1973). Ask the students to rate you on a series of descriptive adjectives (given below). For each adjective, the students should indicate "yes" (the adjective is characteristic of you), "no" (the adjective is not characteristic), or "it depends" (it depends on the situation). When the students have finished rating you, have them repeat the ratings, but this time have them rate themselves on the same set of adjectives. Again, the students indicate "yes," "no," or "it depends." The list of adjectives is:

1. assertive
2. calm
3. talkative
4. impulsive
5. energetic
6. optimistic
7. lenient
8. self-confident

You should read the list slowly to the class, asking them to make the rating for each adjective as it is read. The list should be read twice; the first time the students rate you and the second they rate themselves.

When the students have finished, ask them to count the number of times they used the "it depends" alternative for each stimulus person. You will find a greater frequency of "it depends" for self-ratings, that is, people are more likely to make a situational attribution to themselves than they are to others.

3. Warm versus cold is a trait dimension that has been shown to dramatically affect the impression formed of a stimulus person. This classic finding has been labeled the "central traits" effect, and a discussion of why it occurs can be found in many sources. You should prepare two lists of traits, one said to be characteristic of Person A and the other characteristic of Person B. Each student in the class receives only one list, either the A or the B list. In fact the two lists have six traits in common, and only the middle trait (warm vs. cold) is different. If you are unable to prepare the lists ahead of time, you can simply present them to the class on the chalkboard. Have half the class copy each list. When the "other list" is being presented, have those students who aren't supposed to see it cover their eyes. The trait lists are:

Person A	Person B
intelligent	intelligent
skillful	skillful
industrious	industrious

warm	cold
determined	determined
practical	practical
cautious	cautious

After the students have copied their respective lists, ask them to rate their stimulus person using the following six traits: (a) generous, (b) wise, (c) happy, (d) good natured, (e) reliable, and (f) important. For each trait ask the students to make a "yes" or "no" response. You will find that the warm/cold difference will dramatically affect each of the first four traits, but not the last two traits.

4. This exercise should be done as soon as possible after students have received their test scores on an exam. The exercise asks students to explain the score they received. The prediction is that students who have done well on the exam will explain their performance internally, whereas the students who have done relatively poorly will explain their performance more externally. To find out whether this hypothesis is confirmed, attributions to the internal factors (ability and effort) and to the external factors (the test and luck) should be computed. According to self-serving bias successful people should attribute their success to the internal factors, whereas unsuccessful people should attribute their relative failure to the external factors. A questionnaire for your use is presented in Chapter 2 of the Study Guide.

5. In the transparency section of this Instructor's Manual three situations are presented that can be used to illustrate the basic ideas of Kelley's theory of attribution. Each example describes a behavior and then provides consensus, consistency, and distinctiveness information. At the end of each example, the student is asked to choose the best explanation of the behavior. Transparency 2.4 contains low consensus, high consistency, and low distinctiveness information and should result in students making attributions to the person (i.e., Sue). Transparency 2.5 contains high consensus, high consistency, and high distinctiveness information and should result in students making attributions to the situation (i.e., Professor Ward). Transparency 2.6 contains low consensus, high consistency, and high distinctiveness information and no simple attribution is obvious.

6. In Chapter 2 of your students' Study Guide a page entitled "Applying Attribution to Everyday Situations" is presented. Students are instructed to describe the consensus, consistency, and distinctiveness information contained in each of two scenarios. Have the students respond to the scenarios outside of class (homework!) or you might provide time during class. After they have answered the questions, discuss their answers in class. Students appreciate an opportunity to determine whether they understand Kelley's theory.

Film Notes: A Picture Is Sometimes Worth a Thousand Words

Communication: The Nonverbal Agenda, 32009, 1974, color, 30 mins. Pennsylvania State University, Audiovisual Services, Special Services Building, University Park, PA 16802 (814-865-6314). Discusses the importance of being able to recognize the nonverbal messages that one receives and sends. Examples include interviews between an executive and three department heads, and a male-female encounter in a bar. Describes how communication problems between administrators, as well as manager-subordinate relationships, are worked out. From the *Behavior in Business* series. A CRM production.

*Communication: Social Cognition and Attribution, videotape, 28.5 mins. To obtain this tape, consult your Allyn and Bacon sales representative. Dramatization is used to generate an exchange between Robert A. Baron and Margaret Clark concerning attributional processes and nonverbal communication.

Constructing Social Reality, Number 20 in this 1990 videotape series, 30 mins. The Annenborg Project, Holt, Rinehart & Winston, contact Lee Sutherlin, Marketing Manager (817-334-7632). The factors that contribute to our interpretation of reality and how

understanding the psychological processes that govern our behavior can help us to become more empathetic and independent members of society.

I Guess I Got the Job, 21745, 1975, color, 13 mins. Pennsylvania State University, Audiovisual Services, Special Services Building, University Park, PA 16802 (814-865-6314). Two young men are interviewed for the same job. One is completely honest but shows a lack of confidence, and the other adopts interests and attitudes that he thinks will make him look good. From the *Conflict and Awareness* series.

Judging Emotional Behavior, ES-328, 24 mins., Indiana University, Audiovisual Center, Bloomington, IN 47401. Presents the emotional responses of subjects to emotion-eliciting stories. Shows the subjects first without sound, allowing the audience to judge the emotions being expressed; then shows the same sequences with narration to allow the audience to determine the accuracy of their judgments.

Kinesics, 80036, 1964, 73 mins. Pennsylvania State University, Audiovisual Services, Special Services Building, University Park, PA 16802 (814-865-6314). Filmed lecture by Raymond L. Birdwhistell of the

Eastern Pennsylvania Psychiatric Institute on linguistic kinesics. Describes a system of categorizing and defining facial expressions, posturing, and gestures in terms of communicative meaning.

Nonverbal Communication, 21888, 1976, color, 22 mins. Pennsylvania State University, Audiovisual Services, Special Services Building, University Park, PA 16802 (814-865-6314). Overview of research and theory on communication through gesture, body posture, in- tonation, eye contact, and facial expression. Interviews with Hall on interpersonal distance, Argyle on the equilibrium theory of eye contact, Rosenthal on sex differences in the perception of nonverbal behavior, Akaret on gestures and expressions in photographs, and Eibl-Eibesfeldt on biological programming. From the *Social Psychology* series. Stanley Milgram.

Transparencies

2.1 *Correspondent Inference: When Do We Infer the Traits of Others?*

2.2 *Kelley's Theory of Causal Attribution*

2.3 *Discounting and Augmenting: Two Basic Principles of Causal Attribution*

2.4 *Low Consensus, High Consistency, and Low Distinctiveness Produce an Internal Attribution*

2.5 *High Consensus, High Consistency, and High Distinctiveness Produce an External Attribution*

2.6 *Low Consensus, High Consistency, and High Distinctiveness Present Us with Mixed Information*

Critical Thinking/Essay Questions

1. Cite evidence to support the idea that humans show universal facial expressions and that they universally recognize the meaning of facial expressions.
2. How skilled are we in detecting deception in others? What does research suggest regarding the role of experience in changing our ability to detect deception?
3. Summarize the role played by each of the following factors in determining whether we make a correspondent inference:
   a. The degree to which the person had free choice.
   b. The degree to which noncommon effects were produced by the behavior.
   c. Whether the behavior was high or low in social desirability.
4. Summarize how our attributions about someone's behavior are affected by consensus, consistency, and distinctiveness information.
5. How does the depressive attributional style relate to the attributional style of "normal" persons?

Sources for Lecture

Bower, B. (1985). The face of emotion. *Science News,* July 6, *128*, pp. 12–13. The idea that facial expressions cause us to experience various feelings is explored. Particular attention is paid to Robert Zajonc's recent resurrection of Waynbaum's (1906) theory. Other theorists dealing with the facial feedback issue are also discussed.

Driscoll, R. (1982). Their own worst enemies. *Psychology Today,* July, pp. 45–49. The messages sent by severely self-critical people are examined.

Sadalla, E., & Burroughs, J. (1981). Profiles in eating: Sexy vegetarians and other diet-based social stereotypes. *Psychology Today,* October, pp. 51–57. Eating preferences are correlated with how people see themselves and how others see them.

Snyder, C. R. (1985). Excuses, excuses. *Psychology Today,* September, pp. 50–55. Discusses self-handicapping, defensive attributions, and other ways that people preserve their self-image and reduce stress.

Trotter, R. J. (1983). Baby face. *Psychology Today,* August, pp. 14–20. Evidence is presented that infants possess a rich repertoire of inborn emotional expressions.

INSTRUCTOR'S SECTION

Cheng, P. W., & Novick, L. R. (1990). A probabilistic model of causal induction. *Journal of Personality and Social Psychology, 58,* 545ff. Deviations from predictions made from Kelley's covariational model of attribution are usually interpreted as irrational biases. The present study posits a probabilistic, rational inference process instead.

Davidson, R. J., Ekman, P., Saron, C. D., Senulis, J. A., & Friesen, W. V. (1990). Approach-withdrawal and cerebral asymmetry: Emotional expression and brain physiology I. *Journal of Personality and Social Psychology, 58,* 330–334. Observable facial behavior was measured simultaneously with brain electrical activity to assess patterns of hemispheric activation in different regions during the experience of happiness and disgust.

Ekman, P., Davidson, R. J., & Friesen, W. V. (1990). The Duchenne smile: Emotional expression and brain physiology II. *Journal of Personality and Social Psychology, 58,* 342–353. Facial expression, EEG, and self-report of emotion were recorded while Ss watched both pleasant and unpleasant films. Smiling in which the muscle orbiting the eye was active vs. not active was particularly examined.

Izard, C. E. (1990). Facial expressions and the regulation of emotions. *Journal of Personality and Social Psychology, 58,* 487–498. A new developmental model of expression-feeling relations is presented that provides a framework for reevaluating previous research and for understanding the conditions under which expressions are effective in activating and regulating feeling states.

Lupfer, M. B., Clark, L. F., & Hutcherson, H. W. (1990). Impact of context on spontaneous trait and situational attributions. *Journal of Personality and Social Psychology, 58,* 239–249. Examines the role of background information on inferences regarding a target's behavior.

Major, B., Schmidlin, A. M., & Williams, L. (1990). Gender patterns in social touch: The impact of setting and age. *Journal of Personality and Social Psychology, 58,* 634–643. Gender asymmetry, a pattern in which men are more likely to touch women than vice versa, was observed in touching between adults, but not when children were involved. Cross-sex touching was more prevalent among adults, whereas same-sex touching was more prevalent when a child was involved.

McGill, A. L. (1990). The effect of direction of comparison on the selection of causal explanations. *Journal of Experimental Social Psychology, 26,* 93–107. Ss were asked to provide a causal explanation for the difference between one individual's undesirable outcome (recent illness) and a contrasting desirable occurrence (another individual's good health). The study explores how these judgments are made.

Skinner, E. A., Schindler, A., & Tschechne, M. (1990). Self-other differences in children's perceptions about the causes of important events. *Journal of Personality and Social Psychology, 58,* 144–155. Children's (ages eight to fifteen) beliefs about the effectiveness of multiple internal and external causes for producing outcomes in their own lives and in those of their peers were examined. Results suggest that self-other differences are produced by both developmental changes and environmental opportunities.

3

Social Cognition

Thinking About the Social World

Chapter Outline: Getting the Overall Picture

Learning Objectives

1. What is meant by heuristics, and what are the advantages and disadvantages of using them?
2. Describe the representativeness heuristic, and indicate how it sometimes interferes with our ability to use base-rate information.
3. Describe the availability heuristic and errors related to it.

4. Describe the false consensus effect and two reasons why it occurs.

5. Give examples of priming and automatic priming.

6. What is meant by positive and negative framing, and how does the "association" hypothesis explain this?

7. How does personal involvement affect framing?

8. Describe how anchoring influences the estimated fair price for a house and the estimated probability of nuclear war.

9. Describe counterfactual thinking and the circumstances under which it occurs.

10. What circumstances lead people to view unlikely events with suspicion?

11. Describe how implicit theories of stability and change affect judgments of dating partners and women's memories of menstrual symptoms.

12. Compare and contrast the Cannon-Bard theory, the James-Lange theory, and Schachter's two-factor theory of emotion.

13. Describe the facial feedback hypothesis and experimental findings related to it.

14. Summarize the vascular theory of emotion, and describe research supporting the theory.

15. How does one's affective state influence perception of ambiguous stimuli, memory, and creativity?

16. Compare the effects produced by positive and negative affect.

17. Describe four ways in which cognition influences affect, including the effect of expectations discussed in the "Cutting Edge" box.

18. Summarize the implications of the notion that the self is a schema.

19. What role is played by social input in the development of the self-concept?

20. Describe the self-reference effect, and indicate how categorical and elaborative processing contribute to it.

21. List four reasons possible selves are significant.

22. Compare the responses of Japanese and U.S. students to the question, "Who am I?"

23. Using the principles of action identification theory, compare how alcoholics and nonalcoholics describe their own drinking behavior.

Topics for Discussion

1. Chapter 3 opens with a discussion of the notion that information overload is the basic fact of social cognition. Because we are bombarded with thousands of stimuli, it is argued, we need to be efficient in screening, sorting, and storing social information. But an alternative view is that humans simply are not very good at remembering the content of information that is presented to them. Jacoby and Hoyer (1982) had subjects view thirty-second videotapes in U.S. shopping malls and then had them answer twelve true/false questions pertaining to the videotapes. Despite the fact that the videotape was viewed under ideal conditions, was of short duration, and the testing was done immediately after viewing, only 3.5 percent of the respondents answered all twelve questions correctly. Could it be that what we remember is simply not an accurate representation of what we see? (Jacoby and Hoyer's article appears in *Journal of Marketing, 46,* 12–26.)

2. Watch the news for reports of extreme acts of behavior. Can you find evidence that news analysts overemphasize drastic cases in reporting the news? Does reporting of acts of terrorism, for instance, lead us to a distorted perception of the views of the average resident of the terrorists' home countries?

3. Describe the availability heuristic to the class. Ask students to describe instances in which they were affected by this heuristic. Make sure that you have a firm grasp of the heuristic yourself so that you are ready to respond to their

examples. Next, do the same thing with the representativeness heuristic. Describe the heuristic and request students to describe instances in which they were affected by representativeness.

4. An interesting, although perhaps controversial, way to introduce the ideas of covariation and illusory correlation is to examine the relationship between homosexuality and other behaviors. A paper presented at the Midwestern Psychological Association meeting in May 1983 by Paul Cameron argued that homosexuality is disproportionately associated with murder. Cameron based his conclusion on an examination of sexually related mass murders in the United States. Another relationship which is "understood to be true" among some fire investigators (personally communicated to the author by a state arson investigator) is that arson is associated with homosexuality. Consider these examples in contrasting the difference between actual covariation and illusory correlation.

5. People have fairly detailed conceptions of the characteristics possessed by various groups. For example, we possess a well-developed schema for the elderly. One aspect of this schema is a notion that there are specific occupations appropriate for the elderly. There is evidence that some occupations are age typed. Prepare a list of occupations and ask students to rate them for the most appropriate age of a person in that occupation. What are the processes underlying judgments of age appropriateness for individual occupations? Do people use the availability heuristic, that is, do they search their memories for instances of incumbents of various ages? Do people consider the importance of various work skills? What other factors do they consider? Another aspect of this schema is our view of how a grandmother looks and acts. Brewer, Dull, and Lui (1981) published an interesting article in the *Journal of Personality and Social Psychology* (*41*, 656–670) in which they explored the traits attributed to a grandmother.

Classroom Exercises/Demonstrations

The chapter summarizes a variety of biases that contaminate our thinking. A useful way to introduce this chapter is to have students experience some of these biases first-hand. What follows are brief exercises to introduce some of these biases. You may want to present these to the class early in your consideration of social cognition as some of the examples are presented in the text.

1. *The availability heuristic.* We often use ease of recall as a basis for judging the frequency of events. Just because we can more readily recall one category of events, however, does not necessarily mean that the category is more frequent. Pose the following question to the class: Does the letter *k* appear more often as the first letter of a word or as the third letter? Most people judge that *k* appears more often at the beginning of a word, but in fact *k* is three times more likely to appear as the third letter. Why the error? The reason seems to be that our relative ease of recall of words beginning with *k* convinces us that they are also more frequent.

2. *The representativeness heuristic.* Tell the students that you have a series of thumbnail descriptions of one hundred individuals, thirty of whom were engineers and seventy of whom were lawyers. From this sample, the following description was drawn at random: John is a thirty-nine-year-old-man. He is married and has no children. A man of high ability and motivation, he promises to be quite successful in his field. He is well liked by his colleagues. What is the probability that John is a lawyer? People generally will respond to this question by saying it is fifty-fifty as to whether he is a lawyer or an engineer. What they have done is ignore the base-rate information and instead relied upon useless anecdotal information.

3. *The false consensus effect.* To illustrate this effect, you need to have students respond to some informational questions. An obvious source is exam questions. Tell the students whether they answered the particular question right or wrong. Then have them indicate the percentage of students in the class whom they believe correctly answered that particular question. For the questions they answered correctly, students should overestimate the percentage of correct responses. For the questions they answered wrong, they should underestimate the percentage.

4. Chapter 3 discusses the self-reference effect and summarizes it in Figure 3.18. (Figure 3.18 is reproduced as a transparency at the end of this Instructor's Manual chapter.) You can have the students do an exercise that demonstrates the effect rather convincingly. The exercise can be done either in class with the instructor serving as the experimenter or outside of class with students serving as the experimenters. Half of the subjects are instructed to read a list of trait adjectives and decide whether each of the words describes themselves. The other half of the subjects reads the same list of trait adjectives and indicates whether each of the words contains an *e*. After the subjects have gone through the entire list of adjectives, they are given a surprise recall test.

You will find that people who have gone through the list deciding whether the word describes the self will recall more of the words than people who simply decide whether each word has an *e*. This is because the words related to self are processed more deeply than the other words. When I do this exercise in class I find that students are impressed by the analogy between the exercise and their own study habits. Oftentimes studying becomes an exercise of "just reading words." To learn material, it must be processed deeply; one way to accomplish this is to be able to relate it to something already well known. What is better known than the self?

A list of thirteen trait adjectives to use in conducting the exercise is found in your students' Study Guide. Two identical lists are presented on the assumption that your students may want to gather data from friends by having one person do the task under each instructional set. You can then have the students bring their data to class and combine the data to see whether you have demonstrated the self-reference effect.

Film Notes: A Picture Is Sometimes Worth a Thousand Words

Cognitive Processes, Number 10 in this 1990 videotape series, 30 mins. The Annenborg Project, Holt, Rinehart & Winston, contact Lee Sutherlin, Marketing Manager (817-334-7632). An exploration into the higher mental processes—reasoning, planning, and problem solving—and why the "cognitive revolution" is attracting such diverse investigators, from philosophers to computer scientists.

Communication: Social Cognition and Attribution, videotape, 28.5 mins. To obtain this tape, consult your Allyn and Bacon sales representative. Dramatization is used to generate an exchange between Robert A. Baron and Margaret Clark on the principles of social cognition.

Information Processing, 31761, 1971, color, 29 mins. Pennsylvania State University, Audiovisual Services, Special Services Building, University Park, PA 16802 (814-865-6314). Psychologist Donald A. Norman and comedian David Steinberg use a cocktail party to reveal basic principles and far-reaching ramifications of human information processing. Includes short- and long-term memory, the Stroop phenomenon, mnemonics, retrieval strategies, and problem solving. From the *Psychology Today* series. A CRM production.

Judgment and Decision Making, Number 11 in this 1990 videotape series, 30 mins. The Annenborg Project, Holt, Rinehart & Winston, contact Lee Sutherlin, Marketing Manager (817-334-7632). A look at the process of making judgments and decisions, how and why people make good and bad judgments, and the psychology of risk taking.

Remembering and Forgetting, Number 9 in this 1990 videotape series, 30 mins. The Annenborg Project, Holt, Rinehart & Winston, contact Lee Sutherlin, Marketing Manager (817-334-7632). A look at the complex process of memory: How images, ideas, language—even physical actions, sounds and smells—are translated into codes, represented in memory, and retrieved when needed.

The Self, Number 15 in this 1990 videotape series, 30 mins. The Annenborg Project, Holt, Rinehart & Winston, contact Lee Sutherlin, Marketing Manager (817-334-7632). How psychologists systematically study the origins of self-identity and self-esteem, social determinants of self-concepts, and the emotional and motivational consequences of beliefs about oneself.

Transparencies

3.1 *Self-Schemata and Memory*
3.2 *Mental Simulations and Sympathy for Victims* (Fig. 3.8)
3.3 *Mood and Social Judgments: A Field Study* (Fig. 3.15)
3.4 *How Cognition Sometimes Shapes Affect* (Fig. 3.16)

Critical Thinking/Essay Questions

1. What is the representativeness heuristic, and how is it related to the base-rate fallacy?
2. Describe the false consensus effect, and give a reason it occurs.
3. Summarize ways in which the thinking of depressives is different from that of normal subjects.
4. Describe the facial feedback hypothesis, and discuss the relationship between the hypothesis and the Cannon-Bard, James-Lange, and Schachter two-factor theories of emotion.
5. How does whether one is experiencing positive or negative affect influence perception of ambiguous stimuli and memory?

Sources for Lecture

Allman, W. F. (1985). Staying alive in the 20th century. *Science '85,* October, pp. 34–41. Compares how the experts' assessments of various risks in everyday life are related to the assessment of the general public. Provides excellent examples of the irrationality of human thought.

Langer, E. J. (1982). Automated lives. *Psychology Today,* April, pp. 60–71. Langer discusses the tendency to engage in "mindlessness"—to do things and to make decisions without really thinking.

Le Brecque, M. (1980). On making sounder judgments. *Psychology Today,* June, pp. 32–42. Provides a review of some common errors in human thinking and guidelines for minimizing such errors.

Offir, C. W. (1975). Floundering in fallacy: Seven quick ways to kid yourself. *Psychology Today,* April, 66–68. Discusses common fallacies in human thinking.

Rubin, D. C. (1975). The subtle deceiver: Recalling your past. *Psychology Today,* September, pp. 38–46. Our ability to remember the past details of our lives is hampered by our present lives and our beliefs about ourselves.

Slovic, P., Fischhoff, B., & Lichtenstein, S. (1980). Risky assumptions. *Psychology Today,* June, pp. 44–48. Presents examples of how errors in human thinking get us into trouble, focusing especially on the overconfidence and vividness effects.

Update: Current Articles from Professional Sources

Brown, J. D. (1990). Evaluating one's abilities: Shortcuts and stumbling blocks on the road to self-knowledge. *Journal of Experimental Social Psychology, 26,* 149–167. Research has found that Ss eagerly seek information about their abilities. Whether this is related mainly to self-enhancement or to self-assessment motives was explored. The search for ability relevant feedback was strongest when positive information was expected, but even those led to believe feedback might disclose incompetence sought information.

Dunning, D., Griffin, D. W., Milojkovic, J. D., & Ross, L. (1990). The overconfidence effect in social prediction. *Journal of Personality and Social Psychology, 58,* 568–583. In predicting a specific peer's response to a variety of stimulus situations, subjects consistently proved to be highly overconfident. The levels of accuracy achieved in predictions about roommates, for example, fell far short of levels required to justify their confidence levels. Implications are discussed.

Kitayama, S. (1990). Interaction between affect and cognition in word perception. *Journal of Personality and Social Psychology, 58,* 209–217. Investigated the hypothesis that the accuracy of perception of a briefly presented word depends on both the affective tone of the word and activation of the corresponding memory code. Results are interpreted in terms of attentional mechanisms in conscious perception.

Larsen, R. J., & Kasimatis, M. (1990). Individual differences in entrainment of mood to the weekly calendar. *Journal of Personality and Social Psychology, 58,* 164–171. Two questions are addressed: (1) do people's moods exhibit a weekly cycle? and (2) are there individual differences in the degree to which weekly variation is shown? Evidence is found to support a yes answer to both questions.

Ruble, D. N., et al. (1990). Transition to motherhood and the self: Measurement, stability, and change. *Journal of Personality and Social Psychology, 58,* 450–463. Different ways of conceptualizing and measuring change in attitudes during transition to motherhood are examined. Such transitions are often times of upheaval in self-definition and in relationships with significant others, and thus are of considerable interest to researchers interested in the self.

4

Attitudes

Evaluating the Social World

Chapter Outline: Getting the Overall Picture

I. Forming Attitudes: The Roles of Learning and Experience
  A. Social Learning: Acquiring Attitudes from Others
   1. Classical Conditioning: Learning Based On Association
   2. Instrumental Conditioning: Learning to Express the "Right" Views
   3. Modeling: Learning by Example
  B. Direct Experience: Acquiring Attitudes from Life

II. Attitudes and Behavior: The Essential Link
  A. Attitude Specificity
  B. Attitude Components
  C. Attitude Strength, Vested Interest, and the Role of Self-Awareness
  D. Attitude Accessibility: The Force That Binds
  E. Television and Attitudes About Nuclear War

III. Persuasion: The Process of Changing Attitudes
  A. Persuasion: The Traditional Approach
  B. Delayed Attitude Change: Four Decades of Research on the "Sleeper Effect"
  C. Persuasion: The Cognitive Approach
   1. The Elaboration Likelihood Model: Two Routes to Persuasion
   2. The Heuristic Model of Persuasion
   3. Other Aspects of the Cognitive Approach: Understanding the Effects of Mood and Individual Differences

a. Why Are People in a Good Mood Easier to Influence?
b. Individual Differences and Two Kinds of Processing: Attitude Function and Persuasion

IV. When Attitude Change Fails: Resistance to Persuasion
  A. Reactance: Protecting One's Personal Freedom
  B. Forewarning: Prior Knowledge of Persuasive Intent
  C. Selective Avoidance
  D. Attitude Change and Age: Are There Really "Impressionable Years"?

V. Cognitive Dissonance: How We Sometimes Change Our Own Attitudes
  A. Dissonance and Attitude Change: The Effects of Forced Compliance
   1. Dissonance and the "Less Leads to More" Effect
  B. Dissonance: Does It Really Stem From Inconsistency?
  C. Leading Questions, Attitude Certainty, and Attitude Change: The Impact of Superattitudinal Statements
  D. Putting Dissonance to Work: Effort Justification and the Effectiveness of Psychotherapy

Learning Objectives

1. Define *attitude,* and summarize implications of the definition.
2. Explain the roles of classical conditioning, instrumental conditioning, and modeling in the formation of attitudes.
3. Compare attitudes acquired through direct experience with those acquired through indirect, vicarious experience.
4. Describe the "unsettling conclusion" reached by Wicker (1969).
5. Why is it that general, global attitudes do not predict behavior as well as specific ones?
6. Compare the affective and cognitive components of attitudes, and indicate when each component will be related to behavior.
7. Describe how the attitude-behavior link is affected by attitude strength, vested interest, and self-awareness.
8. Describe the role played by attitude accessibility in mediating the attitude-behavior link.
9. Describe the impact of the TV show "The Day After" on attitudes about nuclear war among watchers and nonwatchers of the program.
10. List eight findings from traditional persuasion research.
11. Describe the sleeper effect, and compare the disassociation and differential decay explanations of it.
12. Compare the explanations for persuasion offered by the traditional and the cognitive perspective.
13. Using the elaboration likelihood model, compare the central and peripheral routes to persuasion.
14. Describe the study by Axsom, Yates, and Chaiken (1987), and indicate how it supports the heuristic model.
15. Describe the study by Mackie and Worth (1989), and indicate why people in a good mood are sometimes easier to influence.
16. Compare the effectiveness of attractive and expert communicators when the target of the communication is a high and low self-monitor.
17. Define reactance, and describe circumstances that produce negative attitude change.
18. Why are we better able to resist persuasive messages when we have prior knowledge of persuasive intent?
19. How does selective avoidance help us to resist persuasion?
20. Describe the "impressionable years" hypothesis and supporting research.
21. Define cognitive dissonance, and indicate the four ways we can get rid of dissonance in the forced compliance situation.
22. Describe the less leads to more effect and the circumstances under which it occurs.
23. Summarize research suggesting that dissonance stems from accepting personal responsibility for negative consequences (and not simply from inconsistency).
24. Describe how a standard leading question can produce attitude change. When is the superattitudinal approach necessary?
25. What is the effort justification effect, and how has it been used to enhance the effectiveness of psychotherapy?

Topics for Discussion

1. As an alternative to dissonance theory, Charles Kiesler has proposed that the reason we change our attitudes in the direction of counterattitudinal behaviors is that we become committed when we perform an action. Whereas dissonance theory is concerned only with the effects created by our counterattitudinal behaviors, Kiesler has proposed that acting in a manner consistent with what we believe can also have important consequences for our attitudes. Dissonance theory considers attitude-consistent actions irrelevant because they do not arouse any dissonance. Kiesler's ideas are presented in a 1971 book, *The Psychology of Commitment,* published by Academic Press.

Like dissonance theory, Kiesler has proposed that only some kinds of behavioral acts will result in a person's becoming committed. Some of the factors determining one's degree of commitment are as follows:

1. *The explicitness of the behavior.* Publicly expressing an opinion is a stronger commitment than expressing your views to a stranger.
2. *The importance of the behavior.* Expressing an opinion to someone important is a stronger commitment than expressing your views to a stranger.
3. *The degree of irrevocability.* Expressing an opinion in a written statement is a stronger commitment than expressing your views orally.
4. *Number of actions.* Expressing an opinion over and over again is a stronger commitment than expressing it only once.

5. *Degree of volition*. Expressing an opinion of your own free will is a stronger commitment than expressing it because someone makes you do it.

6. *Effort*. Going to a lot of trouble to express an opinion is a stronger commitment than when you can express it easily.

2. Have the students write down their attitudes on some important topic and also have them list the people who and experiences that contributed to the development of this attitude. You may want to direct their thinking toward some important issue, such as affirmative action, abortion, or racial prejudice so that the entire class will be thinking about the same issue. After the students have made their lists, introduce the factors that social psychologists have concluded to be important in attitude formation. Do the students have examples of classical conditioning, instrumental conditioning, modeling, and direct experience that they can relate to the class discussion?

3. Analyze the credibility of current political figures. This is especially relevant in a presidential election year. Analyze the contribution of expertise, attractiveness, similarity, trustworthiness, and so on. What is the basis for attributing each of these characteristics to a political figure?

4. A time-consuming, but potentially valuable, exercise is to have the class construct an attitude questionnaire. During one class period have the students write a set of items relevant to a particular topic. A large number of items (perhaps one hundred) is needed. Next, select the best forty or so items and have the students administer these to their friends. Determine which items best discriminate between people who are above or below average on the measured attitude. (The topic should be interesting to students. Allow them to choose the topic from among women's rights, fraternities, raising tuition, or any other issue that is important to them.)

5. Lewittes and Simmons published an article in 1975 suggesting that we often engage in impression management when performing a sexually motivated behavior. They suggest that one reason people say one thing and do another is that they sometimes must do things in public that they consider embarrassing. For example, some people find it embarrassing to buy contraceptives at the pharmacy counter. Likewise, college students buying *Playboy, Penthouse,* and similar magazines at a university bookstore show discomfort. Lewittes and Simmons found that those buying magazines such as *Playboy* purchased more additional items, such as other magazines or candy, and more often asked for a bag for their purchases. Finally, a Dallas cable television franchise conducted a survey to find out what kinds of services people wanted and didn't want. Adult programming was rated very low in the survey, but 60 percent of the subscribers signed up for the adult channel. When asked to make public statements for the survey, most disapproved the sex and nudity of the adult channel; when they could privately sign up for it, most did so. (Lewittes and Simmons's article appears in the *Journal of Social Psychology, 96,* 39–44.)

Classroom Exercises/Demonstrations

1. Ryckman and Sherman (1974) asked college students to rate the trustworthiness of a variety of occupations on a scale of 1 to 4. A rating of 1 meant that the members of the particular profession were seen as most trustworthy. A rating of 4 indicated that the members of the occupation were seen as least trustworthy. Your students can repeat the procedure conducted by Ryckman and Sherman (published in *Journal of Applied Social Psychology, 4,* 351–364). Having rated these occupations, ask the students to explain the basis of their judgments. What characteristics do they associate with trustworthiness? What is the reason for some occupations being rated low in trustworthiness? The occupations to be rated are found in Chapter 4 of your students' Study Guide.

2. Make a list of buildings on your campus. Have the students rate these buildings on two different dimensions, once for likability and once for familiarity or how often they've been there. Each of these ratings can be done on a 5-point scale. Gather up the ratings and determine their degree of correlation. Is there support for the frequency of exposure/liking hypothesis? Do students report liking those buildings with which they are most familiar?

3. Have students bring in advertisements from newspapers and magazines so that you can analyze the techniques of persuasion being used in them. In a 1985 article in *Teaching of Psychology* (12[1], 42–3), Vivian Makosky suggests there are three major persuasion techniques that can be identified in this way. In addition, she suggests several variations on the exercise. One variation is to compare the appeals made in men's magazines with those in women's magazines. Another variation is to compare the appeals in *Vogue* with those in *Family Circle*. Still another variation is to analyze what it is that turns people off in certain ads. Whatever avenue you choose, it is clear that advertising is a rich source of material for testing hypotheses on attitude change.

4. Chapter 4 presents a detailed discussion of the difference between the central and the peripheral route to persuasion. Have students describe examples of television ads that use the two routes. The ads using the central route are presented directly to the viewer, whereas ads using the peripheral route are embedded in distraction. Can the students come up with examples of these types of ads? Are those using the central route based on better arguments than those using the peripheral route?

5. Chapter 4 looks at differences between high self-monitors and low self-monitors in terms of the type of communicator that appeals to each. The Self-Monitoring Scale, authored by Mark Snyder, is presented in Chapter 12 of your students' Study Guide. An interesting extension of the exercise presented in Chapter 12 is to see whether you can replicate the attitudinal effect, that is, to see whether high self-monitors really are more influenced by a source's attractiveness whereas low self-monitors are more affected by the expertise of the source. Prepare a persuasive appeal and vary the source of the message. Half the time it should come from an expert, half from a nonexpert. Half the time it should come from an attractive communicator, half from a less attractive source. Can you replicate the self-monitoring effect?

Film Notes: A Picture Is Sometimes Worth a Thousand Words

Persuasion Box, 1-306, film, 21 mins. Western Illinois University Audiovisual Services, Macomb, IL 61455 (309-298-2417). This film shows how attitudes are changed in everyday life; special emphasis is given to the language of persuasion in advertising and in the mass media.

The Psychology of Mass Persuasion, 727-GK, 35 mm. filmstrip with accompanying audio cassette, 39 mins. Human Relations Media, 175 Tompkins Avenue, Pleasantville, NY 10570. Provides an analysis of mass persuasion in modern society. Looks at who the mass persuaders are and the techniques they use.

Social Animal, 3-156, 1963, 29 mins. Audiovisual Services, Western Illinois University, Macomb, IL 61455. One of the topics covered is the classic experiment by Festinger and Carlsmith (1959) showing the consequences of publicly stating something contrary to one's belief. Cognitive dissonance interpretation is presented.

Social Psychology, 31762, 1971, color, 33 mins. Pennsylvania State University, Audiovisual Services, Special Services Building, University Park, PA 16802 (814-865-6314). Documentary footage of the busing of black children to previously all-white schools in a middle-class suburb is used to explain the social comparison theory, how attitudes are formed and changed, and the nature of racial prejudice. Commentary by psychologists Kenneth B. Clark, Thomas Pettigrew, David Sears, and Thomas Cottle. From the *Psychology Today* series. A CRM production.

Transparencies

4.1 *Cognitive Dissonance Theory in a Nutshell*
4.2 *The Forced Compliance Paradigm for Studying the Effects of Engaging in Attitude-Discrepant Behavior*

4.3 *Dissonance: The Price of Inconsistency*
4.4 *Rewards and Forced Compliance*

Critical Thinking/Essay Questions

1. How is the acquisition of attitudes accounted for by classical conditioning, instrumental conditioning, and modeling?
2. Summarize the factors that determine whether behavior will be predictable from attitudes.
3. Compare the traditional approach with the cognitive approach to attitude change.
4. Summarize the elaboration likelihood model of attitude change. Distinguish between the central and peripheral routes to attitude change. How does this model account for the fact that the effect of distraction during a persuasive message depends on whether we are listening to weak or strong arguments?
5. What is meant by cognitive dissonance? Summarize an experimental demonstration of a cognitive dissonance effect, being sure to indicate as precisely as possible the way in which cognitive dissonance theory accounts for the results.

Sources for Lecture

Ball-Rokeach, S.J., Rokeach, M., & Grube, J. (1984). The great American values test. *Psychology Today,* November, pp. 34–41. Can television be persuasive? An experimental program aired in 1979 found that it can when it challenges people to reflect on the consistency of their attitudes, values, and behavior.

Benson, P.L. (1981). Religion on Capitol Hill: How beliefs affect voting behavior in the U.S. Congress. *Psychology Today,* December, pp. 47–57. An interesting examination of the attitude-behavior relationship.

Cialdini, R.B. (1984). The triggers of influence. *Psychology Today,* February, pp. 40–45. The author examines several popular forms of social manipulation that persuade without appearing to be manipulative. Because of our tendency to respond automatically to many social situations, well-informed manipulators can trigger reactions in us for their own purposes.

Colman, A. (1980). Flattery won't get you anywhere. *Psychology Today,* May, pp. 80–82. Sometimes flattery works and sometimes it backfires. It all depends on the status of the flatterer and the self-image of the person being persuaded.

Diamond, E., & Bates, S. (1984). The political pitch. *Psychology Today,* November, pp. 23–32. The authors examine the problems and pitfalls of political advertising. It is concluded that commercials are effective for some targets, for some issues, under some conditions.

Kipnis, D., & Schmidt, S. (1985). The language of persuasion. *Psychology Today,* April, pp. 40–46. Should we use a "hard" persuasion strategy such as a command or a "soft" strategy such as compromise? The answer is that it depends on some other variables.

MacLachlan, J. (1979). What people really think of fast talkers. *Psychology Today,* November, pp. 112–117. Those who talk fast are often seen as more intelligent and convincing. Implications for the advertising industry are discussed.

Poindexter, J. (1983). Shaping the consumer. *Psychology Today,* May, pp. 64–68. Describes how companies unobtrusively monitor consumers' purchases and use the information to tailor commercial messages to consumer habits.

Poindexter, J. (1983). Voices of authority. *Psychology Today,* August, pp. 53–61. Lee Iacocca and other chief executives of U.S. corporations seem to be succeeding as communicators in advertising. This article examines why.

Schmidt, S.M., & Kipnis, D. (1987). The perils of persistence. *Psychology Today,* November, pp. 32–34. Many different ways of getting your way are examined by the authors, including assertiveness, bargaining, reasoning, friendliness, higher authority, and coalition.

Update: Current Articles from Professional Sources

Howard, D. J. (1990). Rhetorical question effects on message processing and persuasion: The role of information availability and the elicitation of judgment. *Journal of Experimental Social Psychology, 26,* 217–239. Four experiments examined the effects of asking rhetorical questions using a radio commercial as the stimulus material. Views drawn from two different theoretical models are contrasted.

Shavitt, S. (1990). The role of attitude objects in attitude functions. *Journal of Experimental Social Psychology, 26,* 124–148. Attitudes serve various functions, including utilitarian, social identity, and self-esteem maintenance functions. This study found that attitudes toward objects that engage different functions respond to different types of persuasive appeals.

5

Prejudice and Discrimination

The Costs of Hating Without Cause

Chapter Outline: Getting the Overall Picture

I. Prejudice and Discrimination: What They Are and How They Differ
    A. Prejudice: Choosing Whom to Hate
    B. Discrimination: Prejudice in Action
        1. Subtle Forms of Discrimination: Prejudice in Disguise
        2. Tokenism: Small Benefits, High Costs
        3. Reverse discrimination: Giving with One Hand, Taking Away with the Other
    C. Direct Intergroup Conflict: Competition As a Source of Bias
    D. The Us-Versus-Them Effect: Social Categorization As a Basis for Prejudice
    E. Cognitive Sources of Prejudice: Stereotypes, Selective Processing, and Illusory Correlation
        1. Stereotypes: What They Are and How They Operate
        2. Early Experience: The Role of Social Learning
        3. Illusory Correlation: Perceiving Relationships That Aren't There
    F. A Biological Basis for Prejudice? Genetic Similarity Theory

II. Combating Prejudice: Some Plans of Action
    A. Direct Intergroup Contact: The Potential Benefits of Acquaintance
    B. Breaking the Cycle of Prejudice: On Learning Not to Hate
    C. Recategorization: Redrawing the Boundary Between Us and Them
    D. Cognitive Interventions: Countering the Effects of Stereotypes

III. Prejudice Based on Gender: Its Nature and Effects
    A. Gender Stereotypes: The Cognitive Core of Prejudice Toward Females
        1. Gender Stereotypes: Some Unsettling Effects
    B. Discrimination Against Females: Subtle but Often Deadly
        1. The Role of Expectations
        2. The Role of Self-Confidence
        3. Denying Credit Where Credit Is Due: Attributions About Male and Female Achievement
    C. Sexism in Work Settings: Some Room for Optimism

Learning Objectives

1. Be able to review prejudice and discrimination in the past and at present.
2. Learn the definition of prejudice, how attitudes of this kind function as schemata, and the relationship between the three components of the prejudiced attitude as well as how it may strengthen or fade.

3. How is prejudice a reflection of the limits of the cognitive system? Be able to define discrimination and indicate its degrees of severity.

4. Know the procedure of the Rothbart and Hallmark (1988) study (decisions when one assumes the role of "defense minister").

5. What is a subtle form of prejudice?

6. What is tokenism and how did it affect subjects in Chacko's (1982) study (young women in management)? What are the negative effects of tokenism?

7. What is reverse discrimination and how is it reflected in the study by Chidester (1986; conversation with microphones and headphones)?

8. By outlining the Fajardo (1985) study (evaluations of essays by black and white students), be able to consider how reverse discrimination can backfire.

9. Learn the principles of realistic conflict theory. How does it relate to the escalation of opposition between one group and the next? How does the Hovland and Sears (1940) study demonstrate this theory?

10. Know the procedure of the Robbers' Cave Study. How did competition create animosity between the groups of boys, and how did "superordinate goals" destroy the ill feelings?

11. Appreciate how us-versus-them effect leads to prejudice. By reference to Meindl and Lerner's (1985) study in Canada, show how self-esteem plays a role in us versus them and how, in turn, self-esteem needs lead to social competition.

12. Be able to outline the social learning theory of prejudice. How do the media play a role in the social learning of prejudice?

13. Learn what constitutes a stereotype, how it affects the information to which we attend, and how we interpret and remember that information. How is it self-confirming?

14. Know the procedures of Bodenhausen's (1988) study of how stereotypes affect juror bias. How did the time at which information activating stereotypes was introduced and whether subjects rated each piece of information affect results?

15. Understand the definition of illusory correlation and how it plays a role in prejudice.

16. Learn the significance of the perception that out-groups are homogeneous and in-groups are differentiated. Be able to describe the Linville, Fischer, and Salovey (1989) study (subjects rated groups on friendliness, etc.). How does the differential familiarity hypothesis explain results?

17. Appreciate the genetic similarity theory, and how this theory would expect the existence of prejudice. What evidence from the animal kingdom does Rushton invoke to support the theory and what is its current status?

18. Is there hope that parents will work to lessen prejudice? How did the eye-of-the-storm demonstration affect children's appreciation of prejudice? Learn why intergroup contact can reduce prejudice, conditions that must be met if reduction is to occur, and the "jigsaw method."

19. What were the mixed results of Finchilescu's (1988) study of integrated and segregated South African nursing programs?

20. Learn why us versus them disappeared from an Italian city. How was this same phenomenon shown in the Gaertner et al. (1989) study (subjects assigned to three-person teams for competition)?

21. How might attribute-driven, as opposed to category-driven, processing lessen stereotyping?

22. Be able to describe the Indian study of gender and occupational prestige, the general tendency for people to assign valued traits mostly to men, and the tendency for managers and executives to be seen as possessing "male" traits.

23. Why are women typically confined to low-paying jobs? Be able to show that the answer lies in part in lower expectations and in part in lower self-confidence on the part of women (refer to McCarty, 1986). What are the roles of luck and skill in evaluating men's and women's achievement?

24. Learn the four reasons why women are currently doing better on the job than in the past.

Topics for Discussion

1. During World War II, dehumanization promoted vicious hatred between Japanese and Americans. The Japanese thought that Americans were less than human and Americans regarded them in the same way. As a result, Americans unconstitutionally imprisoned and harassed hundreds of thousands of American citizens of Japanese descent and the Japanese starved and tortured to death several thousand American POWs.

The final scene of the great antiwar film, *Paths of Glory,* starring Kirk Douglas, can help students understand the role of dehumanizing the targets of bias in the promotion of prejudice against them. In that scene, battle weary World War I French soldiers are gathered at a night club awaiting the entertainment for the evening. Finally, the proprietor emerges from backstage with a young German woman in tow. The soldiers roar with laughter as she cowers at the sight of them. Derisive comments about her reverberate around the room. Much to their delight, she is terrorized. As the men drink up, the proprietor forces the woman to sing. Her halting whisper of a voice causes the soldiers to jeer even louder. In response, her utterances increase in volume. Slowly, the soldiers come to realize that she is singing a sentimental song familiar to them. The noise begins to subside and one or two soldiers start to sing along with the woman. Instantly, she is transformed from daughter of the German "beast" to human being. Soon all the men are singing along, and many are crying.

When the soldiers and a representative of the enemy joined together in song, they were able to appreciate the tragedy of their common circumstances, and, in turn, one another's humanity. *Paths of Glory* can be rented from many videotape stores (or they can find it for you; if not, your audiovisual people probably can). Play that last scene for the students and ask them why the soldiers initially reacted so violently to a harmless noncombatant, only to join her suddenly in a show of tender emotions. Point out the implications for perceptions of homogeneity of the out-group and for the effect of a joint enterprise on dissolution of those perceptions. Help them understand why it is so easy to hate people who are regarded as less than human and so difficult to hate those same people once their humanity is appreciated.

2. *Cultural diversity* is becoming a catchphrase on many campuses. Why? Sometime during the next century, the many U.S. ethnic groups of non-European heritage will total more people than the current U.S. majority, just as non-Russians now outnumber Russians in the Soviet Union. Just as in the current Soviet Union, extraordinary diversity will characterize the United States. We need to understand diversity better than the Soviets have or we could suffer their possible fate: fragmentation of the country.

You might start on a less serious note by showing students how common gestures vary in meaning from culture to culture (see "Sources for Lecture" for a reference). Tapping the head means "I'm thinking" in Argentina and Peru, but elsewhere it means "He's crazy." Have the students imagine using this gesture in the presence of the wrong audience. The forearm jerk, one hand on the hollow of an elbow joint causing the clenched fist of the other hand to thrust upward about eyeball level, means "——— you" in Mediterranean countries and in the United States, but is a compliment equivalent to a wolf whistle in England. Placing the thumb under the index finger and thrusting the thumb upward, palm outward is an obscene gesture in some European and Mediterranean countries, but is such a good luck symbol in Brazil and Venezuela that it is reproduced in form of paper weights and golden amulets worn around the neck. Imagine using these gestures in the wrong place! How about the "impudent third finger"? Since the time of the Romans it has meant much the same around the world.

Then, consider some less trivial and more meaningful

cultural differences in the United States. If we learned about these differences, we could avoid some conflicts and appreciate the fact that some distasteful behaviors—from the majority of Americans' point of view—are not so bad once understood. For example, consider the old African maxim, "If you throw a rock into a pack of dogs, the one that yelps is the one that was hit." Knowing this proverb helps to understand why a black person who says "whites are racists"—but doesn't mean all whites—is suspicious of a white person who responds with denial. To many white Americans, two people who are vehemently yelling at each other are getting ready to fight; to many black Americans, the two are just "woofing" (as long as they continue, everything is fine). If you start a discussion on racism in your class, black students, usually taught it is good to air emotions, will likely want to argue things out. However, white students, the majority of whom are taught it is embarrassing to express strong emotions publicly, will probably clam up. Little wonder it may not go well . . . unless the two opposite tendencies are discussed first.

Other examples include the observation that some Anglos will march up to the boss and ask for a raise, but some Hispanics, who are equally loyal and hard-working employees, will wait to be given the raise, because they believe the boss is supposed to reward their loyalty spontaneously. A Japanese boss will not chastise an errant employee in front of his or her peers—it would cause the employee to lose face and reflect badly on the peers. However, some American bosses will not hesitate to dress down an employee in front of peers (neither will the Japanese boss, if he or she and the employees have had several drinks together after work!). We "ground" naughty children to their rooms; the Japanese put them outside. Use these and other examples, provided by yourself or students, as a basis for a discussion on cultural diversity. However, be cautious: Students must learn to approach people from a different cultural background as unique individuals, while bearing broader cultural differences in mind so that misunderstandings are avoided. Trying to "learn" someone else's culture can be counterproductive; stereotypes are the only characteristics likely to be learned.

3. If smooth relations between men and women and one cultural group and another are to characterize the future, we must learn to monitor the assumptions behind what we say. The following are several examples that may or may not expand on what you already know, but can serve to illustrate unfortunate assumptions.

College and university administrators are sometimes heard to say, "We are looking for qualified minority [or women] faculty." The phrase *qualified minority* implies that most minority academics are not qualified; therefore, one must search hard for the few qualified ones. The word *minority* may also be offensive, because it lumps all the diverse U. S. ethnic groups together as if they were the same. Different cultural groups are very proud of their unique identities (even the word *Hispanic* is problematic, because of the phenomenal diversity among the groups that are classed under this label).

Referring to "natural ability" as an explanation of why members of certain groups are disproportionately represented among the most successful in a certain field can be less than flattering (e.g., blacks in sports and Asians in high-tech areas). It implies that these successful people didn't have to do anything to succeed except show up, an affront to their perception that they have had to work very hard, probably harder than others.

Referring to women or members of certain ethnic groups as "hired through our affirmative action program" can be insulting. It implies that these individuals were less qualified than others who were candidates for the same job. In fact, the spirit of affirmative action is "all other things being equal, consider ethnic identification or gender when deciding whom to hire." Businesses would be cutting their own throats if they hired less-qualified people, instead of acting according to the aforementioned spirit. Calling on women or members of certain ethnic groups to "tell us what your people think" can be upsetting. For groups as large as women or blacks, for example, no one member can represent all the others, because great diversity exists *within* any large group.

If you use these examples, or other similar ones, it is likely that women and members of different cultural groups in your class will provide many more. The result could be a very enlightening discussion.

4. There is some debate concerning how much women earn, relative to men. Published figures vary from forty-plus cents for every dollar a man makes to seventy-plus cents for every dollar a man makes. One projection based on government statistics indicates that by the year 2000 women will be making only about seventy-five cents for every dollar that men make. To get a lively exchange going, ask your students to assume that these figures are correct, and ask them to come up with reasons. Of course, one of the answers you can expect is sexism. Ask those who provide that answer to indicate exactly what they mean. Are the jobs that women are assigned thought to be less valuable? When women make less, but do the same work as men, is their work viewed as less well done? Are the bosses who decide on salaries mostly men? Or, has the confidence of women been so undermined that, in fact, they do less well? Other possibilities include the idea that women take off to have babies and that puts them behind men on the promotion ladder. If this one comes up, you may want to ask why does this time off necessarily count against women's seniority; after all, men get sabbaticals and leaves of absence without loss of seniority. It might be appropriate to ask why husbands of women who take birth leave couldn't assume some of the early child-care chores so these women could return to work more quickly. In other words, if birth leave is a real problem, it could be solved. Another possibility is the notion that women make less because of a lesser commitment to their jobs, relative to their family lives. This one might be challenged by the following interrogatives: Why is it necessary that women be the ones who are more committed to family than jobs, rather than men? couldn't it be men? couldn't both men and women show more balanced commitments? A discussion that begins with "why do women make less than men?" could lead to several insights.

Classroom Exercises/Demonstrations

1. The following is a set of excerpts from a questionnaire on racism that was actually distributed in the classrooms of the Ann Arbor, Michigan, high schools (a duplicate of it, without the answers expressed in percentages, is found in the corresponding Student Guide chapter). It has been altered slightly to be more appropriate to college students. You could give it to your students and compile their answers as percentages (see "Sources for Lecture" for the reference to this work).

Is There Racism at This School?

This is an anonymous survey written by students. Circle or mark all relevant responses—remember there is no ONE right answer. Any comments are encouraged. This is not a test. The survey will probably take about 15 to 20 minutes.

1. Here are some definitions of racism; check those that you agree with and leave blank those you disagree with.
   <u>88</u> Racism is when people aren't given or allowed equal opportunities because of their racial or ethnic background (For example, black, Asian, Jewish, white, Hispanic, Arab, etc.)
   <u>56</u> Racism is whenever people are discriminated against.

<u>79</u> Racism is when people are segregated according to which racial or ethnic background they are from.

<u>82</u> Racism is when people hate, dislike, or fear other people because of their racial or ethnic background.

<u>80</u> Racism is something that degrades, demoralizes, or hurts people because they are from a certain racial or ethnic group.

<u>13</u> Other, please write your own definition: _____

2. Is there racism at your school? Yes(85)/No(6)/Other(9) If you answered yes, please answer the following questions.

   a. In your school, how is racism shown? (Check all that apply.)

<u>62</u> Ethnic slurs	<u>29</u> Threats against a person
<u>64</u> Offensive remarks	<u>21</u> Threats against a group
<u>22</u> Physical assault	<u>31</u> Exclusion
<u>38</u> Physical intimidation	<u>54</u> Social segregation
<u>64</u> Mocking stereotypes	<u>7</u> Other (be specific) _____

   b. How do you know about racist incidents at your school? (Check all that apply.)

<u>31</u> You've been in the incident	<u>56</u> You witnessed an incident
<u>57</u> Someone told you of one	<u>8</u> I know of no racist incidents at my school
<u>47</u> Rumors	<u>10</u> Other _____

3. To what extent do you feel racism to be a serious problem in your school? (Rate on a scale of 1 to 5: 1 = very serious, and 5 = not a problem at all.) Circle your choice 1(6) 2(21) 3(39) 4(24) 5(7)

4. What causes racism? (Check all that apply.)

<u>40</u> Feelings of inadequacy	<u>45</u> Peer pressure	<u>70</u> Stereotypes
<u>68</u> Ignorance	<u>75</u> Upbringing	<u>51</u> Fear
<u>56</u> Past experiences	<u>28</u> Media	<u>6</u> Other _____

5. Check the words or symbols you think are racist.

<u>54</u> swastika	<u>75</u> "Jap" (Japanese)	<u>80</u> "chink"
<u>93</u> "nigger"	<u>64</u> "JAP" (Jewish)	<u>34</u> "skinhead"
<u>74</u> "white boy"		

6. If you think some social groups are racially segregated, is it because (Check if you agree; leave blank those you disagree with)

<u>63</u> people come from different backgrounds	<u>39</u> people from the same race or ethnic group have more in common
<u>45</u> people stay with friends from their own neighborhoods	<u>16</u> Other (please explain) _____
<u>57</u> people have racist feelings	<u>8</u> I don't think social groups are racially segregated

7. Have you ever seen racism in any of these forms? (Check if yes, leave blank if no.)

<u>25</u> Discrimination in textbooks	<u>10</u> Faculty presenting class material in a discriminatory way
<u>31</u> Faculty ignoring or singling out minority students	<u>21</u> Not enough minority faculty members
<u>22</u> Faculty being more negative to minority students	<u>11</u> Other _____

8. Do you think that minority students discriminate against whites? (Circle one.) Yes(72)/No(5)/I don't know(15)

9. Do you and your friends discuss racism?   Yes(65)/No(26)

10. Do you hold racist feelings?   Yes(23)/No(49)/Other(10) (explain "other") _____

The following questions are completely *optional*. The reason they are asked is not to be personal, but to find out if certain groups of people feel more or less strongly about racism. (82% answered these questions)

Sex: Male / Female

Year in school: 1st, 2nd, 3rd, 4th, 5th

What is your racial identity? (Ex. Black, Caucasian) _____

What is your ethnic identity? (Ex. Italian, Jewish) _____

Source: Polakow-Suransky, S., & Ulahy, N. (1990). Students take action to combat racism. *Phi Delta Kappan*, April, *71*, 601–606. Reprinted with permission of Shael Polakow-Suransky.

INSTRUCTOR'S SECTION

2. Have your students complete the "gender makes a difference" and "race makes a difference" scales found in the Student Guide chapter corresponding to this one. One of the Manual authors has found that student responses pile up in the middle-to-little-difference end of the race scale. They have trouble seeing that race affects their reactions. However, gender is another matter. Students' responses tend to pile up at the gender-makes-a-difference end of the scale. If your students react the same way, ask them why it is relatively obvious to them that they act differently with people of a different gender. (If your students show a very different pattern, write or call us; we'll be curious and help with the interpretation.) Some of the answers you will get will relate to courtship. Men and women, maybe especially the young, single ones, are heavily invested in appearing attractive to the opposite gender. It may also seem important to reaffirm one's own gender identity when confronting the opposite sex. But why the necessity of these reactions? Does it have to be this way? Perhaps you can lead your students to consider the possibility that one's first reactions to a stranger should be founded on appreciation of that person's unique, human characteristics, regardless of gender.

If you have more than one social psychology section, give these scales to one class before they read the text material and one after they have read the text material and participated in relevant classroom events. Results might be interestingly different. Alternatively, one of your classes might complete the scales under the additional instruction, "Respond to these scales according to what you think should be the case, rather than what is the case," and the other class would get no instruction or, "Respond to these scales according to what really is the case, not what should be." Any of these procedures could lead to fruitful exchanges.

3. Before students read this chapter and before it is discussed in class, have students estimate their expected starting salaries and salaries after ten years on the job. A scale is provided in the Student Guide chapter corresponding

to this one. Compare the sexes on estimates to see if results analogous to those of Jackson and Grabski (1988) are produced. If women estimate lower salaries, ask them why. Do the women claim to be realistic and the men assert that they are just reflecting reality? Perhaps you can see in the men's comments that they are playing at, or actually displaying, so-called masculine confidence. Women's responses may reflect lack of confidence, either because it is expected or because it is real. To discover if there is a real difference in confidence, ask the students, "If sexism were dead and gone, would you make different estimates of expected salary?" Perhaps some of the women will say they would raise their estimates, thus indicating that their low estimates resulted from the *expectation* that they will be subjected to discrimination.

4. How do women fare as leaders? Divide your class into approximately equal groups, each group not exceeding five members. Make sure that the number of women in each group is proportional to their number in the class. Appoint men as leaders for half the groups and women for the other half (if asked about the basis of your choices, say that you are choosing arbitrarily). First, have each member complete a map of each person's first name and seating position (maps are included in the Student Guide chapter corresponding to this one). Give each group a social psychology topic to discuss from among those in currently assigned chapters. Have members gain recognition from the leader before they speak and instruct leaders to make a brief comment about each speaker's contribution. Allow at least fifteen minutes for discussion. If you don't normally have class discussion of this sort, say that you are trying a new learning technique. After the discussions, have each member vote for the member who made the greatest contribution to the discussion. There is a suggestion in the literature that you will find leaders getting the most votes, but male leaders do better than female leaders (see Butler & Geis in "Update"). You may also find that female leaders do no better than rank-and-file members.

Film Notes: A Picture Is Sometimes Worth a Thousand Words

The Asianization of America, FC-1912, videotape, (cost to buy: $149; cost to rent: $75), 52 mins. Films for the Humanities and Sciences, Inc., P. O. Box 2053, Princeton, NJ 08543 (800-257-5126). Asians are the nation's fastest growing group. Stereotypes have been revised: love/hate, then condescension, has given way to admiration and jealousy. This tape looks at where it will lead.

Fable of He and She, CSC-2561, film, 15 mins. Indiana University, Audiovisual Center, Bloomington, IN 47401. Cartoon characters portray sex stereotypes,

and in so doing show the absurdities to which we all may be driven by them.

Perceiving and Believing, PB130, videotape, (cost to buy: $89), Insight Media, 121 West 85th Street, New York, NY 10024-4401 (800-233-9910). Ed Asner hosts a video that features dramatic and comic vignettes that show the error of referring to others as "them." Simplistic perceptions and unfair prejudgments are also considered.

Prejudice, videotape, 28.5 mins. To obtain this videotape, consult your Allyn and Bacon sales representative. Robert A. Baron and Margaret Clark use dramatizations as a point of departure for a discussion on prejudice.

Sex Role Development, ESC-1303, film, 30 mins. Indiana University, Audiovisual Center, Bloomington, IN 47401. The influence that sex roles and stereotypes have on people's lives, the way people learn those stereotypes, and new models for behavior are considered in this film.

Prejudice: The Eye of the Storm, PB22, videotape, (cost to buy: $179), 25 mins. Insight Media, 121 West 85th Street, New York, NY 10024-4401 (800-233-9910). Also inquire at Indiana University. This winner of the Peabody Award depicts the classic schoolroom demonstration in which students are divided into blue-eyed and brown-eyed groups, then one group is declared inferior and treated accordingly.

Racism in America, FC-1919, videotape, (cost to buy: $149; cost to rent: $75), 26 mins. Films for the Humanities and Sciences, Inc., P. O. Box 2053, Princeton, NJ 08543 (800-257-5126). The resurgence of bigotry and racially motivated acts of violence and vandalism are graphically depicted.

What's the Difference Being Different? 19511 (videotape) or 1949 (film), (cost to buy: $345; cost to rent: $55), 19 mins. Research Press, Box 3177, Dept. K, Champaign, IL 61821 (217-352-3273). This video (film) shows what multicultural education is all about as it follows an exciting program in the Nashville schools.

Transparencies

5.1 *A Theory of the Relationship Between Racism and Prejudice*

5.2 *Methods of Measuring Prejudice*

5.3 *Theories of Prejudice*

5.4 *The Tendency to View Outgroups as More Homogeneous Than Ingroups: Empirical Evidence*

5.5 *Intergroup Contact: How It Exerts Its Effects*

5.6 *Male and Female Executives: The Stereotype That Failed*

Critical Thinking/Essay Questions

1. Thoroughly describe the relationship between prejudice and discrimination. Under what real-life circumstances will prejudice be expressed or not expressed in discrimination?

2. How do prejudiced attitudes color most of what a bigoted person says and does? Give examples from your own experience, including at least one that involves a subtle form of prejudice.

3. Discuss tokenism and reverse discrimination. Give an example of each from your experience. Tell how both can have benefits and drawbacks for tokens and targets of reverse discrimination.

4. List the principles of realistic conflict theory, then illustrate two of them with examples from your experience.

5. Outline the procedure of the Robbers' Cave experiment. How were us versus them and social competition illustrated by the experiment's results?

6. Use social learning theory as a framework for examining how stereotypes are formed and can become self-fulfilling. Briefly indicate how illusory correlation contributes to stereotypes that would bias jurors in a murder trial where the defendant is black.

7. Pick some group to which you belong and describe the variety of traits that members possess. Do the same for some group to which you do not belong. Look at the difference in descriptions. What do they illustrate?

8. Redesign the eye-of-the-storm demonstration so that it becomes meaningful for a college campus (*hint:* don't use eye or skin color as a basis for discrimination).

9. Choose some habitually conflicting groups and design a way to get them to work together and think differently about each other (*hint:* think of the Italian city study and of the Robbers' Cave experiment).

10. Give some real-life examples of valued traits that are assigned to men and devalued traits that are assigned to women. If you were president of a company, what could you do to redistribute those assignments across your female and male employees?

11. Draw a link between women's low pay and the way their work is credited in terms of luck versus skill. Break that link as you explain why women are doing better on the job today compared to yesterday.

Sources for Lecture

Allen, B. P., & Niss, J. P. (1990). A chill in the college classroom? *Phi Delta Kappan,* April, *71,* 607–609. Following the lead by researchers of elementary and secondary school classrooms, these investigators take probably the first substantive, though tentative, step toward confirming the existence of racism in the college classroom. They also replicate evidence of sexism.

Axtell, R. G. (Ed.) (1985). *Do's and Taboos Around the World.* New York: Wiley Press. This fascinating collection of cultural misunderstandings was compiled for the Parker Pen Company by Roger G. Axtell to help their international staff avoid blunders. It contains many meaningful examples of the need to appreciate cultural diversity.

Carey, J. (1986). Is PMS mental illness? Debate grows. *U. S. News and World Report,* June 26, p. 60. Premenstrual syndrome, the hormonal effects and accompanying cramping and bloating occurring premenstrually, has recently been used in court to excuse violent behavior on the part of female defendants. Will PMS be used in the future as a reason to keep women out of sensitive political and business positions?

Gregor, T. (1979). Short people. *Natural History, 88,* p. 14. If you have suspected that short people are objects of prejudice, you're right, especially if you live in the tropical rain forest of central Brazil.

Harvey, B. (1985). Woman of the eighties: The balancing act. *Psychology Today,* November, p. 80. How does the modern woman handle the new need to achieve and the desire to be mother and homemaker? She tries both.

Polakow-Suransky, S., & Ulaby, N. (1990). Students take action to combat racism. *Phi Delta Kappan,* April, *71,* 601–606. This paper chronicles the study of high school students' prejudices—the study that used the questionnaire found in "Topics for Discussion" above. It shows that students can do something constructive about racism.

Smart-Grosvenor, V. (1983). Obsessed with "racial purity." *Ms.,* June. An obscure Louisiana law, probably dating to the days of slavery, still requires that citizens be classified by "race." Recently, Suzie Guillory Phipps, who thought she was white, discovered she was "colored" when applying for a passport. To make an ugly situation worse, she fought the classification in the courts. Her husband commented, "Hell, she ain't a nigger."

Toch, T., & Davis, J. (1990). Separate but equal all over again. *U. S. News and World Report,* April 23, pp. 37–38. Deja vu. Even in 1990, Louisiana has still not desegregated its colleges and universities. Their case shows that segregation is still very much alive and well.

Update: Current Articles from Professional Sources

Butler, D., & Geis, F. L. (1990). Nonverbal affect responses to male and female leaders: Implications for leadership evaluation. *Journal of Personality and Social Psychology, 58,* 48–59. This study showed that women leaders received more negative affective responses and fewer positive responses than men offering the same suggestions and arguments.

Crocker, J., & Luhtanen, R. (1990). Collective self-esteem and in-group bias. *Journal of Personality and Social Psychology, 58,* 60–67. These researchers postulated that people who are high in trait collective self-esteem should be more likely to react to threats to collective self-esteem by derogating out-groups and enhancing the in-group. Generally, they confirmed this point of view.

Farrell, W., & Jones, C. K. (1988). Recent racial incidents in higher education: A preliminary perspective. *Urban Review—Special Issue: Racial and Ethnic Issues in Higher Education, 20*(3), 265–277. This article gives an overview of minority student experiences and argues that the recent resurgence of racism against minority students on predominantly white campuses was implicitly encouraged by the previous national administration and by majority individuals in leadership roles.

Menchaca, M. (1989). Chicano-Mexican cultural assimilation and Anglo-Saxon cultural dominance. *Hispanic Journal of Behavioral Science, 11*(3), 203–231. This article covers the struggle of Chicanos and Mexicans to maintain their cultural traditions as they are submerged in Anglo culture.

Murstein, B. I., Merighi, J. R., & Malloy, T. E. (1989). Physical attractiveness and exchange theory in interracial dating. *Journal of Social Psychology, 129,* 325–334. The hypothesis that, in interracial courting couples, the black member has to be more physically attractive than the white member was confirmed.

O'Heron, C. A., & Orlofshy, J. L. (1990). Stereotypic

and nonstereotypic sex role trait and behavior orientations, gender identity, and psychological adjustment. *Journal of Personality and Social Psychology, 58,* 134–143. Contrary to other research outcomes, androgynous men and women and cross-sex-typed women were no less well-adjusted than sex-typed individuals. However, low-masculinity men had less secure gender identities. No such gender identity disturbances were found in women.

6

Interpersonal Attraction

Becoming Acquainted, Establishing Friendships

Chapter Outline: Getting the Overall Picture

Learning Objectives

1. Summarize the role played by environmental factors in regulating interpersonal contact.

2. What are the two reasons why propinquity generally fosters interpersonal attraction?

3. Describe negative effects created by repeated exposure.
4. How is interpersonal liking affected by the positive and negative feelings created by such events as transmitting news and listening to music?
5. Summarize the reinforcement-affect model of attraction.
6. Describe characteristics of persons high and low on need for affiliation.
7. Compare the effects of cute or flippant opening lines with innocuous or direct opening lines.
8. How does being in a fear-arousing situation affect people's desire to affiliate?
9. Describe cognitive disregard, and indicate which bodily and behavioral characteristics produce a positive response in others.
10. How are judgments of a person affected if the person has a childlike voice?
11. Discuss stereotypes elicited by clothing, and describe how the behavior of the person wearing the clothes is affected.
12. Describe effects created by physical attractiveness.
13. What attributes are judged to be physically attractive?
14. Summarize research supporting the matching hypothesis.
15. Describe how the proportion of similar attitudes affects liking.
16. Discuss the repulsion hypothesis, and indicate why your text rejects it.
17. What three hypotheses are presented to explain our liking for similar others?
18. List characteristics on which we are attracted to similar others, and note exceptions to the similarity-attraction hypothesis.
19. How is the personality dimension of hypertraditionality related to attraction?
20. Describe how reciprocal positive evaluations create liking.

Topics for Discussion

1. The romantic ideal, the notion that people should marry on the basis of their being "in love," is perhaps more firmly established in the United States than in any other country in the world. Parents still have a great deal to say about the choice of a marriage partner in some countries, and it is even the case that parents arrange marriages in some cultures. An interesting question is the degree to which parents and their children would agree as to the appropriateness of a particular potential mate. Who is in a better position to make a rational choice of a marriage partner—parents or their children? In what ways would their choices be different? Before you begin the discussion, have students indicate their agreement or disagreement with the following statement: "One should not marry against the serious advice of one's parents."

2. Ask students to think of their best friend and to describe how they became friends. Then ask them to describe generally what it is that causes them to choose others as friends. Compare the students' reports to the theories presented in the text. Do they mention propinquity, conditioned emotional responses, similarity, physical attractiveness, reciprocal evaluations, and so on? Are the same factors important early as well as later in a relationship?

3. Researchers disagree about whether love is just an extreme form of liking or whether love and liking are qualitatively different emotions. Zick Rubin distinguishes between liking and loving and has developed separate scales to measure each. Similarly, there is the commonly made distinction between passionate love and companionate love. A good source to read for background information is the book *Liking, Loving and Relating* by Hendrick and Hendrick, published in 1983 by Brooks/Cole. This is the kind of question on which most people have an opinion, so it's important for you to be familiar with the conclusions reached by the experts.

4. Lee has proposed a typology of love that includes six major styles of loving. The styles of loving proposed by Lee (1977) are as follows:

EROS Loving someone primarily because of his or her physical appearance. The Eros lover searches for a person whose physical appearance matches his or her ideal physical type.

LUDUS Playful love. The Ludus lover does not commit to a single relationship, but instead prefers to play the field.

STORGE Loving someone as a result of a slowly developing attachment to that person. The Storge lover moves slowly, carefully, without great passion, to a lasting commitment.

MANIA Intense romantic love. The Mania lover is jealous, thinks intensely and excessively about his or her beloved, and needs repeated reassurance that he or she is loved in return.

AGAPE Altruistic love. Given without expectation of getting anything in return; gentle, caring, and dutiful.

PRAGMA Selecting the "right" person. The Pragma lover looks for someone who has the "right" education, religion, job, and so on.

Lee's typology is presented in an article in *Personality and Social Psychology Bulletin* (3, 173–182). A 1986 article on Lee's typology by the Hendricks is presented in the "Update" section below. Included in the 1986 article is a scale for measuring each of the six types.

5. Does equity theory predict one's level of satisfaction with an intimate relationship? Some theorists have argued that a love relationship in which a partner is concerned about his or her own outcome is flawed. These theorists contend that true love means that the person is concerned only with what they can *give* the partner, and not with what they can *get* from the relationship. On the other hand, equity theorists have maintained that in intimate relationships, just as in other human relationships, people are driven by a desire for equity. In Chapter 6 of the Study Guide, a series of questions is provided for students to assess the degree to which they feel they are being equitably treated in a relationship.

Although a "pure reward" theory might argue that the more one gets for oneself from a relationship, the greater the satisfaction, this doesn't seem to be the case. Instead the most satisfied are those who feel equitably treated. Does your class agree with the equity theory prediction?

Classroom Exercises/Demonstrations

1. An exercise that students can carry out in their everyday environment is to construct a friendship map of their dormitory floor. The maps should be a summary of who is friends with whom. If several students construct maps of their own floors, it would be instructive to combine the information to determine the probability of friendship as a function of propinquity. Are the students surprised to learn how much impact propinquity has on their friendship developments?

2. The text discusses recent work by Craig Hill that proposes that four basic motives underlie the disposition to be affiliative. Hill has developed the Interpersonal Orientation Scale to measure the four motives. The scale is presented in your students' Study Guide in Chapter 6 with permission of Craig A. Hill. You are encouraged to have your students find out how they stand on each of the four motives.

The items for each of the four subscales on the Interpersonal Orientation Scale are as follows:

Items on the Emotional Support Subscale: 1, 4, 9, 15, 17, 23

Items on the Attention Subscale: 5, 8, 16, 19, 21, 22

Items on the Positive Stimulation Subscale: 3, 6, 10, 11, 13, 20, 24, 25, 26

Items on the Social Comparison Subscale: 2, 7, 12, 14, 18

Scores for each subscale are computed by first converting the alphabetic letters on the scales to numeric values: A = 1, B = 2, C = 3, D = 4, E = 5. Then, add the numeric values together for the items listed for each subscale.

3. Some theorists have discussed a phenomenon they call *romanticism*. Romanticism tends to have two components. One is a belief that "love will conquer all" and the other is that one should marry for love. In Chapter 6 of the Study Guide you will find examples of statements used to assess people's degree of romanticism. For each of the five statements, the respondent should indicate his or her degree of agreement. One's score is determined by adding up the responses. Before the responses are added, items 1 and 3 should be reversed (i.e., agreement with items 2, 4, and 5 indicates a romantic attitude, whereas disagreement with items 1 and 3 indicates a romantic attitude). What are the consequences of a belief in romanticism?

4. This exercise is designed to test the hypothesis that similarity and attraction are related. The text devotes much attention to the similarity-attraction hypothesis. This exercise provides very reliable data, and generally serves as an interesting introduction to the chapter.

An Adjective Checklist for use in conducting the exercise is presented in Chapter 6 of the Study Guide. Students are instructed to go through the list of adjectives three times. First, they should go through the list and check those adjectives that describe themselves. Second, they should think of their best friends and check the traits that apply. Finally, in the third column they should check the traits that apply to a person they know, but with whom they could never be friends.

After the students have completed the Checklist, have them count the number of traits in common between self and friend. A trait in common occurs whenever a trait is checked for both self and friend, or whenever a trait is unchecked for both. Likewise, have them count the number of traits in common between self and nonfriend. You will find that students have more in common with their friends than with their nonfriends.

5. Jeffrey Simpson of Texas A & M has published a survey in *Teaching of Psychology* (15[1], 31–33) that assesses past dating behavior and willingness to change partners, both of which are components of commitment to relationships. The dating survey is found in your students' Study Guide. On the basis of their responses to the survey, students are placed into one of three categories. Students who answer "yes" to the first question on the survey (i.e., those who are dating one person exclusively) are referred to as "exclusive daters." Students who answer "no" to the first question but "yes" to the third one (i.e., those who are not dating one person exclusively but who have dated at least two people in the past year) are referred to as "multiple daters." Those who respond "no" to both questions because they are married or because they do not date cannot provide data for classroom analysis. However, Simpson found that only 15 percent to 20 percent of undergraduates enrolled in daytime courses typically fall into this third category. Even though these students cannot provide data for the exercise themselves, they still find the exercise to be interesting and valuable.

Once students have completed the dating survey, the next step is to find out whether commitment in dating relationships is related to the widely studied individual difference dimension of self-monitoring. Two studies published by Snyder and Simpson (1984) in *Journal of Personality & Social Psychology* (*47*, 1281–1291) found that high self-monitors typically adopt an uncommitted orientation to dating relationships, whereas low self-moni-

tors tend to adopt a committed one. The Self-Monitoring Scale is found in Chapter 12 of this Instructor's Manual. After students have completed and scored the Self-Monitoring Scale, determine whether you have replicated the self-monitoring results of Snyder and Simpson. Create four columns on the chalkboard, one for each of the following groups: high self-monitoring/exclusive daters; high self-monitoring/multiple daters; low self-monitoring/exclusive daters; and low self-monitoring/multiple daters. Two comparisons are especially suggested. First, using only exclusive daters, compare the number of months in the relationship for high and low self-monitors. The expectation is that low self-monitors will remain in relationships longer. Second, using only multiple daters, compare the number of partners for high and low self-monitors. The expectation is that high self-monitors will report a higher number of partners. Detailed suggestions regarding how to analyze and present the data to your class is found in the *Teaching of Psychology* article mentioned above.

Film Notes: A Picture Is Sometimes Worth a Thousand Words

Are We Still Going to the Movies? 21730, 1974, color, 14 mins. Pennsylvania State University, Audiovisual Services, Special Services Building, University Park, PA 16802 (814-865-6314). A young couple's relationship is suffering as a result of their disagreement on the amount of sexual involvement to have with each other. Intended to provoke discussion of premarital sexuality and sex roles. From the *Conflict and Awareness* series. Produced by Tom Lazarus.

Beauty Knows No Pain, 31910, 1973, color, 25 mins. Pennsylvania State University, Audiovisual Services, Special Services Building, University Park, PA 16802 (814-865-6314). Coeds aspiring to join the Kilgore College majorettes submit to the ordeal of training and testing. Reactions of both winners and losers show the value that the "Rangerette" ideal holds for them. Produced by Elliott Erwitt.

Divorce: For Better or for Worse, Parts 1 and 2, 50423, 1976, color, 51 mins. Pennsylvania State University, Audiovisual Services, Special Services Building, University Park, PA 16802 (814-865-6314). Divorce is "a kind of death," according to one of the narrators, a form of saying good-bye that entails grief and restructuring of lives and that touches most of us in some way. Film focuses on actual case histories of the divorced and divorcing to show emotional and financial toll, need for legal reform, and stricter regulation of counselors and therapists. From the ABC News "Closeup" series.

Kinds of Love, NET 2037, 29 mins., Audiovisual Center,

Indiana University, Bloomington, IN 47401. In interviews with Father Thurston David and Erich Fromm, misconceptions about love, the relationship between sexuality and love, and love as a religious virtue are discussed.

Love and Sex (from Phil Donahue's "The Human Animal" series), EC-1132, VHS or Beta videotape, color. Falling in love, having sex, making babies—these are easy. Understanding human sexuality is much harder. Phil Donahue takes viewers on an odyssey showing women at a male strip club and a gay rights march, into a hospital room where an unwed teenage mother is giving birth, and into the classroom where teachers and parents are trying to help teenagers come to grips with their sexual selves. Love, monogamy, hetero- and homosexuality are among the topics covered by Donahue, consultants Dr. William Masters of the Masters & Johnson Institute and Dr. June Reinisch of the Kinsey Institute, and by Donahue's best resource, ordinary people. 52 mins.

Love Tapes, MVCS-1034, 1980, videocassette, 30 mins. Pennsylvania State University, Audiovisual Services, Special Services Building, University Park, PA 16802 (814-865-6314). A series of three-minute statements by people from all walks of life who candidly record their feelings about love against background music of their own choosing. Included are Darrell, a black college student, afraid of love; Darlene, unloved as a child, who finds that men treat her callously; Rose, in her eighties, recalling her changing needs; and

Frieda, a disabled professor, who struggles for self-worth. The tapes were recorded as part of an experimental video art project that involved the installation of video recording equipment in museums and other public places. Produced by Wendy Clarke.

Morning After, 1983, color, 17 mins., Filmmakers Library, Inc., 133 East 58th Street, New York, NY 10022. Shows the vulnerability of a seemingly cool, sophisticated man to the breakup of a long-term relationship.

Transparencies

6.1 *The Reinforcement-Affect Model of Attraction*

6.2 *The Three-Factor Theory of Passionate Love*

Critical Thinking/Essay Questions

1. Summarize the effect that repeated exposure to a stranger has on our liking for the stranger. How is the repeated exposure effect related to the propinquity phenomenon?
2. How is interpersonal liking affected by the mood induced by music and news content? How does the reinforcement-affect model account for these results?
3. Describe ways in which behavior and self-esteem are affected by whether one is physically attractive.
4. Summarize the role of personality similarity, behavioral similarity, and need compatibility/need complementarity on liking.
5. Describe the three factors that seem to be necessary for a person to experience passionate love.

Sources for Lecture

Cash, T. F., & Janda, L. H. (1984). In the eye of the beholder. *Psychology Today,* December, pp. 46–52. Attractive women are preferred for dates, friendships, and jobs. On the job, however, women are perceived more positively if they do not look too feminine.

Davis, K. E. (1985). Near and dear: Friendship and love compared. *Psychology Today,* February, pp. 22–30. Friendship and love have much in common, but there are two additional clusters of factors that are typical of love: a "passion cluster" and a "caring cluster."

Fischer, C. (1983). The friendship cure-all. *Psychology Today,* January, pp. 74–78. The California State Department of Mental Health conducted an advertising campaign to convince people to develop their social relationships. This article takes a critical look at the campaign.

Hamburger, A. C. (1988). Beauty quest. *Psychology Today,* May, pp. 29–32. The authors note that cosmetic surgery to improve looks and figures is more common than ever before. What can people expect after undergoing such surgery? Oftentimes, people expect too much!

Lynn, M., & Shurgot, B. A. Responses to lonely hearts advertisements: Effects of reported physical attractiveness, physique, and coloration. *Personality and Social Psychology Bulletin, 10* (3), 349–357. Lynn and Shurgot analyzed personal ads, the lonely hearts classifieds, that appeared in a Columbus, Ohio, monthly. They tabulated the number of responses to each ad to determine what characteristics were most appealing to potential romantic partners.

Meer, J. (1985). The dating game: Ladies' choice. *Psychology Today,* March, p. 16. How a woman can ask for a date and not be seen as making a sexual advance. Meer summarizes research by Muehlenhard et al. suggesting that what she should do is emphasize her intelligence.

Rubenstein, C. (1983). Love and romance: A *Psychology Today* reader survey. *Psychology Today,* February, pp. 60–64. A questionnaire is presented that surveys the current status of love and romance.

Trotter, R. J. (1986). The three phases of love. *Psychology Today,* September, pp. 46–54. Sternberg's three-sided theory of love is summarized. The components? Commitment, intimacy, and passion.

Update: Current Articles from Professional Sources

Bluhm, C., Widiger, T. A., & Miele, G. M. (1990). Interpersonal complementarity and individual differences. *Journal of Personality and Social Psychology, 58,* 464–471. Interpersonal circumplex theory predictions regarding interpersonal complementarity were tested. The research tested whether the fact that friendliness evokes friendly behavior and dominance evokes submission is consistent with this theory, and the circumstances under which this is true.

Collins, N. L., & Read, S. J. (1990). Adult attachment, working models, and relationship quality in dating couples. *Journal of Personality and Social Psychology, 58,* 644–663. A scale was developed to measure the styles of adult attachment. These attachment styles were then related to how the self was viewed and also to the quality of ongoing dating relationships.

Feeney, J. A., & Noller, P. (1990). Attachment style as a predictor of adult romantic relationships. *Journal of Personality and Social Psychology, 58,* 281–291. Securely attached, avoidant, and anxious-ambivalent subjects were studied to see whether this perspective is useful in understanding adult romantic relationships. Attachment style was related to self-esteem and to various forms of love discussed in other theoretical frameworks.

Hendrick, C., & Hendrick, S. (1986). A theory and method of love. *Journal of Personality and Social Psychology, 50,* 392–402. The research extends Lee's theory of six basic love styles: Eros, Ludus, Storge, Pragma, Mania, and Agape. A questionnaire for measuring each of the love styles is presented, along with the correlates of various love styles.

Langlois, J. H., & Roggman, L. A. (1990). Attractive faces are only average. *Psychological Science, 2,* 115ff. Computer-generated composite faces that represented the average value of the population were consistently judged as attractive. This finding was interpreted to be consistent with both evolutionary pressures that favor characteristics close to the population mean and cognitive processes that favor prototypical category members.

7

Close Relationships

Friendship, Love, Intimacy, and Marriage

Chapter Outline: Getting the Overall Picture

I. Interdependent Relationships: Beyond Casual
   A. Varieties of Close Relationships: Friends, Romantic Partners, and Relatives
   B. Passion and Romance: It's So Easy to Fall in Love
      1. Defining and Measuring Passionate Love
      2. Love or Lust?
   C. A Theory of Passionate Love
      1. Learning About Love
      2. Encountering an Appropriate Love Object
      3. Arousal As the Basis of Love
   D. Kinds of Love: Let Me Count the Ways
      1. Companionate Love—A Close, Caring Friendship
      2. A Six-Part Model of Love
      3. Love As a Triangle
      4. Why Do People Differ in the Kinds of Relationships They Form?
   E. Life Without a Relationship: Loneliness
      1. Childhood Sources of Loneliness
      2. Interpersonal Behavior and Loneliness
      3. Overcoming the Causes of Loneliness

II. Establishing and Maintaining Close Relationships: It's Not So Easy
   A. Sexual Intimacy Before Marriage: The Times Are A' Changin'
      1. The Sexual Revolution
      2. Postrevolution Sexuality
      3. Premarital Sex: Effects on Later Marriages?
   B. Marriage: Happily Ever After?
      1. Is Marriage Less Fun Than It Used to Be?
      2. Threats to a Relationship: Jealousy

III. Troubled Relationships: Failure Is Painful
   A. Problems in Relationships
      1. Sources of Male-Female Conflicts
      2. The Discovery of Existing Dissimilarities and the Development of New Ones
      3. Boredom
      4. Replacing Positive Evaluations with Negative Ones
   B. Deterioration of a Relationship: When a Couple Moves Toward Dissolution
      1. Danger Signs in a Relationship
      2. Responding to Relationship Problems
      3. Breakup and Divorce

Learning Objectives

1. Learn some elements of various close relationships. Among the relationships investigated by Berscheid, Snyder, and Omoto (1989b), which was judged

closest by subjects and how was closeness related to breaking up?

2. Under what circumstances does friendship become

love? Be able to contrast friendship with love and to describe passionate love as it relates to sexual desire.

3. Be able to trace the history of the notion of love. What does "gazing into one another's eyes" do to passionate feelings?

4. Be able to describe Buss's evolutionary theory of love.

5. How do males and females differ in the age ranges that are most preferred in a partner? Describe how equity theory explains this difference.

6. Learn the basics of the misattribution theory of love and contrast it with the reinforcement model, as well as the response-facilitation model.

7. Appreciate the problems of love in the workplace. How does sexual harassment rear its ugly head on the job and on campus?

8. Be able to describe companionate love and Hendrick and Hendrick's six types of love, as well as the three sides of the triangle of love. What happens when the triangle is unbalanced?

9. Learn the three ways that people attach themselves to their parents and relate them to loneliness. How is loneliness measured and what is it related to? Be able to describe the childhood sources of loneliness, the cognitive therapy and social skills training methods for overcoming loneliness, and the traits of lonely people, as well as to indicate how interpersonal behavior relates to loneliness.

10. What was the sexual revolution and what's its legacy in terms of attitudes, behavior, and permissiveness? How do men and women differ in how they regard sexual relationships and in the sexual interactions they prefer?

11. How does premarital sex later affect marriage? What proportion of people want to get married and what proportion are happy they did? Learn how men and women have taken to women's role as "co-breadwinner."

12. Learn how jealousy is defined, how it affects jealous people's relationships, their feelings, thoughts, and behaviors. To whom does the jealous person direct his or her jealousy-related feelings, thoughts, and behaviors?

13. Be able to contrast the Soviet Union and its former satellite nations and the Netherlands with regard to what makes inhabitants jealous.

14. What are the sources of conflict between romantic partners? How does Buss explain these differences? How do hidden and late-blooming dissimilarities affect relationships?

15. What does boredom do to a relationship and how is it overcome? Appreciate what factors cause positive evaluations of spouses to be replaced with negative ones and how attributions change in a deteriorating marriage.

16. What are the stages through which relationships go?

17. What may keep relationships together even though they are not going well? What are the categories of responses to disharmony in a relationship and how does self-esteem determine which category people choose?

18. Be able to give some examples of what happens when love is strong or weak and the relationship ends. How does what people observe about others' relationships affect their own relationships?

19. What did the Lauers find regarding what makes marriages work when they investigated 351 mostly happily married couples? Learn what strategy is likely not to pay off when trouble happens and appreciate how reexamining the factors that may have led to marriage in the first place can rekindle a barely smoldering relationship.

20. What is the prevalence of divorce and when is it most likely to happen? How are children affected by divorce? When people divorce, what happens in the remarriage realm?

🔲 *Topics for Discussion*

1. Prenuptial agreements have become familiar to the public since several famous media stars revealed that they sought to avoid large settlements in the event of divorce by drawing up marriage-dissolution papers before their vows were taken. A related phenomenon may be the wave of the future: marriage contracts. See A. K. Shulman, A marriage agreement, in A. Jaggar and D. Rothenberg, eds., *Feminist frameworks* (New York: McGraw-Hill, 311–315). One of the components of such a contract might be division of labor: who will do what housework and which child-care duties. Prime the students with this information. Then give each student about twenty minutes to write up what would be an ideal contract from his or her point of view. Next, have students indicate the aspects of marriage they have covered in their contracts and write them on the chalkboard (e.g., sexual fidelity, allocation of house space, provisions for continuation of hobbies and interests, and so on). After having determined what aspects are included in students' contracts, ask students to provide examples of provisions they have included in their contracts that relate to these aspects (tell them they may not wish to reveal sensitive information). With this information in hand, a lively discussion should ensue.

2. The fact that chance may play a role in deciding whom one marries may be unsettling to students. They are apt to think that someone is predestined to be their "one and only" or that they will carefully sort through candidate partners to find the one that suits them best. In fact, as Albert Bandura (1982) pointed out some time ago (*American Psychologist, 37,* 747–755), pure chance will in great part determine whom one marries. Ask several students to indicate how their parents came to know each other well enough to end up married. Write the examples on the chalkboard until you have several that involve pure chance (e.g., "My dad was driving home from a business meeting and had a car wreck. He was hurt bad and spent several weeks in a hospital outside a small town he had never heard of before. While there he met my mother; she nursed him back to health. Six months later, they were married"). Now go back to these examples of chance and point them out to students. Be ready for arguments about the difference between chance and destiny!

3. How do parents figure into a romantic relationship? There is a thing called the "Romeo and Juliet Effect": interference by parents may actually drive lovers closer together (see Driscoll et al., [1972], *Journal of Personality and Social Psychology, 24,* 1–10). Ask students to indicate their direct and indirect experience with parental interference in romantic relationships. Determine whether there is a pattern fitting the Romeo and Juliet effect. If you refer only to cases of interference that occurred *before* marriage, you will probably find support for the effect. If you

do, identify the effect and inform students that their experience confirms it. If you do not, students will be interested in the observation that their experience is an exception to the Romeo and Juliet "rule." In any case, it will be informative to have students speculate concerning why parental interference tore apart, bonded together, or had no effect on the romantic relationships in their experience (e.g., if increased closeness occurred, did the parties involved misattribute the arousal because of parental meddling to love?).

4. To get at the notion of what constitutes a friend, it is helpful to discover what is not a friend (see friendship chapter in Allen, [1990] *Personal adjustment,* Pacific Grove, CA: Brooks/Cole, for details). Have students discuss each of the following, indicating the nature of each and telling why each is not "true friendship." Then, end the discussion by concluding what is true friendship. Acquaintance (passersby, coworkers, schoolmates), neighbors, confederates (two people engaged in some joint enterprise in which each bears a symbiotic relationship with the other but has little connection outside of the pursuit: robbing banks; selling cars; working for the homeless), pals (they have some activity in common such as beer buddies, horse lovers, or shopping companions), close kin, convenience friends (trade babysitting chores, borrow from one another, share rides to work), and mentor (usually an older person who "shows the ropes" to an up-and-coming neophyte).

Classroom Exercises/Demonstrations

1. According two recent *Psychology Today* surveys, it is young people, adolescents and young adults, not elderly people, who are the loneliest (also see Allen, [1990], *Personal adjustment,* Pacific Grove, CA: Brooks/Cole). And loneliness is a personality trait that matters: as indicated in the text, it is related to important matters such as health. You can get your students to open up about the issue. You might begin by having them indicate what it is like to be lonely. An exercise included in the Student Guide chapter corresponding to this one can help. Students could do the Robert Weiss exercise in class before an exchange of experiences begins. After the exercise and any student testimonials, ask students why young people are the most lonely. Relate loneliness to shyness and introversion. Have students come up with solutions to the problem.

2. Jealousy is literally fascinating to students. One of the manual authors has always preceded class discussion on the topic by having students complete the Mathes Jealousy Scale (included in the Student Guide in the chapter that corresponds to this one). After completing it, they have a reasonably good grasp of the nature of jealousy. A spirited interchange follows. Have students pick out the components of jealousy, such as possessiveness and sus-

piciousness. Then ask them to indicate how jealousy disrupts romantic relationships. Also, inquire whether there is a good side to jealousy (Mathes believes that the nonegocentric side of jealousy—fear of losing the rewards associated with a relationship—may actually be good for relationships). Students sometimes linger after class wanting to know more and many of them have asked for additional copies of the scale.

To calculate their scores, instruct students to put minuses in front of the scale numbers assigned to Items 5, 6, 11, 16, 18, 19, and 21, then add numbers algebraically. The higher the score, the more the jealousy.

3. Early in the process of considering friendship, have students complete the What Kind of a Friend Is Your Friend Scale found in the Student Guide chapter corresponding to this one. This exercise will sensitize them to the meaning of friendship and prime them for the classroom exchange to follow. To set the stage for further consideration of friendship, gently ask students to volunteer information concerning how well their friendship rated. You may see a gender difference here: women's friendships may well come out better. Also, there may be some surprise value: some students' friendships may not fare as

well as they expected. If so, it will be a propitious occasion for considering how to make friendships better.

Students who checked all the items are surely true friends. However, certain items are critical. For those who checked Items 4 and 6, whether they checked the others does not matter so much. They may consider themselves involved in true friendship. Those who failed to check one of these items, or especially those who checked neither item, have reason to wonder whether they have a true friendship.

4. The next exercise is to be introduced after students have read text information about friendship and have considered friendship in class. At this point, it is time to consider ideal friendship. You can see how much students have learned about friendship—more important, they can find out for themselves—by having them complete the Rate Your Friendship Scale. Have them imagine an ideal friend, then complete the scale with that friend in mind. The goal is to score as high as is possible. The higher the score, the more students have grasped the qualities of true friendship. Again, the scale is found in the Student Guide chapter corresponding to this one.

The Rate Your Friendship Scale is a test of quality of friendship. Have students count the leftmost scale as 8, then number to the right so that the rightmost point is 1. Next, for each scale, have them write down the value of the scale points that they have checked. Finally, have them add their scale scores over the ten scales. If they score 70 to 80, their grasp of the qualities of friendship is very good. Those who score 10 to 20 have a poor grasp. 60 to 70 and 30 to 20 may also be interpreted as high and low scores, respectively.

Film Notes: A Picture Is Sometimes Worth a Thousand Words

Are We Still Going to the Movies? 21730, film 14 mins. Pennsylvania State University, Audiovisual Services, Special Services Building, University Park, PA 16802 (814-865-6314). A young couple's relationship is suffering as a result of their disagreement on the amount of sexual involvement.

Divorce: For Better or for Worse, Parts 1 & 2, 50423, film, 51 mins. Pennsylvania State University, Audiovisual Services, Special Services Building, University Park, PA 16802 (814-865-6314). The focus is on actual case histories of divorced and divorcing couples and the emotional as well as financial toll that divorce exacts.

*Friendship, videotape, 28.5 mins. To obtain this tape, see your Allyn and Bacon sales representative. A dramatization leads Robert A. Baron and Margaret Clark to an in-depth discussion of friendship, especially as it differs for men and women.

Kinds of Love, Net 2037, film, 29 mins. Audiovisual Center, Indiana University, Bloomington, IN 47401. In interviews with Father Thurston David and Eric Fromm, misconceptions about love, the relationship between sexuality and love, and love as a religious virtue are discussed.

Love and Sex, FC1132, videotape (cost to rent: $75; cost to buy: $179), 52 mins. Films for the Humanities and Sciences, P.O. Box 2053, Princeton, NJ 08543 (800-257-5126). This is possibly the best of Phil Donohue's excellent "The Human Animal" series. Here love and sex, including their joys and heartbreaks, are covered in poignant fashion.

Love Tapes, MVCS-1034, videotape, 30 mins. Pennsylvania State University, Audiovisual Services, Special Services Building, University Park, PA 16802 (814-865-6314). An interesting and varied sample of people talk candidly about their experiences with love.

Morning After, film, 17 mins. Filmmakers Library, Inc., 133 East 58th Street, New York, NY 10022. Shows the vulnerability of a seemingly cool, sophisticated man to the breakup of a long-term relationship.

The Sexual Brain, EC1738, videotape (cost to rent: $75; cost to buy: $149), 28 mins. Films for the Humanities and Sciences, P.O. Box 2053, Princeton, NJ 08543 (800-257-5126). The battle of the sexes that sometimes ends in marriage, sometimes in friendship, and sometimes in mutual rejection starts with the brain. This tape ends with questions about the structural and reproductive roots of the differences between the sexes.

Transparencies

7.1 *Reinforcement-Affect Theory: How Some Relationships May Start*

7.2 *An Unromantic Explanation of Passionate Love*

7.3 *Levinger's Theory That Relationships Pass Through Five Stages from Beginning to End*

7.4 *Sternberg's "Triangular Model of Love"*

7.5 *Relationships Among Findings in the Lauer's Study of 351 Married Couples*

Critical Thinking/Essay Questions

1. Consider the Berscheid, Snyder, and Omoto (1989b) study of close relations among college students. What kind of relationship was closest for these students and what kind lasted longest? Was there a gender difference in perceived closeness of closest relationships?

2. Contrast friendship and romantic love. What does each have that the other lacks? Also contrast romantic love in general with the more specific variety of love, passionate love.

3. Give the major characteristics of misattribution theory, reinforcement theory, and response-facilitation theory. Pick out one aspect of each that makes it different from the others.

4. Take a look at love in the workplace. How can attempts to establish passionate relationships at work go astray? Indicate how love between mutually consenting workers may create problems in the workplace.

5. Describe the six types of love that can result when one or two sides of Sternberg's triangle dominate the others. How do these compare with Hendrick and Hendrick's six types of love?

6. Indicate how the stage is set for loneliness during childhood. What are lonely people like in terms of traits and social behavior and what can be done to change them in a way that is likely to lessen loneliness?

7. Some say the sexual revolution has come and gone. What was beneficial about it and what was detrimental? Contrast the revolution period with today's orientation to sexual matters.

8. Describe the way marriage has changed over the last two decades. How have men and women's views of marriage changed in different directions? What must be shared among spouses in the future if the trend toward marital problems is to be halted?

9. Describe a jealous person. What will that individual's characteristics be? How will her or his behavior interfere with romantic relationships and friendships? What aspects of this person will be most in need of change?

10. What happens when boredom sets in during the course of a marriage? What makes it happen and how can it be corrected? What are the factors that cause dissimilarities to arise during marriage and can the development of negative attributions be short-circuited?

11. What are the sources of disharmony in a relationship and how does self-esteem relate to them? Contrast a relationship that ends well and one that doesn't. What's the major difference?

12. What makes for long-lasting, happy marriages? How can reexamination of the very factors that lead to spouses selecting each other possibly save their marriages?

13. Examine divorce and remarriage. How likely is divorce? Is divorce more or less likely in the case of a second marriage compared to a first? Indicate a major effect of divorce on children.

Sources for Lecture

Budiansky, S. (1987). All by your lonesome. *U.S. News and World Report*, May 4, p. 71. This report summarizes research on what it is like to be isolated.

Fuhr, J. (1987). Standardization of divorce mediation. *Conciliation Courts Review*, 25, 65–67. Mediation between spouses in the event of divorce proceedings is becoming a hot issue in psychology. Mediation can sometimes stop divorce before it is final. If not, it can lead to more amenable agreements. This article concentrates on the child custody aspect of divorce settlement.

Roberts, M. (1988). Be all that you can be. *Psychology Today*, March, pp. 28–29. As the text indicates, one of the major problems facing lonely people is lack of the kinds of skills that allow success in general and social success in particular. This article indicates which, among the several self-improvement methods available, really does work.

Tan, N-T. (1988). Developing and testing a family mediation assessment instrument. *Mediation Quarterly*, Spring, 53–67. The focus here is on an instrument to assess couples who present themselves for mediation. It reveals some dimensions that are important to the mediation process.

Tavris, C. (1988). Coping with jealousy. *Psychology Today*, November, p. 302. Carol Tavris is well known for her theorizing about anger. More recently, she has turned her attention to jealousy. Here she provides useful information about coping with jealousy.

INSTRUCTOR'S SECTION

Update: Current Articles from Professional Sources

Caspi, A., & Herbener, E. (1990). Continuity and change: Assortative marriage and the consistency of personality in adulthood. *Journal of Personality and Social Psychology, 58,* 250–258. Selecting a marital partner who is similar to oneself promotes consistency of personality organization over the middle adult years.

de Jong-Gierveld, J. (1987). Developing and testing a model of loneliness. *Journal of Personality and Social Psychology, 53,* 119–128. A model of loneliness involving the factors of social network, background variables, personality traits, and evaluative aspects was well fitted to the data of this study.

Feeney, J. A., & Noller, P. (1990). Attachment style as a predictor of adult romantic relationships. *Journal of Personality and Social Psychology, 58,* 281–291. This strong research replicates and extends Philip Shaver and colleagues' earlier work and, thereby, lends considerable credibility to the same.

Mikulincer, M., Florian, V., & Tolmacz, R. (1990). Attachment styles and fear of personal death: A case study of affect regulation. *Journal of Personality and Social Psychology, 58,* 273–280. Attachment styles have many implications. In this study, ambivalent subjects exhibited stronger overt fear of death than did secure and avoidant subjects, and both ambivalent and avoidant subjects showed stronger fear of death at a low level of awareness than secure subjects.

INSTRUCTOR'S SECTION

8

Social Influence

Changing Others' Behavior

Chapter Outline: Getting the Overall Picture

I. Conformity: How Groups Exert Influence
   A. Factors Affecting Conformity: Cohesiveness, Group Size, Social Support, and Gender
      1. Cohesiveness and Conformity: Accepting Influences from Those We Like
      2. Conformity and Group Size: Why "More" Isn't Always "Better" with Respect to Social Influence
      3. The Effects of Support from Others: When Having an Ally Helps
      4. Gender Differences in Conformity: Evidence Against Their Existence
   B. The Bases of Conformity: Why We Often Choose to Go Along
      1. The Desire to Be Liked: Normative Social Influence
      2. The Desire to Be Right: Informational Social Influence

   C. The Need for Individuation and the Need for Control: Why, Sometimes, We Choose Not to Go Along
   D. Minority Influence: One More Reason Why the Majority Doesn't Always Rule

II. Compliance: to Ask—Sometimes—Is to Receive
   A. Ingratiation: Liking As a Basis for Influence
   B. Multiple Requests: Two Steps to Compliance
      1. The Foot-in-the-Door: Small Request First, Large Request Second
      2. The Door-in-the-Face: Large Request First, Small Request Second

III. Obedience: Social Influence By Demand
   A. Destructive Obedience: Some Basic Findings
   B. Destructive Obedience: Why Does It Occur?
   C. Destructive Obedience: Resisting Its Effects

Learning Objectives

1. Learn what conformity means and how social norms play a role in it. How does conformity prevent social chaos but not necessarily be helpful?
2. Be able to describe Asch's experimental method for studying conformity. What percent of his subjects conformed at least once and what percent not at all?
3. Appreciate the difference between public compliance and private acceptance.

4. Be able to discuss the importance of cohesiveness in determining whether group members will conform. How did Crandall's (1988) study of sorority members show the effects of cohesiveness on the adoption of binge eating?
5. Understand the Social Influence Model (SIM) that explains the relationship between the number of influence sources and the number of targets.

6. Be able to explain why and under what conditions having an ally when one is in the minority helps in resisting conformity pressure.

7. What do the early studies say about gender differences in conformity? How does confidence in knowing appropriate behavior explain why one gender conformed more than the other in early studies (refer to Sistrunk and McDavid [1971]).

8. Know why the presumed status of women may be the reason some studies have shown more conformity by them. What are the implications of the observation that both sexes use the same tactics in attempts to influence others?

9. Appreciate the observation that normative social influence—the desire to be liked—and informational social influence—the desire to be right—are two of the reasons that we tend to go along with everyone else.

10. Be able to describe the procedures of Zimbardo's prison experiment, including dress of both prisoners and guards and treatment of prisoners. How did the prisoners and guards react to these procedures? What are the criticisms of the study?

11. Be able to explain the role of the need for uniqueness and of the desire for control in the tendency sometimes to disagree with the group. How did Burger (1987) experimentally illustrate the effects of desire for control?

12. What famous figures in history had unanimous majorities against them, but doggedly stuck with their unusual ideas anyway? Be able to outline the four "rules" that minorities must follow if they are going to influence the majority successfully. How does attribution theory help us to understand minority influence?

13. How do minorities exert influence even when they don't change their overt behavior?

14. Be able to define *compliance* and its most obvious variety, *ingratiation*. Know the target-directed and impression-management methods of getting others to comply and the conditions in which they are likely to work or to backfire.

15. Understand what the foot-in-the-door method entails and the conditions under which it is likely to work or not to work. What are the two prominent explanations why the method works and what is the evidence to support their efficacy (mention the investigation of children)?

16. Know what goes into the door-in-the-face technique, and the two explanations why it works.

17. Does one of the two major compliance techniques have an advantage over the other? How does the time interval between requests, whether the two requests are made by the same or different persons, and the legitimacy of the requester influence the effectiveness of the two methods differently (use the Patch [1986] study to illustrate)?

18. Be able to explain how TNA ("That's not all!") works by outlining the procedure and results of Burger's (1986) cookie-cupcake sale study. Why does TNA work?

19. Know the definition of obedience and the basic procedure that Stanley Milgram used to study it.

20. What did Milgram find in his basic study and in the variations of it? What are the three primary reasons why people obey, and the four avenues to resistance?

21. Be able to outline the changes that have occurred in Eastern Europe, what people did to bring about these changes, and what social psychological principles they demonstrated in bringing about the change.

Topics for Discussion

1. One day in class, begin to reseat class members arbitrarily. Giving no reason, curtly order some to sit in the front row and others to sit in the back, while placing some on the aisle and some in the center. Reshuffle again, until someone asks, "Why?" Discuss what was going through subjects' minds as they were arbitrarily pushed and pulled about and why they complied. Was it thoughtless obedience? to save you embarrassment? to save themselves embarrassment by avoiding the question, "Why?" some hypothesis about your reasons? or, responses to pressure that seemed to be exerted by students who were obeying quickly and efficiently? More generally, ask students what aspects of your characteristics and other students' behavior led to initial obedience. Also, ask students under what circumstances might all or most of them refuse immediately or continue to obey without asking why (one of our former colleagues, a behavior modification expert, ordered opposite-sexed students who were signed up for a weight-loss/behavior modification class to disrobe in preparation for a weigh-in. They began to comply so quickly and in such large numbers that the colleague had trouble stopping them with assurances that it was just a joke!).

2. Begin a lecture by speaking in an unusually low voice, almost approaching a whisper. Tape the session without students' knowledge by placing a tape recorder where only you can see it. Elicit questions and comments from class members (subtly record the tape counter numbers at which given students' voices are recorded; also record the counter number when you terminate the taped session). As the lecture continues, slowly begin to raise your voice until it is well above its normal level, again asking for questions and comments. First, ask students if they were aware of anything unusual. Play the tape to demonstrate conformity to your voice level. Before revealing what is reflected on the tape, ask students if they are, at this point, aware of conforming to subtle pressure applied by you. Some will say yes; then ask them to indicate the form of their conformity. If they have trouble, cue them by making reference to your voice amplitude. Pick out a few students you have on the tape and ask each if he or she showed conformity. If a given one denies it, play the tape back for her or him. Now you are ready to talk about the sometimes unconscious nature of conformity. Playing the very beginning and the very ending of the tape will make your point and stimulate further discussion.

3. A class discussion of the ethical implications associated with various sales techniques should be enlightening. Methods such as the door-in-the-face and the foot-in-the-door could be considered legal confidence games. The way to avoid being duped by these methods is to understand at a commonsense level how users of them deceive us. Just what are the deceptions involved with such methods? The answers come from a real-life understanding of the theoretical explanations why these methods work. By probing students for off-the-top-of-the-head explanations, you can make them arrive at the theories themselves. Using the foot-in-the-door technique as an example, if a student says, "He [the requester] is getting me to grant a small request so I'll look at myself and think, 'I must be a pretty good person to help somebody out like this,'" point out the implications for self-perception. If another exclaims, "After I grant the first small request and she [the requester] heaps lavish praise on me, she will expect that I'll get addicted to granting requests, then, zap, the big one comes," point out how this statement fits the positive view of helping explanation. Use a similar strategy for the foot-in-the-door technique. By probing for everyday explanations that fit the relevant theories, you will allow your students to gain a first-hand appreciation of sales techniques. More important, this level of awareness will allow them to resist these methods.

4. Have students discuss subtle methods of ingratiation that are not explicitly covered in the text, but follow the principles of ingratiation, such as encouraging another person to talk about himself. Salespeople use these methods as well. Cue students concerning the talk about self method by asking, "If you wanted to get someone to feel good about themselves in your presence so you will get credit you can use at request time, but want to be sure that you don't look like a flatterer, what could you do to pump up his or her ego?" If they don't come to the let-them-talk-about-themselves method right away, give them a clue: "What would asking them questions about themselves do?" Pointing out feelings in common with a client is a favorite example: on a hot and humid day, a salesperson says to her client, "Gee, I feel hot and sticky today. How about you, Mr. Mark?" You might cue this technique by asking students, "What social rule have you learned so far in this course that is a powerful cause of people liking each other?" The answer you are looking for is, of course, similarity. When some student identifies similarity in so many words—it's okay to expand on what they say a bit—ask students how they would establish similarity during a conversation with the "mark." Move them toward pointing out trivial similarities—"so you're a midwesterner too!"—that they can easily establish prior to a request. Have students think of additional methods of ingratiation, including ones that backfire, for example, pointing out too many of one's negative traits during a self-disclosure session designed to make one look humble, or slavishly conforming to the "mark's" opinions. This exercise might make students conscious of their probably unconscious attempts to manipulate others, and of their occasional victimization. To make sure they learn to protect themselves and avoid exploitive behavior, be sure to lead them in poking fun at these underhanded methods.

Classroom Exercises/Demonstrations

1. Before you get into the conformity material—and also before students read about it—tell your students that you would like to replicate an experiment on "aesthetics." You are interested in comparing your previous results obtained from former students enrolled in this class during a recent semester with those produced by your present students. Have them turn to the Study Guide chapter corresponding to this one, where they will find a set of numbered symbols grouped in ten different sets. For each set, labeled A through J, pick one symbol at random (give the number of the column in which it is found) and tell students that it is the one picked as most interesting and intriguing by at least 80 percent of former students (be sure to note which you picked for each set). Then ask them to pick the symbol they think is the most interesting and intriguing, and circle it. Do this for all ten sets. Then ask students to exchange sheets and to score each other's sheets. Beginning with set A, call out the "previous students' favorite" that you actually picked at random and tell them to circle the letter for the set (A) if the students whose sheets they are scoring made the same choice as the "previous students." Do the same for sets B through J. Then collect the sheets and count the number of sheets that have at least six of the ten letters circled. After explaining that the

SOCIAL INFLUENCES

symbols were actually picked at random—you invented the other class's responses and there is no evidence that any of the symbols are more interesting and intriguing than the others—you can report to the class the percentage of students who "agreed" with the phantom "previous students'" responses (the number of students "agreeing" at least six out of ten times divided by the total number of students). At least 33 percent of students should have gone along in a majority of the ten cases. Explain to them how the previous students were "exerting pressure on them" to make the same choices as they supposedly made. Ask them for reflections and be ready to entertain the subject of deception in social psychological experiments (you may have to explain that telling the absolute truth and asking them to "pretend that some other students had made the [actually random] responses" would have generated only attempts to *appear* uninfluenceable, rather than genuine responses.

2. Dr. Vivian Parker Makosky (1985) has identified three basic appeals used in advertising (in *Teaching of Psychology, 12,* 42–43). A straightforward and, according to her experience, fascinating demonstration for students, this exercise involves locating magazine ads that represent examples of each kind of appeal, or combinations of them. One of these appeals is the "appeal to or creation of needs." It is based on Maslow's hierarchy of needs. "Aren't you hungry for Burger King now?" (physiological needs); "Get a piece of the rock" (safety and security needs); "Brush your breath with Dentine" (belongingness and love); and "When E. F. Hutton speaks . . ." (self-esteem and status needs) are all examples of Makosky's different appeals. Appeals to cognitive, aesthetic, and self-actualization needs are much less common. Examples of "social and prestige suggestion" appeals—buy it because all kinds of people do—include the "Pepsi generation" ad, the Wrigley's Spearmint Gum ad, and other ads "featuring lots of people, in different types of clothes and/or settings, often of different ages and races . . ." (Makosky, 1985, *Teaching of Psychology, 12,* 43). Examples of "prestige suggestion" appeals—buy it because famous people do—are Michael Jordan for Wheaties, Michael J. Fox for Pepsi, and various famous athletes for light beer.

Another kind of appeal is "loaded words and images." "This technique is the most subtle because it is not what is said so much as how it is said, or what you are seeing while it is being said." (Ibid., 43). Examples include ads with attractive, athletic people touting snacks such as Snickers candy bars; the use of buzz words such as "natural" for beauty products or foods, and "light" for foods to seem dietetic; and the creation of an overall aura that becomes associated with certain products, such as Harvey's Bristol Cream Sherry symbolizing a sophisticated life-style; BMW, the emblem of wealth and status; and Ford (or Chevy) trucks, the epitome of masculine good times.

Because each of the three categories of appeals has subcategories, it is possible, and productive, to divide the class into groups, with each bringing to class examples of some subcategory. The groups can then discuss their example ads in class, pick the ads that best illustrate their subcategory, decide why these ads are appropriate examples of their subcategory, and report to the class on their conclusions.

Other questions for groups to consider are: What kinds of ads appeal to men and what kinds to women? What kinds of ads may be true turn-ons and what kinds may actually backfire? What kinds of ads are most effective for what kinds of products? What kinds of ads are most effective for which age groups?

3. Before getting into Milgram's research, briefly describe his basic study to students. Alternatively, show them one segment from Milgram's film (see "Film Notes" below) involving one subject in the standard experiment. In either case, don't reveal the proportion who obeyed. Rather, have students estimate how many out of one hundred would obey and whether they would obey (let *obey* be defined as "going all the way to the last switch, the 450 volt switch"). (The Study Guide chapter corresponding to this one contains the needed response sheet.)

Ask students whether they had previously heard of or read about Milgram's work. Separate the responses into those who have and those who have not. Calculate the number of people out of one hundred who obey and compare with 65 percent for both groups. You will almost certainly find that students think that less than 65 percent of others would obey and that an even fewer number of them would obey, regardless of the group. However, students with prior information should come closer to correctly estimating the proportion of others who would obey, but such knowledge should not affect their estimates of their own behavior very much (predicted results are based on one of the Manual authors' use of this demonstration).

4. Illustrate the two-feet-in-the-door technique. In one of your non–social psychology classes, pass out index cards and ask students to write their phone numbers on the cards. Have them place them in a box by the door as they leave if they are willing to donate two out-of-class hours of their time to a colleague's research project; however, there will be no compensation.

In your social psychology class, ask your students to stay beyond class time just a couple of minutes to help you with your research. Then, write a phone number on the board and a time to call that is convenient to you or your assistant. Make sure that this process takes only a couple of minutes. To those who call, ask the same question you asked the first class. Compare the number of cards you collected with the number of affirmative answers given by the social psychology students who called. More social psychology students than students from the first class should have volunteered given your technique. Revelation of results and explanation of the foot-in-the-door technique should generate lively classroom discussion.

Film Notes: A Picture Is Sometimes Worth a Thousand Words

Conformity, videotape, 28.5 mins. To obtain this video, consult your Allyn and Bacon sales representative. Robert A. Baron and Margaret Clark use dramatizations as points of departure for a discussion of conformity and other forms of social influence.

Conformity and Independence, 21885, film, 23 mins. Pennsylvania State University, Audiovisual Services, Special Services Building, University Park, PA 16802 (814-865-6314). This video includes much in only 23 minutes: Sherif's experiments on norm formation, Asch's conformity research, Milgram's experiment on action conformity, and some prominent theorists discussing their ideas.

Obedience, U-60027, film, 50 mins. University of Iowa, Audiovisual Dept., Iowa City, IA 52242. Perhaps the most significant media presentation ever produced about social psychology. Filmed excerpts from Milgram's actual obedience research contain an element of suspense, several surprises, and a nearly profound conclusion.

The Power of the Situation, 19, videotape, 30 mins. The Annenborg Project, Holt, Rinehart & Winston, 1990, contact Lee Sutherlin, Marketing Manager (817-334-7632). All about how our beliefs and behavior can be influenced and manipulated by other people and by subtle situational forces.

Transparencies

8.1 *Asch's Line-Judging Task: Example Lines*
8.2 *The Sexes and Conformity*
8.3 *Methods of Gaining Compliance*
8.4 *The Tendency to Obey: Some Key Contributing Factors*

8.5 *The Social Influence Model (SIM)*
8.6 *Bisanz and Rule's Complete List of Means for Gaining Compliance*

Critical Thinking/Essay Questions

1. Give some everyday examples of conformity. Include some that are beneficial, some that are not, and at least one that involves conformity by a large majority.

2. Indicate some factors that promote group cohesiveness. When group cohesiveness is high, is the discrepancy between public compliance and private compliance likely to be great or small?

3. Explain why directing influence attempts to several targets instead of just one lowers the impact of those attempts. When one is in the minority, but the number of allies one has increases, what happens to one's impact on others?

4. Discuss the reasons women have been seen as more conformist and the reasons that perception is incorrect. As women gain in status within a group, what happens to usual assumptions about their degree of influenceability?

5. Contrast normative social influence and informational social influence by providing real-life examples of each. Build a case for one or the other being a significant factor in the Zimbardo prison experiment.

6. Describe some famous people in history (other than those included in the text) who constituted minorities of one on some important issue. Be sure that at least one of them was unique and that one exerted influence without creating obvious behavioral change during their own time.

7. Come up with a scheme to ingratiate yourself with a boss (one that is different from those discussed in the book).

8. Contrast the foot-in-the-door and the door-in-the-face techniques. Also, provide at least one real-life example for each that illustrates when each would likely fail.

9. Indicate how the "That's not all!" (TNA) method overlaps with the "door" techniques and is different from them.

10. Describe how you would alter the basic Milgram-obedience procedure to lower obedience to near-zero. The smaller the change you make and still have a good argument for near-zero obedience, the better your answer.

Sources for Lecture

Allen, B. P. (1990). *Personality Adjustment*. Pacific Grove, CA: Brooks/Cole (p. 390). Several excerpts from newspaper articles summarize instances of deindividuation on the highway, analogous to that which occurred in the Zimbardo prison experiment.

Cookson, P., & Rersell, C. (1986). The price of privilege. *Psychology Today*, March, pp. 31–35. Only the rich can afford the elite prep school. Money may be their children's ticket into the school, but once there, they must buy acceptance and success at the price of stifling conformity.

Cooper, M., & Soley, L. C. (1990). All the right sources. *Mother Jones*, Feb.-March, pp. 20–26, 45–48. Is the news media even-handed and unbiased or, as many suspect, subtly designed to infuse the public mind with the points of view that are favored by whoever happens to be in power? This article, based on a two-year study, finds that the "experts" typically interviewed by the major networks are more often spokesmen for the status quo than unbiased analysts.

Pines, M. (1981). Unlearning blind obedience in German schools. *Psychology Today*, May. Have the German people learned from the lessons of World War II? Apparently, they have.

Remley, A. (1988). From obedience to independence: parents used to raise their children to be dutiful. *Psychology Today*, October, p. 54. The times have changed. Now, parents are raising their children to be self-reliant, rather than obedient.

Science News. (1990). Teenagers' drug use drops, Feb. 24, p. 125. A new norm may be developing: Drug use is out. A survey of 17,000 high school seniors shows that use of most hard drugs is down. Pressure to conform to a new norm may be part of the reason.

Sheridan, C., & King, R. (1974). Obedience to authority with an authentic victim. *Proceedings of the American Psychological Association Convention*, 165–166. What happens when a learner is actually shocked? Who obeys the most, males or females? See this paper for the answers.

Update: Current Articles from Professional Sources

Campbell, J. D., & Fairey, P. (1989). Informational and normative routes to conformity: The effect of faction size as a function of norm extremity and attention to the stimulus. *Journal of Personality and Social Psychology*, 57, 457–468. When the group norm was clearly wrong, normative rather than informational mechanisms became more important and faction size became important.

Kamins, M. A. (1989). The enhancement of response rates to a mail survey through a labeled probe. *Journal of the Market Research Society*, 31, 273–283. Probing subjects in a foot-in-the-door (FITD) experiment to elaborate on their answers to FITD manipulation questions enhanced effects, especially if subjects were labeled "cooperative and helpful."

Kilbourne, B. K. (1989). A cross-cultural investigation of the foot-in-the-door compliance induction procedure. *Journal of Cross-Cultural Psychology*, 20(1), 3–38. The foot-in-the-door (FITD) procedure was tried in France, West Germany, and the Netherlands. It worked only in the Netherlands.

Schlenker, B. R., & Trudeau, J. V. (1990). Impact of self-presentations on private self-beliefs: Effects of prior self-beliefs and misattribution. *Journal of Personality and Social Psychology*, 58, 22–32. According to this article, people took more responsibility for their self-presentations (methods that may help explain the door-in-the-face technique), viewed them as more justifiable, and changed their later self-appraisals more if previously they had strong rather than weak self-beliefs.

Wallace, B. (1990). Imagery vividness, hypnotic susceptibility, and the perception of fragmented stimuli. *Journal of Personality and Social Psychology*, 58, 354–359. Hypnosis is the form of social influence that has been studied for the greatest number of years. In this still very active area of research, the index of influenceability is hypnotic susceptibility. This study showed that high susceptibility is associated with strong performance on a gestalt closure task.

Wang, T., Brownstein, R., & Katzev, R. (1989). Promoting charitable behavior with compliance techniques. *Applied Psychology: An International Review*, 38(2), 165–183. In the case of charitable contributions, door-in-the-face beat foot-in-the-face.

9

Working With and Against Others

Prosocial Behavior, Cooperation, and Conflict

Chapter Outline: Getting the Overall Picture

Learning Objectives

1. Describe the seizure procedure used by Latane and Darley to demonstrate the bystander effect, and describe how diffusion of responsibility accounts for the fact that help decreases as the number of bystanders increases.
2. List the five decisions that an individual must make before performing a prosocial act, and describe how each decision is affected by the presence of other bystanders.
3. In what ways are we inhibited from noticing a victim?
4. Describe how fear of social blunders, ambiguity, and pluralistic ignorance affect our interpretation of emergency situations.
5. What is the link between number of bystanders and the degree of perceived responsibility?
6. How does the competence of the bystander relate to offering assistance?
7. Why do acquaintanceship, opportunity for future interaction, and alcohol consumption relate positively to helping?
8. Describe studies demonstrating the impact of helpful models on prosocial behavior.
9. Describe circumstances where a positive emotional state produces increased helpfulness and decreased helpfulness.
10. Describe circumstances where a negative emotional state produces increased helpfulness and decreased helpfulness.
11. How do personal characteristics of the victim and attributions about the victim's plight affect helping?
12. Summarize the altruism-empathy hypothesis and the results of the supportive ease of escape study.
13. Describe the negative state relief model, the empathic joy hypothesis, and summarize results relevant to each.
14. Summarize evidence for and against Rushton's genetic similarity hypothesis.
15. Examine the concepts of cooperation and competition, and summarize the summer camp study.
16. Describe the social dilemmas captured in the take-some game, the give-some game, the variable game, and the commons dilemma.
17. Describe the prisoner's dilemma game, and give the three ways it differs from the social dilemma.
18. How is each of the following factors related to whether a person cooperates or competes?
    a. Reciprocity/unconditional cooperation
    b. Attributions/perceived motives of others
    c. Communication
    d. Threats
    e. Group size
    f. Whether one is a cooperator, competitor, individualist, or equalizer
19. Define *conflict* and indicate how zero-sum games meet this definition.
20. Describe how competition for scarce resources, revenge, attributions, and faulty communications are related to conflict.
21. Compare the effectiveness of tough and conciliatory bargaining and the effects of adopting a negative and positive frame.
22. Examine the three integrative agreement strategies for managing conflict.
23. Explain how third-party intervention, escalative intervention, and superordinate goals are used in conflict management.

Topics for Discussion

1. In 1904, industrialist Andrew Carnegie founded the Carnegie Hero Fund with an endowment of $5 million. The purpose of the Fund is to reward heroes who risk their own lives in efforts to save the lives of others. In the past eighty-six years more than 63,000 people have been nominated for heroism awards, but only 7,313 (about 11 percent) have been chosen to receive them. Of those chosen for awards, 91 percent have been males. Each recipient is awarded $2,500, accompanied by a bronze medal inscribed with the New Testament verse: "Greater love hath no man than this, that a man lay down his life for his friends." More than 1,500 Carnegie heroes, or roughly 21 percent, died performing their rescues, the most common cause being drownings or fires. In these cases additional monetary compensation is often provided in the form of pensions for beneficiaries, funeral expenses, and scholarships for surviving dependents.

Candidates are excluded from awards if they are obligated to act because of their occupation, such as firefighter or lifeguard. A person who rescues a family member is also excluded, unless the rescuer is severely injured or killed. A candidate is not excluded for failing to save the person's life; the awards are for those who risk their *own* lives in an effort to save others.

Discuss the issue of heroism with the class. In conjunction with the exercise, watch the news for actions that are described as "heroic." Students respond positively to current examples. Ask the students to define *heroism,* and get them to list the criteria they would use to grant Carnegie awards. Finally, compare the definition of *hero* with the text's definition of *prosocial behavior*.

2. Who is more likely to help others in need, urban dwellers or people who live in small towns? Where are you more likely to be helped, in the city or in the country? Depending on where your college or university is located and on the rural to urban ratio of your students, these have the potential to provoke interesting discussion. Perhaps your students can gather some data to compare rural and urban settings for themselves.

Most of the social psychological research indicates that small-town residents are more likely than city dwellers to help. The kinds of help studied have varied considerably, including such actions as helping people who called the wrong phone number, giving back overpayments to customers, mailing lost letters, buying greeting cards from the Multiple Sclerosis Society, helping to pick up dropped envelopes, and correcting inaccurate directions. If you want to read on this topic, studies by Amato (1983) in the *Journal of Personality and Social Psychology* (45, 571–586) and by Korte and Kerr (1975), also in the *Journal of Social Psychology* (95, 183–184), would be helpful.

3. The question of sex differences in both helping and aggression has been studied by Eagly and her colleagues using the technique of meta-analysis. It is not necessary to go into the details of meta-analysis to benefit from a consideration of this topic, but the two articles by Eagly do provide thought-provoking issues for class discussion. The article on gender and helping is in the *Psychological*

Bulletin (100, 283–308). The article on gender and aggressive behavior is in the same issue, pages 309–330.

4. The research conducted by social psychologists has generally dealt with helping that occurs in response to an immediate, short-term need. In order to conduct experimental studies, a "victim" is created and various aspects of the situation are systematically varied to determine their impact on helping. A logical question is whether the results of these short-term studies adequately explain long-term helping, particularly long-term helping carried out despite great danger and cost to the helper. An example is found in the behavior of persons who hid Jews from the Nazis in occupied countries during World War II. To have been caught in this kind of humanitarian effort could have resulted in death for the helper. Is this type of long-term, carefully planned altruism caused by different factors than the help that occurs in emergency situations?

5. The legal system has struggled to define the responsibilities of bystanders to emergency situations. Many states have passed "Good Samaritan" laws that prevent lawsuits against a person who assists in an emergency. Other states have passed laws making it illegal to engage in bystander neglect. One who fails to help a person in need of emergency assistance in Minnesota, for example, can be fined $100. Have the students investigate the laws that apply to the helping situation in your state. Can you be sued if you try to help but do the wrong thing? Under what circumstances can you be found guilty of neglect? Are the laws fair? What changes would you recommend?

Classroom Exercises/Demonstrations

1. The text's definition of *prosocial behavior* seems straightforward, but the provision that there must be no obvious benefit to the helper sometimes makes it difficult to apply. In Chapter 9 of the Study Guide you will find descriptions of several situations that may or may not show prosocial behavior. Have the students respond to these items individually and then poll the class to find out how many students considered each item to be prosocial. You will find that there is considerable disagreement whether most of the situations represent prosocial behavior. Go through the items one at a time, asking students who indicated that the situation was not prosocial behavior to explain why. The ensuing discussion should help students to develop a better idea of the meaning of prosocial behavior, and also to appreciate the difficulty of determining underlying motivation for behavior. A question you might raise is whether the "no obvious benefit to the helper" clause is a necessary part of the definition. Would a definition specifying that prosocial behavior simply benefits the recipient be more appropriate?

2. Rushton et al. (1981) devised a scale to measure help-

fulness in which subjects provide an estimate of the frequency with which they have performed various concrete helping acts. The Self-Report Altruism Scale is a twenty-one-item scale requiring respondents to estimate the number of times they have performed such acts as making change for another, donating blood, holding the door open for someone, and so forth. The scale is scored by adding the responses to the twenty-one items.

3. For students to appreciate the social dilemmas discussed in Chapter 9 of the text, it is useful to experience the dilemmas firsthand. Because the games are difficult to grasp, the best classroom strategy is to follow the outcome tables presented in the text. It is useful to have Table 9.2 on the board so that those participating in the exercise can refer to it as needed. In addition to the columns of information already included in Table 9.2, understanding is enhanced by adding another column labeled "Group Outcome." This column has been added to the table, and the expanded table is reproduced as Transparency 9.4 in this Instructor's Manual.

The first step in playing the give-some game is to

WORKING WITH AND AGAINST OTHERS

have each class member prepare two slips of paper, with "Keep $8" written on one slip and "Give $3 to each of you" written on the other slip. Next, have the students rearrange themselves so that each student is a member of a five-person group. Make sure that everyone understands what is to be done before you begin. Then, you should give some predetermined signal that tells each person to hold up one of the two slips of paper. This is the mechanism by which each person makes his response. Each person responds independently of the other group members, that is, no one should know what response the others are making until all have responded. At the completion of the first trial, each person should determine his or her outcome and also be aware of the outcomes received by the others. Next, have the group members repeat the entire process.

You will probably observe a decline in the number of cooperative responses over repeated trials of the game. Discuss with the students why this is the case, and see if you can get them to verbalize the analogy between how they have played this game and the broader social dilemmas that face our society today.

4. An effective way to teach students about the prisoner's dilemma game is to have them play a few trials of the game in class. Each student in the class should be paired with a partner. One member of the pair should be arbitrarily assigned to be Person 1, the other Person 2. Each person should prepare two slips of paper, with one slip marked "A" and the other marked "B." These slips of paper will be used by the subjects to make their responses. The outcome matrix to be used in the interaction should be drawn on the board so it is available to all the students. (A transparency can be made from the transparency master at the end of the manual if you are so inclined, or simply draw the matrix in Transparency 9.3 on the chalkboard.)

First, have the students respond simultaneously. Each person decides which response he or she is going to make independently of the partner. At some signal from you, the students show their partners which choice they have made. In order to know what one's outcome is on a particular trial, a person must know both his or her own response and the response of the partner. For example, if both persons made response A, then both received 8 points. Likewise, if Person 1 chose B and Person 2 chose A, then Person 1 receives 10 points and Person 2 receives 1 point. Have the students play several trials of simultaneous responding. Second, have the students respond in alternation. One member shows his response to the partner before the partner responds. The game is different when one person knows the other's response first.

Film Notes: A Picture Is Sometimes Worth a Thousand Words

Aspects of Behavior, 1971, color film, also now available on videotape (cost to rent: $55; cost to buy: $260), 30 mins. CRM Films, 2233 Faraday Ave., Carlsbad, CA 92008 (800-421-0833). The social psychology section is about 10 mins. This film includes an excellent portrayal of the smoke-filled room study by Latane and Darley. Interviews with Latane and Darley on the bystander effect and with Milgram on city living are also included.

*Helping and Prosocial Behavior, videotape, 28.5 mins. To obtain this tape, consult your Allyn and Bacon sales representative. Using dramatizations as a stimulus, Robert A. Baron and Margaret Clark discuss the mechanisms behind helping or not helping.

Invitation to Social Psychology, 1975, color. The portion on helping is approximately 5 mins. Harper & Row Media, 10 East 53rd Street, New York, NY 10022. John Darley and Bibb Latane discuss bystander apathy.

Social Animal, 3-156, 29 mins. Western Illinois University Audiovisual Services, Macomb, IL 61455 (309-298-2417). This film contains a major segment on conflict development and resolution with the trucking game as the focus.

Social Modification of Organically Motivated Behavior, silent, 12 mins. Indiana University, Audiovisual Center, Bloomington, IN 47401. Hungry rats display both altruistic and competitive behavior.

When Will People Help? The Social Psychology of Bystander Intervention, 1976, color, 25 mins. Harcourt, Brace, Jovanovich, 757 Third Avenue, New York, NY 10017. Daryl Bem is narrator for reenactments of some of the early Latane and Darley studies, including the smoke-filled room study and the seizure study.

Transparencies

9.1 *Good Samaritan Roadmap*
9.2 *Helping As a Function of Empathy and Empathic Arousal*

9.3 *Outcome Matrix for Prisoner's Dilemma Game*
9.4 *Table of Outcomes for the Give-Some Game*

Critical Thinking/Essay Questions

1. What are the decisions that an individual must make to become an intervener on behalf of a victim? Describe how social influence processes affect each of the decisions. Be sure to describe the specific factors influencing *each* stage.
2. Compare the willingness to help of a bystander who is in a positive emotional state with the willingness of a bystander who is in a negative emotional state. What factors besides the mood state are related to the helping?
3. Compare predictions made by the negative state relief model with those made by the empathic joy hypothesis.
4. In what ways are social dilemmas different from the prisoner's dilemma?
5. Describe a scenario where a person would most likely cooperate. Second, describe a scenario where a person would most likely compete.

Sources for Lecture

Darley, J. M., & Latane, B. (1968). When will people help in a crisis? *Psychology Today,* December, pp. 54–57, 70–71. The authors describe their classic work on the bystander effect. The steps an intervener must go through are examined in order to explain when help will be given.

DeVore, I., & Morris, S. (1977). The new science of genetic self-interest. *Psychology Today,* February, pp. 42–51, 84–88. The selfishness "built into our genes" is described from a sociobiological point of view.

Fogelman, E., & Weiner, V. L. (1985). The few, the brave, the noble. *Psychology Today,* August, pp. 60–65. During World War II some people risked their lives to save Jews from Nazis. Why? Some were motivated by deep moral values, whereas others were motivated by personal attachments or identification with the victim.

Kohn, A. (1988). Beyond selfishness. *Psychology Today,* October, pp. 34–38. The author notes that we start helping others early in life, though we're not always consistent. What makes us helpful sometimes and sometimes not?

Luks, A. (1988). Helper's high. *Psychology Today,* October, pp. 39–42. The author asserts that people feel physically and emotionally good when they help others. In the same manner that running promotes inner calm, helping is said to promote good health.

Pines, M. (1979). Good Samaritans at age two? *Psychology Today,* June, pp. 66–77. Altruistic behavior is examined in very young children. Some babies as young as one are capable of comforting others who are in pain or are crying. More sophisticated behaviors are demonstrated before age three.

Shotland, R. L. (1985). When bystanders just stand by. *Psychology Today,* June, pp. 50–55. The author reviews the literature on personal and situational factors that determine whether a bystander will help a crime victim.

Update: Current Articles from Professional Sources

Batson, D. C., et al. (1989). Religious prosocial motivation: Is it altruistic or egoistic? *Journal of Personality and Social Psychology, 57,* 873–884. Two studies explored the motivation to help associated with three different ways of being religious. In both studies it was concluded that the motivation associated with extrinsic-means religion and intrinsic-end religion seemed egoistic. On the other hand, the motivation associated with quest religion seemed to be more nearly altruistic.

Beggan, J. K., Messick, D. M., & Allison, S. T. (1988). Social values and egocentric bias: Two tests of the might over morality hypothesis. *Journal of Personality and Social Psychology, 55,* 606–611. Two studies determined that cooperators and noncooperators perceive the cooperation-competition distinction differently. Cooperators see it as an evaluative, good-bad dimension, whereas noncooperators see it as a strong-weak dimension.

Begum, H. A., & Ahmed, E. (1986). Individual risk taking and risky shift as a function of cooperation-competition proneness of subjects. *Psychological Studies, 31,* 21–25. This study examined risk taking as a function of proneness to cooperation or competition. Results show that both individual risk taking and shifting toward risk in a group were related to cooperation or competition proneness of the subjects. Here's another chance to make use of the Choice Dilemmas Questionnaire presented as an exercise/demonstration in Chapter 11.

Koestner, R., Franz, C., & Weinberger, J. (1990). The family origins of empathic concern: A 26-year longitudinal study. *Journal of Personality and Social Psychology, 58,* 709–717. Parenting dimensions derived from maternal interviews when subjects were age five predicted empathic concern when subjects were age thirty-one. Specific parenting dimensions are discussed.

Miller, P. A., et al. (1989). Mothers' emotional arousal as a moderator in the socialization of children's empathy. *New Directions for Child Development,* Summer, 44, 65–83. This study examined the effectiveness of child-rearing practices in organizing and structuring four- and five-year-olds' affective capacities to respond to the feelings and needs of others. The affective intensity of the mothers' response to audiotaped vignettes of distressed or happy children was placed into one of six categories. Significant relationships were found between mothers' reactions to the vignettes and the reactions of their children to filmed depictions of distressed children.

Mills, R. S., Pedersen, J., & Grusec, J. E. (1989). Sex differences in reasoning and emotion about altruism. *Sex Roles, 20,* 603–621. Men and women responded to three dilemmas involving a choice between self and other and were asked to decide what they would do. Subjects usually made the self-sacrificing choice, and women and men made this choice equally often. Sex differences were found, however, in the type of reasoning used to account for the choice.

10

Aggression

Its Nature, Causes, and Control

Chapter Outline: Getting the Overall Picture

Learning Objectives

1. Be able to define aggression, indicate the significant questions that have been raised about it, and the theoretical perspectives that have been taken with regard to it.
2. Learn the drive point of view with regard to aggression, as well as the negative affect and learned social behavior positions regarding aggression.
3. Be able to outline the teacher/learner method of studying aggression and the controversies that surround this technique.
4. Appreciate the limitations of the frustration-aggression hypothesis and the strengths of the revision posed by Berkowitz (1989).
5. Be able to indicate how direct provocation affects aggression, with reference to Baron (1988). What are the conditions in which direct provocation may not be reciprocated?
6. Learn the effects of exposure to media violence on subsequent aggression, beginning with the "Bobo doll" studies and emphasizing Josephson's (1987) study and the long-term correlational studies.
7. Be able to outline the classic Berkowitz and Le Page (1967) gun-cue study and the limitations of it.
8. What mechanisms underlie the effect of media violence on aggression?
9. Be able to outline Zillmann's excitation transfer theory and how Zillmann's cognitive factors determine whether residual arousal will affect subsequent aggression.
10. Appreciate how Zillmann's two-component model that explains the U-shaped relationship between sexual stimulation and subsequent levels of aggression works.
11. Know how violent pornography and violence against women outside a sexual context can affect subjects' behaviors and attitudes toward women.
12. Appreciate the lowered restraint hypothesis concerning the effects of alcohol consumption on aggression, with reference to Taylor and Sears's (1988) study involving social pressure.
13. Be able to contrast Type As and Bs and discuss the Evans et al. (1987) study on Type A and B drivers in India, as well as Dodge and Coie's (1987) schema concerning reactive, proactive, and overreactive aggression.
14. Do males and females differ in tendency to aggress? If so, what is it about their training that may explain any difference?
15. Be able to discuss the factors that interplay to produce aggression.
16. Know how well or poorly punishment and catharsis help to prevent subsequent aggression.
17. Under what conditions do apologies for transgressions help to prevent subsequent aggression?
18. How do nonaggressive models help to lower aggression?
19. How does training in social skills help to lower aggression?
20. How does the generation of incompatible responses help to lower aggression?

Topics for Discussion

1. Recently, four men raped a 21-year-old mother of two for 120 agonizing minutes while fellow patrons at a New Bedford, Massachusetts bar cheered the attackers and taunted the victim. No one helped the young woman, but two men were accused of assisting the rapists. At first there was an outpouring of sympathy for the victim. From 2,500 to 4,000 people joined a candlelight procession in protest of the outrage and a local women's group began organizing a rape crisis center and sensitivity training for policemen. Letters arrived expressing sympathy and containing money for the victim. However, the local mood changed. Even though the victim's identity was unknown, callers to a local talk show claimed that she was actually a prostitute who "got what she deserved."

There are at least two interesting topics for discussion suggested by the now-infamous gang rape. First, the label "prostitute" suggests the victim was looking for sex and, thus, she got what she was seeking. That is, rape is a sexual act. If rape is sexual, then some women might be getting what they are looking for. But, if rape is an act of violence, as feminists and some recent research suggest, would any reasonable person assert that there are those who look to be humiliated, beaten, and dehumanized? Second, the attribution "prostitute" might support the just-world hypothesis. In the just world, you get what you deserve and deserve what you get (see the writings of psychologist Melvin J. Lerner). By believing in the just-world hypothesis, New Bedford citizens could reason, "a bad thing happened to the rape victim, because she is a bad and careless person; I'm good and careful and thus need not worry." In this second case, discussion could center on how belief in the just world promotes violence by destroying sympathy for victims of aggression.

2. Discuss the many ways that parents teach aggression

to their children. Besides what is implied by information in the text, consider subtle methods such as permitting aggressive acts and thus tacitly approving of aggression. Also, consider the subtle ways parents communicate that aggression is appropriate for boys but not for girls.

3. Discuss methods of controlling aggression in addition to those included in the text. For example, imagine a parent recoiling in horror at discovering his or her two children mutually masturbating. Would people aggress very often if every time they did, witnesses reacted with similar repugnance? What would happen if people stopped patronizing violent movies and clicked off their TVs when violent programs were scheduled? What if football and hockey game attendance dropped dramatically? What if public figures were as roundly condemned and as thoroughly ruined for acts like punching a photographer as were some members of the British government when they were being photographed after a sexual scandal was revealed)?

4. Discuss alternatives to aggression for getting your way, for protecting yourself or others, and for reaching your goals. Is aggression the most efficient means to any end? Is aggression sometimes counterproductive? Can students name circumstances in which aggression is the only option?

5. July 30, 1987: A teenage motorist was shot while driving away from an argument involving his passenger. The death brought fifty California police agencies onto the freeways in a show of force. August 3, 1987: Between August 3 and June 18, there had been sixteen shootings on the nation's highways. On August 3, in Sun Valley, a tanker truck was hit by gunfire coming from occupants of a green Chevy panel-van. Soon after the tanker incident, another car was hit. In a separate incident, a van was the source of gunfire. Still later that day, a motorist reported drawing fire from a van with tinted windows.

These actual incidents further illustrate the authors' point that there is a connection between driving and aggression. Philip Zimbardo's theory of deindividuation suggests that the driver and passengers of one vehicle constitute an antagonistic group for drivers and passengers of other vehicles. Further, tinted windows, enclosed vans, and sunglasses made occupants of different vehicles anonymous to each other. Add the frustration that results from driving under congested and competitive conditions, the noise of the crowded freeway, fatigue after a day's work (most shooting incidents have occurred in the afternoon), the presence of alcohol in the systems of some drivers, and all the ingredients for aggression on the highway are present. Describe the above incidents to students and ask them if they know of others. Then ask them to come up with the conditions, listed above, that contribute to aggression on the highway. Finally, offer them the opportunity to suggest ways to avoid aggression among motorists.

Classroom Exercises/Demonstrations

1. Under the guise of conducting an impression formation demonstration, have all class members stand up in front of the class and present name, home town, major, and favorite hobbies. For each presentation, have other students write their impressions of the speaker. In each case have students identify themselves and the speaker by name. Then, collect them. A few days later, pass each student an "impression" that actually you and a member of the class, who has agreed to act as collaborater, created. The collaborater's name will appear on each impression. For half the students, the bogus impression would be positive, and for the others, negative. Collect these from students at the end of class so they can't compare notes.

Sometime later announce that, in the interest of studying persuasive communication, a student (the collaborater) has volunteered to read her or his paper just completed for a persuasive communication class. Students would then evaluate that student using the favorability scale presented in the Study Guide. You can sum over agreement scores for each student and compare mean agreement for the two groups (calculate the two means and display them or compare them with a simple t-test). Separating the evaluations of the communicator into those made by students given a positive evaluation by him or her and those made by students given a negative evaluation will allow you to demonstrate how provocation can lead to aggression expressed in the form of a negative evaluation.

2. For the sake of this exercise we will assume that the test items from our bank are entirely fair and reasonable and that you are faultless as a professor (at least we are spreading the charitable assumptions around!). Consider the appreciation of mitigating circumstances in alleviating the need to respond to others' aggressive acts. After all, aggression is often a response to someone else's hostile acts. Recruit a student you know reasonably well. On test day, have the student come up during a test to complain about items moderately loudly. At the end of the test, have the student slam her or his test down and stomp out of the room, complaining loudly about the unfair items and unreasonable professor as he or she departs. Exclaim, "Wonder what is wrong with him [or her]?"

Next class, have students respond to the Understanding Aggression Form (it might be a good idea to have the student who attacked your test be absent until this exercise is over). This device, found in the Study Guide, is designed to create insights concerning mitigating circumstances. Have them use the form to analyze the angry student's reactions to the test. After students have finished the form, tally the results on the board under the categories used on the form: (1) reasons for the aggression relating to the target of aggression [you, in this case]; (2) reasons relating to the aggressor's relationships with people other than the target; (3) reasons relating to the aggressor's feelings about himself or herself and his or her skills and efforts. Use a representative sampling of responses in each category; otherwise, there will be too many reactions to write on the board and too much for students to appreciate. When the total picture is displayed on the board, step back and state, "Here are three possible categories of reasons for the student's behavior toward me after the last test. If you knew that I had decided to retaliate against the student in some way—I may scold the student the next time I see him [or her]—which category would you guess that I had assumed contains the real reasons for the student's behavior?" Students should tend to choose the reasons in Category 1. If they don't, you may ask questions such as, "Why would I retaliate if I know that the student's aggression had nothing to do with me; it was caused by his [or her] quarrel with a lover" (or test anxiety; or lack of self-confidence). The point is to show students that targets of aggression are unlikely to resort to aggression themselves if they know that the person who attacked them has aggressed against them for reasons having nothing to do with them. The form is duplicated in the Study Guide.

3. Psychologist Ludy T. Benjamin of Texas A&M University has devised a method for providing insightful answers to the question, "What is aggression?" (See Benjamin, [1985], Defining aggression . . . *Teaching of Psychology, 12,* 40–42.) The method allows students to define aggression for themselves through an ingenious exercise. Students simply check all of twenty-five statements that they believe indicate aggressive acts (included in the Study Guide). Collect their lists, shuffle them, and redistribute

them to the class (with this procedure, students don't necessarily call out their own responses and can thereby avoid embarrassment). For each statement, get a show of hands of how many students thought the statement indicated aggression. Write on the board only those statements that at least 80 percent saw as indicating aggression or at most 20 percent saw as indicating aggression (the number of hands divided by the number of students present). Now you can take up issues such as whether aggression involves harm to living as opposed to non-living things (Items 9 and 23); accident versus intention (8 and 11); actual damage versus no physical damage (10, 13, and 18); self-defense (3, 13, and 14); duty or job responsibility (3, 4, 19, 20, and 22); predation and instinctual behavior (1, 2, and 25); survival (1, 6, and 16); acts involving animals (7, 16, 17, and 18); covert acts (11 and 14); inaction (12 and 15); self-injury (24); and killing for sport (17 and 25).

4. As your text indicates, Type A behavior in and of itself is not what puts possessors of it at risk for health problems. Rather, the problem is a single trait that is part of the constellation of Type A traits: hostility. Psychologist Redford Williams of Duke University has developed a measure of hostility that may predict health problems, especially those related to the cardiovascular system (included in the Study Guide). Have students complete his questionnaire. Those who answer two of the three questions with "often" or "always" may consider themselves at risk for cardiovascular problems. You could simply collect the questionnaires and tally the number of students who are at risk. This should provide a benchmark so that students could evaluate how they stand relative to other students (make it anonymous, of course). Then, have them respond to William's "Twelve Steps to a More Trusting [and Healthy] Heart." Students could check all statements that represent steps that they feel confident they could take. This will sensitize students to hostility avoidance and reassure students who scored at-risk on the questionnaire that they have a way to deal with their problem.

Film Notes: A Picture Is Sometimes Worth a Thousand Words

*Aggression, videotape, 28.5 mins. To obtain this tape, see your Allyn and Bacon sales representative. Robert A. Baron, an expert on the topic, and Margaret Clark use dramatizations on a basis for a discussion on aggression.

Aggression or Love?, ESC-1055, film, 24 mins. Indiana University, Audiovisual Center, Bloomington, IN 47401. The possible biological and evolutionary roots of aggressive behavior are examined and the question is raised, "Can love cure aggression?"

Black on Black Violence, FC1932, videotape, 26 mins. Films

for the Humanities and Sciences, Inc., P.O. Box 2053, Princeton, NJ 08543 (800-257-5126). A U.S. black male has a one in twenty-nine chance of being murdered; for white men, the odds are one in 186. This video explores the reasons for the difference.

Human Aggression, film, 22 mins. Associated Films, Inc., 512 Burlington Ave., La Grange, IL 60525 (312-352-3377). This film features several well-known aggression researchers and some other public figures. Activities of an actual youth gang provide the opener.

The Question of Violence, CS-1942, film, 59 mins. (two

reels). Indiana University, Audiovisual Center, Bloomington, IN 47401. The social, historical, and psychological factors that seem to underlie violence in modern life are the subject of this film.

Rape: An Act of Hate, FC1055, videotape, 30 mins. Films for the Humanities and Sciences, Inc., P.O. Box 2053, Princeton, NJ 08543 (800-257-5126). Veronica Hamel of "Hill Street Blues" seeks to determine why people rape and to help potential victims protect themselves.

Sexual Assault, three videotapes, 30 mins. each. NETCHE Videotape Library, P.O. Box 83111, Lincoln, NE 68501. These three tapes explore rape from the point of view of the victim, the assailant, and the police officer, respectively.

Sexual Harassment: From 9 to 5, FC1711, videotape, 26 mins. Films for the Humanities and Sciences, Inc., P.O. Box 2053, Princeton, NJ 08543 (800-257-5126). The motivations for sexual harassment and rape have much in common. In this video, some businessmen couldn't understand that "No!" meant "No!" until they were sued. How employees are taught the difference between romance, harassment, and sexual extortion is a major feature.

Violence in the Family, PB81, videotape (cost to buy: $159), 55 mins. Insight Media, 121 West 85th Street, New York, NY 10024-4401 (800-233-9910). Those who don't believe that violence starts at home will be convinced by this video.

Transparencies

10.1 *What Is Sexual Harassment?*
10.2 *Theoretical Conceptions of Aggression*
10.3 *Aggression: Causes and Cures*
10.4 *Media Violence: Mechanisms Underlying the Effects*
10.5 *Aggression According to the Neoassociationists*
10.6 *The Effects of Violent and Nonviolent Pornography on Males' Aggression Toward Females*

Critical Thinking/Essay Questions

1. Define *aggression* and discuss the theoretical perspectives on it, including Freud's view, the notion of fighting instinct, sociobiological theory, the drive notion, aggression as a response to aversive events and aggression as a learned social behavior.

2. Discuss the teacher-learner method of studying aggression and the controversies that surround it.

3. What is wrong with the idea that frustration is a major cause of aggression? Explain why the direct provocation notion provides a better account of why aggression occurs. Include a consideration of attributions of responsibility and mitigating circumstances.

4. List the three kinds of studies that have been used to investigate the possible effects of media presentations on aggression and provide an example of each. Given that the media does affect aggressiveness, why does it do so? What controversies surround the method for determining whether aggressive cues are a source of aggressiveness?

5. Consider Zillmann's ideas about excitation transfer and how they may explain how a chain of events involving heighten arousal may or may not end up in increased aggressiveness.

6. Use Zillmann's two-factor theory to explain how sexual arousal influences aggressiveness. How does violent pornography compare with nonviolent pornography in its effects on males' aggressiveness toward females?

7. Explore how alcohol affects aggressiveness. How does alcohol affect the brain in ways that will produce heightened aggression? How does social pressure to increase aggressiveness influence the difference between alcohol and no alcohol conditions in an aggression experiment?

8. How do Type As and Type Bs differ in general and in terms of the level and kinds of aggression they show? How do Type A drivers differ from Type B drivers? Finally, how do sex (gender) and hostile attributional bias influence aggressiveness?

9. Discuss the reasons punishment and catharsis are limited as means of lessening aggression. By contrast, discuss the merits of apologies, nonaggressive models, social training, and incompatible responses as means of reducing or controlling aggression.

Sources for Lecture

Allen, Bem P. (1990). *Personality, Social, and Biological Perspectives on Personal Adjustment*. Pacific Grove, CA: Brooks/Cole. A chapter on aggression in this book contains, among other items of possible interest, violence ratings of popular TV series and of the networks themselves.

Associated Press. (1990). Illinois psychiatrist works overtime combating TV violence. Released on April 4. Champaign, Illinois, psychiatrist Thomas Radecki, founder of the National Coalition on Television Violence, is Freddy Krueger's number one enemy. He and a small group of "peaceniks" who work long hours for little pay are devoting their lives to fighting violence on TV and in other media. They rate TV programs, movies, cartoons, and other media outlets that feature violence, air their views on such shows as "Larry King Live" and "Donahue," and lobby to end violence in the media.

Horn, J. (1985). Fighting migraines with the Force. *Psychology Today*, November, p. 74. Type-A-like boys who are described as "brightest," "head of the class," and "best athlete" have numerous problems. They are likely to be highly aggressive and some report migraine headaches. But, alas, biofeedback doesn't work with these high-strung kids. However, conjuring up the Jedi ritual from the *Star Wars* movies allows them to relax. May the Force be with them.

Moody, J. (1990). Simon decries violence in children's TV shows. January 26. Released by States News Service. Unsuccessful presidential candidate Paul Simon is having little success trying to convince the Senate to pass legislation that would force the networks to decrease the violence of their programing (NBC was rated number one in violence: 77 percent of their prime-time programing was seen as violent). Senator Simon claims that TV misrepresents reality and makes reference to evidence supporting his position. However, the American Civil Liberties Union worries that Simon's proposed legislation to restrict what TV may show will violate the First Amendment of the Constitution.

Steele, C. (1986). What happens when you drink too much? *Psychology Today*, January, pp. 48–52. Drinking makes people's responses more extreme. Compared to sober people, drinkers were more aggressive, looked at sexual slides longer, gambled more, disclosed more about themselves, and took greater risks.

Ubell, E. (1990). The deadly emotions. *Parade*, February 11, pp. 4–6. This article supports the notion that hostile people's hostility is worse for them than for their victims, but sounds an optimistic note: formerly hostile people can learn to be laid-back.

Update: Current Articles from Professional Sources

Anderson, C. A. (1989). Temperature and aggression: Ubiquitous effects of heat on the occurrence of human violence. *Psychological Bulletin, 106,* 74–96. Psychologist Anderson, a persistent critic of laboratory studies of heat and aggression, reviews the literature and confirms his earlier view: in real-life settings heat increases aggression in linear fashion, but results of laboratory studies are inconsistent.

Derman, K., & George, W. H. (1989). Alcohol expectancy and the relationship between drinking and physical aggression. *Journal of Psychology, 123,* 153–161. There was a stronger relationship between drinking and physical aggressiveness among males who expected that alcohol would raise aggression than among those who had no such expectation.

Farrington, D. P. (1989). Early predictors of adolescent aggression and adult violence. *Violence and Victims, 4,* 79–100. This British study showed that the most important predictors of violence in eight- to ten-year-old children were economic deprivation, family criminality, poor child rearing, school failure, hyperactivity-impulsivity, attention deficit, and antisocial child behavior.

Koss, M. P. (1990). The women's mental health research agenda: Violence against women. *American Psychologist, 45,* 374–380. Koss is an expert on rape. In this article, she presents evidence that the scope of violence against women is much broader than most people believe. Then, she says what must be done about violence against women.

Machover, J., & Sanders, S. (1986). A test of sex differences in aggressive response to hypothetical conflict situations. *Journal of Personality and Social Psychology, 50,* 1045–1049. Males were more likely to be physically aggressive, although verbal aggression was the most probable response to conflict overall. However, reports of aggressiveness were retrospective to age thirteen.

Petty, G. M., & Dawson, B. (1989). Sexual aggression in normal men: Incidence, beliefs, and personality characteristics. *Personality and Individual Differences, 10,* 355–362. Endorsement of the acceptability of using force in sexual encounters; the self-reported likelihood to rape if certain of being undetected; and the personality characteristics of aggression, impulsivity, and dominance were discriminated between college males who were high in use of force in sexual encounters and those who were low in use of force.

Rushton, J. P., Fulker, D., Neale, M., Nias, D., & Eysenck, H. (1986). Altruism and aggression: The heritability of individual differences. *Journal of Personality and Social Psychology, 50,* 1192–1198. This research reveals that substantial proportions of variance in aggressiveness and altruism are attributable to the genes.

INSTRUCTOR'S SECTION

11

Groups and Individuals
The Consequences of Belonging

Learning Objectives

1. List the six criteria that must be met for a collection of people to be classified as a group, and summarize how feelings of "groupness" were produced among subjects in the Insko et al. research.
2. What are the bases of group formation?
3. Summarize the five stages of group development.
4. Describe the types of roles found in groups and the problems of role ambiguity and role conflict.
5. Describe ways in which high-status people differ from lower status individuals.
6. How do prescriptive and proscriptive norms affect group members?
7. What factors determine whether a group will be cohesive, and how does cohesiveness affect the group?
8. What were the "confusing" findings in early studies on how the presence of others affects performance?
9. Summarize Zajonc's drive theory of social facilitation.
10. Compare the mere presence and evaluation apprehension hypotheses.
11. Summarize the cockroach results, and indicate their significance.
12. Compare the performance of individuals and groups on each of the following types of tasks:
    a. Additive
    b. Conjunctive
    c. Disjunctive
    d. Compensatory
13. Describe experiments that document the existence of social loafing.
14. Summarize the three techniques for reducing social loafing.
15. Contrast the reactions of subjects to free riders in the United States with those in Japan.
16. Describe how a group's final decision is reached under each of the four social decision schemes.
17. Describe how straw polls influenced decisions reached by groups in the research by Davis et al. (1989).
18. Compare the risky shift and group polarization hypotheses.
19. Describe how the social comparison and persuasive arguments views account for group polarization.
20. Discuss characteristics of groupthink and how to avoid it.
21. Why is it that groups usually repeat information shared by most members rather than examining unshared information? How can this be avoided?
22. Describe aspects of personality that are related to becoming a leader.
23. Compare charismatic leadership with other styles, and describe why charismatic leaders often succeed.
24. Compare male and female leaders on each of the following:
    a. Concern with task accomplishment versus concern with maintenance of interpersonal relationships
    b. Democratic versus autocratic style
25. According to contingency theory, what determines a leader's success?
    a. Compare low and high LPC leaders.
    b. When is each type of leader successful?
    c. What is the current status of contingency theory?
26. Compare autocratic and participatory styles of leadership, and describe circumstances where each leadership style is likely to succeed.

Topics for Discussion

1. Students who are sports fans are well aware of the home court advantage in competitive sports. Playing at home is generally correlated with winning. Greer (1983) studied the performance of basketball players at Illinois and at Kansas State to determine the impact of noisy fan demonstrations on performance. Greer found that turnovers and scoring favored the home team regardless of crowd noise. The factor most affected by crowd noise was the number of fouls called against the visiting team. For fifteen seconds following noisy crowd demonstrations, the number of fouls called against the visiting team increased. Perhaps some of your students would like to replicate Greer's phenomenon. (Greer's research is found in *Social Psychology Quarterly, 46,* 252–261.)

2. Research by Jackson and Padgett (1982) has suggested evidence for a social loafing effect in songs written by John Lennon and Paul McCartney of the Beatles. The social loafing effect hypothesis was that the songs cowritten by Lennon and McCartney would be of lower quality than the songs written by either of them alone. Jackson and Padgett concluded that there is evidence of a social loafing effect, but only for those songs written after 1967. (For a full explanation, consult the research reported in the *Personality and Social Psychology Bulletin, 88*, 672–677.)

3. Challenge students to come up with examples of tasks that are additive, disjunctive, conjunctive, and compensatory. A way to help them understand the nature of these types of tasks is to have them produce illustrative examples.

4. Ask the students to report on their experience in extracurricular activity groups. The students might comment on such things as the emergence of leadership in the group, polarization effects, social loafing, and social facilitation. Second, you might encourage the students to attend a meeting of a group of which they are not currently members so that they can observe the group's functioning. By observing a group of which they are not a member the students may be better able to gain insight into the group.

Encourage the students to write down their impressions of the group and to share them with the other class members.

5. Before peace talks for ending the Vietnam War could get underway in earnest, negotiators had to settle the issue of what shape the negotiating table would be. Negotiators for the United States and South Vietnam wanted to present the appearance of a two-sided negotiation, whereas the North Vietnamese wanted the appearance that four equal parties were negotiating—the Americans, the South Vietnamese, the North Vietnamese, and the National Liberation Front. The United States considered the National Liberation Front to be sponsored by North Vietnam and thus not an independent party. The final compromise, reached after eight months of negotiating, involved a round table without dividing lines. Sometimes the roles people play in a group are determined by structural factors, such as seating pattern.

Classroom Exercises/Demonstrations

1. One topic discussed in Chapter 11 is the notion of what constitutes a group. One way to get students thinking about this question is to present them with several situations and have them determine whether the people described there are a group or simply a collection of individuals. Several situations of this type are presented in Chapter 11 of the Study Guide. In addition to their yes/no responses, have students write down the reasons for their decisions. Afterward, you can determine the number of students who thought each situation described a group and ask them to discuss their judgments. The text's definition of a group is as follows: "two or more interacting persons who share common goals, have a stable relationship, are somehow interdependent, and perceive that they are in fact part of a group." Do the students' judgments support the text's definition?

2. This exercise not only demonstrates the nature of polarization effects, but it gives students a chance to interact with fellow students in a small-group setting. Students respond twice to each of six items from the Choice Dilemmas Questionnaire (CDQ), one time on their own and the second time after a three-minute discussion. Before the class period, the instructor should prepare enough copies of the CDQ for each student in the class to have one copy. (Six CDQ items are presented in Chapter 11 of the Study Guide.) The following instructions should be read to the class before the exercise is begun:

> On the page(s) that I have given you, you will find descriptions of situations that might occur in everyday life. In each situation a person is faced with a choice between two courses of action. The person can continue his or her present course of action, or the person can embark on a new, more adventurous course. Your task is to decide how certain you would want to be before you would advise the person to try the new course of action.

> For each situation, your task is to indicate the minimum probability of success that you would demand before recommending that the person attempt the new course of action. Note that you are not asked to indicate what the chances of success would actually *be*; rather, you are asked to indicate the smallest chance of success that you would accept and still advise the person to go ahead and try the new course of action. If you say one in ten, you are telling the person to try the new course of action even if there is only one chance in ten of succeeding. On the other hand, if you say nine in ten, you are telling the person to try the new course of action only if very sure of succeeding.

> Read each situation carefully before giving your judgment. Try to place yourself in the position of the person in each situation and then indicate the smallest chance of success that you would accept and still advise the person to try the new course of action.

After everyone in the class has finished responding, the students should divide up into discussion groups of four or five persons. Groups are instructed that their task is to spend three minutes discussing the Alan situation (i.e., the first CDQ situation.) Tell them that at the end of three minutes you will interrupt to ask them to write down their response to the Alan situation. You should emphasize to them the importance of keeping an open mind and of considering all points of view during the discussion. After the three minute discussion, ask each person again to write down on his or her questionnaire the minimum probability of success that he or she would demand.

After completing the first situation, the groups should discuss the next situation for three minutes. At the end of the three minutes, again ask people to respond to the item. After the groups have completed their six discussions, ask each group to prepare a summary of their data. For each situation, have them obtain a prediscussion and a post-discussion sum. They should add together the responses of each group member so that it can be determined whether their group changed in a risky direction, a cautious direction, or stayed the same. It is expected that groups will show a risky shift on the Peter, Henry, and George situations. It is expected that groups will show a cautious shift on the Betty and Mark/Susan situations. The Alan situation is somewhat ambivalent, although risky shifts are more prevalent than cautious shifts. These predictions are based on the assumption that groups cause shifts in the direction of the initial response tendencies of the group members. (See Fig. 11.14 in the text.)

3. Gary Stasser of Miami (Ohio) University has provided a task for illustrating the vagaries of collective information exchange en route to a collective judgment. It uses standard playing cards and requires that a group decide whether there are more black or red cards in an oversized deck constructed from two or more standard decks. Of course, the experimenter or instructor can control which color is more frequent in the deck as well as the degree to which the more prevalent color dominates. The procedure involves dealing a set number (eleven works well but this can be varied to simulate high versus low information conditions) of cards to each member of a group. Then, as an analog of obtaining prediscussion preferences in typical group decision-making exercises, each member privately chooses either red or black as their judgment (guess) based on the information in their own hands. Ratings of certainty of judgment and a record of the actual contents of their hands is also obtained for later purposes. After these private responses are obtained, the group "discusses" by members playing, in turn, cards face up on the table. Play is continued in round-robin fashion until about fifteen cards are displayed on the table. (The number of cards played can be varied to simulate short or long discussions.) After the predetermined number of cards is played, "discussion" is stopped and the group, without further revelation of the contents of their individual hands, reaches a collective judgment based on their pooled information (i.e., the cards on the table). Of course, the cards that individuals retain in their hands can still influence their individual judgments and, thus, their votes or stated preferences in reaching the group's decision.

Even though the task is simple and the "discussion" mechanical, it does capture some of the dynamics of information exchange. First, members must actively decide what kind of information they are going to share. Second, like most group discussions, not all of the information available to members is shared. Third, the task is cooperative in that the collective goal is to reach the correct or best decision.

There are many kinds of data that one can quickly summarize from this task. For example, one can compare members' certainty of judgment before and after "discussion"; rated certainty is typically higher afterward, suggesting that individuals feel that they have benefited from the information exchange and are able to make a better judgment as a result. One can also compare the groups' decisions with reality. It is educational to point out in this context that whereas this task allows one to judge the correctness of the decisions, many real-life contexts do not.

The outcome that generates the most class discussion is usually the comparison of what cards are played with the cards in members' hands. Almost without exception, the color that is dominant in the hands before discussion is overrepresented on the table. For example, suppose there are five members who are dealt the following hands:

	Member				
	A	B	C	D	E
number of red cards	6	4	6	3	5
number of black cards	5	7	5	8	6

Three of the five members' hands favor black and, summing across members' hands, we see that thirty-one (56 percent) of the fifty-five cards dealt are black. A typical outcome is that 70 percent to 80 percent of the cards played on the table would be black in the above case, and the group (as well as individual members) would end up confidently concluding black (which may or may not be right).

Such a result illustrates the tendency for shared information to overrepresent the biases that may exist in members' information before discussion. Moreover, it is instructive to ask members how they decided what to play. They often say, "I played the color that I had the most of," or, "I played the color that I thought was most likely to be correct." Members who find themselves in the "minority" (e.g., members A and C in the above example) often say, "I played red at first because I had more of those, but when others seemed to be favoring black, I decided that they could be right and didn't want to mislead the group—so I started playing black." There are many manipulations one can implement using this task. Thus, it lends itself to illustrating research methods in addition to examining some of the dynamics of information exchange. It requires few materials and is easily explained to participants. Moreover, groups can be run through several trials by using different decks. (Thanks to Gary Stasser for providing this exercise.)

4. What attributes do people perceive to be important in today's political leaders? A way to begin a discussion of the topic is to have students rate the list of characteristics found in Chapter 11 of their Study Guide. The rating students should make is how much they believe these attributes are needed in today's leaders.

Film Notes: A Picture Is Sometimes Worth a Thousand Words

Diagnosing Group Operation, 1961, 30 mins. Audiovisual Services, Kent State University, Kent, OH 44242. An analysis of group functions using Bale's categories.

Dynamics of Leadership, 5 films from 1961, 30 mins. each. Audiovisual Services, Kent State University, Kent, OH 44242. The five films analyze group structure, operations, communication, and leadership.

Experimental Studies in Social Climates of Groups, 32519, 1953, 30 mins. Pennsylvania State University, Audiovisual Services, Special Services Building, University Park, PA 16802 (814-865-6314). Classic study by Kurt Lewin in which a hidden camera observes three boys' clubs operated under autocratic, democratic, and laissez-faire principles. Shows how boys react when conditions of leadership are changed to another method. K. Lewin, R. Lippitt, and R. White.

Four More Days, color, 32 mins. New York University Film Library, 26 Washington Place, New York, NY 10003. The film presents the prisoner-guard experiment by Philip Zimbardo.

*Group Decision Making and Leadership, videotape, 28.5 mins. To obtain this tape, consult your Allyn and Bacon sales representative. After examining a business group's discussion concerning whom to hire, Robert A. Baron and Margaret Clark get inside the workings of group decision making.

Group Dynamics: Groupthink, 21762, 1973, color, 22 mins. Pennsylvania State University, Audiovisual Services, Special Services Building, University Park, PA 16802 (814-865-6314). Presents the eight symptoms of groupthink as proposed by Dr. Irving L. Janis in his book, *Victims of Groupthink.* Offers examples of group decision-making processes that influenced historical events such as Pearl Harbor, the Korean War, and the Bay of Pigs, and describes how effective leadership can prevent a decision-making group from falling into groupthink. From the *Behavior in Business* series. A CRM production.

Individual Motivation and Behavior, 30531, 1963, 30 mins. Pennsylvania State University, Audiovisual Services, Special Services Building, University Park, PA 16802 (814-865-6314). Why do people join groups, and why do some members block or dominate group action? Professor Knowles offers comments before and after practical demonstration and discusses the motivation of each person who participates in the demonstration. One person wants to go home, another hates arguments, another wants everyone to like him, and one believes that others are trying to dominate him. From the *Dynamics of Leadership* series. Produced by NET.

Leadership: Style or Circumstance?, 32006, 1974, color, 30 mins. Pennsylvania State University, Audiovisual Services, Special Services Building, University Park, PA 16802 (814-865-6314). Considers the difference between Fiedler's relation-oriented and task-oriented leadership. Interviews with presidents of Baskin-Robbins and Deluxe General, Inc., show that each style can be effective, and that it is important to gear leadership training programs to the specific group to be led or to the task to be accomplished. From the *Behavior in Business* series. A CRM production.

Problem Solving Strategies: The Synthetics Approach, 1980, color, 27 mins. Now also available on videotape (cost to rent: $55; cost to buy: $260) CRM Films, 2233 Faraday Ave., Carlsbad, CA 92008. The film shows several strategies for improving the quality of group problem solving.

Social Group, videotape, 30 mins. Western Illinois University Television Services, Macomb, IL 61455 (309-298-1880). From the *Understanding Human Behavior* series, this entry explores how social groups form and function.

Transparencies

11.1 *The Drive Theory of Social Facilitation*
11.2 *The Distraction-Conflict Theory of Social Facilitation*

11.3 *Contingency Model of Leadership Effectiveness*

Critical Thinking/Essay Questions

1. Summarize the assumptions underlying Zajonc's drive theory of social facilitation, the predictions the theory makes about behavior, and the conclusions drawn from research findings.

2. Compare the performance of individuals and groups on additive, conjunctive, disjunctive, and compensatory tasks.

3. Compare the exchange of shared versus unshared information in a group.

4. Describe the group polarization effect. Compare the explanations for group polarization put forth by the social comparison theory and by the persuasive arguments theory.

5. Describe the great person theory of leadership, and summarize evidence supporting and contradicting this view.

Sources for Lecture

Burrows, W. E. (1982). Cockpit encounters. *Psychology Today,* November, pp. 43–47. What makes for efficient task performance by the small group working in the cockpit to fly an airplane?

Ciulla, J. B. (1986). Corporate leadership: Try a little tenderness. *Psychology Today,* March, pp. 70, 75. Five recent books are reviewed, all of which essentially take the view that the feared, powerful Machiavellian leader has been replaced by a problem solver who empowers his or her followers.

Fiedler, F. A. (1969). Style or circumstance: The leadership enigma. *Psychology Today,* March, pp. 38–43. Fiedler's leadership theory states that both personal style and the situation are important in determining the leader's success. He examines task-oriented and relationship-oriented styles and discusses the conditions under which each is effective.

Fiedler, F. A. (1987). When to lead, when to stand back. *Psychology Today,* September, pp. 26–27. Here Fiedler probes directive and nondirective leadership styles and also looks at the role played by leader intelligence.

Goleman, D. (1985). Following the leader: Sometimes it's folly to go along with the boss. *Science 85,* October, pp. 18–20. How could E. F. Hutton continue its practice of illegally overdrawing its bank accounts without someone blowing the whistle? Goleman explains in terms of groupthink.

Hall, J. (1971). Decisions, decisions, decisions. *Psychology Today,* November, pp. 51–54, 86–88. Group deci-sions *can* be superior to those of individuals. The achievement of satisfactory group solutions is explored.

Janis, I. L. (1971). Groupthink. *Psychology Today,* November, pp. 43–46, 74–76. Janis himself discusses his well-known work on groupthink. The symptoms of groupthink are highlighted, with excellent examples of each symptom.

Latane, B., Williams, K., & Harkins, S. (1979). *Psychology Today,* October, pp. 104–106, 110. Again, the people who did the work tell us about it! These authors review their research on social loafing and question the value of working as a team in a group.

Markes, M. L. (1986). The question of quality circles. *Psychology Today,* March, pp. 36–46. The basic feature of quality circle programs is that small groups of people who perform similar work meet on a regular basis to analyze work problems and propose solutions to them. The article analyzes their success.

McCall, W. M., & Lombardao, M. M. (1983). What makes a top executive? *Psychology Today,* February, pp. 26–31. Two behavioral scientists from a leading think tank map the pitfalls along the corridor to the executive suite.

McCullough, D. (1983). Mama's boys. *Psychology Today,* March, pp. 32–38. Many famous historic leaders adored their mothers and were adored in return. Is the mother-son relationship crucial to leaders?

Update: Current Articles from Professional Sources

Butler, D., & Geis, F. L. (1990). Nonverbal affect responses to male and female leaders: Implications for leadership evaluations. *Journal of Personality and Social Psychology, 58,* 48ff. Female confederates who assumed leadership in four-person discussion groups elicited more negative nonverbal affect responses than male leaders offering the same initiatives. Offers this as a concrete social mechanism underlying the devaluation of female leaders.

Crocker, J., & Luhtanen, R. (1990). Collective self-esteem and ingroup bias. *Journal of Personality and Social Psychology, 58,* 60–67. Studied collective self-esteem, which is that part of the individual's self-concept that derives from membership in a social group. People high in collective self-esteem react to threats to the group by derogating outgroups and enhancing the ingroup.

Insko, C. A., et al. (1990). Individual-group discontinuity as a function of fear and distrust. *Journal of Personality and Social Psychology, 58,* 68–79. The fact that intergroup relations tend to be more competitive than interindividual relations was investigated. Within-group discussion of distrust for the other group was important in reducing cooperation in the intergroup situation.

Nemeth, C., et al. (1990). Exposure to dissent and recall of information. *Journal of Personality and Social Psychology, 58,* 429ff. Two experiments test the theory that consistent minorities induce different cognitive processes in the group than do consistent majorities. Results show that exposure to information from a consistent minority sometimes leads to better recall than exposure to a consistent majority.

Robinson-Staveley, K., & Cooper, J. (1990). Mere presence, gender, and reactions to computers: Studying human-computer interaction in the social context. *Journal of Experimental Social Psychology, 26,* 168–183. Men and women completed a difficult computer task and a series of questionnaires in the presence or absence of another person. Men and women were differentially affected by the presence of another, although gender differences seemed to be a function of differences in expectations for success.

Sanna, L. J., & Shotland, R. L. (1990). Valence of anticipated evaluation and social facilitation. *Journal of Experimental Social Psychology, 26,* 82–92. Subjects anticipating successful performance and thus a positive evaluation from an audience performed better with the audience than alone. Subjects anticipating poor performance and thus a negative evaluation showed impaired performance with the audience.

INSTRUCTOR'S SECTION

12

Personality and Social Behavior

Chapter Outline: Getting the Overall Picture

Learning Objectives

1. Be able to describe how the concepts of personality and situational determinants developed, and describe the difference between personality and social psychology.
2. Learn how the notion of personality traits relates to that of personality. Be able to define personality and relate the concept to individual differences.
3. Know the history of the use of personality traits. Be able to list and describe the five basic personality traits.
4. Learn about our tendency to see ourselves as complex and unpredictable and to see others as relatively simple and consistent (predictable).
5. Be able to show how real life differs from laboratory studies of the interplay of situational effects and personality.
6. Be able to describe Walter Mischel's revolutionary idea and to indicate how social and personality psychology might be integrated.
7. Know how the Headey and Wearing (1989) study revealed the interplay between the five basic traits and situational factors in the determination of subjective well-being.
8. Be able to elaborate on the metatrait hypothesis by providing examples and to relate it to the traited versus untraited notion.
9. Know the conditions under which personality factors are likely to have an important effect on behavior.
10. Be able to define the concept of authoritarian personality in terms of the basic characteristics that authoritarians exhibit, to tell how the measure of authoritarianism developed, and to indicate what the F-scale predicts.
11. Know the concepts of reliability, validity, construct validity, self-concept and self-esteem.
12. Know the childhood determinants of self-esteem and the health implications of negative self-esteem.
13. Be able to discuss the attributes that are related to self-esteem, the role of positive and negative evaluations, positive self-statements, and situational factors in determining self-esteem.
14. How do illusions and overgeneralizations help people maintain their level of self-esteem?
15. Know what self-efficacy is and what happens to individuals when their self-efficacy is low. How does the level of self-efficacy affect performance?
16. What is the relationship between self-efficacy and the ability to tolerate pain?
17. Be able to describe high and low self-monitoring people, the Lennox/Wolfe (1984) criticism of the original self-monitoring scale, and the consistency level of those scoring high and low on the scale.
18. Know the interpersonal behavior of high and low self-monitoring people and the relationship of extreme scores to maladjustment.
19. Appreciate external and internal locus of control, along with the concepts of expectancy and value. How is the I-E Scale constructed and how do feelings of control affect the sense of well-being?
20. Be able to show how internals and externals get to be the way they are and how the two differ behaviorally.
21. How do social activists differ from others in terms of locus of control and feeling about personal power and social injustice? What factors change locus of control?
22. Be able to contrast erotophobia and erotophilia and tell how these characteristics are measured. How do these dispositions affect sexual expression, health, and contraception use? What can we do about unwanted teen pregnancies?

Topics for Discussion

1. "Yes, I'm aggressive . . . sometimes. It depends on the situation." Bring up the "problem" of behavior being unstable across situations and the implication of stated inconsistency for the interaction between traits and situations. Ask students to reflect on their own behavior and indicate which traits they show in what situations.

2. How can we see so much stability of behavior when it apparently doesn't exist? It could be that stability is in the eye of the beholder. Discuss the mechanisms we adopt to convince ourselves that behavior is cross-situationally consistent. Among the methods we use are forgetting that we tend to see a given person in the same situation, a poverty of terms to label situations, but a plethora of words to use as labels for traits, and a bias toward attributing others' behavior to traits rather than situations. Other methods cited by W. Mischel and colleagues include mistaking temporal consistency (same behavior in the same situation on different occasions) for cross-situational consistency and perceiving and remembering mainly behaviors that correspond to the labels we first hang on a given person (first impressions determine later perceptions of behaviors).

3. Fatalism is an affliction suffered by many. Of course, that orientation is virtually the same thing as being an external. Ask students how many are fatalists, before they read about externals. To convince them of the seriousness of their position, have them discuss health and survival as it relates to fatalism. Some students will reveal neglect of health and dangerous behavior *because* they believe what will be will be or when your time is up, your life is over. Have other students join in to indicate how health problems and unrealistically dangerous situations can be avoided.

4. Perhaps the very essence of being a Type A personality is the concept of doing it now. Of course, it is ironic that the propensity for getting a task done as soon as it is assigned is the stuff that both success *and* heart attacks are made of (to convince students that heart attacks are relevant to them, inform them that attacks do occur for people in their twenties and are fairly frequent for people in their thirties, and the rate for females climbs at an alarming rate at later ages). Elicit suggestions for the best of both worlds, enjoying the success associated with the concept of doing it now and avoiding the problems resulting from the same. You might help by offering the following: make a list of priorities, revising it as needed; start immediately on the number one item and work steadily on it until it is completed, *but do not set a deadline;* when the number one task is complete, start on number two, *but again, no deadline.* Suggest that the list be kept short, and assure students that starting immediately and working steadily will allow them to ignore deadlines imposed by other people.

Classroom Exercises/Demonstrations

1. Give your students an I-E scale. If it is good to be internal and not so good to be external, students should know where they stand. The scale, found in the Study Guide, was contrived by one of the Instructor's Section authors to be more appropriate to college students and more like real life. Though the scale is patterned after the original, it has not itself been validated; have students interpret with care. However, after interpretations, the information in the text about externals and internals will come alive. Students may want to share insights they gained as a result of putting together text information with knowledge of their I-E scores.

One point is given for choosing each of the following alternatives. The higher the score, the more external the scorer. 1.a; 2.b; 3.a; 4.b; 5.a; 6.b; 7.a; 8.b; 9.b; 10.a; 11.a; 12.a; 13.b; 14.a; 15.a; 16.a; 17.b; 18.b; 19.a; 20.a; 21.a; 22.a; 23.b; 24.a; 25.a.

2. Mark Snyder's Self-Monitoring Scale, found in the Study Guide, is probably the fastest growing test in the United States, in terms of the number of times it's been used over the brief period of its existence. The Scale relates to everything, from the kind of ads that will work best to who is consistent and who is inconsistent across social situations. Students will enjoy finding out whether they are high or low in self-monitoring (or inbetween), because it will tell them a great deal about themselves. If a given student knows that he or she is high or low on the Scale, the text information concerning high and low self-monitoring will take on new and more urgent meaning. Perhaps some students will want to share with the class what it is like to be high or low in self-monitoring. Award one point toward being a high self-monitor for each item answered as follows: 1.f; 2.f; 3.f; 4.f; 5.t; 6.t; 7.t; 8.t; 9.f; 10.t; 11.t; 12.f; 13.t; 14.f; 15.t; 16.t; 17.f; 18.t; 19.t; 20.f; 21.f; 22.f; 23.f; 24.t; 25.t.

3. How does what happens to you influence how you view yourself? This is a question asked of many subjects. (See Allen, B., & Potkay, C. [1983]. *Adjective Generation Technique.* New York: Irvington.) Should students answer the question about themselves, they will have gone a long way toward self-understanding. They will also have personal information about the interplay between self-view (personality) and situational effects ("what happens to you"). Have students use the log sheet they will find in the Study Guide chapter corresponding to this one. They simply follow the straightforward instructions accompanying the sheet. The easiest way to score the words is to assign a positive or negative valence to each word, depending on how favorable or unfavorable it is, and then an overall valence, according to whether positive or negative valences are most frequent. Also, a positive or negative valence could be assigned to each description of "what happened to you." The descriptions should be done first for a block of perhaps ten days (have them make several copies of the log sheet). Then they can be scored and the possible correspondence between the two ratings can be observed. More objective ratings would occur if students placed code numbers on their log sheets and then had fellow students score the words and "happenings" blind.

4. Although social circumstances may be the most potent determinants of aggression, there is no denying that some people are disposed to aggression by virtue of their personalities. Charles Spielberger and his colleagues have recently developed a measure of anger trait, a tendency for some people to be chronically angry and thus disposed to aggression and health hazards. Have students complete the scale, found in the Study Guide. It may provide them with some insights concerning the source of some of their social and health problems. Perhaps some students who scored high will want to share their reflections on how being angry has shaped their lives. Scores of 21 or above are at or above the 75th percentile for both sexes. Scores 15 to 12 for females and 14 to 11 for males are at the 25th percentile or below.

Film Notes: A Picture Is Sometimes Worth a Thousand Words

A Day in the Life of Jonathan Mole, film, 30 mins. CRM/McGraw-Hill Films, 110 Fifteenth Street, Del Mar, CA 92014. How personal characteristics and social circumstances interplay to produce a bigoted person is graphically depicted.

Evaluating Personality, PB114, videotape (cost to buy: $179), 30 mins. Insight Media, 121 West 85th St., New York, NY 10024-4401 (800-233-9910). This tape investigates various personality evaluation methods.

Personality, film, 25 mins. CRM/McGraw-Hill Films, 110 Fifteenth Street, Del Mar, CA 92014. A college student's personality is analyzed according to traditional trait-personality notions.

The Self, #15, videotape, 30 mins. The Annenborg Project, Holt, Rinehart & Winston, 1990, contact Lee Sutherlin, Marketing Manager (817-334-7632). This one is all about how psychologists systematically study the origins of self-identity and self-esteem, social determinants of self-concepts, and the emotional and motivational consequences of beliefs about oneself.

Shyness: Reasons and Remedies, PB30, videotape (cost to buy: $129), 30 mins. Insight Media, 121 West 85th St., New York, NY 10024-4401 (800-233-9910). This video studies the causes of shyness and how it affects our personal and social well-being.

Transparencies

12.1 *Some Factors That Make a Difference in Subjective Well-Being*

12.2 *Personality and Social Psychology*

12.3 *Personality Development and Measurement*

12.4 *Interaction of "Strength of Situation" and the Personality Factor "Authoritarianism"*

12.5 *Integrative Research Using Both Social and Personality Variables*

12.6 *Five Robust Personality Traits*

12.7 *Nine Components of the Authoritarian Personality*

Critical Thinking/Essay Questions

1. Define and contrast personality and situational determinants, as well as personality and social psychology. Also, relate personality trait to personality and list the five basic personality traits.

2. Use subjective well-being as an example of how social (situations) psychological and personality perspectives can be integrated to account for a psychological factor.

3. Describe the circumstances in which personality variables are useful and when they are not.

4. Describe an authoritarian. Make up a hypothetical person who displays the major characteristics of authoritarians.

5. What would a personality test be like if it had reliability and construct validity?

6. Tell what deflates self-esteem and design a program that would inflate self-esteem.

7. Outline the relationship between self-efficacy and Type A behavior as it relates to success among college faculty.

8. Construct an imaginary party setting and indicate how two hypothetical party goers, one high and one low in self-monitoring, would behave differently in this setting. Come up with as many differences as you can.

9. How do externals and internals differ in ways that have practical implications (for example, well-being, health, social activism).

10. How do erotophobics and erotophiliacs differ in orientation to sex? How did they get to be the way they are? What are the implications of differences relating to health?

Sources for Lecture

Fischman, J. (1987). Type A on trial. *Psychology Today,* February, pp. 42–50. Like your text, this article concludes that Type A in and of itself is not a determinant of heart disease. Instead, it is traits like anger, impatience, aggravation, and irritation that are bad for the heart. The loss of faith is traced in these pages.

Fischman, J. (1987). Getting tough. *Psychology Today,* December, pp. 26–28. The personality characteristic of "hardiness" grew out of 1970's research linking sickness to emotional stress. Perhaps hardiness is a buffer against life's stresses and the illness they cause.

Horn, J. (1986). Measuring a man by the company he keeps. *Psychology Today,* March, p. 12. Mark Snyder, Ellen Berscheid, and Peter Glick asked high and low self-monitors what kind of information they wanted about potential dates. The lows went for personality information and the highs for physical attractiveness profiles.

Roberts, M. (1988). School yard menace. *Psychology Today,* February, pp. 52–56. Is bullying a personality trait? Or does the school yard bring out meanness in some children? Bullies are usually boys and usually come from families that neglect, reject, or abuse children, or create an environment of violence.

Trotter, R. J. (1987). Stop blaming yourself. *Psychology Today,* February, pp. 31–39. The title says it all. People whose explanatory style reflects learned helplessness blame themselves and suffer the health consequences.

Update: Current Articles from Professional Sources

Adame, D. D., Johnson, T. C., & Cole, S. P. (1989). Physical fitness, body image, and locus of control in college freshman men and women. *Perceptual and Motor Skills, 68,* 400–402. For both men and women there was an association between physical fitness, body image, and locus of control.

Bachorowski, J., & Newman, J. P. (1990). Impulsive motor behavior: Effects of personality and goal salience. *Journal of Personality and Social Psychology, 58,* 512–518. The results of this experiment provide evidence that both impulsive and anxious subjects may display poor motor inhibition on a task used traditionally as a measure of behavioral impulsivity. The outcome is linked to introversion-extroversion.

Bluhm, C., & Widiger, T. A. (1990). Interpersonal complementarity and individual differences. *Journal of Personality and Social Psychology, 58,* 464–471. This study pursued the interplay between situational factors and individual differences. It was found that affiliative behavior was due largely to situational effects and control behavior was due largely to individual differences.

Peterson, C., & Stunkard, A. J. (1989). Personal control and health promotion. *Social Science and Medicine, 28,* 819–828. Famous obesity researcher Stunkard and his colleague reported on how personal control (PC), an individual's belief about the degree that he or she can bring about good events and avoid bad events, affects health. High PC was associated with intellectual, emotional, behavioral, and physiological vigor in the face of challenging situations and events; low PC was associated with maladaptive passivity and poor morale.

Speake, D. L., Cowart, M. E., & Pellet, K. (1989). Health perceptions and life-styles of the elderly. *Research in Nursing and Health, 12*(2), 93–100. Results showed that perceived health status and health locus of control were significant predictors of healthy life-styles.

13

Interacting with the Environment

Chapter Outline: Getting the Overall Picture

I. Adapting to an Environment Shaped by Human Beings
   A. World Population Growth: Steadily Increasing Demands on Planetary Resources
   B. Living in Cities: Effects of an Urban Environment
      1. The Growth of Impoverished Megacities
      2. Cities: Attraction and Fear
      3. The Overstimulation of Cities
   C. Life at Home: Arranging a Private World
      1. Large-Scale Housing Projects
      2. Creating a Home Environment

II. What Are We Doing to the Environment?
   A. The Greenhouse Effect: A Dramatic Alteration of Our World
   B. Motivating Environmentally Responsible Behavior
      1. Reminding People to Act in Accordance with Their Attitudes and Beliefs
      2. Reinforcing Responsible Environmental Behavior
      3. Legislating Attitudinal Change

III. What Is the Environment Doing to Us?
   A. Noise: Volume and Predictability

   1. Effects of Unpredictable Noise
   2. Noise As a Health Risk
   3. Behavioral Effectiveness
   4. Social Effects
   B. Meteorological Effects
   1. Temperature and Behavior
   2. Atmospheric Electricity
   C. The Air We Breathe
   D. Nuclear Threats: Radioactive Waste and Atomic Accidents
   1. Nuclear Waste
   2. Accidents at Nuclear Power Plants

IV. Interpersonal Environment: Effects of Close Encounters with Other People
   A. Crowding
   1. Densely Packed Versus Feeling Crowded
   2. Extended Exposure to Crowded Conditions
   3. Crowding in Prisons
   B. Personal Space and the Effects of Intrusions
   1. Effects of Sex, Age, and Culture
   2. Personal Space Variations Across Situations
   C. Territorial Behavior

Learning Objectives

1. Understand what environmental psychology means and list the environmental issues involving behavior that will be significant in the future.

2. Explore the growth of the human population throughout history. Appreciate the geometric progression of population growth, using the Grand Vi-

zier of Persia's ploy as an example. What will become of the excess population if people refuse to restrain population growth?

3. Examine the growth of the megacity. How have people come to feel about cities? Discover what generates fear in city residents. Is there necessarily a correlation between violence rates and city growth?

4. Appreciate the paradox involved in the coincidence of good living conditions in and the pathology of cities. On a regional basis, where are the most serious social pathological problems? What is stimulus overload and how is it relevant to life in the city?

5. Is there any truth to our beliefs about differences in the friendliness and receptivity between small town and big city residents? Understand how friendliness and receptivity can vary within cities and the reasons for the failure of high-rise housing projects.

6. Learn what the notion of home is and how space in the home is allocated and privacy regulated.

7. Why do even young children pick savannas when given an option of environments?

8. How do we view what we are doing to our environment? Become aware of the greenhouse effect, the gases that contribute to it, and how alterations to human behavior can lessen the warming trend.

9. Be able to discuss the discrepancy between the tendency for people to be proenvironment while remaining relatively inactive when it comes to environmental change. Be able to recognize what constitutes an environmental activist.

10. When will prompts designed to promote responsible treatment of the environment likely be effective? Learn what is the best way to word a prompt.

11. Learn the point of the Ferrari and Baldwin (1989) study of prompts employed to get parents to use grocery cart seat belts.

12. Explore the different methods for rewarding antilitter behavior. Determine how the problem of the cost of rewards can be solved.

13. Determine the sequence of events that prompts antilitter legislation, behavior change, and, finally, attitude change.

14. What is environmental stress? Learn some of the hazards of living in a technological environment.

15. Learn how fear of technology is an all-or-none phenomenon. What is the surprising effect of the media on technological fears?

16. Appreciate the effects of unpredictable noise, the health risks and social effects of noise, and how airport noise affects people. How did the initial lab studies on noise and aggression contradict common beliefs about the relationship between the two factors, and how have subsequent natural studies supported that belief?

17. Learn the effects of ions on behavior. Appreciate the psychological effects of air pollution and how people react to long-term exposure. What is the effect of other people's smoke on us and how do smokers respond to nonsmokers' negative reactions to them? Learn how ground-level ozone affects us.

18. Understand the reaction of people to the prospect of a nuclear dump site near them and to the threat of other toxic sites nearby. Appreciate radiation phobia and the effect of the incident at Three Mile Island on nearby residents.

19. What are the advantages of the winding line as opposed to the straight line? Determine the difference between density and crowding and between social and spatial density. What happens as social density increases, especially in university and school settings?

20. Determine the difference between Easterners and Westerners in reaction to social density and learn prisoners' reactions to it, as well as methods for coping with it and the effect of perception of control.

21. Understand what personal space is and how age, sex, culture, and police officers' mistakes are involved with it. Learn Hall's four common rules regulating interactions at different distances.

22. Determine the differences between primary, secondary, and public territories and relate the prior residence effect to the home field advantage. How do people mark territories and what happens when people share territories?

Topics for Discussion

1. People seem unaware that they contribute to pollution. Have students list all of the cases they can think of where a typical person contributes to pollution (e.g., driving an automobile, drinking out of cans, using nonbiodegradable wrappings). Consider substitute behaviors that would lower individual pollution. Pay special attention to easy avenues to nonpolluting behaviors.

2. The notion of radiation phobia raises some important issues. So long as people lump all things nuclear together and find them all to be equally bad, some benefits of nuclear physics will be retarded and progress toward eliminating the truly threatening applications will be slow. There are positive manifestations of nuclear physics. For example, Rosalyn S. Yalow won a Nobel Prize for the development of radioimmunoassay, a technique that involves treating biologic substances with radiation so that the presence of certain immunological entities can be detected. It is estimated that this technique has saved many thousands of lives and the numbers will eventually reach the millions. She can now be seen on TV in antismoking ads. Yalow is one of those who points out cigarettes are much more dangerous than nuclear power plants. The use of radiation to preserve foods almost indefinitely is another example of positive uses of radiation.

If students need to know that all things nuclear are not bad, they also need to know that some products of nuclear physics are worse than others. Compare nuclear weapons facilities with nuclear power plants. Nuclear power plants are relatively well regulated. Before the Chernobyl incident, there were few deaths worldwide directly attributable to power plant radiation exposure. In the United States the number is very small (see Allen, [1990]. *Personal adjustment*. Pacific Grove, CA: Brooks/ Cole, for a further discussion). By contrast, nuclear weapons facilities are relatively poorly regulated and have been associated with many deaths (see the readings suggested at the end of this chapter).

Armed with this information, you might start the discussion by asking if there is anything good about the application of nuclear physics. Then, guide students to understanding that some things nuclear are more threatening than others. If students can appreciate that nuclear weapons are the real threat, they may act. Consider this discussion an exercise in critical thinking.

3. Have students spend a day violating others' personal spaces (getting too close to some strangers). You may need to award extra credit for this brazen endeavor. To make it easy on them, instruct them to approach strangers a little too closely under the pretense of asking for directions or the time of day. Students should record reactions, noting the sex, age, and circumstances of the "violated" person. Using these records, have students relate their experiences as "violators" during class. There is likely to be some humor in these reports and much stimulation of remembered "violations." All should gain insight into the dynamics of personal space regulation.

4. Abortion is an explosive issue that you may wish to avoid. However, you are guaranteed a lively discussion if you bring up the topic. The problem is avoiding offense. Carl Sagan and Ann Druyan have attempted to develop a strategy that allows choice and at the same time is prolife (see "Sources for Lecture"). You will need to read their article, but, to give you a summary of it, consider a world in which birth control was widely and conscientiously used. In such a world, people would be exercising their choice of when or whether they will have children. At the same time, because conception is avoided by the use of birth control, the issue of killing the embryo or fetus does not arise.

To start this discussion, begin with the question posed as the title of the Sagan-Druyan article: "Is It Possible to Be Pro-life and Pro-choice?" To avoid problems, you may want to work very hard to keep your point of view out of the discussion. Consider acting as a facilitator and moderator only: as you know, even endorsement of birth control can be offensive to some people. Rather than endorsing it, consider raising it as an issue and refer to the text authors' point that the world's population could conceivably become so great that human life itself could not be sustained.

5. What can we do about the greenhouse effect? First, students need to understand what causes it. Start this discussion after students have read the text, or provide the information yourself. Here is a short summary. CO_2, methane, chlorofluorocarbons (CFCs), nitrous oxides, and other gases form a blanket around the earth, letting light through, but trapping heat much like a greenhouse. So far, CO_2 is the major contributor; methane and CFCs are increasing fast, as are nitrous oxides (as you recall, CFCs also deplete the ozone layer, thereby increasing ultraviolet-B, with accompanying increases in the probability of skin cancer, cataracts, and the destruction of plankton, the beginning of the food chain in the world's oceans). Excess CO_2 results primarily from the burning of fossil fuels such as oil, gasoline, and coal. Nitrous oxides are also emitted from the burning of fossil fuels and from certain fertilizers. Excess methane results from forest fires, landfills, rice paddies, and the digestive tracts of ruminant animals such as cattle. CFCs are found in aerosols that propel the contents of spray cans, solvents that are used to clean computer components (microchips and circuit boards), as well as refrigerants and foams.

Equipped with this information, students are ready to suggest ways they can contribute to reductions in greenhouse gases. Encouraging the planting of trees to help in the intake of CO_2 is a way to reduce the gas. We can drive less by carpooling and taking public transportation. We can demand that our politicians seek regulations that ensure cleaner burning of coal and oil to reduce nitrous oxides. We can decrease methane by demanding tighter control of landfills and by eating less red meat (then there will be less cattle).

Aerosols have declined because of regulation. This observation suggests that we can do more to reduce CFCs. We can demand that other solvents be used to clean computer components (there are some available). We can also reduce CFCs by decreasing our dependency on air conditioners and refrigerators. Finally, we can demand the use of containers made of something other than styrofoam. Here is a chance to empower students by helping them discover that there are actions they can take to save the environment.

1. "In every life, a little rain must fall." Are temperature, ozone level, and ion content the only weather factors that affect social behavior? How about precipitation or its opposite, a sunny day? On a beautiful, sunny day have students describe themselves in five words. Have them do the same on a rainy day as well as on two partly cloudy days. Students can "score" their words to show that a little sunshine can make a difference in how people describe themselves. Simply have them exchange descriptions and place positive signs (+) by words that are favorable, and negative signs (−) by unfavorable words (don't score words that are neither favorable nor unfavorable). Then consider a description favorable if it has more positive signs than negative signs. Favorable descriptions should be more prominent on beautiful, sunny days, and unfavorable descriptions on days when it is raining or overcast. In class, ask students why they described themselves in the way they did on assigned days. Point out the precipitation factor in weather as a determinant of descriptions. It should be the case that "beautiful days make for beautiful descriptions": we really are influenced by the weather. (See Allen & Potkay [1983], *Adjective Generation Technique* [AGT]. New York: Irvington, for more information about the "describe yourself with words" method.)

2. The late Milton Rokeach's value conflict test might be altered to fit pollution. Give the students the value scale (found in the Study Guide chapter corresponding to this one) and ask them to rank the items from 1 (most important) to 18 (least important). Then compare the mean ranks of items substituted for "equality" and "freedom" in positions 6 and 8 from the top. Perhaps your students will find a clean environment for future generations more important than freedom to exploit the environment now. Whether or not they do, it will be interesting to discover how environmental issues stack up against the more personal issues found on the scale. Ask them to volunteer which three items they ranked highest. The information they provide may inspire some students to ask others why they ranked issues such as "an exciting life" and "a sense of accomplishment" above "a clean environment in the future."

3. Ignoring the threat of nuclear war is behavior that could lead to the catastrophic destruction of our environment. Many students have recently described nuclear war using the Adjective Generation Technique (AGT) (see Exercise 1, above). Based on recent research—see parenthetical statement below—it is likely that your students will provide similar descriptions. In any case, they will be interested in how they compare with other students from earlier years. Ask them to follow the instructions on the AGT sheet found in the Study Guide. Using the list found below, call out the words in any order and, for each, ask students to indicate whether they have used the word. Tally the results on the board. Compare your tally with that for the twenty-three most-used words in the table below. For each word, does the number of words over the number of students match the proportions of subjects in the 1985, 1986, and 1988 samples that generated the word? Perhaps more interesting is the possibility that the average *number of words* generated by your students reflects the continued decline shown at the bottom of the table below. Your students' responses may reflect the stable horror at the thought of nuclear war that the subjects in the table showed. Your students may also confirm that nuclear war is becoming less salient—it is coming less readily to mind and our perceptions of it are becoming less rich, as indicated by declining numbers of words in descriptions with each succeeding year. You may also wish to compare the Favorability, Anxiety, Femininity, and Concrete-Vividness reflected in the words your students generated with that found in the words of the subjects. (The table below summarizes studies done over three years and reported by Bem Allen at the Convention of the Society for Personality Assessment, San Diego, 1990. Any results obtained from this exercise would be of interest to this Instructor's Section author Allen).

Adjective Generation Technique (AGT): Descriptions of Nuclear War[&]

	Rank-%[@]	Rank-%	Rank-%	Freq.[*]	Freq.[#]	Freq.[^]	FAV	ANX	FEM	CNRT
	1985 Study	1986 Study	1988 Study	1985 Study	1986 Study	1988 Study				
Death	1–40	4–24	1–42	105	24	49	33	467	179	252
Destruction	2–29	9–18	6–21	75	18	24	71	457	175	285
Scary	3–24	1–46	2–28	62	46	33	157	419	251	238
Destructive	4–23	2–39	4–26	60	39	30	71	445	175	347
Horrible	5–20	18–10	8–16	53	10	19	92	429	206	342
Unnecessary	6–18	6–21	11–13	46	21	15	157	346	278	397
Frightening	7–16	7–21	7–17	43	21	20	163	407	294	335
Fearful	8–16	10–16	10–15	42	16	18	154	452	406	345

	Rank-%@	Rank-%	Rank-%	Freq.*	Freq.#	Freq.^	FAV	ANX	FEM	CNRT
	1985 Study	1986 Study	1988 Study	1985 Study	1986 Study	1988 Study				
Painful	9–16	8–21	19–10	42	18	12	83	440	283	220
Deadly	10–16	5–24	5–21	41	24	25	75	448	142	335
Sad	11–15	14–11	16–12	40	11	14	106	369	437	210
Bloody	12–12			32			79	450	160	140
Devastating	13–12	22–8	21–9	31	8	11	138	455	204	338
Disastrous	14–12		17–11	31		13	81	471	211	363
Fire	15–11	20–9	20–9	30	9	11	198	469	209	125
Threatening	16–10	17–10		27	10		138	412	190	327
Inhuman	17–10			25			60	412	257	322
Powerful	18–9	21–8		23	8		445	276	131	280
Ugly	19–8	16–10	22–9	22	10	10	89	390	306	180
Exploding	20–8	19–10	13–13	21	10	15	196	467	232	205
Killing	21–8	15–11		21	15		68	495	142	210
Wasteful	22–8	11–13	15–12	21	13	14	102	390	252	307
Terrifying	23–8		12–13	20		15	89	437	253	310
Stupid		3–24	3–27		24	32	115	351	304	350
End		13–13	9–16		13	19	128	390	282	327
Chaos		23–8	14–13		8	15	177	395	245	305
Terrible		12–13	23–8		13	8	98	420	210	327
Useless			18–10			12	87	363	338	300

*1985 N = 262

#1986 N = 100

^1988 N = 117

&High scores reflect high FAV (favorability), ANX (anxiety), and FEM (femininity). Values are on a scale 0–600. Values on the cnrt (concrete-vivid) scale are 0–500. Low values represent high concreteness-vividness.

In an analysis where the dependent variable was proportion (%@ above) of subjects in a given sample generating a given word multiplied by the value for the word on FAV, ANX, FEM, and cnrt and the "independent" variable was years ('85, '86, '88), neither the multivariate F nor univariate Fs were significant: The values for words that people use to describe nuclear war are quite stable over years. However, a separate analysis looking at the number of words generated by subjects as the dependent variable and years as the "independent" variable found a linear decrease in the number of words generated as a function of time. This result may mean that nuclear war became somewhat less salient over time. The means for this analysis are presented below.

$$
\begin{array}{ccc}
1985 & 1986 & 1988 \\
9.79 & 8.70 & 8.03^{\$}
\end{array}
$$

$^{\$}$F = 10.883, df = 2/476, p < .0001

4. According to psychologist Paul Slovic (see *Science,* April 17, 1987, *236,* pp. 280–285), a key to understanding environmental risks and reacting appropriately to them is to assess them accurately. Unfortunately, certain risks, called *dread risks,* are resistant to accurate assessment: they are unfamiliar, involve fears of catastrophic future events and fatal consequences, and are perceived to be uncontrollable precursors of disaster. All of these characteristics of dread risks are reinforced by the media. In view of these characteristics, one can see why dread risks are inaccurately assessed: what is mysterious is especially frightening and what is terribly fearful seems highly likely to occur. Thus, students should overestimate the incidence of dread risks relative to other risks. Test this hypothesis, with regard to diseases, by asking students to guess the number of cases of each of several diseases, using the incidence of syphilis as a benchmark (information found in *Morbidity and Mortality Weekly Report,* May 18, 1990, *39*[19]). AIDS fits the dread risk criteria well and should be greatly overestimated, relative to other diseases. Students can provide their responses on a form found in the Study Guide. It is similar to the table printed below, except that all statistics, except that on syphilis, are missing. (See Allen [1990], *Personal Adjustment.* Pacific Grove, CA: Brooks/Cole, for more details).

Number of Cases of Various Diseases Accumulated During the First Nineteen Weeks of 1990	
Measles	7216
Rabies (humans)	0
Gonorrhea	239,884
AIDS	16,056
Botulism (contamination of food)	1
Tetanus	20
Syphilis	17,539
Tuberculosis	7,141
Leprosy	59
Typhoid fever	128

Film Notes: A Picture Is Sometimes Worth a Thousand Words

Air for Breathing, 3-328, color, 29 mins. Audiovisual Services, Western Illinois University, Macomb, IL 61455 (309-298-2417). This film is a study of pollution in the United States. It covers pollutants and control.

The City and the Self, 50324, color, 52 mins. Pennsylvania State University, Audiovisual Services, Special Services Building, University Park, PA 16802 (814-865-6314). Study of human relations in the city based on psychological concepts formulated by Stanley Milgram. Examines city dwellers' perceptions of their cities and their behavior in created situations.

Environment, NSC-1299, color, 16 mins. Indiana University, Audiovisual Center, Bloomington, IN 47401. This film outlines current environmental problems.

Invisible Walls, 21175, 12 mins. Pennsylvania State University, Audiovisual Services, Special Services Building, University Park, PA 16802 (814-865-6314). Reactions to violations of "personal spaces" are captured on film.

Noise: The New Pollutant, 31321, 30 mins. Pennsylvania State University, Audiovisual Services, Special Services Building, University Park, PA 16802 (814-865-6314). The harmful effects of prolonged exposure to high levels of noise are illustrated.

People by the Billions, GS-910, 28 mins. Indiana University, Audiovisual Center, Bloomington, IN 47401. This film examines the current population explosion, considers past remedies for overpopulation, and suggests two methods to deal with the present problem.

Planet Earth #7 Fate of the Earth, 1064UC, color videotape, 60 mins. Television Services, Western Illinois University, Macomb, IL 61455 (309-298-1880). This extraordinary video explores the global environmental consequences of the "nuclear winter" and the "ultraviolet spring."

The Price of Pollution, color videotape, 60 mins. NETCHE Videotape Library, P. O. Box 83111, Lincoln, NE 68501. Famed environmentalist Barry Commoner discusses the wages of our sin, pollution.

Transparencies

13.1 *How Personal Space and Territory Differ*
13.2 *Reactions to Invasion Depend on One's Cognitions*
13.3 *Social Density and Spatial Density*
13.4 *Environmental Behavior Can Be Changed by Legislation*
13.5 *Three Gases Contributing to the Greenhouse Effect*

Critical Thinking/Essay Questions

1. Describe the early human and tell why it appeared unlikely during their time that their progeny would some day dominate the world. Explain the Grand Vizier's notion of geometric progression.
2. Describe what city dwellers fear the most and why they have these fears. Do good living conditions in cities ensure low pathology of those cities?
3. Compare urban and small-town living. How does friendliness and receptivity vary across these habitats? Why do even young children pick savannas when given an option of environments?
4. List and discuss current environmental problems. What means would you suggest to mobilize people to do something about these problems?
5. Design a program to induce citizens to take action against litter. Trace the sequence of events that proceeds from legislation to behavior change to attitude change with regard to antilitter behavior.
6. Indicate how noise affects health, academic functioning, and social relations. What kind of noise is the most damaging kind? Tell how lab and real-life studies have differed in conclusions concerning the effect of heat on aggression.
7. Trace the psychological effects of air pollution, in-

cluding that produced by smokers. Define *nuclear phobia* and tell how people react to being near a site that may be contaminated with radiation.

8. List and illustrate the effects of crowding on college students in residence halls, prisoners, and people standing in lines. Indicate the differences between social and spatial density.

9. How do Easterners and Westerners differ in reactions to social density? Define *personal space* and indicate how age, sex, and culture play a role in it. What are the rules for regulating interactions at various distances?

10. List and define the three kinds of territories and what happens when territoriality is ignored. How do people mark territories, and what is the prior residence effect?

Sources for Lecture

Abas, F. (1989). Rocky flats: a big mistake from day one. *Bulletin of the Atomic Scientists,* December, 19–24. Chemist John M. Matuszek's comment that it is safer to live near a low-level nuclear waste dump than reside in Denver is interesting. He is probably right for the wrong reasons: Denver is downwind from the most infamous of several frightening nuclear weapons plants. The Rocky Flats story is a tale of things to come: we will have to face a multibillion dollar cleanup during the '90s and early 2000s.

Cohen, S. (1981). Sound effects on behavior. *Psychology Today,* October. Teacher says, "It's not the noise in here, it's your attitude." Actually, it may well be the noise, but attitudes toward noise matter also.

Ehrlich, P., & Ehrlich, A. (1986). World population crisis. *Bulletin of the Atomic Scientists,* April, 13–19. Two world-famous biologists present shocking statistics concerning the present and future population crises. They state that the birth of a U.S. baby is 200 times more disastrous than a birth in a third world country, because a U.S. baby will live to consume so much more.

Knight, R., & Auster, B. B. (1990). A date with chaos. *U. S. News and World Report,* April 30, pp. 30–32. We are not the only ones with environmental problems. If anything, the Soviets have a worse mess to clean up. This article indicates that responding to environmental problems will have to be one of Gorbachev's highest priorities.

Kunz, A. (1989). Highest disregard. *Mother Jones,* December, pp. 33–36, 44–48. Scientist Sherwood Rowland succeeded in convincing politicians and business figures that spray can propellants were destroying the ozone layer. Now he is battling the electronics industry over their use of solvents that destroy the ozone layer. So far, he has made little headway.

Raloff, J., & Thomsen, D. (1986). Chernobyl may be worst nuclear accident. *Science News,* May 3, p. 276. Three Mile Island was a minor event compared to Chernobyl. What were the psychological effects of the Soviet disaster? Just as in the case of nuclear war, first we must know the physical effects. This article describes how the accident came to be.

Revkin, A. C. (1988). Endless summer: living with the greenhouse effect. *Discover,* October, pp. 50–61. This is a comprehensive and highly readable article that maps out (literally) where and how the greenhouse gases will bring their effects. It also contains information concerning sources of the effect and how it might be short-circuited.

Sagan, C., & Druyan, A. (1990). Is it possible to be pro-life and pro-choice? *Parade,* April 22, pp. 4–8. The answer is yes, according to this famous scientist and wife Druyan, an activist who marshals the forces of science for the good of people.

Science News. (1986). Long-UV light may cause cancer . . . and destroy natural anti-carcinogens. May 3, p. 281. So you want to look good? Get a suntan. But what about ultraviolet radiation (UV) in sunlight? Go to the tanning spa where lamps emit long rather than the short UV that is prominent in sunlight. However, new evidence raises the cost of exploiting the vanity-environment connection. Long UV may cause cancer itself and may destroy natural anticarcinogens.

Update: Current Articles from Professional Sources

Aronson, E. (1990). Applying social psychology to desegregation and energy conservation. *Personality and Social Psychology Bulletin, 16,* 118–132. This article shows how action research has been used to deal with energy conservation.

Omoto, A. M., & Snyder, M. (1990). Basic research in

INSTRUCTOR'S SECTION

action: Volunteerism and society's response to AIDS. *Personality and Social Psychology Bulletin, 16,* 152–165. Here is a fine illustration of the action research model in action. What makes people volunteer and what they experience when they do is the focus.

Seligman, C. & Syme, G. J. (Eds.) (1989). Managing the environment. *Journal of Social Issues, 45*(1), 1–184. These several articles in a special issue of the *JSI* contain a wealth of information about social psychological research into environmental issues. Environmental planning, applied behavior analysis and social marketing, attitudes, environmental design, environmental law, energy conservation and much more are considered.

Turco, R. P., Toon, O. B., Ackerman, T. P., Pollack, J. B., & Sagan, C. (1990). Climate and smoke: An appraisal of nuclear winter. *Science,* January 12, pp. 247, 166–174. There is no better model of climatic disaster than the aftermath of nuclear war. In this update, the TTAPS team who popularized the notion of nuclear winter further supports their position. They write of cold temperatures in the summer and ozone depletion resulting from nitrogen oxides propelled by nuclear blasts into the stratosphere, where they would displace and then destroy the ozone layer.

INSTRUCTOR'S SECTION

14

Applying Social Psychology

Health, Law, and Politics

Chapter Outline: Getting the Overall Picture

I. Health: The Social-Psychological Determinants
  A. How Stress Precipitates Illness
    1. Life Stress and Illness
    2. Moderating the Effects of Stress
    3. The Role of Personality in the Development of Health Problems
    4. Social Support As a Health Benefit
  B. Behavioral Factors That Help Prevent Illness
    1. Perceived Vulnerability to Illness
    2. Motivating Preventive Behavior: The Protection-Motivation Model
    3. Stopping Cigarette Smoking Before It Begins
  C. The Anatomy of an Illness Episode: From Recognizing Symptoms to Seeking Professional Help
    1. Attending to Physical Symptoms
    2. Diagnosing Your Symptoms
    3. Responding to Symptoms
  D. Once You Know You're Ill: Problems with Medical Care
    1. Interacting with a Doctor
    2. Coping with the Procedures of Diagnosis and Treatment

II. Social Psychology and the Legal System
  A. External Effects on Courtroom Behavior: The Media

  B. Eyewitness Testimony: How Accurate Is It?
  C. Potential Biases: Police, Attorneys, and the Judge
    1. The Police: Questions Seldom Reveal "Just the Facts"
    2. The Attorney As Advocate or As Foe
    3. How Impartial Is the Judge?
  D. Defendants and Jurors: They're Only Human, Too
    1. Are Defendants Treated Equally?
    2. Biases on the Jury

III. Psychology and Politics: Liking and Leadership
  A. Political Attitudes and Actions: The Media and Personal Involvement
    1. Political Activism
    2. Media Effects
  B. Psychology and Voter Behavior
  C. Choosing a Candidate: Whom Do You Like?
    1. Repeated Exposure
    2. Physical Appearance: Voting for Candidates Who Look Right
    3. What's in a Name?
    4. Similarity: Voting for Candidates Who Agree with Us
  D. Choosing a Leader: Who Has the Right Stuff?
    1. Characteristics of a Leader
    2. Leadership Styles

INSTRUCTOR'S SECTION

Learning Objectives

1. Learn how applied social psychology and action research compare and how they relate to health psychology.
2. Consider the processes of stress and coping and how they relate to physical disease (Illustrate by reference to psychoneuroimmunology in Magloire's 1988 study of secretory immunoglobulin A).
3. What is the level of stress among students that is high enough for a fifty-fifty chance at illness? How do fitness and hardiness compare and relate to health?
4. Learn to relate the factors of control and optimism and pessimism to stress and illness. What is it about Type As that makes them prone to health problems?
5. Appreciate the role of valuing good health in achieving it. What is social support and what are the health implications in the lack of it? Outline how husbands in the delivery room can alleviate or increase the stress of childbirth, especially according to their level of erotophobia and their wives' degree of dependency on them.
6. Learn how the illusion of invulnerability influences health and longevity. What is the effect of the availability heuristic on "doing the right thing" in the health arena?
7. Learn Rogers' (1983) four informational needs that are critical to taking action against some possible threat. How well and in what areas have the steps worked?
8. Be able to indicate why it is tough to stop smoking and how the false consensus effect deters adolescents from stopping. What surprising factor predicts smoking among young adults better than smoking during the teens?
9. What are the sources of variability among and within people in noticing symptoms, and what is the role of attributional errors in noticing symptoms? Appreciate how people tend to classify problems, with emphasis on the influence of personality factors.
10. Be able to draw up plans to communicate with a physician about one's problems and know the limits of both parties in the ability to "frame" while communicating. What strategies can people adopt to better tolerate medical procedures?
11. Know what forensic psychology is and how the media influences our opinions about which crime problems are the most serious. How accurate are eyewitnesses, what role does their level of certainty play, and how might their accuracy be improved?
12. Know the role of the leading question, the knowledgeable questioner, and the questioning style of the attorney or judges in biasing witnesses.
13. Is there truth to the notion that some judges are lenient and some harsh in their sentencing?
14. How does physical attractiveness, gender (sex), race, and other sources of bias influence juries? In the context of leniency bias, know how guilt or innocence verdicts affect death sentences.
15. Know how the order of charges by the judge to the jury in a murder trial affects juries' decisions.
16. In what areas do social psychologists contribute to the justice system by serving as expert witnesses?
17. What orientations are related to political activism?
18. Is the media as politically biased as many people think? What is the "third person effect?"
19. Is it the hard facts or more superficial factors that determine for whom we vote? Know the role of repeated exposure, optimism/pessimism, and factual orientation to the "state of the union" in getting a politician elected. What is the mistake of the ruminating politician?
20. How does attractiveness affect the appeal of a politician, and what's in a name when it comes to deciding for whom one will vote? Be able to detail the role of a voter's similarity to a candidate in that individual's likelihood of voting for the candidate.
21. What are—in the eyes of the prospective voter—the perceived characteristics of an effective leader? How do presidents differ in their leadership styles? Know what the charismatic politician is like.

Topics for Discussion

1. The simple act of wearing a seat belt could save up to 15,000 lives a year. Yet, not too long ago, most Illinois legislators didn't wear theirs when they drove away from a congressional session during which they voted for mandatory seat-belt use. What causes people to scoff at the effectiveness of a simple behavior, or even if they believe it is effective, still avoid performing it?

First, ask students who don't use seat belts why they don't buckle up. Deal with the misinformation and misbeliefs first. Enlist members of the class to help convince their unbelted colleagues that it is better to be belted than to be plowing into the dashboard or other hard objects. Inform them that cases in which being thrown from a car during a wreck saved a life are a small minority. At this point, you might mention that we need to deal in terms of the probability of saving our own life, not absolutes (everyone will know at least one exception to any life-saving suggestion you or anyone else might make).

Second, deal with the reasons for not wearing a belt, given that one does accept the effectiveness of them. Students are likely to say that buckling up slows them down. Ask students to estimate the time it takes to buckle up. At least one of them should guess that it takes about three seconds, because that is how long it takes an experienced belt user. If some mention that it wrinkles their clothes, ask other students what's unreasonable about that point of view. If you are fortunate, some students will reply something to the effect that wrinkled clothes seem a small price to pay to avoid mangled bodies. Finally, close by asking students whether they would rather take charge of their health and well-being, or leave it up to medical science, technology, or just plain fate.

2. Tapes or films of the famous John F. Kennedy–Richard M. Nixon TV debate of 1960 are readily available (if your college doesn't have a copy, your audiovisual people can probably borrow it from another college). Play as much of it as you think is necessary to give students the flavor of each candidate's strategy, appearance, manner, and orientation to the facts. In the eye of the viewing public, Kennedy was the clear winner. In terms of getting facts straight and speaking to the issues, some experts on debate saw Nixon as the winner. Get the students to indicate who they thought won and why. Most will likely say that Kennedy won. Their reasons will be various, but call attention to those that relate to JFK's handsome looks and cool demeanor. Perhaps you can also get them to notice that he spoke in generalities more than Nixon, who was often strictly factual. In contrast, Nixon's upper lip was sweating and he looked pale, unhealthy, and nervous. Being substantive didn't pay off, but looking good and in charge did. Note the implications of this debate for the importance of optimism, attractiveness, apparent leadership ability, charisma, and saying what people want to hear rather than speaking about substantive issues.

3. Some degree of stress is a fact of every person's life (well, almost everyone). The first step in dealing with stress is to identify its sources. Have students talk about what aspects of college life "stress them out" the most. You may even want to tally these sources on the board, keeping a count of which ones are experienced by how many students. Knowing that others have the same kinds of problems helps students feel less unusual. That knowledge alone lowers anxiety, the first step toward successfully locating a way to deal with stress. Next, have students suggest how they deal with the various sources of stress, or the stress itself. When the problems are personal, it is surprising how the simplest solutions fail to occur to even the brightest of people. You may even want to have the students vote on which coping method mentioned in conjunction with a given source of stress is the most effective. Consensus can be a powerful determinant of beliefs, and when people believe strongly enough in a method, they will often make it work.

4. The death penalty is supported by a majority of Americans, but remains controversial. Whatever you feel about it personally, you can preside over a productive discussion of it. The Nobel Prize–winning organization Amnesty International (AI) is currently conducting an international campaign to abolish the death penalty. They argue that it does not deter murder (often a crime of passion); it is more expensive than keeping murderers in prison for life (housing prisoners is costly, but the legal costs of appeals are even more so); and it is discriminatory, even beyond the fact that all-white juries have sent many blacks to death row (the U. S. Supreme Court has acknowledged the observation that people who kill white persons are significantly more likely to get the death penalty; i.e., blacks killing whites and whites killing whites get the ultimate penalty, not those who kill blacks).

The counterarguments are that only legally sanctioned execution will ensure murderers don't end up on the streets again (too many murderers are released after only short stays in prison); consideration of victims and their families dictates that murderers are executed (family anguish ends only with execution); and the deterrence value of execution has not been properly tested because the death penalty has been too rarely meted out (few convicted murderers end up on death row and few of those currently on death row are being executed).

Let students hash out these arguments in class; prompt them if they should forget some of the points made above. Then raise the critical question: what can social psychologists do to help resolve these issues? For example, can it be shown in the lab that all-white juries are more likely to hang a black person accused of murder, especially if the victim is white? Can studies be designed to show that penalties for resorting to violence deter the use of violence? (For example, during an aggression experiment in which subjects can shock someone who has offended them, will a relatively severe penalty for using shock deter its use?)

Classroom Exercises/Demonstrations

1. What are the life events that generate the most stress? As it turns out, most events involve close relationships, an observation that may be beyond students' awareness. To help them home in on events that may cause stress—the

necessary first step in avoiding health-threatening stressors—have students examine the Holmes & Rahe Social Readjustment Scale [1967], *Journal of Psychosomatic Research, 11*, 213–218). After exploring the scale thoroughly—it is included in the corresponding chapter of the Study Guide—ask them to find the top five most stressful events and rank them, giving a rank of 1 to the most stressful event. Then instruct them to locate the bottom five, giving a rank of 43 to the least stressful, a rank of 42 to the next least stressful, and so on. After the ranking is done, reveal the entire ranking by use of the table below. Have them comment on the degree to which their rankings have approximated the actual rankings based on a one hundred-point scale (marriage was the standard, set at 50). Keep them going until it is clear to them that close personal relationships are the major source of the most stressful events.

The Social Readjustment Scale

Events	Score	Rank
Death of a spouse	100	1
Divorce	73	2
Marital separation	65	3
Jail term	63	4.5
Death of close family member	63	4.5
Personal injury or illness	53	6
Marriage	50	7
Fired from job	47	8
Marital reconciliation	45	9.5
Retirement	45	9.5
Change in health of family member	44	11
Pregnancy	40	12
Sex difficulties	39	14
Gain of new family member	39	14
Business readjustment	39	14
Change in financial state	38	16
Death of close friend	37	17
Change to different line of work	36	18
Change in no. of arguments with spouse	35	19
High mortgage	31	20
Foreclosure of mortgage or loan	30	21
Change in responsibilities at work	29	23
Son or daughter leaving home	29	23
Trouble with in-laws	29	23
Outstanding personal achievement	28	25
Spouse begins or stops work ["wife" originally]	26	26.5
Begin or end school	26	26.5
Change in living conditions	25	28
Revision of personal habits	24	29
Trouble with boss	23	30
Change in work hours or conditions	20	32
Change in residence	20	32
Change in schools	20	32

Events	Score	Rank
Change in recreation	19	34.5
Change in church activities	19	34.5
Change in social activities	18	36
Small mortgage or loan	17	37
Change in sleeping habits	16	38
Change in number of family get-togethers	15	39.5
Change in eating habits	15	39.5
Vacation	13	41
Christmas	12	42
Minor violation of law	11	43

Source: Allen, [1990] *Personal adjustment.* Pacific Grove, CA: Brooks/Cole, used with permission.

2. Students are likely to be plagued with misconceptions concerning which physical diseases are the most dangerous to them. There is much one can do about health hazards, but efforts are often wasted because they are focused on the wrong dangers. For example, cardiovascular disease is by far the biggest killer of Americans, and there is much one can do to avoid these disorders (e.g., exercise and diet control). However, cancer, a much more feared category of disorders, kills only about half as many as cardiovascular disease and may be less controllable through behavioral intervention. If students see the two disease categories as equivalent in likelihood of cutting their lives short and equivalent in terms of possibilities for prevention, they may not assume there is anything they can do to save themselves.

Have them consider the list of disorders below, without numbers and ranks (only the list is reproduced in the corresponding Study Guide chapter). With accidents as the benchmark (its number alone is included in the Study Guide version) students could estimate the annual number of deaths attributed to each source and rank the top five killers, giving a rank of 1 to the most deadly. Then, reveal to them what really are the big five killers. Finally, elicit comments until it is obvious that most of the top five are preventable with appropriate behavioral interventions. Time permitting, you may want to query them concerning what social psychological methods might be used to get people moving in the direction of prevention. Methods for preventing smoking among youth are particularly relevant here.

Actual U.S. Fatalities and Ranks for Several Diseases and for Accidents

Disease (or accidents)	Fatalities	Rank
Smallpox	0	
Tuberculosis	3690	
Accidents	93,990	4

Disease (or accidents)	Fatalities	Rank
Stroke	147,390	3
Diabetes	38,950	
Cancer	465,440	2
Infectious hepatitis	677	
Heart disease	763,380	1
Syphilis	410	
Chronic lung disease	75,220	5
Measles	5	

Source: Allen, B. (1990). *Personal adjustment.* Pacific Grove, CA: Brooks/Cole, used with permission.

3. Hold an election to convince students that attractive candidates are most likely to win when other factors are held constant. Find a copy of a yearbook that is old enough so your students won't recognize the photos, but recent enough so that photos won't reflect out-of-style clothes and hair. Look through it until you find a block of photos that are all posed the same (seniors will probably work). Next, pick out the most attractive three males and three females you can find. Then pick out the most unattractive three males and three females you can find (you may wish to cross-validate by asking opinions of colleagues). Copy the pages containing these twelve photos on transparency plastic and cut the twelve photos from their surround. These are your twelve "candidates" for a hypothetical student government presidential election. Next, locate a half-dozen innocuous campus issues (e.g., the student fee for parking should not be further increased). Then select three of the positions on the issues and assign them to one of the attractive "candidates." Select another candidate of the same sex from among the unattractive photos and assign the same positions on the same issues. Repeat this process until you have six matched pairs, each constituted by one attractive and one unattractive photo, both of the same sex, and each espousing the same position on the same issues.

Now you are ready for the "election." Randomly assign the names on the ballot included in the Study Guide to the photos—with the restriction that sex-appropriate names be assigned. Then, present the transparencies of the photos in random order, mentioning the name and positions on the issues associated with each photo. Have the students take notes on each candidate and then "vote" by marking the ballot in the Study Guide. The simplest method is to have them vote for one candidate, collect the ballots, and see who received the most votes (very likely one of the attractive candidates). To be more sure of obtaining the expected result—attractive candidates receive more votes—have them rank the candidates, giving a rank of 1 to the most favored candidate, a 2 to the next most favored, and so on. Then, average ranks for "attractive" and "unattractive" candidates separately. Viewing these average ranks may be enough, but you may want to perform a test of differences in average ranks, with "attractive" and "unattractive" being the conditions.

4. Judges' instructions to members of a jury may have great impact on jury decisions, as noted in the text. To illustrate this point, divide the class into "jury panels" of about six (four, if the class is small; eight to twelve if the class is large). Then, read the following case to all students:

> Robert Edward Farness stands accused of killing a fellow patron at a local bar. Eye-witness testimony indicates that Farness was talking to a woman, for whom he had provided a drink, when the victim approached and began attempting to convince the woman that she should leave Farness and accompany him. Farness and the victim began to shout at one another; it was clear from what they were yelling that they knew one another and had had conflicts before. At the height of the argument, Farness was heard to shout, "I told you I'd kill you if you bullied me again!" At that point, the victim broke off the neck of a beer bottle and began to thrust the jagged edge at Farness. Farness grabbed a chair, swung it at the victim, and dislodged the broken bottle from the victim's grasp. Witnesses then testified that Farness continued to bludgeon the victim with the chair, even after it was clear that he was no longer in danger. By the time Farness was restrained, the victim was so badly injured that he died on the way to the hospital."

Next, give half the groups a written copy of the following judge's instruction to the jury: "You are instructed that, should you find the accused guilty, you must provide a sentence of life in prison without parole." Give this instruction to the remaining groups: "You are instructed that, should you find the accused guilty, you may provide sentences ranging from a minimum sentence of ten years in jail—parole considered after five years—and a maximum sentence of life in prison without parole."

Now have the "juries" deliberate for twenty minutes or so and then return a "guilty" or "not guilty" decision. Ask them to reach a unanimous decision, if they can, but record the outcome of each vote they take before the final vote (require at least three votes). You should find that, at the minimum, "juries" given the first instruction have more difficulty reaching a decision, as reflected in more and closer votes. Chances are you will also find that "guilty" decisions are less frequent with the first instruction than with the second. (Ballots are provided in the Study Guide chapter.)

Film Notes: A Picture Is Sometimes Worth a Thousand Words

Crime & Human Nature, FC-1327, videotape (cost to rent: $75; cost to buy: $149), 26 mins. Films for the Humanities and Sciences, Inc., P.O. Box 2053, Princeton, NJ 08543 (800-257-5126). Anthropologists Ashley Montague and other experts join Phil Donahue in addressing issues that relate to the structure of our current laws.

The Death Penalty, FC-1938, videotape (cost to rent: $75; cost to buy: $149), 26 mins. Films for the Humanities and Sciences, Inc., P.O. Box 2053, Princeton, NJ 08543 (800-257-5126). Argues that new evidence suggests that death sentences are imposed arbitrarily and that little evidence exists to support the contention that the death penalty is a deterrent to murder.

Fidelity of Report, 11439, film, 6 mins. Pennsylvania State University, Audiovisual Services, Special Services Building, University Park, PA 16802 (814-865-6314). Watch a robbery and see how witnesses describe it.

*Group Decision Making and Leadership, videotape, 28.5 mins. See your Allyn and Bacon sales representative to learn how you may obtain this tape. Robert A. Baron and Margaret Clark discuss issues of leadership that relate well to those that are relevant to politics.

Health and Lifestyles: Positive Approaches to Well-Being, film, 28 mins. Iowa Films, Media Library, University of Iowa, Iowa City, IA 52242. This film is designed to motivate viewers to take responsibility for their own health by making informed decisions.

Heart Attack: Prevention, film, 19 mins. Iowa Films, Media Library, University of Iowa, Iowa City, IA 52242. A case study of the personality traits and life-style factors that make a person a prime candidate for coronary heart disease is presented.

Justice on Trial, 1977, film, 49 mins. CRM/McGraw-Hill Films, 110 Fifteenth Street, Del Mar, CA 92014. Interviews with top authorities on how disparities in sentencing have put the very concept of justice on trial.

Mind, Health and Human Behavior, 23, videotape from the Annenborg Project, 26 mins. Holt, Rinehart & Winston, contact Lee Sutherlin, Marketing Manager (817-334-7632). A biopsychosocial model of health is offered to replace the traditional biomedical model.

Stress Reduction: Strategies That Work, PB124, videotape (cost to buy: $189), 30 mins. Insight Media, 121 West 85th Street, New York, NY 10024 (800-233-9910; 212-721-6316). The latest information on beating the stress that is associated with certain personalities is presented here.

Twelve Angry Men, commercial videotape (1957, United Artists) available for rental at many video stores, 95 mins. This film is perhaps the most respected attempt by Hollywood to look behind the dynamics of jury deliberation. It is outstanding.

Transparencies

14.1 *Unfair Punishment: Different Sets of Biases*
14.2 *Applied Psychological Research*
14.3 *Hardiness, Fitness and Health*

14.4 *Protection-Motivation Theory*
14.5 *Decisions and Choices to Make When the Symptoms of Illness Develop*

Critical Thinking/Essay Questions

1. Define applied social psychology and discuss how it is implemented through action research. Indicate how you might confirm that an antistress program conducted in a factory is working.

2. Tell how hardiness might be achieved and indicate how it would affect health. Describe how optimism and valuing health can contribute to good health.

3. By using the case of "husbands in the delivery room," illustrate how social support can be beneficial, and how attempts at it may backfire.

4. Indicate how meeting Rogers's four critical informational needs can counter the effect of the illusion of invulnerability and the availability heuristic.

5. Briefly outline a program to prevent adolescents from starting to smoke. Be sure to deal with the factors that contribute to smoking among youth, such as false consensus. How would you also instruct them concerning interpretation of disease symptoms?

6. Set up a hypothetical conversation with your physician concerning a back problem. How would you phrase your statements concerning symptoms so that the physician was aided in her or his diagnosis? What would you have the physician say to you concerning any medical procedures that might be necessary?

7. Briefly set up a crime scene (for example, in front of several witnesses, a thief steals a purse and runs away).

What factors on the scene and what other factors that may occur before witnesses are asked to recall the event may interfere with witness accuracy?

8. How do factors like leading questions, knowledgeable questioners, attractiveness of the accused, leniency biases of jurors, and judges' instructions to members of the jury affect jury decisions?

9. Outline a program to generate activism concerning use of biodegradable garbage bags and recycling.
10. Write a brief description of an optimal strategy that an unknown politician should use to get elected to the U.S. Senate. Be sure to include factors such as a possible name change, optimism-pessimism, appearing similar to voters, charisma, and leadership style.

Sources for Lecture

Carey, J., & Silberner, J. (1987). Fending off the leading killers. *U.S. News and World Report,* August 17, pp. 56–65. This article is a cogent summary of what one can do to save one's own life. It is a testimonial to the role of behavior in health. The end of the article is a "heart health" test.

Ellsworth, P. (1985). Juries on trial. *Psychology Today,* July, pp. 44–46. A 1968 case is used to introduce the issue of "death-qualified" juries. The relationship between social psychological research and court cases since then is discussed.

Geller, E. S. (1985). Seat belt psychology. *Psychology Today,* May, pp. 12–13. Geller discusses the low level of seat-belt use in the United States today. Several programs for increasing use, each based on psychological principles, are discussed.

Kaplan, S. M. (1985). Death, so say we all. *Psychology Today,* July, pp. 48–53. The author describes the emotional turmoil experienced by jurors who sat through a lengthy and traumatic trial that resulted in a death-sentence recommendation.

Mahoney, H. (1987). When the law is not enough. *Ms,* September, p. 85. Judges can make some horrible mistakes, beyond misinstructing or otherwise biasing a jury. In this case, a young woman's plea for protection for her husband was ignored by a judge, who told her to "act as an adult." She was subsequently murdered by her husband.

McAuliffe, K. (1987). Legally clean, but questions remain. *U.S. News and World Report,* November 16, pp. 71–72. The kinds of pesticides that pose cancer risks and the foods on which they are found are covered in this article. Readers will, therefore, find the information they need to form a basis for personal action.

Update: Current Articles from Professional Sources

Chassin, L., Presson, C. C., & Sherman, S. J. (1990). Social psychological contributions to the understanding and prevention of adolescent cigarette smoking. *Personality and Social Psychology Bulletin, 16,* 133–151. This is an excellent summary of the many studies that have sought to uncover the best methods for preventing smoking among youth before it begins. Social psychologists have moved away from emphasizing the negative consequences of smoking among teens to designing techniques that address the social and interpersonal underpinning of adolescent smoking behavior.

Dakof, G. A., & Taylor, S. E. (1990). Victims' perceptions of social support: What is helpful from whom? *Journal of Personality and Social Psychology, 58,* 80–89. These researchers report that particular actions were perceived by cancer patients as helpful coming from some members of patients' social support networks, but not when coming from other members.

Pennington, N., & Hastie, R. (1990). Practical implications of psychological research on juror and jury decision making. *Personality and Social Psychology Bulletin, 16,* 90–105. Social psychological research has much to say about the decision-making process in the jury room. This article is an excellent summary of that work.

Taylor, S. E., Bruunk, B. P., & Aspinwall, L. G. (1990). Social comparison, stress and coping. *Personality and Social Psychology Bulletin, 16,* 74–89. One way to deal with stress is to compare oneself with others whose situation is even worse. This summary article goes into social comparison processes and relates the same to coping with stress.

Wells, G. L., & Luus, C. A. E. (1990). Police lineups as experiments: Social methodology as a framework for properly conducted lineups. *Personality and Social Psychology Bulletin, 16,* 106–117. Many are the cases wherein the wrong person is fingered in the police lineup. The usual police lineup procedures illustrate several of the same biases that plague social psychological research. Researchers' methods for dealing with these biases can help make justice more likely.

15

Social Psychology in Work Settings

Applications of Its Principles, Methods, and Findings

Chapter Outline: Getting the Overall Picture

Learning Objectives

1. Why is it that the Hawthorne studies are classics in both social psychology and industrial/organizational psychology?
2. Explain why people report being satisfied with their current jobs, and yet often indicate they would change jobs if they could.
3. Why are there differences in product quality between the United States and Japan?

4. Describe how dissonance processes are involved in escalation of commitment.
5. Summarize the basic ideas underlying equity theory.
6. What are the three tactics by which people can reduce feelings of inequity?
7. Describe studies dealing with effects of inequity in pay.
8. Compare procedural and distributive justice, and in-

dicate how referent cognitions are related to perceptions of procedural justice.

9. Describe how performance appraisals are affected by attributions.

10. How are managers' performance appraisals affected by whether the subordinate is an ingroup or outgroup member?

11. Summarize the role played by attributions in organizational conflict, with particular emphasis on the "my hands are tied" strategy.

12. How is the rating one receives in a job interview affected by the interviewer's mood?

13. Why is it that negotiators in a good mood are able to reach more favorable agreements?

14. Under what conditions does positive affect increase willingness to take a risk? Under what conditions does positive affect decrease risk-taking?

15. Describe the effects of positive affect on job satisfaction and absence from work.

16. What three techniques are suggested as ways to induce positive affect among individuals at work?

Topics for Discussion

1. Technology has changed the nature of many jobs, including that of the secretary/office manager. Consider a hypothetical law office in which the three oldest secretaries were hired in the middle 1950s, when their jobs were primarily being stenographers who used shorthand skills. In the middle 1980s the law firm purchased personal computers to replace the traditional dictaphones that had been in use in the office since the 1950s. The reactions of the office staff to the new computers was mixed. One secretary ignored the new computers and did her work the traditional way. Another reluctantly switched over, but was not happy with the new technology. The third secretary enthusiastically endorsed the new computers and became a highly skilled computer user.

Have students assume that they are given the task of supervising the office secretarial staff. Have them consider how they would handle the problem of diverse reactions to this new technology. Should all of the secretarial staff be expected to adapt to the changeover equally well? Should the evaluation of these secretaries take into account their adaptability? Could some kind of division of duties be worked out so that each could make maximum use of their individual skills?

2. An example of a unique working environment is found in the case of the United Parcel Service (UPS). The entire company is run on stopwatches, for time-study engineers have established tough time standards for the daily tasks performed by company employees. To compensate for this highly paced and regimented work process, the workers are rewarded with high salaries and shares of ownership in the company. Thus, the workers do not see themselves as working for a faceless, impersonal organization, but see themselves as working for themselves. Therefore, they can identify with company objectives that are based on cost-cutting efficiencies.

Ask the students to consider employee needs and to come up with needs that are likely to go unmet with UPS's approach. What do people want out of work? Is bringing home a big paycheck the only consideration?

3. Have students determine whether equity principles predict student satisfaction. Have them ask fellow students how many hours they spent preparing for a particular test, what grade they received, and how satisfied they are with the outcome. Then, have the student do the same thing for him- or herself. What determines student satisfaction? Is it the absolute value of the grade received? Is it the grade relative to how much time and effort they put into the test? To what degree do comparisons with another person's outputs-to-inputs ratio enter in? What kind of person do they choose as a comparison? Do they choose someone who gets good grades with seemingly little effort or do they choose someone who gets considerably less return than themselves for study time?

4. American Airlines negotiated a two-tier contract with its union in order for the company to meet the cost-cutting demands imposed by increased competition. The two-tier concept allows senior employees to retain high salaries but establishes lower pay scales for newer employees. The text focuses on the negative effects created by the two-tier system, such as lower worker morale, higher turnover and absenteeism, lower productivity, poor work quality, and a weakening of the union's strength. However, it is possible to find positive long-range effects as well. For example, the corporation may become more cost effective, and thus be able to grow, offering more jobs and greater job security. Eventually the company may be able to return to equal pay for equal work, but at a cost that is more affordable to the company. Have the students debate the merits of two-tier wage systems. Are they fair? Should they be used? How do students imagine they would personally react to such a system?

5. Ask your students what they are looking for in their future jobs. How important are pay, working conditions, freedom, personal satisfaction, and so forth? To what degree has the future job been a factor in their selection of a major? Another way to approach this issue is by asking what aspects of their jobs their parents find least and most satisfying.

Classroom Exercises/Demonstrations

1. To conduct a performance appraisal, it is necessary to know what is expected of the person on the job, that is, a job analysis must usually precede a performance appraisal. This exercise asks students to do a job analysis of a job found on or near campus. Caution students to find a job about which they can obtain information by interviewing job holders and others familiar with the job. Jobs that might be interesting to analyze include the following:

Department chair	Newspaper reporter
Librarian	Athletic coach
Professor	Residence hall assistant
Computer operator	Pizza delivery person

Once they have determined what the job involves, have them develop a procedure to evaluate a person performing the job. Perhaps they can determine how these people are currently evaluated. What aspects of the performance appraisal do the students think need to be improved?

2. The text talks about employee turnover by emphasizing negative consequences that result when a company loses an employee. Negative consequences include costs of recruiting and training the new employee, productivity loss during the replacement period, and disruption of social and communication processes. However, there are positive consequences that occur as well. For example, new knowledge and technology are often provided by replacements. Poorer performers are often displaced and increased opportunities for internal mobility are provided. Many other advantages and disadvantages of turnover can also be found. Have students debate the advantages and disadvantages of turnover.

3. To what degree do different jobs require people with different personalities? This exercise is designed to get students to think about the difficulty of specifying the type of person "needed" to perform a particular job. Students should consider themselves to be the personnel manager of a large department store. The store is in the process of hiring two people and wants to be sure to get people suited to the jobs. The two available jobs are as follows:

Department Manager. The department manager has full responsibility for keeping merchandise shelves in the department stocked, for managing inventory, and for supervising and developing the department sales staff. In addition, the department manager spends about half of his or her time on the sales floor working with customers.

Stockroom Manager. The stockroom manager has full responsibility for receiving incoming shipments of merchandise, properly storing it in the stockroom, and delivering needed merchandise to the sales floor as requested by department managers.

Have students develop a personality profile for the person needed for each position. This profile should specify the key personality traits likely to lead to success on the particular job. How difficult is it to develop an optimal personality for a particular job? How likely is it that a prospective employee will match the profile? Even if there is a match, is this an indication that the employee can expect success?

Film Notes: A Picture Is Sometimes Worth a Thousand Words

Building More Effective Teams: The Organization Development Approach, 32331, 1978, color, 26 mins. Pennsylvania State University, Audiovisual Services, Special Services Building, University Park, PA 16802 (814-865-6314). Peter Block, a leading organization development consultant, discusses the use of behavioral science concepts and techniques in dealing with problems that different organizations face. Group sessions with thirty managers of a major educational authority are documented. Problems are identified, confronted, and, to a large extent, solved.

Career Development: A Plan for All Seasons, 32325, 1978, color, 27 mins. Pennsylvania State University,

Audiovisual Services, Special Services Building, University Park, PA 16802, (814-865-6314). Presents, in documentary style, one company's approach to helping its employees enrich their working lives through a career development program. Dr. Beverly Kaye, a consultant in career development, directs workshops designed to help Collins Food International employees understand the ingredients of a fulfilling career and to help them develop skills necessary to achieve one for themselves. From the *Business and Management* series. A CRM production.

Group Decision Making and Leadership, videotape, 28.5 mins. To obtain this tape, consult your Allyn and

Bacon sales representative. After examining a business group's discussion concerning whom to hire, Robert A. Baron and Margaret Clark get inside the workings of group decision making.

Women in Management: Threat or Opportunity?, 32001, 1974, color, 27 mins. Pennsylvania State University, Audiovisual Services, Special Services Building, University Park, PA 16802 (814-865-6314). Examines how the women's movement has affected business firms, where many men have traditionally perceived women in terms of roles rather than as individuals. In some areas, affirmative action programs, initiated primarily to meet government quotas and avoid lawsuits, have been followed by attempts to help business people cope with new relationships. Visits training sessions initiated by the Weyerhaeuser Lumber Company. From the *Behavior in Business* series. Directed, written, and produced by Barbara Jampel. A CRM production.

Transparencies

15.1 *Escalation of Commitment: An Overview*
15.2 *Equity and Inequity in Social Exchange*
15.3 *Referent Cognitions and Perceived Fairness*

15.4 *Attributions About Ingroup Versus Outgroup Subordinates*

Critical Thinking/Essay Questions

1. Explain the role of dissonance processes in the escalation of commitment.
2. Summarize the basic ideas underlying equity theory, and describe the tactics used to reduce feelings of inequity.
3. Describe how performance appraisals are affected by attributions.
4. Assume that you are an office worker who is about to be evaluated by your supervisor. What factors will determine whether you feel the evaluation is fair? Include in your answer factors such as equity, procedural justice, your supervisor's attributions, whether you are an in-group or out-group member, and whether your supervisor was in a good or bad mood when evaluating you.
5. Assume that you are a personnel officer in a large company. One day the chief personnel officer asks you whether you think it would be worth the company's effort to try to create more positive affect among the company's employees. How would you answer her? What effects result from people being in a good mood? Would it be beneficial to the company and its employees to institute a "mood enhancement" program?

Sources for Lecture

Rice, B. (1985). Performance review: The job nobody likes. *Psychology Today,* September, pp. 30–36. The methods used to assess how well workers do on their jobs are discussed. The general dissatisfaction of workers and supervisors is discussed, along with common biases and how to correct them.

Rice, B. (1985). Why am I in this job? *Psychology Today,* January, pp. 55–59. A discussion of interest and ability testing to help clients determine whether to make a career change. Issues involved in career counseling are discussed.

Rosen, C., Klein, J. K., & Young, K. M. (1986). When employees share the profits. *Psychology Today,* January, pp. 30–36. Employee stock-ownership plans have grown dramatically in the last ten years. This article examines how these plans affect employee attitudes and satisfaction.

Update: Current Articles from Professional Sources

Avolio, B. J., Waldman, D. A., & McDaniel, M. A. (1990). Age and work performance in nonmanagerial jobs: The effects of experience and occupational type. *Academy of Management Journal, 33,* 407–422. This study examines the degree to which age and years of work experience predict supervisory ratings of work performance. Experience was a better predictor than age.

Holtgraves, T., & Srull, T. K. (1990). Ordered and unordered retrieval strategies in person memory. *Journal of Experimental Social Psychology, 26,* 63–81. The strategy one uses in trying to recall information about stimulus persons will affect what is remembered. An ordered recall strategy (i.e., recalling everything about one target before trying to recall information about another target) is particularly discussed. Presents implications for managers' evaluations of employees.

Greenhaus, J. H., Parasuraman, S., & Wormley, W. M. (1990). Effects of race on organizational experiences, job performance evaluations, and career outcomes. *Academy of Management Journal, 33,* 64–86. Compared to white managers, black managers felt less accepted in their organizations, perceived themselves as having less discretion in their jobs, were more likely to have reached career plateaus, and were less satisfied.

Kim, K. I., Park, H., & Suzuki, N. (1990). Reward allocations in the United States, Japan, and Korea: A comparison of individualistic and collectivistic cultures. *Academy of Management Journal, 33,* 188–198. Studies reward allocation preferences across countries, finding a strong universal tendency to distribute rewards to members based on their contributions. Groups from the United States and Japan, however, exhibited a stronger preference for equity than the group from Korea.

Sweeney, P. D., McFarlin, D. B., & Inderrieden, E. J. (1990). What determines satisfaction with income and pay level? *Academy of Management Journal, 33.* Both social comparisons and a variety of self-comparisons were found to be important.

INSTRUCTOR'S SECTION

SOCIAL PSYCHOLOGY

SOCIAL PSYCHOLOGY
Understanding Human Interaction
S I X T H   E D I T I O N

Robert A. Baron
Rensselaer Polytechnic Institute

Donn Byrne
University at Albany/State University of New York

Allyn and Bacon

Boston ▪ **London** ▪ **Toronto** ▪ **Sydney** ▪ **Tokyo** ▪ **Singapore**

Series Editor: Susan Badger
Series Editorial Assistant: Dana Lamothe
Production Administrator: Susan McIntyre
Editorial-Production Service: Nancy Benjamin
Text Designer: Melinda Grosser for *silk*
Cover Administrator: Linda Dickinson
Composition Buyer: Linda Cox
Manufacturing Buyer: Megan Cochran

To Sandra who warms my heart and brightens my dreams. R.A.B.

To Kathryn with love. D.B.

Photo Credits

Chapter One   Page 2: "Pas Mele," by Bill Barrett/Photo courtesy of Worth Street Studios, N.Y. Page 9L: M. Greenlar/The Picture Group. 9R: J. Riznicki/The Stock Market. Page 10: G. Palmer/The Stock Market. Page 12: Adler/Shooting Star. Page 20: H. Lloyd/The Stock Market. Page 29: S. Connors/The Picture Group. *Chapter Two*   Page 40: "The Couple," by Gregory Hawthorne. Acrylic. Page 45: D. Dempster/Allyn & Bacon. Page 46L: K. Straiton/The Stock Market. Page 46R: V. Moos/The Stock Market. Page 51L: A. Avakian/Woodfin Camp & Associates. Page 51R: Envision Stock. Page 57: Robert Harding Picture Library/

(Photo credits continue on page 682, which constitutes an extension of the copyright page.)

Copyright © 1991, 1987, 1984, 1981, 1977, 1974 by Allyn and Bacon
A Division of Simon & Schuster, Inc.
160 Gould Street
Needham Heights, MA 02194

Library of Congress Cataloging-in-Publication Data

Baron, Robert A.
   Social psychology : understanding human interaction / Robert A.
Baron, Donn Byrne.—6th ed.
      p.   cm.
   Includes bibliographical references and index.
   ISBN 0-205-12602-2
   1. Social psychology.   I. Byrne, Donn Erwin.   II. Title.
HM251.B437 1991
302—dc20   90-44793
                                                              CIP

Printed in the United States of America
10 9 8 7 6 5 4 3 2 1   95 94 93 92 91 90

CONTENTS

PREFACE:
Twenty Years of Hard Listening—
Thoughts on Becoming a "Classic"

The world was a very different place when, in 1971, we began work on the first edition of *Social Psychology: Understanding Human Interaction*. Consider: gasoline was selling for under forty cents a gallon, Richard Nixon was in the White House, the conflict in Vietnam raged; and no one had yet heard of Watergate, space shuttles, the greenhouse effect, Mikhail Gorbachev, or AIDS. In many ways it seems like another age; and social psychology, too, was very different from what it is today. The "cognitive revolution," which has altered our field in crucial ways, was just then stirring. And many lines of research described in this new edition were as yet unknown—or were mere intellectual glimmers in the minds of their future creators.

Despite all this change, our book has kept pace and remained immensely popular. Indeed, almost 1,000,000 students have learned about social psychology from this text (or from its briefer companion, *Exploring Social Psychology*) during the past two decades. Needless to say, we are deeply gratified by this widespread, continuing acceptance. As we move into a third decade of writing *Social Psychology*, though, it seems appropriate to ask what it is about our text that has made it such a long-time favorite—a book that is frequently described as a publishing "classic." The answer, at least from our point of view, seems clear: as suggested by the title of this Preface, we *listen*, and listen hard! In other words, we do our very best to obtain the advice and feedback of our colleagues and students, and then make concerted efforts to incorporate this feedback into our text.

The result of trying to be "good listeners," we believe, is a text that truly represents input from hundreds of talented, helpful persons. In our view, it is this commitment to listening that accounts for the fact that you are now reading the sixth edition, and that writing *Social Psychology* has become a career-long project for both of us.

Now, permit us to summarize what this process of *hard listening* told us this time around, and how we have altered the text to take account of *your* input and suggestions. Please note that the changes below were based, in large measure, on the results of a survey to which *more than five hundred social psychologists* kindly responded. It is the combined views of these colleagues (perhaps including your own) that are reflected in the following pages.

Up-to-Date Content The sixth edition represents a major shift in content—perhaps the largest overall change in this respect in several editions. Among the most important of these changes are the following:

Inclusion of Three New Chapters A new chapter on intimate relationships (Chapter 7, Close Relationships: Friendship, Love, Intimacy, and Marriage). This chapter describes how relationships form, develop, and then, sometimes, dissolve, and also considers important aspects of love and sexuality.

A new chapter on applications of social psychology in work settings (Chapter 15, Social Psychology in Work Settings: Applications of Its Principles, Methods, and Findings). This chapter describes the many ways in which principles and findings of social psychology contribute to our understanding of important aspects of behavior in work settings.

A new chapter dealing with several important forms of interpersonal behavior, ranging from *helping* others on the one hand to *conflicting* with them on the other (Chapter 9, Working With and Against Others: Prosocial Behavior, Cooperation, and Conflict). Much of the material in this chapter is new, and the discussion of interpersonal conflict is entirely new to this edition.

Coverage of Literally Dozens of New Topics Within chapters, too, a tremendous amount of new material has been inserted. Here is a partial listing of some of the new topics covered:

Chapter 1: Theories—Their Potential Dangers in Research / The Multicultural Perspective in Social Psychology

Chapter 2: The Face-in-the-Crowd Phenomenon / Gait as a Nonverbal Cue / Context Effects in Attribution / Gender Differences in the Self-Serving Bias

Chapter 3: Automatic Priming / Counterfactual Thinking and Mental Simulation / Framing and Anchoring / Implicit Theories of Stability and Change / Vascular Theory of Emotion / Greatly Expanded Coverage of Affect-Cognition Links / The Self, Self Schemas, Possible Selves / The Self-Reference Effect

Chapter 4: Attitude Change and Age / Cognitive Perspective on Persuasion / Mood and Persuasion / Dissonance and Responsibility for Negative Outcomes / Leading Questions and Attitude Change

Chapter 5: Recategorization and the Reduction of Prejudice / Ingroup Differentiation and Outgroup Homogeneity / Stereotypes and Biased Processing of Social Information / The Role of Expectations in Discrimination against Females / Genetic Similarity Theory: Does Prejudice Have a Biological Basis?

Chapter 6: Propinquity versus Privacy / The Mum Effect / A Model of Social Skills / Successful and Unsuccessful "Opening Lines" / The Repulsion Hypothesis / Personality Similarity

Chapter 7: NEW CHAPTER
The Nature of Love / Establishing and Maintaining Close Relationships / Troubled Relationships / Sexual Harassment versus Romance in Workplaces / Jealousy

Chapter 8: Sex Differences in the Use of Influence Tactics / The Need for Individuation and Resistance to Conformity / Age and the "Foot-in-the-Door" Tactic / The "That's Not All" Technique / Disobedience to Authority and the Demise of Communism in Eastern Europe

Chapter 9: NEW CHAPTER
Ego versus Empathy as the Motive for Prosocial Behavior / A Sociobiological Explanation for Altruism / Interpersonal Conflict / Destructive versus Constructive Criticism

Chapter 10: The Cognitive-Neoassociationist View of Aggression / Destructive Criticism as an Elicitor of Aggression / Violent Video Games and Aggression / The Interplay between Cognition and Emotion in Aggressive Behavior / Hostile Attributional Bias: Perceiving Evil Intent in Others / Cognition Interventions: The Role of Apologies

Chapter 11: How Groups Develop and Change / Standards for Evaluating Performance and the Reduction of Social Loafing / Straw Polls and Group Decisions / The Information Sampling Model of Group Decision Making / Charismatic Leaders /

Gender Differences in Leadership Style

Chapter 12: Five Robust Factors of Personality / Subjective Well-Being / Metatrait Hypothesis / Self-Esteem / Self-Efficacy

Chapter 13: Greenhouse Effect and Global Warming / Mega-Cities / Psychosocial Pathology / Motivating Environmentally Responsible Behavior / Home Environments

Chapter 14: Psychology and Politics / Stress among College Students / Hardiness and Fitness as Moderators of Stress

Chapter 15: NEW CHAPTER
Dissonance and Work-Related Decisions / Perceived Fairness in Work Settings / Attributions: Their Role in Performance Appraisals / Positive Affect in Work Settings / Contrasting Attitudes about Product Quality in the United States and Japan

New Themes: Gender and a Multicultural Perspective

In response to feedback from our colleagues, we have also expanded our coverage of two themes within the text: *gender* and *multicultural comparisons*. The emphasis on gender is suggested by the addition of special sections dealing with this topic in virtually all chapters. A few examples:

Gender Differences in the Self-Serving Bias (Chapter 2)

Women's Implicit Theories about Menstrual Symptoms (Chapter 3)

Gender Stereotypes and Sexism (Chapter 5)

Gender Differences in Effects of Height (Chapter 6)

Gender Differences in Preferences about Partner's Age (Chapter 7)

Gender Differences in Responding to Sexual Intimacy (Chapter 7)

Gender Differences in Conformity (Chapter 8)

Gender Differences in Aggression (Chapter 10)

Gender Differences in Leadership (Chapter 11)

Gender Differences in Personal Space (Chapter 13)

A cross-cultural or multicultural perspective has been incorporated into the text through discussion of this topic in several chapters, and through the inclusion of special sections, *Social Psychology: A Multicultural Perspective*, throughout the text. These sections include:

Friendship and Dating in the United States and Hong Kong (Chapter 1)

Self-Concepts in Japan and the United States (Chapter 3)

Interracial Multi-Contact in South Africa (Chapter 5)

Response to Childlike Voices in the United States and Korea (Chapter 6)

Jealousy in the United States, Hungary, Yugoslavia, Ireland, the Soviet Union, the Netherlands, and Mexico (Chapter 7)

Resisting Authority on Behalf of Freedom (Chapter 8)

Aggression by Type As and Type Bs in the United States and India (Chapter 10)

Coping with Free Riders in the United States and Japan (Chapter 11)

Adapting to Population Density among British, Southern Europeans, and Asians (Chapter 13)

Husbands in the Delivery Room in Israel and Canada (Chapter 14)

Attitudes about Product Quality in the United States and Japan (Chapter 15)

High-Interest Special Features

We have also made numerous changes in instructional aids and special features in order to make the book more useful and appealing to students. These include:

Special Sections Four distinct types are included. Three types have been retained from the fifth edition, because feedback from colleagues indicated that they were viewed as both effective and useful: **Focus on Research: Classic Contributions; Focus on Research: The Cutting Edge;** and **On the Applied Side.** We should note, though, that in terms of content, virtually all special sections themselves are new to this edition.

A fourth type of special section, **Social Psychology: A Multicultural Perspective**, is entirely new to this edition, and reflects the major cross-cultural themes described above.

Please note: all four types of special sections occur at logical points within chapters and do *not* interrupt the flow of text material. On the contrary, all are introduced in the text, and are integrated into the materials and topics that precede them.

Expanded Summary and Review Each chapter now concludes with an expanded Summary and Review section. These are more complete and detailed than in previous editions, and are divided into discrete sections corresponding to the major segments of the chapter. We have found them to be very helpful for students who want to review the materials covered, and to form a useful schema, or cognitive framework, for each chapter.

Full-Color Illustrations All illustrations in the text are now printed in full color. This greatly enhances their visual appeal, and makes all graphs and charts much more effective from the standpoint of conveying important information.

Together, these changes enhance the appeal of the text to students, and make the book more accessible and easier to use.

Supplements

All good texts should be supported by a complete package of ancillary materials, both for the student and for the instructor. For the student, we offer a *Study Guide*, written by Bem P. Allen and Gene F. Smith. It gives students practice with short answers, definition, matching, multiple choice, and completion questions. Self tests are accompanied by answers cross-referenced to appropriate discussions in the text.

For instructors, we also offer an instructor's edition with bound-in teaching notes, transparency masters, test bank, computerized test bank, and video library, as well as custom-published ancillaries. Please feel free to contact your Allyn and Bacon sales representative for more information.

A Concluding Comment, and a Look to the Future

This preface has focused, appropriately, on past efforts—steps we have taken to improve our text. Looking back, we can state, once again, that we have spared no effort to enrich and enhance the book in many different ways. We fully realize, though, that in a crucial sense, this task is never done: even as we complete work on this edition, we are thinking about and planning the next one. For this reason, we fervently invite your comments, your advice, and your recommendations. We don't claim that our egos can't be bruised by such feedback—on the contrary, they certainly can! But if there's something you feel can be improved, *we want to know about it*!

So, please give us a call or send us your feedback in any format you wish. Doing so definitely won't be wasted effort because, as we said at the start (and as those who know us personally can affirm), we *really will listen*.

ABOUT THE AUTHORS

Robert A. Baron

ROBERT A. BARON is currently Professor and Chair of the Department of Psychology, Rensselaer Polytechnic Institute. A Fellow of the APA since 1978, he received his Ph.D. from the University of Iowa (1968). Professor Baron has held faculty appointments at the University of South Carolina, Purdue University, the University of Minnesota, University of Texas, and Princeton University. He has received numerous awards for teaching excellence at these institutions. Professor Baron has also been a Research Associate at the Fels Research Institute and a Visiting Fellow at the University of Oxford (England). He served as a Program Director of the National Science Foundation from 1979 to 1981. Professor Baron has published more than eighty articles in professional journals, and eighteen invited chapters. He has served on the editorial boards of numerous journals (e.g., *Journal of Personality and Social Psychology, Journal of Applied Social Psychology*) and is currently an associate editor for *Aggressive Behavior* and the *International Journal of Conflict Management*. He is the author or co-author of nineteen books, including *Human Aggression, Psychology: The Essential Science*, and *Behavior in Organizations*. At present, Professor Baron's major research interests focus on applying the principles and findings of social psychology to behavior in work settings (e.g., the causes and management of organizational conflict; impact of the physical environment on work behavior). Professor Baron is a long-time runner; his hobbies include woodworking, enjoying fine food, and music.

Donn Byrne

DONN BYRNE is currently Professor of Psychology and Director of the Social-Personality Program at the University at Albany, State University of New York. He received the Ph.D. degree in 1958 from Stanford University and has held academic positions at the California State University at San Francisco, the University of Texas, Stanford University, the University of Hawaii, and Purdue University. A past president of the Midwestern Psychological Association and a Fellow of the American Psychological Society and the Society for the Scientific Study of Sex, he has authored fifteen books, thirty invited chapters, and over one hundred and thirty-five articles in professional journals. He has served on the Editorial Boards of *Experimental Social Psychology, Journal of Applied Social Psychology, Sociometry, Journal of Sex Research*, and *Review of Personality and Social Psychology*. He was invited to deliver a G. Stanley Hall lecture at the 1981 meeting of the American Psychological Association in Los Angeles and a State of the Science address at the 1981 meeting of the Society for the Scientific Study of Sex in New York City. He was an invited participant in Surgeon General Koop's Workshop on Pornography and Health in 1986, received the Excellence in Research Award from the University at Albany in 1987, and the Distinguished Scientific Achievement Award from the Society for the Scientific Study of Sex in 1989. His current research interests include interpersonal attraction and the prediction of sexually coercive behavior. In his leisure time he enjoys literature, the theatre, and travel.

ACKNOWLEDGMENTS: SOME WORDS OF THANKS

Writing is a solitary task, best performed alone. Converting authors' words into a finished book, though, requires the efforts and assistance of many persons. In preparing this text, we have been aided by a large number of dedicated, talented people. We can't possibly thank all of them here, but we do wish to express our appreciation to those whose help has been most valuable.

First, our sincere thanks to the colleagues listed below, who read and commented on various portions of the manuscript: Dr. David Meissner, Alfred University; Professor Galen Bodenhausen, Michigan State University; Dr. Marjorie Krebs, Gannon University; Professor Adrian Rapp, North Harris County College; Professor Lynda Dodgen, North Harris County College; Professor Blair Johnson, Syracuse University; Dr. Robert D. Johnson, Arkansas State University; Professor Rosina Chia, East Carolina University; Professor Jack Dovidio, Colgate University; Professor Wade Harrison, Northern Arizona University; and Dr. B. Tara Rao, Ferris State University. In addition, of course, we are indebted to the many colleagues who kindly completed our preliminary survey; to a large degree, data from that survey guided major changes in the book.

Second, we want to thank Susan Badger, our editor at Allyn and Bacon, Her expertise, energy, and élan (!) were major assets in virtually every step of the process; working with her has truly been a pleasure.

Third, our sincere thanks to our Project Manager, Susan McIntyre, who oversaw innumerable, crucial aspects of production. We were fortunate indeed to have her—and her considerable talent—as an important part of the team.

Fourth, our thanks to several other people who contributed to various aspects of the production process: to Nancy Benjamin for adeptly handling myriad details in the day-to-day process of production, to Laurel Anderson for yet another job of outstanding photo research, to Melinda Grosser for a very attractive design, and to Linda Dickinson for a very striking cover.

Fifth, our thanks to the following colleagues for providing reprints and preprints of their work (Bram Buunk, Bill Fisher, Phil Rushton), and to several others for their aid in a variety of ways too numerous to mention (Barbara Becker, Warren Chiu, Linda Pearson, Lisa Schulte, Ruth Van Wangenen). Last but certainly not least, our sincere appreciation to George Smeaton for his assistance with respect to several aspects of Chapter 9.

Sixth, we want to take this opportunity to thank those colleagues who, over the years, have provided us with reprints and preprints of their work. By doing so, they have helped keep this text on the very *cutting edge* of social psychology. We look forward to their continued help in this respect in the future.

Finally, we wish to thank Bem P. Allen and Gene F. Smith for their outstanding work on the Instructor's Section, and for their help in preparing the Test Bank and Study Guide.

To all these truly outstanding people, and to many others, too, our warm personal regards.

Reviewers of the Sixth Edition   Galen Bodenhausen, Michigan State University; Rosina Chia, East Carolina State University; Lynda Dodgen, North Harris Community College; Jack Dovidio, Colgate University; Blair Johnson, Syracuse University; Robert Johnson, Arkansas State University; Marjorie Krebs, Gannon University; David Meissner, Alfred University; Taramanohar Rao, Ferris State University; and Adrian Rapp, North Harris Community College.

Reviewers of the Previous Edition   Robert S. Baron, University of Iowa; Russell Clark, III, Florida State University; Herbert Fink, SUNY–Brockport; Jeffrey Fisher, University of Connecticut; Robert Gifford, University of Victoria; Daniel Gilbert, University of Texas–Austin; Steven Prentice-Dunn, University of Alabama; and Daniel Wegner, Trinity University.

Survey Respondents   Charles Ackerson, Dowling College; Frederic Agatstein, Rhode Island College; Robin Akert, Wellesley College; Charles Alexander, Rock Valley College; Sheldon Alexander, Wayne State University; Bem Allen, Western Illinois University; Rhianon Allen, Long Island University; Richard Archer, Southwest Texas State University; Charles Bahn, John Jay College of Criminal Justice; Bruce Bainum, Pacific Union College; R. Baumeister, Case Western Reserve University; Gordon Bear, Ramapo College; Percy Black, Pace University; Thomas Blass, University of Maryland; J. R. Bloomingdale, Washington College; Jeanine Bloyd, Spoon River College; Susan Boland, Drury College; George Boeree, Shippensburg University; Arthur Bohart, California State University; N. Branscombe, University of Kansas; John Braun, University of Bridgeport; Steven Breckler, Johns Hopkins University; June Breninger, Columbia Christian College; Robert Bringle, Indiana University–Purdue University; John Bruni, Jr., Western Kentucky University; Janet Weigel Bruno, Black Hawk College; Robert Buckhout, Brooklyn College; Albert Bugaj, University of Wisconsin–Richland; Shelly Chaiken, New York University; William Chambers, Shorter College; Jerome Chertkoff, Indiana University at Bloomington; Paul Cherulnik, Southeast Missouri State University; Shirley Chrisman, Saint Leo College; Emily Claspell, Chaminade University of Honolulu; Edward Clemmer, Emerson College; Winona Cochran, Bloomsburg University; Ronald Cohen, Bennington College; Alfred Cohn, Hofstra University; Steven G. Cole, Texas Christian University; James Collins, Corpus Christi State University; W. D. Crano, Texas A & M University; Carol Creedon, Reed College; David Cressler, Portland State University; Salvatore Cullari, Lebanon Valley College; James Dabbs, Georgia State University; Kenneth DeBono, Union College; Darlene DeFour, CUNY Hunter College; Linda DeRosier, Rocky Mountain College; David Dodd, Eastern Illinois University; William Dragan, Cornell College; Karen Duffy, SUNY–Geneseo; Thomas Eckle, Modesto Junior College; S. Ellyson, Youngstown State University; James Emshoff, Georgia State University; Robert O. Engbretson, Southern Illinois University; Charles Evans, LaGrange College; Ronald Evans, Washburn University of Topeka; Ann Ewing, Mesa Community College; Lorraine Fahey, Stevens Institute of Technology; Chris Falvey, Grand Valley State University; Michael Flaherty, Eckerd College; Bill Fleming, Nazareth College; John Fleming, University of Minnesota; Linda Foley, University of North Florida; Earl Folse, Nicholls State University; Becky Francis, West Virginia State College; Robin Franck, Southwestern College; Lyle Frank, Blackfeet Community College; Arthur Frankel, Salve Regina College; Stephen Franzoi, Marquette University; Marcia Freer, Doane College; William Rick Fry, Youngstown State University; Solomon Fulero, Sinclair College; Eleanor Gaer, Glassboro State College; Russell Geen, University of Missouri; Florence Geis, University of Delaware; Edward

Gelb, Keystone Junior College; Keith Gerritz, Wilmington College; L. W. Giesbrecht-Bettoli, Tennessee Tech University; Eugene Gliden, Linfield College; Richard Gillies, Cosumnes River College; Rod Gillis, University of Miami; D. Glascoe, University of Utah; Jeffrey Goldstein, Temple University; Randall Gould, Cuesta College; Edith Greene, University of Colorado; Larry Gregory, New Mexico State University; A. F. Gromoll, Millikin University; Michael Haggerty, Mallinckrodt College; Amy Halberstadt, Vassar College; Lily Halstead, Barb College; Richard Halverson, Luther College; Gordon Hammerie, Adrian College; W. Bruce Haslam, Weber State College; George Hearn, Los Angeles College; Robert Heper, Community College of Rhode Island; Rex Hieser, University of Wisconsin–Marinette; Spencer Hildahl, Wells College; Larry Hjelle, SUNY–Brockport; Bert Hodges, Gordon College; George Holden, University of Texas–Austin; Robert Holt, George Mason University; E. Hough, Rutgers University; Teri Hudson, Diablo Valley College; Karen Huffman, Palomar College; Jay Hull, Dartmouth College; Eugene Indebaum, SUNY–Farmingdale; Jacquelyne Jackson; St. Mary's College; Thomas Jackson, Fort Hays State University; Norine Jalbert, Western Connecticut State University; Anthony Johnson, LaGrange College; David Johnson, John Brown University; Jerry Johnson, University of Hawaii–Hilo; Robert Johnson, Arkansas State University; Ruth Ann Johnson, Augustana College; Donn Kaiser, Southwest Missouri State University; Kathy Kalab, Western Kentucky University; Sheldon Kalick, University of Massachusetts–Boston; George Kent, Bridgewater College; Mo Kian, Edinboro University; Andrew Kinney, Mohawk Valley Community College; Richard Klein, Adelphi University; Linda Kline, Murray State University; Gregory Kolden, Colby College; Marjorie Krebs, Gannon University; Ken Kressell, Rutgers University; Neil Kressell, William Patterson College; Kathleen L'Armand, Widener University; Jan LeFrancois, Converse College; Christopher Leone, University of North Florida; L. W. Littig, Howard University; Rolando Diaz Loving, National University of Mexico; Kevin MacDonald, California State University–Long Beach; Margaret Madden, Franklin Pierce College; Santiago Madril, Cochise College; John Mahoney, Virginia Commonwealth University; Richard Mamolen, Edmonds Community College; Grace Martin, Armstrong State College; James May, North Adams State College; L. K. McBride, Willamette University; Lynn McCutcheon, Northern Virginia Community College; Peter McDonald, North Georgia College; Robert McKelvain, Harding University; Ralph McKenna, Hendrix College; Charles McMullen, Tompkins Cortland Community College; Gregory Meissen, Wichita State University; Richard Miller, Navarro College; Robert Miller, Palomar College; Rowland Miller, Sam Houston State University; Barbara Moburg, Skagit Valley College; M. Moore, Webster University; Brian Mullen, Syracuse University; Linda Nelson, California Polytechnic–San Luis Obispo; Steve Nida, Franklin University; John O'Connor, Western Kentucky University; Paul Olczak, SUNY–Geneseo; Timothy Osberg, Niagara University; Don Osborn, Bellarmine College; Chris O'Sullivan, University of Kentucky; Robert Pellegrini, San Jose State University; James Phillips, Oklahoma State University; Jack Powell, University of Hartford; Anthony Pratkanis, University of California–Santa Cruz; Perry Prestholdt, Louisiana State University; Wendall Pribyl, Muscatine Community College; Melvyn Price, Oklahoma City University; Dick Proctor, Andrews University; Thomas Radecki, Siena Heights College; Robert Radlow, San Diego State University; Donald Rajecki,

Indiana University–Purdue University; Susan Ratwik, Lake Superior State College; Robert Reenes, Augusta College; Harry Reis, University of Rochester; D. R. Richardson, University of North Carolina; Marc Riess, Middlebury College; Stephanie Riger, Lake Forest College; Janet Riggs, Gettysburg College; Ron Rogers, University of Alabama; Joan Rollins, Rhode Island College; Barry Ruback, Georgia State University; Karen Salley, Southern Oregon State College; Jeffrey Sanders, Towson State University; Nicholas Santilli, John Carroll University; Michael Scheier, Carnegie Mellon University; Constance Schick, Bloomsburg University; Pat Schoenrade, University of Kansas; Janet Schofield, University of Pittsburgh; Gregory Schmutte, American International College; John Scileppi, Marist College; Robert Seaton, College of Du Page; Charles Seidel, Mansfield University; Susan Shapiro, Mount Marty College; Eugene Sheehan, University of Northern Colorado; Mary Sheridan, Hawaii Pacific College; Linda Silka, University of Lowell; Eleanor Smith, University at Albany; Gene Smith, Western Illinois University; Vicki Smith, Northwestern University; Anthony Sorem, College of St. Benedict; Shirlynn Spacapan, Harvey Mudd College; Charles Stangor, University of Maryland; Frank Stanicek, South Suburban College; Walter Stephan, New Mexico State University; Lloyd Stires, Indiana University of Pennsylvania; Ellen Sullins, Bard College; Harold Takooshian, Fordham University; Jerome Tobacyk, Louisiana Tech University; Stephen Thayer, CCNY; Vaida Thompson, University of North Carolina; Joe Trimble, Western Washington University; Vernon Tyler, Western Washington University; William Wallace, University of Montevallo; Ann Weber, University of North Carolina–Asheville; Carolyn Wells, Texas Southern University; C. K. Whalen, University of California–Irvine; Debbie White, Collin County Community College; Lawrence White, Beloit College; Michael White, Ball State University; Edmond Willis, Central College; David Wilson, Culver-Stockton College; Midge Wilson, DePaul University; Wayne Winborne, New York University; L. A. Witt, Western Illinois University; Guy Wylie, Western Nebraska Community College; Jan Yettl, USCS–Spartanburg; and William Zachry, University of Tennessee.

SOCIAL PSYCHOLOGY

The Field of Social Psychology: How We Think About and Interact with Others

Gee," Val Hatton, a salesperson at Meteor Motors, says, a look of deep sorrow on her face, "I know you're disappointed, but what can I do? My hands are tied."

She has just informed Tom Owen that the deal to which he'd agreed has been rejected by the sales manager. Tom is crushed. This is his first new car, and he had been really pleased with the price and total package they'd negotiated. Tom's friend Jeff, who has come along, is also upset.

"I think you need to go home and think about it," Jeff comments. "This new deal is really a lot worse than the one you had before."

"Yeah, it is," Tom agrees, looking forlornly at the sheet of paper in front of him. "I really want that stereo tape player, but the sales manager crossed it off."

"I know," Val replies. "He told me that we just can't include the stereo at that price—we'd hardly be making any profit. Believe me, I tried to get him to go for it, but he wouldn't. Once he makes up his mind, he's just impossible. But look, it's still a good deal—one of the best I've offered all month. You know what a popular model this is; we can hardly keep any on the lot, they sell so fast."

"Well . . . ," Tom says, a look of uncertainty in his eyes, "I really love that color."

"I know you do," Val responds sympathetically. "And if you pass this one up, I don't know when we'll get another. That Buccaneer Blue is really hot right now. We were lucky to get this one from the distributor. Take my advice: Grab it while you can."

"Look, Tom," Jeff interrupts, "I don't want to get in your way or anything, but I really feel you should think it over. That's a big difference in price; you can't make a decision right now."

"But I want to get it over with," Tom replies. "And you know how much I need a car." Turning to Val, he asks, "Isn't there anything you can do? Can't you help me out?"

"Well, I'll tell you what. How about if I throw in those special floor mats? I know you'll like them a lot more than the ones you can buy at K mart. How about it?"

Tom hesitates for a moment and then, stretching out his hand, says, "Okay, it's a deal. I really want the car!"

"You won't regret it," Val answers, smiling. "I know you'll be really happy with it. Now, if you'll just sign here, here, and here . . ."

"So how'd your term project come off?" Lauri Miller asks her roommate, Sharon, as she enters their room and drops her books on her desk.

"Great!" Sharon replies. "I think we'll get an *A* for sure. Professor Planck liked it a lot, I could tell."

"Well, that's good," Lauri says with a smile. "It's sure lucky you had Todd Bilsky as your partner."

"Todd? Are you kidding?" Sharon answers sharply. "He didn't do that much. I could have gotten along without him altogether."

Lauri seems surprised. "Really? I thought he was a big expert on that stuff. And besides, didn't you tell me that he thought up the basic idea for the whole thing?"

"Well, I guess he did have *something* to do with the idea. But it was me who worked it out and refined it."

"That's not what Bev Stadler says. I was just talking with her, and she was saying what a great job Todd did, how he claims it was all *his* hard work that made the project a success."

"What nerve!" Sharon bristles. "That's just like a man! I do all the important stuff and he wants to take all the credit. Ooh! That makes me so mad!"

"Take it easy, take it easy; no big deal. You'll both get the same grade anyway, right?"

"Yeah, but it's the principle of the thing. I know that *I'm* the one who made it a success. I don't want him going around saying *he* did."

Lauri looks thoughtful. Then, after a brief pause, she remarks: "You know, I think there's some kind of message in all this. There's Todd, trying to take all the credit, and there you are, doing the same thing. Isn't that the way it usually works out? When things go right, we're all right up there taking our bows. But when they go wrong, watch out; we try to pin the blame on anyone handy."

"I don't know what you're talking about," Sharon replies coldly. "If you knew all about it like I do you'd realize that *I* did all the hard work, not Todd. He just came along for the ride. If he thinks otherwise, he's just really mixed up. I'm sure going to set him straight when I see him tomorrow! Anyway, I don't want to talk about it anymore. Let's discuss dinner; I'm starving!"

Let's start with a basic fact: *Other people play a crucial role in our lives.* At different times and in different contexts, they are the source of many of our most satisfying forms of pleasure (love, praise, assistance) and many of our most important forms of pain (criticism, annoyance, rejection). We spend a great deal of our time interacting with them, thinking about them, and trying to understand them (refer to Figure 1.1 on p. 6).

The two incidents presented above illustrate this powerful concern with the social side of life. While reading the first episode, you may well have asked yourself such questions as these: Why did Tom agree to buy the car under terms that were far less favorable than the ones he had initially negotiated? Did the salesperson and sales manager use some tactic that set him up for this decision? Why didn't he listen to his friend's advice about thinking it over? We have all taken part in some form of negotiations and been on the receiving end of attempts by others to influence us; so these questions are certainly relevant to our own personal experience.

Similarly, while reading the second incident, you may have wondered whether Sharon was truly being accurate in her assessment of her own and her partner's contributions. Did she really do most of the work, or was she merely reflecting a general bias to perceive our own efforts as greater than those of others? And was Todd falling prey to the same error in his own assessment of who deserved the credit?

If you have ever taken a step back from the stream of your own social encounters and pondered these kinds of questions, you are in good company. Over the centuries, poets, philosophers, playwrights, and novelists have filled countless volumes with their thoughts about the nature of human social affairs—how we think about and interact with others. Since many were geniuses, their work is often quite insightful. Thus, there seem to be important nuggets of truth in such principles as "Misery loves company" (Schachter, 1959), "Soft words turneth away wrath" (Ohbuchi, Kameda, & Agarie, 1989), and "Laughter is the best medicine" (Baron, 1978, 1984).

In many cases, however, such *informal knowledge* offers a somewhat confusing picture. For example, consider the following illustration. "The wisdom of the ages" suggests that prolonged separation can strengthen bonds of affection: "Absence makes the heart grow fonder." At the same time, though, it tells us

"You're being awfully nice."

FIGURE 1.1   Like the young woman in this cartoon, we spend a great deal of time thinking about other persons. Why is her friend being so nice? What has he got up his sleeve? Most of us confront questions like these every day. (Drawing by Cline; © 1985 The New Yorker Magazine, Inc.)

that separation can yield the opposite effect: "Out of sight, out of mind." Which view is correct? Can both be right? Common sense offers no clear-cut answers.

As a second example of such difficulties, consider the recommendations of informal knowledge with respect to handling provocations from others. On the one hand, we are urged to "turn the other cheek." On the other, we are told that vengeance and counterattacks are effective: "An eye for an eye and a tooth for a tooth." Can both these proposals be useful? Perhaps, but once again common sense offers no clue. We could go on to list other examples of a similar nature, but by now the main point is probably clear. Often, the so-called wisdom of the ages offers a confusing and contradictory picture of human social relations.

At this point, we should note that we certainly don't mean to imply that such information is completely worthless. On the contrary, it can serve as a rich source of suggestions for further study, and it sometimes provides reasonable "first guesses" about the nature of social relationships. By itself, though, informal knowledge cannot stand alone; it fails to provide an adequate basis for fully understanding the complex nature of the social side of human life.

How, then, can we obtain more conclusive—and accurate—information about this topic? How, in short, can we replace speculation, intuition, and unsystematic observation with something more definitive? One answer—and a compelling one, we believe—is provided by the field of **social psychology.** As will soon become apparent, this answer turns out to be both elegant and sophisticated. In simplest terms, though, it rests on the following assertion: *Accurate and useful information about even the most complex aspects of social behavior and social thought can be acquired through the use of basic methods of science.* In short, *social psychologists* suggest that our understanding of the ways in which we think about and interact with others can be greatly enhanced if we replace the informal methods used by poets, philosophers, playwrights, and novelists with more systematic ones that have proved invaluable in other fields of science. From the perspective of the 1990s, this assertion may strike you as being quite obvious. After all, if scientific methods have worked so well in studying other aspects of the natural world, why not apply them to social behavior and social thought as well? You may be surprised to learn, then, that a science-oriented field of social psychology did not emerge until the present century and that it has flourished primarily during the past four decades. Despite its recent appearance, however, social psychology has already made impressive progress. Perhaps the breadth and potential value of the information it has uncovered are best suggested by a list like the one in Table 1.1. Please note that the questions it contains represent only a small sample of the many topics currently being studied by social psychologists. Indeed, it is hard to imagine a single list that could represent all, or even most, of these issues.

Modern social psychology: An indication of its breadth

TABLE 1.1   A sample of the questions currently being studied by social psychologists

Question	Chapter in Which It Is Covered
When we imagine events or outcomes that didn't actually occur, does this change our thoughts about the ones that really *did* happen?	Chapter 3
Are there any situations in which leaders are unnecessary in groups?	Chapter 11
Does smiling actually make us feel happier? Does frowning make us feel sadder?	Chapter 2
What is the best way to ask a favor from another person?	Chapter 8
Is there one kind of love or many? Why do some relationships last while others fail soon after they begin?	Chapter 7
When people say things they don't believe, do they actually come to accept them?	Chapter 4
Is there a link between sexual arousal and aggression?	Chapter 10
Does imagining what we might be like in the future have any effect on our current behavior or our current self-concept?	Chapter 3
Why do people often "throw good money after bad"—stick to poor decisions even when it is clear that they have failed?	Chapter 15
How important is physical attractiveness in determining our liking for others?	Chapter 6
Do individuals differ in the extent to which they show consistent behavior over time and in different situations?	Chapter 12
Does being in a good mood increase our tendency to help others? Do such feelings influence the way we think (e.g., our judgments or decisions)?	Chapters 9, 3

We trust that the list in Table 1.1 has whetted your appetite for more information about social psychology and its findings. If so, please be patient. We will consider all these topics—plus many others—in later chapters. Before turning to that material, however, we want to provide you with some background information. Our reason for doing so is straightforward: Research findings indicate that people have a much better chance of understanding and retaining new information if they are first provided with a framework for holding it (Wyer & Srull, 1986). With this thought in mind, we will use the remainder of this chapter for completing three preliminary tasks.

First, we will present a formal *definition* of social psychology—our view of what it is and what it seeks to accomplish. This knowledge will help orient you to the field and give you an overview of what it is all about. Second, we will offer a brief summary of social psychology's *history*—how it began, how it developed, where it is today, and where, we feel, it may be going. This information will assist you in understanding why social psychologists choose to study certain topics and why they approach them in specific ways. Finally, we will examine some of the basic methods used by social psychologists to answer intriguing questions. A working knowledge of these *research methods* will help you to understand later discussions of specific research projects and will also assist you in comprehending precisely how the body of knowledge that constitutes modern social psychology has been obtained.

Social Psychology: A Working Definition

Proposing a formal definition of almost any field is a complex task. In the case of social psychology, these difficulties are increased by two factors: (1) the field's great diversity, and (2) its rapid rate of change. Despite the broad sweep of topics they choose to study, though, most social psychologists seem to focus the bulk of their attention on one central task: understanding the behavior and thought of individuals in social contexts. In short, social psychologists are primarily concerned with understanding how and why individuals behave, think, and feel as they do in situations involving other persons. Taking this central focus into account, our working definition of social psychology is as follows: *Social psychology is the scientific field that seeks to understand the nature and causes of individual behavior in social situations.* In other words, social psychology seeks to understand how we think about and interact with others. We will now clarify several aspects and implications of this definition.

Social Psychology Is Scientific in Nature

In the minds of many persons, the term *science* refers primarily (or even solely) to specific fields, such as chemistry, physics, and biology. Such persons will, of course, find somewhat puzzling our suggestion that social psychology, too, is scientific. How can a field that seeks to investigate the nature of love, the causes of conflict and aggression, and everything in between be scientific in the same sense as nuclear physics or biochemistry? The answer is surprisingly simple. In reality, the term *science* does not refer to a select group of highly advanced fields. Rather, it refers to a general set of methods—techniques that can be used to study a wide range of topics. In deciding whether a given field is or is not scientific, therefore, the crucial question is, Does it make use of such procedures? To the extent that it does, it can be viewed as scientific orientation. To

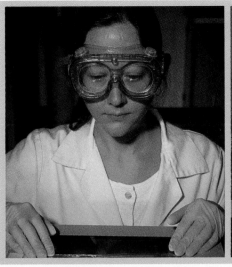

 Science versus nonscience: Different methods, different values

FIGURE 1.2   In scientific fields, such as social psychology, data are gathered systematically and all hypotheses are tested over and over again before being accepted as accurate (left). In nonscientific fields, such as astrology or fortune-telling, in contrast, data are gathered informally and assertions or hypotheses are merely accepted at face value, in the absence of any systematic test of their validity (right).

the extent that it does not, it can be identified as falling outside the realm of science.

What are these techniques and procedures? We'll comment on them in detail in a later section. For now, we will merely note that they chiefly involve efforts to gather systematic information about various phenomena of interest, plus an attitude of skepticism: All "facts" and assertions about the natural world should be tested, retested, and then tested again before they are accepted as accurate. Compare this approach with methods used in various fields that are not generally regarded as scientific (e.g., astrology, fortune-telling, graphology). As you can readily see, the approach and methods are radically different (refer to Figure 1.2).

So, *is* social psychology scientific? Our reply is, definitely yes. Although the topics that social psychologists study are certainly very different from those included in older and more established fields, the methods that they employ are very similar in nature and orientation. For this reason, it makes good sense to describe social psychology as basically scientific in nature.

Social Psychology Focuses on the Behavior of Individuals

Societies may vary widely in terms of their overall level of bigotry, but it is individuals who hold stereotypes about specific groups, experience negative feelings toward them, and seek to exclude them from their neighborhoods, jobs, or schools. Similarly, it is specific persons who give aid to others, commit acts of violence, and fall in or out of love (see Figure 1.3, p. 10). In short, social behavior and social thought rest, ultimately, with individuals—not with collec-

The behavior of individuals in social contexts: Social psychology's major focus

FIGURE 1.3 Because it is *individuals* who engage in specific acts of social behavior, social psychology focuses on factors that influence individual behavior in social contexts.

tivities. Therefore, social psychologists have chosen to focus most of their attention on the actions and thoughts of individuals in social situations. They realize, of course, that such behavior always occurs against a backdrop of sociocultural factors (e.g., the norms and values of a given society). But their major interest lies in understanding the factors that shape the actions and thoughts of individual human beings within social settings.

Social Psychology Seeks to Understand the Causes of Social Behavior and Thought

In a key sense, the heading of this section states the most central aspect of our definition; it specifies the very essence of our field. What it means is that social psychologists are principally concerned with understanding the wide range of conditions that shape the social behavior and thought of individuals—their actions, feelings, beliefs, memories, and ideas—with respect to other persons. The task of identifying the many factors that shape our social behavior and social thought is complex, to say the least. So many variables play a role in this regard that social psychologists truly have their work cut out for them. While the number of specific factors influencing social reactions is large, however, most fall into four major categories: (1) the behavior and characteristics of other persons; (2) basic *cognitive processes,* such as memory and reasoning—processes that underlie social cognition, our thoughts, beliefs, ideas, and judgments about others; (3) ecological variables (direct and indirect influences of the physical environment); and (4) the cultural context in which social behavior and thought occur, and biological aspects of our nature that are relevant to social behavior. Perhaps a few words about each of these categories will help clarify their essential nature.

The Actions and Characteristics of Others   Consider these incidents:

- You are at a party when you notice an attractive person giving you a look that can only be described as inviting.
- Another driver recklessly cuts you off in traffic.
- You are standing in line in a supermarket when the checker suddenly turns out her light and puts a Closed sign in front of your groceries.

Will these actions by other persons affect your behavior and thought? Absolutely. Together, they help illustrate how often and how strongly we are influenced by the actions of other persons.

Now, be honest: Do you ever react differently to attractive people than to unattractive ones? To elderly people than to young ones? To members of racial or ethnic groups different from your own? Again, your answer is probably yes, for we are often strongly affected by the outward characteristics of others. These factors, too, often play an important role in social behavior and social thought.

Cognitive Processes   Next, imagine the following situation: You are asked to write a letter of recommendation for a coworker. What do you remember about this person? How do you combine the information you recall into judgments about her? This example illustrates that in order to understand how we think about other persons, it is often necessary to focus on the basic *cognitive processes* that underlie such thoughts, inferences, and judgments. In short, we must take memory, our information-processing capacities, and various sources of error that can distort inferences and judgment into careful account in our efforts to understand many aspects of human social behavior (Wyer & Srull, 1986).

Ecological Variables: Impact of the Physical Environment   Are people really more prone to wild, impulsive behavior during the full moon than at other times (Rotton & Kelly, 1985; refer to Figure 1.4, p. 12)? Do we become more irritable and openly aggressive when the weather is hot and steamy than when it is cool and comfortable? Such questions call attention to the significant impact of the physical environment on social behavior. Research findings indicate that many factors of this type are important (e.g., crowding, noise, air pollution; cf. Bell, Fisher, & Baum, 1990), and so they certainly fall within the realm of modern social psychology.

Cultural and Biological Factors   Finally, we should note that social behavior does *not* unfold in either a cultural or a biological vacuum. With respect to the former, such factors as cultural norms (social rules concerning how people should behave in specific situations), membership in various groups, and shifting societal values can influence many aspects of social behavior and social thought—everything from political attitudes through choice of marriage partners and preferred number of children. Moreover, because such factors can vary greatly from one culture to another, it is important to take them into account when investigating social behavior around the world. As we'll note below, attention to the effects of culture is an increasingly important trend in modern social psychology.

Turning to biological factors, it is clear that these, too, may play a role in key aspects of social behavior. Growing evidence suggests that many of our

 The physical environment and human behavior: One unverified suggestion

FIGURE 1.4 Do phases of the moon really influence human behavior? While many other aspects of the physical environment (e.g., heat, noise, crowding) do produce such effects, systematic research has yielded little evidence for the occurrence of "moon madness" or any of the other influences often attributed to the presence of a full moon.

preferences, behaviors, and even cognitive abilities are affected to some extent by our biological inheritance (Arvey, Bouchard, Segal, & Abraham, 1989). Please note: The fact that genetic variables play a role in some aspects of social behavior in no way implies that such effects are dominant or that they can't be modified. Far from it; after all, people with vision defects—which are in large part genetically determined—can readily correct such problems with appropriate lenses. Thus, suggesting that genetic factors play a role in some aspects of social behavior in no way implies that these behaviors cannot be changed. Still, the impact of biological factors should not be overlooked, for they appear to play an important role in at least some key aspects of social behavior.

Social Psychology: Summing Up

To conclude: Social psychology focuses mainly on understanding the causes of social behavior and social thought—on identifying factors that shape our feelings, behavior, and thought in social situations. It seeks to accomplish this goal through the use of essentially scientific methods, and it takes note of the fact that social behavior and social thought are influenced by a wide range of factors.

The remainder of this text is devoted to summarizing the findings acquired by social psychology in its quest for such knowledge. This information is fascinating, and we're certain you will find it of interest. But please be warned: It is also full of surprises and will challenge many of your current ideas about people and relations between them. Thus, it's probably safe to predict that after exposure to this field, you'll never think about social relations in quite the same way as before. If you value such change and look forward to gaining new insights, read on.

Social Psychology: A Capsule Memoir

When, precisely, did social psychology begin? This question is difficult to answer, for speculation about social behavior has a long history, stretching back to antiquity (Allport, 1985). Any attempt to present a complete survey of the historical roots of social psychology thus quickly bog us down in endless lists of names and dates. Because we definitely wish to avoid that pitfall, this discussion will be quite limited in scope. We will focus mainly on the emergence of social psychology as an independent field, its growth in recent decades, where it stands at present, and where we believe it will go next.

The Early Years: Social Psychology Gets Started

Few fields mark their beginnings with formal ribbon-cutting ceremonies. Instead, they develop gradually, as growing numbers of scholars or scientists become interested in specific topics or develop new methods for studying existing ones. This pattern was certainly true for social psychology. No bottles of champagne were uncorked to mark its entry on the scientific scene, and so it is difficult to choose a specific date for its official arrival. Perhaps the years between 1908 and 1924 qualify as the period during which social psychology first emerged as an independent entity. In each of these years, an important text containing the words *social psychology* in its title was published. The first, by William McDougall (1908), was based largely on the view that social behavior stems from innate tendencies, or *instincts*. This view is currently rejected by almost all social psychologists, so it is clear that the field had *not* assumed its modern perspective at that time.

The second volume, by Floyd Allport (1924), is a different story. That book is much closer—surprisingly so, given the early date of its publication—to the modern orientation of the field. In this book, Allport argued that social behavior stems from many different factors, including the presence of other persons and their specific actions. Further, his book contained discussions of actual research that had already been conducted on such topics as social conformity, the ability to recognize the emotions of others from their facial expressions, and the impact of audiences on task performance. Because all these topics have been studied by social psychologists in recent years, the following conclusion seems justified: By the middle of the Roaring Twenties, social psychology had appeared on the scene and begun to focus on many of the issues and topics it still seeks to study today.

The two decades following publication of Allport's text were marked by rapid growth. New issues were studied, and systematic methods for investigating them were devised quickly. Important milestones in the development of the new field during this period include research by two of its founders—Muzafer Sherif and Kurt Lewin. Sherif (1935) studied the nature and impact of *social norms*—rules indicating how individuals should or ought to behave—and so contributed many insights to our understanding of pressures toward *conformity*. Lewin and his colleagues (Lewin, Lippitt, & White, 1939) carried out revealing research on the nature of leadership and related group processes. In short, by the close of the 1930s social psychology was an active, growing field that had already contributed much to our knowledge of human social behavior. (To gain an idea of what was happening in the world during the years when social psychology took shape, please refer to Figure 1.5.)

Social Psychology's Youth: The 1940s, 1950s, and 1960s

After a pause necessitated by World War II, social psychology continued its growth during the late 1940s and 1950s. During this period, the field expanded its scope in several directions. Social psychologists focused attention on the influence that groups and group membership have on individual behavior (Forsyth, 1983). And they examined the link between various personality traits and social behavior. Perhaps the most significant event of the period, however, was the development of the theory of **cognitive dissonance** (Festinger, 1957). This theory proposed that human beings dislike inconsistency and will strive to reduce it. Specifically, the theory argues that people find inconsistency between their attitudes or inconsistency between their attitudes and their behavior disturbing and seek to eliminate it. While these ideas may not seem very surprising, they actually lead to many unexpected predictions. For example, they suggest that offering individuals small rewards for stating views they don't really hold

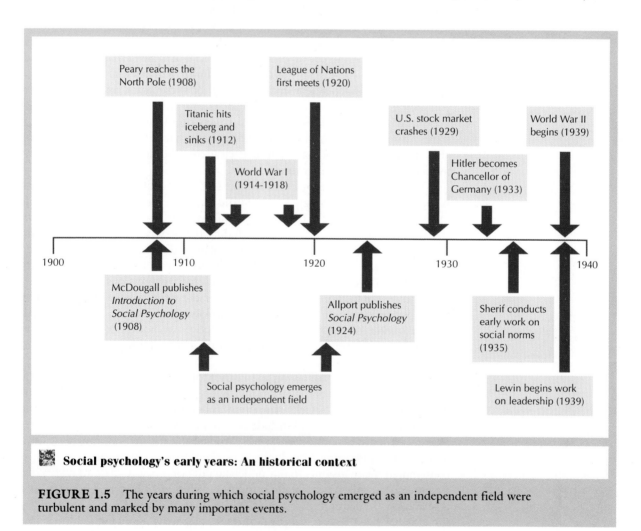

Social psychology's early years: An historical context

FIGURE 1.5 The years during which social psychology emerged as an independent field were turbulent and marked by many important events.

CHAPTER ONE   THE FIELD OF SOCIAL PSYCHOLOGY

Major topics of research in social psychology during the 1960s

TABLE 1.2   During the 1960s, the scope of research in social psychology expanded greatly

Topic	Description/Key Questions
Social perception	The process through which we attempt to understand other persons. (How do we form first impressions of others? How do we identify their major traits?)
Interpersonal attraction	The basis for our liking or disliking of others. (Does attraction stem from similarity or dissimilarity? How important is physical attractiveness as a determinant of attraction?)
Prosocial behavior	The tendency to offer help to others. (Why do people help or fail to help during emergencies? Do people help others out of a sense of social responsibility?)
Group decision making	The process through which groups make decisions. (Are groups more or less likely to take risks than individuals are? Do groups make decisions that are more or less accurate than those made by individuals?)

can often be more effective in getting them to change their opinions than offering them larger rewards for the same actions—a principle sometimes described as the *less-leads-to-more* effect. Festinger's theory captured the interest of many social psychologists and remained a major topic of research for several decades. (We will return to this topic in Chapter 4.)

In an important sense, the 1960s can be viewed as the time when social psychology came into its own. During this turbulent decade of rapid social change, the number of social psychologists rose dramatically and the field expanded to include virtually every aspect of social interaction you might imagine. So many lines of research either began or developed during these years that we could not possibly list them all here. A sample of the questions and issues receiving major attention is presented in Table 1.2. As you can see, social psychology certainly moved into many new areas during this period.

The 1970s and 1980s: A Maturing Field

The rapid pace of change did not slacken during the 1970s; if anything, it accelerated. Many lines of study begun during the 1960s were continued and expanded. Several new topics rose to prominence or were studied from a new and more sophisticated perspective. Among the most important of these were

SOCIAL PSYCHOLOGY: A CAPSULE MEMOIR   **15**

attribution (How do we infer the causes behind others' behavior?), *gender differences* and *sex discrimination* (To what extent does the behavior of women and men actually differ in various situations? What forces work against full equality for females?), and *environmental psychology* (What is the impact of the physical environment—such factors as heat, crowding, noise, and pollution—on social behavior?).

In addition, two larger-scale trends took shape in and continued to expand during the 1980s. Since these trends are of great significance to our understanding of modern social psychology, we will describe them here.

Growing Influence of a Cognitive Perspective As we noted earlier, social psychologists have long been aware that cognitive factors—attitudes, beliefs, values, inferences—play a key role in social behavior. Starting in the late 1970s, however, interest in such topics took an exciting new form. At present, many social psychologists believe that our understanding of virtually all aspects of social behavior can be greatly enhanced by focusing on the cognitive processes that underlie them (e.g., Markus & Zajonc, 1985; Wyer & Srull, 1986). Consistent with this view, they have applied a cognitive perspective to a wide range of social processes, including stereotypes (Schaller & Maass, 1989), self-evaluation (Markus & Wurf, 1987), group decision making (Kaplan & Miller, 1987), and persuasion (Petty & Cacioppo, 1986). What this approach involves, briefly, are efforts to apply basic knowledge about such issues as (1) how memory operates, (2) how reasoning occurs, (3) how new information is integrated into existing mental frameworks, and (4) how available information about others is combined into judgments or evaluations of them. To cite just one example, from this perspective the formation and persistence of stereotypes are understood within the context of certain aspects of memory (tendencies to recall only certain types of information) and aspects of social reasoning (tendencies that lead individuals to reach false conclusions about others). We will discuss these and related topics in Chapters 2, 3, and 4.

The results of research conducted within this perspective have been impressive. Major insights into key aspects of social behavior have been gained, and new phenomena previously ignored have been brought sharply into focus (Fiske & Taylor, 1984; Srull & Wyer, 1988). Thus, it is far from surprising that the volume of work concerned with cognitive factors and processes has risen steeply in recent years.

Growing Emphasis on Application: Exporting Social Knowledge The 1970s and 1980s were also marked by a second major trend in social psychology: growing concern with the application of social knowledge (e.g., Spacapan & Oskamp, 1988). An increasing number of social psychologists have turned their attention to questions concerning *personal health* (e.g., What factors help individuals resist the adverse impact of stress? Are certain life-styles linked to heart attacks and related diseases?), the *legal process* (e.g., How valid is eyewitness testimony? What information is most influential in shaping the decisions of jurors?), and many aspects of behavior in *work settings* (e.g., What factors lead employees to conclude that they are being fairly or unfairly compensated? Do personal factors like applicants' appearance affect the outcome of job interviews?). Whatever its specific focus, such research attempts to apply the findings and principles of social psychology to the solution of practical problems. This theme is certainly not new in social psychology; Kurt Lewin, one of the founders of the field, strongly recommended such research and often stated that "there's nothing as practical as a good theory," by which he meant that theories of social behavior and thought developed through systematic research often turn out to be extremely useful in solving practical problems. Interest in applying the knowledge of social psychology to practical issues has, however, definitely increased in recent years, with many beneficial results. (For one example of such research, please see the special section below.)

ON THE APPLIED SIDE

Perceived Fairness in Work Settings: Why (Sometimes) Bigger Offices Yield Higher Output

Most people want to feel they are being treated fairly by others. In fact, few will long tolerate situations in which they decide they are receiving less from others than they deserve. What factors, precisely, lead people to conclude that they are being treated fairly or unfairly by others? Social psychologists have conducted a great deal of research on this question (Leventhal, 1980). This research has in turn led to the formulation of sophisticated theories of *perceived fairness* or *equity* (Adams, 1965; Greenberg & Cohen, 1982). Moreover, and most relevant to our present concerns, *these theories have been applied to a wide range of practical situations and problems* (Greenberg, 1986, 1990). As an example of such research, we'll consider an intriguing field study conducted by Greenberg (1988)—a social psychologist who has spent years applying the principles and findings of this field to practical issues in many settings.

Participants in this investigation were employees at a large insurance company. Because of construction within the company's building, it was necessary to reassign several groups of persons—underwriter trainees, associate underwriters, and underwriters—to temporary offices. As their titles suggest, the three groups differed in terms of status, a fact that was reflected in their original offices. Underwriters had the largest offices, a door they could close for privacy, and no officemates. Associate underwriters had smaller offices, no door, and one officemate. Finally, underwriter trainees had five officemates, less space, and, of course, no door.

To determine whether predictions derived from equity theory would be verified in this natural setting, Greenberg obtained the cooperation of the company's top managers, who agreed to reassign the three groups of employees to new temporary offices *at random*. This random assignment meant that some of the workers in each group were assigned to a new office that was equivalent to the one they had before, while others found themselves in offices that were either larger or smaller (higher or lower in status) than the ones from which they moved.

Equity theory will be discussed in detail in Chapter 11. For the moment, therefore, we merely wish to note that it predicts that people will experience feelings of unfairness (inequity) when they perceive that the ratio between what they contribute to a relationship and what they receive from it is less favorable than that of other persons. Thus, feelings of inequity will be maximum when

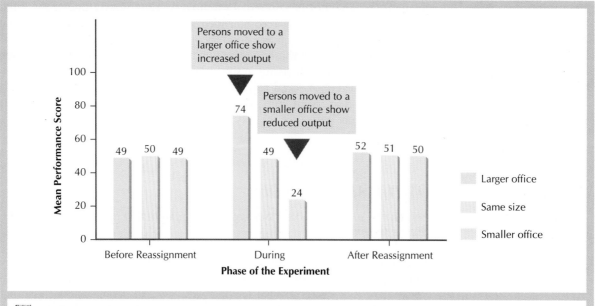

Office size, work output, and equity

FIGURE 1.6 Employees who, during construction, were moved to an office larger than the one they had initially occupied showed increased work output. In contrast, those moved to an office smaller than the one they had initially occupied showed reduced output. These findings are consistent with predictions derived from *equity theory.* (Source: Based on data from Greenberg, 1988.)

individuals perceive that they contribute much more but receive much less than others do.

Applying this theory to the present situation, what would we expect? Greenberg (1988) reasoned that employees who found themselves in smaller offices than they'd had before would experience feelings of inequity. As a result, they would work less hard in order to reduce their contributions. Thus, their output would fall. In contrast, people who found themselves in larger offices than they'd had before would feel overpaid, with the result that they would increase their effort on the job and raise their output.

As you can see from Figure 1.6, this is precisely what occurred. Employees who were placed in offices equivalent to their original ones showed no change in output (number of cases processed); those moved to smaller offices showed a drop in output; and those moved to larger ones actually showed an increase. (These effects largely disappeared when subjects were returned to their original offices.) Interestingly, the increase in output among "overcompensated" persons was smaller than the drop in performance among "undercompensated" employees—a finding that suggests our tolerance for underpayment is much less than our tolerance for overpayment.

Greenberg's results, and those obtained in many related studies, suggest that organizations would be wise to pay careful attention to the principles of equity theory when deciding how to distribute various rewards (e.g., pay, office size, and other perks) among employees. By following these principles, businesses can help ensure that their employees feel fairly treated. By ignoring them, in contrast, they run the risk of generating unnecessary—and costly—reductions in motivation and productivity. In sum, equity theory, which was originally developed, tested, and refined by social psychologists, has been found to have important implications for work settings and for any other context in which individuals enter into some kind of exchange with others.

The 1990s and Beyond: A Look at the Future

Earlier, we noted that *diversity* is a prime characteristic of social psychology. Given this fact, predictions about its future are uncertain to say the least. Still, at the risk of being proven wrong by future events and trends, we are willing to offer the following guesses about how social psychology will change and develop in the coming decades.

Cognition and Application: The Adventure Continues The first of our predictions is perhaps the one on firmest ground: The two major trends described above—the growing influence of a cognitive perspective and an increasing interest in application—will continue. Knowledge about cognitive processes (memory, decision making) is fast accumulating. Given this fact, it seems only natural for social psychologists to use that knowledge in their efforts to understand social behavior and especially social thought. Such work has already yielded valuable results, and we are confident it will continue to do so in the decades ahead.

We predict that interest in applying the principles and findings of social psychology, too, will continue. Increased concern with such application appears to be a natural outgrowth of increasing maturity and sophistication in almost any field. Thus, as social psychology advances, efforts to apply its growing knowledge base to a number of practical issues will continue and perhaps expand.

The Internationalization of Social Psychology: Adoption of a Multicultural Perspective While social psychology has always existed in many different countries, its early growth and development took place primarily in the United States. Even today, a large majority of practicing social psychologists live in North America. Because of this, a substantial proportion of all research in social psychology has been conducted in the United States and Canada. Do the findings of these studies generalize to other cultures? Are the principles established in such research applicable to people all around the world? We predict that for several reasons, interest in such questions will increase in the years ahead. First, growing international trade and travel have raised the consciousness of tens of millions of persons—including social psychologists—with respect to differences among various cultures. Second, the United States has itself become increasingly diverse in terms of the ethnic and cultural background of its citizens (refer to Figure 1.7, p. 20), thereby spurring interest in the nature and impact of such differences. Third, in recent years, social psychologists have shown increasing interest in this question: Which aspects of human behavior are *culture-specific*—the result of conditions existing in various cultures—and which ones, as part of our shared human heritage, occur in all parts of the globe and across many cultures? In an important sense, it is the growing interest in

Ethnic diversity: One basis for a multicultural perspective in social psychology

FIGURE 1.7 In recent decades, ethnic diversity has increased in the United States. Such diversity has in turn spurred interest in *multicultural perspective* among social psychologists.

this question that lies behind the recent spurt in research conducted from a *multicultural* perspective. Together, these three trends seem to guarantee the further development of a social psychology that is truly multicultural in its approach and content. (For an example of recent research conducted from a multicultural perspective, please see the special section below.)

SOCIAL PSYCHOLOGY: A MULTICULTURAL PERSPECTIVE

Friendship and Dating in the United States and Hong Kong: Differences and Similarities

According to Rudyard Kipling, a poet and author of the nineteenth century, "East is East and West is West, and never the twain shall meet." In other words, in Kipling's view the gulf between the customs, values, and behavior of people from the Orient and those of people from the Western Hemisphere was so huge that it could never be bridged. Time and the tide of human affairs have certainly proved Kipling wrong. Despite large differences in culture, religion, and politics, contacts between the East and the West have grown ever closer during the past hundred years and especially in recent decades. One result of this contact is a convergence between these diverse cultures, at least on some dimensions. People in Japan, Korea, and many other countries have adopted numerous practices from the West, and millions of people in Western cultures have come to enjoy and appreciate Eastern art, food, and manufactured goods. Such convergence in no way implies that East has *become* West or vice versa, however. On the contrary, critical differences in social behavior and social attitudes persist. What are these differences? And in what ways is social behavior in these diverse cultures similar? Research projects have begun to provide answers to such questions (e.g., Bond & King, 1985).

In one study, Wheeler (1988) focused on similarities and differences between college students in the United States and in Hong Kong with respect to friendship and dating. Not surprisingly, he found numerous differences in these forms of social behavior. For example, students in the United States reported having more interactions with others during the course of a day. They have more spare time for social interaction than their counterparts in Hong Kong. Perhaps more interesting, Hong Kong students reported having more interactions with others in groups that include persons of both sexes, while students in the United States reported having more interactions with persons of the same or opposite sex. Further, while students in Hong Kong described most of these interactions as involving the performance of various tasks, those in the United States described them as involving primarily recreation.

Turning to sex differences in the two cultures, Wheeler observed the following patterns: In the United States, females reported having more interactions with members of the opposite sex than did males; in Hong Kong, precisely the opposite was true. This finding takes on added interest when its relationship to competence in dating situations is considered. Here, females scored higher in the United States, while males scored higher in Hong Kong. In other words—and not surprisingly—within each culture, the sex that engaged in more interactions with the opposite sex reported being more at ease and competent in dating situations than the other sex did (refer to Figure 1.8).

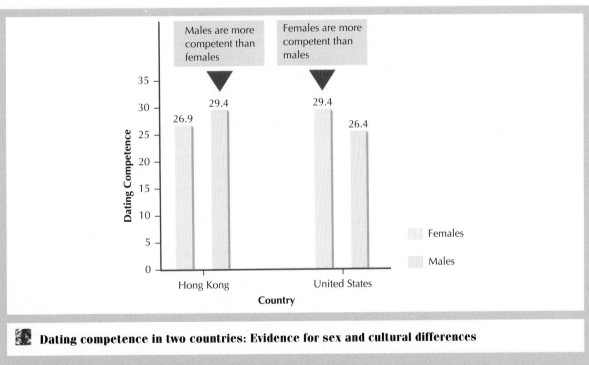

Dating competence in two countries: Evidence for sex and cultural differences

FIGURE 1.8 In the United States, females report higher dating competence than males. In Hong Kong, males report higher dating competence than females. These differences reflect contrasting amounts of social experience in opposite-sex groups. In the United States, females have more experience of this type than males. In Hong Kong, the opposite is true. (Source: Based on data from Wheeler, 1988.)

In addition, and perhaps most intriguing, Wheeler reported differences in the behavior of the two sexes that were consistent *across* the two cultures. For example, in both Hong Kong and the United States, females reported having a larger number of interactions with same-sex persons than did males. Further, females rated such interactions as more pleasant. That this difference was observed in both cultures suggests that it may be quite general in scope and independent of very different socialization practices.

In sum, Wheeler's research points to the existence of many similarities and also many differences in the social behavior of students in the two cultures. Through research such as this, social psychologists seek to determine which aspects of social behavior and thought are related to specific facets of various cultures and which, in contrast, are quite universal around the world and so seem to reflect our common human heritage.

Social Psychology as an Importer as Well as an Exporter of Knowledge   In the past, social psychology has served as a source of basic knowledge about social behavior for many other fields. As we will see in later chapters, the findings reported by social psychologists have been used as the basis for important advances in such applied fields as education, counseling, and management (Baron & Greenberg, 1990; Gerstein, White, & Barke, 1988) and have served as the basis for important research in other social and behavioral sciences (e.g., sociology and political science). Now, however, there are signs that this *exportation* of knowledge may soon be matched by a degree of *importation* as well.

A growing number of social psychologists are beginning to draw on the findings and principles of other fields—including all the ones listed above—in formulating and conducting their own research. They realize that such fields, because they have collected data in different ways, from different populations, and in different contexts than traditional social psychology has, often have much to offer. To mention just one example, the field of *counseling psychology* (which seeks to help individuals cope with a wide range of personal problems) deals with a very diverse group of persons—a group much more varied in age, occupation, and background than those typically studied by social psychologists. Similarly, counseling psychologists often study individuals over prolonged periods of time (e.g., weeks or months) rather than for just a few hours, as is typical in much social psychological research. Because of such differences in approach and methods, the findings reported by counseling psychologists may shed important light on various issues and questions of interest to social psychologists (Gerstein et al., 1988).

Similar arguments can be made for the value, to social psychology, of several other fields as well. The fact that growing numbers of social psychologists are indeed making use of such connections is illustrated by the founding, several years ago, of a journal entitled the *Journal of Social and Clinical Psychology*. This publication provides a concrete example of the emergence of what we suspect may be a new *interdisciplinary* perspective in our field.

Those, then, are our major predictions. Will they prove to be accurate? Only time will tell. Regardless of their fate, however, there is one additional prediction we are willing to make with considerable confidence: No matter how social psychology changes in the years ahead, it will remain an active, vital field, one with an impressive potential for contributing in essential ways to human welfare and human potential.

Answering Questions about Social Behavior and Social Thought: Research Methods in Social Psychology

By now, you should have a basic grasp of (1) what social psychology is, (2) how it developed, and (3) where, perhaps, it is going next. With that information in place, it is appropriate for us to turn to another essential issue: How do social psychologists attempt to answer questions about social behavior and social thought? How, in short, do they seek to add to our knowledge of these basic topics? To provide you with a useful overview of this process, we will touch on three related issues. First, we will describe two key *methods of research in social psychology*. Next, we will examine the role of *theory* in such research. Finally, we will consider some of the complex *ethical issues* that arise in the context of systematic research on social behavior.

The Experimental Method: Knowledge through Intervention

If a large sample of social psychologists were asked to name the method of research they most prefer, the majority would probably reply with the term **experimentation.** Unfortunately, our past experience suggests that many persons view this procedure as somewhat mysterious and complex. In fact, that is far from the case. In its essential logic, experimentation is surprisingly straightforward. To help you understand its use in social research, we will first describe the basic nature of experimentation and then comment on two conditions that are essential for its success.

Experimentation: Its Basic Nature A researcher who decides to employ the experimental method generally begins with a clear-cut goal: determining whether (and how strongly) a specific factor (variable) influences some aspect of social behavior. To find out, she or he then (1) varies the presence, or strength, of this factor in a systematic manner and (2) tries to determine whether those variations have any impact on the aspect of social behavior or social thought under investigation. The central idea behind these procedures is this: If the factor varied does exert such effects, individuals exposed to different amounts, or levels, of the factor should show different patterns of behavior. Exposure to a small amount of the factor should result in one level or pattern of behavior, exposure to a larger amount should result in another pattern, and so on.

Generally, the factor systematically varied by the researcher is termed the **independent variable,** while the aspect of behavior studied is termed the **dependent variable.** In a simple experiment, then, subjects in different groups are exposed to contrasting levels of the independent variable (e.g., low, moderate, high). The behavior of these persons is then carefully examined and compared to determine whether it does in fact vary with different levels of the independent variable. If it does, and if two other conditions we will mention below are met, the researcher can tentatively conclude that the independent variable does indeed affect the aspect of behavior or cognition being studied.

Perhaps a concrete example will help you to form a clearer picture of this process. Let's consider an experiment designed to examine the *hypothesis* (an as-yet-unverified suggestion) that repeated exposure to pornographic materials (e.g., X-rated videotapes) causes individuals to become dissatisfied with their own sex lives and with their current sexual partners. (Presumably this would be the case, because virtually no real-life partner could live up to either the amazing physiques or the astounding levels of sexual drive demonstrated by the participants in X-rated materials.)

In such research, the independent variable would be the amount of exposure to pornographic materials, while the dependent variable would be some measure of subjects' satisfaction with their own sex lives and with their current partners (e.g., they could rate such satisfaction on a specially designed questionnaire). Thus, in such a study, one group of subjects might be exposed to ten hours of X-rated videotapes (two hours per day for five days), a second group might be exposed to five hours of such tapes (one hour per day for five days), and a third group—a control condition—would see no X-rated tapes. (Subjects in this third group would also watch five hours of videotapes, but the content of those tapes would be nonsexual.)

After watching the videotapes, subjects in all three groups would complete a questionnaire designed to measure their satisfaction with their current sex lives and with their current sexual partners. Items on the questionnaire might, for example, ask subjects to rate the extent to which they derive pleasure from their sexual activities, their sexual partners' physical appearance, and their sexual partners' sexual performance. Such ratings might be made on a seven-point scale, with one end of the scale indicating low satisfaction and the other high satisfaction. (As we'll soon note, it is important that subjects assigned to the three treatment conditions *not* differ on this measure before the start of the study. If they do, serious complications can occur with respect to making sense out of any results that are later obtained.)

If exposure to pornographic materials does indeed affect sexual satisfaction, a pattern of results such as those shown in Figure 1.9 might be obtained. As you can see, these results suggest that exposure to X-rated videotapes does indeed reduce sexual satisfaction. Moreover, the greater such exposure, the larger this reduction. (Actually, several studies have been conducted to investigate this relationship, and they support the conclusion offered here—that exposure to pornographic material does indeed seem to reduce satisfaction with one's sex life and with one's sexual partners; Zillmann & Bryant, 1988.)

At this point we should note that the example just presented describes an extremely simple case—the simplest type of experiment social psychologists ever conduct. In many instances, researchers wish to examine the impact of several independent variables at once. For example, in the study just described, the sex of the persons exposed to the videotapes might also be considered, in order to determine whether males or females react in similar or different ways to exposure to pornography. Or, the specific content of the videotapes might be systematically varied so that some subjects watch tapes that depict sexual relations between mutually consenting adults while others watch tapes showing sexual relations involving an element of force or violence. When several variables are included in an experiment, a larger amount of information about the topic of interest can usually be obtained. Even more important, potential *interactions* between variables can be examined—that is, we can determine whether the impact of one independent variable is affected in some manner by one or more other variables. For example, in the experiment described above we might find

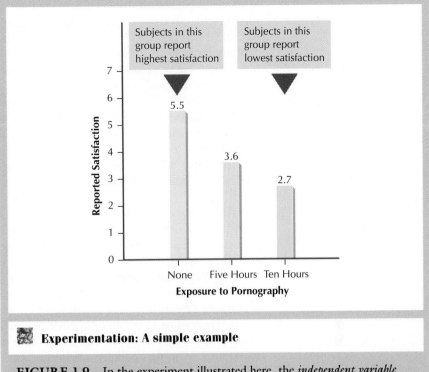

Experimentation: A simple example

FIGURE 1.9 In the experiment illustrated here, the *independent variable* was the amount of exposure to X-rated videotapes (none, five hours, ten hours). Results indicate that increasing amounts of exposure to such materials reduced subjects' reported satisfaction with their sex lives and with their current sexual partners.

that exposure to sexual relations involving force or violence reduces satisfaction with one's own sex life (perhaps because the negative reactions generated by viewing such scenes reduce viewers' interest in many sexual activities), while exposure to sexual relations between mutually enthusiastic partners has the opposite effect (it enhances viewers' satisfaction with their own sex lives). Because social behavior is usually affected by many factors operating at once, knowledge of such interactions is often crucial. We will refer to many such interactions in later portions of this book.

Successful Experimentation: Two Basic Requirements Earlier we noted that before we can conclude that an independent variable has affected some form of behavior, two important conditions must be met. Because a basic understanding of these conditions is essential for evaluating the usefulness of any experiment, we will now describe them.

The first involves what is usually termed the **random assignment of subjects to groups.** According to this principle, each person taking part in a study must have an equal chance of being exposed to each level of the independent variable. The reason for this rule is simple: If subjects are *not* randomly assigned to each group, it may prove impossible to determine whether differences in their later behavior stem from differences they brought with them to the study, from the impact of the independent variable, or from both. For instance, continuing with our study of pornography, imagine that all the participants exposed to the X-rated tapes were persons currently receiving therapy for various psychological problems, while those in the control condition (those viewing nonsexual tapes) were persons not undergoing therapy. Assume that persons in the two groups exposed to pornographic tapes reported lower satisfaction with their sex lives. Is this due to watching the tapes? Or is it due to the personal problems these participants have that may be interfering with their sexual enjoyment? Obviously, it is impossible to tell. To avoid such problems, it would be necessary to ensure that persons with and without current psychological problems have an equal chance of being assigned to each of the experimental groups—ten hours of X-rated tapes, five hours of X-rated tapes, or no X-rated tapes.

The second condition we referred to above may be stated as follows: Insofar as possible, all other factors that might also affect subjects' behavior, aside from the independent variable, must be held constant. To see why this is so, consider the following situation. In the sample study on pornography, imagine that when showing the X-rated tapes, the assistant who presents the tapes (and who is extremely attractive) flirts seductively with the subjects and compliments their appearance several times. In contrast, when showing the nonsexual tapes, the assistant maintains a cool and impersonal manner. Further, please note that this is *not* part of the study; the researcher who designed it did not instruct the assistant to act in these different ways and would be quite upset to hear of the situation. Once again, subjects exposed to the pornographic tapes report lower satisfaction with their current sexual partners than those in the control condition do. Why? Perhaps this is a result of exposure to the X-rated tapes. But it might also be the result of the assistant's provocative behavior (which, by the way, would be entirely inappropriate and should *never* occur during actual research). Some subjects, at least, might be flattered by the attentions of the attractive assistant, and might conclude that they are not fully appreciated by their current lovers, who don't often compliment them in this manner. Thus, it could be this factor—not exposure to the tapes—that accounts for the drop in subjects' reported satisfaction. In short, the independent variable of interest—exposure to sexual materials—is **confounded** with another variable that is not part of the research: provocative behavior on the part of the assistant. The potential effects of each cannot be separated or disentangled (refer to Figure 1.10).

In the case we have just described, confounding between variables is relatively easy to spot. Often, though, it can enter in more subtle and hidden ways. For this reason, researchers wishing to conduct successful experiments must always be on guard against it. Only when such confounding is prevented can the results of an experiment be interpreted with confidence.

The Correlational Method: Knowledge through Systematic Observation

Earlier we noted that experimentation is usually the preferred method of research in social psychology (we'll indicate below why this is so). Sometimes, though, it simply cannot be used, for two basic reasons. First, systematic variations in some factor of interest may lie beyond an experimenter's control. Imagine, for example, that a researcher has reason to believe that prejudice is fostered by vivid accounts in the mass media of violent crimes performed by members of various minority groups. Such reports strengthen stereotypes and so help to fan the flames of bigotry. Clearly, the researcher would find it ex-

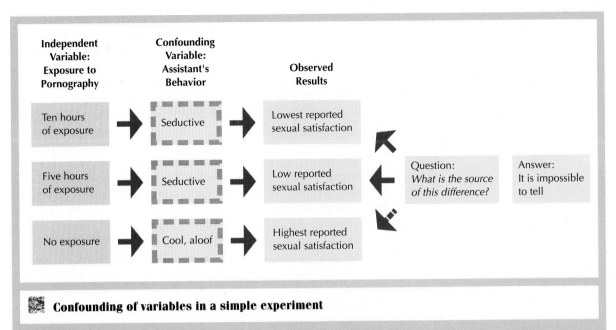

Independent Variable: Exposure to Pornography	Confounding Variable: Assistant's Behavior	Observed Results
Ten hours of exposure	Seductive	Lowest reported sexual satisfaction
Five hours of exposure	Seductive	Low reported sexual satisfaction
No exposure	Cool, aloof	Highest reported sexual satisfaction

Question: *What is the source of this difference?*

Answer: It is impossible to tell

Confounding of variables in a simple experiment

FIGURE 1.10   In a study of the effects of exposure to pornography on reported sexual satisfaction, some subjects were exposed to ten hours of X-rated videotapes, some to five hours, and others to none. In addition—and unknown to the researcher who planned the study—the assistant who showed these tapes acted seductively toward subjects in the two pornography conditions but in a cool and aloof manner toward subjects in the control (no pornography) condition. As a result, the independent variable is *confounded* with the assistant's behavior. This means that it is impossible to determine whether differences in the dependent measure (reported sexual satisfaction) are due to the effects of the independent variable, to the confounding variable (differences in the assistant's behavior), or to both.

tremely difficult to test this hypothesis through experimental means: How could she or he induce newspapers, television stations, and magazines to alter the contents of their reports in a systematic manner?

Second, ethical constraints may prevent a researcher from conducting what might otherwise be a feasible experiment. Although it may be possible to vary some factor of interest, doing so could violate ethical standards accepted by social psychologists or by society generally. For example, imagine that a researcher suspects that specific kinds of events serve as triggers for dangerous riots. Certainly it would not be permissible for the researcher to stage such events in some locations but not in others in order to determine whether collective violence actually erupts more frequently under the first set of circumstances. Similarly, consider the dilemma faced by a social psychologist who wishes to test the hypothesis that certain kinds of beliefs about one's partner are especially damaging to romantic relationships. Could this researcher try to induce such beliefs among one group of couples but not among another in order to determine whether breakups are more common in the first group than in the second? Obviously, conducting such a study would be unethical, for it would endanger the happiness or well-being of the unknowing participants.

Faced with such difficulties, social psychologists often adopt an alternative technique of research known as the **correlational method.** In this approach, efforts are made to determine whether two or more variables are related by engaging in careful observation of both. If changes in one are found to be consistently associated with changes in the other, evidence for a link between them is obtained. Please note: With the correlational method, in contrast to experimentation, *no attempt is made to vary one of the factors in a systematic manner in order to observe the effect of such variations on the other variable;* rather, *naturally occurring* variations in both are observed to determine whether they tend to occur together in some fashion.

Perhaps the best way of illustrating the correlational method and how it differs from experimentation is to return to the topic discussed earlier—the effects of exposure to pornography on observers' reported sexual satisfaction. If we wished to study this issue by means of the correlational method, procedures would be relatively simple. We would first ask a large group of subjects to rate their sexual satisfaction and, at the same time, to indicate how often they were exposed to various kinds of X-rated materials. We would then relate their answers to the two categories of questions through statistical means. If exposure to pornography did indeed lead to reduced sexual satisfaction, a *negative correlation* would exist between reported viewing of such materials and reported sexual satisfaction. (Negative correlations indicate that as one variable increases, the other decreases.)

Note again that in such an investigation we would not attempt to control or vary the amount of pornography to which individuals were exposed. Rather, we would simply relate their reports concerning exposure to such materials to measures of their current sexual satisfaction.

The correlational method offers several useful advantages. For one thing, it can be employed to study behavior in many real-life settings. For another, it is often highly efficient and can yield a large amount of interesting data in a short time. Moreover, it can be extended to include many different variables at once. For example, in the research mentioned above, such variables as subjects' age, sex, occupation, number of previous lovers or marriages, family background (e.g., number of brothers and sisters, income of parents), and several aspects of their personalities could all be included in the study. Through a statistical technique known as *regression analysis,* the extent to which each of these variables is related to (predicts) sexual satisfaction can be assessed. Finally, as we noted earlier, the correlational method can be used for research in situations in which practical or ethical constraints render experimentation impossible. Unfortunately, though, the correlational method suffers from one major drawback that greatly lessens its appeal to social psychologists: *In contrast to experimentation, the findings it yields are often somewhat uncertain with respect to cause-and-effect relationships.* The fact that changes in one variable are accompanied by changes in another in no sense guarantees that a causal link exists between them—that changes in the first caused changes in the second. Rather, in many cases the fact that two variables tend to rise or fall together simply reflects the fact that both are caused by a third, perhaps less visible variable.

Sometimes this last point is obvious. For example, suppose we measured both the weight and the salaries of a large group of executives. What might we find? One possibility is a *positive correlation*—the higher the weight of these persons, the higher their salaries. Does this mean that weight gain produces a higher income? Obviously not. In fact, both variables are related to a third— *age.* As people grow older, many tend to gain weight; and as people age, they advance in their careers and obtain higher salaries.

Do high temperatures cause aggression? An illustration of the fact that correlation does not necessarily imply causation

FIGURE 1.11 More riots and violent crimes occur during the hot summer months than at other times. Does this mean that uncomfortable heat causes irritability and aggression? Not necessarily. It is also possible that high temperatures are associated with other factors (e.g., increased consumption of alcohol, longer days, more people out on the streets) and that these, not high temperatures themselves, cause increased aggression. Only systematic research can resolve this issue. (See Chapter 13 for a discussion of actual research on this topic.)

In other cases, however, it may be more difficult to recognize the fact that correlation—even strong correlation—does not necessarily equal causation. Have you ever heard the phrase *the long, hot summer*? It refers to the fact that most riots and related civil disturbances tend to take place during the warm summer months (see Figure 1.11). Does this fact mean that high temperatures *cause* riots, perhaps by somehow making people irritable and short-tempered? Perhaps. This suggestion seems to make good sense, and indeed, several recent studies of the link between temperature and violence suggest that this may be so (e.g., Anderson, 1987, 1989; Cotton, 1986). Yet it is also possible that the relationship between heat and violence stems from other factors. For example, days are longer during the warm summer months, thus affording people greater opportunity to become involved in acts of aggression. Similarly, there is some indication that people consume more alcoholic beverages (e.g., beer) during the warm summer months, and so perhaps *this* factor, not heat itself, is the cause of increased violence.

By now the main point should be clear. The existence of even a strong correlation between two factors should not be interpreted as a definite indication that they are causally linked. Such conclusions are justified only in the presence of additional confirming evidence.

The Role of Theory in Social Psychology: Major Benefits and a Few Potential Dangers

Over the years, we have often heard our students ask, "How do social psychologists come up with such interesting ideas for their research?" As you can probably guess, there is no simple answer, for several factors play a role. Some research projects are suggested by informal observation of the social world around us. Social psychologists take note of some puzzling aspect of social behavior or social thought and plan investigations to increase their understanding of that aspect. On other occasions, the idea for a research project is suggested by the findings of an earlier study. Successful experiments in social psychology do not simply answer questions; they often raise additional ones as well. Thus, the problem facing social psychologists is usually *not* that of coming up with interesting ideas for research. Rather, it is choosing among the many intriguing possibilities. Perhaps the single most important basis for research in social psychology, however, is formal **theories.**

In simple terms, theories represent efforts by scientists in any field to answer the question, Why? Theories involve attempts to understand precisely *why* certain events or processes occur as they do. Thus, theories go beyond mere observation or description of various aspects of social behavior; they seek to *explain* them. The development of comprehensive, accurate theories is a primary goal of all science (Howard, 1985; Pepper, 1959), and social psychology is no exception. Accordingly, a great deal of research in our field is concerned with efforts to construct, test, and refine such frameworks. But what precisely are theories, and how are they used in social psychological research? Perhaps the best way to clarify such issues is, again, by means of a concrete example.

Imagine that a social psychologist is interested in the following question: When people are in a good mood, are they more willing or less willing to take risks? Common sense seems to suggest that people who are feeling good will be high rollers and will take more or larger risks. When the researcher attempts to test this possibility, however, he finds a mixed pattern of results. Sometimes people in a good mood do take greater risks, but sometimes they actually take smaller ones than people who are in a neutral mood. What's going on here? On the basis of such data and other work on the impact of mood on behavior and cognition, the researcher begins to formulate a preliminary theory: Perhaps people in a good mood seek to maintain this pleasant state. Thus, if taking risks will help them reach that goal, they will indeed be more willing to take risks than people in a neutral mood. If, in contrast, taking risks threatens the persistence of their positive feelings, the opposite may be true: People in a good mood will take smaller risks than those who are experiencing neutral emotions. The researcher now predicts (again, on the basis of previous research and existing theories) that the key factor in this relationship may be the potential for actual loss. If people in a good mood believe that the risks involved can lead to substantial losses, they will refrain from such behavior. If, instead, they view the potential for losses as minor or nonexistent, then being in a good mood may make them feel expansive and so increase their risk-taking tendencies.

In sum, the social psychologist now has a preliminary theory concerning the effect of mood on risk taking. In older and more advanced fields such as physics or chemistry, theories are often phrased as mathematical equations. In social psychology, however, they are usually phrased as verbal statements or assertions, such as those above. Regardless of how they are stated, theories consist of two main parts: (1) several basic concepts (e.g., risk taking, mood, potential losses) and (2) statements concerning relationships between them (e.g., "Being in a good mood will increase risk taking when potential losses from such risks are small but will reduce risk taking when potential losses are large").

Once a theory has been formulated, a critical process begins. First, predictions are derived from the theory. These are formulated in accordance with basic principles of logic and are known as *hypotheses*. For example, one such prediction from the theory of mood and risk taking described above is as follows: People who have just received some kind of good news (and so are in a good mood) will be more likely to purchase a lottery ticket than people who have not received good news. (This would be the case because the only loss associated with taking that kind of risk is not winning, and lottery tickets are relatively inexpensive.)

Next, such predictions are tested in actual research. If they are confirmed, confidence in the accuracy of the theory is increased: The theory is viewed as providing a useful explanation for the phenomena with which it deals. If, instead, such predictions are disconfirmed, confidence in the theory is weakened. Then the theory itself may be altered so as to generate new predictions. These latter predictions are subjected to test, and the process continues. If the modified predictions are confirmed, confidence in the revised theory is increased; if they are disconfirmed, the theory may be modified again or, ultimately, rejected. (Please see Figure 1.12 for a summary of this process.)

Please note, by the way, that theories are useful from a scientific point of view only to the extent that they lead to *testable* predictions. Indeed, if theories

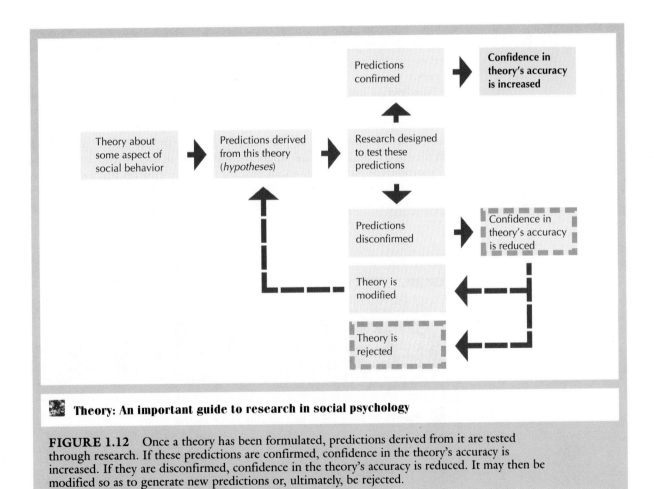

Theory: An important guide to research in social psychology

FIGURE 1.12 Once a theory has been formulated, predictions derived from it are tested through research. If these predictions are confirmed, confidence in the theory's accuracy is increased. If they are disconfirmed, confidence in the theory's accuracy is reduced. It may then be modified so as to generate new predictions or, ultimately, be rejected.

fail to generate hypotheses that can be examined in actual research, they cannot be viewed as scientific in nature (see Figure 1.13).

Theories: Some Potential Dangers On the basis of our comments thus far about theories, you may well conclude that they are an unmixed blessing. Theories both stimulate and guide research. And as they are tested and refined, they add appreciably to our understanding of the natural world around us—a key goal of all science. In general, this is true. We should note, however, that there is a potential disadvantage to theories as well. According to Greenwald and his colleagues (Greenwald & Pratkanis, 1988; Greenwald, Pratkanis, Leippe, & Baumgardner, 1986), the primary danger inherent in theories involves operation of the **confirmation bias**—in essence, a tendency on the part of researchers to become personally involved with and committed to theories they have proposed or support. As a result of such involvement, it becomes harder for the researchers to evaluate the theories objectively in terms of the weight of existing evidence. Indeed, researchers who slip into this pitfall may soon find themselves working hard to confirm their theories rather than merely to test them (cf. Johnson & Eagly, 1989). For example, such researchers may ignore data that are inconsistent with their pet theories while overemphasizing data that agree with those theories' predictions. They may also (either consciously or unconsciously) design their studies in such a manner that the likelihood of obtaining a particular pattern of findings—one consistent with the theories—is increased. (See Figure 1.14 for a summary of these potential dangers.)

Needless to say, to the extent this type of process operates, theories *can* pose a danger to progress in social psychology or any other field. After all, the overall result is the apparent confirmation of theories that may actually be false. Is confirmation bias truly a serious danger? Do researchers really "fall in love" with their theories to the point where the soundness of their scientific judgment is compromised? At present, social psychologists disagree on this issue. Most, however, do believe that the dangers outlined above, while real, pose far less of a threat to scientific accuracy than Greenwald and his colleagues suggest (Green-

Theories: They must be testable to be useful

FIGURE 1.13 Contrary to Lucy's belief, only theories that can be subjected to direct test are useful from the point of science. (Reprinted by permission of UFS, Inc.)

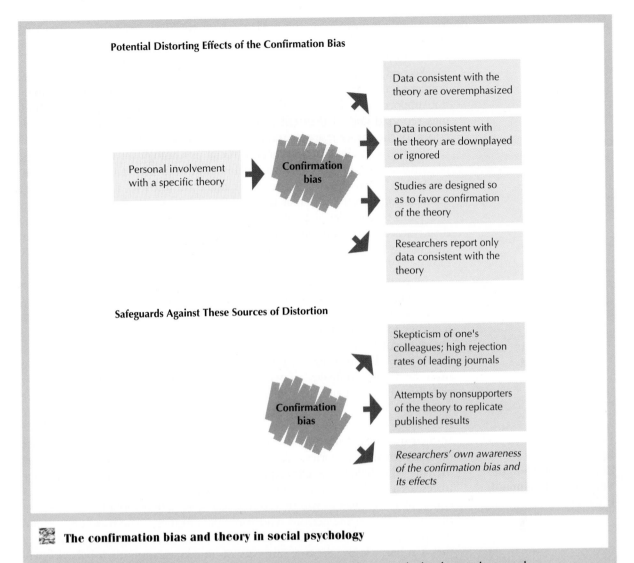

Potential Distorting Effects of the Confirmation Bias

Personal involvement with a specific theory

Confirmation bias

Data consistent with the theory are overemphasized

Data inconsistent with the theory are downplayed or ignored

Studies are designed so as to favor confirmation of the theory

Researchers report only data consistent with the theory

Safeguards Against These Sources of Distortion

Confirmation bias

Skepticism of one's colleagues; high rejection rates of leading journals

Attempts by nonsupporters of the theory to replicate published results

Researchers' own awareness of the confirmation bias and its effects

The confirmation bias and theory in social psychology

FIGURE 1.14   When researchers become deeply committed to a particular theory, they may be subject to the impact of a strong *confirmation bias*—a tendency to seek data supporting the theory (upper panel). While such effects may sometimes occur, many safeguards are built into the publication system in social psychology and tend to counter their presence (lower panel).

wald, Solomon, Pyszczynski, & Steinberg, 1988; Moser, Gadenne, & Schroder, 1988). This is the case for several reasons.

First, while individual researchers (or groups of researchers) may indeed become ego-involved with specific theories, not all their colleagues share the same kind of involvement. Thus, when they submit their research projects to leading journals for publication, these papers may be reviewed by persons who do not share their bias or ego involvement. The result: Researchers must overcome the healthy scientific skepticism of such reviewers. Only if they can convince the reviewers that their research is sound will their papers be published.

Since leading journals in the field reject up to *90 percent* of the papers they receive, the review process provides an important safeguard against operation of the confirmation bias.

Second, even after research reports offering support for specific theories are published, they are subject to careful review and criticism by colleagues who do not support those theories. Other researchers may attempt to *replicate* the findings reported and, if they fail to do so, will seek to publish papers that are critical of the earlier research and the theories on which it was based.

Finally, virtually all researchers in social psychology are fully aware of the potential impact of the confirmation bias and take steps to guard against it. Thus, they often ask persons who are not committed to a given theory (or perhaps don't even know that it exists) to collect crucial data. Similarly, they take pains to consider alternative hypotheses and explanations when planning their research. Recent findings suggest that such steps can go a long way toward countering the impact of tendencies toward theory confirmation (Gadenne & Oswald, 1986).

Of course, none of these safeguards entirely eliminates the potential dangers that can result when researchers "fall in love" with their theories. Consequently, social psychologists (and all other scientists) must remain on guard against the tendency to seek confirmation of theories they support. Sometimes, given one's commitment to such frameworks and the understandable desire to see one's efforts rewarded, resisting such bias may prove difficult. Still, such tendencies must be firmly controlled if we are to have knowledge of social behavior and thought based on *fact* rather than on personal conviction or the desire to be right.

The Quest for Knowledge and the Rights of Individuals: Seeking a Reasonable Balance

In their use of experimentation and systematic observation and in their reliance on comprehensive theories, social psychologists do not differ from researchers in many other fields. One technique, however, does seem to be relatively unique to research in social psychology: **deception.** Basically, this technique involves efforts by researchers to withhold or conceal information about the purposes of their studies from the persons who participate in them. The reasoning behind this procedure can be stated simply: Many social psychologists are convinced that if subjects know the true purposes of an investigation, their behavior will be changed by that knowledge. The research itself then will then be doomed to fail; it will have little chance of adding to our knowledge. (See Figure 1.15 for an amusing illustration of this principle.)

On the face of it, this is an eminently reasonable suggestion. For example, imagine that in a study designed to examine the effect of an extreme initial offer on subsequent bargaining, subjects are informed of this purpose. They may then react differently to their opponent's first offer than would otherwise be the case (Northcraft & Neale, 1987). Similarly, imagine that subjects participating in a study of the impact of an apology on subsequent aggression are told of this purpose (Ohbuchi, Kameda, & Agarie, 1989). Will an apology from someone who has previously angered them have the same impact it would have had if they were not provided with this information? Probably not.

Because of such considerations, many social psychologists feel that deception—at least on a temporary basis—is essential for their research (Suls & Rosnow, 1988). Thus, deception is common in projects conducted by social psychologists (Gross & Fleming, 1982). The adoption of this technique is not,

"Sure, I _could_ tell you what I want you to say, but then you'd just say it because I _told_ you to say it, so it wouldn't count."

 Why temporary deception is often necessary in social psychological research

FIGURE 1.15   As this cartoon illustrates, individuals' behavior can often be changed by knowing how they are expected to act in a given situation. When extended to research on social behavior or social thought, this principle suggests why many social psychologists believe that withholding information from subjects about the purpose of studies is necessary for obtaining valid results. (Drawing by Lorenz; © 1985 The New Yorker Magazine, Inc.)

however, without its costs. Deceiving research participants or withholding information from them, no matter how justified, raises important ethical issues.

First, it is possible that at least some persons exposed to such treatment will resent having been led astray. They may then adopt a negative attitude toward social research generally. Second, deception, even when temporary, may result in some type of harm to the persons exposed to it (Kelman, 1967). For example, they may experience discomfort, stress, or negative shifts in self-esteem. Finally, there is the very real question of whether scientists committed to the search for knowledge should place themselves in the position of deceiving persons kind enough to assist them in this undertaking.

In short, the use of deception does indeed pose something of a dilemma to social psychologists. On the one hand, it seems essential to their research. On the other, its use raises serious problems. How can this issue be resolved? At present, opinion remains divided. Some of our colleagues feel that deception, no matter how useful, is inappropriate and must be abandoned (Baumrind,

1979). In contrast, many others (perhaps a large majority) believe that temporary deception *is* acceptable, provided that certain safeguards are followed (Baron, 1981). The most important of these are **informed consent** and thorough **debriefing.**

Informed consent involves providing research participants with as full a description of the procedures to be followed as is feasible, *prior to* their decision to take part in a given study. In short, by following this principle, researchers ensure that subjects know what they are getting into and what they will be asked to do before making a commitment to participate. In contrast, debriefing *follows* rather than precedes each experimental session. It consists of providing participants with a full explanation of all major aspects of a study, including its true goals and the hypotheses under investigation, and an explanation of the need for temporary deception so that research participants should leave the session in *at least* as favorable or positive a state as when they arrived.

Do informed consent and thorough debriefing help to eliminate, or at least reduce, the potential dangers of deception? Research on this issue suggests they do. First, when surveyed, an overwhelming majority of subjects report that they view temporary deception as acceptable and do not resent its use (Rogers, 1980). Second, individuals who have participated in studies involving deception actually tend to report more positive feelings about the value of social psychological research than persons who have not taken part in such projects (Smith & Richardson, 1983). Third, effective debriefing appears to eliminate many negative effects experienced by subjects as a result of temporary deception (Smith & Richardson, 1985). Of course, even in light of such findings it is unwise to take the safety or appropriateness of deception for granted (Rubin, 1985). Rather, it appears that the guiding principles for all researchers wishing to use deception in their studies should remain as follows: "DANGER: Complex ethical issues ahead. Proceed with extreme caution and with the safety and well-being of research participants firmly in mind."

Using This Book: A Displaced Preface

Before concluding this introduction to social psychology, we'd like to comment briefly on several features of this text. Such information could have been placed in the preface, but since many readers tend to skip such messages from authors we have decided to present it here.

First, we should mention several steps we've taken to make our text easier and more convenient for you to use. Each chapter begins with an outline of the major topics covered and ends with a detailed summary. Key terms are printed in **boldface** and defined in a glossary at the end of each chapter. All figures and graphs contain special labels designed to call your attention to the key findings presented. Finally, a list of sources for further information concludes each chapter.

Second, we wish to indicate that we've included three distinct types of special sections throughout the text. The first type, labeled **Focus on Research,** describes specific studies performed by social psychologists. These sections appear in two forms: (1) those subtitled *Classic Contributions,* which describe studies now widely viewed as classic in the field, and (2) those subtitled *The Cutting Edge,* which focus on recent projects carried out at what we feel are the frontiers of knowledge in social psychology.

The second type of special section is titled **On the Applied Side** (please see the one on pages 17–19). These sections highlight the practical implications of social psychology—ways in which its knowledge and principles can contribute to the solution of a wide range of practical problems.

Finally, a third type of special section is titled **Social Psychology: A Multicultural Perspective.** In keeping with recent developments in the field, these sections describe efforts by social psychologists to compare the social behavior or social thought of individuals in different cultures. Often, the goal of such projects is to determine which findings and principles of social psychology apply to people living in diverse cultures and which ones apply only to people belonging to a given society.

It is our hope that these features of our text will help make your first encounter with social psychology more interesting and valuable than might otherwise be the case. We also hope they will help us to communicate our own excitement with the field to you, for despite more than fifty years of combined teaching and research in social psychology, we remain enthusiastic about it and its potential. To the extent that we succeed in these tasks—and only to that extent—we will feel that we, as authors, teachers, and representatives of social psychology, have succeeded.

SUMMARY AND REVIEW

The Nature of Social Psychology

Social psychology is the scientific field that seeks to understand the nature and causes of individual behavior in social situations. It uses scientific methods to obtain new information about how we interact with and think about other persons.

The Development of Social Psychology

Speculation about social behavior and thought has continued since antiquity; however, a science-oriented field of social psychology emerged only during the present century. Once established, that field grew rapidly, and at present it investigates every conceivable aspect of social behavior and social thought.

Two recent trends in the field have involved the growing influence of a *cognitive perspective*—efforts to apply knowledge about cognitive processes to the task of understanding social behavior—and an increasing emphasis on *applying* the principles and findings of social psychology to a wide range of practical problems.

While predictions about the future are always risky, it seems likely that in the decades ahead social psychology will also be marked by the adoption of an increasingly *international perspective* and by a greater importation of knowledge from several fields.

Research Methods in Social Psychology

In conducting their research, social psychologists often employ **experimentation** and the **correlational method.** Experimentation involves procedures in which one or more factors (variables) are systematically varied to examine the impact of such changes on one or more aspects of social behavior or thought. The correlational method involves careful observation and measurement of two or more variables to determine whether changes in one are accompanied by changes in the other.

In selecting the topics of their research and in planning specific studies, social psychologists are often guided by formal **theories.** These are logical frameworks that seek to explain various aspects of social behavior and thought. Predictions from theories are tested in research. If they are confirmed, confidence in the accuracy of the theory is increased. If they are disconfirmed, such confidence is reduced. Theories generally play a crucial and beneficial role in the research of social psychologists. Investigators who conduct *theory-testing research,* however, must always be on guard against the **confirmation bias**—a tendency to overemphasize data supporting the theories they favor and to ignore or downplay data inconsistent with such views.

Social psychologists often withhold information about the purpose of their studies from the persons participating in them. Such temporary deception is deemed necessary because knowledge of the hypotheses behind an experiment may change participants' behavior in important ways. Although the use of deception raises important ethical issues, most social psychologists believe that it is permissible, provided that proper safeguards, such as **informed consent** and thorough **debriefing,** are adopted.

KEY TERMS

Cognitive dissonance An unpleasant state that occurs when individuals discover inconsistencies between two of their attitudes or between their attitudes and their behavior.

Confirmation bias A tendency on the part of human beings to seek support or confirmation for their beliefs. Scientists must always be on guard against such tendencies. If they are not, they may overlook data that are inconsistent with theories they support and at the same time may emphasize data that *are* consistent with such frameworks.

Confounded (variables) Occurs when factors other than the independent variable in an experiment vary across the experimental conditions. When such confounding occurs, it is impossible to determine whether results stem from the effects of the independent variable or from the other, confounded variables.

Correlational method (of research) A method of research in which two or more variables are systematically observed and measured to determine whether changes in one are accompanied by changes in the other.

Debriefing Procedures at the conclusion of a research session in which participants are given full information about the nature of the research and the hypothesis or hypotheses under investigation.

Deception A technique whereby researchers withhold information about the purposes or procedures of a study from persons participating in it. Deception is used in situations in which information about such matters might be expected to change subjects' behavior, thus invalidating the results of the research.

Dependent variable That variable which is measured in an experiment. In social psychology, the dependent variable is some aspect of social behavior or social thought.

Experimentation A method of research in which one factor (the independent variable) is systematically changed to determine whether such variations affect a second factor (the dependent variable).

Independent variable That variable which is systematically varied by the researcher in an experiment.

Informed consent A procedure by which subjects are told, in advance, about the activities they will perform during an experiment. The subjects then take part in the study only if they are willing to engage in such activities.

Random assignment of subjects to groups A basic requirement for conducting valid experiments. According to this principle, research participants must have an equal chance of being exposed to each level of the independent variable.

In short, they should be randomly assigned to one of the conditions within the study.

Social psychology A scientific field that seeks to understand the causes of individual behavior in social situations.

Theories Efforts by scientists to explain natural phenomena. Theories consist of (1) a set of basic concepts and (2) assertions regarding relationships between those concepts.

FOR MORE INFORMATION

Baron, R. A., & Greenberg, J. (1990). *Behavior in organizations: Understanding and managing the human side of work,* 3rd ed. Boston: Allyn and Bacon, Inc.

This text provides a broad introduction to the field of organizational behavior/psychology. By skimming through it, you can get a good idea of how the findings and principles of social psychology are being applied to a wide range of practical problems in work settings.

Cialdini, R. (1990). *Influence: Science and practice,* 2nd ed. New York: Random House.

The process of *influence* has always been of major interest to social psychologists. In this witty and insightful book, the author describes many of the tactics people use to change others' behavior or thought. Findings from systematic laboratory research as well as informal observations made by the author in a wide range of applied settings are included.

Jones, E. E. (1985). Major developments in social psychology during the past five decades. In G. Lindzey and E. Aronson (Eds.), *Handbook of social psychology,* vol. 1. New York: Random House.

In this chapter, an eminent social psychologist describes what he perceives to be the major trends in theory and research in social psychology during the past fifty years. After reading this excellent summary, you'll have a good idea of how social psychology has grown and developed.

Social Perception:
Understanding Others—
and Ourselves

Nonverbal Communication: The Language without Words

Attribution: Understanding the Causes of Behavior

Self-Attribution: The Process of Knowing Ourselves

SPECIAL SECTIONS

I don't know how he does it, but he sure does it!" Kelly Bender declares to her assistant, Cindy Graubman. "Just look at these numbers—he's brought in more contributions from alumni in the first three months than anyone else has ever done in a whole year! What's he got, some kind of magic formula?"

"Maybe," Cindy replies. "Or maybe he just hypnotizes them! How else can you explain it?" (At this remark, both women, who are members of the university's fund-raising office, laugh. They are discussing Dan O'Connor, a new member of their team.)

"Could be, just could be," Kelly replies with a chuckle. "That smile of his probably *can* put some people in a trance; I know it sure has an effect on me! But there's got to be more to it than that. We've had other charmers work for us, and they haven't done this well. What *does* he do to get all those contributions?"

"I'm not sure, but I have some ideas," Cindy answers. "You've put your finger on one of them: He's just plain likable. Everyone he meets seems to think he's one heck of a great guy."

"Right. That's why we hired him in the first place. But *why* is he so likable? That's what interests me."

"Well, for one thing, he kind of revs people up. I guess it's all that enthusiasm. He doesn't just say "Good morning," like most people. He says *"Good morning!"* with a big smile and a wave. Makes you feel like you've made his day just by being there."

"Yeah, that's right. I've noticed the same thing. He's very expressive. When he thanks you, he really thanks you; when he's disappointed, you feel like you want to cry, he looks so pitiful."

"Okay, so being expressive is part of it. But there's more, too. I think it's also the way he always seems so sincere. You know the old saying, 'Butter wouldn't melt in his mouth'? That's Dan all over."

"Too true!" Kelly agrees, nodding her head. "It's like you just know he wouldn't exaggerate or lead you astray. That's probably one reason he finally got that big donation from Mrs. Johnson. She's always been so cagey—'We'll see, we'll see. And tell me again how you plan to use my gift?'"

"Yeah, that's her, all right. But three visits from Dan, and she just seemed to *melt*. I'll bet that baby face of his didn't hurt him any."

"I'm sure it didn't; you'd have to be made out of steel to resist. But you know, this conversation is starting to make me a little queasy. Maybe, just maybe, he's too good to be true. Someone like Dan isn't going to hang around bringing in donations for a university for very long. He's not even one of our alumni. Just where do you think he's headed?"

"I don't know," Cindy answers, "but I saw him with Chuck Fenley yesterday—you know, one of Senator Padillo's top aides. They were awfully chummy. You don't suppose he's going to leave us for politics, do you?"

"I sure hope not!" Kelly exclaims, shaking her head. "We can't afford to lose someone like Dan when times are this bad. And Padillo's never been much of a friend to education; you know how he votes. It'd be terrible if Dan joined his staff."

"Well, you never know," Cindy comments. "People are hard to figure out, even when you've known them for years. And honestly, we don't know that he's planning to leave. Let's give him the benefit of the doubt."

"Normally I'd say yes," Kelly replies, "but I don't know. I've got this kind of internal alarm system that goes off when trouble is headed my way. And wow—is it ever ringing now!"

Admit it. Other people are often something of a mystery. They say and do things we don't expect, have motives we don't readily understand, and seem to see the world through very different eyes from our own. Yet, because they play such a key role in our lives, this is one mystery we can't afford to leave unsolved. For this reason, we often engage in efforts to understand other persons—to gain insight into their motives and traits. Like the two women in the story above, we try to figure out what other persons are really like, why they do and say the things they do. Then, in light of such knowledge, we try to determine the best ways of interacting with (or avoiding!) them. The process through which we seek such information is known as **social perception** and has long been a major topic of research in social psychology.

While our efforts to understand the people around us (and ourselves, too) take many different forms, two aspects of this process seem to be most important. First, we try to understand other persons' current feelings, moods, and emotions—how they are feeling here and now. Such information is often yielded by *nonverbal cues* from their facial expressions, eye contact, body posture, and movements. Second, we attempt to understand the more lasting causes behind others' actions—their stable traits, motives, and intentions. Information relating to this second task is acquired through **attribution**—a complex process in which we observe others' behavior and then attempt to *infer* the causes behind it from various clues (see Figure 2.1; Jaspars, 1983; Trope, 1986).

Because nonverbal communication and attribution provide us with somewhat different kinds of information about others, we will consider them separately here. Please note, however, that the two processes usually occur simultaneously and are closely interrelated. For example, we can sometimes identify others' stable likes and dislikes from their emotional reactions in a wide range of situations. Similarly, we frequently use information about others' intentions or motives as guides to interpreting their current nonverbal cues. If, for instance, we conclude that someone is trying to deceive or persuade us, we may interpret their smiles and other signs of friendliness very differently from how we would in the absence of such attributions.

In addition to attempting to understand others, we often devote considerable effort to the task of understanding ourselves—identifying our own feelings, emotions, and traits. We will consider the process of self-perception in the final section of this chapter. At first glance, this might appear to be a simple and straightforward task. Actually, though, understanding ourselves turns out to be

Attribution in action

FIGURE 2.1   Like Charlie Brown, we often infer the causes behind others' behavior from subtle clues. (Reprinted by permission of UFS, Inc.)

far more complex than common sense suggests. So be ready for some intriguing surprises about the nature of self-perception and its relationship to both social behavior and social thought (Olson, 1988; Ross & Olson, 1981).

Nonverbal Communication: The Language without Words

In many situations, social behavior is strongly affected by temporary factors or causes. Shifting moods, fleeting emotions, fatigue, various drugs—all can influence the ways in which we think and behave. Most persons, for example, are more willing to do favors for others when in a good mood than when in a bad one (Isen, 1987). Similarly, many people are more likely to lose their tempers and lash out at others when feeling irritable than when feeling mellow (Anderson, 1989). Finally, several forms of behavior, as well as basic cognitive processes, are strongly affected by drugs, fatigue, and illness (e.g., Taylor & Sears, 1988).

Because such temporary factors often exert important effects on social behavior and social thought, it is useful to know something about them. But how can we obtain such knowledge? How can we know whether others are in a good or a bad mood; whether they are experiencing anger, joy, or sorrow; or whether they are under the influence of some drug that may affect their judgment? One answer is straightforward: We can ask them directly. Unfortunately, this strategy fails in many situations. Sometimes others are willing to reveal their inner feelings or moods, and sometimes they are not. Indeed, they may actively seek to deceive or mislead us in this regard (e.g., DePaulo, Stone, & Lassiter, 1985). In such cases, it is not necessary to give up in despair and view this task as a hopeless one. On the contrary, there is another, highly revealing source of information about these temporary causes of behavior: others' *nonverbal cues*. In short, we can learn much about others' current moods and feelings from a silent language that often accompanies but can be quite independent from their spoken words. Such **nonverbal communication** is very complex, and has been studied from several different perspectives. In this discussion, however, we will focus on two major issues: (1) the basic channels through which nonverbal communication takes place and (2) its role in social perception and ongoing social interaction.

Nonverbal Communication: The Basic Channels

If you go to a commercial bookstore, you will see many books like the ones pictured in Figure 2.2. Each one has an enticing cover, and each promises to teach you, in a few easy lessons, how to understand others' innermost feelings and desires. Beware: *Such claims are wildly overstated*. People do indeed reveal much about their current moods, preferences, and emotions through nonverbal communication; however, the process of reading and deciphering such information is far more complex and subtle than these popular books suggest. One reason this is so is that nonverbal communication occurs through many different *channels* simultaneously. Several decades of research suggest that the most revealing of these channels, from the perspective of social perception, involve facial expressions, eye contact, and body movements and posture (so-called *body language*).

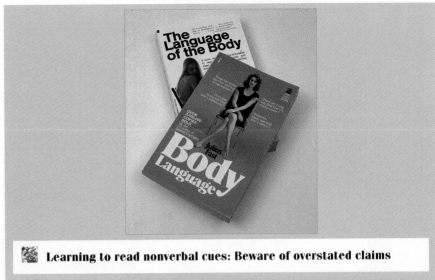

Learning to read nonverbal cues: Beware of overstated claims

FIGURE 2.2 Popular books claim that they can make readers experts in interpreting nonverbal cues by means of a few short lessons. In fact, though, deciphering this unspoken language is a complex task.

Unmasking the Face: Facial Expressions as Guides to Others' Emotions   More than two thousand years ago the Roman orator Cicero stated, "The face is the image of the soul." By this he meant that human feelings and emotions are often reflected on the face and can be read there from specific expressions. Modern research suggests that Cicero (and many other observers of human behavior) were correct in this belief: It *is* possible to learn much about others' current moods and feelings from their facial expressions. In fact, it appears that six different basic emotions are represented clearly on the human face: happiness, sadness, surprise, fear, anger, and disgust (Buck, 1984; Izard, 1977). Please note: This in no way implies that human beings are capable of demonstrating only six different facial expressions. As you know from your own experience, emotions occur in many combinations (e.g., anger along with fear, surprise along with happiness). Further, each of these reactions can vary greatly in intensity. Thus, while there seem to be only six basic themes in facial expressions, the number of variations on them is large.

The fact that facial expressions do indeed often reflect our inner feelings raises another intriguing question: Are such expressions universal among members of our species? If you traveled to a remote part of the world and visited a group of people who had never before met an outsider, would their facial expressions in various situations resemble your own? Would they smile when happy, frown when sad, and so on? Further, would you be able to recognize their facial expressions as signs of such emotions? The answer to all these questions appears to be *yes*. People living in widely separate geographic areas do seem to demonstrate similar facial expressions in similar emotion-provoking situations. And they show an impressive ability to recognize one another's expressions accurately (Ekman & Friesen, 1975). Moreover—and more impor-

 The universality of facial expressions

FIGURE 2.3   People from different cultures show similar facial expressions when experiencing the same emotions (e.g., happiness, fear, anger). Further, such expressions need no interpreter; they can be readily recognized by persons from other cultures.

tantly—this is true even when they have had no direct contact with one another. Thus, it appears that when experiencing basic emotions, human beings all over the world tend to show similar facial expressions and that the meaning of such expressions, too, is universal (see Figure 2.3). (For additional evidence pointing to the conclusion that there is a close link between facial expressions and underlying emotions, please see **The Cutting Edge** section below.)

FOCUS ON RESEARCH: THE CUTTING EDGE

Facial Muscle Activity, Brain Activity, and Subjective Experiences of Emotion: Where Mind and Body Meet

The fact that people all over the globe demonstrate similar facial expressions when experiencing particular emotions suggests that the link between these two factors must be a very basic (perhaps biologically determined) one. Additional evidence for this strong emotion-to-expression link is provided by research suggesting that minute changes in the electrical activity of facial muscles is closely related to underlying emotional experiences (e.g., Cacioppo et al., 1986; Fridlund, 1990). Such effects have recently been demonstrated in a sophisticated investigation conducted by Cacioppo, Martzke, Petty, and Tassinary (1988).

Subjects in this study were female students who were asked by an interviewer to talk about themselves in as frank and self-disclosing a manner as possible. Under these instructions, the subjects discussed topics ranging from their family background and physical attributes to their perceived strengths or weaknesses and traumatic events they had experienced. While the subjects spoke, electrical activity in a facial muscle that underlies the brow (the corrugator supercilii) was recorded. Subjects' faces were videotaped during the interviews; afterward, participants were shown the tapes and asked to indicate just what they had been thinking, feeling, or imagining at various times. In addition, they rated their feelings at these times along several dimensions (merry/gleeful/amused; sad/downhearted/blue; irritated/angry/mad). When electrical activity in the subjects' facial muscles was related to these reports, strong links emerged. Specifically, at times when their corrugator supercilii muscles showed certain types of electrical activity (clusters of muscle reactions), subjects reported feeling sadder, more fearful, and less warmhearted than at other times. In short, the greater the activity in these muscles, the more negative their reported emotional states (refer to Figure 2.4).

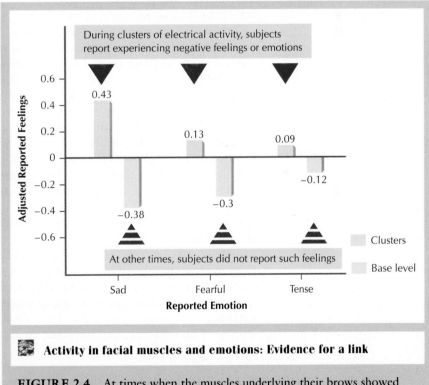

Activity in facial muscles and emotions: Evidence for a link

FIGURE 2.4 At times when the muscles underlying their brows showed specific types of electrical activity (clusters of reactions), subjects reported experiencing negative emotions or thinking sad thoughts. These findings suggest that there is a basic and important link between emotional experiences and facial expressions. (Source: Based on data from Cacioppo, Martzke, Petty, & Tassinary, 1988.)

It is important to note that this electrical activity was not accompanied by readily recognizable facial expressions. Judges who tried to identify subjects' emotional reactions from the video portion of the tapes (without sound) were unsuccessful in that task. Thus, the minute electrical activity recorded was not associated with clear facial expressions.

Additional evidence, however, points to the existence of important links between overt facial expressions and underlying physiological processes. In one especially intriguing study on this relationship, Ekman, Davidson, and Friesen (1990) recorded the brain activity of female subjects as they watched brief films containing pleasant or unpleasant content. (The pleasant films showed such scenes as a puppy playing with flowers; the unpleasant films depicted such scenes as the medical treatment of persons with serious burns.) Subjects' facial expressions as they watched the films were videotaped so that the relationship between two kinds of overt smiles and patterns of underlying brain activity could be examined. One type of smile is known as the *Duchenne smile*. Smiles of this type involve the activity of specific muscles near the eye which, when contracted, pull the facial skin into the "crinkly" pattern associated with genuine smiles—ones that are spontaneous and reflect underlying positive feelings. The other type of smile does not involve such muscle activity, and is often voluntary in nature; such smiles do not necessarily reflect positive feelings and are "managed" rather than spontaneous in nature.

On the basis of previous evidence, Ekman, Davidson, and Friesen (1990) predicted that subjects would show more Duchenne smiles in response to the positive than the negative films and that, moreover, this type of smiling would be associated with reports of positive emotions by subjects. Both of these predictions were confirmed. In addition, and more to the point, they also hypothesized that Duchenne (genuine) smiles would be accompanied by a pattern of greater activity in the left hemisphere of the brain than in the right hemisphere; other smiles, in contrast, would be associated with precisely the opposite pattern. This prediction, too, was supported. (Please note: other research findings indicate that positive feelings are associated with increased activation in the left side of the brain whereas negative feelings are often associated with increased activity in the right side.)

Together, the findings reported by Cacioppo and his colleagues (1988), Ekman and his associates (1990), and others indicate that there are important—if complex—links between subjective experiences of emotion and patterns of activity in facial muscles and in several areas of the brain. Given such relationships, it is far from surprising that facial expressions and other nonverbal cues often provide important guides to the emotions of others in many different situations.

Why Facial Expressions Are Universal: Survival Value and the Face-in-the-Crowd Phenomenon If facial expressions and our ability to readily identify them are indeed universal throughout our species, another interesting question follows: Why is this the case? One answer, offered by several researchers (e.g., Zajonc, 1985), is that the ability to transmit emotional signals in this fashion from one person to another has survival value. For example, through this process one person can warn others of impending danger (by outward signs of fear) or can help prepare them for aggression against outside attackers (through facial signs of anger). If this reasoning is correct, then it should be especially easy for individuals to recognize facial expressions that signal potential danger—for example, angry faces. That people can in fact easily do so is suggested by findings reported by Hansen and Hansen (1988).

These investigators showed subjects photos of crowds (nine faces) in which all of the individuals but one showed the same expression. In one condition, eight of the faces in the crowd were angry, while the remaining person showed a neutral or happy expression. In another condition, all faces in the crowd but one were happy and the remaining face showed a neutral or angry expression. Finally, in a third condition, all but one of the crowd members showed a neutral expression and the remaining person showed signs of happiness or anger. Hansen and Hansen predicted that subjects would find angry faces more quickly in both neutral and happy crowds than they would find happy faces in corresponding crowds. As shown in Figure 2.5, this is precisely what happened. Moreover, not only were subjects able to detect angry faces in neutral or happy crowds

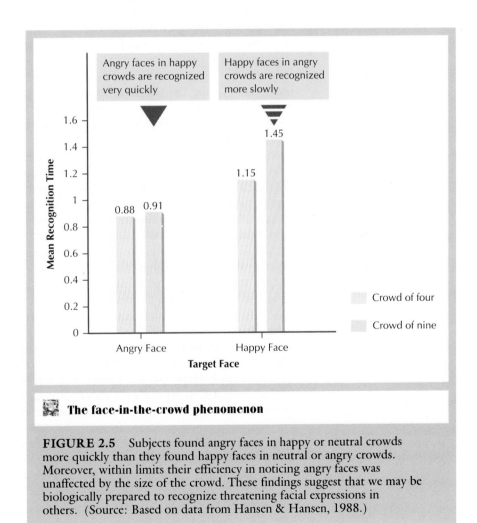

The face-in-the-crowd phenomenon

FIGURE 2.5 Subjects found angry faces in happy or neutral crowds more quickly than they found happy faces in neutral or angry crowds. Moreover, within limits their efficiency in noticing angry faces was unaffected by the size of the crowd. These findings suggest that we may be biologically prepared to recognize threatening facial expressions in others. (Source: Based on data from Hansen & Hansen, 1988.)

faster; they also made fewer errors in finding such faces than in finding happy faces in neutral or angry crowds.

In a follow-up study, Hansen and Hansen varied the number of distracting faces in the crowd. They reasoned that if the detecting of angry faces is an especially easy task for human beings (perhaps because of its adaptive value), the number of faces present should have little if any effect on a person's noticing them—that is, subjects should be able to find them as quickly in crowds of nine as in crowds of four. In contrast, the size of the crowd should affect subjects' ability to detect happy faces: As the crowd increases, speed should decrease. This hypothesis, too, was confirmed.

Together, these findings suggest that as human beings, we may be biologically programmed to process certain kinds of information about facial expressions more readily than other kinds. Specifically, we seem to be especially efficient at detecting those facial expressions which pose the greatest potential threat to our safety and well-being: ones reflecting anger. If this is indeed the case, then perhaps we are also highly adept at recognizing shifts from facial signs of anger to facial neutrality or happiness; after all, the person who conceals his or her anger may be the most dangerous potential enemy of all. Further research will provide evidence on this and many other intriguing possibilities concerning our ability to notice and remember others' facial expressions (e.g., Agostinelli et al., 1986).

Gazes and Stares: The Language of the Eyes   Have you ever had a conversation with someone who was wearing dark glasses? If so, you know that this situation is uncomfortable: Since you can't see the other person's eyes, you are uncertain about how she or he is reacting. Taking note of such events, ancient poets often described the eyes as "windows to the soul," and in one important sense they were correct. We *do* often learn much about others' feelings from their eyes. For example, we interpret a high level of gazing from another as a sign of liking or friendliness (Kleinke, 1986). In contrast, if others avoid eye contact with us, we may conclude that they are unfriendly, don't like us, or are simply shy (Zimbardo, 1977).

While a high level of eye contact from others is usually interpreted as a sign of liking or positive feelings, there is one important exception to this general rule. If another person gazes at us continuously and maintains such contact regardless of any actions we perform, she or he can be said to be **staring**—a decidedly unpleasant experience, one that makes most persons nervous and tense (Strom & Buck, 1979). It is thus not surprising that when confronted with such treatment, many persons seek to withdraw from the situation in which staring occurs (Greenbaum & Rosenfield, 1978). Further, stares are often interpreted by both people and animals as a sign of hostility or anger (Ellsworth & Carlsmith, 1973). Given such effects, it is clear that staring is one form of nonverbal behavior that should be used with caution in most situations.

Body Language: Gestures and Movements   Before reading further, try this simple demonstration. First, try to remember some incident that made you angry—the angrier the better. After thinking about this event for about a minute, try to remember another incident—one that made you feel sad (again, the sadder the better). Now consider your behavior: Did you change your posture or move your hands, arms, or legs as your thoughts shifted from the first event to the second? The chances are good that you did, for our current moods or emotions are often reflected in the posture, position, and movement of our bodies. Nonverbal cues from such sources are usually termed **body language** and can provide us with several useful kinds of information about others.

First, as just noted, body language often reveals much about other persons' emotional states. Large numbers of movements—especially ones in which a particular part of the body does something to another (e.g., scratching, rubbing)—suggest emotional arousal. The greater the frequency of such behavior, the higher others' level of arousal or nervousness seems to be (Knapp, 1978).

Second, more specific information about others' feelings is often provided by *gestures*. These fall into several categories, but perhaps the most important are **emblems**—body movements carrying a highly specific meaning in a given culture. For example, in several countries, holding one's hand with the thumb pointing up is a sign of "Okay," or "Everything's all right." Similarly, seizing one's nose between the thumb and index finger is a sign of displeasure or disgust. Emblems vary greatly from culture to culture, but all human societies seem to have at least some signals of this type for greetings, departures, insults, and the description of various physical states (see Figure 2.6).

Finally, body movements and posture can reveal much about others' physical states (e.g., their vigor, age) and perhaps about the extent to which they possess several different traits (cf. Berry & McArthur, 1986). Evidence pointing to these conclusions has been reported in several intriguing studies on **gait** conducted by Montepare and Zebrowitz-McArthur (1988). In an initial investigation on this topic, these researchers had males and females in four age-groups (five to seven, thirteen to fourteen, twenty-six to twenty-eight, and seventy-five to eighty years old) walk back and forth at a pace they felt was

Gestures: One form of nonverbal communication

FIGURE 2.6   Various gestures (known as *emblems*) have specific meaning within a given culture. Several that are common in the United States and other Western nations are shown here.

comfortable. The walkers were videotaped as they performed this everyday activity; these tapes were later shown to subjects who rated the walkers on various dimensions related to their gait, traits, age, and sex. To ensure that only information about the walkers' gait would be available to subjects when they made these ratings, the walkers wore dark shirts and pants, and reflective tape was attached to their main limb joints (e.g., inside and outside of both wrists, elbows, knees, and ankles). When the videotapes were then shown to subjects, the brightness was adjusted so that all they saw were moving points of light corresponding to the pieces of reflective tape.

Subjects watched the videotapes and made judgments about the walkers on two occasions. The first time, they rated the walkers in terms of a number of traits (e.g., submissive-dominating, physically weak–physically strong, timid-bold, sad-happy, unsexy-sexy). On the second occasion, they rated the walkers' gait in terms of several characteristics (e.g., amount of hip sway, knee bending, forward or backward lean, slow or fast pace, stiff or loose-jointed gait, short or long strides). In addition, subjects estimated the walkers' age and tried to guess whether they were female or male.

Results indicated that gait was indeed an important nonverbal cue. First, as predicted, subjects' ratings of the walkers' traits and gaits did vary with the age of these persons. Ratings of sexiness increased from children to adolescents and young adults but then decreased for older adults. Similarly, ratings of the walkers' hip sway, knee bending, stride length, bounce, and loose-jointedness decreased with age (see Figure 2.7). Further analyses revealed that possession of a youthful gait (one characterized by hip sway, knee bending, arm swing, loose-jointedness, and more steps per second) was strongly related to ratings of the walkers' happiness and power. Thus, persons with a youthful gait—regardless of their actual age—were rated more positively, along several dimensions, than persons with an older gait.

In subsequent research, Montepare and Zebrowitz-McArthur (1988) showed subjects the same videotapes used previously, but with the brightness turned up so that subjects could see the walkers, rather than merely points of light related to their limbs. Even with this richer array of nonverbal cues to examine, however, subjects' ratings of the walkers were still influenced by the walkers' gait. Again, walkers with a youthful gait were rated as more powerful and happier than those with an older gait, despite the fact that other cues concerning their actual age were readily available. These findings, as well as those in related research (McArthur & Baron, 1983), suggest that an individual's gait is an important determinant of the impression she or he makes on others. Having a bounce in one's step and a smoothness to one's body motions, it seems, can be a definite plus in many situations, especially in societies that place a heavy premium on youth and the physical vigor it implies.

Nonverbal Cues and Social Interaction: Self-Presentation and the Detection of Deception

Because they are an important source of information about others, nonverbal cues play a role in several forms of social interaction. For example, they are used by many individuals as a tactic of **self-presentation**—a means of enhancing the impressions they make on others (Schlenker, 1980; Wortman and Linsenmeier, 1977). Thus, individuals wishing to induce favorable reactions in others often seek to do so by controlling their own nonverbal behavior. While interacting with target persons (the ones they wish to impress) they smile frequently, lean forward, maintain a high level of eye contact, and nod in agreement with the

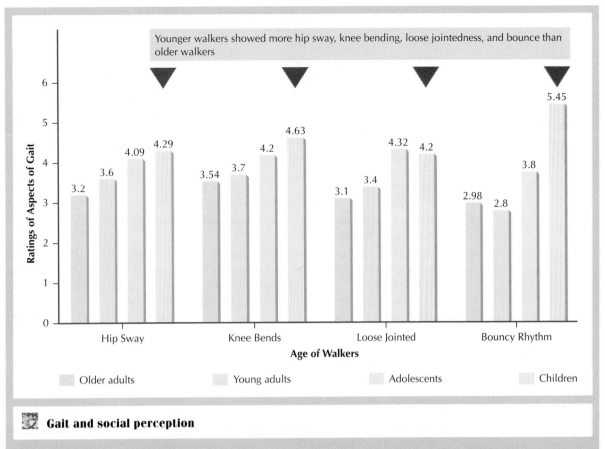

Younger walkers showed more hip sway, knee bending, loose jointedness, and bounce than older walkers

Gait and social perception

FIGURE 2.7 The younger walkers were, the more hip sway, knee bending, bounce, and loose-jointedness they showed. Together, these and several other features seem to characterize a *youthful gait*. Persons showing such a gait, in turn, are rated as sexier, happier, and stronger physically than those showing a less youthful gait. (Source: Based on data from Montepare & Zebrowitz-McArthur, 1988.)

target person's statements. That such tactics actually succeed is indicated by the findings of many studies, conducted in widely divergent contexts (e.g., Riggio, 1986). For example, persons who emit nonverbal cues suggestive of friendliness and related traits often receive higher ratings during job interviews than persons who do not (e.g., Baron, 1986; Rasmussen, 1984). Similarly, they are liked to a greater degree in first meetings with others in purely social contexts (e.g., Friedman, Riggio, & Cassella, 1988).

Another aspect of social behavior in which nonverbal cues play a significant role is the *detection of deception*—efforts to determine when others are being truthful and when they are trying to mislead us. Research on this topic suggests that in attempting to perform this crucial task, we rely heavily on nonverbal cues. Moreover, by relying on such cues we are indeed fairly (if not impressively) successful in recognizing deception when we encounter it (e.g., DePaulo, Stone, & Lassiter, 1985). What kinds of nonverbal cues are most helpful in this regard? Four seem especially helpful.

First, we rely on **microexpressions**—fleeting facial expressions lasting only a few tenths of a second. Such reactions appear on the face very quickly after an emotion-provoking event, before the persons showing them can get their "masks" in place (Ekman & Friesen, 1975). As a result, such expressions can be quite revealing about the feelings and emotions they are actually experiencing.

Second, we rely on changes in the nonverbal characteristics of people's speech. When individuals lie, the pitch of their voices often rises slightly (Zuckerman et al., 1981). Such shifts can be a useful clue to deception. Similarly, when others' speech is filled with many pauses and *sentence repairs*—instances in which they start a sentence, interrupt it, and then start it again—these are also useful signs that they are not being completely truthful (Stiff et al., 1989; see Figure 2.8).

Third, we can often detect deception from eye contact. When individuals avoid our gaze or blink frequently, this can be a sign that they are engaging in deception (Kleinke, 1986).

Finally, deception is often signaled by *adapters*—instances in which individuals move their hands and touch various body parts while speaking. The more of these there are, the more likely the person is to be lying.

Which of these cues is most important? Existing evidence suggests that in general, we rely more on visual cues—ones we can see—than on cues relating to verbal elements (aspects of a person's speech, such as pauses; Zuckerman et al., 1981). At one point, it was assumed that this was so because the presence of visual cues distracts attention from verbal cues. Recent evidence, however, suggests that individuals seem to make use of both kinds of information in deciding whether another person is being truthful or deceptive (Stiff et al., 1989). Yet, it appears that we tend to rely on visual cues because in many situations involving potential deception, we have little experience with the other person and so cannot tell whether verbal cues to deception (e.g., voice pitch, pauses) are a part of her or his normal style or the result of deception. In such cases, we fall back on our knowledge of what liars typically look like, thus relying primarily on visual cues.

Nonverbal cues: An important clue to deception

FIGURE 2.8 Nonverbal aspects of speech (aspects unrelated to its verbal meaning) are often helpful in identifying deception. (By permission of Mell Lazarus and Creators' Syndicate, Inc.)

Now for the key question: Can individuals learn to recognize deception through practice at this task? Common sense suggests that they should be able to do so, but research evidence casts doubt on this possibility. For example, consider an intriguing study on this topic by DePaulo and Pfeifer (1986). They asked two groups of subjects—undergraduate students and experienced law enforcement officials with years of practice in detecting deception—to listen to tapes in which the speakers told two truths and two lies. Subjects tried to determine which of the statements were true and which were false. Results were clear—and discouraging: The inexperienced students and experienced law enforcement officials (members of the Secret Service, military police) did not differ in their accuracy; both groups did slightly better than chance in detecting deception. Does this result mean that people cannot learn to recognize deception when they encounter it? Not necessarily. While the law enforcement officials had much practice in attempting to recognize deception, they did not have formal training in that skill. Moreover, much of their experience occurred under conditions that would not be expected to aid them in sharpening their deception-detecting abilities (e.g., they did not receive feedback on the accuracy of their judgments, or they received it only after relatively long delays). Under these conditions, they would have little basis for identifying those cues most helpful in detecting deception and might develop their own personal theories about what gestures or expressions are signals of deceit—theories that could be quite misleading. Thus, the possibility remains that formal and systematic training in using the kinds of cues outlined above *can* help individuals improve their ability to recognize deception. Efforts to develop such training programs are now under way, and it seems likely that they will be available for practical use in the near future (e.g., DePaulo et al., 1985; Siegman & Feldstein, 1987).

Attribution: Understanding the Causes of Behavior

Accurate knowledge about others' current moods or feelings can be useful in many ways. Yet where social perception is concerned, such knowledge is only part of the picture. In addition, we usually want to know more: to understand others' lasting traits and to know the causes behind their behavior—why, precisely, they have acted as they have. The process through which we attempt to gain such information is known as **attribution,** and it has been a topic of major interest in social psychology for several decades (e.g., Jones, 1990).

Theories of Attribution: Frameworks for Understanding How We Seek to Interpret Others

Because attribution is complex, several theories designed to explain its operation have been proposed (e.g., Heider, 1958). Here, we will focus on two that have been especially influential, plus recent efforts to expand and refine them (cf. Trope, 1986).

From Acts to Dispositions: Using Others' Behavior as a Guide to Their Lasting Traits The first of these theories—Jones and Davis's (1965) theory of **correspondent inference**—focuses on the following question: How do we use information about others' behavior as a basis for inferring that they possess various traits or characteristics? In other words, the theory is concerned with how we decide, on the basis of others' overt actions, that they possess specific traits or dispositions they carry with them from situation to situation and that remain fairly stable over time.

At first glance, this task might seem relatively simple. Others' behavior provides us with a rich source of information on which to draw, so if we observe it carefully, we should be able to learn a lot about them. Up to a point, this is true. The situation is complicated, however, by the following fact: Often individuals act in certain ways not because doing so is consistent with their own traits or preferences but because external factors (including ones outside their control) leave them little choice. For example, imagine that you observe a clerk refusing to accept a customer's personal check—does this mean the clerk is suspicious and mistrustful of strangers? Not necessarily. She may merely be obeying strict company rules concerning payment for merchandise. Indeed, it is entirely possible that she is a very trusting person and that if it were up to her, she would accept the check. The situation is such, though, that she cannot act on that preference. In such cases—which are quite common—using others' behavior as a guide to their lasting traits or motives can be misleading.

How do we cope with such complications? Jones and Davis's theory provides an answer (cf. Jones & Davis, 1965; Jones & McGillis, 1976). According to their framework, we accomplish this difficult task by focusing our attention on certain types of actions—those most likely to be the most informative.

First, we consider only behaviors that seem to have been freely chosen. Ones that were somehow forced on the persons in question tend to be ignored, or at least discounted. Second, we pay careful attention to actions that produce **noncommon effects**—outcomes that would not be produced by any other action. The advantage offered by such behaviors is easy to grasp. For example, imagine that in the company where you work, someone you know only slightly has just decided to leave to accept another job. Further, suppose that this job (1) pays much more than the person's current position, (2) involves much more interesting kinds of work, and (3) is located in a beautiful part of the country. Does the fact that this person accepted the new job tell you anything about his personal traits? Probably not. There are so many good reasons for taking the new job that you can't tell why this person has decided to leave. Now, in contrast, imagine the same situation with the following change: The new job (1) pays much more, (2) involves very boring work, and (3) is located in a highly undesirable geographic spot. Would your coworker's decision to accept it now tell you anything about his personal characteristics? Clearly, it would. You could now conclude that this person values money more than many other things, such as doing interesting work or living in a nice place. By comparing these situations, you should be able to see why we can usually learn more about others from actions or decisions on their part that yield noncommon effects than from ones that yield no such consequences.

Finally, Jones and Davis suggest that we also pay greater attention to actions by others that are low in *social desirability* than to actions that are high on this dimension. In other words, we learn more about others' traits or characteristics from actions they perform that are somehow unusual or out of the ordinary than from actions that are very much like those performed by most other persons (see Figure 2.9). For example, if you watched the sales clerk mentioned above operate the register or wrap up customers' purchases, you would not learn much about her as a unique individual. These actions, after all, are part of her job. But if you saw her urging a customer to go to another store where

Unusual behavior: A useful clue to others' traits

FIGURE 2.9 We learn much more about other persons' traits or characteristics from behaviors they perform that are unusual and low in social desirability than from behaviors that are typical of most other persons.

merchandise is cheaper, you would learn something of interest—such behavior would be unusual and definitely *not* part of her job description!

In sum, according to the theory proposed by Jones and Davis, we are most likely to conclude that others' behavior reflects their stable traits (i.e., we are likely to reach *correspondent inferences* about them) when that behavior (1) occurs by choice; (2) yields distinctive, noncommon effects; and (3) is low in social desirability.

Kelley's Theory of Causal Attribution: How We Answer the Question, Why? Consider the following events.

- You ask a classmate to lend you his notes and he refuses.
- You come home and discover that suddenly your spouse is not speaking to you.
- Much to your surprise (and chagrin), you learn you have failed to receive a promotion you were expecting.

What question would arise in your mind in each of these situations? The answer is clear and can be stated in one word: *Why?* You would want to know *why* your classmate won't lend you his notes, *why* your spouse is angry with you, and *why* you didn't get the promotion. In countless life situations, this is the central attributional task we face. We want to know why other people have acted as they have, or why events have turned out in a particular way. Such knowledge is crucial, for only if we understand the causes behind others' behavior can we adjust our own actions accordingly and make sense of the social world. Obviously, the number of specific causes behind others' behavior is large—almost infinite. To make this task more manageable, therefore, we often begin with a preliminary question: Did others' behavior stem mainly from *internal* causes (their own characteristics, motives, intentions), mainly from *external causes* (some aspect of the social or physical world), or from a combination of the two? For example, you might wonder whether your classmate refused to lend you his notes because he is a supercompetitive person who doesn't want you to do well on the upcoming exam (an internal cause), because he has several other tests and needs to start studying for this one right away (an external circumstance), or for both reasons. Revealing insights into how we carry out this initial attributional task are provided by a theory proposed by Kelley (Hilton & Slugoski, 1986; Kelley, 1972; Kelley & Michela, 1980).

According to Kelley, in our attempts to answer the question *Why?* about others' behavior, we focus on information pertaining to three major dimensions. First, we consider **consensus**—the extent to which others react in the same manner to some stimulus or event as the person we are considering. Second, we consider **consistency**—the extent to which the person reacts to this stimulus or event in the same way on other occasions. And third, we examine **distinctiveness**—the extent to which he or she reacts in the same manner to other, different stimuli or events. (Please don't confuse consistency and distinctiveness. Consistency refers to the extent to which an individual reacts similarly to the same stimulus or event at different times. Distinctiveness refers to the extent to which he or she reacts in a similar manner to different stimuli or events. If an individual reacts in the same way to a wide range of stimuli, distinctiveness is low.)

Kelley's theory suggests that we are most likely to attribute another's behavior to internal causes under conditions in which consensus and distinctiveness are low but consistency is high. In contrast, we are most likely to attribute another's behavior to external causes under conditions in which consensus, consistency, and distinctiveness are all high. Finally, we usually attribute behavior to a combination of these factors under conditions in which consensus is low but consistency and distinctiveness are high. Perhaps the reasonable nature of these suggestions is best illustrated by a simple example.

Imagine that during some important business negotiations, one side makes an offer to the other. Upon receiving it, the head of this team loses his temper, shouts angrily about the offer being unreasonable, and stalks off, thus bringing the negotiations to a halt. Why has he acted this way—because of internal causes or because of external causes? In other words, is the recipient a person with a bad temper, supersensitive to every imagined slight, or was the offer really so low as to be insulting? According to Kelley's theory, your decision (as an outside observer) would depend on the three factors mentioned above. First, assume that the following conditions prevail:

1. No other negotiator is angered by the offer (consensus is low).
2. You have seen this negotiator lose his temper during other sessions (consistency is high).
3. You have seen this negotiator lose his temper in other settings as well (distinctiveness is low).

In this case, Kelley's theory suggests that the negotiator lost his temper because of internal causes: He is a difficult person with a low boiling point (see the upper portion of Figure 2.10).

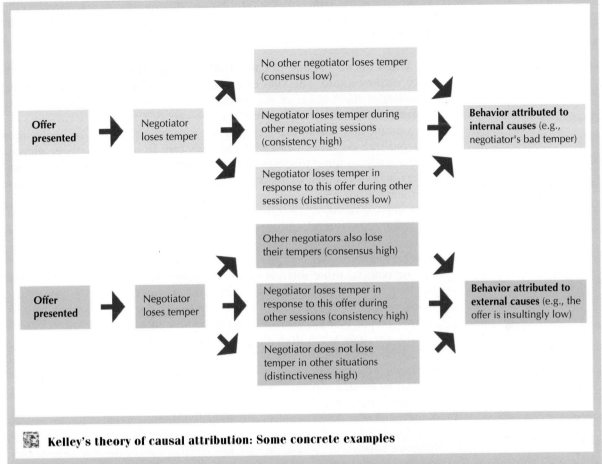

| | Kelley's theory of causal attribution: Some concrete examples |

FIGURE 2.10   Under the conditions shown in the top portion of this figure, we would attribute the negotiator's behavior to internal causes (e.g., this person has a bad temper). Under the conditions shown in the lower portion, in contrast, we would attribute this behavior to external causes (e.g., an offer presented by the opponent that was so low as to be insulting).

Now, in contrast, assume that the following conditions exist:

1. Several other negotiators also express anger at the offer (consensus is high).
2. You have seen this negotiator lose his temper during other negotiating sessions on receipt of similar offers (consistency is high).
3. You have not seen him lose his temper in other contexts (distinctiveness is high).

Here, you would attribute his behavior to external causes—the offer really was an unreasonable one (refer to the lower portion of Figure 2.10).

As we noted earlier, Kelley's theory is reasonable, a fact that becomes eminently clear when it is applied to specific social situations. Further, the theory has been confirmed by the findings of many studies (e.g., Harvey &

Weary, 1984; McArthur, 1972). We should note, though, that research on this framework also suggests the need for certain modifications. Several of these are described below.

When do we engage in causal attribution? The path of least resistance strikes again The kind of causal analysis described by Kelley requires considerable effort. After all, paying close enough attention to others' behavior to gather information about consensus, consistency, and distinctiveness is a far-from-simple task. Given this fact, it is not surprising to learn that people tend to avoid such cognitive work whenever they can. In many situations, they are all too ready to jump to quick and easy conclusions about the causes behind others' actions (Lupfer, Clark, & Hutcherson, 1990). They can do this because they know from past experience that certain kinds of behavior generally stem from internal factors while other kinds usually derive from external ones (Hansen, 1980). For example, most people believe that success is generally the result of ability and effort—two internal causes. Thus, when they encounter someone who is experiencing success they quickly assume that this outcome derives from one or both of those internal causes. In contrast, most people assume that laughing or being amused is largely the result of external causes—exposure to a funny film or situation. Thus, when they see another person laughing they quickly assume that he or she is doing so because of external causes.

So, precisely when does the kind of careful analysis described by Kelley occur? Primarily under two conditions: (1) when people are confronted with unexpected events (ones they cannot quickly and easily explain in terms of what they know about a specific situation, a specific person, or people generally) and (2) when they encounter unpleasant outcomes or events (Bohner, Bless, Schwarz, & Strack, 1988). In sum, Kelley's theory appears to be an accurate description of causal attribution *when it occurs.* It may not describe people's behavior in many situations, though, because they simply don't want to bother; they'd rather save such cognitive effort for occurrences that are unusual or unexpected.

Context effects: Background and causal judgments Suppose that you read about a violent crime—to what cause will you attribute this disturbing behavior? Your answer will depend, to a large degree, on background information. If you learned that the person who committed the crime had just been released from a mental hospital, you would probably select her mental imbalance as the primary cause. If you learned that she was a paid assassin working for organized crime, you would probably conclude that this was just one more paid assignment for her. Finally, if you learned that the killer was a jealous wife who found her husband in the arms of another woman, you would probably attribute the crime to her jealousy.

This simple example calls attention to an important point about causal attributions: They do not occur in a vacuum. On the contrary, when attempting to identify the causes of others' behavior we take into account the context in which it occurred and use this information as a guide to selecting those factors which appear most important. Thus, to cite another example, consider the case of a married woman who becomes pregnant. She may attribute this outcome to a failure to use birth control on one occasion. In contrast, a doctor who runs a fertility clinic might attribute that outcome to high fertility on the part of the woman and her husband. In short, different persons faced with the same outcome may identify different causes as a result of their different perspectives (Einhorn & Hogarth, 1983).

This point has important implications for Kelley's theory. Specifically, it suggests that in different contexts the same behavior may be attributed to different causes and that sometimes contextual (background) factors may be more important than consensus, consistency, or distinctiveness in shaping causal attributions. That this is actually the case is indicated by research conducted recently by McGill (1989).

In one of her studies on the effects of context on attributions, McGill presented subjects with a description of an imaginary event (Bill yelled at the waiter), plus information concerning distinctiveness and consensus. In one condition, this information suggested that both were low (No one else yells at this waiter; Bill yells at all other waiters), whereas in another, both consensus and distinctiveness were high (Almost everyone else yells at this waiter; Bill yells at no other waiters).

Another feature of the study involved providing subjects with a context for Bill's irritable behavior. In one case, subjects learned that he yelled at the waiter during an important job interview with a law firm interested in hiring someone who could handle pressure very well. In another, they learned that he yelled at the waiter during an evaluation of the waiting staff by management at a restaurant. In a third condition, no background information was provided. McGill predicted that in the third condition (no background information), predictions from Kelley's theory would be confirmed: Subjects would attribute Bill's behavior primarily to internal causes (something about Bill) when consensus and distinctiveness were low, but to external causes (something about the waiter) when consensus and distinctiveness were high. When background information was provided, however, this would not necessarily be the case. Instead, the combination of low consensus and low distinctiveness would produce attributions to internal causes only in the context of the job interview (where the focus was on personality), while the combination of high consensus and high distinctiveness would produce attributions to external causes only in the context of the restaurant management episode (where the focus was primarily on the waiter's performance). As shown in Figure 2.11 (p. 62), this is precisely what happened.

In sum, it appears that people use information about consistency and distinctiveness as a basis for reaching causal attributions, but only when no information about context or background is available. When such information *is* present, however, it may tip the balance strongly toward internal or external causes, regardless of what consensus and distinctiveness information suggest. Clearly, this point is important to consider with respect to Kelley's theory.

Discounting and augmenting: Multiple potential causes and the impact of contextual factors Suppose that you see one of your neighbors shouting angrily at her child. What would you conclude about the cause of this behavior? One possibility is that she has an uncontrollable temper and is a poor parent who will soon cause serious psychological damage to her offspring. Now, however, imagine that you learn that she was shouting at her child because he ran out in front of traffic on a busy street. Would you remain convinced that your neighbor was an irritable, bad-tempered parent? Probably not. You now realize that there are at least two possible causes for her behavior: a bad temper

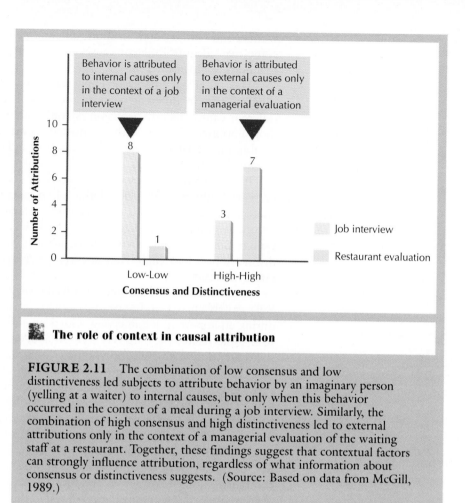

Behavior is attributed to internal causes only in the context of a job interview

Behavior is attributed to external causes only in the context of a managerial evaluation

Job interview

Restaurant evaluation

Number of Attributions

Consensus and Distinctiveness

Low-Low   High-High

The role of context in causal attribution

FIGURE 2.11 The combination of low consensus and low distinctiveness led subjects to attribute behavior by an imaginary person (yelling at a waiter) to internal causes, but only when this behavior occurred in the context of a meal during a job interview. Similarly, the combination of high consensus and high distinctiveness led to external attributions only in the context of a managerial evaluation of the waiting staff at a restaurant. Together, these findings suggest that contextual factors can strongly influence attribution, regardless of what information about consensus or distinctiveness suggests. (Source: Based on data from McGill, 1989.)

and a dangerous action by the child. This example illustrates the **discounting principle** (sometimes called the *subtraction rule*), which suggests that the importance of any potential cause of another person's behavior is reduced (discounted) to the extent that other potential causes also exist (refer to Figure 2.12).

Now, imagine a somewhat different situation. You see your neighbor shouting angrily at her child, but this time the minister from her church is also present. Now what will you conclude? Almost certainly, you will decide that your neighbor is indeed a person with a bad temper. After all, she is shouting at her child in front of someone who might be expected to inhibit such actions. This example illustrates a second attributional principle—**augmenting,** which suggests that when a factor that might facilitate a given behavior and a factor that might inhibit it are both present and the behavior occurs, we assign added weight to the facilitative factor. We do so because that factor has succeeded in producing the behavior even in the face of important inhibitory barriers (refer to Figure 2.12).

Both augmenting and discounting play an important role in attribution, especially when we can't observe others' actions over extended periods of time

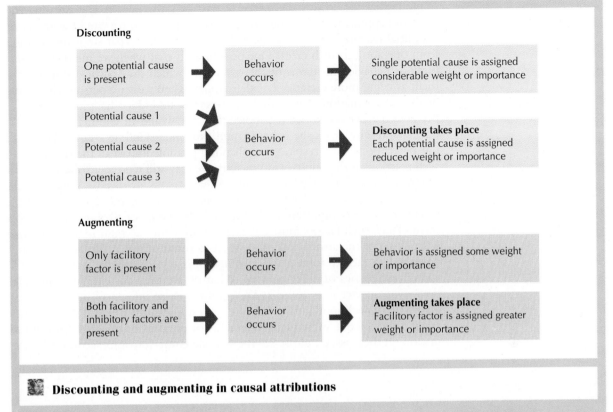

Discounting

One potential cause is present → Behavior occurs → Single potential cause is assigned considerable weight or importance

Potential cause 1
Potential cause 2 → Behavior occurs → **Discounting takes place** Each potential cause is assigned reduced weight or importance
Potential cause 3

Augmenting

Only facilitory factor is present → Behavior occurs → Behavior is assigned some weight or importance

Both facilitory and inhibitory factors are present → Behavior occurs → **Augmenting takes place** Facilitory factor is assigned greater weight or importance

Discounting and augmenting in causal attributions

FIGURE 2.12 The *discounting principle* suggests that we attach less importance to a given cause of some behavior when other potential causes are also present. The *augmenting principle* suggests that when a given behavior occurs in the presence of factors that facilitate and factors that inhibit its occurrence, we assign added weight to the facilitating cause.

or in several situations (i.e., when information on consistency and distinctiveness is lacking). Thus, they should be taken into account when applying Kelley's theory. It is also important to note that contextual factors can play an important role with respect to discounting (the subtraction rule). To see why this is so, consider the following incident: An individual demonstrates an ambiguous emotional reaction—one you can't readily identify (e.g., a mixture of happiness and fear). How do you interpret this behavior? Trope, Cohen, and Maoz (1988) suggest that your interpretation will depend strongly on contextual information. If the situation is one in which you would expect the person to be happy, you will label the reaction "happiness"; if, instead, it is a situation in which you would expect the person to be fearful, you will label the reaction "fear."

Now, suppose you were asked to rate the individual's personality: To what extent is she or he *generally* a happy or fearful person? The discounting principle suggests that if someone seems happy in a happy situation or fearful in a fear-inducing situation, we will be less likely to view her or him as generally happy or fearful; after all, the situation, not the individual's personality, may have produced those reactions. In fact, though, recent evidence (Trope et al., 1988) suggests that we do just the opposite: We view the person as possessing the traits of happiness or fearfulness to a *greater* extent than we would were he or his initial reactions unambiguous. Why do we do so? What stops discounting from operating in such cases? One possibility is that when we interpret unambiguous behaviors in terms of the context in which they occur, we may view them as being more extreme. In other words, when we see a person who seems happy in a situation that would be expected to induce happiness, we may perceive the person as being happier than we would in another context; we understand why he or she is happy, and this understanding seems to magnify our perceptions. As a result, even when the possible impact of the situation on such reactions is discounted (subtracted), we may still tend to attribute them to internal dispositions (e.g., the traits of the persons involved). Whatever the precise mechanism involved, it is clear once again that the context in which behaviors occur is important in determining the nature of attributions based on them. Thus, such factors must be taken carefully into account in any complete description of the attribution process. (As a result of the attribution processes described so far, we form a series of *inferences* concerning the traits, motives, and characteristics of other persons. What do we then do with such information? One answer is as follows: We combine these inferences into an overall *impression* of each individual. How are such impressions formed? And do they really influence our subsequent judgments or evaluations of others? For information on these issues, please see the **Classic Contributions** section below.)

FOCUS ON RESEARCH: CLASSIC CONTRIBUTIONS

Primacy or Recency? Evidence That First Impressions Really Do Count

First impressions, it is widely believed, are very important. Most persons assume that the initial impressions they make on others tend to persist. Further, they realize that such impressions may be quite resistant even in the face of later contradictory information. It is for this reason, of course, that most of us prepare especially carefully for first dates, job interviews, and other situations in which we will meet others for the first time (see Figure 2.13). After all, we assume that others' reactions to us in these encounters can strongly shape our future relationships—and our futures! Is common sense correct in attaching so much significance to first impressions? The answer provided by several decades of research is at least a qualified yes (e.g., Anderson, 1981; Burnstein & Schul, 1982; Wyer, 1988). The first research on this issue was performed by Solomon Asch (1946) shortly after World War II. Asch's work was influential in focusing the attention of social pyschologists on the process of impressions formation and has become a true classic in the field.

In his initial studies, Asch used a straightforward procedure. Subjects in two different groups were given one of the following descriptions of a hypothetical person:

intelligent-industrious-impulsive-critical-stubborn-envious
envious-stubborn-critical-impulsive-industrious-intelligent

Making a good first impression: Often, no effort is spared

FIGURE 2.13 Most people believe that *first impressions* are very important. Because they do, they take great pains to look their best when meeting others for the first time.

Obviously, the two lists of traits are identical in content; they differ only in sequence. Whereas the first list moves from positive traits to negative ones (i.e., from *intelligent* to *envious*), the second list does just the opposite. If the impressions we form of others are more strongly affected by information we receive first (by *primacy*), then it would be predicted that when asked to indicate their impression of the hypothetical person, subjects in the first group would report more favorable reactions. In fact, that is exactly what happened. For example, subjects exposed to the first list rated the imaginary person as more sociable, humorous, and happy than those in the second group did.

Why did these differences occur? Asch suggested that the order was important because the adjectives subjects read first changed the meaning of those they read later. For example, having learned that someone was intelligent and industrious (the first list), they interpreted the later, more negative adjectives within this context. Thus, the fact that the hypothetical person was *critical* simply implied that this person made good use of his or her high intelligence. Similarly, the fact that this person was *stubborn* merely suggested that he or she stuck to views or positions that, because of high intelligence, were likely to be correct. In contrast, having learned that the imaginary person was envious and stubborn, subjects viewed the fact that he or she was also intelligent as suggestive of unprincipled shrewdness.

Another and more modern interpretation of Asch's findings is somewhat simpler, suggesting that the primacy effects Asch observed occur because once we have some initial information at our disposal, we just don't bother to pay a lot of attention to additional input. After all, we already have enough information to form an impression; why deal with any more? As we noted above in our discussion of causal inference, and as we'll see in more detail in Chapter 3, this tendency to operate as *cognitive misers*—to do the least amount of cognitive work we can in thinking about others—is a powerful factor in much of social thought (Fiske & Taylor, 1984).

Whatever the exact mechanisms involved, Asch's research called social psychologists' attention to the importance of **impression formation** as a key aspect of social perception. The line of research he started has continued to the present and provides valuable insights into the ways in which we make use of the products of attribution (inferences about others' traits) in our efforts to make sense of the social world.

Attribution: Some Basic Sources of Bias

Our comments about attribution thus far seem to imply that it is a highly rational process, one in which individuals seeking to identify the causes of others' behavior follow an orderly cognitive process. In general, this view *is* correct; attribution is logical in several respects. We should note, however, that attribution is also subject to several forms of bias—tendencies that can lead us into serious errors concerning the causes of others' behavior. Several of these errors are described below.

The Fundamental Attribution Error: Overestimating the Role of Dispositional Causes

Imagine that you witness the following scene: An individual arrives at a meeting thirty minutes late. On entering the room, he drops his notes and they scatter all over the floor. While attempting to pick them up, he falls over and breaks his glasses. How would you explain these events? The chances are quite good that you would reach conclusions such as these: This person is disorganized, clumsy, and generally incompetent. Are such attributions accurate? Perhaps. But it is also possible that the individual was late because of unavoidable delays at the airport, dropped his notes because they were printed on extremely slick paper, and fell down because his shoes were wet from the rain outside and the floor is quite slippery. That you would be less likely to mention such potential causes reflects what is often termed the **fundamental attribution error**—our strong tendency to explain others' actions in terms of dispositional (internal) rather than situational (external) causes. In short, we tend to perceive others as acting as they do because they are "that kind of person," rather than because of the many situational factors that may have affected their behavior.

This tendency to overemphasize dispositional causes while underestimating the impact of situational ones seems to arise from the fact that when we observe another person's behavior, we tend to focus on his or her actions: the context in which these occur often fades into background. As a result, the potential impact of situational causes receives less attention. A second possibility is that we do notice such situational factors but tend to assign them insufficient importance or weight (cf. Gilbert & Jones, 1986).

Whatever the precise basis for the fundamental attribution error, it has important implications. For example, it suggests that even if individuals are made aware of the situational forces that adversely affect disadvantaged groups in society (e.g., poor diet, broken or nonexistent family life), they may still perceive the members of those groups as "bad" and responsible for their own plights. Clearly, then, the fundamental attribution error can have significant social consequences.

The Actor-Observer Effect: You Fell; I Was Pushed   Another and closely related type of attributional bias can be readily illustrated. Imagine that while walking along the street, you see someone stumble and fall. How would you explain this behavior? Probably in terms of this person's characteristics. You might assume that he is clumsy. Now, suppose the same thing happens to you—would you explain your own behavior in the same terms? Probably not. Instead, you might well assume that you tripped because of situational causes—wet pavement, slippery heels on your shoes, and so on.

This tendency to attribute our own behavior to external or situational causes but that of others to internal ones is known as the **actor-observer effect** (Jones & Nisbett, 1971) and has been demonstrated in several different studies (Peterson, 1980). It seems to stem in part from the fact that we are quite aware of the situational factors affecting our own actions but, as outside observers, less aware of such factors when we turn our attention to the actions of others. Thus, we tend to perceive our own behavior as arising largely from situational causes but the behavior of others as deriving mainly from their traits or dispositions (Fiske & Taylor, 1984).

Up to this point, we have been discussing the actor-observer effect as it pertains to current situations. What happens when people think back over the past and try to remember their own prior behavior? Do they continue to focus on situational causes? A recent study by Frank and Gilovich (1989) suggests they may not. These researchers had male and female subjects engage in a brief "get acquainted" conversation with a stranger of their own sex. After the conversation, they rated their own behavior along several dimensions (e.g., friendliness, dominance, nervousness). Three weeks later, they returned and were asked to remember this conversation and to rate their behavior once again. In addition, on this second occasion subjects were also asked to indicate how they imagined the scene while recalling it: from their own visual perspective or as an outside observer would have seen it. Frank and Gilovich reasoned that if subjects remembered the scene from their own perspective, they would show a tendency toward increasingly situational attributions. However, if they remembered it as an outside observer (picturing the conversation as a third person would have seen it), then the opposite would be true—they would show a shift toward explaining their own behavior in dispositional (trait) terms. As you can see from Figure 2.14 (p. 68), that is exactly what happened. Most subjects remembered the scene from their own perspective, and these persons reported more situational attributions on the second occasion than on the first. Some subjects, however, remembered the scene from an outside observer's perspective, and they shifted toward more dispositional attributions. Together, these findings suggest that the difference in perspective noted above does indeed play a role in the occurrence of this interesting form of attributional bias.

The Self-Serving Bias: "I Can Do No Wrong, But You Can Do No Right"   Suppose that at some future time, you write a report for your boss. After reading it, she provides very positive feedback. To what will you attribute this success? The actor-observer effect would seem to suggest that you will explain it in terms

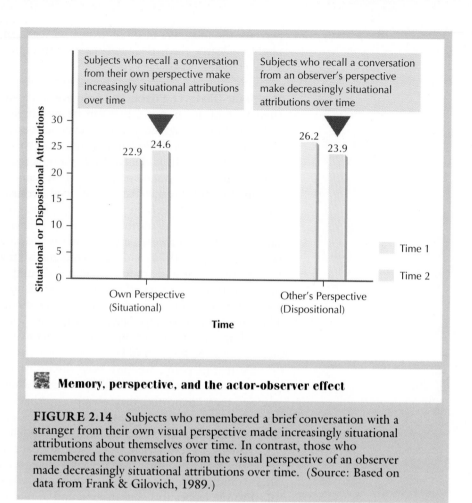

Subjects who recall a conversation from their own perspective make increasingly situational attributions over time

Subjects who recall a conversation from an observer's perspective make decreasingly situational attributions over time

Memory, perspective, and the actor-observer effect

FIGURE 2.14 Subjects who remembered a brief conversation with a stranger from their own visual perspective made increasingly situational attributions about themselves over time. In contrast, those who remembered the conversation from the visual perspective of an observer made decreasingly situational attributions over time. (Source: Based on data from Frank & Gilovich, 1989.)

of situational factors (e.g., the task was easy, your boss is lenient). But would that be the case? We doubt it. If you are like most persons, the chances are good that you will explain your success in terms of *internal* causes—your high level of talent, the exceptional amount of effort you expended on the report, and so on.

Now, in contrast, imagine that your boss is unhappy with your report and criticizes it harshly. How will you explain *this* outcome? Here it is likely that you will focus mainly on situational factors—the difficulty of the task, your boss's incredibly high standards, and so on. In short, the actor-observer bias may well be outweighed in this context by yet another form of attributional bias: our tendency to take credit for positive behaviors or outcomes but to blame negative ones on external causes. This tendency is generally known as the **self-serving bias** (Miller & Ross, 1975), and its existence has been confirmed by the results of numerous experiments (e.g., Baumgardner, Heppner, & Arkin, 1986; O'Malley & Becker, 1984).

Why does this "tilt" in our attributions occur? Two possibilities exist. First, the self-serving bias allows us to protect or enhance our self-esteem. If we are responsible for positive outcomes but are not to blame for negative ones, our feelings about our own worth may be bolstered (Greenberg, Pyszczynski, & Solomon, 1982). Second, the self-serving bias permits us to enhance our public image—to look good to others. Regardless of its precise origins, this type of attributional error is common and can be the cause of much interpersonal friction. For example, it leads the persons who work together on a joint task each to perceive that *they*, not their partner, have made the major contribution. Similarly, it leads individuals to perceive negative actions on their part as relatively mild and excusable but identical actions on the part of others as unforgivable trespasses. To the extent that such reactions occur, the effects of the self-serving bias can be quite serious from the standpoint of interpersonal relations. (Do males and females differ in their tendency to fall prey to the self-serving bias? And do such differences play a role in their intimate relations with others? For information on these issues, please see the **Multicultural Perspective** section below.)

SOCIAL PSYCHOLOGY: A MULTICULTURAL PERSPECTIVE

Gender Differences in the Self-Serving Bias: Attributions of Italian Men and Women about Their Sexual Experiences

Because it is a source of potential error in our attributions, the self-serving bias can prove quite costly. Yet as should be clear, it also serves an adaptive function, both bolstering our egos as we bask in the warm glow of successes for which we take personal credit and protecting them as we avoid or minimize responsibility for failures and other negative occurrences. Given such benefits, it seems reasonable to expect that the self-serving bias will exist as a strong tendency in both males and females. In fact, however, some research findings suggest that it may be stronger among men than among women (e.g., Deaux & Farris, 1977; Hansen & O'Leary, 1985). This difference has not been observed in all research (e.g., Frieze, Whitley, Hanusa, & McHugh, 1982; Sohn, 1982), but it *has* been reported frequently enough to merit special attention.

In what settings are such differences most likely to emerge? According to two researchers, Maas and Volpato (1989), they might be especially likely to arise with respect to behaviors that are highly ego-involving (very important to the persons concerned). One area of life that meets this requirement is sexual relations. Here, it is possible that when asked to consider past sexual experiences, males will be more likely to demonstrate the self-serving bias than females. Specifically, it is possible that males will be more likely than females to take credit for satisfying experiences but will also be more likely than females to blame unsatisfying experiences on external causes (e.g., their partners). Is this actually the case? A series of studies conducted by Maas and Volpato (1989) with Italian subjects indicates that it is.

In one of their studies, these researchers asked men and women in three age-groups (under nineteen, twenty to forty-five, and over forty-five) to recall a satisfying and an unsatisfying sexual experience. For each, participants were then asked to rate the extent to which various factors were relevant to the experience. These factors included internal causes (participants' own sexual skill or effort), situational factors (the general ease or difficulty of obtaining sexual satisfaction, especially favorable or unfavorable circumstances on that occasion), and the sexual relationship (general incompatibility or compatibility with the partner, good or poor sexual communication on that occasion). It was predicted that men would display the self-serving bias more strongly than women. Results offered at least partial support for this prediction. For satisfying sexual experiences, there were no differences between the sexes. However, for unsatisfying ones, males did in fact blame their partners to a greater extent than females did. Indeed, females actually attributed more responsibility for such experiences to themselves than to their partners (please see Figure 2.15). Additional findings indicated that for males, there was no relationship between the tendency to engage in the self-serving bias and subjects' reported history of past sexual satisfaction (e.g., how frequently they achieved orgasm). For women, however, such a relationship *was* obtained: The lower their tendency to engage in the self-serving bias, the poorer their reported sexual satisfaction.

In a follow-up study, Maas and Volpato (1989) repeated the same basic procedures with married or cohabiting couples. (In the first study, both married

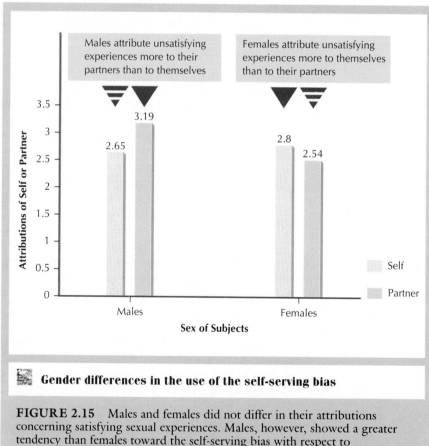

Gender differences in the use of the self-serving bias

FIGURE 2.15 Males and females did not differ in their attributions concerning satisfying sexual experiences. Males, however, showed a greater tendency than females toward the self-serving bias with respect to unsatisfying sexual experiences. They blamed such experiences on their partners to a greater extent than did females. (Source: Based on data from Maas & Volpato, 1989.)

CHAPTER TWO   SOCIAL PERCEPTION

and single persons participated.) In addition, the researchers asked subjects to rate the extent to which the experiences they recalled were satisfying or unsatisfying. This latter question was asked to determine whether males and females recalled experiences that were approximately equal in these respects. Results indicated that subjects' ratings of their experiences were in fact equal. Thus, differences in this factor could not explain other findings of the study—findings that replicated the results of the initial study. Once again, males showed a stronger tendency than females to engage in the self-serving bias.

Given that these findings support those obtained in studies conducted in the United States (e.g., Frank & Maas, 1985), it appears that differences between men and women in this respect are quite general in scope. Precisely why males should be more likely than females to show the self-serving bias with respect to sexual behavior remains an open question. Regardless of the origins of such differences, though, it is clear that they may play an important role in many long-term intimate relationships. For example, if males attribute unsatisfying experiences to their partners, they may feel somewhat justified in seeking new (or additional) ones: after all, it is their partners—not themselves—who are responsible for their lack of sexual fulfillment. Correspondingly, if females tend to accept the blame for unsatisfying experiences, their self-confidence and self-esteem may suffer needlessly, and such declines in confidence may reduce the likelihood of mutually satisfying sexual relations still further. To the extent that such effects occur, gender differences in the self-serving bias may constitute an important cause of friction in relationships that might otherwise be quite successful.

Putting Attribution Theory to Work: Some Practical Applications

Kurt Lewin, one of the founders of modern social psychology, often remarked, "There's nothing as practical as a good theory." By this he meant that once we have obtained scientific understanding of some aspect of social behavior, we can put this knowledge to practical use. Where attribution is concerned, this has truly been the case. Basic knowledge of this aspect of social perception has been put to practical use in a wide range of contexts, several of which are described below.

Attribution and Marital Dissatisfaction We have already noted that attributions (especially the self-serving bias) can play a role in sexual satisfaction. Here, we wish to add that attributions also exert more general effects on long-term relationships such as marriage. Research findings suggest that couples experiencing dissatisfaction are more likely than other, happier couples to attribute negative actions by a spouse to stable traits and characteristics (e.g., the partner's personality; Holtzworth-Munroe & Jacobson, 1985). As a result, they see little hope of change. In contrast, couples not experiencing marital distress tend to attribute negative actions by their spouses to external, temporary causes. For example, they may believe that their spouses are being insensitive or difficult because of stress, illness, or similar causes. He or she will return to a more positive pattern of behavior once these factors change. To the extent unfavorable patterns of attribution play a role in marital discord, it may be possible to alleviate such problems—and perhaps to save many long-term relationships— by inducing shifts in these social perceptions. (See Chapter 7 for more information about the nature and development of long-term relationships.)

Attribution and Interpersonal Conflict   Conflict is an all-too-common part of daily life. Individuals frequently take actions that thwart the real or perceived interests of others. Others then respond in kind, and patterns of costly, escalating conflict are soon established (Pruitt & Rubin, 1986). Breaking this pattern is difficult, but attribution theory suggests several potentially useful strategies for doing so (Baron, 1990a). One reason why initially mild conflicts tend to get quickly out of hand is that the persons involved make negative attributions concerning the causes of each other's actions. Each side attributes malevolence and deviousness to the other, with the result that the conflict itself is intensified. Efforts to break this cycle of increasingly negative attributions, then, may prove very helpful. That such efforts are indeed successful is suggested by the findings of a growing body of evidence (Baron, 1990a; Bies et al., 1988). For example, it has been found that when individuals offer explanations for confrontational actions that focus on such causes as role obligations (i.e., claims that they are required by their current role to take these actions) or their sincere belief that such actions are fair and justified, anger and subsequent conflict on the part of opponents are reduced (Baron, 1985, 1988). For such effects to occur, however, these causal explanations must be believed. If instead they are rejected as false, conflict may be increased rather than decreased (refer to Figure 2.16). In general, though, providing one's opponent with a reasonable explanation concerning the factors behind specific actions seems to be an effective means of avoiding or reducing costly conflicts.

Attribution and Coping with Personal Problems   Attribution theory has also been used to assist individuals in coping with a wide range of personal problems. In short, it has been applied to the development of several forms of

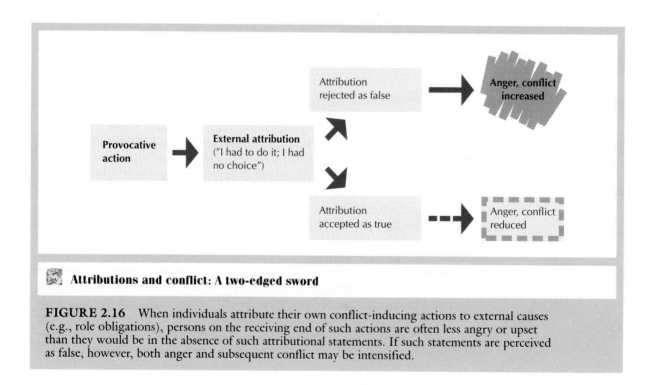

Attributions and conflict: A two-edged sword

FIGURE 2.16   When individuals attribute their own conflict-inducing actions to external causes (e.g., role obligations), persons on the receiving end of such actions are often less angry or upset than they would be in the absence of such attributional statements. If such statements are perceived as false, however, both anger and subsequent conflict may be intensified.

CHAPTER TWO   SOCIAL PERCEPTION

individual therapy. One use of these procedures has focused on students experiencing difficulties in their college studies (Wilson & Linville, 1982). A key problem faced by such persons is that they attribute these difficulties to lasting internal causes (e.g., their own lack of ability). When they are induced to shift their attributions so that they now perceive their low grades as stemming mainly from external or temporary causes (e.g., adjustment to college), important benefits follow. Their grades improve, and they are less likely to drop out of school than comparable students not exposed to such attribution-based treatment. Similar procedures have been applied to helping individuals in work settings (e.g., Brockner & Guare, 1983). Here, a key problem interfering with success for many persons seems to be lack of confidence or low self-esteem. Again, this problem stems from the tendency to show a pattern opposite to that of the self-serving bias: Such individuals blame themselves for failures but refuse to take personal credit for success. Procedures aimed at reversing this pattern appear to improve both morale and performance of such persons (Brockner & Guare, 1983). (Can attribution theory also be applied to the treatment of an even more serious problem—personal depression? For evidence that it can, please see the **On the Applied Side** section below.)

SOCIAL PSYCHOLOGY: ON THE APPLIED SIDE

Attributions and Depression; or, How to Dig Your Own Emotional "Black Hole"

Depression is the most common psychological disorder. Indeed, it is estimated that at any given time more than 10 percent of all people are suffering from it to some degree (Alloy, 1990). Although many factors play a role in depression, one that has received much attention in recent years is what might be termed a *self-defeating* pattern of attributions. In contrast to most persons, who evidence a self-serving bias, depressed persons tend to adopt an opposite pattern. Like the employees with low self-esteem mentioned earlier, they tend to attribute negative life events to stable, internal causes (their own personality, lack of ability, etc.) while attributing positive life events to temporary, external causes (lucky breaks, being in the right place at the right time, etc.; see Figure 2.17, p. 74). As a result, such persons come to perceive that they have little or no control over what happens to them—that they are mere chips in the winds of unpredictable fate. Little wonder that they become depressed and tend to give up on life.

But this is only part of the picture. Attribution theory offers other insights into the cognitive and social nature of depression. First, it appears that depressed and nondepressed individuals differ in their perceptions of *consensus* with respect to positive and negative life events. Specifically, depressed persons perceive that negative events are more likely to happen to them but that positive events are more likely to happen to others (Crocker, Alloy, & Kayne, 1988). In contrast, nondepressed persons perceive the opposite as being true: They believe they are more likely than others to experience positive events but less likely than others to experience negative ones.

Second, depressed individuals express less confidence in their attributional judgments than nondepressed persons do (Weary et al., 1987). In other words,

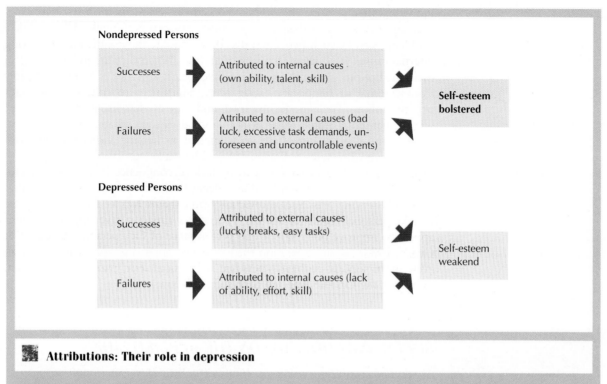

Nondepressed Persons

Successes → Attributed to internal causes (own ability, talent, skill) →

Failures → Attributed to external causes (bad luck, excessive task demands, unforeseen and uncontrollable events) →

Self-esteem bolstered

Depressed Persons

Successes → Attributed to external causes (lucky breaks, easy tasks) →

Failures → Attributed to internal causes (lack of ability, effort, skill) →

Self-esteem weakend

Attributions: Their role in depression

FIGURE 2.17 Depressed individuals often demonstrate a *self-defeating* pattern of attributions. Instead of attributing successes to internal causes and failures to external ones (upper panel), they do the reverse (lower panel). Thus, they refuse to take credit for successes but do blame themselves for failures.

they feel that they have less understanding of other persons and the social world generally than do nondepressed individuals. Third, and contrary to the preceding fact, moderately or deeply depressed persons show reduced motivation to engage in the difficult cognitive work required by causal attribution (Marsh & Weary, 1989). Interestingly, this pattern does not hold for *mildly* depressed persons, who actually demonstrate an increase in such motivation relative to nondepressed persons, perhaps because they have not yet given up on the possibility of making sense of the social world around them. Finally, we should note that depressed individuals do not seem to process social information differently from nondepressed ones. For example, depressed individuals do not encode ambiguous feedback more negatively (Dykman, Abramson, Alloy, & Hartlage, 1989). Differences between depressed persons and others arise only when information relevant to the contrasting cognitive frameworks (schemas) of these two groups is processed. Then, the more negative schemas held by depressed persons (e.g., more negative views of themselves and their traits) may tip the balance against them in several ways.

So where does all this leave us? With an array of potentially useful strategies for alleviating deep depression. To the extent that depression stems from self-defeating attributions, negative cognitive frameworks, and feelings of incompetence with respect to understanding other persons or the social world, interventions designed to alter these factors will prove effective. In fact, several forms of treatment focused on changing the ways in which depressed people think about themselves and others have already been developed and put to practical use (Abramson et al., 1990; Beck, Rush, Shaw, & Emery, 1979). These forms of therapy do not mention repressed urges, inner conflicts, or traumatic events early in life, but they *do* work. Indeed, they appear to be greatly superior in effectiveness to older and more traditional forms of treatment. Since it provides the basis for those newer forms of treatment, attribution theory can be viewed as having contributed in highly concrete ways to the alleviation of one important and common cause of human suffering.

Self-Attribution: The Process of Knowing Ourselves

So far in this chapter, we have focused primarily on the ways in which we come to understand others. In this final section, we will turn to a related question of equal importance: How do we come to know and understand *ourselves*? At first glance, you might assume that the process of **self-perception** is a relatively simple task. After all, our own feelings, motives, and intentions are open to our direct inspection at any time. It should therefore be easy to obtain information about these matters by turning our attention inward (Carver & Scheier, 1981). To some degree, this is true. But think again: There are at least two important complications in this process. First, we are often unaware of at least some of the factors affecting our own behavior (Nisbett & Ross, 1980). We may know that we acted in a given manner but are uncertain—or even wrong—about *why* we did so. Second, it is often difficult to evaluate our own traits, abilities, or attitudes without reference to the persons around us. Are we intelligent or dull, sexy or not sexy, charming or boring? Usually, we can't tell merely by looking inward or into a mirror. Instead, we must rely on social information to answer such questions.

Most likely, you are not surprised by the suggestion that we learn much about ourselves from others. But now consider the following proposal: In many cases, even our perceptions of our own internal states are strongly affected by external factors. In short, our understanding of our own feelings and emotions is strongly influenced by external conditions around us. Two major theories in social psychology are based on this proposal. We will consider each of them below and will also indicate their implications for some key practical questions.

Schachter's Theory of Emotion: Misattribution and Knowing What to Feel

Schachter and his colleagues (Schachter, 1964; Schachter & Singer, 1962) reasoned as follows: The labels we attach to feelings of arousal will be determined, to a large degree, by external factors. In general, we will label such arousal as one emotion or another depending on the situation around us. If we feel aroused in the presence of an attractive person, we may label our feelings "attraction" or "sexual excitement." If, instead, we feel aroused while watching a horror movie, we will probably label our feelings "fear." In short, we will perceive ourselves as experiencing the emotion that external cues suggest we *should* be feeling (see Figure 2.18, p. 76). Obviously, we can sometimes be mistaken in our interpretations of complex situations and of the causes of our arousal, hence the term *misattribution*.

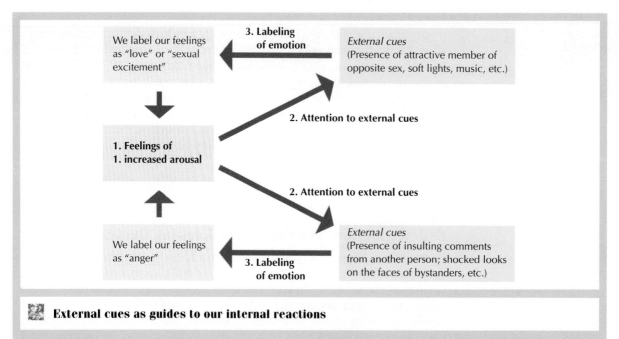

| We label our feelings as "love" or "sexual excitement" | 3. Labeling of emotion ← | External cues (Presence of attractive member of opposite sex, soft lights, music, etc.) |

External cues as guides to our internal reactions

FIGURE 2.18 According to a theory proposed by Schachter (1964), the labels we attach to arousal are often strongly influenced by external cues. Thus, we label such feelings in accordance with what the world around us suggests we *should* be experiencing.

To determine whether this reasoning was accurate, Schachter and Singer conducted a famous experiment in which subjects were told that the researchers wished to examine the effects of a vitamin compound known as "Suproxin." Participants were then given injections of epinephrine, a drug that produces heightened arousal. One group (the *epinephrine-informed* condition) was given accurate information concerning the effects of this drug. They were told that it would increase their heart rate and produce flushing of the face. In contrast, a second group (the *epinephrine-ignorant* condition) was not provided with such information. Both groups were then exposed to the actions of an accomplice who either behaved in a highly euphoric manner (e.g., shot crumpled papers at a wastebasket, built and flew paper airplanes) or demonstrated signs of extreme anger while filling out a questionnaire. (His anger was readily understandable. The questionnaire contained such items as "With how many men other than your father has your mother had extramarital relationships?") After witnessing these actions, subjects rated their own present mood. It was expected that those in the epinephrine-ignorant group would lack a ready explanation for their own increased arousal. Thus, they would interpret their own feelings in a manner consistent with the accomplice's actions. In short, they would report feeling happy when he acted euphorically but would report feeling angry when he behaved angrily. In contrast, subjects in the epinephrine-informed group were expected to attribute their arousal to the drug; thus, they would be unaffected by the accomplice's actions. Results provided support for both predictions.

These results were later replicated in many related studies (e.g., Reisenzein, 1983). In addition, later studies extended Schachter and Singer's theory in several intriguing ways. For example, several researchers reasoned that if individuals could be induced to attribute arousal to some relatively neutral source unrelated to a task they were performing, their experienced emotions (e.g., anxiety) could be reduced (e.g., Olson & Ross, 1989). Such effects were clearly demonstrated in a study conducted by Olson (1988). He asked subjects (male and female students) to read a speech into a video camera—a task known to produce high levels of arousal. In three conditions, subjects were told that they would hear subliminal noise through headphones while reading the speech. The first group was told that the noise was arousing; the second group, that it was relaxing; and the third group, that it would have no effect on them. Subjects in two additional groups heard no mention of such noise. In one case, they were given accurate information about how the task would make them feel (aroused), while in the other no information of this type was provided. Olson predicted that subjects told the noise was arousing would make fewer errors while delivering the speech (a sign of reduced anxiety) than those in the no-effect control condition. This would be the case because they would attribute their feelings of arousal to the noise rather than the potentially embarrassing task. In contrast, subjects told the noise was relaxing would make more errors; they would attribute their arousal to the task. As shown in Figure 2.19, this was precisely the pattern of findings obtained.

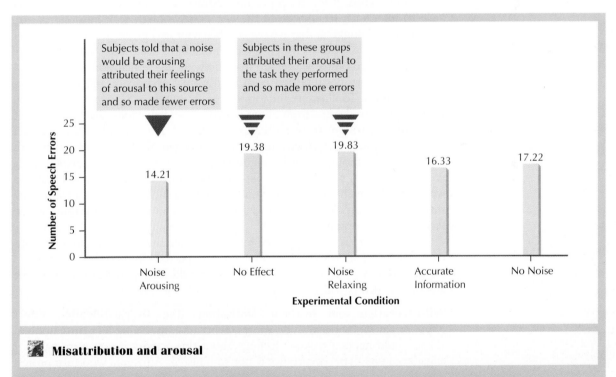

Misattribution and arousal

FIGURE 2.19   Subjects told that a subliminal noise they supposedly heard was arousing made fewer errors while delivering a speech than subjects told that such noise would be relaxing or would have no effect. These results suggest that attributing arousal to some neutral source unrelated to a current task can reduce the intensity of experienced emotions. This pattern is consistent with Schachter's theory of emotion. (Source: Based on data from Olson, 1988.)

While some aspects of Schachter's theory remain controversial (Marshall & Zimbardo, 1979), it appears that the central tenet of the theory is indeed correct. Our perceptions of our own internal states—including pain, anger, fear, and even sexual arousal—can be strongly affected by external cues. In sum, in determining how we feel, we often pay attention to information from external sources, as well as to feedback from within our own bodies.

Bem's Theory of Self-Perception: Behavior as a Source of Self-Knowledge

A second influential view concerning the nature of self-perception is one first proposed by Bem (1972). Bem agrees with Schachter in suggesting that often we do not know our own attitudes, feelings, or emotions directly. Instead of focusing on external sources of such knowledge, however, Bem points to another potential source: observations of our own behavior. If we have acted in some manner, we seem to reason, then we must hold an attitude or feeling consistent with such behavior. What we do, in short, serves as a useful guide to what is happening inside. Further, according to Bem, we draw such inferences about ourselves in much the same manner as we do about other persons. Thus, the process through which we come to know ourselves is very similar to the process through which we come to know others.

At this point, we should emphasize that Bem assumes that we rely on observations of our own behavior to infer our feelings or attitudes primarily in situations in which our internal cues concerning such matters are weak or ambiguous. Thus, if we are powerfully attracted to another person, we don't have to infer such feelings from the fact that we often seek him or her out. Similarly, Bem suggests that we use our behavior as a guide to our attitudes or emotions only in cases in which these actions have been freely chosen. If they have been forced on us, we refrain from drawing any conclusions.

Bem's theory is supported both by informal experience and by many research findings. To illustrate the former, recall times in your own life when you were surprised to learn—from observing your own behavior—that your feelings were different (often stronger) than you believed. For example, have you ever started to eat and then discovered, once you began, that you were much hungrier than you thought? Or have you ever been in a situation in which, once you gave voice to your irritation with another person, you discovered that you were actually much angrier than you believed? In such cases, Bem's contention that we really don't know our inner feelings or views as well as we think we do seems very appropriate.

Bem's theory is also supported by several different lines of research. Perhaps the most intriguing of these involves the unexpected effects of being rewarded for performing some action we enjoy and would have performed even in the absence of such payoffs.

Self-Perception and Intrinsic Motivation: The Overjustification Effect
Suppose you enjoy performing some activity (e.g., pursuing a favorite hobby). What would happen to your feelings about this activity if you were paid for engaging in it? (This occurrence is not so unusual: Amateurs who turn professional face precisely this situation.) Bem's theory suggests an interesting possibility. It predicts that at least under some conditions, the persons involved would actually experience a *drop* in their intrinsic motivation to perform the activity. The reasoning behind this prediction is as follows. Upon observing their own behavior, such *overrewarded* persons might conclude that they chose

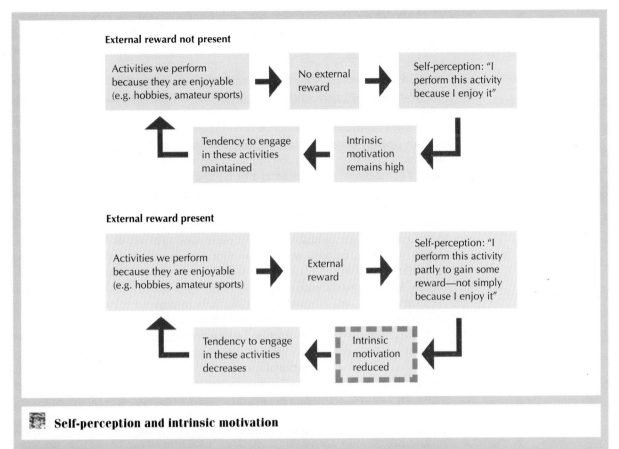

External reward not present

Activities we perform because they are enjoyable (e.g. hobbies, amateur sports) → No external reward → Self-perception: "I perform this activity because I enjoy it"

Tendency to engage in these activities maintained ← Intrinsic motivation remains high ←

External reward present

Activities we perform because they are enjoyable (e.g. hobbies, amateur sports) → External reward → Self-perception: "I perform this activity partly to gain some reward—not simply because I enjoy it"

Tendency to engage in these activities decreases ← Intrinsic motivation reduced ←

Self-perception and intrinsic motivation

FIGURE 2.20 When individuals perform an activity they enjoy in the absence of external rewards, their intrinsic interest in it is maintained (upper panel). When they receive extrinsic rewards for performing this activity, however, their self-perceptions about why they do so may change. Then, their intrinsic motivation may be reduced (lower panel).

to engage in the activity partly to obtain the external rewards provided. To the extent they reached this conclusion, they would then perceive their intrinsic interest as lower than was formerly the case. In short, such persons might shift from explaining their behavior in terms of purely intrinsic motivation ("I engage in this activity [e.g., playing golf] because I like it") to accounting for their actions partly in terms of external rewards ("I engage in this activity partly because it yields various external rewards [e.g., cash prizes]"). In other words, such persons may now have too many good reasons (justifications) for performing the activity to continue to view it as intrinsically motivated (see Figure 2.20). This is known as the **overjustification effect.**

Note, by the way, that the discounting principle, which we discussed earlier, is also relevant here. Since the persons paid for performing an activity they enjoy now have two potential causes to explain their behavior (their liking for it and the external reward), they may discount the role of the former. The result? They experience a decline in intrinsic motivation.

Support for this reasoning has been obtained in many experiments (e.g., Deci, 1975; Lepper & Greene, 1978; Pretty & Seligman, 1984). In these and other studies, subjects provided with extrinsic rewards for engaging in some task they initially enjoyed later demonstrated lower-quality performance and reduced tendencies to perform these activities voluntarily than did other subjects not given such rewards. Thus, it appeared that the intrinsic interest of rewarded subjects in such tasks had in fact been reduced.

More recently, however, it has been found that such overjustification effects do not always occur. Several factors may operate to prevent reductions in intrinsic interest or motivation. First, when external rewards are offered as a sign of competence rather than as a bribe, they may increase rather than reduce much motivation (Rosenfield, Folger, & Adelman, 1980). Second, even if external rewards *are* perceived as a bribe for performing some activity, reductions in intrinsic motivation may be avoided, provided that steps are taken to counter the negative feelings induced by such perceptions (Pretty & Seligman, 1984). Third, when the external rewards provided to individuals are both large and satisfying, they can maintain rather than reduce intrinsic motivation (Fiske & Taylor, 1984). In sum, providing individuals with external rewards for activities they enjoy does not necessarily reduce their interest in these activities. Such effects tend to occur, but through appropriate steps they can be avoided.

The research we have described so far focused on the impact of extrinsic rewards on the performance of various activities. Before concluding, it is important to address one additional question: What are the effects of such rewards on attitudes? In short, what happens when we reward individuals for stating views they already believe or taking an action consistent with them? Applying Bem's theory here, it seems clear that this situation will be somewhat confusing and unsettling for the persons involved. On the one hand, they enjoy the reward they have received; on the other, they are left wondering why it was provided (Crano & Sivaeck, 1984). How will they seek to explain this unexpected event? According to Crano and his colleagues (Crano et al., 1988), one possibility is as follows: After receiving a reward for behaving in a manner consistent with their own views, such persons may lower their estimates of the extent to which their views are shared by others. They may conclude that fewer persons than they formerly believed hold such views; to the extent that this is the case, it makes sense for someone to reward them for expressing such views—after all, they are relatively uncommon. Further, since they now view their attitude as less popular, they may be more readily swayed to change it.

Evidence for the occurrence of precisely such effects have been reported by Crano, Gorenflo, and Shackelford (1988). These researchers provided a surprise payment to one group of subjects after these subjects read a speech fully consistent with their own views—a speech arguing against a recent tuition increase. In contrast, subjects in another group did not receive this payment. After reading the speech, half the subjects in this second group were asked to read and evaluate another communication, one presenting the opposite point of view—that is, supporting the tuition increase (the remaining half did not read this communication). Finally, all subjects were asked to estimate the proportion of other students who would also be opposed to the tuition increase and to indicate their own views toward this issue. It was predicted that those who had received the surprise payment and read the communication arguing in favor of the tuition increase would report lower consensus (agreement by other students with their view) and more favorable attitudes toward the tuition increase than those in the other conditions. Results offered clear support for both these predictions.

It appears, then, that providing individuals with rewards for behaving in ways consistent with attitudes they already hold can produce shifts in their self-perceptions, and hence in their attitudes and behavior. Again, such findings are not readily predicted from common sense but are consistent with—and can be derived from—Bem's theory.

Self-Handicapping: The Potential Benefits of Fuzzy Self-Perceptions

It seems reasonable to assume that accurate self-knowledge (accurate self-perception) is always a plus. In general, this is true; understanding ourselves, our feelings, and our attitudes is usually helpful in several ways. There are some situations, however, in which we seem to prefer a degree of uncertainty in this respect. If you have ever remarked, right before an exam, that you are not feeling well or had been kept awake all night by noisy neighbors, you are acquainted with the kinds of situations we mean. In such circumstances, we attempt to protect our self-esteem (or public image) by calling attention to external causes that might reasonably explain subsequent failures. When we note that we are not in tip-top health or that we didn't get enough sleep, we provide ourselves with an out: If we don't do well in the situation, we can point to these factors as explanations for our lack of success (refer to Figure 2.21). Certainly, they are much easier on our ego than explanations that focus on our lack of ability, talent, or effort! This attributional tactic is known as **self-handicapping** and appears to be quite common (e.g., Baumgardner & Arkin, 1987; Jones & Berglas, 1978). As you can see, it rests on introducing a degree of uncertainty into the situation by calling attention to multiple potential causes of behavior. To the extent that many causes exist, the role of each is discounted—and it is this uncertainty, of course, that lets us off the hook.

Self-handicapping in action

FIGURE 2.21   If potential failures can be attributed to external causes, they are less damaging to our egos or self-image. The lack of opportunities for such **self-handicapping** is what the character in this cartoon finds disturbing. (Reprinted with special permission of King Features Syndicate, Inc.)

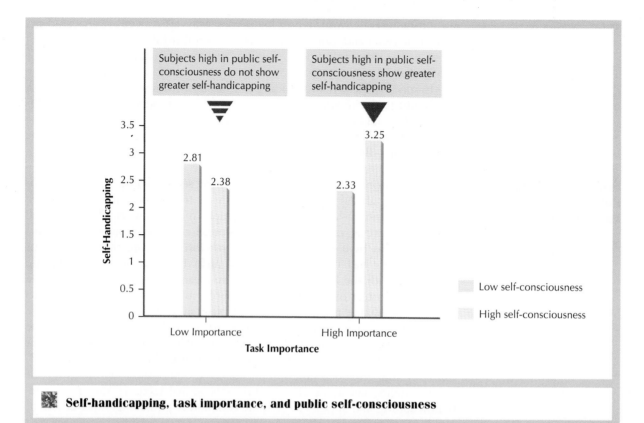

FIGURE 2.22 Subjects high in public self-consciousness engaged in self-handicapping to a greater extent than those low in such self-consciousness, but only in the context of an important task. (Source: Based on data from Sheppard & Arkin, 1989b.)

But when, precisely, *do* individuals engage in self-handicapping? And are some persons more likely to use this strategy than others? Recent studies on self-handicapping have begun to provide answers to such questions (e.g., Sheppard & Arkin, 1989a; Snyder & Smith, 1986). Among the factors found to facilitate the use of self-handicapping are social anxiety (Sheppard et al., 1986), test anxiety (Harris, Snyder, Higgins, & Schrag, 1986), unexpected (and incomprehensible) success (Kolditz & Arkin, 1982), and a high level of task importance (Sheppard & Arkin, 1987). At the same time, self-handicapping is reduced when a situation already has a handicap built in—that is, when factors that might interfere with excellent performance are already present (Sheppard & Arkin, 1989a).

Turning to personal characteristics that predispose individuals to adopt self-handicapping, a study by Sheppard and Arkin (1989b) is quite revealing. These researchers reasoned that individuals high in *public self-consciousness* (persons very concerned with their public image) would be more likely to engage in this strategy than persons low in public self-consciousness (Fenigstein, Scheier, & Buss, 1975). To test this hypothesis, subjects previously identified as high or low in this trait were told that while performing an upcoming task, they could choose to listen to one of five types of music. It was further explained that the music ranged from a type that would strongly enhance performance to a type that would strongly inhibit performance. Another aspect of this study involved the supposed importance of the task. Half the subjects were informed that the task they would soon perform was a valid predictor of college and career success, while the others were told that it was a new and unvalidated test. After selecting one of the five types of music, subjects performed a test requiring them to make judgments of spatial relations.

Sheppard and Arkin (1989) predicted that when the task was described as an important one, subjects high in public self-consciousness would engage in self-handicapping to a greater extent than those low in public self-consciousness. However, this would not be true when the task was unimportant. As shown in Figure 2.22, this was exactly what happened. Subjects high in public self-consciousness selected music that was more likely to interfere with their performance than subjects low in public self-consciousness did, but only in the condition involving an important task. In addition—and consistent with previous studies—males tended to engage in self-handicapping to a greater extent than females. This may have been due to a greater tendency on the part of males to use performance on the kind of task employed (judgments of spatial relations) as a basis for making attributions about ability. Alternatively, females may have perceived that there was little reason to engage in self-handicapping on this task, since it was not one on which they expected to excel. Whatever the reason, females have been found to be somewhat less likely to engage in self-handicapping than males in several different contexts.

To conclude: Self-handicapping, like other biases in attribution, can distort perceptions of social reality. Given the frequency with which most persons find their egos on the line, however, it is far from surprising that self-handicapping is a common tactic in many settings. While it can't prevent potential failures, it can at least soften their blow. This, it seems, is too valuable a benefit for most people to ignore.

SUMMARY AND REVIEW

Nonverbal Communication

Social perception is the process through which we attempt to understand other persons and ourselves. To obtain information about the temporary causes of behavior (e.g., others' emotions or feelings), we focus on *nonverbal cues*. These are provided by others' facial expressions, eye contact, and body posture or movements. Facial expressions are quite universal in the human species; similar expressions occur in response to various emotions all over the world and are readily recognized across different cultures. Electrical activity in certain facial muscles and in the brain has been found to reflect individuals' subjective thoughts or feelings. Nonverbal cues play an important role in social interaction. They are often used for *impression management* and can provide important clues to the presence of attempts at deception.

Attribution: Understanding the Causes of Behavior

Knowledge about the most lasting causes of others' behavior is acquired through **attribution.** In this process, we infer others' traits, motives, and intentions from observation of their behavior. In order to determine whether their behavior stems mainly from internal or external causes, we focus on information relating to **consensus, consistency,** and **distinctiveness.** In addition, causal attributions are often strongly affected by contextual factors (e.g., knowledge about the specific situation in which behavior occurs). Detailed causal analysis of others' behavior requires considerable cognitive effort. Thus, it is performed only under certain conditions (e.g., when actions by others are unexpected or unusual). Attributions are affected by *discounting* (a tendency to discount one potential cause of behavior when others are also present) and *augmenting* (a tendency to emphasize the importance of factors that might cause a specific behavior when factors that might inhibit it are also present). Attribution is far from a completely rational process. It is subject to a number of biases, including the **fundamental attribution error**, the **actor-observer effect,** and the **self-serving bias.** The last refers to a tendency to emphasize internal causes for success (e.g., our own ability) but external causes for failure (e.g., bad luck, a difficult task). Males demonstrate stronger tendencies to engage in the self-serving bias than females do, and this is true with respect to sexual experiences as well as other forms of behavior.

Attribution theory has been put to practical use in several contexts. It helps explain marital discord and escalating spirals of interpersonal conflict. Attributions also play a significant role in depression. Several forms of therapy based on attribution theory have proven helpful in treating this important psychological disorder.

Self-Perception: Understanding Ourselves

The task of understanding the causes of our own behavior is more difficult than it appears. Schachter's theory of emotion suggests that we label feelings of arousal in accordance with external information; misattribution of arousal to neutral causes can reduce emotional reactions. Bem's theory of self-perception suggests that we infer our attitudes from our overt actions. This theory helps explain why providing individuals with external rewards for engaging in activities they enjoy often reduces their interest in these activities (the **overjustification effect**). While individuals usually seek increased self-perception, they also attempt to protect their self-esteem from the effects of potential failure through **self-handicapping.** This involves calling attention to external factors, such as poor health or lack of sleep, that could explain failure if it occurs.

KEY TERMS

Actor-observer effect The tendency to attribute our own behavior mainly to situational causes but others' behavior mainly to internal (dispositional) causes.

Attribution The process through which we seek to identify the causes of others' behavior and so gain knowledge of their stable traits and dispositions.

Augmenting The tendency to attach greater importance to a potential cause of behavior if the behavior occurs despite the presence of other, inhibitory causes.

Body language Cues provided by the position, posture, and movement of others' bodies or body parts.

Consensus The extent to which actions by one person are also shown by others.

Consistency The extent to which an individual responds to a given stimulus or situation in the same way on different occasions (i.e., across time).

Correspondent inference (theory of) A theory describing how we use others' behavior as a basis for inferring their stable dispositions.

Discounting principle The tendency to attach less importance to one potential cause of some behavior when other potential causes are also present.

Distinctiveness The extent to which an individual responds in a similar manner to different stimuli or different situations.

Emblems Gestures that have a specific meaning within a given culture.

Face-in-the-crowd phenomenon Our tendency to notice angry, threatening faces in the midst of neutral or happy faces more readily than we notice happy or neutral faces in the midst of threatening ones.

Fundamental attribution error The tendency to overestimate the impact of dispositional cues on others' behavior.

Gait The characteristic way in which people walk.

Impression formation The process through which we combine diverse information about other persons into a unified impression of them.

Microexpressions Brief and incomplete facial expressions that occur on people's faces quickly after exposure to a specific stimulus and before active processes can be used to conceal them.

Noncommon effects Effects produced by a particular cause that could not be produced by any other apparent cause.

Nonverbal communication Communication between individuals that does not involve the content of spoken language. It relies instead on an unspoken language of facial expressions, eye contact, and body language.

Overjustification effect Reductions in intrinsic motivation produced by receiving external rewards for performing actions one enjoys.

Self-handicapping An attributional strategy for protecting one's self-esteem by calling attention to the existence of external causes for potential failures.

Self-perception The process through which we seek to know and understand our own feelings, traits, and motives.

Self-presentation Techniques designed to create a favorable impression of their user in others (target persons).

Self-serving bias The tendency to attribute positive outcomes to internal causes (e.g., one's own traits or characteristics) but negative outcomes or events to external causes (e.g., chance, or task difficulty).

Social perception The process through which we seek to know and understand other persons.

Staring A form of eye contact in which one person continues to gaze steadily at another regardless of what the recipient does.

FOR MORE INFORMATION

Harvey, J. H., & Weary, G. (Eds.). (1989). *Attribution: Basic issues and applications*. San Diego: Academic Press.

This collection of chapters, each prepared by an expert researcher, provides updated information on major theories of attribution, recent research findings, and how knowledge about this key aspect of social perception has been applied to many practical problems.

Jones, E. E. (1990). *Interpersonal perception*. New York: W. H. Freeman.

An insightful review of many aspects of social perception, prepared by one of the leading researchers in this important area of social psychology. The chapters on attributions, self-presentation, and self-perception expand on topics covered in the present chapter.

Ross, M., & Fletcher, G. J. O. (1985). Attribution and social perception. In G. Lindzey and E. Aronson, (Eds.), *Handbook of social psychology*. New York: Random House.

A comprehensive discussion of many aspects of social perception. While the chapter is intended mainly for professional social psychologists, it is clearly written and contains a great deal of interesting information.

Siegman, A. W., & Feldstein, S. (Eds.). (1987). *Nonverbal behavior and communication*. Hillsdale, NJ: Erlbaum.

This book contains chapters by experts on various aspects of nonverbal communication. Included are fascinating discussions of body movement and gestures, nonverbal aspects of speech, and the ways in which nonverbal cues regulate conversations and even group process. This is an excellent source to consult if you'd like to know more about nonverbal communication.

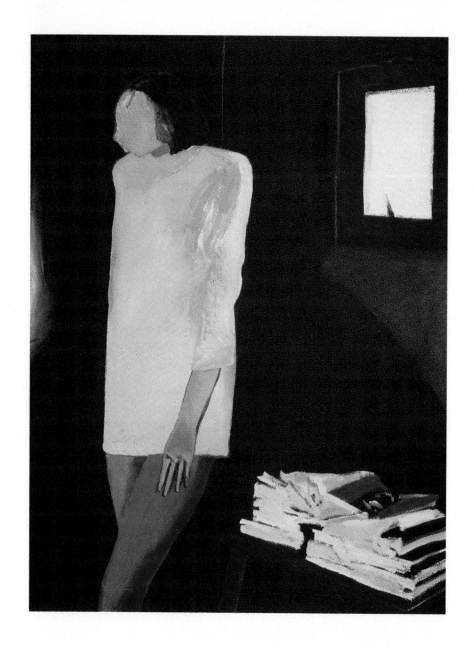

Social Cognition: Thinking About the Social World

Come on, Joe, who are you kidding?" Angela Foster remarks, shaking her head. "She *can't* be better than everyone else in your department. I just don't buy it."

"But she *is*," Joe Padrone replies heatedly. "You don't really think I'd be putting her up for promotion ahead of guys like John Burke and Eddie Stevens if she weren't, do you?"

"I'm not saying that you don't *think* she's better," Angela replies. "I just think that maybe you're being influenced more than you realize by all that affirmative action stuff. We both know the pressure is on to promote more women. How can you separate that from your ratings?"

"But I can," Joe contends. "I've been in this business a long time, and I've had to rate lots of people. Believe me, she's really top-notch."

"We all know she's good," Len O'Leary interrupts, "but is she really better than all the rest? You've got to admit that it looks a little strange. There are eighteen people working for you, and only one of them is a woman. Now, just when we're knee-deep in all these guidelines and directives, who happens to come out on top? Karen Farley. What a coincidence!"

"But I'm telling you: That stuff didn't influence my judgment. It's her record that counts with me. And thinking back over the past two years, that really looks good."

"Oh yeah?" Angela asks. "Then what about that Tri-City deal? She blew it and cost us a bundle. You must remember that?"

At this, Joe looks a little confused. "Well . . . yeah . . . she did. But just think about all those successes she's had. Even taking the Tri-City bungle into account, I still consider her first-rate."

"Yeah, but Joe," Len chimes in, "haven't you been saying right along that you expected her to do well—that you just *knew* that anyone who came out of that tough training program would be first-rate? Maybe you're letting *that* influence you."

"No way!" Joe exclaims angrily. "Sure, I expected her to do good work—everyone with an MBA from Tech can really cut it. But what's that got to do with anything? I'm rating her performance, not my predictions about it."

"But how can you separate the two?" Angela asks. "Everyone knows that we tend to see what we expect to see. You expected her to do well, so you rate her really high. And there's another thing: Everyone around here knows how much you like Karen personally. You and Millie have practically adopted her. You can't look me in the eye and tell me *that* isn't affecting your decision."

At those words, Joe rises to his feet. "That does it. I'm not going to listen to any more. It doesn't matter what I say—you two have already made up your minds. Well, I'll tell you this: If you don't come around, I'm going to take it over your heads. Someone around here is bound to listen." And with that remark, he walks stiffly out of the room.

"Whew!—we're in for it now," Len says, shaking his head in disbelief. "Maybe we were too rough on him."

"No way," Angela replies. "He's just too close to the situation to see it clearly. Sure, Karen's good. But she doesn't deserve to be promoted over people like Eddie Stevens. He's been with us for ten years; if he doesn't get the nod this time, it'll just wipe him out. No, Joe just can't handle this one. His thinking is confused, and what's even worse, he can't see that it is. Ugh—what a mess!"

Thinking about others, and about the social world generally, is one of life's major tasks. As noted in Chapter 2, we often wish to understand other persons—to identify their key traits, comprehend their major motives, recognize their current feelings. Similarly, we spend a considerable amount of time thinking about *ourselves,* trying to grasp the nature of our own feelings, traits, or motives and comparing our present selves to other versions we can readily imagine (e.g., what we might like to become, could become, or are afraid of

Social cognition: A basis for social judgments

FIGURE 3.1 We spend a great deal of time thinking about others, partly so that we can make various kinds of judgments about them or their behavior.

becoming; Markus & Nurius, 1986). We engage in such thought for many reasons, but one of the most important is suggested by our opening story: We think about others because we must make various kinds of judgments about them. We must decide whether we like or dislike them, whether they have performed some task poorly or well, whether they are telling the truth or are lying, and whether they are suited for some role or job (see Figure 3.1).

In order to make such judgments, we must somehow notice, sort, remember, and use a wealth of information. And this task, it turns out, is even more complex than it sounds. After all, when making even relatively simple judgments about others, we have a wealth of potential information at our disposal. We know what they look like, what they've said at various times, and how they've acted in different situations. We also have our own expectations about them, and we may compare their current words or actions to these internal standards or predictions. Finally, we have feelings about them; total neutrality toward others is rare. How, then, do we make use of such information? Intriguing answers are being provided by an important area of social psychology known as **social cognition** (cf. Higgins, 1987; Miller, Turnbull, & McFarland, 1990; Ross, 1989). Social cognition is concerned with understanding the processes through which we notice, interpret, remember, and then use information about the social world. The kinds of questions investigated by social psychologists interested in this topic can be readily illustrated using the incident described above:

1. Why did Joe remember mainly positive information about Karen, while tending to forget (or at least overlook) negative facts about her past performance?

2. Was Joe's judgment really affected by his desire to meet the guidelines of affirmative action and promote more women? Or was the fact that he rated Karen higher than seventeen men in his group merely a coincidence? And why did Angela and Len have such strong doubts on this score, despite Joe's comments?

3. Were Joe's ratings of Karen affected by his expectations concerning her performance or by his personal liking for her?

As we'll see in later sections of this chapter, research on various aspects of social cognition offers revealing answers to these and many other questions concerning social thought and human judgment.

In the remainder of this chapter, we'll examine key aspects of social cognition. First, we'll consider several shortcuts and strategies people use to help them make sense of the social world (e.g., **heuristics**). While these methods often succeed in simplifying social cognition and reducing the effort it requires, their ultimate impact is similar to that of other types of shortcuts: They lead us to errors and difficulties we might not at first anticipate. Second, we'll consider the complex interplay between **affect** (temporary shifts in moods or feelings) and *cognition*. We'll see that this relationship is indeed a two-way street, with feelings influencing cognition, and cognition, in turn, shaping affect. Finally, we will examine the *self*—our cognitive representations of our own characteristics and traits (Kihlstrom et al., 1988). As we'll soon see, our self-concept encompasses not only knowledge of our current self but also conceptions of what we might become in the future (i.e., a host of *possible selves*).

Mental Shortcuts: Heuristics and Other Strategies of the "Cognitive Miser"

People, it is often noted, prefer the path of least resistance. In other words, when faced with various tasks, they select those approaches which will allow them to reach their goals with the least amount of effort. As we mentioned in our discussion of causal attribution (see Chapter 2), this preference applies to cognitive as well as to physical work. In fact, it is a guiding principle of social cognition. All things being equal, most people will do the least amount of mental work they can get away with in most situations (cf. Taylor & Fiske, 1984). In other words, we can be described as **cognitive misers**—creatures unwilling to expend more than the minimum amount of cognitive effort required in a given situation (refer to Figure 3.2 for an amusing illustration of this point). Of course, this is not always true. There are situations in which individuals willingly engage in complex and effortful forms of social thought (cf. Tetlock & Boettger, 1989). Still, such instances are more likely to be the exception than the rule, and usually people seek to minimize cognitive effort whenever feasible.

This fact points to the following conclusions: In many cases, people adopt various strategies designed to reduce cognitive effort and to decrease the possibility of **information overload**—having to deal with more information than they can handle. To be successful, however, such strategies must have two properties. First, they must provide a quick and simple way of dealing with large amounts of social information. Second, they must work—they must be reasonably accurate much of the time. After all, if a given cognitive strategy always leads to wrong decisions or serious errors, it will probably be dropped

"Surely not guilty. Next case."

Minimizing mental effort in social cognition: One example

FIGURE 3.2   In thinking about others, we often do the least amount of mental work we can. Like the character in this cartoon, we act as "cognitive misers." (Drawing by C. Barsotti; © 1988 The New Yorker Magazine, Inc.)

and replaced by another. So, selecting and using various cognitive strategies involves striking a good working balance between these two features—accuracy (or reliability) and speed (or simplicity).

In social psychology, efforts to understand such mental shortcuts have focused on two major topics: **heuristics** and **biases.** Heuristics are simple decision-making rules we often use to make inferences or draw conclusions quickly and easily. Biases, in contrast, refer to the errors and distortions that often appear in social thought. Since these often derive from the use of heuristics, the two topics are related, and we'll consider them together in this section.

Heuristics in Social Cognition: Mental Rules of Thumb

Suppose you want to estimate the dimensions of a room but don't have a tape measure handy. What will you do? One possibility involves pacing off its length and width by placing one foot almost exactly in front of the other. Since the distance from the heel to the toe of an adult's foot is approximately twelve inches, you would be able to get rough estimates of the numbers you want through this "quick and dirty" method. Similarly, we make use of many different mental *heuristics* in our efforts to think about and use social information. We will now describe several of the most important ones.

Representativeness: Judging by Resemblance   Imagine that you have just met your next-door neighbor for the first time. On the basis of a brief conversation with her, you determine that she is very neat in her habits, has a good vocabulary, reads many books, is somewhat shy, and dresses conservatively. Later you realize that she never mentioned what she does for a living. Is she a business executive, a librarian, a waitress, an attorney, or a dancer? One quick way of making a guess is to compare her with typical members of each of these occupations. In other words, you could simply ask yourself how well she resembles people you have met in each of these fields. If you proceeded in this fashion, you would probably conclude that she is a librarian; after all, her traits seem to resemble those of other librarians more closely than the traits of dancers, attorneys, or waitresses. In this instance, you would be using the **representativeness heuristic.** In other words, you would make your judgment on the basis of a relatively simple rule: *The more similar an individual is to typical members of a given group, the more likely he or she is to belong to that group.*

Are such judgments likely to be accurate? Since membership in particular groups affects the behavior and mannerisms of the people in them (see our discussion of this topic in Chapter 11) and since individuals are attracted to specific groups because they share various interests or characteristics with their members, the representativeness heuristic *is* often accurate. However, as you probably know from your own experience, there are exceptions to this general rule. Some librarians are extroverted and lead exciting social lives; some dancers are shy and read lots of books. And some professors (believe it or not) climb mountains, practice skydiving, and even run for political office in their spare time (refer to Figure 3.3). Because of such exceptions, the representativeness heuristic, though useful, can sometimes lead to serious errors. In addition, and perhaps more importantly, reliance on this heuristic can lead us to overlook other forms of information that could potentially be quite useful. The most important information of this type relates to *base rates*—the frequency with which some event or pattern occurs in the general population. The ten-

The representativeness heuristic in action

FIGURE 3.3   Are any of the people shown here librarians, professors, or accountants? Probably you find this idea laughable; since the persons shown don't seem to resemble typical librarians, professors, and accountants, you quickly conclude that they do not belong to this occupational group. In other words, you rely on the *representativeness heuristic* in making these judgments. Since some librarians, professors, and accountants *do* sometimes engage in these activities, your conclusions may be false.

dency to overlook such information when relying on the representativeness heuristic was illustrated some years ago by a famous study conducted by Tversky and Kahneman (1973).

Subjects in this study were told that an imaginary person named Jack had been selected from a group of one hundred men. They were then asked to guess the probability that Jack was an engineer. Some subjects were told that thirty of the men were engineers (thus, the base rate for engineers was 30 percent). Others were told that seventy of the men were engineers. Half the subjects received no further information. The other half, however, also received a personal description of Jack that either resembled the common stereotype of engineers (e.g., they are practical, like to work with numbers) or did not. When subjects received only information relating to base rates, their estimates of the likelihood that Jack was an engineer reflected this information: They thought it more likely that Jack was an engineer when the base rate was 70 percent than when it was 30 percent. However, when they received personal information about Jack, they tended to ignore the base-rate information and instead made their estimates primarily on the basis of whether Jack seemed to resemble the stereotype of an engineer. In sum, subjects tended to overlook a valuable form of information and to operate in terms of representativeness alone. This tendency to ignore useful base-rate information is known as the **base-rate fallacy.**

Availability: What Comes to Mind First?   Which is more common—words that start with the letter *k* (e.g., *king*) or words that contain *k* as the third letter (e.g., *awkward*)? Tversky and Kahneman (1982) put this question to more than a hundred people and came up with a revealing set of findings. In the English language there are more than twice as many words having *k* as the third letter than the first. Yet despite this fact, a majority of the subjects guessed incorrectly, assuming that more words begin with *k*. Why was this the case? In part, because of their use of another heuristic—**availability.** According to this heuristic, the easier it is to bring instances of some group or category to mind, the more frequent these are judged to be. This heuristic, too, makes good sense—after all, common events or objects *are* usually easier to think of than less common ones because we have had more experience with them. However, relying on availability in making such judgments can also lead to errors, such as the one involving words with the letter *k*. As another example, consider the case of a professor who is grading students on the basis of class participation. As she assigns grades, she thinks: *Hm . . . let's see . . . how often did Frank participate? Did he speak up more than Ellen?* Does the ease with which the professor can recall each student's comments reflect the actual frequency with which the students contributed? Not necessarily. Perhaps she is more likely to remember comments that were made forcefully, with lots of conviction. To the extent that this is so, she will assign higher grades to those students who express themselves with greatest conviction—not necessarily to those who participate most.

Another illustration of the impact of the availability heuristic is provided by the fact that many people are much more frightened of flying than of driving. One reason for this is that media coverage of air crashes is often extensive and vivid. Because it is, such events are relatively easy to remember—much easier to remember than the two-inch article buried on page thirty-four of the second section describing yet another fatal auto accident. In other words, accounts of air crashes are much more available in memory. For this reason, many people view them as being more frequent and alarming than the actual numbers warrant.

The False Consensus Effect: Availability and the Tendency to Assume That Others Think as We Do   Be honest: On a scale ranging from one (strongly against) to seven (strongly in favor of), what is your view about the death penalty for convicted murderers? Now, out of a hundred other students, how many do you think share your view? (That is, how many are on the same side of the neutral point [4] as yourself?) If you are like most people, the number you indicated is higher than what would be revealed by an actual survey. In other words, you assume that people agree with you to a greater extent than they actually do. This is known as the **false consensus effect,** and it has been observed in numerous contexts. For example, male high school students who smoke estimate that 51 percent of their fellow male students smoke, but non-smoking male students estimate that only 38 percent of their male peers smoke (Sherman et al., 1984). In a similar manner, students tend to overestimate the proportion of other students who agree with their attitudes about drugs, abortion, seat-belt use, university policies, politics, and even Ritz crackers (Nisbett & Kunda, 1985; Suls, Wan, & Sanders, 1988). In short, the false consensus effect is quite common (although in an absolute sense, it is not very large).

What is the basis for this tendency to assume that others think as we do? Two factors seem to play a role. First, most people want to believe that others agree with them because this enhances their confidence that their own actions, judgments, or life-styles are normal or appropriate (Sherman, Presson, & Chassin, 1984; Marks & Miller, 1987). Here, the false consensus effect serves a self-enhancing function.

Second, the effect seems to stem, at least in part, from reliance on the availability heuristic. Such reliance can occur in two distinct ways: (1) Some people find it easier to notice and later remember instances in which others agreed with them than instances in which others disagreed. As a result of this distortion in processing social information, such people find it easier to bring instances of agreement to mind. Then, these are perceived as more frequent than instances of disagreement. (2) Since most persons tend to choose friends and associates who share their views (see our discussion of attraction in Chapter 5), they are actually exposed to many instances of agreement. This, too, leads to higher availability for agreement than disagreement and contributes to the occurrence of the false consensus effect.

We should note, by the way, that the false consensus effect is common but far from universal. It is comforting to assume that others share our attitudes and perhaps even our undesirable attributes (e.g., the inability to resist rich desserts). For highly desirable attributes, however, people may be motivated to perceive themselves as unique (e.g., Goethals, 1986; Suls & Wan, 1987). Thus, when the desire to "stand out from the crowd" in some positive way is stronger than the desire to be similar to others, the false consensus effect may fail to occur (Campbell, 1986).

Priming: Some Effects of Increased Availability   During the first year of medical school, many students experience what is known as the *medical student syndrome*: They begin to suspect that they (or their friends or families) are suffering from serious illnesses. An ordinary headache, for example, may cause such students to worry about the possibility that they have a brain tumor. A mild sore throat may create anxiety that some rare but fatal infection is present. What accounts for such effects? Two factors seem crucial. Medical students are exposed to descriptions of such diseases day after day in their classes and assigned readings. As a result, such information is high in availability. Thus, when a mild symptom occurs, it is readily brought to mind, with the result that the students tend to imagine the worst about their current health. Such effects are termed **priming**. Specifically, priming involves any procedures that heighten the availability of certain categories of information so that they can be readily brought to mind. Many instances of priming occur in everyday life. For example, after watching an especially frightening horror movie, many people react strongly to stimuli that previously would have had little impact on them (*What's that creak on the stairs? Where does that strange shadow come from?*). Similarly, after viewing a television show filled with sexual remarks and content, some people will be more likely to perceive innocuous comments or gestures by others as come-ons than they might otherwise. (See Figure 3.4 for another example of priming.)

The occurrence of priming effects has been demonstrated in several studies (e.g., Higgins & King, 1981; Wyer & Srull, 1980). For example, in one of the earliest experiments on this topic (Higgins, Rohles, & Jones, 1977) subjects were exposed to lists of positive traits (e.g., adventurous, independent) or negative traits (e.g., reckless). Then, in what they thought was a separate task, they were asked to form an impression of an imaginary person. They formed these impressions on the basis of descriptions of his behavior that were either

Priming: A concrete example

FIGURE 3.4 *Priming* occurs when some stimulus or event increases the availability of certain types of information in memory. In this instance, the sign on the back of the truck has activated thoughts of the driver's mother-in-law. (Source: Reprinted with special permission of King Features Syndicate, Inc.)

relevant to the previously viewed traits (e.g., sailing across the Atlantic, climbing mountains) or unrelated to them. Results indicated that subjects' impressions of the imaginary character were indeed affected by the trait words, but only when these words were relevant to the descriptions of his behavior. Thus, subjects' impressions were more favorable if they had previously seen positive traits (e.g., adventurous) than if they had previously seen negative ones (e.g., reckless). In short, their social judgments were affected by priming—by words that had activated different aspects or categories of their memories.

More recent research on priming suggests that it is pervasive. In fact, this phenomenon even seems to occur when individuals are unaware of the priming stimuli (e.g., Bargh & Pietromonaco, 1982). Such **automatic priming,** as it is usually termed, is demonstrated quite clearly in a revealing study by Erdley and D'Agostino (1988).

These researchers first asked subjects to perform a vigilance task—one in which they indicated whether two dark flashes presented for brief periods of time in a tachistoscope appeared on the right or the left side of a central focus point. In reality, the flashes consisted of pairs of words; however, the words were presented so briefly that subjects could not read them. For one group of subjects, some of the words were related to the trait of being *mean* (e.g., *selfish, rude, difficult*), while the other words in each pair were unrelated to this trait (e.g., *what, little, many, number*). For a second group, some of the words were related to the trait of *honesty* (e.g., *honorable, truthful, sincere*), while the others were unrelated. For a third group, some of the words were related to honesty and the others to meanness, while for a fourth (control) group, the words were unrelated to either trait.

Following exposure to the pairs of words, subjects read a description of an imaginary person (Donna) that was ambiguous with respect to honesty and meanness: The character was described as engaging in some behaviors that were somewhat honest and in others that were somewhat mean. Finally, after reading this description, subjects were asked to rate this person on a series of trait dimensions. Some of these were related to honesty (e.g., sincere, truthful, deceitful), some to meanness (kind, considerate, mean, selfish), and others were unrelated to either (interesting, intelligent, boring, nervous). It was predicted that subjects primed for meanness (exposed to words related to this trait) would rate the target (imaginary) person higher in this trait than subjects in the control condition. Similarly, subjects primed for honesty (exposed to words related to this trait) were expected to rate the target person higher in honesty. However, such effects were *not* predicted to occur with respect to ratings on dimensions unrelated to the primed traits. Results offered support for all these predictions (see Figure 3.5). In the case of meanness, subjects exposed to pairs of mean and control words (e.g., *selfish/water*) and to pairs of mean and honest words (e.g., *selfish/sincere*) rated the imaginary person as higher in meanness than those in the control group. For honesty, however, such effects occurred only for subjects exposed to pairs of honest and control words. As predicted, though, these priming effects occurred only for ratings on traits related to honesty or meanness; they did not occur for ratings with respect to unrelated traits.

Together, these findings suggest that such subliminal (automatic) priming effects occur because exposure to the priming words increases the availability in memory of certain trait categories. The results obtained by Erdley and D'Agos-

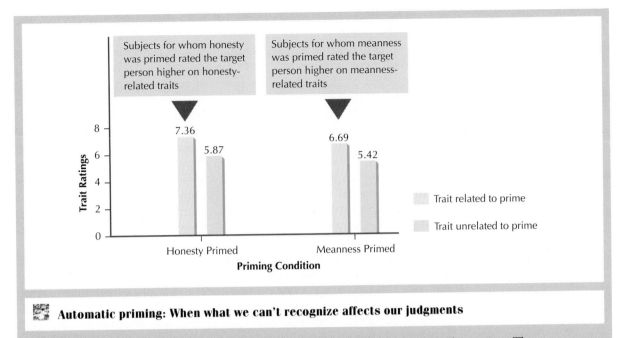

Subjects for whom honesty was primed rated the target person higher on honesty-related traits

Subjects for whom meanness was primed rated the target person higher on meanness-related traits

Automatic priming: When what we can't recognize affects our judgments

FIGURE 3.5 Subjects were exposed to words related to two traits: honesty and meanness. The words were shown to subjects so quickly that they could not read or recognize them. Yet, they rated an imaginary character as being higher on traits related to honesty and meanness. Similar *automatic priming effects* did not occur with respect to traits unrelated to the ones that had been primed (i.e., honesty, meanness). (Source: Based on data from Erdley & D'Agostino, 1988.)

tino (1988) offer little support for an alternative explanation—one suggesting that such priming elicits global affective reactions (i.e., good or bad feelings with respect to the target person). Whatever the precise mechanism involved, however, it is clear that even exposure to stimuli we can't consciously recognize can influence the availability of information stored in memory and so our later judgments about others. Priming, it appears, is indeed a powerful phenomenon.

Framing and Anchoring: How Posing the Question Sometimes Determines the Answer

Suppose that you learned of a survey indicating that fully 75 percent of all persons who purchased a particular brand of automobile reported being highly satisfied with it. How would you rate its overall quality on a scale of one (very low) to seven (very high)? Now, in contrast, imagine that you read about a survey indicating that 25 percent of all persons who purchased this automobile reported being dissatisfied with it. How would you rate the car's quality now?

Clearly, the two surveys yielded identical results: In both cases, three-quarters of customers are satisfied and one-quarter dissatisfied. Yet if you are like most people, you might well assign higher ratings to the automobile in the first case than in the second. Such effects are known as **framing** and have been observed with respect to a wide range of stimuli and dimensions. Framing refers to the fact that our judgments about various objects or issues are often strongly affected by the way in which information about them is presented. When positive attributes are emphasized, our evaluations are higher than when negative attributes are emphasized (Levin 1987; Neale & Bazerman, 1985). For example, if negotiators are urged to think about the benefits of making concessions in order to reach an agreement with their opponents, they tend to evaluate offers from them more favorably and actually make more concessions than if they are urged to think about the potential costs of such moves (Neale & Bazerman, 1985).

Why do these effects occur? One explanation (Levin, 1987) suggests that they stem from the fact that when stimuli are described (framed) in positive terms, favorable associations to them are evoked. Individuals tend to think about positive experiences they have had with the object or product (e.g., they remember how beautiful it looked, gleaming in the showroom), about other positive information concerning it (that enticing ad they saw recently), and so on. This process in turn leads them to make relatively positive judgments about the object. In contrast, when stimuli are described in negative terms, unfavorable associations are elicited and the end result is lower evaluations.

If this reasoning is correct, it seems possible that increasing individuals' personal involvement with their judgments might reduce the occurrence of framing. This would be the case because under conditions of high involvement, individuals would think about all sides of the issue no matter how it was framed. A study by Levin, Schnittjer, and Thee (1988) was designed to assess this possibility. In this investigation, male and female subjects were asked to evaluate the effectiveness of a new medical technique for treating a specific type of cancer. Half the subjects received information suggesting that the technique had a 50 percent success rate (*positive frame*), while the other half learned that it had a 50 percent failure rate (*negative frame*). To vary subjects' personal involvement with the situation, this framing information was presented in three different contexts. One-third of the subjects were asked merely to evaluate the effectiveness of this new technique (*low involvement*). A second group was asked to imagine that they were a doctor faced with the task of recommending or not recommending the technique to a patient (*moderate involvement*). Finally, a third group was asked to imagine that they had to decide whether to recommend the technique to a member of their own family. This last context, of course, constituted the highest level of personal involvement with the situation. (Incidentally, we will return to the effects of involvement in our discussion of persuasion in Chapter 4; Johnson & Eagly, 1989.)

Results were both surprising and revealing. While subjects in the three groups did report the expected different levels of involvement with the tasks, strong framing effects occurred in all three conditions (see Figure 3.6). Subjects in the low-involvement group rated the medical technique as being more effective in the positive than in the negative framing condition. Similarly, those in the moderate- and high-involvement groups reported stronger recommendations for the use of the technique in the positive than in the negative framing condition. These and related findings suggest that framing is a strong phenomenon, one whose effects cannot be readily eliminated.

Framing, though, is only part of the total picture where the impact of the initial representation of information about an object or issue is concerned. Another closely related effect, known as **anchoring,** also exists. To understand the nature of this effect, consider the following incident. Suppose you are looking for a good used car. Finally, you find one you think you want. How do you decide what it is worth? The rational approach is to look in the "blue

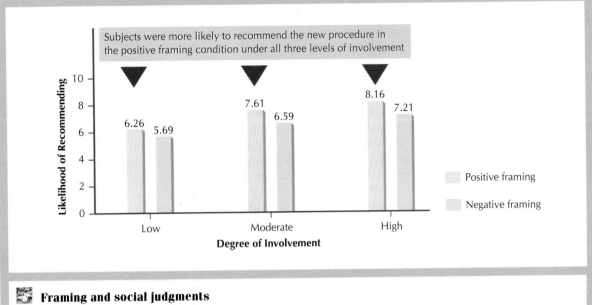

FIGURE 3.6 Subjects were more likely to recommend use of a new medical procedure when it was described as being successful half the time (positive frame) than when the same procedure was described as being unsuccessful half the time (negative frame). Moreover, this was true even under conditions of high personal involvement in the decision (i.e., when they were recommending the treatment for a member of their own family). (Source: Based on data from Levin, Schnittjer, & Thee, 1988.)

book," a publication that lists the average prices paid for various used cars in recent months. But would you actually proceed in this fashion? Perhaps—but only *perhaps*. Since we tend to follow the path of least resistance and since few of us have the "blue book" handy, you might well proceed in a different manner. You would ask the seller what she or he wants for the car and then proceed to bargain from there. At first glance, this strategy seems reasonable. But think again: If you adopt it, you allow the seller to set a *reference point*—a figure from which your negotiations will then proceed. If this price is close to the one in the "blue book," well and good. But if it is considerably higher, you may end up paying more for the car than it is really worth.

Surprisingly, such reference points, or *anchors,* have been found to strongly affect our judgments. In part, this is due to the fact that once they are established, our adjustments to these anchors tend to be too small to counter their initial impact. In other words, if the seller asks a very high price, we bargain to get it lowered but tend to quit before the agreed-on price is where it would have been if we had used the "blue book" instead. How powerful and general are such effects? Growing evidence suggests that they may be much stronger than many people think. An intriguing field study by Northcraft and Neale (1987) illustrates this fact quite dramatically.

These researchers hypothesized that anchoring effects would occur even in a practical and important economic context—with respect to negotiating the price of a house. To test this prediction, they conducted research in which two groups of subjects—one students and the other actual real estate agents—were quoted supposed asking prices for houses. In various conditions, these prices were considerably lower, slightly lower, slightly higher, or much higher than the actual asking price. For example, in one case, the actual asking price for a house was $134,900. Subjects were told, however, that the asking price was either $119,900, $129,900, $139,900, or $149,900, respectively.

After learning of the supposed asking prices, subjects were permitted to visit the homes and inspect them. Then they were asked to indicate what they thought would be a fair price for each. Results indicated that the figures subjects suggested were strongly affected by the anchor (the supposed asking price) they had received. The higher the anchor, the higher were subjects' estimates of the value of the houses (see Figure 3.7). Moreover—and this is the surprising part—this was as true for experienced real estate agents as for students.

Additional research suggests that anchoring and adjustment effects occur in many other contexts as well. For example, in one intriguing study on this topic, Plous (1989) asked almost fifteen hundred students to estimate the likelihood of nuclear war. Before providing these estimates, some subjects were exposed to a low anchor: They were asked whether the chances of nuclear war were

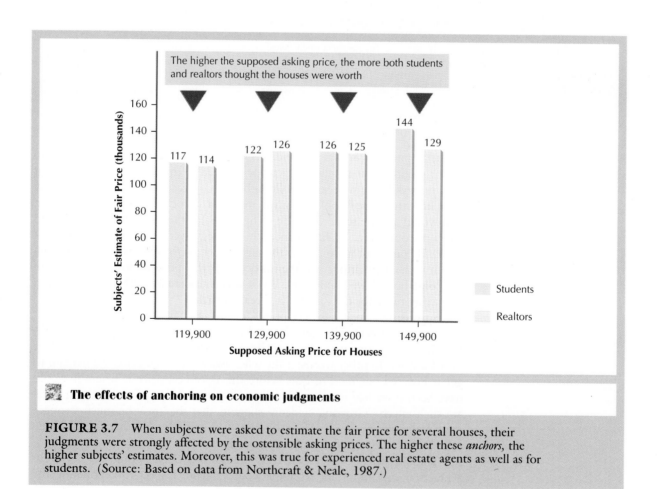

The effects of anchoring on economic judgments

FIGURE 3.7 When subjects were asked to estimate the fair price for several houses, their judgments were strongly affected by the ostensible asking prices. The higher these *anchors*, the higher subjects' estimates. Moreover, this was true for experienced real estate agents as well as for students. (Source: Based on data from Northcraft & Neale, 1987.)

greater or less than *1 percent*. Others were given a high anchor: They were asked whether the chances were greater or less than *90 percent*. Finally, others were given no anchor—they were never asked to respond to this initial question. Subjects in all three groups then proceeded to provide a personal estimate of the exact chances of a nuclear war between the United States and the Soviet Union. Results were clear: Those exposed to the low anchor reported the lowest estimates (10.8 percent), those exposed to the high anchor reported the highest estimates (25.7 percent), and those in the no-anchor control condition were in between (19.1 percent).

Taken together, the findings reported by Plous (1989), Levin and his colleagues (1988), and many others suggest that our judgments are often influenced by information that should, from a strictly rational point of view, have no impact on them. Apparently, our susceptibility to framing and anchoring represents one more potential cost of our strong desire for efficiency and minimal cognitive effort in our attempts to deal with the social world.

Counterfactual Thinking and Mental Simulation: The Effects of Considering "What Might Have Been"

Imagine the following events: Ms. Caution never picks up hitchhikers. Yesterday, however, she gave a stranger a ride. He repaid her kindness by robbing her. Now, in contrast, consider the following events: Ms. Risk frequently picks up hitchhikers. Yesterday she gave a stranger a ride. He repaid her kindness by robbing her. Which of these two persons will experience greater regret?

If you answered, "Why Ms. Caution, of course," your thinking in this instance is very much like that of other persons. An overwhelming majority of individuals identify Ms. Caution as feeling more regretful (Kahneman & Miller, 1986). Yet take a step back from the situation and think about why this is the case. Both individuals have suffered precisely the same negative outcome—they have been robbed. Why, then, do we perceive Ms. Caution as experiencing more regret? The answer involves some intriguing facts about the nature of social thought and the judgments and reactions resulting from it. In essence, it appears that our reactions to various events depend not only on the events themselves but on what those events bring to mind (Kahneman & Miller, 1986). When we have some experience, we do not think only about the experience itself. We also engage in *mental simulation* with respect to it. This often results in **counterfactual thinking**—bringing alternative events and outcomes to mind. In this particular instance, we may think, *If only Ms. Caution had not broken her usual rule against picking up hitchhikers, she'd be okay.* Alternatively, we may imagine, *If Ms. Risk read the papers and thought about how dangerous it is to pick up hitchhikers, she might act differently.*

But why, precisely, does such counterfactual thinking lead us to believe that Ms. Caution will experience more regret? In part, because it is easier to imagine alternatives to unusual behavior (e.g., Ms. Caution's picking up the hitchhiker) than to imagine alternatives to usual, normal behavior (e.g., Ms. Risk's picking up the hitchhiker). So, we conclude that Ms. Caution experienced more regret because it is easier for us to imagine her acting in a different way—sticking to her rule—than to imagine Ms. Risk acting differently. After all, Ms. Risk always picks up hitchhikers; it was just her bad luck that the practice finally caught up with her. In a sense, she has been asking for trouble all along and finally found it.

This reasoning leads to the interesting prediction that negative outcomes that follow unusual behavior (behavior that elicits mental simulations that are

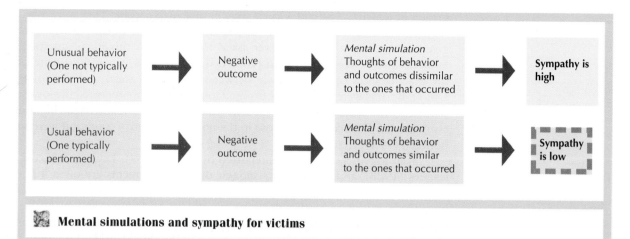

| Unusual behavior (One not typically performed) | → | Negative outcome | → | *Mental simulation* Thoughts of behavior and outcomes dissimilar to the ones that occurred | → | **Sympathy is high** |
| Usual behavior (One typically performed) | → | Negative outcome | → | *Mental simulation* Thoughts of behavior and outcomes similar to the ones that occurred | → | **Sympathy is low** |

Mental simulations and sympathy for victims

FIGURE 3.8 Negative outcomes that follow unusual behavior readily elicit *mental simulations* of events different from the ones that actually occurred. Thus, they will generate high levels of sympathy for the victims (upper panel). In contrast, negative outcomes that follow usual behavior will elicit mental simulations of events similar to the ones that actually occurred. As a result, sympathy for the victims will be lower (lower panel). (Source: Based on suggestions by Kahneman & Tversky, 1982.)

primarily *dissimilar* to it) will generate more sympathy than ones that follow usual behavior (behavior that elicits mental simulations that are primarily *similar* to it; refer to Figure 3.8). Precisely such effects have been demonstrated in many recent studies (Kahneman & Tversky, 1982). For example, in one such investigation, Miller and McFarland (1986) asked subjects to read a description of a victim of a crime to determine how much money he should receive as compensation for his injuries. All subjects read about a male victim who lost the use of his right arm as the result of a gunshot wound that occurred when he walked in on a robbery in a neighborhood convenience store. One group of subjects (*normal behavior condition*) learned that on the night he was shot, the victim had gone to a store he visited frequently. Another group (*abnormal behavior condition*) learned that he had gone to a store he rarely visited for a "change of pace." (Please note: in this context *abnormal* merely means unusual.) After reading the descriptions, all subjects indicated how much the victim should receive in compensation (from no money to $1 million). As predicted, subjects assigned greater compensation to the victim when his wound occurred at a store he rarely visited than when it occurred at a store he visited frequently. In other words, when subjects could readily imagine alternative events (e.g., the man did not visit this store and was not wounded), they felt more sympathy for him and awarded him a larger compensation.

As you can see, counterfactual thinking is closely related to the availability heuristic. The ease with which we can imagine alternative events ("what might have been") depends, to some extent, on how available alternative outcomes are. The more readily such alternatives can be brought to mind, the stronger our reactions to the present situation.

Additional research on counterfactual thinking suggests that it is also closely related to judgments of causality. (Recall our discussion of *attribution* in Chapter

2.) In particular, it appears that we will perceive events as causing an outcome to the extent that we can readily imagine changes in that event that would undo the outcome. Returning to the example above, imagine that on the night in question, there was only one holdup, in the store the man chose to visit. How important was his decision as to which store to visit? Most people would reply, "Very important." They would do so because had the man visited the other store, he would not have been shot, so they can readily imagine changes that would lead to other outcomes. But now imagine that on the night in question, both stores had holdups. Now how important was the man's decision about which store to visit as a cause of his being shot? Most people would rate that decision less important, since he might well have been shot no matter where he went on that violent and dangerous evening and since it is harder to imagine events that would undo the harm he experienced.

Direct evidence for such effects has been reported recently by Wells and Gavanski (1989), who asked male and female subjects to read one of two versions of a story involving a handicapped couple. In both versions, the couple phoned for a cab but the driver refused to take them to their destination because he thought their wheelchairs would not fit into the taxi. The couple then took their own car and were involved in a fatal accident in which they drove off a damaged bridge. In one version of the story, the taxi driver was described as having reached the bridge before it was damaged, so that he made it safely across. In the other version, he was described as crashing off the damaged bridge, too.

After reading one version of the story, subjects were asked to rate the extent to which the taxi driver's refusal to take the couple had caused their deaths, and the extent to which the taxi driver should feel responsible for this tragic outcome. It was predicted that when the driver, too, was in an accident, imagining a different event (his agreeing to take the couple) would not change the outcome. In contrast, it was expected that when the driver was not in an accident, imagining that he agreed to take the couple would change the outcome. As a result, subjects would rate his behavior as more causal in the second condition than in the first and would assign more responsibility to him. As shown in Figure 3.9 (p. 104), this was precisely what happened. Subjects rated the driver's behavior as playing more of a role in the couple's tragic end, and the driver as feeling greater responsibility, when he was not portrayed as being in an accident, too, than when he was presented as being in an accident. Since in an absolute sense the driver had no direct role in the couple's tragic end in either case, these findings lend strong support to the view that our reasoning about the causes of various events and outcomes is strongly influenced by counterfactual thinking—by our thoughts about "what might have been."

Mental Simulation and Coincidence: When Are Unlikely Events Viewed as Suspicious? In the opening story of this chapter, we described a situation in which a manager had recommended a woman for promotion over seventeen other members of his department, all of whom were male. Two other persons in his company questioned his motives. After all, they reasoned, it seemed suspicious that the only woman in the group just "happened" to be better than all the males. Indeed, they attributed the manager's recommendation to his desire to comply with affirmative action pressures or—even worse—to his personal liking for the woman in question.

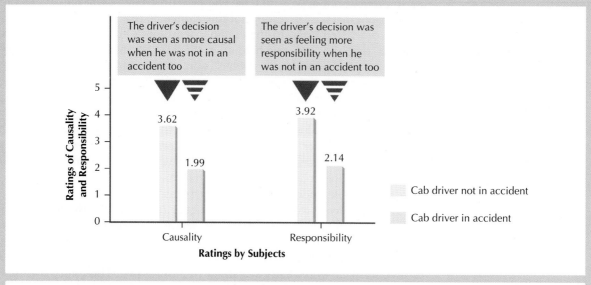

The driver's decision was seen as more causal when he was not in an accident too

The driver's decision was seen as feeling more responsibility when he was not in an accident too

Ratings of Causality and Responsibility

3.62

1.99

3.92

2.14

Causality

Responsibility

Ratings by Subjects

Cab driver not in accident

Cab driver in accident

Counterfactual thinking and causal attributions

FIGURE 3.9 A taxi driver refused to take a disabled couple as fares. As a result, they took their own car and suffered a fatal accident. Subjects were more likely to view the driver's decision as a cause of this tragic event when he was not involved in an accident himself than when he, too, was involved in an accident. This is because it is more difficult to imagine events different from the ones that occurred in the second instance than in the first. These findings point to the important role of *counterfactual thinking* in causal attributions. (Source: Based on data from Wells & Gavanski, 1989.)

If you think about your own life experiences, you will probably realize that such events are far from rare. On many occasions when we encounter an improbable event, we become suspicious about its occurrence. Was it really due to chance? Or were other factors involved? An insightful analysis of such situations has recently been offered by Miller, Turnbull, and McFarland (1989). These researchers suggest that when we encounter unlikely events, we consider the absolute number of ways in which they could have occurred. If these are very low, we become suspicious. If they are somewhat higher, however, we may be more likely to accept them as chance events. In other words, the more easily we can bring similar events to mind, the less suspicious the event in question appears to be. Perhaps a concrete example will help.

Imagine that you have a young child. She asks permission to take a cookie from the cookie jar. The jar contains two types of cookies: chocolate chip and peanut butter. You know that there are only twenty cookies in the jar and that nineteen of them are peanut butter. You also know that your daughter strongly prefers chocolate chip. You are tired of having so many peanut butter cookies left over, and so you tell her to close her eyes when reaching into the cookie jar. She agrees but returns with the chocolate chip cookie anyway. Are you suspicious about her peeking? Absolutely. After all, the odds are greatly in favor of her having selected a peanut butter cookie. Now imagine the same situation with one change: You have a giant cookie jar, containing 200 cookies. Ten are chocolate chip and 190 are peanut butter. Again your daughter returns with a chocolate chip cookie. Are you as suspicious? According to Miller and his colleagues (1989), probably not: Since there are ten chocolate chip cookies, you know that there are ten ways in which she could have selected this type, even with her eyes closed (see Figure 3.10).

All this makes intuitive sense, but as you can see, the probability of choosing a chocolate chip cookie by chance is *precisely the same in both cases*. So, our tendency to become more suspicious in the first case suggests that our thinking in such cases is not entirely rational. We allow our mental simulations—images of various ways in which unlikely events could have occurred—to influence our social judgments.

To obtain direct evidence for the occurrence of such effects, Miller, Turnbull, and McFarland (1989) conducted a study in which subjects were presented with almost precisely the kind of cookie jar problem just described. They learned that the jar contained either one chocolate chip and nineteen oatmeal cookies or ten chocolate chip and 190 oatmeal cookies. As predicted, subjects were much more suspicious that the child had peeked while reaching into the jar in the first condition than in the second. In a follow-up study, Miller and his

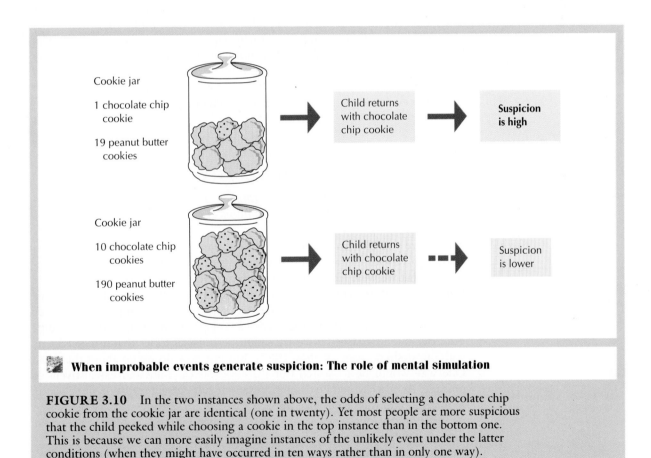

When improbable events generate suspicion: The role of mental simulation

FIGURE 3.10 In the two instances shown above, the odds of selecting a chocolate chip cookie from the cookie jar are identical (one in twenty). Yet most people are more suspicious that the child peeked while choosing a cookie in the top instance than in the bottom one. This is because we can more easily imagine instances of the unlikely event under the latter conditions (when they might have occurred in ten ways rather than in only one way). (Source: Based on suggestions by Miller, Turnbull, & McFarland, 1989.)

colleagues employed a situation similar to the one in this chapter's opening story. Here, subjects were told that a supervisor had either one male and nine females or ten males and ninety females in his department. Yet, he had given the highest marks on an examination used for promotion purposes to a man. Again, subjects reported being more suspicious that the exam was unfair in the one male/nine females condition than in the ten males/ninety females condition. Miller and his colleagues (1989) found similar results in several other studies in which different but conceptually related situations were employed (e.g., one in which the owner of a rental-car company said that only two of his twenty or twenty of his two hundred cars had ever had any mechanical problems; as you can probably guess, subjects reported more suspicion about this claim in the two out of twenty condition).

These findings suggest that people will find it much more difficult to convince others that an improbable event is due to chance under some circumstances than under others. Specifically, they will have an especially difficult time in this respect when there are only a few ways in which the low-probability event could have occurred (e.g., if there is only one chocolate cookie or one man or woman in the department). This may be one reason why individuals who find themselves in such situations tend to become defensive and feel compelled to make such remarks as "No, really—it's just a coincidence!" In this and many other situations, our tendency to engage in mental simulation can have important effects. Indeed, our thoughts about "what might have been" may often be just as important as what actually happened in shaping our subsequent social judgments and decisions. (It is not entirely surprising that we are "cognitive misers" in thinking about others. But what about cases in which we think about ourselves—does the same tendency toward expending the least effort exist? For evidence on this issue, please see **The Cutting Edge** section below.)

FOCUS ON RESEARCH: THE CUTTING EDGE

Implicit Theories about Stability and Change: The Case of Women's Memories of Their Own Menstrual Symptoms

What were you like two months ago? Five years ago? Have you changed with respect to various characteristics, or have you remained quite stable? Remembering what we were like in the past is an important part of social thought. For instance, we try to remember what we were like and how we felt in order to attain insight into our current preferences and views, to compare our former selves with our children or other persons younger than we are, and to manipulate our public images (by constructing personal histories that are consistent with our desired image; Korda, 1987). But just how do we go about this task? One way would be to search our memories as carefully and exhaustively as possible. Another would be to simply examine our current status on dimensions of interest, and then to invoke implicit theories concerning stability or change on those dimensions—views suggesting that change is or is not likely. We could then extrapolate our past selves quite readily by applying such theories.

Given our tendency to act as "cognitive misers," there are convincing reasons for assuming that we often adopt the latter strategy. Are our attitudes today what they were six months ago? Most people assume that attitudes don't change very rapidly, so according to this implicit theory, the answer is easily obtained: yes, probably they were. Are we different in various respects as a result of having undergone some special form of professional training (e.g., medical or law school)? Most people would assume that since such programs are designed to produce change, the answer is again, yes: We *are* different now than we were when we began such training.

Ross (1989) has recently argued quite persuasively for the existence of such implicit theories about stability or change and for their substantial role in the construction of personal histories and personal memories. He has also called attention to the fact that the operation of such implicit theories may result in important forms of memory distortion. Consider a case in which an individual's implicit theory suggests a high degree of stability on some characteristic. If, in fact, there has been considerable change, he or she will tend to exaggerate (overestimate) the similarity between his or her past and present selves. Conversely, if an individual's implicit theory suggests change but little has occurred, the person may underestimate the amount of similarity that actually exists.

As noted by Ross, many findings lend support to the suggestion that we often construct our personal histories with the aid of and in the context of such implicit theories of change or stability. For example, consider a study in which dating couples rated each other on several dimensions on two separate occasions several months apart (McFarland & Ross, 1987). Some students became more favorable toward their partners during this time, while others became less favorable. But since, in general, the students didn't expect much change in this regard, they tended to underestimate these shifts. Specifically, when asked to remember their earlier impressions, they recalled these as more consistent with their current opinions than was actually the case.

Perhaps the most intriguing evidence for the operation of such implicit theories, however, is provided by a study concerned with women's memories of symptoms relating to their menstrual cycle (McFarland, Ross, & DeCourville, 1989). Women in North America generally accept the view that they experience several symptoms with the onset of menstruation (e.g., increased irritability, depression, pain). Given this view, it would be expected that when asked to recall their symptoms at the time of menstruation, many women will overestimate them, because their implicit theory about menstruation suggests the occurrence of pronounced changes in affect and various symptoms during the menstrual cycle. Accordingly, when asked to report their feelings on these kinds of dimensions, women may refer to this theory and so report larger changes (e.g., stronger symptoms) than they actually experienced.

In order to investigate this possibility, McFarland, Ross, and DeCourville asked young women to keep daily diaries in which they reported on their use of several legal drugs, various life events, and their physiological and affective states. (Subjects were *not* told that the study had anything to do with the menstrual cycle.) Separate items in the diaries assessed the presence or absence of various physical symptoms (cramps, headaches, backaches, and weight gain) as well as changes in affect (mood swings, restlessness, irritability, and depression). Subjects also completed a special questionnaire designed to measure their implicit theories concerning the impact of the menstrual cycle. Replies to this questionnaire revealed the extent to which they believed changes in symptoms and mood occurred during the cycle.

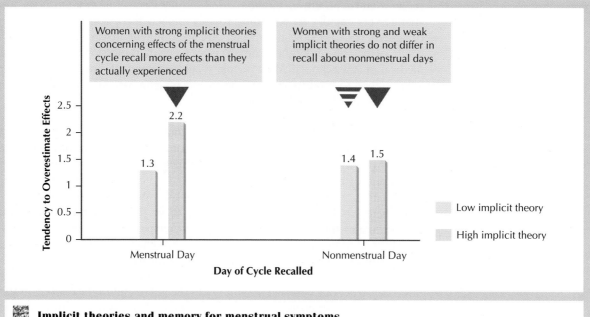

Women with strong implicit theories concerning effects of the menstrual cycle recall more effects than they actually experienced

Women with strong and weak implicit theories do not differ in recall about nonmenstrual days

Low implicit theory

High implicit theory

Implicit theories and memory for menstrual symptoms

FIGURE 3.11 Female subjects kept daily diaries of their moods and physical symptoms throughout their menstrual cycle. Later, they were asked to recall the effects menstruation had on them. Findings suggest that subjects' recall was guided by their implicit theories concerning the effects of menstruation. The stronger they believed such effects to be, the greater subjects' tendency to overestimate menstrual symptoms, relative to their actual diary reports of these effects. (Source: Based on data from McFarland, Ross, & DeCourville, 1989.)

At the end of several weeks, subjects were asked to recall their diary entries for a day either during menstruation or at another point in their cycle. It was hypothesized that for women in the first group, their replies would be guided by their implicit theories about menstruation. Thus, the greater their belief that menstruation had a major impact on them, the greater their tendency to recall more symptoms and negative reactions than they had actually reported. For women asked to recall their diary entries for a day not during menstruation, however, such effects were not expected to occur. After all, implicit theories about menstrual symptoms would not apply to such days. As you can see from Figure 3.11, results supported these predictions, both for self-reported pain and for self-reported negative shifts in mood states.

These findings, as well as those obtained in several other lines of research, suggest that personal memories are indeed often subject to bias stemming from the operation of implicit theories of stability and change. When we try to remember what we were like or how we felt in the past, we often rely on a mental strategy (the use of implicit theories) that saves us considerable cognitive effort. Such benefits, however, may sometimes be offset by the same kind of cost encountered with other mental shortcuts: reduced overall accuracy.

Affect and Cognition: How Thought Shapes Feelings and Feelings Shape Thought

Imagine the following situation: You are sitting in your room studying when your thoughts turn to an experience you had last night in a restaurant. You were there with a group of ten people and when the bill came, you noticed that it seemed quite high. As you reviewed it, you realized that a 15 percent tip had been added to the total. When you discovered this addition, you were somewhat annoyed, since no one had informed you of this policy and you were about to add another 15 percent to the total bill. When you mentioned it to the waiter, he was unsympathetic, saying that you should have known that all "nice" restaurants add a tip for groups of more than six. You told him—in no uncertain terms—that some restaurants do this and others don't and that the policy should be clearly stated on the menu. At this, the waiter made a rude comment and walked off. Now, as you think back over his surly behavior, you feel your pulse quicken. Soon, you are experiencing intense anger all over again.

Situations like this suggest that cognitive processes—our current thoughts, memories we recall (and perhaps ones of which we are not directly conscious [see pages 106–108])—frequently exert strong effects on our emotional states (Isen, 1987). Indeed, such internally generated factors seem to generate emotional reactions that are fully as intense as those produced by external causes (e.g., events we experience, the words or deeds of others). Social psychologists are well aware of such effects, and have devoted careful attention to them. More frequently, however, they have focused on the reverse: the impact of emotions on various aspects of social thought (Fiedler & Forgas, 1988). Since much of this work has addressed the effects of mild, temporary shifts in feelings, rather than those of intense, long-lasting emotions, the term *affect* seems more suitable than the term *emotion* in describing such work (Isen, 1987). Thus, we'll use the former term throughout most of this discussion.

Research on the impact of affect on cognition has yielded many intriguing results (cf. Isen & Baron, 1990). It is now clear that even very mild shifts in people's current feelings can influence many aspects of cognition. Before turning to such evidence, however, we'll first consider several contrasting views about the nature of emotion, and one intriguing explanation for how even mild shifts in affect can produce such effects.

The Nature of Emotion: Contrasting Views and Some Recent Advances

Because feelings are a central part of everyday life, many different views about the nature of emotions have been offered over the centuries. Within psychology, however, three approaches have received the most attention. The first, known as the **Cannon-Bard theory,** is the commonsense perspective. It suggests that when we are exposed to emotion-provoking (eliciting) events or stimuli, we quickly experience both the physiological signs of emotion *and* the subjective feelings we label as fear, anger, joy, and so on. In other words, the two happen concurrently, and both types of reaction stem from the same eliciting events. For example, imagine that one day you switched on the radio and learned that you had won the lottery. Your pulse and blood pressure would soar, and you would be swept by waves of surprise and elation.

In contrast, the **James-Lange theory** proposes that our subjective emotional experiences are actually the *result* of our relatively automatic, physiological reactions to various events. According to this view, we experience anger, fear, joy, or sorrow *because* we become aware of a racing heart, tears streaming down our face, and so on. Returning to the lottery example, the James-Lange theory suggests that you would experience elation *because* you quickly feel (and become aware of) all the physiological signs of this emotion. As James himself noted in another example, if you see a bear while in the woods, you begin to run. Then you experience fear because of the feelings of intense arousal produced by running away.

We have already considered the third view—Schachter's **two-factor theory**—in Chapter 2. As you may recall, that theory suggests that any form of arousal—whatever its source—initiates a search for the causes of such feelings. The causes we then identify play a key role in determining the label we place on our arousal, and so in the emotion we experience. Thus, if we feel aroused in the presence of an attractive person, we may label our arousal as "love" or "attraction." If we feel aroused after a near miss in traffic, we label it as "fear" or perhaps "anger" (toward the other driver, who was clearly at fault!).

Which of these views is most accurate? For many years, evidence seemed to favor the commonsense Cannon-Bard approach. More recently, however, the pendulum has swung in the opposite direction, as growing evidence for some form of the James-Lange theory (and for some aspects of Schachter's theory) has accumulated. Perhaps the most dramatic support for the suggestion that we experience various emotions because of bodily changes is provided by studies that have tested the **facial feedback hypothesis** (e.g., Matsumoto, 1987).

The Facial Feedback Hypothesis: Do We Feel What We Show?   The facial feedback hypothesis suggests that changes in our facial expressions sometimes *produce* changes in our emotional experiences, rather than merely reflecting them. In other words, if we smile, we feel happy; if we frown, we feel sad; and so on (see Figure 3.12). Two versions of this hypothesis exist. The *strong* version suggests that facial expressions are sufficient to induce emotional reactions. In contrast, the *weak* version suggests that facial expressions merely intensify or

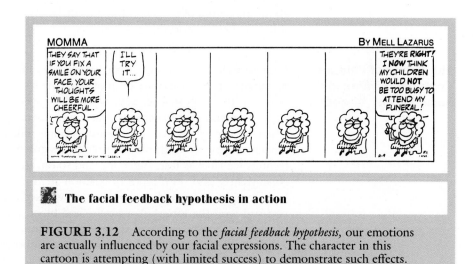

The facial feedback hypothesis in action

FIGURE 3.12   According to the *facial feedback hypothesis,* our emotions are actually influenced by our facial expressions. The character in this cartoon is attempting (with limited success) to demonstrate such effects. (Reprinted by permission of Mell Lazarus and Creators Syndicate, Inc.)

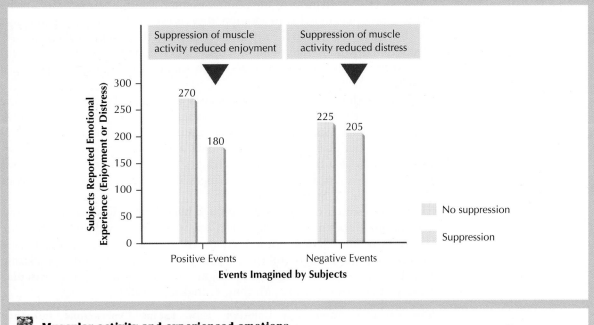

Muscular activity and experienced emotions

FIGURE 3.13 When subjects suppressed tension in muscles normally active during smiling, they reported less enjoyment of positive events they imagined. Similarly, if they suppressed tension in muscles active during frowning, they reported less distress to negative events they imagined. These findings offer some support for the *facial feedback hypothesis*. (Source: McCanne & Anderson, 1987.)

reduce such reactions (Rutledge & Hupka, 1985). While there are many complexities in examining this hypothesis, the results of several studies offer support for its accuracy.

In one such study, McCanne and Anderson (1987) asked female subjects to imagine positive and negative events (e.g., "You inhcrit a million dollars," "You lose a really close friendship"). While imagining these events, subjects were told to either enhance or suppress tension in certain facial muscles. One of these is active when we smile or view happy scenes. The other muscle is the one that is active when we frown or view unhappy scenes. Measurements of electrical activity in both muscles indicated that after a few practice trials, most subjects could carry out this task quite successfully. They could enhance or suppress muscle tension when instructed to do so and, moreover, could do so without any visible change in facial expression.

After imagining each scene, subjects rated their emotional experiences in terms of enjoyment or distress. The researchers reasoned that if the facial feedback hypothesis was correct, subjects' ratings would be affected by their efforts to enhance or suppress muscle tension. For example, if subjects enhanced activity in muscles associated with smiling, they would report more enjoyment of positive events. If they suppressed such activity, they would report less enjoyment. Similarly, if they enhanced tension in muscles associated with frowning, they would report more distress when imagining the unhappy events. Results offered partial support for these predictions. As shown in Figure 3.13, subjects did report less enjoyment of the positive events when they suppressed activity in the appropriate muscles. In addition, they showed a slight tendency to report less distress in response to the negative events when they suppressed the muscles involved in frowning. Interestingly, subjects also reported less ability to imagine and experience scenes of both types when suppressing activity in their facial muscles.

These findings suggest that there may be a substantial grain of truth in the James-Lange theory and modern views related to it (cf. Zajonc, Murphy, & Inglehart, 1989). Subjective emotional experiences do often arise directly in response to specific external stimuli, as the Cannon-Bard view suggests. However, they can also be generated by changes in (and awareness of) our own bodily states—even, it appears, by changes in our current facial expressions (Strack, Martin, & Stepper, 1988).

While research on the facial feedback hypothesis offers support for this contention, it does not by itself explain *how* such effects might occur. In other words, such research does not indicate the mechanism through which changes in facial expressions might influence affective states. Fortunately, this perplexing issue has recently been addressed by Zajonc and his colleagues in the **vascular theory of emotion** (Zajonc, Murphy, & Inglehart, 1989).

The Vascular Theory of Emotion: How Facial Expressions Influence Affect Consider the following phrases: *hotheaded, boiling mad, hot under the collar.* All refer to anger, and all describe it in terms related to temperature: When we are angry, we feel hot. (As we'll note in later chapters, this relationship may operate in the other direction, too: When people are exposed to uncomfortably high temperatures, they often *become* more irritable and aggressive [e.g., Anderson, 1989].) This suggestion of a link between unpleasant warmth and negative emotions raises an intriguing question: Are positive and negative feelings (affect) somehow related to changes in the temperature of the brain? Such a possibility has recently been suggested by Zajonc, Murphy, and Inglehart (1989) in a modern version of the *vascular theory of emotional efference.* (We say "modern" because an early version of this theory was proposed by Waynbaum [1907] more than eighty years ago.)

Zajonc and his colleagues (1989) suggest that changes in facial expressions influence the vascular system of the head—the veins and arteries that serve the brain. Specifically, they propose that facial expressions can enhance or restrict cooling of the venous blood supply of the brain in two ways: mechanically, by pressing on these veins, and indirectly, by regulating the amount of air that enters the nasal cavities and so cools the blood in these veins. Further, they suggest that such changes can produce slight alterations in the temperature of the brain, thereby affecting neurochemical events within it that are related to positive and negative feelings. Small drops in brain temperature are assumed to generate positive feelings; small increases, negative feelings. These predictions are derived from and consistent with several observations. For example, restriction of the nasal passages during common colds restricts the cooling capacity of the nasal passages, and at such times, most people report experiencing considerable discomfort. Similarly, when individuals' noses are packed with gauze during medical procedures, they often report strong negative emotions, including panic (Vig, 1985). Such evidence, however, is indirect and far from convincing. Much more conclusive support for the vascular theory has come from a series of carefully conducted studies by Zajonc and his colleagues (1989).

In one of these investigations, male students were asked to repeat seven different vowel sounds (e.g., *i, e, o, a, ah*) over and over again. While they repeated the sounds, temperature readings at two separate points on their foreheads (points previously found to be related to internal brain temperature) were recorded. After repeating the vowels, subjects were asked to rate their liking for them and to indicate whether saying these vowels put them in a good or a bad mood. Results were striking. A vowel sound known to restrict the entry of air into the nasal passages (*u*, a sound common in German but not in English) raised forehead temperature and also received the most negative ratings. In contrast, two vowels known to expand air access to the nasal passages (*e* and *ah*) lowered forehead temperature and received the most positive evaluations.

In an even more provocative study, Zajonc and his colleagues (1989) asked subjects to breathe air that was either at room temperature (22.2°C; approximately 72°F), relatively warm (32.2°C; approximately 90°F), or relatively cool (18.9°C; approximately 66°F). Subjects were told that the air they breathed contained mild scents and that their task was to rate these scents. In fact, only the room-temperature air contained any scent. (A mild odor of the spice oregano was introduced in this condition.) Subjects' forehead temperatures were measured as they sniffed the air. Subjects then rated the supposed scents on several dimensions (liking, familiarity, pleasantness). Results again offered support for the vascular theory. As expected, the warm air raised forehead temperature and the cool air reduced it. More importantly, subjects reported liking the cool, scentless air more than they liked the warm, scentless air. The air containing a mild aroma of oregano was rated in between (refer to Figure 3.14).

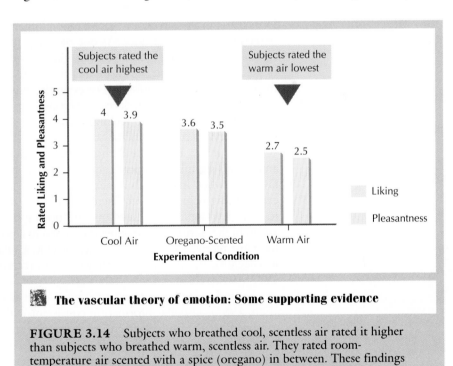

The vascular theory of emotion: Some supporting evidence

FIGURE 3.14 Subjects who breathed cool, scentless air rated it higher than subjects who breathed warm, scentless air. They rated room-temperature air scented with a spice (oregano) in between. These findings offer support for the *vascular theory of emotion*. (Source: Based on data from Zajonc, Murphy, & Inglehart, 1989.)

Together, these and other findings reported by Zajonc, Murphy, and Inglehart (1989) offer support for the vascular theory of motor efference. This theory in turn suggests a mechanism through which facial expressions may influence affective states. Apparently, several expressions can change the temperature of the blood supply serving the brain and so the temperature of the brain itself. These shifts then seem to influence neurochemical events that play a role in the occurrence of positive and negative feelings. We should hasten to add that many details remain to be determined and that the data reported by Zajonc and his colleagues, valuable as they are, should certainly not be viewed as definitive. On the contrary, additional evidence is clearly needed before this theory can be accepted as verified. Further, there is no suggestion in the vascular theory that changes in brain temperature are the only—or even the most important—source of positive and negative affect.

Such reservations aside, the vascular theory does offer some intriguing benefits. For example, it helps explain why (as noted in Chapter 2) facial expressions are so universal in form and meaning around the globe. If such expressions are linked to affective states through shifts in brain temperature and associated neurochemical events, it would be surprising if they were *not* universal. The human brain, after all, operates in the same fashion everywhere, and neurochemistry is largely impervious to limits of culture and language.

In sum, the vascular theory suggests that crucial, if subtle, links exist between face and brain. Certainly, our facial expressions often reflect our current emotions and affective states. However, the relationship may operate in the other direction as well, so that what we feel really *is* influenced by the expressions we show to the outside world.

How Affect Influences Cognition

Does being in a positive or negative mood influence the way we think? Informal observation suggests it does. As one old song puts it, when we are happy "we see the world through rose-colored glasses"—everything takes on a positive tinge. And most people are aware that they think differently when feeling happy than when they feel depressed. For example, when we are experiencing positive feelings (affect), difficult tasks or situations seem easier to handle than when we are experiencing negative feelings. Are these subjective impressions correct? Growing evidence suggests they are.

First, it has been found that affective states influence the perception of ambiguous stimuli. In general, such stimuli are perceived (and evaluated) more favorably when individuals are experiencing positive affect than when they are experiencing negative affect (Isen & Shalker, 1982). For example, when asked to interview applicants whose qualifications for a job are ambiguous, subjects assign higher ratings to these persons when in a positive mood (e.g., when they have just received favorable feedback or won a small prize) than when they are in a negative mood (e.g., when they have just received negative feedback; Baron, 1987, 1990).

Second, positive and negative affect exert a strong influence on memory (Isen, 1987). Usually, information consistent with our current moods is easier to remember than information inconsistent with it. Moreover, mood seems to exert such effects both at the time of *encoding* (when information is first entered into memory) and at the time of *retrieval* (when such information is recalled). Such effects are clearly illustrated by a study conducted by Forgas and Bower (1987).

In this investigation, subjects were first induced to experience positive or negative affect through feedback about their performance on a test supposedly assessing their personality and level of social adjustment. Subjects in the positive-mood condition were told that their scores were much better than average (i.e., that their scores were higher than average on social adjustment). In contrast, those in the negative-mood condition were told that their scores were much poorer than average. Subjects in both groups then read realistic descriptions of four persons. These descriptions related to the imaginary persons' likableness and competence. Equal amounts of positive and negative information were supplied about each character. (An example of a positive statement: "In grade school Bob was always very good at sports." An example of a negative statement: "Cindy is short and very plain looking.")

After reading these descriptions, subjects rated the stimulus persons on several dimensions (e.g., intelligent–unintelligent, happy–unhappy, hard to work with–good to work with). In addition, they were then asked to recall and write down everything they could remember about each of the four characters. Not surprisingly, subjects who were in a good mood reported more favorable impressions of the four characters than those who were in a negative mood. In addition, it was found that subjects were better at remembering information consistent with their mood at the time they read about the four persons than they were at remembering information inconsistent with this mood. Why is this the case? One possibility is that it is easier to form associations with information that is consistent with our current moods than with information that is inconsistent with these affective states. Then, when we try to recall both types of information, the former is more readily accessible in our memory (Isen, 1987). Whatever the precise mechanism, there seems little doubt that mood-consistent information is easier to remember than mood-inconsistent information, at least among adults. (Recent findings suggest that the same effects may not occur among children, perhaps because their cognitive capacities are quite different from those of adults; Forgas, Burnham, and Trimboli, 1988.)

Positive and negative affect have also been found to influence the way in which information is organized in memory. People experiencing positive affect seem to include a wider range of information within various memory categories than those in a neutral or negative mood (Isen & Daubman, 1984). People experiencing positive affect provide more unusual associates to neutral words and rate objects that are not very typical of a given category as more representative of it than people who are not in a positive mood. (For example, the former rate the word *elevator* as more typical of the category *vehicle* than the latter do; Isen et al., 1985.)

Finally, there is some indication that people in a good mood are more creative. At least, they are more successful in performing tasks involving creative problem solving (searching for novel approaches, exploring new uses for familiar objects) than people in a neutral mood (Isen, Daubman, & Nowicki, 1987).

One cautionary note: In most of the research described here, it has been found that positive affect exerts a stronger, more consistent influence on cognitive processes than negative affect. This finding may derive from the fact that when people experience negative feelings, they quickly engage in strategies designed to help alleviate such feelings. Thus, efforts to put people in a negative mood have weaker, more temporary effects than ones designed to put them in a positive mood. If so, then it might be suggested that negative affect is equal to positive affect in terms of its impact on cognition and that it is simply difficult to demonstrate this fact under laboratory conditions. However, the results of an ingenious field study conducted by Forgas and Moylan (1987) argue strongly against this conclusion.

These researchers approached individuals leaving movie theaters in a large city and asked them to indicate their views on a wide range of issues (e.g., their satisfaction with two prominent politicians; the likelihood of various future events, such as the future performance of the economy; the severity of punishment for various crimes). In addition, subjects were asked to rate their satisfaction with their private, social, and working lives and their current mood. Subjects were approached after viewing one of three types of films: happy films (e.g., *Back to the Future*), sad films (e.g., *Killing Fields*), and aggressive films (e.g., *Rambo*). Thus, they were expected to be in contrasting affective states as a result of this recent experience. Subjects in a control group were approached on their way into the theaters, before they had seen any movie.

As anticipated, subjects reported being in a more positive mood after seeing a happy movie than after a sad or aggressive one. In addition, these differences were reflected in their responses to most of the questions asked. Subjects who had seen happy movies rated political leaders more positively, reported more optimism about future events, and recorded more satisfaction with their own lives than those who had seen the sad or aggressive movies. Further (and also consistent with predictions), subjects who had seen the sad or aggressive movies supported stronger punishments for various crimes than those who had seen the happy movies. Finally, and most germane to the question of whether positive affect and negative affect differ in their impact, effects of seeing the happy movies were generally stronger than those of seeing the sad or aggressive movies. Relative to the control group (who had not yet seen any of the films), the happy movies produced strong, positive shifts in subjects' judgments and views. The effects produced by the sad or aggressive movies were considerably weaker (see Figure 3.15). Thus, it appears that even under these realistic conditions and following exposure to movies that induced strong shifts in current moods, positive affect exerted stronger effects than negative affect.

In sum, existing evidence suggests that even relatively mild shifts in affect can exert significant effects on many aspects of cognition—including ones related to important forms of social judgment (see Chapter 15 for further discussion of this topic). Clearly, we are still a long way from a full understanding of the complex interplay between affect and cognition. The evidence already at our disposal, though, points firmly to the following conclusion: Efforts to develop comprehensive knowledge of one cannot reasonably proceed without efforts to develop corresponding knowledge of the other.

How Cognition Influences Affect

Most research on the relationship between affect and cognition has focused on how feelings influence thought. However, there is also compelling evidence for the reverse—the impact of cognition on affect. We have already mentioned one aspect of this relationship in discussing the theories proposed by Schachter and Bem (see Chapter 2). As you may recall, both these theories suggest that often, we don't know our own feelings or attitudes directly. Rather, since these internal reactions are often ambiguous, we must look outward—at our own behavior or other aspects of the external world—for clues about their essential nature. In

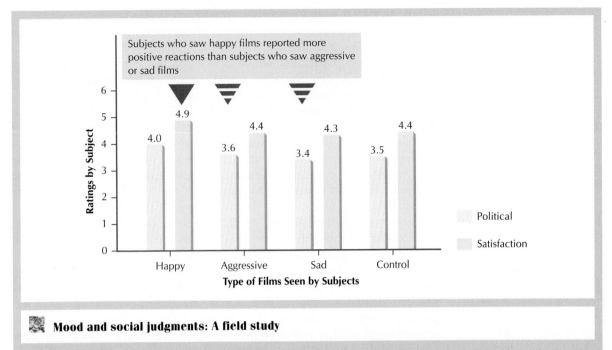

Subjects who saw happy films reported more positive reactions than subjects who saw aggressive or sad films

Mood and social judgments: A field study

FIGURE 3.15 Persons leaving movie theaters who had just seen happy movies reported more positive feelings about a wide range of issues (e.g., political leaders, future events) and greater satisfaction with their own lives than persons who had just seen sad or aggressive movies. In addition, comparisons with a control group (people about to enter theaters, who had not yet seen any movie) suggested that the happy films had much stronger effects on subjects' moods than the sad or aggressive films. (Source: Based on data from Forgas & Moylan, 1987.)

such cases, the emotions or feelings we experience are strongly determined by the interpretation or cognitive labels we select.

A second way in which cognition can affect emotions is through the activation of schemas containing a strong affective component. For example, if we label an individual as belonging to some group, the schema for this social category may suggest what traits he or she probably possesses. In addition, it may also tell us how we *feel* about such persons. Thus, activation of a strong racial, ethnic, or religious schema or *stereotype* may exert powerful effects on our current feelings or moods (please see our discussion of stereotypes in Chapter 5).

Third, our thoughts can often influence our reactions to emotion-provoking events by causing us to interpret or appraise them in various ways. For example, imagine that while you are standing in line outside a theater, a woman bumps up against you. Will you react with anger? This depends strongly on your interpretation of her act. If you conclude that she is trying to push ahead of you, the chances are good that you will become angry and perhaps push back. If, instead, you conclude that she merely tripped over an irregularity in the sidewalk, you probably won't experience such feelings or take defensive action. As we'll note in Chapter 10, growing evidence suggests that our interpretations of provocative actions by others often play a key role in our emotional reactions and in our tendencies to behave aggressively (Zillmann, 1988).

Finally, an important link between cognition and affect or emotion is suggested by our reactions in situations where we try our best to suppress exciting thoughts. Such instances are far from rare; most people have had the experience of trying to push an amusing thought or image from their minds in a situation where humor and overt laughter are inappropriate (e.g., during an important meeting or at a sad gathering such as a funeral). What happens when we attempt to suppress such emotion-laden thoughts? As you probably know from your own experience, the result is uncertain, to say the least. Sometimes we succeed in suppressing such thoughts. On many occasions, however, the more we try to avoid thinking about them, the more strongly they force their way into consciousness—with predictable results! Moreover, even if we succeed in suppressing exciting thoughts initially, they have an annoying habit of reappearing later and arousing our emotions all over again.

Evidence for precisely such effects has recently been reported by Wegner, Shortt, Blake, and Page (1990). These researchers asked male and female students to alternately suppress and express thoughts about sex and three less exciting topics (e.g., dancing, their mother, a Dean at their college). While subjects suppressed or expressed their thoughts about these topics, a measure of their level of arousal (skin conductance) was obtained. Thus, the effects of trying to suppress exciting thoughts could be assessed in this manner. As shown in Figure 3.16, subjects were not successful in controlling their thoughts or their own arousal. Whether they expressed their thoughts about sex or tried not to think about this topic, their arousal was higher than it was during a base-level period when they were free to think about anything they wished. (Not surprisingly, subjects showed little arousal when expressing or suppressing thoughts about any of the other topics.) In follow-up studies, Wegner and his colleagues found that while subjects were not successful in suppressing thoughts about sex initially, they improved at this task so that after only a few minutes, they managed to reduce their level of arousal to that of the baseline period. However, with the passage of time, exciting thoughts about sex returned, and increased emotional arousal once again.

Together, these findings suggest that trying to avoid thoughts about an exciting topic may not be a very effective strategy. In fact, efforts to do so may set up a cycle in which the exciting thoughts become even more provocative as a result of being suppressed. This increases the strength of the motive to suppress them, so that soon the reactions evoked become highly intense. Thoughts about an illicit lover or unwanted habits such as smoking or drinking seem to provide clear examples of this process. Trying *not* to think about such matters may simply add to the emotion they evoke until, finally, the persons involved can think about little else! In such cases, certainly, the link between cognition and affect or emotion may be much deeper and more profound than many of us would initially predict.

In sum, there can be little doubt that cognition often does strongly influence affect. What we think can indeed sometimes determine what we feel. (For additional evidence concerning the impact of cognition on affect, please see the following **The Cutting Edge** section.)

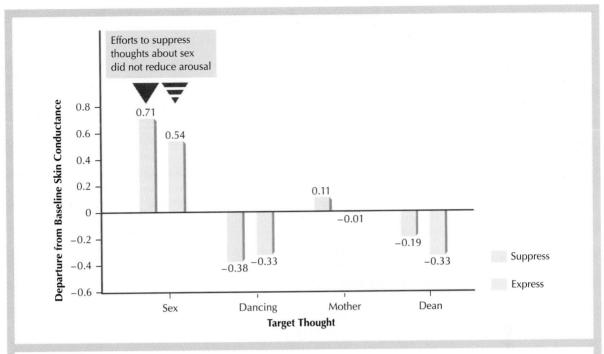

Efforts to suppress thoughts about sex did not reduce arousal

Trying to suppress exciting thoughts: Evidence that it's not very successful

FIGURE 3.16 When subjects tried to suppress thoughts about sex, their level of arousal (as measured by skin conductance) was as much above base level as it was when they were told to freely express such thoughts. These findings suggest that trying to suppress thoughts about an exciting topic is not usually a very effective strategy. Indeed, efforts along these lines may sometimes actually increase rather than reduce emotional arousal. (Source: Based on data from Wegner et al., 1990.)

FOCUS ON RESEARCH: THE CUTTING EDGE

Do We Feel What We Expect to Feel? The Impact of Expectations on Affective Experiences

Several of your friends have raved about a new television show. They claim it is the funniest program they have seen in years. Since you usually agree with your friends, you decide to give it a try. Will you find it funnier and like it more because you expect to have such reactions? In other words, can your expectations about some event influence your affective reactions to it? If so, this would provide strong evidence for the impact of one aspect of cognition on affect. In fact, convincing evidence for precisely such effects has recently been provided by Wilson and his colleagues (Wilson et al., 1989). They reasoned that often when people hold expectations about how they will react to a new event or stimulus, these expectations will shape their perceptions (and their feelings). Thus, for example, if people expect to like an event, they *will*, even if they might not like it in the absence of such expectations. In other words, if a discrepancy exists between the value of the stimulus and individuals' expectations, the expectations will often dominate and shape their affective reactions. Indeed, they may not even notice that the discrepancy exists. Only if this gap between expectations and reality is quite large will people recognize it and adjust their affect accordingly.

To investigate these suggestions, Wilson and his colleagues exposed subjects to three cartoons known, on the basis of raters' reactions, to be quite funny. After seeing these cartoons, subjects viewed three others that were known to be much less amusing. Before seeing the cartoons, one group of subjects (the *expect-to-like* group) was told that they were lucky—the cartoons they had chosen (ostensibly by choosing one pile of slides from among others)—were ones previous subjects had found to be very funny. Those in another condition, in contrast, were not given any expectations about the cartoons (the *no-expectation* group). While subjects watched the cartoons, their facial expressions were videotaped. These tapes were later shown to judges who rated the amount of mirth they showed while watching each cartoon. In addition, subjects rated each cartoon on a scale ranging from "not at all funny" to "extremely funny." The amount of time they took to evaluate each cartoon was also measured.

Wilson and his colleagues predicted that subjects in the expect-to-like condition would rate the second three cartoons (the ones that were not very funny)

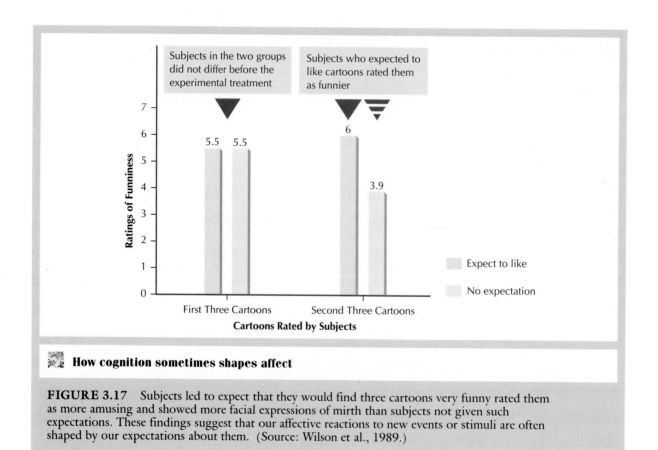

How cognition sometimes shapes affect

FIGURE 3.17 Subjects led to expect that they would find three cartoons very funny rated them as more amusing and showed more facial expressions of mirth than subjects not given such expectations. These findings suggest that our affective reactions to new events or stimuli are often shaped by our expectations about them. (Source: Wilson et al., 1989.)

as funnier and would show more facial expressions of mirth while viewing them than subjects in the no-expectation condition. In addition, the researchers predicted that subjects in the expect-to-like condition would spend less time examining the second three (nonfunny) cartoons than those in the no-expectation condition. This would be the case because, given their clear expectations, they would already "know" their feelings about these cartoons and feel little need to consider them with care. As shown in Figure 3.17, results offered clear support for these predictions.

These findings suggest that in many instances, our reactions to new events or stimuli are strongly determined by our expectations about them—a notion that offers both advantages and disadvantages. On the plus side, there is a substantial saving in cognitive effort. After all, if we "know" how we will react to a new situation, it's not necessary to evaluate it or our affective reactions very carefully. On the negative side, however, we may find it difficult to recognize that various experiences don't quite fit our expectations. For example, it may take us longer to realize that we really like (or don't like) something (or someone) than would otherwise be the case. Thus, as is true of virtually all the strategies we adopt as "cognitive misers," gains in efficiency must be carefully weighed against potential costs in terms of errors and inaccuracy. The fact that we often get what we expect in terms of affective reactions, therefore, is definitely something of a mixed blessing.

The Self: What We Are . . . and What We Might Be

Who are you? When confronted with this question, many people's first tendency is to answer, "Why, *me,* of course!" Alternatively, they reply with their name: "I'm Bob—who did you think?" Whatever the reply, this simple question—and our reactions to it—calls attention to the fact that we spend a great deal of time and effort thinking about the object that is, in an important respect, the very center of our social universe: *ourselves.* As we noted in Chapter 2 (in our discussion of self-perception), such thinking is closely related to other forms of social thought. The key difference, though, is that now it is *us* rather than other persons who are the focus of attention and the subject of careful scrutiny. Because of this and because we acquire our self-identity, or **self-concept,** primarily through social interaction with others, the **self** has long been a topic of primary interest in social psychology (cf. Higgins, 1987; Markus & Wurf, 1987; Suls & Greenwald, 1986). In this final section, we'll review current knowledge about the self, primarily from the perspective of social cognition. In other words, we'll focus on the self as a special type of cognitive framework, one that strongly influences our processing of social information (e.g., Klein, Loftus, & Burton, 1989), our motivation, our affective states, and even our emotional well-being (cf. Van Hook & Higgins, 1988).

Defining the Self: A Schema-Based View

Suppose you were asked to describe your current self-concept; what kind of information would you provide? Most people would answer by describing their physical appearance, listing their major traits, and explaining their central goals and motives. Some would go on to provide specific examples or evidence for these characteristics. And some, at least, might call attention to disparities between the way they are at present and what they would like to become. In short, for most people, the self-concept is a complex collection of highly diverse information. Yet somehow it is all held together. We don't, after all, think of ourselves as consisting of separate pieces; rather, we view ourselves as relatively unified human beings. What is the "glue" that holds this information together? What allows us to combine so much diversity into a fairly unified self-image? According to social psychologists who have studied this issue in detail, the answer lies in a concept known as the **schema** (Markus, 1977).

Schemas are cognitive frameworks—organized collections of information about some object. (The term *object* can refer to virtually anything—other people, their traits, physical objects, issues, or even ourselves.) Such frameworks are developed through experience and, once they exist, exert powerful effects on the processing of information related to them. For example, they determine which stimuli are selected for attention, which stimuli are remembered, and what kinds of inferences are drawn about them (e.g., Greenwald & Pratkanis, 1984; Higgins & Bargh, 1987). The direction of such effects is not always easy to predict. For instance, some evidence suggests that information *consistent* with schemas is easier to remember than information inconsistent with them (e.g., Bodenhausen & Lichtenstein, 1987), while other findings point to the opposite conclusion: information *inconsistent* with existing schemas is easier to recall (Hastie & Kumar, 1979). Which effect is more accurate? Recent evidence suggests that both may occur but that which one is more likely depends on the stage of development of a given schema (cf. Stangor & Ruble, 1989). Early in the process, when a schema is first being formed, information inconsistent with it may be easier to notice and remember. Once the schema is fully developed, however, it exerts powerful effects on perception, so that such information is largely ignored. Then, information consistent with the schema tends to have an important edge in terms of processing, and the schema grows stronger and stronger (refer to Figure 3.18). As we'll note in Chapter 5, this process may play a key role in persistent forms of prejudice.

Schemas, then, can be viewed as *mental scaffolds*—existing cognitive structures that give form and shape to our thoughts and to new social information. By providing such structure, they assist us in making sense out of a potentially confusing social world. However, schemas can also act as self-confirming filters, ensuring that we interpret the world in certain ways and that our thoughts run along certain well-defined channels.

Now, to return to our main point: what role do schemas play with respect to the self? According to many experts, self-knowledge is organized into the kinds of cognitive frameworks we have been discussing. In other words, the self can be viewed as a special type of schema—a **self-schema** (Markus, 1977; Markus & Nurius, 1986). Specifically, the self is a cognitive framework that organizes and guides the processing of information related to ourselves. Self-schemas reflect all our past self-relevant experiences, all knowledge and memories we have about ourselves, and all information about what we were like in the past, what we are like now, and what we may be like in the future. In a sense, they are the sum of everything we know or can imagine about ourselves.

Origins of the Self-Concept: The Role of Social Input

As we have just noted, our self-concept reflects the sum of all our self-relevant experience. But what experiences, specifically, are most crucial in shaping this knowledge about ourselves and our major characteristics? While many contrasting views about the self have been proposed, there is general agreement on one

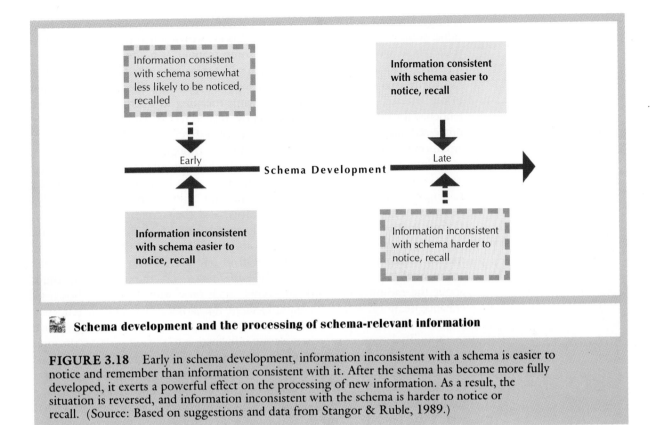

Schema development and the processing of schema-relevant information

FIGURE 3.18 Early in schema development, information inconsistent with a schema is easier to notice and remember than information consistent with it. After the schema has become more fully developed, it exerts a powerful effect on the processing of new information. As a result, the situation is reversed, and information inconsistent with the schema is harder to notice or recall. (Source: Based on suggestions and data from Stangor & Ruble, 1989.)

key point: the self-concept emerges primarily from information provided by other people—that is, from *social input.*

Writing more than a hundred years ago, William James (1890) noted that without the feedback and evaluations provided by other persons, we would, in a sense, cease to have a personal identity. Similarly, Charles Cooley (1964) and other sociologists have employed the phrase *the looking-glass self* to emphasize that to a large extent, our self-concept is a reflection of information provided by the persons around us. Of course, not everyone we meet has an equal impact on our self-concept. Only those whose reactions and evaluations are important to us can shape our conceptions of ourselves in this manner. Thus, while strangers or casual acquaintances may have little impact on our self-concept, close friends, members of our families, respected teachers, and many other persons can and do mold our ideas about who and what we are.

In sum, the self-concept is truly the result of a continuing social process. In our own eyes, it seems, we are largely what other people perceive us to be.

Cognitive Effects of the Self: The Self-Reference Effect

If the self is the center of our social universe and if we possess well-developed self-schemas, a straightforward prediction follows: We should be more efficient in processing information that is somehow relevant to ourselves than information that is irrelevant. Self-relevant information should be more likely than other information to become the center of our attention, to be entered into memory, and to be easily recalled. Is this actually the case? Several studies suggest that it

THE SELF

is (e.g., Higgins & Bargh, 1987; Kuiper & Rogers, 1979). In these investigations, subjects found it easier to recall various words when they were asked to relate these words to themselves in some manner (e.g., by considering the question, "Does it describe you?") than when they were asked to perform other tasks unrelated to the self (e.g., to answer the question, "Is this word printed in big letters?" or "Does it have the same meaning as another word?"). This tendency for information that is somehow related to the self to be more readily processed and remembered is known as the **self-reference effect,** and it calls attention to the importance of the self in social thought.

While existence of the self-reference effect is certainly interesting, a related issue is also worth considering. Why, precisely, does it occur? What is it about relating information to the self that enhances our ability to process it effectively? A series of experiments by Klein, Loftus, and their colleagues (e.g., Klein, Loftus, & Burton, 1989) have offered valuable insights in this respect. In one especially revealing study, Klein and Loftus (1988) reasoned that relating information to the self might aid later recall in one of two ways. First, it might enhance what psychologists term *elaborative processing*—the tendency to think about the meaning of words or events. Such processing has been shown to enhance memory. Second, it might facilitate *categorical processing*—the tendency to place stimuli in specific categories. This, too, has been shown to improve memory. To determine whether relating information to the self operates through either (or both) of these mechanisms, Klein and Loftus presented three different groups of subjects with thirty words. The first group was told to think of a definition for each word (the *elaborative-processing* task). The second group was told to place each word under one of five categories (e.g., things associated with a day by the sea, things associated with parties—the *categorization* task). Finally, subjects in a third group were asked to indicate whether each word brought to mind an important personal experience (the *self-reference* group). The words on each list were either related to one another or unrelated. (Examples of related words: *Canada, Mexico* [countries], *jazz, opera* [music]. Examples of unrelated words: *aspirin, gym, library, boat*.) After completing one of the three tasks, subjects were given an unexpected recall task: They were asked to write down as many of the words as they could remember.

Klein and Loftus predicted that for the unrelated words, the categorical-processing task would be especially helpful for memory, because in the absence of such processing, relations between the words would not be readily apparent. In contrast, for the related words, the elaborative-processing task was predicted to be helpful. Here, subjects would recognize the relationships between the words so that thinking about their definitions would provide something "extra" not already built into the list. Klein and Loftus further reasoned that if the self-reference effect stems mainly from elaborative processing, the self-reference task should have the same effects as the elaborative task (i.e., it would enhance performance on the list of related words). However, if the self-reference effect stems mainly from categorical processing, the self-reference task should have the same effect as the categorical-processing task. Results were clear: The self-reference task had both types of effects. For the unrelated words, it produced levels of performance equal to those of the categorization task, while for the related words, it produced levels of performance equal to those of the elaborative-processing task. In sum, our ability to process information related to the self more readily than we process other information seems to derive from the

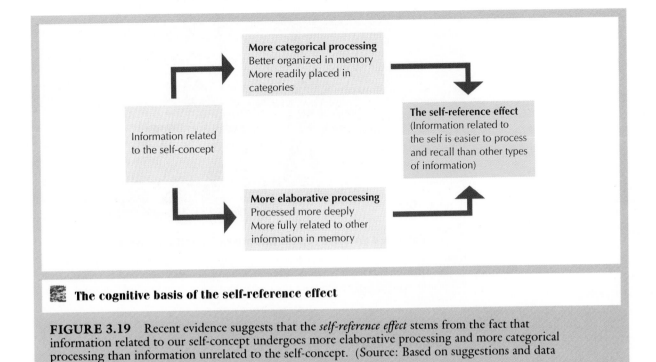

The cognitive basis of the self-reference effect

FIGURE 3.19 Recent evidence suggests that the *self-reference effect* stems from the fact that information related to our self-concept undergoes more elaborative processing and more categorical processing than information unrelated to the self-concept. (Source: Based on suggestions and data from Klein & Loftus, 1988.)

operation of two powerful mechanisms. We think about such information more deeply than we do other information, and we categorize it more effectively. Little wonder, then, that the self-reference effect occurs; indeed, it would be surprising if it did not (see Figure 3.19).

Possible Selves: Our Many Potential "Me's"

When people speak about their self, they often describe it in static terms. "This is me," they seem to say, "so don't expect anything different." Yet while they imply that the self is unchanging, most people also realize that they are quite capable of change. They understand that they are different today, in some respects, from what they were like in the past, and they recognize that they may well change again in the future. Indeed, it is the rare individual who has not daydreamed, at some time, about various possible selves—what she or he might be like under other circumstances, how she or he might change by getting married or divorced, entering another career, or moving to another country. In short, we do not seem to possess only a single, unchanging self. Rather, we are all somewhat aware of a whole succession of **possible selves** as well.

This fact has been eloquently emphasized by Markus and her colleagues (e.g., Markus & Nurius, 1986). Markus contends that the self-concept we possess at any given time is really only a *working self-concept,* one open to change as we encounter new experiences and receive an unending array of feedback and other forms of information about ourselves. In addition, of course, we can—and frequently do—imagine alternative selves: the self we would like to become (e.g., slimmer, more attractive, more accomplished; see Figure 3.20, p. 126), the self we would not like to become (e.g., plumper, less attractive, locked into

Enhanced possible selves: Incentives for self-improvement

FIGURE 3.20 One reason individuals engage in various efforts at self-improvement is that they can imagine alternate—and improved—possible selves.

a dead-end job). And we often ponder *ideal selves* (what, ideally, we should be like) and *ought selves* (what, in the eyes of others or according to social norms, we should be).

Do such possible selves have any significance? According to Markus and Nurius (1986), they do. First, they can play an important role in our motivation. One reason individuals are motivated to work long and hard for various goals is that they can conceive of themselves as reaching them. They can envision themselves as college graduates, physicians, attorneys, scientists, successful entrepreneurs, proud parents, and so on. If individuals cannot imagine themselves in these states, there is little reason to strive for them. In short, possible selves may serve as *incentives*—goals toward which individuals strive. In this manner, they may play a key role in human motivation.

Second, possible selves help account for the frequent lack of agreement between individuals' self-perceptions and how they are viewed by others. In other words, individuals may see themselves as possessing certain traits while others do not share this view. Such discrepancies may arise, at least in part, because outside observers cannot take into account individuals' possible selves. Individuals see themselves in terms of what they would like to be and are—they hope—becoming. The persons around them, however, can only see behavior related to the current self; hence, a pronounced gap in social perceptions may develop.

Third, possible selves influence our affective states. Discrepancies between what we would like to be and our current state can be quite painful and indeed can lead to considerable emotional turmoil (Van Hook & Higgins, 1988). Moreover, imagining a positive or negative possible self may elicit strong emotions directly, as we consider the benefits or costs associated with these potential selves.

Finally, the nature of a person's repertoire of possible selves can be a significant source of individual differences. In this context, optimists are those who see mainly positive changes in the self ahead: They, like the external world, will get better. Pessimists, in contrast, are those who extrapolate current shortcomings into the future and predict further negative changes relating to their self-concept.

Perhaps the value of the concept of possible selves is best illustrated by a concrete piece of research. In one such study, Porter, Markus, and Nurius (1984) asked thirty victims of a major life crisis (e.g., the death of a loved one) to describe their current and future possible selves. Some of the subjects indicated that they had largely recovered from their life crisis, while others indicated that they had not. The current self-concepts of these two groups did not differ: Both reported that they were currently fearful, resentful, depressed, and not in control. However, when the possible selves described by these individuals were compared, striking differences emerged. Those who reported being largely recovered described their future possible selves in much more positive terms than those who reported little progress. For example, the recovered subjects described possible selves that were happy, had lots of friends, were confident and secure, and were optimists. The poor-recovery group, in contrast, reported future selves that would be unpopular, unimportant, weak, unable to fit in, depressed, and failures. Clearly, in this case, examining possible selves as well as current ones provided valuable added information about the subjects.

In sum, the notion that we possess many possible selves rather than a single, unchanging self-concept is an intriguing one. It provides new insights into the nature of the self and helps clarify its relationship to motivation, affect, and overt behavior. Realizing that individuals have many possible selves in addition to their current working self-concepts certainly complicates the picture somewhat. Still, this realization captures the richness of human experience with respect to the self more fully than earlier, static conceptions. On this basis alone, the idea is certain to be the focus of considerable research attention in the years ahead. (Do self-concepts differ from one nation to another? For evidence on this issue, please see the **Multicultural Perspective** section below.)

SOCIAL PSYCHOLOGY: A MULTICULTURAL PERSPECTIVE

Self-Concepts in Japan and the United States: The Role of Cultural Context in Descriptions of the Self

During the nineteenth century it was widely assumed that the cultures of "the East" (Asia) and "the West" (Europe) were so different that, in certain respects, they were separated by a permanent, unbridgeable gap. While this extreme (and somewhat pessimistic) view no longer holds sway, it is clear, even today, that Eastern and Western nations do indeed differ profoundly with respect to values, beliefs, and customs (Bond and Tak-sing, 1983). Some of these differences are directly relevant to our current discussion of the self. It has frequently been contended, for example, that Eastern and Western cultures differ with respect to their location on a dimension ranging from *individualistic* at one end to *collectivistic* at the other (Triandis, 1989). Individualistic societies, such as those in Europe and the United States, emphasize the importance of individual goals and stress the uniqueness of individuals with respect to many traits and characteristics. Collectivistic societies, in contrast, emphasize the importance of group goals and pay less attention to individual differences in terms of traits. Applying this difference to the self-concept, it has been suggested that persons from many Eastern cultures show less tendency to differentiate themselves clearly from others—less tendency to search for the unique differences that are so important to many persons in the West. Is this actually the case? A recent study carried out by Cousins (1989) suggests that this is not really so.

In his study, Cousins asked students in the United States and Japan to complete a questionnaire designed to assess the self-concept. One version of the questionnaire merely asked respondents to answer the question, "Who am I?" by filling in twenty blanks. Another version, however, asked subjects to describe themselves in various contexts (e.g., at home, at school, with close friends). Cousins predicted that when given the first, no-context form of the question-

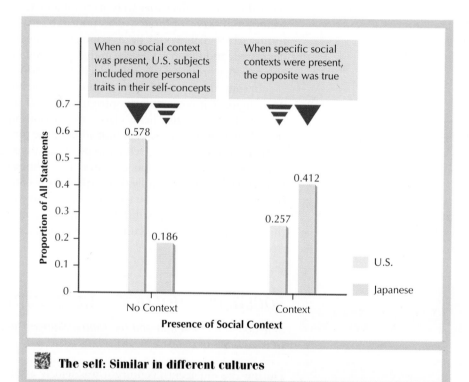

The self: Similar in different cultures

FIGURE 3.21 When asked "Who am I?" without any accompanying social context, students in the United States described themselves in terms of personal attributes to a greater extent than students in Japan. However, when the students were asked the same question with respect to specific social contexts (e.g., "Who am I at home . . . at school . . . with close friends . . ."), such differences disappeared. These findings suggest that persons in both countries possess equally rich and well-developed self-concepts. Because of cultural factors, however, they answer questions about self-concept differently. (Source: Based on data from Cousins, 1989.)

naire, Japanese students would indeed describe themselves in more concrete terms than Americans. For example, the Japanese students were expected to refer more to their physical appearance and their social roles but to mention abstract traits less frequently. This would be the case because in Japanese culture, individuals are seen (more clearly than in U.S. culture) as tied closely to a network of social relationships and contexts; they are not viewed (as in the United States) primarily from the standpoint of individual, abstract traits (e.g., aspects of personality). When a context for self-descriptions was provided, however, Cousins predicted that these differences would disappear. Under these conditions, it was expected that Japanese students would report self-concepts as rich in traits and individual characteristics as would Americans.

As shown in Figure 3.21, these predictions were confirmed. In the version of the questionnaire that provided no social contexts, U.S. students were much more likely than Japanese students to include specific traits or attributes in their self-concepts. However, this difference was actually reversed with the version of the questionnaire that included mention of concrete social contexts. Additional findings also indicated that the self-concepts of Japanese students were just as rich and complex as those of Americans. For example, even on the no-context version of the questionnaire, Japanese students were more likely to describe themselves in highly abstract terms (e.g., as a human being, an organic life-form).

In sum, there is little evidence in Cousins's research for pronounced differences in the self-concepts of American and Japanese students. Both groups seem equally aware of their unique traits and characteristics, and both seem to possess equally rich conceptions of their individual identities. Not surprisingly, though, cultural factors do influence how these students describe their self-concepts and how they interpret the question, "Who am I?"

Action Identification: Do People Really Know What They Are Doing?

What are you doing right now? One answer is, "Reading [and, we hope, enjoying] this book." Another is, "Getting ready for the next exam." A third might be, "Working toward my degree," or even "Stretching my mind." While all these answers describe what you are doing, they involve different levels of analysis. The first reply, "Reading this book," is the simplest and most direct; the last two (e.g., "Stretching my mind") are more abstract. According to the theory of **action identification,** proposed by Vallacher and Wegner (1987), people always have *some* idea about what they are doing. These ideas, however, may vary in abstractness or complexity, just as the possible replies above do. The theory also holds that when an action can be identified at both a higher and a lower level, the higher level will become dominant. Moreover, it suggests that as behaviors become better learned and so smoother and more automatic, there is a tendency to identify them at higher levels.

The theory also suggests that the way in which individuals identify their own actions has important implications. Higher-level identifications may make actions more stable and therefore somewhat harder to change. This, in turn, is relevant to several types of personal problems. For example, when individuals engage in self-destructive actions, such as excessive use of alcohol, we often say they "don't know what they're doing." The theory of action identification, however, contends that they *do* know—that in fact, their tendency to identify such actions at relatively high levels may contribute, at least in part, to the persistence of these self-destructive actions. If this is indeed the case, then individuals showing such problems would be expected to identify (explain) their actions (e.g., excessive drinking) in higher-level terms than others. This reasoning has recently been examined by Wegner, Vallacher, and Dizadji (1989).

These researchers asked students and clients at an alcohol treatment center to indicate, by noting the extent to which various statements described their actions, what they were doing when they drank alcoholic beverages. The statements ranged from ones involving low-level action identifications (e.g., "lifting a glass," "swallowing liquid," "holding a glass in my hand") to ones involving higher-level action identifications (e.g., "hurting myself," "relieving tension," "getting drunk," "rewarding myself"). The students were divided into groups of those who used alcohol rarely, moderately, and heavily; these groups, plus the treatment center clients, were compared with one another in terms of their answers to the questionnaire. Results supported the prediction that the alcohol-abusing clients would describe their actions in terms of higher-level identifications (see Figure 3.22). In addition, there was some indication that those students who reported heavy use of alcohol also tended to identify drinking in terms of such factors as "rewarding myself" and "relieving tension."

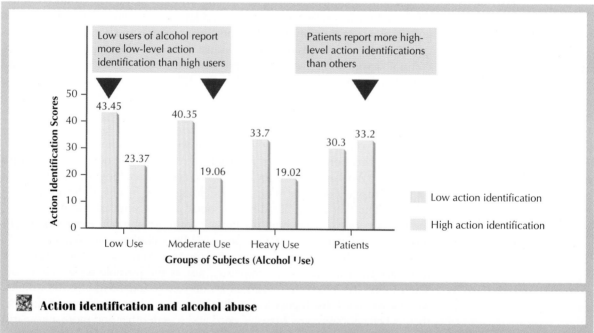

Action identification and alcohol abuse

FIGURE 3.22 Persons undergoing treatment for alcohol abuse and students who reported drinking heavily described their use of alcohol in terms of higher-level action identifications than other persons. For example, they were more likely than others to state that they were "relieving tension" or "hurting themselves" but less likely to state that they were "swallowing liquids" or "holding a glass." This tendency toward the use of high-level action identification may in turn contribute to the inability of heavy alcohol users to regulate such behavior. (Source: Based on data from Wegner, Vallacher, & Dizadji, 1989.)

These findings and those of related studies (e.g., Wegner & Vallacher, 1986, 1987) suggest that people's ideas about what they are doing at any given time can strongly affect their behavior. In short, what we *think* we are doing can influence what we *actually* do—sometimes with serious consequences for our personal health and well-being.

SUMMARY AND REVIEW

Heuristics and Other Mental Shortcuts

Social cognition is concerned with understanding the processes through which we notice, interpret, remember, and later use information about the social world. In order to minimize the effort involved in these complex tasks, people often use a number of "mental shortcuts." Some of these involve the use of *heuristics*—mental rules of thumb that permit rapid decisions about various stimuli. For example, the frequency of a stimulus can be judged in terms of *availability*—the ease with which instances of it can be brought to mind. Other mental shortcuts include *framing* and *anchoring*. Both terms refer to the fact that the way information is presented (e.g., in a positive or a negative light) can strongly affect judgments about it.

Social judgments are affected not only by actual events or stimuli but by our *mental simulations* about them. For example, we engage in *counterfactual thinking,* imagining the opposite of some event that has occurred or conditions that might have produced different outcomes. Such thinking has been shown to influence our judgments about whether improbable events are or are not coincidences and about the causes behind specific outcomes. Individuals also hold *implicit theories* concerning change or stability in their behavior. These, too, influence various judgments.

Affect and Cognition

Sharply contrasting views of the nature of emotions have been proposed. The *Cannon-Bard theory* suggests that emotion-provoking stimuli evoke both physiological reactions and subjective emotional states. In contrast, the *James-Lange theory* suggests

that emotional experiences stem primarily from our recognition of changes in our bodily states. Schachter's *two-factor theory* proposes that it is the cognitive label we attach to physiological arousal that is crucial. Another view, the *vascular theory of emotion,* suggests that changes in affect (positive or negative feelings) can be produced by facial expressions, which influence airflow through the nasal passages and so indirectly influence brain temperature. Small rises in brain temperature produce negative affect, while small drops generate positive affect.

Mild shifts in affect have been found to influence interpretation of ambiguous stimuli, memory, creative problem solving, risk taking, and many other forms of behavior. Positive affect appears to have stronger effects in this regard than negative affect. Cognition also influences our affective states. The emotions we experience are determined, at least in part, by the labels we attach to arousing events, and our emotional reactions to provocative actions by others depend, in part, on our interpretation of the causes behind these actions. Finally, if we expect to like or dislike some stimulus or event, our affective reactions to it will usually be consistent with such expectations.

The Self

Our *self-concept* consists of all the knowledge we possess about ourselves. It can be viewed as a special type of **schema**—a cognitive framework, developed through experience, that organizes information about some object (in this case, ourselves). Information relevant to the self is remembered more readily than other forms of information. Apparently, this *self-reference effect* occurs because such information is processed more deeply and is better organized than other types of information. While we all possess a current self-concept, we are also aware of other potential selves—what we have been in the past and what we might become in the future. Some of these possible selves (the desirable ones) operate as incentives, spurring us on to efforts to attain them.

Research on the theory of **action identification** suggests that people do have some idea of what they are doing at any given time. However, they may define their current actions at relatively low (specific) or high (abstract) levels. Behaviors that are identified at relatively high levels may be more difficult to change than ones identified at relatively low levels. Consistent with this view, alcoholics describe their problem drinking in terms of abstract ideas such as "hurting myself" or "relieving tension." In contrast, persons who consume very little alcohol describe this activity in lower-level terms (e.g., "holding a glass," "drinking a liquid").

KEY TERMS

Action identification Individuals' interpretation or labeling of their own behavior (their understanding of what they are doing at a given time).

Affect Temporary and relatively mild shifts in feelings or mood.

Anchoring The tendency for a starting value (e.g., in negotiations) to unduly influence judgments or decisions.

Automatic priming A process that occurs when stimuli of which individuals are not consciously aware alter the availability of various categories of information in memory.

Availability heuristic A strategy for making judgments on the basis of how easily specific kinds of information can be brought to mind. Information that can be readily remembered is viewed as more frequent or important than information that cannot be readily remembered.

Base-rate fallacy The tendency to ignore or underuse information relating to the relative frequency with which various events or stimuli actually occur.

Biases With respect to social cognition, a term referring to tendencies to process information in such a way that false conclusions or inferences are drawn.

Cannon-Bard theory A theory of emotion suggesting that various events elicit both physiological reactions and the subjective reactions we label as emotions.

Cognitive misers A phrase that describes the human tendency to expend the least amount of cognitive effort possible in attempting to understand the social world.

Counterfactual thinking The tendency to evaluate events by thinking about alternatives to them (e.g., "what might have been"). The more readily such alternatives come to mind, the stronger our reactions to the events that actually occurred.

Facial feedback hypothesis The suggestion that changes in facial expression can induce shifts in emotions or affective states.

Fallacies Errors in human social judgment that result from the systematic use of various mental shortcuts or strategies.

False consensus effect The tendency to assume that others behave or think like we do to a greater extent than is actually true.

Framing Effects on judgment or decisions stemming from the way in which information related to these decisions is presented.

Heuristics Rules or principles that allow individuals to make social judgments rapidly and with reduced effort.

Information overload A process that occurs when our ability to process information is exceeded.

James-Lange theory (of emotion) A theory contending that emotional experiences result from our perceptions of shifts in bodily states. For example, according to this theory we become fearful because of awareness of such physiological reactions as increased heartbeat and shortness of breath.

Possible selves Mental representations of what we might become, or should become, in the future.

Priming Occurs when stimuli or events increase the availability of specific types of information in memory.

Representativeness heuristic A strategy for making judgments based on the extent to which current stimuli or events resemble ones we view as being typical.

Schema An organized collection of beliefs and feelings about some aspect of the world. Schemas operate like mental scaffolds, providing structure for the interpretation and organization of new information we encounter.

Self All of our knowledge, feelings, and ideas about ourselves as unique individuals.

Self-concept A system of affective and cognitive structures (schemas) about the self that lends coherence to individuals' self-relevant experiences.

Self-reference effect The tendency for information related to the self to be processed more efficiently (in several respects) than other forms of information.

Self-schema A special type of schema containing information about the self.

Social cognition A subfield of social psychology concerned with the manner in which individuals interpret, analyze, remember, and use information about the social world.

Two-factor theory (of emotion) The view that arousal initiates a search for the causes of such arousal. The labels then attached to such feelings strongly determine the emotion experienced.

Vascular theory of emotion (or emotional efference) A theory of emotion suggesting that positive affect and negative affect stem at least in part from changes in the pattern of blood flow to the brain and resulting increases or decreases in brain temperature.

FOR MORE INFORMATION

Fiedler, K., & Forgas, J. P. (Eds.). (1988). *Affect, cognition, and social behavior.* Toronto: Hogrefe.

Chapters in this volume deal with the complex relationship between affect and cognition. The unit on the role of affect in social judgments is especially interesting and is closely related to topics covered in this chapter.

Fiske, S. T., & Taylor, S. E. (1984). *Social cognition.* Reading, MA: Addison-Wesley.

A clear, thorough review of research on social cognition. Many basic aspects of our thinking about others (e.g., attribution, memory for social information) are examined.

Kahneman, D., Slovic, P., & Tversky, A. (Eds.). (1982). *Judgment under uncertainty: Heuristics and biases.* Cambridge, England: Cambridge University Press.

A collection of articles and chapters focused on heuristics, biases, and fallacies. If you want to learn more about the ways in which we make use of mental shortcuts and err in our efforts to understand the social world, this is "must" reading.

Srull, T. K., & Wyer, R. S. (1988). *Advances in social cognition: A dual model of impression formation.* Hillsdale, NJ: Erlbaum.

In this book, leading experts on an important aspect of social cognition—how we combine information about others into impressions of them—describe recent theory and findings related to this topic. Some of the chapters make for difficult reading, but the ideas and data presented are fascinating and make the effort of understanding them well worthwhile.

Attitudes: Evaluating
the Social World

So what do you think?" Todd Hiller asks his friends Dave Cox and Rick Ervin as they leave the large auditorium in which one of the candidates for U.S. Senator has just finished speaking.

"What do I think?" Dave replies. "Easy. It's the same old bull all over again. I knew she was a bleeding-heart liberal before we came, but man, I never imagined she'd lay it on *that* thick."

"Right," Rick adds. "Spend, spend, spend—that's all they ever think about. Where do they think the money's going to come from for all those wonderful programs? I'll tell you where—from *us*. And I say to Ms. Steinmetz and her crew: Thanks all the same, but no thanks.

Find some other sucker this time. I'm tired of footing the bill."

Todd looks shaken. He pauses for a moment, then continues. "Gee, you know, I kind of felt the same way before listening to her, but now I don't know. I mean, *something* has to be done about all those homeless people."

"Yeah, I agree," Dave replies. "And I can tell you what it is. Put 'em back in prison or the loony bin, where they belong. You been downtown lately? The streets are loaded with them. Ugh!"

"Hey," Todd responds, a note of irritation in his voice. "Those are *people* you're talking about. You can't just write them off like that. They've got rights too."

"Sure they've got rights," Rick answers. "The right to get a job, the right to pay taxes, and the right to get the heck off the streets! What a racket. These characters have always been around, and always lived in the same way, but nobody worried about them until one of those smart cookies in the media dreamed up a new phrase—*the homeless*. What a scam!"

"You guys are starting to get to me!" Todd shouts. "How can you be so blind? I didn't realize it until I heard her speech, but Steinmetz is right: A lot of those people have real problems, and they need help. How can you lump them all together as bums?"

"Oh, it's easy," Dave says, his voice dripping sarcasm. "I can lump them all together just the way I lump my trash together twice a week before I throw it out. Stop, will you? I can't stand any more of that liberal baloney. You're only falling for it because you just heard it dished out in person by a real, live, honest-to-goodness candidate. Come off it; it's almost like she hypnotized you."

"No, that's not why he's swallowing it," Rick interjects. "I think it's because of that raise. He's been after it for months, and now he's just on a high. You know how it is: When someone's feeling good, they're always a pushover—you can get them to agree with practically anything."

"That has nothing to do with it!" Todd exclaims angrily. "I just recognize good sense when I hear it. And if you two jerks can't do the same, then so long!" And with these words, he storms off, leaving his two friends stopped dead in their tracks.

"Whew," Rick comments, waving his hand. "I always thought he was okay. Now he turns out to be a closet liberal. What a drag."

"You could have fooled me," Dave agrees. "I don't know . . . maybe it's that left-wing college he went to. I thought we had him reeducated, but I guess when people get these ideas in their heads at a certain age, they just can't shake them— once indoctrinated, always indoctrinated."

"Yeah, I'm sure glad that never happened to *us*," Dave remarks, as the two friends start off down the street.

We don't know what your reactions to this incident are, but we're pretty confident of one thing: You don't feel entirely neutral about it. On the contrary, you probably side quite strongly with either Dave and Rick, the two persons who expressed conservative views, or with Todd, who supported a liberal position. Why? Many social psychologists would reply, "Because you already possess **attitudes** relevant to this situation." You hold attitudes about the issues in-

"Nobody else has complained about flies in the soup."

FIGURE 4.1 *Attitudes* lead individuals to react in certain ways to events or situations they encounter. (Drawing by Chas. Addams; © 1989 The New Yorker Magazine, Inc.)

volved (e.g., homeless persons and the treatment of them, government spending, taxes, politicians in general or female politicians in particular). These attitudes in turn lead you to react in specific ways to the incident reported (see Figure 4.1).

But what precisely *are* attitudes? Although numerous definitions have been suggested, one that captures the essence of several of them is as follows: *Attitudes are general evaluations people make about themselves, other persons, objects, or issues* (cf. Petty & Cacioppo, 1986). In other words, attitudes involve lasting likes and dislikes, preferences and aversions, toward specific aspects of the external world. This definition is useful, for attitudes *do* involve affective reactions and must persist over time to be of any practical (or theoretical) importance. However, recent evidence suggests that to be truly comprehensive, this definition must be broadened in two respects. First, it should reflect the fact that attitudes involve more than just positive and negative feelings (Pratkanis, Breckler, & Greenwald, 1989). Memories of past experiences with attitude objects, mental images of them, and several other aspects of cognition also play a part (Breckler & Wiggins, 1989b).

Second, a comprehensive definition of attitudes should reflect the fact that they serve important *functions* for the persons who hold them. In other words, attitudes do not exist in a social vacuum; rather, they develop for important reasons and serve various functions (Shavitt, 1990; Snyder & DeBono, 1989). For example, attitudes guide behavior toward valued goals and away from aversive events. Similarly, they assist individuals in processing complex information about the social world. Thus, once attitudes are formed, they help individuals to interpret new information and to reach decisions more efficiently than would otherwise be the case. Taking these points into account, we offer the following definition: *Attitudes are enduring mental representations of various features of the social or physical world. They are acquired through experience and exert a directive influence on subsequent behavior* (Breckler & Wiggins, 1989b). Perhaps a concrete example will help you grasp the scope and implications of this definition.

Consider a woman who holds a negative attitude toward a particular brand of automobile. What does this imply? In part, that as a result of previous experiences with such cars, she has acquired a mental representation of them. This representation reflects the fact that cars she has owned of this brand broke down a lot and ran up expensive repair bills. Thus, it contains an emotional or affective component: She doesn't like cars with this manufacturer's nameplate, and she experiences negative feelings whenever she encounters one. In addition, her representation reflects (and summarizes) all the information she has acquired about such autos (how they look; reports about their quality in consumer magazines; what other people have said about them). Finally, the representation influences (guides) her behavior: She avoids buying such cars or even driving them (e.g., she avoids rental-car companies that rent autos of this brand; see Figure 4.2).

In sum, attitudes are internal representations of various aspects of the social or physical world—representations containing affective reactions to the attitude object and a wide range of cognitions about it (e.g., thoughts, beliefs, judgments). Attitudes reflect past experience, shape ongoing behavior, and serve essential functions for those who hold them.

This definition suggests that attitudes are certainly an important component of social behavior and social thought. This has been recognized by social psychologists for several decades. Indeed, writing more than fifty years ago, Gordon Allport (1935), one of the founders of our field, noted that *attitude* is social psychology's most central concept. Many present-day social psychologists would agree. In fact, the volume of research concerned with attitudes and their effects has recently increased sharply (e.g., Pratkanis, Breckler, & Greenwald, 1989). In order to reflect this important work, we will proceed as follows. First, we'll examine the process through which attitudes are *formed* or *developed*. Next,

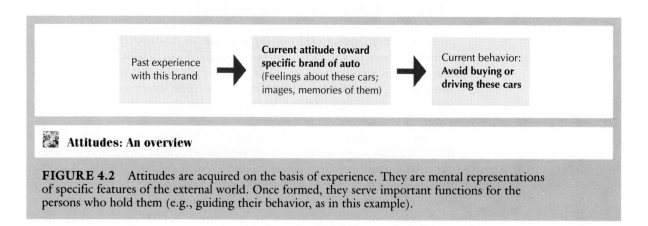

Attitudes: An overview

FIGURE 4.2 Attitudes are acquired on the basis of experience. They are mental representations of specific features of the external world. Once formed, they serve important functions for the persons who hold them (e.g., guiding their behavior, as in this example).

we'll consider how attitudes are sometimes *changed* through *persuasion* and related processes. (The word *sometimes* should be emphasized, for as we'll note in another section, changing attitudes that are important to those holding them is far from easy.) Third, we'll consider *cognitive dissonance*—a process with far-reaching implications for social behavior and social thought that, surprisingly, sometimes leads individuals to change their own attitudes. Finally, we'll examine the relationship between attitudes and behavior. This link is more complex than you might expect, so be prepared for some surprises about its nature.

Forming Attitudes: The Roles of Learning and Experience

Heroes and heroines may be born, but liberals, conservatives, environmentalists, and football fans are clearly made. Few psychologists would suggest at present that babies enter the world with political preferences, racial bigotry, or religious views already fully formed. Rather, such attitudes are acquired over a long period of time, through the impact of several different processes. What are these processes, and how do they operate? It is on these issues that we will now focus.

Social Learning: Acquiring Attitudes from Others

One source of our attitudes is obvious: We acquire them from other persons through the process of **social learning.** In other words, we acquire many of our views from situations in which we interact with others or merely observe their behavior. Such social learning occurs in diverse ways, but here we will examine three processes that often play a role in this process.

Classical Conditioning: Learning Based on Association   It is a basic principle of psychology that when one stimulus regularly precedes another, the one that occurs first may soon become a signal for the one that occurs second. In other words, when the first stimulus is presented, individuals come to expect that the second will follow. As a result, they may gradually demonstrate the same kind of reactions to the first stimulus as they do to the second, especially if the second stimulus is one that induces fairly strong reactions when encountered. Consider, for example, a man whose shower emits a low hum just before the hot water runs out and becomes an icy stream. At first, he might show little reaction to the hum. After it is followed by freezing water on several occasions, though, he might well experience strong emotional arousal (fear!) when it occurs. After all, it is a signal for what will soon follow—something quite unpleasant.

What does this process—known as **classical conditioning**—have to do with attitudes and their formation? Potentially, quite a bit. Imagine a young child who sees her father frown and demonstrate signs of displeasure each time he meets members of a particular minority group. At first, the child is quite neutral toward members of this group; their defining characteristics (e.g., skin color, style of dress, accent) have little or no effect on her. Yet her father's emotional signs of disapproval are quite upsetting to the child. The result: Gradually, she begins to experience negative reactions to the group in question (refer to Figure 4.3, p. 140). In short, the child has acquired a tendency to respond negatively to such persons. Such affective reactions may then form the core of a developing negative attitude toward members of this group. (We'll consider such attitudes in Chapter 5, when we discuss *prejudice*.) In sum, classical conditioning can play a role in the development of attitudes, and some of these, at least, have a high degree of social importance (cf. Rajecki, 1989).

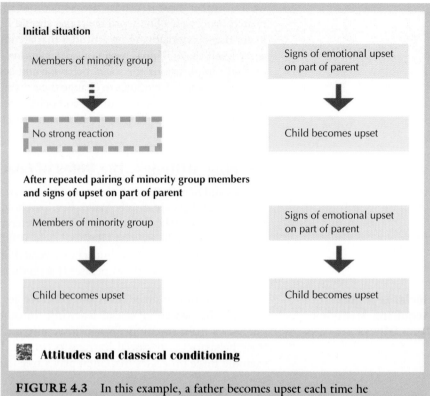

Initial situation

Members of minority group

↓

No strong reaction

Signs of emotional upset on part of parent

↓

Child becomes upset

After repeated pairing of minority group members and signs of upset on part of parent

Members of minority group

↓

Child becomes upset

Signs of emotional upset on part of parent

↓

Child becomes upset

Attitudes and classical conditioning

FIGURE 4.3   In this example, a father becomes upset each time he encounters members of a specific minority group. At first, his young daughter has little if any emotional reaction to minority group members. After the father's emotional upset has been paired with minority group members on numerous occasions, however, the child acquires a negative emotional reaction to such persons. This reaction can then serve as the core of a developing racial or ethnic prejudice.

Instrumental Conditioning: Learning to Express the "Right" Views   Have you ever heard a three-year-old state, with great conviction, that he is a Republican or a Democrat? Or that Fords (Hondas) are far superior to Chevrolets (Toyotas)? Clearly, children of this age have little if any comprehension of what such statements mean. Yet they make them all the same. Why? The answer is obvious: They have been praised or rewarded in various ways by their parents for stating such views. As we're sure you know, behaviors that are followed by positive outcomes are strengthened and tend to be repeated. In contrast, behaviors that are followed by negative outcomes are weakened, or at least suppressed. Thus, a second way in which attitudes are acquired from others is through the process of **instrumental conditioning.** By rewarding their children for stating the "right" views—the ones they themselves favor—parents and other adults play an active role in shaping their offspring's attitudes. It is for this reason that, until they reach their teen years, most youngsters express political, religious, and social views highly similar to those held by their families. Given the power of positive reinforcement to shape behavior, it would be surprising if they did not.

Modeling: Learning by Example   A third process through which attitudes are formed can operate even when parents have no desire to transmit specific views to their children. This third process involves **modeling**—instances in which individuals acquire new forms of behavior merely through observing the actions of others. It is often said that "little pitchers have big ears," and where attitude formation is concerned, this is certainly true. In many cases, children hear their parents say things not intended for their ears, or they observe their parents engaging in actions the parents tell them not to perform. For example, a father who smokes may warn his daughter against smoking even as he lights a cigarette or pipe. Similarly, a mother may leave her own room a mess even as she urges her son to be tidy and clean *his* room. What message do children take away from such instances? The evidence is clear: That they should do as their parents *do,* not as they *say*. In sum, attitudes are often acquired through processes that permit individuals (especially children) to learn reactions from others; thus, attitudes may be transmitted *socially,* from one person—or generation—to another.

Direct Experience: Acquiring Attitudes from Life

While individuals often acquire attitudes from others through social learning, this is not the only source of such views. Attitudes are also formed as a result of direct, personal experience. For example, how do you know that you like or dislike various foods? Probably because you have tasted them. Similarly, how do you know that you like or dislike different kinds of music? Again, because you have heard them and discovered that you found them pleasant or unpleasant. Of course, this is not always the case: Sometimes people *assume* that they will react negatively to various experiences and so avoid actually having them. This may or may not be correct, but in a practical sense, it doesn't matter; they will never have the experiences that would allow them to determine what their actual reactions might be.

Interestingly, research findings suggest that attitudes formed through direct experience with attitude objects are stronger, in several respects, than either the kind of "anticipated" attitudes just described or attitudes borrowed from others (i.e., through indirect experience; Fazio & Zanna, 1981). For example, individuals who form their attitudes about an object through direct experience with it have been shown to respond more quickly when asked to express their reactions to the object than those individuals who form such attitudes indirectly (by watching someone else handle it) (Fazio et al., 1982). Quick responses of this type are usually interpreted as a sign of attitude strength. Similarly, attitudes stemming from direct experience are also held more confidently and are more resistant to change than attitudes formed through indirect experience (Fazio & Zanna, 1978; Wu & Shaffer, 1987).

In sum, while new experiences can prove costly (they can be unpleasant as well as pleasant, and perhaps even dangerous or harmful), the attitudes that result from them are stronger in a number of respects than ones resulting from vicarious experiences. One practical message in such findings is clear: If you hold strong attitudes about some issue, object, or person and want someone else to share them, you should arrange for him or her to have direct experience with the attitude object. In the absence of such experience, the person's attitudes will probably be only pale reflections of your own more passionate views.

Attitudes and Behavior: The Essential Link

Do attitudes shape behavior? Your first answer is likely to be, "Of course." After all, you can remember many incidents in which your own actions were strongly shaped by your opinions. Besides, you might reason, social psychologists wouldn't define attitudes as a central concept of their field and spend so much time studying them if various attitudes didn't predict behavior. Yet until quite recently, evidence about the strength of the link between attitudes and behavior was anything but encouraging. Many studies seemed to suggest that this link was sometimes more apparent than real. For example, consider a classic study on this topic conducted years ago by LaPiere (1934). He toured the United States with a young Chinese couple, stopping at more than 250 hotels, motels, and restaurants. In all that time, he and his friends were refused service only once. When LaPiere wrote to the same businesses several months later and asked whether they would serve Chinese patrons, fully 92 percent reported they would not. (Remember, this study was conducted in the 1930s, a time when it was not unusual for people to admit openly to strong racial or ethnic prejudice.)

To make matters worse, about twenty years ago one social psychologist (Wicker, 1969) reviewed all the evidence existing at the time on the link between attitudes and behavior and came to an unsettling conclusion: Attitudes and behavior are at best only weakly related. And often, there is virtually no relationship between them. Social psychologists were stunned. The belief that attitudes predict behavior had always been offered as one strong basis for investigating attitudes systematically (Greenwald, 1989). Had researchers really been wasting their time pursuing ghosts or shadows? Fortunately, additional evidence gathered after the publication of Wicker's review soon indicated otherwise. Attitudes and behavior *are,* in fact, often closely linked. This is not always the case, however, and the relationship between them is more complex than first meets the eye. Thus, the basic question becomes: When do attitudes predict behavior and when are they uninformative in this regard? Several factors that play an important role in this respect will now be described.

Attitude Specificity

Consider two of your own attitudes. Suppose, for example, that you like pickles on your hamburger (a specific attitude) and that you oppose racial discrimination (a general attitude). Which attitude will be more strongly related to your actual behavior? Probably you don't always take every opportunity to work for racial equality—you don't participate in every demonstration, sign every petition, or actively seek to discourage every instance of discrimination at work or in school. This translates into a relatively weak relationship between your attitude and your behavior: Your actions can't be predicted very accurately from your views about discrimination. In contrast, if you like pickles you will probably order them almost every time you have a hamburger. Here, your behavior is indeed highly consistent with your attitude. While you would probably say that racial equality is more important to you than pickles, the link between your attitudes and your behavior is stronger with respect to the latter—that is, with respect to the specific attitude rather than to the more general one.

A large proportion of attitude research has focused on general attitudes, such as those pertaining to religion, politics, or various social groups, in part because these views are perceived—and rightly so—as the most important ones. However, as noted by Ajzen and Fishbein (1977), this emphasis on general, global attitudes may have been responsible in part for the relatively weak link between attitudes and behavior noted by Wicker (1969). After all, why should general attitudes be successful in predicting specific behaviors with a high degree of certainty? Such a link is probably weak at best and quite tenuous in many cases. Perhaps one more example will help clarify this point.

Consider a woman who holds what she believes are liberal social views. She favors government programs to help people she describes as being "disadvantaged," is against harsh punishment for criminals, and approves of additional aid to education. Now she is asked to vote on a broad-based increase in taxes; if the measure passes, the amounts she pays in income, sales, and property taxes will all increase sharply. What does she do? If she is like many people, she votes "No, no, a thousand times no!" Is she a hypocrite? Not necessarily. It's just that her specific attitudes—her positive feelings toward the new car she wants to buy, her negative views about waste in her local government—are more strongly linked to her behavior than her more general attitudes. So the link between attitudes and behavior is indeed significant, provided that we choose to focus on specific, relatively narrow attitudes rather than more general ones.

Attitude Components

You love pizza; just the thought of one—hot, bubbling, and emitting enticing aromas of cheese and spices—brings a smile to your lips. You also have several thoughts about why you love it so much: You know that it tastes good, is really quite nourishing, and is both filling and inexpensive. In short, your mental representation of pizza (your attitude toward it) involves both feelings (an affective component) and various forms of knowledge (a cognitive component). Which of these exerts a stronger impact on your behavior and is a better predictor of it? Probably your feelings.

Now, consider a situation in which you must choose between two college courses. One sounds more interesting than the other, but you know that the duller-sounding course will count toward more important degree requirements and is more closely related to your major. Again, your attitudes toward these courses involve both affective and cognitive components. Which component will be more closely related to your choice? Here, it seems reasonable to predict that the cognitive component will predominate.

These examples help illustrate another key point about the attitude-behavior relationship: the various components of attitudes are not always highly consistent (e.g., the affective component may be very positive—you are in love!—while the cognitive component is not so favorable—you have doubts about the relationship's future). More to the point, when these components are consistent, one of them may be more closely related to specific forms of behavior than the other. That this is indeed the case is indicated by a recent study conducted by Millar and Tesser (1989).

These researchers asked male and female subjects to work on various puzzles (e.g., determining which of several patterns most closely matched a target pattern; supplying the missing word in incomplete sentences). To measure the cognitive and affective components of subjects' attitudes toward these puzzles, the researchers next asked them how they felt while performing each type (a measure of the affective component) and *why* they felt that way (a measure of the cognitive component). Subjects in two groups were then told either that the puzzles were useful in developing their analytic ability or that they would be used to measure their social sensitivity. Millar and Tesser (1989) reasoned the first condition would lead subjects to view working on the puzzles as a form of instrumental behavior (it had a specific external purpose), while the second condition would lead them to view the activity as a form of consummatory behavior (something they did for its own enjoyment). The researchers then predicted that the cognitive component of subjects' attitudes would be more closely related to instrumental behavior than the affective component, while the opposite would be true for consummatory behavior. Moreover, this was expected to be especially true when the affective and cognitive components were not highly consistent. To test this hypothesis, subjects were then given an opportunity to work on each type of puzzle; the amount of time they worked on each was the measure of their behavior.

Results supported the hypothesis. When the two attitude components were not highly consistent, subjects' affective reactions were more closely related to consummatory behavior than their cognitive reactions. Similarly, subjects' cognitive reactions were more closely related to instrumental behavior than their affective ones were (refer to Figure 4.4). When consistency between the two components was high, these differences were much smaller. So, various components of attitudes predict different types of behavior to different degrees. The ability of attitudes to predict behavior can often be maximized by taking this fact into account.

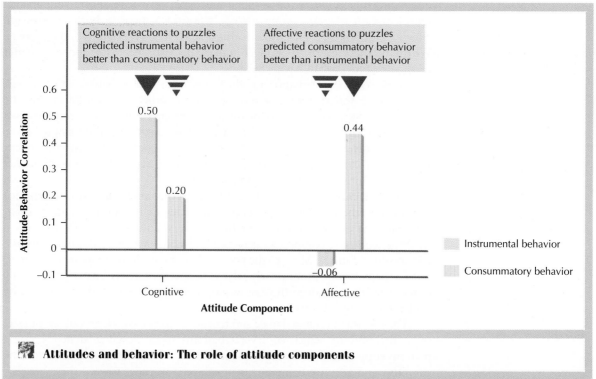

Attitudes and behavior: The role of attitude components

FIGURE 4.4 Subjects' affective reactions to puzzles on which they worked were more closely related to consummatory than to instrumental behavior regarding these puzzles. In contrast, subjects' cognitive reactions to the puzzles were more closely related to their instrumental than to their consummatory behavior. These findings suggest that different components of attitudes are maximally effective in predicting different forms of behavior. (Source: Based on data from Millar & Tesser, 1989.)

Vested interest and the attitude-behavior link

FIGURE 4.5 When individuals have a *vested interest* in some issue, their behavior with respect to that issue can often be predicted quite accurately from their attitudes about it.

Attitude Strength, Vested Interest, and the Role of Self-Awareness

Obviously, strong attitudes predict behavior better than weak ones. There are several less obvious factors related to attitude strength, however. One is direct experience. At the beginning of this chapter, we noted that attitudes formed through direct personal experience are stronger than ones acquired passively by observation. It is not surprising, then, that attitudes of the first type are generally stronger predictors than attitudes of the latter type (Fazio et al., 1982).

A second factor to consider concerns the extent to which individuals have a **vested interest** in the attitude object. By a "vested interest," we mean that the events or issues in question have a strong effect on the person's life. Having a vested interest (which seems closely related to *outcome-relevant involvement* as described by Johnson and Eagly [1989]) increases the strength of the attitude-behavior link (see Figure 4.5). This fact is demonstrated quite clearly in a study conducted by Sivaeck and Crano (1982), who contacted students and pretended to solicit their help in campaigning against a proposed state law that would raise the drinking age from eighteen to twenty. Nearly all students were opposed to the law, regardless of their own age. Some of them, however, had a vested interest—the ones young enough so that passage of the law would impinge directly on their future social lives. Students who were a little older had no vested interest; even if the law passed, they would already be over twenty by the time it took effect. Which group do you think agreed to campaign against the law? The younger students, of course. The older students, while equally opposed to it in principle, lacked any vested interest. Their attitudes did not lead to the corresponding behavior.

A third factor determining the strength of the attitude-behavior link involves *self-awareness*. As we noted in Chapter 3, heightened self-awareness increases the degree of consistency between attitudes and behavior (e.g., Pryor et al., 1977). There are two reasons for this: (1) Self-awareness increases our access to our own attitudes; we can report them more accurately when we are self-aware than when we are not. Obviously, the more readily we can bring various attitudes to mind, the greater the possibility that they will affect our behavior at a given moment. (2) In situations in which overt behaviors are required, self-awareness can bring specific attitudes more sharply into focus, thus enabling them to guide the actions that follow. Enhancing self-awareness, it appears, is akin to saying to someone: "Before you act, stop for a moment and think about who you are and what you believe to be true. In light of these thoughts, what course of action suits you best?" Such reflection makes it more likely that behavior will follow from existing attitudes and less likely that it will be determined mainly by external, situational factors. The result: The link between existing attitudes and overt behavior is strengthened.

Attitude Accessibility: The Force That Binds

In our discussion of social cognition in Chapter 3, we called attention to the concept of *availability*—the ease with which specific kinds of information can be brought to mind. A similar concept is useful in understanding the relationship between attitudes and behavior: **attitude accessibility.** This refers to the ease with which specific attitudes can be remembered and brought into consciousness (Fazio, 1989). In an important sense, attitude accessibility allows us to tie together the diverse factors and findings covered so far in this discussion. Attitude strength, specificity, vested interest, and even self-awareness can all be better understood in terms of their relationship to attitude accessibility. In each case, the kinds of attitudes that have been found to be closely related to behavior are the ones that would probably be most accessible—for example, strong, specific, and personally relevant ones (Krosnick, 1988, 1989). Thus, attitude accessibility may be crucial to understanding why attitudes sometimes predict behavior accurately and why sometimes they do not.

A helpful illustration of the importance of attitude accessibility in the attitude-behavior link is provided by a study conducted by Fazio and Williams (1986). This experiment consisted of three distinct parts. In the first, residents of a small midwestern town were interviewed and asked about their attitudes toward the two candidates in the 1984 U.S. presidential campaign, Ronald Reagan and Walter Mondale. The accessibility of these attitudes was assessed by measuring the amount of time subjects took to indicate the extent to which they agreed or disagreed with a set of attitude statements about the candidates. (Previous research has shown that the time it takes to report one's attitude reflects how accessible these attitudes are. The faster the response, the more accessible the attitudes.) Two months later, the same subjects received a letter inquiring about who they thought had been more impressive in a recent TV debate between the candidates. Finally, in a third phase, subjects were phoned one day after the election and asked to indicate how they had voted.

Not surprisingly, subjects generally reported that the candidate they favored had performed better than his opponent. However, the association between subjects' initial preferences and their perceptions of how well each candidate had done in the debate was stronger for subjects whose initial attitudes were highly accessible—subjects who had reported these attitudes relatively quickly, with little hesitation. Moreover, a similar pattern emerged with respect to actual voting: While subjects did generally vote for the candidate they favored initially, the relationship between previously stated political preferences and actual voting was stronger for subjects whose attitudes were more accessible.

Attitude accessibility and political polling

FIGURE 4.6 The more accessible attitudes are, the more strongly they predict behavior. Taking this factor into account may help political pollsters in their efforts to predict the outcome of elections.

These findings suggest that attitude accessibility is a valuable concept in understanding the relationship between attitudes and behavior. In addition, they also contain a practical message for political pollsters: To predict the outcome of elections more accurately, it may be useful to measure not only people's attitudes but also the extent to which these attitudes are accessible. The more accessible such views are (and therefore the stronger, more relevant, and involving), the more useful they may be in predicting actual behavior on voting day (refer to Figure 4.6). (Can attitudes be changed by the mass media? And what about behavior—can it, too, be influenced by events appearing on television or cinema screens? Please see the **On the Applied Side** section below for evidence suggesting that such effects do in fact occur.)

ON THE APPLIED SIDE

Television and Attitudes about Nuclear War: When the Mass Media Induce Mass Change

Each year, corporations, politicians, and many others interested in shaping public opinion spend huge sums to purchase time on television—the medium they believe is most effective for this purpose. As a result, anyone who watches more than a few minutes of TV is literally bombarded with commercials, speeches, and various messages designed to alter attitudes. A growing body of evidence suggests that television does indeed exert powerful effects on the persons who watch it. It is a major source of information about the outside world for children and adults alike, and has been found to shape a wide range of attitudes and many forms of behavior, ranging from helping, on the one

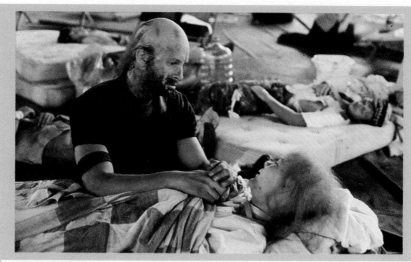

Television and attitudes: A dramatic example

FIGURE 4.7 *The Day After*, a TV movie showing the effects of a future nuclear war, was watched by tens of millions of persons. Evidence gathered by social psychologists suggests that it exerted strong effects not only on the attitudes of many who watched it but also on the attitudes of persons who did not.

hand, to aggression and violence, on the other (cf. Baron & Richardson, in press; Liebert & Sprafkin, 1988). Perhaps even more impressive, recent findings suggest that television can influence the attitudes and behavior of even those who do not watch it in various indirect ways. Dramatic evidence for this conclusion is provided by recent research concerned with the impact of a made-for-television movie entitled *The Day After* (e.g., Schofield & Pavelchak, 1989).

The movie, concerned with the consequences of a nuclear war, vividly depicted the destruction, social disintegration, and other effects that would follow from such a disaster. The movie was widely advertised and was watched by a large proportion of the TV-viewing audience—tens of millions of persons in the United States alone (see Figure 4.7). What impact did this movie have on viewers and on those who did not watch it? A study carried out by Schofield and Pavelchak (1989) suggests that the impact was both general and far-reaching.

These researchers conducted a survey of attitudes concerning nuclear war two weeks prior to the telecast of *The Day After* and again one and three weeks after it was shown. The survey asked respondents to indicate their views concerning the likelihood of nuclear war, their perceived chances of surviving such a war, their emotional feelings about such an event, and their intentions to perform various actions designed to prevent its occurrence (e.g., writing to their congressional representatives, signing petitions, volunteering to assist antinuclear organizations). Results indicated that significant changes occurred both among people who watched the movie and those who did not. For both groups, belief in the likelihood of nuclear war was higher after broadcast of the movie than before it (52.4 percent versus 46.7 percent). Similarly, both groups reported being more concerned about nuclear war and more depressed about the prospects of such an event following broadcast of the movie than before it was shown. Only in their stated intentions to engage in antinuclear activities did viewers differ from nonviewers; here, although persons in both groups reported stronger intentions to engage in such activity after broadcast of the movie, this shift occurred primarily among viewers rather than nonviewers.

That this vivid, unsettling movie was able to change the attitudes and behavioral intentions of those who saw it is far from surprising; the movie drove home the tragic consequences of nuclear war with great effectiveness. What is puzzling is that *The Day After* was also able to influence the attitudes of nonviewers. How did such effects arise? Although definitive evidence is not yet available, it seems likely that several factors came into play. First, the movie was highly publicized. Thus, even people who did not watch knew about it and had a general idea of its content. This information may in itself have been sufficient to get them to think about nuclear war and its effects. Their attitudes may then have shifted as a result. Second, the movie was viewed by millions of persons and given expansive coverage in numerous newspapers and magazines. As a result, considerable informal discussion of it occurred. In this way, persons who did not see it may have learned about its content from those who did and been influenced. Finally, the movie, quite apart from its specific content, was a stimulus to the discussion of nuclear war in general. Again, increased exposure to discussions of this topic may have induced shifts in the attitudes of those who did not actually view the movie.

In sum, it appears that television, by altering the attitudes of millions of persons, can sometimes serve as a source of major social change. We can only hope that when it is used in this manner, the changes it yields will be ones that contribute to human welfare.

Persuasion: The Process of Changing Attitudes

In the closing years of the twentieth century, the business of changing attitudes (or, at least, of trying to change them) is definitely a big one. If you have any doubts about this, simply switch on your TV or radio or flip through the pages of any popular magazine. Almost at once, you will be bombarded by attempts to alter some of your attitudes. In enticing, ingenious, and humorous ways, commercials and ads proclaim the advantages of various products and urge you to buy them (see Figure 4.8, p. 150). Political candidates plead for your financial support and your vote. Public service organizations caution you against smoking, drinking, speeding, and eating the wrong foods. And in many nations, governments use the mass media to rally support for new policies, laws, or regulations. In short, efforts to change your attitudes are all-pervasive and can be avoided only with considerable difficulty. To what extent are such attempts at **persuasion** successful? And what specific factors determine whether they succeed or fail? It is to these issues that we turn next.

Persuasion: The Traditional Approach

In most cases, efforts at *persuasion* involve the following elements: Some *source* directs some type of message (*communication*) to those whose attitudes he or she wishes to change (the *audience*). Taking note of this fact, much early research on persuasion focused on these elements, addressing various aspects of the question, *Who* says *what* to *whom* and with what effect? More specifically, such research sought to identify those characteristics of communicators (sources), communications (persuasive messages), and audiences which, together, would serve to maximize the impact of efforts at persuasion (Hovland, Janis, & Kelley,

Persuasion in action: An example

FIGURE 4.8 Advertisements for various products constitute a common and often ingenious form of persuasion. The Pepsi/Coke war has spawned some especially entertaining ads.

1953). The findings of this early research were complex and not always entirely consistent. Among the most notable, however, were these:

1. Experts are more persuasive than nonexperts (Hovland & Weiss, 1951). The same arguments carry more weight when delivered by people who seem to know what they are talking about and to have all the facts than when made by people lacking such expertise.

2. Messages that do not appear to be designed to change our attitudes are often more successful than ones that seem intended to manipulate us (Walster & Festinger, 1962). In other words, we don't trust—and we refuse to be influenced by—those who deliberately set out to persuade us. This is one reason why many efforts at persuasion adopt the kind of soft-sell approach shown in Figure 4.9.

3. Popular and attractive communicators (sources) are more effective in changing attitudes than unpopular or unattractive ones (Kiesler & Kiesler, 1969). This is one reason why politicians devote so much effort to the task of enhancing their personal appeal to voters.

"Look. I could just sell you a car, but that doesn't happen to be my primary objective."

Persuasion: The soft sell

FIGURE 4.9 People often resist intentional efforts at persuasion. For this reason, many would-be persuaders rely on less direct measures, or—as shown here—even deny any desire to exert such influence. (Drawing by Weber; © 1984 The New Yorker Magazine, Inc.)

4. People are sometimes more susceptible to persuasion when they are distracted by some extraneous event than when they are paying full attention to what is being said (Allyn & Festinger, 1961). This is why political candidates often arrange for "spontaneous" demonstrations during their speeches.

5. Individuals relatively low in self-esteem are often easier to persuade than those high in self-esteem (Janis, 1954). Lacking in self-confidence, the former are more susceptible to social influence from others.

6. When an audience holds attitudes contrary to those of a would-be persuader, it is often more effective for the communicator to adopt a *two-sided approach,* in which both sides are presented, rather than a *one-sided approach.* Apparently, strongly supporting one side of an issue while acknowledging that the other side has a few good points in its favor serves to disarm audiences and make it harder for them to resist the source's conclusions.

7. People who speak rapidly are generally more persuasive than those who speak slowly (Miller et al., 1976). This idea is contrary to the popular view that people distrust fast-talking salespersons and politicians. One reason rapid speech is more persuasive is that it seems to convey the impression that the communicator knows what he or she is talking about (i.e., is high in expertise).

8. Persuasion can be enhanced by messages that arouse strong emotions (especially fear) in the audience, particularly when the message provides specific recommendations about how a change in attitudes or behavior will prevent the negative consequences described in the fear-provoking message (Leventhal, Singer, & Jones, 1965). Such fear-based appeals seem to be especially effective in changing health-related attitudes and behavior (Robberson & Rogers, 1988).

At this point we should insert a note of caution: While most of these findings have withstood the test of time and appear to be accurate, some have been modified, to a degree, by more recent evidence. For example, while people low in self-esteem *are* often easier to persuade than those high in self-esteem, this difference may be smaller than originally believed (Baumeister & Covington, 1985). Those high in self-esteem, too, may be persuaded, but they don't want to admit it. As a result, they seem to experience much less attitude change than people with low self-esteem when in fact this difference is quite small. Still, the findings described above appear to represent useful generalizations about persuasion, and they form an important part of our knowledge about this process. (For a discussion of an additional—and intriguing—finding uncovered by early research on persuasion, see the **Classic Contributions** section below.)

FOCUS ON RESEARCH: CLASSIC CONTRIBUTIONS

Delayed Attitude Change: Four Decades of Research on the "Sleeper Effect"

Common sense suggests that the greatest impact of a persuasive message will occur immediately after it is presented. And indeed, in most research that has measured the effects of efforts at persuasion across time, this is the pattern that has been obtained (e.g., Gillig & Greenwald, 1974). Yet some of the earliest research on attitude change and persuasion reported a different pattern. For example, in 1933, Peterson and Thurstone exposed children to silent movies about different ethnic groups in an attempt to reduce prejudice (negative attitudes) toward these groups. For three of the films used, the impact on attitudes was greatest immediately and then decreased over time. For one film, however, the opposite occurred: Attitude change was actually greater six months later than immediately after the film was shown.

Similar, puzzling results were obtained by Hovland, Lumsdaine, and Sheffield (1949) in an entirely different context. These researchers measured the impact of films designed to enhance the attitudes of American soldiers toward their British allies during World War II. The films were quite effective, and Hovland and his colleagues expected that their impact would decrease over time. Yet much to the researchers' surprise, the influence of the films on attitudes was greater nine weeks after their presentation than it was only one week afterwards.

These and related findings led Kelman and Hovland (1953) to propose an intriguing explanation for this **sleeper effect**—for the occurrence of increased persuasion (attitude change) over time. Reasoning from a learning perspective (an approach that was very popular in the study of attitudes at that time), they suggested that when people are first exposed to a persuasive message, they form two types of associations: (1) ones between the message's argument and its conclusion and (2) ones between other cues (e.g., information about the source's credibility) and the message's conclusion.

The first type of association tends to persist over time more strongly than the second type. Thus, delayed attitude change can occur as follows: Assume that at the time a persuasive message is presented, people also receive information that casts doubts on the credibility of the source (e.g., they learn that the source is low in expertise or wishes to manipulate them). As a result, they reject the message's conclusion and demonstrate relatively little attitude change. Over time, however, the association between such *discounting cues* and the message weakens, while the association between the message's argument and its conclusion remains relatively strong. The result: People remember the message's argument and its conclusion more strongly than they remember their doubts about its source, and attitude change actually increases (see Figure 4.10, p. 154).

This *disassociation* explanation seemed convincing and soon gained widespread acceptance. But there was a large, unpleasant fly in the ointment: Try as they might, subsequent researchers could not readily replicate the sleeper effect itself. In other words, it proved extremely difficult to demonstrate the kind of delayed attitude change described above. Were social psychologists seeking an imaginary phenomenon? Or does the sleeper effect really exist?

More recent research strongly supports the latter point of view. For example, Gruder and his colleagues (Gruder et al., 1978) succeeded in demonstrating the sleeper effect with respect to an interesting issue: adoption of a four-day workweek. Subjects in this investigation first read a persuasive message arguing against this social change. Some read only the message itself, while others received both the message and a discounting cue—they learned that the conclusion of the message was false. (Individuals in a third, no-message control group never read the persuasive message.) Five weeks later, subjects returned and reported their attitudes once again. Results were clear: Those who had received

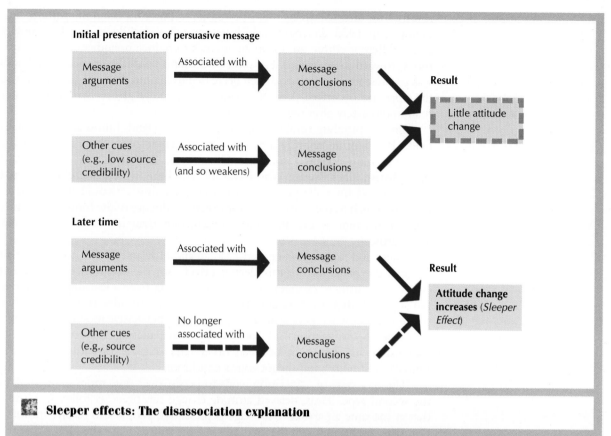

Initial presentation of persuasive message

Message arguments → Associated with → Message conclusions

Other cues (e.g., low source credibility) → Associated with (and so weakens) → Message conclusions

Result: Little attitude change

Later time

Message arguments → Associated with → Message conclusions

Other cues (e.g., source credibility) → No longer associated with → Message conclusions

Result: Attitude change increases (*Sleeper Effect*)

Sleeper effects: The disassociation explanation

FIGURE 4.10 According to the *disassociation* explanation, sleeper effects occur because over time, the association between *discounting cues* (e.g., low source credibility) and the message's conclusion weakens. In contrast, the association between the message's argument and its conclusion remains relatively strong. As a result, attitude change is minimal at first, but increases over time. (Source: Based on suggestions by Kelman & Hovland, 1953.)

the discounting cue along with the message actually showed a significant shift in attitude in the direction advocated by the message. In other words, they demonstrated a strong sleeper effect.

Why did Gruder and his colleagues obtain a sleeper effect when so many other researchers had failed to do so? They pointed to several conditions present in their research that appear to be necessary for the occurrence of such effects. These include a strong discounting cue (one that virtually eliminates the impact of the persuasive message), a strong and convincing message, and sufficient time for the message and discounting cue to become dissociated. Additional findings reported by Pratkanis, Greenwald, Leippe, and Baumgardner (1988) suggest that other factors, too, are important. In a series of seventeen different studies, these researchers found that sleeper effects occur only when people (1) take careful note of the key arguments in the message and (2) receive the discounting cue after the message has been presented. (In many of the unsuccessful earlier studies, the cue had been presented before the persuasive message.)

On the basis of these and other findings, Pratkanis and his colleagues (1988) have proposed a different interpretation of the sleep effect—one more in keeping with modern social psychology than the disassociation view offered by Kelman and Hovland (1953). Briefly, Pratkanis and his colleagues suggest that both the persuasive message and the discounting cue contain information that can influence recipients' attitudes. The impact of the discounting cue, however, is often weaker than that of the message itself. Over time, the influence of both decreases, but in some cases, at least, the impact of the discounting cue decreases (decays) somewhat faster. Thus, the sleeper effect occurs because of such *differential decay* of impact, not as a result of disassociation between the discounting cue and the message. Whatever its precise origins, the sleeper effect does seem to exist and to play a role in persuasion. Its history in social psychology provides a compelling illustration of how the careful use of scientific methods, coupled with growing theoretical sophistication, can add to our knowledge about even very subtle and complex aspects of social thought.

Persuasion: The Cognitive Approach

The traditional approach to understanding persuasion (sometimes called the *Yale approach,* since much early work within this framework was conducted at Yale University) has certainly proved useful. Research conducted from this perspective provided much information about the "when" and "how" of persuasion—it indicated when such attitude change is most likely to occur and how, in practical terms, it can be produced. Unfortunately, however, this approach was less helpful with respect to the *why* of persuasion; it did not offer as many insights into why people change their attitudes in response to persuasive messages.

This issue has been brought into sharp focus in a more modern approach known as the **cognitive perspective** (cf. Chaiken, 1987; Petty & Cacioppo, 1986). Within this approach, the key question has shifted from, Who says what to whom with what effect? to, What cognitive processes determine when someone is actually persuaded? In other words, this newer perspective focuses on what many researchers term a *cognitive response analysis*—efforts to understand (1) what people think about when they are exposed to persuasive appeals and (2) how their thoughts and related cognitive processes determine whether and to what extent they experience attitude change (Greenwald, 1968; Petty, Ostrom, & Brock, 1981). While several theoretical models currently reflect this approach, we'll consider two that have proven to be quite influential.

The Elaboration Likelihood Model: Two Routes to Persuasion What happens when individuals receive a persuasive message? According to Petty and Cacioppo (1986), they think about it, the arguments it makes, and (perhaps) the arguments it has left out. It is these thoughts—not the message itself—that then lead either to attitude change or to resistance.

Does this mean that we think deeply and carefully about all the persuasive messages we receive? Not at all. As you probably know from your own experience, this is certainly not the case. Careful, logical thinking is hard work, and as we noted in Chapter 3, human beings do not engage in it without strong reason to do so. Thus, when we receive a persuasive message, Petty and Cacioppo (1986) suggest, the effort we expend in thinking carefully about it depends on how important or relevant it is to us. Only if we have strong reasons for analyzing the message carefully and fully will we do the cognitive work required to engage in such processing.

But how does persuasion actually occur? According to the **elaboration likelihood model (ELM),** two different processes can be involved, and which one is selected depends on the amount of *elaboration* (careful scrutiny) individuals direct to persuasive messages they receive. If they give substantial attention to the message and its arguments, persuasion can occur through the **central route.** This route involves careful, thoughtful consideration of the issue and arguments. Here, attitude change occurs to the extent that the arguments are indeed convincing and the facts marshaled in their behalf are strong. In contrast, if the arguments are weak and unconvincing, little attitude change will follow.

The second way in which persuasion can occur is through what Petty and Cacioppo (1986) term the **peripheral route.** Here, change occurs in the absence of careful thought. It is, in a sense, an "automatic" response to *persuasion cues*—information related to the expertise or status of the would-be persuader, or presentation of a two-sided communication, which seems fairer and more balanced than a one-sided message (e.g., Sorrentino et al., 1988). The peripheral route is also the more likely route to persuasion when audience members are distracted and can't pay full attention to a careful analysis of the speaker's message (e.g., Petty, Wells, & Brock, 1976). An overview of the ELM model and the two routes to persuasion it suggests is presented in Figure 4.11.

At this point, we should note that persuasive messages may be relevant or important to us for several reasons. As Johnson and Eagly (1989) recently noted, we may find such messages personally involving because they are relevant

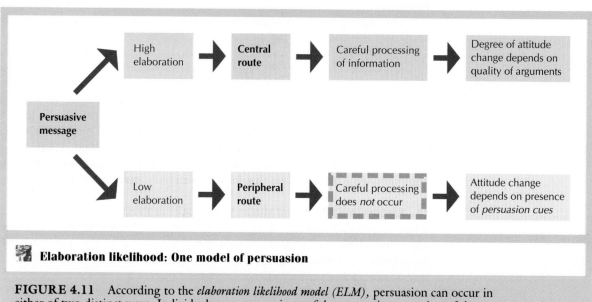

Elaboration likelihood: One model of persuasion

FIGURE 4.11 According to the *elaboration likelihood model (ELM),* persuasion can occur in either of two distinct ways. Individuals may engage in careful, systematic processing of the information contained in persuasive messages, in which case persuasion occurs through the *central route.* Alternatively, individuals may respond largely to *persuasion cues* (e.g., information about the source's credibility or status). In this case, persuasion occurs through the *peripheral route.* (Source: Based on suggestions by Petty & Cacioppo, 1986.)

to our basic values or because they are related to important outcomes (e.g., something that may happen to us as a result of our attitudes and decisions that follow from them). Research findings suggest that in the former case, involving persuasive messages will indeed lead to considerable processing, but primarily to bolster and support our current attitudes—*not* to weigh or evaluate carefully the information being presented. Thus, even when we find a message important or personally involving, we will not necessarily enter the central route and think systematically about its content.

Despite such limitations, the ELM appears to be of considerable value because it helps explain, in modern, cognitive terms, the impact of the many variables that have been found to affect persuasion. For example, consider the following illustration. Research findings indicate that people are persuaded to a greater degree by sources high in credibility (expertise, status) than by sources lower in credibility, even when the arguments offered are relatively weak. The ELM model can explain such findings by calling attention to the fact that in such cases, persuasion is occurring through the peripheral route, in which the quality of an argument is relatively unimportant. In other words, when individuals receive a persuasive message from a highly credible source, they don't bother to carefully process and evaluate the arguments presented. Rather, they respond in a relatively automatic manner, accepting the message largely on the basis of its source.

Similarly, the ELM helps explain why people are often more persuaded by information from multiple sources than by information from a single source (Harkins & Petty, 1987). According to the ELM, this **multiple-source effect** occurs because information receives greater scrutiny when it is presented by multiple sources. Then, if the arguments presented are strong, greater attitude change may follow.

The Heuristic Model of Persuasion   A closely related view of persuasion is the **heuristic model,** proposed by Chaiken (1987). (As you may recall from Chapter 3, heuristics are mental shortcuts—rules of thumb we find useful in processing social information.) Chaiken suggests that when a situation is personally involving (e.g., when it deals with attitudes important to the people in question), systematic processing of input occurs. Thus, individuals engage in the kind of careful, cognitive analysis described above with respect to the central route to persuasion. In contrast, when personal involvement is low, individuals rely on various heuristics to determine whether or not to change their attitudes. For example, they are more persuaded by expert than nonexpert and likable than nonlikable sources, by a greater rather than a smaller number of arguments, and by arguments bolstered by the presence of statistics than by arguments not supported in this manner (e.g., Chaiken, 1980; Eagly & Chaiken, 1984). So again, persuasion can occur through either of two mechanisms, depending on the circumstances involved.

A good illustration of the value of the heuristic model is provided by a study conducted by Axsom, Yates, and Chaiken (1987). These researchers were interested in an intriguing question: When individuals overhear the reactions of an audience to a persuasive message, does this influence the extent to which they, too, are persuaded? In other words, if you heard audience members cheer wildly (or boo loudly) after a political speech, would hearing these reactions influence the extent to which you, too, were persuaded? On the basis of the heuristic model, Axsom, Yates, and Chaiken (1987) predicted that audience reaction would be influential when the individuals in question had little involvement in the issue. Under these conditions, they would rely on simple heuristics, such as *If other people think it's right (wrong), then it probably is.* In contrast, when the issue is important to the persons involved, audience reactions would make little difference: Systematic processing would occur, and persuasion would depend on such factors as the quality of the arguments.

To test these predictions, the researchers had subjects listen to a recording of what was supposedly a previous debate over whether probation should be used as an alternative to imprisonment for convicted criminals. Some subjects were given information designed to increase their involvement in this issue (e.g., they were told it was very important), while others were given information designed to reduce their personal involvement (e.g., they were told to just relax while the tape was playing). The quality of the arguments, too, was varied so that some subjects heard high-quality arguments favoring probation while others heard weak arguments. The tape also contained either cheers and enthusiastic clapping by an audience or a few weak claps and cries of derision. After listening to one version of the tape, subjects indicated their attitudes about probation.

As you can see from Figure 4.12, results offered support for predictions derived from the heuristic model. Under conditions of low involvement, subjects were more in favor of probation after hearing an enthusiastic audience

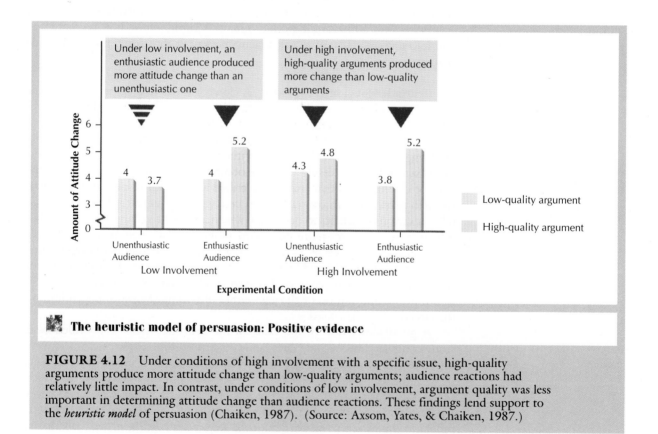

The heuristic model of persuasion: Positive evidence

FIGURE 4.12 Under conditions of high involvement with a specific issue, high-quality arguments produce more attitude change than low-quality arguments; audience reactions had relatively little impact. In contrast, under conditions of low involvement, argument quality was less important in determining attitude change than audience reactions. These findings lend support to the *heuristic model* of persuasion (Chaiken, 1987). (Source: Axsom, Yates, & Chaiken, 1987.)

than after hearing an unenthusiastic one. Argument quality made little difference; instead, subjects whose involvement was low seemed to follow the heuristic *If others agree, then I should too.* In contrast, under conditions of high involvement, subjects were influenced primarily by argument quality: The better these arguments were, the more they favored the use of probation, regardless of the audience's apparent reaction.

In sum, both the ELM and the heuristic model offer important insights into persuasion. Both help explain *how* persuasive messages induce attitude change, and both call attention to the fact that persuasion can occur along either of two distinctively different routes. Clearly, such models constitute a marked advance in our understanding of this important process.

Attitude Function, Attitude Object, and Persuasion At several points in this chapter, we have noted that attitudes can serve any of several different functions for the persons who hold them. Often, they help the attitude-holders to organize and interpret diverse sets of information (*knowledge function*). They can also permit individuals to express their central values or beliefs (*self-expression* or *self-identity function*). And attitudes sometimes help those who hold them to maintain or enhance their self-esteem (*self-esteem function*) by, for example, comparing themselves favorably with other persons or groups.

The functions served by attitudes are important from the point of view of a cognitive analysis of persuasion. Persuasive messages containing information relevant to specific attitudes—and, especially, information relevant to the functions served by those attitudes—will be processed differently (perhaps more carefully) from persuasive messages that do not contain such information. To the extent this is true, the precise conditions required for successful persuasion should vary with the functions served by various attitudes.

Convincing evidence for a relationship between attitude function and persuasion has recently been provided by Shavitt (1990). She reasoned that because of their basic nature, certain objects are associated with attitudes serving primarily one kind of function. For example, Shavitt noted that some objects (e.g., air conditioners) serve primarily a *utilitarian function*—people buy and use them because of the rewards they provide. Thus, attitudes about them should focus on this function. In contrast, other objects (e.g., perfume) serve a *social identity function*—they permit individuals to express their identity and values, or the reference groups to which they would like to belong. To put it more concretely, people buy some products, like an air conditioner, because, presumably, they enjoy the comfort these provide. In contrast, they buy other products (e.g., perfume) at least in part because these products allow them to transmit a particular kind of personal "image."

Given such differences, Shavitt reasoned that persuasive appeals that focus on the appropriate attitude function for a given object will be more successful than those that focus on other attitude functions. Specifically, persuasive messages that emphasize the features of a product should be more successful in changing attitudes about air conditioners and coffee than about perfume or greeting cards. In contrast, persuasive messages that emphasize the image various products yield should be more persuasive for perfume and greeting cards.

To test these predictions, she exposed female subjects to four pairs of ads— one ad about each of two brands of each of four products. In each ad pair, one focused on features (e.g., the flavor and aroma of a brand of coffee) while the other focused on what the product indicated about the purchaser's taste and values (e.g., how use of a brand of coffee would indicate one's good judgment to others). Results offered strong support for the hypothesis. For the utilitarian products (air conditioners, coffee), subjects strongly preferred the brands that had been promoted by ads focused on their features. For the self-identity products (perfume, greeting cards), however, subjects strongly preferred the brands that had been promoted on the basis of their "snob appeal." In short, the persuasive appeals whose content matched the function of the product (and hence attitudes about it) were more effective than those that did not. These findings indicate that where persuasion is concerned, the functions served by attitudes are an important factor to consider. Messages that draw a bead on these functions may be processed more carefully, and so exert greater impact, than ones that do not.

Other Aspects of the Cognitive Approach: Understanding the Effects of Mood and Individual Differences   Before concluding this discussion of the cognitive approach to persuasion, we should call attention to two additional ways in which it contributes to our understanding of persuasion. Each of these involves the influence of affect (mood) on persuasion and the role of individual differences in this process.

Why are people in a good mood easier to influence? Would-be persuaders frequently adopt a strategy of "Put them in a good mood first, then try to persuade them." Is this strategy effective? As we saw in Chapter 3, affective states seem to influence a wide range of behavior and several cognitive processes, so at first glance, this strategy seems reasonable. Moreover, informal observation suggests that such tactics sometimes succeed in realms of life as unrelated as sales of various products and sexual seduction. Why is this the case? The cognitive approach to persuasion offers a compelling answer: Perhaps when people are in a good mood, they are less able to engage in careful, systematic processing than when they are in a neutral mood. As a result, they may be more easily influenced, especially by strong and convincing arguments. An ingenious study by Mackie and Worth (1989) offers support for this reasoning.

In this experiment, male and female subjects read a persuasive message arguing against their own views (whatever these were) about a key issue: the use of government controls to reduce acid rain in the northeastern United States. Half the subjects read this message after experiencing an event designed to put them in a good mood (they learned they had been randomly selected to receive a two-dollar cash prize and actually did receive it). The remaining subjects received the message while in a neutral mood (they were not told about the prize and did not receive it). Within each of these conditions, half the subjects received strong arguments in favor of a view different from their own, while the remainder received weak arguments. Finally, half the subjects were told they could look at the persuasive message (shown on a computer screen) for as long as they wished; the remainder were told they could look at it only briefly, just long enough to read it once.

After reading the message, subjects reported their attitudes toward the acid-rain issue. Mackie and Worth (1989) predicted that those in a positive mood would be prevented from engaging in systematic processing of the arguments presented. Thus, in the limited-time condition (where they could read the

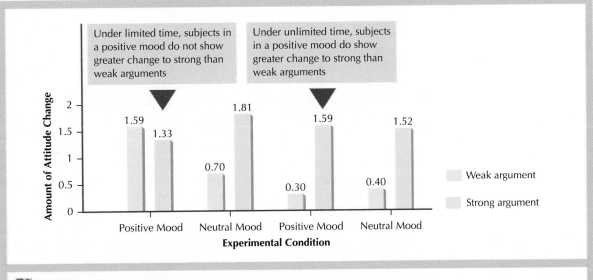

Positive affect and persuasion

FIGURE 4.13   When subjects had unlimited time to read a persuasive message, they demonstrated greater attitude change in response to strong than to weak arguments even when they were in a good mood. Under conditions of limited time, however, those in a good mood were not more strongly affected by strong than by weak arguments. These findings suggest that persons experiencing positive affect are less capable of engaging in careful, systematic information processing than persons in a neutral mood.   (Source: Based on data from Mackie & Worth, 1989.)

message only once), subjects would show the same amount of attitude change, regardless of whether the arguments were weak or strong. In contrast, both subjects in a neutral mood and those in a positive mood when given unlimited time to read the message were expected to show greater attitude change in response to strong arguments than to weak ones. As shown in Figure 4.13, this is precisely what happened. In addition—and also as predicted—when subjects were given an opportunity to look at the message for as long as they wished, those in a positive mood chose to do so for a longer period than those in a neutral mood (78.37 seconds versus 69.49 seconds). This latter finding suggests that people in a good mood are motivated to engage in systematic processing of a persuasive message but are prevented from doing so in their pleasant mood, which reduces their capacity for such active thought in several ways (e.g., it causes them to think about a wider range of ideas and experiences, thus occupying more of the mind's limited capacity; Isen, 1987). In sum, being in a good mood does reduce the ability to engage in systematic processing, and this, in turn, can sometimes enhance susceptibility to persuasion.

Individual differences and two kinds of processing: Attitude function and persuasion   Earlier, we noted that individuals are more likely to engage in active, systematic processing of persuasive messages when they find the content of such messages involving than when they do not (cf. Petty & Cacioppo, 1986; Johnson & Eagly, 1989). This point raises the question, Do individual differences play a role in this process? Do different people, because of their personal characteristics, find certain types of situations or issues more involving than others? Growing evidence suggests they do (e.g., Sorrentino et al., 1988). For example, consider **self-monitoring**—an intriguing aspect of personality we'll examine in detail in Chapter 12. Persons high in self-monitoring are very concerned with making a good impression on others. Accordingly, they may find situations in which they receive communications from attractive sources to be especially involving, particularly when they have the opportunity to meet these communicators. In contrast, such persons may find situations in which they receive persuasive appeals from expert sources relatively uninvolving. In other words, persons high in self-monitoring may engage in systematic processing in response to persuasion from attractive sources but in peripheral (heuristic) processing in response to persuasion from expert sources. Just the opposite would be true for persons low in self-monitoring, who are less interested in making favorable impressions on others and more concerned that their behavior reflect their inner attitudes and values. These predictions have been confirmed in research by DeBono and Harnish (1988). Their findings and those of other studies suggest that individual differences do indeed play a role in persuasion. Some people *are* easier to influence than others in certain contexts, and such differences can be traced to several personal characteristics and the effects these factors have on the information-processing strategies people adopt.

When Attitude Change Fails: Resistance to Persuasion

Given the frequency with which we are exposed to various persuasive messages, one point is clear: If we changed our attitudes in response to even a small fraction of these messages, we would soon be in a pitiable state. Our views on a wide range of issues would change from day to day or even from hour to hour; and, reflecting this fact, our behavior, too, would show a strange pattern of shifts, reversals, and rereversals. Obviously, this does not happen. Despite all the charm, charisma, and expertise would-be persuaders bring to bear on us, our attitudes remain remarkably stable. Rather than being pushovers where persuasion is concerned, we are a "tough sell" and can withstand even powerful efforts to change our attitudes. Why? What factors provide us with such an impressive ability to resist? As you might guess, the answers to these questions are complex and involve many processes. In this section, we will describe several of the most important of these.

Reactance: Protecting One's Personal Freedom

Have you ever found yourself in a situation in which, because you felt that someone was trying to exert undue influence on you, you leaned over backward to do the opposite of what he or she wanted? If so, you are already familiar with the operation of **reactance.** This refers to the negative reactions we experience whenever we feel that someone is trying to limit our personal freedom. Research findings suggest that when we perceive this to be the case, we tend to shift in a direction exactly *opposite* to that being urged on us—an effect known as **negative attitude change** (e.g., Brehm, 1966; Rhodewalt & Davison, 1983). Indeed, so strong is the desire to resist undue influence that in some cases individuals shift away from a view being advocated even if it is one they might normally accept.

The existence of reactance is one principal reason why hard-sell attempts at persuasion often fail. When individuals perceive such appeals as direct threats to their personal freedom (or to their public image of being a free, independent human being), they are strongly motivated to resist. And such resistance, in turn, virtually guarantees that many would-be persuaders are doomed to fail.

Forewarning: Prior Knowledge of Persuasive Intent

On many occasions when we receive a persuasive message, we know full well that it is designed to change our views. Indeed, situations in which a communicator manages to catch us completely unprepared are probably quite rare. Does such advance knowledge, or **forewarning,** of persuasive intent help us to resist? Research evidence suggests that it does (e.g., Cialdini & Petty, 1979; Petty & Cacioppo, 1981). When we know that a speech, taped message, or written appeal is designed to alter our views, we are often less likely to be affected by it than if we do not possess such knowledge. The basis for such beneficial effects seems to lie in the impact that forewarning has on key cognitive processes. When we receive a persuasive message, especially one contrary to our current views, we often formulate *counterarguments* against it (see Figure 4.14). Knowing about the content of such a message in advance, then, provides us with extra time in which to prepare our defenses. Similarly, forewarning may also give us more time in which to recall relevant facts and information from memory—facts that may prove useful in refuting a persuasive message (Wood, 1982). Again, such effects are more likely to occur with respect to attitudes we consider to be important, for they are more readily accessible from memory (Krosnick, 1989). For these and related reasons, to be forewarned *is* to be forearmed, at least in cases in which we care enough about the topic in question to engage in active processing about it.

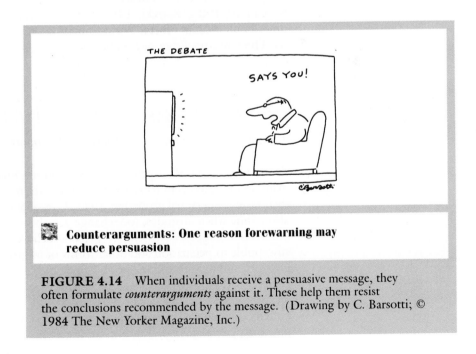

Counterarguments: One reason forewarning may reduce persuasion

FIGURE 4.14 When individuals receive a persuasive message, they often formulate *counterarguments* against it. These help them resist the conclusions recommended by the message. (Drawing by C. Barsotti; © 1984 The New Yorker Magazine, Inc.)

Selective Avoidance

Still another way in which we resist attempts at persuasion is through **selective avoidance**, a tendency to direct our attention away from information that challenges our existing attitudes. In the context of social cognition (see Chapter 3), selective avoidance is one of the ways in which attitudes (a type of schema) guide the processing of incoming information. For example, consider the act of television viewing. Growing evidence suggests that people do not simply sit in front of the tube and absorb whatever the media decide to throw at them. Instead, they change channels, push the mute button, or cognitively tune out when confronted with information (e.g., news coverage) counter to their existing views. The opposite effect occurs as well: When we encounter information that supports our views (e.g., commentary consistent with our attitudes), we tend to give it increased attention. We stop changing channels and both watch and listen carefully. Together, these tendencies to tune out information that contradicts our attitudes but to tune in information consistent with them constitutes the two sides of *selective exposure*—deliberate efforts to obtain information that supports our views. Through this mechanism, we can protect our current attitudes against persuasion and assure that they remain unchanged for long periods.

To conclude: Because of the operation of reactance, forewarning, and selective avoidance, our ability to resist persuasion is considerable. Of course, attitude change *does* occur in some cases; to deny that it does would be to suggest that all forms of advertising, propaganda, and political campaigning are worthless. But the opposite conclusion—that we are helpless pawns in the hands of powerful, expert communicators—is equally false. Resisting persuasion is an ancient human art, and recent events in Eastern Europe, where very few citizens were convinced of the benefits of Communist rule despite four decades of continuous propaganda, indicate that it is certainly alive and well today. Thus, persuasion is often much easier to plan or imagine than it is to achieve (Chaiken & Stangor, 1987; Rajecki, 1989). (Are attitudes easier to influence at some times of life than at others? For information on this intriguing question, please see **The Cutting Edge** section below.)

FOCUS ON RESEARCH: THE CUTTING EDGE

Attitude Change and Age: Are There Really "Impressionable Years"?

Youth, it is often said, is prone to excess. During their teens and early twenties, many individuals seem to swing from one extreme to another with respect to their tastes in personal grooming, style of dress, and many other matters. Is this also a time when attitudes, too, change greatly—and perhaps readily? Informal observation suggests it is. Many persons believe that our attitudes are most susceptible to persuasion and other forms of influence when we have left childhood behind but are still young. In short, they accept the accuracy of what has been termed the *impressionable-years hypothesis*—the suggestion that our attitudes are profoundly shaped during this period but then settle down to a lifelong pattern of stability. Is this hypothesis correct? Or is a competing view—the *increasing-persistence hypothesis*—more accurate? This latter hypothesis suggests

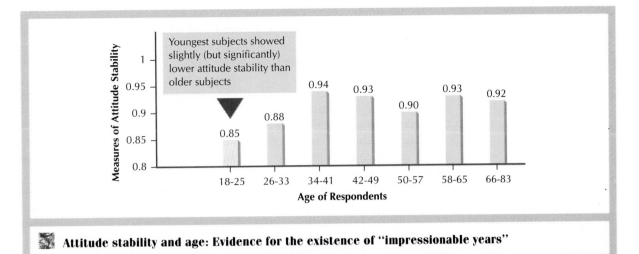

Attitude stability and age: Evidence for the existence of "impressionable years"

FIGURE 4.15 Among individuals ranging in age from eighteen to eighty-three, those in the youngest group demonstrated the lowest amount of stability in political and social attitudes. These findings offer support for the *impressionable-years hypothesis*. (Source: Based on data from Krosnick & Alwin, 1989.)

that we are most susceptible to persuasion when we are young but then become increasingly resistant as we age, until, by midlife, we are downright petrified! A series of studies conducted by Krosnick and Alwin (1989) shed considerable light on these issues.

In this research, Krosnick and Alwin examined survey data from literally thousands of persons who had responded to a wide range of questions about their political and social views at different times during a thirty-year period. One sample of subjects completed surveys at the time of the 1956 U.S. presidential election, again during the 1958 election, and finally at the time of the 1960 election. Another sample responded at the time of the 1972 U.S. presidential election, again in 1974, and once more at the time of the 1976 presidential election. In the 1956–1960 study, respondents were asked about their views concerning such issues as school integration, U.S. financial aid to other nations, and federal financial aid to schools. In the 1972–1976 study, subjects were asked questions about their political affiliation, their attitudes toward various groups (e.g., labor unions, the military), and their attitudes toward racial policy (e.g., school busing).

Subjects were divided into seven different age-groups (eighteen to twenty-five, twenty-six to thirty-three, thirty-four to forty-one, and so on), and statistical analyses were performed to determine the extent to which their attitudes remained stable during the period covered by each survey (approximately four years). The results were clear: As predicted by the impressionable-years hypothesis, attitude stability was lower in the youngest sample (ages eighteen to twenty-five) than in any of the others (see Figure 4.15). There was no support for the increasing-persistence hypothesis, however. As individuals grew older, they did not show the increasing stability this view predicts.

To determine whether these findings could be replicated at still another time and within a shorter period, Krosnick and Alwin repeated the same basic procedures before and after the 1980 U.S. presidential election. Again, a large sample of individuals responded to a wide range of questions about their political and social views. Results were virtually identical to those of the first study. Once again, subjects in the youngest age-group showed significantly lower stability than older participants, and there was little if any support for the view that people become increasingly resistant to change as they grow older.

Together, the data reported by Krosnick and Alwin suggest that we do indeed pass through a period that can be described as the *impressionable years*. During our late teens and early twenties, we are more open to change and to shifts in our attitudes than we are at later times in our lives. This point suggests that the experiences we have, the people we meet, and the friendships we form during this period may have profound effects on views we then continue to hold for many decades. Moreover, since social conditions change rapidly in the modern world, it also seems likely that persons who pass through this stage of life at different points in history (e.g., during the 1950s versus the 1980s) will form contrasting attitudes. Indeed, the attitudes formed by these groups of age-mates (or *cohorts*, as psychologists term them) may be so different from one another that they contribute, along with other factors, to the proverbial *generation gap* that each group of young adults discovers anew. To the extent that they do, the existence of a period of maximum attitude flexibility has profound social implications worth considering with care.

Cognitive Dissonance: How We Sometimes Change Our Own Attitudes

Imagine the following situation: You have always been in favor of affirmative action (special programs for hiring and promoting minority group members). Now, however, you learn that because of this policy, one of your friends has been passed over for promotion, even though she has more experience and better qualifications than the minority candidate who *was* promoted. While you are in favor of affirmative action, you also believe that people should be promoted on the basis of merit. How do you feel? If you are like most people, you find this situation disconcerting. After all, you have come face to face with the fact that two of your attitudes are inconsistent—they just don't fit together, at least not in this situation.

In the terminology of social psychology, you would be experiencing a state known as **cognitive dissonance** (Festinger, 1957). This is the feeling, usually unpleasant, that arises when we discover inconsistency between two of our attitudes or between our attitudes and our behavior. We have already illustrated inconsistency between two attitudes in the example above, in which favorable attitudes toward affirmative action ran smack up against attitudes toward promotion on the basis of merit (see Figure 4.16). But there are many other causes of dissonance as well. It occurs whenever individuals must choose between two attractive alternatives. After all, rejecting one job, school, or lover in favor of another is inconsistent with the positive features offered by the rejected option. Most relevant to our present discussion, though, is that dissonance is generated

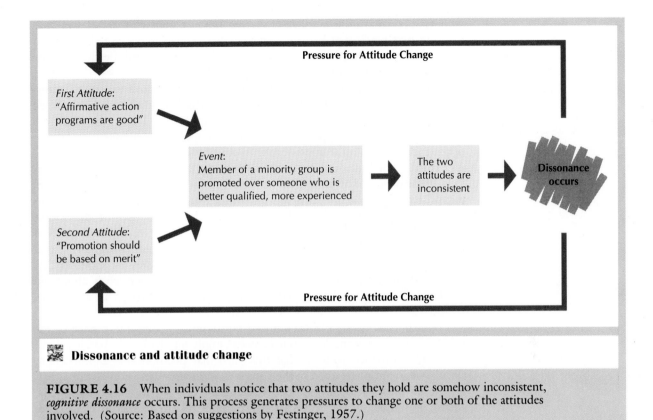

Pressure for Attitude Change

First Attitude: "Affirmative action programs are good"

Event: Member of a minority group is promoted over someone who is better qualified, more experienced

The two attitudes are inconsistent

Dissonance occurs

Second Attitude: "Promotion should be based on merit"

Pressure for Attitude Change

Dissonance and attitude change

FIGURE 4.16 When individuals notice that two attitudes they hold are somehow inconsistent, *cognitive dissonance* occurs. This process generates pressures to change one or both of the attitudes involved. (Source: Based on suggestions by Festinger, 1957.)

whenever individuals say things they don't mean or behave in ways that are inconsistent with their underlying attitudes and values. In such cases, the dissonance produced can have a startling effect: It can lead the people involved to change their attitudes so that these more closely reflect their words and deeds. In other words, saying or doing things that are inconsistent with their attitudes sometimes causes individuals to change the attitudes themselves. How can this be so? For some intriguing answers, please read on.

Dissonance and Attitude Change: The Effects of Forced Compliance

There are many occasions in everyday life when we must say or do things inconsistent with our real attitudes. For example, Aunt Helen gives you one of her paintings—again. Although you dislike it, you must do the right thing and thank her warmly for her thoughtfulness. Similarly, at an important meeting your boss turns to you and asks your opinion of her new strategic plan. Since you value your working relationship with her (and your job!), you praise the plan, even though you think it is seriously flawed. In these and countless other situations, we find that our words and our attitudes are clearly inconsistent. What happens in these situations, which social psychologists describe as involving *forced compliance* (we are forced by various circumstances, to comply in ways that run counter to our own views)?

Since dissonance is a motivational state (people who experience it are motivated to reduce it), something has to give (change). Several possibilities exist. First, individuals can change their attitudes so that these are now consistent

167

with their behavior. For example, you may convince yourself that Aunt Helen's painting isn't really that bad, or that your boss's plan is better than you first believed. Doing so would be an instance of self-generated attitude change—the kind of effect referred to in the title on page 166.

Second—and this option is somewhat harder—individuals experiencing dissonance can change their cognitions about their behavior. (The behavior itself can't be changed, since it has already been completed.) Thus, you might tell yourself that offering support to your boss in important meetings is really part of your job, and so quite consistent with your basic attitudes.

Third, dissonance can be reduced by acquiring *new information*—specifically, information that is consistent with the attitudes or actions that seem inconsistent. For example, people who smoke cigarettes usually know that this action is harmful to their health. They often try to reduce the dissonance generated by such counterattitudinal behavior by eagerly seeking evidence that smoking is truly not all that bad. They read reports of studies suggesting that smoking has few or no ill effects (even though these studies are sponsored by large tobacco companies). And they repeatedly remind themselves about old Uncle Herb, who lived to ninety-six despite smoking two packs a day (see Chapter 14).

Fourth, dissonance can be reduced by minimizing the importance of the inconsistency. For example, in our earlier example involving affirmative action, you might convince yourself that this particular promotion is unimportant, since your friend plans to leave the company soon anyway.

In which of these ways do people actually seek to reduce dissonance? The answer is simple: in the way that is least effortful. In this as in most other situations, we follow the path of least resistance and seek to reduce dissonance by changing what is easiest to change. And since acquiring new information and minimizing the important of outcomes that really *are* important are quite difficult, the easiest route may well involve changing our own attitudes. This, in brief, is why saying or doing things inconsistent with our attitudes sometimes leads to changes in them.

Dissonance and the Less-Leads-to-More Effect   So far, we have described the nature of forced compliance and indicated how it can lead individuals to change their own attitudes. There is one complication we have not yet considered, however: How strong are the reasons for saying or doing something inconsistent with your attitudes to begin with? If these reasons are very good, little or no dissonance will be generated. After all, if the last person to disagree publicly with your boss was fired on the spot, you have strong grounds for praising her plan even if you don't like it. Similarly, if Aunt Helen has promised to leave you her original Picasso because you appreciate fine art, you have powerful grounds for biting your tongue when she gives you one of her own "masterpieces." In short, the better the reasons for saying what you don't believe, the less dissonance you will experience, and so the weaker the pressure to change your actual views. Social psychologists describe this paradoxical prediction as the **less-leads-to-more effect**—the more inducements there are for engaging in attitude-discrepant behavior, the weaker the pressures toward attitude change.

Surprising as it may seem, this effect has actually been confirmed in many different studies (e.g., Riess & Schlenker, 1977). For example, in the first and most famous of these experiments (Festinger & Carlsmith, 1959), subjects were offered either a small reward (one dollar) or a large one (twenty dollars) for telling another person that some dull tasks they had just performed were very interesting. (One of the tasks consisted of placing spools on a tray, dumping them out, and repeating the process over and over again.) After engaging in this attitude-discrepant behavior (telling another subject that the tasks were interesting when they knew that they were not), subjects were asked to indicate their own liking for the tasks. As predicted by the less-leads-to-more effect, subjects actually reported greater liking for the dull tasks when they had received the small reward than when they had received the large one (see Figure 4.17).

While this and several other studies lend support to predictions based on dissonance theory, we should note that the less-leads-to-more effect occurs only under certain conditions (Sogin & Pallak, 1976). First, it occurs only in situations in which people believe they have a choice as to whether or not to perform the attitude-discrepant behavior. Second, small rewards lead to greater amounts of attitude change than large ones do only when people believe that they were

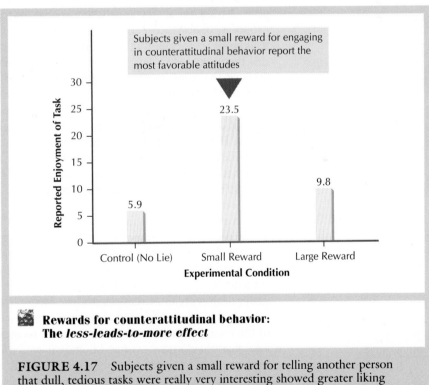

Rewards for counterattitudinal behavior: The *less-leads-to-more effect*

FIGURE 4.17 Subjects given a small reward for telling another person that dull, tedious tasks were really very interesting showed greater liking for these tasks (i.e., greater attitude change) than those given a larger reward for the same action. This finding indicates that where attitude change is concerned, *less* (small rewards) is sometimes *more* (can produce greater amounts of change). (Source: Based on data from Festinger & Carlsmith, 1959.)

personally responsible for both the chosen course of action and any negative effects produced (Goethals, Cooper, & Naficy, 1979). And third, the less-leads-to-more effect does not occur when people view the payment they receive as a bribe rather than well-deserved pay for services rendered. These and related findings suggest that there are significant limits on the impact of forced compliance and that it does not always lead individuals to change their own attitudes. Still, we should note that often, the conditions just outlined *do* exist— often people do have (or think they have) freedom of action. And they frequently accept responsibility for their own behavior even when doing so produces negative consequences. As a result, the strategy of offering others just barely enough reward to induce them to say or do things contrary to their beliefs can often be effective in inducing attitude change—and self-generated change at that.

Dissonance: Does It Really Stem from Inconsistency?

Ever since the concept of cognitive dissonance was first developed, more than thirty years ago, social psychologists have assumed that *inconsistency* is its most basic feature. It has been reasoned that people dislike inconsistency and strive to reduce it when it arises. In recent years, however, a radically different interpretation of dissonance has been offered by Cooper and his colleagues (Cooper & Fazio, 1984; Cooper & Scher, in press). This more recent framework suggests that inconsistency is *not* the essential ingredient in dissonance. Rather, it proposes, dissonance—and the motivation to reduce it—stems primarily from feelings of responsibility for negative events or outcomes. The reasoning behind this theory is as follows. Whenever people notice they have brought about an aversive (harmful) event, they are motivated to determine whether they were responsible for this outcome or whether, perhaps, it stemmed from factors beyond their control. In other words, they are motivated to engage in a special type of self-attributional search (recall our discussion of this topic in Chapter 2). If they conclude that they were indeed personally responsible for the outcome, dissonance is generated and all the effects described above (e.g., efforts to reduce it) then follow. Sometimes, of course, saying or doing things we don't believe can produce negative outcomes and so generate dissonance. But Cooper and his colleagues argue that such attitude-discrepant behavior is not necessary for the occurrence of dissonance. What *is* essential, they maintain, is that people accept responsibility for producing aversive events.

Are these suggestions accurate? Some evidence provides support for them. For example, in one recent study, Scher and Cooper (1989) had male and female students write essays that either supported or refuted their actual views. The essays dealt with an increase in student fees, so when subjects wrote against this change, their essays favored their own views, while when they wrote in favor of the increase, their essays were opposite to their real views. All subjects were told that their essays would be shown to a policy committee interested in student reactions to the proposed increase. Information concerning the supposed impact of the essays, however, was varied systematically. Half the subjects were told that their essays would be presented in such a manner that they would probably be effective in influencing the committee in the intended direction (e.g., toward rejecting the fee increase, if the essay argued for this position). The others were told that their essays would be presented in such a manner that they would probably influence the committee in a direction *opposite* that urged by the essay (e.g., toward raising the fees, if the essay argued against this change). Scher and Cooper reasoned that from the students' viewpoint, aversive outcomes would be produced (1) when they engaged in counterattitudinal behavior (wrote essays favoring the fee increase) *and* learned that their essay would influence the committee in this direction and also (2) when they wrote essays favoring their own views (against the fee increase) but learned that their essays would influence the committee in the *opposite* direction. Thus, attitude change in the direction of raising the fees was predicted in both cases. Here is the crucial point: If dissonance stems primarily from inconsistency, then attitude change should occur only in the first condition (when students wrote counterattitudinal essays). If, however, it stems from personal responsibility for aversive consequences, such change should occur in both groups. As you can see from Figure 4.18, the latter prediction was confirmed.

These findings and those of related studies (cf. Cooper & Scher, in press) suggest that dissonance may involve something other than inconsistency. Pro-

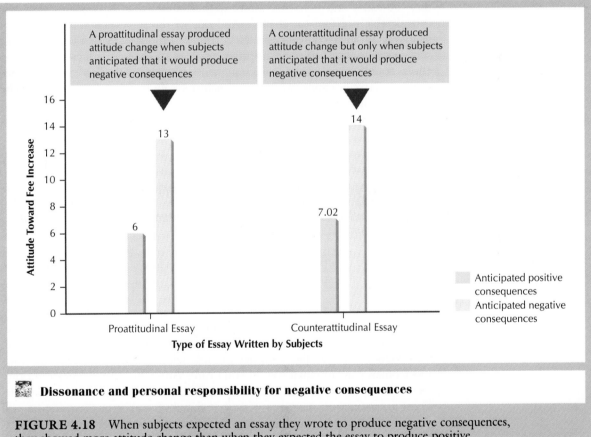

A proattitudinal essay produced attitude change when subjects anticipated that it would produce negative consequences

A counterattitudinal essay produced attitude change but only when subjects anticipated that it would produce negative consequences

Dissonance and personal responsibility for negative consequences

FIGURE 4.18 When subjects expected an essay they wrote to produce negative consequences, they showed more attitude change than when they expected the essay to produce positive consequences. Moreover, they did so regardless of whether the essay supported their own views (was proattitudinal) or refuted them (was counterattitudinal). These findings suggest that dissonance may stem from personal responsibility for producing negative effects, not simply from inconsistency. (Source: Based on data from Scher & Cooper, 1989.)

ducing negative events and feeling personally responsible for them appear to be as important as—and perhaps more important than—disliking inconsistency. Having said that, we wish to note that in our view, the case for changing our basic conception of dissonance is far from complete or fully convincing. Recent research does call attention to several factors that may influence dissonance and the attitude change it often produces, but such research does not seem to account for all the intriguing findings generated in studies that have defined dissonance in the traditional, inconsistency-based manner (cf. Baumeister, 1986). Further, it seems possible to interpret personal responsibility for aversive outcomes within the context of traditional dissonance theory. After all, most persons have a relatively positive self-image; discovering that they personally have been responsible for causing negative outcomes is in a sense inconsistent with that image. Accordingly, attitude change in such cases may stem, at least in part, from inconsistency.

Until such complexities are fully resolved, we believe it is reasonable to continue to view dissonance as deriving from and centering on the effects of inconsistency. To repeat: When people discover that their various attitudes or their attitudes and behaviors don't fit neatly together, they may experience considerable pressure for change. And one of the important things that may give way in such contexts is their attitudes. (Inducing individuals to make statements contrary to their attitudes can lead to change in these views. Can efforts to induce people to make statements *consistent* with their views produce similar effects? For some surprising conclusions about this issue, please see **The Cutting Edge** section below.)

FOCUS ON RESEARCH: THE CUTTING EDGE

Leading Questions, Attitude Certainty, and Attitude Change: The Impact of Superattitudinal Statements

Attorneys and others often use leading questions to change people's views. The basic idea behind such questions is simple: They contain a premise that, once granted, leaves the target person no choice—he or she must respond in the manner desired by the questioner. Doing so often involves making statements that are inconsistent with the target person's current attitudes. Once such statements are made, dissonance comes into play and may induce actual shifts in these views. For example, consider the following question: Why should men and women play an equal role in child care? Any reply to this question other than "They shouldn't" grants the assumption that such a division is desirable. Thus, a person who disagrees with this view but replies to the question will probably make some statement that is contrary to his or her actual (conservative) views. In short, to reply is to be trapped into making a counterattitudinal statement.

Leading questions of this type have been found to succeed in inducing attitude change among people who are uncertain of their views and are therefore willing to reply (Swann & Ely, 1984). However, such questions have generally failed to induce attitude change among people who are highly certain of their opinions, and so refuse to answer in the way the questioner would prefer. Can such persons, too, be induced to alter their opinions? Swann, Pelham, and Chidester (1988) suggest they can. Suppose that such individuals are presented with leading questions that support their views but are extreme. What will they do? Since they don't wish to appear extreme, they may voice some measure of disagreement with the question and answer in a more moderate manner. This situation is truly paradoxical: Such persons find themselves disagreeing with statements that are basically consistent with their views. As a result, dissonance may be induced, and they may experience pressure to shift farther in this direction—away from views they initially supported.

To determine whether such effects actually occur, Swann and his colleagues first identified a group of female students who held conservative views about women's roles. For example, these students agreed with such statements as "If my husband and I both worked, I would realize that his job came first" and "I would expect my husband to be head of the house simply because he's a man." In addition, the researchers measured the certainty with which these women held such views. Subjects in two groups were then exposed to one of two leading-question procedures. In the standard approach, they were asked to reply to ten questions that encouraged them to make statements inconsistent with their conservative views (e.g., "Why do you think women make better bosses than men?" "What do you like most about taking the initiative in a dating relationship?"). In a second approach, subjects were exposed to leading questions that encouraged them to give extremely conservative replies (e.g., "Why do you think men always make better bosses than women?" "Why do you sympathize with the feelings of some men that women are better kept barefoot and pregnant?"). Swann and his colleagues reasoned that subjects would be reluctant to agree with these latter extreme views and would thus make statements of a more moderate nature in replying to them. In short, since they held conservative views, this procedure would lead them to make counterattitudinal replies.

On the basis of the reasoning outlined previously, Swann and his colleagues predicted that the standard leading-question approach would be more successful in changing the attitudes of subjects who were relatively uncertain of their views, while the second (superattitudinal) approach would be more successful with subjects who were high in attitude certainty. As you can see from Figure 4.19 (p. 174), this prediction was supported. Subjects low in attitude certainty demonstrated more attitude change in response to the standard leading questions than to the superattitudinal ones, while subjects high in attitude certainty showed the opposite pattern. (Subjects in a third, control condition were never asked any leading questions and showed no significant attitude change.)

In sum, it appears that leading questions can induce attitude change even among individuals who hold their views with great conviction. To influence such persons, however, it is necessary to employ leading questions that, because they are extreme, induce these persons to reject them and protect their self-images by making relatively moderate statements. When they do, they open the door to dissonance and so, of course, to important changes in their own views.

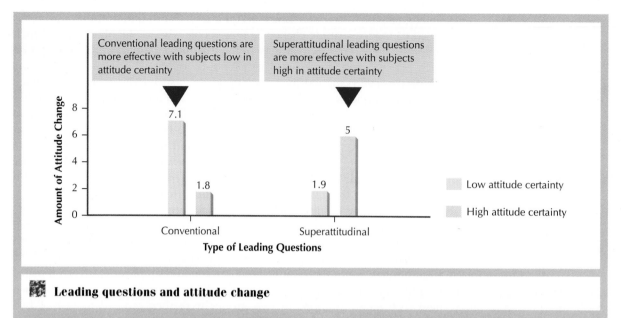

Leading questions and attitude change

FIGURE 4.19 Conventional leading questions, which encouraged subjects to make statements inconsistent with their views, were more effective than "superattitudinal" leading questions in changing their views when attitude certainty was low. The opposite was true when subjects' attitude certainty was high. (Source: Based on data from Swann, Pelham, & Chidester, 1988.)

Putting Dissonance to Work: Effort Justification and the Effectiveness of Psychotherapy

Think about various goals you have sought in your life. Which of them did you value most highly once they were attained? Probably the ones for which you had to work hardest. In general, the greater the effort we must expend in attaining some goal or outcome, the more value we attach to it. Why is this the case? One possibility, of course, is that those things for which we must work hard really *are* higher in intrinsic worth. Various versions of dissonance theory (Abelson, 1982; Cooper & Fazio, 1984), though, offer another explanation. They suggest that we may evaluate goals or outcomes requiring great effort more favorably because of the effort itself. The reasoning behind this proposal— sometimes known as the **suffering-leads-to-liking effect**—is as follows: If we expend a great deal of effort in attaining some goal but then evaluate it negatively, dissonance is produced. After all, the fact that we worked so hard to gain it is inconsistent with such negative reactions. One way of reducing these feelings is then to convince ourselves that we really didn't invest much effort in attaining the goal. Given that long years of study, hours of hard work, or great expense are difficult to ignore, however, this solution is often not feasible. In contrast, another means of eliminating dissonance is far easier to employ: We can raise our evaluations of the goal or outcome in question. In short, we can perceive it more favorably and in this way justify our past actions.

The occurrence of precisely such effects has been observed in a number of experiments (e.g., Aronson & Mills, 1959; Gerard & Mathewson, 1966). In these investigations, the harder people worked to reach some goal (e.g., entry into a social group), the more favorably they evaluated it, even if the goal turned out to be rather disappointing. Such effects are certainly thought-provoking and offer useful insights into the nature of attitudes and attitude change. Here, however, we wish to focus on practical applications of this principle.

How can the *suffering-leads-to-liking,* or **effort justification,** effect be put to practical use? One answer involves its role in psychotherapy—efforts by psychologists to assist individuals in overcoming a wide range of personal problems. The effort justification principle suggests that the more effort individuals invest in such procedures, the more valuable they will perceive them as being. And since commitment to therapy and belief in its efficacy are often crucial factors in its ultimate success, such shifts in attitude can be of considerable value. This reasoning leads to the prediction that steps designed to convince individuals that a specific form of therapy is effortful may increase its benefits. Precisely such effects have been noted in a number of recent studies.

In one such investigation, Axsom and Cooper (1985) exposed overweight women to a "therapy" consisting of various cognitive tasks (e.g., making perceptual judgments of stimuli presented for very brief intervals). These tasks were either high or low in effort; in neither case, however, could they be expected to aid in weight loss. Yet, over a three-week period, subjects in the high-effort condition actually lost more weight than those in the low-effort condition. And this difference actually increased over the next six months. Apparently, after exerting considerable effort in their bogus "therapy," subjects felt committed to restricting their diets and so lost weight.

Additional evidence suggests that actual expenditure of effort is not necessary for such effects to occur; merely expecting to exert effort is sufficient. The point is demonstrated by a study recently conducted by Axsom (1989). In this experiment, male and female subjects who had reported being frightened of snakes were first asked to go as close as they could to a live snake caged in a glass aquarium. The distance at which they stopped was recorded. Next, subjects read a description of a basic form of therapy designed to help them overcome their fear. (This form of therapy involves gradual extinction of the fear and anxiety such persons experience when they see—or merely imagine—a snake, and it has proven highly effective in treating such phobias.) For one group of subjects, the description indicated that the therapy was extremely effortful; for the other group, that it was relatively easy. Dissonance theory suggests that effort justification will occur primarily when people have freely chosen to engage in an effortful task. Thus, to test this prediction, the researchers reminded half the subjects that they were free to withdraw after reading the description of the therapy. The others were not reminded of this option.

Following these procedures, subjects were again asked to approach the snake as closely as possible. Finally, they were asked to complete a questionnaire designed to measure their motivation to change their fear of snakes and their interest in receiving further therapy. Axsom (1989) predicted that subjects in the high-effort, high-choice condition would show the greatest change from the first to the second test of their willingness to approach the snake and would

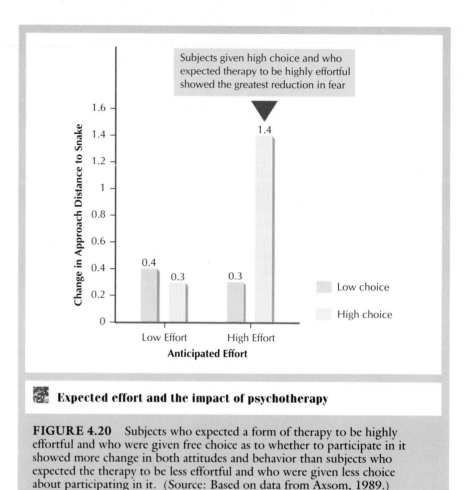

Subjects given high choice and who expected therapy to be highly effortful showed the greatest reduction in fear

Expected effort and the impact of psychotherapy

FIGURE 4.20 Subjects who expected a form of therapy to be highly effortful and who were given free choice as to whether to participate in it showed more change in both attitudes and behavior than subjects who expected the therapy to be less effortful and who were given less choice about participating in it. (Source: Based on data from Axsom, 1989.)

also report the highest motivation to change. As shown in Figure 4.20, results supported these predictions. The most change occurred among those subjects expected to experience the greatest amount of dissonance and the strongest pressures toward effort justification. These persons became more willing to approach the snake merely because they had committed themselves to an effortful course of action. Presumably, such commitment led them to value the treatment and to expect it to help them; consequently, they showed positive change even before the treatment was conducted. (Similar *anticipatory change* is often reported with actual psychotherapy; just the act of seeking help seems to be sufficient to yield some benefits to those who seek it.)

In sum, our tendencies toward effort justification can do more than merely lead us to evaluate certain goals or outcomes more highly; in some cases, at least, they can contribute to improvements in our well-being and psychological adjustment.

The Nature and Formation of Attitudes

Attitudes are enduring mental representations of various features of the social or physical world. They are acquired through experience and exert a directive influence on subsequent behavior. Attitudes serve important functions for the persons who hold them (e.g., they aid in the processing of social information and permit individuals to express their basic values).

Attitudes can be acquired indirectly, from other persons, through *social learning*. This process involves three basic forms of learning: classical conditioning, instrumental conditioning, and modeling. Attitudes can also be acquired directly, through personal experience. Such attitudes tend to be stronger than ones acquired through social learning.

Attitudes and Behavior

Attitudes are related to behavior, but this relationship is far from simple. Specific attitudes predict behavior better than general ones. Similarly, strong attitudes, or ones in which people have a *vested interest,* are more closely related to behavior than weak or irrelevant ones. The cognitive component of attitudes predicts certain types of behavior (e.g., instrumental actions) better than the affective component. The opposite is true for other forms of behavior (e.g., consummatory actions). Most if not all of these effects can be understood in terms of *attitude accessibility*—the ease with which various attitudes can be remembered and brought into consciousness.

Persuasion

Persuasion is the process of changing attitudes through the presentation of various types of information. The traditional view of persuasion focused primarily on identifying crucial characteristics of communicators, communications, and audiences. It uncovered many intriguing phenomena, including the *sleeper effect*. A newer, *cognitive approach* focuses on the cognitive processes that underlie persuasion. Two important models that adopt this perspective are the *elaboration likelihood model (ELM)* and the *heuristic model*. Both suggest that persuasion can occur in two distinct ways: (1) through careful processing of attitude-relevant information or (2) in a relatively automatic manner, in response to various persuasion cues (e.g., cues concerning the expertise of would-be persuaders). The cognitive perspective explains many aspects of persuasion (e.g., why people in a good mood are easier to influence than others).

Resistance to Persuasion

Several factors play a role in our strong ability to resist persuasion. These include *reactance* (efforts to protect or restore personal freedom), *forewarning* (advance knowledge of persuasive intent on the part of others), and *selective avoidance* of information inconsistent with our attitudes.

Cognitive Dissonance: Changing Our Own Attitudes

When individuals discover inconsistency between two attitudes they hold or between their attitudes and their behaviors, they experience **cognitive dissonance.** Dissonance is motivating and leads to efforts to reduce it. When individuals say or do things inconsistent with their attitudes, they then attempt to reduce the dissonance generated by changing these attitudes. The fewer good reasons they have for having engaged in attitude-discrepant behavior in the first place, the greater the dissonance and so the stronger the pressures for change—a phenomenon known as the *less-leads-to-more effect*. Under some conditions, people can be induced to change their attitudes through *leading questions*. These are questions phrased in such a manner that replying to them grants an assumption inconsistent with existing attitudes. The dissonance produced in such situations may then facilitate attitude change. Dissonance also explains why the harder individuals work for various goals, the more highly they value them; this *suffering-leads-to-liking effect* has been used to enhance the effectiveness of various forms of psychotherapy.

Attitude accessibility The ease with which specific attitudes can be remembered and brought into consciousness.

Attitudes Mental representations of various features of the social or physical world. They are acquired through experience and exert a directive influence on subsequent behavior.

Central route (to persuasion) Attitude change resulting from systematic processing of information presented in persuasive messages.

Classical conditioning A basic form of learning in which one stimulus, initially neutral, acquires the capacity to evoke reactions through repeated pairing with another stimulus. In a sense, one stimulus becomes a signal for the presentation or occurrence of the other.

Cognitive dissonance An internal state that results when individuals notice inconsistency between two or more of their attitudes or between their attitudes and their behaviors.

Cognitive perspective (on persuasion) An approach that attempts to understand persuasion by identifying the cognitive processes that play a role in its occurrence.

Effort justification The tendency to justify past effort by evaluating those outcomes or consequences which have required considerable effort more highly than those which have required less effort. (See also *suffering-leads-to-liking effect*.)

Elaboration likelihood model (ELM) A theory suggesting that persuasion can occur in either of two distinct ways, differing in the amount of cognitive effort or elaboration they require.

Forewarning Advance knowledge that one is about to become the target of an attempt at persuasion. Forewarning often increases resistance to the persuasion that follows.

Heuristic model A theory suggesting that persuasion can occur either through careful cognitive analysis of persuasive messages or through the operation of simple *heuristics* suggesting, for example, that we should accept influence from experts more readily than from nonexperts.

Instrumental conditioning A basic form of learning in which responses that lead to positive outcomes or that permit avoidance of negative outcomes are strengthened.

Less-leads-to-more effect Refers to the fact that offering individuals small rewards for engaging in counterattitudinal behavior often produces more dissonance, and so more attitude change, than offering them larger rewards.

Modeling A basic form of learning in which people acquire new forms of behavior through observing others.

Multiple-source effect The tendency for people to be persuaded to a greater degree by information from multiple sources than from one source.

Negative attitude change Attitude change in a direction opposite to that recommended in a persuasive communication.

Peripheral route (to persuasion) Attitude change that occurs in response to persuasion cues—information concerning the expertise or status of would-be persuaders.

Persuasion The process through which one or more persons attempt to alter the attitudes of one or more others.

Reactance Negative reactions to threats to one's personal freedom. Reactance often increases resistance to persuasion.

Selective avoidance A tendency to direct attention away from information that challenges existing attitudes. Such avoidance increases resistance to persuasion.

Self-monitoring A personality characteristic involving individual differences with respect to the willingness to change one's behavior to match various situations, awareness of one's effects on others, and the ability to regulate one's nonverbal cues and other factors that influence others' impressions.

Sleeper effect An increase in attitude change over time, so that a persuasive message actually generates more attitude change sometime after it has been presented than immediately afterward.

Social learning The process of acquiring new forms of behavior (including attitudes) from others.

Suffering-leads-to-liking effect The tendency to evaluate those outcomes or consequences which have involved high degrees of effort more fa-vorably than those which have involved lower degrees of effort. (See *effort justification*.)

Vested interest The extent to which various events or issues have a strong effect on the lives of persons holding attitudes about them.

FOR MORE INFORMATION

Petty, R. E., & Cacioppo, J. T. (1986). *Attitude change: Central and peripheral routes to persuasion*. New York: Springer-Verlag.

This book provides an insightful, sophisticated analysis of the cognitive processes that play a role in persuasion. The elaboration likelihood model (ELM) is described clearly and in considerable detail.

Pratkanis, A. K., Breckler, S. J., & Greenwald, A. G. (Eds.). (1989). *Attitude structure and function*. Hillsdale, NJ: Erlbaum.

This book provides a cutting-edge examination of the nature and impact of attitudes. Each chapter has been prepared by expert researchers, so an exceptionally up-to-date treatment of attitudes is provided. A "must" for anyone interested in the nature and function of attitudes.

Rajecki, D. W. (1989). *Attitudes* (2nd ed.). Sunderland, MA: Sinauer Associates.

A broad introduction to current knowledge about attitudes. A wide range of topics, from methods of attitude research to attitude change induced through group discussions. All in all, an interesting and valuable text.

Prejudice and Discrimination:
The Costs of Hating
Without Cause

So, how do you like it down there?" Shana Gillen asks her friend Pat Marber. (By "down there," she means Tennessee, where Pat moved from New York six months ago to take a new job.)

"Pretty well. It's sure different from the East, but then I knew it would be. Altogether, I guess I'm pretty happy there."

Shana looks surprised. "You really like it? I thought that by now you'd be dying to get back. I mean, how can you stand living around those people? Ugh!"

"What do you mean?" Pat asks. "They seem pretty nice to me."

"Oh come on, who are you kidding? I've seen lots of movies; and once, when I was a kid, I went to Georgia. Those southerners—they're all alike: Slow, dull, out of it. They'd drive me nuts inside of a week."

"I don't know what you mean!" Pat exclaims. "Sure, they talk different, and maybe a little slower than we do up here, but that doesn't mean anything. And whatever gave you the idea they're any dumber than people up here? I've never found a spot that has a monopoly on *stupidity;* there's always plenty to go around."

At this comment, both friends laugh, but Shana isn't satisfied yet.

"Well, what about all that 'holier-than-thou' stuff?" she asks. "Doesn't it bug you that everyone there is so religious? I've heard they really don't want anything to do with you unless you're a regular churchgoer."

"That's baloney," Pat answers. "Not one person where I live or work has ever asked me to go to church or even talked to me about religion. There do seem to be a lot of churches around—more than up here—but that doesn't bother me. Live and let live, I always say."

"I think you're just painting me a rosy picture," Shana comments. "It's *got* to be hard to take in some ways. And how about your boss—didn't you say he was from *Mississippi?* I can't even imagine working for someone from there. I'll bet sometimes you think he's moving in slow motion."

"You wanna make a bet? Mr. Harrison is one of the sharpest people I've ever known. Sure, sometimes he's so polite I can't figure out what he really means. But let me tell you, we could use some of his manners up here. Just yesterday I was in Macy's and this sales clerk . . ."

Shana cuts her off. "Okay, okay, I get the picture. It's just peaches and cream, with no pits or fuzz. But there's one thing you *can't* deny: those people down there are the most bigoted, most prejudiced anywhere. Just think about how they treated blacks for so long. Separate water fountains, back-of-the-bus. You won't catch *me* living around people like that, not if *I* can help it!"

"That's interesting," Pat replies. "You call *them* prejudiced! I wish I had a tape recorder; you'd be surprised if I played back some of the stuff you've said in the past few minutes. If that's an example of how superior things are up here, forget it; I'm staying down in Tennessee!"

P*rejudice, discrimination*—in the late twentieth century these terms have taken on an increasingly sinister meaning. In fact, it is difficult to get through a single week without learning of some new act of violence stemming from intolerance or bigotry. Racially motivated murders in Brooklyn; angry demonstrations (and harsh police reaction) in South Africa; bloody riots in the Baltic states as native Estonians or Latvians clash with ethnic Russians—these are just a few examples of what seems to be an endless stream of disturbing, prejudice-driven events.

Yet when asked if they are prejudiced against others, most persons—perhaps an overwhelming majority—have a ready answer: Absolutely not! Like Shana in the story above, they are all too ready to perceive prejudice and bigotry in others but fail to recognize such tendencies in themselves. And of course, this is one reason that the cycle of hatred continues. It is always those "others" who are dangerous, who harbor evil intentions, and who are not to be trusted;

members of our own group, in contrast, are vastly superior in these and many other ways (Hogg & Abrams, 1988; Stephan, 1985).

But what, precisely, are **prejudice** and **discrimination?** And what factors contribute to their existence? Perhaps even more important, how can they be countered or reduced? Given the great diversity of the human species and the fact that close and frequent contact between persons of different racial, ethnic, and national backgrounds is decidedly on the rise, these are vital questions. Indeed, it seems reasonable to suggest that overcoming prejudice and discrimination is one of the most crucial tasks confronting humanity today. The alternative—permitting these negative forces to persist or increase—would condemn us to an ever-rising tide of hatred and violence. If nothing else, then, the present chapter—and social psychology's commitment to understanding the roots of prejudice and discrimination—is certainly timely.

To provide you with some revealing and useful information about these topics, we will proceed as follows. First, we will examine the nature of *prejudice* and *discrimination,* indicating what these concepts are and how they differ. Second, we will consider the roots of prejudice and discrimination—the many reasons they occur and tend to persist. Third and perhaps most important, we will examine various strategies for reducing their presence, or at least their impact. Finally, because it has been the subject of an especially large amount of research by social psychologists, we will also focus on the nature and impact of one particular form of prejudice—that based on gender (**sexism**).

Prejudice and Discrimination: What They Are and How They Differ

In everyday speech, many persons seem to use the terms *prejudice* and *discrimination* as synonyms. Are they really the same? Most social psychologists draw a clear distinction between them. *Prejudice* refers to a special type of attitude—generally, a negative one—toward the members of some distinct social group. In contrast, *discrimination* refers to negative *actions* toward those individuals. Since this is an important difference, let's consider it more closely.

Prejudice: Choosing Whom to Hate

We'll begin with a more precise definition: *Prejudice is an attitude (usually negative) toward the members of some group, based solely on their membership in that group.* In other words, a person who is prejudiced toward some social group or category tends to evaluate its members in a characteristic manner (usually negatively) merely because they belong to that group. Their individual traits or behavior plays little role; they are disliked (or possibly liked) simply because they belong to a specific social group. (See Figure 5.1, p. 184.)

When prejudice is defined as a special type of attitude, two important implications follow. First, as we noted in Chapter 4, attitudes often function as *schemas*—cognitive frameworks for organizing, interpreting, and recalling information (Fiske & Taylor, 1984). Thus, individuals who are prejudiced toward particular groups tend to process information about these groups differently from the way they process information about other groups. Specifically, information consistent with their prejudiced views may receive more attention, be rehearsed more frequently, and, as a result, tend to be remembered more accurately than information that is not consistent with these views (Bodenhausen,

Prejudice: A precursor for violence

FIGURE 5.1 Prejudice is responsible for a great deal of violence in the late twentieth century.

1988; Wyer, 1988). To the extent that this is the case, prejudice becomes a kind of closed cognitive loop and, in the absence of truly dramatic experiences that refute its accuracy, it can only grow stronger over time (refer to Figure 5.2).

Second, to the extent that prejudice is an attitude, it involves the three basic components of attitudes described in Chapter 4. It encompasses *affective* (feeling), *cognitive* (belief), and *behavioral* aspects. The affective component refers to the negative feelings or emotions prejudiced persons experience when in the presence of, or even just thinking about, members of specific groups. Direct evidence for such reactions has been obtained in several studies designed to assess emotional reactions to members of one's own versus a different racial group. Results indicate that many persons do indeed experience greater anxiety and emotional arousal when interacting with members of another race than when interacting with members of their own racial group (e.g., Stephan & Stephan, 1988). The cognitive component involves beliefs and expectations about members of these groups, plus (as noted above) the ways in which information about them is processed, stored, and recalled. Finally, the behavioral component involves tendencies to act in negative ways—or intentions of doing so—toward the groups who are the object of prejudice. When those tendencies or intentions are translated into overt actions, they constitute *discrimination*—the next major topic we will consider.

Before turning to discrimination, however, we should make one additional point. When most people think about prejudice, they tend to focus on the emotional or affective component described above. They emphasize the strong negative feelings and irrational hatreds that so often characterize racial, ethnic, or religious prejudice. Such reactions are certainly important and play a key role in many forms of prejudice. Yet it is crucial to note that prejudice also has roots in certain aspects of *social cognition*—the ways in which we notice, store, recall, and then use information about others. Growing evidence suggests that our capacity to accomplish such tasks has definite limits: We can handle only so much information at a given time. Because of this, we frequently follow the

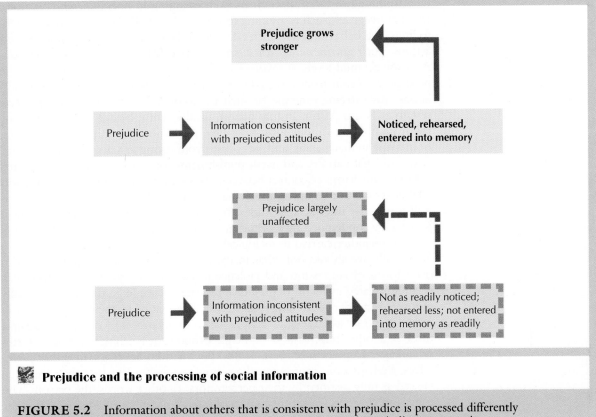

Prejudice and the processing of social information

FIGURE 5.2 Information about others that is consistent with prejudice is processed differently from information that is not consistent with such views. As a result, prejudice may constitute a closed cognitive loop that tends to grow stronger over time.

path of least resistance, taking shortcuts and applying simple rules of thumb to the task of understanding others (Fiske, 1989). As a result, we tend to place diverse people in convenient, if inaccurate, categories; to jump to false conclusions about them; and to rely on existing cognitive frameworks (e.g., schemas, memories), rather than striving to adjust these so as to reflect social reality more closely (Devine, 1989). Because of these and other tendencies, prejudice is often as much a reflection of the limits and operation of our cognitive systems as it is of deep-seated hatred, strong emotions, and pervasive ill will. Although we will return to this point in more detail below, please keep it in mind as you read the pages that follow. This view constitutes a marked shift—and an important advance—in our understanding of prejudice, and we wish to call it strongly to your attention early on.

Discrimination: Prejudice in Action

As we noted in Chapter 4, attitudes are not always reflected in overt actions. In fact, there is frequently a substantial gap between the views individuals hold and their actual behavior. Prejudice is no exception to this rule. In many cases, persons holding negative attitudes toward the members of various groups find that they cannot express those views directly. Laws, social pressure, fears of retaliation—all serve to deter them from engaging in openly negative actions. In other instances, such restraining forces are absent. Then, the negative beliefs, feelings, and behavioral tendencies described above may find expression in overt actions. Such *discrimination* (or *discriminatory behaviors*) can take many forms. At relatively mild levels, it involves simple avoidance. At stronger levels, it can produce exclusion from jobs, educational opportunities, or specific neighborhoods. An extreme example of such exclusion is provided by the *apartheid* system in South Africa. In that nation, until recently, blacks were excluded by law from holding various jobs, from entering various schools and universities, from living in many areas, and, of course, from voting in key elections. In short, powerful legal barriers and harsh punishments for crossing them were erected to limit many forms of contact between black citizens and white ones. The roots of this system are complex, involving the unique history of South Africa, as well as negative interracial attitudes. Yet, there can be little doubt that apartheid is generally condemned by world opinion as an especially appalling illustration of racial prejudice carried to its logical conclusions.

Finally, we should note that in the most extreme cases, prejudice leads to overt forms of aggression and violence toward its targets. Such instances can occur as isolated incidents of prejudice-driven violence (e.g., the kinds of racially motivated murders that have occurred in large cities in the United States in recent years) or as large-scale actions taken by members of one group against those of another (e.g., attacks on neighborhoods or lynchings and other forms of violence; Hepworth & West, 1988). Such actions are tragic in and of themselves. Perhaps even more unsettling, however, is the fact that they are often viewed as fully justified by their perpetrators. In other words, the persons who engage in violence against the targets of intense prejudice often believe that the victims *deserve* such treatment. An unsettling illustration of this process, in a slightly different context (that of international relations), is provided by an ingenious study conducted by Rothbart and Hallmark (1988).

In this study, male and female students were asked to imagine that they were the defense ministers of two fictitious countries, Takonia and Navalia. They were informed that these countries were involved in an arms race and that both were developing devastating new weapons. They were then asked to consider various policy options their nation could adopt and to rate the effectiveness of each option in getting the other country to reduce or eliminate its new weapons. These strategies ranged from one that was highly coercive (their country would build up its supply of new weapons and threaten to use them unless the other country cut back on *its* weapons) to one that was highly conciliatory (their country would unilaterally stop producing new weapons and would also cut back its existing forces by 20 percent in the hope that the other country would take similar actions). It was predicted that because of their roles as defense minister of the two opposing nations, subjects would view coercion as more effective in changing the other country's behavior than conciliation. The opposite, however, was predicted to be true for their own country; here, subjects were expected to view conciliation as more effective than coercion in changing their country's behavior. As you can see from Figure 5.3, results offered clear support for the researchers' predictions.

In a follow-up study, Rothbart and Hallmark asked subjects merely to imagine that they were citizens of the two countries. This variation was adopted to see whether the same effects would be obtained even under conditions where

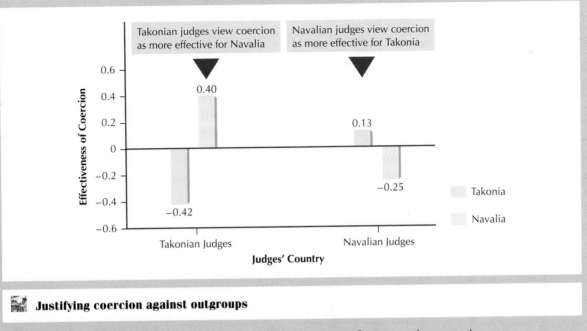

Justifying coercion against outgroups

FIGURE 5.3 When asked to play the role of defense ministers of two opposing countries, subjects viewed coercion as more effective in changing the behavior of their opponent than in changing the behavior of their own nation. These findings suggest that many persons perceive harsh actions as more justified when used on outgroups than when used on their own ingroup. (Source: Based on data from Rothbart & Hallmark, 1988.)

participants did not experience pressure to be a "tough" minister of defense. Results were highly similar to those in the initial study. Once again, subjects viewed coercion as more effective (and hence more justified) when used on the other country but viewed conciliation as more effective when directed toward their own nation. Together, the findings of both experiments point to two conclusions. First, many persons do indeed view harsh, coercive actions as more effective and justified when directed toward persons outside rather than inside their own group. Second, such effects do not require active hatred or hostility toward the outgroup in order to occur; they seem to stem, at least in part, from simple identification with one group relative to another. We will discuss the effects of such *social categorization* processes in more detail in a later section (see pages 194–196). We introduce them here to show that in many cases, prejudice stems not from the deep-seated animosities or hatreds that common sense suggests but (at least in part) from the ways in which we think about and attempt to make sense of the social world.

Subtle Forms of Discrimination: Prejudice in Disguise Bigots, like other persons, prefer to "have their cake and eat it, too." They prefer, if possible, to harm the targets of their prejudice without any cost to themselves. How do they seek to accomplish this goal? One answer involves the use of several *subtle forms of discrimination*—ones that permit their users to conceal the underlying negative views from which they stem. A number of these subtle forms exist, ranging from overpraising an accomplishment or overcriticizing a mistake (Gaertner & Dovidio, 1986) to displaying distant, unfriendly nonverbal behavior (e.g., standing slightly too far away, failing to make appropriate eye contact; Neuberg, 1989). Here, though, we will focus on two that seem to be most common: **tokenism** and **reverse discrimination.**

Tokenism: Small benefits, high costs   Imagine that you were hired for a job you really wanted and at a higher starting salary than you expected. At first, you would be happy about your good fortune. Now, assume that one day you learn that you got the job mainly because you belong to a specific group— one underrepresented at the company and one to which the company felt compelled to add so as to fend off legal action by a government agency. How would you react? In all probability, your reactions would be like those of the person shown in Figure 5.4—you would be upset. After all, few persons would enjoy discovering that they were hired solely as a *token* member of a specific racial, ethnic, or religious group, rather than on the basis of their qualifications. Direct evidence for such negative reactions to tokenism in work settings has been reported in recent research. For example, in one such study, Chacko (1982) asked young women holding management-level jobs to rate the extent to which several factors (their ability, experience, education, and sex) played a role in their being hired. In addition, subjects were asked to complete questionnaires designed to measure their commitment to their organizations (favorable

"We need a token man, and I guess you're it."

🖼 **Tokenism in action**

FIGURE 5.4   As suggested by this cartoon, serving as a *token* can be an unpleasant and disconcerting experience. (Drawing by Koren; © 1985 The New Yorker Magazine, Inc.)

attitudes toward their companies and satisfaction with their supervisors and work). When participants who rated their ability as the most important factor in being hired were compared with those who rated their sex as most important, unsettling differences emerged. Those who felt they were mere tokens reported a significantly lower degree of commitment and satisfaction than those who felt they had been hired on the basis of their ability.

Of course, tokenism occurs in many other contexts as well. More generally, it refers to trivial, positive actions toward the targets of prejudice that are then used as an excuse or justification for later discrimination. "Don't bother me," prejudiced persons who have engaged in tokenism seem to say; "haven't I done enough for those people already?" (e.g., Dutton & Lake, 1973; Rosenfield et al., 1982). Wherever it occurs, tokenism seems to have at least two negative effects. On the one hand, it lets bigoted people off the hook; they can point to tokenistic actions as proof that they are not really prejudiced or that they have followed the letter if not the spirit of antidiscrimination laws. On the other hand, it can be damaging to the self-esteem and confidence of the targets of prejudice, including those few persons who are selected as tokens or who receive minimal aid. Clearly, then, tokenism is one subtle form of discrimination worth preventing.

Reverse discrimination: Giving with one hand, taking away with the other A second type of subtle discrimination occurs in situations in which persons holding at least some degree of prejudice toward the members of a social group lean over backward to treat those group members favorably—more favorably than they would were the individuals not members of that particular group. Such effects have been observed in several contexts. For example, Chidester (1986) had subjects engage in a brief "get acquainted" conversation with a stranger who was described as being either black or white. (The conversation took place through microphones and headphones.) When subjects later evaluated their partners in this conversation, they reported more favorable reactions when this person was supposedly black than when he or she was supposedly white. (In fact, all participants were white; only subjects' beliefs about the race of their partner were varied.) Unless one assumes that the white subjects actually held more favorable views of blacks than of members of their own race, these findings point to the occurrence of "lean over backward" or "demonstrate my lack of prejudice" reactions among participants.

At first glance, such behavior may not seem to fit our definition of discrimination; after all, it yields positive rather than negative outcomes for its victims. On one level, this is certainly true; people exposed to reverse discrimination do receive raises, promotions, and other benefits. But on another level, such favorable treatment may prove harmful, especially over the long run. A clear illustration of the potential damage stemming from reverse discrimination is provided by a study conducted by Fajardo (1985).

In this investigation, teachers were asked to grade essays prepared in advance and deliberately written so as to be poor, moderate, or excellent in quality. Information attached to the essays indicated that they were prepared either by white or by black students. If reverse discrimination existed, it would be expected that the teachers (all of whom were white) would rate the essays more favorably when they were supposedly prepared by black rather than by white students. Results indicated that this is precisely what happened. Moreover, as

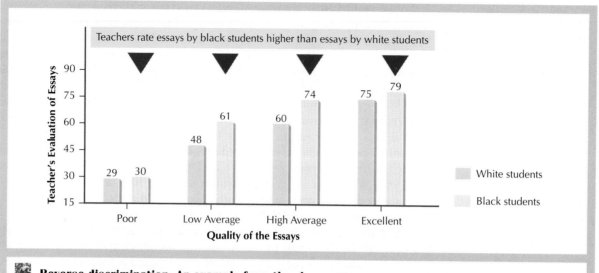

Teachers rate essays by black students higher than essays by white students

Teacher's Evaluation of Essays

90
75
60
45
30
15

Poor: White 29, Black 30
Low Average: White 48, Black 61
High Average: White 60, Black 74
Excellent: White 75, Black 79

Quality of the Essays

White students
Black students

Reverse discrimination: An example from the classroom

FIGURE 5.5 White teachers rated essays supposedly written by black students higher than they rated identical essays supposedly written by white students. Thus, these teachers demonstrated *reverse discrimination* in their behavior. This tendency was strongest when the quality of the essays was most uncertain (when the essays were average in overall quality). (Source: Based on data from Fajardo, 1985.)

shown in Figure 5.5, the tendency of white teachers to favor black students was strongest under conditions where the essays were of moderate quality—in short, where there was greatest uncertainty as to the rating students should receive. As you can readily see, assigning favorable ratings to mediocre work by black students can indeed help them in the short run. But it can also set them up for later problems. It may lead some students, at least, to develop inflated opinions of their own abilities and unrealistic expectations about the likelihood of future success. The anguish that follows when such hopes collide with reality can be devastating. Similarly, reverse discrimination may be a subtle (and perhaps largely unconscious) tactic on the part of teachers for minimizing close contact with minority students—after all, few students who receive consistently high grades request special help. In these and several other ways, then, reverse discrimination can be as harmful as the more obvious forms of discrimination it sometimes replaces.

In Search of the Roots of Prejudice: Contrasting Views of Why It Occurs

That prejudice exists is all too obvious. Indeed, it seems to have been present in all human societies throughout recorded history. This point raises an important question: How does prejudice originate? Why do so many persons hold negative views about those belonging to specific social groups? Many different answers have been proposed. Here, we will consider several of these contrasting views.

Direct Intergroup Conflict: Competition as a Source of Bias

Unfortunately, the things people value most—good jobs, nice homes, high status—are always in short supply: There's never quite enough to go around. This fact serves as the foundation for what is perhaps the oldest explanation of prejudice—**realistic conflict theory**. According to this view, prejudice stems from competition between various social groups over valued commodities or opportunities. In short, prejudice develops out of the struggle over jobs, adequate housing, good schools, and other desirable outcomes. The theory further suggests that as such competition continues, the members of the groups involved come to view each other in increasingly negative ways (White, 1977). They label each other "enemies," view their own group as morally superior, and draw the boundaries between themselves and their opponents ever more firmly. The result, of course, is that what starts out as simple competition, relatively free from animosity and hatred, gradually develops into full-scale, emotion-laden prejudice (refer to Figure 5.6).

Evidence for the occurrence of this process has been obtained in several different studies suggesting that as competition persists, the individuals or groups involved come to perceive each other in increasingly negative ways. Even worse, such competition often leads to direct and open conflict. Perhaps the most dramatic evidence for this process is provided by a classic study in social psychology conducted by Hovland and Sears (1940). These researchers examined the relationship between the number of lynchings of blacks in four-

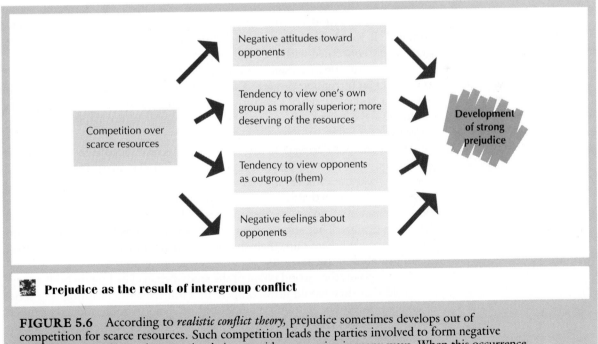

Prejudice as the result of intergroup conflict

FIGURE 5.6 According to *realistic conflict theory,* prejudice sometimes develops out of competition for scarce resources. Such competition leads the parties involved to form negative views of one another and to *perceive* their own side as superior in many ways. When this occurrence is coupled with strong negative emotions, overt prejudice emerges.

teen states in the American South and two indexes of economic conditions: farm value of cotton and acre value of cotton. (Cotton was the most important crop in the South at that time.) Their data covered a forty-nine-year period, and results seemed clear: The more negative economic conditions were, the greater the incidence of this type of violence by whites against blacks. (The correlations they reported were -0.72 and -0.63 for number of lynchings and the two economic indexes, respectively.)

These findings have often been interpreted as suggesting that under adverse economic conditions, competition for increasingly scarce economic resources increases. Such competition in turn increases prejudice toward outgroup members (in this case, prejudice on the part of whites toward blacks) and so increases the incidence of prejudice-related violence. Interestingly, a recent reanalysis of Hovland and Sears's data using the much more sophisticated statistical techniques available today and a more accurate measure of economic conditions has confirmed these results (Hepworth & West, 1988). Thus, it appears that increased competition between various groups during periods of economic decline may indeed be one of the factors contributing to prejudice and interracial violence. (For additional evidence concerning the impact of intergroup conflict on prejudice, please see the **Classic Contributions** section below.)

FOCUS ON RESEARCH: CLASSIC CONTRIBUTIONS

Conflict and Prejudice in a Summer Camp: The Robber's Cave Experiment

Dwight D. Eisenhower was president, the economy was humming along smoothly on all cylinders, and—at least for the moment—domestic tranquility prevailed. It was America in the mid-1950s. Yet even then, social psychologists were deeply concerned with the topic of prejudice. To acquire new insights into the nature of this process, Sherif and his colleagues (Sherif et al., 1961) decided to conduct an intriguing project. Their study involved sending eleven-year-old boys to a special summer camp in a remote area where—free from external influences—the nature of conflict and its role in prejudice could be carefully observed.

When the boys arrived at the camp, they were divided into two separate groups and assigned to different cabins located quite far apart (see Figure 5.7). For one week, the campers in each group lived and played together, engaging in such enjoyable activities as hiking, swimming, and various other sports. During this initial phase, the boys quickly developed strong attachments to their own groups. They soon chose names for their teams (the Rattlers and the Eagles), stenciled them onto their shorts, and made up separate flags with their group's symbol on them.

At this point, the second phase of the study began. The boys in both groups were told that they would now compete in a tournament consisting of a series of competitions. The winning team would receive a trophy, and its members would earn prizes (pocket knives and medals). Since these were outcomes the boys strongly wanted, the stage was set for intense competition. Would such conflict generate prejudice? The answer was quick in coming. As the boys competed, the tension between the groups rose. At first, it was limited to verbal

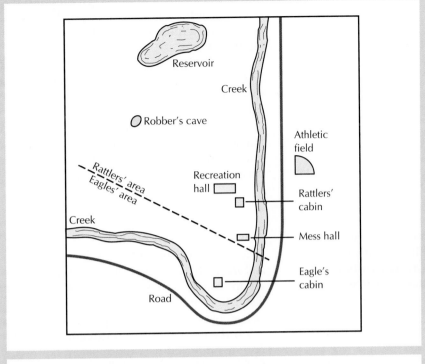

The setting for the Robber's Cave experiment

FIGURE 5.7 The summer camp that served as the site of the famous *Robber's Cave* experiment. Note the distance between the cabins of the two opposing groups (the Rattlers and Eagles) and the division of the camp into two separate territories (one for each team). (Source: Based on information in Sherif et al., 1961.)

insults, teasing, and name-calling. Soon, though, it escalated into more direct acts—for example, the Eagles burned the Rattlers' flag. The next day the Rattlers retaliated by attacking the rival group's cabin, overturning beds, tearing out mosquito netting, and taking personal property. Such actions continued until the researchers intervened to avoid any serious consequences. At the same time, the two groups voiced increasingly negative views of each other. They labeled their opponents "sissies," "bums," and "cowards," while heaping praise on their own group at every turn. In short, after only two weeks of conflict the groups developed all the key components of strong prejudice toward each other.

Fortunately, the story (and the research project) has a happy ending. In the study's final phase, Sherif and his colleagues attempted to reduce the negative reactions described above. Merely increasing the amount of contact between the groups failed to accomplish this goal; indeed, it seemed to fan the flames of anger. However, when conditions were altered so that the groups found it necessary to work together to reach *superordinate goals*—ones they both desired—dramatic changes occurred. After working together to restore their water supply (previously sabotaged by the researchers), pooling their funds to rent a

IN SEARCH OF THE ROOTS OF PREJUDICE

movie, and jointly repairing a broken-down truck, tensions between the groups largely vanished. Indeed, after six days of such experiences, the boundaries between the groups virtually dissolved, and many cross-group friendships were established.

We should hasten to note that there are major limitations to this research. The study took place over a relatively short period, the camp setting was a special one, and, perhaps most important, the boys were quite homogeneous in background—they did not belong to distinctly different social groups. Even given these restrictions, however, the findings reported by Sherif and his colleagues are compelling. They offer a chilling picture of how what starts out as rational competition over scarce, desired resources can quickly escalate into full-scale conflict and strong negative attitudes.

The Us-versus-Them Effect: Social Categorization as a Basis for Prejudice

A second perspective on the origins of prejudice begins with a basic fact: People generally divide the social world around them into two distinct categories—*us* and *them*. In short, they view other persons as belonging to either their own group (usually termed the **ingroup**) or another group (the **outgroup**). Such distinctions are based on a number of dimensions, including race, religion, sex, age, ethnicity, and even occupation, to name just a few.

If the process of **social categorization** stopped there, it would have little bearing on prejudice. Unfortunately, however, it does not. Sharply contrasting feelings and beliefs are usually attached to members of one's ingroup and members of various outgroups. Persons in the former (us) category are viewed in favorable terms, while those in the latter (them) category are perceived more negatively. These latter persons are assumed to possess undesirable traits, are perceived as being more alike (i.e., more homogeneous) than members of the ingroup, and are often strongly disliked (Linville, Fischer, & Salovey, 1989; Schaller & Maass, 1989; Wilder, 1986).

That strong tendencies to divide the social world into these contrasting groups exist has been demonstrated in many studies (e.g., Stephan, 1985; Tajfel, 1982; Turner et al., 1987). In these investigations, subjects generally expressed more negative attitudes toward members of outgroups and treated them less favorably than members of their own group. Further, these findings held true even when these categories were purely arbitrary, when they had no existence beyond the experiment, and when the persons involved never met face to face. Moreover, on the other side of the coin, additional research suggests that when individuals shift the boundaries of this *us-versus-them* distinction so that persons previously on the "wrong" side of the ingroup-outgroup boundary are now viewed as being inside, prejudice toward them tends to disappear as well (Gaertner et al., 1989). Together, these findings suggest that in some settings at least, prejudice may well stem from a basic aspect of the way in which we think about the social world: a strong tendency to perceive others as belonging either to our own group or to some other group of outsiders.

But why, precisely, is this the case? What happens when we define others as different that leads us to view them in biased and mainly negative ways? An intriguing answer has been provided by Tajfel and his colleagues (e.g., Tajfel, 1982), who suggest that individuals seek to enhance their self-esteem by becoming identified with specific social groups. This tactic can succeed, however, only to the extent that the persons involved perceive these groups as somehow superior to other, competing groups. Since all individuals are subject to the same forces, the final result is inevitable: Each group seeks to view itself as somehow better than its rivals, and prejudice arises out of this clash of social perceptions (see Figure 5.8). Tajfel terms this process *social competition* to distinguish it from the kind of intergroup conflict over scarce resources that was described earlier. (Please see Figure 5.8 for a summary of this process.)

Support for the accuracy of these suggestions has been obtained in several experiments. For example, in one study on this topic Meindl and Lerner (1985) hypothesized that experiencing a failure would increase individuals' needs for enhancing their self-esteem and that as a result, their tendencies toward social categorization (dividing the world into *us* and *them*) would increase. Specifically, Meindl and Lerner predicted that persons who have just experienced failure will evaluate members of an outgroup more extremely than those who have not had such an experience. To test this possibility, English-speaking Canadians were exposed or not exposed to conditions designed to threaten their self-esteem. Subjects were then asked to express their opinions toward French-speaking Canadians. (In the lowered self-esteem condition, subjects were asked to get a chair, and while taking it, they "accidentally" caused a large pile of computer cards to fall to the floor. Needless to say, the chair had been placed so that its slightest movement caused the cards to fall.) Results offered support for the hypothesis. Subjects who had caused the accident (and so experienced reduced self-esteem) did rate members of the outgroup more extremely than

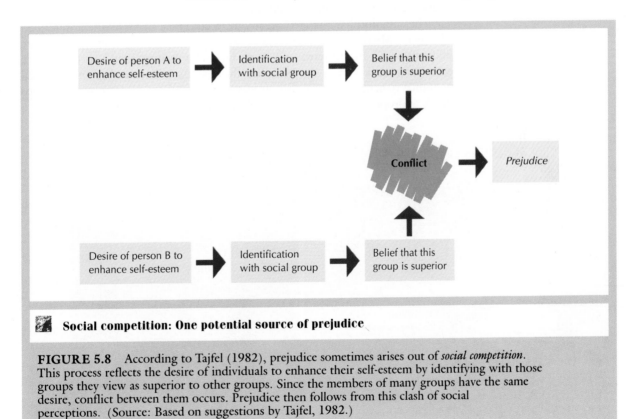

Social competition: One potential source of prejudice

FIGURE 5.8 According to Tajfel (1982), prejudice sometimes arises out of *social competition*. This process reflects the desire of individuals to enhance their self-esteem by identifying with those groups they view as superior to other groups. Since the members of many groups have the same desire, conflict between them occurs. Prejudice then follows from this clash of social perceptions. (Source: Based on suggestions by Tajfel, 1982.)

those who had no such accident. These and related findings offer support for the view that our tendency to divide the social world into two camps often plays a role in the development of important forms of prejudice.

Early Experience: The Role of Social Learning

A third explanation for prejudice is one you will find quite straightforward. It suggests that such reactions are *learned* and that they develop in much the same manner—and through the same basic processes—as other attitudes (refer to Chapter 4). According to this **social-learning view** of prejudice, children acquire negative attitudes toward various social groups because they hear such views expressed by parents, friends, teachers, and others and because they are directly rewarded (with praise and approval) for adopting them. In addition to direct observation of others, *social norms*—rules within a given group suggesting what actions or attitudes are appropriate—are also important (Pettigrew, 1959). As we will note in Chapter 8, most persons choose to conform to most social norms of groups to which they belong most of the time. The development and expression of prejudice toward others often stem from this tendency.

While persons with whom children have direct contact are central in both social learning and pressures toward obeying social norms, the mass media, too, are important. Until quite recently, members of racial and ethnic minorities were shown infrequently in movies or on television. Further, when they did appear, they were usually cast in low-status or comic roles. Given repeated exposure to such materials for years or even decades, it is not at all surprising that many children came to believe that the members of such groups must be inferior. After all, why else would they always be shown in this manner?

The situation has changed greatly in recent years, in the United States and elsewhere. Members of various racial and ethnic minorities now appear more frequently and are depicted in a more favorable manner than was true in the past (refer to Figure 5.9). Whether these shifts will contribute to reduced prejudice remains uncertain, but at least there appear to have been a few steps in the appropriate (counterprejudicial) direction.

The mass media and prejudice

FIGURE 5.9   In recent years, the mass media (e.g., television, movies) have begun to show blacks and other minority groups more frequently and in a more favorable manner than was true in the past.

Cognitive Sources of Prejudice: Stereotypes, Selective Processing, and Illusory Correlation

A fourth source of prejudice is in some ways the most unsettling of all. As we noted earlier, it involves the view that prejudice stems, at least in part, from the ways in which we think about others and process information about them— that is, from various aspects of *social cognition*. We will now consider several forms of evidence pointing to this conclusion.

Stereotypes: What They Are and How They Operate   Consider the following groups: African-Americans, Asian-Americans, Jews, and homosexuals. Suppose you were asked to list the traits most characteristic of each—would you experience much difficulty? If you are like most people, you would not. Rather, you would be able to construct a list of traits for each group quite easily. The reason you could do so lies in the existence of numerous **stereotypes.** As we noted in Chapter 3, these are cognitive frameworks consisting of knowledge and beliefs about specific social groups. Stereotypes suggest that all members of such groups possess certain traits or characteristics, hence your ease in constructing the lists described above (Higgins & Bargh, 1987; Wyer, 1988).

Like other cognitive frameworks, stereotypes exert strong effects on the ways in which we process incoming information. For example, information relevant to a particular stereotype is processed more quickly than information not related to it (Dovidio, Evans, & Tyler, 1986). Similarly, stereotypes lead the persons holding them to pay attention to specific types of information—usually, input consistent with the stereotypes. Alternatively, if information inconsistent with a stereotype does manage to enter consciousness, it may be actively refuted, perhaps by recalling facts and information that *are* consistent with the stereotype (O'Sullivan & Durso, 1984). Moreover, stereotypes also determine what we remember—usually, again, information that is consistent with these frameworks.

Now, consider the relevance of such effects to prejudice. Once an individual has acquired a stereotype about some social group, he or she tends to notice information that fits readily into this cognitive framework and to remember "facts" that are consistent with it more readily than "facts" that are inconsistent with it. As a result, the stereotype becomes, to a large degree, self-confirming; even exceptions to it make it stronger, for they simply induce the person in question to bring more supporting information to mind.

Evidence for the ways in which stereotypes bias social thought is provided by the findings of numerous studies (e.g., Hamilton & Trolier, 1986; Wyer, 1988). An especially clear illustration of their impact is provided by research conducted by Bodenhausen (1988). In the first of two related studies, Bodenhausen asked students to play the role of jurors in an imaginary court case. Some subjects received information designed to activate a negative stereotype toward Hispanics—the defendant was named Carlos Ramirez; he came from Albuquerque, New Mexico. Others received more neutral information, unrelated to existing stereotypes—the defendant was named Robert Johnson; he came from Dayton, Ohio. Half the subjects learned the defendant's name before receiving evidence about the case, while the others learned his name only after reading the evidence. Bodenhausen suggested that the impact of stereotypes on subsequent social judgments and behavior derives from the fact that stereotypes bias the processing of information received after their activation. Specifically, he suggested that stereotypes (a) change recipients' interpretation of such in-

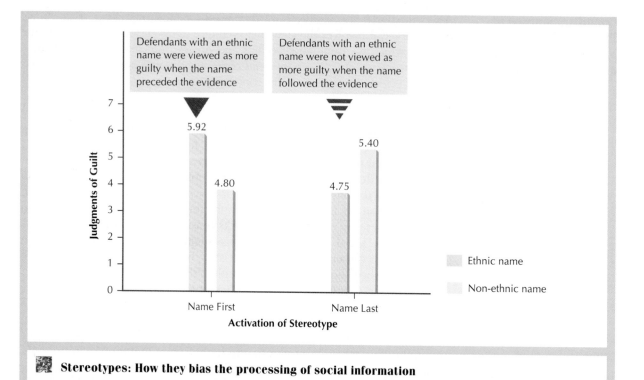

Defendants with an ethnic name were viewed as more guilty when the name preceded the evidence

Defendants with an ethnic name were not viewed as more guilty when the name followed the evidence

Stereotypes: How they bias the processing of social information

FIGURE 5.10   Subjects who learned that a defendant in an imaginary case had an ethnic name rated him as more guilty than subjects who learned that the defendant had a nonethnic name, but only when they received this information before evidence about the case. These findings suggest that stereotypes affect social judgments by biasing the manner in which information about others is processed. (Source: Based on data from Bodenhausen, 1988.)

formation, (b) cause them to devote more effort to processing stereotype-consistent than stereotype-inconsistent information, or (c) both.

After learning the defendant's name and reading information about the case, subjects in all conditions rated the likelihood that the man was guilty. Bodenhausen predicted that the defendant would be rated as more guilty when he had an ethnic name, but only when subjects had learned this fact *before* reviewing the evidence. As shown in Figure 5.10, that is precisely what occurred.

While this initial study provided strong evidence for the view that stereotypes cause individuals to engage in biased processing of social information, it did not indicate clearly whether such bias involves a shift in the interpretation of new information or selective attention to (and rehearsal of) stereotype-supporting input. To determine which of these effects was dominant, Bodenhausen conducted a second study. Here, participants were asked to rate each piece of evidence, as it was received, in terms of its favorability or unfavorability to the defendant. Bodenhausen reasoned that this step would prevent the kind of selective attention just described. Thus, if subjects still rated the defendant with the ethnic name as more guilty, that would provide evidence for the view that stereotypes change the meaning or interpretation of information received after their activation. If, however, such effects did not occur, evidence would be obtained for the alternate view that stereotypes affect the amount of attention and rehearsal directed to such information. Results offered clear support for this second interpretation. Asking participants to rate each piece of evidence as it was received completely eliminated their tendency to rate the defendant with the ethnic name as more guilty.

These findings and related evidence (e.g., Greenberg and Pyszczynski, 1985; Wyer, 1988) suggest that stereotypes do indeed lead to biased processing of social information. Once they are activated, it appears, we tend to focus on input consistent with them while tending to ignore other, contradictory information. As we noted earlier, the result is that stereotypes become largely self-confirming in nature, and continued prejudice is ensured. Still, there is a ray of hope in this distressing picture: Techniques, even relatively simple ones, that force us to pay attention to *all* relevant information may help to overcome this "tilt" in our cognitive systems. In short, in the absence of interventions the impact of stereotypes is both pervasive and strong—but by no means impossible to overcome.

Illusory Correlation: Perceiving Relationships That Aren't There We have already considered another cognitive source of prejudice and discrimination in Chapter 3, where we discussed the topic of **illusory correlation**—our tendency to perceive associations (correlations) between variables that do not in fact exist (Hamilton & Gifford, 1976). Illusory correlation seems to stem, at least in part, from the co-occurrence of relatively rare and therefore distinctive events. When two such events occur together, the combination is especially unusual and so is more readily noticed, more quickly encoded into memory, and easier to recall than other kinds of events.

What does this have to do with prejudice? A great deal. For example, consider the following facts. Even in the 1990s, violent behaviors are still relatively rare (except among some persons living in truly devastated urban environments). Similarly, for most white persons in the United States, contact with minority group members is also relatively rare. For this reason, when individuals read or hear about a violent crime committed by a minority person, this event is quite distinctive. Since people find it easier to recall such incidents than similar ones involving majority group members (e.g., whites), they tend to perceive a stronger association between racial identity and violent behavior than is actually the case. Please note: We are not suggesting that no such relationship exists. In fact, in the United States the members of some minority groups do commit a higher proportion of violent crimes than would be expected solely on the basis of their proportion of the total population. Illusory correlation, however, leads many persons to assume that the relationship between racial or ethnic identity and violence is even higher than it actually is. (The existence of such relationships should not, of course, be overinterpreted. Many factors, including past and present prejudice, contribute to such differences.)

Recent evidence suggests that the tendency to perceive illusory correlations between membership in a given group and various undesirable forms of behavior can be reduced in several ways (e.g., Schaller & Maass, 1989). To the extent that they occur, however, illusory correlations contribute to the persistence of negative stereotypes and to both prejudice and discrimination in many real-life settings. (For discussion of another aspect of social cognition that figures prominently in prejudice, please see **The Cutting Edge** section below.)

FOCUS ON RESEARCH: THE CUTTING EDGE

Ingroup Differentiation, Outgroup Homogeneity: "They All Seem Pretty Much the Same—Until You Get to Know Them"

One remark people with a strong prejudice toward some group often make goes something like this: "You know what they're like; they're all the same." What such comments imply, of course, is that the members of some outgroup are much more similar to one another (i.e., are more homogeneous) than the members of one's ingroup. This tendency to perceive persons belonging to groups other than one's own as all alike is known as the **illusion of outgroup homogeneity** (Linville et al., 1989; Quattrone, 1986). The mirror-image reflection of this tendency is known as the **ingroup differentiation hypothesis** and refers to our tendency to perceive members of our own group as showing much larger differences from one another than those in other groups. Strong evidence for the occurrence of both effects, together with revealing insights into why they occur, has recently been provided by Linville, Fischer, and Salovey (1989).

In a series of related studies, these researchers sought to determine whether individuals perceive members of outgroups as showing smaller *variability* (i.e., less tendency to spread out around the group's mean) and smaller differences from one another than do members of their own ingroup. The first of these experiments focused on the perceptions of elderly people and college students. Each group was asked to rate both its own and the other group on several dimensions (friendliness, motivation, typical mood, attractiveness, etc.). Subjects made these ratings by indicating how one hundred persons in each group (college students, elderly persons) would be distributed along each dimension, assuming that there were seven categories on each scale. (For example, with respect to ratings of friendliness, subjects indicated how many of the hundred persons would fall into each of the following categories: very unfriendly, unfriendly, somewhat unfriendly, neutral, somewhat friendly, friendly, and very friendly.) As you can see from Figure 5.11, results offered strong support for the tendency to perceive members of other groups as much more homogeneous than members of their own group. College students perceived elderly persons as being much less variable and much more like one another than they did other college students. And precisely the opposite pattern was found for the elderly participants: They perceived college students as being much more homogeneous than senior citizens.

Similar results were found in a second study, in which college students in the United States and Ireland rated one another on several dimensions. Again, the students in each country perceived those in the other country as less differentiated than were those in their own. Why do such effects occur? Linville and her colleagues propose that the answer lies mainly in differential familiarity. Most persons are simply much more familiar with members of their own group than those of outgroups. As a result, they are more aware of differences between

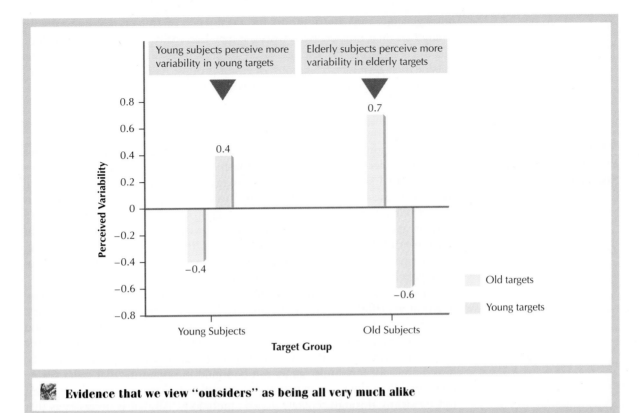

Young subjects perceive more variability in young targets

Elderly subjects perceive more variability in elderly targets

Old targets

Young targets

Evidence that we view "outsiders" as being all very much alike

FIGURE 5.11   College students perceived other young persons as much more variable than elderly persons in several traits. In contrast, elderly subjects demonstrated the opposite pattern. Together, these findings provide evidence for the existence of a strong tendency to perceive that persons with whom we are familiar (our own ingroup) are more differentiated than persons with whom we are less familiar (outgroups). (Source: Based on data from Linville et al., 1989.)

members of their own group. Is there any evidence for this *differential familiarity* hypothesis? In fact, there is. In an additional study, Linville, Fischer, and Salovey asked the members of a college class to rate other members of the class along a number of dimensions (e.g., likability, SAT scores, typical mood, friendliness) on several occasions: near the beginning of the semester, at the midpoint, and near the end. The researchers reasoned that if differential familiarity plays a key role in perceptions of outgroup homogeneity (and ingroup differentiation), the students' ratings of their classmates would shift toward increased differentiation as their contact with one another increased. Results indicated that this was indeed the case. Over the semester, students in the class came to perceive one another as showing greater variability and greater differentiation.

Given these findings and those reported in related research (e.g., Linville et al., 1986), it appears reasonable to conclude that the tendency to perceive members of other groups as being very much alike is real. Moreover, that tendency seems to stem from the fact that we are simply more familiar with the members of our own group than with the members of other groups. As you can readily see, this tendency to perceive persons belonging to outgroups as homogeneous can contribute to the persistence of stereotypes, and perhaps strengthen their impact. Even worse, it may lead many individuals to conclude that there is really no strong reason to seek increased contact with people outside their own racial, religious, or ethnic groups: As far as they're concerned, they already know what such persons will be like.

A Biological Basis for Prejudice? Genetic Similarity Theory

Before concluding this discussion of the many potential causes of prejudice, we should consider one that is simultaneously intriguing, unsettling, and controversial. Stated simply, this perspective suggests that prejudice has a biological basis—that the tendency to dislike members of groups other than our own is part of our inherited human nature. This approach derives from *sociobiology*, a field suggesting that many aspects of behavior can be understood in terms of our powerful drive to contribute our genes to the next generation. Indeed, in its extreme form sociobiology suggests that virtually everything we do can ultimately be understood in terms of its relationship to this central drive.

How can this perspective account for the existence of prejudice? According to Rushton (1989), the answer lies in what he terms **genetic similarity theory.** This theory holds that genes can best ensure their own survival in the next and future generations by encouraging the reproduction of others possessing the same (or closely related) genes. Such persons do not necessarily have to be directly related, for similar genes can be found in organisms that cannot trace their origins to the same ancestor. For example, similar genes may have arisen independently through separate genetic mutations. All that is necessary is that the genes possessed by the persons involved be similar. The theory also contends that human beings can recognize genetic similarity through both physical and behavioral similarity. Presumably, people who resemble one another or who show similar patterns of traits are more likely to share common genes than persons who do not show such similarity.

Some evidence is consistent with Rushton's (1989) proposals. Persons from the same ethnic group do tend to share more genes than those from different ethnic groups (Reynolds et al., 1987). According to genetic similarity theory, this factor might cause individuals to behave more benevolently toward members of their own group, who possess similar genes, than toward persons from other groups. Indeed, since reproduction by persons belonging to outgroups might interfere with reproduction by persons having related genes (e.g., the offspring of the former would compete for available resources), strong hostility toward outgroup members could well develop.

In support of this reasoning, Rushton cites evidence suggesting that fear and mistrust of strangers are common among animals, even when the strangers have never been the source of any harm (Rushton, 1989, p. 516). He suggests that such reactions may be genetically determined among human beings as well, and as such, are a contributing factor in many forms of prejudice (refer to Figure 5.12).

Are these views correct? Most social psychologists don't think so. They reject the suggestion that prejudice is, in a sense, a built-in part of our basic human nature. On the contrary, most believe that such reactions stem primarily from the other causes and factors described in this chapter—social conflict between groups, social categorization, early (and later) socialization, and several

Fear of strangers: Genetically determined?

FIGURE 5.12 Human beings often show signs of fear and mistrust when meeting others from outside their group for the first time. Some psychologists interpret such responses as evidence for the view that negative reactions to "outsiders" is determined, at least in part, by biological (i.e., genetic) factors.

cognitive processes. This position does not, however, imply that *some* genetic contribution to the roots of prejudice is impossible. After all, there does seem to be a powerful tendency for human beings to prefer to associate with (e.g., form friendships with, marry) persons similar to themselves. (We'll consider this point in detail in Chapter 6, as part of our discussion of interpersonal attraction.) That tendency in turn may well reflect some genetic component. But at present there appear to be no strong grounds for assuming that genetic factors play a unique or even large role in the occurrence of human prejudice. While our genes may determine many of our physical characteristics and even contribute to some aspects of our personalities, there is as yet insufficient evidence to conclude that they also cause us to hate. Genetic similarity theory, then, should be viewed as a thought-provoking but as yet unverified perspective on the age-old problem of prejudice.

Combating Prejudice: Some Plans of Action

Whatever the specific origins of prejudice, there can be no doubt about the following point: it is a brutal, negative force in human affairs. Wherever and whenever it occurs, it is a drain on precious human resources. Reducing prejudice and countering its impact are therefore important tasks—crucial ones in the 1990s, when racial, ethnic, and religious prejudice threatens to tear whole societies and potentially the entire planet apart. Do any effective strategies for accomplishing these goals exist? Fortunately, they do. And although none by itself can totally eliminate prejudice or discrimination, together they are capable of making substantial dents in these problems. The most promising of these tactics will now be reviewed.

Breaking the Cycle of Prejudice: On Learning *Not* to Hate

Are children born with all their prejudices firmly in place? Or do they acquire them through experiences at home, in school, or elsewhere? At present, it would probably be difficult to find someone willing to support the first view, for a vast body of knowledge on human development maintains that bigots are made, not born (Berk, 1989). Children acquire prejudice and related reactions from their parents, other adults, and their peers. Given this fact, one useful technique for reducing prejudice follows logically: Somehow we must discourage parents from providing their offspring with training in bigotry and must encourage them instead to assist in the development of more positive views about others.

Having stated this principle, we must now admit that putting it into practice is anything but simple. How, for example, can we induce parents who are themselves highly prejudiced to encourage accepting, prodiversity views among their youngsters? One possibility involves calling parents' attention to their own prejudiced views. As we noted at the start of this chapter, few persons are willing to describe themselves as prejudiced; instead, they view their *own* negative attitudes toward various groups as entirely justified. A key initial step, therefore, is to convince parents that the problem exists. Once they come face to face with their own prejudice, many do seem willing to modify their words and their behavior. True, some diehard fanatics actually want to turn their children into hate-filled copies of themselves (refer to Figure 5.13). Most, however, genuinely wish to provide their children with a more positive view of the social world. For this reason, campaigns designed to enhance parents' awareness of prejudice and its harmful effects and to discourage them from demonstrating prejudice in their own words or deeds can yield desirable results.

In addition, schools and teachers can play a positive role. A dramatic illustration of this point was provided some years ago by Jane Elliot, an Iowa schoolteacher. In an attempt to help her all-white class of third-graders understand the nature of prejudice, Ms. Elliot divided the class into two groups on

Prejudice: One way in which it is acquired

FIGURE 5.13 Some parents actively seek to encourage prejudice among their children. Most, however, do not consciously seek such outcomes. Even though they don't, they may communicate their own prejudiced views to their offspring.

the basis of eye color. On the first day of the demonstration, brown-eyed children were assigned an inferior status. They were ridiculed by the teacher, who described them as being duller, lazier, and sloppier than blue-eyed children. They were denied classroom privileges and, as a sign of their low status, were made to wear special collars. This treatment continued for several days and then was reversed, so that the blue-eyed students now became the victims of prejudice.

Not surprisingly, the youngsters in both groups found the experience of being the victims of discrimination quite upsetting. In fact, the proceedings lowered students' performance on standard classroom tasks. The purpose of the demonstration was to provide the children with an opportunity to experience the evils of prejudice and discrimination in a protected environment; Ms. Elliot hoped that in this way, the children's own likelihood of evidencing these tendencies in their own behavior would be reduced. (A vivid pictorial record of the demonstration is presented in the documentary film *The Eye of the Storm*.)

Direct Intergroup Contact: The Potential Benefits of Acquaintance

American society has sometimes been described as a melting pot, a place in which persons from diverse backgrounds meet, interact, and somehow blend. Is this actually the case? Only to a limited degree. In reality, patterns of social contact within the United States (and within other heterogenous societies as well) tend to be predominantly *within-group* in nature. White persons interact primarily with whites, blacks with blacks, Christians with Christians, Jews with Jews, and so on. Even in the 1990s, many residential neighborhoods are segregated by race, religion, and ethnic background; and most American cities show a distinct pattern in which blacks and other minorities live within the central-city boundaries, while the surrounding suburbs are predominantly white (Hacker, 1983; refer to Figure 5.14).

Intergroup contact in the United States: How much really occurs?

FIGURE 5.14 Contrary to the view that the United States is a "melting pot," different ethnic, racial, and religious groups often live in segregated communities. As a result of this pattern, they have little direct contact with one another.

This state of affairs raises an intriguing question: Can prejudice be reduced by somehow increasing the degree of contact between different groups? The idea that it can is known as the **contact hypothesis,** and there are several good reasons for predicting that such a strategy might prove effective (Pettigrew, 1981). First, increased contact between persons from different groups can lead to growing recognition of similarities between them. As we will see in Chapter 6, perceived similarity can in turn generate enhanced mutual attraction. Second, while stereotypes are indeed resistant to change, they can be altered when sufficient information inconsistent with them is encountered. As persons from different groups get to know one another on a personal basis, this information may be forthcoming, with the result that the stereotypes begin to crumble. Third, increased contact may help counter the illusion of outgroup homogeneity described earlier. For these and other reasons, it seems possible that direct intergroup contact may be one effective means of combating prejudice. Is it? Existing evidence suggests that it is, but only when it occurs under certain conditions (Cook, 1985).

First, the groups interacting must be roughly equal in social, economic, or task-related status. If, instead, they differ sharply in such respects, communication may be difficult and prejudice can actually increase. Second, the contact situation must involve cooperation and interdependence so that the groups work toward shared goals (as in the *Robber's Cave* experiment described earlier). Third, contact between the groups must be informal so that they can get to know one another on a one-to-one basis. Fourth, contact must occur in a setting in which existing norms favor group equality. Fifth, the groups must interact in ways that permit disconfirmation of negative, stereotyped beliefs about one another. And sixth, the persons involved must view one another as typical of their respective groups; only then will they generalize their pleasant contacts to other persons or situations (Wilder, 1984).

When contact between initially hostile groups occurs under these conditions, prejudice between them does seem to decrease (Cook, 1985; Riordan, 1978). Such effects have been demonstrated by Aronson and his colleagues in a series of studies employing increased contact as a means of reducing racial prejudice (Aronson, Bridgeman, & Geffner, 1978). The procedure they used, known as the *jigsaw method,* was simple. Racially mixed groups of six students worked together on a specific lesson. Each member of the group was required to master a single portion of the lesson and present it to the others. Successful group performance could be attained only if each person performed adequately. Thus, all members had to cooperate in order to attain a shared group goal. The results achieved with this simple procedure were impressive. Following exposure to the jigsaw method (and the cooperative intergroup contact it involved), students showed reduced racial stereotyping and increased liking for members of the other race.

Additional evidence (e.g., Cook, 1984) also suggests that friendly, cooperative contact between persons from different social groups can indeed promote respect and liking between them. In view of these findings, it appears that when used with care, direct group contact can be an effective tool for combating cross-group hostility and prejudice. When people get to know one another, it seems, many of the anxieties, stereotypes, and false perceptions that have previously kept them apart seem to vanish (or at least diminish) in the warmth of new friendships. (Is intergroup contact effective in reducing prejudice even in a society in which such feelings are extreme? For evidence on this question, please see the **Multicultural Perspective** section below.)

SOCIAL PSYCHOLOGY: A MULTICULTURAL PERSPECTIVE

Interracial Contact in South Africa: Evidence for Some Limited Gains

In the United States and many other multiracial countries, integration and cross-race contact are viewed as positive outcomes by many persons. In South Africa, however, the opposite is true. As we noted previously, until recently official government policy (termed *apartheid*) was designed to minimize contact between blacks and whites in all spheres of life. Will increased contact succeed in reducing racial prejudice even in this type of setting? A study on this issue by Finchilescu (1988) offers something of a mixed answer.

This investigation was conducted with nursing students in four different hospitals in South Africa. Two of the hospitals had racially integrated training programs (one involving white and Indian nurses, the other involving Indians and Africans). The remaining two hospitals did not provide such cross-race contact. In each hospital, the student nurses were asked to complete questionnaires designed to measure their attitudes toward racial integration in the training of nurses and about the characteristics and work ability of nurses belonging to different racial groups.

With respect to attitudes about integrated training, results were quite encouraging. Nurses in the two hospitals with interracial programs reported stronger support for such training and such contact than did nurses in the two segregated hospitals (refer to Figure 5.15, p. 208). Thus, there was some evidence that interracial contact yielded beneficial effects. Unfortunately, however, such benefits were not apparent with respect to other interracial attitudes. Contrary to expectations, nurses in the two integrated hospitals did not report more favorable views toward nurses of other races than those in the two hospitals without integrated training programs. Instead, with few exceptions, each racial group tended to report more positive attitudes toward its own members than toward persons of other races.

Why did intergroup contact fail to lessen at least some aspects of racial prejudice? Finchilescu suggests that this finding may reflect the fact that while personal contact between individuals can enhance attitudes about specific persons or about interacting with them, it may not readily change more general views, including ones about entire racial or ethnic groups. In other words, as a result of their positive experiences during interracial training, subjects may have formed more positive views toward student nurses of other races in the context of training but shown minimal tendency to generalize these views to such persons in other contexts or to other racial groups generally.

In any case, Finchilescu's results suggest that interracial contact can be a force for positive change even in a culture in which segregation and racial prejudice are official societal policy. To the extent that this finding is confirmed

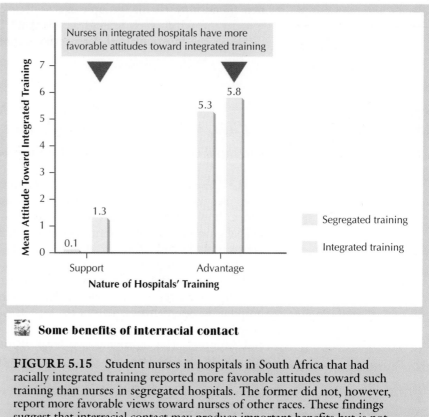

Nurses in integrated hospitals have more favorable attitudes toward integrated training

Segregated training

Integrated training

Some benefits of interracial contact

FIGURE 5.15   Student nurses in hospitals in South Africa that had racially integrated training reported more favorable attitudes toward such training than nurses in segregated hospitals. The former did not, however, report more favorable views toward nurses of other races. These findings suggest that interracial contact may produce important benefits but is not completely effective in eliminating racial prejudice. (Source: Based on data from Finchilescu, 1988.)

in additional research, it offers grounds for at least guarded optimism concerning the possibility of overcoming even powerful and long-entrenched forms of prejudice.

Recategorization: Redrawing the Boundary between "Us" and "Them"

In the town of Siena, Italy, different neighborhoods (wards) form tight-knit groups. Residents identify strongly with these groups, which date back to the Middle Ages, and are proud of their unique history and symbols (various wards are represented by such signs as a turtle or a seashell). Once a year, each neighborhood enters several horses in a citywide race, and the struggle for victory in this event is fierce. Indeed, for many days before the event itself, crowds of young people from various neighborhoods gather in the street to hurl jeers and taunts at one another. These often become so intense that violent fights erupt, often with tragic consequences. During the race itself, almost any action that might bring victory is acceptable, and jockeys frequently engage in tactics banned on most racetracks throughout the world.

To an outsider, these events seem puzzling. After all, Siena is a small city, and the persons involved all speak the same language, share the same ethnic background, and practice the same religion. Yet because they choose to divide their social world into competing groups, hostility and conflict between them run high. But now consider what happens when sports teams from Siena play against teams from other Italian cities. During such events, neighborhood distinctions disappear, and all Sienese join together to support and root for *their* teams. What has happened? In terms of the principles discussed in this chapter, the citizens of Siena have shifted the location of their boundary between "us" and "them." Most of the time, this boundary falls between neighborhoods. When their city competes with others, however, it is moved outward and falls between Siena and other towns (refer to Figure 5.16).

Such shifts in the boundary between "us" and "them" are a common part of social life. Most persons have had the experience of rooting for their school's

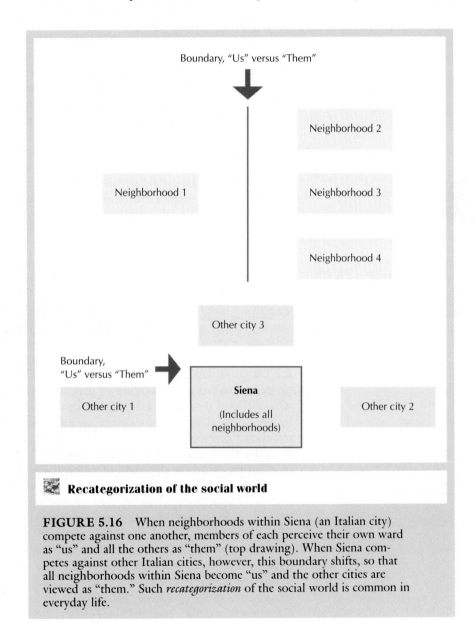

Recategorization of the social world

FIGURE 5.16 When neighborhoods within Siena (an Italian city) compete against one another, members of each perceive their own ward as "us" and all the others as "them" (top drawing). When Siena competes against other Italian cities, however, this boundary shifts, so that all neighborhoods within Siena become "us" and the other cities are viewed as "them." Such *recategorization* of the social world is common in everyday life.

team when it plays against teams from other schools but of forgetting such distinctions and rooting for their state's or city's team, whatever school it comes from, when it plays in higher-level competitions. Can such shifts, or **recategorization,** be used to reduce prejudice in other contexts? Research conducted recently by Gaertner and his colleagues (1989) indicates that it can.

In this ingenious study, groups of six subjects first worked as two competing, three-person teams on the task of solving a difficult problem. (The problem involved first imagining that their plane had crashed in the woods of northern Minnesota in January and then deciding which of various items salvaged from the plane were most valuable in terms of survival.) After reaching a consensus on the problem, subjects worked on the same problem once again. This time, however, they worked under one of several different conditions. In one (the *two-groups* condition), the original division into two groups of three persons each was maintained. Subjects were seated so that three members of one group faced the others, and they merely described their previous group consensus to each other. In another (the *one-group* condition), subjects worked as a single group of six persons. Here, subjects were seated so that the members of the former groups alternated (a member from one group, a member from the other, and so on). Further, they were told to work together to arrive at a new consensus for all six persons. Finally, in a third condition (the *separate-individuals* group), each subject first worked on the problem alone in a separate cubicle. Then, all six entered a single room and, while seated with their backs to one another, described their individual solutions.

Following these procedures, subjects rated one another on various dimensions (e.g., liking, cooperativeness, honesty). It was predicted that persons in the two-group condition would continue to view themselves as members of two distinct three-person groups. Thus, they would rate members of their own ingroup higher than those of the other, competing group. In contrast, it was expected that in the one-group and separate-individuals conditions, subjects would no longer view themselves in this manner. As a result, tendencies toward intergroup bias (prejudice) would decrease. As you can see from Figure 5.17, this is precisely what happened. Subjects in the two-group condition showed a stronger tendency to rate members of their own initial group more favorably than did those in the one-group or separate-individuals conditions. While both the one-group and separate-individuals treatments were effective in reducing prejudice, further analyses indicated that these reductions stemmed from somewhat different mechanisms. In the one-group condition, the reductions seemed to involve the development of more favorable attitudes toward former ingroup members, while in the separate-individuals group, they involved decreased attractiveness toward former ingroup members.

Can this principle of recategorization (or, in the case of the separate-individuals group, *de*categorization) be put to practical use? Gaertner and his colleagues believe it can. Indeed, they suggest that the induction of common ingroup membership (as in the one-group condition) can initiate a process in which reductions in intergroup bias generate increased positive contacts between groups. These contacts in turn reduce such bias still further. Previous research indicates that even relatively simple steps, such as forming new subgroups composed of members from competing groups, can be useful in starting this process (Brewer, Ho, Lee, & Miller, 1987; Vanbeselaere, 1987). Given such evidence, plus the findings reported by Gaertner et al. (1989), it

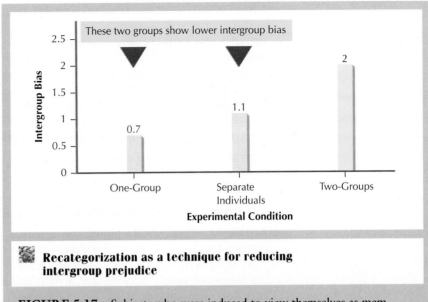

These two groups show lower intergroup bias

Recategorization as a technique for reducing intergroup prejudice

FIGURE 5.17 Subjects who were induced to view themselves as members of a single group (one-group condition) or as separate individuals not belonging to specific groups (separate-individuals condition) showed less intergroup bias than individuals who viewed themselves as members of two distinct groups. These findings suggest that *recategorization* (or decategorization) is a useful procedure for lessening intergroup prejudice. (Source: Based on data from Gaertner, Mann, Murrell, & Dovidio, 1989.)

seems reasonable to suggest that strategies based on shifting individuals' perceived boundaries between "us" and "them" constitute a very promising approach to the problem of intergroup bias.

Cognitive Interventions: Countering the Effects of Stereotypes

Earlier, we noted that stereotypes play an important role in prejudice. Indeed, the tendency to form impressions of others on the basis of their membership in various groups or categories *(category-driven processing)* appears to be a key factor in the occurrence and persistence of several forms of prejudice (Fiske, 1989). If so, interventions designed to reduce the impact of stereotypes—to induce individuals to pay careful attention to others and to understand them in terms of their unique attributes rather than the groups to which they belong—might prove highly effective in lessening the various forms of prejudice.

Precisely this approach has been taken by Fiske and her colleagues in a continuing series of related studies (e.g., Erber & Fiske, 1984; Neuberg, 1989). The results of these studies indicate that when individuals are motivated to pay close attention to others, they tend to perceive them in terms of their personal attributes rather than their race, ethnic background, or gender. How can individuals be motivated to engage in such attribute-driven processing of social information? Recent findings suggest that such procedures as making their fates dependent on a stranger's performance or merely telling them that it is very important to be accurate in forming an impression of this person can do the trick. Presumably, these conditions enhance subjects' motivation to be accurate, and this in turn reduces their tendency to rely on stereotypes (i.e., category-driven forms of processing). Another way of looking at these findings is as follows: When individuals form impressions of a stranger, they can engage in a wide variety of strategies, ranging from total dependence on stereotypes (the least effortful route) to total dependence on the unique characteristics of the target person (the most effortful route; Fiske & Neuberg, 1990). Conditions that tip the balance in favor of attribute-based strategies tend to reduce reliance on stereotypes, and in this respect can be an important means of reducing several forms of prejudice.

Prejudice Based on Gender: Its Nature and Effects

A majority of the world's population is female. Yet despite this fact, in many cultures females have often been treated as though they were a minority group. They have been excluded from economic and political power; they have been the subject of strong negative stereotypes; and they have faced overt discrimination in many spheres of life (e.g., work settings, social organizations, various realms of higher education). As we move into the 1990s, this situation appears to be changing, at least to a degree (see Figure 5.18). Overt discriminatory practices have been banned by legislation in many nations, and there has been at least some weakening of negative stereotypes concerning women. Still, there can be little doubt that prejudice based on sex persists in some contexts (e.g., Glick, Zion, & Nelson, 1988; Steinberg & Shapiro, 1982). For example, consider a study performed by Kanekar, Kolsawalla, and Nazareth (1988), who asked several hundred students at Indian universities to rate the prestige of sixteen occupations. For each occupation, subjects provided two ratings: one for males and another for females. As shown in Figure 5.19, the occupations differed greatly in terms of overall prestige. In addition, there was evidence of

Full equality for females: Some progress is apparent

FIGURE 5.18 While females have certainly not yet attained fully equal treatment in many societies, there has been considerable progress toward this goal in recent decades.

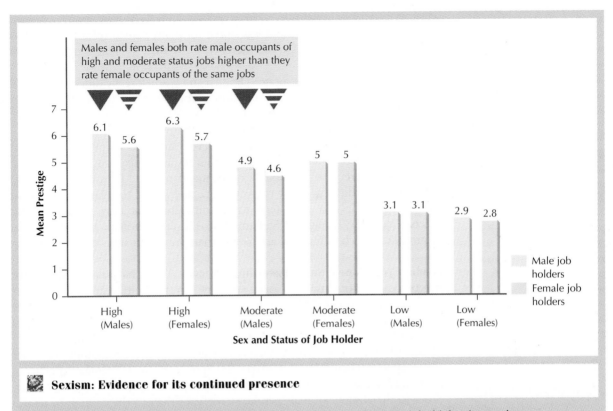

Males and females both rate male occupants of high and moderate status jobs higher than they rate female occupants of the same jobs

Mean Prestige

6.1, 5.6, 6.3, 5.7, 4.9, 4.6, 5, 5, 3.1, 3.1, 2.9, 2.8

High (Males), High (Females), Moderate (Males), Moderate (Females), Low (Males), Low (Females)

Sex and Status of Job Holder

Male job holders
Female job holders

Sexism: Evidence for its continued presence

FIGURE 5.19 Both males and females rated male occupants of various jobs higher in prestige than female occupants of the same jobs. This tendency was most visible with respect to occupations that were viewed as moderate or high in status. (Source: Based on data from Kanekar, Kolsawalla, & Nazareth, 1988.)

a clear bias favoring males. Especially for occupations high in prestige, ratings were higher for male than for female jobholders. Moreover, this same pattern was observed among female as well as male subjects. Such findings suggest that sexism—prejudice based on gender—is far from a memory; on the contrary, it is still very much with us in many respects.

Because prejudice based on gender affects more individuals than any other single kind (more than half the human race!), and because it produces negative outcomes for both men and women, we will consider it here in some detail.

Gender Stereotypes: The Cognitive Core of Prejudice toward Females

As we noted earlier, females have often been the object of strong, persistent stereotypes. To an extent, so have males: They, too, are perceived as being "all alike" in their possession of certain traits. Usually, however, stereotypes about females are more negative in content than those about males are. For example, in many cultures males are assumed to possess such desirable traits as decisiveness, aggressiveness, ambition, and logical patterns of thought. In contrast, the corresponding stereotype for females includes such less desirable characteristics as passivity, submissiveness, high emotionality, and indecisiveness (Deaux & Lewis, 1984). Some positive characteristics, too, are included (e.g., nurturance, sensitivity, personal warmth). However, by and large, the traits assigned to females are less desirable and less suited for many valued roles (e.g., leadership, authority) than the gender stereotype for males (Heilman, Martell, & Simon, 1988).

Are such stereotypes accurate? Do men and women really differ in the ways these stereotypes suggest? This question is complex, for such differences between the sexes, even if observed, may be more a reflection of the impact of stereotypes and their self-confirming nature than of basic differences between men and women. Existing evidence, however, seems to point to the general conclusion: Where differences between the sexes are concerned, common sense (and gender stereotypes) probably overstates the case. Males and females do indeed seem to differ in some respects (e.g., males tend to be more aggressive than females; the two sexes tend to use different techniques for influencing others; Carli, 1989; Eagly & Steffen, 1986). Overall, though, the number and magnitude of such differences are far less than prevailing stereotypes suggest.

Gender Stereotypes: Some Unsettling Effects   As we have noted previously, stereotypes do not exist in a social vacuum. On the contrary, they often exert powerful effects on judgments and evaluations of the persons to whom they are applied. Gender stereotypes are no exception—they influence the perceptions and behavior of large numbers of persons throughout the world. In the case of females, the impact of such stereotypes is largely negative. For example, consider what happens when these stereotypes are applied in work settings. In general, the traits assumed to be necessary for success in many high-level jobs are much closer to the content of male gender stereotypes than to the content of female gender stereotypes. After all, aren't managers or leaders supposed to be bold, assertive, tough, and decisive? Few persons expect—or want—them to be kind, sensitive, emotional, and passive. The result is that to the extent that females are subject to traditional gender stereotypes, they face a difficult uphill climb in efforts to launch and advance their careers.

Evidence for the negative impact of gender stereotypes on females in work settings has been reported by Heilman and her colleagues in several related studies. These experiments have repeatedly found that females are perceived as less suited for jobs traditionally filled by males and that any characteristics serving to emphasize or activate female gender stereotypes tend to intensify such negative effects (e.g., Heilman & Martell, 1986). For example, females who are physically attractive are perceived as being more feminine and therefore less suited for managerial roles than females who are less physically attractive. Encouragingly, the impact of gender stereotypes can be reduced if clear evidence for a woman's ability or competence is provided (Heilman, Martell, & Simon, 1988). Nevertheless, it appears that even in such cases, stereotypes concerning occupations themselves (e.g., the view that nurses are—or should be—women; the view that surgeons should be men) can remain and lead to discrimination based on sex (Glick, Zion, & Nelson, 1988). Thus, even if they manage to avoid the negative effects of gender stereotypes, females may still face difficulties that reduce their chances for success at work.

Discrimination against Females: Subtle but Often Deadly

In the 1990s, overt discrimination on the basis of sex has been made illegal by court rulings and legislation. As a result, it is much more difficult for businesses, schools, and social organizations to reject applicants for jobs or admission simply because they are female (or male). Despite this fact, women continue to occupy a relatively disadvantaged position in society. They are concentrated in relatively low-paying, low-status jobs (e.g., about 40 percent are employed as clerical and service workers), and their average salary remains lower than that for males. Why is this the case? One possibility is that sufficient time has not yet passed for women to receive the full benefits of legal and social changes that occurred during the 1970s and 1980s. Another possibility, one supported by growing research evidence, is that while overt barriers to female advancement have largely disappeared, other, more subtle forces continue to operate against women in many contexts.

The Role of Expectations One such factor impeding the progress of females involves their own expectations. In general, women seem to hold lower expectations about their careers than men. Women expect to receive lower starting and peak salaries than men (Major & Konar, 1984). And they view lower salaries for females as being somehow fair. This last fact, an unsettling one, was reported by Jackson and Grabski (1988), who asked male and female shoppers at large suburban malls to indicate what they considered to be fair pay for male and female employees (or employees whose gender was unspecified) holding various jobs. The jobs varied in status so that they were high (e.g., mathematics professor, nursing professor), moderate (e.g., police officer, bank teller), or low (e.g., hospital orderly, gas station attendant). Results indicated that for jobs high and moderate in status, females indicated lower fair salaries than did males (refer to Figure 5.20, p. 216). Why do females hold these lower expectations? Perhaps because they know, from actual experience, that on average, females earn less than males. Another possibility is that females perceive a weaker connection between work and monetary outcomes than do males. They value other aspects of work (e.g., friendly relations with coworkers) more highly than males do (Jackson & Grabski, 1988). Whatever the basis for such differences, as a general rule, people tend to get what they expect in life. Thus, the lower expectations held by females may be one factor operating against them in many instances.

The Role of Self-Confidence Confidence, it is often said, is the single best predictor of success. People who expect to succeed often do; those who expect to fail find that these predictions, too, are confirmed. Unfortunately, women tend to express lower self-confidence than men in many achievement-related situations. That they have not yet attained full equality with men in many work settings, therefore, may stem, at least in part, from this factor. Evidence that this is indeed the case has been reported by McCarty (1986).

In a laboratory study on this issue, McCarty asked male and female students to work on tasks involving creativity. Subjects performed three such tasks (e.g., devising unique uses for ordinary objects, such as a pencil or wire hanger) and received feedback on each one. Some learned that they had done very well, others that they had done quite poorly. A third group received no feedback. Results indicated that female participants in the study reported lower levels of self-confidence than males before working on the tasks. More importantly, while positive feedback increased women's self-confidence, it remained lower than men's. Finally, men who received no feedback reported self-confidence as high as that of women who had received positive feedback.

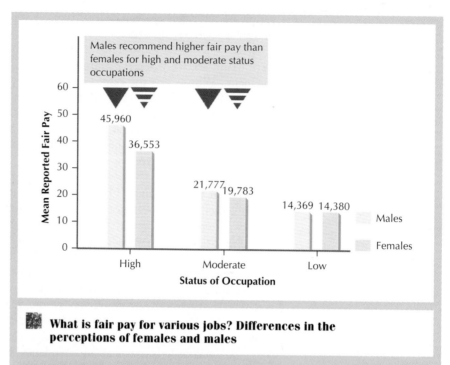

Males recommend higher fair pay than females for high and moderate status occupations

45,960
36,553
21,777 19,783
14,369 14,380

Males
Females

Mean Reported Fair Pay

High   Moderate   Low

Status of Occupation

What is fair pay for various jobs? Differences in the perceptions of females and males

FIGURE 5.20   When asked to describe what would be fair pay for various jobs, females reported lower figures than males. This was true for occupations of high and moderate status but did not occur for ones low in status. Since expectations concerning pay often affect actual salaries, it is possible that the differences shown are one factor in the lower average pay received by females as compared with males. (Source: Based on data from Jackson & Grabski, 1988.)

These findings suggest that positive feedback about task performance may be especially important for women. Even in the absence of such feedback, men express relatively high degrees of self-confidence. However, women report similar levels of confidence only in the context of encouraging feedback. Since positive feedback is not readily available in many situations, this factor may be another subtle force operating against females.

Denying Credit Where Credit Is Due: Attributions about Male and Female Achievement   A third factor that tends to operate against females in many contexts involves differences in attributions concerning successful performance by males and females. Several studies suggest that some persons, at least, tend to attribute success by males to internal factors, such as effort or ability, while attributing similar performance by females to external causes such as luck or an easy task (Deaux, 1982; Nieva & Gutek, 1981). For females, the results of this tendency can be devastating: If a man succeeds at some task, it is assumed that he worked hard or that he possesses a high level of ability. If a female attains the same level of performance, however, it is assumed that she "lucked out" or that the task wasn't very difficult. Since important rewards such as raises and promotions usually depend on such evaluations, these tendencies clearly operate against achievement by females in many business settings. Fortunately, they do not seem to occur in all contexts. In particular, when the attention of the persons making such evaluations is directed firmly to the actual performance of those being judged, such bias may vanish (Izraeli, Izraeli, & Eden, 1985). In other contexts, though, the tendencies may persist and exert damaging effects on the careers of deserving female employees.

Negative Reactions to Female Leaders: When Nonverbal Cues Can Hurt
Suppose you stopped a hundred people at random and asked them the following question: "Can women be as successful as men in leadership roles?" What, in the 1990s, would you find? Probably, a large majority would answer "yes" or "of course." In other words, most people would report little if any prejudice against females. But stop and consider: Do such comments reflect their real views? Or would many of these same persons actually behave differently toward male and females leaders when they encounter them? A study conducted by Butler and Geis (1990) points to the latter conclusion.

These researchers reasoned that even at present, many people—both women and men—find leadership by females to be unexpected: It just doesn't seem to fit with sex-role stereotypes that they hold, perhaps without realizing it. Since violations of expectations often induce negative affect, Butler and Geis (1990) predicted that when confronted with female leaders, many persons will demonstrate negative nonverbal cues—facial expressions of displeasure or rejection. Such cues, in turn, can be very damaging. They are readily visible to other group members who may then interpret them as signs that female leaders are incompetent or unsuccessful in this role. The result, of course, may be devastating for emerging female leaders in a wide range of groups.

To determine if individuals really do demonstrate more negative facial expressions toward female than male leaders, Butler and Geis had groups of four persons (two males and two females) discuss a standard survival problem. (This task involves ranking the survival value of nine items after an imaginary crash on the moon.) Two of the persons in each group were naive subjects, while two others (one male and one female) were assistants specially trained to assume leadership roles. In one condition (solo leader), one of these persons assumed the role of leader, making many contributions and taking charge of the discussion. In the other (co-leaders), they both acted as leaders. During the group discussions, observers recorded facial signs of pleasure or displeasure to the leaders on the part of the subjects. Since one assistant was male and the other was female, contrasting reactions to male and female leaders could then be assessed. Both assistants stuck to carefully rehearsed scripts, so their behavior was consistent across groups and experimental conditions.

It was predicted that emergent female leaders would elicit more negative nonverbal cues from subjects than would emergent male leaders. As you can see from Figure 5.21 (p. 218), this is precisely what happened. Regardless of whether there were two leaders or one, female leaders received more negative nonverbal cues than male leaders. Moreover, male leaders also received more positive nonverbal cues per minute than did female leaders. Disturbingly, these findings emerged even though subjects strongly disclaimed any bias against females. The fact that they still showed contrasting facial reactions to virtually identical actions by female and male leaders, therefore, points to the existence of yet another subtle, yet potentially important, barrier to equal achievement by females.

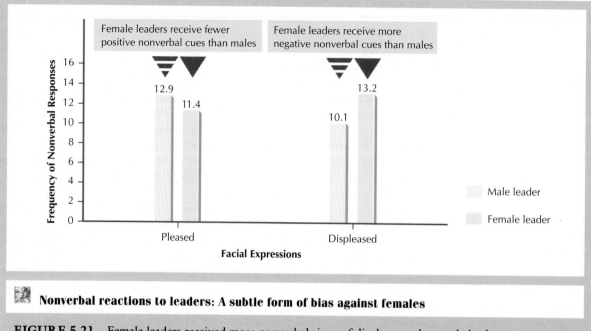

Nonverbal reactions to leaders: A subtle form of bias against females

FIGURE 5.21 Female leaders received more nonverbal signs of displeasure than male leaders from other group members. Conversely, female leaders received fewer nonverbal signs of pleasure than male leaders. (Source: Based on data from Butler & Geis, 1990.)

Sexism in Work Settings: Some Room for Optimism

There is no doubt that in the past, the aspirations and careers of large numbers of women were adversely affected by prejudice based on gender. The costs, in terms of both wasted potential and personal disappointments, were certainly high. In recent years, though, the situation seems to have altered considerably. Growing numbers of females have been hired for or promoted to managerial positions. Indeed, at present more than 30 percent of managers are females, compared with less than 10 percent twenty years ago. Increasing numbers of females are rising to high-level positions in large organizations and are gaining an increased share of the power and prestige that were once the sole domain of males. Perhaps even more encouraging, growing evidence suggests that sexist attitudes, too, are on the wane. Several diverse findings point to this conclusion.

First, women are no longer viewed as "unsuitable" for leadership positions simply because they are female. This fact is illustrated clearly by a recent study conducted by Goktepe and Schneier (1989). The subjects in this study were male and female students belonging to groups who worked together on exercises that were part of a college course in business policy. Students in these groups rated one another in terms of their attractiveness and leader status at two times: halfway through the semester and again near its end. In addition, they completed standard measures of gender-role orientation (e.g., the Bem Sex Role Inventory; Bem, 1974). Results indicated that persons identified as being leaders received significantly higher ratings in terms of attractiveness than nonleaders. Further, leaders, regardless of whether they were males or females, scored higher on traditionally masculine characteristics than did nonleaders. However, there was no difference in the frequency with which males and females emerged as leaders in these groups. Thus, there was little sign of bias against choosing females as leaders, provided that they demonstrated certain traits.

Second, it appears that women no longer receive lower on-the-job evaluations from their supervisors simply because they are female. In a large-scale study on this topic, Peters and his colleagues examined the performance ratings assigned to more than six hundred male and female store managers by their male and female supervisors (Peters et al., 1984). Results showed no evidence of discrimination against females. Indeed, both male and female supervisors actually assigned higher ratings to female managers than to male ones.

Third, recent findings suggest that discrimination based on sex is on the wane in the context of job interviews (Graves & Powell, 1988). Contrary to earlier findings, the sex of applicants appears to have little if any impact on the ratings assigned to them by professional interviewers.

Finally, jobs filled predominantly by females are not currently rated as less deserving of compensation than jobs filled predominantly by males (Grams & Schwab, 1985). Again, this finding is contrary to earlier reports indicating that such bias exists and operates against the fair treatment of females.

Together, all these findings point to substantial shifts toward a reduced incidence of sex discrimination in the world of work. Females, it seems, are receiving more equitable treatment now than in the past. Of course, this trend does not imply that sexism is no longer of major importance in work settings. On the contrary, women and other disadvantaged groups continue to face serious problems in this regard. Yet at least some forms of prejudice do appear to be on the wane and to be less influential—and less harmful—than they were in the past. It is our hope, of course, that such trends will continue and that at some point in the future, the impact of sexism and other forms of prejudice will vanish in work settings and in all other contexts as well.

SUMMARY AND REVIEW

The Nature of Prejudice and Discrimination

Prejudice is a negative attitude toward the members of some specific social group that is based solely on their membership in that group. Such attitudes often serve as *schemas,* strongly affecting the processing of information about groups that are the target of prejudice. **Discrimination** refers to harmful actions directed toward the persons or groups who are the targets of prejudice. It can be overt, ranging from simple avoidance or exclusion to violence, but often occurs in more subtle forms, such as *tokenism* or *reverse discrimination.*

Causes of Prejudice

Several contrasting views have been offered concerning the origins of prejudice. The *realistic conflict* view suggests that prejudice stems from competition for scarce resources between social groups. A second theory suggests that prejudice stems from *social categorization*—strong tendencies to divide the social world into two camps, "us" and "them." A third perspective calls attention to the role of early experience, in which children acquire prejudiced attitudes from their parents, teachers, friends, and others.

Much recent evidence supports the view that prejudice stems from certain aspects of *social cognition*—the ways in which we think about others and attempt to make sense of the social world. In this context, **stereotypes,** various forms of *selective* or *biased processing* of social information, *illusory correlation,* and the tendency to view all members of outgroups as being alike *(outgroup homogeneity)* all contribute to prejudice.

Strategies for Reducing Prejudice

Prejudice can be reduced by encouraging parents to transmit positive rather than negative attitudes about other groups to their children. *Direct intergroup contact* also seems to be helpful in this respect, provided that the contact occurs under appropriate conditions (e.g., roughly equal status on the part of the two groups, a friendly context for their interactions). Another useful technique for reducing prejudice involves somehow inducing individuals to shift the boundary between "us" and "them" so that former outgroup and ingroup members are now viewed as belonging to the same social category.

Prejudice Based on Gender

Sexism, prejudice based on gender, involves acceptance of strong and widespread *gender stereotypes*. These suggest that all males and all females share basic traits that distinguish the two sexes from each other. Overt discrimination against females has been made illegal in many nations. Several subtle forces, however, operate against female achievement in many contexts. These forces include lower expectations and self-confidence on the part of females and a tendency on the part of some persons to attribute female success to external causes (e.g., luck, an easy task).

Growing evidence suggests that sexism is on the wane in work settings. Females emerge as leaders as frequently as males do in work groups; performance appraisals and job interviews show little evidence of prejudice against females; and jobs filled predominantly by females are no longer viewed as being less deserving of compensation than jobs filled predominantly by males. Sexism has not entirely vanished, however, and continues to prevent the fair treatment of females in at least some settings.

KEY TERMS

Contact hypothesis The view that increased contact between members of various social groups can be effective in reducing prejudice between them. Such efforts seem to succeed only when contact takes place under specific, favorable conditions.

Discrimination Negative behaviors directed toward members of social groups who are the object of prejudice.

Genetic similarity theory A theory suggesting that individuals tend to favor reproduction by others possessing genes similar to their own.

Illusion of outgroup homogeneity The tendency to perceive members of outgroups as more similar to one another (as less variable) than the members of one's own ingroup are.

Illusory correlation The perception of a stronger association between two variables than actually exists because each is a distinctive event and the co-occurrence of such events is readily entered into and retrieved from memory.

Ingroup The social group to which an individual perceives herself or himself as belonging ("us").

Ingroup differentiation hypothesis The view that individuals perceive greater variability among members of their ingroup than they do among members of various outgroups.

Outgroup Any group ("them") other than the one to which individuals perceive themselves as belonging.

Prejudice Negative attitudes toward the members of specific social groups.

Realistic conflict theory The view that prejudice sometimes stems from direct competition between various social groups over scarce and valued resources.

Recategorization Shifts in the boundary between an individual's ingroup ("us") and some outgroup ("them"). As a result of such recategorization, persons formerly viewed as outgroup members may now be viewed as belonging to the ingroup.

Reverse discrimination The tendency to evaluate or treat persons belonging to outgroups (especially ones that are the object of strong ethnic or racial prejudice) more favorably than members of one's own ingroup.

Schemata Cognitive frameworks developed through experience that affect the processing of new social information.

Sexism Prejudice based on gender.

Social categorization The tendency to divide the social world into two separate categories: our ingroup ("us") and various outgroups ("them").

Social-learning view (of prejudice) The view that prejudice is acquired through both direct and vicarious experiences in much the same manner as other attitudes.

Stereotypes Beliefs to the effect that all members of specific social groups share certain traits or characteristics. Stereotypes are cognitive frameworks that strongly influence the processing of incoming social information.

Tokenism Instances in which individuals perform trivial positive actions for members of outgroups toward whom they feel strong prejudice. Such tokenistic behaviors are then used as an excuse for refusing to take more meaningful beneficial actions toward these groups.

FOR MORE INFORMATION

Dovidio, J. F., & Gaertner, S. L. (Eds.). (1986). *Prejudice, discrimination, and racism.* Orlando, FL: Academic Press.

This book contains chapters prepared by various experts on the topics of prejudice and discrimination. Several call attention to the fact that racial prejudice has not actually decreased or disappeared in recent years—it has simply shifted to more subtle forms.

Gutek, B. A. (1985). *Sex and the workplace.* San Francisco: Jossey-Bass.

A thoughtful analysis of sexual harassment and related issues in work settings. Various chapters examine the causes of sexual harassment, the attitudes of women and men toward such behavior, and techniques for coping with this serious problem.

Shaver, P., & Hendrick, C. (Eds.). (1987). *Sex and gender.* Newbury Park, CA: Sage.

A collection of chapters by experts on gender, sex roles, and sexism. The discussions of gender development are especially interesting. A valuable source to consult if you'd like to know more about these topics.

Stephan, W. G. (1985). Intergroup relations. In G. Lindzey and E. Aronson (Eds.), *Handbook of social psychology* (Vol. 2). New York: Random House.

A thorough review of current knowledge about intergroup relations. Many processes that play a role in the development of prejudice, as well as several techniques for combating such reactions, are carefully examined.

Interpersonal Attraction: Becoming Acquainted, Establishing Friendships

Meeting and Evaluating Strangers: Physical Proximity and Emotional State

Propinquity: The "Invisible" Matchmaker / Affect: The Role of Emotions

When Former Strangers Become Close Acquaintances

Need for Affiliation: Dispositional Differences and External Influences / Physical Characteristics: Judging Books by Their Covers

Establishing Friendships

Similarity: Liking Those Who Are Like Ourselves / Reciprocity: If You Like Me, I Like You

SPECIAL SECTIONS

ON THE APPLIED SIDE
Opening Lines: Cute, Innocuous, or Direct?
SOCIAL PSYCHOLOGY: A MULTICULTURAL PERSPECTIVE
Responding to a Stranger's Voice: Judgments about Those Who Sound Childlike in the United States and Korea
FOCUS ON RESEARCH: THE CUTTING EDGE
Hypertraditionality and Attraction to the Opposite Sex

It was Saturday morning. Phil woke up after a good night's sleep and felt on top of the world. He was sure he had aced the anthropology exam the day before, the sun was shining, the sky was blue, and there was absolutely nothing he *had* to do all weekend. He could stay in bed, go for a swim, or even read a book just for fun. He thought, *Why not just get out of bed and see what develops?*

After a surprisingly good dorm breakfast, he walked slowly down the hill to the tennis courts to see if anyone was around to play a couple of sets. On the way, he glanced at the front page of the college paper and was pleased to see his name in one of the stories. The story listed ten juniors who would receive special fellowships for their final undergraduate year, and there he was—Phil Johnson. He was so pleased that he couldn't help whistling as he walked toward the courts.

When he got there, Phil noticed a guy from his chemistry lab sitting on the grass, idly twirling his racket. Phil didn't know his name, but he looked pleasant enough. Walking up to his classmate, he said, "Hi. I'm Phil Johnson. We're both in Klineberg's lab."

"Yeah, I know. You're the one who always gets the top *A* on every project. I won't hold that against you, though, if you're willing to play tennis with an amateur. I'm Rick Tangora."

Phil laughed, and they walked through the iron mesh door to an empty court. Rick seemed like someone he would enjoy knowing. Later, after the game, it might be a good idea to get together for a beer and lunch. It was time he made some new friends.

One of the basic research interests in social psychology over the past century has been the way we react to other people, making many acquaintances, becoming friends with a few individuals, and actively disliking others. Each of us evaluates others in positive and negative terms, and they evaluate us in return (Park & Flink, 1989). Some will like you while others will not, as Figure 6.1 suggests.

As you go about your life at school, at work, or in various daily activities, you interact with other human beings. You come into brief contact with many people, and you will get to know some of them. You may be surprised to learn that who you know and how well you like them are determined by some very specific and increasingly predictable factors. These interpersonal reactions appear to be based in large part on emotions; positive emotions result in liking, while negative emotions lead to feelings of dislike.

In the story about Phil, we saw an example of one way in which emotions operate. He had a good night's sleep, and woke up to find many things going well for him. Some of his positive feelings then transferred to a fellow student he recognized from his chemistry lab. As a result, he made a friendly approach. Negative emotions operate just as strongly, but in the opposite direction. Have you ever had a terrible day when everything went wrong? If Phil had awakened with a headache, found two painful pimples on his chin, believed that he had flunked the anthropology exam, eaten a miserable breakfast of soggy waffles and half-cooked bacon, read bad news in the paper, and walked outside on an uncomfortably hot and humid morning, would he have responded to Rick in the same friendly way? As we will see, a lot of research provides strong evidence that he would not.

The study of **interpersonal attraction** focuses on responses to other people that range from love to hate (see Figure 6.2). In this chapter, we will examine the initial steps people take to establish relationships. We will first describe how most interpersonal contacts are determined by factors that are related only indirectly to the people involved. You most often meet others

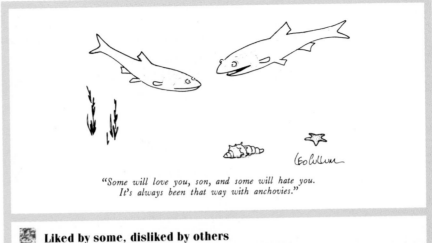

"Some will love you, son, and some will hate you. It's always been that way with anchovies."

Liked by some, disliked by others

FIGURE 6.1 As this young fish is being taught, some people love anchovies, and some hate them. The same is true for each person, and attraction research seeks to discover why a given person is liked by some people and disliked by others. (Drawing by Leo Cullum; © 1989 The New Yorker Magazine, Inc.)

because you are brought into close *physical proximity* with them by such impersonal environmental determinants as the location of seats in a classroom, rooms in a dormitory, or desks in an office. Seemingly random contacts result in your becoming acquainted with some of these individuals. This process is most likely to occur if you are in a positive *emotional state,* regardless of the reason for feeling good. Contacts are much less likely to be followed by friendly overtures if you are experiencing negative emotions. Next, we will outline the factors that lead you to move beyond simple acquaintanceship, in which you respond to those who look familiar by nodding and saying hello. Whether you progress further in getting to know someone depends on how motivated you and this acquaintance are to form *affiliations* and on how each of you reacts to the *external characteristics* of the other (physical attractiveness, accent, skin color, height, etc.). In the final section of this chapter, we explore the formation of *friendships* in which you and another person discover that you are *similar* in a number of respects and communicate *mutually positive evaluations* of each other. In Chapter 7, we will show how this process can continue when closer relationships (including romantic ones) are developed and maintained, as well as how relationships sometimes fail.

Meeting and Evaluating Strangers: Physical Proximity and Emotional State

Among the more than five billion people now living, any one individual will probably interact with only a very small percentage of them. Of this smaller sample, there remain thousands of potential friends, enemies, and lovers. Still, we tend to form emotionally meaningful relationships with just a small number

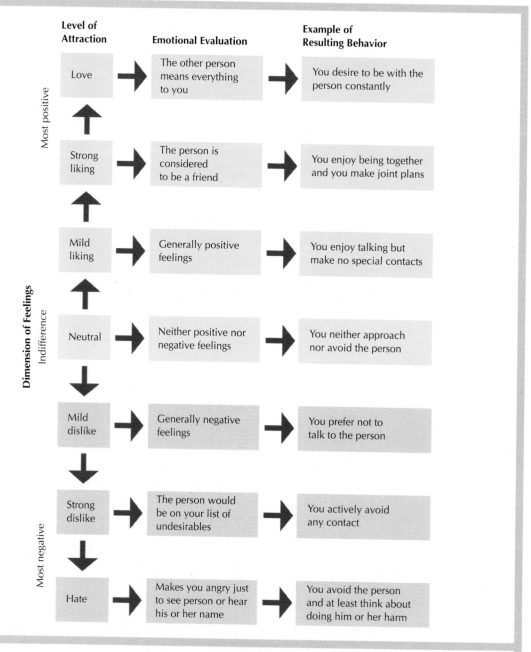

Interpersonal attraction: Liking and disliking other people

FIGURE 6.2 *Interpersonal attraction* refers to the evaluation one person makes of another along a positive-negative attitudinal dimension that ranges from hate at one extreme to love at the other. Research on attraction concentrates on the emotional and behavioral responses limited to that portion of the scale involving like and dislike.

of persons at any given time. For social psychologists, two questions have been central to a great deal of research: (1) On what basis do we narrow our social world to a manageable number of acquaintances; and (2) On what basis do we place each of them along the attraction continuum from love to hate? Some of the first steps in getting to know other people have little or nothing to do with their specific characteristics, or ours either. Two people are likely to become acquainted if they are brought into contact through simple physical proximity, or **propinquity,** and if each happens to be experiencing positive rather than negative **affect** at the time.

Propinquity: The "Invisible" Matchmaker

A common first step in forming a relationship is a series of unplanned encounters determined by where two individuals happen to be and the physical details of their mutual surroundings. For example, two students are assigned adjoining seats in a classroom, two people by chance rent apartments in the same building and on the same floor, or two people on the way to work each morning use the same bus stop at the same time of day. On the basis of such casual, accidental contacts, the other person becomes someone who is recognized, and human beings clearly are more comfortable around those they have seen before than total strangers. Following a series of exposures to someone new, most people find it emotionally and socially acceptable to say hello and to exchange casual remarks about a newsworthy event, the weather, or whatever. Even infants respond less positively to a stranger than to a person they have encountered previously (Levitt, 1980).

The Power of the Environment in Controlling Interpersonal Contact In studies spanning more than a half-century, it has been well established that when any aspect of the environment increases the propinquity of two individuals on a regular basis, the odds are that they will gradually come to know and like each other (Caplow & Forman, 1950; Newcomb, 1961). In universities, students become acquaintances on the basis of classroom seating assignments (see Figure 6.3, p. 228) or the location of their dormitory rooms, and these environmental factors are much better predictors of social relationships than the fact that two people have the same major, religion, or hobbies. When classroom seats are assigned according to the alphabet, students primarily get to know those whose last names begin with the same letter or with a nearby letter (Segal, 1974). All of this may seem obvious or trivial until you stop to realize that those you meet and those who become your friends (or perhaps even your future spouse) do so in part because of an instructor's seating chart, the way a computer is programmed to assign dormitory rooms, or the first letters of your last names. A couple who donated a large sum of money to a New York university in 1990 mentioned that they met in an economics class at that institution during the 1930s; they were seated alphabetically, so Edward George met and married Frances Gildea.

Propinquity operates very consistently. In housing units for married students, any two couples whose apartment doors are within twenty-two feet of each other will probably get to know one another socially. If the doors are eighty-eight or more feet apart, the best bet is that the couples will not ever become acquainted (Festinger, Schachter, & Back, 1950).

Because much of the research has been done in college settings, you may think that propinquity operates only in schools or only among those in a

 Classroom neighbors become acquaintances

FIGURE 6.3 *Propinquity* is an important determinant of who we get to know. In college, for example, classroom seating assignments help determine which students will and will not know one another by the end of the term. Students sitting side by side in a class are very likely to become acquainted. As the distance between the assigned seats increases, the probability of becoming acquainted drops rapidly.

particular age-group. In fact, these effects seem to be universal. For example, in a housing project for the elderly in a large city, the residents became friends if they were given rooms on the same floor—precisely the same pattern found in college dorms (Nahemow & Lawton, 1975). Environmental variables operate similarly in an apartment complex for young adults. The closer two people live, the better their chance of becoming close friends (Ebbesen, Kjos, & Konecni, 1976).

Why Are We Affected by Propinquity?   There are two reasons that propinquity shapes our interpersonal lives. First, most of us have learned that it is inappropriate, awkward, or even dangerous to interact with total strangers. What would you think if a man you have never seen before walked up to you, introduced himself, and said he wanted to be your friend? Probably you would react negatively, and you might assume that the person was odd, drunk, wanted to sell you something or get your vote, or was even someone who intended you harm. Our parents wisely taught us not to speak to strangers, and most of us learned that lesson well.

Part of the explanation, then, is that we rely on propinquity to bring us together because we are not comfortable in deliberately approaching strangers or in having them approach us. The second aspect of propinquity's power goes beyond that, however. Environmental variables operate to bring people together over and over again. As Zajonc (1968) and his colleagues have found in many experiments, **repeated exposure** to almost any strange stimulus leads to an increasingly positive evaluation of that stimulus. When subjects view line drawings over and over, or words in a language they don't know, or strangers, liking increases as the number of exposures increases (Moreland & Zajonc, 1982). Advertising pays off for the same reason—the more we come in contact with a brand name, a new product, or even a candidate in an election, the more positively we respond. Even if a stranger only *resembles* someone we know and like, we perceive him or her as familiar (White & Shapiro, 1987).

These effects are not necessarily obvious to those whose behavior is affected. Familiarity influences our interpersonal responses even when we are unaware of the fact. An experiment provides evidence as to how this process operates (Bornstein et al., 1987). Subjects interacted with two confederates (accomplices) in a discussion of a neutral topic. Before the interaction, however, they were exposed to a photograph of one of these individuals at a speed so rapid that they were unaware of it. Despite not being conscious of the previous exposure, subjects responded to a "familiar" confederate more positively than to one whose picture had not been flashed on the screen.

The Perils of Propinquity: Can Familiarity Breed Contempt?   Though there is abundant evidence indicating the positive effects of exposure, sometimes the opposite effect occurs. For example, repeated exposure to a stranger who acts unpleasantly each time he or she is encountered results in less and less liking for that person (Swap, 1977). You may have had the experience of being assigned an obnoxious roommate; contact with that person day after day certainly does not have a positive effect. In this instance, your initial feelings of dislike simply become more intense with repeated exposure.

Beyond interacting with someone who is unpleasant, even positive or neutral interactions can be aversive under some conditions. Though close physical proximity usually facilitates liking, it also interferes with one's **privacy.** Most of us don't want others to know everything about what we are doing, have done, or will do. Environmental conditions that bring about repeated contacts with roommates, apartment neighbors, or fellow workers may be perceived as promoting an invasion of privacy.

Further, some individuals value privacy more than others, and we would expect those high in the need for privacy to react most negatively to such invasions. In an experiment designed to test this hypothesis, Larson and Bell (1988) measured the need for privacy among undergraduate subjects. Students with a high need for privacy and those with a low need were asked to interact with a stranger (actually an experimental confederate) to discuss either personal topics (birth control, lying to parents, etc.) or nonpersonal ones (hometown, number of siblings, etc.). Though the topic of discussion had no effect, those highest in privacy needs tended to like the stranger less, to say less, to ask fewer questions, and to interact less positively than those whose need for privacy was low. The high-privacy students behaved in ways that were less natural, more tense, and more awkward than the low-privacy students did. In real-life interactions, we would expect someone with high privacy needs not to respond to interpersonal propinquity in the usual positive way.

There is an additional negative effect of repeated interpersonal contacts. When people have a job to do, seating arrangements that promote face-to-face contact and verbal interactions are positive in terms of attraction for fellow workers, but productivity suffers (Dixit, 1985). In this instance, the motives of employees to make friends and behave in a social fashion are in conflict with the employer's desire to get as much work done as quickly as possible in order to maximize profits. Propinquity furthers one of those goals but not the other.

Affect: The Role of Emotions

As in the opening story about Phil, positive and negative events in daily life can strongly influence one's mood (Stone & Neale, 1984). In turn, mood influences reactions to others, including attraction. The term **affect** refers to emotions or feelings.

Emotions and Attraction   Experiments have established that positive feelings increase interpersonal attraction toward strangers, while negative feelings decrease attraction. Even good versus bad news on radio and television influences feelings. To test the hypothesis that interpersonal attraction would be affected by news, Veitch and Griffitt (1976) arranged for subjects to hear a news broadcast while they were "waiting for the experiment to begin." What they heard was actually a cassette recording containing a series of false news stories that were either good or bad. Immediately afterward, the subjects received information about a stranger and indicated how they felt about him or her. As predicted, the good news caused a positive emotional reaction, and subjects who had heard that broadcast liked a stranger better than did subjects who had heard the bad news and experienced negative emotions. Other research has confirmed this finding (Kaplan, 1981).

What if the news is not something that is broadcast but information you possess about another person? How do you feel about informing someone that he or she has failed a test or lost a contest? Generally, people are reluctant to transmit bad news to others—this tendency is called the **MUM effect.** Sometimes the bad news is simply not communicated, or it is distorted to make it seem less negative. We realize that negative information arouses negative feelings and that we will be liked less if we pass it on. Taking this reaction to an extreme, ancient kings would execute the messenger who communicated bad news.

As a test of the MUM effect, Bond and Anderson (1987) gave undergraduates the task of informing another student about that person's success or failure on an intelligence test. Further, half the subjects were led to believe that the stranger could see them through a one-way mirror. As shown in Figure 6.4, when subjects thought they were visible, it took them about twice as long to deliver bad news as to deliver good news. This difference disappeared when the stranger could not see them. The investigators concluded that the MUM effect occurs not because of personal discomfort in relaying bad news or feelings of empathy for the recipient but, rather, because each individual wants a positive response from others. So, there is no problem in transmitting bad news anonymously, but there is reluctance to do so when the recipient can see who is relaying the unpleasant information.

Many different manipulations have been used to create positive or negative emotions, and the effect on attraction is the same in each instance. Examples include negative feelings aroused by a hot, uncomfortably humid room (Griffitt, 1970) and happy versus sad movies (Gouaux, 1971). Feelings are also affected by music. In one experiment, female college students were asked to rate male strangers on the basis of their photographs; in the laboratory in which these students worked, pleasant (rock), unpleasant (avant-garde classical), or no music

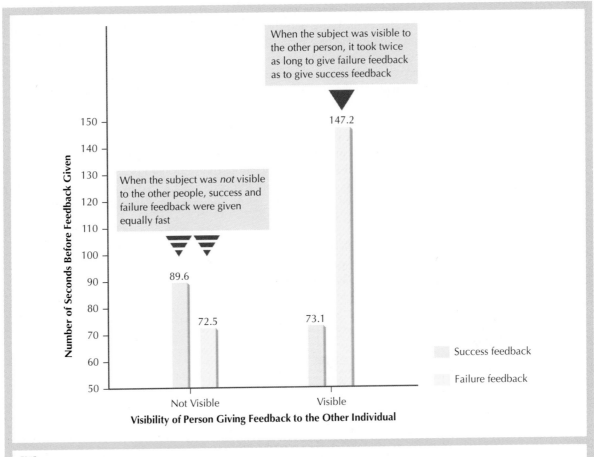

Number of Seconds Before Feedback Given

When the subject was visible to the other person, it took twice as long to give failure feedback as to give success feedback

147.2

When the subject was *not* visible to the other people, success and failure feedback were given equally fast

89.6

72.5

73.1

Success feedback

Failure feedback

Not Visible   Visible

Visibility of Person Giving Feedback to the Other Individual

Keeping MUM about bad news

FIGURE 6.4 The *MUM effect* describes the general reluctance people experience in transmitting bad news. In an experiment in which subjects were instructed to inform a confederate that he or she had just scored in either the top or the bottom twenty percent on an intelligence test, the good news was communicated much more quickly than the bad news when the subject could be seen by the confederate. Apparently, people prefer to avoid or postpone giving a negative message to a stranger only if they are visible to that person. No one wants to be associated with the negative feelings elicited by an unpleasant message and perhaps disliked because of it. (Source: Based on data from Bond & Anderson, 1987.)

was played (May & Hamilton, 1980). Compared with those in the silent condition, subjects liked the strangers better and even thought they were more physically attractive when rock music was playing; the opposite was true for those who heard the unpleasant classical music. Whatever the source of the emotions, once a person feels depressed, other people are liked less well, perceived as different (Swallow & Kuiper, 1987), and evaluated in negative terms (Shapiro, 1988).

Emotions influence interpersonal behavior as well as interpersonal evaluations. These effects were shown in an experiment by Cunningham (1988). Half the male subjects were made to feel happy (by means of a funny movie or a positive evaluation), and the other half were made to feel sad (by means of a depressing movie or a negative evaluation). Afterward, in the waiting room, a female confederate who was identified as another subject interacted in a standard way with each male subject. She was, of course, not informed whether the male had just had a positive or a negative mood manipulation. Males in a positive mood communicated with the female stranger more and disclosed more about themselves than those in a negative mood did. Other research has consistently shown that a person experiencing positive affect (happiness, excitement, curiosity, interest, etc.) is much more likely to engage in social interactions than he or she is when negative emotions are aroused (Clark & Watson, 1988).

Not only are our judgments and behavior affected by our feelings, but also by the emotional states of others. As one example, depressed individuals cause

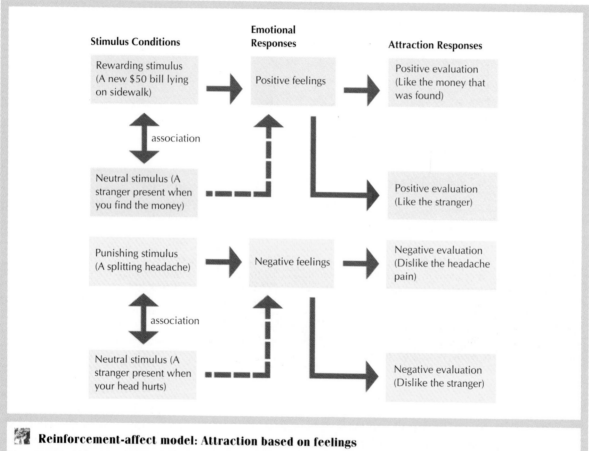

Reinforcement-affect model: Attraction based on feelings

FIGURE 6.5 According to the *reinforcement-affect model*, likes and dislikes are based on whether positive or negative feelings are aroused. We like any rewarding stimulus because of our positive feelings, and we dislike any punishing stimulus because of our negative feelings. When a stranger (or any other neutral stimulus) is present at the same time, that person becomes associated with the positive or negative feelings. This conditioning results in liking for any stranger associated with positive feelings and dislike for any stranger associated with negative feelings.

us to have negative feelings, and so we like them less (Winer et al., 1981). College students tend to reject, dislike, and avoid a depressed roommate more than they would a roommate who is not depressed (Burchill & Stiles, 1988). Interactions with a depressed roommate are personal and relatively negative in tone. Somewhat surprisingly, these interactions bring about a more positive mood for both individuals, possibly because the painful exchanges help "clear the air" and permit them to deal with problems that would otherwise be avoided.

Explaining the Effect of Emotions on Attraction The most plausible explanation of emotions as the basis of attraction involves conditioning. According to one theory of interpersonal attraction, the **reinforcement-affect model,** all likes and dislikes are based on emotional responses (Clore & Byrne, 1974). At the simplest and most obvious level, we like anyone or anything that makes us feel good and dislike whoever or whatever makes us feel bad.

Another aspect of the model is less obvious. As shown in Figure 6.5, we react not only to the person or event responsible for *arousing* our emotions but also to anyone or anything that is simply *associated* with those feelings. This conditioning of emotional responses is the reason you like a person who is simply present when you hear good news on the radio. He or she was not responsible for your pleasant feelings; the news story was. Nevertheless, you associate that person with your emotional state and evaluate him or her accordingly. The conditioning of emotions and its effect on attraction have been demonstrated in numerous laboratory experiments (Bleda, 1976; Byrne & Clore, 1970; Singh, 1974).

Conditioning of affective responses has been studied in a somewhat different context by Rozin, Millman, and Nemeroff (1986). These investigators point out that even brief contact between a neutral object and anything very positive or very negative will lead to a transfer of the emotional response to the neutral object. For example, a laundered shirt that had been worn by a disliked person was rated as less desirable than a laundered shirt that had been worn by a liked person. Even though the shirts did not actually differ, one elicited a positive evaluative response and the other a negative response on the basis of learned associations.

When Former Strangers Become Close Acquaintances

If two people are brought into contact by propinquity and if they are experiencing relatively positive emotions, they are at a transition point—they may become close acquaintances. Acquaintanceship involves recognizing each other, engaging in friendly conversation, and identifying each other by name. Two additional factors become especially important at this point—*affiliative needs* and reactions to observable *physical characteristics*.

Need for Affiliation: Dispositional Differences and External Influences

Surveys indicate that people feel it is *very important* to make new friends, spend time with existing friends, and share personal feelings with those to whom they feel close (Research and Forecasts, Inc., 1981). Wright (1984) has proposed that people are intrinsically motivated to establish enjoyable friendships.

Recent evidence confirming the biological basis of affiliative needs is provided by studies of chimpanzees and monkeys (de Waal, 1989). The tendency to make friends, resolve conflicts, and live in peace seems to be part of our genetic heritage. Many primates even form "old boys networks" or alliances among males, establish lasting male-female relationships, and develop techniques to resolve conflicts through conciliatory behavior as illustrated in Figure 6.6.

Though the desire to form relationships may be "built-in," people differ in how strongly they are motivated to engage in friendly interactions. The phrase for this motivational variable is **need for affiliation.** People fall at different points along a continuum—at one extreme are those who prefer to spend much of their time alone; at the other extreme are those who prefer to interact socially whenever possible. The stronger a person's need for affiliation, the more he or she will respond to such factors as propinquity and positive emotions by interacting positively with a stranger.

Need for Affiliation as a Trait Beginning with the pioneering work of Murray (1938), psychologists have been interested in measuring individual differences in affiliation need and in determining its effect on behavior. Research has revealed, for example, that males high in this need are relatively self-confident, and they spend more time talking to attractive females than do males whose affiliative need is low (Crouse & Mehrabian, 1977). In a college classroom, students high on the affiliation dimension make more friends during the semester than do students with low affiliative needs (Byrne & Greendlinger, 1989).

In recent years, different types of affiliative need have been identified. For example, McAdams and Losoff (1984) focus on **friendship motivation,** the need to establish warm interpersonal relationships. Children who are high in this type of motivation know a great deal about their friends, have stable

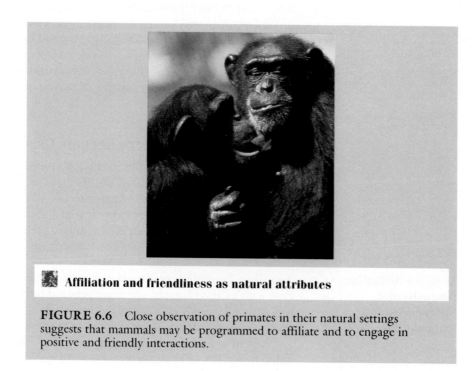

Affiliation and friendliness as natural attributes

FIGURE 6.6 Close observation of primates in their natural settings suggests that mammals may be programmed to affiliate and to engage in positive and friendly interactions.

relationships, and are rated by their teachers as friendly, affectionate, cooperative, happy, and popular.

Going still further in analyzing the need to interact with others, Hill (1987) suggests that four basic motives underlie the disposition to be affiliative: *social comparison* (affiliating in order to reduce uncertainty), *positive stimulation* (wanting interesting, lively contact with others), *emotional support* (wanting to be close to others when feeling low), and *attention* (increasing self-worth by getting praise and attention). Hill's Interpersonal Orientation Scale (see Table 6.1) measures each of these motives. Depending on a person's score on each subscale, affiliative behavior will be more likely to occur in some situations than in others. Those high on the *emotional support* dimension want to affiliate primarily when they are having problems, those high on *attention* want to affiliate only if others serve as an appreciative audience, and so forth.

How Social Skills Can Help or Hinder Affiliation   Individuals differ not only in their motivation to affiliate and to form friendships but also in their *social skills*. Those who are most skilled are perceived as friendly, think well of themselves, are not easily provoked to anger, and find it easy to talk with others (Reisman, 1984). The least skilled are seen as unfriendly, possess negative self-images, easily lose their tempers, and find it difficult to engage in casual conversation.

Why are some people highly skilled socially while others are not? For one thing, birth order plays a role. Compared with firstborns, the youngest siblings are found to be more skillful socially (Ickes & Turner, 1983). Moreover, those who have an older, opposite-sex sibling interact most easily with members of the opposite sex. It appears, then, that people first learn how to interact with others through interacting with their siblings.

Four types of affiliation need

TABLE 6.1   Hill's Interpersonal Orientation Scale measures four types of affiliation motives. The sample items suggest the different reasons people have for affiliating with others.

Type of Need	Sample Test Items that Measure the Need
Social Comparison	When I am not certain about how well I am doing at something, I usually like to be around others so I can compare myself to them.
Positive Stimulation	Just being around others and finding out about them is one of the most interesting things I can think of doing.
Emotional Support	One of my greatest sources of comfort when things get rough is being with other people.
Attention	I like to be around people when I can be the center of attention.

Source: Based on Hill, 1987.

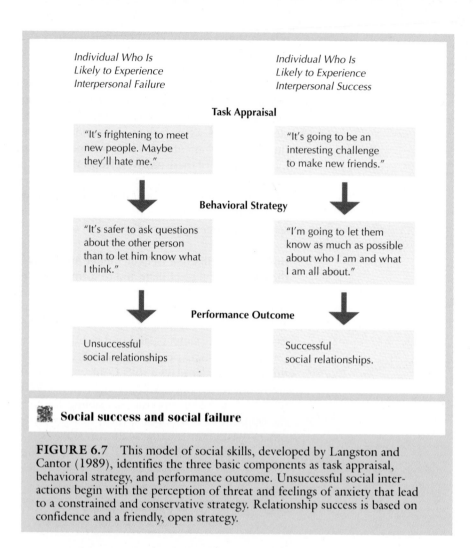

Individual Who Is
Likely to Experience
Interpersonal Failure

Individual Who Is
Likely to Experience
Interpersonal Success

Task Appraisal

"It's frightening to meet new people. Maybe they'll hate me."

"It's going to be an interesting challenge to make new friends."

Behavioral Strategy

"It's safer to ask questions about the other person than to let him know what I think."

"I'm going to let them know as much as possible about who I am and what I am all about."

Performance Outcome

Unsuccessful social relationships

Successful social relationships.

Social success and social failure

FIGURE 6.7   This model of social skills, developed by Langston and Cantor (1989), identifies the three basic components as task appraisal, behavioral strategy, and performance outcome. Unsuccessful social interactions begin with the perception of threat and feelings of anxiety that lead to a constrained and conservative strategy. Relationship success is based on confidence and a friendly, open strategy.

The initial weeks and months of college offer an especially critical period in which to study differences among people's needs to make friends and their success at doing so. Many students who are otherwise very competent and who function quite well feel disappointed and unhappy about leaving high school and their old friends because of unsuccessful social interactions in the new setting (Arkin, Lake, & Baumgardner, 1986). For many, the task of meeting people and establishing relationships is a new and sometimes frightening experience, not encountered since they were first-graders. The resulting social anxiety can be extremely disrupting.

Langston and Cantor (1989) carried out a longitudinal study of students who differed in their interpersonal success in college. The goal was to discover why some students are successful socially while others fail. The investigators proposed a model (see Figure 6.7) that describes the crucial variables. Three processes are identified. First, the person makes a *task appraisal;* those headed for interpersonal failure view the tasks of social life as threatening and anxiety evoking. Second, the individual must develop a *strategy* for dealing with other people. Those who appraise the situation negatively and feel anxious are more likely to develop constrained and conservative strategies in social interactions. For example, when talking with someone new they may ask questions about the other person but reveal very little about themselves or their own opinions (Thorne, 1987). The final result of appraising the task negatively and adopting a constrained strategy is a *performance outcome* in which social relationships are unsuccessful. They lack success because others do not respond positively to someone who holds back and plays it safe. Those with the opposite, successful interpersonal pattern feel confident in appraising the task; adopt a friendly, open, outgoing strategy; and do well in establishing friendships.

One potentially important aspect of becoming acquainted has received little research attention. What should you say when you want to begin interacting with a stranger? For a description of various types of "opening lines" and how they are perceived by males and females, see the following **On the Applied Side** section.

ON THE APPLIED SIDE

Opening Lines: Cute, Innocuous, or Direct?

It has become increasingly acceptable for either men or women to "make the first move" by initiating a conversation with a member of the opposite sex, though males are still more likely to do so than females. There are, however, no general guidelines about what to say. Consider a situation in which propinquity has brought two people into contact, emotions are positive, and both have affiliative needs. What would be a socially skilled way to become acquainted with the other person? Young adolescents on TV sitcoms agonize about what to say, and in the movies clever remarks always get the other person's attention and arouse interest. In addition, you might guess that an insulting opening line ("You don't sweat much for a fat girl" or "Do you have to be a dumb jock to join this frat?") could only elicit rejection.

Kleinke, Meeker, and Staneski (1986) point out that opening lines play a crucial role in expanding or reducing a person's chances of meeting and getting to know potential dates, one of whom may in time become a marriage partner. The "right" approach can mark the beginning of a relationship, and the "wrong" approach can be a social disaster.

These investigators surveyed employees in several firms as well as university students to determine what kinds of lines males and females use and how others respond to these lines. Analysis revealed that the remarks fell into three categories:

cute-flippant	(males) Isn't it cold? Let's make some body heat.
	(females) Hey baby, you've got a gorgeous chassis. Mind if I look under the hood?
innocuous	(males) Where are you from?
	(females) Could you tell me what time it is?

"Hey, good lookin', what you got cookin'?"

TABLE 6.2 When men want to start a conversation with a woman they don't know, research indicates that they should avoid cute-flippant remarks and stick with innocuous or direct opening lines. Females are more negative than males in evaluating a stranger's clumsy attempts to be amusing.

Setting	Most Preferred Opening Lines	Least Preferred Opening Lines
General Situation	Hi.	Your place or mine?
Bar	Do you want to dance?	Bet I can outdrink you.
Restaurant	I haven't been here before. What's good on the menu?	I bet the cherry jubilee isn't as sweet as you are.
Supermarket	Can I help you to the car with those things?	Do you really eat that junk?
Laundromat	Want to go have a beer or cup of coffee while we're waiting?	Those are some nice undies you have there.
Beach	Want to play frisbee?	Let me see your strap marks.

Source: Based on data from Kleinke, Meeker, & Staneski, 1986.

direct   (males) Hi. I like you.
(females) I don't have anybody to introduce me, but I'd really like to get to know you.

Overall, the most preferred lines were innocuous or direct, and the least preferred were cute-flippant. Some sex differences were found. Women tended to be much more negative about the cute-flippant lines and more positive about innocuous lines than men were. It seems that those who work hard to develop amusing lines in order to make a good impression usually produce the opposite effect—especially when the target is a female.

The specific situation also plays a role; a bar and a laundromat are very different social settings. Table 6.2 shows some of the best lines used by males (rated good to excellent) and some of the worst (rated poor to terrible) in various settings. As you can see, once again a cute-flippant remark to a stranger is rated as much less appealing than an innocuous or direct approach.

Considering these findings, why is it that so many people use cute-flippant lines? Kleinke and his colleagues suggested that such lines are common because people fear rejection and defend themselves by using humor. Further, some simply have poor social skills and fail to notice how others react. Another factor is that cute lines are occasionally successful; a very small minority of women said they like openings such as "I'm easy. Are you?" even though most did not. As a result, flippancy is partially reinforced if it is used enough times and if the user doesn't mind a lot of rejection.

Nevertheless, the safest strategy for either sex is to stick with innocuous lines, because they tend not to offend anyone and they also protect the user against rejection. Most importantly, an unthreatening opening remark increases the likelihood that a stranger will respond positively.

When Affiliation Needs Are Aroused by External Events Though need for affiliation has been identified as a dispositional characteristic, external events may also motivate people to affiliate. You have probably been in a situation in which strangers strike up conversations because they share an unusual experience—the stress of a snowstorm, the excitement of a special celebration such as Mardi Gras, or some other out-of-the-ordinary event.

Reactions to the October 1989 earthquake in northern California provided many examples of this phenomenon. One resident of Los Gatos, a hard-hit town near the epicenter, wrote:

> After the earthquake there was a strange mixture of elation and despair. Neighbors gathered for an impromptu party on the lawn. We needed to hold on through the terrifying aftershocks and reassure one another that loved ones whom we couldn't reach would be fine. Our bodies were intact, but the interiors of our homes were a mangled mess of broken glass, splintered furniture and uncertain underpinnings. We united as friends. (Humphriss, 1989, p. 121.)

The psychological basis of such reactions was identified by Schachter (1959), who investigated the effect of fear on affiliation. In an experimental setting, subjects who had been informed they would soon be receiving painful electrical shocks preferred waiting with other subjects rather than remaining alone. If a nonfrightening task was anticipated, subjects either preferred waiting alone or had no preference. Why should fear or anxiety increase the motivation to be with others?

The explanation, confirmed by subsequent research, is that individuals seek out others—even total strangers—in order to talk about the situation, compare their perceptions, and decide what to do (Morris et al., 1976). This behavior is an example of the **social comparison process,** the general tendency to evaluate what we think and do by comparing our reactions with those of other people. Such comparisons reduce uncertainty and anxiety (Suls & Fletcher, 1983; Rofe, 1984).

In some situations a person who is fearful about an upcoming experience can obtain the greatest amount of information from someone who has already gone through the procedure and "knows the score." Here, affiliation could be motivated by the need to obtain accurate knowledge about what will happen rather than by the desire to engage in social comparison with others who are also fearful and uninformed. This situation often occurs in a medical setting in

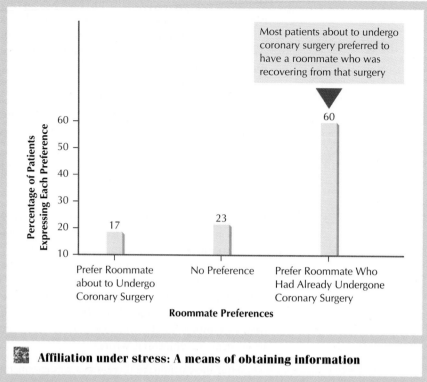

Most patients about to undergo coronary surgery preferred to have a roommate who was recovering from that surgery

Percentage of Patients Expressing Each Preference

60 — 60

Prefer Roommate about to Undergo Coronary Surgery — 17

No Preference — 23

Prefer Roommate Who Had Already Undergone Coronary Surgery — 60

Roommate Preferences

Affiliation under stress: A means of obtaining information

FIGURE 6.8 The desire to affiliate in stressful situations is based in part on the need for information that will help reduce the stress. Among patients about to undergo surgery, there was a strong preference for being assigned a roommate who had already gone through the experience rather than one who had not yet had the operation. (Source: Based on data from Kulik & Mahler, 1989.)

which a patient is about to undergo treatment. Would that individual prefer to be with another patient waiting for the treatment or with one who had already gone through it?

To answer that question, Kulik and Mahler (1989) studied the affiliation preferences of patients who were about to undergo coronary bypass surgery for the first time. Two nights before the scheduled operation, each subject was interviewed and asked about roommate preferences—would the person rather room with another patient scheduled to undergo the same operation, one who was recovering from that operation, or was there no preference? As Figure 6.8 indicates, the investigators found that the majority of these patients wanted a roommate who had already had the surgery. From the data presented, you can see there was an overwhelming preference among these patients to be with someone who was well informed about the frightening operation. As one man observed in explaining his response, "You'd rather talk to a guy that's been through it . . . the doctors know the technicalities but they never feel the pain" (Kulik & Mahler, 1989, p. 188).

Physical Characteristics: Judging Books by Their Covers

We have each learned that "beauty is skin deep," and surely we know that it is meaningless to react to stereotypes based on appearance. Nevertheless, in the early stages of interpersonal contact, most people operate on the basis of positive stereotypes about beauty (Albright, Kenny, & Malloy, 1988), negative stereotypes about physical defects (Fichten & Amsel, 1986), and a host of other prejudices about other observable characteristics as well. Strangers are accepted or rejected because of skin color, age, sex, height, weight, accent, hair color, and so forth (Perdue & Gurtman, 1990), even though these judgments are likely to be worthless in predicting anything meaningful about them, as we indicated in Chapter 5 in discussing prejudice. Although in this section we will summarize research on the effects of **physical attractiveness,** we will first describe how other physical attributes also influence attraction.

Responding to the Superficial Aspects of Strangers   As the cartoon in Figure 6.9 suggests, it is commonplace to like or dislike someone simply because of some irrelevant aspect of his or her outward appearance.

"I'm sorry, I don't like men with a mustache."

Attraction decisions based on physical appearance

FIGURE 6.9   People often respond to strangers on the basis of observable characteristics. Unfair and inaccurate attributions are made about personality and character because of stereotypes about various aspects of physical appearance. Sometimes these stereotypes are culturewide and sometimes (as in this cartoon) they represent one person's specific beliefs. (Drawing by Koren; © 1982 The New Yorker Magazine, Inc.)

Attention to outward characteristics is part of a general screening response known as **cognitive disregard.** According to Rodin (1987), when we find ourselves with people we don't know, we engage in a two-part process. We first exclude all those who are "unsuitable." Anyone categorized this way is not attended to and not remembered afterward. For example, experiments show that undergraduates disregard the elderly and middle-aged, males disregard unattractive females, and those who are middle-aged disregard anyone perceived to be young. If a person fails to meet our criteria, he or she becomes effectively invisible. Only after this exclusion process—based on observable characteristics—has taken place do we decide who we like among the remaining individuals. Cognitive disregard saves time by allowing us to eliminate anyone who is not acceptable as an acquaintance or friend. It also eliminates from consideration some people we might have liked had we taken time to get to know them.

One observable characteristic to which people respond is physique. In an interesting study of how both males and females stereotype strangers based on body type, Ryckman and his colleagues (1989) presented undergraduate subjects with information about *somatotypes*. This once-very-popular system classifies people into three major physical categories (Sheldon, Stevens, & Tucker, 1940); briefly, *endomorphs* are round and fat, *mesomorphs* are muscular, and *ectomorphs* are thin and angular. The subjects were asked to rate the personalities of males and females who fit each of the physical descriptions. As expected, the ratings were strongly affected by physique. Endomorphs were perceived as having the fewest friends and getting teased a lot, as well as being lazy, sickly, ugly, sloppy, sad, dirty, and slow. Mesomorphs were described as being the least kind and intelligent but as having many friends and being healthy, brave, and good-looking. Ectomorphs tended to be judged as falling in the middle on many traits but these thin individuals were also viewed as being the most fearful, intelligent, and neat.

Keep in mind that you cannot predict intelligence, bravery, kindness, or other characteristics just by knowing a person's body build, though these college students clearly responded as if they could. Such beliefs represent stereotypes. Because of these stereotypes, it's obviously an advantage to be born a mesomorph, rather than an endomorph, if you want to make friends and create a good first impression.

Overt behavior also provides cues by which others are judged, however unfairly. Investigators have repeatedly found that males who behave in a dominant way are liked better than those whose behavior is relatively submissive (Sadalla, Kenrick, & Vershure, 1987). Thus, if a male gestures a lot, has a strong tennis serve, and is competitive and authoritative, he is preferred to one who looks down, nods his head in agreement, plays tennis for fun rather than to win, and is disconcerted by a forceful opponent. In contrast, attraction toward a female stranger is not affected by how dominant she is. In other research, males were liked best if they behaved in an extraverted, expressive way, while females made a good impression if they were facially expressive (Riggio & Friedman, 1986).

When overt behavior is easily altered, people tend to act in ways that create a good impression. For example, males and females eat less in the presence of someone of the opposite sex than when they are alone or with a same-sex companion (Pliner & Chaiken, 1990). Both sexes assume that overeating is socially undesirable, and females also believe that they appear more feminine if they consume small amounts of food.

People even respond to the voice pitch of others. That this tendency is not confined to a single culture is illustrated in the following **Multicultural Perspective** section.

SOCIAL PSYCHOLOGY: A MULTICULTURAL PERSPECTIVE

Responding to a Stranger's Voice: Judgments about Those Who Sound Childlike in the United States and Korea

When strangers speak, we evaluate them not only on the basis of what they say but also on their grammar, accent, pitch, and whether the voice is perceived as "pleasant" (Warner & Sugarman, 1986).

A specific attribute of speech is whether it sounds "childlike." If an adult's voice sounds like that of a child, he or she might well be judged as having childish traits and as behaving like a child. Similar attributions have consistently been identified in research on facial appearance (McArthur & Berry, 1987). Baby-faced adults are perceived (by others and even by themselves) as being physically and socially weak, naive, warm, and honest (Berry & Brownlow, 1989).

The phrase *baby face* generally refers to a relatively round head, large eyes, smooth skin, pug nose, and so on, but what is meant by a *childlike voice*? Research conducted by Montepare and Zebrowitz-McArthur (1987) indicates that a voice sounds like that of a child if it is high pitched, lacking in clarity, and tense. These investigators tested the hypothesis that strangers who sounded like children would be treated as being like children. Further, they tested the generality of this stereotype by conducting the research using subjects in both the United States and Korea.

Tape recordings were made by male and female speakers who recited the English alphabet. The subjects were American and Korean college students. The ratings of personality characteristics on the basis of voice were surprisingly similar in the two cultures. As Figure 6.10 (p. 244) shows, students in both countries judged someone who had a childlike voice to be relatively weak, incompetent, and warm. This effect held even when the sex and perceived age of the speaker were controlled.

Why should there be this striking cross-cultural agreement in responding to the childlike quality of a stranger's voice as indicative of personal characteristics? One possibility is that people in different cultures share certain common experiences (McArthur & Baron, 1983). People in all cultures interact with children and learn (1) how children sound when they speak and (2) that children tend to be weaker, less competent, and more interpersonally warm than adults. The learned association between children's speech patterns and children's behavior is then generalized to adults whose speech resembles that of children.

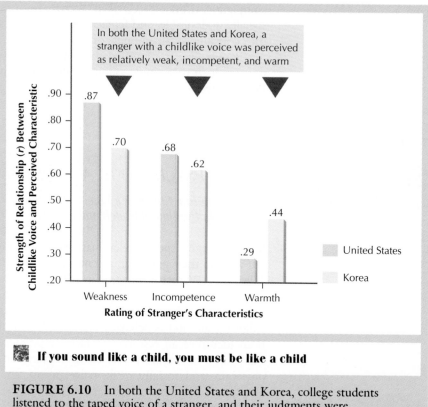

In both the United States and Korea, a stranger with a childlike voice was perceived as relatively weak, incompetent, and warm

If you sound like a child, you must be like a child

FIGURE 6.10 In both the United States and Korea, college students listened to the taped voice of a stranger, and their judgments were influenced by how childlike that person sounded. Across the two cultures, when a person's voice was like that of a child, the person was rated as being relatively weak, incompetent, and warm. There appears to be a learned association between *sounding* like a child and *behaving* like a child. (Source: Based on data from Montepare & Zebrowitz-McArthur, 1987.)

As is true of other stereotypes, such generalizations lead to faulty perceptions and inaccurate predictions about adults whose voices are childlike.

Do a Person's External Characteristics Affect His or Her Actual Behavior?
Before we examine the effects of attractiveness, note that studies of response to physical characteristics leave a basic question unanswered: Given that people accept and reject others and make attributions about them on the basis of stereotypes, do such stereotypes also affect the behavior of those possessing the characteristics? For example, do ectomorphs learn to believe they are more intelligent and begin to act more intelligently? Do those with childlike voices believe they are weak and incompetent and act accordingly? It is difficult and most often impossible to change basic physical qualities such as skin color, beauty, physique, expressive style, or voice pitch in order to answer such questions. Nevertheless, one external characteristic *can* be changed rather easily: the

clothing a person wears. Consequently, we can ask whether observers respond to others on the basis of clothing and whether clothing affects the wearer's behavior.

People *do* respond to clothing in a stereotyped way. For example, more strangers make change for a female at an expired parking meter when she wears a uniform than when she is dressed in either sloppy or professional attire (Bushman, 1988). People also behave differently when wearing specific types of clothing; in one experiment, females dressed as nurses were less aggressive toward a stranger than were females wearing Ku Klux Klan uniforms (Johnson & Downing, 1979). Given such findings, it should be possible to show that specific aspects of clothing are perceived in stereotyped ways and that the stereotypes affect the wearer's behavior.

In a series of investigations, Frank and Gilovich (1988) concentrated on the effect of black clothing on perceptions and on behavior. They pointed out that black is the color of evil and death in most cultures, that the "bad guys" in Westerns wear black hats, and that many negative terms include the word *black,* such as *blacklist, blackball,* and *blackmail.* When subjects were asked to rate professional football and hockey uniforms (not identified as to team or city), teams wearing pants and jerseys that were at least 50 percent black were rated as bad, mean, and aggressive. The stereotypes seem clear, but is it possible that those who put on black uniforms are somehow induced to behave in bad, mean, and aggressive ways?

To test this hypothesis, the investigators obtained several kinds of data. For example, they found that actual football- and hockey-team members who wear black uniforms play more aggressively and receive more penalties than those who wear light-colored uniforms (see Figure 6.11). It seems, then, that when a player wears black, his behavior becomes more aggressive.

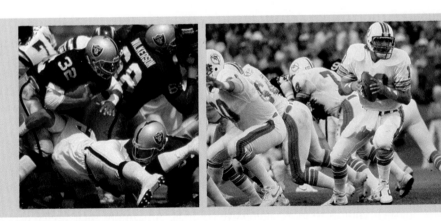

The bad guys wear black

FIGURE 6.11 People respond to others on the basis of not only their physical characteristics but also their clothing. Dark uniforms worn by football or hockey players lead to perceptions of their being aggressive. Even more surprising, these beliefs affect the behavior of those wearing the dark clothing. For example, over the years 1970 to 1986, the Los Angeles Raiders (wearing black) led the National Football League in the number of yards they were penalized, while the Miami Dolphins (wearing white) were penalized the least number of yards during those years.

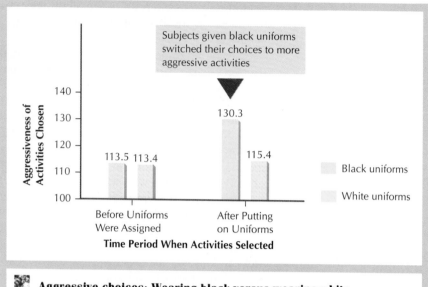

Subjects given black uniforms switched their choices to more aggressive activities

Aggressive choices: Wearing black versus wearing white

FIGURE 6.12   When subjects in an experiment were given uniforms to wear while engaging in a series of activities, the color of the uniform influenced their behavior. Compared with the activities subjects selected *before* receiving a uniform, those given black to wear shifted their choices to more aggressive activities, while those given white uniforms did not. It appears that behavior is affected by our beliefs about appearance, including beliefs about clothing. (Source: Based on data from Frank & Gilovich, 1988.)

The effect of clothing on behavior was shown even more convincingly in an experiment in which male subjects were told they would be competing against one another in several events (Frank & Gilovich, 1988). These events differed in how much aggression they involved; the most aggressive were chicken fights, a dart-gun duel, and burnout, while the least aggressive were basket shooting, block stacking, and a putting contest. Each subject was asked to select the five activities in which he preferred to compete. Subjects were then grouped in teams of three, each person was given either a black or a white uniform to wear over his clothing, and the team was asked to consider the events again and to agree on five. As shown in Figure 6.12, those given white uniforms made the same choices in terms of task aggressiveness as they did before wearing the uniform. Those given black uniforms, however, changed their choices to more aggressive contests. Amazingly, their preferences shifted after only a few minutes of being clothed in a black uniform.

We will now consider physical attractiveness, an observable characteristic that has a powerful effect on interpersonal attraction.

The Effects of Attractiveness   Both males and females are strongly influenced by attractiveness (Cash & Killcullen, 1985; Folkes, 1982; Hatfield & Sprecher, 1986b), though males are more responsive to appearance than females (Feingold, 1989, 1990b). The attractiveness effect has been found in settings ranging from college dances to commercial dating services (Green, Buchanan, & Heuer, 1984).

Attractive individuals are assumed to have many other positive qualities, as suggested in Figure 6.13 (Calvert, 1988). Both sexes believe that those who are attractive are more poised, interesting, sociable, independent, dominant, exciting, sexual, intelligent, well adjusted, socially skilled, and successful than those who are unattractive (Brigham, 1980; Feingold, 1990b; Hassebrauck, 1988; Moore, Graziano, & Miller, 1987). Handsome males are perceived as more masculine, and beautiful females as more feminine, than those who are less attractive (Gillen, 1981). Smeaton (1990) found extremely high correlations between the attractiveness of female strangers and how males rated their desirability sexually and as potential dates or spouses.

A few negative assumptions are also made about those who look "mahvelous." Attractive females, in comparison with other women, are judged to be more vain, more materialistic, and less faithful to their husbands (Cash & Duncan, 1984). Though attractiveness is a plus for male politicians, it is not an asset for female politicians (Sigelman et al., 1986), perhaps because femininity is not deemed appropriate for elected officials. Attractiveness is assumed to result in status and success—people feel that these rewards will simply be given on the basis of appearance, not because the individuals earn it (Kalick, 1988).

Primarily, however, attractiveness is a positive attribute. You may think that appearance is of importance only during the dating years, but this is not so. Even newborn infants are rated as more sociable and so forth if they are attractive rather than unattractive (Karraker, Vogel, & Evans, 1987). Moreover, the stereotypes associating attractiveness with desirable personality traits are also found in ratings of those aged sixty to ninety-three (Johnson & Pittenger,

Making personality judgments based on appearance

FIGURE 6.13 Though you do not know either of these men, which one do you like better? Would you guess that they differ in terms of poise, sociability, and independence, or in being interesting, exciting, sexual, or masculine? If you are like most people, you will choose the person on the left as being higher in each of these qualities, simply because he is more physically attractive.

1984). Altogether, there is a bias favoring attractiveness that operates from birth to old age. It is also true that facial attractiveness is a stable characteristic, at least from early childhood to the late teenage years (Pittenger, Mark, & Johnson, 1989).

Why are attractive people most often viewed in positive terms? Dion and Dion (1987) suggest that such stereotypes are based on a general **belief in a just world,** the assumption that people get what they deserve and deserve what they get. One assumed consequence is that "good" people are given good looks, while "bad" people are not. The Dions found that the more strongly a person believes in a just world, the more he or she also believes that attractive people possess positive traits and will do well in life.

We know that physical appearance is highly valued in our society, but are very attractive individuals actually any different from others in their behavior? In fact, attractive individuals do *not* fit the stereotypes associated with how they look except with respect to social skills and popularity (Feingold, 1990a). Probably because most people respond positively to those who are good-looking, attractive males and females are found to interact well with the opposite sex and to date more than those who are less attractive (Reis et al., 1980). They also adapt well interpersonally (O'Grady, 1989). Surprisingly, self-esteem is not consistently high for those who are the most attractive (Maruyama & Miller, 1981), perhaps because they feel they are often rewarded simply for their looks rather than for their actual worth (Major, Carrington, & Carnevale, 1984).

How Do We Decide That Someone Is Physically Attractive?   Although there is general agreement in a given culture at a given time as to what constitutes attractiveness (Banner, 1983), most of us find it difficult to verbalize exactly what the components are. We just "know it when we see it."

Some investigators have tried to pinpoint the details more precisely than that. For example, Cunningham (1986) gathered photographs of females appearing in college yearbooks and of Miss Universe contestants and asked male undergraduates to rate their attractiveness. Subjects rated two facial types as most attractive. On the one hand, males responded positively to childlike features, including large, widely spaced eyes; a small nose; and a small chin. On the other hand, males also gave high ratings to females with mature features, such as prominent cheekbones, narrow cheeks, high eyebrows, large pupils, and a big smile. These same two facial types were perceived as attractive for black, Oriental, and white females. One curious finding in other research is that there is greater agreement in rating the attractiveness of females than of males, in part because homosexual and heterosexual males differ in their judgments of male attractiveness (Donovan, Hill, & Jankowiak, 1989). Whether homosexual and heterosexual females rate female attractiveness differently has not been investigated.

Beyond facial appearance, women are rated as most attractive if they have medium-size breasts (Kleinke & Staneski, 1980) and are not overweight (Franzoi & Herzog, 1987). A woman whose face is very attractive but whose body is not is rated low in overall attractiveness; when her body is attractive and her face is not, overall attractiveness ratings remain fairly high (Alicke, Smith, & Klotz, 1986). Men are perceived as attractive if they are shaped like Robert Redford—slim legs and waist, broad shoulders, and small buttocks (Lavrakas, 1975)—and are not obese (Harris, Harris, & Bochner, 1982).

A male's height is important in a variety of interpersonal situations. Taller males are preferred as job candidates (e.g., Feldman, 1975) and as management trainees (Farb, 1978). When advertising in the personal columns for dates, males indicating they are tall receive more letters from females than those who do not (Lynn & Shurgot, 1984). Even as children, tall boys are rated as more competent than short ones (Eisenberg et al., 1984).

Until recently, less was known about the effects of female height. Sheppard and Strathman (1989) explored the hypothesis that shortness is as positive for females as tallness is for males. As in previous studies (e.g., Gillis & Avis, 1980), these investigators found that 95 percent of the females preferred to date males taller than themselves, while 80 percent of the males preferred females shorter than themselves. In their actual dating experiences, shorter females had more dates than taller ones, but males' height was unrelated to dating frequency. Altogether, the bias toward short females is strong in that they are preferred as dating partners, have more dates, and are perceived as more attractive than tall females.

The Matching Hypothesis: Selecting Friends and Lovers Who Are as Attractive as Oneself   The positive effects of attractiveness clearly influence beauty contests, the way subjects respond in the studies we have been describing, and the success of males and females who become models and movie stars. In seeking real-life relationships, however, people are afraid of being rejected by those who are more attractive than they (Bernstein et al., 1983). There is also rejection of those who are less attractive than oneself—"I can do better than that." As a result, romantic partners tend to pair off on the basis of similarity of physical attractiveness, a tendency known as the **matching hypothesis** (Berscheid et al., 1971). The selection of similarly attractive partners influences casual dates, engagements, and marriages (Murstein, 1972; Price & Vandenberg, 1979). Further, similarity in appearance actually increases over the years when two people live together (Zajonc et al., 1987).

Note that people may not actively seek out partners whose attractiveness matches their own. Instead, it is possible that the most attractive are "taken" first, so that only the next most attractive remain available, and this process continues until finally the least attractive individuals are left to pair off (Kalick & Hamilton, 1986, 1988). Also note that mismatches do occur (see Figure 6.14, p. 250), but they are the exception. People attempt to explain these exceptions on the basis of **equity theory** (see Chapter 15), which proposes that people in any social exchange, such as a relationship, should contribute rewards equally to avoid unfairness. If one is more attractive than the other, for example, people tend to assume that the less attractive individual in the mismatched pair must be rich, powerful, wise, sexy, or famous in order to make up for his or her "deficiencies" in appearance.

More surprisingly than for opposite-sex pairs, matching for attractiveness also occurs in same-sex friendships (Cash & Derlega, 1978). Male friends are actually more likely to be similar to one another in attractiveness than are female friends (Feingold, 1988; McKillip & Riedel, 1983). One reason that friends are selected on this basis is that one's own perceived attractiveness is affected by the appearance of companions. That is, the way your friends look seems to rub off on you, so that if you are associated with someone unattractive you are perceived as less attractive than if you are with someone who is better looking

When couples differ in attractiveness, how do you explain the relationship?

FIGURE 6.14   People usually select romantic partners who are similar to themselves in physical attractiveness. When they do not, others try to explain the "mismatch" on the basis of some exceptional qualities possessed by the less attractive member of the pair. In "Beauty and the Beast" on TV, Vincent's appearance may not have been traditionally handsome, but his kindness, gentleness, and bravery made it believable that he was loved by the attractive Catherine.

(Geiselman, Haight, & Kimata, 1984; Wedell, Parducci, & Geiselman, 1987).

In summary, however reasonable or unreasonable and however fair or unfair, physical appearance plays a crucial role in determining friendship patterns.

Establishing Friendships

We have seen that once two people are brought together by physical proximity, the probability that they will be attracted to each other is determined by the presence of positive versus negative emotions, by the strength of their affiliative needs, and by stereotypical responses to physical characteristics. The next step toward a closer relationship requires interpersonal communication that is rewarding for both participants (Lea, 1989). It is the content of the communications that determines whether a close acquaintance will become a friend. In this section we will describe the two major aspects of such communication—*similarity* and *reciprocal evaluations*.

Similarity: Liking Those Who Are Like Ourselves

Since the time of Aristotle (who wrote in some detail about friendship), it has been observed that people respond most positively to those who agree with them and most negatively to those who disagree. Though the effects of **attitude similarity** have been studied extensively, attitudes represent just one example of our tendency to like those who most closely resemble ourselves, as Figure 6.15 illustrates.

"We had a hunch they'd be perfect for each other."

 Similarity and attraction

FIGURE 6.15 The tendency of people to like those who are similar to themselves is pervasive. (Drawing by Koren; © 1982 The New Yorker Magazine, Inc.)

In folklore and in fiction, opposites attract, but decades of research support a more ancient proposition—birds of a feather flock together. As former tennis star Bjorn Borg said of his new wife after the ceremony, "She's a great woman. She's just like me" (Milestones, 1989). We don't know what Mrs. Borg had to say, but women are found to be even more positively affected by the similarity of the opposite sex than men are (Feingold, 1989). One reason for this sex difference is that males sometimes react so strongly to an attractive female's face and body that they ignore such details as her attitudes, beliefs, and values.

The Effect of Similar and Dissimilar Attitudes on Attraction   The similarity effect was first documented in correlational studies of the attitudes of actual friends and romantic partners, and experimental investigations in the laboratory (beginning with Schachter, 1951) have firmly established a cause and effect relationship. When a stranger expresses views similar to those of a subject, that stranger is liked; conversely, the expression of dissimilar views leads to dislike.

Such effects are powerful and very consistent, and they are as characteristic of children and the elderly as of college students. Further, the same findings have been reported in investigations in India, Japan, Korea, Mexico, and the United States (Byrne et al., 1971; Park, 1989).

When people interact, they frequently express their attitudes as they talk about school, movies, music, politics, religion, and everything else. Saying what one likes and dislikes and asking the other person about his or her views in each instance are common when two people first begin to interact (Kent, Davis, & Shapiro, 1981). Each person responds to the other on the basis of the **proportion of similar attitudes** expressed. The higher the proportion of similar views, the more the person is liked; the lower the proportion of similarity, the more he or she is disliked (Byrne & Nelson, 1965).

Note that although the proportion of similar attitudes predicts attraction, it is only one aspect of the effect that positive stimulus events have on liking. That is, as the proportion of positive elements increases, evaluations are increasingly positive.

The same principle that determines interpersonal attraction operates in establishing our likes and dislikes of other aspects of our world. For example, Meoli and Feinberg (1989) applied this formulation to predict how well people like shopping malls. Among those in retailing, it was generally believed that a mall's popularity simply reflects the number of stores it contains: the more stores, the more consumers will want to shop there. Instead, the *proportion* of positively evaluated stores was found to have a greater effect on liking a mall than the absolute *number* of stores, as Figure 6.16 indicates. Thus, how much a shopping mall is liked can be predicted on the same basis as interpersonal liking.

The Repulsion Hypothesis Despite decades of research in which the effects of similar and dissimilar attitudes seemed to be firmly established, Rosenbaum (1986) made a startling proposal. He suggested that attitude similarity has *no* effect on attraction; instead, he hypothesized, people respond positively to all strangers and only begin to dislike them if dissimilar attitudes are expressed. This concept was labeled the **repulsion hypothesis.** In several investigations, Rosenbaum was able to demonstrate that while similar attitudes did not have a positive effect on attraction, dissimilar attitudes did have a negative effect.

The new element in Rosenbaum's research that produced such results was what he described as a "no information control condition." For example, if subjects are shown a photograph of a fellow student (no information) and indicate how much this person is liked, attraction is not any greater when subjects are also told that this stranger holds attitudes similar to theirs. If that person is described as holding dissimilar attitudes, however, attraction decreases. Does this finding mean that Rosenbaum is correct about similar versus dissimilar attitudes?

There are two basic reasons to answer no. First, it is simply not possible to create a condition in which no information is given (Byrne, Clore, & Smeaton, 1986). We tend to assume others agree with our own opinions (Dawes, 1989; Mullen et al., 1985)—a phenomenon known as the **false consensus effect,** as discussed in Chapter 3. Second, if the person to be judged is represented by a yearbook photograph that is shown to a group of subjects composed of college students, they know that he or she is also a college student—similar to them in age; probably similar to them in race, educational goals, and academic ability; reasonably attractive; and so forth. All such cues simply add to the effect of assumed similarity (Marks & Miller, 1982). Altogether, the "no information" condition is loaded with (1) information based on assumed similarity and (2) stereotypes based on appearance. For this reason, adding information about attitude similarity doesn't have an effect because the stranger is already perceived as similar.

In an experiment designed to test the repulsion hypothesis directly, Smeaton, Byrne, and Murnen (1989) held constant the number of dissimilar attitudes while varying the number of similar attitudes expressed by a stranger.

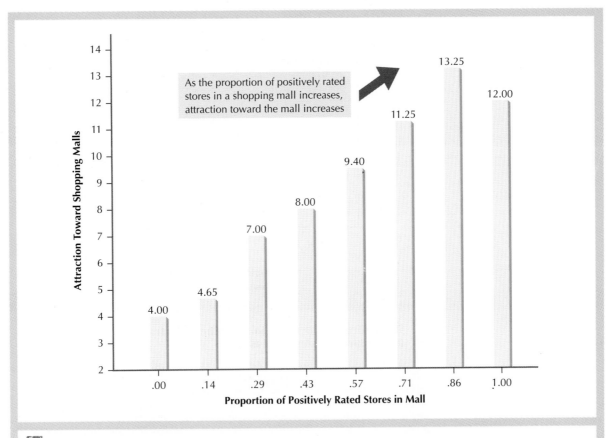

Attraction toward shopping malls

FIGURE 6.16 Attraction research indicates clearly that we like other people on the basis of the proportion of positive attributes associated with them, including the proportion of similar attitudes they express. Other kinds of liking follow the same pattern. In this study, liking for shopping malls was found to increase as the proportion of positively rated stores in the mall increased. (Source: Based on data from Meoli & Feinberg, 1989.)

The repulsion hypothesis predicts no effect on attraction, while the similarity hypothesis predicts increased attraction as the number of similar attitudes increases. The results were clear; as the number of similar attitudes increased, subjects liked a stranger better (see Figure 6.17, p. 254). So although the repulsion hypothesis was an interesting idea, it was not confirmed in this experimental test.

There is, nevertheless, a specific situation in which attraction to an agreeing stranger does not develop. Cramer and his colleagues (1985) found that if an individual is with someone he or she already likes, attraction toward a stranger expressing similar attitudes is blocked. These investigators suggested that the total context in which two people interact is of great importance. From this perspective, attraction is most likely to develop between two people who have similar attitudes if they are alone (no competing positive relationships) and if they are in a neutral setting (no competing positive or negative stimulation).

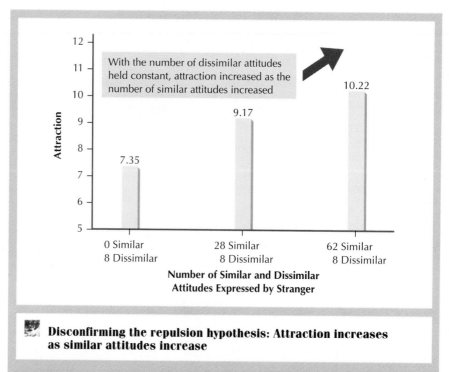

With the number of dissimilar attitudes held constant, attraction increased as the number of similar attitudes increased

Disconfirming the repulsion hypothesis: Attraction increases as similar attitudes increase

FIGURE 6.17 Though Rosenbaum's *repulsion hypothesis* predicts that attraction is influenced only by dissimilar attitudes and not by similar ones, research does not confirm this prediction. When the number of dissimilar attitudes expressed by a stranger is held constant, subjects express more attraction toward that person as the number of similar attitudes increases. In other words, attraction is affected by *both* similar and dissimilar attitudes. (Source: Based on data from Smeaton, Byrne, & Murnen, 1989.)

The investigators speculated that the stark, stainless-steel environments commonly depicted in futuristic science fiction may be ideal for developing positive interpersonal relationships.

Why Do We Like Similar Others?   Many theorists agree that attitude similarity has a positive effect because similar attitudes confirm one's judgments about the world. Through social comparison, we find out whether others "validate" what we have already concluded about politics or religion or whatever by agreeing with us (Festinger, 1954; Goethals, 1986a). In effect, if someone makes the same evaluations you do, that person is providing "evidence" that you are correct. It feels good to learn that your judgment is sound, and you like the person who created that feeling. Disagreement has just the opposite effect; it suggests you are wrong, arouses negative feelings, and causes you to dislike the person responsible.

  Balance theory provides a different explanation of the similarity effect (Hummert, Crockett, & Kemper, 1990). Newcomb (1961) and others propose that human beings organize their likes and dislikes cognitively in a symmetrical arrangement that results in **balance** (Cacioppo & Petty, 1981; Insko, Sedlak, & Lipsitz, 1982). Balance is created when two people like each other and agree about something. When they like each other and disagree, there is **imbalance,** and this unpleasant state motivates each individual to do something to restore balance (Orive, 1988). For example, one person could convince the other to change his or her attitudes, or they could decide to dislike each other. Once two people dislike each other, **nonbalance** is created, and, theoretically at least, they become indifferent as to whether they agree or disagree.

More recently, a third possible explanation (discussed further in Chapter 9) has been provided by Rushton (1989), who hypothesized that people are somehow able to detect the genetic similarity of others and are programmed to prefer those who are most genetically similar to themselves. In one investigation, long-term (nonhomosexual) male friends of European ancestry were compared with respect to ten genetically determined blood characteristics, such as Rh factor and blood type. Friends were found to be similar on significantly more of these factors (54 percent) than were random pairs of males (48 percent). The socio-biological explanation of such findings is that it is crucial to pass on one's own genes to future generations: If you like, become friends with, and come to the aid of those who are most genetically similar to yourself, you are simply trying to ensure that your segment of the gene pool will be safely maintained and eventually transmitted to offspring. As we will point out in Chapter 7, choosing a genetically similar mate is even more important as a way to ensure the survival of your genes.

Despite the attitude similarity effect, we do not *always* reject those who express views that differ from our own. There is a need to validate what we believe, but there are other needs as well. By interacting with someone who holds dissimilar attitudes, we may learn something new and valuable (Kruglanski & Mayseless, 1987) or find that we are special and unique instead of being just like everyone else (Snyder & Fromkin, 1980). Dissimilarity is unpleasant in part because it is an indication that we will probably be disliked by those holding divergent views (Gonzales et al., 1983), but that threat can be eliminated if we know in advance that those who disagree are open to discussing alternative viewpoints and will not automatically respond with rejection (Broome, 1983; Sunnafrank & Miller, 1981).

Other Kinds of Similarity   Whereas attitude similarity most often leads to attraction, the effects of personality similarity or behavioral similarity are found to be less consistent.

For one thing, some personality characteristics are generally liked by everyone, *regardless* of similarity to self. As we discussed earlier, dominant males are viewed positively by those who are dominant *and* by those who are submissive. Competitive individuals, too, are liked by both men and women (Riskind & Wilson, 1982), and people who disclose information about themselves are preferred to those who are unwilling to reveal much (McAllister & Bergman, 1983).

For most characteristics, however, similarity results in liking (Griffin & Sparks, 1990). Among many examples, heterosexual males respond negatively to homosexual males, regardless of agreement on various topics (Aguero, Bloch, & Byrne, 1984). By the time children reach the age of seven or eight, they prefer friends close to their own age (Ellis, Rogoff, & Cramer, 1981), and high school friends are found to be similar in age, sex, religion, and race (Kandel, 1978)—though propinquity could explain at least some of these findings. We also like those who behave as we do when playing games (Knight, 1980) and those who are similar to ourselves in academic and nonacademic skills (Tesser, Campbell, & Smith, 1984). Friends behave in similar ways with respect to smoking, drinking, and engaging in premarital sex (Rodgers, Billy, & Udry, 1984); using marijuana (Eisenman, 1985); and being active in the morning hours as opposed to the evening hours (Watts, 1982). Friends also prefer to engage in similar activities (Jamieson, Lydon, & Zanna, 1987). Perhaps as a result of the tendency to choose similar friends, people find it easier to understand a complex communication written by a friend than one written by a stranger (Fussell & Krauss, 1989).

One of the exceptions to the similarity effect involves those diagnosed as having cancer. They prefer to be with others who are healthy or to be alone rather than to interact with other cancer patients (Rofe, Lewin, & Hoffman, 1987). The explanation is that this disease is sufficiently threatening that patients are motivated to avoid all reminders of their condition. Thus, there is a special aversion to conversations with fellow patients.

Research on **personality similarity** has been less consistent because an individual's responses on a personality test are not necessarily reflected directly in what he or she ordinarily says or does. A person may respond to test items indicating that he or she feels anxious and has physical symptoms of stress, such as headaches and diarrhea. If, however, that person does not behave in an obviously anxious way and does not discuss headaches or gastrointestinal problems, there is no way for others who are similar (or dissimilar) in these respects to know about it. As a result, some investigations report that people with similar scores on such and such a test are no more likely to be friends than those with dissimilar scores. A better test of the effect of personality similarity, as described in the following **Cutting Edge** section, is provided by investigations of personality characteristics that *are* directly reflected in what people say and do. Only then can we discover whether attraction is influenced by similarity of personality characteristics.

FOCUS ON RESEARCH: THE CUTTING EDGE

Hypertraditionality and Attraction to the Opposite Sex

Recent research has identified two conceptually similar personality dimensions, one that applies to males and one that applies to females: **hypermasculinity** and **hyperfemininity**. These terms refer to a series of beliefs, perceptions, and characteristic behaviors that are based on extremely traditional and exaggerated ideas about appropriate behavior for males and females.

Hypermasculinity (sometimes labeled the *macho male personality*) is described by Mosher and Sirkin (1984) as having three components. Males who score high on this dimension express callous beliefs about women and sex ("Get a woman drunk, high, or hot and she'll let you do whatever you want"), perceive violence as manly ("It's natural for men to get into fights"), and enjoy the excitement of risk-taking action ("After I've been through a really dangerous

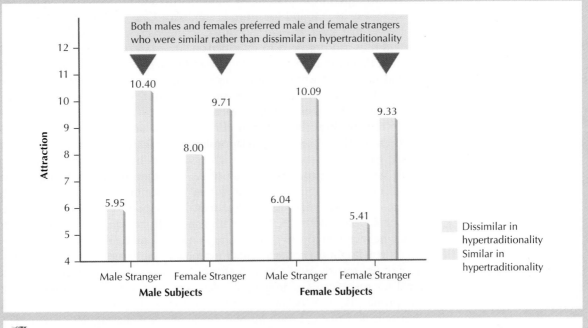

Personality similarity: Attraction to those most like ourselves

FIGURE 6.18 Though early studies of personality similarity and attraction were not clear-cut, it appears once again that similarity is a basic factor in determining who is liked. Both in the laboratory (as in the data shown here) and among real-life couples, males and females are most attracted to others who are similar to themselves in *hypertraditionality*. (Source: Based on data from Smith, 1989.)

experience I feel high"). You can see that these tendencies (and their opposites—low hypermasculinity) are very likely to be expressed overtly, so that others would soon learn if a male were relatively high or relatively low on this dimension of personality.

A corresponding personality dimension among females, labeled hyperfemininity, has been described by Murnen and Byrne (1990). A hyperfeminine woman believes she is successful to the extent that she can maintain a relationship with a man ("Most women need a man in their lives"), uses her sexuality as a primary asset ("I sometimes act sexy to get what I want from a man"), and accepts male aggressiveness ("It's okay for a man to be a little forceful to get sex"). Again, those who are relatively high or relatively low on this dimension would be expected to reveal that fact in what they say and do.

In two investigations of personality similarity, Smith (1989) examined male and female **hypertraditionality** (referring to either hypermasculinity or hyperfemininity) as a determinant of attraction. First, she conducted a simple laboratory experiment in which subjects high or low in hypertraditionality rated either a male or a female stranger on the basis of his or her responses to a personality test; these responses were either similar or dissimilar in hypertraditionality. The results indicated that personality similarity was clearly a strong determinant of attraction toward both same-sex and opposite-sex strangers (see Figure 6.18).

In this experiment, personality similarity determined attraction in precisely the same way as is found for attitude similarity. One reason for such clear-cut results was that subjects were shown the stranger's responses to the personality test and thus did not need to infer personality from behavior. Smith believed, however, that both high and low hypertraditionality are revealed in what people say and do. If so, actual dating couples should be similar in their degree of hypertraditionality—that is, their similarity on this personality dimension should have led to their mutual attraction.

To test this hypothesis, Smith (1989) studied undergraduate couples who had been involved in a dating relationship for at least one month. In separate rooms, each male was measured with respect to hypermasculinity and each female with respect to hyperfemininity. As hypothesized, these dating couples were found to be much more similar in hypertraditionality than would be expected by chance. Hypermasculine men and hyperfeminine women tend to like one another and to establish relationships. To an equal extent, low hypermasculine men and low hyperfeminine women are mutually attracted.

As you might expect, with other personality dimensions that are expressed more or less overtly, similarity is preferable to dissimilarity. Examples are traditional sex roles versus androgynous roles; sensation seeking; depression; coronary-prone, Type A behavior; and cognitive style (Antil, 1983; Lesnick-Oberstein & Cohen, 1984; Morell, Twillman, & Sullaway, 1989; Pursell & Banikiotes, 1978; Rosenblatt & Greenberg, 1988). The personality similarity effect becomes even stronger as the interaction between two individuals increases (Blankenship et al., 1984), in part because many personality traits are not obvious until two people have spent a good deal of time together (Funder & Colvin, 1988).

Reciprocity: If You Like Me, I Like You

Once two people find that they are similar and have many things in common, a friendship is likely to develop. There is one more crucial step in the process, however. The most powerful determinant of your attraction to another person is any indication, in word or deed, that he or she likes you, evaluates you highly, and wants to be with you (Condon & Crano, 1988; Hays, 1984). If you feel the same way about that individual, a close friendship is very likely to follow.

Though reciprocal liking can easily be expressed in words, often the first signs are nonverbal ones. For example, when a female interacts positively with a male by maintaining eye contact, leaning toward him, and engaging in conversation, he tends to be attracted to her even if he knows that she has dissimilar attitudes (Gold, Ryckman, & Mosley, 1984). Almost everyone likes a positive evaluation from others and dislikes any indication of a negative judgment (Coleman, Jussim, & Abraham, 1987). Even if the positive evaluation is inaccurate (Swann et al., 1987) or is a rather obvious attempt at flattery, we are pleased to receive it (Drachman, deCarufel, & Insko, 1978). People respond negatively to negative evaluations, even when they are directed at someone else (Amabile, 1983).

The effects of evaluations are reflected immediately in interpersonal behavior. In one experiment, some subjects were led to believe that they were liked and others that they were disliked by a stranger who had been shown a survey filled out by each subject earlier (Curtis & Miller, 1986). These evaluations "by a stranger" were actually made up by the experimenters. When the subject then engaged in a ten-minute discussion with another subject (supposedly the stranger who had expressed liking or disliking), his or her behavior was strongly influenced by that individual's evaluation. As Figure 6.19 indicates, subjects who expected to be liked made more eye contact with the other person, spoke in a warmer tone, and were more self-disclosing than those who expected to be disliked. Such behavior also led to reciprocal liking at the conclusion of the experiment. Information that the other person had expressed dislike led to less eye contact and so forth and to less reciprocal liking afterward.

Another result of mutual liking is that two individuals indicate their feelings by behaving in a considerate and helpful way. Clark, Mills, and Corcoran (1989) distinguish between friendship (a *communal relationship*), in which there is concern for the other's welfare, and an *exchange relationship,* in which two people can benefit each other in specific ways.

These investigators created an experimental task in which the two kinds of relationships could be compared. Each subject was paired with a friend or a stranger, and then the partner was taken to another room, supposedly to work on a task. Half the subjects were told that the partner would signal if help was needed, and the other half were told that the signal meant the partner was doing well on the task so that the two of them would receive a joint reward. In each case, the signal from the partner was to be a change in the lights in the subject's room, but in fact the lights never changed. The behavior of interest was the number of times each subject looked at the lights. The hypothesis was that a

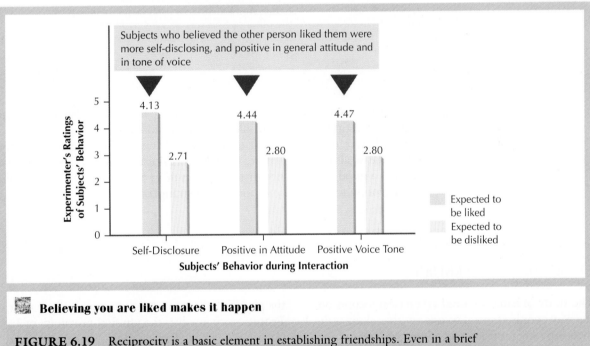

Believing you are liked makes it happen

FIGURE 6.19 Reciprocity is a basic element in establishing friendships. Even in a brief experiment, subjects who believed the other person liked them engaged in more self-disclosure, expressed more positive attitudes, and spoke in more positive tones than subjects who believed the other person disliked them. Such behavior, in turn, led to reciprocal positive behavior from the other person. When you perceive that another person likes you, you behave differently than you do when you perceive dislike, and, as a result, you *are* liked. (Source: Based on data from Curtis & Miller, 1986.)

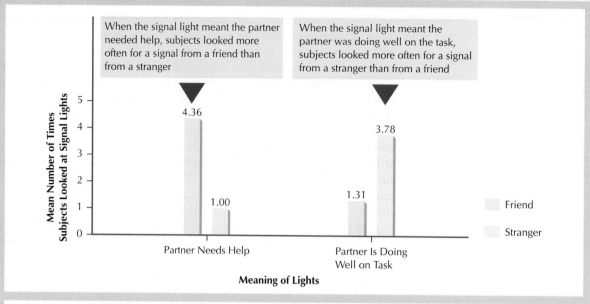

When the signal light meant the partner needed help, subjects looked more often for a signal from a friend than from a stranger

When the signal light meant the partner was doing well on the task, subjects looked more often for a signal from a stranger than from a friend

Keeping track of a friend's needs and of a stranger's success

FIGURE 6.20 When interacting with a friend (communal relationship), people behave differently than they do when interacting with a stranger with whom they have an exchange relationship. In this experiment, subjects looked more often at lights that were to indicate the need for help when the other person was a friend than when the other person was a stranger. The reverse was true when the lights were to signal that the other person was doing well on the task so that the two of them would receive a joint reward. (Source: Based on data from Clark, Mills, & Corcoran, 1989.)

signal for help would lead to more looking if the partner was a friend and that a signal indicating a reward would cause more looking if the partner was a stranger. Figure 6.20 shows that the hypothesis was confirmed. Subjects kept track of the needs of a friend more than the needs of a stranger. When the signal indicated a good performance that would result in a reward, the subjects paid more attention to a communication from a stranger.

SUMMARY AND REVIEW

The study of **interpersonal attraction** focuses on the way people respond to one another along a dimension ranging from hate at one extreme to love at the other.

Meeting and Evaluating Strangers

Among the factors bringing strangers together are the physical aspects of their common environment. **Propinquity** involves the physical proximity of classroom seats, dormitory rooms, apartments, and so on that encourages contact between people who do not know one another. As such contacts increase in frequency, two individuals become familiar to each other and become casual acquaintances. These unplanned contacts lead to a positive response because of the *repeated-exposure* effect. If the interactions consist of negative acts or if *privacy* is violated, propinquity can have the opposite effect. **Affect** is crucial to interpersonal attraction because we like those who arouse positive emotions and dislike those who arouse negative emotions. Through simple conditioning, we also evaluate others on the basis of our emotional state, even when they are not in any way responsible for it.

Becoming Close Acquaintances

Whether casual acquaintances move toward a closer relationship depends in part on the strength of each person's **need for affiliation.** Research suggests that affiliative needs are based on biological tendencies, early experiences, and the adequacy of one's social skills. Affiliation is also motivated by external events that are emotionally arousing, including those which are frightening and stressful. Under such conditions, we seek out others for *social comparison* purposes and to obtain *valid information*. Attraction is also influenced by each person's stereotyped reactions to the *physical characteristics* of the other. People hold stereotypes based on the assumptions made about strangers with respect to physique, behavioral style, voice pitch, clothing, and many other attributes. *Physical attractiveness* has received the most research attention, and it influences attraction and other evaluations from birth to old age. In addition, romantic relationships and even friendships are determined in part by the tendency to select partners who *match* oneself in attractiveness.

Forming Friendships

Attitude similarity is a consistent determinant of attraction. People respond positively to those who express similar attitudes, beliefs, and values; they respond negatively to dissimilarity. Theoretical explanations of the attitude similarity effect include the positive and negative feelings aroused when others provide "evidence" that one is correct or incorrect in interpreting events, the need for *balanced* as opposed to *imbalanced* cognitions, and an inherited preference for *genetic similarity*. Beyond attitudes, similarity of personality and behavior also has a positive effect on attraction. The final, crucial determinant of whether a friendship is or is not formed is the expression of *reciprocal positive evaluations*. People become friends if they each indicate, by what they say and do, that the other person is liked—is someone with whom it is desirable to spend time.

KEY TERMS

Affect Emotions or feelings.

Attitude similarity The degree to which two individuals share the same attitudes.

Balance In Newcomb's theory, the pleasant state that exists when two people like each other and agree about a topic.

Balance theory A cognitive theory of the relationships among an individual's liking for a second individual, his or her attitude toward a given topic, and his or her perception of the second individual's attitude toward that same topic.

Belief in a just world The belief that people get what they deserve and also deserve what they get.

Cognitive disregard Part of the screening process whereby some of the people we meet are excluded from further consideration as acquaintances and friends on the basis of their observable characteristics. Little attention is paid to those who are excluded, and they are not recognized afterward.

Equity theory The formulation that a relationship is perceived as fair if the outcomes each participant receives are proportional to the contributions each makes.

False consensus effect The tendency to believe incorrectly that most people agree with oneself about a given issue.

Friendship motivation The motive to establish warm and friendly interpersonal relationships.

Hyperfemininity A personality dimension involving specific female characteristics. At the highest extreme, the individual believes that success is defined by maintaining a relationship with a man, that sexuality is her primary asset, and that men should adhere to a traditional masculine role.

Hypermasculinity A personality dimension involving specific male characteristics. At the highest extreme, the individual expresses callous sexual beliefs about women, believes that violence is manly, and enjoys danger.

Hypertraditionality The tendency for males to be hypermasculine or females to be hyperfeminine.

Imbalance In Newcomb's theory, the unpleasant state that exists when two people like each other but disagree about some topic. Each is motivated to change some aspect of the interaction in order to achieve balance or nonbalance.

Interpersonal attraction The degree to which we like other individuals. Interpersonal attraction varies along a dimension ranging from hate on one extreme to love on the other.

Matching hypothesis The proposal that individuals with approximately equal social assets (such as physical attractiveness) will select one another as friends, lovers, and/or spouses.

MUM effect The reluctance most people feel about transmitting bad news to others.

Need for affiliation The motive to seek interpersonal relationships and to form friendships.

Nonbalance In Newcomb's theory, the indifferent state that exists when two people dislike each other and don't care whether they agree or disagree about various topics.

Personality similarity The degree to which two individuals are alike with respect to a given personality characteristic.

Physical attractiveness The combination of facial features, bodily shape, and grooming that is accepted in a given culture at a given time as being most appealing.

Privacy The desire to prevent others from knowing everything that one says and does at present (or has said and done in the past or will say or do in the future). Privacy is achieved by arranging one's physical and social world so that it is not totally open to others.

Propinquity Physical proximity. As propinquity between two individuals increases, the probability of their interacting increases. Repeated interactions most often lead to increased familiarity and becoming acquainted.

Proportion of similar attitudes In the array of attitudes expressed by another person, the number of topics on which an individual is in agreement divided by the total number of topics (number of agreements plus number of disagreements).

Reinforcement-affect model A theory proposing that all evaluations are based on positive and negative emotions. These evaluations are directed at the stimulus object responsible for the emotion *and* at any other stimulus that is simply associated with the emotional arousal.

Repeated exposure Zajonc's theory that multiple contacts with any neutral or mildly positive stimulus results in an increasingly positive evaluation of that stimulus.

Repulsion hypothesis Rosenbaum's proposal that attraction is not enhanced by similar attitudes but that, instead, people are repulsed by dissimilar attitudes.

Social comparison process The tendency to evaluate one's abilities, accomplishments, views, behavior, appearance, beliefs, and other attributes by comparing them with those of other relevant people.

FOR MORE INFORMATION

Berscheid, E. (1985). Interpersonal attraction. In G. Lindzey and E. Aronson (Eds.), *Handbook of social psychology* (Vol. 2). New York: Random House.

This chapter presents an overview of the empirical research and theoretical formulations of the topic of interpersonal attraction. Professor Berscheid has done extensive work in this field, and she brings an expert's knowledge to bear in summarizing this very large field of investigation.

Derlega, V. J., & Winstead, B. A. (Eds.). (1986). *Friendship and social interaction*. New York: Springer-Verlag.

A series of contributors cover a broad range of topics centering on friendship. An unusual strength of this book is the concern with the many disciplines that deal with overlapping aspects of these same phenomena. The major elements include friendship formation, the importance of friendships, and the effects of sex and social settings on how friendships function.

Hatfield, E., & Sprecher, S. (1986). *Mirror, mirror . . . The importance of looks in everyday life*. Albany, NY: SUNY Press.

A well-written and extremely interesting summary of research on the effects that physical attractiveness has on interpersonal relationships. The authors' coverage of the scientific literature is illustrated throughout with anecdotes, photographs, and cartoons that consistently enliven the presentation.

Close Relationships:
Friendship, Love, Intimacy,
and Marriage

Steve and Marta sipped their drinks as they waited for the appetizers to be brought to their table. Tonight was their fifth wedding anniversary, and they were having dinner at Chez Jacques to celebrate. Although it should have been a happy occasion, they found themselves struggling to find something to talk about. That had never been a problem in the past, but lately their lives were gradually moving in different directions.

Both were lost in thought. Marta was thinking of those first weeks and months when they'd met and gone out almost every night. She'd shown considerable promise as an artist, and painting was the greatest joy in her life, but suddenly her love affair with Steve seemed far more important. She wanted to be with him, make love with him, and devote the rest of her life to creating something real—not just two-dimensional images on canvas. Now, six years later, her outlook had changed dramatically.

Steve was thinking about how well he was doing. His job took much of his time and was a matter of pride to him. He had become chief accountant at a large department store and made more than his father had ever earned. He and Marta owned a comfortable home, and they had a three-year-old son who was truly a delight to both of them. During their first years together, Marta seemed content to take care of the house and then to be a mother. Over the past year, though, she surprised him with her decision to return to art school, taking a full load of classes.

As for Marta, there was actually more to that decision than a desire for an artistic career. Being honest with herself, she felt that Steve was just plain boring. He said and did the same things month in and month out. Even sex was boring— just something else on his schedule of things to do. Could this possibly be the same man she'd fallen in love with?

Steve was even more dissatisfied. He didn't like placing his son in day-care or eating a frozen dinner because Marta no longer had time to cook. They didn't seem to have much in common anymore, except Tommy. Marta had no interest in hearing anything about his work, and Steve became angry when she talked about Paul, her art teacher, or the male models who posed practically in the nude for her class. *It's possible that she still can be excited about sex,* Steve thought, *but not with me—she's made that clear enough.*

Their silence at the table was becoming awkward, and both were relieved when the waiter arrived with the onion soup. Then, at least, they could talk about how good the food was. They even joked about the pompousness of the waiter, whose ability to speak French was probably limited to the menu.

Beneath the surface of their conversation were concerns that each kept private. Both were unhappy with their marriage, and neither knew exactly why. Divorce seemed out of the question, but going on as they were made no sense. They didn't know what had gone wrong with their relationship or what to do about it. Neither wanted to talk about the situation, and so they spent the rest of the evening making small talk and pretending that everything was all right. Each wondered what would happen next in their lives. Maybe if they just let matters drift, everything would somehow get better.

One of the most important aspects of our lives is the establishment of close *relationships*. Most of the current research (and therefore most of this chapter) concentrates on heterosexual partners, but many of the same issues are equally applicable to gays and lesbians (Schullo & Alperson, 1984). Despite many changes in society and in interpersonal styles, the ideal life for most people includes close friends, love, marriage, and parenthood. Though daily we are exposed in the media or in real life to the realities of loneliness, unhappy relationships, and divorce, most of us continue to maintain the belief that we can find happiness with a spouse, offspring, and friends at least as successfully as the characters depicted on TV's "The Cosby Show." As the story of Steve and Marta suggests, however, attempting to live up to such ideals and beliefs quite often results in disappointment. Nevertheless, no one really expects to fit the description given by the disc jockey shown in Figure 7.1.

Social psychologists are increasingly interested in studying close relationships (Berscheid, Snyder, & Omoto, 1989a; Clark & Reis, 1988). Given the importance of friendship, love, and marriage to most people, why should any of these relationships cause any difficulties? In the following pages, we will attempt to identify some of the reasons for interpersonal success and failure.

We will first describe the difference between a casual friendship and a close relationship, the latter often characterized by one of the many facets of *love*. When an individual wants to establish relationships and cannot, the result is *loneliness,* and we will examine why some people are lonely and what can be done about it. Next, we will turn to a very difficult interpersonal task: *establishing and maintaining* a *close relationship*. Finally, we will explore why, all too often, positive feelings fade and partners find themselves in a *troubled relationship*. Although some problems can be avoided and many relationships can be saved, sometimes the outcome is a permanent and usually painful breakup.

"This next one goes out to all those who have ever been in love, then become engaged, gotten married, participated in the tragic deterioration of a relationship, suffered the pains and agonies of a bitter divorce, subjected themselves to the fruitless search for a new partner, and ultimately resigned themselves to remaining single in a world full of irresponsible jerks, noncommittal weirdos, and neurotic misfits."

A pessimistic view of relationships

FIGURE 7.1   For the vast majority of people in our culture, the ideal life is defined by love and marriage. We know, of course, that reality very often does not conform to the fantasy of "living happily ever after." Nevertheless, few of us want or expect our relationships to follow the pattern described here. (Drawing by Cheney; © 1989 The New Yorker Magazine, Inc.)

Interdependent Relationships: Beyond Casual Friendships

Even among those of the same sex, casual friendships are not the same as close friendships. Close friends spend time together more often and in a wider variety of situations than casual friends do. Close friendships tend to exclude others, and they provide emotional support that is absent in casual relationships (Hays, 1989). What are the other characteristics of interpersonal closeness?

Varieties of Close Relationships: Friends, Romantic Partners, and Relatives

Friendship and love are similar in some respects, but they are not identical, as Rubin (1973) demonstrated several years ago. Sometimes, one also feels very close to a sibling, a cousin, or some other family member. Perhaps the common element in each type of close relationship is the *interdependence* of the two individuals, as demonstrated in their day-to-day interactions (Kelley et al., 1983). Interdependence exists when two people frequently influence one another's lives and engage jointly in many kinds of activities over an extended period.

To study such interactions, Berscheid, Snyder, and Omoto (1989b) first identified what kinds of relationships people establish. They asked college students to identify the *one person* to whom they felt closest. Three types of relationships were specified most often: 47 percent named a romantic partner, 36 percent a friend, and 14 percent a family member. The remaining 3 percent mentioned someone else, such as a fellow worker.

The investigators then developed an instrument to measure the closeness of these relationships, the **Relationship Closeness Inventory.** This scale asks a series of questions about the individual's interactions with one other person. Subjects indicate how much time the two of them spent together in the past week and what specifically they did (e.g., watched TV, went to a bar, talked on the phone, made love). Subjects are then asked how much the other person influences their thoughts, feelings, and behavior in such specific areas as socializing, spending money, and making career plans. Males and females report equal degrees of closeness, and both sexes perceive romantic relationships as closer than either friendships or family ties.

A major goal in developing this scale was to make it possible to predict which relationships would last and which would not. As it turned out, only romantic relationships are perceived as ending. Friends and family members may become less close over time, but seldom does anyone report that a friendship or a family relationship has ceased to exist. Such interactions may slowly wither and fade; in contrast, romantic partners indicate a dramatic and clear breakup when the relationship ends. Does the Relationship Closeness Inventory predict which romances will last?

In a nine-month longitudinal study, Berscheid, Snyder, and Omoto (1989b) found that relationship success was consistently related to scores on their scale. As Figure 7.2 indicates, couples who remained together through the nine months of the study had the highest closeness scores, followed by those who broke up between the third and sixth months. Couples with the lowest scores broke up quickly—during the first three months of the study.

Most of the research on relationships concentrates on male-female romances because romantic relationships are the most common, the most close, and when they do not succeed, the most painful.

Passion and Romance: It's So Easy to Fall in Love

Some have suggested that a relationship turns to **love** when two friends perceive themselves as potential sexual partners. Large-scale studies of both students and nonstudents suggest, however, that "friendship" is not an accurate description

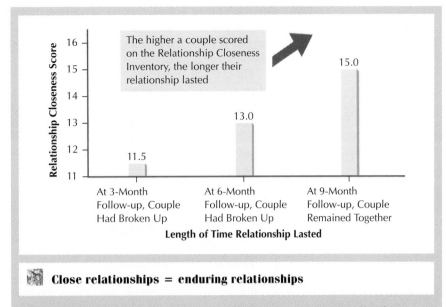

The higher a couple scored on the Relationship Closeness Inventory, the longer their relationship lasted

Close relationships = enduring relationships

FIGURE 7.2 Scores on the *Relationship Closeness Inventory* predict the outcome of relationships over a nine-month period. Scores were highest among couples whose relationships lasted throughout the nine months. Scores were lowest among couples who broke up during the first three months and intermediate among couples who broke up between the third and sixth months of the study. (Source: Based on data in Berscheid, Snyder, & Omoto, 1989b.)

of how love begins. In fact, falling in love is determined by factors quite different from those of "falling in friendship" (Aron et al., 1989).

When individuals are asked to describe their own experiences with love and friendship, their responses indicate that love is most often precipitated by desirable aspects of the other person, such as an attractive appearance and personality, as well as by reciprocal liking (Aron et al., 1989). Love is affected much less strongly by such factors as perceived similarity and propinquity. For friendships, the reverse is true; similarity and propinquity *are* major determinants. These differences between friendship and love provide a clue as to why love may not be the best basis on which to establish a long-term relationship. We will now provide some evidence indicating why this is so.

Defining and Measuring Passionate Love   When you respond to a member of the opposite sex as a possible romantic partner, there is often a sudden, intense, all-consuming response that is usually perceived as love. Such expressions as *falling head over heels in love* suggest that love is an accident, much like slipping on a banana peel (Solomon, 1981). Research in social psychology indicates that this description applies most accurately to **passionate love,** one of several varieties of emotional attraction (Berscheid & Walster, 1974). What exactly is meant by passionate love?

Studies of those who describe themselves as being in love indicate many common characteristics. An individual experiencing passionate love is preoccupied with his or her partner, idealizes that person, responds with sexual attraction and physiological arousal, feels miserable if there are relationship problems, wants to be with the partner, and wants to be loved as well as to love (Hatfield, 1988).

Those in love begin to interact with other friends less frequently than before and to focus all their attention on this one, very special individual (Milardo, Johnson, & Huston, 1983). Hatfield and Sprecher (1986a) devised a scale to measure this kind of emotional relationship, and a portion of it is shown in Table 7.1. In reading the test items, you can see that passionate love combines cognitive, emotional, and behavioral components. Love is expressed in our beliefs, feelings, and overt acts.

Measuring passionate love

TABLE 7.1 The Passionate Love Scale was devised to measure the intense emotion of passionate love. Subjects are told that other terms for this feeling are *infatuation, love sickness,* and *obsessive love.* The sample items shown here represent only a portion of the total scale.

Please think of the person whom you love most passionately *right now.* If you are not in love right now, please think of the last person you loved passionately. If you have never been in love, think of the person whom you came closest to caring for in that way.

1. I would feel deep despair if _____ left me.
2. Sometimes I feel I can't control my thoughts; they are obsessively on _____ .
3. I feel happy when I am doing something to make _____ happy.
4. I would rather be with _____ than anyone else.
5. I'd get jealous if I thought _____ were falling in love with someone else.
6. I yearn to know all about _____ .
7. I want _____ —physically, emotionally, mentally.
8. I have an endless appetite for affection from _____ .
9. For me, _____ is the perfect romantic partner.
10. I sense my body responding when _____ touches me.
11. _____ always seems to be on my mind.
12. I want _____ to know me—my thoughts, my fears, and my hopes.
13. I eagerly look for signs indicating _____ 's desire for me.
14. I possess a powerful attraction for _____ .
15. I get extremely depressed when things don't go right in my relationship with _____ .

Responses to each item are made along the following scale:

Not at all true			Moderately true			Definitely true		
1	2	3	4	5	6	7	8	9

Source: Adapted from Hatfield & Sprecher, 1986a, p. 391.

Love or Lust?   Hatfield and Rapson (1987) have also pointed out the parallels between *sexual desire* and *passionate love*. Perhaps these phrases are used to describe the same kind of interpersonal response; it is simply more acceptable to say, "I love you" than to say, "I lust for you."

Though passionate love can occur at any age, a familiar question among adolescents is, How do you know if you are *really* in love? Advice columnists sometimes answer that question by saying, "If you have to ask, you're not in love." Perhaps the best way to answer the question is to understand what psychologists believe to be the underlying elements responsible for this kind of love.

A Theory of Passionate Love

One very popular theory of intense love proposes three conditions that are necessary for its occurrence (Hatfield & Walster, 1981). Specifically, an individual must have learned that love is an appropriate response, an acceptable target for love must be encountered, and emotional arousal must occur and be attributed to "love."

Learning about Love   First, you must be raised in a culture that teaches you to believe in love and to expect it to happen to you (Dion & Dion, 1988). Both in fiction ("they fell in love and got married") and in real life ("Mommy and Daddy got married because we were in love"), most of us have been exposed to examples of love. Further, we learn that love leads to living happily ever after and to having offspring. Because we have heard stories and sung songs of love since childhood, we are well prepared to feel it ourselves "when the right person comes along" (Dion & Dion, 1975). This notion may seem natural to those of us living in such a culture, but love is a relatively recent invention in human history and not something that is universally accepted, even in the 1990s.

The concept of love originated in Europe during the Middle Ages. Originally, it was described as a pure and holy emotion that was separate from sexual desire. Not until the end of the seventeenth century in England was love considered to be the cornerstone of an ideal marriage (Stone, 1977). In India, movies about couples who marry because of love (rather than because their parents arranged the union) have only become common in the last several years (Kaufman, 1980). According to a 1986 report, in the Soviet Union only 50 percent of the women and 33 percent of the men say they marry for love; most indicate they marry because of loneliness, shared interests, or pregnancy. In contrast, most Americans (87 percent) say they believe love is crucial to a good marriage. In any event, one reason we fall in love is that we have learned it is what we are expected to do.

Encountering an Appropriate Love Object   The second condition necessary for love is the presence of an appropriate person as the target for this emotion. For most people, the object of their love must be a physically attractive member of the opposite sex. There is also some evidence that genetic similarity plays a role in such attraction (Rushton, 1989b; Rushton & Nicholson, 1988).

Given no additional knowledge about what the other person is like, people of various ages report that it is common to come into brief contact with a stranger and experience "love at first sight" (Averill & Boothroyd, 1977). Even in a laboratory setting, when opposite-sex strangers are instructed to gaze into each other's eyes for two minutes, they report feelings of passionate love for each other (Kellerman, Lewis, & Laird, 1989).

Some theorists, including Buss (1988), identify an "appropriate love object" as one meeting criteria established through evolutionary biology. Buss proposes that we engage in acts of love because in the history of our species, certain acts led to the birth of offspring who themselves successfully reproduced. From this perspective, loving behavior survived in our genetic makeup because it led to the selection of mates who could reproduce *and* nurture their children. Among the implications of this approach are male-female differences in resources, the criteria for mate selection, the appropriate cues for evaluating potential mates, and the kind of love acts that attract a mate. The genetically based differences between males and females are summarized in Figure 7.3.

Buss (1989) tested these proposals by examining mate preferences among over ten thousand males and females in a cross-cultural study conducted in

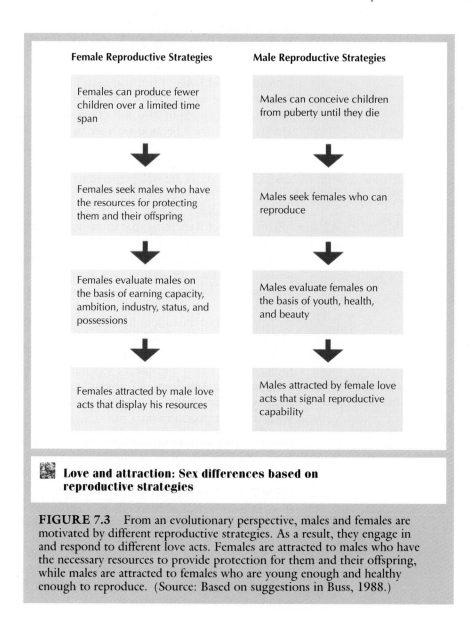

Female Reproductive Strategies

Females can produce fewer children over a limited time span

Females seek males who have the resources for protecting them and their offspring

Females evaluate males on the basis of earning capacity, ambition, industry, status, and possessions

Females attracted by male love acts that display his resources

Male Reproductive Strategies

Males can conceive children from puberty until they die

Males seek females who can reproduce

Males evaluate females on the basis of youth, health, and beauty

Males attracted by female love acts that signal reproductive capability

Love and attraction: Sex differences based on reproductive strategies

FIGURE 7.3 From an evolutionary perspective, males and females are motivated by different reproductive strategies. As a result, they engage in and respond to different love acts. Females are attracted to males who have the necessary resources to provide protection for them and their offspring, while males are attracted to females who are young enough and healthy enough to reproduce. (Source: Based on suggestions in Buss, 1988.)

countries located on six continents and five islands. The findings provided striking support for the prediction that females throughout the world place the highest value on cues indicating a male's *resource acquisition* (earning capacity, ambition, industriousness, and maturity) while males most value those cues indicating a female's *reproductive capacity* (youth and attractiveness).

One of the sex differences just described involves preferences about the age one's partner should be. Kenrick and Keefe (1990) reported that in both the United States and India, males advertising for a partner express a preference for females younger than they, a preference that increases as men grow older. Females, however, prefer male partners their own age or older. This same pattern holds true for actual marriages. Why should this be so?

One explanation is based on an economic exchange model (see Chapters 6 and 15 for a discussion of *equity theory*). In a society in which males have the advantage in economic resources and power, they are able to "trade" these assets for the major assets possessed by females—physical attractiveness and youth. In contrast, an evolutionary model based on differential reproductive strategies is favored by Kenrick and Keefe (1990). Unconsciously, each sex is motivated to maximize reproductive success. Most males remain fertile throughout their lives, from puberty until they die, but females are able to conceive offspring only during the years between puberty and menopause. Males, then, are most likely to be successful in reproducing if they are attracted to young females, even when they themselves are no longer young. Females, however, are attracted to older males who are powerful and successful because such males can best take care of them and their offspring. There is no definitive evidence that supports either the economic exchange or the evolutionary model, but the ideas are provocative and can serve as the impetus for further investigations of mate preference.

Attributing Arousal to Feelings of Love Third, intense infatuation is most likely to occur if you are in a state of emotional arousal when the other person is present. Considerable evidence supports Schachter's theory (see Chapter 2) that the specific emotional label we apply to physiological arousal depends on external cues that tell us how we *should* feel. In a variety of laboratory and field studies, arousal has been created while subjects are exposed to an opposite-sex stranger. As a result, subjects express romantic feelings, attraction, and sexual interest. These reactions occur even though the arousal involves fear (Dutton & Aron, 1974), sexual excitement (Istvan, Griffitt, & Weidner, 1983), embarrassment (Przybyla, Murnen, & Byrne, 1985), or frustration and anger (Driscoll, Davis, & Lipetz, 1972). From this perspective, love is simply a misattribution in which various kinds of arousal are labeled as "love."

This three-factor theory of passionate love is summarized in Figure 7.4 (p. 274). Hatfield's (1983) review of the literature suggests that men and women are very similar in wanting both love and sex in a relationship; they also want both intimacy and control. The sexes differ in some respects, however. Men fall in love more easily than women do, while women fall out of love more easily than men do (Rubin, Peplau, & Hill, 1981).

Though the *misattribution* explanation of the effect of arousal on attraction to an opposite-sex stranger has been a popular one, two additional theoretical proposals have also been made. The *reinforcement model* states that attraction increases because a decrease in negative feelings becomes associated with a

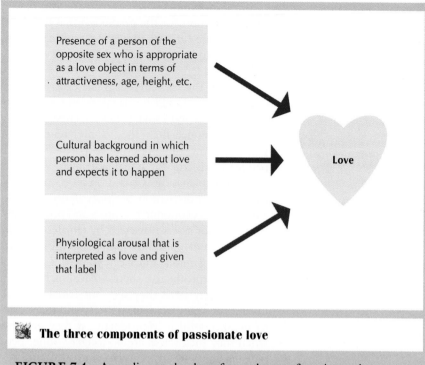

Presence of a person of the opposite sex who is appropriate as a love object in terms of attractiveness, age, height, etc.

Cultural background in which person has learned about love and expects it to happen

Physiological arousal that is interpreted as love and given that label

Love

The three components of passionate love

FIGURE 7.4   According to the three-factor theory of passionate love, you are most likely to experience this emotional reaction to another person if (1) you live in a culture that provides models of love in fiction and in real life, (2) you meet someone who appears to be an appropriate and desirable love object, and (3) you are emotionally aroused and interpret your feelings as indicating "love." It may not sound romantic, but many social psychologists view passionate love as based on learned beliefs, specific cues in the present situation, and the mislabeling of physiological arousal.

stranger. For example, in an anxiety-arousing situation, the presence of another person is reinforcing because anxiety decreases for the reasons described in Chapter 6's discussion of affiliation. Because negative emotional arousal can also increase attraction toward a same-sex stranger, it seems that the concept of associated reinforcement might be a better explanation than misattribution (Kenrick & Johnson, 1979; Riordan & Tedeschi, 1983).

A third possibility, supported by the work of Allen and his colleagues (1989), is a *response-facilitation model*. Using Hull's (1943) learning theory, these investigators proposed that arousal facilitates each individual's dominant response in any given situation. Because arousal leads to increased attraction toward an attractive stranger and to decreased attraction toward an unattractive stranger (White et al., 1981), it is suggested that arousal simply increases the strength of the dominant response in each instance. In a series of experiments, Allen and his colleagues (1989) obtained evidence that is inconsistent with the misattribution model, in that focusing the subject's attention on the source of the arousal did not result in less attraction toward the stranger. Other evidence was inconsistent with the reinforcement model, in that nonthreatening arousal (physical exercise) was also found to increase sexual attraction toward a stranger. These investigators concluded that the response-facilitation model best explains the various findings. If they are correct, the three-factor theory of passionate love would still apply, but the theoretical explanation of the arousal effect would be modified.

Before describing other types of love, we will focus on one setting in which romance commonly occurs—the workplace—in the following **Cutting Edge** section.

FOCUS ON RESEARCH: THE CUTTING EDGE

Romance in the Workplace: From Harassment to True Love

If you consider some of the factors that facilitate attraction (such as propinquity and similarity), it becomes obvious that people who work for the same organization are very likely to become acquainted and to form friendships. They come in contact with one another day after day, and they have a great deal in common by virtue of the kind of work they do. These same factors operate whether the organization is a fast-food franchise, a large business, a university, or whatever. Further, if two people share emotional experiences that occur from time to time at work, positive relationships would be expected.

Although few would object to work-related friendships between two men or two women, potential problems arise when the friends are of the opposite sex. Quinn (1977) observed some years ago that organizations are a "natural environment for romantic relationships" (p. 30). As the number of women in the work force steadily increases (U.S. Bureau of the Census, 1984), that statement becomes more and more significant. If passionate love occurs regularly in organizations (see Figure 7.5, p. 276), do you believe this development is good or bad for the individuals involved or for their employer?

The most objectionable form of romantic attraction occurs when one employee is attracted to a coworker and makes unwelcome sexual advances. The person making the advances is almost always a male (95 percent) who is married (67 percent). Though such interactions have been recognized since at least the beginning of the industrial revolution, the phrase **sexual harassment** was not coined until the 1970s. Harassment can be mild (sexual teasing and joking), moderate (pressuring a female for dates), or severe (forceful attempts at sexual acts). Only since 1980 has this kind of sexually offensive behavior been unlawful in the United States (Diamond et al., 1981).

More than two-thirds of working females are subjected to unwanted approaches by males each year, and most say they dislike the experience (Schneider, 1982). As you might guess, the targets are most often relatively young females whose status in the organization is low. On college campuses, about one out of five female students report harassing experiences from a male instructor at least once during their college years (Glaser & Thorpe, 1986).

Most people would agree that unwanted advances and the use of one's power to attempt sexual coercion are unacceptable. If, however, the attraction

Romance on the job: A common experience

FIGURE 7.5 When people work in the same organization, many factors operate to foster mutual attraction—propinquity, similarity, shared emotional experiences, and so forth. It is not surprising that the workplace has been described as "a natural environment for romantic relationships."

is mutual, is there any problem? Opinions range from the view that any romance creates a conflict of interest between the couple and the organization (Collins, 1983) to the position that intimate relationships are of no concern to anyone but the two persons involved (Schrank, 1984).

To pinpoint the consequences of romance on the job, Dillard and Broetzmann (1989) conducted a large-scale survey of individuals who had experienced mutual sexual attraction in the work setting. The subjects were males and females employed in both large and small organizations. Their responses revealed that romance led to many behavioral changes at work, but the motivation for the relationship was an important consideration. For those motivated by love and the desire to find a long-term partner, romance resulted in more positive attitudes about their jobs. Those motivated by job concerns (advancement, prestige, security, etc.) were absent from work more often after a romance began. In addition, sex differences were found. Females were more likely than males to respond to a love affair with both positive and negative effects. They were more enthusiastic about their work but also more likely to arrive late and leave early.

Altogether, there are no simple rules that apply to romance in the workplace. Attraction, desire, and love seem to be inevitable, and the outcome for the individuals ranges from offensive harassment to mutual passion. For the organizations, the effects include lawsuits (in harassment cases), tardiness, and absenteeism—but also, under the right circumstances, happier employees.

Kinds of Love: Let Me Count the Ways

There is general agreement that passionate love is only temporary. People are unable to remain infatuated indefinitely. The question, then, is whether there are other kinds of love that *can* be sustained over time. Luckily, the answer is yes.

Companionate Love—A Close, Caring Friendship   Though love may begin with intense emotions and light up the night like skyrockets, it can either end in a disappointing fizzle or mature into **companionate love.** This latter phrase refers to "the affection we feel for those with whom our lives are deeply entwined" (Hatfield, 1988, p. 205). This kind of love resembles a very close friendship in which two people are attracted to each other, have a great deal in common, and express reciprocal liking and respect (Avery, 1989; Caspi & Herbener, 1990; Neimeyer, 1984). Each *cares* about the partner's well-being and happiness (Rubin, 1974; Steck et al., 1982). Interestingly, males and females can sometimes remain friends after a passionate relationship breaks up, especially if they were also friends *before* the romance (Metts, Cupach, & Bejlovec, 1989).

Unfortunately, we seem to find songs and stories about passionate love more interesting and exciting than those about companionate love. For a relationship to last, partners must be friends as well as lovers. This is a crucial aspect of real life, one well presented fictionally by the film *When Harry Met Sally. . . .*

A Six-Part Model of Love   Other theorists propose that there are several additional kinds of love (Lasswell & Lobsenz, 1980; Lee, 1973, 1988). Basing their work on these formulations, Hendrick and Hendrick (1986) suggest that there are six different types of love, and they have developed measures of each type. Table 7.2 presents some of the test items that assess the different forms love can take.

Males score higher than females in both passionate and game-playing love, while females score higher than males in friendship, logical, and possessive love (Hendrick et al., 1984). As you might guess, partners in romantic relationships tend to resemble each other in the kind of love they feel (Hendrick, Hendrick, & Adler, 1988). Passionate love and selfless love are positively related to satisfaction with the relationship; game-playing love is negatively related to satisfaction. The importance of the kind of love expressed in a relationship was shown in a follow-up study of romantic couples. Those who avoided breaking up were high in passionate love and low in game-playing love.

Love as a Triangle   According to Sternberg (1986, 1988), love is best understood in terms of three components conceptualized as a **triangular model of love.** Figure 7.6 (p. 279) illustrates how the three basic components combine in various ways to produce quite different kinds of loving relationships.

The first component is **intimacy**—the closeness two people feel and the strength of the bond holding them together. Partners are high in intimacy to the extent that each is concerned with the other's welfare and happiness. Each values the other, and they regard one another highly, count on each other in times of need, and possess mutual understanding. They share their selves and their possessions, give and receive emotional support, and engage in intimate communications.

Love is truly a many-splendored thing

> **TABLE 7.2** Hendrick and Hendrick's (1986) description of love includes six distinct varieties that go beyond the passionate and companionate (friendship) types. That people differ in the kind of love they feel further complicates the task a couple undertakes in working out a mutually satisfying relationship.

Basic Love Styles	Sample Items Measuring Each Style
1. Passionate love	My lover and I were attracted to each other immediately after we first met.
	My lover and I became emotionally involved rather quickly.
2. Game-playing love	I have sometimes had to keep two of my lovers from finding out about each other.
	I can get over love affairs pretty easily and quickly.
3. Friendship love	The best kind of love grows out of a long friendship.
	Love is really a deep friendship, not a mysterious, mystical emotion.
4. Logical love	It is best to love someone with a similar background.
	An important factor in choosing a partner is whether or not he [she] will be a good parent.
5. Possessive love	When my lover doesn't pay attention to me, I feel sick all over.
	I cannot relax if I suspect that my lover is with someone else.
6. Selfless love	I would rather suffer myself than let my lover suffer.
	Whatever I own is my lover's to use as he [she] chooses.

Passion, the second component, includes romance, physical attraction, and sexual interactions. Sternberg suggests that other needs—such as self-esteem, affiliation, dominance, and submission—may contribute to passion.

The **decision/commitment** component is based on cognitive factors and has a short-term and a long-term aspect. In the short-term, a person decides that he or she loves someone. The long-term aspect involves the commitment to maintain a loving relationship.

Sternberg further describes the triangles of love as varying in two ways. Love varies in *intensity,* which is represented by the size of a triangle—the larger the triangle, the more intense the love. The shape of the triangle indicates the extent to which love is *balanced,* as depicted in Figure 7.7 (p. 280).

The importance of each of the three components varies as a function of several factors. For example, passion plays a larger role in short-term relationships, whereas intimacy and commitment are essential in a lasting relationship. The three components are balanced when all three are roughly equal. They are unbalanced when one of the components is stronger than the other two. For example, in the three unbalanced triangles in Figure 7.7, passion is emphasized in the first, as when physical attraction is the major reason for the relationship. In the second, intimacy is crucial. In the third, decision/commitment is the major focus, as when rational, logical reasons form the basis for maintaining the relationship.

Why People Differ in the Kinds of Relationships They Form   Considering the many kinds of love and relationships that people experience, is there any way to understand why a given person approaches love in a particular way?

Hazan and Shaver (1987) propose that the romantic relationships each person forms as an adult are strongly influenced by his or her childhood inter-

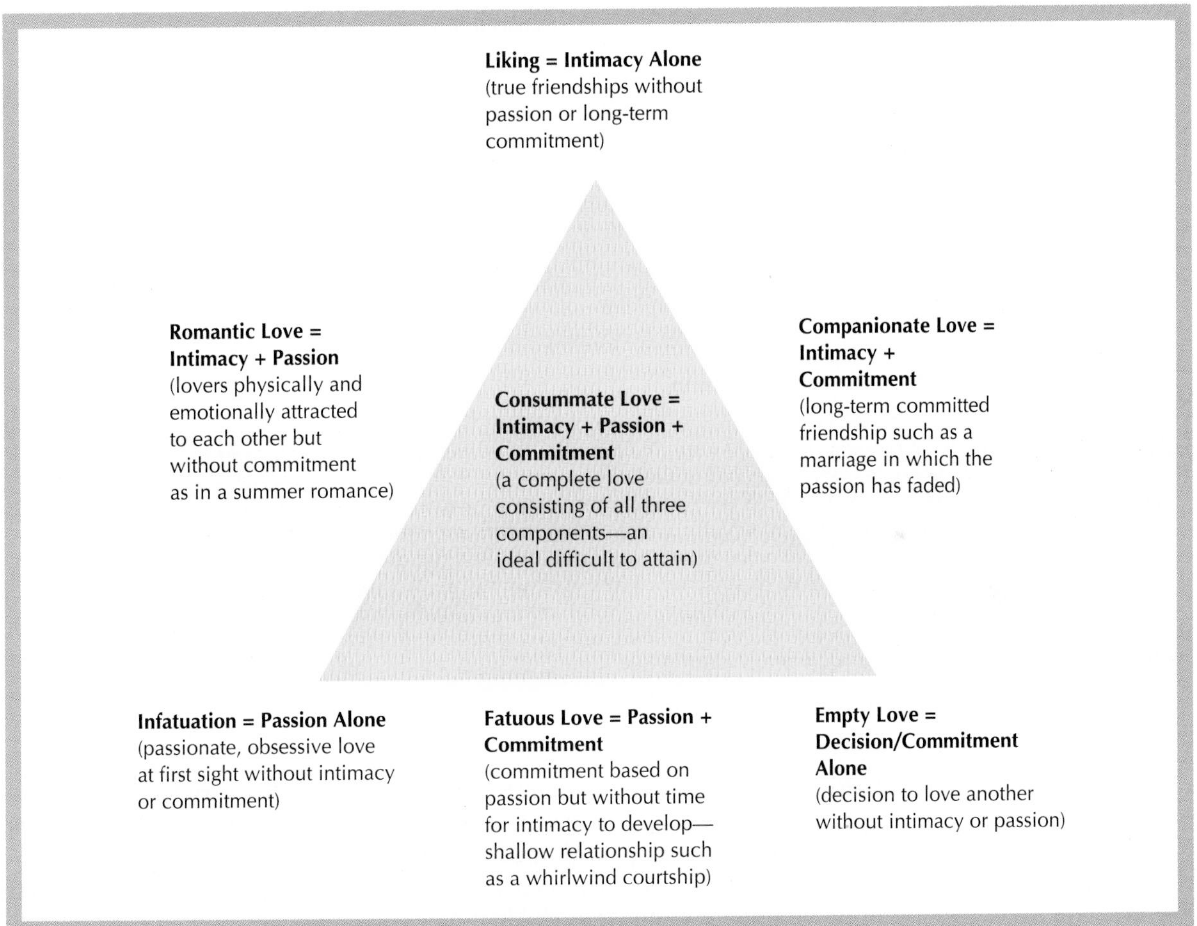

Liking = Intimacy Alone
(true friendships without passion or long-term commitment)

Romantic Love = Intimacy + Passion
(lovers physically and emotionally attracted to each other but without commitment as in a summer romance)

Consummate Love = Intimacy + Passion + Commitment
(a complete love consisting of all three components—an ideal difficult to attain)

Companionate Love = Intimacy + Commitment
(long-term committed friendship such as a marriage in which the passion has faded)

Infatuation = Passion Alone
(passionate, obsessive love at first sight without intimacy or commitment)

Fatuous Love = Passion + Commitment
(commitment based on passion but without time for intimacy to develop—shallow relationship such as a whirlwind courtship)

Empty Love = Decision/Commitment Alone
(decision to love another without intimacy or passion)

 Three components of love → seven kinds of love

FIGURE 7.6   In Sternberg's *triangular model of love,* the three components are intimacy, passion, and decision/commitment. As shown here, each can occur alone or in combination with the others. As a result, there are seven quite different kinds of love relationships. (Source: Adapted from Sternberg, 1988, p. 122.)

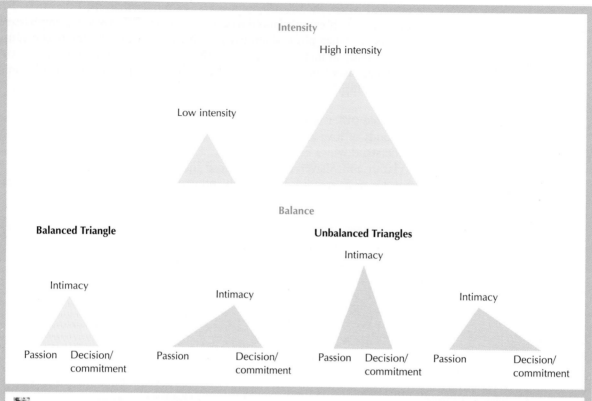

Balanced and unbalanced love triangles

FIGURE 7.7 In the triangular model of love, the *intensity* of an individual's experience of love is indicated by the size of the triangle. The larger the triangle, the more intense the love. The shape of the triangle indicates the extent to which the three components are *balanced*. A triangle with three equal sides represents balanced love, in which all three components are equally strong. On the bottom row are three unbalanced triangles. On the left, passion plays the greatest role, and some predominantly sexual relationships fit this pattern. Next, intimacy is the strongest component, the friendship of the two lovers being most important. On the right is a love emphasizing decision-commitment—being together in a permanent relationship is of greater importance than sex or friendship. (Source: Adapted from Sternberg, 1986.)

actions with parents. These investigators sampled college students and newspaper readers to ask about their most important romance and also about childhood relationships with their parents.

The investigators identified three types of individuals. Those who were *securely attached* said that as children they perceived their parents as loving and warm. As adults, they expressed the belief that it is easy to get close to others, and their relationships were good. They reported few problems, their romances were long lasting, and they had the fewest divorces of the three types.

The *avoidant* group said their parents were rejecting. As adults, they reported feeling uneasy and untrusting when people became too close to them. Their relationships were described as a series of emotional highs and lows.

The third group was characterized as *anxious/ambivalent*. They reported mixed relationships with their parents—sometimes loving and sometimes cold and rejecting. These individuals wanted their partners to be close, found it hard to be giving, and worried a lot about their lovers leaving them.

We need to know much more about how childhood experiences are transferred to adult relationships and about the ways in which some individuals overcome negative experiences with parents. For example, securely attached individuals report the most positive early family relationships, those who are avoidant have a childhood history of separation from their mothers, and the anxious/ambivalent adults describe their fathers as being relatively unsupportive (Feeney & Noller, 1990). Such research provides an unusual opportunity to understand the roots of love in developmental experiences.

Life Without a Relationship: Loneliness

Despite the emphasis in our society on establishing relationships and falling in love, not all people have these experiences. For those who don't, the result can be **loneliness:** the unmet desire to engage in close interpersonal relationships (Peplau & Perlman, 1982). Recent research has concentrated on why some people are lonely and on what to do about it (Hojat & Crandall, 1987; Marangoni & Ickes, 1989).

Measuring Loneliness   In 1980, Russell, Peplau, and Cutrona constructed the **UCLA Loneliness Scale** to assess the extent to which individuals feel lonely. Here, subjects use a four-point scale ranging from "never" to "often" to respond to such items as "I feel left out" and "I have a lot in common with the people around me." Someone who is lonely would tend to indicate *often* in response to the first item and *never* in response to the second.

Scores on this instrument have been found to be associated with feelings of depression, anxiety, dissatisfaction, unhappiness, and shyness (Russell, 1982). Similar findings hold for groups as divergent as college students and senior citizens (Perlman, Gerson, & Spinner, 1978). It should be noted that loneliness is not a necessary component of old age, but those elderly individuals who *are* lonely (because of physical impairments or other reasons) feel much like lonely young people do (Mellor & Edelmann, 1988).

Those who are most lonely differ from the nonlonely in a number of reported behaviors. Lonely individuals are, for example, more likely to eat dinner by themselves and to spend the weekend without companionship (see Figure 7.8, p. 282). They engage in few social activities and tend not to have dates (Russell, Peplau, & Cutrona, 1980). When asked to name their friends, those high in loneliness list as many people as do those who are not lonely, but closer examination reveals that these "friendships" involve low levels of intimacy and often are not reciprocated (Williams & Solano, 1983). Also, the greater one's loneliness, the less the chance for social support when things go wrong; in effect, there's no one to talk to or to confide in (Berg & McQuinn, 1989).

Childhood Sources of Loneliness   It is not unusual to have periods of loneliness while growing up, especially if one's parents move from one location to another or if a serious childhood illness requires a long absence from school. These difficulties are usually temporary, and they are not a major cause of adult loneliness.

🔲 **Loneliness: Wanting a relationship and being unable to establish one**

FIGURE 7.8 Loneliness is felt when a person wants to establish relationships but cannot do so. Adolescence is an especially vulnerable time, because it is during these years that friendships and relationships with the opposite sex become crucial.

The primary cause seems to be the failure to learn appropriate social skills during childhood (Rubin, 1982). Few of us receive formal instruction in the best way to make and keep friends, to reinforce others, to deal with disagreements, and to be sensitive to others' feelings (Putallaz & Gottman, 1981; Rubin, 1980). Some children have good role models in their parents or older siblings, and some develop good skills by accident. Without such advantages, other children never quite get the knack of interpersonal behavior. What often happens is that such individuals either become aggressive or withdraw into loneliness.

In adolescence, loneliness can reach a peak (Brennan, 1982). As young people begin the process of separation from their parents and attempt to form outside relationships, failure can be experienced acutely. Those who are lonely feel alienated from parents, teachers, and peers (Brennan & Auslander, 1979).

Interpersonal Behavior and Loneliness The basic problem of inadequate social skills remains characteristic of those who are lonely in late adolescence and adulthood. Such persons are often shy and don't know how to behave appropriately or fail to do so even when they have the knowledge (Bruch et al., 1989; Hill, 1989). When they interact with a stranger in an experimental setting, those high in loneliness, compared with the nonlonely, refer to the other person less, are less inclined to follow up on topics introduced by the stranger, and ask fewer questions (Jones, Hobbs, & Hockenbury, 1982). In essence, they lack interest in others, and one consequence is that they are rejected. Their behavior drives away potential friends.

A history of such rejections leads those who are lonely to expect interpersonal failure (Jones, Freeman, & Goswick, 1981). Lonely individuals disclose very little about themselves, or they make inappropriate disclosures (Berg & Peplau, 1982; Solano, Batten, & Parish, 1982). Their unhappy experiences with others results in cynicism, pessimism, and the feeling that they have little control over their lives (Jones, 1982). Members of the opposite sex are a special problem. Loneliness is associated with the belief that love is not a necessary basis for marriage with the expectation that one's own marriage will end in divorce (Jones, Hansson, & Smith, 1980).

Those who feel lonely and shy assume that others are the same way, as the *false consensus effect* would predict (see Chapter 5). Harris and Wilshire (1988) asked subjects who were or were not shy to rate their friends and relatives and also soap opera characters for shyness. As Figure 7.9 indicates, shy individuals are much more likely than those who are not shy to perceive this trait in both real and fictional others. This perception tends to undermine any motivation to change, because the person thinks, *Everyone else is just like me.*

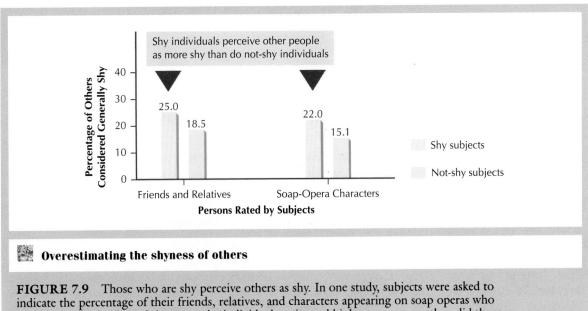

Overestimating the shyness of others

FIGURE 7.9 Those who are shy perceive others as shy. In one study, subjects were asked to indicate the percentage of their friends, relatives, and characters appearing on soap operas who were generally shy. In each instance, shy individuals estimated higher percentages than did those who were not shy. (Source: Based on data in Harris & Wilshire, 1988.)

Overcoming the Causes of Loneliness Unless major steps are taken to change behavior, loneliness persists from year to year, and lonely individuals believe—accurately—that improvement will not occur. Common responses are engaging in wish-fulfilling fantasies, becoming absorbed in an occupation, and using alcohol or drugs (Paloutzian & Ellison, 1979; Revenson, 1981). Some lonely individuals turn to music as a substitute for interpersonal contacts, but this outlet actually increases loneliness, perhaps because of the content—themes of separation, heartache, and sadness (Davis & Kraus, 1989). In that these coping strategies only make things worse, what can be done? Two techniques, often used together, are **cognitive therapy** and **social skills training.**

Cognitive therapy is designed to change the way a person thinks about himself or herself in social situations (Young, 1982). For example, if a man feels that he is dull and boring, the therapist may convince him that this self-perception is untrue or may work to alter the man's belief that being witty and exciting is necessary to making friends. If a woman feels that social situations are stressful because others are always evaluating her (Asendorpf, 1989), she can learn that she is *not* the center of everyone's attention.

Beyond changes in thought processes, behavioral changes are also important, and social skills can be taught (Rook & Peplau, 1982). A lonely individual can be shown, by means of videotapes, how others deal with social situations. The person can then practice such skills and observe himself or herself on tape. Specific interactions, such as initiating a relationship, can be encouraged. Some people need to be taught how to begin a conversation, speak easily on the telephone, give compliments, and even improve their physical appearance with changes in hairstyle, clothing, or makeup.

The results of such efforts can be remarkable, even in a short period of time. Once an individual thinks about social situations in a new way, learns how best to interact with other people, and changes his or her style, the resulting interpersonal successes can eliminate loneliness.

Establishing and Maintaining Close Relationships: It's Not So Easy

We all know that many relationships, no matter how happily and hopefully they begin, run into problems. Love affairs come to an end. Couples stay together unhappily. Divorce is all too common. What goes wrong, and what can be done to prevent relationship failure? In this section we will describe some of what has been learned about this very important topic.

Sexual Intimacy before Marriage: The Times They Are A' Changin'

Despite centuries of formal disapproval, love has increasingly come to mean that the couple will engage in sexual intercourse prior to marriage. Below, we will examine current evidence that suggests possible changes in sexual attitudes and behavior and will explore what is known about the effect of premarital intimacy on marital success.

🔲 **Premarital sex: The revolutionary norm**

FIGURE 7.10   In the decades following World War II, sexual attitudes and behaviors became dramatically more permissive, especially in North America and in Western Europe. A major component of this "sexual revolution" was the much greater acceptance of premarital intercourse as the norm for both sexes.

The Sexual Revolution   Among the most dramatic and widespread changes in attitudes and behavior over the decades following World War II have been those involving sexuality. Especially in Western Europe and in North America, research has documented a steady and consistent shift toward greater tolerance for the sexual practices of others, including the acceptance of premarital sexual intercourse for both males and females (see Figure 7.10).

These attitudinal changes were also accompanied by behavioral changes. By the early 1980s, the traditional male-female differences in early sexual experience had disappeared, and females were at least as likely as males to engage in premarital sex (Clement, Schmidt, & Kruse, 1984). Among university students, both sexes approve of premarital intercourse in a serious relationship, and both believe it's important to feel loved and needed, though male-female differences are evident in other respects (Carroll, Volk, & Hyde, 1985). For most females, an emotional involvement is a prerequisite for sex all or almost all of the time (85 percent), but this is true for only 40 percent of males. Similarly, twice as many males (84 percent) as females (42 percent) report having had sexual relations without any emotional involvement. Very similar sex differences have been reported in Australia (McCabe, 1987), where females also were found to view love and sex as closely linked. Males agree that love should be accompanied by sex, but they also believe that sex is desirable even without love.

Differing male and female attitudes about love and sex are also revealed in what each wants to occur in a sexual relationship. Hatfield and her colleagues (1989) hypothesized that women would express the need for more indications of love and intimacy, whereas men would focus on their desire for more arousing sexual activity. Among undergraduates in dating relationships and newly married couples, precisely such sex differences were found. Figure 7.11 indicates those male-female differences which were consistent for both the sample of dating undergraduates and the newly married couples. Women wanted their partners to talk lovingly more often than they did. Men in both groups ex-

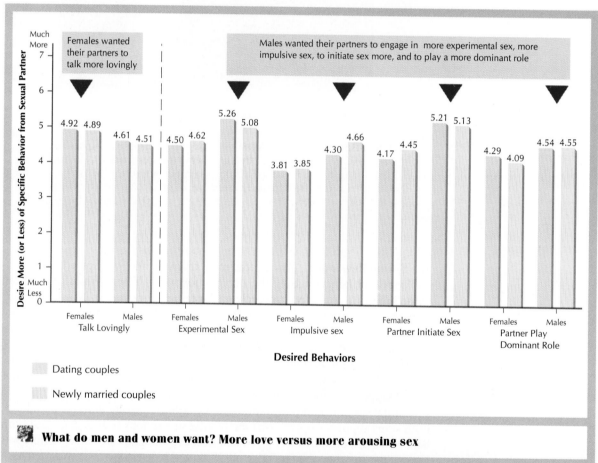

What do men and women want? More love versus more arousing sex

FIGURE 7.11 Whatever the explanation—learned social norms or evolutionary selection—males and females express somewhat different desires in a sexual relationship. Among both married and unmarried couples, women indicate that they want more expressions of love from their partners than men do. Males, more than females, indicate that they want more arousing and varied sexual interactions. (Source: Based on data in Hatfield et al., 1989.)

pressed the desire for sexual interactions that were more experimental, rough, fast, and impulsive, and they wanted more sexual initiative and dominance from their female partners.

One consequence of the sexual revolution was that sexual intimacy became an expected and accepted part of any serious relationship. In a study of college couples, for example, only 17 percent reported not having engaged in intercourse (Christopher & Cate, 1985). Most (44 percent) had begun having intercourse when they decided to become "known as a couple"; 32 percent, when they were just beginning to consider becoming a couple; and 7 percent, on the first date.

More recently, however, the sexual revolution has begun to show signs of weakening.

Postrevolution Sexuality   Even in the late 1970s and early 1980s, there were warning signs suggesting that totally permissive sexuality was not necessarily the perfect answer in matters of love and happiness. For one thing, many individuals became sexually active for external reasons. That is, their partners wanted sex, there was peer pressure to lose one's virginity, and society was perceived as equating sexual freedom with normality (DeLamater, 1981). Among females especially, many reported feeling guilty, anxious, and exploited by males (Weis, 1983). Both males and females frequently found their actions in conflict with the values taught by their religion and by their parents (McCormack, 1980). Somewhat surprisingly, those who were most experienced sexually were perceived by their peers as less suitable marriage partners (Hudson, 1980; Istvan & Griffitt, 1980).

These subjective reactions to permissive sexual attitudes and behavior were enhanced by two very frightening and completely objective consequences of sexual intimacy. Among teenagers in the United States (and elsewhere), increased sexual activity was accompanied by the failure to practice effective contraception (Byrne & Fisher, 1983). As a result, more than a million unwanted teenage pregnancies occurred in this country each year (Alan Guttmacher Institute, 1981). Moreover, the personal and societal tragedies of such pregnancies are only partially communicated by the statistics. Unwanted conceptions result in abortion (46 percent); children born to young, unwed mothers (26 percent); forced and usually unsuccessful teenage marriages (13 percent); and miscarriage (15 percent).

Even more chilling than the threat of unwanted pregnancy is the increasing fear of **sexually transmitted disease (STD)** (see Figure 7.12, p. 288). Studies indicate a very high rate of such curable infections as **gonorrhea** and **chlamydia** (Judson, 1982), but there is a much greater fear of two viral STDs for which no cure has yet been found. The less serious one, **genital herpes,** is characterized by periodic outbreaks of painful blisters on the genitals and elsewhere. This disease infects about one out of ten Americans, and new cases develop at the rate of five hundred thousand each year (Connell, 1983). The more serious one, **acquired immune deficiency syndrome (AIDS),** leads to a breakdown of the immune system and to death. AIDS was unknown in the United States until 1978, but by 1989, the U.S. Centers for Disease Control reported ninety thousand cases and more than fifty thousand deaths. AIDS has a long incuba-

AIDS: A contributor to changes in sexual attitudes and sexual behavior

FIGURE 7.12   Though there are probably many reasons for the current shift away from the permissive sexuality of the past few decades, the fear of disease seems to be one of the central factors. Obviously, the most frightening of the many sexually transmitted diseases is AIDS, because there is no cure and because it results in death. Shown here are the AIDS quilts, assembled in memory of the victims of the disease.

tion period, and it is estimated that about one out of every two hundred Americans has already been infected (Raeburn, 1989).

Perhaps as a result of these subjective and objective consequences of permissive sexuality, current attitudes about premarital intimacy have shifted in a conservative direction. One indicator is an increase in sex guilt among college females between the mid-1970s and mid-1980s (Gerrard, 1986). At the same time, rates of premarital intercourse have begun to drop (Gerrard, 1987). The specific effects of fear about STDs is reflected in immediate changes in sexual practices once an individual is informed about the dangers of AIDS. Some take steps to engage in "safer sex," such as using condoms, and others reduce the number of sex partners (McQuay, 1985).

Maugh (1990) summarized the results of a survey of 1,500 adults conducted by sociologists at the University of Chicago. Among the findings were a reported increase in sexual abstinence (22 percent had no sex during the past 12 months), a decrease in the number of different partners (an average of 1.2 sexual partners per year), and a decrease in extramarital sex (only 1.5 percent of married individuals had a sexual encounter outside of marriage in the previous year).

Obviously, no one can predict whether sexual attitudes and behaviors will become more or less restrictive in the years ahead. For the time being, at least, "going to bed" no longer seems to be the automatic response to falling in love. Guilt and fear have combined to change the recent patterns of romantic behavior.

Premarital Sex: Effects on Later Marriages?   Whatever one's judgments about the morality or the safety of premarital sexual experience, another question is whether such behavior is harmful or beneficial to later sexual and marital satisfaction.

Investigations indicate that those who engage in premarital sex, including cohabitation, have neither more nor less satisfactory marriages than those who avoid intimacy (Bentler & Newcomb, 1978; Newcomb, 1979). Learning to get along with a partner and to communicate with him or her appear to be far more important for later harmony in a relationship than whether intercourse begins before or after the wedding (Markman, 1981).

Marriage: Happily Ever After?

Despite what may be happening in our society or in the world at large, marriage is still the goal of most young people. More than 90 percent of eighteen-year-olds say they expect to marry, and only 3 percent indicate no interest in such a relationship (Thornton & Freedman, 1982). These expectations accurately predict behavior, because most people do get married. The challenge, as we shall see, is to find happiness in a relationship and to find ways to prevent a relationship from dissolving.

Is Marriage Less Fun Than It Used to Be?   Several years ago, advice columnist Ann Landers (1977) asked her readers, "If you had it to do over again, would you marry the person to whom you are now married?" During the following ten days, more than fifty thousand people replied; 55 percent said yes, and 45 percent said no. Though this sample was self-selected and probably not representative of the total population, the reactions suggest that a great many individuals are not pleased with their marital choices. What is known about marital contentment?

A consistent finding over the years is that those who are married are happier than those who never married or who are divorced, separated, or widowed. In the past fifteen years, however, the association between marriage and happiness has become weaker among both men and women. Married couples may be more content than single individuals, but not as much so as in past decades

Being married versus being single: A sex difference

FIGURE 7.13 Though married individuals are still found to be happier than those who are not married, the difference has decreased in recent years. One reason seems to be that married *women* are less happy than in the past, in part because of conflicts between the demands of being a wife and mother and the demands of holding down an outside job. In contrast, single *men* are happier than was previously the case, in part because sexual partners are now more available outside marriage.

(Glenn & Weaver, 1988). These data also indicate that those who have never married, especially males, now report being happier than similar males did fifteen years ago. In contrast, married females report being less happy now than their counterparts did in the past (see Figure 7.13). Why?

Several factors seem to be operating. For one thing, the life-styles of those who are married and those who are not have become increasingly similar. Despite the conservative shift discussed earlier, sexual relationships are still readily available and generally acceptable outside a formal marriage (Reed & Weinberg, 1984).

Another change is an increase in economic opportunities for women and the effect of new occupational patterns on the relationship between the sexes. To an increasing degree, women are entering many types of careers and achieving financial independence. Although in many ways the multiple responsibilities and opportunities for women represent a positive step, they do not necessarily lead to happier relationships.

One clear effect of greater female independence is that a husband is no longer essential to a woman's survival. Adjusting to these changes presents difficulties, but men do not appear to be upset by the simple fact that their wives are employed. In a study of English husbands, for example, Newman and Cochrane (1987) found that men accepted the idea of a working wife and did not react negatively to a woman's having high occupational prestige and income.

A crucial problem, however, arises with respect to household duties. When males ages eighteen to fifty were surveyed, 75 percent admired and wanted a spouse who would be a good mother, do all the housework, and earn money outside the home as well (Scott, 1979). Women, in contrast, increasingly view housework as something to be *shared* equally, along with power, within the relationship (Weeks & Gage, 1984). For both sexes, perceived control over the assignment of household and child-care duties is associated with marital satisfaction (Madden, 1987). These are not trivial concerns, and many couples report continuing disagreements in dealing with such issues. An additional source of stress and hostility for working women occurs when they fail to receive sufficient social support from their husbands and work supervisors (Houston & Kelly, 1989).

Threats to a Relationship: Jealousy   In the course of daily life, people inevitably come into contact with potential alternatives to their romantic partners. Some reject the possibility of switching partners, but others do not. What differentiates those who remain in a relationship from those who are tempted? Johnson and Rusbult (1989) hypothesized that commitment to an ongoing relationship would cause individuals to devalue a potential alternative partner, especially if that person were very attractive. In several studies, evidence supported this prediction. A committed partner avoids the threat of a breakup by deciding that the tempting outsider is not sufficiently intelligent or attractive and that he or she has a poor sense of humor.

The possibility of attraction toward someone new is a common problem in relationships, as is the response by one's partner—**jealousy** (White & Mullen, 1990). Jealousy is defined as an "aversive emotional reaction evoked by a relationship involving one's current or former partner and a third person" (Buunk & Bringle, 1987, p. 124).

When a relationship involves very little love or commitment, a partner's interactions with a rival are not particularly upsetting (Bringle & Boebinger, 1990). In contrast, commitment means that love and sex are confined exclusively within the partnership. When there is a perceived rival for the partner's affection, strong negative emotions are aroused (Salovey & Rodin, 1986). Smith, Kim, and Parrott (1988) asked undergraduates to specify how they feel when jealousy occurs, and more than half named the sixteen unpleasant emotions shown in Figure 7.14 (Smith, Kim, & Parrott, 1988).

Jealousy endangers a relationship, and the jealous person feels decreased self-esteem (Mathes, Adams, & Davies, 1985; White, 1981). Much like passionate love in reverse, jealousy elicits a flood of all-consuming negative thoughts, feelings, and behaviors (Pines & Aronson, 1983). The jealous person evaluates the rival negatively on such important attributes as intelligence, warmth, sincerity, and honesty but the evaluation on less important attributes such as popularity is positive (Schmitt, 1988). It is helpful when the offending partner apologizes, but not if he or she attempts to make excuses or to justify the attraction toward a rival (Hupka, Jung, & Silverthorn, 1987). A jealous response to a lover's sexual affair with someone else is most likely to result

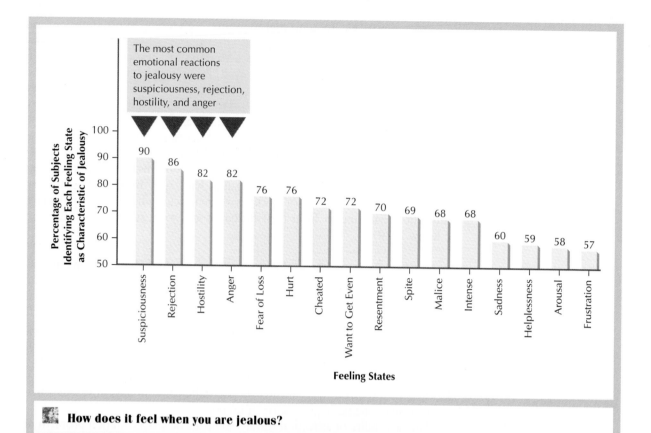

The most common emotional reactions to jealousy were suspiciousness, rejection, hostility, and anger

How does it feel when you are jealous?

FIGURE 7.14 Though it has long been quite clear that jealousy is an unpleasant emotional state, the specific content has only recently been identified. More than half the subjects in one investigation indicated each of the feelings shown here. Jealousy combines anger, hurt, depression, and the desire for revenge. (Source: Based on data from Smith, Kim, & Parrott, 1988.)

in a breakup if the relationship already involves dissatisfaction and conflict (Buunk, 1987).

Jealousy has similar effects even if there is no "other person." Individuals may be jealous of an imaginary rival, someone in the partner's past, or even an unknown *potential* threat. Such jealousy is most likely to occur in individuals who perceive themselves as inadequate and who are dependent and overconcerned about sexual unfaithfulness (White, 1981).

Perhaps because of examples presented in movies and on television, some people deliberately attempt to elicit jealousy in their partners by such tactics as flirting or talking about former lovers (White, 1980). Among college students, such behavior is reported by one in three females and one in five males, but it is a dangerous game to play. When jealousy is induced, a relationship is more likely to suffer than to benefit.

The specific incidents that are most likely to arouse jealousy are not universal—they differ from culture to culture, as we discuss in the following **Multicultural Perspective** section.

SOCIAL PSYCHOLOGY: A MULTICULTURAL PERSPECTIVE

Arousing Feelings of Jealousy: Differences across Nations

Anthropologists have observed that jealousy occurs more frequently in some cultures than in others and that groups differ with respect to what kind of behavior arouses it (Mead, 1977). Jealousy seems not to be an instinctive response to a partner's interest in—or even sexual relations with—someone else. Instead, the reaction depends on the meaning each culture assigns to such behavior (Hupka, 1981).

Among the limited amount of research on such differences is Christensen's (1973) study of cultural differences in reacting to extramarital affairs. About 90 percent of American midwesterners disapproved of extramarital sex, as did 50 percent of Belgians; in Denmark, however, only 10 percent viewed sex outside of marriage negatively. Americans, by the way, still disapprove; a relatively recent poll conducted in liberal San Francisco found that more than 80 percent of those questioned evaluated adulterous sex as wrong (Lawson, 1988).

The specific causes of sexual jealousy were studied by Buunk and Hupka (1987), who sampled more than two thousand university students in Hungary, Ireland, Mexico, the Netherlands, the Soviet Union, the United States, and Yugoslavia. Each subject was asked about his or her reactions to situations in which a lover interacts in some way (kissing, dancing, etc.) with another individual.

These investigators' findings are summarized in Table 7.3. You can see that those living in different countries react quite differently to each potentially

National differences in cues eliciting jealousy

TABLE 7.3 In a study of jealousy in seven industrialized nations, differences were found with respect to the type of behavior by one's partner that elicited jealous feelings. The reasons for these differences are a matter for future research. The responses of Irish subjects are not shown here, because their jealous feelings were neither the weakest nor the strongest in response to any of these behaviors.

Behavior	Strongest Sexual Jealousy in	Weakest Sexual Jealousy in
Flirting	Yugoslavia	Hungary
Kissing	Hungary	Yugoslavia
Dancing	Soviet Union	Netherlands
Hugging	Hungary	United States
Sexual relationship	Soviet Union	Mexico
Sexual fantasies	Netherlands	Yugoslavia

Source: Based on data from Buunk & Hupka, 1987.

threatening situation. For those in Yugoslavia, the most intense feelings of jealousy are aroused when a lover is flirting, but Yugoslavians are least jealous about a lover kissing or having sexual fantasies about someone else. Hungarians, in contrast, are most jealous about kissing and hugging and least jealous about flirting. Students in the Soviet Union are most jealous about a lover's dancing or engaging in sex with a rival. In the Netherlands, a lover's sexual fantasies arouse the most jealousy; dancing, the least. In the United States, hugging is the least upsetting, and in Mexico, students are less jealous about a lover's sexual activities than students in any of the other countries are. In Ireland, responses to each situation tended to fall midway between most and least jealous, compared with responses in other nations.

A general finding was that acceptance of a lover's freedom to behave autonomously in interacting with others was greatest in those countries with the highest gross national product per capita, the most democratic governments, and the most individualistic values (Buunk & Hupka, 1986).

In this multicultural investigation, two sex differences were found, and these were consistent across all seven countries. Women were more jealous when a lover kissed another female than men were when a lover kissed another male. Men, however, felt more jealous about a lover's sexual fantasies than women did.

Given these striking differences across nations and between males and females in perceiving a lover's behavior as a threat, the next task is to determine how such differences arise. We know that jealousy is a common emotion experienced by people differing in language, politics, and religion. It will be fascinating to discover precisely how people learn that specific acts of a loved one are acceptable or unacceptable.

Troubled Relationships: The Pain of Failure

Though jealousy can clearly poison a relationship, most marital unhappiness does not result from anything so specific as a partner's attraction to a rival. Social psychologists and others are just beginning to identify some of the causes of marital discontent and to suggest possible remedies (Byrne & Murnen, 1988).

Problems in Relationships

How do a loving bride and groom become an unhappily married couple? Some problems are universal, but couples differ in how well they manage them. For example, by their very nature, intimate relationships create conflicts between each partner's desire for independence versus the desire for closeness, the need to be open and honest versus the need for privacy, and wanting predictable interactions versus wanting to experience novelty (Baxter, 1990). Other kinds of problems arise only for some couples. In this section we will examine some of the most common sources of discontentment in relationships.

Sources of Male-Female Conflicts   Although males and females react similarly in disliking certain behaviors of their partners, they differ strikingly in some respects. Buss (1989) asked several hundred individuals to describe the source of their conflicts with romantic partners; Table 7.4 summarizes the responses.

Sex differences in causes of conflict

TABLE 7.4 In a relationship, partners who are unfaithful or abusive upset both males and females. In addition, several sex-specific behaviors are also upsetting. Explanations for these differences include a sociobiological emphasis on different reproductive strategies for the two sexes and a socialization emphasis on differences in what males and females learn about appropriate sex roles.

Behaviors That Upset Both Males and Females
Unfaithfulness
Physical abuse
Verbal abuse

Male Behaviors That Upset Females
Trying to demand or force sex
Ignoring a female's opinions and treating her as inferior or stupid
Hiding his emotions, acting tough, drinking or smoking excessively
Neglecting her, ignoring her, failing to say he loves her
Being thoughtless or rude, teasing her

Female Behaviors That Upset Males
Sexual rejection, being unresponsive
Moodiness, acting bitchy
Self-absorbed with her appearance and clothing

Source: Based on data in Buss, 1989.

Buss (1989) explains these sex differences in evolutionary terms. He proposes that whenever a person of one sex behaves in a way that interferes with the partner's inherited reproductive strategy, conflict results. These differences are most pronounced in sexual interactions. Others believe that such findings simply reflect differences in learned sex roles (Goleman, 1989). Whatever the ultimate explanation of how they originate, differences between males and females create specific problems in most heterosexual relationships.

The Discovery of Existing Dissimilarities and the Development of New Ones When two people discover over time that they are dissimilar in various attitudes, values, and preferences, negative feelings are aroused. This development can easily occur in marriages based on passionate love. When "love is blind," overpowering emotions make it difficult or impossible to pay attention to or care about such seemingly irrelevant details as a lover's similarity to oneself.

Dissimilarities can be fatal to a relationship, but their discovery during the dating process is much less devastating than *after* the couple has married (Hill, Rubin, & Peplau, 1976).

Sometimes, dissimilarities are perceived clearly, but one individual believes the partner will eventually change. It is usually a safe bet, however, that any characteristic of the other person that is unacceptable before marriage is unlikely to be changed by the magic of matrimony (see Figure 7.15, p. 296).

TROUBLED RELATIONSHIPS: THE PAIN OF FAILURE

Ignoring dissimilarities and hoping for change

FIGURE 7.15 Even when important dissimilarities are recognized beforehand, two individuals may nevertheless enter into a relationship because of expectations that the other person will change over time. As Kvack will discover, such changes rarely occur. (Reprinted with special permission of King Features Syndicate, Inc.)

Some dissimilarities arise only *after* marriage, and they cannot be avoided. For example, one person may change his or her religious views, politics, drinking behavior, or sexual preferences, while the other does not. Thus, initial similarity can turn to dissimilarity (Levinger, 1980, 1988). Consider a situation in which a man marries a woman who plans to be a homemaker but who later decides to further her education or pursue a career. Though the male's commitment to a career is generally assumed, the female's newfound interest in a life outside the home can be a source of discontent (Nicola & Hawkes, 1986).

Other dissimilarities are hard to avoid because they are not relevant to a dating couple. Two people may simply have no reason to discover that they differ in attitudes about saving money versus spending it, raising children, setting the thermostat at night, or being responsible for cleaning the bathroom. When such differences become apparent, marital dissatisfaction may well result.

Boredom For some but not all individuals, a long-term relationship becomes uncomfortable because of boredom. Couples find themselves doing and saying the same things in the same way day after day, year after year. Even some dating couples who break up identify the general problem in terms of boredom (Hill, Rubin, & Peplau, 1976).

Though boredom has not often been investigated (Skinner, 1986), casual observation suggests that married couples frequently adopt unchanging routines and gradually perceive that they are "in a rut." Given what we know about affect and attraction, it can be seen that the negative feelings generated by boredom would easily become associated with one's partner. Further, spouses often make attributions that it must be the partner's fault that life became dull. Rather than letting themselves drift into boredom, couples might wish to take steps to avoid this particular danger. Of course, for individuals who feel comfortable and secure when things remain the same, an unvaried routine is not a problem.

When boredom does occur, it might be overcome by a husband and wife who together seek new stimulation in the form of vacations, joint educational efforts, unfamiliar dining experiences, new hobbies that are enjoyed by both, new sexual techniques, and so on. Different couples might find quite different solutions. Sex therapist Dagmar O'Connor suggests that sexual boredom in marriage can be overcome by engaging in more sexual fantasies and by recapturing one's adolescent feelings about sex. She says that, for many people, "the best time they had was petting in the back seat of a car, and then they got married and gave that up for 'serious lovemaking.' A lot of times my work is getting them back to that back seat of the car to have a good time" (Goldberg, 1985, p. C-3). The alternative—doing the same things the same way with little variation—can lead to dissatisfaction.

Replacing Positive Evaluations with Negative Ones   In the previous chapter, we described the importance of reciprocal evaluations. One of the most curious and most self-defeating aspects of a long-term relationship occurs when partners shift from positive to negative reciprocity (see Figure 7.16, p. 298).

In much of what they say and do, dating couples and newlyweds express their positive feelings about each other frequently. They make an effort to be together, they hold hands, they demonstrate their love, they say kind things, they help each other, they indicate how much the other person is appreciated, they make it obvious that each finds the other sexually desirable, and so forth.

As two people settle into daily married life, their attention may gradually shift to the tasks that must be performed inside and outside the home, time pressures, problems to solve, and a multitude of pressing requirements. As a result, many of the verbal and behavioral niceties begin to drop away. One example is provided by a study of male air traffic controllers and their wives. On days when the airport work load is heavy and difficult, these men tend to come home, withdraw from interactions with their spouses, and retreat into a solitary world of television and newspapers (Repetti, 1989).

It's as though most people decide, "I don't have to tell you I love you; I married you, didn't I?" Other behavior may also change; as the song lyrics suggest, "You don't bring me flowers anymore." Few individuals consciously decide to stop being as nice to their partners as they were initially; instead, their positive interactions gradually occur less frequently.

While the absence of explicit positive reciprocity may well decrease mutual attraction, an even worse pattern occurs among married couples. Over time, reciprocal negative evaluations are expressed more often. In close relationships, both males and females frequently assume that they have a license to nag and criticize each other. These instances of negative reciprocity obviously have a dampening effect on feelings of love and affection.

Once a relationship begins to deteriorate, each individual attributes good behaviors by the partner to external causes and bad behaviors to internal factors (Harvey, 1987). In general, when partners are dissatisfied, each emphasizes the negative behavior of the other person and minimizes the positive behavior (Baucom, Sayers, & Duhe, 1989). Conflictful words and deeds lead to their own circular reciprocity (Margolin, John, & O'Brien, 1989). As a result, when one partner withdraws, the other withdraws; when one is verbally aggressive, the other follows suit. In contrast, happy partners make attributions that en-

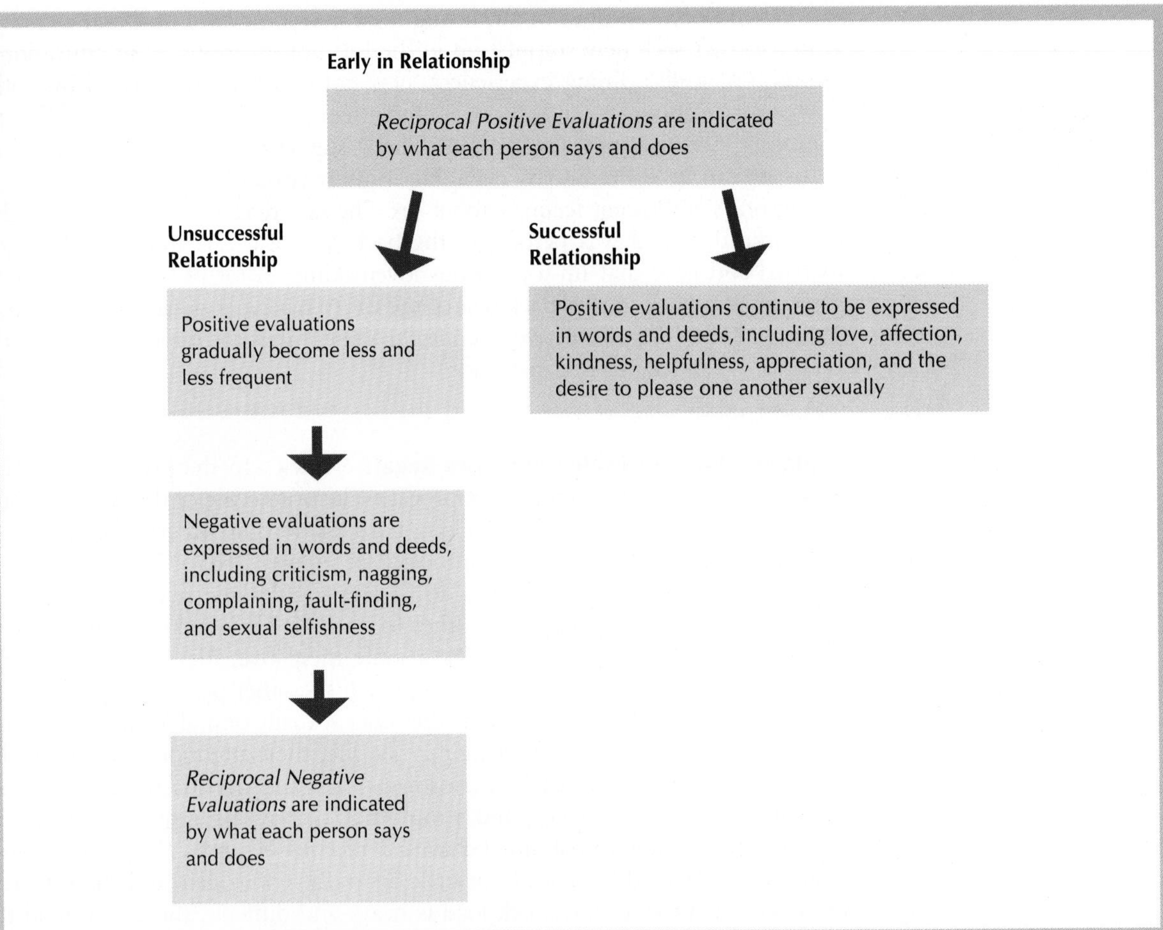

Early in Relationship

Reciprocal Positive Evaluations are indicated by what each person says and does

Unsuccessful Relationship

Positive evaluations gradually become less and less frequent

Negative evaluations are expressed in words and deeds, including criticism, nagging, complaining, fault-finding, and sexual selfishness

Reciprocal Negative Evaluations are indicated by what each person says and does

Successful Relationship

Positive evaluations continue to be expressed in words and deeds, including love, affection, kindness, helpfulness, appreciation, and the desire to please one another sexually

 Positive versus negative evaluations: Success versus failure

FIGURE 7.16 In successful relationships, reciprocal positive evaluations continue to be expressed over time. In unsuccessful relationships, such positive evaluations are expressed less and less frequently; they are replaced by reciprocal negative evaluations.

hance the relationship (Grigg, Fletcher, & Fitness, 1989), and positive acts elicit positive acts.

Deterioration of a Relationship: When a Couple Moves toward Dissolution

Levinger (1980) describes relationships as passing through five possible stages: initial attraction, building, continuation, and—for some—deterioration and ending. Table 7.5 provides examples of the factors operating at each stage. And whereas much of the past research on attraction and on relationships concentrated on the first two stages, a great deal of current research interest is concentrated on the final three stages.

Danger Signs in a Relationship Among the many friends you have had since your preschool days, most have probably slipped quietly out of your life. People

TABLE 7.5 Levinger (1980) proposed that relationships progress through five stages, from initial attraction to a problem period (deterioration) that can result in dissolution. At each stage are positive factors that cause the relationship to develop and to maintain itself and negative factors that can prevent the relationship from developing or cause it to fail.

Stage of Relationship	Positive Factors	Negative Factors
Initial Attraction	Propinquity and repeated exposure	Absence of propinquity and repeated exposure
	Positive emotions	Negative emotions
	High affiliative need and friendship motivation	Low affiliative need and friendship motivation
Building a Relationship	Equivalent physical attractiveness	Nonequivalent physical attractiveness
	Similarity of attitudes and other characteristics	Dissimilarity of attitudes and other characteristics
	Reciprocal positive evaluations	Reciprocal negative evaluations
Continuation	Seeking ways to maintain interest and variety	Falling into a rut and becoming bored
	Providing evidence of positive evaluation	Providing evidence of negative evaluation
	Absence of jealousy	Jealousy
	Perceived equity	Perceived inequity
	High level of mutual satisfaction	Low level of mutual satisfaction
Deterioration	Much time and effort invested in relationship	Little time and effort invested in relationship
	Work at improvement of relationship	Decide to end relationship
	Wait for improvement to occur	Wait for deterioration to continue
Ending	Existing relationship offers some rewards	A new life appears to be the only acceptable solution
	No alternative partners available	Alternative partners available
	Expect relationship to succeed	Expect relationship to fail
	Commitment to a continuing relationship	Lack of commitment to a continuing relationship

move to new locations, enter different schools, or develop divergent interests, and many friends simply become memories (Rose, 1984). When a relationship involves love, however, it is much harder to drift apart peacefully. Instead, there are often painful emotions, hurt feelings, and anger.

One of the reasons romantic relationships do not end easily is that they involve the investment of one's time, the exchange of powerful rewards, feelings of mutual commitment, and the perception that there are fewer and fewer acceptable alternative partners (Simpson, 1987). Availability of other partners plays a special role in relationships. When someone perceives few candidates to take the partner's place, he or she views the current relationship more positively and makes a greater commitment and time investment than when alternative partners are plentiful (Jemmott, Ashby, & Lindenfeld, 1989).

Deterioration begins, however, when at least one member of a couple perceives that the interactions are less desirable than they were previously. What does one do when a relationship begins a downward slide?

Responding to Relationship Problems The response to disharmony can be either active or passive (Rusbult & Zembrodt, 1983). Actively, individuals may decide to end the relationship ("exit" behaviors) or to work at improvement ("voice" behaviors). Passively, one can wait for improvement to occur ("loyalty" behaviors) or for things to get worse ("neglect" behaviors). This framework is outlined in Figure 7.17.

According to research conducted by Rusbult, Morrow, & Johnson (1990), individual differences in self-esteem (see Chapter 12) are associated with the two negative alternatives. These investigators found that among college students, older adults, and also gay and lesbian couples, those high in self-esteem were most likely to respond to deterioration with active exit behavior, while those low in self-esteem tended to engage in passive neglect. As these investigators suggest, an individual with positive self-regard responds to troubled relationships by searching for "greener pastures;" those with low self-regard take the ineffective path of least resistance and wait for the situation to get worse. These responses (exit and neglect) constitute the most destructive choices, and they are the major causes of distress (Rusbult, Johnson, & Morrow, 1986).

Whether a breakup is long and painful or a relatively rapid source of relief depends on how strongly the two people feel about each other (Lee, 1984). When love is very strong and the relationship fails, there is considerable unhappiness, fear, and loneliness. One or both individuals may be badly hurt when love turns to hate, and each partner blames the other for the failure. One young woman described her own experience with the painful dissolution of a relationship:

> We had a most awful scene yelling and screaming at each other, and that's where the situation ended. We both wanted out, but were both angry with the other for causing the hurt. I wanted out because he was still seeing his former wife. He, of course, denied this, but said that he wanted out because I wasn't giving him enough breathing space—always accusing him of cheating when not with me. (Baxter, 1984, p. 40.)

When the initial emotional bonds are weak, the ending of a relationship can be much simpler and much less upsetting. Both partners just agree that it's over, as in the following instance:

300 CHAPTER SEVEN CLOSE RELATIONSHIPS

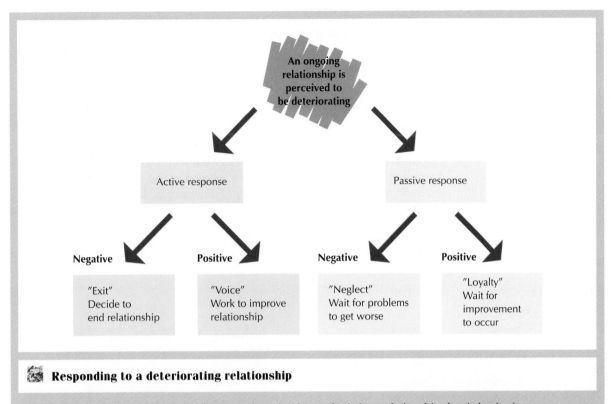

An ongoing relationship is perceived to be deteriorating

Active response | **Passive response**

Negative | **Positive** | **Negative** | **Positive**

"Exit"
Decide to end relationship

"Voice"
Work to improve relationship

"Neglect"
Wait for problems to get worse

"Loyalty"
Wait for improvement to occur

Responding to a deteriorating relationship

FIGURE 7.17 When an individual perceives that he or she is in a relationship that is beginning to fail, the response can be *active* or *passive*. Within each of these patterns, the person can assume that everything will work out (positive) or that a breakup will occur (negative). With a positive assumption, the person can work actively to improve the situation or wait passively for improvement. With a negative assumption, the person can act to end a bad situation or simply wait for things to get worse. If the relationship is worth saving, an active, positive response to the problem is the most adaptive. (Source: Based on suggestions by Rusbult & Zembrodt, 1983.)

My lover was a married man who was visiting overnight on his way through Portland. We had a bad night, with a lot of unstated tension by both of us. On the way to the airport next day, we hardly spoke at all. When we did speak it wasn't concerning our relationship. We both knew that it was over and we would probably never see each other again (and that we were both relieved that it was over). (Baxter, 1984, p. 40.)

Once the deterioration process is under way, a breakup is likely to occur. Sometimes one or both partners expect the relationship to fail because they have observed the failure of other relationships, such as their parents'. Sometimes things are so bad that the only reasonable solution for each individual is to start over with a new life. If three specific factors are present, however, a relationship has the potential to be maintained: a high level of satisfaction for each partner, the past investment of time and effort to build the relationship, and the absence of new lovers (Rusbult, 1980, 1983; Rusbult, Musante, & Soloman, 1982; Simpson, 1987).

What can two people do to save a troubled relationship? Several ideas are suggested in the following **Applied Side** section.

ON THE APPLIED SIDE

Rekindling Love

Though much of the research on marriage has focused on problems, it is helpful to remember that as many marriages succeed as fail. It can be instructive to examine these enduring relationships. For example, Lauer and Lauer (1985) surveyed 351 couples who had been married fifteen years or longer. The vast majority of these pairs said they were happily married. When asked to explain why their marriages had lasted, the most common responses (shown in Figure 7.18) stressed feelings of friendship, commitment, similarity, and positive affect.

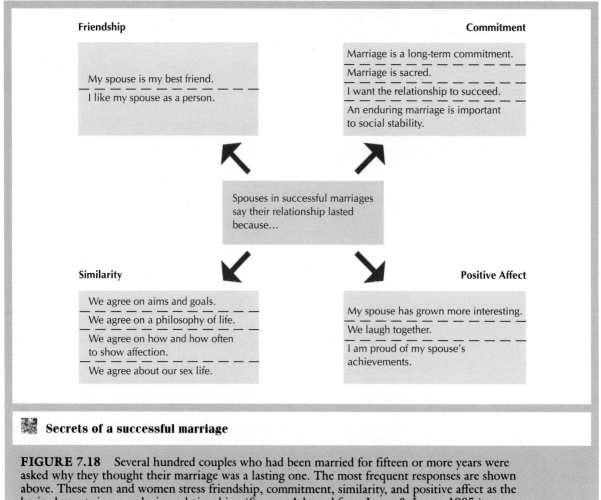

Friendship

My spouse is my best friend.
I like my spouse as a person.

Commitment

Marriage is a long-term commitment.
Marriage is sacred.
I want the relationship to succeed.
An enduring marriage is important to social stability.

Spouses in successful marriages say their relationship lasted because…

Similarity

We agree on aims and goals.
We agree on a philosophy of life.
We agree on how and how often to show affection.
We agree about our sex life.

Positive Affect

My spouse has grown more interesting.
We laugh together.
I am proud of my spouse's achievements.

Secrets of a successful marriage

FIGURE 7.18   Several hundred couples who had been married for fifteen or more years were asked why they thought their marriage was a lasting one. The most frequent responses are shown above. These men and women stress friendship, commitment, similarity, and positive affect as the basic elements in an enduring relationship. (Source: Adapted from Lauer & Lauer, 1985.)

In other words, the couples spontaneously described not passionate love but a relationship built on companionate love.

Is it possible to reverse the deterioration process and recapture the period when two people were in love and strongly attracted to each other? As Rusbult and her colleagues have suggested, those who passively wait for the situation to improve (loyalty) are apt to be disappointed (see Figure 7.19, p. 304). If there are basic problems to be faced and solved and if basic changes are necessary, waiting and hoping are not effective strategies. The active alternative (voice) requires hard work on the part of each partner. If the perception is simply that "it's all her fault" or "it's all his fault," little can be accomplished; if, however, a couple agrees that "we need to improve," much can be done.

When two people are in a committed relationship such as marriage, there presumably was a time when they found each other physically attractive, fun to be with, and sexually desirable. They shared similar attitudes, values, and interests and communicated their positive feelings to each other. If such was the case, their job now is to discover whether those elements are still part of the relationship and, if not, whether they can be reconstructed (Holmes & Boon, 1990). What are the principal issues on which to focus? The factors responsible for creating attraction and love that were discussed in this and the previous chapter would seem to be the best place to begin.

1. *Propinquity and affect.* In marriage, propinquity is usually ensured, but remember that repeated exposure involving negative interactions leads not to increased liking but to the reverse. The problem is not that physical proximity is lacking but that the interactions are not positive ones. Further, too much propinquity can mean a loss of privacy. Both partners need some time and space without intrusions.

Early in a relationship, couples seek pleasurable activities to enjoy together. In a marriage, it is easy to neglect the search for fun. Time at home often means cooking, cleaning, doing yard work, paying bills, making repairs, feeding the dog, taking care of offspring, having the car serviced, going to the dentist, and so on. Most of these chores and duties can't be avoided, but they can be shared in an equitable way (Castaneda, Hendrick, & Flanary, 1986). In addition, it is crucial to set aside time for enjoyable activities as a couple. As indicated earlier, attempts to counteract boredom are important. Partners can add variety to their lives in ways ranging from how they spend weekends to how they interact sexually.

2. *Affiliation and attractiveness.* Presumably, the relationship would not have formed initially were both individuals insufficiently motivated to seek affiliation. In a long-term relationship, however, friendship can be taken for granted. It is possible for couples to remain friendly and to interact as friends.

Attractiveness may in part be trivial, and it is partly beyond one's control. It *is* possible—and probably wise—to select attractive clothing and hairstyles, remain clean, shave, wear makeup, avoid obesity, and generally be as physically appealing as one's genes will allow. A good guide is whether you would go on a first date looking or smelling as you now do and dressed as you now are. If not, you may be subjecting your partner to you at your worst.

3. *Similarity and reciprocity.* We have already stressed the importance of knowing as much as possible about the other person early in the attraction process.

Maintaining a relationship requires making an effort

FIGURE 7.19 Though not many wedding cakes depict the bride and groom as shown in this cartoon, these figures portray what often happens as two people settle into a relationship and ignore the factors that created attraction and love in the first place. Social psychological research provides a great many suggestions about positive steps to take to recapture the couple's original positive feelings. (Drawing by Stuart Leeds; © 1987 The New Yorker Magazine, Inc.)

If unanticipated dissimilarities develop, about the best one can do is evaluate their central relevance to the relationship and consider compromise or avoidance. For a married couple, some dissimilarities can be crucial—marriage-relevant beliefs have more effect on dissatisfaction than do other beliefs (Jones & Stanton, 1988). If, for example, one partner wants to engage in particular sexual acts while the other finds those same acts repugnant and immoral, and if neither has any desire to change or compromise, not much can be done. This source of dissatisfaction is likely to continue and to have a negative effect on the couple's sexual interactions and on the total relationship (Smith et al., 1990). There are also areas of dissimilarity that are irrelevant and need not ever be discussed. If a husband and wife disagree strongly about their government's policy in Central America, why discuss it and make each other angry? Because neither of them has the power to set or change foreign policy, they might benefit by avoiding the topic entirely.

Earlier in this chapter we pointed out the importance of mutual evaluations. A conscious effort can be made to express that which is positive and to minimize stressing that which is negative.

These suggestions represent only a commonsensical extension of well-established factors identified in the study of attraction and love. Applying them in one's own everyday interactions is, however, more difficult than it sounds. The reward for such effort is the creation of a happy and satisfying relationship with a loved one. Those who don't bother to make that effort simply increase the odds that they will find themselves among the many unhappy couples on the road to a painful separation.

Breakup and Divorce About 2.4 million American couples marry each year, while an additional 1.2 million American couples are divorced. The rate of divorce has been rising steadily for many decades in this country, and in recent years the rate of increase has been greatest among African-Americans.

The critical years for divorce are during the second to sixth years of marriage when the spouses are in their thirties or early forties (Glick, 1983). Though some assume that urban life increases all social problems (see Chapter 13), the divorce rate is actually higher in rural settings than in big cities (Kelley, 1985a).

While both males and females suffer emotionally when a marriage falls apart, economic suffering is more likely to be a consequence for women than for men. For both sexes, those who do not remarry commonly respond with loneliness, depression, and long-lasting anger (Fischman, 1986; Renshaw, 1982).

When children are involved, they become the innocent victims of their parents' failure (Brody, Neubaum, & Forehand, 1988). Even four years after a divorce, children are found to evaluate their parents' separation in very negative terms (Kurdek et al., 1981). Because children generally remain with the mother following a divorce, they share in any economic hardships she faces. When parents divorce, their children, especially boys, frequently develop both academic and social problems (Guidubaldi et al., 1987). Even when the offspring are teenagers, they often respond to what happened with anxiety, negative self-perceptions, and the feeling that they lack control over their lives (Slater & Calhoun, 1988; Slater & Haber, 1984).

The most positive aspect of divorce is that most people seek out new partners and marry again (Goode, 1981). Remarriage is more likely for males than females, and males tend to remarry more quickly. If the second marriage also ends in divorce, those who go on to a third marriage are likely to stay married. In the United States, over two million people have been married three or more times, and that number is rising rapidly (Brody, Neubaum, & Forehand).

Research on relationships can help people make better decisions about entering romantic partnerships and provide an understanding of what is required to maintain a long-term relationship.

SUMMARY AND REVIEW

A crucial aspect of our lives is the establishment of close, loving *relationships*.

The Many Varieties of Love

Passionate love is an intense, sometimes sudden, emotional experience in which one's thoughts, feelings, and behaviors are concentrated on one individual. It appears that a person "falls in love" this way most easily if he or she has been raised to believe in such a phenomenon, comes into contact with an appropriate target person, and experiences physiological arousal during the interaction. Romantic affairs can begin anywhere, and the workplace is one common setting for both romance and *sexual harassment*. A close, caring friendship with a member of the opposite sex, **companionate love,** is less intense and more likely to last than is passionate love. Hendrick and Hendrick provide evidence that there are six types of love, while Sternberg has formulated a *triangular model of love* based on intimacy, passion, and decision/commitment.

Establishing and Maintaining Relationships

Love often means *sexual intimacy,* and couples in the twentieth century have faced dramatic changes over the past decades, first with increased permissiveness and more recently with a conservative shift in attitudes about premarital sex. The ultimate interpersonal goal for most people is *marriage,* but few realize the hard work required to make this relationship work. Threats to relationships include *jealousy* about a real or imagined rival.

When Relationships Fail

Among the many factors that contribute to trouble within a relationship and potentially to its breaking up are the discovery or development of *dissimilarities,* the experience of *boredom,* and the gradual substitution of negative for positive *reciprocity* in the couple's interactions. The hurt and anger of a deteriorating relationship often interferes with active attempts to improve the situation. Although many actions can help prevent dissolution, they are likely to be effective only if the relationship provides satisfaction for both partners, if both have invested time and effort in building the relationship, and if alternative partners are not easily available. The emotional pain of breaking up and the long-lasting effects on the two individuals and on any offspring they may have make it extremely important to attempt to maintain positive interactions and to counteract problems when they arise.

KEY TERMS

Acquired immune deficiency syndrome (AIDS) A viral STD for which there is no cure. To date, AIDS is fatal.

Chlamydia A common bacterial STD that causes a painful skin lesion.

Cognitive therapy Psychotherapy in which the emphasis is on altering the client's maladaptive thought processes.

Companionate love Love that rests on a firm base of friendship, common interests, mutual respect, and concern for the other person's happiness and welfare.

Decision/commitment In Sternberg's triangular model of love, the cognitive elements involved in deciding to form a relationship and in being committed to it.

Genital herpes A viral STD caused by herpes simplex type 2. To date, no cure has been found, but the symptoms that accompany its repeated outbreaks can be alleviated.

Gonorrhea A bacterial STD characterized by a mucous discharge and painful urination. The symptoms are more noticeable in males than in females.

Intimacy In Sternberg's triangular model of love, the closeness or bondedness of the two partners.

Jealousy The thoughts, feelings, and actions that are instigated by a real or imagined rival. Such a rival is a threat to the relationship and to one's self-esteem.

Loneliness The personality disposition that characterizes those who want to form relationships but fail to do so. The lonely individual feels unhappy and isolated, lacking the social skills to overcome the problem.

Love An emotional state involving attraction, sexual desire, and concern about another person. Love represents the most positive level of attraction. Several quite different kinds of love have been described by various theorists.

Passion In Sternberg's triangular model of love, the sexual drives and sexual arousal associated with the interpersonal relationship.

Passionate love An intense and often unrealistic emotional response to another person. This response is interpreted by the individuals involved as "true love," while observers often interpret it as "infatuation."

Relationship Closeness Inventory A scale that measures the closeness of two individuals in a romantic, friendly, or family relationship.

Sexual harassment Unwelcome sexual advances or requests for sexual acts, usually from a male in a position of power within an organization to a female in a lower-status position.

Sexually transmitted disease (STD) An infection that is transmitted by means of sexual contact.

Social skills training A therapeutic intervention that teaches individuals what to do and say in interpersonal interactions.

Triangular model of love Sternberg's formulation that conceptualizes love relationships in terms of the relative emphasis placed on intimacy, passion, and decision/commitment.

UCLA Loneliness Scale A personality test that assesses the extent to which an individual feels lonely and isolated from others.

FOR MORE INFORMATION

Duck, S., & Perlman, D. (Eds.). (1986). *Understanding personal relationships: An interdisciplinary approach.* London: Sage.

A compilation designed to integrate the work on personal relationships conducted by social psychologists, sociologists, clinical psychologists, and those interested in family studies. The book constitutes an optimistic report on the progress being made in a rapidly growing field of research interest.

Hojat, M., & Crandall, R. (1989). *Loneliness: Theory, research, and applications.* Newbury Park, CA: Sage.

An up-to-date summary of the study of loneliness. Topics include the development of loneliness, attributional models, loneliness among the elderly, and therapeutic approaches.

Hendrick, C. (Ed.). (1989). *Close relationships.* Newbury Park, CA: Sage.

Chapters written by leading investigators covering close friendships, romantic relationships, and marriage. Among the issues addressed are behavior and satisfaction in marriage, emotional communication, trust, jealousy, and date rape.

Sternberg, R., & Barnes, M. (Eds.). (1988). *The psychology of love.* New Haven, CT: Yale University Press.

These chapters, written for the nonprofessional, present recent theories and findings on the nature of love.

CHAPTER
Eight

Social Influence: Changing
Others' Behavior

A̲s he finishes clearing the last of the dishes from their table, Todd Geier, a waiter at the Pine Hills restaurant, asks the three female diners, "Can I interest any of you ladies in dessert?"

The reactions of the three women are almost immediate. Pam Linder shudders visibly. "No, no . . . not for me," she answers quickly, as if recoiling from some imminent danger. "I couldn't possibly!"

"Hm . . . ," Stephanie Barrick comments, as she considers the possibility. "Let's see, I *did* have that roll with my salad, and I also drank a Pepsi. No, I better skip it. I'm over my quota already."

Now it's Linda Roper's turn. Her response, too, is rapid: "What have you got?" she asks, with obvious interest. And then, after hearing the waiter's recital of the available temptations, she opts for "Death by Chocolate," the richest, most calorie-laden choice on the menu.

While she is eating it, her two friends show varying degrees of discomfort. Pam has turned pale and tries to avoid even looking in Linda's direction as she consumes her dessert with signs of pleasure. In fact, Pam, after a few moments, murmurs something about fixing her hair and rushes from the table. Stephanie, too, looks uncomfortable but reacts somewhat differently. It is clear that she'd dearly love some of the dessert, too, but feels guilty about having any.

"Gee, this is really great!" Linda remarks, fork poised in midair. "The name is right on target. It's so good I practically feel weak in the knees. Are you sure you don't want any?"

"I'd love to, but you know how it is," Stephanie replies. "I really want to lose those three pounds, and that won't help any!"

"But why do you want to lose weight? You look great. And doesn't Bob always say that he likes you a little on the plump side?"

"Yeah, he does. But I don't know—it seems so important to stay slim these days. Everyone works at it so hard, too."

"People work at it, all right," Linda agrees, "and what they get for their efforts, mainly, is a lot of misery. Not me—I'm not buying it. I'm never going to look like one of those models on TV, so why torture myself trying?"

"You're probably right," Stephanie agrees, "but I'm always afraid that if I start thinking that way, I'll end up being a blimp. Not everyone's as lucky as you. We can't eat anything we want without gaining an ounce. Honestly, it ought to be illegal!"

At this comment, both friends laugh. But their amusement is cut short by Pam's return to the table. "Gee, aren't you done yet?" she comments, noting that her friend is still consuming her rich dessert. Pam's discomfort and impatience are so obvious that Linda pauses for a moment and then, with a sigh, pushes the plate away.

"Yeah, I'm done. I'm too full to hold that last mouthful. Let's go. We'll just make it back to the office on time if we leave right now."

Have you ever witnessed or participated in a scene like this one? Living in the 1990s, the chances are good that you have. Everyone, it seems, wants to be slim. And while this goal is sought somewhat more intensely by women than by men, the thin-equals-beautiful notion seems to be accepted by many members of both sexes.

Now, take a step back from this widespread attitude and ask yourself the following question: Why, precisely, do so many people want to be thin? Your answer is probably some variation on the following theme: Because they believe it will make them more attractive. In short, you realize that modern standards of beauty (at least, in many Western nations) include *slimness* as one of their central characteristics. At present, this belief is so pervasive that we more or less take it for granted. Yet if you ever watch old movies or leaf through old magazines, you probably realize that such views have not always been widely accepted. During the 1940s and 1950s, for example, popular ideas of feminine beauty emphasized a well-rounded shape, even to the point of plumpness. And going back still further, we find that slimness was highly valued during the 1920s, when flappers worked hard to attain a slender shape. (Incidentally, popular ideas about male attractiveness, too, have changed over time. These shifts have generally focused on hairstyles and aspects of personal grooming rather than on a man's overall figure.)

The fact that ideas about beauty and attractiveness change radically is not a new one in this text; we discussed it in detail in Chapter 6. Here, however, we wish to emphasize the fact that whatever these ideas happen to be at a given time and in a specific culture, *most people do their best to live up to them.* They accept the definition of beauty offered by their own society and try hard to approach it as closely as possible. The fact that they do illustrates the central theme of the present chapter: In many instances, our perceptions, attitudes, and actions are strongly affected by other persons, either individually or collectively. In short, our behavior and thoughts are very different from what they would be if we lived in total social isolation. The process through which others affect us in this manner is known as **social influence,** and as you already realize, it alters much more than just our ideas concerning beauty. Indeed, social influence is so pervasive and so powerful in its impact that few things we do, think, or feel are unaffected by it (refer to Figure 8.1, p. 312).

In this chapter we will focus on several key aspects of social influence—the many ways in which our thoughts or actions are changed by others. First, we'll consider **conformity,** instances in which individuals alter their behavior in order to adhere to existing *social norms*—widely accepted ideas or rules indicating how people *should* behave in certain situations. This process was illustrated by the behavior of two of the characters in our opening story. Both Pam and Stephanie have apparently accepted the thin-equals-beautiful rule (norm) described above. As a result, their actions are quite different from what they might be in the absence of such acceptance. The third character, Linda, has overtly rejected this norm, and partly for this reason her behavior in this situation is unlike that of her two friends.

In contrast to conformity, a second major form of social influence—**compliance**—is exerted directly by individuals rather than by beliefs or norms. Compliance involves efforts by one person to alter the behavior of one or more others through direct requests or similar tactics. Many techniques for enhancing compliance—for increasing the likelihood that a target person will say yes—exist. We will consider several of them below.

Finally, in a third form of social influence—**obedience**—one person simply orders others to change their behavior in specific ways. Usually, the persons who issue such orders have some means of enforcing submission to them—they hold *power* over those on the receiving end. Surprisingly, though, direct orders can sometimes be effective even when the persons who employ them actually have little or no authority over the recipients.

For each of these main types of social influence, we'll examine why they seem to work—why they are effective in changing others' behavior. In addition, we'll examine factors that determine their degree of effectiveness in this regard—conditions that influence their success in changing the actions of target persons.

"A fantastic evangelist was on TV, and I sent him everything."

Social influence in action

FIGURE 8.1 While the effects of social influence are not always as dramatic as those shown here, this process affects many aspects of our lives. (Drawing by W. Miller; © 1987 The New Yorker Magazine, Inc.)

Conformity: How Groups Exert Influence

Have you ever found yourself in a situation in which you felt you stuck out like the proverbial sore thumb? If so, you have already had firsthand experience with pressures toward *conformity*. In such situations, you probably felt a strong desire to "get back into line"—to fit in with the other people around you. Such pressures toward conformity seem to stem from the fact that in many situations, both spoken and unspoken rules indicate how we ought to behave. These rules are known as **social norms** and, in some instances, can be quite detailed and precise. For example, governments often function through constitutions and written laws; athletic contests are usually regulated by written rules; and signs in many public places (e.g., along highways, in parks and airports) frequently describe expected behavior in considerable detail.

In contrast, other norms are unspoken, or implicit. Most of us obey such unwritten rules as "Don't stare at strangers on the street" and "Don't arrive at parties or other social gatherings exactly on time." We are often strongly influenced by current and rapidly changing standards of dress, speech, and personal grooming. Regardless of whether social norms are explicit or implicit, people obey most of them most of the time. For example, few people visit restaurants without leaving at least some tip for their server. And virtually everyone, regardless of personal political beliefs, stands when the national anthem is played at sports events and other public gatherings.

At first glance, this strong tendency toward conformity—toward going along with society's expectations about how we should behave in various situations—may strike you as objectionable. After all, it does prevent people from "doing their own thing." Actually, though, there is a strong basis for the existence of so much conformity: Without it, we would quickly find ourselves in the midst of social chaos. Imagine what would happen outside movie theaters or voting booths and at supermarket checkout counters if people did not follow the simple rule, "Form a line and wait your turn." (By the way, this rule is not universal. In fact, as shown in Figure 8.2, it is entirely absent in some cultures—with predictable results.) Similarly, consider the danger to both drivers and pedestrians if there were no clear and widely followed traffic regulations. In many situations, then, conformity serves a useful function. But please note: This idea in no way implies that conformity is always helpful. At times, norms governing individual behavior appear to have no obvious purpose; they simply exist. For example, Western-style dress (suits and ties for men, dresses or suits for women) has become the standard for business dress around the world, despite the facts that (1) business can obviously be conducted in any style of clothing and (2) Western-style garb was designed for use in cool European climates and is inappropriate in many other locations. The norm requiring that such clothing be worn can therefore be viewed as inflicting needless discomfort on millions of persons for no obvious, compelling reason.

Whatever their precise origins, it is clear that powerful pressures toward conformity exist in many settings. It is surprising to learn, therefore, that conformity, as a social process, was not studied in detail until the 1950s. At that time, Solomon Asch (1951) carried out a series of experiments that added much to our knowledge of this important form of social influence. (For a description of his research, please see the following **Classic Contributions** section.)

Social norms: An important factor in human behavior

FIGURE 8.2 In some nations, there are norms suggesting that people waiting outside theaters or using public transportation should form a line and wait their turn (left photo). In other nations, however, such norms are absent, with predictable results (right photo).

FOCUS ON RESEARCH: CLASSIC CONTRIBUTIONS

Group Pressure and Personal Judgments: What Do You Do When Your Own Eyes and Other Persons Disagree?

Suppose that just before an important exam, you discover that your answer to a homework problem is different from that obtained by another member of the class. How do you react? Probably with mild concern. Now, imagine that you learn that a second person's answer, too, is different from yours. To make matters worse, it agrees with the answer reported by the first person. How would you feel *now*? The chances are good that your anxiety would rise to high levels. Next, you discover that a third person agrees with the other two. At this point, you know that you are in *big* trouble. Which answer should you accept— yours or the one obtained by your three classmates? There's no time to find out, for at this moment the exam starts. Sure enough, the first questions relate to this specific problem. Which answer should you choose? Can all three of your friends be wrong while you are right?

Life is filled with such dilemmas—instances in which we discover that our own judgments, actions, or conclusions are different from those of others. What do we and others do in such cases? The answer is provided by a series of studies conducted by Asch (1951) that are considered true classics in social psychology.

In his research, Asch asked subjects to respond to a series of simple perceptual problems like the one in Figure 8.3. On each problem, participants indicated which of three comparison lines matched a standard line in length. Several other persons (usually six to eight) were also present during the session, but unknown to the subject, all were accomplices of the experimenter. On pre-arranged occasions (twelve out of eighteen problems) the accomplices offered answers that were clearly wrong (e.g., they unanimously stated that line A matched the standard line in Figure 8.3). Moreover, they gave their answers before the subject gave his. Thus, on such trials subjects faced the kind of dilemma described above. Should they go along with the other persons present, or stick with their own judgments? A large majority of the subjects opted to do the former; indeed, fully 76 percent of those tested in several different studies

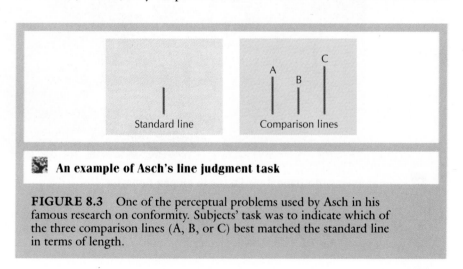

An example of Asch's line judgment task

FIGURE 8.3 One of the perceptual problems used by Asch in his famous research on conformity. Subjects' task was to indicate which of the three comparison lines (A, B, or C) best matched the standard line in terms of length.

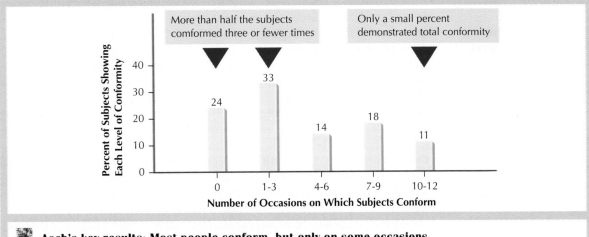

Asch's key results: **Most people conform, but only on some occasions**

FIGURE 8.4 While most subjects in Asch's research conformed on at least one occasion, a majority resisted group pressure most of the time. For example, fully 58 percent conformed three times or less during the twelve critical trials (occasions when the accomplices gave false answers). (Source: Based on data from Asch, 1957.)

went along with the group's false answers at least once. In contrast, only 5 percent of the subjects in a control group—one that responded to the same problems in the absence of any accomplices—made such errors.

Although most subjects conformed at least once, it is important to note that on many other occasions they did resist such influence. As shown in Figure 8.4, almost 24 percent never conformed and many others yielded on only a few of the trials on which the accomplices gave wrong answers. Yet, a large majority did conform to the accomplices' false responses, and the implicit norm these generated, at least part of the time. These results, and those obtained in later studies (Tanford & Penrod, 1984), point to an unsettling conclusion: many persons find it easier to publicly contradict the evidence of their own senses than to disagree openly with the unanimous judgments of other persons—even those of total strangers.

In later research, Asch (1957) repeated the above procedures with one important change: Instead of stating their answers aloud, subjects wrote them on a piece of paper. As you might guess, the incidence of conformity dropped sharply—a finding that points to the importance of distinguishing between *public compliance* (doing or saying what others around us say or do) and *private acceptance* (actually coming to feel or think as they do). Often, it appears, we overtly adhere to social norms or yield to group pressure without changing our private views or interpretations of the social world (Maas & Clark, 1984). Thus, in Asch's research and in many real-life situations, too, individuals may modify their overt actions so as to "get into line" with others, while at the same time keeping their personal views largely intact. We will return to this distinction between public compliance and private acceptance at several points in this chapter.

Factors Affecting Conformity: Cohesiveness, Group Size, Social Support, and Gender

Although Asch's research demonstrated the existence of powerful pressures toward conformity, even a moment's reflection indicates that conformity does not occur to the same degree in all settings or among all persons. This point raises an intriguing question: What factors determine the extent to which people yield to conformity pressure? Many variables play a role in this process, but among these, four have received primary attention: (1) *cohesiveness,* the degree of attraction to the group or persons exerting influence; (2) group *size,* how many persons are exerting influence; (3) the presence or absence of *social support;* and (4) the gender of those who are exposed to conformity pressure.

Cohesiveness and Conformity: Accepting Influence from Those We Like
Consider the following situation. After graduating from college, you go to work for a large corporation. You like your job and feel you have a bright future with the company. There's only one minor problem. In the past, you have considered yourself to be politically moderate with a slight preference for Democratic candidates. Now, however, you discover that most of your coworkers are relatively conservative. They repeatedly voice their opposition to wasteful government programs and criticize judges who in their opinion are too lenient toward criminals. Will your own views change as a result of exposure to these statements? Perhaps. You may find yourself agreeing with your new colleagues more and more as time passes. And even if you do not, you may demonstrate the kind of public compliance noted above, voicing agreement with your coworkers from time to time, even if you don't really share their views.

Now, in contrast, imagine that you have signed up for an evening course in personal self-defense. During the sessions, you hear other members of the class express extremely conservative views about law and order, the right to own guns, and punishing criminals. Will you be influenced by these statements? Probably not. In fact, the chances are good that you will pay little if any attention to such statements. Why do you react so differently in these two contexts? Partly because of contrasting levels of attraction to these different groups of persons. While you like your coworkers very much and want to gain their acceptance, you are fairly neutral toward the people in your self-defense class. Thus, you have strong motivation for agreeing with people where you work but little motivation for adopting the views of students in your evening class. In social psychology, such differences in attraction toward a particular group or its individual members is usually described by the term *cohesiveness.* And there is little doubt about its impact on conformity. In general, when cohesiveness is high (i.e., when we are strongly attracted to a group and want badly to be accepted by it), pressures toward conformity are much greater than when cohesiveness is low (Forsyth, 1983). This is one basic reason why most persons are much more willing to accept social influence from friends or persons they admire than from others.

A compelling illustration of the impact of cohesiveness on conformity is provided by a study conducted by Crandall (1988). In this investigation, members of two different sororities completed questionnaires designed to measure patterns of friendship within these social organizations (i.e., who was friends with whom) and tendencies toward the potentially serious health problem of binge eating. (Binge eating involves periods during which individuals report uncontrollable urges to eat and actually consume tremendous amounts of food. It does not necessarily involve subsequent efforts to purge oneself.) Both questionnaires were completed by members of the two sororities on two occasions: at the start of the academic year and when it was nearly over. This time frame allowed Crandall to determine whether shifts in friendship patterns over time would be related to changes in tendencies toward binge eating. Specifically, Crandall hypothesized that the young women who participated in the study would report becoming more like their friends with respect to binge eating as time passed and bonds of friendship (cohesiveness) deepened.

The results of the study indicated that friendship cliques formed within the two sororities and tended to become stronger over time. (Members of such friendship groups identified one another as "best friends" more uniformly at the end of the year than at the beginning.) Even more important, members of those friendship groups, for whom cohesion was high, tended to become increasingly like one another in terms of binge eating. Initially, friends were no more similar to one another in this respect than they were to other members of the sorority. After approximately seven months had passed, however, their patterns of binge eating grew increasingly similar (refer to Table 8.1).

Additional findings indicated that relatively clear social norms concerning binge eating had emerged and were operating in both sororities. The nature of those norms, however, differed in the two organizations. In one sorority, the more individuals binged, the more popular they were. In the other, women were most popular when they engaged in binge eating with moderate frequency; binging too often or not often enough reduced their popularity.

Together, Crandall's findings provide a clear illustration that the more we like others and wish to gain their approval, the more likely we are to be influenced by them. Moreover, her findings help underscore the fact that pressures toward conformity can affect virtually any aspect of behavior—even something as basic as eating habits.

Conformity and Group Size: Why "More" Isn't Always "Better" with Respect to Social Influence A second factor that exerts important effects on the tendency

---

Cohesiveness and binge eating in two sororities

TABLE 8.1 As cohesiveness (mutual friendship choices) increased, friends in two sororities became more similar in terms of their tendencies to engage in binge eating.

	First Sorority		Second Sorority	
	Fall	Spring	Fall	Spring
Percentage of mutual friendship choices	87.2 → 89.4		82.3 → 85.4	
Similarity in binge eating (correlation)	.00 → .21		−.15 → .40	

Source: Based on data from Crandall, 1988.

to conform is the size of the influencing group. Studies designed to investigate this relationship indicate that up to a point—about three or four members—conformity does increase with rising group size. Beyond this level, however, further increments in group size produce less and additional effect (e.g., Gerard, Wilhelmy, & Conolley, 1968). Why is this the case? One reason seems to be that as group size rises beyond three or four members, persons exposed to social pressure begin to suspect *collusion*. They conclude that group members are neither expressing individual views nor behaving in accordance with individual preferences. Rather, they are working together to exert influence (Wilder, 1977). This conclusion makes a great deal of sense; after all, it is rare to find all the people around us agreeing unanimously with one another; more often, they hold varying opinions and express a wide range of actions and preferences. Hence, when too many people agree, it may be a signal that it is time to be on guard.

Regardless of the reason for this leveling off in conformity pressure as group size mounts, another complication enters the picture. Groups do not always seek to exert influence on a single holdout member. On the contrary, conformity pressure may be directed to several persons rather than to only one. How does this factor operate? One answer is provided by a theory known as the **social influence model,** or SIM (Tanford & Penrod, 1984). This model suggests that the function relating group size to conformity or social influence is S-shaped in form (refer to Figure 8.5). At first, each person added to the group (each additional source of influence) produces a larger increment in conformity pressure than the one before. Soon, however, this function levels off, so that each additional person adds *less* to the total amount of influence than did the preceding ones. The SIM also suggests that as the number of targets of social influence increases, the shape of the function relating group size to conformity becomes flatter (see Fig. 8.5), because the impact of the influencing group is now spread over several target persons rather than a single holdout.

Is the SIM model accurate? Some evidence suggests that it is. When Tanford and Penrod (1984) applied their model to the findings of many previous studies dealing with the impact of group size on conformity, they found that this model predicted the obtained results quite accurately. Thus, the SIM appears to provide a useful description of how pressures toward conformity vary with the size of the group and the number of persons who are the target of such influence.

We should note, however, that recent findings (Tindale, Davis, Vollrath, & Nagao, 1990) suggest that it does not take account of several factors that may also determine patterns of influence within freely interacting groups. Thus, this model will require further development and refinement before it can be viewed as fully verified.

The Effects of Support from Others: When Having an Ally Helps   In Asch's research and in many later studies of conformity, subjects were exposed to social pressure from a unanimous group. All the other persons present seemed to hold views different from their own. Under such conditions, it is hardly surprising that most subjects yielded to social pressure. What would happen, though, if persons facing such pressure discovered they had an *ally*—someone who shared their views, or at least failed to accept the position of the majority? Perhaps under such conditions, conformity would be reduced. That it actually is reduced is indicated by the results of several experiments (e.g., Allen & Levine, 1971; Morris & Miller, 1975). In these studies, subjects provided with an ally or

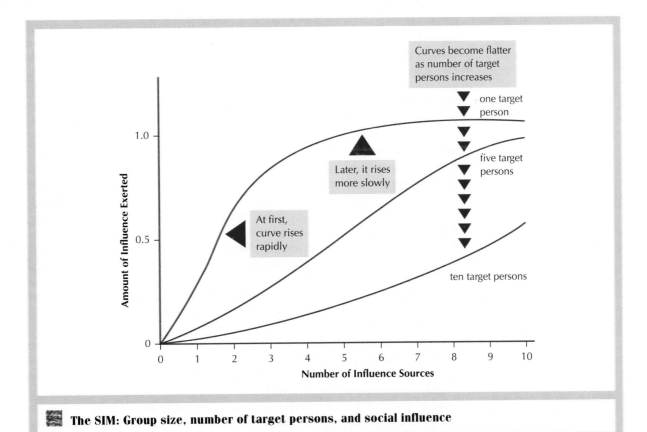

At first, curve rises rapidly

Later, it rises more slowly

Curves become flatter as number of target persons increases

one target person

five target persons

ten target persons

The SIM: Group size, number of target persons, and social influence

FIGURE 8.5 According to the *social influence model* (SIM), social influence initially rises rapidly as group size increases. Soon, however, this function levels off, so that adding more group members has less and less effect. The model also predicts that the curve relating group size to social influence becomes flatter as the number of target persons grows, because the influence exerted is divided among an increasing number of persons. (Source: Based on suggestions by Tanford & Penrod, 1984.)

partner showed much less conformity than ones who did not receive such social support.

Perhaps the importance of such support in reducing conformity is best illustrated by two additional points. First, conformity is reduced even when the partner or ally is someone not competent in the present situation. For example, in one study involving visual judgments, conformity was reduced even by a partner who wore thick glasses and could not see the relevant stimuli (Allen & Levine, 1971). Second, it is not even crucial that the ally share the subject's views. Conformity is reduced even if this person merely differs from the other group members—breaks their united front in some manner.

These and other findings suggest that almost any form of social support can be helpful from the point of view of resisting social pressure. As you might guess, though, certain forms of support are more effective than others. For example, it appears that support received early—before pressures toward conformity have increased—is more effective than support received later (Morris,

Miller, & Spangenberg, 1977). Apparently, learning that someone else shares their views can help strengthen individuals' ability to resist group pressure as it grows. This fact has important implications for many real-life settings. If you ever find yourself in a situation in which pressures toward conformity are rising and you feel that they should be resisted, try to speak out as quickly as possible. The sooner you do, the greater your chances of rallying others to your side and resisting the majority.

Gender Differences in Conformity: Evidence Against Their Existence Suppose that you approached a hundred people at random in some public place (e.g., a large shopping mall) and asked them the following question: "Do women and men differ in terms of their tendencies to conform?" What would you find? Even today, the chances are good that many respondents would identify females as higher in conformity than males. As evidence for this supposed difference, they might note that women are more likely than men to adhere to the changing dictates of fashion or that women are more concerned with being liked and pleasing others.

Are such views correct? Are women truly more susceptible to conformity pressure than men? Early studies seemed to suggest that they are (e.g., Crutchfield, 1955), indicating that women do indeed show greater conformity or yield more to social pressure than men. More recent investigations, however, point to very different conclusions (e.g., Eagly & Carli, 1981), suggesting that there are no differences between the sexes in this respect. What accounts for the sharply contrasting findings in these two groups of studies? One crucial factor involves the nature of the tasks and materials used in the early investigations (those conducted during the 1950s and 1960s). In many of these studies, the tasks employed were more familiar to males than to females. Since individuals generally yield more readily to social influence when they are uncertain about how to behave than when they are more confident in this regard, it is hardly surprising that females demonstrated higher levels of conformity.

That this factor was indeed responsible for the sex differences obtained in early research is indicated by the results of an experiment performed by Sistrunk and McDavid (1971). These researchers found that when females were less familiar than males with the items used, they did in fact show greater yielding to group pressure. However, when the tables were turned so that the items used were less familiar to males, it was *they* who showed greater conformity. Thus, in efforts to compare the sexes in terms of susceptibility to social pressure, we must be careful to avoid confounding gender with an additional, unrelated factor—familiarity with the items or tasks about which such pressure is exerted.

Additional evidence for the conclusion that the sexes do not differ in conformity is provided by two other lines of research. The first has focused on the following possibility: One reason why many persons continue to believe that females are easier to influence than males is that in general, females have lower status (Eagly, 1987). Since persons holding low status *are* often easier to influence than those holding higher status, this difference between the sexes may at least partly account for the popularity of the view that females are more susceptible to conformity pressure. Support for this reasoning has been obtained in several studies conducted by Eagly and her colleagues (e.g., Steffen & Eagly, 1985). In one such investigation, for example, Eagly and Wood (1982) asked men and women to read a brief story in which one employee of a business attempted to influence the views of another employee of the opposite sex. In half the cases, the would-be influencer was male and the target person was female; in the remainder, the reverse was true. In half the stories, job titles were included, thus informing subjects of the status of the persons involved. In the remaining instances, no such information was included.

After reading the story, subjects were asked to indicate the extent to which the target person would be influenced. It was hypothesized that when no information on status was provided, subjects would tend to assume that females held lower status than males and would thus predict greater compliance by female targets than by male targets. When information on status was provided, however, this factor—not sex—was expected to affect subjects' judgments. Both hypotheses were confirmed: When information on status was absent, subjects predicted greater yielding by females; when information on status was present, they predicted greater yielding by low- than by high-status targets, regardless of gender.

Finally, evidence that the sexes do not differ in conformity is provided by research addressing the specific tactics used by women and men to influence others (Rule, Bisanz, & Kohn, 1985). The results of such investigations suggest that the two sexes tend to use the same tactics for influencing others and to move from one tactic to another in the same order. For example, in one of these studies, Bisanz and Rule (1989) asked male and female students to read descriptions of situations in which either a man or a woman was attempting to influence another person (a friend or the student's father). Subjects were also provided with a list of various influence tactics that might be used in such situations (see Table 8.2 on p. 322). They were then asked to rate how likely they would be to employ each of these tactics and to what extent they approved of their use. As shown in Figure 8.6, both male and female subjects assigned very similar ratings to the various tactics. These findings do not directly address

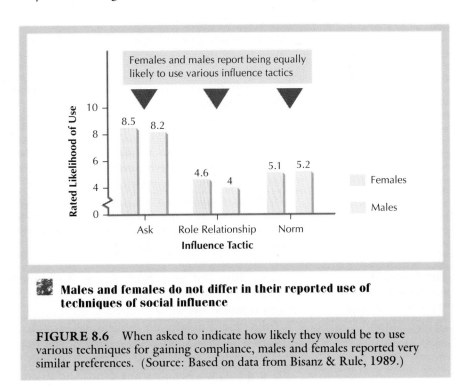

Males and females do not differ in their reported use of techniques of social influence

FIGURE 8.6   When asked to indicate how likely they would be to use various techniques for gaining compliance, males and females reported very similar preferences. (Source: Based on data from Bisanz & Rule, 1989.)

Different methods for gaining compliance

TABLE 8.2 Various techniques for gaining compliance.

Name of Technique	Description
Ask	Simply present request
Present information	Offer facts or evidence to persuade target person
Mention personal benefits	Indicate how target will benefit from complying
Mention relationship	Mention existing relationship between requester and target
Bargain	Offer to do something for target in return
Invoke norm	Indicate that others would comply
Make moral appeal	Make appeal to a moral value (e.g., "It's the right thing to do")
Butter up	Make target feel good in some manner (e.g., flattery)
Emotional appeal	Beg, plead, throw a tantrum, sulk
Criticize	Attack target for not complying
Deceive	Mislead target to gain compliance
Threaten	Threaten target to gain compliance
Force	Use force to gain compliance

Based on information from Bisanz & Rule, 1989.

the possibility that males and females will react differently to such tactics when they are on the receiving end of them. However, they do indicate that the two sexes think about and actually use social influence in ways that are quite similar. In view of this fact, there seem to be few if any grounds for assuming that they differ in the tendency to conform.

At this point, we should note that this absence of major sex differences extends to other aspects of social influence as well (Eagly, 1987). Contrary to popular belief, females do *not* demonstrate greater tendencies to yield to attempts to change their behavior or attitudes than males do. Moreover, consistent with the findings reported by Rule and her colleagues, when females hold positions of authority they tend to exert influence and to behave in much the same manner as males (Eagly & Johnson, 1990). In general, then, it appears that differences between the sexes with respect to many aspects of social influence are more illusory than real.

The Bases of Conformity: Why We Often Choose to "Go Along"

As we have just seen, many factors determine whether and to what extent conformity will occur. Despite such variations, one fact is clear: Conformity is very common. As we noted before, most people conform to most norms most of the time. But why do they do so? Why do people so often choose to go along with the expectations of others, the rules of society, or the norms of various groups to which they belong? Certainly, there are no simple answers to these questions. Many factors contribute to our strong tendency to conform.

CHAPTER EIGHT   SOCIAL INFLUENCE

The most important of these, however, seems to involve two basic needs possessed by all human beings: the desire to be liked and the desire to be right (Insko, 1985).

The Desire to Be Liked: Normative Social Influence   How can we induce others to like us? This is one of the eternal puzzles of social life. As we noted in Chapter 6, many strategies can prove effective in this regard. One of the most successful, though, is to appear to be as similar to others as possible. From our earliest days we learn that agreeing with the persons around us and behaving much as they do cause them to like us. Parents, teachers, friends, and others often heap praise and approval on us for demonstrating such similarity. One important reason we conform, therefore, is simple: We have learned that doing so can yield the approval and acceptance we so strongly crave. Conformity stemming from this source is known as **normative social influence,** since it involves altering our behavior to meet others' expectations. Clearly, it is a common aspect of daily life.

The Desire to Be Right: Informational Social Influence   If you want to determine the dimensions of a room, you can measure them directly. Similarly, if you want to know the population of a particular city, you can look it up in an atlas. But how can you establish the "accuracy" of various political views or decide which hairstyle others will find most attractive? There are no simple physical tests or handy references to consult. Yet most of us have just as strong a desire to be right about such matters as about questions relating to the physical world. The solution is obvious: To answer such questions, or at least to obtain information about them, we turn to other people. We use *their* opinions and *their* actions as guides for our own. This second important source of conformity is known as **informational social influence,** and it, too, is a basic part of everyday life. In countless situations we choose to act and think as others do because doing so assures us that we are "right"—or at least not too out of line with others.

Together, normative and informational social influence provide a strong basis for our tendency to conform—to act in accordance with existing social norms and with the social roles they often dictate. In short, there is nothing mysterious about the compelling and pervasive occurrence of conformity; it stems directly from basic needs and motives that can be fulfilled only when we do indeed decide to "go along." (For a chilling illustration of the powerful impact of social norms and pressures toward conformity, please see the **Classic Contributions** section below.)

FOCUS ON RESEARCH: CLASSIC CONTRIBUTIONS

Testing the Limits of Social Influence: Life in a Simulated Prison

Imagine the following events. One peaceful Sunday, you hear a loud knock on your door. When you answer, you find yourself facing several police officers. Without a word of explanation, they place you under arrest and take you downtown, where you are photographed, fingerprinted, and booked. You are then blindfolded and driven to a prison whose location you can only guess.

Once there, you are stripped of all your clothes and forced to wear an uncomfortable, shapeless garment and a tight nylon cap. All your personal possessions are removed, and you are given an ID number in place of your name. Then you are locked in an empty cell. Guards in the prison wear identical uniforms and reflective sunglasses that make eye contact with them impossible. And they carry obvious badges of authority, such as clubs and whistles.

As a prisoner, you are expected to obey a long list of rules. You must remain silent during rest periods and after "lights out." You must eat only at mealtime and must address other prisoners only by their ID numbers, and guards as "Mr. Correctional Officer." And you must ask permission before performing even the simplest acts, such as writing, smoking, or going to the bathroom.

How would you react to such conditions? Would you obey the rules, or rebel? And what if you were a guard—would you treat prisoners in a fair and kindly manner, or harass and humiliate them? These intriguing questions were actually examined by Philip Zimbardo and his colleagues in a famous (but controversial) study known as the *Stanford Prison Experiment* (Haney, Banks, & Zimbardo, 1973). In this study, male college students who had volunteered for a psychological study of prison life were arrested and confined to a mock prison in the basement of the Stanford University psychology building. The "guards," too, were paid volunteers, and in fact assignment to one of these two roles was completely random.

The major purpose of the study was to determine whether subjects would soon come to behave very much like real guards and real prisoners. In other words, in one sense Zimbardo and his colleagues wished to establish whether both implicit and explicit social norms concerning these roles would shape subjects' behavior in important and obvious ways.

The results of the investigation were both dramatic and unsettling. Although the study was originally planned for a two-week period, it was necessary to end it after only six days. The reason was simple: Even during this brief interval, major—and alarming—changes occurred in the behavior of both the prisoners and the guards. At first, prisoners were rebellious and even attempted to take over the prison. Once their uprising was crushed, however, they became increasingly passive and depressed. Indeed, several began to show signs of serious emotional disturbance (e.g., uncontrollable fits of crying and screaming).

While the prisoners were becoming increasingly depressed and lethargic, the guards became increasingly brutal. They harassed the prisoners constantly, forced them to derogate one another, and assigned them to tedious, senseless tasks (e.g., moving cartons back and forth between closets in an endless manner).

In short, subjects came to act more and more like actual prisoners and actual guards in real prisons. The norms established by the researchers, plus knowledge of these roles brought to the study by subjects, exerted what seemed to be a very powerful effect on their behavior.

At this point, we should note that the findings of the Stanford Prison Study are viewed by many social psychologists as quite controversial. Several critics have called attention to the fact that participants in the study knew full well that they were volunteers in a research project. Thus, their behavior may merely have reflected their beliefs about how they should or ought to behave rather than any impact of the prison setting (Banuazizi & Movahedi, 1975). In reply to such criticism, other researchers have noted that even if subjects were in fact playing the roles of prisoners and guards, they were, in this respect, no different from individuals who actually enter these roles for the first time in real prisons. Such persons, too, bring expectations concerning appropriate behavior with them and then attempt to put these into practice (Thayer & Saarni, 1975).

As you can readily see, these are complex issues, which can be resolved only through the conduction of additional systematic research. Regardless of whether we choose to accept the specific findings of the Stanford Prison Study as valid, they do call attention to a key fact we wish to emphasize: In many situations, the pressures to yield to existing social norms can be powerful indeed. Thus, resisting them often requires strong convictions and the conscious decision to "stand the heat" that may quickly follow when we choose to stand apart from the crowd.

The Need for Individuation and the Need for Control: Why, Sometimes, We Choose *Not* to Go Along

Having read our discussion of normative and informational social influence, plus our description of the Stanford Prison Experiment, you may now have the distinct impression that pressures toward conformity are all but impossible to resist. If that's so, take heart. While such pressures are indeed powerful, they are definitely *not* irresistible. In many cases, individuals—or groups of individuals—decide to dig in their heels and say "No!" This was certainly true in Asch's research where, as you may recall, most of the subjects yielded to social pressure, but only part of the time. On many occasions, they stuck to their own judgments, even in the face of a disagreeing, unanimous majority. What accounts for this ability to resist even powerful pressures toward conformity? Research findings point to the importance of two key factors.

First, as you probably already realize, most persons have a strong desire to maintain their uniqueness or individuality. They want to be like others, but not to the extent that they lose their personal identity. In short, along with the needs to be right and to be liked, most of us possess a desire for **individuation**—for being differentiated, in some respects, from others (e.g., Maslach, Santee, & Wade, 1987; Snyder & Fromkin, 1980). It is partly because of this motive that individuals sometimes choose to disagree with others or to act in idiosyncratic ways. Although they realize that such behavior may be costly in terms of gaining others' approval or acceptance, their desire to maintain a unique identity is simply stronger than various inducements to conformity.

A second reason why individuals often choose to resist group pressure involves the desire to maintain control over the events in their lives (e.g., Burger & Cooper, 1979). Most persons want to believe they can determine what happens to them, and yielding to social pressure sometimes runs counter to this desire. After all, going along with a group implies behaving in ways one would not ordinarily choose, and this can be interpreted as a restriction of personal freedom and control. Direct evidence for the powerful impact of this factor has been reported by Burger (1987) in several related studies.

In one of these experiments, male and female students were asked to rate each of ten cartoons in terms of how funny they found them to be. Half the participants rated these cartoons while alone; the other half, after hearing the ratings provided by several other persons. As in Asch's research, these individuals were all accomplices of the researcher. The accomplices rated the cartoons as being quite funny (an average rating of almost seventy on a hundred-point

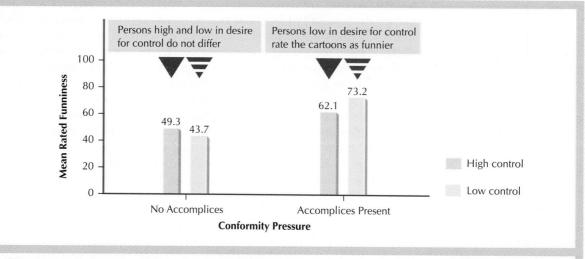

Persons high and low in desire for control do not differ

Persons low in desire for control rate the cartoons as funnier

Conformity and the desire for personal control

FIGURE 8.7   In the absence of social pressure, subjects low and high in the desire for personal control did not differ in their judgments of several cartoons. After hearing the judgments of several accomplices who rated the cartoons as being quite funny, however, persons low in need for personal control rated them more favorably than those high in need for personal control. Thus, subjects low in need for personal control showed stronger tendencies to conform to the false group judgments. (Source: Based on data from Burger, 1987.)

scale), despite the fact that other people had previously rated them as quite dull. Prior to rating the cartoons, all subjects had completed a questionnaire designed to measure the strength of their desire for personal control (the *Desirability of Control Scale;* Burger & Cooper, 1979). It was predicted that those high in the desire for personal control would show less yielding to the accomplices' influence than those low in such desire. As you can see from Figure 8.7, this prediction was confirmed. In the absence of the accomplices, subjects high and low in the desire for personal control did not differ in their ratings of the cartoons; both groups rated them as not very funny. In the presence of social influence from the accomplices, however, subjects low in the desire for personal control rated the cartoons as funnier than those high in such desire and thus yielded to pressures toward conformity to a greater extent.

In sum, while pressures toward conformity often win out and induce people to behave in ways they would not otherwise choose, this is not always the case. On some occasions, at least, our desires to maintain our uniqueness and to exert control over our lives help us to resist even strong social influence.

Minority Influence: One More Reason the Majority Doesn't Always Rule

As we have just noted, individuals can—and often do—resist group pressure (Wolfe, 1985); lone dissenters or small minorities can dig in their heels and refuse to go along. Yet even this is not the total story, for sometimes such persons or groups can also turn the tables on the majority and *exert* rather than merely receive social influence. History provides numerous examples. Such giants of the scientific world as Galileo, Pasteur, and Freud faced virtually unanimous majorities who harshly rejected their views. Yet, over time, these individuals won growing numbers of colleagues to their side until ultimately their opinions prevailed. More recent examples are provided by the success of environmentalists. Initially, such persons were viewed as wild-eyed radicals, operating at the fringes of society. Over time, however, they have succeeded in changing strongly held attitudes and laws, with the result that society itself has been altered through their efforts (refer to Figure 8.8).

How do minorities manage to exert social influence on majorities? Research findings suggest that to do so successfully, several conditions must be met (Moscovici, 1985). First, the members of such groups must be consistent in their opposition to majority opinions. If they waffle or show signs of yielding to the majority view, their impact is reduced. Second, for a minority to affect a larger majority its members must avoid appearing rigid and dogmatic (Mugny, 1975). A minority that merely repeats the same position time and time again is less persuasive than one that demonstrates a degree of flexibility in its stance. Third, the general social context in which a minority operates is important. If a minority argues for a position that is consistent with current social trends (e.g., argues for conservative views at a time of growing conservatism), its chances of influencing a majority are greater than if it argues for a position that is out of step with such trends. Finally, *single minorities*—minorities that differ from the majority only with respect to beliefs or attitudes—are more effective in exerting influence than *double minorities*—ones that differ in both attitudes and group membership. In the United States, for example, members of a black radical group holding extreme political views would constitute a double minority; members of a white radical group holding similar views would represent a single minority.

In sum, under appropriate conditions, committed, consistent minorities can indeed change the views of even large majorities—a fact that in turn raises

Sometimes minorities influence majorities

FIGURE 8.8 In the 1960s, environmentalists constituted a tiny minority in Western societies. By the 1980s, however, some of their views had been adopted by a majority of all citizens. This is a dramatic illustration of the manner in which small but committed minorities can sometimes exert influence on much larger majorities.

the question, Why is this the case? One possible answer is provided by key aspects of attribution theory (Maas & Clark, 1984). As you may recall from Chapter 2, we tend to view others' behavior as stemming from internal causes when (1) consensus is low (other people don't act in the same way), (2) consistency is high (the person in question acts in the same manner across time), and (3) distinctiveness is low (the person acts in the same manner in other situations). Such conditions apply quite well to the actions of highly committed minorities. Such persons adopt an unpopular stand, maintain it consistently, and act in accordance with it across many situations. The result: Their actions are viewed as stemming from deep conviction and commitment. Little wonder, then, that their views are often taken seriously and considered with care by the majorities around them.

At this point we should note that even when minorities are consistent and highly committed to their positions, they may fail to exert much influence. The power of majorities is so strong that most people continue to comply with the norms the majorities establish even in the presence of vocal, eloquent minorities. While minorities may fail to change overt behavior in many cases, however, they can still produce important effects. For example, they may induce large numbers of persons to think more deeply or carefully about the issues in question (Nemeth, 1986). Observers confronted with an unpopular but highly committed minority may ask themselves such questions as *How can they be so wrong, yet be so sure of themselves?* and *Why are they willing to go to so much trouble for a lost cause?* Such thinking may in turn lead some persons to consider ideas and alternatives they would otherwise have ignored. Some of these, in turn, may suggest new and creative solutions to the problems emphasized by the minority. As we noted in Chapter 4, such cognitive effort can often serve as an initial step to attitude change. In sum, even when minorities fail to sway majorities, they can serve a useful function; in this respect, at least, there is much truth in the saying, "Long live the loyal opposition!"

Compliance: To Ask—Sometimes—Is to Receive

How many times a day do you receive requests from others? If you kept a record, you'd probably be surprised at the total, for friends, coworkers, acquaintances, family members, lovers, and roommates frequently ask us to change various aspects of our behavior. Advertisers, politicians, and many others also get into the act, so that finally, the list of people attempting to exert such influence is large indeed (refer to Figure 8.9).

Social psychologists term this type of influence **compliance**, and in its most basic form it is quite straightforward. Persons seeking compliance express their wishes and hope these will be granted. In many instances, however, the situation is more complex. Rather than presenting their requests "cold," persons seeking compliance begin with preliminary steps designed to tip the balance in their favor—tactics they hope will increase the likelihood of the target's saying yes. While many different procedures are used for this purpose, here we'll concentrate on several which appear to be most successful.

Ingratiation: Liking as a Basis for Influence

Earlier we noted that most people have a strong desire to be liked by others. While this motive probably stems from several different sources, one of the

Efforts at gaining compliance: A common part of daily life

FIGURE 8.9   Each day, we are exposed to many attempts to gain our *compliance*—efforts to induce us to say yes to various requests.

most important is this: We realize that if others like us, they are more willing to do things for us. They are more likely to help us with various tasks, to evaluate us favorably, and to say yes to our requests. Recognition of this basic fact lies behind a common technique for gaining compliance: **ingratiation** (Jones, 1964). What this concept involves, in essence, are efforts by individuals to enhance their attractiveness to a target person so that she or he will then be more susceptible to their requests (Liden & Mitchell, 1988; Wortman & Linsenmeier, 1977).

What techniques are effective from the point of view of ingratiation? Several are useful. First, individuals seeking to ingratiate themselves to others can employ *target-directed* tactics (Liden & Mitchell, 1988), those which concentrate on inducing positive feelings in the target person. Presumably, such feelings will transfer to the ingratiator and increase liking for him or her (refer to our discussion of attraction in Chapter 6). Included among target-directed tactics are *flattery,* expressing *agreement* with the target person's views, showing *interest* in the target (e.g., appearing to hang on her or his every word), and directing positive nonverbal cues toward the target person (e.g., smiling, leaning in her or his direction; Wortman & Linsenmeier, 1977; refer to Figure 8.10, p. 330).

Other tactics involve *impression management* or *self-presentation*—efforts by the ingratiator to create a favorable impression on the target person (Schlenker, 1980). This can involve efforts to enhance one's personal appearance through dress or grooming (Baron, 1986; Berscheid, 1985), presenting information suggesting that the ingratiator possesses desirable characteristics (e.g., sincerity, competence, intelligence, friendliness), or merely associating oneself with positive events or people the target person already likes. In this last category, ingratiators can engage in name-dropping, thereby linking themselves to important or respected persons, and can casually introduce evidence of their past accomplishments into the conversation. Additional tactics include *self-deprecation*—providing negative information about oneself as a means of promoting the

Flattery: An effective route to compliance

FIGURE 8.10 As suggested by this cartoon, *flattery* is often an effective technique for gaining compliance. (Copyright 1986 Universal Press Syndicate. Reprinted with permission. All rights reserved.)

image of modesty—and *self-disclosure*—offering personal information about one-self even if it is not requested. This latter tactic fosters the impression that the ingratiator is honest and likes the target person (Tedeschi & Melburg, 1984).

Do such tactics work? A growing body of evidence suggests that if used with skill and care, they do. For example, in one laboratory study on this topic, Godfrey, Jones, and Lord (1986) asked pairs of unacquainted subjects to carry on two brief conversations with each other. After the first conversation, one subject in each pair was asked to try to make the other person like him or her as much as possible; the others were not given such instructions. After the conversations, subjects rated each other on a number of dimensions. In addition, videotapes of their conversations were carefully coded and analyzed by two trained raters. Results indicated that subjects told to ingratiate themselves with their partners succeeded in this task: They were indeed rated as more likable after the second conversation than after the first. In contrast, subjects in the control group did not show such gains. Further, some of the factors behind this success were apparent in the tapes. The ingratiating subjects reduced the amount of time they spoke and showed more agreement with their partners from the first to the second conversation. Again, subjects in the control group failed to show such changes.

Other studies point to the success of ingratiation in applied contexts. It is now well established that job applicants who dress and groom appropriately and who emit positive nonverbal cues (e.g., smile frequently, maintain eye contact with the interviewer) receive higher ratings than applicants who do not engage in such actions (e.g., Arvey & Campion, 1982). Additional evidence suggests, however, that as in other contexts involving ingratiation, these tactics can be overdone. For example, Rasmussen (1984) found that when job applicants with poor credentials emit many positive nonverbal cues, they are down-rated relative to applicants who do not engage in such behavior. This finding may stem from the fact that interviewers then attribute such cues to efforts on the part of a less-qualified applicant to distract them and shift their attention from poor credentials. Similarly, Baron (1986) found that female job applicants

330   CHAPTER EIGHT   SOCIAL INFLUENCE

who wore perfume *and* emitted many positive nonverbal cues were rated less favorably than those who employed only one of these tactics. Again, the use of too many ingratiatory tactics seemed to backfire and reduce rather than enhance interviewers' reactions to the applicants.

Multiple Requests: Two Steps to Compliance

Suppose you wanted a fairly large favor from one of your friends. Would you simply approach this person and make your request? Perhaps, but it is more likely that you would try to prepare the ground before seeking compliance. One way in which you might do so would be to make an initial request for something different from what you really want. You would then somehow use that request as an entering wedge for gaining the compliance you really seek—in short, you would follow up with your actual request. Several variations on this *multiple-request* strategy exist, and under appropriate circumstances all can be effective.

The Foot-in-the-Door: Small Request First, Large Request Second Experts in gaining compliance—skilled salespersons, confidence artists—often start their campaigns for gaining compliance with a trivial request. They ask potential customers to accept a free sample, or potential "marks" to do something that seems entirely without risk (e.g., to hold a receipt or the key to a safe-deposit box; refer to Figure 8.11). Only after these small requests are granted do they move on to the requests they really want—ones that can prove quite costly to the target persons. In all such instances, the basic strategy is much the same: somehow induce another person to comply with a small initial request and thereby increase the chances that he or she will agree later to a much larger one. Is this approach—often called the **foot-in-the-door technique**—really successful? Evidence from numerous studies suggests that it is (Beaman et al., 1983).

In what is perhaps the most famous study concerned with this topic, (Freedman & Fraser, 1966), homemakers were phoned by a male experimenter

The foot-in-the-door technique in operation

FIGURE 8.11 Use of the *foot-in-the-door technique* is quite common. Salespersons and others wishing to gain compliance often start with a small request. Once this is granted, they move to a larger request—the one they always intended to make.

who identified himself as a member of a consumers' group. During this initial contact, he asked subjects to answer a few simple questions about the kinds of soap they used at home. Several days later, the same person called again and made a much larger request: Could he send a crew of five or six persons to the subject's home to conduct a thorough inventory of all the products he or she had on hand? The experimenter explained that the survey would take about two hours and that the crew would require freedom to search in all closets, cabinets, and drawers. As you can see, this was truly a huge request. In contrast, subjects in a one-contact control group were called only once and were presented with the large, second request "cold." Results were impressive: Only 22.2 percent of those in the one-contact condition agreed, but fully 52.8 percent of those in the two-contact, foot-in-the-door group complied. While results have not been as strong in several later studies (Beaman et al., 1983), existing evidence suggests that the foot-in-the-door tactic *is* effective in producing enhanced compliance in many settings and in response to a wide range of requests—everything from signing a petition (Baron, 1973) through contributing to charity (Pliner et al., 1974). But how, precisely, does it operate? Why does agreeing to a small initial request increase one's likelihood of saying yes to a later and much larger one? Two possibilities exist.

First, it may be that after consenting to a small request, individuals come to hold a more positive view of helping situations generally. They now perceive such situations as less threatening or costly than they would otherwise. As a result, they are more willing to comply with later—and larger—requests (Rittle, 1981).

Second, once individuals agree to a small initial request, they may experience subtle shifts in their own self-perceptions, coming to view themselves as the kind of person who does that sort of thing—one who offers help to people who need it. Thus, when contacted again and presented with a much larger request, such persons agree in order to be consistent with their enhanced self-image.

Although both explanations have received some support from research findings (DeJong & Musilli, 1982; Rittle, 1981), a study conducted by Eisenberg, Cialdini, McCreath, and Shell (1987) offers impressive and convincing evidence for the accuracy of the second (self-perception) view. This study was based on the fact that prior to age seven, children do not possess sufficient cognitive capacity to use their past behavior and inferences about it as predictors of their future behavior. In short, they are not capable of reasoning "I was helpful before; therefore, I will probably be helpful again." Since they lack the capacity for such reasoning, they experience few if any pressures to be consistent in their behavior.

On the basis of these facts, Eisenberg, Cialdini, and their colleagues reasoned that children younger than age seven would not demonstrate susceptibility to the foot-in-the-door effect. Children age seven and above, however, would indeed be affected by it. To test this prediction, the researchers exposed children in three age-groups (five to six, seven to eight, and ten to eleven) to (1) a small initial request or (2) no initial request. The initial request involved donating, to poor children described as having no toys, coupons that could be used to win prizes. Subjects received six coupons, and virtually all complied with the experimenter's request that they donate one of these to the poor youngsters.

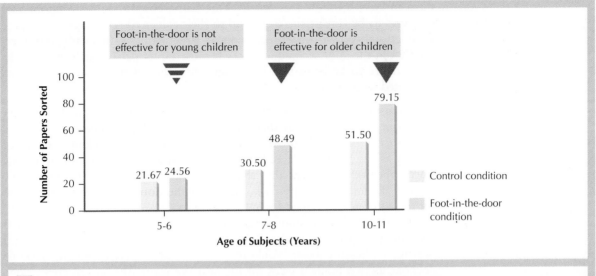

Evidence for the self-perception explanation of the foot-in-the-door effect

FIGURE 8.12   Young children (ages five to six) were not affected by the foot-in-the-door tactic. However, older children (ages seven to eight and ten to eleven) were affected by this tactic. These results stem from the fact that children below the age of seven are not yet able to draw inferences about themselves from their own behavior or to use their past behavior to predict future actions. (Source: Based on data from Eisenberg et al., 1987.)

In a second session held one or two days later, children were given a choice of either playing with an array of attractive toys or helping "sick children in the hospital" by sorting colored paper into four color-coded piles. Doing the latter, rather than playing with the toys, constituted the second, larger request. (It involved considerable effort and giving up the opportunity to play with the attractive toys.)

The results offered support for the hypothesis that the foot-in-the-door effect would not occur among the youngest children. For the five- to six-year-olds, there was no difference between the foot-in-the-door group and the control condition (children who were not exposed to the initial request) in terms of willingness to expend effort for the "sick children." Among the older children, in contrast, those in the foot-in-the-door group sorted more papers than those in the control condition; this difference was significant for the ten- to eleven-year-olds and approached significance for the seven- to eight-year-olds (see Figure 8.12).

An additional aspect of the study involved having the children complete a questionnaire designed to assess their preference for consistent behavior. It was expected that the stronger subjects' preference for consistent behavior, the stronger would be the foot-in-the-door effect. This prediction, too, was confirmed.

Together, the findings reported by Eisenberg, Cialdini et al. (1987) support the self-perception interpretation of the foot-in-the-door effect. Apparently, exposing people to small initial requests that they are unlikely to refuse leads them to view themselves as *helpful*. This factor, coupled with strong internal pressures to be consistent (to live up to their enhanced self-image), then produces greater compliance with subsequent, larger requests. In a sense, therefore, the foot-in-the-door technique works because target persons help it to work: Their desire to be consistent is stronger than their desire to avoid the costs associated with saying yes.

The Door-in-the-Face: Large Request First, Small Request Second   Another compliance-gaining strategy that is also based on multiple requests is in a sense the reverse of the foot-in-the-door technique. Here, persons seeking compliance start by asking for a very large favor—one the target is almost certain to refuse. Then, when refusal occurs, they shift to a smaller request, the favor they really wanted all along. This approach, known as the **door-in-the-face technique** (or the *rejection-then-retreat tactic*), also appears to be quite effective.

In one well-known study designed to investigate this strategy, Cialdini and his colleagues (Cialdini et al., 1975) stopped college students on the street and presented a huge request: Would they serve as unpaid counselors for juvenile delinquents two hours a week for the next *two years*? As you can guess, none agreed to this proposition. When the experimenters then scaled down their request to a much smaller one—would the same students take a group of delinquents on a two-hour trip to the zoo?—fully 50 percent agreed. In contrast, less than 17 percent of those in a control group agreed to this smaller request when it was presented alone, rather than after a giant initial request.

The use of the door-in-the-face technique can be observed in many real-life situations. Negotiators often begin with a position that is extremely favorable to themselves but very unfavorable to their opponents. When this initial proposal is rejected, they back down to a position much closer to the one they really hope to obtain. Similarly, television writers who wish to get certain lines or scenes past network censors often sprinkle throughout their scripts certain words or situations they know will be cut. They then agree to the elimination of many of these while still retaining the key lines they wanted all along (Cialdini, 1988).

Why does this tactic sometimes succeed? Two explanations have been proposed. The first relates to the notion of *reciprocal concessions*. When someone who starts with a very large request backs down to a smaller one, the target persons may view that action as a concession on the requester's part. Target persons then feel obligated to make a matching concession of their own. As a result, they become more willing to comply with the requester's second, scaled-down proposal.

Another possibility involves concern over *self-presentation*—presenting ourselves in a favorable light to others. If we refuse a large and unreasonable request, doing so appears justifiable and our image doesn't suffer. But if we then also refuse a much smaller request from the same source, we may appear unreasonable. Thus, we may often yield to the door-in-the-face technique because of our concern that failing to do so will cause us to look rigid or intransigent to others (Pendleton & Batson, 1979).

Comparing the Foot-in-the-Door and the Door-in-the-Face: The Role of Source Legitimacy   Research findings, as well as informal observations of daily life, indicate that both the foot-in-the-door and the door-in-the-face techniques sometimes succeed. Is one of these tactics preferable to the other? In general, the answer seems to be no. Neither has a clear, overall advantage. Several factors, however, suggest that the foot-in-the-door technique may operate successfully in a somewhat wider range of situations.

First, consider the issue of time between the initial and later requests. Since shifts in self-perception tend to persist, the foot-in-the-door technique should succeed even when the first and second requests are separated by substantial time periods (several hours or more). In contrast, the door-in-the-face technique may fail under such conditions, because the tendency to make a reciprocal concession to the requester after he or she backs down may quickly dissipate. Existing evidence suggests that this is indeed the case (e.g., Cann, Sherman, & Elkes, 1975).

Second, it appears that the foot-in-the-door tactic can succeed even when the initial and subsequent requests are made by two different persons. Again, this is due to the fact that shifts in self-perception, once induced, tend to persist. Thus, internal pressures toward being consistent (i.e., toward helping others) may enhance compliance even when the second request is made by a different person. With the door-in-the-face technique, in contrast, target persons should feel little or no obligation to make concessions to someone different from the person who proposed the large initial request, and this technique may therefore succeed only when the two requests are made by the same individual.

Third, the foot-in-the-door technique may succeed regardless of the legitimacy of the requester, whereas the door-in-the-face tactic may work only when the requester is judged to be high on this dimension. This would be the case because pressures to be consistent by agreeing to a second, larger request should operate regardless of source legitimacy. In contrast, individuals might feel little obligation to make reciprocal concessions to a source of influence that is low in legitimacy. Direct evidence for these predictions is provided by a study conducted by Patch (1986). In this investigation, male and female subjects whose phone numbers were chosen randomly from a telephone directory were called and exposed to one of three conditions: foot-in-the-door, door-in-the-face, or control (one large request). In the foot-in-the-door condition, subjects were called once and asked to comply with a very small request (answering a few short questions about their television-viewing habits). Later, they were called again and asked if they would comply with a larger request (completing a fifty-item questionnaire on their viewing habits and opinions about violence on television). In the door-in-the-face condition, subjects were called once and asked if they would keep a journal on all the programs they watched for the next two weeks and then allow an individual to come and interview them in their homes. After refusing this request, they were then asked to comply with the same second request described above (completing a fifty-item questionnaire). Subjects in the control group were asked to comply only with the second, larger request.

To half the subjects, the caller identified himself as belonging to Parents for Good Television Programming, a nonprofit organization concerned with the public welfare; this was the *high-legitimacy* condition. The remaining subjects— those in the *low-legitimacy* condition—learned that the caller was a member of Multimedia Programming Associates, a consulting group working for commercial television interests.

Patch predicted that the foot-in-the-door tactic would succeed in raising compliance with the second, larger request, regardless of the legitimacy of the

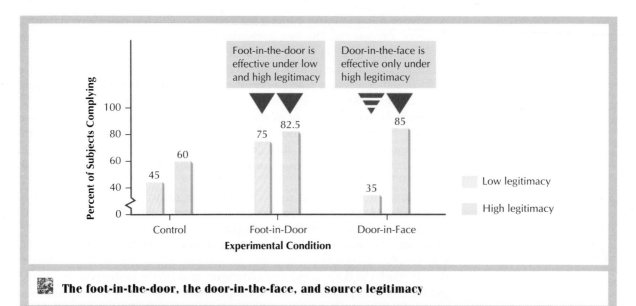

The foot-in-the-door, the door-in-the-face, and source legitimacy

FIGURE 8.13 The door-in-the-face technique is more effective when the requester is high rather than low in legitimacy. In contrast, the foot-in-the-door technique operates effectively under both conditions. These findings confirm the view that these procedures induce compliance through different mechanisms. (Source: Based on data from Patch, 1986.)

source, but that the door-in-the-face procedure would be more effective when source legitimacy was high. As you can see from Figure 8.13, that is precisely what happened. Both multiple-request conditions increased compliance relative to the control group. However, the foot-in-the-door technique was successful under both high and low source legitimacy, while the door-in-the-face technique succeeded only when source legitimacy was high.

Using the foot-in-the-door technique

FIGURE 8.14 While he may not succeed in gaining compliance with his second request, this little boy definitely understands the use of the foot-in-the-door tactic. (Reprinted with special permission of North America Syndicate, Inc.)

In sum, while both techniques are useful in gaining compliance, existing evidence suggests that the foot-in-the-door tactic is applicable in a somewhat broader range of contexts than the door-in-the-face tactic. For this reason, the character shown in Figure 8.14 may well be on the right track—even if his efforts at gaining compliance fail in this particular instance!

(For information on another effective tactic for gaining compliance from others, please see the **Cutting Edge** section below.)

FOCUS ON RESEARCH: THE CUTTING EDGE

Sweetening the Deal: The "That's Not All" Technique

A television program popular during the 1950s ("The Milton Berle Show") contained a segment that many people found highly amusing. A man would come onto the stage and set up a small platform. He would then roll up his sleeves, and begin to offer members of the audience what he described as "incredible deals." During this comedy routine, he would mention a deal and then immediately indicate how he would sweeten it by throwing in something extra. "Tell you what I'm gonna do," he'd comment. "You say that's not enough? You say you want more for your money? Well, then, listen to this . . ."

The deals offered in this comic routine were preposterous, but the technique itself is an intriguing one. Have you ever been in a situation in which someone tried to sell you something but then, before you could answer yes or no, offered to add some bonus to the deal? Auto dealers sometimes do this, offering to add an option to the car in question as a "closer." Similar techniques are used in many other settings, too. Does this approach, sometimes termed the **"that's not all" (TNA) technique,** really work? Evidence gathered by Burger (1986) suggests it does.

In an initial study on this tactic, Burger conducted a bake sale on a college campus. Cupcakes were displayed on a table, but no price was indicated. In one condition of the study (the *that's-not-all* condition), when potential buyers asked the price, they were given this information and then, before they could respond, were also shown a bag containing two cookies; the seller noted that the price included the cookies. In a second (control) condition, in contrast, subjects were shown the cookies and told that these were included in the deal before being given the price. Results indicated that the TNA technique worked. Seventy-three percent of subjects in this group bought the cupcakes, while only 40 percent of those in the control condition did so.

In a follow-up study, subjects in the TNA condition were told that the cupcakes were priced at $1.25. Then, before they could respond, the seller indicated that he would lower the price to $1.00, since he was planning to close his booth soon. In a control condition, in contrast, subjects were simply told that the cupcakes were priced at $1.00. Finally, in a third *(bargain)* condition, the seller indicated that the cupcakes were now $1.00, although formerly they had been $1.25. This third group was included to determine whether any increased tendency among subjects in the TNA condition to buy the cupcakes was attributable merely to the fact that these items were now a bargain (their price had been reduced).

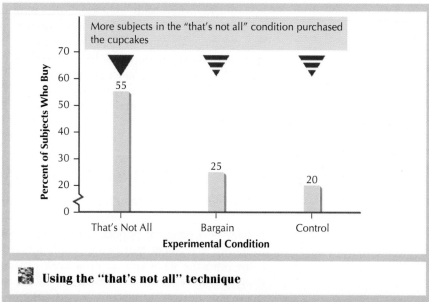

Using the "that's not all" technique

FIGURE 8.15 A high percentage of prospective customers actually bought some cupcakes when the seller "sweetened the deal" by first naming one price and then lowering it. Fewer customers bought the cupcakes when they learned that the price had been lowered previously (the *bargain condition*) or when only the low price was mentioned. These findings provide support for the effectiveness of the *that's not all (TNA) technique*. (Source: Based on data from Burger, 1986.)

As shown in Figure 8.15, the TNA technique was effective once again. More than 50 percent of subjects in this condition bought the cupcakes; the corresponding percentages were much lower in both the control and the bargain conditions. This latter finding suggests that the TNA technique is effective not merely because it offers items at a bargain price but because there is something about "sweetening the deal" in midstream that generates increased compliance.

Why does the TNA technique work? One possibility involves the *norm of reciprocity*. As we noted in our discussion of the door-in-the-face technique, when another person makes a concession, we often feel obligated to reciprocate. Applying this idea to the TNA technique, target persons may feel an increased obligation to say yes when the requester lowers the price, throws in a bonus, or takes some similar action. Support for this view is provided by the fact that the TNA technique succeeds only when subjects perceive the seller's addition of a bonus as a personal gesture; if it is viewed as something he or she had to do, the tactic fails.

Whatever its precise basis, the TNA technique can be quite effective. Moreover, as we noted previously, it appears to be in widespread current use. For this reason, you should be on guard whenever someone attempts to induce you to say yes by offering more than they did initially. The chances are good that in such situations, the new "improved" deal is the one the requester had in mind all along.

Obedience: Social Influence by Demand

What is the most direct technique one person can use to change the behavior of another? In one sense, the answer is as follows: he or she can *order* the target person to do something. Although this approach is less common than either conformity pressure or tactics for gaining compliance, it is far from rare—business executives issue many orders to their subordinates, military officers shout commands they expect to be followed at once, and parents, police officers, and coaches, to name just a few, seek to influence others in this manner. Obedience to the commands of sources of authority is hardly surprising; such persons usually possess some means of enforcing their directives (e.g., they can reward **obedience** and punish resistance). More surprising, though, is the fact that even persons lacking in such power can sometimes induce high levels of submission from others. The clearest and most dramatic evidence for the occurrence of such effects has been reported by Stanley Milgram in a series of famous—and controversial—experiments (Milgram, 1963, 1974).

Destructive Obedience: Some Basic Findings

In his research, Milgram wished to learn whether individuals would obey commands from a seemingly powerful stranger requiring them to inflict what appeared to be considerable pain on another person—an innocent stranger. Milgram's interest in this topic derived from the occurrence of tragic real-life events in which seemingly normal, law-abiding persons actually obeyed such directives. For example, during World War II, troops in the German army obeyed commands to torture and murder unarmed civilians. Similarly appalling events have occurred in many other cases and at many other points in history (e.g., the infamous My Lai massacre during the Vietnam War, the slaughter of many thousands of civilians in Haiti by the infamous Tonton Macoutes of the late Papa Doc Duvalier).

To gain insights into the nature of such events, Milgram designed an ingenious, if unsettling, laboratory simulation. Subjects in his research were informed that they were participating in a study of the effects of punishment on learning. Their role was to deliver electric shocks to another person (actually an accomplice) each time he made an error in a simple learning task. These shocks were to be delivered by means of thirty switches on the equipment shown in Figure 8.16, p. 340. Subjects were told to move to the next higher switch each time the learner made an error. Since the first switch supposedly delivered a shock of 15 volts, it was clear that if the learner made many errors, he would soon be receiving powerful jolts. Indeed, according to the labels on the equipment, the final shock would be 450 volts. In reality, of course, the accomplice (the learner) *never received any shocks during the experiment*. The only real shock ever used was a mild demonstration pulse from one button (number three) to convince subjects that the equipment was real.

During the session, the learner (following prearranged instructions) made many errors. Thus, subjects soon found themselves facing a dilemma: Should they continue punishing this person with what seemed to be increasingly painful shocks? Or should they refuse to go on? The experimenter pressured them to choose the former path, for whenever they hesitated or protested, he made one of a series of graded remarks, beginning with "Please go on," escalating to "It is absolutely essential that you continue," and finally shifting to "You have no other choice; you *must* go on."

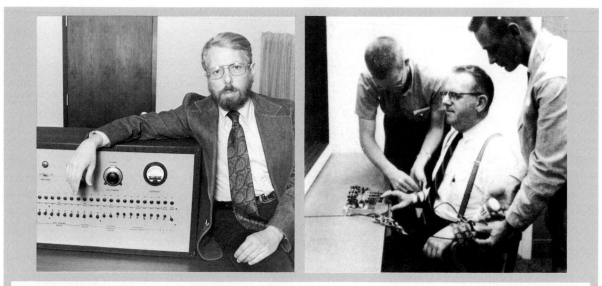

Milgram's procedures for studying obedience

FIGURE 8.16 The photo on the left shows Stanley Milgram with the apparatus he used in his famous experiments on obedience. The photo on the right shows the experimenter (right front) and a subject (rear) attaching electrodes to the learner's (accomplice's) wrists. (Source: From the film *Obedience,* distributed by the New York University Film Library, Copyright 1965 by Stanley Milgram. Reprinted by permission of the copyright holder.)

Since subjects were all volunteers and were paid in advance, you might predict that they would quickly refuse the experimenter's orders. But, in reality, fully *65 percent showed total obedience,* proceeding through the entire series to the final 450-volt level (see Figure 8.17). In contrast, subjects in a control group who were not exposed to such commands generally used only very mild shocks during the session. Of course, many persons protested and asked that the session be ended. When ordered to proceed, however, a majority yielded to the experimenter's social influence and continued to obey. Indeed, they continued to do so even when the victim pounded on the wall as if in protest against the painful treatment he was receiving (refer to Figure 8.17).

In further experiments, Milgram (1965a, 1974) found that similar results could be obtained even under conditions that might be expected to reduce such obedience. When the study was moved from its original location on the campus of Yale University to a run-down office building in a nearby city, subjects' level of obedience remained virtually unchanged. Similarly, a large proportion continued to obey even when the accomplice complained about the painfulness of the shocks and begged to be released. Most surprising of all, many (about 30 percent) continued to obey even when they were required to grasp the victim's hand and force it down on the shock plate. That these unsettling results were not due to special conditions present in Milgram's laboratory is indicated by the fact that similar findings were soon reported in studies conducted in several different nations (e.g., Jordan, West Germany, Australia) and with children as well as adults (e.g., Kilham & Mann, 1974; Shanab & Yahya, 1977). Thus, these results seemed to be alarmingly general in scope.

Destructive Obedience: Why Does It Occur?

The results obtained by Milgram and others are disturbing. The parallels between the behavior of subjects in these studies and atrocities committed against civilians during times of war or civil uprising seem clear. (For example, consider the willingness of Chinese troops to fire on civilians during the spring of 1989.) But why, precisely, do such effects occur? Why were subjects in these experiments—and many persons in tragic situations outside the laboratory—so willing to yield to the commands of various authority figures? Several factors appear to play a role.

First, in many situations the persons in authority relieve those who obey of the responsibility for their own actions. "I was only carrying out orders" is the defense many offer after obeying harsh or cruel directives. In life situations, this

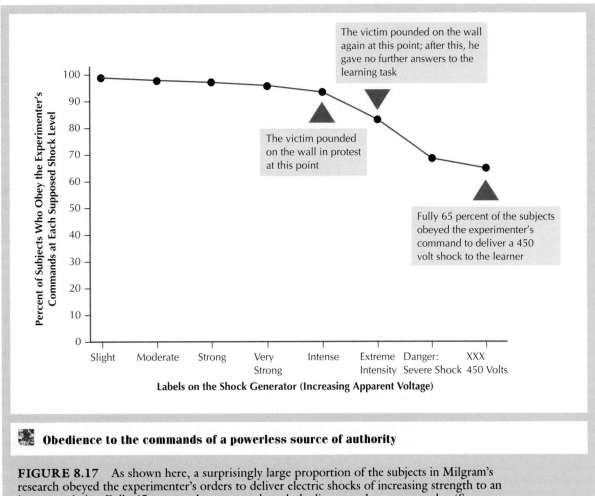

Obedience to the commands of a powerless source of authority

FIGURE 8.17 As shown here, a surprisingly large proportion of the subjects in Milgram's research obeyed the experimenter's orders to deliver electric shocks of increasing strength to an innocent victim. Fully 65 percent demonstrated total obedience to these commands. (Source: Based on data from Milgram, 1963.)

Outward signs of authority: One factor in obedience

FIGURE 8.18 One reason many persons obey commands from authority figures is that such figures possess readily visible signs of their power.

transfer of responsibility may be implicit. In Milgram's experiments, in contrast, it was quite explicit. Subjects were told at the start that the experimenter (the authority figure), not they, would be responsible for the victim's well-being. Given this fact, it is not surprising that many tended to obey.

Second, persons in authority often possess visible badges or other signs of their status and power. These consist of special uniforms, insignia, and titles (refer to Figure 8.18). Faced with such obvious reminders of who's in charge, most people find it difficult to resist. The powerful impact of such cues has been demonstrated by Bushman (1984, 1988) in several related experiments. For example, in one of these investigations, a female accomplice of the researcher ordered pedestrians to give a nickel to a young man who needed it for a parking meter. In one condition, she was dressed in a uniform (although its precise nature was ambiguous). In a second condition she was dressed as a business executive, and in a third, she was dressed as a panhandler. Not surprisingly, a higher percentage of subjects complied (72 percent) in the first condition than in the others (48 and 52 percent, respectively). Other data, collected by asking subjects who complied why they did so, indicated that the uniform had the expected effect: Subjects in this condition reported that they complied simply because they had been ordered to do so by someone in authority. These findings and those of related studies suggest that the possession of outward signs of authority, even if they are largely irrelevant to the present situation, play an important role in the ability of authority figures to elicit high levels of obedience to their commands.

A third reason for obedience in many situations in which the targets of such influence might resist involves its gradual nature: Initial commands are relatively small and innocuous; only later do they increase in scope and come to require behavior that is dangerous or objectionable. For example, police or military personnel may at first be ordered to question, arrest, or threaten potential victims. Gradually, however, demands are increased to the point where the persons involved are commanded to beat, torture, or even kill unarmed civilians.

Similarly, subjects in the laboratory study described earlier were first required to deliver only mild and harmless "shocks" to the victim. Only as this person continued to make errors on the learning task did the intensity of these "punishments" rise to harmful levels.

In sum, several factors contribute to the high levels of obedience witnessed in both laboratory studies and in real life. Together, these factors merge into a powerful force—one that most persons find difficult to resist. Unfortunately, the consequences of this compelling form of social influence can be disastrous for many innocent and largely defenseless victims.

Destructive Obedience: Resisting Its Effects

Now that we have considered some of the factors responsible for the strong tendency to obey sources of authority, we will turn to a related question: How can this type of social influence be resisted? Several strategies seem to be effective.

First, individuals exposed to commands from authority figures can be reminded that they, not the authorities, are responsible for any harm produced. Under these conditions, sharp reductions in the tendency to obey have been observed (e.g., Hamilton, 1978; Kilham & Mann, 1974).

Second, the tendency to obey can be reduced by providing individuals with an indication that beyond some point, unquestioning submission to destructive commands is inappropriate. For example, they can be exposed to the actions of *disobedient models*—persons who refuse to obey an authority figure's commands. Research findings suggest that this strategy, too, is quite effective in reducing obedience (Milgram, 1965b; Powers & Geen, 1972).

Third, individuals may find it easier to resist influence from authority figures if they question those figures' expertise and motives. Are such persons really in a better position to judge what is appropriate and what is inappropriate? What motives lie behind their commands—selfish gain, or socially beneficial goals? By asking such questions, persons who might otherwise obey may find support for independence rather than submission.

Finally, simply knowing about the power of authority figures to command blind obedience may in itself be helpful. Growing evidence (e.g., Sherman, 1980) suggests that when people learn about the research findings of social psychology, they may change their behavior to take this knowledge into account. With respect to obedience, there is some hope that knowing about this process can enhance individuals' ability to resist. To the extent this is the case, then even exposure to findings as disturbing as those reported by Milgram can be of positive social value. As they become widely known, they may produce desirable shifts within society.

In sum, the power of authority figures to command obedience is certainly great but *not* irresistible. Under appropriate conditions, it can be countered and reduced. As in many other spheres of life, there *is* a choice. Choosing to resist the dictates of authority can, of course, be dangerous. Those holding power wield tremendous advantages in terms of weapons and technology. Yet, as recent events in China, Poland, and elsewhere demonstrate, the outcome is by no means certain when committed groups of citizens decide to resist. The human spirit, it appears, is not so easily extinguished as many sources of authority would like to believe. (Can the recent events in Eastern Europe be understood in terms of the factors just described? For a discussion of this issue, please see the following **Multicultural Perspective** section.)

SOCIAL PSYCHOLOGY: A MULTICULTURAL PERSPECTIVE

The "Meltdown" of Communism in Eastern Europe: Resisting Authority on Behalf of Freedom

When 1989 began, the Iron Curtain, first described by Winston Churchill in the late 1940s, was still totally intact. In Berlin, the forbidding and seemingly impenetrable wall symbolized the permanence of the division between the two halves of Europe, while in Poland, Czechoslovakia, Romania, and many other nations, the Communist party seemed to have a total and unshakable grip on the levers of power. By the end of that year, however, an entirely different situation had emerged. In Berlin, the wall had been breached, permitting the free flow of people and commerce between the Eastern and Western halves of the city—and between the states they represented—for the first time in almost thirty years (see Figure 8.19). And soon these countries moved toward full reunification. In Poland and Czechoslovakia, the Communist governments had been replaced by coalitions pledged to free elections, while in Hungary, the Communist party had renamed itself "Socialist" and surrendered its claims to absolute power. Perhaps most dramatic, the people of Romania first rid themselves of their Communist dictator, Nicolae Ceausescu, and then, in a stunning move, established a provisional government that voted to *outlaw* the Communist party. Even within the Soviet Union itself, the winds of change blew strong, with the Baltic states of Estonia, Latvia, and Lithuania moving toward reestablishment of the independence they enjoyed in the years before World War II. All in all, it was a dramatic year, certain to live forever in the annals of world history.

Refusing to obey: Sometimes it can yield positive results

FIGURE 8.19 Many factors contributed to the willingness of millions of people in Eastern Europe to defy the authority of their governments in 1989 and 1990. Among these were several variables that have been shown, in actual research, to weaken the tendency to obey orders from sources of authority.

Many factors contributed to these dramatic events. The emergence of Mikhail Gorbachev as the leader of the Soviet Union certainly played a key role, as did the continuing decline in the Communist-controlled economies of all these nations. Yet the changes just described could not have occurred without the heroic actions of countless individuals who decided to shoulder the risks involved in resisting the authority of their own entrenched governments. In East Germany, Poland, Czechoslovakia, and elsewhere, citizens took to the streets in huge demonstrations, national strikes, and other actions designed to topple governments they found intolerable. And in Romania, thousands of civilians, as well as units of the armed forces, defied established authority and took up arms against a regime that had oppressed them for decades. Close examination of these events suggests that in many cases, the acts of defiance were encouraged by the factors described earlier in our discussion of resisting obedience. For example, in all these nations, courageous leaders who refused to obey and so served as *disobedient models* rose to the fore. (Lech Walesa, the Polish leader of Solidarity, is perhaps the most famous of these.) Similarly, in all these nations, large numbers of citizens concluded that the established governments did not have their best interests at heart. Rather, they were corrupt instruments for guaranteeing a life of ease and luxury for those who ran them— top-level Communists. Finally, millions of people in Eastern Europe decided that those who governed them did not really know what they were doing: After forty years of Communist rule, people's lives were harder and less fulfilling than ever. In response to these conditions and to the new policy of nonintervention announced by Mikhail Gorbachev, the peoples of Eastern Europe quickly took control of their own destinies and the cause of freedom triumphed at last.

Together, these dramatic events suggest that no matter how great their authority or military might, tyrants cannot long remain in power when large numbers of citizens refuse to obey. For us, it is hard to imagine a more cheering or optimistic note on which to conclude than this one.

SUMMARY AND REVIEW

Conformity

Conformity occurs when individuals change their attitudes or behavior to comply with *social norms*— expectations about how they should behave in various situations. Conformity increases with *cohesiveness*—liking for the sources of such influence—and with the number of persons exerting conformity pressure, but only up to a point. Conformity is reduced by the presence of *social support*—one or more individuals who share the target person's views, or at least depart from the majority's position in some manner. Contrary to early findings, current evidence indicates that there are no significant differences between males and females in the tendency to conform. Continued popular belief in such differences stems partly from the fact that females frequently hold lower-status positions in society than males. In their own use of various tactics for gaining social influence, males and females are virtually identical.

Compliance

Compliance involves direct efforts by individuals to change the behavior of others. Many techniques can be used to increase the likelihood that target persons will in fact say yes. *Ingratiation* involves efforts by requesters to increase their attractiveness to target persons. Presumably, if such attempts are successful, compliance, too, will increase. Ingratiation involves a wide range of specific tactics, such as *flattery,* the expression of *agreement* with the target persons, and *self-deprecation* and *self-disclosure.*

Other tactics for gaining compliance involve *multiple requests.* One such procedure is the **foot-in-the-door technique.** Here, requesters begin with a small initial request and then, when it is accepted, shift to a larger one. Recent evidence suggests that this technique is successful because agreeing with an initial request leads individuals to perceive themselves as being helpful. They then comply with follow-up requests in order to be consistent with this changed self-image. A related technique involves opposite procedures: Those seeking compliance begin with a large request and then, when it is refused, back down to a smaller one. This tactic, known as the **door-in-the-face technique,** works because target persons feel obliged to reciprocate the requester's concession with one of their own. While both the foot-in-the-door and the door-in-the-face techniques can be successful in increasing compliance, the foot-in-the-door seems applicable to a somewhat wider range of situations.

An additional technique for gaining compliance involves "sweetening the deal"—offering individuals something extra before they decide to accept or reject a request. This strategy is known as the **"that's not all" (TNA)** technique and in some situations is quite effective.

Obedience

The most direct form of social influence is **obedience**—direct orders from one person to another. Research findings indicate that many persons will obey commands from an authority figure even when such persons have little power to enforce their orders. These tendencies toward obedience stem from several causes (e.g., authority figures gradually escalate the scope of their orders; they wear uniforms or have other visible signs of their power). Fortunately, obedience can be reduced through various procedures. These include reminding individuals that they, not the authority figure, will be responsible for harmful outcomes; exposing the targets of obedience to disobedient models; and inducing such targets to question the motives or legitimacy of those in authority.

KEY TERMS

Compliance A form of social influence involving direct requests from one person to another.

Conformity A form of social influence in which individuals change their attitudes or behavior in order to adhere to existing social norms.

Door-in-the-face technique A procedure for gaining compliance in which requesters begin with a large request and then, when it is refused, retreat to a smaller one (the one they actually desired all along).

Foot-in-the-door technique A procedure for gaining compliance in which requesters begin with a small request and then, when it is granted, escalate to a larger one (the one they actually desired all along).

Individuation The desire to differentiate oneself from others by emphasizing one's uniqueness or individuality.

Informational social influence Social influence based on the desire to be correct (i.e., to possess accurate perceptions of the social world).

Ingratiation A technique for gaining compliance in which requesters first induce target persons to like them and then attempt to change their behavior in some desired manner.

Normative social influence Social influence based on the desire to be liked or accepted by other persons.

Obedience A form of social influence in which one person simply orders one or more others to perform some action(s).

Social influence Efforts on the part of one person to alter the behavior or attitudes of one or more others.

Social influence model (SIM) A model of social influence designed to account for the impact that group size, number of target persons, and several other factors have on the acceptance of in-fluence in a wide range of settings.

Social norms Rules indicating how individuals are expected to behave in specific situations.

"That's not all" (TNA) technique A technique for gaining compliance in which requesters offer additional benefits to target persons before they have decided whether to comply with or reject specific requests.

FOR MORE INFORMATION

Cialdini, R. B. (1988). *Influence: Science and practice* (2nd ed.). New York: Random House.

An insightful account of the major techniques people use to influence others. The book draws both on the findings of systematic research and on informal observations made by the author in a wide range of practical settings (e.g., sales, public relations, fund-raising agencies, organizations). This is the most readable and informative account of knowledge about influence currently available.

Milgram, S. (1974). *Obedience to authority.* New York: Harper & Row.

More than sixteen years after it was written, this book remains the definitive work on obedience as a social psychological process. The untimely death of its author only adds to its value as a lasting contribution to our field.

Hendrick, C. (Ed.). (1987). *Group processes.* Newbury Park, CA: Sage.

This book contains chapters dealing with several of the topics covered in this chapter (e.g., majority and minority influence, how groups affect the behavior of their members). Each chapter is written by an expert on the line of research and concept covered. This is a useful source to consult if you'd like to know more about key aspects of social influence.

Working With and Against Others: Prosocial Behavior, Cooperation, and Conflict

Prosocial Behavior

Cooperation and Competition

Interpersonal Conflict

SPECIAL SECTIONS

It's Friday afternoon, and as soon as this class is over, I'm jumping in my car and heading home to spend the weekend with Sean and Tom, Dave thought. *Has it really been three months since I last saw those two? Before college we got together almost every night.*

Dr. Sorenson, Dave's American history professor, was delivering another of his sleep-inducing lectures. On that particular Friday, it seemed to Dave that the class was even duller than usual. At the beginning of the hour, things seemed a little promising, because Dr. Sorenson came in pushing an audiovisual cart with a monitor on top and a VCR on the bottom shelf; whatever was on the tape, it had to be better than listening to Sorenson. As the lecture dragged on, however, Dave decided that the class period would end before the tape was played—time was running out.

But then Dr. Sorenson looked down at his watch, abruptly ended his lecture, and hastily reached for the tape. "If we get this thing started right away, there should just be enough time to finish it before the bell rings," he muttered, half to himself. He quickly bent down toward the VCR to insert the tape. In his haste, he didn't notice the corner of a metal coatrack that was positioned midway between his head and the VCR. A very loud thud was heard throughout the classroom as the top of Dr. Sorenson's bald head struck the sharp corner.

Nervous laughter broke out in the class. Then a student asked, "Dr. Sorenson, are you all right?"

For several seconds, the instructor remained bending over, clutching his head and saying nothing. Finally, in a very strained voice he responded, "Everything's okay . . . don't worry about me . . . it sounded much worse than it really was."

When he turned around to say this, blood was streaming through his fingers as they pressed against his head. A student in the front row shouted, "You're bleeding!"

At that, the professor looked at his hands and became very pale. Without saying a word, he pushed the start button on the VCR and rushed out of the classroom.

A student sitting just behind Dave asked, "Can you believe how much he was bleeding? I wonder if he really is all right?"

Other students began talking, ignoring the videotape:

"Maybe someone should check on him—he looked like a ghost when he left."

"What if he passes out on the floor somewhere out there?"

"Except for us, there's hardly anyone in the building this late on a Friday afternoon. It could be a while before anyone finds him."

The students nervously looked around at one another. Surely someone would volunteer to go out to see if Dr. Sorenson needed help. Dave's mind was racing: *Maybe I should go out, but I'm no expert on first aid, and I don't know if I could handle the sight of all that blood. Besides, what if it's only a minor problem? After all, he did say he was okay, and I would really feel stupid running out there if he was just getting a drink of water. There are thirty-five other people here, and I don't see anyone else jumping up. It's probably not that big of an emergency. Besides, he's a professor—he'd probably resent having a student come out to take care of him.*

Just then, the students' uncertainty was resolved because Dr. Sorenson walked back in. He was still holding his head, but it was no longer bleeding. He asked, as if nothing had happened, "How's the video?"

The students were clearly relieved, and ripples of laughter broke out. Once again, Dave's thoughts returned to the weekend that was about to begin: *It sure will be great to see Sean and Tom again. Maybe I'll tell them how I almost made a fool of myself today.*

Horney (1945) identified three classes of human social interaction: (1) moving toward people, (2) moving away from people, and (3) moving against people. Moving toward people involves behaviors carried out to please or help them. Moving away from people includes indifference and insensitivity to others. Moving against people is characterized by competitiveness, conflict, and aggression.

A large body of psychological research has focused on the circumstances under which these three kinds of interpersonal behavior are most likely to occur. What causes us sometimes to move toward others to offer help and to perform acts of kindness? Why do we sometimes move away from others by looking the other way when we encounter someone in need? Why do we sometimes move against others to engage in divisive and even violent conflict?

These questions will be discussed in this chapter. Specifically, we will examine *prosocial behavior*—acts that help other people; *cooperation*—behavior that is mutually beneficial to the person carrying it out and to others; *competition*—behavior that benefits the individual engaging in it at the expense of others; and *conflict*—confrontations between individuals or between groups.

Prosocial Behavior

A frequent theme in the 1988 presidential campaign of George Bush was the extent to which Americans give of themselves in order to help others in need. Bush used the phrase *a thousand points of light* to describe this phenomenon. Yet the fact that people help others is more than campaign rhetoric. Nearly half the adult population of the United States, or about ninety million people of various ages, ethnic backgrounds, and economic levels, voluntarily participate in charitable activities each year. Examples include visiting homebound senior citizens, delivering food and clothing to the homeless, serving as "buddies" for terminally ill AIDS victims, assisting runaway youth in urban shelters, and entertaining hospitalized children. A New York City accountant even volunteered to clean and bandage the infected rat bite of a homeless person each day (Hamill, 1986).

We sometimes encounter the need for help directly, as in the story about Dr. Sorenson's classroom accident. Do we then engage in **prosocial behavior** to help the person, or do we find a reason not to help? If you came across the situation shown in Figure 9.1, what would you do?

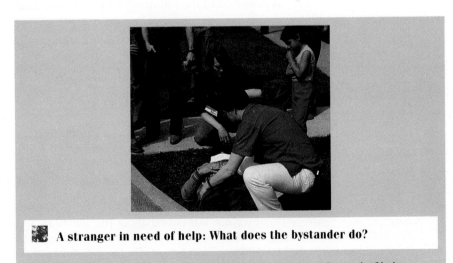

A stranger in need of help: What does the bystander do?

FIGURE 9.1 When an individual encounters someone in need of help, a series of decisions must be made, beginning with awareness that a problem exists and culminating in the final decision to help or not to help.

At times, the response to someone in need goes beyond simple helpfulness. **Altruism** refers to truly selfless acts that can include heroism in that they involve risk for the helper. An example of such a response occurred on January 13, 1982, when Air Florida flight 90 crashed into the icy water of the Potomac River in Washington, D.C. The ultimate act of heroic sacrifice was carried out by a man whose identity was never determined. When a life ring was thrown to him from a helicopter, he passed it on to other victims who were more badly hurt than he. By the time the rescue helicopter returned to pull him to safety, he had died beneath the frigid water (Gaily, 1982).

Despite many examples of helpfulness and courage, there are also examples of help being withheld even though a victim is desperately in need. This response was once labeled "bystander apathy," but research has made it clear that those who fail to help are not really apathetic. Probably the best-known example of failure to help occurred on March 13, 1964, at 3:20 A.M. Catherine (Kitty) Genovese was returning from her job as a manager of a bar. As she walked across the street from her car to the apartment house where she lived, a man with a knife came up to her. She ran; he chased, caught, and stabbed her. Genovese screamed for help, and lights came on in the windows of many apartments that overlooked the street. The attacker retreated temporarily but then came back to his bleeding victim. Again Genovese screamed for help, but this time her attacker did not retreat. Almost three-quarters of an hour after the attack began, Genovese lay dead from multiple stab wounds. Although thirty-eight persons reported hearing Genovese's screams, not one offered any assistance, and none even bothered to call the police (Rosenthal, 1964). Was this failure to help an isolated example of a few unusually heartless individuals? In fact, the failure of bystanders to respond is a common occurrence. In the twenty-five years since Kitty Genovese was violently murdered, similar incidents have been reported throughout the world.

For social psychologists, the central problem has been to explain why people sometimes help and sometimes do nothing. The beginning of this research is described in the following **Classic Contributions** section.

FOCUS ON RESEARCH: CLASSIC CONTRIBUTIONS

Let George Do It: Diffusion of Responsibility in an Emergency

It is not at all unusual for social psychological research to grow out of a real-life incident. The goal is to discover why such things happen. Research on the **bystander effect** came about as a direct result of Kitty Genovese's murder. John Darley described how the project was initiated, as he and Bibb Latané conversed over lunch:

> Everyone was talking about [the incident], and so were we. And, as we started to talk about it, we began to realize that this was something that could be analyzed in terms of the theories we knew and were teaching. We probably sketched out the experiments on a tablecloth that day. (Krupat, 1975, p. 257.)

Were there a psychological hall of fame, that tablecloth should clearly be in it. The experiment Darley and Latané designed was both inventive and the first step in an important program of research and theory. They initially proposed **diffusion of responsibility** as the explanation for the nonresponsiveness of bystanders facing an emergency. To test this idea, the experimenters created a bogus emergency involving a stranger in distress in the presence of varying numbers of bystanders. The hypothesis was that as the number of potential helpers increased, responsibility for helping would be diffused; as a result, the likelihood of helping would decrease.

When the undergraduate subjects arrived at the laboratory, they were told that they would discuss with fellow students some of the problems faced by those attending college in a high-pressure urban environment. Supposedly to avoid any embarrassment about revealing personal problems, each subject would be alone in a room, communicating through an intercom system. Further, the experimenter would not listen to any of the conversations. Subjects were also told that each participant was to talk for two minutes and then each would comment on what the others had said.

Some subjects were told that they were one of two discussants, others that they were one of three, and still others that six students were taking part. In reality, only one subject was present at each session, and the other "participants" were in fact tape recordings. Thus, a controlled emergency could be staged and the number of apparent bystanders manipulated.

In the "discussions," the first person to speak was the tape-recorded individual who was to be the emergency victim. He said, in a manner that sounded embarrassed, that he was prone to seizures, especially during stressful situations such as exams. The other participant or participants each gave a two-minute talk about college problems with the victim responding last. He began with a few calm, coherent statements and then began to "experience a seizure."

> I er I think I need er if if could er er somebody er er help because I er I'm er h-h-having a a a real problem er right now and I er if somebody could help me out it would er er s-s-sure be good . . . because er there er er a thing's coming on and and I could really er use some help so if somebody would er give me a little h-help uh er er er er er c-could somebody here er help er uh uh uh (choking sounds) . . . I'm gonna die er er I'm gonna die er help er er seizure (chokes, then is quiet). (Darley & Latané, 1968, p. 379.)

The investigators observed the percentage of subjects who responded within five minutes (by coming out of the small room to look for the emergency victim). They also measured the time that elapsed before such a response was made. As Figure 9.2 (p. 354) indicates, the number of perceived bystanders dramatically influenced helping behavior. As the number increased, the percentage of subjects attempting to help decreased and (for those who did respond) more time passed before a response was made.

In this experiment, when a fellow student seemed to have a serious problem, the typical subjects were very responsive. When they thought there were no other bystanders, the vast majority acted to provide help, and they did so quickly (in less than a minute). As the number of bystanders increased, however, helpfulness sharply decreased. Why? One suggestion was that when an individual is one of multiple witnesses to an emergency, he or she is in a no-win situation: It's uncomfortable to observe someone suffering, but it's also unpleasant to overreact and appear foolish to the other bystanders. A typical solution is to hold back and wait for someone else to take the responsibility. Under these

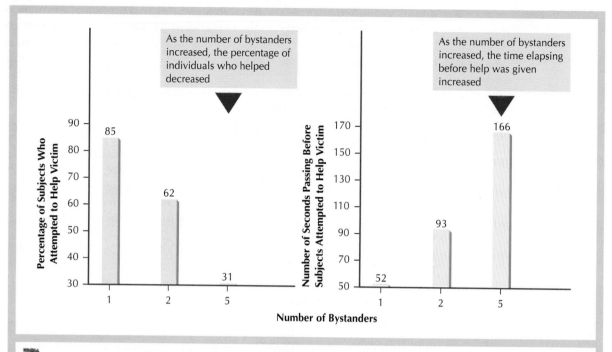

As the number of bystanders increased, the percentage of individuals who helped decreased

As the number of bystanders increased, the time elapsing before help was given increased

Diffusion of responsibility: Help decreases as number of bystanders increases

FIGURE 9.2 In an experiment dealing with prosocial behavior, subjects heard what appeared to be a fellow student having a seizure. The subject was supposedly the only bystander to this emergency, one of two bystanders, or one of five. As the number of bystanders increased, the percentage of subjects who tried to help the victim decreased. Moreover, for those who helped, the time elapsing before help was offered increased as the number of bystanders increased. (Source: Based on data from Darley & Latané, 1968.)

circumstances, although the bystanders seem apathetic they are actually emotionally upset and confused about what to do. These findings and these explanations initiated a large body of work on prosocial behavior.

Responding to an Emergency: Five Crucial Decisions

Latané and Darley (1970) conducted a series of interrelated experiments on the bystander effect, formulating a model of helping behavior. They conceptualized a helping response as the culmination of a series of cognitive choices (see Figure 9.3). In an emergency situation, an individual must make several preliminary decisions before a helpful response can occur. Unless the appropriate choice is made at each step, no help will be given.

To appreciate the details of the model, you may find it useful to imagine yourself in the class described at the beginning of the chapter. If you had been there, would you have done anything to help your professor? If you are at all similar to the students in the class of one of our colleagues when that painful (and embarrassing) incident actually occurred, it is quite likely that you would

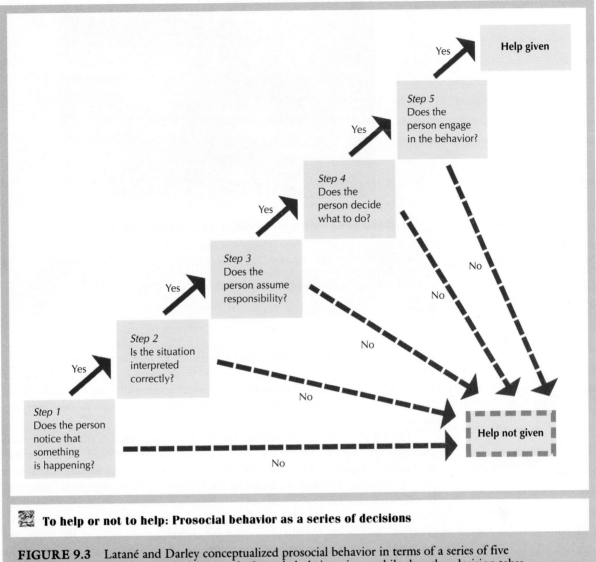

To help or not to help: Prosocial behavior as a series of decisions

FIGURE 9.3 Latané and Darley conceptualized prosocial behavior in terms of a series of five decisions. At each point, one decision results in no help being given, while the other decision takes the individual one step closer to the prosocial act. (Source: Adapted from Byrne & Kelley, 1981.)

not have. In his class of thirty friendly, well-adjusted students, no one left the room to discover whether the professor needed assistance when he injured his head. Presumably, these students did not make the necessary preliminary decisions at each step of the model. What determines such responses?

Noticing the Emergency The first decision is whether to notice the emergency. In Dr. Sorenson's classroom, noticing the incident was inescapable, but there are other situations when this is not the case. What if you walked out of a movie theater and saw a woman lying on the sidewalk with her eyes closed (see

If you don't notice the problem, you can't provide help

FIGURE 9.4 The crucial initial step in prosocial behavior is to notice the emergency. For people who are busy, preoccupied, or not attending to their surroundings for whatever reasons, it is easy to be unaware that an emergency exists.

Figure 9.4). You could easily pass by without paying any attention, perhaps because you are in a hurry to get back to your warm room on a cold winter night. Such responses are common on busy city sidewalks—pedestrians fail to notice those reclining in doorways and beside garbage cans, merely stepping around them.

The proposal that preoccupation with other concerns can affect whether an emergency is noticed was tested by Darley and Batson (1973). Seminary students participated in the study, and they were instructed to present a talk in a nearby building. For half the subjects, the talk was to be on the good Samaritan parable in Luke 10:25–37—about two high-status and presumably busy individuals who fail to offer assistance to a man lying half-dead on the ground. In contrast, a low-status individual (the good Samaritan) notices the man and helps him. The remaining subjects were asked to give a talk on jobs most enjoyed by seminary students. These subjects were further told that they were (1) ahead of schedule and had plenty of time, (2) right on schedule, or (3) late for their speaking engagement. On the way to give their speech, all subjects passed a confederate of the experimenters who was slumped in a doorway, coughing and groaning. Although the topic of the anticipated speech had no effect on helping, time pressures did. As Figure 9.5 indicates, help was offered by 63 percent of the subjects who believed they were ahead of schedule, 45 percent of those who believed they were right on schedule, and only 10 percent of those who believed they were late. The investigators noted that on several occasions the seminarians who were on their way to talk about the good Samaritan literally stepped over the victim slumped on the ground in their haste to make their appointments.

Interpreting the Situation as an Emergency If the emergency is noticed, the next decision involves the observer's interpretation of the incident. Is it really an emergency, or is it something more mundane? On a recent David Letterman show, the host showed a tongue-in-cheek film clip of his response to an "emergency situation": While walking down a street on a hot summer day, he encountered a locked car with a Baby on Board sign on the window. Fearing that a baby might be suffocating in the car, he smashed open a window and broke into the car. After searching through the car and finding there was no baby, he exclaimed with a tone of relief, "Boy, am I glad I was wrong about this!" Had this incident been real, Letterman, instead of being glad, would have been greatly embarrassed—and probably charged with property damage as well.

To avoid such consequences, most people are unlikely to take any drastic action unless they have convincing evidence indicating an emergency. If you heard loud screams coming from the dorm room below yours on a Saturday night, would you rush downstairs to offer help? You probably wouldn't. In that situation, you might easily believe the sounds were the result of too much beer at a party or of a blaring TV set and think nothing of it.

Getting back to the plight of Dr. Sorenson, could his comment that "it sounded much worse than it really was" cause his students to interpret the situation as a nonemergency? Surely students could see that he was bleeding from a head injury. Wouldn't the potential seriousness of such an injury override

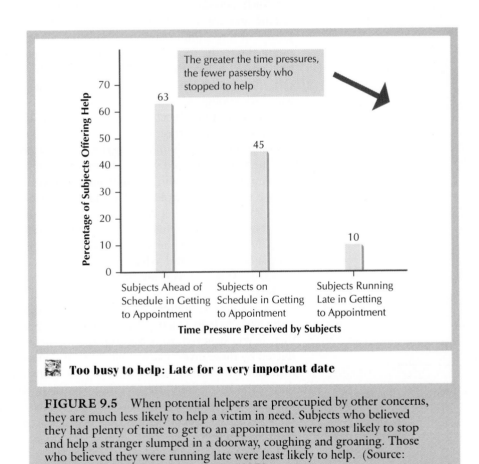

Too busy to help: Late for a very important date

FIGURE 9.5 When potential helpers are preoccupied by other concerns, they are much less likely to help a victim in need. Subjects who believed they had plenty of time to get to an appointment were most likely to stop and help a stranger slumped in a doorway, coughing and groaning. Those who believed they were running late were least likely to help. (Source: Based on data from Darley & Batson, 1973.)

his comments? Probably not, according to what has been found in a number of studies.

Many emergency situations involve some degree of ambiguity. People are not sure exactly what is going on, and they tend to hold back, waiting for additional information. And the more ambiguous the situation, the less likely it is that help will be offered (Bickman, 1972; Clark & Word, 1972). Because people may be reluctant to help in the first place, they are especially attentive to any information that suggests there is no need to be concerned (Wilson & Petruska, 1984).

When an emergency is witnessed by two or more persons, each bases his or her interpretation of the event on the reactions of the others. The difficulty is that in our culture we have learned it is socially appropriate to maintain a calm demeanor in an emergency. We are not "supposed" to scream and tear our hair. The result is that everyone pretends to be calm and then utilizes the apparent calmness of others in the group as an indication that the emergency is not serious. As a consequence, multiple bystanders conclude that the situation is much less serious than each would as a single bystander. This reliance on the responses of others is another example of the social comparison process, discussed in Chapter 6.

Such *pluralistic ignorance* was demonstrated in another experiment by Latané and Darley (1968). Here, subjects sat in a room either alone or in groups of three, filling out questionnaires. Shortly after they began, smoke was pumped into the room through a vent. The experimenters recorded how much time passed before the smoke was reported. If no one reacted within six minutes, the experiment was terminated—by that point, the smoke in the room was thick enough to obscure the subjects' vision. Among those working alone, 75 percent of the subjects reported the smoke, half of them responding within two minutes. In contrast, 62 percent of those in three-person groups continued working the entire six-minute period. In only one of the three-person groups was the smoke reported within the first four minutes.

Ambiguity may also account for outsiders' hesitating to intervene in response to domestic violence. Consider a situation in which you hear sounds from your neighbor's open window: There is shouting, the sound of crashing objects, and a female yells, "I hate you! I don't ever want to see you again!" Would you interpret the situation as an emergency and call the police? Most people would not. But what if there were the same sounds and the woman shouted, "Whoever you are, just get out of my house!" Now would you call for help?

According to findings by Shotland and Straw (1976), you would be much more likely to help a victim if you believed the person did not know the attacker than if you believed a relationship existed between the two. In a study conducted by these investigators, male subjects witnessed a staged fight between a man and a woman. In one condition, the woman screamed to her attacker, "I don't even know you!" In the other condition, the woman screamed, "I don't even know why I ever married you!" The results? Three times as many interventions took place when the fight was between strangers than when it involved a husband and wife.

Assuming Responsibility At the third decision point in the model, the bystander either does or does not assume responsibility to act. Though you may notice and correctly interpret an emergency situation, unless you believe it is your responsibility to do something you are unlikely to help. For example, if you were at a swimming pool and observed a swimmer calling for help in plain view of the lifeguard, you would be unlikely to jump in the water to provide help (see Figure 9.6). Instead, you would probably decide that helping a swimmer in distress is the responsibility of the lifeguard.

In other emergency situations when a group is present, the group leader is perceived to be responsible for taking action (Baumeister et al., 1988). For example, had a student, rather than Dr. Sorenson, injured his or her head in class, the professor, not fellow students, would be expected to do something about it. When there is no preestablished leader, who is supposed to deal with emergencies? Or if it is the leader who requires help, who is supposed to provide it? Who is responsible? Quite often, no one assumes the responsibility. When many bystanders are present, each one is a potential helper, and, as we have seen, this diffusion of responsibility decreases helping behavior.

The direct link between the number of bystanders present and the degree of perceived responsibility was documented by Schwartz and Gottlieb (1980). In this investigation, subjects observed an emergency either in the presence of another person or alone. Consistent with previous studies, less help was offered when the subject was with a second individual. When asked afterward about why they responded as they did, 80 percent of the subjects who were alone specifically mentioned that they believed they were personally responsible for offering help; only 17 percent of the subjects who were with another bystander indicated any feelings of personal responsibility for offering help.

Deciding How to Help: The Competence of the Bystander   When an emergency is noticed and correctly interpreted and the bystander accepts responsibility for

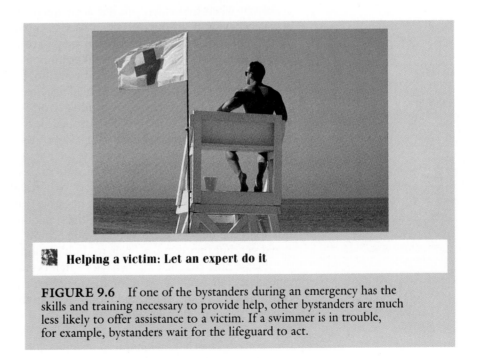

Helping a victim: Let an expert do it

FIGURE 9.6   If one of the bystanders during an emergency has the skills and training necessary to provide help, other bystanders are much less likely to offer assistance to a victim. If a swimmer is in trouble, for example, bystanders wait for the lifeguard to act.

offering help, a fourth decision must be made: *How* should the victim be helped? Once a bystander answers that question, a related one arises immediately: *Do I possess the skills to do what needs to be done?* Consider the swimming pool example. Even if you were the only person at the pool besides the victim, you would be extremely unlikely to dive in if you didn't know how to swim. If, however, you were an excellent swimmer and had been trained in lifesaving skills, you would be much more likely to try to help even if other bystanders were present.

The hypothesis that the competence of a bystander can overcome the diffusion of responsibility among multiple bystanders was supported by the research of Cramer et al. (1988). These experimenters found that when a bystander was present, registered nurses were more likely to offer assistance to an accident victim than college students were. When no bystander was present, however, the college students, despite a lack of medical training, were just as likely to offer assistance as were the nurses.

Deciding Whether to Help   The last decision in the model is whether or not to act. In a group situation, this decision is influenced to a large extent by possible costs, including rejection by the victim, getting one's clothes dirty, and the fear of making a social blunder. Emergencies often require behavior that is unusual, unexpected, and incompatible with our everyday roles. For example, by jumping up and offering assistance to an injured professor, a student runs the risk of being viewed as an apple-polisher by the other students and possibly as a pest to the professor, who may prefer being left alone. The most feared social blunder is that of responding inappropriately. This fear can be minimized, however, if the bystanders can discuss with one another just what is going on. For this reason, there is much less inhibition of prosocial behavior among bystanders who are acquainted than among those who are not (Latané & Rodin, 1969; Rutkowski, Gruder, & Romer, 1983).

Even when bystanders are not acquainted, there is less inhibition of prosocial behavior if an opportunity exists to interact with one another in the future and explain any behavior that may have appeared foolish (Gottlieb & Carver, 1980). As is the case with other inhibitory emotions, the fear of social blunders can also be greatly reduced by alcohol (see Figure 9.7).

To test the effect of alcohol on helping, Steele, Critchlow, and Liu (1985) placed subjects in a situation combining strong pressures both to help and to withhold help. Help was found to be more likely to occur when the bystanders had consumed a modest amount of alcohol than when they had consumed none. With more alcohol, the subjects were even more willing to help. Steele and his colleagues hypothesize that alcohol causes a kind of "cognitive myopia" in that the intoxicated person perceives only the victim's need and is unaware of possible inhibiting factors such as negative consequences that might follow or the presence of any ambiguities in the situation. Steele adds, "Now you may not want the help of a drunk . . . I don't know about the quality of the help you'd get, but they're more likely to do it" (quoted in Kent, 1990, p. 13).

Please note that helping behavior often occurs not in response to an acute emergency but as a long-term commitment to socially responsible action. People contribute their time, skills, and money to help those in need. Even so, the five decision steps are relevant. For example, to provide help to starving children in a distant country, you must become aware of the problem, interpret the children's needs correctly, assume responsibility for taking action, decide what to do, and then actually provide the necessary help.

🔲 **A positive effect of alcohol: Greater willingness to provide help**

FIGURE 9.7   Because alcohol reduces inhibitions and conflicts, a victim is more likely to receive help from bystanders who have been drinking than from those who have not. Research suggests that these Mardi Gras revelers would be more likely to provide help to a stranger than would totally sober individuals.

Helping: Role Models, Emotions, and the Victim's Responsibility

Beyond the effect of multiple bystanders, helping is also influenced by modeling, by the potential helper's emotional state, and by attributions about why the victim needs help.

Exposure to Helpful Models   Have you ever watched a street musician playing a guitar for a group of onlookers who contribute no money until one person tosses the first quarter into the instrument case? This single act is usually followed by a shower of coins and bills from the audience. In a study of similar behavior, Macauley (1970) found that the presence of contributing models greatly increases contributions placed into street-side Salvation Army collection boxes.

Just as the hesitation of others can cause people to hold back rather than help, the presence of helpful models can induce helping. Bryan and Test (1967) found male motorists to be much more likely to offer to change a woman's flat tire if they had recently observed a male helping another woman than if they had not been exposed to a helpful model.

The model for prosocial acts need not be someone actually present when the help is needed. Those appearing on television also influence what we do. As we'll see in Chapter 10, television violence can instigate real-life violence among children. Could the opposite also be true? That is, could television with prosocial themes increase the likelihood of prosocial behavior?

Sprafkin, Liebert, and Poulous (1975) showed six-year-old subjects either an episode of "Lassie" containing a rescue scene, a "Lassie" episode without a prosocial theme, or an episode from "The Brady Bunch" series that was humorous but did not involve prosocial acts. Later, while taking part in a competitive game, the children came into contact with puppies that seemed to be experiencing discomfort. Despite the fact that helping the puppies interfered with their chance to win a prize, those who had been exposed to the prosocial TV program spent much more time attempting to help the animals than did those who had been exposed to the other programs.

Still other studies have found that preschool children exposed to the prosocial content of "Mister Rogers' Neighborhood," "Sesame Street," and similar programming (see Figure 9.8) are more likely to engage in prosocial behavior than those who do not see these shows (Coates, Pusser, & Goodman, 1976; Forge & Phemister, 1987; Friedrich & Stein, 1973, 1975; Stein & Friedrich, 1972). Such studies consistently suggest that television is able to exert a very positive influence on the social development of children.

Positive and Negative Emotions: Mood and Helpfulness   Although intuitively you might expect good moods to foster good deeds, the effects of the helper's mood on his or her willingness to help are not that simple. Happy people are often more helpful than unhappy people, but sometimes the opposite is true. Several other variables must be taken into account before one can predict the effect of mood on helping in any specific situation.

Children sometimes wait for their parents to be in a really good mood before asking for something. The assumption underlying this strategy has been supported by a number of experiments. Whether the pleasant mood is induced by succeeding on a task (Berkowitz, 1972); finding money or receiving cookies (Isen & Levin, 1972); watching a happy movie (Underwood et al., 1977); being exposed to good news (Veitch, DeWood, & Bosko, 1977), soothing music (Fried and Berkowitz, 1979), or sunshine (Cunningham, 1979); or listening to a recording of Steve Martin (Wilson, 1981), the result is an increase in the likelihood of offering assistance to others.

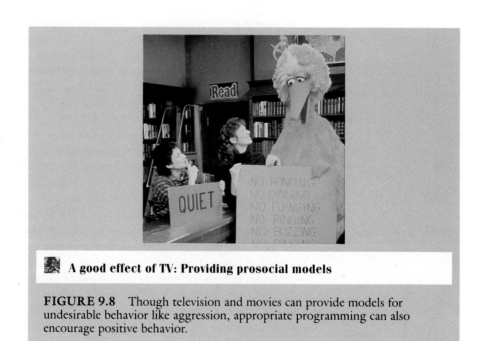

A good effect of TV: Providing prosocial models

FIGURE 9.8   Though television and movies can provide models for undesirable behavior like aggression, appropriate programming can also encourage positive behavior.

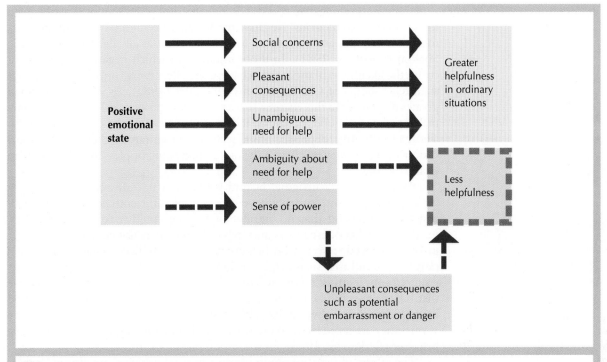

	Social concerns		
Positive emotional state	Pleasant consequences		Greater helpfulness in ordinary situations
	Unambiguous need for help		
	Ambiguity about need for help		Less helpfulness
	Sense of power		

Unpleasant consequences such as potential embarrassment or danger

Positive emotions: Sometimes more helpful, sometimes less helpful

FIGURE 9.9   A positive emotional state can lead to an increased or a decreased likelihood that an individual will engage in prosocial behavior. Positive feelings lead to greater helpfulness if social concerns are involved, the consequences of helping are pleasant, and the need for help is unambiguous. Positive emotions lead to less helpfulness if the need is ambiguous. Less helping also occurs if unpleasant consequences are involved; the happy individual feels powerful enough to refuse to help.

Yet despite the consistency of such research, contradictory findings have sometimes been reported as well (Shaffer & Graziano, 1983). A key factor accounting for the negative effect on prosocial acts that is sometimes found for positive emotions is the anticipated level of rewards and costs associated with helping. Acts that are potentially embarrassing or risky are inhibited by positive emotions (Forest et al., 1980; Isen & Simmonds, 1978; Rosenhan, Salovey, & Hargis, 1981), but acts associated primarily with rewards are fostered by such emotions (Cunningham, Steinberg, & Grev, 1980).

One explanation is that happy people are reluctant to do anything that might spoil their mood (Isen, 1984). In addition, a good mood induces a sense of personal power *(I can do anything!),* and this includes the power to say no to helping a stranger. According to Cunningham et al. (1990), those in an elated mood are most affected by social concerns associated with a request for help; for example, those in a positive mood respond well to interpersonal encouragement to help, and they are most likely to volunteer to help with a social task. (For a summary of the relationship between positive emotions and helping behavior, see Figure 9.9.)

The effects of negative moods on prosocial acts are even more variable than those of positive emotions. Negative moods have been found to foster helping, to inhibit helping, and sometimes to have no effect at all (Barden et al., 1981; Shelton & Rogers, 1981). In those instances in which negative emotions increase the likelihood of prosocial behavior, the effect is explained by the negative state relief model of Cialdini and his colleagues (1982). As we will discuss in greater detail later in this chapter, these researchers propose that because helping makes people feel good, people do it as means of escaping their negative moods. Those in a negative, depressed mood seem to concentrate on their own personal concerns, and so they will help if the task is interesting or pleasant (Cunningham et al., 1990).

As you can well imagine, helpful behavior is not always a remedy for a negative mood. You probably have experienced sufficiently strong feelings of anger or depression that no amount of helping could make you feel better. Further, the relief offered by some types of helping may not be worth the bother involved. Indeed, research on helping as a way to relieve negative emotional states has found that such helping is most apt to occur when (1) the behavior required appears to be relatively easy and effective, (2) there is reason to believe that bad feelings can be minimized by the behavior, and (3) the negative mood is not very intense (Berkowitz, 1987). When the negative emotions are very strong, they are more likely to predispose individuals to aggression or avoidance behavior (Berkowitz, 1983).

The effects of negative emotions on prosocial behavior are also influenced by the focus of those emotions. Thompson, Cowan, and Rosenhan (1980) found that helping is inhibited when a person focuses on his or her own misfortune, while helping increases when the focus is on the misfortune of someone else. These investigators suggested that directing one's attention toward the problems of others elicits empathy that motivates prosocial acts.

Further, negative emotions foster helping behavior when the person feels *personally responsible* for his or her mood (Rogers et al., 1982). (For a summary of these various factors involving negative emotions, see Figure 9.10.)

Characteristics of the Person in Need of Help According to Blount (1986, p. 81), "Panhandlers are as much a part of New York culture as investment bankers." Blount concludes that this situation forces New Yorkers to devise a personal policy for determining which individuals do and do not deserve money—for example:

> I only give money to old men. Young people can earn it and old women yell at you if you don't give it to them.

> I give [money] to old women because it's so sad. . . . Unless they're better dressed than I am. There's one on the corner of Bergdorf's who's got a different outfit on every day. Who is she kidding?

Although these particular selection strategies may well be unique to the New York City residents interviewed, it is likely that each of us perceives certain types of people to be more deserving of assistance than others.

As you might expect, attraction to an individual (see Chapter 6) greatly influences our decision to offer that person assistance. Despite the biblical command to love one's enemies, we seem to be more disposed to help people we like (Clark et al., 1987; Eisenberg, 1983; Schoenrade et al., 1986). Prosocial

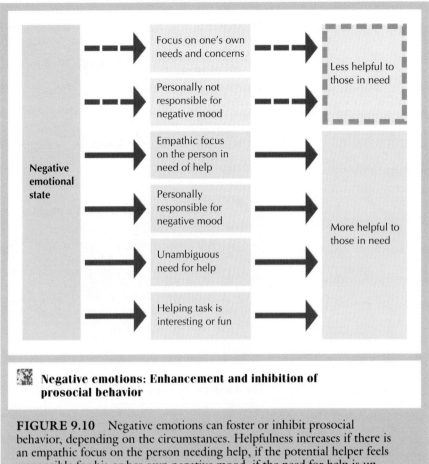

Focus on one's own
needs and concerns

Personally not
responsible for
negative mood

Less helpful to
those in need

Negative
emotional
state

Empathic focus
on the person in
need of help

Personally
responsible for
negative mood

Unambiguous
need for help

Helping task is
interesting or fun

More helpful to
those in need

Negative emotions: Enhancement and inhibition of
prosocial behavior

FIGURE 9.10 Negative emotions can foster or inhibit prosocial
behavior, depending on the circumstances. Helpfulness increases if there is
an empathic focus on the person needing help, if the potential helper feels
responsible for his or her own negative mood, if the need for help is unambiguous, and if the helping task is interesting or fun. Negative emotions lead to less helpfulness if the person's focus is on his or her own
needs and concerns and if the person does not feel responsible for the
negative mood.

behavior is clearly fostered by the various factors that increase liking, such as
physical attractiveness (Benson, Karabenick, & Lerner, 1976) and similarity to
self (Dovidio, 1984).

Sometimes, specific victims are helped on the basis of the reciprocity
norm—people do nice things for those who are nice to them (Gouldner, 1960).
In a similar way, individuals are more likely to help those who have helped them
in the past (Goranson & Berkowitz, 1966; Kahn & Tice, 1973). Studies have
even shown that those in helping occupations, such as nurses, are more likely
to be helped than individuals of the same social status who are not in helpgiving professions, such as bookkeepers (Yinon & Dovrat, 1987; Yinon, Dovrat,
& Avni, 1981). Even though we may not personally ever have been helped by
the former, we apparently feel they deserve reciprocation simply because their
help is potentially available to us.

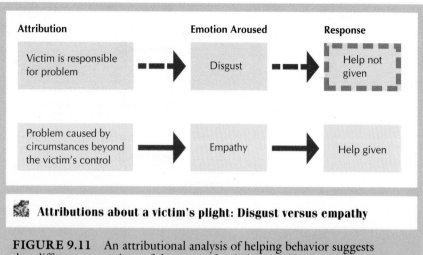

Attribution	Emotion Aroused	Response
Victim is responsible for problem	Disgust	Help not given
Problem caused by circumstances beyond the victim's control	Empathy	Help given

Attributions about a victim's plight: Disgust versus empathy

FIGURE 9.11 An attributional analysis of helping behavior suggests that different perceptions of the cause of a victim's problems lead to different emotional responses. If the victim is perceived as responsible for the problem, disgust is aroused and help is not given. If, however, external circumstances are perceived as responsible for the problem, empathy is aroused and help is given. (Source: Based on suggestions by Weiner, 1980.)

The Victim's Responsibility for the Problem Implicit in the familiar saying "You've made your bed, now lie in it" is the assumption that people are expected to find their own solutions to problems created by their own irresponsibility or carelessness. In part on the basis of assumptions about a just world (see Chapter 6), the victim is blamed for his or her predicament.

Such a reaction has been borne out in studies reporting that people are more likely to help those individuals whose plight is attributed to uncontrollable, external causes rather than those perceived to be personally responsible for their problem (Meyer & Mulherin, 1980; Reisenzein, 1986; Schmidt & Weiner, 1988). A model formulated by Weiner (1980) proposes that help-inhibiting disgust is elicited by individuals deemed responsible for their plight, whereas help-fostering empathy is elicited by individuals perceived as the victims of unfortunate circumstances (see Figure 9.11).

What Motivates Prosocial Behavior? Egoism versus Empathy

An issue attracting considerable attention among those studying prosocial behavior is the question of *why* people help others. Can such behavior be purely altruistic—carried out strictly because of concern for the victim—or is it always selfishly motivated? This issue, like so many other theoretical debates, is unlikely to be decided conclusively. Nevertheless, attempts to provide supporting evidence for each view are thought-provoking and interesting to follow. We will present findings from both sides and let you be the judge.

The Empathy-Altruism Hypothesis: Helping for the Sake of Helping Although prosocial behavior appears on the surface to be selfless, it is possible that people help others in order to receive recognition, financial reward, admittance to heaven, and other positive outcomes. In Mario Puzo's *The Godfather,* for example, the Mafia head achieved and maintained his power over his organization not through iron-fisted coercion but by performing favors for individuals under the implicit assumption that at some point those favors would be returned. Such egoistic motivation has been the basis of many psychological theories of apparent altruism (e.g., Campbell 1975; Hoffman, 1981; Midlarsky, 1968; Piliavin et al., 1981; Schwartz & Howard, 1982).

Opposing this depiction of selfishly motivated prosocial acts is the **empathy-altruism hypothesis** proposed by Batson and his colleagues (1981). According to this view, some (but by no means all) prosocial behavior is motivated solely for the purpose of increasing the welfare of the recipient (Batson et al., 1989). The empathy-altruism hypothesis is outlined in Figure 9.12.

To determine whether prosocial behavior could be based purely on empathic concern, Batson and his colleagues (Batson et al., 1981; Batson et al., 1983; Toi & Batson, 1982) devised an ingenious experimental procedure in which they manipulated the level of empathic concern for the recipient and the difficulty of escape for the help giver. Subjects in the experiment were each informed that they were to observe; on closed-circuit TV, a second subject performing a task while that person received random electrical shocks. Because the role of observer versus performer was seemingly determined by a chance drawing, subjects were led to believe that they themselves could easily be the one receiving the shocks. In reality, the "victim" was an experimental confederate whose videotaped performance included no actual shocks. As presented in the videotape, almost immediately the victim showed signs of great discomfort and indicated she'd had a traumatic experience with electricity as a child but was nevertheless willing to go on with the experiment. At that point, the experimenter would hesitate for a moment and then ask the subject if he or she was willing to trade places with the victim. Empathic concern for the victim was manipulated by informing the subjects that her values were similar (high

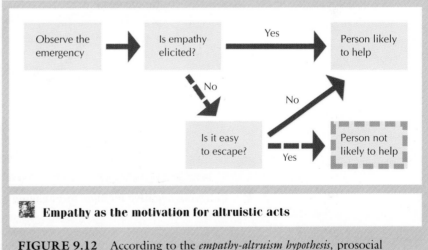

Empathy as the motivation for altruistic acts

FIGURE 9.12 According to the *empathy-altruism hypothesis*, prosocial acts are motivated by concern about the welfare of the victim. Without feelings of empathy, the bystander escapes from the scene if doing so can be accomplished easily. (Source: Based on suggestions from Batson et al., 1981, 1983; Toi & Batson, 1982.)

empathy) or dissimilar (low empathy) to theirs. Ease of escape was manipulated by informing subjects either that they could leave after witnessing only two random shock trials (easy escape) or that they were required to witness ten such trials (difficult escape). The results? When empathy was low, ease of escape minimized prosocial behavior, but when empathy was high, ease of escape had no effect. Thus, contrary to the egoistic perspective, empathic concern was found to foster prosocial behavior even when it would have been much easier for subjects simply to leave.

Critics argued that the helping behavior in that situation may have been motivated by social evaluation concerns (Archer, 1984; Archer et al., 1981). To explore that possibility, Fultz and his colleagues (1986) demonstrated that the same results could be obtained using a design that permitted the subjects to believe that neither the experimenter nor the victim would ever know if they declined to help.

The Egoistic Perspective: The Negative State Relief Model   Earlier we described how negative moods do not always inhibit helping behavior and indeed can even increase its likelihood. An explanation for this finding is provided by the **negative state relief model** (Cialdini et al., 1973, 1981; see Figure 9.13). This model indicates that individuals experiencing negative emotions are moti-

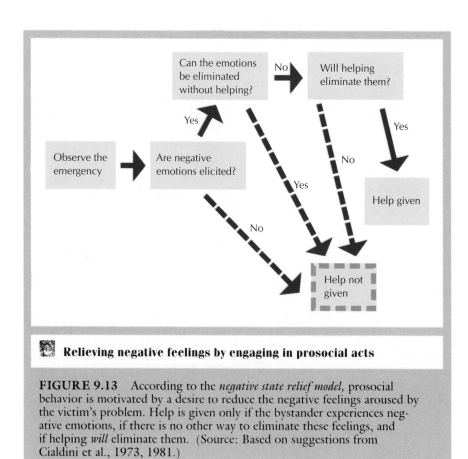

Relieving negative feelings by engaging in prosocial acts

FIGURE 9.13   According to the *negative state relief model*, prosocial behavior is motivated by a desire to reduce the negative feelings aroused by the victim's problem. Help is given only if the bystander experiences negative emotions, if there is no other way to eliminate these feelings, and if helping *will* eliminate them. (Source: Based on suggestions from Cialdini et al., 1973, 1981.)

vated to help in order to achieve relief from such emotions. The negative emotions need not be preexisting when an emergency is encountered; in many cases, the emergency situation is itself a source of unpleasant emotions that individuals are motivated to reduce (Fultz, Schaller, & Cialdini, 1988).

Cialdini and his colleagues (1987) argue that the prosocial behavior observed in studies supporting the empathy-altruism hypothesis is motivated simply by the subject's desire to escape his or her own sad feelings. In support of this contention, they cite two experiments that found that (1) an empathic orientation toward a victim increased sadness; (2) when the effects of empathy and sadness were examined separately, helping was increased by sadness but not by empathy; and (3) when subjects were led to believe that, because of the temporary effects of a "mood-fixing" drug (a placebo) they had been given, helping could not affect their emotions, empathic concern for a victim had no effect on helping.

In a follow-up study, Schaller and Cialdini (1988) found that when subjects expected to be exposed to a mood-elevating comedy tape, those in the high-empathy condition helped no more than those in the low-empathy condition. Taken together, these various findings suggest that helping behavior fostered by empathic concern for a victim is motivated by the subject's desire to minimize personal sadness. When sadness cannot be minimized by helping or when it can be minimized without helping, helping does not occur.

An Empathic Rebuttal   Though the findings from the Cialdini research seemed conclusive, Batson and his colleagues (1989) responded by presenting the results of three experiments that directly contradicted the findings of Schaller and Cialdini (1988). Briefly, the new research indicated that anticipating a mood-enhancing experience did not negate the positive effect of empathy on helping, regardless of whether the helping was done publicly or anonymously. Moreover, a study by Schroeder et al. (1988) found that the effects of empathy on helping were not affected by a subject's belief that his or her mood resulted from a "mood-fixing" placebo.

Empathic Joy: An Alternative Egoistic Interpretation of Helping   Just when the debate seemed to have reached a stalemate, a "dark horse" hypothesis appeared on the scene. According to Smith, Keating, and Stotland (1989), helping in response to empathy is motivated by neither a selfless concern for the welfare of others nor the reduction of personal sadness but, rather, the joy one experiences when observing that another person's needs have been met (see Figure 9.14, p. 370).

Such joy can even be experienced when the victim's needs are met by other bystanders. If you have ever seen the movie *It's a Wonderful Life*, you undoubtedly experienced this kind of positive feeling when the character played by Jimmy Stewart was rescued from financial ruin by the unsolicited contributions he received from the people he had helped throughout his life. When the joyful state (sometimes referred to as *helper's high*) results from one's own actions, it is associated with calmness, feelings of self-worth, and a physical sensation of warmth (Luks, 1988).

To compare the validity of the **empathic-joy hypothesis** with that of the empathy-altruism and negative state relief hypotheses, Smith, Keating, and

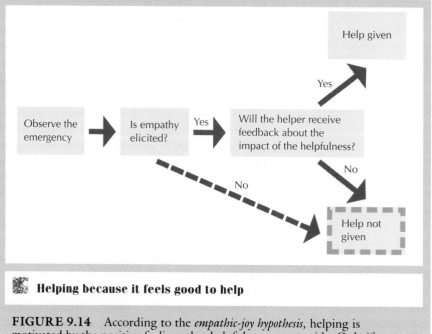

Help given

Observe the emergency → Is empathy elicited? — Yes → Will the helper receive feedback about the impact of the helpfulness? — Yes → Help given — No → Help not given

No → Help not given

Helping because it feels good to help

FIGURE 9.14 According to the *empathic-joy hypothesis*, helping is motivated by the positive feelings that helpfulness can provide. Only if a bystander will receive feedback about the impact of his or her actions will prosocial behavior occur. (Source: Based on suggestions from Smith, Keating, & Stotland, 1989.)

Stotland (1989) conducted an experiment in which they manipulated whether or not subjects received feedback about their helping. The rationale was that although one must observe the positive effects of one's help to derive any joy from it, feedback is unnecessary when one's motivation either is purely altruistic or reflects the need to relieve a negative state. Subjects were shown a videotape of a female college student who indicated that she was considering leaving the university because of stress and feelings of isolation. The participants were informed that they could offer her advice on how to cope with college life. Half were told that if they gave advice, they would see a follow-up tape on which the student would report how effective the advice was; the remainder believed they would have no further contact with the woman whether or not they gave advice. Empathy was manipulated in terms of the similarity between the subject and the person needing help. The investigators found that empathy fostered helping only when subjects anticipated being able to see the fruits of their advice. In other words, joy was a necessary component of prosocial action.

Obviously, the results of a single experiment do not conclusively invalidate the other two explanations of the motivation behind helping. Still, if this finding is replicated in future research, the empathic-joy hypothesis may prove to be a useful way to bring together the competing theoretical explanations.

It might seem that the psychological explanations of prosocial behavior just discussed more or less exhaust the possibilities. But in fact there is another, biologically based theory of altruism. It is described in the following **Cutting Edge** section.

FOCUS ON RESEARCH: THE CUTTING EDGE

Do We Help Others in Order to Preserve Our Genes?

If you were in a busy shopping center and suddenly saw your brother lying unconscious next to the exit, would you stop and help him? Of course. If the person were a stranger but nevertheless similar to you in age and race, would you stop and help? Probably. Why? According to the intriguing yet controversial theoretical analysis of Rushton (1989a), the answer lies in your genes. While other aspects of this formulation were noted in earlier discussions of prejudice (Chapter 5), friendship (Chapter 6), and love (Chapter 7), we will now describe the underlying reasoning in greater detail.

Studies of species such as ants and aphids indicate that the greater the genetic similarity of two individuals, the more each engages in altruistic acts when the other needs help (Ridley & Dawkins, 1981; Wilson, 1975). From the viewpoint of the "selfish gene," genetic survival can best be ensured by helping family members so that they will be able to live and reproduce. Those who are related to one another share common genes, so it is genetically advantageous to each for all such relatives to reproduce (Rushton, Russell, & Wells, 1984).

Because siblings are 50 percent similar with respect to their genes, by taking any kind of risk to protect the safety of a brother or sister you are increasing the odds that at least half your genes will be passed on to future generations even if you yourself fail to reproduce. This formulation goes beyond the individual to account for behaviors that lead to *maximizing inclusive fitness*. That is, each individual is motivated not only to live long enough to pass on his or her individual genes but also to enhance the reproductive odds for those who share some of those same genes.

What does any of this have to do with altruistic acts directed toward unrelated friends or total strangers? Rushton (1989a) argues that we seek out lovers and spouses who are genetically similar to ourselves; we mate not with random strangers but with a partner who has genes similar to our own. We somehow perceive this underlying similarity and respond positively to it. The result is that offspring who are more similar to us genetically than would occur with random pairing are produced and our segment of the gene pool is thus enhanced. As noted earlier, this preference for genetic similarity also affects attraction.

You can see how the genetic argument holds for a stranger in distress (see Figure 9.15, p. 372). By helping people we like (i.e., those genetically similar to us), we are helping preserve the genes that we have in common.

A major problem with this proposal is the question of how we determine who is most genetically similar or dissimilar to ourselves. Though Rushton concedes there is no clear answer to this question, he does suggest a few possibilities. First, he says, in that we are familiar with the appearance and behavior of our close relatives, we may assume that those who look and act similar to them may be genetically similar to us. Second, he cites a study of several thousand British and Australian twins indicating attitudes may in part be genetically determined (Martin et al., 1984); one conclusion is that attitude similarity leads to attraction not because of positive affect, balance, and so on

Helping those with genes like yours

FIGURE 9.15 Which stranger would you help? According to Rushton's (1989a) genetic explanation of altruism, you would help the stranger most similar to yourself, because the two of you probably share common genes. This explanation assumes that altruism is based on behavior that results in preserving the helper's portion of the gene pool.

but because such attitudes indicate genetic similarity. Third, he argues that we also make inferences about genetic similarity on the basis of familiarity and propinquity. Because we are most familiar with and live closest to those whose genes we share, we simply assume that anyone who lives and works near us (and thereby becomes familiar) is genetically similar. Given the way in which prejudice and segregation operate, assumptions about the genetic similarity of our neighbors may be at least partially accurate.

As interesting as these ideas are, Rushton's theory has attracted a good deal of criticism. Critics point out, for example, that short of giving blood tests to those we meet, it is very difficult to determine the degree to which we are genetically similar (Anderson, 1989; Dunbar, 1989). Then too, the findings indicating attraction to those who are genetically similar may only mean that we like those who resemble our parents (Daly, 1989; Gangstad, 1989). The sociobiologist would reply that we like those who resemble our parents not on the basis of some unconscious Freudian motive but because such preferences have been beneficial in preserving genes.

Regardless of the final answer, the genetic theory of prosocial behavior is intriguing.

Cooperation and Competition

Whatever the underlying motivation to provide help to others, the act itself is beneficial to the person being helped. A related behavior is **cooperation,** in which mutual helpfulness is clearly beneficial to all participants.

In almost every situation in which two or more persons interact, the participants can often be observed cooperating with one another in order to obtain some mutually desired outcomes. Players on a basketball team pass the ball to one another and physically block opponents trying to cover their teammates—acts that increase the odds of someone on the team having an open shot (see Figure 9.16). College students frequently share class notes before a test so that each can benefit from material he or she might have missed or misunderstood. Roommates work together to keep their living area clean and the refrigerator stocked. In short, cooperation is a familiar part of our lives.

There are also numerous situations in which individuals fail to cooperate. Instead, they engage in **competition** to determine who can get the biggest share of some resource for themselves. With competitive behavior, an individual appears to be motivated solely by selfishness, greed, and the desire to win. Rather than passing the ball, a basketball player sometimes takes foolish shots in an attempt to obtain a high individual scoring total. In group study sessions, there are inevitably some students who jot down everyone else's notes but have none of their own to share with others. And anyone who has lived with a roommate is well aware of the possibility of noncooperation in that setting: Dishes pile high in the sink as each person plays a waiting game to find out who will finally break down and wash them all; shared supplies of food, beverages, and other household goods are depleted and never restocked. Indeed, in his college days a colleague lived through an entire hot summer in the Midwest without ice cubes, because neither he nor his roommates were willing to refill the trays after using some of the ice.

Although it may seem that cooperation is always more desirable than competition, that is not necessarily true. The fact that businesses compete with one another for our money provides us with an array of goods and services unavailable in countries with noncompetitive economic systems. Competition can also motivate people to do their very best. Among salespeople, for example, a bonus paid to the person with the most sales can motivate the entire staff to work harder. How do these examples differ from instances of harmful competition?

Cooperation: Working together to reach a common goal

FIGURE 9.16 In many situations, people engage in cooperative behavior in order to reach a shared goal. The aim is for the group to succeed.

Healthy competition consists of working toward one's own self-interest in ways that benefit others as well. The more each individual car salesperson sells, the more financially healthy the dealership as a whole. In contrast, harmful competition occurs when people work toward their own personal gain in ways that cause problems for others.

The Robber's Cave experiment of Sherif and his colleagues (1961), described in Chapter 5, is a classic study of cooperation and competition. Divided into two groups, the young campers were placed in competitive situations, and the members of each group soon became hostile and aggressive toward those in the opposing group. This very unpleasant interpersonal situation was then reversed when the experimenters introduced tasks with *superordinate goals* that forced the boys to work together, thus creating friendly relationships across group boundaries. In part because of the enormous expenditure of time and effort required to carry out such research, those interested in studying cooperation and competition have turned to more limited interactions in the laboratory.

In this section we will examine why people often cause harm to others by behaving selfishly and how cooperation can be encouraged in such situations.

Social Dilemmas

A **social dilemma** is a situation in which selfish behavior results in individual gain but can result in collective disaster (Dawes, 1980). For each individual caught in a social dilemma, competitive behavior will lead to a greater payoff than cooperation will, but all are better off if every individual cooperates rather than competes.

When each resident of an apartment restocks the food he or she takes from the refrigerator, there is always an available food supply for all to share. But if one person defects from the restocking rule, that person eats at the expense of the remaining cooperators—and if no one cooperates, the refrigerator soon resembles Mother Hubbard's cupboard. Other examples of common social dilemmas include such behaviors as giving money to support public broadcasting, voting in an election, and protecting the environment. In each case, the cooperative behavior brings little or no immediate reward and may actually involve some cost. Failure to cooperate is profitable but would harm the entire community if everyone behaved selfishly (see Figure 9.17).

Games That Simulate Social Dilemmas   Mathematical models are used to formulate games that reproduce social dilemmas in the laboratory. Although math models may sound intimidating, the resulting games are among the most involving experiments in all of social psychology. According to Dawes (1980), tears, profanity, and verbal threats are common among the subjects participating in cooperation experiments. To help you understand how college students can become emotionally involved in social dilemma games, we will describe two common types.

The **take-some game,** shown in Table 9.1, gives students the opportunity to profit at the expense of others (Dawes, 1980). In one version of the game, subjects in groups of three are each given the opportunity to hold up either a red or a blue chip. If a participant holds up a red chip, he or she receives $3.00 but the other two group members are each fined $1.00. Each player who holds up a blue chip is awarded $1.00 with no fine. Therefore, if every player holds up a blue chip, everyone earns $1.00, but if everyone holds up a red chip, no

FRANK AND ERNEST · by Bob Thaves

TAKE A NUMBER FOR SERVICE

FOR FASTER SERVICE TAKE A NUMBER FROM SOMEONE WHO GOT HERE BEFORE YOU.

Competition: Individuals act to help themselves

FIGURE 9.17   When an individual decides to compete rather than cooperate, he or she has responded to a social dilemma in a way that brings personal rewards while harming others. If everyone were to behave as the second sign in this cartoon suggests, all would suffer. (Reprinted by permission of NEA, Inc.)

money will be paid out, because the three fines will negate each person's payoff. Despite the advantages of cooperative behavior in this situation, the typical player is found to hold up a red chip because he or she risks only a $1.00 fine while standing to gain a $2.00 profit at the other players' expense.

This laboratory game situation is analogous to that faced by industrial managers deciding whether or not to invest in pollution control. On the one hand, if every factory in a city were to curb its emission of pollutants, the quality of life for all residents, the managers included, would improve. On the other

The take-some game: Do you cooperate or not?

TABLE 9.1   In a three-person *take-some game*, used to study social dilemmas, players face a choice of cooperating or profiting at the expense of others. The greatest gain is made by a player who does not cooperate when the other two players *do* cooperate. The greatest loss is experienced by a cooperating player who interacts with two noncooperating individuals.

Number of Players Who Cooperate	Money Received by Noncooperators	Money Received by Cooperators
3	—	$1.00
2	$2.00	0
1	$1.00	−$1.00
0	0	—

hand, a selfish, noncooperative decision has its advantages. The pollution emitted by one factory would not seriously affect its owners and employees, and the money saved by not investing in pollution control could increase profits. Sometimes it pays to be a bad guy so long as everyone else is a good guy.

A second laboratory task is the **give-some game** (see Table 9.2), which provides players with the opportunity to contribute to the public good (Dawes, 1980). In a version devised by Bonacich (1972), each member of a group of five players is given the choice of either taking $8.00 or giving $3.00 to each of the other players. If all cooperate, each will receive $12.00, but each defector significantly reduces the payoff for cooperating. By contrast, defecting guarantees at least $8.00 and, with enough cooperators, can lead to a substantially higher payoff. Again, refusing to cooperate can be personally beneficial.

A real-life situation analogous to this game is that of the group project in a course in which group members each receive the same grade based on the total project. The more each individual contributes, the better the overall grade, but a defector can, in many cases, receive a good grade even if he or she does nothing—that is, be so rewarded simply on the basis of the work done by other group members.

A variation of these games is the **minimal contributing set game** designed by Rapaport and Bornstein (1987) as a way to study *step-level public goods dilemmas*. Unlike group grades on projects that could vary from *F* to *A*, step-level public goods are distributed in an all-or-nothing fashion: There is total success or total failure. For example, victories in sporting events or elections depend on the number of points scored or votes cast; if there are enough, everyone on the team or in the political party benefits regardless of whether or not they contributed to the outcome. In the experimental game, players are

 The give-some game: Either cooperation or noncooperation can pay

TABLE 9.2 In the *give-some game*, used to study social dilemmas, five players must each decide whether or not to cooperate. If all five cooperate, each receives $12.00; if none cooperates, each receives $8.00. The biggest gain occurs for one person who fails to cooperate while all the others do cooperate; the greatest loss, for one person who cooperates while the other four players do not.

Number of Players Who Cooperate	Money Received by Noncooperators	Money Received by Cooperators
5	—	$12.00
4	$20.00	$ 9.00
3	$17.00	$ 6.00
2	$14.00	$ 3.00
1	$11.00	0
0	$ 8.00	—

given a sum of money that they can keep or donate to the group. If the number of contributors exceeds some minimal level set by the experimenter, everyone in the group receives a financial bonus regardless of whether or not he or she contributed any money. A subject is most likely to make contributions if he or she perceives that cooperating will be critical to group success (Rapaport & Bornstein, 1988).

The Commons Dilemma   Still another social dilemma task frequently used in cooperation research has been labeled the **variable game** (Dawes, 1980). In one version of this game Edney (1979a, b), the researcher, provides a group of subjects with a bowl containing metal nuts, the goal being for each participant to obtain as many nuts as possible. Each subject can remove any number of nuts at any point, but every ten seconds the experimenter will double the number of nuts in the bowl. If all the nuts have been removed, the experimenter will add no more. The most constructive long-term behavior is to remove only modest numbers, so that the total number of nuts will increase, benefiting the entire group. But in fact the average subject grabs as many as possible, and the bowl is emptied in the first ten seconds.

This game is based on what Hardin (1968) referred to as "the tragedy of the commons." As we'll discuss further in Chapter 13, human beings are over-taxing the earth's capacity to replenish itself. Hardin drew the analogy of colonial American cattle owners overgrazing shared pastureland—each attempting to obtain as much milk and meat as possible. Because each owner behaved selfishly, the pastures were destroyed, resulting in less milk and meat for all.

One experiment duplicated the commons situation in Japan. In this study, Sato (1987) presented subjects with a simulated forest from which they could harvest trees and receive money. The longer they waited to do so, the larger the trees grew and the more money they were worth. Analogous to the behavior of American students grabbing the metal nuts, the subjects in Sato's investigation rushed to remove most of the trees before they grew to their maximum size and maximum value.

The Prisoners' Dilemma   Beyond the social dilemma games, cooperation is also studied in a task known as the **prisoners' dilemma.** The name is derived from the following hypothetical situation (Rapaport, 1973): Two fugitives are arrested and locked in separate cells. Though the district attorney lacks sufficient evidence to guarantee a major felony conviction, enough evidence is available to convict each prisoner of a minor crime. In an attempt to convict at least one of them as a felon, the district attorney goes to each prisoner separately and offers the following deal. If the suspect admits that he and his fellow prisoner committed the felony and the other person does not confess, the prisoner will go free and his partner will receive a ten-year sentence. If the partner confesses but the prisoner does not, the opposite will occur. If both confess, they will each receive a five-year term. Finally, if neither confesses, they will both be convicted of a minor crime and will each get a one-year sentence. Figure 9.18 (p. 378) summarizes these possibilities.

Obviously, the key to cooperation in this situation is trust. Each prisoner wonders, "If I take the risk of the big penalty in order to help my partner, will he take a similar risk for me or will he work toward his own interest and leave me high and dry?"

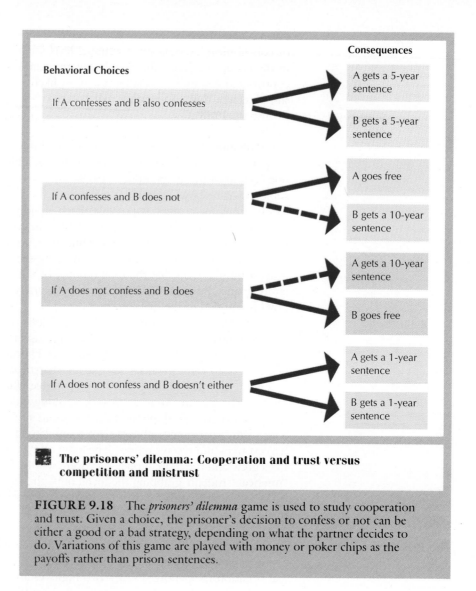

Behavioral Choices

Consequences

If A confesses and B also confesses	A gets a 5-year sentence
	B gets a 5-year sentence
If A confesses and B does not	A goes free
	B gets a 10-year sentence
If A does not confess and B does	A gets a 10-year sentence
	B goes free
If A does not confess and B doesn't either	A gets a 1-year sentence
	B gets a 1-year sentence

The prisoners' dilemma: Cooperation and trust versus competition and mistrust

FIGURE 9.18 The *prisoners' dilemma* game is used to study cooperation and trust. Given a choice, the prisoner's decision to confess or not can be either a good or a bad strategy, depending on what the partner decides to do. Variations of this game are played with money or poker chips as the payoffs rather than prison sentences.

Studying Responses to the Prisoners' Dilemma   Research on behavior in such situations is based on two-person games in which the monetary rewards for cooperative versus competitive responses for each individual are dependent on whether the other person engages in competitive or cooperative behavior. Typically, these games are played repeatedly by the two players and the overall pattern of responses is examined.

Just as occurs in international situations in which leaders must decide to trust or distrust the other side, opponents often take advantage of subjects who are trusting and cooperative in these laboratory experiments (Reychler, 1979).

Differentiating Prisoners' Dilemmas from Social Dilemmas   According to Dawes (1980), three important characteristics differentiate the prisoners' dilemma from the social dilemma.

1. In the prisoners' dilemma, the harm resulting from competitive responses is directed specifically at the other player, whereas in social dilemmas harm is diffused throughout a group.

2. Competitive responses in the prisoners' dilemma are public, whereas those who fail to cooperate in social dilemmas are often anonymous.

3. Unlike those facing social dilemmas, players in prisoners' dilemma games can attempt to affect opponents' responses. Because the game is played repeatedly, players can punish competitive responses with competitive responses of their own and can reward cooperative responses with cooperation.

When Do People Cooperate?

Because individuals obviously engage in both cooperative and competitive behavior, it is important to be able to predict when one or the other response is more likely to occur. Several crucial factors have been identified.

Reciprocity As indicated in our earlier discussion of prosocial behavior, the reciprocity norm has a powerful impact on human behavior. With respect to cooperation and competition, people tend to cooperate with cooperators and to compete with competitors (Black & Higbee, 1973; Rosenbaum, 1980). There are, however, notable exceptions to this rule.

First, individuals differ in how strongly they adhere to the reciprocity norm. Haley and Strickland (1986) found that when a partner initially promised to cooperate but then actually behaved competitively, depressed individuals were far more likely to respond with extreme levels of competitiveness than nondepressed individuals were (see Figure 9.19). The results of this investigation

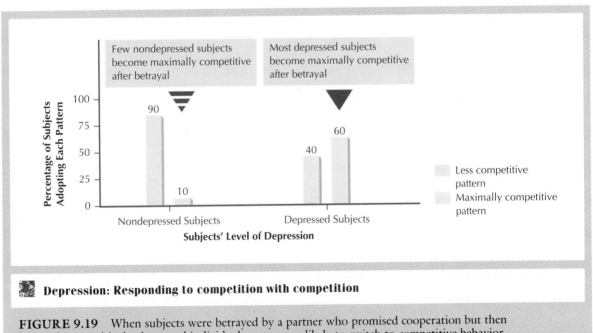

Depression: Responding to competition with competition

FIGURE 9.19 When subjects were betrayed by a partner who promised cooperation but then behaved competitively, depressed individuals were more likely to switch to competitive behavior themselves than were nondepressed individuals. (Source: Based on data from Haley & Strickland, 1986.)

suggest that among those who are depressed, betrayal activates their negative personal and interpersonal schemas, thereby minimizing trust and maximizing competitiveness.

Second, as indicated above, cooperative behavior offered freely without any requirement of cooperation on the part of others may invite exploitation. In one study, 129 out of 143 participants in a prisoners' dilemma game responded to total cooperation from an opponent with exploitation (Shure, Meeker, & Hansford, 1965). In this instance, nice guys really did finish last.

Third, perceptions of how cooperative or competitive another person is can be distorted by the self-serving bias described in Chapter 3. As a result, we often overestimate our own degree of cooperativeness and underestimate that of other persons (Youngs, 1986).

Attribution and Social Exchange: Reacting to the Perceived Motives of Others
A given cooperative act by another person can be interpreted in many ways. On the one hand, that person might be genuinely attempting to help both of you obtain a reward you both desire. On the other hand, he or she might be setting you up in order to take advantage of you. These two alternative explanations involve different attributions about the basis of the other person's behavior (see Chapter 2). When others cooperate, we are more likely to respond cooperatively if we believe their cooperation is sincerely motivated than if we attribute their acts to a devious strategy that will eventually cause us harm (Brickman, Becker, & Castle, 1979; Enzel, Hansen, & Lowe, 1975; see Figure 9.20).

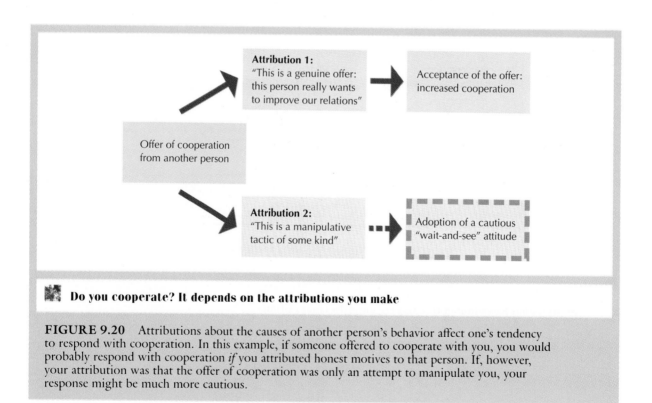

Do you cooperate? It depends on the attributions you make

FIGURE 9.20 Attributions about the causes of another person's behavior affect one's tendency to respond with cooperation. In this example, if someone offered to cooperate with you, you would probably respond with cooperation *if* you attributed honest motives to that person. If, however, your attribution was that the offer of cooperation was only an attempt to manipulate you, your response might be much more cautious.

Although you may not be surprised that our decision to cooperate with another person is affected by our attributions about that person's motivation, you might not be aware that in some situations the relationship can be reversed: One's own competitiveness or cooperativeness can influence the attributions made about others. For example, if you are very cooperative, you are not as likely to attribute the cooperation of others to ulterior motives (Messe & Sivacek, 1979). This tendency to interpret the behavior of others as reflecting our own motivations has been attributed to the **false consensus effect** (see Chapter 6). What's more, both cooperators and noncooperators perceive those who respond in the opposite way from themselves as "ignorant" (van Lange, Liebrand, & Kuhlman, 1990).

The fact that attributions play a key role in determining how we respond in social exchange situations means, unfortunately, that we often make incorrect attributions. We may reject potentially useful help because we are overly suspicious, and we can be suckered by con artists and others who pretend to be working for our benefit.

Communication   Intuitively, effective communication would seem to be necessary in order to coordinate cooperative behavior. Indeed, studies using variable games have shown that groups allowed to communicate behaved more cooperatively and, as a result, were able to amass more resources than groups not allowed to communicate (Braver & Wilson, 1986; Dawes, McTavish, & Shaklee, 1977; Edney & Harper, 1978; Harper, 1977; Orbell et al., 1988).

Similar findings have been obtained in studies using the step-level public goods game (Rapaport & Bornstein, 1989). Here, discussion seems to foster group identity, which in turn minimizes both selfish plundering of the group's resources and taking a "free ride" on the contributions of other members (Bornstein et al., 1989; Kramer & Brewer, 1984; Orbell et al., 1988).

Threats   Some types of communication do not foster cooperation. Particularly ineffective is the use of **threats,** which consist of warnings that failure to behave in a specific manner will result in dire consequences. For example, if a dorm neighbor is driving you crazy with loud music when you are trying to study, you could barge into that person's room and announce that the next time he or she wants to study, you'll turn up your own music. Although such threats are a common response to unwanted behavior, they are usually ineffective (see Figure 9.21, p. 382).

The problem is that threats lead to counterthreats and a general pattern of retaliation in which both parties lose (Deutsch & Krauss, 1960; Youngs, 1986). How would your dorm neighbor respond to your threat? It might well be some version of the line shared by Clint Eastwood and former president Reagan: "Go ahead, make my day!"

Group Size   In discussing bystander intervention, we pointed out that the more people present in an emergency situation, the less responsibility falls on each individual to offer assistance. Could group size affect behavior in dealing with a social dilemma as well? In the case of public goods dilemmas, this seems very likely. When many other people are involved, it is easy to assume that the critical total will be reached without your individual effort. Besides, one vote or one positive act is not likely to have much impact.

Threats: A common but ineffective form of communication

FIGURE 9.21 Threats represent one of the most common responses to unwanted behavior—whether one is dealing with children, criminals, or other nations. Nevertheless, this kind of communication is an ineffective way to bring about cooperation.

The existence of a negative relationship between group size and cooperation has been consistently found in experiments (Bonacich et al., 1976; Marwell & Schmidt, 1972). Isac and Walker (1986) suggested, however, that group size per se does not affect cooperation. Instead, they identified **marginal per-capita return (MPCR),** the amount each individual will benefit if the public good is obtained, as the crucial factor. Because MPCR normally diminishes as group size increases, a negative relationship is typically found between group size and cooperation. When MPCR is held constant by increasing the benefits of cooperation as group size is increased, group size exerts no effect on cooperation (Rapaport, Bornstein, & Eref, 1989).

Personal Orientation: Cooperators, Competitors, Individualists, and Equalizers
Although cooperation and competition are reliably affected by the situational factors discussed above, it is also true that some people are either very competitive or very cooperative regardless of the situation they are in.

In one interesting study, Derlega and Grzelak (1982) concluded that most of us exhibit one of four general patterns of social exchange.

The primary motive of **competitors** is to win. As one of history's all-time great competitors, football coach Vince Lombardi once said, "Winning isn't everything—it's the *only* thing." For such individuals, the main concern is how well they are doing compared with everyone else in the interaction. Even if they do badly, that is not a problem so long as everyone else does worse.

Cooperators are motivated to maximize the rewards obtained by everyone involved in a social exchange. For them, winning is not very satisfying, because somebody else must lose.

Individualists are chiefly concerned with maximizing their own gains. How well others are doing in any given situation makes no difference to them.

For **equalizers,** the main goal is to minimize the differences in the reward levels obtained by everyone in a social exchange situation.

As you might suspect, not everyone falls neatly into one of the four categories; many individuals exhibit combinations of these patterns (see Figure 9.22). In particular, two combinations are relatively common: (1) the individualist-competitor, who wants to do as well as possible but is also interested in outperforming others, and (2) the individualist-equalizer, who, by contrast, wants to do as well as possible without getting too far ahead of others.

The behavioral effects of such orientations were demonstrated by McClintock and Allison (1989). Subjects who had been classified on the basis of test responses were later mailed a request to volunteer up to ten hours of their time to a worthy cause. As predicted, the cooperators were willing to contribute more time to the cause than either the individualists or the competitors.

Gender and Cooperation-Competition Knight and Dubro (1984) examined the frequency of each of the personal orientation patterns among males and females. Among males, the competitor orientation was most common, and it occurred much more frequently than among females. The cooperative orientation, in contrast, was much more common among females than among males. These findings suggest that there may be substantial differences between males and females in responding cooperatively versus competitively.

In a give-some game situation, women were found to be slightly more cooperative than men, but the effect of gender was much smaller than the effect

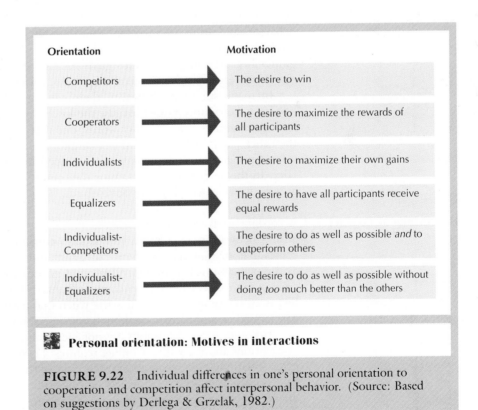

Personal orientation: Motives in interactions

FIGURE 9.22 Individual differences in one's personal orientation to cooperation and competition affect interpersonal behavior. (Source: Based on suggestions by Derlega & Grzelak, 1982.)

of group size (Stockard et al., 1988). It was also found, however, that whether or not females cooperated, they were more likely than males to report being oriented toward harmonious group relations. This latter finding suggests that while the women in this study may have been inclined to cooperate, they were not willing to cause disharmony by pushing the matter.

When an individual is assigned to carry out a project for a class in a two-person group, is the work affected by the partner's gender? What if the partner contributes little or nothing to the outcome—does the gender of the person make a difference?

These questions were addressed by Kerr and MacCoun (1985), who hypothesized that because traditional sex roles dictate that it is appropriate for men to provide for women rather than vice versa, both males and females would be more willing to allow a male partner to do most of the work on a group task than to allow a female partner to do so. Further, the investigators predicted that both sexes would be more annoyed with a free-riding male than with a free-riding female. Both hypotheses were confirmed. The findings suggest that women neither expect nor are expected to work on group projects as hard as their male partners do. This stereotype-based pattern seems to rest on lower expectations for women and could tend to limit their aspirations and foster dependency on men.

Interpersonal Conflict

With both social and prisoner dilemmas, the possibility exists that cooperative behavior can lead to greater payoffs for the individuals involved than if they all worked for their own benefit. Such situations are known as **nonzero-sum games** because one participant's gains minus the other participants' losses do not always equal zero. It is therefore possible for everyone to win.

In many situations, however, there can be only one winner. These are known as **zero-sum games** because the loser's losses subtracted from the winner's gains equals zero. In other words, one party cannot gain without causing the other party to lose. Common examples are sports contests, lawsuits, and wars. Cooperation is impossible, and competition often escalates into a **conflict.** In this section we will examine the origins and effects of conflict, as well as ways in which conflicts can be resolved.

Definitions of Conflict

According to Raven and Kruglanski (1970), conflict is the state of tension arising between two or more individuals or groups because they desire outcomes that are mutually incompatible. Pruitt and Rubin (1986) define conflict as the perception held by individuals and groups that the outcomes they are seeking cannot be achieved simultaneously. According to Thomas (1990), conflict is an ongoing process that starts when one party believes the other party has harmed or will harm something he or she values.

Although these definitions are not identical, they share several important assumptions about conflict. Conflict requires: (1) opposing interests (zero-sum game situations), (2) recognition on the part of the conflicting parties that they have opposing interests, (3) beliefs on both sides that the other has caused or intends to cause harm to its interests, (4) an ongoing interaction between the parties, and (5) direct actions carried out by one or both sides that harm the interests of the other side.

Causes of Conflict

To those involved in a conflict, the cause is usually clear—it's the other guy's fault. Are there more objective ways to identify the cause?

Competition for Scarce Resources   Whenever there is a finite amount of a highly desired resource, conflict is almost certain to arise. Among roommates, space is such a resource, for if one roommate clutters the living space with clothes, books, and papers, there is less available space for others. Marital conflicts can arise about how to spend a limited income, racial conflicts may center on job opportunities or political power, and territorial conflicts can and do lead to wars.

Within organizations, such resources as money, office space, equipment, personnel, and various perks are both scarce and valued. As a result, conflicts between individual employees and between groups within organizations are so frequent and costly that they occupy an estimated 20 percent of the average manager's time (Thomas & Schmidt, 1976).

Revenge   The reciprocity norm is not limited to positive interchanges. It also operates in negative interactions—"an eye for an eye"—and is the basis for an important source of conflict: revenge. In many instances, there is no competition for a resource. Instead, each is trying to "set the record straight" by punishing the other for perceived injustices.

When an act makes one party lose face by appearing foolish, there is a strong negative reaction to the person responsible. The resulting grudge can cause the aggrieved individual to spend months or even years plotting revenge (Baron & Richardson, 1991). In organizations, revenge may take the form of strikes, insubordination, or even the disclosure of company secrets (Raelin, 1984).

Attributions   Just as attributions about another person's cooperative behavior determine reciprocation, attributions about another person's harmful behavior determine how one responds. Was it a misunderstanding or an accident, or did the other person deliberately intend to do harm? Suppose you say hello to someone, and the person says nothing in return. Is that person deliberately trying to snub you? What if after you walk past this individual, a friend who had observed the two of you says, "You know, I really feel bad for Heather, her grandmother just died. They were really close." Now your feelings of anger turn to sympathy. As in research on aggression (see Chapter 10), attributions influence how we respond to the negative acts of others (Johnson & Rule, 1986).

Consider another situation: You and two other students are working on a difficult project. The three of you divided the tasks equally, you and one of your partners completed your portions of the project flawlessly, and now, if the third partner can do the same, you've got an *A* cinched. But two days before the remaining portion is due, the third partner calls you up and asks you to do his share and to put his name on it because he needs to go home to attend his grandmother's funeral. Would you feel empathy toward this individual, or would you suspect he was lying? Because either explanation is plausible, your confidence in each is reduced—an example of the **discounting principle** discussed in Chapter 2. In Chapter 15, such reactions will be discussed in greater detail.

Research on attribution and conflict indicates that perceived insincerity arouses considerable anger and the decision to avoid the individual in the future or to be confrontational should further conflicts occur (Baron, 1988). If the other person provides adequate reasons for his or her negative acts and is perceived as sincere, there is much less anger and a decrease in perceived unfairness (Bies, Shapiro, & Cummings, 1990).

Faulty Communication The results of two recent surveys have shown that faulty communication was the largest source of conflict within work groups of employees (Baron, 1988b; Baron & Bingley, 1989). Have you ever been angered by a comment that you later learned was made without any hostile intent? Depending on your mood, it is even possible to interpret compliments as criticisms if they aren't worded strongly enough. For example, if you expect to be told your new outfit looks "great," being told that it looks "okay" can be viewed as a negative remark.

Going one step further, attempts at constructive criticism can easily be misinterpreted as a personal attack. Criticism is least likely to incite conflict when it is specific, prompt, and considerate (Ilgen, Fisher, & Taylor, 1979; Ilgen, Mitchel, & Fredrickson, 1981; Liden & Mitchel, 1985). All too often, however, these conditions are not met, and the effects of such destructive criticism will be described in Chapter 10. It sometimes happens that our fear of offending others causes us to avoid saying anything critical until we are too angry to hold back. After the victim stifles his or her anger over a series of provocative incidents, one more small remark or action becomes "the last straw," and there is an angry outburst. The perpetrator, in turn, is surprised by this reaction and perceives the other person as overreacting in an unjustified fashion to this one isolated event (Baumeister, Stillwell, & Wotman, 1991). In effect, the two participants in such interpersonal conflicts often have very different views about what caused the problem and who is to blame.

Managing Conflict

If you were asked to list the pros and cons of conflict, the con list would almost certainly be longer. Conflict can be costly to a relationship and to an organization. Among other things, conflicts within a group can be a major handicap when dealing with external ones. When a conflict continues to build, the results are increasingly negative, with homicide and war being the most extreme examples.

There are, however, benefits to be gained from controlled conflicts. Problems that might not otherwise be noticed are exposed and can be addressed. Conflict facilitates innovation and change. And conflict between groups can increase loyalty, motivation, and performance within a group.

Because conflict is common and because it can be beneficial, rather than attempting to eliminate it, the key is to *manage* its occurrence, though individuals vary in how they believe conflicts should be resolved (Grace & Harris, 1990). In a relationship or an organization, the strain caused by attempting to avoid all conflict is likely to be greater than that which would be produced by proper management. By "management," we mean carrying out procedures that maximize the potential benefits of conflict and minimize its costs. What are those procedures?

Bargaining   By far the most common means of managing conflict effectively is **bargaining** (Lewicki & Litterer, 1985). Basically, this method involves an exchange of offers and counteroffers between the conflicting parties that will lead to an agreement acceptable to both. If such an agreement is not reached, however, the result may be a deadlock that intensifies the conflict.

What determines whether agreements can or cannot be reached? The tactics of bargaining are crucial. For example, when negotiating over the price of a car, is it better to take a "tough" stance by making an extreme offer containing few concessions, or is it better to take a conciliatory approach that involves a more reasonable first offer coupled with sizable concessions? Research has shown that the answer depends on the availability of other offers. The tough strategy is effective when few alternatives are available to the person on the receiving end of the strategy (Lawler & MacMurray, 1980; Yukl, 1974). In such cases, a tough strategy may lower an opponent's expectations, thereby causing him or her to be satisfied with less. In contrast, when many alternatives are available, a conciliatory approach is much more likely to result in agreement (Shelom, Walker, & Esser, 1985). Among other considerations, this "soft" strategy creates a good first impression unlike the negative effects caused by a tough stance (Esser, 1989).

In the bargaining process, if you dwell on your potential losses you are adopting a **negative frame,** but if you focus on your gains you are adopting a **positive frame** (see Chapter 3). Research has shown that adopting a positive frame results in far more concessions from an opponent than can be obtained from adopting a negative frame (Neale & Bazerman, 1985). A negative frame encourages inflexibility, because concessions are perceived as losses. With a positive frame, though, concessions are perceived as merely the price one pays to achieve the desired goal. In other words, it is better to view the proverbial glass as half-full rather than half-empty.

In addition to the helpful effect of positive cognitions, positive affect also can improve how individuals respond to conflict. Even simple interventions such as humor, mild flattery, or a small gift induce positive feelings and make collaboration more likely than competition (Baron et al., 1990).

Walton and McKersie (1965) noted that individuals may choose to view conflicts as (1) win-lose (zero-sum game) situations, in which one person's gains are always equal to the other person's losses, or (2) win-win situations, in which it is possible for both parties to succeed. In fact, many conflicts that on the surface appear to be win-lose situations can become win-win situations with the use of **integrative agreement strategies**—techniques that attempt to find ways in which both parties can benefit from the agreement.

Pruitt and Rubin (1986) describe several common integrative agreement strategies. *Nonspecific compensation* refers to one side getting what it wants on a specific issue, while the other is compensated by a concession on some unrelated issue. You might ask the person in an adjoining dorm room to keep his music turned down on weeknights; in return, you offer him your lecture notes for a class. Another strategy is *logrolling,* whereby each party makes a concession on a low-priority issue in return for a concession on a high-priority issue. If your date has a mild preference for Chinese food but loves horror films, whereas you have a passion for pizza and a slight preference for comedy films, you could give up the comedy film in exchange for the pizza, and your date could give up the Chinese food in exchange for the horror film. A third tactic is *cost cutting*—one party gets what it desires but the other party's costs are reduced. The salesperson may not lower the price of the car, but the customer is given an extended period on the loan so that her monthly payments are less than they would be had the price simply been lowered.

When integrative strategies are used to settle conflicts, not only do both parties benefit, but threats and tough stances decrease while the open exchange of accurate information increases. In conflict situations, it is advisable to ask yourself, *Can we both win?* You may be surprised how often the answer is yes.

Third-Party Interventions   Regardless of the strategy used or the frames adopted, there are times when no agreement can be reached. In such instances, outside assistance may be helpful (Lewicki & Litterer, 1985; Sheppard, 1984). The assistance usually comes in the form of either **mediation** or **arbitration.**

In mediation, an outside party is asked to assist both sides in reaching an agreement. The mediator cannot impose any binding decisions, because compliance is voluntary, but instead attempts to clarify issues and facilitate communication between the disputants. Professional mediators use a variety of tactics, depending on the details of the specific dispute (Lim & Carnevale, 1990). In arbitration, both parties agree to submit their dispute to an impartial arbitrator who will formulate a settlement. And whereas in *binding arbitration* both parties are required to accept the arbitrator's decision, in *voluntary arbitration* either party is free to reject the settlement.

Mediation is effective when the mediator can control the future of the disputants (Hamilton, Swap, & Rubin, 1981), probably because mediators with such power can offer the disputants inducements for settling. In addition, conflicts involving great differences between the disputants' positions are more likely to be resolved through mediation than smaller, less important disputes are (Hiltrop & Rubin, 1982). In major disputes, either side would lose face by backing down, but this situation doesn't happen if the mediator is responsible.

Escalative Interventions   On the face of it, intensifying a conflict in order to solve it may seem a little like attempting to put out a fire with gasoline. According to Van de Vliert (1984; 1990), however, this notion is not nearly as crazy as it sounds.

The specific strategy employed by Van de Vliert is to intensify the conflict by such tactics as emphasizing to each side the incompatibility of their goals, increasing direct contacts between the parties, and urging both participants to express their negative feelings about each other. Once the conflict is intensified to the point at which it is almost intolerable, the negotiator helps both sides to channel their aroused emotions into working out integrative agreements. Van de Vliert (1990) has shown that such interventions can be effective in resolving both marital and organizational conflicts.

Introducing Superordinant Goals   As with the young campers in Sherif's experiment, people belonging to one's own group are usually viewed favorably, whereas those outside one's group are lumped together and viewed negatively (Linville, 1982). How can this tendency to form group distinctions be countered? A familiar theme in science fiction is the development of harmony between warring nations when both are confronted by the common threat of interplanetary invaders. The same principle can be applied in real life: Disputes between members of an organization tend to be overlooked if a competing organization is perceived as the common enemy.

Even without a common enemy, the members of any large group probably share some **superordinant goals**—goals that tie the interests of the various subgroups together, as we discussed in Chapter 5. Focusing on such goals can be an effective way of bridging the us-versus-them distinctions that affect many conflict situations.

In brief, conflicts need not lead to disaster. They can serve useful functions, and they can be managed and even resolved to the satisfaction of both sides.

SUMMARY AND REVIEW

Altruism

Prosocial behavior refers to acts of helping that have no obvious benefit to the helper. Latané and Darley (1970) suggest that helping in an emergency depends on making a series of decisions, beginning with noticing the situation and ending with the decision to help. The process is influenced by helpful models, positive and negative emotions, the attractiveness of the recipient, and the degree to which the recipient is perceived to be responsible for the problem. Explanations for helpfulness include the **empathy-altruism hypothesis,** the **negative state relief model,** the **empathic-joy hypothesis,** and the genetic model.

Cooperative versus Competitive Behavior

The extent to which people either work together toward a common goal or work against one another toward individual goals has been studied in simulated games that consist of **social dilemmas** and the **prisoners' dilemma.** Research using various games has shown that cooperation is influenced by the reciprocity norm, attributions about

the motivation underlying the other person's cooperation, types of communication employed, the size of the group facing a dilemma, and individual differences in orientation toward cooperation or competition.

Conflict between Individuals and Groups

Conflict refers to interactions in which individuals or groups attempt to obtain mutually incompatible outcomes. Conflict occurs when there are opposing interests, recognition by the conflicting parties that their interests are incompatible, belief on each side that the other has caused or intends to cause harm to its interests, an ongoing interaction between the parties, and actions by one or both sides that harm the other side's interests. Conflict can be caused by competition over scarce resources, the desire for revenge, and attributions about the behavior of others. Conflict can be managed through bargaining or negotiation, through third-party interventions like arbitration or mediation, by a skillful escalation of the conflict, and through the introduction of superordinant goals.

Altruism Selfless acts that benefit only the person in need, sometimes involving risk for the individual who behaves altruistically.

Arbitration In bargaining, a form of third-party intervention in which the person who intervenes provides a solution.

Bargaining A form of social exchange in which individuals trade offers and counteroffers in an attempt to reach an agreement acceptable to both participants.

Bystander effect The finding that effective responses to an emergency are less likely to occur (and more likely to be delayed if they do occur) as the number of bystanders increases.

Competition A form of social exchange in which individuals attempt to maximize their own outcomes, often at the expense of others.

Competitors Individuals whose primary concern in social exchange is to do better than their opponent or opponents.

Conflict A direct confrontation between individuals or groups whereby one or both sides perceives that the other has thwarted or will thwart its interests.

Cooperation A form of social exchange in which two or more persons coordinate their behavior in order to reach a shared goal.

Cooperators Individuals whose primary concern in social exchange is to maximize the outcome for all participants.

Diffusion of responsibility The proposition that when multiple bystanders are at the scene of an emergency, the responsibility for taking action is shared among all members of the group. As a result, each individual feels less responsible than if he or she were alone.

Discounting principle The tendency to reduce the importance assigned to one potential cause of a given behavior when other potential causes are present.

Empathic-joy hypothesis The proposal that prosocial behavior is motivated by the joy aroused by helping someone in need.

Empathy-altruism hypothesis The proposal that prosocial behavior is motivated solely for the purpose of benefiting the recipient.

Equalizers Individuals whose primary concern in social exchange is that all participants receive the same benefits.

False consensus effect The tendency to believe that most people agree with oneself about a given issue.

Give-some game Used to study social dilemmas, a task in which each participant can keep a sum of money for himself or herself or give a portion of it to the others. The biggest payoff comes to an individual who behaves selfishly while the other participants behave cooperatively.

Individualists Those whose primary concern in social exchange is to maximize their own benefits.

Integrative agreement strategies That solution to a conflict in which both parties can succeed.

Marginal per-capita return (MPCR) The amount of benefit received by each individual if enough of the others behave cooperatively in a social dilemma situation.

Mediation In bargaining, a form of third-party intervention in which the one who intervenes tries to help the two sides reach an agreement.

Minimal contributing set game Used to study social dilemmas, a task in which a participant can keep a sum of money or donate it to the group. If the total amount contributed reaches a sufficiently high level, all participants get a bonus.

Negative frame A tendency to focus on the potential costs in a bargaining situation.

Negative state relief model The proposal that prosocial behavior is motivated by the desire to attain relief from a negative emotional state.

Nonzero-sum games Situations in which gains minus losses do not always equal zero.

Positive frame A tendency to focus on potential gains in a bargaining situation.

Prisoners' dilemma A situation in which each of two participants can be punished or rewarded for cooperative or competitive behavior, the outcome depending on whether the other participant engages in cooperative or competitive behavior.

Prosocial behavior Acts that benefit others but have

no obvious benefits for the person who carries them out.

Social dilemma A situation in which selfish behavior can result in gain for the individual but loss for the group.

Superordinant goals Those goals shared by individuals and by groups which can override the concerns that led to conflict.

Take-some game Used to study social dilemmas, a task in which each participant holds up a chip that either (1) rewards himself or herself and costs the others or (2) provides a smaller reward for himself or herself and no costs to the others.

Threats A form of communication in which one individual informs another that negative consequences will follow if that person does not respond in a certain fashion.

Variable game Used to study social dilemmas, a task in which each participant has access to a common pool of resources. At varying intervals, the experimenter increases the size of the pool by a fixed percentage. If the participants limit themselves, the pool is maintained indefinitely; if they are greedy, the pool disappears.

Zero-sum games Situations in which the gains minus the losses always equal zero.

FOR MORE INFORMATION

Blalock, H. M., Jr. (1989). *Power and conflict*. Newbury Park, CA: Sage.

The author brings together research and theory on conflict resolution that involves various kinds of social conflict, ranging from interpersonal confrontations to international ones.

Eisenberg, N. (1985). *Altruistic emotion, cognition, and behavior*. Hillsdale, NJ: Erlbaum.

Two of the crucial factors determining altruism—emotions and cognitions—are the central focus of this book. Specific topics include sympathy, conceptions of altruism, and moral decision making.

Lewicki, R. J., & Litterer, J. A. (1985). *Negotiation*. Homewood, IL: Richard D. Irwin.

This is a clear, concise, and well-written summary of current knowledge concerning the process of negotiation. Described are basic aspects of this form of communication, persuasion, and the personalities of negotiators, along with practical tactics for negotiators.

Pruitt, D. G., & Rubin, J. Z. (1986). *Conflict*. New York: Random House.

A very readable summary of research in the areas of conflict escalation, stalemate, and settlement is presented by two experts in this field. Specific topics include definitions of conflict, sources of conflict, problem solving, and third-party interventions. Numerous real-world examples are used to clarify the concepts introduced in the book.

Aggression: Its Nature, Causes, and Control

Did you see this article?" Jean Pilowski asks her husband, Frank. "Ugh—it really gives me the creeps."

"Which one—the story about that gang and the old couple?"

"Yeah, that's it. How could fifteen- and sixteen-year-old kids do things like that, especially to helpless old people? It says here that the man was kicked so many times, almost all his ribs were broken. And one of the gang actually burned his initials onto the woman's forehead with a lit cigarette. It makes me feel kind of sick."

"What do you expect? You let scum like that run around free and that's what happens. They ought to be locked up for life—or worse."

"But what makes them *do* things like that? The old couple gave them all their money, but then the kids went for them anyway, like they enjoyed hurting just for its own sake."

"They probably did, the sadistic little monsters! That's how they get their kicks—hurting people who can't fight back," Frank replies. "Anyway, I think it's all in their genes. Look at their parents—assuming you can find them. I'll bet they were out doing the same kind of thing when *they* were young. This stuff runs in families; human garbage, I call it."

"I don't know," Jean says thoughtfully. "How can it be that simple? Think of the kind of life these kids have had. That's important, too. Maybe if they came out of a different environment they'd be more like other teenagers."

"Next you'll be blaming it all on violence on TV!" Frank answers sarcastically. "What should we do, kiss them on both cheeks and let them go?"

"No, I'm not saying that. We have to protect people like this poor old couple. You can't put these kids back on the street; they'd just do the same kind of thing again. But I just don't believe they're *born* bad. I mean, take a step back and think about what it would be like to be one of them. You've got no family life—maybe no family; you spend your time living in filth, boiling hot in the summer and freezing in the winter. The only people you see with any money are pimps, thieves, and drug dealers. So your heroes are people like that, or maybe gang leaders, and you kind of take violence for granted. How can you expect those kids to be like the ones in our neighborhood?"

"You can't. But I don't expect them to go around beating and torturing grandparents, either. You don't have to be middle class to know right from wrong. So, I repeat: Kids like that are human garbage and ought to be treated like it. Nothing you're going to do will ever change them, so let's just get them out of circulation!"

"You're wrong, Frank," Jean replies heatedly. "I think you *can* work with them and help. . . . They don't have to be like this all their lives. But anyway, now that we're on the subject, maybe we should go ahead and put those extra locks on the doors. The way things are these days, there's no sense taking any chances. . . ."

Who is correct? Is aggression an inherited tendency, as Frank suggests? Or is it shaped by external factors and past experience, as Jean believes? Reading a current newspaper or listening to the evening news, it's tempting to side with Frank—to assume that some people *are* simply violent by nature. Rape, murder, war, terrorism, child abuse—each day we learn of unsettling new instances of human cruelty and violence. Despite the frequency of such events, however, social psychologists generally believe that human **aggression**—the intentional infliction of some form of harm on others—is anything *but* inevitable (Baron, 1977; Lysak, Rule, & Dobbs, 1989). They have concluded, largely on the basis of extensive research findings, that aggression is a complex form of behavior, one whose roots are equally complicated and diverse. Thus, the fact that aggression is extremely frequent in many parts of the world is *not* an indication that it is part of our inherited human nature (see Figure 10.1).

Aggression: Frequent but *not* inevitable

FIGURE 10.1 Violence is disturbingly common in many parts of the world. Despite this fact, however, social psychologists do not view it as an unavoidable, innate part of human behavior.

If aggression is not universal in our species and is not an inevitable part of our human nature, where *does* it come from? What factors influence its occurrence? And how can it be controlled? It is on questions such as these that social psychologists have focused their attention. To provide you with an overview of their major findings, we'll proceed as follows.

First, we'll describe several different *theoretical perspectives* on aggression—contrasting views about the nature and origins of such behavior. Some of these views are mainly of historical interest, but others represent the cutting edge of our current knowledge about this topic. Next, we'll review various *social* causes of aggression—factors related to the words or actions of others (or our interpretations of them) that seem to initiate or intensify aggressive reactions. To complete the picture, we'll then turn to several *personal* causes of aggression—characteristics or traits that seem to predispose specific persons toward more than their fair share of aggressive encounters. Finally, in order to end on a fairly optimistic note, we'll examine various techniques for the *prevention and control* of human aggression. As will soon be apparent, a degree of optimism is justified, for several of these techniques do appear to work.

Theoretical Perspectives on Aggression: In Search of the Roots of Violence

Why do human beings aggress? What makes them turn, with brutality unmatched by even the fiercest of predators, against their fellow human beings? Scholars and scientists have pondered such questions through the ages, and that interest certainly continues today. Over the centuries, many contrasting explanations for the paradox of human violence have been proposed. Here, we'll describe several that have been especially influential.

Aggression as an Innate Tendency

The oldest and probably best-known explanation for human aggression centers on the view that human beings are somehow "programmed" for violence by their biological nature. This is the view supported by Frank, the character in our opening story, and it is sometimes known as the **instinct theory** of aggression. The most famous early supporter of this perspective was Sigmund Freud (1933), who held that aggression stems mainly from a powerful *death wish,* or *instinct (thanatos),* possessed by all persons. According to Freud, this instinct is initially aimed at self-destruction but is soon redirected outward, toward others. Freud believed that the hostile impulses it generates increase over time and, if not released periodically, will soon reach high levels capable of generating dangerous acts of violence. It is interesting to note that a death instinct was not originally part of Freud's theories. Rather, he added it after witnessing the atrocities and wholesale human slaughter of World War I. Freud also suggested that directly opposed to the death wish is another instinct, *eros,* focused on pleasure, love, and procreation. The complex relationship between these two powerful forces fascinated Freud and is reflected in modern research on the potential links between sex and aggression (see pages 415–416).

A related view was proposed by Konrad Lorenz, a Nobel Prize–winning scientist. Lorenz (1966, 1974) suggests that aggression springs mainly from an inherited *fighting instinct* that human beings share with many other species. Presumably, this instinct developed during the course of evolution because it yielded important benefits. For example, fighting serves to disperse populations over a wide area, thus ensuring maximum use of available natural resources. Further, because it is often closely related to mating, fighting helps ensure that only the strongest and most vigorous individuals will pass their genes on to the next generation.

A third perspective suggesting that aggression is at least partly innate has been provided in recent years by the field of **sociobiology** (Rushton, 1989; Wilson, 1975). According to sociobiologists, all aspects of social behavior, including aggression, can be understood in terms of evolution. Basically, sociobiology contends that those behaviors which help individuals to pass their genes on to the next generation will become increasingly prevalent in the species' population. Since aggression aids the males of many nonhuman species in obtaining mates, principles of natural selection will, over time, favor increasing levels of aggression (at least among males). Sociobiology further contends that since human beings, too, evolved in the context of natural selection, our strong tendencies toward such behaviors can be understood in this context. In short, they are now part of our inherited biological nature.

Is there any basis for these sociobiological views? Do biologically inherited tendencies toward aggression actually exist among human beings? Most social psychologists doubt that they do, primarily for two important reasons. First, they note that instinct views such as the ones proposed by Freud and Lorenz are somewhat circular in nature. These views begin by observing that aggression is a common form of behavior. On the basis of this fact, they then reason that such behavior must stem from universal, built-in urges or tendencies. Finally, they use the high incidence of aggression as support for the presence of such instances and impulses. As you can see, this is questionable logic!

Second—and perhaps more important—several findings argue against the existence of universal, innate human tendencies toward aggression. Comparisons among various societies indicate that the level of at least some forms of aggression varies greatly. For example, more murders are committed each year in individual cities in the United States than in entire nations (with ten times their population) in Europe and the Orient. Similarly, the incidence of aggression seems to change over time in different societies (cf. Baron & Richardson, in press). If aggression is indeed a universal human tendency based largely on genetic factors, such differences and shifts would not occur.

For these and other reasons, social psychologists generally reject *instinct theories* of aggression. This does not imply, however, that they also reject any role of biological factors in such behavior. On the contrary, there is increasing awareness among social psychologists of the importance of such factors in a wide range of social behavior (Rushton, 1988). Further, recent evidence points to the conclusion that some biological factors do indeed predispose specific individuals toward aggression (Mednick, Brennan, & Kandel, 1988). For example, several studies suggest that individuals arrested for violent crimes are considerably more likely than those not arrested for such crimes to have suffered mild neurological damage during the prenatal period (Baker & Mednoff, 1984; Denno, 1982). These and related findings indicate that biological factors do indeed play a significant role in at least some instances of aggression. This is still a far cry, however, from the suggestion that human beings possess a universal, inherited *instinct* toward aggression. Theories such as those offered by Freud, Lorenz, and others should therefore be viewed as intriguing but largely unverified proposals concerning the origins of human violence.

Aggression as an Elicited Drive: The Motive to Harm or Injure Others

An alternative view concerning the nature of aggression, and one that continues to enjoy some support among psychologists, suggests that such behavior stems mainly from an externally elicited *drive* to harm or injure others. This approach is reflected in several different **drive theories** of aggression (cf. Berkowitz, 1988, 1989; Feshbach, 1984). Such theories suggest that various external conditions (e.g., frustration, loss of face) arouse a strong motive to engage in harm-producing behaviors and that this aggressive drive leads in turn to the performance of overt assaults against others. By far the most famous of these drive theories is the well-known **frustration-aggression hypothesis.** According to this view, frustration leads to the arousal of a drive whose primary goal is that of harming some person or object. This drive, in turn, leads to attacks against various targets—especially the source of frustration. Berkowitz (1989) has recently offered a sophisticated revision of this hypothesis; we'll consider it in detail in a later section.

Because they suggest that external conditions rather than innate tendencies are crucial in the occurrence of aggression, drive theories seem somewhat more optimistic about the possibility of preventing such behavior than instinct theories. Since being frustrated or thwarted in various ways is a common aspect of everyday life, however, drive theories, too, seem to leave us facing continuous—and often unavoidable—sources of aggressive impulses.

Aggression as a Reaction to Aversive Events: The Role of Negative Affect

Think of times you have behaved aggressively. Now, try to remember how you felt on those occasions. The chances are good that you will recall feeling upset, irritated, or annoyed. In short, you probably experienced some type of *negative affect* in situations in which you aggressed against others. This relationship between negative, unpleasant feelings and overt aggression serves as the basis for a third theoretical perspective on aggression, one sometimes known as the **cognitive neoassociationist view** (Berkowitz, 1984, 1988). This theory sug-

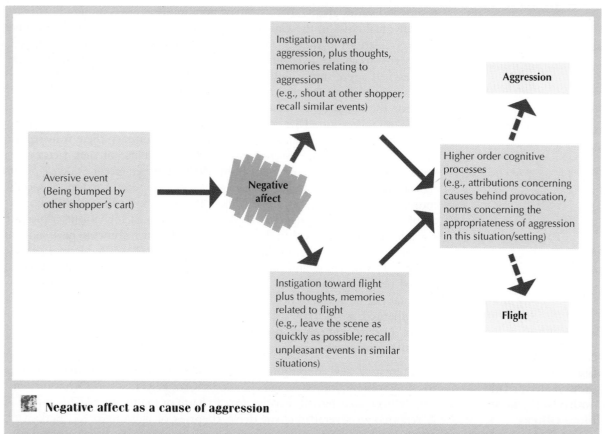

Negative affect as a cause of aggression

FIGURE 10.2 According to the *cognitive neoassociationist view*, aversive experiences produce negative affect (e.g., feelings of annoyance, irritation). These negative feelings activate tendencies toward both aggression and flight. Which of these two reactions occurs depends on memories, thoughts, and other cognitive processes. (Source: Based on suggestions by Berkowitz, 1988, 1989.)

gests that exposure to aversive events (ones we prefer to avoid) generates negative affect (unpleasant feelings). These feelings, in turn, automatically activate tendencies toward both aggression and flight (efforts to escape from the unpleasant situation), as well as physiological reactions and thoughts or memories related to such experiences. Whether overt aggression then follows depends on several factors, such as higher levels of thought and cognition. For example, consider an individual shopping in a supermarket who is bumped by another shopper's cart. This experience is painful, and the shopper reacts with tendencies toward aggression, plus thoughts and memories related to similar unpleasant events. Then, the other shopper apologizes profusely, explaining that she lost her footing on a wet spot on the floor. At this point, the angry shopper reappraises the situation and decides that the incident was truly an accident. As a result, her anger subsides, and aggression is unlikely (refer to Figure 10.2).

Considerable evidence offers support for the accuracy of this theory. Individuals exposed to a wide range of unpleasant, aversive events do tend to behave more aggressively than those not exposed to such conditions, even when their aggression cannot possibly eliminate the causes of such negative affect (Berkowitz, 1989). Further, negative affect, induced in several different ways, encourages aggressive thoughts and memories (e.g., Rule, Taylor, & Dobbs, 1987). Thus, the cognitive neoassociationist view seems to offer useful insights into the origins and nature of aggressive behavior. Unfortunately, unpleasant events and the negative feelings they generate are an all-too-common part of daily life. Consequently, this modern approach is similar to earlier ones in at least one respect: It too suggests that instigations to aggression, if not aggression itself, are an ever-present fact of life.

Aggression as Learned Social Behavior

Another important perspective on aggression, the **social learning view,** is more of a general framework than a fully developed theory. This approach (Bandura, 1973; Baron & Richardson, in press) emphasizes the fact that aggression, like other complex forms of social behavior, is largely *learned.* Human beings, it argues, are *not* born with a large array of aggressive responses at their disposal. Rather, they must acquire these responses in much the same way they acquire other complex forms of social behavior—either through direct experience or by observing the behavior of others (i.e., *social models,* Bandura, 1973). Thus, depending on their past experience, people in different cultures learn to attack others in different ways—by means of kung fu, blowguns, machetes, or revolvers. But this is not all that is learned where aggression is concerned. Through direct and vicarious experience, individuals also learn (1) which persons or groups are appropriate targets for aggression (e.g., in many societies, males learn that physical attacks against females are strongly prohibited), (2) what actions by others either justify or actually require aggressive retaliation, and (3) in what situations or contexts aggression is or is not appropriate behavior.

The social learning perspective, then, suggests that whether or not a specific person will aggress in a given situation depends on a vast array of factors, including his or her past experience, current reinforcements associated with aggression, and many variables that shape the person's thoughts and perceptions of the appropriateness and potential effects of such behavior (refer to Figure 10.3). Such a view is far more complex than one suggesting that aggression

One kind of training for aggression

FIGURE 10.3 According to the *social learning view*, aggression is a learned form of social behavior. The character is this cartoon (Beetle) is now learning that aggression is approved in his environment—provided that it succeeds! (Reprinted with special permission of King Features Syndicate, Inc.)

stems primarily from an aggressive instinct or an aggressive drive. However, it is also much more likely to be accurate. In one sense, it is also somewhat more optimistic. After all, if aggression is primarily learned, it should be open to direct modification and change. Because of these advantages, the social learning perspective forms the basis for much of our current understanding of aggression and underlies several other theories we will consider in this chapter. Admittedly, it is more complex than earlier views. However in social psychology as in all science, *accuracy*—not simplicity—is the guiding principle.

Social Determinants of Aggression: How Others' Actions, or Our Understanding of Them, Cause Aggression

Think back to the last time you lost your temper and aggressed in some fashion. What made you blow your cool? The chances are quite good that your anger and subsequent aggression stemmed from the actions of another person. In other words, something someone said or did caused you to become angry, to view aggression as justified, and then to actually give vent to your annoyance in some concrete form. In fact, this is a very common pattern. Aggression often stems from various *social* conditions that either initiate its occurrence or increase its intensity. As you can probably guess, many factors play a role in this regard. We'll examine several of the most important below. Before doing so, however, we will consider a closely related question: How can human aggression—especially physical aggression—be studied systematically without any danger of harm to the persons involved? For information on this issue, please see the **Classic Contributions** section that follows.

FOCUS ON RESEARCH: CLASSIC CONTRIBUTIONS

Studying Aggression in the Laboratory: The Researcher's Dilemma

Researchers wishing to investigate human aggression under carefully controlled conditions face the following paradox: How can they study this important but potentially dangerous form of behavior under safe conditions—ones that prevent any potential harm to research participants? A simple but elegant solution to this puzzle emerged in the early 1960s: Why not inform research participants that they could deliver physical pain or discomfort to another person when in fact they could not? Under such conditions, participants' intentions to inflict harm on others could be studied without any risk of actual harm to the supposed victim. Since aggression is generally defined as involving intentional harm to others, such procedures might well capture the essence, if not the precise form, of aggression in many real contexts. Several variations on this approach were soon developed (e.g., Berkowitz, 1962). The one that gained widest use, however, was devised by Arnold Buss (1961). Buss's method was as follows.

When subjects arrived for their appointments, they were told they would be participating, along with another person, in a study concerned with the effects of punishment on learning. It was further explained that to investigate

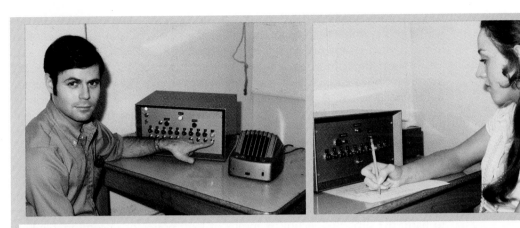

 The aggression machine: One technique for studying aggression under controlled laboratory conditions

FIGURE 10.4   Equipment like this is often used to study aggression under controlled laboratory conditions. Subjects are informed that they can deliver electric shocks (or some other type of aversive stimuli) to another person by pushing buttons on the apparatus. The higher the buttons and the longer they are pushed, the more discomfort the supposed victim will receive. In reality, no unpleasant stimuli are ever delivered to the recipient, who is actually an accomplice of the researcher. (Left photo shows a subject pushing a button on an aggression machine; right photo shows researcher recording subjects' behavior during an experimental session.)

this topic, one of the two persons present would serve as a *teacher* and the other as a *learner*. The teacher (the actual subject) would present various materials to the learner (who was actually an accomplice). On occasions when the learner made a correct response, the teacher would reward him by indicating that his response had been correct. Whenever the learner made an error, however, the teacher would punish him by means of electric shock. These shocks would be delivered by a device similar to the one shown in Figure 10.4 (often known in social psychology as an **aggression machine**) and could vary in strength from very mild to quite intense. The higher the number on each button, the stronger, presumably, the shock to the learner. To convince subjects that the apparatus actually worked in this manner, mild sample shocks were then delivered from several of the buttons.

As you can probably guess, the subject was always chosen to serve as the teacher and the accomplice to serve as the learner. The accomplice then made a prearranged series of errors, thus providing subjects with several opportunities to deliver electric shocks. Since any shock, even the mildest one, would be sufficient to inform the learner that he had made an error, Buss reasoned that the strength of the shocks subjects actually chose to deliver would provide a measure of aggression—their willingness to inflict harm or injury on the accomplice. (A second index of aggression was provided by the length of time subjects depressed each button—the duration of their assault against the learner.) Please note: *The accomplice never actually received any shocks.* Rather, subjects were simply led to believe that shocks were being delivered. In this way, it was possible to measure the willingness of one person to harm another in the absence of any real danger to participants.

If these procedures remind you of the ones used by Milgram to study destructive obedience (see Chapter 8), you are correct: The two approaches are quite similar. There is one crucial difference, however: In Milgram's research, subjects were *ordered* to push buttons of increasing number, hence their actions reflected their willingness to obey such orders. In research using Buss's procedures, in contrast, subjects are free to select any buttons they wish; their actions thus reflect (presumably) their own desire to harm the learner.

In recent years, Buss's procedures have been modified in several respects by other researchers (Baron, Russell, & Arms, 1985; Gustafson, 1989; Zillmann, 1988). In some studies, for example, subjects have been given the opportunity to harm the supposed victim by means of loud noises or uncomfortable heat rather than electric shock. In others, the purpose of the research has been described as that of studying physiological reactions to unpleasant stimuli. This eliminates the need for the *teacher* and *learner* roles and so lessens the possibility that subjects might use high-numbered buttons on the aggression machine in order to help the accomplice master the materials presented. (Doing so would, of course, allow the accomplice to avoid additional shocks.) Despite such changes, however, the basic logic remains the same: Subjects are led to believe that they have multiple opportunities to harm another person when in fact they do not.

That these procedures are relatively safe is obvious. But the key question is this: Do they actually provide a valid means for studying aggression? Some critics have argued that most participants don't "buy" the notion that they can really hurt the victim. Consequently, all that these procedures measure is subjects' tendency to push various buttons on the apparatus; there is no aggressive intent in these actions. In response to such arguments, researchers who use these procedures note several points. First, they cite studies indicating that persons with a prior history of violent behavior often choose stronger levels of shock (or heat or noise) than those without such a history (e.g., Gully & Dengerink, 1983; Wolfe & Baron, 1971). Second, they call attention to the fact that subjects participating in such studies often *do* believe they can harm the supposed victim in some manner (Donnerstein & Berkowitz, 1982). To the extent they do, their behavior can be viewed as aggressive in nature—it stems from conscious intentions to inflict discomfort on another person. Finally, these researchers note that subjects who have been angered or frustrated by the accomplice generally deliver stronger attacks against this person than those who have not been so angered (cf. Baron & Richardson, in press).

Together, these arguments provide some basis for assuming that the methods described above do measure something akin to aggression or aggressive intent. Certainly, though, they are far from perfect; a great deal of "noise" (random error) can enter the picture and distort (or even potentially invalidate) experimental results. Still, these procedures, if used with care, caution, and numerous safeguards, do seem to provide at least a working index of the central concept we wish to measure: people's willingness to inflict harm—physical or otherwise—on another human being.

Frustration: Why Not Getting What You Want (and What You Expect) Can Sometimes Lead to Aggression

Suppose you asked twenty people you know to name the single most important cause of aggression. How would they reply? The chances are good that a majority would answer, "Frustration." And if asked to define frustration, many would reply, "The way I feel when something prevents me from getting something I want and expect to get in a given situation." In short, many persons would indicate that in their experience, aggression often stems from interference with their efforts to reach various goals.

The widespread acceptance of such views derives, at least in part, from the famous **frustration-aggression hypothesis** first proposed by Dollard and his colleagues more than fifty years ago (Dollard et al., 1939). In its original form, this hypothesis made two sweeping assertions: (1) frustration *always* leads to some form of aggression and (2) aggression *always* stems from frustration (Dollard et al., 1939). In short, it held that persons who are frustrated always engage in some type of aggression and that all acts of aggression, in turn, result from frustration. Bold statements like these are always appealing—they are intellectually stimulating, if nothing else. But are they accurate? Does frustration really play such an all-important role with respect to aggression? The answer is almost certainly no. Both portions of the frustration-aggression hypothesis are far too sweeping in scope to be accurate.

First, it is now clear that frustrated individuals do not always respond with aggressive thoughts, words, or deeds. On the contrary, such persons show a wide variety of reactions to frustration, ranging from resignation and despair on the one hand to attempts to overcome the source of their frustration on the other.

Second, it is also apparent that not all instances of aggression result from frustration. People aggress for many different reasons and in response to many different factors. Professional boxers, for example, hit and sometimes seriously injure others because it is their role to do so and because they wish to win valued prizes—not because they are frustrated. Similarly, military personnel during times of war direct powerful attacks against others in response to orders, even in the total absence of frustration. In these and many other cases, aggression stems from factors other than frustration.

In view of these considerations, few social psychologists now accept the suggestion that frustration is the only—or even the most important—cause of aggression. Instead, most believe that it is simply one of a host of factors that can potentially lead to aggression (cf. Baron, 1977). Along these lines, Berkowitz (1989) has recently proposed a revised version of the frustration-aggression hypothesis that seems consistent with a large amount of existing evidence. According to this revised view, frustration is an aversive, unpleasant experience, and leads to aggression because of this. In short, this view holds that frustration sometimes produces aggression because of the basic relationship between negative feelings and aggressive behavior described on pages 397–399.

These suggestions seem quite straightforward and contribute much to our understanding of the role of frustration in aggression. In particular, they help explain why *unexpected* frustration and frustration that is viewed as *illegitimate* (e.g., the result of someone's whims or hostile motives) produce stronger aggression than frustration that is expected or viewed as legitimate. Presumably, this is the case because unexpected or illegitimate frustration generates stronger negative feelings than that which is expected or legitimate.

Going further, Berkowitz (1989) also explains why frustration, even when strong, unexpected, and illegitimate, does not always lead to aggression. He notes that the negative feelings generated by frustration do initially produce tendencies toward aggression. However, these tendencies are soon modified by higher-level cognitive processes. Individuals who have been frustrated may examine the nature of their feelings, attempt to understand *why* they have experienced frustration, consider the relative appropriateness of aggression and other possible reactions, and engage in efforts to control their anger or annoyance. Given the unpredictable outcome of these processes, it is hardly surprising that frustration does not always lead to aggression.

In sum, frustration is indeed one potential cause of overt aggression (Gustafson, 1989). However, it is certainly not the only cause behind such behavior, and is not necessarily the strongest or most important of these. Thus, it does not play the very central role in human aggression that many people assume.

Direct Provocation: When Aggression Breeds Aggression

Imagine that one morning you hand in an important report that your boss has asked you to write. That afternoon, she storms into your office, throws the report onto your desk, and says, "Where did *you* ever learn to write? I've seen better from my eight-year-old son!" After these words, she continues, berating your report in every conceivable way. How do you react? If you are like most people, you probably make excuses or just stand there sullenly; after all, she's the boss and there's not much else you can do. But all the while she's attacking your work, you're thinking such thoughts as *Who does she think she is? How dare she speak to me like that?* and *Just wait—I'll get back at her for this!*

This incident illustrates an important point about aggression: Often, it is the result of verbal or physical **provocation** from others. In short, when we are the victims of some form of aggression from others, we rarely "turn the other cheek"—at least not if we can help it! Instead, we tend to reciprocate such harsh treatment, returning as much aggression as we have received, or perhaps slightly more. Evidence for such effects has been obtained in several studies (e.g., Dengerink, Schnedler, & Covey, 1978; Ohbuchi & Ogura, 1984), but since we began with an example involving verbal provocation, let's consider one study concerned with this topic.

In this investigation (Baron, 1988a), male and female subjects first worked on a complex task—preparing an ad campaign for a new product. Their work was then evaluated by another subject (actually an accomplice), who provided feedback that was quite negative (e.g., he or she assigned a rating of 3 out of 7 to subjects with respect to creativity). The verbal comments accompanying these ratings, however, differed sharply in two conditions. In one group (the *destructive-criticism* condition), the accomplice's written comments were insulting and condescending (e.g., "I don't think you could be original if you tried. Dull stuff"; "I wasn't impressed at all. The whole thing needs to be fixed"). In the other group (the *constructive-criticism* condition), the tone of these comments was much more considerate (e.g., "I think you were too conventional and unwilling to try anything new"; "I think there's a lot of room for improvement").

After receiving this feedback, subjects completed a questionnaire that asked them to indicate how they would be likely to deal with the accomplice on future occasions. As you might expect, those in the destructive-criticism group indicated stronger tendencies to avoid or to compete with this person and weaker tendencies to collaborate with him or her than subjects in the constructive-criticism group (refer to Figure 10.5). These results illustrate the way in which most persons respond to verbal or physical provocation: with present counter-attacks or plans for future ones.

While reciprocity seems to characterize reactions to direct provocation, we should add that this is not always the case. Several factors seem to determine whether and to what extent, individuals choose to respond to provocation in kind, or to overlook such treatment. Perhaps the most important of these factors is the *perceived intentionality* of the provocation. When individuals conclude that provocation from another person was *intended*—purposely performed—they generally become quite angry and engage in strenuous efforts to reciprocate. If, instead, they conclude that provocation was *unintended*—the result of accident or factors beyond others' control—they are much less likely to lose their temper and behave aggressively. In short, *attributions* concerning the causes behind provocative actions by others play a key role in determining how we will react to them.

Evidence for the importance of attributions in determining responses to provocation is provided by several experiments (e.g., Kremer & Stephens,

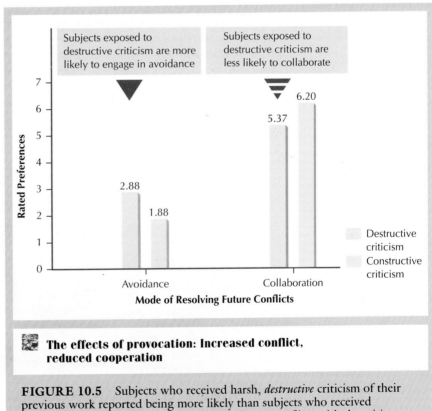

The effects of provocation: Increased conflict, reduced cooperation

FIGURE 10.5 Subjects who received harsh, *destructive* criticism of their previous work reported being more likely than subjects who received reasonable, *constructive* criticism to handle future conflicts with the critic through avoidance (left bars). Those who received the destructive criticism also reported being less likely to collaborate with the critic (right bars). (Source: Based on data from Baron, 1988.)

1983). For example, in one study on this topic, Johnson and Rule (1986) exposed male subjects to strong provocation from an accomplice. The researchers then measured subjects' physiological reactions to such treatment and their later retaliation against this person. Half the subjects were told before being provoked that the accomplice was very upset over an unfairly low grade on a chemistry quiz; the remaining half received this information only after being provoked. Results indicated that this information about *mitigating circumstances* exerted strong effects on subjects' reactions. Those who received the information before being provoked actually showed lower emotional upset (as measured by changes in heart rate) and lower retaliation against the accomplice (as indexed by the bursts of noise they chose to deliver to him) than subjects who received such information only after being provoked.

These and related findings suggest that when we are provoked or angered by another person, we do not automatically dish out what we have received. Often, our reactions reflect our interpretations of the *causes* behind their actions. As is true in many other contexts, our behavior toward others is strongly determined by our thoughts about them.

Exposure to Media Violence: The Effects of Witnessing Aggression

One issue that has repeatedly gripped public attention in recent years is this: Does repeated exposure to filmed or televised violence produce an increase in similar behavior among viewers? This is an important question, with serious social implications. It is not surprising, then, that it has been the subject of literally hundreds of research projects. The findings of these studies have certainly *not* been entirely consistent. Given the complexity of the issues addressed, this is to be expected. However, taken together, they point to the following conclusion: Exposure to media violence may, in fact, be one factor contributing to high and rising levels of violence in the United States and elsewhere (refer to Figure 10.6). Several lines of research conducted in very different ways are consistent with this interpretation.

Media violence: One potential cause of aggression

FIGURE 10.6 A large body of evidence suggests that exposure to media violence can increase aggressive behavior on the part of both children and adults.

First, this interpretation is supported by many short-term laboratory studies. In the earliest of these investigations, Bandura, Ross, and Ross (1963) exposed young children to one of two short films. In one, an adult model aggressed against an inflated toy clown (known as a Bobo doll) in various ways (e.g., she sat on the toy and repeatedly punched it in the nose). In the other, the same model behaved in a quiet, nonaggressive manner. Later, the children in both groups were allowed to play freely in a room containing many toys, including several used by the model. Observations of their behavior revealed that those who had seen the model behave aggressively were much more likely to attack the inflated toy than those who had not witnessed such behavior. These findings suggest that even very young children can acquire new ways of aggressing against others through exposure to filmed or televised violence.

In subsequent laboratory studies, subjects viewed actual television programs or films and were then given an opportunity to attack (supposedly) a real victim rather than an inflated toy (e.g., Liebert & Baron, 1972). Once again, results were the same: Participants (both children and adults) who witnessed media violence later demonstrated higher levels of aggression than participants who were not exposed to such materials did (Liebert, Sprafkin, & Davidson, 1989). Consider a well-conducted study by Josephson (1987). In this investigation, second- and third-grade boys watched either an exciting film about a bike-racing team or excerpts from a popular, violence-filled television program. The latter film contained scenes in which the member of a special police team killed or knocked unconscious a large number of criminals. After the boys watched one of these films, their behavior was observed while they played a game of "floor hockey." Results indicated that for boys who were rated by their teachers as being highly aggressive in the classroom, exposure to the violent programs had the expected effects: Those who watched these shows engaged in more acts of aggression during the hockey game (e.g., hitting others with their hockey stick, elbowing them, insulting them). Such findings were not obtained among groups of boys previously rated as nonaggressive—a finding suggesting that violence in the media is more likely to enhance aggression among persons who already have a strong tendency for such behavior than among those in whom this tendency is relatively weak.

Additional—and in some ways more convincing—evidence for the aggression-enhancing impact of media violence is provided by a second group of studies using different methods. In these *long-term field investigations*, different groups of subjects have been exposed to contrasting amounts of media violence, and their overt levels of aggression in natural situations were then observed (e.g., Leyens et al., 1975; Parke et al., 1977). Again, results indicate that youngsters exposed to violent programs or movies demonstrate higher levels of aggression than those exposed to nonviolent materials.

Third, other investigators have conducted long-term *correlational studies* in which the amount of media violence watched by individuals as children is statistically related to their rated levels of aggression several years—or even decades—later (e.g., Eron, 1982; Huesmann, 1982). Information on the amount of violence watched is based on subjects' reports about the shows they watched plus violence ratings of these programs. Information on subjects' subsequent levels of aggression is acquired from ratings of their behavior by classmates or teachers. The results of such investigations indicate that these two variables are indeed related: The more media violence individuals watch as

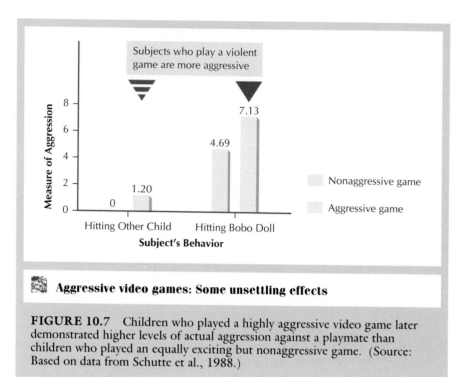

Aggressive video games: Some unsettling effects

FIGURE 10.7 Children who played a highly aggressive video game later demonstrated higher levels of actual aggression against a playmate than children who played an equally exciting but nonaggressive game. (Source: Based on data from Schutte et al., 1988.)

children, the higher their rated levels of aggression as adults. Further, the strength of this relationship seems to increase with age, thus suggesting that the influence of media violence is cumulative over time. The more shows of this kind that individuals watch, the more likely they are to behave aggressively in a wide range of situations.

Finally, we should note that similar effects seem to occur as a result of playing aggressive video games, as well as from merely watching aggressive programs. (In a sense, such games provide players with an opportunity to participate in aggressive activities, or at least representations of them.) In one revealing study on this topic, Schutte and his colleagues (Schutte et al., 1988) had male and female children ages five to seven play one of two exciting video games. In the first, a violent game called "Karateka," the character controlled by subjects hit or kicked various villains in order to destroy them. In the second, a nonviolent game called "Jungle Hunt," the character swung from vine to vine while crossing a jungle. After playing one of these two games, children were observed, in pairs, in a special playroom. Results indicated that those who had played the aggressive game were more likely to hit both their playmate and an inflated doll than those who had played the nonviolent game (see Figure 10.7).

Incidentally, additional findings indicate that even among adults, the greater individuals' tendency to engage in "horse-play" (aggressive play-fighting), the greater their tendency to engage in more harmful acts of aggression (Gergen, 1991). Thus, the relationship between aggressive play and actual aggression may be stronger than many persons suspect.

Again, we should add a note of caution: Not all findings have been consistent with the idea that exposure to media violence (or participation in aggressive video games) increases actual aggression (Freedman, 1984). Moreover, the evidence for relatively short-term effects of viewing violence are more firmly established by research than the potential long-term effects are. Still, existing evidence, when taken as a whole, seems to offer at least moderate support for the conclusion that exposure to media violence can contribute, along with many other factors, to the occurrence of aggressive behavior. (The fact that exposure to media violence can sometimes facilitate similar behavior among viewers is by itself somewhat unsettling. Perhaps even more disturbing, however, is evidence pointing to the conclusion that even inanimate objects can sometimes encourage dangerous instances of aggression. For a discussion of such possibilities, please see the **Classic Contributions** section below.)

FOCUS ON RESEARCH: CLASSIC CONTRIBUTIONS

The Role of Aggressive Cues: Does the Trigger Sometimes Pull the Finger?

Suppose you had a friend who owned a large collection of guns. One evening, you got into an argument with this person while sitting in the room containing his personal arsenal. Would you be more likely to lose your temper and behave aggressively in this setting than elsewhere? In other words, would the presence of racks of weapons on the walls actually facilitate the likelihood of aggression? (Assume, by the way, that all the guns are unloaded!)

According to a noted authority on aggression, Leonard Berkowitz (1969, 1974), this might well be the case. He has proposed that one important determinant of aggression is the presence of what he terms **aggressive cues.** These are stimuli that have been associated or linked with aggression in the past. Berkowitz suggests that these cues serve to elicit aggressive responses from persons who have been angered or otherwise made ready to aggress. Thus, the greater the presence of such cues on the scene, the higher the level of aggression that is likely to occur.

What does this have to do with the gun-collection example presented above? According to Berkowitz, the objects in this collection (guns) have been intimately associated with aggression on numerous occasions. As a result, they become aggressive cues, and their mere presence on the scene may facilitate aggressive behavior *even if they are not themselves used in such actions.* Support for this reasoning was reported more than twenty years ago by Berkowitz and LePage (1967) in a now-famous experiment. In this study, male students were first either angered or not angered by an accomplice and then provided with an opportunity to aggress against him by means of electric shock. (Subjects were given an opportunity to evaluate the accomplice's work by giving him from one to nine shocks. Obviously, the lower their evaluation, the higher the number of shocks.) In one condition (the *no-objects* control), only the equipment used by subjects ostensibly to deliver shocks to the accomplice was present. In two other conditions, in contrast, a .38-caliber revolver and a 12-gauge shotgun were lying on the table near the shock button. In one of these latter groups, it was explained to subjects that the weapons were being used in another study and had no connection with the present experiment (*unassociated-weapons* condition). In the other, it was explained to subjects that the weapons were being

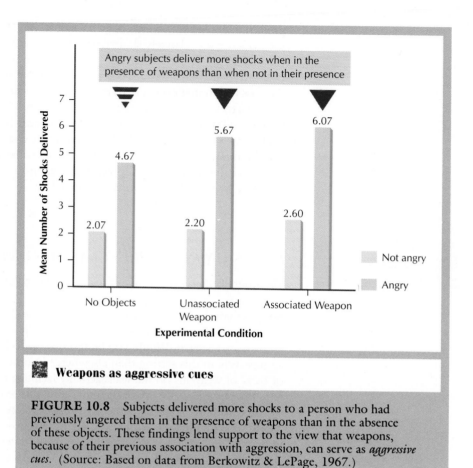

Weapons as aggressive cues

FIGURE 10.8 Subjects delivered more shocks to a person who had previously angered them in the presence of weapons than in the absence of these objects. These findings lend support to the view that weapons, because of their previous association with aggression, can serve as *aggressive cues.* (Source: Based on data from Berkowitz & LePage, 1967.)

used by the accomplice in another study he was conducting (*associated-weapons* condition). Berkowitz and LePage (1967) predicted that the mere physical presence of the weapons would facilitate aggression by the angry subjects but would fail to enhance aggression by those who had not been angered. As you can see from Figure 10.8, this is precisely what occurred. Subjects who had previously been angered by the accomplice delivered more shocks to him in the presence of weapons than in their absence. There was no difference, however, between the associated- and the unassociated-weapons conditions.

These findings seem to suggest that aggression can indeed be facilitated by the presence of weapons, even if the weapons themselves are not used in the subsequent assaults. As Berkowitz himself has put it (1968, p. 22): "Guns not only permit violence, they can stimulate it as well. The finger pulls the trigger, but the trigger may also be pulling the finger."

Unfortunately, the relatively neat picture provided by this initial study has been somewhat complicated by subsequent research (Buss, Booker, & Buss, 1972; Turner & Simon, 1974). These later studies suggest that the *weapons effect* reported by Berkowitz and LePage (1967) may occur only under relatively restricted conditions (e.g., when subjects have absolutely no suspicions concerning the presence of these unusual items in a research laboratory). Regardless of the ultimate validity of the weapons effect, however, there can be little doubt that Berkowitz's more general suggestion that aggression is *pulled* from without rather than merely *pushed* from within has gained widespread acceptance among social psychologists. In this respect, certainly, his research on the impact of aggressive cues has been highly influential.

The Impact of Media Violence: Why Does It Occur?   The finding that exposure to violence on television or in the movies can encourage similar behavior among viewers has important implications. It suggests that steps designed to limit such exposure or to reduce the violent content in TV and Hollywood offerings might help lessen one potential cause of aggression. But assuming that such effects occur, another question arises: *How,* precisely, does exposure to media violence stimulate increased aggression among viewers? Several processes seem to play a role.

First, exposure to media violence weakens viewers' *inhibitions* against engaging in such behavior. After watching many characters—including heroes and heroines—handle many situations through aggression, some viewers feel less restrained about engaging in similar actions themselves. *If they can do it,* such persons seem to reason, *so can I.*

Second, exposure to media violence provides viewers with new techniques for attacking and harming others—ones not previously at their disposal. And such behaviors, once acquired, tend to be used in appropriate contexts.

Third, watching others engage in aggressive actions can influence viewers' cognitions in several ways (cf. Berkowitz, 1984, 1988). Such materials can serve to *prime* aggressive thoughts and memories, making these more readily available in viewers' cognitive systems. (See our discussion of priming in Chapter 3.) Similarly, exposure to aggressive films or television shows can both strengthen and activate aggression-related *scripts*—ideas about what events are likely to happen or are appropriate in a given environment (Huesmann, 1988). For example, after watching media characters deal with interpersonal friction or tension through violence, viewers—especially children—may acquire cognitive scripts suggesting that aggression is indeed likely to occur in such situations. Then, when these viewers are confronted with similar situations in their own lives, such scripts, aggressive thoughts, and related cognitions are activated. To the extent that this is the case, the likelihood of overt aggression, too, may be increased.

Finally, continued exposure to media violence may reduce emotional sensitivity to violence and its harmful consequences. In short, after watching countless murders, fights, and assaults, viewers may become *desensitized* to such materials and show diminished emotional reaction to them (Geen, 1981). They may then find real-life aggression, too, less disturbing and demonstrate reduced empathy toward its victims, even when those victims show signs of considerable pain and suffering (Baron, 1971, 1979). As we will soon see, such effects may be especially damaging when they result from exposure to scenes involving sexual violence (Linz, Donnerstein, & Penrod, 1988).

In sum, media violence seems to enhance the occurrence of overt aggression for several different reasons and through several different mechanisms (see Figure 10.9, p. 412). Given this fact, it is not at all surprising that such materials influence the behavior of children and adults alike.

SOCIAL DETERMINANTS OF AGGRESSION   **411**

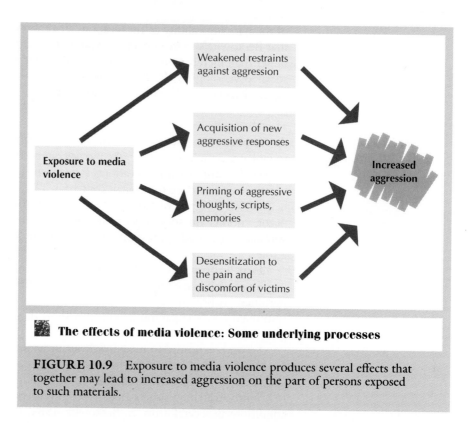

The effects of media violence: Some underlying processes

FIGURE 10.9 Exposure to media violence produces several effects that together may lead to increased aggression on the part of persons exposed to such materials.

Heightened Arousal: Emotion, Cognition, and Aggression

Imagine that you are driving to the airport to meet a friend. A slow-moving truck is in the lane ahead of you, and you begin to pass. As you do so, you hear prolonged honking. You jam on your brakes and just barely avoid colliding with a car that was about to pass *you* on your left. The other driver continues to honk angrily and shakes her fist at you as she drives by. You are very embarrassed and can feel your heart pounding wildly. Now, you arrive at the airport. Since it's almost time for your friend's flight, you park hurriedly and rush through the terminal. When you get to the security check, there is an elderly man in front of you. As he walks through, the buzzer sounds and he becomes confused. The security guard can't make him understand that he must empty his pockets and walk through again. You are irritated by the delay. In fact, you feel yourself growing unbearably angry. *What's wrong with him?* you think to yourself. *Can't he understand simple directions?* You begin to mutter under your breath and shake your head in disbelief. *One more minute,* you think, *and I'll just shove past him.*

What's going on in this situation? Do you think that your recent near miss in traffic played any part in your excessive anger? In short, could the emotional arousal from that incident have somehow transferred to the totally unrelated situation at the security gate? Growing evidence suggests that it could (Zillmann, 1983, 1988). Under some circumstances, heightened arousal—whatever its source—can enhance aggression in response to annoyance, frustration, or provocation. In different experiments, arousal stemming from participation in competitive games (Christy, Gelfand, & Hartmann, 1971), vigorous exercise (Zillmann, 1979), and even some types of music (Rogers & Ketcher, 1979) has been found to facilitate subsequent aggression. Why? A compelling explanation is offered by **excitation transfer theory** (Zillmann, 1983, 1988).

This framework begins by noting that physiological arousal, however produced, dissipates slowly over time. As a result, some portion of such arousal may persist as individuals move from one situation to another. In the example above, some portion of the arousal you experienced as a result of a near miss in traffic might still have been present as you approached the security gate in the airport terminal. Then, when you encountered minor annoyance, such arousal intensified your emotional reactions to it. The result: You became enraged rather than just mildly irritated.

When are such effects most likely to occur? Excitation transfer theory offers two related answers. First, they are most likely to take place when we are relatively unaware of such residual arousal—a common occurrence, since small elevations in arousal are difficult to detect (Zillmann, 1988). Second, these effects are also most likely to occur when we recognize the presence of such arousal but attribute it to events occurring in the current situation. Thus, in the incident we have been describing, if you attributed your residual feelings of arousal to the delay you were experiencing, your anger would be intensified. (Please see Figure 10.10 for a summary of excitation transfer theory as it applies to this situation.)

Emotion, Cognition, and Aggression: Complex Interdependencies While excitation transfer theory offers important insights into the way arousal can influ-

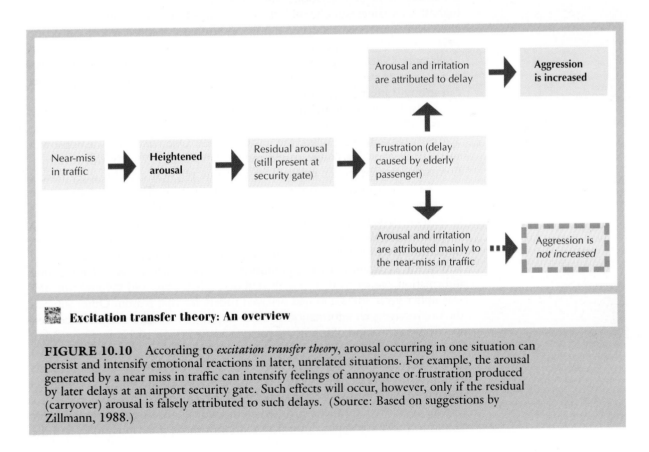

Excitation transfer theory: An overview

FIGURE 10.10 According to *excitation transfer theory*, arousal occurring in one situation can persist and intensify emotional reactions in later, unrelated situations. For example, the arousal generated by a near miss in traffic can intensify feelings of annoyance or frustration produced by later delays at an airport security gate. Such effects will occur, however, only if the residual (carryover) arousal is falsely attributed to such delays. (Source: Based on suggestions by Zillmann, 1988.)

ence aggression, it has recently been expanded in several crucial ways (Zillmann, 1988). The theory now considers how emotion (arousal) and cognition interact in shaping aggressive reactions. Let's first consider the impact of cognition on emotion. How can our thoughts influence arousal and so subsequent aggression? One answer involves the fact that our thoughts can lead us to *reappraise* various emotion-provoking events. Such reappraisal can in turn affect our reactions to those events. A dramatic illustration of this process is provided by a study conducted by Zillmann and Cantor (1976). In this study, subjects were first severely annoyed by a rude experimenter and then given an opportunity to retaliate against him by voting for or against his reappointment as a research fellow. Before retaliating, two groups of participants received mitigating information suggesting that the experimenter was under a lot of stress from important exams and had behaved rudely for that reason. One group of subjects received this information before being annoyed by the experimenter; the second received it only after he had acted rudely. (Subjects in a control condition received no mitigating information.) Results indicated that subjects who received the mitigating information *before* the experimenter annoyed them showed very little arousal following the provocation. Those who received no such information showed the highest level of arousal, while those who received mitigating information only after being annoyed showed an intermediate level. Similar findings were found with respect to retaliation against the accomplice: Subjects who received mitigating information before being provoked showed the lowest level of retaliation, while those in the control group showed the highest level. Interestingly, subjects who received mitigating information only after being provoked retaliated almost as strongly as those who received no information of this type. These findings, coupled with those of other studies (Zillmann, 1988), suggest that cognitive processes can strongly affect arousal in response to various forms of annoyance or provocation and in this manner can strongly affect aggression as well.

Now, let's examine the impact of arousal on cognition. Do high levels of arousal affect our thoughts about others' behavior and so our tendencies to aggress against them? Again, the answer is yes. One study that demonstrates such effects very clearly was conducted by Zillmann (1979). In this investigation, subjects first either engaged in vigorous physical exercise (they rode a stationary bicycle) or did not engage in such exercise. This arrangement produced high levels of arousal in one group and lower levels in the other. Subjects were then strongly provoked by a rude experimenter who made disparaging remarks about them and their performance. Next, and before being given an opportunity to retaliate against the experimenter (again, by rating him and voting for or against his reappointment), some subjects received mitigating information similar to that described above: They were told the experimenter was under great stress and had behaved rudely for that reason. Other subjects did not receive such information. Would subjects' level of arousal influence their reactions to this kind of input? As you can see in Figure 10.11, it certainly did. Those who had not ridden the bicycle and were not highly aroused showed a drop in retaliation when they received an explanation for the experimenter's behavior. In contrast, those who were strongly aroused did not. These findings agree with the informal observation that "When emotions run high, reason flies out the window." In other words, when individuals are strongly aroused, their ability to process complex information about others, their intentions, and the

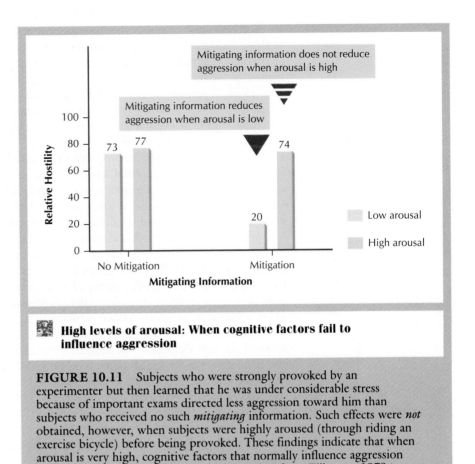

Relative Hostility

Mitigating information does not reduce aggression when arousal is high

Mitigating information reduces aggression when arousal is low

73 77

20 74

Low arousal

High arousal

No Mitigation   Mitigation

Mitigating Information

High levels of arousal: When cognitive factors fail to influence aggression

FIGURE 10.11   Subjects who were strongly provoked by an experimenter but then learned that he was under considerable stress because of important exams directed less aggression toward him than subjects who received no such *mitigating* information. Such effects were *not* obtained, however, when subjects were highly aroused (through riding an exercise bicycle) before being provoked. These findings indicate that when arousal is very high, cognitive factors that normally influence aggression may have little impact. (Source: Based on data from Zillmann, 1979.)

reasons behind their behavior may be reduced. The result may then be an impulsive lashing out at others in what attorneys often describe as "the heat of passion."

In sum, it appears that aggression, like many other forms of social behavior, is influenced by a complex interplay between emotion and cognition. As we noted in Chapter 3, cognition frequently influences emotional reactions and these in turn often shape cognition. In other words, what we think influences what and how we feel, and what we feel influences what and how we think. And this complex pattern of thoughts and emotions determines whether and to what degree we aggress against others.

Sexual Arousal and Aggression: Are Love and Hate Really Linked?

As we have just seen, under appropriate circumstances, arousal stemming from a wide range of sources can sometimes influence aggression. Given this fact, it seems reasonable to pose the following question: Can sexual arousal, too, have such effects? Such a link between sex and aggression has frequently been suggested. For example, Freud (1933) proposed that desires to hurt or be hurt by one's lover are a normal part of sexual relations. Is there any evidence that sexual arousal affects aggression or vice versa? The answer is a definite yes.

The results of several studies indicate that mild levels of sexual arousal, such as those induced by viewing pictures of attractive persons shown either nude or partially clothed, can reduce later aggression against persons who have previously provoked them in some fashion (e.g., Baron, 1974, 1979; Baron & Bell, 1973; Ramirez, Bryant, & Zillmann, 1983). However, stronger levels of sexual arousal, such as those induced by reading highly erotic passages or by watching scenes of explicit lovemaking, have opposite effects: Such activities seem to increase subsequent aggression (e.g., Jaffe et al., 1974; Zillmann, 1984). In short, the relationship between sexual arousal and overt aggression appears to be curvilinear. Mild levels of arousal reduce aggression below that shown in the absence of sexual arousal, while higher levels actually increase aggression above this point. What accounts for this U-shaped function? A *two-component* model proposed by Zillmann (1984) offers one useful answer.

According to this model, exposure to erotic stimuli produces two effects: (1) It increases arousal, and (2) it influences current *affective states*—positive and negative feelings. Whether sexual arousal will increase or reduce aggression then depends on the overall pattern of such effects. Mild erotic materials generate only weak levels of arousal and mainly positive affect. As a result, exposure to such materials tends to reduce subsequent aggression. In contrast, explicit erotic materials generate stronger levels of arousal. Also, since many people find some of the acts demonstrated unpleasant or repulsive, such explicit materials also produce considerable amounts of negative affect. As a result, erotica of this type may increase aggression. The findings of several studies support this two-component theory (e.g., Ramirez, Bryant, & Zillmann, 1983). When subjects in these studies were exposed to sexual stimuli that induced low levels of arousal and positive feelings, their aggression was reduced. When, in contrast, they experienced high levels of arousal along with negative feelings, their subsequent aggression was increased.

In sum, it appears that there is indeed a link between sexual arousal and aggression. However, the nature of this relationship is more complex than at first suspected and, again, relates to the effects of both affect (emotions) and cognition.

The Effects of Violent Pornography: Aggressive Actions, Callous Attitudes

In recent decades, restrictions against the explicit depiction of sexual behavior in films and magazines have all but disappeared in many nations. This fact, coupled with the huge sale of videocassette recorders, has resulted in a situation in which access to such materials is as close as the nearest shopping center. Moreover, some of the X-rated tapes available (as well as other media sources, such as magazines) contain scenes that mix sex with violence. In such materials, women are generally the victims and are shown being raped, tortured, and brutalized in many ways. Given that exposure to media violence can encourage similar behavior among viewers and that high levels of sexual arousal (coupled with negative affect) can also increase aggression, it seems possible that such *violent pornography,* as it is often termed, can be a dangerous combination. Unfortunately, growing empirical evidence suggests that this is actually the case.

First, several recent studies indicate that exposure to such materials increases the tendency of males to aggress against females (Malamuth & Briere, 1986). For example, in one experiment on this topic (Donnerstein, Berkowitz, & Linz, 1987), male subjects were angered by a female accomplice. Then they watched either a pornographic film containing violence against females (e.g., scenes of rape, torture), an X-rated film containing explicit sexual behavior but no violence, or a film showing violence against women but containing no sexual content. When subjects were then given an opportunity to attack the female accomplice (by means of bogus electric shocks), those exposed to violent pornography showed the highest level of aggression. Those who watched the X-rated film containing no violence showed the lowest level, and those who saw the violent film containing no sexual content were in between but closer in level of aggression to those who watched the violent pornography (see Figure 10.12).

Additional findings suggest that exposure to violent pornography may have other harmful effects as well (e.g., Linz, Donnerstein, & Penrod, 1984; Zillmann & Bryant, 1984). These investigations suggest that after prolonged exposure to scenes depicting sexual violence toward females (several hours of viewing such films), both men and women report more callous attitudes toward such actions. They perceive crimes such as rape as less serious, report less sympathy toward rape victims, indicate greater acceptance of false beliefs about rape (e.g., the myth that many women really want to be ravaged), and become more accepting of various bizarre forms of pornography.

Other research, conducted by Linz, Donnerstein, and Penrod (1988), suggests that similar effects can also occur as a result of watching films that do not

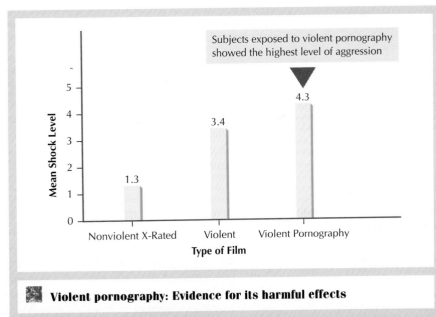

Violent pornography: Evidence for its harmful effects

FIGURE 10.12 Male subjects exposed to an X-rated film containing scenes of aggression against females (*violent pornography*) later showed more aggression against a female accomplice than subjects who watched a violent film containing no sexual content. Subjects who saw an X-rated film containing no violent content were the least aggressive of all. These findings suggest that the combination of explicit sexual content and violence against women is potentially dangerous. (Source: Based on data from Donnerstein, Berkowitz, & Linz, 1987.)

contain explicit sexual behavior. Indeed, this research, along with findings reported by several other investigators, suggests that it is violent content, not explicit sexual behavior, that is crucial. Subjects in this study (male students) watched one of three types of films: X-rated nonviolent movies showing explicit sexual behavior, R-rated violent movies ("slasher" films containing explicit scenes of violence, primarily directed toward women), and R-rated films depicting women as sexual objects, but containing no scenes of explicit sexual behavior (nonviolent teenage-sex films). Subjects in various groups watched either two or five of one of these three types of films. Additional subjects in control groups saw no films. Before and after each film, subjects in the appropriate groups reported on their moods and emotional reactions. Next, all subjects watched a tape of a simulated rape trial. Both before and after viewing the tape of the trial, subjects completed questionnaires designed to measure their acceptance of myths about rape and their sympathy for the victims of this crime.

Results indicated that exposure to the R-rated violent movies (the "slasher" films showing aggression toward women) did produce emotional desensitization among subjects: After watching such films, subjects found them less disturbing than they did initially. Subjects exposed to the X-rated and R-rated films containing sexual content did not show similar trends. Subjects who watched the "slasher" movies were also less sympathetic toward the rape victim and were less able to empathize with rape victims generally than those in the other conditions or control subjects. Contrary to predictions, however, exposure to the "slasher" films and the sexual violence they contained did not increase subjects' acceptance of rape myths or the tendency to approve the use of force in sexual relations.

Taken as a whole, the findings reported by Linz, Donnerstein, and Penrod (1988) suggest that exposure to scenes of violence against women may well exert adverse effects on viewers. After watching such materials, males become desensitized to them and to signs of pain and suffering on the part of victims of real crimes, such as rape. Given the immense popularity of films depicting violence and especially of films containing violence toward females, it seems possible that the long-term social costs of such forms of "entertainment" may be considerable.

Alcohol and Aggression: A Potentially— But Not Necessarily— Dangerous Mix

Common sense suggests that some people, at least, become more aggressive when they consume alcoholic beverages. Bars and nightclubs are notorious as the scene of impulsive acts of violence (refer to Figure 10.13). Moreover, almost 75 percent of persons arrested for violent crimes (e.g., murder, assault) are legally intoxicated at the time they are taken into custody by police (Shupe, 1954). Evidence for an important link between alcohol and aggression is also provided by many laboratory studies. In such experiments, subjects given substantial doses of alcohol—enough to make them legally drunk—often respond more strongly to provocation than persons given drinks containing either no alcohol or so small an amount that it has no appreciable effects (Taylor & Leonard, 1983).

What accounts for such reactions? One possibility is that alcohol acts directly on the brain, releasing relatively primitive areas that govern emotion and rage from control by the cerebral cortex. If this is indeed the case, then people who consume alcohol may find it extremely difficult, if not impossible, to

Alcohol and aggression: Informal evidence for a link

FIGURE 10.13 Bars, nightclubs, and other places in which people consume alcohol are often the scene of aggressive behavior.

control aggressive outbursts (Zeichner and Pihl, 1980), for they are, quite simply, no longer capable of such restraint. Another, less disturbing possibility is that alcohol weakens restraints against aggressive (or sexual) behavior but leaves people able to monitor and regulate their own actions to some degree. Thus, it is only one of several factors that contribute to aggression, and by no means assures that such behavior will occur.

This latter conclusion is supported by a growing body of research evidence (Taylor & Jeavons, 1985). For example, in one interesting study on this topic (Taylor & Sears, 1988), male subjects consumed drinks containing either a large dose of alcohol (1.5 ounces of hundred-proof vodka per forty pounds of body weight) or no alcohol (drinks that smelled of alcohol but actually contained none). After consuming the drinks, subjects competed with another person (who was actually nonexistent) in a reaction-time task. In this task, the slower player on each trial received a shock set for him by his opponent. Thus, subjects' willingness to aggress against the fictitious opponent could be measured in terms of the strength of the shocks they chose for this person. Before the reaction-time trials started, two accomplices entered the room, explaining that they had been assigned by their professor to observe the study. During the session, these accomplices exerted increasing social pressure on the subject to use highly numbered buttons (i.e., to deliver strong shocks to their opponent). The accomplices remarked that using high levels would provide more excitement for both the subject and themselves, and they expressed approval when the subject followed their recommendations (or disapproval when he did not). Then, near the end of the session, one of the accomplices suggested that their comments might be interfering with the session. After that, they sat silently and exerted no further pressure on the subject to behave aggressively.

It was predicted that the intoxicated subjects would be more responsive than the nonintoxicated subjects to the accomplices' social pressure, increasing the strength of the shocks they delivered during its presence. However, when it

SOCIAL DETERMINANTS OF AGGRESSION **419**

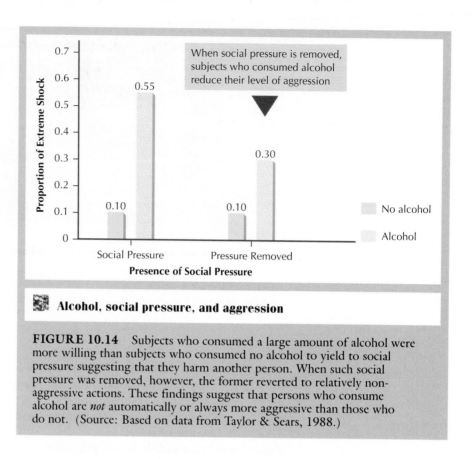

Alcohol, social pressure, and aggression

FIGURE 10.14 Subjects who consumed a large amount of alcohol were more willing than subjects who consumed no alcohol to yield to social pressure suggesting that they harm another person. When such social pressure was removed, however, the former reverted to relatively non-aggressive actions. These findings suggest that persons who consume alcohol are *not* automatically or always more aggressive than those who do not. (Source: Based on data from Taylor & Sears, 1988.)

was removed near the end of the session they would reduce their level of aggression. This is precisely what happened. Intoxicated subjects first increased and then decreased their level of aggression in response to the accomplices' pressure (see Figure 10.14). Nonintoxicated subjects showed little change over the course of the study.

These results and those of several related studies (e.g., Jeavons & Taylor, 1985) suggest that alcohol does not automatically increase aggression by individuals who consume it. Such persons do sometimes become more aggressive, but only in the context of social or situational cues suggesting that such behavior is appropriate (e.g., strong provocation from others, social pressure to behave aggressively). Thus, they are not programmed for violence by the drug they have consumed; actually, they remain capable of demonstrating considerable restraint. This finding in turn has important implications for legal proceedings. It suggests that defenses based on the suggestion that persons accused of violent crimes consumed so much alcohol that they didn't know what they were doing rests on very shaky ground, to say the least.

Personal Causes of Aggression

Are some persons primed, by their personalities or other characteristics, for aggression? Informal observation suggests that this is so (refer to Figure 10.15). While some persons rarely lose their tempers or participate in aggressive encounters, others seem to be forever blowing their tops, often with serious consequences. Many personal factors play a role in such differences; in this section we'll consider three that appear to be of considerable importance.

Personality and Aggression: The Type A Behavior Pattern

Do you know any persons you could describe as (1) extremely competitive, (2) always in a hurry, and (3) especially irritable and aggressive? If so, they stand a good chance of being what psychologists term **Type As** (Glass, 1977). This set of characteristics (known as the *Type A behavior pattern*) sets such persons apart from others who do not share such traits and are described as **Type Bs.** As is true with virtually any individual difference, these represent extremes on a dimension. We should note, however, that recent evidence suggests that the Type A–Type B distinction does seem to be a real dichotomy: Most people do tend to fall into one category or the other (Strube, 1989).

Given the characteristics mentioned above, it seems only reasonable that Type As would tend to be more aggressive, in a wider range of situations, than Type Bs. After all, Type As are highly competitive, easily irritated, and always in a hurry. The results of several experiments indicate that this is indeed the case (Baron, Russell, & Arms, 1985; Carver & Glass, 1978). Moreover, other findings indicate that Type As are truly hostile. They don't merely aggress against others because doing so is a useful means for reaching other goals, such as furthering their own careers or winning in athletic contests. (This is known as **instrumental aggression**). On the contrary, Type As are more likely than Type Bs to engage in **hostile aggression**—aggression whose prime purpose is that

"Miss Jenkins, is anyone out there waiting to tangle with me?"

Personality and aggression

FIGURE 10.15 As suggested by this cartoon, some individuals seem to possess characteristics that predispose them toward high levels of aggression. (Drawing by Modell; © 1983 The New Yorker Magazine, Inc.)

of inflicting pain and suffering on the victims (Strube et al., 1984). Additional evidence suggests that Type As are more likely than Type Bs to engage in such actions as child or spouse abuse (Strube et al., 1984).

Finally, it appears that Type As are more likely than Type Bs to experience conflict with others in work settings. In a recent study on this issue, Baron (1989) asked a large group of managers to report on the frequency with which they experienced conflict with subordinates, peers, or supervisors during the course of their jobs. Persons classified as Type A reported a higher incidence of conflict with peers and subordinates than did persons classified as Type B. Neither group reported much conflict with supervisors—yet another indication that aggression is strongly influenced by such social factors as relative status. (Are Type A individuals more aggressive than Type Bs around the world? Or is this phenomenon restricted to the Western nations in which it was first studied systematically? For evidence on this issue, please see the **Multicultural Perspective** section below.)

SOCIAL PSYCHOLOGY: A MULTICULTURAL PERSPECTIVE

On-the-Job Aggression by Type As and Type Bs: Bus Drivers in the United States and India

Even persons who are generally low in the tendency to aggress seem to change radically in one special context: while driving. When they find themselves in traffic, many persons readily become angry and demonstrate their anger by honking their horns, engaging in risky driving maneuvers, or even making obscene gestures (e.g., Baron, 1976; Kenrick & MacFarlane, 1986). Given that restraints against aggression seem to be relatively weak in the context of driving, it seems possible that this activity might provide a good context in which to look for differences between Type A and Type B individuals. In fact, a study by Evans, Palsane, and Carrere (1987) has adopted this procedure.

These researchers compared the behavior and driving records of bus drivers classified (on the basis of a standard test) as being Type A or Type B. Drivers in two countries—the United States and India—were studied. To obtain evidence about the drivers' on-the-job behavior, records of their previous accidents were obtained from their employers. In addition, assistants boarded the drivers' buses and, unknown to them, observed their behavior during typical workdays.

Results indicated that Type A drivers did in fact behave differently—and more aggressively—than Type B drivers. They had a higher incidence of accidents in both countries. Indeed, the rate of accidents was several times higher among Type A drivers than among Type B drivers. That this difference was due at least partly to differences in aggressive actions on the job was suggested by observations of the drivers' daily behavior. In India, Type A drivers passed other drivers more frequently, stepped on their brakes more often, and blew their horns almost twice as often as Type B drivers (see Figure 10.16). Similar differences were not observed among bus drivers in the United States, perhaps because they worked under much less hectic driving conditions; bus drivers in the United States rarely blew their horns or passed other vehicles. Recall,

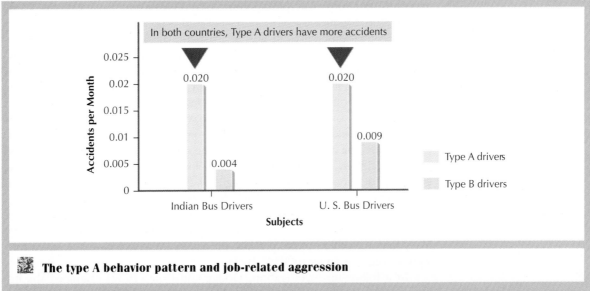

In both countries, Type A drivers have more accidents

The type A behavior pattern and job-related aggression

FIGURE 10.16   Type A bus drivers in India and the United States had more accidents than Type B bus drivers. In addition, in India (but not in the United States), Type A bus drivers were more aggressive on the job: They honked their horns and passed other motorists more frequently. (Source: Based on data from Evans, Palsane, & Carrere, 1987.)

however, that Type A and Type B drivers did differ in accident rates in both countries.

Taken as a whole, the findings reported by Evans and his colleagues suggest that the link between the Type A pattern and aggression is not restricted to a single culture. On the contrary, it appears that Type As are more likely than Type Bs to become involved in aggressive encounters no matter where they live. Clearly, then, this is one personal determinant of aggression worth considering with care.

Perceiving Evil Intent in Others: Hostile Attributional Bias

Earlier, we noted that *attributions* about others' intentions often play an important role in aggression. When individuals perceive ambiguous actions by others as stemming from malevolent intentions, they are much more likely to retaliate than when they perceive the same actions as stemming from other motives (cf. Baumeister, Stillwell, & Wotman, 1991; Johnson & Rule 1986). This fact points to another personal characteristic that sometimes contributes to the occurrence of aggression: The tendency to perceive hostile intent in others even when it is totally lacking. Presumably, individuals differ greatly in their tendency to make such attributional errors. To the extent that they do make these errors, their likelihood of aggressing, too, may increase.

Evidence that this is actually the case has been provided by several studies (e.g., Dodge, Murphy, & Buchsbaum, 1984). Perhaps the clearest support for the importance of individual differences in this characteristic—known as **hostile**

attributional bias—has been reported by Dodge and Coie (1987). These investigators conducted a series of related studies concerned with the possibility that individual differences in hostile attributional bias would affect the likelihood or intensity of *reactive* aggression—aggression in response to prior provocation. In one of these studies, boys who had previously been rated by their teachers as high in reactive aggression, high in *proactive* aggression (aggression performed without provocation, for purposes of gaining dominance over others or other goals), or relatively nonaggressive were shown videotapes of incidents in which one child provoked another (e.g., one knocked over the other's building blocks). The apparent intentions of the actor in these incidents was varied systematically, so that to outside adult observers, they were clearly hostile, prosocial (designed to help), or ambiguous. Subjects were then asked to explain the intentions of the actor in each incident. As expected, subjects high in reactive aggression made more errors than those high in proactive aggression in describing these intentions. Specifically, those high in reactive aggression were more likely than the other boys to perceive the actor's intentions as hostile when they were ambiguous (refer to Table 10.1).

In a follow-up investigation, Dodge and Coie (1987) examined the hypothesis that this hostile attributional bias would be positively related to a high rate of *overreactive* aggression—tendencies to engage in strong retaliation in response to even mild provocations. To test this hypothesis, the researchers first measured subjects' tendency to falsely attribute hostile intentions to others and then observed their behavior while playing with other children. Results supported the major prediction: The greater subjects' tendency to show hostile attributional bias, the greater their tendency to engage in overreactive aggression.

While these findings were gathered with children, it seems clear that adults, too, differ along this dimension. At one extreme are persons who tend to give others the benefit of the doubt, attributing ambiguous actions to positive or at least neutral motives. At the other extreme are persons who see malevolence and aggressive intentions everywhere—even where they don't really exist. Need-

---

Hostile attributional bias and reactive aggression

TABLE 10.1 Boys rated as high in reactive aggression by their teachers were more likely than other boys to perceive ambiguous actions by others as stemming from hostile intentions. (Numbers shown are the percentage of ambiguous actions by others judged by subjects to be hostile.)

Subjects Rated High in Reactive Aggression	Subjects Rated High in Proactive Aggression	Subjects Rated as Being Relatively Nonaggressive
83	38	53

Source: Based on data from Dodge & Coie, 1987.

less to say, individuals falling into the latter category are more likely to become involved in aggression and conflict than those in the former. Indeed, they perceive such actions as necessary to protect themselves against a hostile and dangerous social world.

Sex Differences in Aggression: Imaginary or Real?

Are males more aggressive than females? Folklore suggests they are. And crime statistics reveal that males are more likely than females to be arrested for violent acts. Does this mean that large and consistent differences between the sexes exist with respect to overt aggression? Research findings provide something of a mixed answer.

After carefully reviewing a broad sample of evidence on this issue, Eagly and Steffen (1986) concluded that males are indeed somewhat more likely than females to engage in overt aggression. The size of this difference, however, appeared to be quite small. Further, it was larger in some contexts than in others. For example, this sex difference in aggression was found to be stronger in studies involving physical forms of aggression than in studies involving nonphysical forms of aggression (e.g., verbal assaults, rating others negatively along certain dimensions). Similarly, the difference was found to be larger in situations in which aggression seemed to be required (e.g., by some social role) rather than freely chosen. In addition, males and females appeared to differ somewhat in their attitudes toward aggression. Males indicated less guilt or anxiety about engaging in such behavior than females, while females reported greater concern over the possibility that aggressing against others could pose a threat to their own safety (e.g., if the victim chose to retaliate). Finally, Eagly and Steffen (1986) found that both sexes directed slightly more aggression against male targets than against female ones.

In sum, it appears that men and women do differ to a degree in their willingness to handle interpersonal relations through aggression. The next question, then, is obvious: What is the source of such differences? Are men somehow programmed for violence by genetic factors (e.g., possession of a Y chromosome)? Or are these differences largely the result of contrasting gender roles—cultural beliefs suggesting that men should be tough and aggressive, while women should be kind and cautious? As Eagly and Steffen (1986) note, little evidence on this issue currently exists. However, given the fact that many other supposedly "innate" differences between the sexes have been found, on close study, to stem mainly from contrasting sex roles and socialization practices for boys and girls, it seems likely that this one, too, rests largely on such foundations. In addition, physical differences between the sexes may play a role. Males tend to be larger than females and to possess greater upper-body strength. As a result, males may find it easier, physically, to engage in certain aggressive actions and may be more likely to succeed in such behavior (i.e., to be rewarded for its performance).

To the extent that sex roles and socialization practices play a role in existing sex differences in aggression, the magnitude of these differences is not set in stone. On the contrary, they may vary with changes in society. For example, if traditional stereotypes concerning *masculinity* and *femininity* continue to wane, sex differences in aggression, too, may decrease. If, however, such stereotypes persist or even strengthen, existing differences between the sexes, too, may be expected to continue.

The Prevention and Control of Aggression: Some Useful Techniques

An underlying theme in this discussion of aggression—perhaps the most important theme—has been this: Aggression stems from the complex interplay between a variety of *external events* (e.g., provocation, frustration), *cognitions* concerning these events (attributions, memories, scripts), and *individual differences* along several key dimensions (e.g., the Type A behavior pattern). As such, aggression is definitely *not* a programmed, automatic response. To the extent that you accept this point of view, you will also find our next proposal to be reasonable: Aggression *can* be prevented, or at least reduced. It is not an inevitable pattern for either individuals or our entire species. On the contrary, several techniques for controlling its occurrence or intensity exist and can be put to practical use (Baron, 1983). In this final section, we'll consider a number of these procedures.

Punishment: An Effective Deterrent to Violence?

Throughout history, most societies have used **punishment** as a means of deterring human violence. They have established harsh punishments for such crimes as murder, rape, and assault (see Figure 10.17). Are such tactics effective? In one sense, of course, they are—persons who are imprisoned or executed for performing violent acts cannot repeat those offenses. But what about deterrence: Will the threat of severe punishment prevent individuals from engaging in aggressive acts in the first place? The pendulum of scientific opinion has swung back and forth on this issue for decades. At present, however, the weight of existing evidence seems to suggest that punishment, if used appropriately, *can* be an effective deterrent to violence. In order for it to succeed, however, several conditions must be met (Bower & Hilgard, 1981).

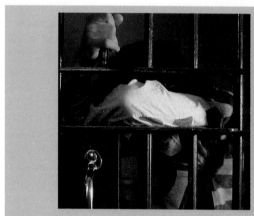

Punishment: Society's response to aggression

FIGURE 10.17 Most societies impose strong penalties on individuals who commit violent crimes against others.

First, punishment must be *prompt*—it must follow aggression as soon as possible. Second, it must be *intense*—it must be of sufficient magnitude to be highly aversive to the potential recipients. Third, it must be *probable*—the likelihood that it will follow aggressive actions must be quite high. Unfortunately, of course, these conditions are precisely the ones lacking from the criminal justice systems of many nations. In many societies, the delivery of punishment for aggressive actions is delayed for months or even years, the magnitude of punishment itself is variable from one locale to another, and it is well known that many violent crimes go unpunished—no one is ever apprehended, tried, or convicted of them. In light of these realities, it is hardly surprising that punishment has often seemed to fail as a deterrent to violent crime. The dice, so to speak, are heavily loaded against its succeeding.

In sum, the fact that punishment does not currently seem to be successful in deterring the rising tide of violence in many nations does not imply that punishment itself is useless. Rather, it implies that this procedure is being used in ways that virtually guarantee its failure. If these conditions were changed, we believe, the potential impact of punishment might well be enhanced. And then the safety and well-being of countless innocent victims might also be better protected.

Catharsis: Does "Getting It Out of Your System" Really Help?

Does "getting it out of your system"—giving vent to feelings of anger—really work where the reduction of aggression is concerned? The belief that it does is widespread. Most people accept some version of the **catharsis hypothesis** (Dollard et al., 1939). They believe that permitting angry persons to blow off steam through participation in vigorous actions produces two benefits: (1) their emotional tension is reduced, and (2) they are less likely to engage in subsequent acts of aggression. Further, most people assume that it is not necessary for such actions to result in harm to others. Any vigorous, emotion-draining activity will do.

Are these suggestions accurate? Existing evidence provides a mixed reply (Feshbach, 1984). First, consider the assumption that participation in vigorous activities can reduce the arousal stemming from frustration or provocation. Here, some findings do suggest that physically exhausting activities can reduce arousal (Zillmann, 1979). Unfortunately, though, such effects appear to be temporary. Arousal stemming from frustration or provocation may reappear when individuals again bring to mind real or imagined wrongs at the hands of others (Zillmann, 1988). Further, the most effective technique for reducing such arousal seems to be attacking the source of one's anger (Hokanson, Burgess, & Cohen, 1963). These points suggest that the benefits of participation in cathartic activities may be quite minimal.

Turning to the idea that the performance of "safe" aggressive actions reduces the likelihood of more harmful ones, the picture is even more uncertain. Research on this topic indicates that overt aggression is not reduced by (1) watching scenes of filmed or televised violence (Geen, 1978), (2) attacking inanimate objects (Mallick & McCandless, 1966), or (3) aggressing verbally against others. Indeed, there is some evidence that aggression may actually be increased by each of these conditions.

Contrary to popular belief, then, catharsis does not appear to be as effective a means for reducing aggression as is widely assumed. Participating in exhausting, nonaggressive activities may produce temporary reductions in arousal and in this way may lower the tendency to aggress in some situations. Thus, such activities can be useful for reducing aggression temporarily—an important gain in some contexts. However, because of the strong impact of cognition on arousal, feelings of anger and irritation may quickly reappear when individuals encounter or merely think about whatever previously annoyed them. For this reason, catharsis may be less effective in producing long-term reductions in aggression than has often been assumed.

Cognitive Interventions: The Role of Apologies

Imagine the following scene: You are waiting for another person with whom you have an appointment. She is late, and as time passes you become more and more upset. Finally, fully thirty minutes after the agreed-on time, she shows up. Before you can say a word, she apologizes profusely: "I'm so sorry. My car wouldn't start. Then I got stuck in a traffic jam on the highway. I'm really upset; please forgive me." Would you be angry and criticize this person severely? Probably not. Her apology—an admission of wrongdoing plus a request for your forgiveness—would go a long way toward diffusing your annoyance. Of course, your reactions would depend strongly on the nature of her excuses. Research findings suggest that excuses that make reference to external events beyond the excuse-giver's control are much more effective than ones that refer to events within the person's control (e.g., "Sorry . . . I just forgot"; Weiner, Amirkhan, Folkes, & Verette, 1987). In sum, common sense and informal observation indicate that apologies can be an effective technique for reducing aggression. This conclusion is also supported by the findings of systematic research.

In a revealing study on this topic (Ohbuchi, Kameda, & Agarie, 1989) female subjects were embarrassed while performing a complex task, through a series of errors committed by an assistant. The assistant made these errors while presenting experimental materials, with the result that the subjects performed poorly and received a negative evaluation from a senior experimenter. To investigate the impact of apologies on subjects' later reactions, the assistant either apologized for his errors or did not apologize. In one condition (*public apology*), he apologized to subjects in front of the experimenter, thus relieving them of the responsibility for their poor performance. In another condition (*private apology*), the assistant also apologized but did so while the experimenter was not present. In a third condition (*no apology*), the assistant offered no apology whatsoever. Finally, to determine whether merely restoring subjects' self-assurance would be as effective in reducing later aggression as an apology, the researchers included a fourth condition (*harm removal*), in which the senior experimenter stated that the subjects' poor performance must be due to errors by the assistant.

After being exposed to one of these sequences of events, subjects rated the assistant on several dimensions (e.g., sincere–insincere, responsible–irresponsible), reported their own affective state (unpleasant–pleasant), and rated the assistant's skills as a psychologist. This last scale constituted a measure of aggres-

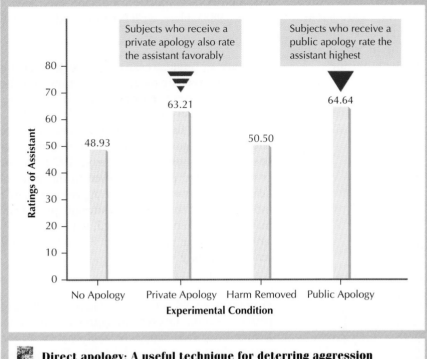

Direct apology: A useful technique for deterring aggression

FIGURE 10.18 Subjects who received an apology from an assistant who had previously provoked them were less aggressive toward him than those who received no apology. Moreover, an apology that rectified the harm done to subjects (i.e., a public apology) was slightly more effective than one that did not remove such harm (a private apology). The mere removal of harm without an apology was also relatively ineffective in deterring subsequent aggression. (Source: Based on data from Ohbuchi, Kameda, & Agarie, 1989.)

sion, because it was explained to subjects that their ratings would influence the assistant's grade.

As you can see from Figure 10.18, results offered strong support for the value of apologies. Subjects who received an apology rated the assistant higher, reported feeling better, and showed less aggression than those in the other conditions. Moreover, mere removal of the harm produced—either by the private apology or by the experimenter's independent recognition of the assistant's errors—was not as effective as the combination of an apology *and* removal of harm (the public-apology group).

These findings and those of related studies (e.g., Baron, 1988b, 1990d) suggest that apologies by sources of provocation can go a long way toward preventing retaliation against them. While it is often difficult to admit wrongdoing and to say "I'm sorry," the value of doing so may make such momentary discomfort well worthwhile.

Other Techniques for Reducing Aggression: Nonaggressive Models, Training in Social Skills, and Incompatible Responses

Many other techniques for reducing overt aggression have been suggested (cf. Baron, 1983). Here, we'll briefly consider three that appear to be quite effective.

Exposure to Nonaggressive Models: Is Restraint Contagious?   As we noted previously, exposure to aggressive actions by others in films or on television can increase aggression among viewers. If this is so, then it seems only reasonable to expect parallel—but opposite—effects from exposure to persons who either demonstrate or urge *restraint* in the face of provocation. That exposure to such *nonaggressive models* actually produces such effects is indicated by the findings of several experiments (e.g., Baron, 1972; Donnerstein & Donnerstein, 1976). In these studies, persons exposed to the actions of nonaggressive models later demonstrated lower levels of aggression than persons not exposed to such models, even if they had been strongly provoked. These findings suggest that it may be useful to plant restrained, nonaggressive models in tense and threatening situations. Their presence may well serve to tip the balance against the occurrence of violence.

Training in Social Skills: Learning to Get Along with Others   One reason many persons become involved in aggressive encounters they would prefer to avoid is straightforward: They are sorely lacking in the basic social skills that would enable them to avoid such events. For example, they do not know how to provide negative feedback to others (i.e., criticism) and thus do so in a way that angers them (Baron, 1988a). Similarly, they do not know how to express their wishes to others, have an abrasive style of self-expression, and are insensitive to outward signs of others' emotional states. As a result, they experience severe, repeated frustration and say or do things that unnecessarily anger those around them. Persons lacking in social skills seem to account for a high proportion of violence in many societies (Toch, 1985). Thus, equipping such persons with the social skills they lack may go a long way toward reducing the incidence of aggression.

Incompatible Responses: Positive Affect as a Means of Reducing Anger   The final aggression-reducing technique we will consider rests on the following basic principle: It is impossible to engage in two **incompatible responses** or to experience two incompatible emotional states at once. Applying this idea to aggression, it seems feasible that both anger and overt aggression can be lessened by inducing reactions or emotional states incompatible with them. That this is indeed the case is indicated by a large body of research evidence. When angry persons are induced to experience emotional states incompatible with anger or aggression (e.g., *empathy, mild sexual arousal,* or *humor*), they do show reduced levels of aggression (Baron, 1983; Ramirez, Bryant, & Zillmann, 1983). This reduction may occur because the positive feelings produced by such reactions lessen the negative emotions stemming from frustration or annoyance and also because such positive affect tends to lower the very high levels of arousal associated with extreme anger. (As we noted previously, high levels of arousal make it difficult for individuals to regulate their own behavior.) Whatever the precise mechanisms involved, one fact seems clear: People in a pleasant or happy frame of mind are usually much less likely to aggress against others. Thus, steps designed to generate such reactions can be a useful strategy for the control of aggression.

SUMMARY AND REVIEW

Theoretical Perspectives on Aggression

Aggression—the intentional infliction of harm on others—has been attributed to many different causes. *Instinct theories,* such as the ones proposed by Freud and Lorenz, suggest that aggression stems from innate urges toward destructive actions. *Drive theories* suggest that aggression stems from externally generated motives to harm or injure others. In contrast, modern perspectives (the *neoassociationist* and *social learning* views) suggest that aggression stems from negative reactions to aversive experiences, memories, cognitions, learning, and present reinforcement or punishments for aggressive actions.

Social Determinants of Aggression

Many acts of aggression are triggered by the words or deeds of persons with whom the aggressor interacts or by social conditions generally. *Frustration,* interference with goal-directed behavior, can facilitate aggression, perhaps because of the negative feelings it generates. *Direct provocations* from others are an important cause of aggression, especially when such actions appear to stem from malevolent intent. Considerable evidence suggests that exposure to *media violence* (in films or television shows) can increase aggression on the part of viewers.

Heightened *arousal* can increase aggression. However, the impact of arousal on aggression depends on the complex interplay between emotions and cognitions. Cognitions sometimes shape emotions and hence aggression. Conversely, emotions affect cognitions, and this, too, can influence aggressive behavior. *Alcohol* can facilitate aggression under some conditions; however, persons who consume this drug remain responsive to social cues and will aggress only when this seems appropriate or justified.

Personal Determinants of Aggression

Type A persons, because of their extreme competitiveness and hostility, are more aggressive in many situations than *Type B* persons. Individuals who perceive hostile intentions behind others' actions even when such intentions are lacking are more aggressive than those who do not demonstrate such *hostile attributional bias.* Males appear to be somewhat more aggressive than females. However, differences between the sexes in this respect have been exaggerated in the past.

The Reduction of Aggression

Several techniques are effective in reducing aggression. *Punishment* can serve as an effective deterrent to aggression if it is delivered swiftly, if it is intense, and if its likelihood of occurrence is high. Participation in *cathartic activities* (i.e., vigorous, nonaggressive behaviors) can sometimes lower arousal and anger. Such reductions appear to be temporary, and anger can readily reemerge when individuals bring to mind thoughts and memories associated with aggression (or past sources of provocation).

Direct *apologies* are highly effective in reducing anger and subsequent aggression. They are much more effective in this respect than efforts to remove the harm done to victims by previous provocation.

Other techniques effective in reducing aggression include exposing aggressors to *nonaggressive models,* training them in basic *social skills,* and the induction of responses that are *incompatible* with anger.

KEY TERMS

Aggression Behavior directed toward the goal of harming or injuring another living being who is motivated to avoid such treatment.

Aggression machine Apparatus used to measure physical aggression under safe laboratory conditions.

Aggressive cues Stimuli that, because of previous association with aggression, acquire the capacity to elicit such behavior.

Catharsis hypothesis The view that providing angry persons with an opportunity to engage in vigorous but noninjurious activities will reduce their level of emotional arousal and lower their tendencies to aggress against others.

Cognitive neoassociationist view A theory suggesting that aversive experiences generate negative affect that in turn activates tendencies toward both aggression and flight. Which of these actions follows depends in part on higher-level cognitive processes.

Drive theories Theories suggesting that aggression stems from external conditions that arouse the motive to harm or injure others. The most famous of these theories is the frustration-aggression hypothesis.

Excitation transfer theory A theory suggesting that arousal produced in one situation can persist and intensify emotional reactions occurring in subsequent situations.

Frustration-aggression hypothesis The suggestion that frustration is a very powerful determinant of aggression.

Hostile aggression Aggression for which the primary goal is harm or injury to the victim.

Hostile attributional bias The tendency to perceive others' actions as stemming from hostile intent even when this is not clearly the case.

Incompatible responses With respect to aggression, responses that are incompatible with anger or overt aggressive actions against others.

Instinct theory A view suggesting that specific forms of behavior (e.g., aggression) stem from innate tendencies that are universal among members of a given species.

Instrumental aggression Aggression directed toward goals other than harm or injury to the victim.

Provocation Actions by others that are perceived as acts of aggression deriving from hostile intentions.

Punishment Procedures in which aversive consequences are delivered to individuals each time they engage in specific actions. Under appropriate conditions, punishment can serve as an effective deterrent to human aggression.

Social learning view A perspective suggesting that aggression is a complex form of learned behavior.

Sociobiology The field that seeks to determine the biological bases of social behavior, primarily in terms of evolution and natural selection.

Type As Persons characterized by high levels of competitiveness, time urgency, and hostility.

Type Bs Persons who do not show the pattern of characteristics demonstrated by Type As (i.e., they are relatively low in competitiveness, time urgency, and hostility).

FOR MORE INFORMATION

Baron, R. A., & Richardson, D. R. (1991). *Human aggression* (2nd ed.). New York: Plenum.

An overview of existing knowledge about human aggression. Separate chapters examine the biological, social, environmental, and personal determinants of such behavior. Additional chapters consider the occurrence of aggression in many natural settings.

Liebert, R. M., Sprafkin, J. N., & Davidson, E. S. (1989). *The early window: The effects of television on children and youth* (3rd ed.). New York: Pergamon.

A clear, concise review of research dealing with the impact of television on children and adults.

Zillmann, D., & Bryant, J. (Eds.). (1989). *Pornography: Research advances and policy considerations.* Hillsdale, NJ: Erlbaum.

A clear, up-to-date discussion of current evidence concerning the effects of pornography on the viewers of such materials. The implications of such findings for social policy (e.g., regulation of the sale of certain types of pornography) are also discussed. All in all, an informative and thought-provoking volume.

CHAPTER
Eleven

Groups and Individuals: The Consequences of Belonging

Well, I'll tell you one thing," Alison Bryant says to her assistant, Bob Eidelson, "he's worked wonders out there."

"No, not wonders," Bob replies, *"miracles."*

(The two executives are discussing John Nowicki, the new head of one of their company's branch operations.)

Chuckling, Alison replies, "Yeah, you might almost say that. We all thought he'd do a good job, but this goes beyond our wildest expectations."

"I'll say," Bob agrees. "And in just six months, too. He moves in and presto! Output jumps, quality rises, and turnover goes way down.

What a record. I don't know what he's doing, but I sure hope he keeps doing it!"

"Right," Alison agrees emphatically. "He sure has done a great job." Then, pausing, she continues, "But just what *is* he doing? What's he doing that's so different from the six other people we sent there?"

"Beats me," Bob answers. "He seems pretty much like all the others. Sure, he's pleasant and bright enough, but I've never seen anyone faint when he comes into the room."

"Well, maybe not faint," Alison comments, "but there *is* something kind of special about him."

"What do you mean?" Bob asks.

"For one thing, think about the way he exudes confidence. It seems to practically flow out of him."

"Yeah, I guess so," Bob agrees. "And it doesn't come across as arrogance, either. He kind of gives the impression that he's confident in himself *and* in you."

"Right. People really react positively to that."

"Hmm . . ." Bob mutters while stroking his chin, "now that you mention it, there *are* some things about him that I've noticed, too. Like the way he's so relaxed when talking to you—kind of puts you at ease."

"That's him, all right," Alison agrees. "And how about the way he always seems to know just where he's going? With John, you get the idea that he's got all his goals lined up in a row and that they're darned good ones, too."

"So what we're saying, I guess, is that it's not one single thing he does that makes him special. It's lots of different things."

"Yup," Alison says, nodding her head. "And the payoff is that people like him, respect him, and want to do their best for him."

"Hey, maybe we should bring him in here to do some seminars on leadership," Bob exclaims. "I think maybe we can *all* learn something from this guy!"

Have you ever known an exceptional leader like John, the character in this story? If so, you probably realize that such a person can be extremely valuable to the people with whom he or she works (or plays). Groups fortunate enough to have first-rate leaders function more smoothly, make more progress toward chosen goals, and have an important advantage over ones that have less effective leaders. *Leadership,* however, is just one of many central processes occurring in **groups**—collections of two or more interacting persons. Once individuals join various groups, they are subjected to a wide variety of forces and processes, including some they neither expected nor desired. In short, belonging to a group can change members' behavior, attitudes, and thoughts in important and subtle ways.

It is on such *group influence*—the effects of group membership on individual behavior—that we will focus in this chapter. First, to set the stage for further discussion, we'll consider the basic nature of groups: what they are and how they function. Second, we'll consider the impact of groups on *task performance*. Here, we'll examine the ways in which our performance on various tasks can be affected by the presence of others or their potential evaluations—a process known as **social facilitation.** We'll also address the complex question of whether groups or individuals perform various tasks more efficiently. Third, we'll turn to **decision making** in groups, examining both the process through which groups move toward consensus and several factors that may distort or bias the decisions they reach. Finally, we'll return to the topic of our opening story, **leadership,** touching on the question of whether leaders are born or made (including the issue of *charisma*). We'll also consider modern theories concerning the factors that make them relatively effective or ineffective.

Groups: Their Nature and Function

Look at the photos in Figure 11.1. Which show social groups? To answer this question, we must first define the word *group* in concrete terms. According to most social psychologists, groups consist of *two or more interacting persons who share common goals, have a stable relationship, are somehow interdependent,* and *perceive that they are in fact part of a group* (Paulus, 1989). In other words, the term *group* does not apply to mere collections of individuals who happen to be in the same place at the same time but have no lasting relationship to one

Groups versus mere collections of unrelated persons

FIGURE 11.1 Which of these photos show social *groups?* Applying the definition offered in the text, it is easy to see that the top two illustrate real groups, while the bottom photo does not.

another. Rather, this term is restricted to those collections of persons which meet certain criteria.

First, such persons must *interact* with each other, either directly or indirectly. Second, they must be *interdependent* in some manner—what happens to one must affect what happens to the others. Third, their relationship must be relatively *stable;* it must persist over appreciable periods of time (e.g., weeks, months, or even years). Fourth, the individuals involved must share at least some *goals* that they all seek to attain. Fifth, their interactions must be *structured* in some manner so that, for example, each performs the same or similar functions each time they meet. Finally, the persons involved must *perceive* themselves as members of a group—they must recognize the existence of a lasting relationship between them.

Applying this definition to the photos in Figure 11.1, it is easy to see that the people in the top two illustrations are members of groups. In contrast, those in the bottom photo are not; they are simply persons who happen to be in the same place at the same time, but who have no real relationship to one another.

Do individuals actually apply these criteria in deciding whether they do or do not constitute a social group? Research conducted by Insko and his colleagues (Insko et al., 1988) provides compelling evidence that they do. In order to determine just what conditions are necessary for individuals to perceive themselves as belonging to a group, these researchers had subjects (female and male students) play a game in which they could choose, on each of several trials, either to cooperate or to compete with others. (This was a *prisoner's dilemma game,* similar to the one described in Chapter 9.) Six individuals, divided into two sets of three, participated in each session. They then played the game under one of five conditions. In one condition *(interdependence),* members of each set were seated in individual cubicles and could not even see one another. In a second condition *(contact),* all three individuals in each set were placed in a single room. Thus, they could see one another. However, they were forbidden to talk during the session. In a third condition *(discussion),* in contrast, subjects were instructed to discuss their choices in the game. In each of the conditions described so far, subjects in one set played the game with an opponent from the other set as individuals. In two final conditions, they operated as teams, playing against the other three persons. In the first of these conditions *(consensus)* the members of each set were told to reach a consensus about their choices in the game. All members of the set then had to stick to this agreement while playing against their opponents from the other set. In the second *(group-all)* of these conditions, the members of the two sets were brought together and played as teams against each other.

Under which of these conditions did subjects come to think of themselves as a group? To find out, Insko and his colleagues observed subjects' behavior during the game and also had them complete various questionnaires. Previous research indicated that when persons are part of a group, they act more competitively toward opponents than when they play as individuals. Thus, it was reasoned that those conditions which produced such feelings would generate fewer cooperative choices by subjects than those conditions that did not. As you can see from Figure 11.2, the results were clear: Subjects in the consensus and group-all conditions made considerably fewer cooperative choices than those in the other conditions. Thus, they behaved as team members and sought to defeat members of the opposing group.

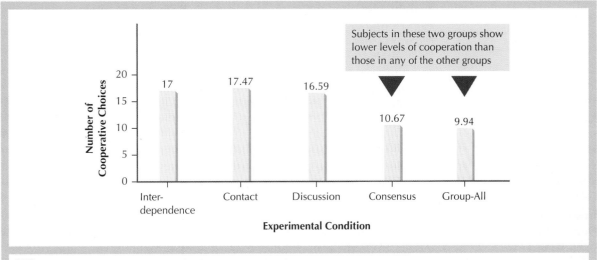

Subjects in these two groups show lower levels of cooperation than those in any of the other groups

What makes a group a group? Experimental evidence

FIGURE 11.2 Subjects in the *consensus* and *group-all* conditions acted like true groups: They demonstrated lower levels of cooperation than those in the other conditions and rated themselves higher in terms of acting like a group. These findings suggest that individuals perceive themselves as belonging to a group only under specific conditions (e.g., the need to reach consensus concerning various actions). (Source: Based on data from Insko et al., 1988.)

Additional findings lend support to the view that these two conditions were the ones that produced feelings of "groupness" among subjects. When asked to rate the extent to which they perceived members of their own set as a group and those of the other set as another group, subjects in the consensus and group-all conditions provided higher ratings than those in the other conditions. Similarly, subjects in these two conditions reported that they had less control over their own earnings than those in the other conditions—a pattern that would be expected if subjects perceived their behavior as being strongly determined by their group membership.

In sum, the findings reported by Insko and his colleagues suggest that feelings of belonging to a group do indeed emerge out of conditions similar to those suggested by the definition of *group* offered above. Only when individuals have the opportunity to interact with others, perceive that their fates are somehow interdependent, share common goals, and then coordinate their actions to reach these, do they conclude that they belong to a functioning group. And only then is their behavior influenced by such membership so that they act differently than they would if operating as unrelated individuals.

Group Formation: Why Do People Join?

At present, you probably belong to several different groups. Why did you join them in the first place? Existing evidence on this issue suggests that individuals generally enter groups for several reasons. First, groups help us satisfy important psychological or social needs, such as those for belonging or for receiving attention or affection (Robbins, 1989). Second, groups help us achieve various goals that we could not attain as individuals. Belonging to various groups helps us perform tasks we could not perform alone. In addition, group membership often provides us with knowledge and information that would not otherwise be available to us. For example, individuals are often denied access to sensitive or restricted information held by a group until they are admitted to full membership. Only then are they permitted to share such knowledge.

Finally, group membership also contributes to the establishment of a positive *social identity*—it becomes part of the self-concept (refer to Chapter 3). Simply put, the more prestigious, restrictive groups to which an individual is admitted, the more her or his self-concept is bolstered. In sum, there are many important reasons for joining groups, and so it is not at all surprising that most persons seek entry to many groups over the course of their lives.

Group Development: How Groups Change over Time

If you have ever participated in the formation of a new group, you already realize that groups do not spring into existence fully formed and "ready for business." On the contrary, they seem to move through several stages of development en route to full-fledged existence (Tuckman & Jensen, 1977). The major steps in this process are summarized in Table 11.1. As you can see, the initial phase, known as *forming,* is one in which group members get to know one another and begin to establish some basic ground rules (preliminary norms) for their operations.

Group development: Some basic stages

TABLE 11.1 Many groups seem to move through the stages of development described here. Depending on many factors, specific groups may skip or combine one or more stages.

Stage	Description
Forming	Group takes shape; initial ground rules established. Members become acquainted.
Storming	Members compete for attractive roles and positions within the group; considerable conflict may occur.
Norming	Members develop a common perspective about how the group will operate; adopt shared rules. Feelings of attachment to the group intensify.
Performing	Group now concentrates on carrying out its major tasks and moving toward shared goals.
Adjourning	Once goals have been attained, members may have little reason for remaining in some groups; thus, they may disband. In other cases, however, attraction to the group remains and it persists.

Source: Based on suggestions by Tuckman & Jensen, 1977.

Once these ground rules are determined, a second phase—*storming*—often follows. Here, members jockey for position and contend for desirable roles within the group. As we'll note later in this chapter, many people believe that they can serve as effective leaders, so one of the key steps occurring during this phase is the emergence of one or more actual leaders for the group.

If the conflicts of the storming stage are resolved, the group enters a third phase of development, known as *norming*. (If storming is not handled effectively, the group may, in contrast, break apart and cease to function as a group.) Norming involves the development of a common, shared perspective—a feeling of "we-ness" within the group. Rules (norms) concerning how the group will operate are more fully established, and a sense of shared responsibility for dealing with the group's problems develops. Once this phase is complete, the group moves into a fourth stage—*performing*. Here, energies are focused on specific tasks and jobs, and progress toward these goals is often made. As long as groups are relatively successful in achieving their goals, they may remain in existence. However, if all goals have been met, the group may enter a final phase—*adjourning*—in which it disbands. Adjourning is especially likely to occur in groups that have been formed for a specific purpose (e.g., fund-raising groups, special task forces). Groups may also disintegrate if key members leave, if unresolvable conflicts develop, or if disagreement over long-term goals emerges.

One concluding note: Although the pattern we have described is accurate for many forming groups, it is by no means universal. All groups are unique, and their development may combine or even omit some of these stages. In general, though, this simple model is helpful in understanding how many diverse groups evolve during the early stages of their existence.

How Groups Function: Roles, Status, Norms, and Cohesiveness

That groups often exert powerful effects on the behavior and cognitions of their members is obvious. Indeed, we will devote much of this chapter to describing such effects. Before turning to specific types of *group influence*, however, we should address a more basic issue: How, precisely, do groups affect their members? A complete answer to this question involves many processes, including several we have examined in previous chapters (e.g., conformity, persuasion, attraction). There is, however, general agreement that four aspects of groups are crucial in this regard: **roles, status, norms,** and **cohesiveness** (Forsyth, 1983; Paulus, 1989).

Roles: Differentiation of Function within Groups   Think of a group to which you have belonged—anything from the Scouts to a professional association related to your occupation. Now, consider the following question: Did everyone in that group act in the same way or perform the same functions? Your answer is probably no. On the contrary, a considerable degree of differentiation may well have existed. Specific persons probably worked at different tasks and were expected to accomplish different things for the group. In short, they played different *roles*. Sometimes roles are assigned in a formal and specific manner— for example, an individual may be chosen by a group to serve as its leader, secretary, or treasurer. In other cases, individuals gradually acquire certain roles without being formally assigned to them. Leaders often emerge in this manner (Ellis, 1988). And within a given group, different persons gradually come to

 Status: A key dimension of group structure

FIGURE 11.3 Groups exert strong effects on their members' behavior by regulating *status* (members' relative standing within the group). The photos here illustrate various outward signs of high status—a reward for which many persons will work long and hard.

fulfill either *task-oriented roles* (they focus on getting the group's major jobs done) or *relations-oriented roles* (they focus on reducing interpersonal friction and maintaining good relations between members).

Roles help to clarify the responsibilities and obligations of the persons belonging to a group. In addition, they are a key way in which groups shape the behavior and thoughts of their members. They do have a "down side," however. First, individuals may experience *role ambiguity*—uncertainty about precisely what is expected of them. New employees, for instance, frequently experience such feelings of uncertainty, and these can be quite stressful (Baron & Greenberg, 1990). Similarly, group members can experience *role conflict*— pressures stemming from the fact that they must play two or more roles concurrently. Such conflict is readily apparent among new parents, who may often find that their roles as parents conflict quite strongly with their roles as employees actively pursuing careers. Role conflict, too, can be extremely stressful, with all this implies for the health and adjustment of the persons who experience it.

Status: The Prestige of Various Roles Have you ever worked for a large organization? If so, you already realize that while everyone belonging to a group has a role, not all roles are equal with respect to prestige. On the contrary, huge differences in relative social position or rank—**status**—are associated with such roles as Chief Executive Officer, Manager, Data Processor, and Janitor. High status is clearly an outcome that many people desire. Thus, by controlling this factor and offering it as a reward for various actions, groups can exert powerful effects on their members (refer to Figure 11.3). As you might expect, high-status members of a group or organization are often more influential than low-status members. Similarly, high-status persons can initiate communication with low-status persons whenever they wish to do so and can adopt an informal manner (e.g., calling such persons by their first name). In contrast, low-status persons can initiate communication with high-status ones only on special occasions and must generally use formal titles when addressing such persons unless specifically invited to drop these by the high-status persons (McLaughlin, Cody, & Rosenstein, 1983).

Norms: The Rules of the Game   A third factor responsible for the powerful impact of groups on their members is one we have already considered—*norms*. As you may recall from Chapter 8, norms are rules—implicit or explicit—established by various groups to regulate the behavior of members. Norms tell group members how to behave *(perscriptive norms)* or how *not* to behave *(proscriptive norms)* in various situations. Most groups insist on adherence to their norms as a basic requirement for membership. Thus, it is not surprising that individuals wishing to join or remain in specific groups generally follow these rules of the game quite closely. If they do not, they may soon find themselves on the outside looking in.

Cohesiveness: The Effects of Wanting to Belong   Consider two groups. In the first, members like one another very much, strongly desire the goals their group is seeking, and feel they could not possibly find another group that would better satisfy their needs. In the second, the opposite is true: Members don't like one another, do not share common goals, and are actively seeking other groups that might offer them a better deal. Which group would exert stronger effects on its members? The answer is obvious: the first. The reason for this difference lies in the fact that **cohesiveness**—all pressures or forces causing members to remain part of a group—is much higher in the first group than in the second. In other words, individuals in the first group want to retain their membership much more strongly than those in the second.

What factors influence cohesiveness? Research findings suggest that four are most important. First, the greater the cost of getting into a group to begin with, the higher members' attraction to it. As dissonance theory suggests (refer to Chapter 4), the harder we must work to attain a goal (in this case, group membership), the higher our evaluation of it. Second, groups facing an external threat or severe competition are generally higher in cohesiveness than ones not confronting such conditions (Sherif et al., 1961). Apparently, such external pressures lead group members to pull together and enhance the value of their membership in the group. Third, groups that have a past history of success are generally more cohesive than ones that do not (Shaw, 1981). And fourth, groups that are relatively small tend to be higher in cohesiveness than ones that are very large (presumably because small groups afford members greater opportunity to interact directly and get to know one another).

At first glance, you might assume that high cohesiveness is always a plus where groups are concerned. In fact, however, it is something of a mixed blessing. On the one hand, high cohesiveness can enhance productivity and morale among group members. On the other, it can unleash forces that tend to expose groups to serious problems. For example, high levels of cohesiveness can cause group members to adopt an uncritical or unquestioning approach to the group's views. As we'll note in a later section (pages 462–464), this development can prove quite dangerous, for it leaves little room for correcting various errors.

In sum, several aspects of groups determine the extent to which they can and do influence their members. Since these aspects play an important role in group influence, keeping them in mind is well worthwhile as we consider some of the specific ways in which groups shape the behavior and thought of individuals.

Groups and Task Performance: The Benefits—and Costs—of Working with Others

Some activities, such as studying, balancing one's checkbook, or writing love letters, are solitary ones, best done alone. Most tasks we perform, however, are done either with others or in their presence. This point raises an intriguing question: What impact, if any, do groups exert on task performance? To answer this question, it is necessary to consider two separate but related issues: (1) What are the effects of the mere presence of others on individual performance? and (2) Are groups more, or less, efficient in carrying out various tasks?

Social Facilitation: Performance in the Presence of Others

Imagine that you must make a speech in front of a large audience. You have several weeks to prepare, so you write the speech and then practice it alone over and over again. Now, finally, the big day has arrived. You are introduced and begin to speak. How will you do? Will your performance be better or worse than when you delivered the speech to the four walls of your own room? In short, will the presence of an audience facilitate your performance or interfere with it (refer to Figure 11.4)? Early research concerned with this issue (Triplett, 1898) yielded a confusing pattern of results: Sometimes performance was *improved* by the presence of an audience, and sometimes the opposite was true. How could this puzzle be resolved? An insightful answer was offered by Zajonc (1965).

The presence of others and task performance: A plus or a minus?

FIGURE 11.4 Do individuals perform better or worse when in the presence of others? Research on this issue indicates that both outcomes are possible. (Copyright 1985: Universal Press Syndicate. Reprinted with permission. All rights reserved)

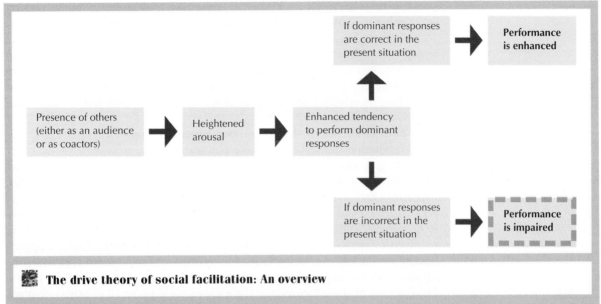

The drive theory of social facilitation: An overview

FIGURE 11.5 According to the *drive theory of social facilitation,* the presence of others increases arousal. This in turn enhances the performance of dominant responses. If these responses are correct, performance is enhanced. If they are incorrect, performance is impaired.

The Drive Theory of Social Facilitation: Other Persons as a Source of Arousal Before describing Zajonc's (1965) theory (now known as the **drive theory of social facilitation**), we should clarify a point. The phrase *social facilitation* is used by social psychologists to refer to any effects on performance resulting from the presence of others. Thus, it includes decrements as well as improvements in task performance.

Now, back to Zajonc's theory. The basic idea behind his theory is as follows: The presence of others produces increments in level of arousal. As you can see, this suggestion agrees closely with informal experience. The presence of other persons—especially when they serve as an audience—does seem to generate signs of increased arousal (e.g., feelings of tension or excitement). But how do such increments in arousal then affect performance? According to Zajonc, the answer involves two facts.

First, it is a basic principle of psychology that increments in arousal enhance the performance of *dominant responses*—ones an individual is most likely to perform in a given situation (one example: the tendency to smile back at others when they smile at us). Thus, when arousal increases, the tendency to perform strong, dominant responses increases too. Second, such dominant responses can be either correct or incorrect for any task currently being performed.

When these two facts are combined with the suggestion that the presence of others is arousing, two predictions follow: (1) The presence of others will facilitate performance when an individual's dominant responses in a situation are correct and (2) the presence of others will impair performance when a person's dominant response in the situation are incorrect. (Please see Figure 11.5 for a summary of these suggestions.) Stated in slightly different terms, the presence of others will facilitate the performance of strong, well-learned responses but may interfere with the performance of new, as yet unmastered ones.

Initial studies designed to test these predictions generally yielded positive results (e.g., Matlin & Zajonc, 1968: Zajonc & Sales, 1966). Subjects were in fact more likely to emit dominant responses when in the presence of others than when alone, and performance on various tasks was either enhanced or impaired depending on whether these responses were correct or incorrect in each situation (Geen & Gange, 1977).

Additional research, however, soon raised an important question: Does social facilitation stem from the mere physical presence of others? Or do other factors (e.g., concern over others' possible evaluations) also play a role? Support for the latter possibility was provided by the results of several interesting studies suggesting that social facilitation occurred only when individuals believed their performance could be observed and evaluated by others (e.g., Bond, 1982; Bray & Sugarman, 1980; Cottrell et al., 1968). Such findings led some researchers to propose that social facilitation actually stems either from **evaluation apprehension**—concern over being judged by others—or from related concerns over *self-presentation*—looking good in front of others (Carver & Scheier, 1981). Thus, it may be these factors, not the mere physical presence of others, that are crucial in determining the impact of an audience or coactors on task performance.

Further support for the view that social facilitation involves concern over evaluations from others is provided by a recent study performed by Sanna and Shotland (1990). The results of this experiment indicate that subjects who performed a memory task in front of an audience did better than subjects who performed alone, but only when they anticipated a *positive* evaluation from the audience. When they anticipated a *negative* evaluation, in contrast, the opposite was true: Subjects who worked alone performed better than those who worked in front of an audience. These results indicate that the valence (direction) of expected evaluations, not merely expectation of being evaluated by others, plays a key role in the occurrence of social facilitation.

At first glance, such suggestions seem quite reasonable. Most of us *are* concerned with the impressions we make on others and do care about their evaluations of us. Further, such concerns might be motivating or arousing in many situations. However, other evidence points to the conclusion that social facilitation effects can sometimes occur even in situations in which these factors do not seem to play a role (e.g., Markus, 1978; Schmitt et al., 1986). For example, in one intriguing study on this issue, Schmitt and his colleagues (Schmitt et al., 1986) had subjects perform both a simple task and a more complex one under one of three conditions: while alone in the room, while in the presence of another person who wore a blindfold and earphones (the *mere-presence* condition), or in the presence of another person who could directly observe their performance *(evaluation-apprehension)* condition. The simple task was that of typing their own names. The complex one involved typing their names backward and inserting ascending numbers between each letter. The researchers reasoned that if the mere presence of others was arousing, social facilitation effects would occur in this condition. As you can see from Figure 11.6, this was indeed the case. Subjects in the mere-presence condition performed the simple task faster but the complex task more slowly than those in the control (alone) condition. Moreover, those who could be observed by another person (the evaluation-apprehension condition) performed the simple

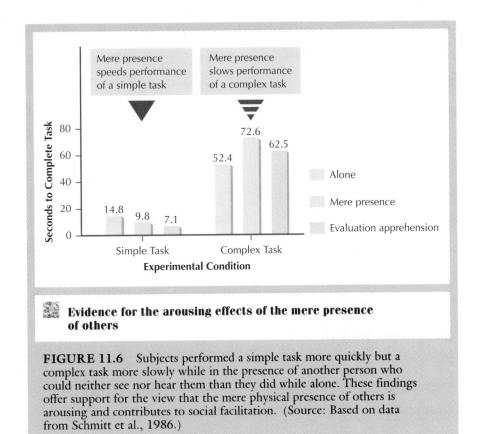

Mere presence speeds performance of a simple task

Mere presence slows performance of a complex task

Seconds to Complete Task

80

60

40

20

0

14.8

9.8

7.1

52.4

72.6

62.5

Simple Task

Complex Task

Experimental Condition

Alone

Mere presence

Evaluation apprehension

Evidence for the arousing effects of the mere presence of others

FIGURE 11.6 Subjects performed a simple task more quickly but a complex task more slowly while in the presence of another person who could neither see nor hear them than they did while alone. These findings offer support for the view that the mere physical presence of others is arousing and contributes to social facilitation. (Source: Based on data from Schmitt et al., 1986.)

task most quickly of all. Together, these findings suggest that the mere presence of others is arousing and that the possibility of being evaluated increases such arousal still further. (For additional evidence suggesting that arousal and social facilitation is sometimes due to the mere presence of others, please see the **Classic Contributions** section below.)

FOCUS ON RESEARCH: CLASSIC CONTRIBUTIONS

Is the Mere Presence of Others Arousing? Evidence from an Unusual Subject Population

That human beings are strongly affected by the presence of an audience is far from surprising. People are concerned with evaluations of their performance by others, and for good reason: Many positive and negative events depend on such evaluations. But what about animals; do they, too, demonstrate social facilitation? If so, this fact would argue strongly against the view that such effects stem mainly (or solely) from evaluation apprehension. After all, it makes little sense to assume that animals share our concern with "looking good" to one another. In fact, several studies suggest that social facilitation does indeed occur among

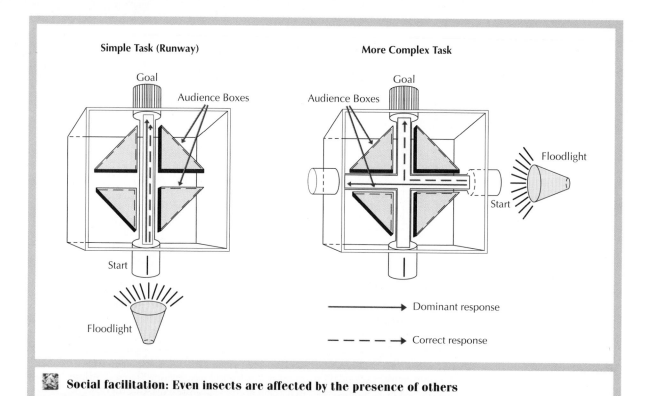

Simple Task (Runway)   More Complex Task

Goal   Goal

Audience Boxes   Audience Boxes

Floodlight

Start

Start

Floodlight

———————▶ Dominant response

– – – – – ▶ Correct response

Social facilitation: Even insects are affected by the presence of others

FIGURE 11.7   Do cockroaches show social facilitation? Results obtained with this apparatus suggest that they do. Roaches ran through the simple maze (left) faster while in the presence of an audience (in the marked boxes) than when alone. However, they ran through the more complex maze (right) slower when in the presence of an audience than when alone. (Source: Adapted from Zajonc, Heingartner, & Herman, 1969.)

animals (e.g., Rajecki, Kidd, & Ivins, 1976). In fact, even insects seem to respond to the presence of an audience. Perhaps the most surprising demonstration of this latter fact has been provided by Zajonc, Heingartner, and Herman (1969).

These researchers employed a very unlikely group of subjects—common household cockroaches—as their subjects. The roaches were placed in one of the two mazes shown in Figure 11.7. As you can readily see, the top maze is quite simple. Subjects' dominant response (running straight ahead) is the correct one: It leads to the dark bottle and escape from the bright floodlight. (Roaches, as you probably know, dislike bright lights.) The bottom maze, however, is more complex. Here, subjects' dominant response is incorrect, for a right-hand turn is needed to escape from the bright light. Zajonc's theory offers straightforward predictions for performance in both mazes. It suggests that the presence of an audience will facilitate performance in the first maze, where subjects' dominant responses are correct ones. However, it will interfere with performance in the second maze, where subjects' dominant responses are errors. To test these predictions, the investigators had the roaches perform both tasks while alone in the apparatus or in the presence of four other roaches that were placed in the audience boxes (refer to Figure 11.7). Results offered support for both predictions: The presence of an audience facilitated performance of the simple task but interfered with performance of the more complex one.

These findings and those of other studies conducted with several animal species (e.g., Rajecki et al., 1976) raise serious questions for an interpretation of social facilitation based solely on evaluation apprehension. It seems quite awkward, after all, to attribute concerns over "looking good" or "making favorable impressions" to cockroaches! In view of this fact, it appears that a satisfactory explanation for social facilitation must rest on simpler psychological mechanisms—ones common to both human beings and animals. Do such mechanisms exist? And if they do, what are they like? For some answers, please read on.

One Potential Resolution: Distraction-Conflict Theory   How can the diverse and seemingly contradictory findings described above be explained? One compelling answer is provided by **distraction-conflict theory,** developed by Baron, Sanders, and Moore (e.g., R. S. Baron, 1986; Sanders, 1983).

Like other explanations of social facilitation, this theory assumes that the effect of audiences and coactors (others performing the same task as subjects) stems from heightened arousal. In contrast to earlier views, however, distraction-conflict theory suggests that such arousal stems from conflict between two tendencies: (1) the tendency to pay attention to the task being performed and (2) the tendency to direct attention to an audience or coactors. The conflict produced by these competing tendencies is arousing, and such arousal, in turn, enhances the tendency to perform dominant responses. If these are correct, performance is enhanced; if they are incorrect, performance is reduced (refer to Figure 11.8, p. 450).

A considerable body of evidence offers support for this theory. For example, audiences produce social facilitation effects only when directing attention to them conflicts in some way with task demands (Groff, Baron, & Moore, 1983). When paying attention to an audience does not conflict with task performance, social facilitation fails to occur. Similarly, individuals experience greater distraction when they perform various tasks in front of an audience than when they perform them alone (Baron, Moore, & Sanders, 1978). Finally, when individuals have little reason to pay attention to others present on the scene (e.g., when such persons are performing a different task), social facilitation fails to occur. When individuals have strong reasons for paying close attention to others, social facilitation occurs (Sanders, 1983).

Distraction-conflict theory offers two additional advantages worth considering. First, since animals as well as people can experience the type of conflict shown in Figure 11.8, the theory can account for the occurrence of social facilitation among animals. Second, with certain modifications (R. S. Baron, 1986), the theory can explain the occurrence of social facilitation without reference to the notion of arousal. The reasoning is as follows: The presence of an audience (or coactors) threatens the persons involved with *information overload*—they have more things demanding their attention than they can readily handle. As a result, they focus their attention primarily on those cues most central to the task at hand. Such focused attention can enhance performance on

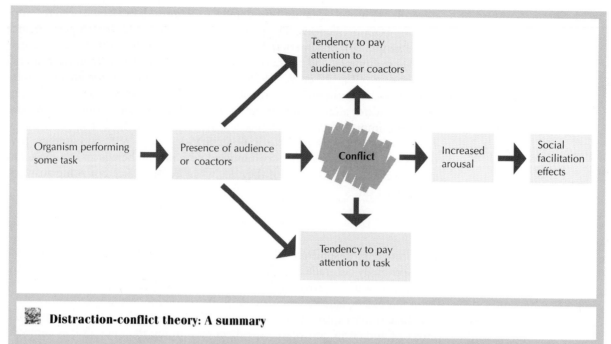

Tendency to pay
attention to
audience or coactors

Organism performing
some task

Presence of audience
or coactors

Conflict

Increased
arousal

Social
facilitation
effects

Tendency to pay
attention to task

Distraction-conflict theory: A summary

FIGURE 11.8 According to *distraction-conflict theory,* the presence of others produces competing tendencies to (1) pay attention to these individuals and (2) pay attention to the task being performed. The conflict generated by these competing tendencies yields increased arousal, which in turn produces social facilitation.

simple tasks but may reduce it on complex ones requiring attention to a wide range of stimuli. In short, a modified form of distraction-conflict theory can explain social facilitation effects in terms of our limited information-processing capacity.

To conclude: While distraction-conflict theory may not provide a final answer to the persistent puzzle of social facilitation, it is quite promising in this respect. In any case, the theory has added substantially to our understanding of what many social psychologists consider to be the simplest type of group effect.

Groups versus Individuals: Which Has the Edge in Task Performance?

At the start of this discussion, we noted that many tasks people perform involve working with others. One reason for this is the nature of the tasks themselves: Many simply cannot be performed by one person alone (refer to Figure 11.9). Another basis for this reliance on groups where tasks are concerned is as follows: There is a general, widespread belief that people can accomplish more by working with others than by working alone. In one sense, this suggestion must be true; several people working together do generally accomplish more than any one of them in isolation. But more to the point, are groups *really* more efficient than individuals—do they accomplish more *per member* than persons working alone? The answer, it turns out, is fairly complex. On the one hand, working in groups does indeed offer certain advantages. It allows individuals to pool their knowledge and skills. Similarly, it allows for an efficient division of labor, so that specific persons perform those tasks for which they are best equipped.

On the other hand, however, working in groups has important costs as well. When cohesiveness is high, members may spend a lot of time engaging in pleasant but nonproductive interactions. Further, strong pressures to adhere to existing norms may interfere with the development of new and better procedures for completing essential tasks. The likelihood of conflict between members, too, is increased, and this can interfere with effective performance (cf. Thomas, 1990). In sum, group settings offer a mixed bag of potential pluses and minuses where task performance is concerned. What determines the final balance between these factors? Research findings suggest that the single most important factor involves the type of task being performed.

Type of Task and Group Performance One useful framework for understanding the different types of tasks performed by groups has been proposed by Steiner (1972, 1976). According to this perspective, most tasks fall into one of three categories.

First are **additive tasks,** ones in which the contributions of each member are combined into a single group product. For example, when several persons combine their efforts to lay the foundation for a house, to move a heavy object, or to sell a specific product, the tasks being performed are additive ones. The group's output is based on the sum of their individual efforts and the extent to which these are usefully coordinated.

Second are **conjunctive tasks.** Here, the group's final product is determined by its weakest link—the poorest-performing member. A clear example of this type of task is provided by a team of mountain climbers. The entire team can advance only as fast as its slowest member.

Third are **disjunctive tasks.** Here, too, the group's product is determined by a single member. In this case, though, it is the best or most competent

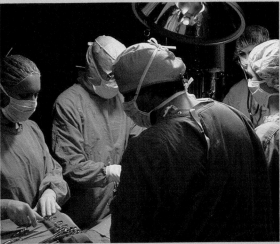

Groups: An essential ingredient in the performance of many tasks

FIGURE 11.9 Many tasks can be completed only by groups of individuals working together in a coordinated manner.

person who sets the limit. Many complex problem-solving tasks faced by groups are disjunctive—the correct solution will be obtained only if one member discovers it and can then convince the others of its accuracy. For example, consider a group of attorneys trying to determine a legal way of preparing a specific contract; a workable solution will be found only if at least one member of the group can generate it and then gain the acceptance of the others.

Last are **compensatory tasks,** ones in which the contribution of the various members are averaged together to form a single group outcome. For example, consider a group of economic forecasters, trying to predict next year's rate of inflation. The group outcome is the average of all their predictions. Presumably, since the rosy predictions of optimists in the group will be offset by the dire predictions of pessimists, the final prediction will tend to be more accurate than the judgments of any individual member.

Now, to return to our basic question: How do groups and individuals compare with respect to performance on each of these types of tasks? Many factors play a role in the performance of both individuals and groups, so a complete answer would require many pages. A useful rule of thumb, however, is as follows: On both additive and compensatory tasks, groups usually outperform individuals—in fact, they often do better than the best individual member. In such cases, then, the whole is indeed greater than the sum of its parts. (But see the next section for a discussion of one important exception to this conclusion, at least where additive tasks are concerned.) On conjunctive tasks, groups generally perform more poorly than individuals, since overall performance is determined by the weakest member. Finally, on disjunctive tasks, groups tend to do better than the average individual, because the ultimate outcome is determined largely by the talents and contributions of the best (most effective) member. (Please see Figure 11.10 for a summary of these conclusions.)

Social Loafing: Letting Others Do the Work in Group Tasks

Suppose that you and several other people are helping a friend to move. In order to lift the heaviest pieces of furniture, you join forces, with each person lending a hand. Will all of the people helping exert equal effort? Probably not. Some will bear down and take as much of the load as possible, while others will simply hang on, appearing to help without really doing much.

This pattern is quite common in situations in which groups perform *additive tasks*. Some persons work hard, while others engage in **social loafing:** doing as little as they can get away with. Why do such effects occur? Apparently because in many additive tasks, it is difficult if not impossible to identify the contributions of each participant. The group outcome depends on the efforts of all members, and the efforts exerted by each cannot be separated or identified.

Direct evidence for the occurrence of social loafing has been gathered in many experiments. For example, in one of the first of these projects, Latané, Williams, and Harkins (1979) asked groups of male students to clap or cheer as loudly as possible at specific times, supposedly so that the experimenter could determine how much noise people make in social settings. Subjects engaged in clapping and cheering either alone or in groups of two, four, or six persons. The results were clear: The magnitude of the sounds made by each subject decreased sharply as group size rose. In other words, each participant expended less and less effort as the number of other group members increased. Additional research suggests that such social loafing is quite general in scope, occurring in both sexes, in several different cultures, and under a wide range of work con-

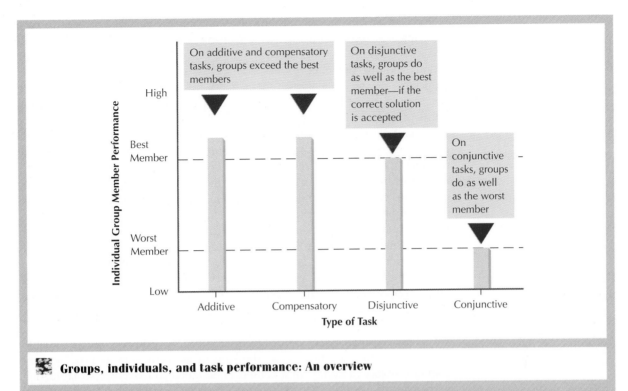

On additive and compensatory tasks, groups exceed the best members

On disjunctive tasks, groups do as well as the best member—if the correct solution is accepted

On conjunctive tasks, groups do as well as the worst member

High

Best Member

Worst Member

Low

Individual Group Member Performance

Additive   Compensatory   Disjunctive   Conjunctive

Type of Task

Groups, individuals, and task performance: An overview

FIGURE 11.10 Groups often outperform individuals on compensatory tasks. They are superior on additive tasks, too, provided that social loafing doesn't occur. And although groups are about equal to individuals on disjunctive tasks, they are often less productive on conjunctive tasks.

ditions (e.g., Brickner, Harkins, & Ostrom, 1986; Harkins, 1987; Harkins & Petty, 1982). Moreover, it occurs with respect to cognitive tasks as well to tasks involving physical effort (Weldon & Mustari, 1988). In one study on this topic (Weldon & Gargano, 1988), subjects (students of both sexes) were asked to evaluate a number of part-time jobs on several key dimensions (e.g., flexibility of hours, friendliness of coworkers, task variety). Some subjects were told that they were the only evaluator of these jobs, while others were told that they were one of sixteen judges who would rate the jobs. Several measures of subjects' cognitive effort on this task were obtained by determining how much of the available information they used in making their judgments. As expected, participants who thought they were the only evaluator of the jobs worked significantly harder than subjects who thought they shared this responsibility with fifteen other persons.

Reducing Social Loafing: Some Useful Techniques The fact that social loafing occurs so generally is somewhat discouraging. It suggests that many persons will "goof off" and do less than their fair share when working in groups. Since so many important tasks are performed under group conditions, the implications for society are quite unsettling. Can anything be done to counter such tendencies? Fortunately, additional evidence points to several techniques that may prove useful in this respect.

The most obvious of these involves making the output or effort of each participant readily identifiable (e.g., Williams, Harkins, & Latane, 1981). Under these conditions, individuals cannot conceal minimal effort within the group, and the tendency to sit back and let others do the work is greatly reduced.

Second, social loafing can be reduced by increasing group members' commitment to successful task performance (Zaccaro, 1984). Here, pressures to work hard serve to offset temptations to engage in social loafing. Moreover, the larger the group, the stronger such pressures will be. Thus, output per group member may actually *increase* rather than decrease as group size rises.

Third, several recent studies suggest that social loafing can be reduced by conditions that provide individuals with an opportunity to evaluate their own contributions or the contributions of the entire group relative to those of other groups (Harkins & Szymanski, 1988; Szymanski & Harkins, 1987). In other words, social loafing seems to occur not simply because individuals believe their contributions cannot be identified but also, at least in part, because they feel these cannot be evaluated, either by themselves or by others. Conditions affording the opportunity for such evaluation greatly reduce tendencies toward social loafing. Evidence for this suggestion has recently been provided by Harkins and Szymanski (1989).

These researchers had groups of three subjects (male and female students) perform a simple cognitive task: thinking of as many uses as possible for a common object (a knife). In a condition designed to maximize social loafing, participants were informed that their lists of uses would be combined with those of other members of the group and that, moreover, they would receive no feedback on the total. In two other conditions, subjects were also told that their individual output would be combined (pooled) with that of other group members. In one case (the *pooled scores–standard* condition), however, subjects were informed that at the end of the session, they would be told the average output of previous groups; thus, they knew they could compare their group's performance with this standard. In the other case (the *pooled scores–no standard* condition), no mention of receiving such information was made. Finally, in one other experimental group, subjects were told that their performance would be scored individually and that they would receive information about the average performance of other individuals who had performed the same task previously (the *individual scores–standard* condition).

Harkins and Szymanski (1989) predicted that tendencies toward social loafing would be reduced by providing subjects with an opportunity to compare the output of their group with that of other groups, and in fact this is what occurred. As shown in Figure 11.11, subjects in the pooled scores–standard condition generated as many uses for a knife as those in the individual score–standard condition, and far more uses than those in the group designed to maximize social loafing.

These findings and those of several other studies (e.g., Harkins, 1987; Zaccaro, 1984) suggest that tendencies toward social loafing are not an unavoidable part of task performance by groups. On the contrary, such tendencies *can* be reduced under appropriate circumstances. Further, in order to reduce social loafing it is not necessary to convince individuals that their outputs will be readily identifiable. Providing them with a standard against which to evaluate their contributions or even those of the entire group may be sufficient. (How

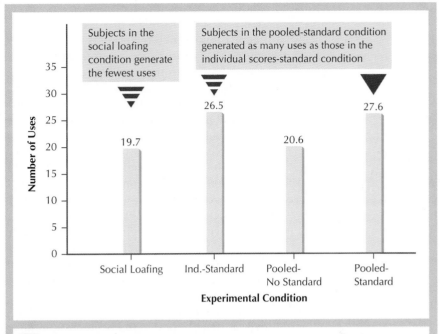

Social loafing and the ability to evaluate group performance

FIGURE 11.11 Subjects who learned that their scores would be pooled with those of others (and therefore would not be individually identifiable) did not demonstrate social loafing when they also received a standard against which to compare their group's performance (the pooled scores–standard condition). These findings suggest that the inability to evaluate one's performance (either individually or collectively) is an important cause of social loafing. (Source: Based on data from Harkins & Szymanski, 1989.)

do individuals react when they feel that others with whom they work are engaging in social loafing? And do such reactions differ in various cultures? For evidence on these issues, please see the **Multicultural Perspective** section below.)

SOCIAL PSYCHOLOGY: A MULTICULTURAL PERSPECTIVE

Coping with Free Riders: Contrasting Reactions to Social Loafing in the United States and Japan

In additive tasks, the contributions of all group members are combined to yield a single group outcome. Given this fact, it is not surprising that in such situations, available rewards are often shared equally among all participants. This arrangement presents no difficulties so long as all group members perceive that their respective contributions have been about equal. The situation changes radically, however, if one or more members conclude that they have been the victims of social loafing—that they have exerted more effort on the task than others. In such cases, the persons involved experience anger and, if they cannot increase their share of the rewards, may choose to escape from a bad situation by withdrawing from the group (e.g., Messick & Brewer, 1983).

Will such tendencies vary across different cultures? There are compelling reasons for assuming they will. In some cultures (ones whose orientation is described as *individualistic*), there is strong commitment to the belief that rewards should reflect performance: The more people contribute, the more they should receive. In others (described as *collectivistic*), however, a different belief prevails: It is assumed that all individuals should receive equal rewards, in order to maintain group harmony and cooperation (Leung & Bond, 1984). On the basis of such differences, it seems reasonable to predict that, for example, persons in individualistic Western cultures (e.g., the United States) will be more likely to withdraw from groups in which they feel they are the victims of social loafing by "free riders" than persons in collectivistic cultures (e.g., China, Japan). However, there is an important complication in this seemingly neat picture. True, persons in collectivistic cultures prefer equal division of available rewards. They do so, however, because in such cultures, there are extensive systems designed to protect against free riders (group members who engage in social loafing). These systems involve careful, mutual monitoring of ongoing performance to ensure that all are contributing equally, plus strong sanctions against social loafing. Under such conditions, persons from collectivistic cultures might indeed be less likely to withdraw from groups because of free riding by others; after all, the free riding itself would be unlikely to occur. If, however, the protective systems just described are absent, the opposite might be true: Persons from such cultures, who have learned to rely on protective systems, might have less trust in fair play by others than persons from individualistic cultures. Thus, they might be more ready to withdraw from situations in which social loafing can occur.

Evidence that this is actually the case is provided by a revealing cross-cultural study conducted by Yamagishi (1988). In this investigation, male and female subjects in the United States and in Japan worked on a simple letter-matching task in groups of three. The conditions of the game were such that subjects could *not* observe and monitor one another's behavior. Thus, the protective systems described above, designed to guard against free riders, were not present. However, the experimenter explained that rewards would be divided equally among team members. On each trial, subjects were given the choice of either remaining in the group or withdrawing from it. If they chose the latter course, their earnings on that trial would depend only on their own performance. The cost of exiting was also varied so that in one condition it was low (points earned by subjects were worth the same amount of money whether they remained in the group or not) and in another it was high (points had less value when subjects chose to withdraw from the group).

On the basis of the reasoning outlined above, Yamagishi (1989) predicted that Japanese subjects would actually choose to withdraw from the group on more trials than Americans. As you can see from Figure 11.12, this prediction was confirmed, especially when the costs of exiting were high. These findings suggest that Japanese subjects disliked the possibility of free-rider (social-loafing) effects so strongly that they chose to withdraw on many trials, even in the

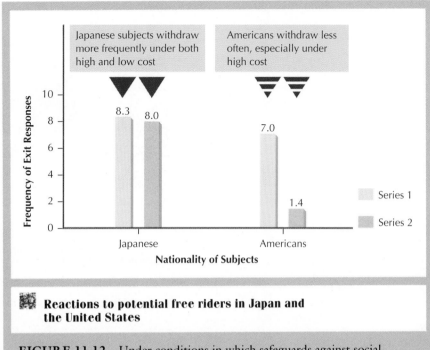

Japanese subjects withdraw more frequently under both high and low cost

Americans withdraw less often, especially under high cost

Reactions to potential free riders in Japan and the United States

FIGURE 11.12 Under conditions in which safeguards against social loafing were not present, Japanese students were more likely than American students to withdraw from a group in which rewards were shared equally among all members. This was especially true when the costs of withdrawing from the group were high. These findings suggest that Japanese subjects are less trusting with respect to others' efforts under such conditions than Americans are. (Source: Based on data from Yamagishi, 1988.)

high-cost condition. In contrast, American subjects were deterred from withdrawing from the group when this action was costly.

In sum, it appears that people from cultures as different as those of Japan and the United States react negatively to the possibility of social loafing by others. No one, regardless of her or his cultural background, seems to like the idea of being exploited by persons who do less than their fair share of the work.

Decision Making by Groups: How It Occurs, the Outcomes It Yields, and the Pitfalls It Faces

Groups are called on to perform a wide range of tasks—everything from conducting delicate surgical operations through harvesting the world's crops. One of the most important activities they perform, however, is making decisions. Governments, large corporations, military units, and virtually all other social entities entrust key decisions to groups. As a result, most of the laws, policies, and business practices that affect our daily lives are determined by committees,

"There you have it, gentlemen—the upside potential is tremendous, but the downside risk is jail."

Group decision making: Not always on target

FIGURE 11.13 Why do decision-making groups like this one sometimes make disastrous choices? Several factors (e.g., groupthink, group polarization) seem to play a role. (Drawing by Mankoff; © 1985 The New Yorker Magazine, Inc.)

boards of directors, and similar groups—not by single individuals. There are several reasons for this fact, but perhaps the most crucial is this: Most people believe that groups, by pooling the expertise of their members and by avoiding extreme courses of action, can usually reach better decisions than individuals can.

Are such assumptions accurate? Do groups actually make better (i.e., more accurate) decisions than individuals? In their efforts to deal with this practical question, social psychologists have focused on three major—and closely related—topics: (1) How do groups actually go about moving toward consensus and reaching decisions? (2) Do decisions reached by groups differ in any way from decisions reached by individuals? and (3) What accounts for the fact that groups sometimes make truly disastrous decisions—ones that are so bad they seem hard to explain? (Refer to Figure 11.13.)

The Decision-Making Process: How Groups Move toward Consensus

When groups first begin to discuss some issue, their members rarely voice unanimous agreement. Rather, they support diverse views and favor competing courses of action. After some period of discussion, however, a decision is usually reached. This is not always the case—for example, juries become hung, and other decision-making groups, too, may experience deadlock. In most cases, though, *some* decision is reached. Is there any way of predicting this final outcome? In short, can we predict the decision a group is likely to reach from information about the views initially held by its members? Growing evidence suggests we can (e.g., Kerr & McCoun, 1985).

Social Decision Schemes To summarize some very complex findings in simple terms, it appears that the final decision reached by groups can often be predicted quite accurately by relatively simple rules known as **social decision schemes.** These rules relate the initial distribution of member views or preferences to the group's final decisions. For example, one—the *majority-wins scheme*—suggests that in many cases, the group will opt for whatever position is initially supported by a majority of its members. According to this rule, discussion serves mainly to confirm or strengthen the most popular view. In contrast, a second decision scheme—the *truth-wins rule*—indicates that the correct solution or decision will ultimately come to the fore as its correctness is recognized by growing numbers of members. A third decision scheme, one adopted by many juries, is the *two-thirds-majority rule*. Here, juries tend to convict defendants if two-thirds of the jurors initially favor this decision (Davis et al., 1984). Finally, some groups seem to follow a *first-shift rule*. That is, they tend, ultimately, to adopt a decision consistent with the direction of the first shift in opinion shown by any member.

Surprising as it may seem, the results of many studies indicate that these straightforward rules are quite successful in predicting even complex group decisions. Indeed, they have been found to be accurate in this regard up to 80 percent of the time (e.g. Stasser, Taylor, & Hanna, 1989). Of course, different rules seem to be more successful under some conditions than others. Thus, the majority-wins scheme seems best in situations involving *judgmental tasks*—ones that are largely a matter of opinion. In contrast, the truth-wins rule seems best in predicting group decisions on *intellective tasks*—ones for which there *is* a correct answer (Kirchler & Davis, 1986).

Procedural Processes: The Effects of Straw Polls While the decisions reached by groups can often be predicted from knowledge of members' initial positions, it is clear that many other factors play a role in this complex process. Among the most important of these are several aspects of the group's *procedures*—the rules it follows in addressing its agenda and managing the flow of interaction between members, as well as related issues (Stasser, Kerr, & Davis, 1989). One procedure adopted by many decision-making groups is the **straw poll,** in which members indicate their present positions or preferences. While straw polls are nonbinding and leave members free to change their views, it seems possible that simply learning about the current distribution of opinions within a group could have strong effects on them. That this is actually the case is indicated by the results of a study conducted by Davis and his colleagues (Davis et al., 1988).

In this study, subjects first viewed a videotape of a mock trial and indicated their views about the guilt of the defendant. On the basis of these initial preferences, they were assigned to six-person groups in which three members believed that the defendant was guilty and three believed this person was not guilty. Straw polls were then conducted in these groups either immediately (a few minutes after the groups convened) or after five minutes of discussion. In two conditions, the polls were conducted *sequentially,* with one juror at a time indicating his or her opinion. In one case, the three jurors favoring a not-guilty verdict were polled first; in the other, the three jurors favoring a guilty verdict were polled first. In a third condition, all jurors indicated their opinions *simultaneously* (by holding up cards reading "Guilty" or "Not Guilty"). The key question addressed was what impact, if any, these straw polls would have on the fourth juror in each group—the swing vote in this situation.

Results indicated that the straw polls did have important effects. First, relative to the simultaneous condition, a substantial proportion of jurors who favored a guilty verdict were influenced to switch to a not-guilty verdict after hearing three other jurors report this preference. Moreover, this happened regardless of whether the straw poll occurred immediately or only after a delay. Similarly, a substantial proportion of jurors who favored a not-guilty verdict were swayed to switch to a guilty verdict after hearing three other group members state this latter view. However, this was true only when the straw poll was held immediately; when it was held later, no jurors showed such a shift. This pattern of findings seems to reflect the fact that jurors enter this type of situation with a tendency to be lenient—to avoid convicting innocent defendants. This norm seemed to strengthen as discussion continued, thus helping jurors to avoid switching from a not-guilty to a guilty verdict, even after hearing several other persons favor the latter view.

The findings reported by Davis and his colleagues (1988) and by several other researchers (e.g., MacCoun & Kerr, 1988) suggest that the procedures adopted by a group can strongly affect the decisions it reaches. In particular, these findings indicate that straw polls do more than merely reflect the current opinions of group members; under some conditions, at least, they can shape these opinions as well. The implications for conducting fair trials seem clear: In order to protect the rights of defendants, straw polls among jurors should be delayed until after considerable deliberation has occurred, and should then be conducted in a simultaneous rather than sequential manner. Other procedures (e.g., sequential voting, early polling) leave the door open for patterns of influence among jurors that may lead to hasty—and potentially false—decisions.

The Nature of Group Decisions: Moderation or Polarization?

Truly important decisions are rarely entrusted to individuals. Instead, they are generally made by groups composed of individuals whose training, expertise, and background seem to qualify them for this crucial task. Indeed, even kings, queens, and dictators usually consult with groups of advisers before taking major actions. As we noted earlier, the key reason behind this strategy is the belief that groups are far less likely than individuals to make serious errors—to rush blindly over the edge. Is this belief really true—are groups actually better at making decisions than individuals? Research conducted by social psychologists offers some surprising answers.

Groups versus Individual Decisions: A Shift toward Risk or a Shift toward Polarization?   About thirty years ago, a graduate student named James Stoner decided to examine this question in his master's thesis. In order to do so, he asked college students to play the role of advisers to imaginary persons supposedly facing decisions between two alternatives: one that was attractive but relatively high in risk and another that was less appealing but quite conservative (Stoner, 1961). For example, in one of these situations, a character had to choose between a low-paying but secure job and a higher-paying but uncertain one.

During the first part of Stoner's study, each subject made individual recommendations about these situations. Then, they met in small groups and discussed each problem until a unanimous agreement was attained. Stoner expected that the decisions recommended by groups would be more conservative than those offered by their individual members. Surprisingly, however, just the opposite was true: Groups actually recommended riskier decisions than individuals. The size of this difference was small, but it had important implications. After all, if groups make riskier decisions than individuals, the strategy of entrusting key decisions to committees, juries, and so on may be a poor one. In fact, it may prove downright dangerous!

Impressed by these possibilities, many researchers conducted additional studies on this so-called **risky shift** (e.g., Burnstein, 1983; Lamm & Myers, 1978). At first, these experiments seemed to confirm Stoner's initial findings. Soon, however, a more mixed pattern of results emerged. In some cases, group discussion actually seemed to produce shifts toward *caution* rather than risk (e.g., Knox and Safford, 1976). How could this be? How could group discussion produce both shifts toward caution and shifts toward risk? Gradually, a clear answer emerged. What had at first seemed to be a shift toward risk was actually a more general phenomenon—*a shift toward polarization*. Group discussion, it appeared, led individual members to become more extreme, not simply more risky or more cautious. In short, it enhanced or strengthened initial views. Thus, if an individual group member was mildly in favor of a course of action prior to the group discussion, he or she might come to favor it more strongly after the group deliberations. Similarly, if an individual was mildly opposed to some action prior to the discussion, he or she might come to oppose it even more strongly after the exchange of views. Since such shifts occur in the direction of greater extremity, this effect is known as **group polarization** (please see Figure 11.14).

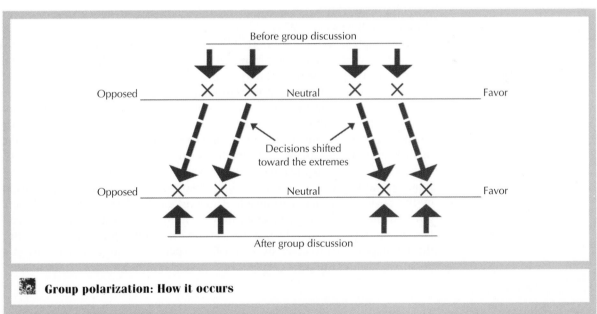

Group polarization: How it occurs

FIGURE 11.14 After taking part in a group discussion, group members often shift to views that are more extreme (in the same general direction) than the ones they held initially. Such shifts are known as *group polarization*.

As we noted earlier, the tendency for groups to become increasingly extreme in their views has important—and unsettling—implications. Thus, it is not surprising that group polarization has been the subject of a considerable amount of research (Burnstein, 1983). Much of this research has focused on two questions: (1) Why, precisely, does group polarization occur? and (2) What is it about group discussions that tends to intensify the initial beliefs of individual members?

Group Polarization: Why It Occurs   Although several explanations for group polarization have been proposed, two have received most support: the *social comparison* and *persuasive arguments* view.

The social comparison approach suggests that prior to group discussion, most persons assume that they hold "better" views than the other members. They assume that their views are more extreme in the right (valued) directions. Since it is impossible for everyone to be above average in this respect, many individuals experience a rude awakening during group discussion: They discover that their own views are not nearly as far above average as they assumed. The result? They shift to more extreme positions (Goethals & Zanna, 1979).

The persuasive arguments approach offers a contrasting explanation for the occurrence of polarization. In essence, it suggests that group members gradually convince themselves of the correctness of their initial views and so come to adopt these even more strongly. The result, of course, is a shift toward extremity. More specifically, the persuasive arguments approach suggests that during group discussion, most of the information presented by group members supports their own views. Thus, if even a slight majority of the members lean in a particular direction, most of the arguments tend to favor this view. Gradually, then, the view that predominated initially gains greater and greater support (Vinokur & Burnstein, 1974).

Both explanations are supported by research findings, and so it seems likely that both play a role in the occurrence of group polarization. In addition, several other cognitive processes, too, may be involved (Mackie, 1986). Regardless of the precise basis for group polarization, it has important implications. The occurrence of polarization may lead many decision-making groups to adopt positions that are more and more extreme—and therefore more and more dangerous. In this context, it is interesting to speculate about the potential role of such shifts in disastrous decisions by political, military, or business groups that should, by all accounts, have known better (e.g., the decision by President Johnson and his advisers to escalate U.S. involvement in Vietnam; the decision by the Soviet government to invade Afghanistan; the decision by the Chinese government to crush the democracy movement in Peking's Tiananmen Square). Did group polarization influence these events? It is difficult to say for sure. But the findings of many carefully controlled experiments suggest that this is a possibility well worth considering.

Decision Making by Groups: Some Potential Pitfalls

The tendency of many decision-making groups to drift toward polarization is serious and can interfere with their ability to make accurate decisions. Unfortunately, this process is not the only one that can exert such negative effects.

Several others, too, seem to emerge out of group discussions and can lead such groups into disastrous courses of action. Among the most important of these are **groupthink** and the apparent inability of groups to pool their expertise by discussing unshared information.

Groupthink: When Too Much Cohesiveness Can Be a Dangerous Thing
Common sense suggests that a high level of cohesiveness among group members is beneficial. After all, if members are strongly attracted to a group, their motivation—hence the group's performance—should be enhanced. Up to a point, this seems to be true. Yet when very high levels of cohesiveness are coupled with several other conditions (e.g., the presence of a dynamic, influential leader; a complex or difficult decision; emergency conditions involving strong time pressures), an unsettling process known as **groupthink** may emerge (Janis, 1982). This term refers to a mode of thinking, by group members, in which concern with maintaining group consensus overrides the motivation to evaluate all potential courses of action as accurately and realistically as possible. In short, groupthink involves a shift from primary concern with making the best decision to primary concern with reaching and maintaining consensus.

Once groupthink develops within a group, several trends—all potentially catastrophic from the standpoint of effective decision making—soon follow. Group members come to view their group as invulnerable, one that is incapable of making mistakes. Similarly, they engage in *collective rationalization,* discrediting or ignoring any information counter to the group's current views. Third, they conclude that their group is not only right, it is also morally superior and that all others (especially those who do not share its views) are confused, evil, or worse. Once groupthink develops, pressures on members to go along with the group's stated views become intense. These are further strengthened by the growing illusion that the group is truly unanimous—not only is dissent unnecessary; there *is* no dissent!

Do group members merely voice acceptance of the group's views when groupthink develops (i.e., show *compliance*)? Or do they actually come to accept and believe them (i.e., demonstrate *internalization*)? A recent analysis of groupthink by McCauley (1989) suggests that both may occur. Further, McCauley's research points to the conclusion that groupthink is most likely to develop in situations involving external threats to the group (e.g., hostile actions by another, opposing group). Several other factors considered important in the occurrence of groupthink (e.g., time pressures, complex or difficult decision situations) seem to play a somewhat weaker role in this respect.

Whatever its specific causes, groupthink seems common where the deliberations of important decision-making groups are concerned. To mention just a few famous examples, a compelling case can be made for the role of groupthink (or closely related processes) in such costly decisions as that by President Nixon and his advisers to attempt a cover-up of the illegal activities known as Watergate and the decision by President Kennedy and his advisers to support the ill-fated Bay of Pigs invasion of Cuba (Janis, 1982; McCauley, 1989). A more recent example is the decision by NASA officials to launch the space shuttle *Challenger* despite warnings from engineers that low temperatures at the launch site might have damaged crucial seals. The result, of course, was tragic.

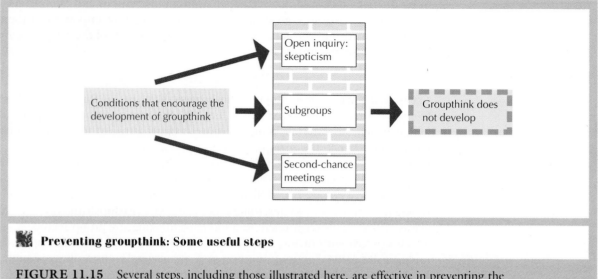

Preventing groupthink: Some useful steps

FIGURE 11.15 Several steps, including those illustrated here, are effective in preventing the occurrence of groupthink.

In sum, groupthink, like tendencies toward polarization, helps explain why seemingly intelligent, rational, and highly experienced groups sometimes reach decisions that are catastrophic in every respect. Certainly, then, groupthink is a process worth avoiding. What steps are useful in this regard? Several seem helpful (refer to Figure 11.15).

First, groups wishing to avoid the development of groupthink should promote *open inquiry* and *skepticism* among their members. Group leaders should encourage careful questioning of each alternative or policy and should, if necessary play the role of devil's advocate, intentionally finding fault with various options as they are discussed. Second, the use of *subgroups* can be helpful. Such groups consider different aspects of a problem, and any final decision is then based on discussion of their recommendations. Since the subgroups work independently, spirited disagreements between them are far from rare, and this dissent can, of course, halt any drift toward premature consensus and groupthink. Third, once a decision is reached, *second-chance meetings,* in which group members are asked to express any lingering doubts, can be extremely helpful. Such meetings provide a setting in which pressures toward conformity and consensus are reduced. This gives new ideas and criticism a chance to emerge and may effectively counter tendencies toward groupthink.

In sum, groupthink is certainly a real danger faced by decision-making groups, especially under some conditions. However, through steps such as those outlined above, the drift toward such premature closure can be halted or even reversed. Constant questioning of group decisions, as well as disagreement among members, is certainly less comfortable and pleasant than total consensus. Where effective decision making is concerned, however, it may be much more valuable.

Why Group Members Often Tell One Another What They Already Know: Sampling of Shared and Unshared Information during Group Discussions   As we noted earlier, one reason many key decisions are entrusted to groups is the belief that members will pool their resources—share ideas and knowledge unique to each individual. In this way, the decisions they reach will be better informed—and presumably more accurate—than those that would be reached by individuals working in isolation. Is this actually the case? Do groups really share the knowledge and expertise brought to them by individual members? A series of sophisticated studies conducted by Stasser and his colleagues (Stasser & Titus, 1985, 1987; Stasser, Taylor, & Hanna, 1989) suggests that in fact such pooling of resources may be the exception rather than the rule.

These studies were undertaken to test the validity of a model of group discussion known as the **information sampling model** (Stasser & Titus, 1985). This model suggests that because information shared by many members is more likely to be mentioned during group discussion than information held by only a single member, decision-making groups are more likely to discuss—and discuss again—information shared by most members than information known to only a single member. More specifically, the model predicts that the larger the group, the greater the advantage of shared over unshared information. Further, and even more discouraging, the model also indicates that efforts to increase the pooling of resources by structuring group discussions will usually fail. This happens because such efforts will enhance each member's recall of available information and this, in turn, will actually increase the discussion of shared information.

To test these predictions, Stasser, Titus, and Hanna (1989) asked male and female students to read descriptions of several imaginary candidates for student body president, and then to discuss their qualifications. They conducted these discussions in groups of three or six persons. The percentage of information about the various candidates shared by all group members was varied so that participants shared 33 percent, 66 percent, or 100 percent of this information. Finally, a third variable in the study involved the structuring of group discussions. Half the subjects were told to review all of the important information about the candidates before trying to reach a decision. The remainder were not given such instructions. Group discussions were recorded and then carefully analyzed to determine how much information shared by all group members and how much unshared information was actually discussed.

As you can see from Figure 11.16 (p. 466), results offered support for the information sampling model and its somewhat discouraging predictions. More shared than unshared information was discussed, and as expected, this tendency was greater for groups of six than for groups of three. Further, the advantage of shared over unshared information was greater for groups that conducted structured rather than unstructured discussions.

These findings have important implications for many decision-making groups. They suggest that in general, such groups are much better at rehashing and repeating information already shared by most members than at bringing new, unshared information into focus. Further, these tendencies seem to increase as groups grow larger. Thus, while adding members may increase the potential pool of expertise, it is no guarantee that such information will actually be used. Finally, and perhaps most disconcerting of all, efforts to maximize the supposed

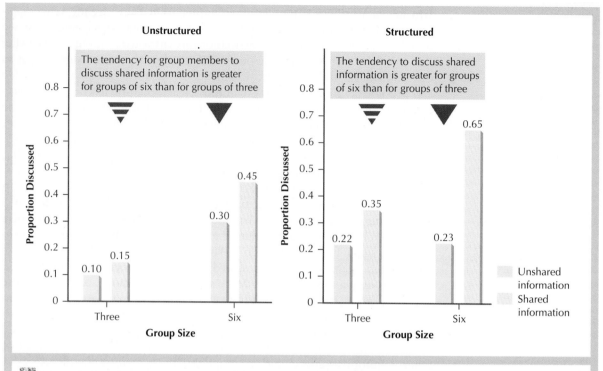

Unstructured

The tendency for group members to discuss shared information is greater for groups of six than for groups of three

Structured

The tendency to discuss shared information is greater for groups of six than for groups of three

Unshared information
Shared information

Do groups pool their resources? Some discouraging findings

FIGURE 11.16 Groups of six persons were less likely to exchange unshared information (information known to only one member) than groups of three persons (left graph). Moreover, this difference was greater when groups were told to structure their discussions (so as to maximize such sharing of information) than when they did not receive such instructions (right graph). Together, these findings lend support to the *information sampling model* of group decision making. (Source: Based on data from Stasser, Taylor, & Hanna, 1989.)

advantages of groups by urging members to focus on information exchange may actually backfire, serving to magnify rather than reduce the tendency to return to shared information over and over again.

Can anything be done to overcome these problems? Stasser and his colleagues suggest that they may be minimized by reducing the amount of information with which groups must deal. If decisions can be boiled down to a relatively small number of key issues, useful exchange of information between members may be enhanced. Other procedures specifically designed to encourage the consideration of unshared information may also prove helpful. For example, if members are reminded of differences in their individual expertise, they may tailor their comments so as to reflect such expertise. The result may then be the presentation of additional, unshared information. Attempts along these lines may require a considerable amount of effort. However, given the tendency of groups to spend much of their time discussing things they already know, it may well prove worthwhile in many situations.

Leadership: Its Nature and Impact in Groups

Suppose you surveyed persons belonging to a wide range of groups (businesses, sports teams, social clubs, military units) and asked them to name the single most important factor in determining the success of their group. What would you find? The chances are good that many—perhaps a majority—would reply, "Effective leadership." This answer reflects the widespread belief that leadership is a key ingredient in group activities. Indeed, many persons believe that a group without an effective leader is worse than no group at all; they would do better, in terms of reaching key goals, on their own. But what, precisely, *is* **leadership?** Like love, it is something most persons feel they can readily recognize but find difficult to define. For social psychologists, however, this process does have a clear focus: *influence*. Thus, many experts on this topic agree that leadership is *the process through which one member of a group (its **leader**) influences other group members toward the attainment of specific group goals* (Hollander, 1985).

In the remainder of this discussion we will consider several issues related to this process. First, we'll consider the question of who, precisely, becomes a leader—why some persons but not others rise to positions of authority. Second, we'll examine evidence concerning *gender differences* in leadership. Finally, we'll examine two views concerning the basis of leaders' effectiveness—why some leaders but not others are effective in their roles.

The Trait Approach: Are Leaders Born or Made?

Are some people born to lead? Common sense suggests this is so. Prominent leaders of the past such as Alexander the Great, Queen Elizabeth I, and Abraham Lincoln do seem to differ from ordinary human beings in several respects. For example, they all seem to have possessed extremely high levels of ambition coupled with clear visions of precisely where they wanted to go. To a lesser degree, even leaders lacking in such history-shaping fame seem different from followers. Top executives, some politicians, and even sports heroes or heroines seem to possess an aura that sets them apart from others (see Figure 11.17, p. 468). On the basis of such observations, early researchers interested in leadership formulated a view known as the **great person** or **trait theory**. According to this approach, great leaders possess key traits that set them apart from most other human beings. Further, the theory contends that these traits remain stable over time and across different groups. Thus, it suggests that all great leaders share certain characteristics regardless of when and where they lived or the precise role in history they fulfilled.

Certainly, these are intriguing suggestions. You will probably be surprised to learn, therefore, that they have *not* been strongly confirmed. Decades of active research (most conducted prior to 1950) failed to yield a short, agreed-on list of key traits shared by all leaders (Geier, 1969; Yukl, 1981). Although a few consistent findings did emerge (e.g., leaders are slightly taller and more intelligent than their followers), these were hardly dramatic in nature or in scope. Indeed, the overall results of this persistent search for traits associated with leadership were so disappointing that most investigators gave up and reached the following conclusion: Leaders simply do not differ from followers in clear and consistent ways.

While this conclusion is still widely accepted today, we should note that there has recently been renewed interest in the possibility that leaders and

 Leadership: Is it primarily a matter of traits?

FIGURE 11.17   Do all successful leaders share key traits? The *great person* or *trait theory of leadership* suggests that this is so. (Pictured here, left to right, are: Nelson and Winnie Mandela, and Mikhail Gorbachev.)

followers do differ in at least some measurable respects. Several types of evidence have contributed to this trend. First, research indicates that persons possessing certain patterns of motives (e.g., a high need for power coupled with a high degree of self-control) are more successful as business leaders than persons showing other patterns are (McClelland & Boyatzis, 1982). Second, political leaders appear to differ from nonleaders in ways we might expect (e.g., they are higher in self-confidence, achievement motivation, and dominance; Costantin-ini & Craik, 1980). Third, growing evidence suggests that several personal characteristics or traits (e.g., dominance, intelligence) are related to leader emergence in many situations (Lord, DeVader, & Alliger, 1986). As an example of the research pointing to this conclusion, let us consider a study by Ellis (1988).

This investigation sought to relate one important aspect of personality, *self-monitoring,* to the tendency to become a leader in actual groups. As we will note in more detail in Chapter 12, self-monitoring is actually a multifaceted, rather than a simple or unitary, dimension. Basically, however, it relates to two major factors: (1) *social sensitivity,* or sensitivity to others' reactions, and (2) *acting,* or the ability to modify or adjust one's behavior to various situations. Thus, high self-monitors are persons who are able to "read" others' reactions to various events effectively and are also able to change their own behavior so as to generate favorable responses from others. Low self-monitors, in contrast, are less capable of accomplishing both tasks.

Which group—low or high self-monitors—is more likely to emerge as a leader? Ellis predicted that high self-monitors would have a significant edge in this respect. To test this possibility, he had business students who worked together as teams in a college course rate one another in terms of contribution to the group, influence in the group, and leadership. Results offered clear support for a link between self-monitoring and such ratings. The higher individuals were in self-monitoring, the higher their ratings as a leader. Interestingly, these findings were much stronger for males than for females, presumably because leadership of a work group, even now, is still viewed by many as primarily a masculine activity. Putting such sex differences aside, though, it appears that self-monitoring, one important aspect of personality, is indeed related to emergence as a leader.

Finally, there is growing evidence that **charismatic leaders**—ones capable of generating tremendous loyalty, respect, and admiration among their followers—do indeed differ from other leaders (and from nonleaders) in several important respects. (For a summary of recent evidence on this issue, see the **Cutting Edge** section below.)

Please don't misunderstand: None of the findings just described suggest that all leaders share the same traits or that possession of these characteristics is required for leadership at all times and in all places. However, they do suggest that personal factors *can* play a role in leadership under some conditions and that in this respect, certainly, there may be a small grain of truth in the trait approach.

FOCUS ON RESEARCH: THE CUTTING EDGE

Charismatic Leaders: Style and Substance

Down through the ages, some leaders have been exceptionally successful in changing the attitudes or behavior of their followers. Indeed, it is no exaggeration to say that such persons have often served as key agents of social change, transforming entire societies through their visions of a new order (Bass, 1988). These individuals are often described as being **charismatic leaders,** and they have constituted a persistent puzzle for scientists interested in the nature of leadership. What sets these persons apart from other leaders? How do they induce large numbers of human beings to accept their views and directives so willingly? While no firm answers to such questions yet exist, growing evidence suggests that charisma is a real phenomenon and is, moreover, one that can be readily understood from the perspective of modern social psychology (Conger & Kanungo, 1988). In particular, it appears that charisma is largely the result of specific patterns of behavior on the part of leaders, patterns that in turn generate specific attributions about them among followers.

What specific forms of behavior contribute to followers' tendencies to attribute charisma to leaders? Among the ones suggested by careful analysis of this topic are (1) a compelling indictment of current conditions within a society or organization—one suggesting that these conditions are intolerable; (2) an emotional (and emotion-provoking) vision of another, far better state; and (3) a willingness to take risks and adopt unconventional actions in order to reach these goals. When these actions by leaders are coupled with outstanding social skills (e.g., a high ability to "read" the reactions of others quickly and accurately; expertise in impression management and related activities), the profound impact of charismatic leaders becomes understandable. In essence, they are individuals with a powerful message, a stirring personal style, and the interpersonal skills necessary for translating this combination into a major force for change.

When we think of charismatic leaders, we usually do so in connection with political movements or the clash of military forces. Increasing evidence suggests, however, that charismatic leaders play an important role in more prosaic settings as well. For example, they may make major contributions to the productivity and therefore the success of many organizations. Such effects are clearly illustrated by the results of a laboratory study conducted recently by Howell and Frost (1989).

These researchers had male and female subjects work on an "in-basket" task in which each acted as a manager and responded to a number of items a manager might find in her or his in-basket (e.g., letters, reports, memos). Subjects worked on these tasks under the direction of leaders specifically trained to demonstrate one of three contrasting styles: *charismatic, structuring,* or *considerate.* (The leaders were professional actors and actresses, carefully rehearsed to play these roles.) The *charismatic* leaders carefully stated an overarching goal, communicated high expectations for performance, and expressed great confidence in their subordinates. Moreover, these leaders demonstrated high levels of dynamism and energy (e.g., they paced back and forth or sat on the edge of their desk while giving directions; they used an engaging but relaxed tone of voice). The *structuring* leaders, in contrast, conveyed the impression that they were primarily concerned with the task at hand. They provided directions in a cool, factual tone; sat behind their desks; and generally acted in a purely businesslike manner. Finally, the *considerate* leaders conveyed an impression of frien-

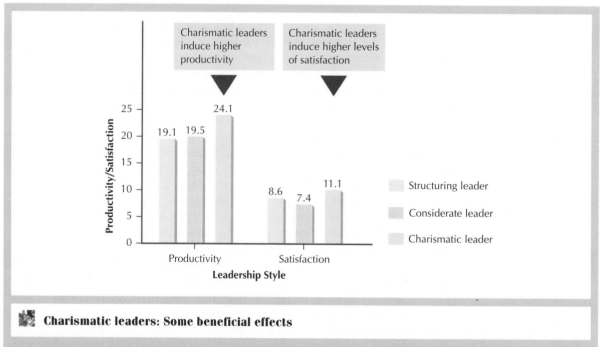

Charismatic leaders: Some beneficial effects

FIGURE 11.18 Leaders trained to demonstrate a charismatic style induced higher levels of productivity and satisfaction among group members than did leaders trained to demonstrate a structuring or considerate style. These findings suggest that charisma involves a discrete set of behaviors that can be acquired by many, if not all, persons. (Source: Based on data from Howell & Frost, 1989.)

dliness toward the subjects and generally indicated a high level of interest in them and their satisfaction with the task. (These latter two styles of leadership were included in the study because they have been found, in a large amount of previous research, to reflect basic dimensions along which actual leaders vary considerably. A given leader, it appears, can be high or low on structuring and high or low on showing consideration toward followers; Baron & Greenberg, 1990. We will return to these dimensions in a discussion of gender differences in leadership, below.)

Howell and Frost (1989) predicted that overall, charismatic leaders would produce the most favorable results; they would generate high levels of productivity and high levels of satisfaction among subjects. As shown in Figure 11.18, this was generally the case. These findings suggest that leaders who demonstrate a style many persons would describe as charismatic offer substance as well as style: Not only do they capture and hold the interest and enthusiasm of followers—they encourage high levels of effort and output among them as well.

Since the actors and actresses who served as leaders in this investigation were trained to demonstrate the three contrasting styles, it appears that charisma is not the innate or unalterable characteristic many persons believe. On the contrary, charisma is more accurately viewed as a specific pattern of behavior that some—perhaps even many—individuals can acquire. To the extent that this idea proves true, one potential answer to the quest for productivity, so important to many organizations, follows logically: Don't launch a spirited search for new and more charismatic leaders. Rather, concentrate on arming the leaders you already have with enhanced social skills.

Gender Differences in Leadership: Do Male and Female Leaders Really Differ in Style?

Before leaving the subject of the role of personal characteristics in leadership, it is important to consider one additional question: Do male leaders and female leaders differ in their style or approach to leadership (see Figure 11.19, p. 472)? The authors of many popular books (e.g., Loden, 1985) have contended that the sexes do indeed differ in this respect. Specifically, such authors have suggested that female leaders often adopt a style emphasizing cooperativeness and a less directive approach, while males exhibit a more "I'm in charge," directive strategy. In contrast, social scientists have generally contended that there are no consistent or major differences between the sexes in terms of leadership style (e.g., Nieva & Gutek, 1981). Which of these conclusions is more accurate? Clearly, this is a complex subject with no simple answers. However, a recent analysis of existing evidence on gender differences in leadership style (Eagly & Johnson, in press) goes a long way toward clarifying matters.

These researchers examined the results of more than 150 separate studies of leadership by means of a highly sophisticated *meta-analysis*. (As you may recall from earlier discussions, this is a statistical procedure for evaluating the effects of one or more variables across many different studies.) Three types of studies were included: *laboratory studies* (in which subjects interacted with a stranger), *assessment studies* (in which measures of subjects' leadership style were obtained), and *organizational studies* (in which leadership behavior in actual organizational settings was assessed). Eagly and Johnson (in press) reasoned that any differences between males and females would be more apparent in the first two types of studies than in the third type. This would be the case because

Gender differences in leadership: Do they really exist?

FIGURE 11.19 Do female leaders and male leaders differ in style? A recent *meta-analysis* of existing evidence suggests they may, but not necessarily in ways that traditional sex-role stereotypes suggest.

in actual organizations, leadership roles would require similar behavior from males and females. As a result, any differences between them would soon disappear. In laboratory and assessment studies, in contrast, any differences between males and females would not be subject to such role requirements.

Potential differences between male and female managers were examined on two dimensions: (1) concern with task accomplishment versus concern with maintenance of interpersonal relationships (initiating versus consideration, as discussed above) and (2) participative (democrative) versus directive (autocratic) style. Sex-role stereotypes suggest that female leaders might show more concern with interpersonal relations and tend to behave more democratically than male leaders. Results, however, did not confirm such stereotypes. With respect to the first dimension (an emphasis on tasks versus relations), there was little indication of substantial differences between the sexes. Such differences *were* observed in the laboratory and assessment studies, but they were small in magnitude. Further, they indicated that females were slightly higher than males on *both* task and relations emphasis—a finding contrary to what sex-role stereotypes would predict. Perhaps even more important, no differences on this dimension existed in the studies conducted in real organizations.

Evidence for significant sex differences did emerge, however, for the second dimension (democratic versus autocratic style). Here females adopted a more democratic or participative style than males in all three groups of studies. What accounts for this difference? Eagly and Johnson (in press) suggest that it stems at least in part from the fact that women are higher than men in interpersonal skills. Because of this, they find it easier than men to adopt a participative approach—one in which subordinates are invited to take part in the decision-making process. Females' superior interpersonal skills make it easier for them to invite such input and also to reject it gracefully when doing so is necessary. As a result, a participative leadership style is somewhat more congenial—and perhaps also more effective—for females.

These suggestions, of course, are somewhat speculative. However, they are consistent with existing evidence concerning differences in the interpersonal skills of males and females (Rosenthal, Hall, DiMatteo, Rogers, & Archer, 1979). Whatever the precise mechanisms involved, it appears that male and female leaders do differ in some respects. These differences are not closely related to widely held sex-role stereotypes, but they do seem to exist. It remains for further research to identify the precise situations in which such differences play an important role and in which they constitute an advantage (or disadvantage) to each gender.

Leader Effectiveness: Two Influential Views

All leaders are definitely *not* equal. Some are effective and contribute to high levels of performance and satisfaction on the part of their followers. Others are much less successful in these respects. Why is this the case? What factors determine leaders' success in directing their groups? This has been a central issue in much research concerned with leadership (Vecchio, 1987), but as yet, no definitive answers have emerged. However, the two theories described below—Fiedler's **contingency theory** (Fiedler, 1978; Fiedler & Garcia, 1987) and Vroom and Yetton's **normative theory** (Vroom & Yetton, 1973)—have added considerably to our understanding of this issue.

Contingency Theory: Matching Leaders and Tasks   Fiedler labels his approach the *contingency theory,* and this term is quite appropriate, for its central assumption is this: A leader's contribution to successful performance by his or her group is determined both by the leader's traits and by various features of the situation. To fully understand leader effectiveness, both types of factors must be considered.

With respect to characteristics possessed by leaders, Fiedler identifies *esteem* (liking) *for least preferred coworker,* or LPC, as most important. This refers to a leader's tendency to evaluate favorably or unfavorably the person with whom she or he has found it most difficult to work. Leaders who perceive this person in negative terms (low LPC leaders) seem primarily concerned with successful task performance. In contrast, those who perceive their least preferred coworker in a positive light (high LPC leaders) seem mainly concerned with good relations with subordinates.

Which of these types of leaders is more effective? Contingency theory's answer is, "It depends." And what it depends on, of course, is several situational factors. Fiedler suggests that whether low LPC or high LPC leaders are more effective depends on the degree to which the situation is *favorable* to the leader—provides him or her with control over subordinates. This, in turn, is determined largely by three factors: (1) the nature of the leader's relations with group members (the extent to which he or she enjoys their support), (2) the degree of structure in the task being performed (the extent to which task goals and subordinates' roles are clearly defined), and (3) the leader's "position power" (his or her ability to enforce compliance by subordinates). Combining these three factors, the leader's situational control can range from very high (positive relations with members, a highly structured task, high position power) to very low (negative relations, an unstructured task, low position power; refer to Figure 11.20, p. 474).

Now, to return to the central question: When are different types of leaders most effective? Fiedler suggests that low LPC leaders (ones who are task ori-

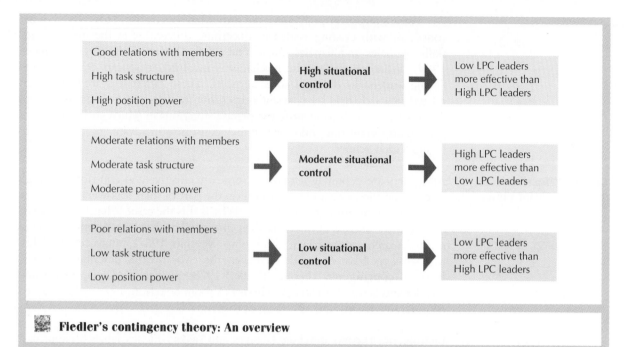

Good relations with members High task structure High position power	→	**High situational control**	→	Low LPC leaders more effective than High LPC leaders
Moderate relations with members Moderate task structure Moderate position power	→	**Moderate situational control**	→	High LPC leaders more effective than Low LPC leaders
Poor relations with members Low task structure Low position power	→	**Low situational control**	→	Low LPC leaders more effective than High LPC leaders

Fiedler's contingency theory: An overview

FIGURE 11.20 According to Fiedler's *contingency theory,* leader effectiveness is determined by a complex interplay between leader characteristics (where they stand on the LPC dimension) and the degree of situational control they enjoy. Low LPC leaders are more effective than high LPC leaders under conditions of low or high situational control. The opposite is true under conditions of moderate situational control.

ented) are superior to high LPC leaders (ones who are people oriented) when situational control is either very low or very high. In contrast, high LPC leaders have an edge when situational control falls within the moderate range. The reasoning behind these predictions is as follows: Under conditions of low situational control, groups need considerable guidance to operate effectively. Since low LPC leaders are more likely to provide such structure, they will usually be superior in these cases. Similarly, low LPC leaders have an edge under conditions that offer leaders high situational control. Here, such leaders realize that conditions are very favorable and that task performance is assured. As a result, they often adopt a relaxed, hands-off style that is appreciated by subordinates. In contrast, high LPC leaders, feeling that they already enjoy good relations with subordinates, may shift their attention to task performance. Their attempts to provide guidance in this respect may then be perceived as needless meddling, with the result that performance suffers.

To repeat: Fiedler's theory predicts that low LPC (task-oriented) leaders will be more effective than high LPC (relations-oriented) leaders under conditions of either low or high situational control. In contrast, high LPC leaders will have an edge under conditions in which situational control is moderate.

Contingency Theory: Its Current Status Have these predictions been supported by research findings? Existing evidence presents something of a mixed picture. On the one hand, most laboratory studies performed to test various aspects of contingency theory have yielded positive results (Strube & Garcia, 1981). On the other hand, the findings of studies conducted with naturally existing groups have not been as favorable (Peters, Hartke, & Pohlmann, 1985). Such investigations have sometimes yielded results contrary to what contingency theory predicts. In addition, the theory has been criticized on several important grounds. A degree of ambiguity exists with respect to the placement of specific situations along the dimension of situational control (Ashour, 1973). Unless situations can be accurately classified as low, moderate, or high in this respect, predictions about leader effectiveness are difficult to make. Similarly, some critics have questioned the adequacy of the procedures used to measure leaders' standing along the LPC dimension and even the validity of this dimension itself (cf. Peters, Hartke, & Pohlmann, 1985).

Taking such criticism as well as existing evidence into account, the following tentative conclusions seem justified. Contingency theory has indeed added to our understanding of key aspects of leadership and leader effectiveness. Several questions about its accuracy remain, however, and require careful further attention. In sum, it should be viewed more as a theory still undergoing refinement than as one offering a fully developed framework for understanding all aspects of leader effectiveness.

Normative Theory: Decision Making and Leader Effectiveness One of the central tasks performed by leaders is making decisions. Indeed, a defining characteristic of leadership positions is that they are places where "the buck stops" and concrete actions must be taken. Yet leaders do not operate in a social vacuum; even when they possess considerable power and authority, there is no guarantee that their decisions will be accepted or implemented by followers. Thus, leadership is always something of a two-way street in which leaders influence followers and followers, in turn, exert some degree of influence over leaders.

Given this fact, an intriguing question arises: In making decisions, how much participation by followers should leaders permit? According to the **normative theory** of leadership, this is an important determinant of leader effectiveness (Vroom & Yetton, 1973). Leaders who permit an appropriate amount of participation by followers will generally be more effective, over the long run, than leaders who permit either too much or too little. But how much participation is enough? Vroom and Yetton's theory suggests that the answer depends on several issues relating primarily to the importance of the quality of the decision and the importance of its acceptance by subordinates. For example, consider a situation in which a high-quality decision is crucial (the stakes are high), the leader has enough information or expertise to make the decision alone, and acceptance by subordinates is not essential (the decision will work even without their support). Here, a relatively *autocratic* style of decision making is best. It is efficient and will cost little in terms of getting the decision implemented. In contrast, consider a situation in which a high-quality decision is necessary, the leader has enough information to make the decision alone, but acceptance by subordinates *is* crucial—the decision won't work without their active support. Here, a more *participative* style would be preferable.

Vroom and Yetton's theory suggests that by answering a series of such questions, leaders can arrive at the appropriate decision-making style—one that affords subordinates just the right amount of participation to maintain their morale while retaining the highest degree of efficiency possible. In general, these guidelines and suggestions seem to work: Leaders who adapt their style of decision making to existing conditions are generally more successful than those who are either uniformly autocratic or uniformly participative in style (Vroom & Jago, 1978). However, additional evidence suggests the need for certain adjustments in the theory.

First, it appears that most persons prefer a participative approach by their leader even under conditions in which normative theory recommends an autocratic style (Heilman et al., 1984). Second, it appears that specific leader characteristics may play an important role in determining the relative effectiveness of various decision-making strategies. A study by Crouch and Yetton (1987) provides strong support for this latter conclusion.

These investigators focused on an aspect of normative theory known as the *conflict rule*. This suggests that in situations in which conflicting opinions exist among subordinates over the means of reaching some goal and acceptance of the decision is important, a participative approach is best. Crouch and Yetton reasoned that this might indeed be true when leaders are high in the ability to handle interpersonal conflict. However, when they are low in this ability, a more

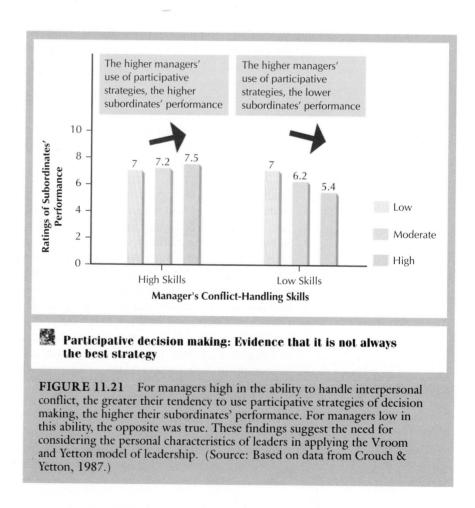

Participative decision making: Evidence that it is not always the best strategy

FIGURE 11.21   For managers high in the ability to handle interpersonal conflict, the greater their tendency to use participative strategies of decision making, the higher their subordinates' performance. For managers low in this ability, the opposite was true. These findings suggest the need for considering the personal characteristics of leaders in applying the Vroom and Yetton model of leadership. (Source: Based on data from Crouch & Yetton, 1987.)

autocratic approach, that avoids direct contact (and the opportunity for open conflict) among subordinates, might be preferable.

To test these predictions, the researchers asked a large group of employees to rate their managers' skills in conflict management. Ratings included items designed to assess each manager's skills in encouraging suggestions, maintaining an open mind, and being willing to listen to input from others. In addition, the managers rated the job performance of their subordinates. Finally, the same managers completed another measure that assessed their tendencies to use participative rather than autocratic styles of decision making. Crouch and Yetton predicted that for managers relatively high in conflict-handling skills, the greater the tendency to use participative decision making, the higher their subordinates' performance; however, for managers low in conflict-handling skills, the opposite would be true. As shown in Figure 11.21, both predictions were confirmed. These findings suggest that managers in the first group (those having good conflict-handling skills) would be wise to adopt participative strategies for reaching decisions, while managers in the second group might attain greater success by means of more autocratic approaches.

In sum, normative theory appears to offer useful guidelines to leaders for choosing the most effective approach to decision making. However, adjustments in the model designed to take account of strong preferences for participative procedures and the personal skills of leaders seem necessary. With the addition of such changes, the Vroom and Yetton model, like contingency theory, adds appreciably to our understanding of those factors which make specific leaders effective "pluses" or ineffective "minuses" for the groups they lead.

SUMMARY AND REVIEW

The Nature and Function of Groups

Groups consist of two or more individuals who share common goals, whose fates are interdependent, who have a stable relationship, and who recognize the group's existence. Groups exert influence on their members through *roles* (members' assigned functions within the group), *status* (their relative standing or influence), *norms* (rules concerning appropriate behavior), and *cohesiveness* (forces acting to keep members within the group, e.g., their attraction to it).

Groups and Task Performance

Individuals' performance of various tasks is often affected by the presence of others or by the potential evaluation of their work. Such effects are known as **social facilitation,** although they can in-

volve reduced as well as enhanced task performance. Social facilitation appears to stem from arousal induced by the presence of others. *Distraction-conflict theory* suggests that such arousal stems from conflict between paying attention to others and paying attention to the task at hand.

Groups are more efficient in performing certain types of tasks than are individuals (e.g., additive and compensatory tasks). However, they are less efficient than individuals in performing other types of tasks (e.g., disjunctive ones). In some cases where groups might prove relatively efficient, their output is hindered by **social loafing**—the tendency of some members to "take it easy" and let others do most of the work. Social loafing stems from such persons' beliefs that their effort will be pooled with that of others and from the fact that for various reasons, such effort cannot be evaluated. Several techniques (e.g., making individual's work identifiable, providing standards for self-evaluation) are effective in countering tendencies toward social loafing.

Decision Making in Groups

Groups make many key decisions. These can sometimes be predicted by *social decision schemes*—simple rules relating the initial views of members to a group's final decision. Procedures such as *straw polls* can influence the views of individual members, and hence the decisions reached by groups.

As a result of their deliberations, groups often demonstrate **group polarization,** a tendency to shift toward more extreme views. Two other potential difficulties faced by decision-making groups are **groupthink,** a tendency to become concerned more with maintaining consensus than with choosing the best alternative, and an inability to pool unshared information.

Leadership

Leaders are group members who exert influence on group members in the direction of specific goals. The **great person** or **trait theory** of leadership suggests that specific persons become leaders because they possess crucial traits. Presumably, these traits are much the same in all cultures and at all times. Although little evidence for this view exists, recent research suggests that leaders do differ from followers in certain respects (e.g., in terms of their major motives, their possession of certain traits and social skills). **Charismatic leaders** demonstrate specific patterns of behavior (e.g., high energy, a strong commitment to clear-cut goals, expressions of confidence in themselves and followers). In addition, they possess high levels of specific social skills (e.g., self-presentation). Male and female leaders do not differ in their relative concern with task performance and interpersonal relations. However, female leaders tend to adopt a more democratic leadership style than males.

According to Fiedler's **contingency theory,** leader effectiveness stems from a complex interplay between leaders' characteristics and the situations they confront. Vroom and Yetton's **normative theory** proposes that one important determinant of such effectiveness is decision-making style—the extent to which leaders permit participation by followers in key decisions. Leaders who permit the most appropriate level of participation by followers in a given situation are more effective than leaders who permit too little or too much participation.

KEY TERMS

Additive tasks Tasks for which the group product is the sum or combination of the efforts of individual members.

Charismatic leaders Leaders who induce among followers high levels of loyalty, respect, and admiration.

Cohesiveness All forces acting on group members to remain part of a group.

Compensatory tasks Tasks in which the group product is the average of all members' contributions.

Conjunctive tasks Tasks in which the group product is determined by the performance of the poorest member.

Contingency theory A theory suggesting that leader effectiveness is determined by a complex interplay between the leader's characteristics and the favorability of the situation (situational control) for the leader.

Decision making (group) The processes through which groups move toward consensus and reach decisions.

Disjunctive tasks Tasks in which the group product is determined by the contribution of the best member.

Distraction-conflict theory A theory suggesting that social facilitation stems from the conflict produced when individuals attempt, simultaneously, to pay attention to other persons and to the task being performed.

Drive theory of social facilitation A theory suggesting that the mere presence of others is arousing and increases the tendency to perform dominant responses.

Evaluation apprehension Concern over being evaluated by others. Such concern can increase arousal and so contribute to social facilitation.

Great person or *trait theory (of leadership)* A theory suggesting that all great leaders share key traits that suit them for positions of authority.

Group polarization The tendency of group members to shift, as a result of group discussion, toward more extreme positions than those they initially held.

Groups Two or more persons who interact with one another, share common goals, are somehow interdependent, and recognize that they belong to a group.

Groupthink The tendency of members of highly cohesive groups to adhere to the shared views so strongly that they ignore information inconsistent with those views.

Information sampling model A theory of group decision making suggesting that group members are more likely to discuss shared than unshared information. This tendency increases with group size.

Leaders Those individuals who exert the most influence on other members of groups. Such influence can be profound, involving shifts in a wide range of attitudes, perceptions, and behavior.

Leadership The process through which leaders influence other group members toward attainment of specific group goals.

Norms Rules within a group indicating how its members should (or should not) behave.

Normative theory A theory suggesting that leaders are most effective when they adopt the style of decision making (from autocratic to participative) which is most appropriate in a given situation.

Risky shift The tendency for individuals to recommend riskier courses of action following group discussion than prior to its occurrence.

Roles The set of behaviors that individuals occupying specific positions within a group are expected to perform.

Social decision schemes Rules relating the initial distribution of member views to final group decisions.

Social facilitation Effects on performance resulting from the presence of others.

Social loafing The tendency of group members to exert less effort on a task than they would if working on it alone.

Status Relative social position or rank within a group.

Straw poll A procedure in which group members indicate their current preferences regarding a decision. Because these statements are not binding on them, members are free to shift to other positions.

FOR MORE INFORMATION

Fiedler, F. E., and Garcia, J. E. (1987). *Leadership: Cognitive resources and performance*. New York: Wiley.

A clear, well-written overview of current knowledge about several aspects of leadership. Particular attention is directed to the question of how leaders' cognitive abilities influence their success in wide-ranging situations.

Hendrick, C. (Ed.). (1987). *Group processes*. Newbury Park, CA: Sage.

A collection of chapters dealing with various aspects of group process (e.g., group decision making, leadership, minority influence). Each chapter is quite complete and was prepared by established experts in the field.

Paulus, P. B. (Ed.). (1989). *Psychology of group influence*. Hillsdale, NJ: Erlbaum.

This book deals with many of the topics considered in this chapter (e.g., social facilitation, social loafing, leadership). If you'd like to know more about these aspects of behavior in group settings, this is an excellent source to consult.

Personality and
Social Behavior

The Behavioral Effects of Personality Dispositions

Conceptualizing Individual Differences / Traits and Situations as Joint Determinants of Human Behavior / Measuring Personality Dispositions

Self-Concept as a Central Disposition

Self-Esteem: Evaluating Yourself / Self-Efficacy: Estimating Your Ability to Get Things Done / Self-Monitoring: Sensitivity to the Reactions of Other People

Individual Differences in Beliefs and Attitudes

Locus of Control: Beliefs about Internal versus External Responsibility / Erotophobia: Generalized Attitudes about Sexuality

SPECIAL SECTIONS

FOCUS ON RESEARCH: CLASSIC CONTRIBUTIONS
Authoritarian Beliefs and Attitudes: Measuring the Predisposition to Fascist Ideology
FOCUS ON RESEARCH: THE CUTTING EDGE
Maintaining Positive (or Negative) Self-Esteem: Illusions and Overgeneralizations
ON THE APPLIED SIDE
Social Activism: Beliefs about Personal Power and Social Injustice

When Ruth was very young, she was described by almost everyone who knew her as a happy, easygoing child. She was cheerful, often smiling and laughing, and she seldom caused her parents any trouble. As a toddler, Ruth was a joy to have around because she entertained herself for hours at a time playing with her toys, watching cartoons on television, and, as she grew older, drawing pictures in a special notebook (her "picture diary") and banging on the piano keys to make "music."

When Ruth entered school, her kindergarten teacher was enthusiastic about having her in class. The parent-teacher meetings were a pleasure, because the discussions were always about Ruth's wonderful social adjustment and the positive way she interacted with her classmates. These characteristics remained constant throughout her school years. She continued to make friends easily, and it was a rare event when she was not invited to a party or elected to a class or school office. In high school and college, she dated often, and one of her envious classmates, Carla, once said that Ruth must be a tramp because she wasn't pretty enough to attract all those boys otherwise. Ruth only laughed when someone told her about Carla's accusation. She knew her dates found her fun to be with, and, no, it wasn't sex that drew them to her.

Ruth married soon after graduating from college and adjusted well to the role of wife and mother. She seldom seemed upset about anything, and her three sons were devoted to her. At one family gathering, when Ruth was in her early forties, an elderly aunt remarked, "Look at Ruth over there! She makes everyone smile, no matter how grumpy they usually are. That girl hasn't changed one bit since she was two years old."

Ashley's parents were surprised when the high school counselor called to ask whether they could arrange to meet with her. Their daughter had never caused them any worry. She came home from school, did her homework, helped with the house cleaning and the cooking, and always had perfect manners. What in the world could the counselor want to talk about?

The meeting took place late one afternoon; Mr. and Mrs. Walters had no inkling of what was to come. The counselor seemed a little embarrassed but quickly came to the point: "As you undoubtedly know, Ashley is not doing very well in her classes this semester. After three years of better-than-average work, she has begun her senior year with a dismal performance."

Mr. Walters broke in, "Actually, we had no idea."

"I feel that a good part of the problem is her new group of friends. I'm almost certain they're drinking a lot. Who knows what else? The immediate concern, though, is that Ashley is pregnant. You may know that already, but I had to be sure."

The parents could scarcely believe what they had just heard. *Their* Ashley? Pregnant, drinking, having trouble with her classes? There had to be some mistake. Their daughter wasn't like that at all.

The two young women in these stories represent two extremes—one with stable, unchanging characteristics and one who changes as her situation changes. Many individuals, such as Ruth, seem to behave consistently from situation to situation and from one time period to another—they remain predictably the same. We all know people who follow that pattern, and it is easy to understand how the concept of **personality** developed. There must be something about the individual (possibly inherited, possibly learned in early childhood) that acts to guide the person's behavior.

In contrast, we also encounter other individuals, such as Ashley, who behave very differently in different situations and at different points in their lives. A person may interact in one way with parents and in quite another way with friends. An obnoxious youngster may become an affectionate, caring adult. A gentle child may grow up and commit murder. What is that kind of person *really* like? Given such observations, it is easy to understand how the concept of **situational determinants** of behavior developed. From this viewpoint, people are like kites in the wind, influenced by whatever breeze is blowing at a given moment.

These alternative views and their implications have a long history in both philosophy and psychology. They constitute the foundations for two approaches to the study of human behavior—**personality psychology,** which focuses primarily on internal dispositions that lead to consistent behavior across situations, and **social psychology,** which focuses primarily on external factors that lead otherwise different individuals to respond in a consistent way to particular events. Traditionally at least, personality psychologists have placed more emphasis on the role of traits, and social psychologists have placed more emphasis on the role of situations. As this chapter will demonstrate, current research and theory provide evidence that both approaches are useful and that these two conceptualizations of human behavior can be integrated into a single framework that predicts behavior more accurately than either approach alone.

In this chapter, we will first discuss how *personality dispositions* function and how they interact with situational variables in influencing behavior. Next, we will describe three important dispositional aspects of the *self-concept*—self-esteem, self-efficacy, and self-monitoring. Then, we will provide examples of research on individual differences in *beliefs and attitudes* with descriptions of locus of control and of erotophobia.

The Behavioral Effects of Personality Dispositions

Much of the research described in the previous chapters has shown convincingly that people respond to specific situational factors in predictable ways. For example, people like strangers who express attitudes similar to their own, and when one person attacks another verbally or physically, anger and aggression are common responses. We also know, however, that not *everyone* responds in exactly the same way, as Figure 12.1 (p. 484) illustrates.

The fact that different individuals may respond differently to the same situation is most often explained as the result of their different **personality traits.** We have already discussed several instances of how such traits operate, including racial prejudice in Chapter 5, need for affiliation in Chapter 6, loneliness in Chapter 7, Type A behavior pattern in Chapter 10, and leadership ability in Chapter 11. The general idea is that people bring certain characteristics to each situation; these characteristics, in turn, result in different responses. We will now describe some of the ways such traits are conceptualized and measured.

Conceptualizing Individual Differences

The original personality theories were constructed by psychotherapists like Freud and Jung long before personality and social psychology were active research fields. Consequently, most of the theories were based on clinical obser-

Personality: Different responses to the same situation

FIGURE 12.1   Interest in personality variables stems from the fact that in response to the same stimulus situation, individuals respond in different ways (as the fish do in this cartoon). The assumption is that the differences are based on internal dispositions—known as personality traits or personality variables. (Reprinted courtesy Penthouse Magazine © 1990.)

vations, speculations, and creative ideas, rather than on the kind of empirical research that typifies today's behavioral science. These early formulations are of considerable historical interest, and some of their major constructs continue to be of value as a source of hypotheses. We will concentrate our discussion, however, on current approaches to personality.

Personality Research: Minitheories Based on Traits   When modern psychologists began investigating personality variables, most concentrated on a limited number of specific traits rather than on all aspects of personality. An individual's **personality** is defined as the combination of those relatively enduring traits which influence behavior in a predictable way in a variety of situations. What are these traits, and how do we identify them?

Most of the trait variables of current interest were first identified long before the field of social psychology began. When people were observed to differ in some relatively consistent way, words were created to describe individual differences in dozens of characteristics, such as shyness, intelligence, honesty, and generosity. Allport and Odbert (1936) identified 171 different traits in Webster's unabridged dictionary. These descriptive terms have appeared for centuries in fiction, in histories, and in how people describe one another in their daily interactions (Hampson, 1983). Many such traits have been useful in research, and a multitude of personality tests have been constructed to measure them.

Some psychologists (e.g., Eysenck, 1986; Zuckerman, Kuhlman, & Camac, 1988) feel that a trait-by-trait approach to understanding personality is a mistake. They propose that we first establish what the basic traits are and then investigate personality as a whole. Nevertheless, personality psychologists most often conduct research based on a single trait that is useful in predicting specific social behaviors. There has also been only limited agreement as to what constitutes the "basic traits." Very recently, however, there has been a growing interest in a five-trait model of personality. What are these five traits?

"Five Robust Factors" In research with roots in the original Allport and Odbert dictionary study, McCrae (1989) and others have become convinced that all the descriptive terms can be reduced to just five basic personality dimensions. These five factors appear repeatedly in analyses of trait research (Borkenau, 1988; Costa & McCrae, 1988; Digman, 1989, 1990; Peabody & Goldberg, 1989). They also appear cross-culturally, as in a study of Filipinos using each subject's native language—either English or Tagalog (Church & Katigbak, 1989). Summarizing such research, Digman and Inouye (1986, p. 116) conclude:

> A series of research studies of personality traits has led to a finding consistent enough to approach the status of a law. The finding is this: If a large number of rating scales is used and if the scope of the scales is very broad, the domain of personality descriptors is almost completely accounted for by five robust factors.

These five basic traits are measured by the NEO Personality Inventory (Costa & McCrae, 1985). These dimensions—*extraversion, agreeableness, will to achieve, emotional stability,* and *openness to experience*—are presented in Table 12.1.

Five robust personality dimensions

TABLE 12.1 Five robust personality traits have been identified, and some investigators suggest that these should be considered the basic personality dispositions.

Five Basic Personality Dimensions	Characteristics of Those Who Are High versus Those Who Are Low on Each Dimension
Extraversion	Talkative, frank, adventurous, and sociable *versus* silent, secretive, cautious, and reclusive
Agreeableness	Good-natured, not jealous, gentle, and cooperative *versus* irritable, jealous, headstrong, and negativistic
Will to achieve (or conscientiousness)	Fussy, responsible, scrupulous, and persevering *versus* careless, undependable, unscrupulous, and willing to quit
Emotional stability (or neuroticism)	Poised, calm, composed, and not hypochondriacal *versus* nervous, anxious, excitable, and hypochondriacal
Openness to experience (or culture)	Artistically sensitive, intellectual, polished, and imaginative *versus* insensitive, narrow, crude, and simple

Source: Based on suggestions by Borkenau, 1988.

If in fact only five dimensions underlie what is meant by personality traits, future personality-social research will look quite different from the work with which we are currently familiar. An important caution is that the "big five" traits are based primarily on *descriptive* terms. When the data consist of individual differences in *behavior*, the five-factor model is much less satisfactory (Botwin & Buss, 1989).

Despite the promise of the five basic factors, as yet no well-established, agreed-on formulation exists to tie together all the research and theorizing on personality traits. In the following section we will describe the role played by traits (including the five robust factors) in the study of behavior.

Traits and Situations as Joint Determinants of Human Behavior

Whether or not personality variables even exist and whether or not they are useful elements in scientific research have been matters of controversy from time to time in psychology.

Early Conceptions of Traits   Personality psychologists originally assumed that people behave consistently across situations and over time. Some people are hostile no matter what the setting; some are friendly to everyone. Small children who are stubborn become stubborn adults; youngsters who are competitive develop into competitive grown-ups. One of psychology's founding fathers, William James, observed at the turn of the century that a person's tendencies were "set like plaster" by the age of thirty. We know now, however, that while some people are quite consistent over time, others undergo dramatic changes (Ozer & Gjerde, 1989).

James and his early colleagues were not alone; most people tend to overestimate the degree of consistency in the responses of others (Kunda & Nisbett, 1986; Reeder, Fletcher, & Furman, 1989). In judging themselves, in contrast, people perceive much complexity and unpredictability (Sande, Goethals, & Radloff, 1988).

One reason we believe others are consistent is that people generally spend their time in particular types of situations, and so predictable behavior based on situational factors may be misinterpreted as predictable behavior based on personality factors (Caspi, Bem, & Elder, 1989). When conducting an experiment, an investigator randomly assigns subjects to conditions, and everyone in a given stimulus condition is exposed to the same situational variable. In real life, we select our own situations, and we prefer those which match our inclinations (Staats & Burns, 1982; see Figure 12.2). For example, extraverted people spend their leisure time in social settings (Diener, Larsen, & Emmons, 1984), energetic people select settings in which they can be physically active (Gormly, 1983), and Type A students prefer college courses that require a lot of effort and provide feedback on performance (Feather & Volkmer, 1988). Further, when possible, people even arrange their environment to fit their personalities (Osborn, 1988). It seems that if we observe people behaving consistently in self-chosen activities, it is impossible to determine whether the behavior occurs because of traits or because of situational influences.

To the extent that personality traits do influence behavior, the task of psychologists is to devise instruments to measure stable traits. Accordingly, numerous personality tests were developed in the first half of this century. The creators of these instruments assumed that test scores would provide a way to

 Behavioral consistency across situations: Do traits determine behavior or choice of situations?

FIGURE 12.2   In real life, we often observe an individual behaving in the same way in different situations. One explanation of the consistent behavior is that personality variables determine behavior across all situations. It is also possible that personality factors influence the choice of situations. Generally, people seek out situations that match their inclinations.

predict behavior, and most of the early tests were *global measures* designed to learn as much as possible about an individual's basic personality. Examples include *projective tests* that used ambiguous stimuli like inkblots (Rorschach, 1921) and drawings (Morgan & Murray, 1938) and *objective tests* on which subjects responded to a long series of statements in terms of agree/disagree or true/false (Hathaway & McKinley, 1940).

Whatever the specific instrument, the goal was clear: Measure an individual's personality dispositions, and use the test scores to predict his or her characteristic behavior.

Problems with the Trait Approach   The popular application of personality tests in organizational and clinical settings naturally led to research evaluating how well the tests functioned. It gradually became clear that these instruments were not very impressive as predictors of what people would actually do. Early critics such as Rotter (1954) concluded, on the basis of research evidence, that even the best and most widely used personality tests did not perform well.

One solution to the weakness of personality measures was an attempt to build better tests. A more revolutionary proposal was made by one of Rotter's former students, Walter Mischel (1968, 1977), who argued that behavior is *not* consistent; rather, behavior is primarily a function of situational factors, not internal dispositions. If so, perhaps the concept of personality was only a myth.

One implication of this "situational revolution" was that research should focus on the situational determinants of behavior rather than on traits (Snyder & Ickes, 1985).

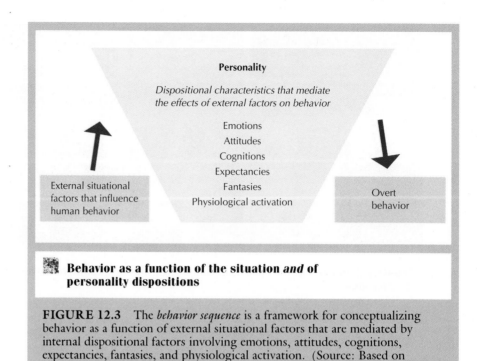

Personality

*Dispositional characteristics that mediate
the effects of external factors on behavior*

Emotions
Attitudes
Cognitions
Expectancies
Fantasies
Physiological activation

External situational
factors that influence
human behavior

Overt
behavior

**Behavior as a function of the situation *and* of
personality dispositions**

FIGURE 12.3   The *behavior sequence* is a framework for conceptualizing
behavior as a function of external situational factors that are mediated by
internal dispositional factors involving emotions, attitudes, cognitions,
expectancies, fantasies, and physiological activation. (Source: Based on
suggestions by Byrne & Schulte, 1990.)

Integrating Social and Personality Psychology   It was ironic that antitrait arguments were most strongly advanced at a time when social psychologists were
beginning to explore the value of including personality variables in their research in order to enhance the predictive power of situational factors (Funder
& Ozer, 1983; Silverstein, 1988). Rather than abandoning personality traits,
psychologists began integrating them in experimental social research. Clarke
and Hoyle (1988) suggest that the objective is to explain the relationship
between situations and behavior by including internal processes. These
processes consist of **personality dispositions** that are responsible for characteristic responses to a given situation.

Personality dispositions include all of the psychological processes that are
described throughout this book—emotions, attitudes, cognitions, and so on.
When we speak of dispositions, we mean simply that individuals respond in
consistent ways. For example, we each experience a variety of emotional responses in our everyday lives, but some people are characteristically more anxious than others across situations. People also differ in their basic attitudes,
such as those involving sexism and racism, and in their cognitions, such as the
details of their self-schemas.

From this perspective, a personality theory is simply a map or a flowchart
that outlines the kinds of dispositions likely to be useful in understanding
human behavior. Let's examine one version of such a map.

In Figure 12.3, personality variables are defined as dispositions that mediate
the effects of external events on human behavior, sometimes called the **behavior
sequence** (Byrne & Schulte, 1990). The dispositions are grouped into six

processes, in that people are found to differ in their characteristic *emotions, attitudes, cognitions, expectancies, fantasies,* and level of *physiological activation.*

The figure may make it appear as if behavior always occurs in response to external factors mediated by dispositional variables. In fact, some situations are so powerful that psychological mediation is irrelevant (e.g., the blow of a rubber hammer below your knee causes a reflexive jerk of your leg). Some external factors elicit emotions, cognitions, or whatever, but no external behavior follows (e.g., an erotic movie may strongly affect how you feel or what you think about without affecting what you do). Further, some sequences begin internally and lead to overt behavior (e.g., fantasizing about your favorite food can result in physiological activation that motivates eating or the search for food). Finally, as noted often in this book, the internal factors influence one another (e.g., emotions influence cognitions and vice versa, attitudes influence expectancies and vice versa, fantasies influence physiological activation and vice versa).

Dispositions may be determined by genetics, may be based on learning, or may involve both genetic and experiential determinants. In addition, many dispositions can be modified on the basis of experience. Democrats can become Republicans, criminals can become ministers, positive beliefs about the future can change to negative ones, and on and on. The possibility of modifying such dispositions is what underlies much of education, psychotherapy, advertising, and other enterprises as well.

When we look at the combined behavioral effects of external, situational variables and internal, dispositional variables, the result is the **integrative approach** to understanding human behavior (Feshbach, 1984b; Kenrick, 1986; Malloy & Kenny, 1986). A general depiction of the integrative approach is provided in Figure 12.4 (p. 490).

Subjective Well-Being: An Example of the Integrative Approach   We each have experienced what it is like to be "on top of the world." Everything is going right, and we feel good about ourselves. In the words of a beer commercial on TV, "It doesn't get any better than this." Some of us have also experienced the feeling that life is "the pits." Nothing is going right; we feel bad about ourselves; "there's nowhere to go but up." These positive and negative extremes are the end points of a dimension along which we evaluate our lives—**subjective well-being.**

Headey and Wearing (1989) describe the sense of well-being as consisting of three dimensions: (1) *Cognitive life satisfaction* is measured by asking a series of questions, such as "How do you feel about your life as a whole?" and "How do you feel about the sense of purpose and meaning in your life?" Subjects respond on a scale ranging from "delighted" to "terrible." (2) *Positive affect* and (3) *negative affect* are measured by asking about each person's emotional reactions during the past few weeks. Subjective well-being is highest for those who are satisfied with their lives and who report experiencing positive rather than negative emotions. Low subjective well-being is characterized by dissatisfaction with one's life and by reporting negative rather than positive emotions.

The research question is, What determines feelings of well-being? Some have proposed that personality differences are the primary factors responsible for this self-perception (Costa & McCrae, 1984) and that people consistently feel good or bad about themselves over the years on the basis of internal dispositions. Others propose that external events play a critical determining role

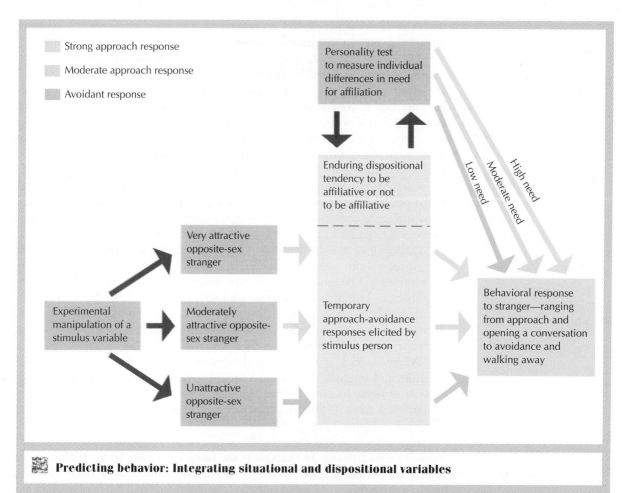

Strong approach response

Moderate approach response

Avoidant response

Personality test to measure individual differences in need for affiliation

Enduring dispositional tendency to be affiliative or not to be affiliative

Low need

Moderate need

High need

Experimental manipulation of a stimulus variable

Very attractive opposite-sex stranger

Moderately attractive opposite-sex stranger

Unattractive opposite-sex stranger

Temporary approach-avoidance responses elicited by stimulus person

Behavioral response to stranger—ranging from approach and opening a conversation to avoidance and walking away

Predicting behavior: Integrating situational and dispositional variables

FIGURE 12.4   To an increasing extent, personality and social research integrates the traditional emphasis of personality psychology on dispositional variables with the traditional emphasis of social psychology on situational variables. Behavioral prediction is improved because both types of factors are considered simultaneously.

(Argyle, 1987). Studies have reported significant effects for negative (Henderson, Byrne, & Duncan-Jones, 1981) and for positive (Headey, Holmstrom, & Wearing, 1984) life events. In contrast, Brickman, Coates, and Janoff-Bulman (1978) argue that life events have little effect, because research indicates that people quickly adapt to both favorable happenings, such as winning a lottery, and unfavorable happenings, such as becoming partially paralyzed.

To examine personality and situational factors simultaneously, Headey and Wearing (1989) studied hundreds of Australian subjects. These individuals were interviewed once every two years from 1981 to 1987. At each session, subjective well-being was determined. Situational factors consisted of recent favorable (e.g., got married) and unfavorable (e.g., serious problems with one's children) life events. Measures parallel to three of the five robust factors—*extraversion, neuroticism,* and *openness to experience*—were administered on each occasion.

Over the six years of the study, subjective well-being was found to be fairly stable; that is, the same people tended to be satisfied or dissatisfied with their lives over the years and to report similar levels of positive versus negative affect at each interview. Nevertheless, many people reported changes in well-being. The data indicated that both personality and situational events affected subjective well-being. The authors proposed a **dynamic equilibrium model** to describe the specific way the various factors function to determine how people feel about themselves. Figure 12.5 depicts the operation of this model at high and low levels of subjective well-being.

Those highest in subjective well-being tend to be high in extraversion, low in neuroticism, and open to experience. They indicate that they repeatedly experience favorable happenings involving friends (e.g., I made many new

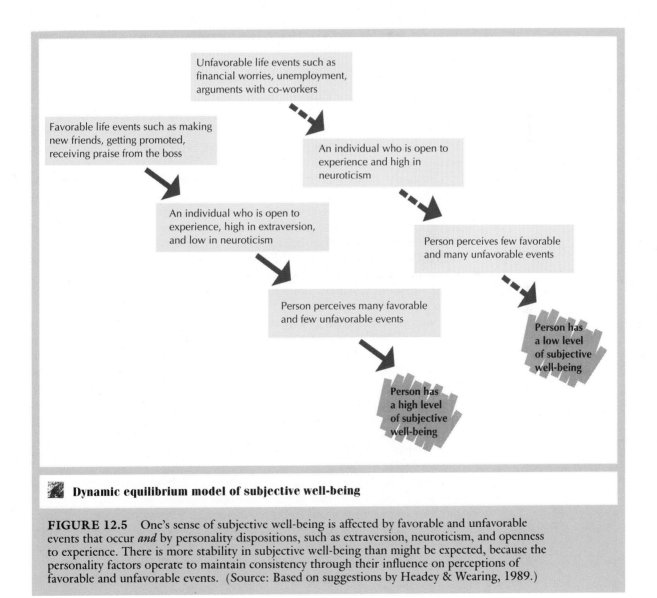

Dynamic equilibrium model of subjective well-being

FIGURE 12.5 One's sense of subjective well-being is affected by favorable and unfavorable events that occur *and* by personality dispositions, such as extraversion, neuroticism, and openness to experience. There is more stability in subjective well-being than might be expected, because the personality factors operate to maintain consistency through their influence on perceptions of favorable and unfavorable events. (Source: Based on suggestions by Headey & Wearing, 1989.)

friends, my friendships became closer) and job-related events (e.g., I was pro- moted, my boss praised my work). Those lowest in subjective well-being are usually high in neuroticism, but they are also open to experience. They indicate that they repeatedly experience unfavorable happenings, primarily related to their work (a financial crisis or financial worry, unemployment, being fired, or having arguments at work). In part, personality factors lead to particular kinds of life events, and, in part, personality factors influence how the events are perceived.

Over and above these personality effects, however, the occurrence of good and bad life events also influenced the subjective well-being of the Australian subjects. The investigators suggested that the personality variables operate to maintain stability and a sense of equilibrium. Whenever life events become excessively positive or negative, however, they can overcome this equilibrium and change the person's subjective well-being. Altogether, it appears that how a person feels about himself or herself depends both on stable personality dispositions *and* on what is happening in his or her life.

When Are Personality Variables Useful? Social psychological research does not *always* include personality variables; rather, it is necessary to identify the circumstances in which they provide useful information (Kenrick & Funder, 1988). Four guidelines suggest when traits are likely to improve our ability to predict behavior in given situations.

First, the more specific and limited the trait, the better it will predict behavior. We pointed out in Chapter 4 that specific attitudes are better behav- ioral predictors than general attitudes. An analogous rule holds true for person- ality traits. For example, a general characteristic like sociability tends to be less helpful in predicting social behavior than a specific characteristic like dating anxiety does. The more specific the trait, the more consistent the behavior across relevant situations. Thus, although people may behave differently in different social situations, their reactions to dating may be quite consistent over time (Mischel, 1985).

Second, some people behave consistently with respect to some traits, while other people behave consistently on different traits. This general proposition is known as the **metatrait hypothesis.** The personalities of different individuals consist of different sets of traits, and so a given dimension applies to some people but not to others (Baumeister & Tice, 1988; Zuckerman et al., 1989). Tice (1989) points out that few people have attitudes about *every* issue. If you have no opinion about regressive taxation, for example, that attitude plays no role in your behavior. Analogously, not all traits need be relevant to every- one. If that is so, the next problem is to determine which traits apply to which people.

One possibility is to ask people whether they exhibit a given trait. Kenrick and Stringfield (1980) had subjects list those traits on which they were most and least consistent from situation to situation. For the consistent traits, there was agreement among parents, friends, and the individual as to how the person behaved. For those traits on which the individual said he or she was inconsis- tent, parents, friends, and relatives reported very different kinds of behavior. Those who are inconsistent on a given dimension have also been found to respond differently in private than in public (Koestner, Bernieri, & Zuckerman, 1989).

Another way to determine trait relevance is to seek extremes on a dimension. On a given dimension, those at the low and high extremes behave with greater consistency than those who fall in the midrange (Paunonen, 1988). In addition, those with extreme scores (compared with those in the middle) tend to perceive the trait as an important aspect of their self-descriptions, and they engage in trait-related behavior more frequently.

A related methodology involves a statistical means of identifying those who are "traited" versus those who are "untraited" on any given personality dimension (Tellegen, 1988). Briefly, those who are traited respond to test items in a more consistent fashion than those who are untraited (Baumeister & Tice, 1988). As a result, the behavior of traited individuals is more predictable than that of untraited individuals in relevant situations.

Third, the effect of personality traits is greater when situational influences are weak than when they are strong. Monson, Hesley, and Chernick (1982) propose an inverse relationship between situational effects and personality effects. For example, a strong situational variable like attitude similarity affects attraction to such a degree that personality traits play a minor role (see Chapter 6). When there are weak situational determinants or many conflicting determinants, personality traits may be crucial in influencing behavior, as with the effects of violent films on aggression (see Chapter 10).

In general, when situational factors are numerous and complex, personality variables are most likely to operate. An example is provided by a study comparing East Indian males who intended to immigrate to Canada with those who planned to remain in India (Winchie & Carment, 1988). Because no single situational factor is responsible for such a major decision, personality variables predicted immigration behavior. For example, those planning to relocate were found to believe in a predictable world rather than one based on luck, and they were higher in *sensation-seeking* (the tendency to enjoy variety and new experiences) than those planning to remain in their homeland.

Fourth, when personality test items include references to specific situations, they are better able to predict behavior in those situations. As Gergen, Hepburn, and Fisher (1986) point out, most test items are stated in general terms rather than specifying the situational details. For example, you may be asked to agree or disagree with a statement such as "I become very angry." Your response would probably differ a great deal if the item went on to indicate specific conditions, such as "I become very angry when someone can't understand what I mean" versus "I become very angry when someone deliberately insults me." Interestingly, both children and adults rely on dispositions in describing the behavior of others, but they also modify these descriptions with reference to specific situations (Wright & Mischel, 1988).

We will now turn to the question of how personality traits are measured. It may be helpful to keep in mind that a personality test functions in the way suggested in Figure 12.6 (p. 494). That is, the test items elicit responses that reflect differences among individuals in the dispositional factors described earlier—emotions, attitudes, cognitions, expectancies, fantasies, and physiological activation. The test score summarizes the person's responses to the various items and potentially provides a way to predict responses beyond the test.

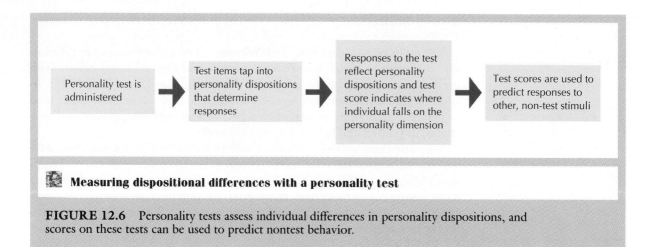

Measuring dispositional differences with a personality test

FIGURE 12.6 Personality tests assess individual differences in personality dispositions, and scores on these tests can be used to predict nontest behavior.

Measuring Personality Dispositions

Personality psychologists often take a common term in the culture, define it in detail, devise a way to measure it precisely, and use the resulting measuring instrument to make specific behavioral predictions. We will describe how this general process operates in the following **Classic Contributions** section.

FOCUS ON RESEARCH: CLASSIC CONTRIBUTIONS

Authoritarian Beliefs and Attitudes: Measuring the Predisposition to Fascist Ideology

It is not unusual for external events to provide the impetus for a given line of psychological research. This was certainly true with respect to the origin of work on the personality trait of **authoritarianism.** In the 1930s and 1940s, fascist ideology was popular in numerous countries, and many people perceived that their social and economic problems would be solved by a strong, racially pure, powerful central government able to direct and control an orderly society of obedient, law-abiding citizens. To many people, the followers of Mussolini in Italy and of Hitler in Germany seemed to represent the wave of the future in a brave new world. These fascist dictatorships (along with the military elite in imperial Japan) launched World War II and provided a frightening picture of a totalitarian environment in which censorship, propaganda, slave labor, torture, death camps, and the bombing and strafing of civilians were commonplace (see Figure 12.7).

After the war, the goal for one group of psychologists—Adorno and his colleagues (1950)—was to seek ways to prevent such events from ever happening again. Their approach was to identify a personality variable, which they labeled *authoritarianism,* that predisposed individuals to respond positively to

 Nazism's appeal and fearful consequences: The basis for psychological research on the authoritarian personality

FIGURE 12.7 Interest in the *authoritarian personality* was created by the rise of fascism in the 1930s and the fearful consequences that followed.

fascism. The long-range agenda was to (1) discover how to raise children so that they would not become authoritarian adults and (2) devise ways to alter the ideology of those possessing authoritarian tendencies. As is frequently the case in personality research, the values and beliefs of the investigators were strongly reflected in their scientific work.

The first step for Adorno and his colleagues (1950) was to agree on the attitudes and beliefs that constituted an authoritarian. They then devised test items to tap these dispositional components of potential fascists. Table 12.2 (p. 496) presents the nine characteristics that were proposed, along with corresponding test items. On each item, subjects indicate the strength of their agreement or disagreement.

To devise an effective test based on these preliminary items, the investigators administered them to large numbers of subjects and analyzed the responses statistically in order to identify those which measured a common construct. Items that did not correlate with that central core were discarded or rewritten and given to new groups of subjects. After a series of such steps, the final result was a personality test, the **F Scale,** with *F* standing for "fascism," or California F Scale because it was constructed at Berkeley.

In the following decades, the F Scale was used in hundreds of studies, and most of the findings have been consistent with the original theoretical description of this disposition. For example, the higher an individual's authoritarianism score, the more he or she holds sexist attitudes (Rigby, 1988), prefers to vote for conservative political candidates (Byrne & Przybyla, 1980), behaves in a conforming and self-protective fashion (Browning, 1983), believes the statements of TV newscasters and newspaper columnists (Levy, 1979), and obeys the orders of an authority figure to administer punishment to a stranger (Elms & Milgram, 1966). Authoritarianism is repeatedly found to affect the way children are raised, in that there is considerable emphasis on discipline and obedience (Byrne & Kelley, 1981). In addition, when both parents are high in authoritarianism, their offspring are very likely to be low in self-esteem (Buri et

THE BEHAVIORAL EFFECTS OF PERSONALITY DISPOSITIONS   **495**

TABLE 12.2   The study of authoritarianism began with an attempt to identify the basic characteristics of individuals who are predisposed to accept fascist ideology. Adorno and his colleagues identified nine components of the authoritarian personality and then constructed test items designed to tap each of the components, examples of which are shown here. Subjects respond to the items along a scale ranging from strong agreement to strong disagreement.

Characteristics of Authoritarian Personality	Test Items Constructed to Measure Characteristic
Conventionalism	A person who has bad manners, habits, and breeding can hardly expect to get along with decent people.
Submission to a strong leader	Obedience and respect for authority are the most important virtues children should learn.
Aggression	Homosexuals are hardly better than criminals and ought to be severely punished.
Destruction and cynicism	The true American way of life is disappearing so fast that force may be necessary to preserve it.
Power and toughness	People can be divided into two distinct classes: the weak and the strong.
Superstition and stereotypy	Science has its place, but there are many important things that can never possibly be understood by the human mind.
Anti-intraception	The businessman and the manufacturer are much more important to society than the artist and the professor.
Projectivity	Most people don't realize how much our lives are controlled by plots hatched in secret places.
Sex	The wild sex life of the old Greeks and Romans was tame compared to some of the goings-on in this country, even in places where people might least expect it.

al., 1988). In summary, the F Scale has proved to be a useful predictor of many social behaviors.

Determining Whether a Personality Test Is Reliable and Whether It Is Valid   Once a test has been constructed, it must be evaluated with respect to both its ability to measure the disposition in a consistent way *and* its ability to predict the appropriate behavior. A good test must do both.

Reliability is the consistency of a measuring instrument. A reliable test has internal consistency (all the items measure the same construct), consistency over time, consistency with other measures of the same construct, and consistency of scoring. These different aspects of reliability are described in Figure 12.8.

Validity indicates the extent to which a test measures what it was designed to measure. The four types of validity are described in Figure 12.9 (p. 498). When a test is used to select individuals for a specific job (e.g., personnel testing in industrial psychology) or for admission to special training (e.g., SAT scores

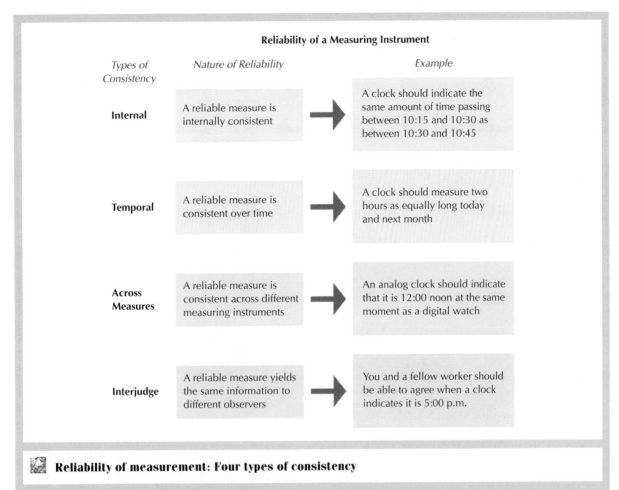

Reliability of a Measuring Instrument

Types of Consistency	Nature of Reliability	Example
Internal	A reliable measure is internally consistent	A clock should indicate the same amount of time passing between 10:15 and 10:30 as between 10:30 and 10:45
Temporal	A reliable measure is consistent over time	A clock should measure two hours as equally long today and next month
Across Measures	A reliable measure is consistent across different measuring instruments	An analog clock should indicate that it is 12:00 noon at the same moment as a digital watch
Interjudge	A reliable measure yields the same information to different observers	You and a fellow worker should be able to agree when a clock indicates it is 5:00 p.m.

Reliability of measurement: Four types of consistency

FIGURE 12.8   The reliability of an assessment device refers to its consistency of measurement. Any measuring device, whether a clock or a personality test, must be high with respect to all four types of reliability in order to be useful.

used in educational selection), two types of validity are most important: The accurate prediction of relevant criterion behavior, such as job performance, and a substantial correlation with relevant current behavior, such as grade point average. A third type of validity is primarily relevant in education when achievement is assessed, as when high school seniors are tested for their knowledge of history; this type of test must have content validity, sampling a representative array of appropriate subject matter.

For most personality tests, such as the F Scale, only a fourth type, **construct validity,** is meaningful. A test has high construct validity to the extent that it accurately predicts a variety of interrelated behaviors that form a meaningful conceptual pattern. The hypotheses that guide such research are either *deduced* from a theory or *induced* from observations (Ozer, 1989). Rather than a single number that indicates its "validity coefficient," the construct validity of

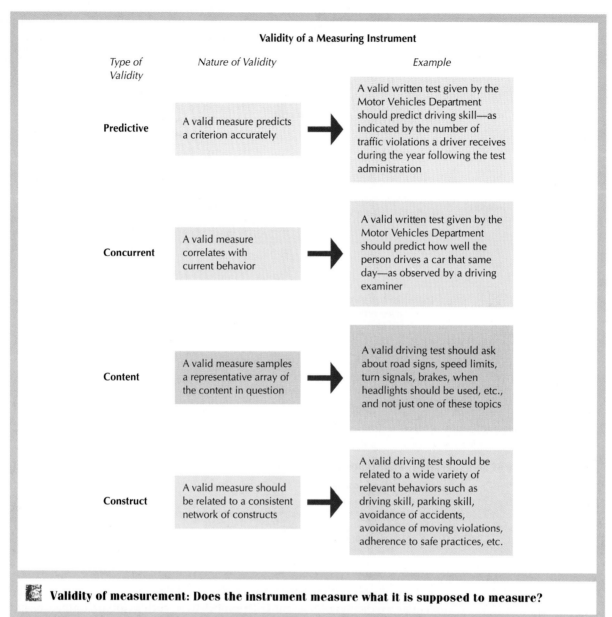

Validity of a Measuring Instrument

Type of Validity	Nature of Validity	Example
Predictive	A valid measure predicts a criterion accurately	A valid written test given by the Motor Vehicles Department should predict driving skill—as indicated by the number of traffic violations a driver receives during the year following the test administration
Concurrent	A valid measure correlates with current behavior	A valid written test given by the Motor Vehicles Department should predict how well the person drives a car that same day—as observed by a driving examiner
Content	A valid measure samples a representative array of the content in question	A valid driving test should ask about road signs, speed limits, turn signals, brakes, when headlights should be used, etc., and not just one of these topics
Construct	A valid measure should be related to a consistent network of constructs	A valid driving test should be related to a wide variety of relevant behaviors such as driving skill, parking skill, avoidance of accidents, avoidance of moving violations, adherence to safe practices, etc.

Validity of measurement: Does the instrument measure what it is supposed to measure?

FIGURE 12.9 To be useful, a test must be valid, meaning that it must accurately measure what it is intended to measure. The most relevant type of validity in personality research is *construct validity*.

a personality test is indicated by multiple research findings providing evidence that this instrument predicts relevant behavior well and that it is *not* related to irrelevant variables. The construct validity of the F Scale, for example, is indicated by hundreds of findings that make conceptual sense.

We will now discuss a few selected examples of additional personality variables that have been of interest in social psychological research.

Self-Concept as a Central Disposition

For many personality theorists, such as the late Carl Rogers, the self-concept represents the single most important aspect of one's total personality (Benesch & Page, 1989; Lynch, Norem-Hebeisen, & Gergen, 1981). It is true, as Figure 12.10 illustrates, that people are more concerned about themselves than about others. The extent to which people engage in self-focusing behavior has been studied extensively (e.g., Fenigstein, 1987; Wicklund & Gollwitzer, 1987), and women show a greater tendency to self-focus than men do (Ingram et al., 1988).

In Chapter 3 we discussed the self-concept as a cognitive framework that provides a way to organize what we know about ourselves and to process self-relevant information. Such **self-schemas** also involve specific components that operate as personality dispositions. We will discuss three of these components—individual differences in the way people evaluate themselves, in their beliefs about how effectively they can work to reach desired goals, and in the extent to which they are concerned with the effects of their behavior on others.

Self-Esteem: Evaluating Yourself

Much of the research on individual differences in self-concept has concentrated on how people evaluate themselves—**self-esteem**. In part, self-esteem depends on how closely an individual's perceived self-characteristics match his or her concept of an ideal self (Moretti & Higgins, 1990). Of all the attitudes we hold, this central attitude about self is probably the most important. Consider for a moment whether you feel relatively positive or relatively negative about who you are. In effect, do you like yourself? As we will show, research indicates that positive self-regard is beneficial in a great many ways.

The self: A central concern

FIGURE 12.10 Self-concept is a crucial aspect of human functioning in part because people are greatly concerned about themselves, including who they are, how good they feel about themselves, how effectively they function, the impression they make on others, and so forth. As this cartoon illustrates, people focus more attention on themselves than on others. (Drawing by Modell; © 1979 The New Yorker Magazine, Inc.)

Self-esteem can function as a *trait;* that is, people consistently differ in their self-evaluations. In addition, self-esteem can function as a *state,* in that external circumstances can raise or lower one's evaluations of self.

Self-Esteem as a Personality Trait   Some of the interest in self-esteem as a trait focuses on the child-rearing practices that produce positive versus negative self-views. For example, Kaplan and Pokorny (1971) found that married adults were lower in self-esteem if their childhood experiences had included such negative events as their father's death, the hospitalization of a parent for mental illness, or the remarriage of a parent. In other research with adults, low self-esteem was found to be associated with such unpleasant childhood experiences as worries about school grades, fears of parental punishment, and the self-perception of being physically unattractive (Kaplan & Pokorny, 1970). Also, children tend to evaluate themselves in part on the basis of how they believe their parents evaluate them, but they are not very accurate about what their parents think (Felson, 1989).

Such research provides evidence that a variety of negative events and negative perceptions can convince a young person that he or she is less worthwhile than others. More recent research indicates that high self-esteem is based on positive feelings about oneself, self-perceptions of one's strengths as well as weaknesses, and the tendency to evaluate the strengths as more important than the weaknesses (Pelham & Swann, 1989).

The negative health effects of stressful life events (failure on an exam, loss of a job, etc.) are discussed in Chapter 14. It should be noted here, however, that even positive events (marriage, a promotion, etc.) have a negative health effect for those *low* in self-esteem (Brown & McGill, 1989). It seems that for these individuals who are negative about themselves, positive events are inconsistent with their self-concepts. This inconsistency is stressful and results in illness.

An individual's self-esteem is associated with a great many other attributes. As you might expect, those low in self-esteem report more negative emotions, such as depression (Strauman & Higgins, 1988). In contrast, those high in self-acceptance often perform better academically, with the effect varying as a function of age and educational demands (Skaalvik & Hagtvet, 1990), believe that those who expend the most effort have the highest ability (Baumgardner & Levy, 1988), are better adjusted psychologically (Davids & Lawton, 1961), are less afraid of failure (Smith & Teevan, 1971) and of death (Buzzanga et al., 1989), express anger appropriately (Worchel, 1958), and engage in self-enhancing behaviors, such as evaluating their own group's work positively (Brown, Collins, & Schmidt, 1988). High self-esteem is also associated with the tendency to attribute failure to external rather than internal causes (Fitch, 1970) and to perform better following either success or failure (Shrauger & Rosenberg, 1970).

Positive and negative evaluations have different effects on those high versus low in self-esteem. Because people with low self-esteem are less certain of their self-worth, they are more affected by and concerned with social evaluations. Baumgardner, Kaufman, and Levy (1989) find that individuals with low self-esteem react by complimenting sources of positive feedback and derogating sources of negative feedback—attempts at self-enhancement. Those high in self-esteem, in contrast, can cope with both kinds of feedback, and their social skills are better. As a result, they are aware that it is neither socially desirable to derogate the source of negative feedback nor necessary to compliment the source of positive feedback.

The stability of one's self-esteem also affects behavior. For example, anger and hostility are experienced most by those with high but unstable self-esteem and least by those with stable high self-esteem. Individuals with either stable or unstable low self-esteem fall between these two extremes (Kernis, Grannemann, & Barclay, 1989).

Generally, however, those with high self-esteem function better in interpersonal situations than do those with low self-esteem. This does not mean, however, that positive self-statements are socially helpful. Holtgraves and Srull (1989) report that others do not respond positively when an individual spontaneously says good things about himself or herself, such as "My IQ as a child was 133." Favorable self-statements have a positive effect only when they are made in response to a direct question ("What was your IQ when you were tested?"). Nevertheless, Finch and Cialdini (1989) find that people regularly strive to present somewhat irrational positive information about themselves by basking in reflected glory. Examples include wearing one's school sweatshirt only when that institution has a winning team or pointing out a connection between oneself and someone who is famous ("Frank Lloyd Wright grew up just a few miles from where I was born").

Situational Effects on Self-Esteem Despite the general stability of our self-esteem, many situations can make us feel—at least temporarily—better or worse about ourselves (see Figure 12.11). For example, self-esteem drops when children first leave elementary school to enter junior high, but gradually returns to

When good things happen, self-esteem increases

FIGURE 12.11   Self-esteem is affected by external events, and it tends to increase following experiences of success and accomplishment.

normal during the seventh grade (Eccles et al., 1989). Then, self-esteem rises even more in the years between adolescence and young adulthood (O'Malley & Bachman, 1983).

In an experimental setting, evaluations of an individual's performance as good have been found to raise self-esteem; a bad evaluation, to lower it (Flippo & Lewinsohn, 1971; Videbeck, 1960). Failure does not affect self-esteem if the subject believes he or she has been drinking alcohol, in which case the poor performance is attributed to the drinks (Isleib, Vuchinich, & Tucker, 1988), a finding that is consistent with our discussion of self-handicapping in Chapter 2. Mood induction, too, affects self-esteem; it is raised by a positive mood and lowered by a negative one (Esses, 1989).

In field studies, actual success experiences raise self-esteem. Examples include learning how to swim in summer camp (Koocher, 1971), being positively evaluated by a partner after the first date (Coombs, 1969), participating successfully in several weeks of strength training (Holloway, Beuter, & Duda, 1988), and having pleasant experiences in college (Weir & Okun, 1989). For low-achieving high school males, participation in a twenty-six-day Outward Bound program led to an increase in self-esteem, an improvement that lasted at least eighteen months (Marsh, Richards, & Barnes, 1986a, b).

The reverse is also true: Such real-life problems as the death of a close friend or a serious illness in the family can lower self-esteem (Kaplan, 1970). A study of young Dutch girls (ages eleven to sixteen) unexpectedly found lower self-

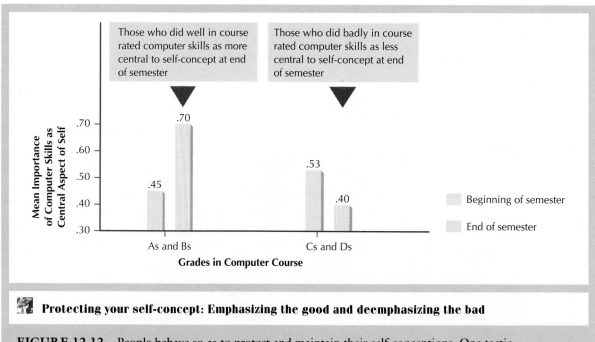

Protecting your self-concept: Emphasizing the good and deemphasizing the bad

FIGURE 12.12 People behave so as to protect and maintain their self-conceptions. One tactic for those with high self-esteem is to perceive positive information about self as more crucial than negative information. In one investigation of how this process operates, students who received *A*s or *B*s in a computer course were compared with those receiving *C*s or *D*s. The central importance of computer skills to self increased for those with good grades and decreased for those with bad grades. (Source: Based on data from Hill, Smith, & Lewicki, 1989.)

esteem among those enrolled in professional ballet schools than among non-dancers; this finding was attributed to the frequency of negative evaluations and criticism common in ballet classes (Bakker, 1988).

Interestingly, people are often able to protect themselves from negative information by shifting the importance they place on various aspects of their self-image. If negative information is received about some skill, for example, that skill is devalued, permitting the person to feel as positively as possible about himself or herself. Hill, Smith, and Lewicki (1989) reported that the central importance of "computer skills" as a self-attribute increased among students receiving *A*s and *B*s in an introductory computer science course and decreased among students receiving *C*s and *D*s. Figure 12.12 shows these shifts.

In addition to personal self-esteem, people also differ in evaluating the groups to which they belong—*collective self-esteem*. For example, how positively or negatively do you rate your gender, race, religious denomination, nationality, fellow college students, and so forth? Crocker and Luhtanen (1990) found that those highest in collective self-esteem concerning a group to which they belonged react to threats to that group by derogating outsiders and enhancing fellow members.

In the **Cutting Edge** section that follows, we will describe research that provides insight into how positive and negative self-attitudes are maintained in everyday life.

FOCUS ON RESEARCH: THE CUTTING EDGE

Maintaining Positive (or Negative) Self-Esteem: Illusions and Overgeneralizations

We know that positive experiences tend to raise self-esteem, while negative events tend to lower it. Nevertheless, those who are ordinarily positive about themselves seem to be surprisingly able to withstand negative events while maintaining a positive view of themselves. In an analogous way, those with low self-esteem manage to retain a negative self-perception despite positive experiences. How is such consistency possible? Recent evidence indicates that those low in self-esteem and those high in self-esteem process information in different ways.

Though it may at first seem odd, Taylor and his colleagues (1989) propose that normal mental functioning is characterized by the ability to maintain positive illusions to counter negative information. That is, we function best if we hold extremely positive self-conceptions even if they are unrealistic, have an exaggerated belief in our ability to control events even though this notion is incorrect, and hold optimistic views about what the future holds even though that assessment is inaccurate. Lily Tomlin, in her role as Trudy the Bag Lady, humorously sums up the importance of holding illusions:

> I refuse to be intimidated by reality anymore. After all, what is reality anyway? Nothin' but a collective hunch. . . . I made some studies, and reality is the leading cause of stress amongst those in touch with it. . . . Now, since I put reality on a back burner, my days are jam-packed and fun-filled. . . . When I think of the fun I missed, I try not to be bitter (Wagner, 1986).

Illusions are adaptive and beneficial because they enable people to maintain a positive view of the world. When negative information is encountered, those high in self-esteem simply screen it out (e.g., an unpleasant remark by a casual acquaintance is explained away, forgotten, or reinterpreted) so long as it has no implications for future behavior. When negative information is relevant, however, such persons use it to make an adaptive response (e.g., when a tooth is causing pain, they make a dental appointment). Snyder (1989) characterizes this tendency as involving hope for that which is good and finding excuses for that which is bad.

When, however, a person's perception of life events is extremely accurate, the result is depression (Baumeister, 1989). This idea helps explain why a very negative experience—such as being the victim of a terrible crime, a serious illness, or a natural disaster—can be devastating. The person's illusions are shattered, and it is no longer possible to maintain an unrealistically positive view of life (Janoff-Bulman, 1989).

Low self-esteem and negative feelings are also maintained over time. Burns and Seligman (1989) compared the way a group of elderly subjects (average age: seventy-two) currently explained negative events with how they had done so in letters and diaries they'd written a half-century earlier. The type of explanation used by an individual remained stable over this period. Not only was a negative, hopeless pattern (e.g., "I'm really no good for anything," "I feel

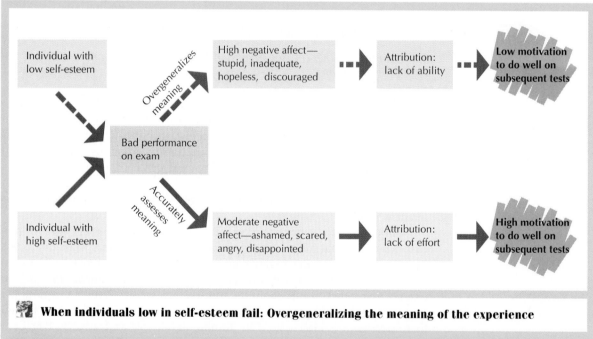

When individuals low in self-esteem fail: Overgeneralizing the meaning of the experience

FIGURE 12.13 Students who did well on a course examination expressed positive affect afterward, while those who did badly expressed negative affect. Those low in self-esteem reported more negative affect than did those high in self-esteem. Those low in self-esteem who did badly also overgeneralized the meaning of the negative experience as reflecting on their ability to do well now and in the future; in addition, failure decreased their motivation to perform better on future exams. (Source: Based on data from Kernis, Brockner, & Frankel, 1989.)

powerless") consistent across five decades, but this pattern has also been shown to be associated with depression (Sweeney, Anderson, & Bailey, 1986), poor physical health (Peterson, Seligman, & Vaillant, 1988), and low achievement (Seligman & Schulman, 1986). This negative view of oneself becomes a consistent maladaptive way of responding to negative life events, with negative consequences.

These findings are consistent with other research indicating that people with low self-esteem react badly to failure and to negative feedback of all kinds. One reason for the devastating effects of aversive experiences on people who have low self-esteem is their tendency to *overgeneralize* on the basis of failure. Kernis, Brockner, and Frankel (1989) reported, for example, that a student who did not do well on one midterm exam in an organizational behavior course concluded "I am not suited for a career in management" rather than "I did poorly on this particular test." These investigators found that such overgeneralization is characteristic of individuals with low self-esteem.

Kernis and his colleagues (1989) studied a large group of male and female undergraduates enrolled in introductory psychology who did either relatively well or relatively badly on the first exam. The students low in self-esteem experienced more negative affect than those high in self-esteem did when they received low test scores. Specifically, the former described their feelings in the terms indicated in Figure 12.13. In addition, those low in self-esteem responded to their poor performance by being less motivated to do well on subsequent tests; they also blamed their test scores on lack of ability rather than lack of effort. Altogether, low self-esteem and the tendency to overgeneralize the meaning of a single low grade were strongly related.

As with high self-esteem, an individual's low self-esteem is perpetuated by the way he or she processes information. The tendency to overgeneralize traps the person in a vicious cycle of negative self-perceptions and self-defeating cognitions. To summarize, one's level of self-esteem is maintained by overly positive illusions at one extreme and overly negative generalizations at the other extreme.

Self-Efficacy: Estimating Your Ability to Get Things Done

One of the elements of each person's self-concept is a constellation of beliefs and expectancies about his or her ability to deal effectively with tasks and to accomplish what needs to be done. Bandura (1977) labeled this component of one's self-concept **self-efficacy.**

When self-efficacy is low, one result is a negative mood. In a study of seriously ill patients with kidney disease, perceived self-efficacy and mood were assessed (Devins et al., 1982). The findings indicated that the lower the individual's self-efficacy, the greater the feelings of depression and helplessness, and the lower the self-esteem. Adjusting to the experience of having an abortion is also related to self-efficacy; coping is better when self-efficacy is high (Mueller & Major, 1989).

Self-Efficacy and Performance In working at various kinds of tasks, those high in self-efficacy are found to perform best (Garland et al., 1988). A central element seems to be the presence of a clear image of good performance and its outcome. In the Soviet Union, an athlete is shown videotapes of his or her best

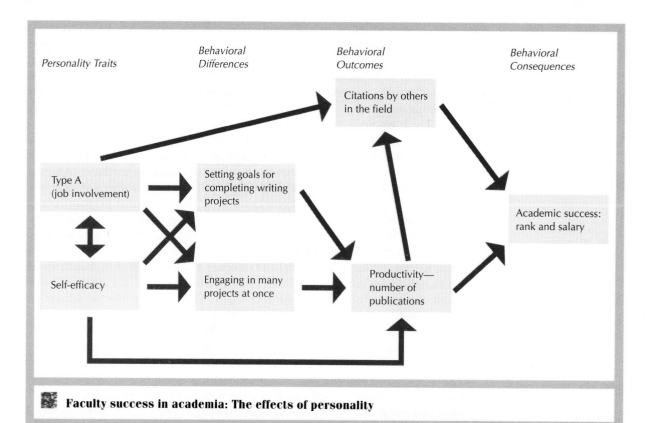

Behavioral
Differences

Behavioral
Outcomes

Behavioral
Consequences

Citations by others
in the field

Type A
(job involvement)

Setting goals for
completing writing
projects

Self-efficacy

Engaging in many
projects at once

Productivity—
number of
publications

Academic success:
rank and salary

Faculty success in academia: The effects of personality

FIGURE 12.14 Personality variables are found to be useful in predicting the success (rank and salary) of faculty members at a research-oriented institution. Those high in Type A characteristics and in self-efficacy engage in behaviors that directly or indirectly lead to success. (Source: Based on data from Taylor et al., 1984.)

performance, edited to make it look even better (Feltz, 1982). Presumably, this practice helps the competitor form a strong image of the necessary behavior. The result is an increased feeling of self-efficacy and an improved performance.

Performance by university professors (as indicated by rank and salary) has been found to be positively related to self-efficacy and to another personality disposition, Type A behavior (see Chapters 10 and 14). Taylor et al. (1984) predicted that males and females in various disciplines in academia would be most successful if they were high on both dimensions. As Figure 12.14 shows, these personality characteristics affect a variety of behaviors that are necessary for academic success. Those high in the job involvement aspects of Type A behavior also tend to be high in self-efficacy. One or both of these variables were found to predict such actions as setting goals and engaging in multiple projects; those behaviors, in turn, led to high levels of productivity and to a professor's work being cited by others. Finally, rank and salary were found to be directly affected by productivity and citations (along with a different kind of variable, age). The investigators pointed out that in other fields involving less freedom to set goals and to work at one's own pace, these personality measures may have little to do with success.

An important aspect of self-efficacy for those working in a university setting is that much of the crucial behavior is done alone (e.g., writing grant applications, scientific articles, and books). One situational determinant of a person's perceived ability to accomplish his or her goals is group size. Feelings of efficacy decrease in large groups (Kerr, 1989). In general, people can get more done if a problem is subdivided into small parts that can be worked on separately by small subgroups or by single individuals.

Self-Efficacy and the Ability to Tolerate Pain   Surprisingly, perceived self-efficacy actually increases pain tolerance. Litt (1988) used a *cold-pressor test* in which subjects place an arm in ice-cold water for a series of trials to determine how well they can tolerate this unpleasant experience. Self-efficacy perceptions were also manipulated. Those highest in self-efficacy were able to tolerate the pain of the cold water for longer periods of time than those low in perceived self-efficacy. How, you may wonder, could self-perceptions influence the ability to tolerate pain? Further research indicated a fascinating physiological process.

Bandura and his colleagues (1988) induced perceptions of high or low mathematical self-efficacy in subjects and then gave them mathematical problems to perform. Those with high perceived self-efficacy felt much less stress and less autonomic arousal than those with low perceived self-efficacy. Further, these researchers discovered that self-efficacy enables people to cope with stressors because it activates the production of *endogenous opioids* that block the transmission of pain and thus allow the individual to function more effectively. In other words, when a person has confidence in his or her ability, the body releases a safe, natural painkiller that enhances performance and reduces stress.

Self-Monitoring: Sensitivity to the Reactions of Other People

Snyder and his colleagues have identified **self-monitoring** as a major component of self-related behavior (Gangestad & Snyder, 1985; Snyder & Ickes, 1985). Individuals high in self-monitoring regulate their behavior on the basis of the immediate situation. They pay attention to what is appropriate in a given social setting and then behave accordingly. Those low in self-monitoring, in contrast, are inclined to act on the basis of internal factors rather than in response to the external situation.

Measuring Self-Monitoring Tendencies   Differences along this dimension are assessed on the **Self-Monitoring Scale** (Snyder, 1974). With this instrument, subjects respond to a series of items such as the following (high self-monitors tend to agree with the first two and to disagree with the second two):

> When I am uncertain how to act in social situations, I look to the behavior of others for cues.

> In different situations and with different people, I often act like very different persons.

> My behavior is usually an expression of my true inner feelings, attitudes, and beliefs.

> I would not change my opinions (or the way I do things) to please someone else or to win their favor.

Lennox and Wolfe (1984) criticized the Self-Monitoring Scale as overly broad. To correct this feature, they constructed a revised scale that measures only two dimensions: sensitivity to the expressive behavior of others ("I can usually tell when I've said something inappropriate by reading it in the listener's eyes") and the ability to modify one's self-presentation ("I find that I can adjust my behavior to suit different people and different situations"). Despite this and other proposals to modify the scale (e.g., Briggs & Cheek, 1988; Montag & Levin, 1990), Snyder and Gangestad (1986) defend its construct validity.

Earlier in this chapter, we discussed the consistency of behavior across situations and across time. As you might guess from the description of self-monitoring, low self-monitors are much more consistent than high self-monitors (Shaffer, Smith, & Tomarelli, 1982). In some respects, those who score low on the scale behave according to trait theory while high self-monitors respond to situational demands. Another aspect of their differences is that private attitudes and public behaviors correspond for low self-monitors but not for high self-monitors (Zanna & Olson, 1982). What differences in social behavior might we expect as a function of differences in self-monitoring?

Interpersonal Behavior   When they engage in casual conversations, low self-monitors are more likely to speak in the first person (*I, me, my,* etc.), while high self-monitors speak in the third person (*he, she, they,* etc.), according to research conducted by Ickes, Reidhead, and Patterson (1986). The explanation is that those who score high in this dimension are most concerned about what others do and how they react; low scorers, in contrast, concentrate on their own behavior and reactions.

The importance of others to high self-monitors was shown in an experiment in which subjects were asked to play the role of a morally reprehensible person (Jones, Brenner, & Knight, 1990). In response to feedback from a simulated audience, high self-monitors were most positive when they succeeded in playing a "bad guy." Low self-monitors responded most positively when they failed in pretending to be such a person.

On what basis do you decide which friends you want to be with when you engage in a particular activity? Whom do you ask to play tennis, for example? Research suggests that if you are a high self-monitor, your choice will be based on how well the other person plays tennis; if you are a low self-monitor, your choice is based on how much you like the other person (Snyder, Gangestad, & Simpson, 1983).

Self-monitoring also affects dating relationships. Do you interact with your partner regardless of the activity you engage in, or do you go from partner to partner on the basis of what you are going to do? Snyder and Simpson (1984) expected low self-monitors to prefer being with their dating partners no matter what and high self-monitors to select partners on the basis of the activity (sailing, bowling, tennis, etc.). As you can see in Figure 12.15, this is precisely the pattern found among undergraduates.

One way to view these very different responses to a dating partner is in terms of commitment. High self-monitors do not appear to feel especially committed to one person. In fact, when Snyder and Simpson (1984) asked subjects about giving up their current dating partner in favor of someone else of the opposite sex, high self-monitors expressed a preference for someone new, while low self-monitors indicated a desire to stay with their present partners. On the basis of such findings, it is not surprising that those high in self-monitoring date nearly twice as many different partners over a year's period as those low in self-monitoring. These findings raise the possibility that low self-

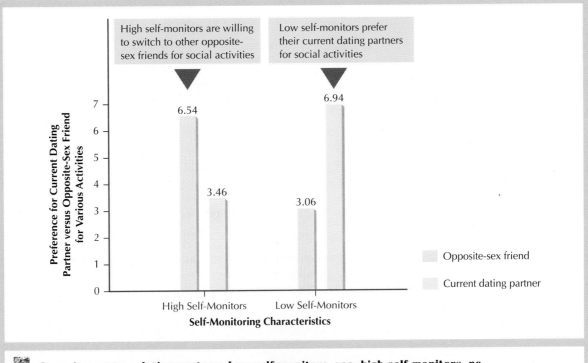

High self-monitors are willing to switch to other opposite-sex friends for social activities

Low self-monitors prefer their current dating partners for social activities

Opposite-sex friend

Current dating partner

Commitment to a dating partner: Low self-monitors, yes; high self-monitors, no

FIGURE 12.15 Those high in *self-monitoring* and those low in this dimension respond quite differently to their opposite-sex partners. Low self-monitors express more commitment and prefer to be with their partners, regardless of the activity involved. High self-monitors, in contrast, are much less committed to their partners and actually prefer to be with different people for various activities. (Source: Based on data from Snyder & Simpson, 1984.)

monitors might be more committed as marriage partners and less likely to divorce; however, additional research is needed to pursue that question.

The seemingly superficial response to a dating partner led to another kind of prediction about high self-monitors: that outward appearance is more important to them than it is to low self-monitors, a hypothesis that was confirmed (Glick, 1985; Snyder, Berscheid, & Glick, 1985). In an experimental setting, Glick, DeMorest, and Hotze (1988) asked subjects to determine which pairs among a group of males and females would be most compatible. High self-monitors tended to match pairs in terms of attractiveness, while low self-monitors matched them on the basis of sense of humor, personality, and common interests.

High self-monitors attend to surface qualities even in evaluating consumer products; they prefer attractive products to a greater extent than do low self-monitors (DeBono & Snyder, 1989). Zuckerman, Gioioso, and Tellini (1988) found that, in a similar way, high self-monitors preferred advertising based on a product's image and extrinsic rewards ("Heineken—you are moving up") versus advertising based on quality and intrinsic rewards ("Heineken—you can taste the difference").

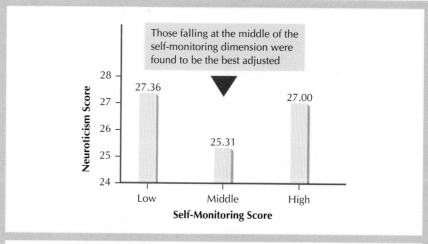

Those falling at the middle of the self-monitoring dimension were found to be the best adjusted

Adjustment and self-monitoring: The golden mean is best

FIGURE 12.16   The extremes of self-monitoring behavior consist of individuals who are either too responsive to the present situation (high self-monitors) or too unresponsive to it (low self-monitors). As indicated by a measure of neuroticism, the best adjusted individuals are those falling in the middle of the self-monitoring dimension. (Source: Based on data from Miller & Thayer, 1988.)

Maladjustment and Self-Monitoring   Would you guess that high self-monitors are better adjusted or less well adjusted than low self-monitors?

Miller and Thayer (1988, 1989) suggested that individuals at either extreme of this dimension would be less well adjusted than those scoring near the middle of the scale. High self-monitors fluctuate from situation to situation like chameleons, while low self-monitors remain rigidly the same, regardless of whether doing so is appropriate. To test this *curvilinear* hypothesis of the relationship between self-monitoring and adjustment, the investigators assessed undergraduates with respect to self-monitoring and neuroticism. As shown in Figure 12.16, the hypothesis was confirmed: The middle scorers were found to be less neurotic than those falling at either extreme of the self-monitoring dimension.

Individual Differences in Beliefs and Attitudes

Literally hundreds of personality dimensions have been included in social psychological research, and it is obviously impossible to discuss all of them in one chapter. Instead, we will summarize research concentrating on two such variables: **locus of control** and **erotophobia**.

Locus of Control: Beliefs about Internal versus External Responsibility

One recurring theme in social psychological research is the extent to which people perceive themselves as in control of events. In some situations, you obviously do have control—you can decide whether or not to turn on your TV set and which channel to watch. In other situations, you obviously do not have control—as a passenger on an airplane, your safety depends entirely on the actions of other people, including mechanics, air traffic controllers, and the pilot.

Where control is less obvious, some individuals generally believe that their own actions play a large role in maximizing good outcomes and minimizing bad outcomes, a concept termed **internal locus of control.** Others believe that what happens to them depends on luck, fate, and other uncontrollable outside forces, an idea known as **external locus of control** (see Figure 12.17). Locus of control was first identified as a personality dimension by Rotter (1966), and its effect on many aspects of social behavior has been described by Strickland (1989).

Measuring Individual Differences in Locus of Control   According to Rotter's theoretical system, behavior occurs as a function of the individual's *expectancy* that a given act will result in reinforcement (or punishment) and the *value* or importance he or she assigns to that particular reinforcement (or punishment). People are assumed to act so as to receive highly valued rewards and to avoid extremely unpleasant punishments.

Rotter (1966) proposed that each of us develops a broad set of beliefs about who or what controls such rewards and punishments in our lives. Some

"*When I grow up, I hope to win the lottery.*"

Externality: Success depends on luck, not skill and effort

FIGURE 12.17   An individual whose locus of control is external assumes that rewards and punishments occur as a function of external events over which he or she has no control. This little boy seems to assume that internal factors play no role in financial success, and so the best he can do is hope to be lucky. (Drawing by Mulligan; © 1984 The New Yorker Magazine, Inc.)

develop an internal orientation, believing that skill, hard work, foresight, and responsible behavior will lead to positive outcomes. Others develop an external orientation, believing that events are determined by chance, the actions of others, or unknown and uncontrollable factors.

To measure individual differences on this dimension, the **I-E Scale** requires subjects to choose between two alternatives on each item. For instance, in the following examples, do you believe item a or item b to be more true?

(1) _____ a. Many of the unhappy things in people's lives are partly due to bad luck.

_____ b. People's misfortunes result from the mistakes they make.

(2) _____ a. In the case of the well-prepared student there is rarely such a thing as an unfair test.

_____ b. Many times exam questions tend to be so unrelated to course work that studying is really useless.

As with most personality characteristics, research on locus of control has focused on how these belief systems develop and on how they affect behavior. Some investigators have proposed that a series of I-E scales dealing with specific situations would yield better predictions (Coombs & Schroeder, 1988). In a similar vein, Bryant (1989) has presented a four-factor model of perceived control. People differ not only in their perceived ability to avoid negative events and to obtain positive events but also in their perceived ability to cope with negative events when they can't be avoided and to savor positive events when they are obtained. According to this view, subjective distress is experienced when avoiding and coping aren't perceived as controllable, while those who perceive themselves as being able to obtain positive outcomes and to savor them are most likely to report a sense of subjective well-being.

Developing Expectancies about Control An internal locus is most likely to develop if a child's mother expects and encourages independent behavior beginning at an early age (Chance, 1965). In addition, parents of internals (those with an internal locus of control) are found to be protective, affectionate, and approving of their offspring (Katkovsky, Crandall, & Good, 1967). It seems that the parents of internals expect a lot from their children and are affectionately involved in rewarding their activities. The most important thing the child learns is that reinforcements are *contingent* on behavior.

Externals, in contrast, experience more restrictive parental control, rejection, and hostile criticism (Davis & Phares, 1969; Johnson & Kilmann, 1975). Additionally, in large families the last-born child tends to be more external than his or her siblings (Walter & Ziegler, 1980), possibly because the youngest and smallest family member has less experience with independence and fewer opportunities to exert control.

Behavioral Effects of Internal versus External Locus of Control Most often, internality is found to be a more positive asset than externality. Among children, for example, those who are external are found to be neurotic, impulsive, and hyperactive (Linn & Hodge, 1982; Raine, Roger, & Venables, 1982); among adults, those who are external tend to be depressed (Burger, 1984). A cross-cultural study found that among residents of the United States, India, and Hong Kong, those who were externally oriented also engaged in such self-destructive behaviors as smoking, excessive drinking, and unsafe driving (Kelley et al., 1986).

Internality is positively related to school performance, cognitive development, and various kinds of achievement in several cultures (Bar-Tal & Bar-Zohar, 1977; Findley & Cooper, 1983; Shute, Howard, & Steyaert, 1984; Tyler, Labarta, & Otero, 1986). Even in graduate school, internals do well; they are more likely than externals to complete their requirements and obtain a Ph.D. (Otten, 1977).

In the United States, the academic difficulties of various disadvantaged groups seem to rest in part on their tendency to develop an orientation involving external locus of control (Lefcourt, 1982). Even among students identified as leaders in their third- and sixth-grade classes, whites are more internal than blacks (Brown et al., 1984).

In competitive situations, those who are most external tend to give up; in cooperative situations, however, they do as well as internals (Nowicki, 1982). Job satisfaction is higher among internals than among externals (Cummins, 1989). In social interactions, internals are more likely than externals to take steps to influence the outcome, in that they resist pressures to conform (Lefcourt, 1982) and, among females, use more cosmetics than externals do (Cash, Rissi, & Chapman, 1985). Among the consequences of these differences in interpersonal behavior is that internals have more frequent and more satisfying interactions with members of the opposite sex (Catania, McDermott, & Wood, 1984).

As the following **Applied Side** section shows, beliefs about one's power to control events play a crucial role in influencing individuals to engage in social activism.

ON THE APPLIED SIDE

Social Activism: Beliefs about Personal Power and Social Injustice

Why do some individuals leave their comfortable, everyday lives to become active participants in attempting to bring about changes in society? In most instances, such behavior involves a degree of sacrifice and sometimes danger. The action can range from something relatively simple, such as helping to prepare a Thanksgiving meal for nursing home residents, to something quite dramatic, such as attempting to change (or even overthrow) one's government (see Figure 12.18, p. 514).

One answer is that those with an internal locus of control believe their actions can bring about a worthwhile outcome, and so they act. For example, Gore and Rotter (1963) found that black college students who in 1961 were willing to participate in civil rights activities—attending a rally, signing a petition, or taking a "Freedom Ride" across the South—were higher in internality than those who were not interested in participating. Other research also confirmed that black activists were more internally oriented than black students who were not involved in the fight for civil rights (Strickland, 1984).

At the same time, those who are most internal hold positive beliefs about the motives and the fairness of people in positions of authority, such as the

Engaging in social action to improve society: Difficulties and dangers

FIGURE 12.18 In order to take part in some action to bring about improvements in society (social activism), an individual must be highly motivated to act. Social action includes simple steps, such as signing a petition; more time-consuming behavior, such as doing volunteer work for the Special Olympics; and potentially life-threatening activity, such as attempting to bring about major changes in society as the student demonstrators in Beijing are doing.

police, military personnel, and teachers (Heaven, 1988). Internals, more than externals, believe in a just world (see Chapter 6).

Altogether, it appears that those who become socially active must have two characteristics: the belief that they have the power to affect outcomes (internality) and the belief that something is wrong with current societal practices (injustice).

O'Neill et al. (1988) tested the general hypothesis that people participate in social activism when they believe in both personal power and social injustice. These investigators used a modified version of the I-E Scale, along with an Injustice Scale that contained such items as "Our courts often let the guilty go free while they convict innocent people." In a construct validity study, those scoring high on the Injustice Scale were less likely to blame the victim in a case of acquaintance rape than were those scoring low. In effect, then, those who feel that the world is frequently unjust are more likely to side with the victim.

To study social activism, the investigators selected a group of people who were highly involved in taking action—board members who directed a transition house for battered women. Other subjects were those not involved in social action, including single mothers who applied for help from Big Brothers/Big Sisters and a group of introductory psychology students.

As summarized in Figure 12.19, the data supported the hypothesis that socially active people are more likely than others to believe in their power to control events *and* to believe that injustice is common in our society. The investigators pointed out that either dispositional variable alone may be insufficient to precipitate action. Thus, many who are disadvantaged may be firmly convinced that they live in an unjust world, yet also express defeatism and believe nothing they do will improve their lives. In contrast, many middle- and upper-class citizens believe that they have the power to bring about change, yet

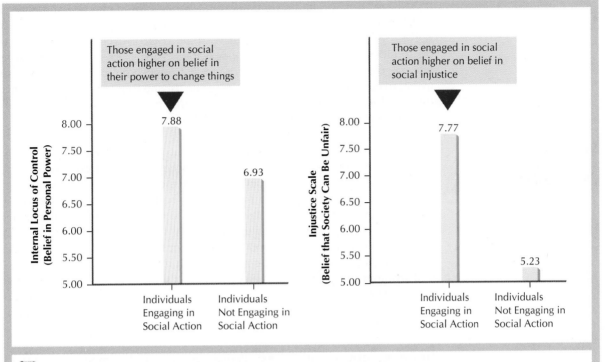

Social activism: Belief in internal control and belief in injustice

FIGURE 12.19 To engage in social activism, an individual must believe (1) that he or she has the power to bring about changes in society *and* (2) that there is injustice in society that should be changed. A comparison of socially active and non-socially active individuals reveals differences in the strength of precisely those beliefs about personal power and social injustice. (Source: Based on data from O'Neill et al., 1988.)

also feel their society is fine as it is. Only when a person's beliefs include both confidence in one's power and a sense of injustice is social activism likely to occur.

Changes in Locus of Control Though locus of control is a relatively stable characteristic (Wolfle & Robertshaw, 1982), anyone's orientation may change as the result of certain experiences. For example, during the childhood years, internality increases with age (Penk, 1969), presumably because those who are older do in fact have greater control over their lives. Similarly, when adults are given a position of responsibility (such as an administrative job), internality increases (Harvey, 1971).

When lives are disrupted by uncontrollable events, the opposite change occurs—people become more external in orientation. Examples include women who have been physically abused by their husbands (Cheney & Bleker, 1982), who have been recently divorced (Doherty, 1983) or who have lost their jobs (Baubion-Broye, Megemont, & Sellinger, 1989). Both males and females increase in externality as they reach old age (Lumpkin, 1986).

Change can also be brought about deliberately. Both children and college undergraduates (Reimanis, 1971) have been taught to perceive themselves as active, optimistic individuals who have some control over what happens to them, rather than seeing themselves as helpless pawns. As they become more internal, college students become more likely to switch out of an unsatisfactory major, to change unpleasant living arrangements, and to inform instructors that they need increased feedback. To the extent that people become better able to control their own lives, internality is an obvious advantage.

Erotophobia: Generalized Attitudes about Sexuality

In Chapter 4, we described how attitudes are acquired on the basis of classical conditioning, instrumental conditioning, modeling, and direct experience. People learn to respond to sexual cues in precisely these same ways. A young child may quickly discover that certain parts of the body should not be exposed or discussed, that a negative response to sexual scenes on TV amuses his or her parents, or that parents kiss or embrace only when they believe no one is looking. A child may also discover at some point that it feels good to touch the forbidden parts of the body. The result of such mixed experiences is a generalized attitudinal response to sexuality that falls at some point along a continuum ranging from extremely positive (**erotophilia**) to extremely negative (**erotophobia**). Differences among individuals in their sexual attitudes have been found to affect a great many sex-related behaviors.

Measuring Attitudes about Sex   Perhaps because of the emotional nature of the topic, many aspects of sexuality (nudity, pornography, prostitution, homosexuality, masturbation, premarital intercourse, contraception, etc.) tend to elicit a generalized positive response in some individuals and a generalized negative response in others. As a result, the two primary measures of sexual attitudes—the **Sex Guilt Scale** (Mosher, 1968) and the **Sexual Opinion Survey** (Fisher et al., 1986)—ask subjects their positive or negative views about a series of sex-related topics; these responses are then added to yield a total score.

As with all personality dimensions, people fall along a continuum, and only a few individuals are positive about *every* aspect of sexuality (erotophiles) and only a few are negative about *every* aspect (erotophobes). Nevertheless, the closer one falls to the erotophobic extreme, the more negative the emotional response to erotic cues (anxiety, guilt, shame, embarrassment, etc.), the more such cues function as punishment rather than reinforcement, and the more the individual attempts to avoid them. Those falling toward the erotophilic extreme are more likely to respond to sex-related material with positive emotions (curiosity, enjoyment, pleasure, excitement, etc.), to react to such cues as rewards, and to engage in approach behavior (Byrne & Schulte, 1990; Griffitt & Kaiser, 1978; Kelley, 1985a; O'Grady, 1982).

Effects of Erotophobia on Sex-Related Behaviors   In an experimental setting, the higher an individual scores in erotophobia, the more negatively he or she responds to sexual films or stories (Kelley, 1985b; Mosher & O'Grady, 1979). Given free choice as to how much time they spend looking at explicit sexual slides, erotophobic individuals prefer shorter viewing times and recall the content less accurately than those who are erotophilic (Becker & Byrne, 1985). In everyday life, sexual attitudes exert a similar effect in determining experiences with and reactions to magazines, movies, television shows, and books containing sexual content.

In imaginative activity, those who are erotophobic create less explicit and more negatively toned erotic fantasies (Kelley, 1985c; Walker, 1983), and they are less aroused by such fantasies (Green & Mosher, 1985). When asked to draw a nude male and a nude female, those who are relatively erotophobic create less explicit drawings with less detail than those who are relatively erotophilic (Przybyla, Byrne, & Allgeier, 1988).

As these various findings suggest, sexual attitudes also affect overt sexual behavior. Among those who are single (and also among those who are married), the greater the erotophobia, the less frequently individuals interact sexually (DiVasto, Pathak, & Fishburn, 1981; Fisher, 1984; Gerrard, 1980; Gerrard & Gibbons, 1982).

Husbands and wives tend to be quite similar in their sexual attitudes, and those who hold different attitudes report greater marital dissatisfaction (Smith et al., 1990). Among parents, sexual attitudes influence what is communicated to their offspring about sexuality. For example, the greater the parents' erotophobia, the less sexual information they provide, including "where babies come from" (Lemery, 1983; Yarber & Whitehill, 1981).

The Effect of Sexual Attitudes on Learning, Health, and the Prevention of Unwanted Pregnancies An individual with erotophobic attitudes experiences anxiety and other negative emotions when he or she encounters sexual cues. These unpleasant feelings can be controlled by avoiding such cues. Although avoidance is often adaptive in that there is no need to place oneself in situations involving, for example, pornography or public nudity, there are other situations in which avoidance can be maladaptive. Specifically, sexual anxieties can interfere with acquiring knowledge, engaging in important health-related behavior, and preventing unwanted conception.

The more erotophobic an individual is, the less factual knowledge he or she has about sex and the less likely he or she is to take an elective course in human sexuality (Fisher et al., 1988). Further, when students do take courses dealing with sex, erotophobia interferes with performance, even though sexual attitudes are unrelated to how well students do in all other kinds of courses (Fisher, 1980). More recent research has shown that those with negative sexual attitudes are able to learn sexual material as well as those with positive attitudes; they have trouble only because they differ in their familiarity with such material (Goldfarb et al., 1988). Sexual information about contraception and AIDS is *not* retained, however, if erotophobia is combined with high self-esteem (Gerrard, Kurylo, & Reis, 1990); those who find this kind of sexual information unpleasant are apparently able to "tune it out" if they also feel self-confident.

Among teachers, the higher the erotophobia score, the more likely an instructor is to omit such anxiety-evoking topics as birth control or abortion from his or her course (Yarber & McCabe, 1984).

Health-related behavior, too, is affected by sexual attitudes. While most people feel uncomfortable dealing with problems involving sexual anatomy or functioning, erotophobic attitudes make such issues even more aversive. As a result, females with negative attitudes engage in self-examination for breast cancer and obtain gynecological checkups less frequently than those with positive attitudes (Fisher, Byrne, & White, 1983). Similarly, erotophobes have been found to avoid actions that help prevent sexually transmitted diseases (Yarber & Fisher, 1983). Among erotophobic mothers, even breastfeeding their infants is experienced as unpleasant, and consequently they are more likely to bottle-feed their offspring (Fisher & Gray, 1988).

The best-documented negative effect of sexual attitudes is their interference with contraceptive use (Kelley et al., 1987). Among sexually active individuals who do not wish to conceive, those who are erotophobic tend to avoid each aspect of behavior that is a prerequisite for effective contraception (see Figure 12.20).

As shown in Figure 12.20, the first step in contraceptive behavior is learning about conception and contraception; here, erotophobia leads the individual

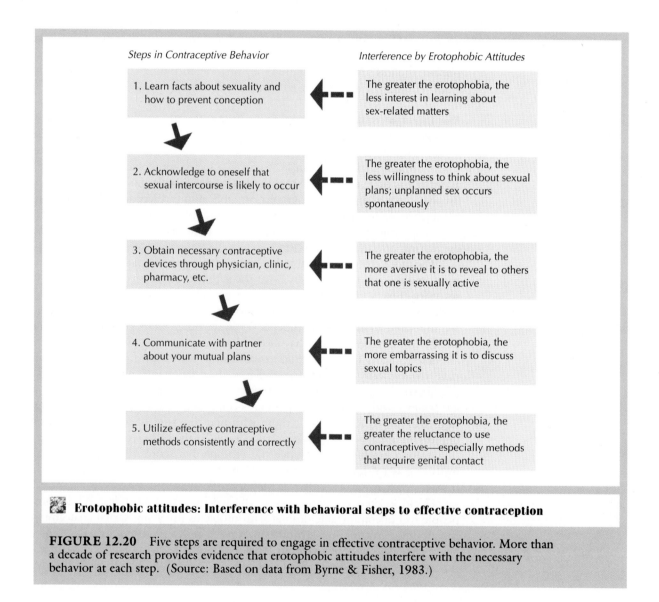

Steps in Contraceptive Behavior	Interference by Erotophobic Attitudes
1. Learn facts about sexuality and how to prevent conception	The greater the erotophobia, the less interest in learning about sex-related matters
2. Acknowledge to oneself that sexual intercourse is likely to occur	The greater the erotophobia, the less willingness to think about sexual plans; unplanned sex occurs spontaneously
3. Obtain necessary contraceptive devices through physician, clinic, pharmacy, etc.	The greater the erotophobia, the more aversive it is to reveal to others that one is sexually active
4. Communicate with partner about your mutual plans	The greater the erotophobia, the more embarrassing it is to discuss sexual topics
5. Utilize effective contraceptive methods consistently and correctly	The greater the erotophobia, the greater the reluctance to use contraceptives—especially methods that require genital contact

Erotophobic attitudes: Interference with behavioral steps to effective contraception

FIGURE 12.20   Five steps are required to engage in effective contraceptive behavior. More than a decade of research provides evidence that erotophobic attitudes interfere with the necessary behavior at each step. (Source: Based on data from Byrne & Fisher, 1983.)

to avoid such knowledge. Second is admitting to oneself that sexual intercourse is going to occur; for erotophobic people, such cognitions are anxiety evoking. Third is obtaining contraceptive devices and supplies through contact with medical or pharmacy personnel, a difficult prospect for those with negative reactions to sex, who may then take the easier path of avoidance. Fourth is communicating about contraception with a partner—a step that is also more unpleasant for erotophobic individuals, who find it more comfortable to interact nonverbally. And fifth is the correct, consistent utilization of contraceptive methods, a practice requiring knowledge and (for most methods) genital contact that once again may be shunned by those holding negative attitudes.

Because the problem of unwanted teenage pregnancies is of great concern to society and to the individuals themselves (Byrne & Fisher, 1983), several efforts have been made to develop intervention programs to encourage changes in sex-related attitudes and behavior.

Intervening to Prevent Unwanted Teenage Pregnancies The most effective programs in preventing unwanted teen pregnancies have recognized that the problem involves two major elements: Not only is it necessary to impart information about sexuality and conception, but it is vital to reduce erotophobic anxiety so that the individual is able to deal with such factual material, retain it, and be in responsible control of his or her sexuality.

One of the first attempts to decrease the number of unwanted pregnancies on campus was designed by Gerrard, McCann, and Geis (1982). They were able to show that the greatest changes in contraceptive behavior occurred among students who received both information about contraception *and* material designed to correct erroneous beliefs based on negative sexual attitudes.

In Canada, a more ambitious program was undertaken by Fisher (1989). The plan was to deal with sexual knowledge and sexual feelings at each step in the contraceptive process—from acquiring information to making decisions about sexual behavior. At the University of Western Ontario, unwanted pregnancies had been occurring at a steady rate during the late 1970s and early 1980s; in any given academic year, approximately 100 males and 100 females found themselves facing unwanted parenthood. Because even one such conception can create an emotional tragedy involving the woman, her partner, their families, and the unborn child, the university instituted a pregnancy prevention program aimed at undergraduates.

Three specific elements were phased in during 1983 and 1984: pregnancy prevention lectures in the dormitories, a videotape depicting college students involved in decision making about sex and contraception, and a book, distributed to all incoming students, covering the same material. The general message was designed to reduce anxiety, provide information, and legitimize either the decision to avoid sexual intercourse or engage in sex using contraceptives. Altogether, the students were given information, were exposed to positive role models who were anticipating possible sexual activity, learned how to obtain contraception, discussed the matter with their partners, and, if they decided to become sexually involved, used contraceptives consistently.

Was the program effective? Beyond increased knowledge or reduced guilt, the most convincing evidence of effectiveness was a change in the pregnancy rate; those data are shown in Figure 12.21 (p. 520). Before the intervention program, pregnancies had occurred at a fairly steady rate of about 10.0 per

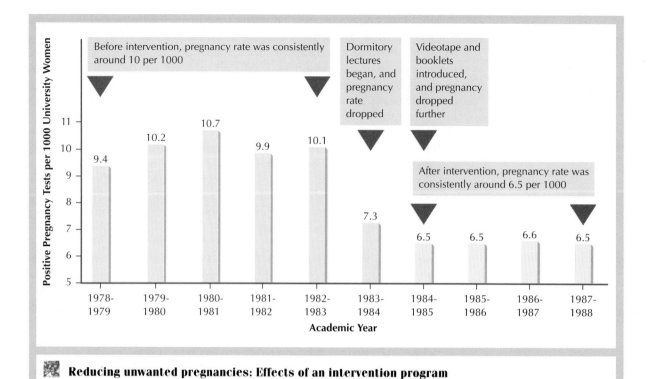

Reducing unwanted pregnancies: Effects of an intervention program

FIGURE 12.21 At the University of Western Ontario, an institutionwide intervention program was developed in an attempt to reduce the incidence of unwanted pregnancies among undergraduate students. When dormitory lectures were introduced, the pregnancy rate dropped, and when videotapes and booklets were introduced, the rate dropped further; over the same years, the rate of unwanted pregnancies in the general population remained constant. The intervention procedures were designed to provide information, reduce negative attitudes and emotions, and introduce responsible role models. (Source: Based on data from Fisher, 1989.)

1,000 female students each year from 1978–1979 through 1982–1983. The year the dormitory lectures began, the rate dropped to 7.3 per 1,000 female students in 1983–1984. When the video and booklets were introduced, the rate dropped to 6.5 in 1984–1985—and, in the succeeding years, has remained steady.

In any large-scale attempt to change behavior, the initial findings leave many questions unanswered. The most critical is whether the data represent the effects of the program or simply changes in sexual behavior in the general population. Control data obtained for Canadian women in the same age-group over those same years indicated *no* change in the rate of unwanted pregnancies over that time period. Thus, the program appears to have been successful. Until additional research is conducted, it is not known whether the results are based on a decrease in sexual activity or an increase in contraceptive use; nevertheless, it seems clear that this effort to address the knowledge gaps and the anxieties associated with negative sexual attitudes was extremely beneficial.

Personality psychology focuses on internal dispositions that are responsible for an individual's consistent behavior across situations, and *social psychology* focuses on situational factors that are responsible for consistent responses to a given stimulus across individuals.

Effect of Personality Traits

Though there are good arguments for different procedures, most investigators have dealt with specific **personality traits** and their effects, rather than attempting to build comprehensive theories of **personality.** In general, personality dispositions moderate the effects of stimulus events on behavior and consist of individual differences in emotions, attitudes, cognitions, expectancies, fantasies, and physiological activation. Despite past disagreements about the importance of traits versus situations, today there is widespread agreement that *both* traits and situations determine human behavior. Personality variables, such as *authoritarianism,* are identified on the basis of applied or theoretical interests, and a test is then constructed to measure the dimension in question. The test must be shown to have adequate **reliability** and **construct validity.**

Self-Concept as a Basic Set of Traits

Self-schemas differ across individuals and function as personality dispositions. **Self-esteem** refers to a person's attitude about himself or herself; self-esteem is relatively stable but can be raised or lowered by external events. It is advantageous to have high rather than low self-esteem. A positive self-concept is maintained in part by *illusions,* while a negative self-concept is maintained in part by the tendency to *overgeneralize* the meaning of negative events. **Self-efficacy** refers to that part of the self-concept involving a person's belief in his or her ability to deal effectively with tasks and to accomplish what needs to be done. High self-efficacy leads to better performance in many activities, in part because it activates physiological changes that reduce pain and make stressors more tolerable. People also differ in their **self-monitoring** tendencies. Those who are high self-monitors regulate their behavior on the basis of the immediate situation, while those low in self-monitoring act on the basis of internal factors. Interpersonally, low self-monitors are more committed to relationships, and high self-monitors are more affected by external qualities, such as attractiveness. Those who fall midway between the extremes of high and low self-monitoring score highest in psychological adjustment.

Beliefs about Control and Attitudes about Sex

Locus of control refers to generalized beliefs and expectancies about whether rewards and punishments are based internally (and are thus under one's control) or externally (and are thus under the control of external factors). When children learn that reinforcements are contingent on their own behavior, internality develops; when they learn that rewards and punishments occur regardless of their own behavior, externality develops. Most research indicates that internality is preferable to externality. Dramatic life changes can shift an individual's locus of control toward greater internality or greater externality.

Generalized attitudes about sexuality range from positive to negative, and **erotophobia** refers to the negative extreme in which many sexual cues elicit negative emotional responses and avoidance behavior. Negative sexual attitudes interfere with learning about sex and with performing health-related behaviors that involve sex—breast self-examinations, gynecological examinations, steps to prevent sexually transmitted diseases, and the use of contraception.

Authoritarianism The personality dimension that ranges from authoritarian attitudes and beliefs on one extreme to equalitarian attitudes and beliefs on the other. Authoritarians are characterized by adherence to conventional values, submission to a strong leader, aggression toward those who deviate, and an emphasis on the importance of power.

Behavior sequence A personality framework that conceptualizes behavior as being determined by situational variables that are in turn moderated by dispositional variables involving emotions, attitudes, cognitions, expectancies, fantasies, and physiological activation.

Construct validity The network of relationships between scores on a personality test and other theoretically relevant behaviors.

Dynamic equilibrium model A proposal involving the effect of personality variables in determining one's response to favorable and unfavorable life events. Such variables operate so as to maintain a relatively stable level of subjective well-being.

Erotophilia One extreme of a personality dimension, involving positive emotions, accepting attitudes, and approach behavior in response to sexual cues.

Erotophobia One extreme of a personality dimension, involving negative emotions, rejecting attitudes, and avoidance behavior in response to sexual cues.

External locus of control The generalized belief that reinforcements are controlled by external factors, such as luck or powerful others, over which the individual has no influence.

F Scale The Fascist Scale, a personality test constructed to measure authoritarianism.

I-E Scale A personality test that measures internal versus external beliefs concerning locus of control.

Integrative approach Research in which the behavioral effects of situational manipulations and personality traits are studied simultaneously.

Internal locus of control The generalized belief that reinforcements are controlled by internal factors, such as ability and effort, over which the individual has influence.

Locus of control The generalized beliefs that the control of one's reinforcements rests either on controllable internal factors or on uncontrollable external factors.

Metatrait hypothesis The proposition that people differ with respect to the traits that make up their individual personalities. One result is that any given personality dimension is relevant to the behavior of some individuals and irrelevant to the behavior of others.

Personality The combination of those relatively enduring characteristics of an individual which are expressed consistently across situations and over time.

Personality dispositions The psychological processes that moderate the effects of stimulus variables on behavior.

Personality psychology That scientific field which seeks to identify and measure relatively enduring personality dispositions and to determine their role in influencing behavior.

Personality trait A dispositional variable along which individuals differ in ways that are stable over time and consistent across situations.

Reliability The consistency with which a measuring instrument assesses a variable.

Self-efficacy The beliefs and expectancies an individual holds that involve his or her ability to deal effectively with a given task in order to accomplish what needs to be done.

Self-esteem An individual's attitude about himself or herself, involving self-evaluation along a positive-negative dimension.

Self-monitoring A personality disposition that ranges from the tendency to regulate one's behavior on the basis of the situation (high self-monitors) to the tendency to regulate one's behavior on the basis of internal factors (low self-monitors).

Self-Monitoring Scale A test devised by Snyder to measure individual differences in self-monitoring.

Self-schema An organized collection of beliefs and feelings about oneself.

Sex Guilt Scale A personality test that assesses the tendency to punish oneself with anxiety whenever one's personal sexual standards are violated in thought or deed. High sex guilt is associated with erotophobia and low sex guilt with erotophilia.

Sexual Opinion Survey A personality test that assesses attitudes about sexuality along a positive-negative dimension ranging from erotophilia to erotophobia.

Situational determinants Those external stimulus events, both simple and complex, which have predictable effects on behavior.

Social psychology That scientific field which seeks to understand and predict the behavior of individuals in social situations.

Subjective well-being The dimension along which we evaluate our lives. It consists of cognitive life satisfaction and the relative frequency of positive and negative emotional reactions.

Validity The extent to which test scores are associated with or able to predict relevant behavior.

FOR MORE INFORMATION

Aronoff, J., & Wilson, J. P. (1985). *Personality in the social process*. Hillsdale, NJ: Erlbaum.

A text that conceptualizes behavior as a function of both enduring dispositions *and* situational demands. This integrative approach is applied to such diverse areas as social perception, information processing, interpersonal attraction, negotiating behavior, and group functioning.

Bandura, A. (1988). Perceived self-efficacy: Exercise of control through self-belief. In J. P. Dauwalder, M. Perrez, & V. Hobbi (Eds.), *Annual series of European research in behavior therapy* (Vol. 2, pp. 27–59). Lisse, The Netherlands: Swets & Zietlinger.

An up-to-date description of research and theory on the concept of self-efficacy, by the psychologist who originally formulated this aspect of self-functioning.

Buss, D. M., & Cantor, N. (Eds.). (1989). *Personality psychology: Recent trends and emerging directions*. New York: Springer-Verlag.

A collection of chapters by personality psychologists who describe several trends in current research in the field. Moving beyond temporal stability and situational consistency, these investigators stress the organized coherence of personality dispositions, new assessment techniques, and advances in theory building.

Interacting with
the Environment

Linda, a student in the seventh grade, was always pleased when she and her classmates went on a field trip, but this one was especially exciting. For several weeks, Mr. Hazelwood had been giving them reading material and special lectures dealing with the many changes that had taken place in the world over the past hundred years—going way back to the beginning of the twenty-first century. Now, they were actually going on a cruise to visit the original New York City.

On an electric school bus, the class members traveled from their hometown in the Adirondacks to a busy seaport in upstate New York, where they boarded the solar-powered tour boat. From there, they moved smoothly down the saltwater gulf that was once the lower part of the Hudson Valley. As they approached the old city, Linda could see strange "islands" visible above the waves. These, of course, were the buildings of Manhattan that were now deserted except for the sea life that inhabited the lower floors, the anglers who sometimes docked their boats at a convenient balcony, and the many birds that used them as nesting places.

Mr. Hazelwood was telling the class once again how millions of people in the distant past lived and worked just below the ocean surface where they now were. Then, the gradual rising of all the earth's oceans totally covered low-lying regions such as Long Island and most of New York City. The complete evacuation of those living in the path of the rising water took decades of work, and many of the people settled in the new New York City that was built on much higher ground in the Catskill Mountains. Many residents moved elsewhere, of course, and so the new city was much smaller than the old one.

As their floating classroom glided smoothly between the rows of buildings, Linda thought about how different her country must have been before so much of the land was covered by water. She would never be able to see historical places like Cape Cod, most of the old cities along the East Coast and the Gulf Coast, or a place like Florida, which must have been fun. Maybe her parents could afford to take her on one of the expensive submarine cruises someday. Otherwise, the best she could do would be to visit places like New Houston, New New Orleans, New Miami, New Charleston, New Baltimore, New Philadelphia, and the rest. Most, like New Washington, D.C. (located near Pittsburgh), had museums displaying pictures and interesting artifacts of the original settings.

Mr. Hazelwood pointed out that the problem was not limited to the United States but part of a worldwide change in sea level as the planet grew warmer each year and the ice packs of the arctic and antarctic slowly melted away. Most islands, such as Japan and Great Britain, were greatly reduced in size, and others, such as the Bahamas, disappeared completely, along with such low-lying countries as Denmark, Belgium, and the Netherlands.

The students were given box lunches, and they ate sandwiches and drank soda as their teacher continued his survey. Besides the rising sea, the warmer climate had many other effects as well. Huge sections of Alaska, Canada, Norway, Sweden, the northern portion of Finland that was still above water, Mongolia, and much of the USSR were now the agricultural centers of the world, and the population of temperate Greenland was booming. Former tourist spots on the Mediterranean and in the West Indies were now far too hot for a vacation. Taking their place were such warm-weather havens as the Wicklow Islands—once a mountain range in Ireland.

Linda interrupted the lecture by raising her hand. "Excuse me, but something is bothering me a lot."

Mr. Hazelwood put down his notes. "What is it, Linda?"

"These changes you're talking about are interesting and all, but why did they have to happen? You told us the major causes were too many people and the way they lived—burning gasoline and things like that. Since everyone knew about the dangers, why didn't they *do* something?"

"That's a good question, Linda, and that's going to be our main topic next week when we get back to school—what could have been done and why people were unwilling to do it. For now, though, let's get on with the tour. Do you see those two rectangles above the water to our south—the ones covered by sea gulls? Those are part of what once was called the World Trade Center. . . ."

Linda looked, but she simply couldn't imagine why anyone had let all this happen. What a waste!

This brief fictional glimpse of the future may or may not be an accurate prediction of what will actually happen, but a growing number of scientists believe that global warming is inevitable. For many, the only remaining questions involve the precise timing of the alterations in climate, sea level, and so forth.

The general issues raised here are not especially controversial. We know that human behavior affects the environment in a great many ways, and that the environment affects human behavior. Social psychologists, among others, have become increasingly interested in identifying and understanding the details of this process.

Environmental psychology focuses on the interaction between the physical world and human behavior (Holahan, 1986; Sanchez & Wiesenfeld, 1987). Much of the initial research in this field dealt with the behavioral effects people have on each other's environments—investigations of crowding, for example. During the 1960s and 1970s, however, interest broadened to include such environmental effects as air pollution, noise, and temperature. One fundamental question has to do with world population growth and the consequences of having our planet populated by more and more people each year.

Quite often, the research on environmental questions is a cooperative venture that includes investigations by psychologists, architects, urban planners, population experts, and others (Sommer, 1980). The overriding goal is to learn how the physical and social environments influence behavior and to devise ways to motivate pro-environmental behavior.

In this chapter, we describe some of the work concerning what is known about *behavior in an environment created by people*, selected examples of *what we are doing to the environment* and how we might behave more wisely, research that identifies *environmental effects on behavior*, and the impact of the *interpersonal environment* on our feelings and our actions.

Adapting to an Environment Shaped by Human Beings

For most of human history, small bands of people lived not much differently from animals. The lives of our remote ancestors centered on obtaining food, avoiding danger, and mating. People lived their brief lives in the natural world, and their major goal was survival. Over a very long period of time, the population grew, and eventually human intelligence and manipulative skills began to pay dividends in the crude technology of weapons, fire, clothing, shelter, and language. As Figure 13.1 illustrates (p. 528), even today some people retain this relatively primitive way of life.

An outsider, observing these earliest human beings, would scarcely have guessed that people would come to dominate the planet and develop politics, religion, science, technology, art, nuclear weapons, and—perhaps—ways to make it impossible for this species to survive. In the following discussion we will first point out problems associated with a growing world population and then describe how our technological skills have made it necessary to adapt to a world of cities and homes which we created ourselves.

The way we were: Daily life during most of human existence

FIGURE 13.1 Until about fifteen thousand years ago, human beings lived in the natural environment, hunting and gathering food. When resources became scarce, they simply moved to a new location. Some groups, such as the Yagua Indians of Brazil, maintain that lifestyle even today. For most human beings, the development of agriculture and the domestication of animals led to settling in permanent locations. As a result, human-built environments were created, and we have been adapting to this artificial world ever since.

World Population Growth: Steadily Increasing Demands on Planetary Resources

In the history of the earth and its inhabitants, ten thousand years represents a minuscule period of time. Looking back to that "recent" date, scientists estimate that only about 5 million human beings populated the entire world (Ehrlich & Ehrlich, 1971). That is a smaller population (by at least 3 million) than now lives in New York City. Over the millennia that followed, the number of people grew to 1 billion by the year 1800 (Demeny, 1974). A hundred and thirty years later, this figure doubled to 2 billion. During the last half of the twentieth century, increases have become rapid and obvious: 2.49 billion in 1950, 3.05 billion in 1960, 3.72 billion in 1970, 4.47 billion in 1980, and more than 5 billion by the time this book is published in 1991 (Dumanoski, 1990). By the year 2000, the planet will hold 6 billion people. The most optimistic forecast is that improved education and increased economic well-being will halt further growth as the earth reaches a stable population of about 12 billion people sometime in the twenty-first century (Sagan, 1989; see Figure 13.2).

As these data indicate, not only is the population becoming larger (at present, by about 240,000 additional human beings each day), it is growing faster and faster as the numbers increase. According to World Watch, 1989 set a new record with 88 million additional people, and the United States has returned to the post-war baby-boom rate of over four million births annually (Borowski, 1990). Even if this nation's growth were to be at an exceptionally slow rate, there will be an additional 20 million residents by 2080 (Bouvier, 1990). Although the present growth rate for the world's population is less than

2 percent per year, that seemingly small figure means a doubling of world population in about forty years, and then again in another forty years, and again, and again, and again. Just 120 years of continued growth at this rate will produce a world population of 40 billion people, and that may be more than the earth can support.

An explanation for this almost unbelievable growth is provided by what Sagan (1989) calls the "secret of the Persian chessboard." According to his version of this old story, the Grand Vizier of Persia invented a war game (known today as chess) played on a board divided into sixty-four squares. The king was so pleased by the new game that he told the vizier to name whatever reward he desired. The shrewd vizier said that he was a humble man, and his request was therefore only a small one. He wanted the king to give him a single grain of wheat on the first square of the board, twice that amount on the second square, twice that on the third square, and so on for all sixty-four squares. The king was amazed his adviser didn't ask for jewels or palaces but relieved that he had only to provide a small reward.

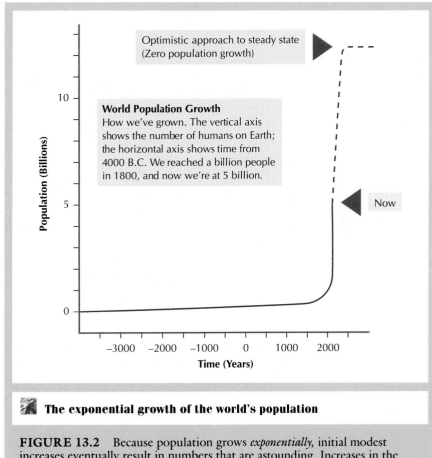

The exponential growth of the world's population

FIGURE 13.2 Because population grows *exponentially,* initial modest increases eventually result in numbers that are astounding. Increases in the food supply and in other necessary resources in time will be outstripped by the number of human beings unless steps are taken to bring the growth to a halt. (Source: Sagan, 1989, p. 15.)

In fact, the doubling process results in an outcome that was not obvious to the king—or to most of us. By the time the last square on the board received its quota, 18.5 quintillion grains of wheat would be required, or about 75 billion metric tons, more than all the king's granaries could possibly hold. Sagan (1989) notes that had the game of chess used a hundred squares instead of sixty-four, the amount of wheat required would have weighed as much as the entire earth. The point is that a *geometric progression* such as this involves an *exponential increase* in numbers. This same mathematical principle governs both *compound interest* (ten dollars invested two hundred years ago at 6 percent interest would be worth more than a million dollars today) and *biological reproduction* (population growth is one example).

The long-range problem associated with a growing population was first stated by an economics professor, Thomas Robert Malthus, in a book titled *Essay on Population,* published in 1798. Malthus contrasted the geometric increase in population with the arithmetic increase in the means to sustain life. The eventual result seemed clear—the population would outgrow the supply of food and other necessities unless people learned to practice "sexual restraint."

If nothing is done to cut the growth rate to zero, Malthus as well as more recent observers predict that the total number of people will nevertheless be reduced through famine, disease, and wars fought over possession of the remaining basic resources, such as drinking water and farmland (Heilbroner, 1974; Umpleby, 1990).

Obviously, we hope that our future is not this bleak. But only the concerted efforts of individuals and of governments can prevent eventual catastrophe. Even if growth can be halted, ways must be found to feed, house, educate, and create meaningful lives for a world population more than twice as large as today's.

Living in Cities: Effects of an Urban Environment

Once human beings progressed beyond the hunting-and-gathering period and learned to plant seeds and cultivate crops, the stage was set for a new kind of living arrangement. Instead of a nomadic life spent largely seeking food, our ancestors now settled down in fixed locations. It became feasible to build permanent structures in which to live and eventually in which to conduct commerce. Walls and fortresses were constructed to protect the residents from external enemies. These small clusters of buildings in various parts of the world represented the beginning of a now-familiar aspect of our existence—urban life.

The Growth of Impoverished Mega-Cities By the end of the present decade, most of the earth's six billion people will live in cities. Increasingly common is the **mega-city,** one with a population of four million or more. In 1950 there were only thirteen mega-cities in the world, a figure that increased rapidly to forty-two by 1985. By the turn of the century, 600 million people are expected to reside in sixty-six mega-cities.

As Figure 13.3 shows, many of these new metropolitan areas will be located in economically deprived nations. Because the birthrate is highest in the least developed countries, only 20 percent of those residing in mega-cities will be in industrialized nations; in 1950, the figure was 65 percent. The result, even now,

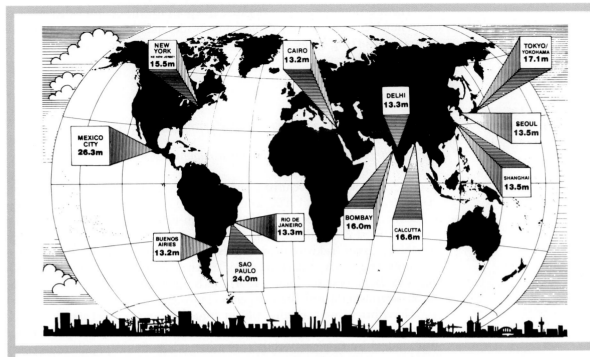

The mega-cities: Poverty in enormous urban centers

FIGURE 13.3   One of the consequences of population growth is a worldwide migration from rural areas and small towns to cities as people seek a better life. Over time, the result is an increase in the number of *mega-cities*—those with populations of four million or more people—primarily located in the world's poorest nations. This map shows the twelve largest urban areas that are predicted for the year 2000. (Source: *Popline*, May 1986, p. 8.)

is a grim urban life for millions of people who are illiterate and unskilled, living in makeshift structures that lack running water, a sewage system, and electricity and being without the services of police officers, firefighters, teachers, and medical personnel.

Most of us can only imagine what such an environment is like and what the effects may be on future generations. We do, however, know something about today's city life in the relatively affluent societies of North America and Europe. What effects does urban life have on people's behavior?

Cities: Attraction and Fear   Environmental studies indicate that human beings are extraordinarily adaptable to quite varied situations, though a price must be paid for that adaptation.

We seem to have conflicting attitudes about cities. Opinion polls regularly indicate widespread negative views, but the proportion of people living in cities continues to increase. Even in the United States, there is currently a population shift, with people moving back to cities and away from the suburbs (Logan & Molotch, 1986).

The overriding reason for negative reactions to cities is fear of an environment in which crime, drugs, alcoholism, suicide, and divorce are common. The following **Cutting Edge** section summarizes recent research questioning the validity of such fear.

FOCUS ON RESEARCH: THE CUTTING EDGE

Do Big Cities Create Pathological Environments?

People frequently perceive urban environments as dangerous, with crime as the central fear (Glaberson, 1990). Though you might assume that those who fear crime the most have been victimized through firsthand experience, this is not the case (Baba & Austin, 1989). Among city residents, fear is greatest when people are dissatisfied with their neighborhood environment. When an area has abandoned buildings, vandalism, and idle teenagers, it is perceived as unpleasant and also dangerous (see Figure 13.4). Such signs suggest deterioration of the social controls on which safety depends (Lewis & Salem, 1981).

Nevertheless, we *know* that violent crimes like murder and assault increase as the population of a city increases—right? Not necessarily. This question was first studied by Guerry (1833) in France, and he found population density unrelated to crime. More recent research has yielded inconsistent findings, with some studies showing that crime increases as population increases, others showing the reverse, and still others indicating no relationship. Many of the findings are surprising. For example, Whyte (1989) provides evidence that an individual

Unsatisfactory neighborhoods arouse fear of crime

FIGURE 13.4 Fear of crime is most often based not on the direct experience of being a victim but on dissatisfaction with one's neighborhood environment. The most fear-inducing setting is an area containing abandoned buildings, vandalism, and teenagers hanging around with nothing to do.

Psychosocial pathology in metropolitan areas: Better climate, higher average income, and better economic conditions

TABLE 13.1 Four indicators of *psychosocial pathology* (combining rates of alcoholism, suicide, divorce, and crime) were compared across the 286 Standard Metropolitan Statistical Areas of the United States. Shown here are the fifteen areas having the highest and the fifteen areas having the lowest rates of psychosocial pathology. It is obvious that the population of a given metropolitan area is not a good predictor of pathology.

Areas with the Highest Rates of Social Pathology	Areas with the Lowest Rates of Social Pathology
Reno, NV *(Highest rate in nation)*	Allentown, Bethlehem, Easton, PA–NJ
Las Vegas, NV	Bismarck, ND
Miami, FL	Patterson, Clifton, Passaic, NJ
Lakeland, Winter Haven, FL	Lancaster, PA
Little Rock, North Little Rock, AR	Sheboygan, WI
Panama City, FL	Akron, OH
Odessa, TX	Utica, Rome, NY
Jacksonville, FL	Provo, Orem, UT
San Francisco, Oakland, CA	Bloomington, IN
Los Angeles, Long Beach, CA	Altoona, PA
West Palm Beach, Boca Raton, FL	McAllen, Pharr, Edinburg, TX
Fort Lauderdale, Hollywood, FL	Rochester, MN
Phoenix, AZ	St. Cloud, MN
Oklahoma City, OK	Grand Forks, ND
Orlando, FL	State College, PA *(Lowest rate in nation)*

Source: Based on data from Levine, Miyake, & Lee, 1989.

is more likely to become a victim of crime in the parking lot of a suburban shopping mall than in the central section of a large city.

Perry and Simpson (1987) decided to examine data from a single city over several years of growth, rather than relying on comparisons across cities differing in size. Criminal data for Raleigh, North Carolina, over a decade revealed that as the population of the city expanded, the rates for murder and aggravated assault *declined,* though rape *did* occur at a higher rate as population increased. It seems that assumptions about city crime need to be reevaluated.

Levine, Miyake, and Lee (1989) devised a broader measure of **psychosocial pathology** by combining the rates of alcoholism, suicide, divorce, and crime in a given community. The frequencies of these four behaviors were found to be highly related. The combined index of psychosocial pathology was compared across the 286 Standard Metropolitan Statistical Areas in the United States. Those places having the most and least pathology are listed in Table 13.1. In looking at the table, a first impression is that, generally, (1) the cities with the most pathology seem to be fairly desirable places to live and (2) the list of cities with the most pathology does *not* include several names you might have expected, such as New York, Chicago, Houston, Detroit, and Atlanta. In fact, these investigators found that overall, social pathology was highest in cities having better climates, higher average incomes, and generally better economic conditions. And while total population and population density were found to be positively associated with the crime rate, the relationship was not particularly strong.

In any event, rather than focusing on crime as a characteristic of cities, one might do better to consider crime and other problems as a regional issue. The highest level of social pathology in the nation was found in the West and the South, the North Central region was next, and the Northeast was lowest in problem behavior. A possible explanation has to do not with cities or population but with migration. Consider the fact that crime rates increase as the percentage of residents born out-of-state increases. It is possible that migration entails the loss of stable interpersonal relationships and normative guidelines, resulting in maladaptive social behavior among those who move (Linsky & Straus, 1986). The migration factor also makes clear why social pathology develops in pleasant climates—people move there because of the good weather.

Altogether, these various studies dating back to the early nineteenth century offer little support for common beliefs about the negative effects of big-city environments.

The Overstimulation of Cities   A notable aspect of city life is the presence of too much information—the sights and sounds of the city, along with the presence of a great many strangers (Milgram, 1970). The pace of life is literally faster in big cities, in that the walking speed of pedestrians increases as city size increases (Walmsley & Lewis, 1989). More generally, the fast-paced environment known as *urban tempo* steadily increases with a city's population (Sadalla, Sheets, & McCreath, 1990). The experience of driving to work in a city is also stressful, as is revealed by increases in blood pressure among commuters (Schaeffer et al., 1988). Interestingly, single drivers show fewer negative effects than members of a car pool, possibly because they feel a greater sense of control. It is clear that city life involves many sources of stimulation. **Stimulus overload** theory proposes that urban dwellers, as a way of coping with the overload, learn to screen out stimuli not directly relevant to themselves.

Because noninvolvement helps individuals to adapt, city dwellers are less friendly and less helpful to strangers than small-town residents are (Korte, 1980, 1981; Krupat & Guild, 1980). The generality of such findings is supported by Amato's (1983) research in fifty-five cities and towns in Australia. On most of the measures of helping behavior he used (giving a donation to charity, responding to a question for a student project, correcting inaccurate directions given to a stranger, helping a stranger who collapsed on the sidewalk), helpfulness decreased as community size increased.

Differences in friendliness are apparent. When a stranger offers to shake hands, fewer city residents respond than residents of small towns (Milgram, 1977). Commuters in a downtown terminal are less likely to make eye contact with a stranger than commuters in a suburban train station (McCauley, Coleman, & DeFusco, 1977). Such findings suggest that city life results in a distant, impersonal style of behavior that decreases interaction with others.

The stimulating environment of a city need not cause unfriendliness, however. Response to strangers depends in part on the pleasantness or unpleasantness of the environmental setting. Russell, Ward, and Pratt (1981) hypothesized that an arousing, pleasant setting would lead to friendly, affiliative behavior, whereas an arousing, unpleasant setting would inhibit friendly behavior. Amato and McInness (1983) tested that proposal in a field study, using city settings that varied on both dimensions. For example, a downtown shopping mall was rated as pleasant and arousing; a downtown construction site, as unpleasant and arousing. In each of several such locations, individuals were given a friendly greeting by a male or a female confederate. The friendliness of the response was defined in terms of eye contact, smiling, nodding, or speaking. As predicted, friendly responses were most common in pleasant, arousing environments and least common in unpleasant, arousing environments (see Figure 13.5). This

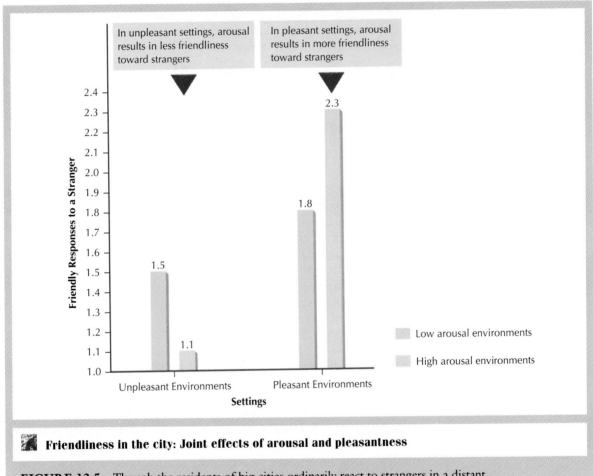

Friendliness in the city: Joint effects of arousal and pleasantness

FIGURE 13.5 Though the residents of big cities ordinarily react to strangers in a distant, uninvolved way, positive surroundings can alter this pattern. When a friendly stranger is encountered in a pleasant and arousing setting, city dwellers respond in a friendly way. The least friendly response to a stranger occurs in settings that are unpleasant and arousing. (Source: Based on data from Amato & McInness, 1983.)

research suggests that unfriendly behavior in cities is a function of unpleasant surroundings rather than simply the city itself.

Life at Home: Arranging a Private World

The one part of the environment where we feel at least partially in control is at home, whether that be a dormitory room, an apartment, a city townhouse, a suburban dwelling, or some other setting. The question for environmental psychology is whether behavior is affected by the details of our living arrangements.

Large-Scale Housing Projects When architects and designers fail to consider the behavioral consequences of their creations, the outcome can be disastrous. A classic example is the failure of the Pruitt-Igoe public housing project in St. Louis, built in 1955 (Newman, 1972). This expensive development consisted of thirty-three eleven-story buildings containing almost three thousand apartments. The award-winning design turned out to be a failure as a place to live. What went wrong?

The buildings of Pruitt-Igoe provided few areas for socialization among residents, thus making it unlikely that friendly social networks would emerge. Numerous stairwells made it difficult for parents to supervise children. Sterile, institution-like features such as wall tiles, narrow hallways, unattractive light fixtures, and radiators were designed to prevent vandalism. Such features send a psychologically damaging message to residents that they are inferior and not to be trusted (Rainwater, 1966). Within three years of construction, the Pruitt-Igoe buildings had been defaced by the occupants and were a hotbed of criminal activity. In 1972, the city of St. Louis solved the environmental design problem by dynamiting the project and thus eliminating it.

Creating a Home Environment A *home* is something more than the physical structure that defines where one lives. Saegert (1985, p. 287) suggests, "Not only is it a place, but it has psychological resonance and social meaning. It is part of the experience of dwelling—something we do, a way of weaving up a life in particular geographic spaces."

Among the functions of a home's interior design is a specification of where activities take place (cooking, bathing, sleeping, etc.) and who has access to which areas at which times. Furniture may be explicitly or implicitly assigned to particular members of the family (e.g., the chair where the father sits in the evening), and rooms may also be linked to specific individuals (Sebba & Churchman, 1983). Bedrooms obviously "belong" to those who sleep there. Some areas (e.g., the living room or hallway) are shared by all family members. Still other areas may be shared, but one person is "in charge" (e.g., the kitchen or the den). These social divisions are useful because they prevent misunderstandings and interpersonal conflict; they also serve another purpose.

According to Altman and Gauvain (1981), the unspoken rules governing the use of a home's space can be viewed as **privacy regulation.** Even in a dormitory room, privacy can be regulated, and that can be very important. Vinsel et al. (1980) found that college freshmen who are able to maintain privacy are more likely to remain in school than freshmen who fail to do so. Most critical is the ability to interact socially when one wishes and to be alone when that is appropriate. Those students who dropped out of college were less likely than those who remained to do such things as shut their dormitory room

 An inborn preference for the savanna?

FIGURE 13.6 Which natural setting do you like best? Most people have a strong preference for scenes of the African savanna. Sociobiological theories propose that this preference is based on the fact that human beings first evolved in such an environment. Even today, we design yards, formal gardens, and parks to resemble such African scenes.

doors, tune out noise in order to sleep or study, take a walk alone, or use the bathroom at a quiet time of day. In effect, some students learn to control their college lives by controlling aspects of the environment while others fail to do so, and this difference appears to be central to success in college.

In homes, cultural and social class variables determine what the rooms are named (Giuliani, 1987). The terms *kitchen* and *bedroom* are almost universal, but such designations as *family room, TV room, living room, recreation room, den,* and *parlor* are based on the individual's background, and these names in turn influence what behavior is appropriate or inappropriate in a given space.

The effects of the world immediately outside our homes have also been studied. Some propose that an evolutionary bias influences human preferences for certain kinds of outdoor environments (Kaplan, 1987). As Figure 13.6 illustrates, even young children select pictures of a savanna (a grassy plain with scattered trees) in preference to pictures of a desert, a rain forest, and so on (Balling & Falk, 1982). The significance of this finding is that human beings are believed to have evolved on the savannas of Africa.

Beyond laboratory studies of environmental preferences, Orions (quoted in Kaplan, 1987) points out that ornamental gardens and similar landscape designs actually consist of savannalike patterns. Note that some individuals live in dwellings where space does not permit a lawn with trees; their solution is to seek out parks that adhere to just that design (Hull, 1989; Joardar, 1989).

What Are We Doing to the Environment?

It may seem obvious, but almost everything humans do has a measurable effect on the environment. We have offspring, drive cars, use hair spray, build power lines, destroy a wooded area to construct a shopping mall, use products whose manufacture produces toxic waste that must be discarded somewhere, treat icy roads with salt that enters the soil to destroy plants and make the underground water supply undrinkable, cut down trees for Christmas, use disposable products ranging from diapers to household appliances, place garbage in landfills or in the ocean, and on and on. Often the effects are neither obvious nor immediate.

It is easy enough to believe that one's own behavior doesn't have enough impact to matter. After all, with billions of people in the world, *my* garbage and the size of *my* family and the exhaust products of *my* car and *my* litter represent too small a portion to make a meaningful difference one way or the other. In a sense, that is true, but when most people feel the same way, their collective behavior *can* and *does* make a great difference, as we indicated in Chapter 9 in discussing the *dilemma of the commons*. A brief overview of the most serious environmental consequences of human activity and a summary of the research designed to change environmental behavior are provided below.

The Greenhouse Effect: A Dramatic Alteration of Our World

Countless studies in recent years offer evidence that, in time, the earth will become a warmer place primarily as a function of human activity. Though experts in the field are by no means unanimous (Stevens, 1989b), for many the arguments are not about *whether* the changes will occur but *when*. If **global warming** (Schneider, 1989) does occur, ice caps will melt, the seas will rise, and portions of the land will be submerged.

Such predicted effects are sufficiently startling that they seem more like science fiction than the sober conclusions of physical scientists. Chhabra (1990) suggests that if you were one of the 205,000 residents of the Republic of Maldives, you probably would not doubt the accuracy of these predictions. This nation consists of some 1,600 islands in the Indian Ocean, most of which lie less than three feet above the sea. Because the water level is rising about one inch every five years, three of the Maldive islands are already submerged, and the remaining ones obviously will disappear over the next few decades. The Maldives are not unique; in other parts of the world, including Bermuda and several islands in the Caribbean, the gradual loss of land has also been documented.

In addition, the reality of such environmental changes is directly observable in the form of three gases that are present in the earth's atmosphere. According to studies of glacial ice, the natural levels of these gases began to increase around the year 1850 as a function of what humans do. Over the past century and a half, the situation has rapidly worsened. Despite increased concern about the environment, large corporations nevertheless frequently refuse to comply with environmental laws (DiMento, 1989), perhaps expressing the attitude shown in Figure 13.7.

The major cause of the **greenhouse effect** is *carbon dioxide,* or CO_2, a gas produced by organic matter. Prior to the middle of the last century, the main sources of carbon dioxide were the exhaled breath of human beings and other animals and the natural decay of dead plants and animals. The production of carbon dioxide has been increased considerably by the burning of coal and oil to provide the power that propels most forms of transportation, warms our homes and businesses, and creates the electricity required to operate a complex society. The concentration of this gas in the atmosphere is currently higher than at any known time in the earth's history (Fischer, 1989). As a result, heat is

"I think we agree, gentlemen, that one can respect
Mother Nature without coddling her."

Environmental safety versus the desire for profit

FIGURE 13.7 Despite rising fears about the effects of a polluted environment on human health and safety, many individuals and some corporate leaders (such as those depicted here) continue to ignore the problem. (Drawing by Lorenz; © 1986 The New Yorker Magazine, Inc.)

trapped in the atmosphere and the climate gradually grows warmer. As Table 13.2 (p. 540) indicates, carbon dioxide is responsible for about half the human-caused global warming.

Though most of the public concern has been focused on carbon dioxide, there is another gas that is twenty to thirty times more powerful in trapping heat to produce the greenhouse effect—*methane* (Stevens, 1989a). Methane is contained in natural gas, but it is also generated in rice paddies, forest fires, landfills, and the digestive tracts of animals such as the 3.3 billion domesticated cattle and other mammals that human beings use for milk, food, hides, and so forth. As a result of human activity, methane in the atmosphere has doubled in the past three hundred years, and the total amount is growing by 1 percent each year (keep in mind the earlier discussion of exponential increases). Methane is responsible for about 25 percent of the warming of our planet caused by humans.

Another fourth of the warming is attributed to *chlorofluorocarbons,* the kind of gas used in refrigerators, air conditioners, and many spray cans. These gases are responsible for the holes observed in the earth's ozone layer. The ozone layer protects us from the most intense of the sun's rays, and that protection is being steadily reduced.

TABLE 13.2 Three gases have been identified as contributing to *global warming* and the *greenhouse effect*. The process can be stopped by reducing the emissions of carbon dioxide and methane and by totally banning the use of chlorofluorocarbons.

Type of Gas	Amount of Contribution to Greenhouse Effect	What Must Be Done to Stabilize the Amount of the Gas in Atmosphere
Carbon dioxide	50 percent	Reduce emissions by 50 to 80 percent through changes in behavior and in technology.
Methane	25 percent	Reduce emissions by ruminants (cattle, sheep, etc.) through changes in their diets.
Chlorofluorocarbons	25 percent	Use of this gas must be totally banned.

Source: Based on data from Stevens, 1989a.

What can be done? The most difficult challenge is the necessary reduction of carbon dioxide emissions by 50 to 80 percent. It is here that much of modern civilization must change, either by the development of better technology (e.g., solar power, hydropower) or by alterations in human behavior (e.g., using public transportation, decorating artificial trees at Christmas), or by some combination of the two. Further, whenever you plant a new tree or replace one that has died, you make a small but significant contribution; a single tree absorbs up to forty-eight pounds of carbon dioxide each year (Grondahl, 1989).

Methane is possibly the easiest to control because a 10 to 20 percent decrease in emissions would bring the atmospheric increase to a halt. To do this, the most promising approach is to reduce the emissions from cud-chewing animals (the *ruminants,* such as cattle, sheep, goats, buffalo, and camels) by feeding them nutrients other than high-fiber vegetation and applying food additives such as hormones.

Chlorofluorocarbons can be controlled by banning certain products and replacing them with alternatives. In recent years, fifty nations have agreed to do just this. The bad news is that further increases in damage to the atmosphere can be stopped only if such gas is totally banned, not simply reduced.

Will people act to halt the progressive warming and hence the alteration of the world we know? No one can answer that question. We can only say that if human behavior does not change, the climate will.

Motivating Environmentally Responsible Behavior

It is ironic that at a time when rapidly changing political events around the world are leading people to proclaim the end of the cold war and a sharp decrease in the threat of nuclear destruction, we must now face the threat of environmental disaster. Further, this latter kind of threat cannot be blamed on "capitalist pigs" or on the "evil empire" of Communists—the enemy is us. And this enemy can be overcome only by modifying behavior (Geller, 1989).

Although most people are verbally pro-environment, only a limited number are actively concerned and involved in environmental protection efforts. Samdahl and Robertson (1989) identified three types of concern: perception of local environmental problems (e.g., air and water pollution, sewage treatment), support for environmental regulations (e.g., laws against dumping hazardous waste, restrictions on pesticides), and ecological behaviors (e.g., setting the thermostat lower in winter, using low-phosphate soap). These investigators had only limited success in predicting who would and would not show such concern. Specifically, those who supported environmental regulations also expressed proregulatory, liberal attitudes favoring passage of the Equal Rights Amendment, protection of homosexuals, and antidiscrimination housing laws.

In another attempt to determine the factors differentiating those who are active in the environmental movement from those who are not, Manzo and Weinstein (1987) found no differences with respect to age, sex, home ownership, or employment. The environmental activists (compared with nonactivists) were more likely to have experienced negative consequences from an environmental problem, to belong to a church, and to volunteer their time in other organizational efforts. The activists were more conservative politically and more likely to believe in the efficacy of activism, and they placed a lower value on financial success. Racial differences have also been reported, with blacks showing less concern than whites (Taylor, 1989).

Individual differences in both concern and activism are important, but the more general question is how best to convince most people to behave in an environmentally responsible way.

Reminding People to Act in Accordance with Their Attitudes and Beliefs
Research over the past few decades has consistently shown that people hold positive attitudes about environmental issues, regardless of the quality of their own surroundings. For example, a British study found that respondents were strongly in favor of taking action to ensure pure air whether they lived in a city that complied with clean-air laws or one that did not (Wall, 1973).

Because of these widespread pro-environmental attitudes and beliefs, it is difficult to obtain accurate information about environmental behavior by simply asking people what they do. For example, water conservation is periodically a problem in many localities, and campaigns are typically launched to encourage citizens to use less water. No one is in favor of wasting water, and few want to admit that they carelessly ignored the problem and made the situation worse. For these reasons, verbal responses may not match what people actually do. A study of the residents of Concord, New Hampshire, following a water-conservation campaign, revealed that self-reports of water use were consistently lower than objective measures of water use (Hamilton, 1985).

A special problem with any kind of conservation effort is that people are often unaware of how much water, electricity, and so forth they use unless they receive direct feedback (Kushler, 1989). To avoid the problem of inaccurate verbal reports and honest errors based on the absence of feedback, other research approaches are required. One solution has been to focus on *littering* in intervention experiments, because this behavior can be easily observed without having to depend on verbal reports. In addition, littering is important in its own right; Americans alone pay $500 million each year to clean it up.

Under some circumstances, prominent reminders (known as **prompts**) are helpful. This strategy is most effective when the response is a relatively simple one requiring little effort—such as depositing litter in trash bags in response to signs indicating what to do (Durdan, Reeder, & Hecht, 1985). In contrast, prompts are of little use when the required response involves effort and discomfort. When President Jimmy Carter tried to encourage energy conservation in the United States by asking citizens to turn down their thermostats during cold weather and wear sweaters to keep warm, few citizens complied (Luyben, 1982). In general, the more difficult the required behavior, the more creative the influence process must be (Costanzo et al., 1986). For example, when homeowners were induced to become involved in reading meters, feeling the temperature difference of the outside of insulated versus uninsulated water heaters, examining the air flow through cracks under doors and around windows, and so forth, over 60 percent of them weatherized their homes (Aronson, 1990).

The nature of the reminder is also important. Consider its tone. Would you be more responsive to a message that said "Smoking is forbidden in this room!" or to one that said "Thank you for not smoking in this room"? In a study of different kinds of prompts in a student cafeteria, Durdan, Reeder, and Hecht (1985) attempted to alter littering behavior. The amount of litter was observed during a baseline period, during a six-week period when prompts were used, and then during a follow-up period when the prompts were removed. The prompts consisted of messages on cards placed on the dining tables, and, as Figure 13.8 shows, the messages varied as to positive versus negative wording

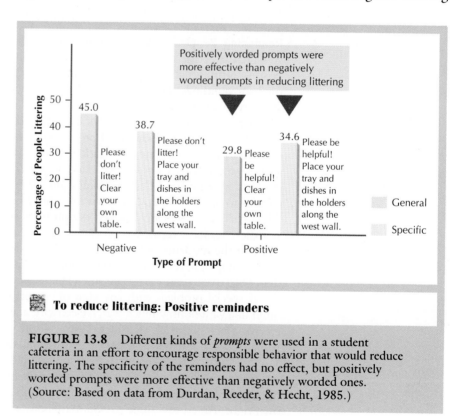

To reduce littering: Positive reminders

FIGURE 13.8 Different kinds of *prompts* were used in a student cafeteria in an effort to encourage responsible behavior that would reduce littering. The specificity of the reminders had no effect, but positively worded prompts were more effective than negatively worded ones. (Source: Based on data from Durdan, Reeder, & Hecht, 1985.)

and whether they were general or specific. During the baseline period, 54.9 percent of the individuals littered; this figure dropped to 36.6 percent when the prompts were present and then increased to 45.6 percent when the prompts were removed. Although positively worded messages were more successful than negatively worded ones, the generality of the prompt had no consistent effect. Among the other variables that affected littering was the size of the group at a given table. An individual eating as a member of a large group was more likely to litter than one with a small group. This finding possibly represents the same kind of diffusion of responsibility noted in studies of prosocial behavior (see Chapter 9).

In another investigation, prompts were employed in a supermarket study designed to encourage the use of seat belts for children riding in shopping carts (Ferrari & Baldwin, 1989). The reason for concern about these seat belts is that in the United States there are more than twenty-two thousand shopping-cart accidents resulting in injuries each year, most of them involving very young children (Friedman, 1986). In a field experiment, observations were made in two supermarkets, first before prompts were used and then while they were in use. Multiple prompts were employed to obtain the greatest possible effect. Fliers were posted depicting a child buckled up in the seat of a cart. These fliers were also placed in each shopper's grocery bag during checkout. The slogan "Buckle-Up Your Baby!" was taped over the doors leading into and out of the stores; employees also wore buttons displaying this slogan. Inside the store entrance was a large poster marked off in inches, indicating the importance of buckling up if the child was forty or fewer inches tall. There were also posters thanking patrons for using the seat belts. Finally, a brief taped message warning of accidents and encouraging the use of seat belts was played every twenty minutes. The effectiveness of these prompts is shown in Figure 13.9 (p. 544).

These and other studies using prompts indicate that reminders can bring about changes in behavior. They work best when the expected behavior is clear and simple, not requiring a great deal of effort or personal sacrifice. To increase the effectiveness of this approach, some investigators have devised ways to *reinforce* the desired environmental behavior.

Reinforcing Responsible Environmental Behavior One problem with many pro-environmental actions is that they require effort and even sacrifice. In effect, engaging in responsible behavior is at least mildly punishing. The only reward people receive is the belief that they are doing the right thing for the environment, for future generations, and so forth. Getting people to change their behavior might require more tangible rewards, and several experiments confirm the effectiveness of using reinforcement for this purpose.

In an investigation of littering in a movie theater, several prompting methods were used, including making trash cans available, projecting an antilittering cartoon on the screen, and passing out litterbags (Clark, Hendee, & Burgess, 1972). As in other research, the prompts reduced littering behavior but the effect was small. The addition of rewards, however, had much greater success. When the movie patrons were given litterbags *and* promised a reward if the bags were filled (either ten cents or free movie tickets), the percentage of litter remaining on the floor decreased from more than 80 percent to less than 10 percent.

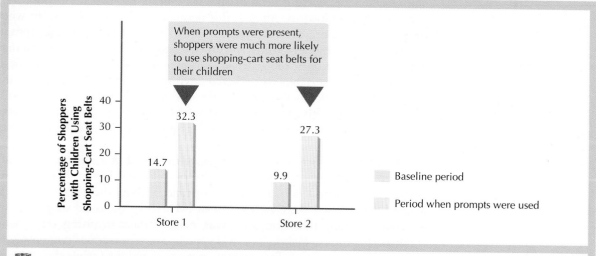

When prompts were present, shoppers were much more likely to use shopping-cart seat belts for their children

Percentage of Shoppers with Children Using Shopping-Cart Seat Belts

Store 1   Store 2

14.7   32.3   9.9   27.3

Baseline period

Period when prompts were used

Reminding shoppers to buckle-up their children

FIGURE 13.9   To encourage adults to protect their children from injury by using the seat belts on grocery carts, investigators used a variety of prompts in two supermarkets. Compared with observations during a baseline period, seat belt use strongly increased while prompts were present. (Source: Based on data from Ferrari & Baldwin, 1989.)

The only drawback to using rewards is the cost. One solution, proposed by Hayes, Johnson, and Cone (1974), is the *marked-item technique*. Here, very attractive rewards are provided, but not for every item, so that the payoff is something like a lottery. In a test of this procedure, marked items were scattered among the litter on the grounds of an institutional setting. Residents were told that some of the litter was marked in a way that could be seen only under a special light; anyone who collected litter that contained a marked item would be given an attractive prize; the result was an increase in litter collection.

These and other investigations provide evidence that the use of reinforcement is quite effective in changing littering behavior. Moving beyond research, the Goldman Environmental Foundation in San Francisco is now providing an annual reward of $360,000 to be divided among six "grass-roots heroes" throughout the world who make significant efforts to preserve or enhance the environment. The hope is that these cash awards will motivate many individuals to become environmental activists.

Legislating Attitudinal Change   A limited but surprisingly effective approach to a specific environmental problem combines mild coercion and a small monetary reward—the *bottle bill*. In many states, customers who purchase beer, soft drinks, mineral water, and the like in bottles or cans must pay a small deposit (usually five cents) on each item. The "reward" is a refund of the deposit when the bottle or can is returned to the store (see Figure 13.10).

Even though some people ignore the refund and continue to throw the beverage containers away, individuals in need of money regularly collect these

Returning bottles and cans: A small but effective reward

FIGURE 13.10 When states enact a *bottle bill*, those purchasing drinks must pay a small deposit on each bottle and can. When the empties are returned, the customers are "rewarded" by receiving a refund of the deposit on each item.

items by gathering the discards from roadsides, college campuses, business establishments, parks, and other locations. The results are overwhelmingly positive, in that littering is decreased. The outcome is a cleaner, more attractive environment, along with increased recycling of cans, a measure that in turn helps preserve the nation's aluminum resources.

Despite the objectively positive outcome, these laws initially elicit negative responses from not only retailers and bottlers but consumers as well. The price paid for beverages is higher because of the deposit, it is necessary to save and wash the containers, and they must then be transported back to the store if the customer wants to collect the refund. Do such negative responses affect long-term attitudes?

The surprising answer is that once the law is passed, public attitudes become very positive over time. Kahle and Beatty (1987) conducted a longitudinal study in Oregon (the state that pioneered the bottle bill two decades ago) and discovered an interesting sequence of events (shown in Figure 13.11, p. 546). The new law leads to changes in behavior (however reluctantly for many), the new behavior becomes habitual, and then attitudes about the bottle bill change to correspond with the altered behavior. This attitudinal change is presumably based on attempts to reduce cognitive dissonance (see Chapter 4) and on shifts in subjective norms about the "right" thing to do. An additional consequence is the tendency to generalize attitudes beyond beverage containers, resulting in increased concern about the environment. It appears that the passage of pro-environmental legislation can be quite effective in changing both behavior and attitudes.

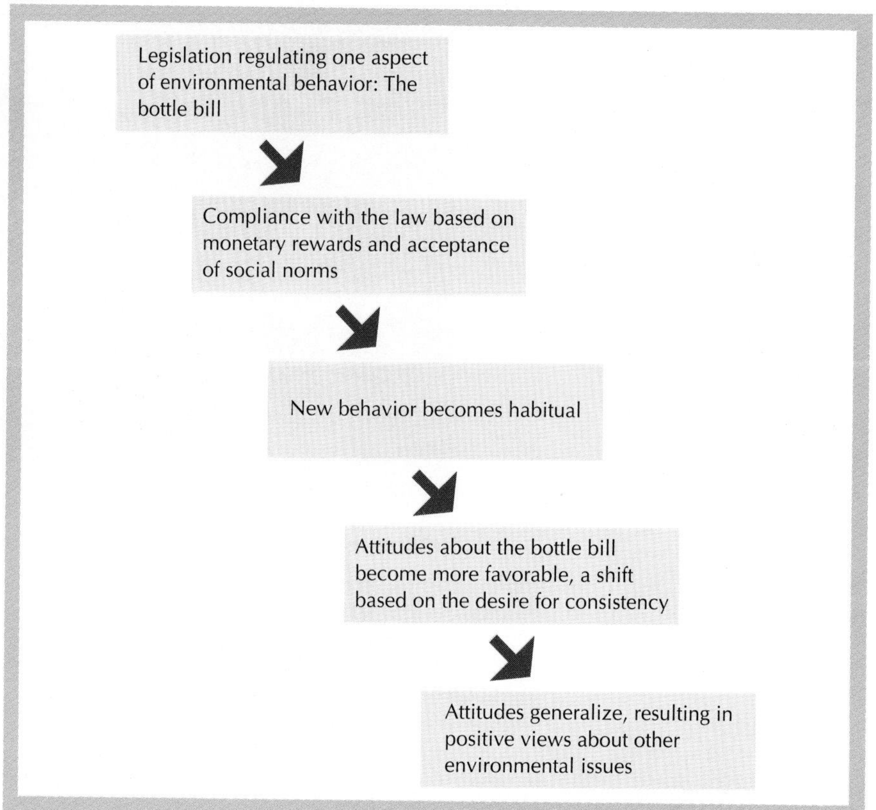

Legislation regulating one aspect of environmental behavior: The bottle bill

Compliance with the law based on monetary rewards and acceptance of social norms

New behavior becomes habitual

Attitudes about the bottle bill become more favorable, a shift based on the desire for consistency

Attitudes generalize, resulting in positive views about other environmental issues

Legislation → Behavior → Attitude change

FIGURE 13.11 Legislation such as a bottle bill can help change environmental behavior by combining new social norms with monetary rewards. When the new behavior becomes habitual, attitudes about the legislation become more favorable. The final step is a generalization of positive environmental attitudes to other issues. (Source: Based on suggestions of Kahle & Beatty, 1987.)

What Is the Environment Doing to Us?

Environmental stress refers to the way we react to perceived threats in the world around us. Each individual attempts to cope with such stress and to adapt by dealing with his or her fear, anxiety, and anger (Lazarus & Folkman, 1984). Though human beings have always been faced with dangerous natural events, such as floods, earthquakes, and tornadoes, technological advances have brought us new dangers.

Before outlining some of the behavioral problems created by specific environmental factors, we will examine the growing concern expressed by people about the potential sources of harm in the world around them. The following **Applied Side** section discusses the emotional and behavioral effects of perceived technological threats.

ON THE APPLIED SIDE

Is Anything Safe? Concern about Technological Hazards

Almost every day, it seems, we learn about a new danger stemming from technology. Most often, a product is developed that has positive benefits but then, after a period of time, a side effect is identified; some aspect of its manufacture or use is found to have unanticipated consequences. Most people agree that modern technology can and too often *does* pose a danger to the environment and to our health (Environmental Task Force, 1984).

To take a recent example, an as-yet-unpublished study by Genevieve Matanoski, an epidemiologist, has established that among fifty thousand telephone workers, leukemia and almost all types of cancer (including breast cancer among men) are highest for those employees regularly exposed to electromagnetic fields (Electric lines linked . . . , 1989). Such fields are generated by power lines, and the fact that many of us live or work in the vicinity of a nationwide network of more than two million miles of these lines is unsettling. Even worse, other research indicates that similar dangers may result from the use of toasters, electric blankets, TV sets, and computer terminals (Toufexis, 1989). As another example, more than 25 percent of those surveyed in a recent investigation reported illnesses resulting from the use of home pesticides (Grieshop & Stiles, 1989).

Possible sources of danger seem ever present and have given rise to what is called *technophobia,* or the fear of living in a technological society. At times, the situation appears beyond repair, and some have advocated giving up all our technological advances and returning to a simpler, safer, more primitive existence.

As realistic as some of the anxiety may be, Pilisuk and Acredolo (1988) suggest that the specific fears are in fact a reflection of a more general concern. People respond to specific media stories about one or another environmental danger for reasons unrelated to the concrete details of a given threat.

These investigators surveyed almost five hundred residents of Northern California and discovered a high level of technological concerns, as shown in Table 13.3 (p. 548). Despite the varied nature of these potential dangers, statistical analysis indicated that for both males and females, a single factor emerged—degree of technological anxiety. This means that people tended to be equally worried or not worried about almost all these dangers.

The next step was to identify any common factors among those who were most fearful of technological hazards. You might think, for example, that those most exposed to the news would have the greatest fears, but such exposure was found to be unrelated to worries about technology. Instead, the investigators found that those who were most upset were women, minority group members, and persons having less education and a relatively low income. In addition, fear was highest among liberals and individuals active in their religious groups.

It seems that public concern about the dangers of living in a technological society may not be based on a given news item or a specific danger. Rather, the ones most fearful are those who have not benefited greatly from technology. The least worried citizens are financially secure white males. A difficult question to be answered in future research is, Who is responding more realistically? That

Technological concerns

> **TABLE 13.3**   Surveys indicate that people are concerned about the dangerous effects of technology. Underlying these specific fears is a generalized concern that is greatest among women, minorities, those who are less well educated and who have lower incomes, liberals, and those who are most involved in religion.

Technological Concerns	Mean Concern Score
	(4 = Highest)
Contaminated drinking water	3.74
Storage of toxic chemicals	3.62
Cancer-causing chemicals	3.62
Pesticide residue in food	3.56
Air pollution	3.54
Nuclear power plant accidents	3.37
Nuclear war	3.36
Car accidents	3.20
Transport of explosives	3.15
Food preservatives	3.15

Source: Based on data from Pilisuk & Acredolo, 1988.

is, are the fearful only expressing their general insecurities, or are the less fearful hiding their heads in the sand—denying genuine dangers because they are prospering?

Noise: Volume and Predictability

Though a jet taking off and a rock group in concert are equally loud, many people find one intolerable and the other a source of pleasure. Whatever your reaction, repeated exposure to either source of high decibel levels can result in hearing loss (Lebo & Oliphant, 1968).

Effects of Unpredictable Noise   Even in the distant past when the big "cities" of the world were relatively small towns by today's standards, one of the more conspicuous features was the noise generated in an urban environment. A newcomer to almost any modern city is acutely aware of the sounds of traffic, horns, sirens, police whistles, construction work, and squealing breaks (see Figure 13.12). Further, urban noise is not only loud but usually *unpredictable*.

Some years ago, psychologists David Glass and Jerry Singer and their associates explored the effects of such noise in laboratory experiments and field studies. Glass, Singer, and Friedman (1969) proposed that it is more difficult to adapt to unpredictable than to predictable noise, because with unpredictability, the individual perceives that he or she is not in control of the environment. In an experiment, subjects were found to be able to adapt to either type of noise in carrying out a proofreading task. Nevertheless, those exposed to unpredictable noise made more errors and showed less tolerance for frustration. The importance of perceived control was tested by informing some subjects that they could press a switch and turn off the sound; though few subjects actually used the switch, the knowledge that they *could* do so reduced the negative effects of unpredictable noise.

The real-life consequences of such exposure were tested by Cohen, Glass, and Singer (1973). Here, the subjects were children living in a thirty-two-story apartment building in New York City that was built directly over a busy highway. These youngsters had adapted to the situation—no one was startled when a loud truck suddenly roared underneath the building. Nevertheless, those children residing on the lowest floors (where the noise was greatest) performed less well than those on the highest floors in tests of auditory discrimination and reading ability. The effects remained even when such factors as social class and air pollution were controlled, and it was concluded that exposure to loud, unpredictable noise was responsible for the effects.

Noise as a Health Risk   In addition to hearing loss, exposure to loud noises at industrial plants or in neighborhoods located near airports is associated with generally poor health—including hypertension (Cohen et al., 1986; Peterson et al., 1981), higher rates of admission to mental hospitals (Meecham & Smith, 1977), and increased risk of death from strokes (Dellinger, 1979). Presumably, high noise levels are harmful because they are arousing and stressful (Topf, 1989).

Behavioral Effectiveness   Children whose homes and schools are near an airport perform less well on math achievement tests and on puzzle-solving tasks

The negative effects of city noise

FIGURE 13.12   Noise is a common aspect of city life. Both its volume and its unpredictability have detrimental physical and behavioral effects.

than do children whose homes and schools are in quiet neighborhoods (Cohen et al., 1986). Adults, too, find noise disrupting (Smith & Stansfeld, 1986). Those regularly exposed to loud aircraft noise make more everyday mistakes than those in quieter environments do. For example, noise leads to confusion about left versus right in giving directions, difficulty in finding items in a supermarket, memory problems, and a tendency to drop things. In one experiment, college students were also found to perform less well on complex tasks under noisy conditions (Nagar & Pandey, 1987).

Individuals differ in their response to noise. Performance on a comprehension task is impaired by noise among introverts, but extraverts are able to tolerate such conditions without negative effects (Standing, Lynn, & Moxness, 1990).

Social Effects   Arousing and stressful noise influences social behavior as well. Unless the need is very great, helping behavior is less likely to occur in a noisy environment (Mathews & Canon, 1975), neighbors interact less in noisy neighborhoods (Appleyard & Lintell, 1972), and noisy conditions facilitate aggressive behavior (Donnerstein & Wilson, 1976).

Meteorological Effects   Though people often assume that behavior is affected by environmental factors such as climate, amount of sunshine, a full moon, and so on, research on meteorological effects has only aroused interest relatively recently.

Temperature and Behavior   As the temperature rises, negative interpersonal responses tend to increase and positive responses to decrease. For example, heat leads to decreased liking for a stranger (Griffitt, 1970) and to less help for someone in need (Page, 1978). When asked if they are willing to be interviewed, people are less likely to agree if the weather is either uncomfortably hot or uncomfortably cold (Cunningham, 1979).

The general belief that aggression increases when the temperature goes up has become part of our collective folk wisdom. The initial studies of the relationship between heat and aggression seemed to contradict that belief. Baron and Ransberger (1978) found that aggression increases with a rise in temperature, but only up to moderately hot conditions. At very high temperatures, aggression begins to decline. These investigators proposed that while moderately warm temperatures cause annoyance and anger, very hot temperatures are sufficiently unpleasant that the individual becomes motivated to seek a more comfortable location, rather than to aggress.

That formulation is interesting, but the bulk of recent evidence points to a positive relationship between temperature and interpersonal aggression (Anderson, 1989; Cotton, 1986; DeFronzo, 1984; Rotton & Frey, 1985b; Harries & Stadler, 1988). For example, Anderson and Anderson (1984) examined the association between the number of aggressive crimes (murder and rape) and the ambient temperature recorded over a two-year period in two large American cities. The results for one of these locations, Houston, are shown in Figure 13.13. As you can see, criminal violence occurred more frequently as the temperature rose. Similarly, in Raleigh, as the average monthly temperature rose, the number of rapes and aggravated assaults also went up (Cohn, 1990; Perry & Simpson, 1987; Simpson & Perry, 1990). If global warming actually does occur, increased human aggression could create more problems than the rising sea level.

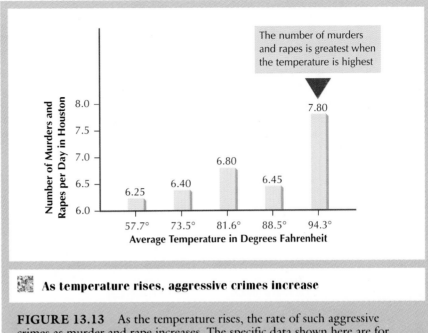

The number of murders and rapes is greatest when the temperature is highest

As temperature rises, aggressive crimes increase

FIGURE 13.13 As the temperature rises, the rate of such aggressive crimes as murder and rape increases. The specific data shown here are for Houston, Texas. (Source: Based on data from Anderson & Anderson, 1984.)

A milder variety of aggression was studied in Phoenix, Arizona. Horn honking (at the driver of a car that remained motionless in response to a green light) was found to increase as the temperature rose over a series of spring and summer days (Kenrick & McFarlane, 1986). In summary, the bulk of the evidence indicates that heat has a negative effect on interpersonal behavior, decreasing liking and helpfulness while increasing aggression.

Atmospheric Electricity Because of lightning, wind, and other conditions, molecules in the air frequently split into positively and negatively charged particles called *ions*. The resulting **atmospheric electricity** (indicated by the number of positive and negative ions) affects social behavior in several ways. Research data show that the frequency of suicides, industrial accidents, and some types of crime increases when the ion level in the atmosphere rises (Muecher & Ungeheuer, 1961; Sulman et al., 1974), quite possibly because of effects on mood.

In more recent laboratory research on this phenomenon, special equipment is used to generate high levels of atmospheric electricity. Negative ions increase general activation levels, adding to the strength of whatever responses are dominant for an individual in a given situation. For example, negative ions increase the aggressiveness of Type A individuals, presumably because they already possess strong aggressive tendencies (Baron, Russell, & Arms, 1985).

In attraction research, the presence of negative ions acts to increase liking for a stranger who has similar attitudes and to decrease attraction for a stranger who has dissimilar attitudes (see Chapter 6); in other words, the usual reactions are intensified (Baron, 1987). These results are shown in Figure 13.14 (p. 552).

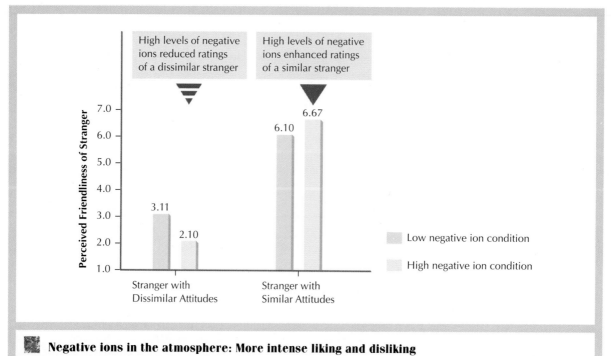

High levels of negative ions reduced ratings of a dissimilar stranger

High levels of negative ions enhanced ratings of a similar stranger

Low negative ion condition

High negative ion condition

Stranger with Dissimilar Attitudes

Stranger with Similar Attitudes

Negative ions in the atmosphere: More intense liking and disliking

FIGURE 13.14   As discussed in Chapter 6, strangers who have similar attitudes are liked better than strangers who have dissimilar attitudes. When negative ions are in the atmosphere, these responses become stronger—similar strangers are liked more and dissimilar strangers are liked less. (Source: Based on data from Baron, 1987a.)

The Air We Breathe

Particles in the exhaust fumes of automobiles and industrial smokestacks pose numerous health problems. In the United States, the Clean Air Act has provided some relief, but the cost of maintaining clean air creates considerable resistance to taking the necessary corrective steps.

Despite the physical and emotional dangers of polluted air (Rotton & Frey, 1985b), people tend to accept pollution psychologically. Over time, they tend not to notice that the air is polluted or to perceive pollution as a problem. Thus, whereas newcomers to a polluted area such as Southern California complain about the smog, long-term residents do not rank it as a pressing community issue (Evans, Jacobs, & Frager, 1982).

At a more personal level, cigarette smoke is a form of pollution that has received considerable attention in recent years. Not only do smokers have increased health risks (see Chapter 14), but nonsmokers who breathe the smoke-filled air caused by others' cigarettes also suffer health problems. These "passive smokers" (such as the nonsmoking wives of heavy-smoking husbands) have a higher rate of lung cancer than the nonsmoking wives of nonsmoking husbands (*Washington Post,* July 28, 1985).

In addition to health risks, cigarette smoke is increasingly likely to instigate negative interpersonal responses from nonsmokers, who may withdraw from the interaction (Bleda & Bleda, 1978) or become hostile (Zillmann, Baron, &

Tamborini, 1981). As suggested in Figure 13.15, some smokers remain oblivious to the negative responses they elicit.

Earlier in this chapter, we noted that ozone in the upper atmosphere serves a protective function; close to the earth, however, it constitutes an unpleasant form of smog. Rotton and Frey (1985b) examined the relationship between family disturbances reported to the police and atmospheric ozone levels over a two-year period. Family disturbances increased as the ozone level rose. One explanation is that pollution arouses negative emotions, thereby lowering the threshold for aggressive behavior.

In general, air that smells bad elicits negative emotions, resulting in less friendly interpersonal behavior (Rotton et al., 1979). In contrast, air containing a pleasant smell is a source of positive affect, with beneficial consequences. Baron (1990c) found that the presence of air-fresheners with pleasant artificial scents led subjects working on a clerical coding task to set higher goals, use more efficient strategies, and engage in more agreeable interpersonal behavior than those whose room did not contain air-fresheners. The addition of such scents to work settings could quite possibly enhance both morale and performance.

Nuclear Threats: Radioactive Waste and Atomic Accidents

Though recent political events have reduced fears of an atomic war, the potential dangers of radioactivity remain a problem.

"Does anyone mind if I smoke?"

Nonsmokers *do* mind if you smoke—and for a very good reason

FIGURE 13.15 Nonsmokers are endangered by exposure to the cigarette smoke of others because they are forced to become "passive smokers" when they breathe the air. Nevertheless, many who smoke seem to be unaware of the negative reaction to their dangerous habit. (Drawing by Koren; © 1982 The New Yorker Magazine, Inc.)

Nuclear Waste All plants that produce atomic power also produce nuclear waste as a by-product. Because this material can be extremely harmful to living organisms and because it remains radioactive for up to three million years, the question of where to dispose of it becomes critical. The most common response is, "Not in my backyard"—or the NIMBY effect. One example occurred when the U.S. Department of Energy wanted to create a national dump site in Nevada; that location was satisfactory to everyone except Nevadans. The state refused to issue the environmental permits needed even to study the proposed site.

The closer a person lives to a given source of danger (such as a toxic landfill), the greater the perceived threat, the greater the distrust of authorities, and the lower the perceived quality of life (Stefanko & Horowitz, 1989). Similarly, when British television broadcast a documentary about safety problems at an English nuclear reprocessing plant, those living nearest to the facility expressed more antinuclear attitudes afterward than did those living elsewhere (van der Pligt, Eiser, & Spears, 1987).

Note that some experts believe fears about radioactive dumps are largely groundless. John M. Matuszek, a nuclear chemist, labels the public's concern as *radiation phobia*. He argues that a person picks up less radiation each year from living near a low-level waste dump than from sleeping in a double bed with his or her spouse, eating bananas or saltwater fish, or residing in Denver (Gesensway, 1989). As is often the case, we are faced with the conflict between deeply felt concerns about safety and official reassurances that we have little to worry about.

Accidents at Nuclear Power Plants A special fear in recent years has been the threat of possible accidents at power plants using nuclear fuel (see Figure 13.16). At the Three Mile Island nuclear plant in Pennsylvania, an accident in 1979 resulted in the collection of radioactive water and gas in the reactor building, some of which leaked into the surrounding atmosphere. Over time, the plant was cleaned up, but the fears of local residents and environmentalists remain even today. A worse accident—at Chernobyl in the Soviet Union in 1986—had devastating effects on the local area and also caused consternation in Eastern Europe, Scandinavia, and beyond. Immediately after that accident, antinuclear attitudes increased in the Netherlands; however, this effect diminished over time (Verplanken, 1989).

Understandably, those living close to such plants (and many living at a distance) remain wary about future accidents and their effects (Richardson, Sorensen, & Soderstrom, 1987). In the Three Mile Island area three years after the accident, residents reported more physical symptoms, such as digestive problems and headaches, and more anxiety than similar individuals not living near the nuclear plant (Baum, Gatchel, & Schaeffer, 1983). In addition, the Three Mile Island residents reported more general problems related to maintaining control of their lives. They indicated lack of concern about what they did, because they felt unable to control major events. As these feelings of loss of control increased, physical symptoms increased as well (Davidson, Baum, & Collins, 1982). It seems that the stress and uncertainty caused by living near such an installation have long-lasting negative consequences.

A special fear: Accidents at nuclear power plants

FIGURE 13.16 Following the accidents at the nuclear plants at Three Mile Island in the United States and at Chernobyl in the Soviet Union, fears of this type of environmental danger increased, especially among those who live near such a facility. Shown here is a radiation victim being treated at Clinic #25, one of the many clinics set up after the accident at Chernobyl.

Some people moved away from Three Mile Island following the accident. Research revealed that those who moved were more likely to associate environmental threat with loss of perceived control than those who remained (Prince-Embury & Rooney, 1989). Interestingly, for those who stayed, perceived control was greatest among those who had the most faith in experts.

The Interpersonal Environment: Effects of Close Encounters with Other People

We have shown throughout this chapter that people are affected by their physical surroundings. Other human beings are also part of the environment, and their presence exerts a powerful influence on our everyday lives.

Crowding

Because of increases in population and the growth of cities and mega-cities, more and more people live and work in close proximity to one another. How is human behavior affected by the presence of others?

One example of such effects is the necessity of standing in line with strangers in various settings. Each American spends about thirty minutes a day lined up with others, totaling some 27 billion hours in line each year (Lindley, 1989). The frustration and discomfort caused by this activity are greatly reduced when banks, amusement parks, and airlines arrange for S-shaped rather than straight lines. People perceive the winding line as more fair and less likely to permit others to slip into line or move ahead of where they are supposed to be.

The earliest investigations of the effects of living in an overcrowded environment were conducted with animals, beginning with Calhoun's (1962, 1971) study of rats. These animals were provided with a sufficient amount of food and water, but their environment was densely packed with fellow rats. The results were devastating and included increases in aggression, cannibalism, and physical illness. Later animal research yielded consistent findings (e.g., Massey & Vanderbergh, 1980). If animals respond in this fashion, are humans also negatively affected by analogous conditions?

Densely Packed versus Feeling Crowded Most psychologists distinguish between **density** and **crowding** (Paulus, 1980; Stokols, 1972). *Density* refers to the number of people in a given space, while *crowding* refers to a subjective judgment that too many people are present. The same degree of density can be acceptable under some conditions (as in a baseball stadium) and unacceptable under other conditions (as in an airport), as illustrated in Figure 13.17. What determines when we do and do not feel crowded?

In general, high density arouses negative feelings when it interferes with a person's goals (Schopler & Stockdale, 1977), creates information overload (Cohen, 1978), or weakens the individual's sense of control (Baron & Rodin, 1978; Baum & Valins, 1979). It is hypothesized that the feeling of crowding occurs when an individual becomes aroused and attributes that arousal to spatial

Density versus crowding: Objective measure, subjective response

FIGURE 13.17 Density is an objective measure of the number of people in a given physical space. Crowding is subjective—a negative response to the perception that there are too many people for comfort. One determinant of whether or not a person feels crowded is the nature of the setting. A given degree of density can be very unpleasant in an airport because it interferes with each traveler's goal-directed activities, yet quite acceptable at a baseball game because it adds to the excitement.

restrictions (Worchel & Teddle, 1976); experimental evidence supports this proposition (Worchel & Brown, 1984). Moreover, when one can categorize members of the crowd into subgroups, feelings of being crowded decrease even though the number of people remains the same (Webb et al., 1986). For example, being surrounded by fifty sailors may make you feel more crowded than being surrounded by twenty-five sailors and twenty-five marines.

Crowding is also affected by the kind of density that is involved. There is a distinction between **social density** and **spatial density** (Baum & Valins, 1977; Paulus, 1980). Social density increases as the number of people in a given space increases; you could be in the same dormitory lounge with two other people or the lounge could be filled with people watching television. Spatial density increases as a given number of people occupy spaces of decreasing size; you could be with twenty other people in the large lobby of a building or with the same group when you all enter a small elevator.

Social density seems to cause more negative responses than does spatial density, especially among males; such responses include unpleasant emotions, physiological arousal, diminished attraction toward strangers, and an inability to perform complex tasks (Paulus et al., 1976; Ross et al., 1973; Singer, Lundberg, & Frankenhaeuser, 1978; Zuckerman, Schmitz, & Yosha, 1977). To some extent, people adjust to crowded conditions. Those who have lived in crowded conditions for many years show more tolerance for crowding in a laboratory experiment than do those without such experience (Nagar, Pandey, & Paulus, 1988).

Extended Exposure to Crowded Conditions   Most laboratory studies are limited to short-term crowding. The effects of long-term crowding can best be studied in real-life settings. For example, serious residential crowding in inner cities results in withdrawal, the breakdown of social support networks (see Chapter 14), and a decline in psychological health (Evans et al., 1989).

Student dormitories are frequently the site for studies of crowding. In one investigation, it was found that when three students (versus two students) are assigned to the same size room (increased social density), the residents feel more crowded, dislike their roommates to a greater degree, feel more dissatisfied with their living conditions, and obtain lower grade point averages (Baron et al., 1976; Gormley & Aiello, 1982; Karlin, Rosen, & Epstein, 1979). Several studies suggest that a major reason for the negative effects of high social density in dormitories is the loss of control over one's social interactions (Baum & Gatchel, 1981; Baum & Valins, 1977).

Research conducted with junior high school populations also indicates the importance of social density. McCain and his colleagues (1985) studied two identical schools, one of which experienced a 43 percent reduction in enrollment while the other did not. The school in which social density was reduced benefited in several ways. For example, the students had more positive attitudes about the institution's environment, and faculty absenteeism decreased.

As you might expect, people differ in their response to crowding, perhaps because of differences in their cultural backgrounds. In the **Multicultural Perspective** section that follows, we examine ethnic differences in adapting to residential crowding.

SOCIAL PSYCHOLOGY: A MULTICULTURAL PERSPECTIVE

Ethnic Differences in Responding to Population Density: The British, Southern Europeans, and Asians

In discussing cities, we described the contradictory findings concerning the effects of population density. One explanation for seemingly inconsistent results is simply that such effects are different in different cultures. We know, for example, that at the same level of social density, some people feel crowded while others do not (Baldassare, 1981; Gove & Hughes, 1983). Can the factors responsible for these differences be identified?

Gillis, Richard, and Hagan (1986) argue that in some cultures, people learn to cope with density and to share their coping techniques with others. As a result, perceptions of crowding are less common, and density does not lead to negative responses.

Support for this view can be found in many cross-cultural studies. For example, Asians in such high-density settings as Hong Kong and Tokyo have lower levels of social pathology than do North Americans living in much less dense settings, such as Los Angeles (see Figure 13.18). A possible reason for this difference is a long-established Asian (including American Indian) custom of adapting to the environment and seeking harmony with it.

In contrast, when Westerners are uncomfortable with the environment, their first response is an attempt to change it. British citizens, for example, emphasize privacy, prefer small towns and rural areas to life in a city, and create formal gardens with clipped hedges and smooth, rolled lawns.

In between the Asian and British extremes are Southern Europeans and others living around the Mediterranean. People from these areas are more gregarious, demonstrative, and comfortable with close interpersonal contact

Population density and behavior: Cultural differences

FIGURE 13.18   People from different cultures have learned different ways of responding to high-density environments. Asians have developed better adaptive behaviors than people from Western cultures.   (Left photo: Tokyo, Japan; right photo: Atlanta, Georgia)

than Northern Europeans but are not as tolerant of density as Japanese citizens, who are regularly packed, sardinelike, onto commuter trains.

Gillis and his colleagues (1986) investigated such cultural differences by studying reactions to residential density in Toronto among high school students of varied backgrounds. The subjects were divided into three groups: British (English, Irish, Scottish, and Welsh), Southern Europeans (primarily Italians but also Greeks, Portuguese, Spanish, and Maltese), and Asians (Chinese, Japanese, Vietnamese, etc.). Information about each student's home included *room density* (number of people sharing the subject's bedroom) and *design density* (single detached house, duplex, row house, or high-rise apartment). Negative reactions to crowding were assessed by questions about physical symptoms, such as sleep problems, loss of appetite, headaches, weight loss, and dizziness. These responses were combined to form an index of *psychological strain*.

The three cultural groups did not differ from one another in overall levels of psychological strain, but females across cultures reported more strain than males. When density is considered, however, the cultural differences become apparent. Among the British subjects, as either room density or design density increased, strain increased. The Southern European subjects revealed the same tendency only for design density, but much less strongly than the British. For the Asian subjects, density was unrelated to strain, and there was even a slight trend indicating the least stress among those living in the residences having the greatest density.

In summary, as hypothesized, the cultural groups differed in their response to density, with the British showing the greatest effects and the Asians the least. Neither sex nor socioeconomic levels were responsible for the ethnic differences. In future research, it would be of interest to identify precisely how those in different cultures are taught to deal with other people in settings that vary in density.

Crowding in Prisons   The prison population of the United States is growing faster than prison capacity, and the result is an increase in crowding, characterized by some as cruel and unusual punishment (*Ruiz* v *Estelle,* 1980).

Studies of prison populations indicate that as the number of prisoners increases, there is a corresponding increase in disciplinary problems, death rates, and suicides (Cox, Paulus, & McCain, 1984). Biochemical analysis provides evidence that the stress of crowded conditions leads to the increased production of adrenal hormones, perhaps accounting for some of the negative behavioral effects (Schaeffer et al., 1988).

Though spatial density does not seem to be a problem (Paulus & McCain, 1983), social density has a strong effect on perceptions of crowding. The key factor, once again, is perceived control over the environment: When control is low, satisfaction declines, and the prisoners feel stressed and develop physical symptoms (Ruback, Carr, & Hopper, 1986).

Personal Space and the Effects of Intrusions

Personal space refers to that area around each individual which is treated as a part of himself or herself. Research has centered on differences among people in the size of this space, situational effects on personal space, and reactions to spatial intrusions by others.

Effects of Sex, Age, and Culture   We tolerate the close physical proximity of friends more comfortably than we do that of strangers (Ashton, Shaw, & Worsham, 1980). Females interact at closer distances with one another than males with members of their own sex (Heshka & Nelson, 1972) but prefer larger distances than males in interacting with opposite-sex strangers (Rustemli, 1986). There are also age differences in personal space, in that young children tolerate much closer interaction distances than older children or adults do (Burgess, 1981; Shea, 1981). In addition, people perceive their own space and the space of others differently; others are seen as more intrusive than oneself (Codol et al., 1989).

Work on such interpersonal distances **(proxemics)** was initiated by Hall (1966), an anthropologist interested in cultural differences. As suggested in the study of cultural differences in responding to residential density, Hall observed that during social interactions Northern Europeans and North Americans place more distance between themselves and others than do Southern Europeans or those living in the Middle East.

The effects of age and culture on interpersonal distance were investigated simultaneously by Pagan and Aiello (1982). They observed the same-sex interactions of Puerto Rican children of different ages who grew up either in Puerto Rico or in New York City. Figure 13.19 shows that interaction distances increased with age for both groups, and the cultural differences began to operate by grade six. Those growing up in New York learned to interact at greater distances from one another than those growing up in Puerto Rico.

Occupational effects are also found. When police officers approach a civilian to ask questions, they stand physically closer to that person than nonofficers do (Winkel, Koppelaar, & Vrij, 1988). As a result, the person whose space is invaded feels threatened and very uncomfortable and engages in defensive behavior, such as moving back or ducking his or her head. The police, in turn, misinterpret these responses as suspicious. This kind of threat and the unnecessary suspicion can presumably be reduced if police officers are trained to interact at greater interpersonal distances.

Personal Space Variations across Situations   Hall (1966) pointed out four common situations in which people interact at different distances. **Intimate distance** (0 to 1½ feet) is appropriate for such interactions as making love or fighting. **Personal distance** (1½ to 4 feet) is common in everyday interactions among people who know one another. **Social distance** (4 to 12 feet) is used for impersonal interactions, such as business transactions. **Public distance** (more than 12 feet) is common in formal settings, as when a speaker addresses an audience. Many studies indicate that when these norms of appropriate distance are violated, people feel uncomfortable (e.g., Albert & Dabbs, 1970; Scott, 1984).

Reliance on such zones of interaction acts as a buffer, protecting us against unwelcome approaches and preventing sensory overload (Nesbett & Steven, 1974). When appropriate interpersonal distances are observed, people feel better able to regulate and control the level of privacy and intimacy in their interactions (Altman, 1975; Patterson, 1976). But when strangers ignore these distance "rules" and intrude on a person's personal space, he or she is likely to have a negative emotional reaction, to become physiologically aroused, and to escape the situation if possible (Konecni et al., 1975; Middlemist, Knowles, &

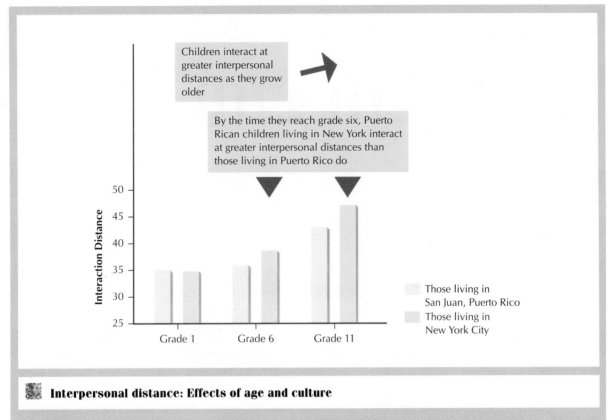

Children interact at greater interpersonal distances as they grow older

By the time they reach grade six, Puerto Rican children living in New York interact at greater interpersonal distances than those living in Puerto Rico do

Those living in San Juan, Puerto Rico

Those living in New York City

Interpersonal distance: Effects of age and culture

FIGURE 13.19 As age increases, children interact at greater interpersonal distances. In addition to this developmental change, those from different cultures also develop different norms for interpersonal distance. In this study of Puerto Rican youngsters, both effects can be observed. (Source: Based on data from Pagan & Aiello, 1982.)

Matter, 1976; Smith & Knowles, 1979). The opposite effects are found when the intrusions are by a close friend or someone who is friendly and helpful (Cowen, Weissberg, & Lotyczewski, 1982; Storms & Thomas, 1977; Willis & Hamm, 1980).

Territorial Behavior

In addition to personal space, people are also protective of physical space defined as theirs—**territory.** We engage in **territorial behavior** by marking off our territory and defending it against unwanted intrusions (see Figure 13.20, p. 562). As with other environmental responses, territorial behavior helps to regulate privacy and maintain control (Altman, 1975).

A **primary territory** is owned and used by an individual or a group for an extended period of time. An example is one's home, where any unwanted intrusions are especially stressful (Taylor & Stough, 1978). A **secondary territory** is used regularly but shared with others—such as the seat you occupy in a classroom for a specific class. A **public territory** (e.g., a public waiting room) is not "owned" by individuals, and a given space is yours temporarily on a first come, first served basis. While in use, public spaces are defended by placing one's belongings there or even just touching them from time to time (Sommer

Territorial behavior: Keep out of my space

FIGURE 13.20   As is true of many animals, human beings mark off specific territories as their own. We also take steps to defend these designated areas against intrusion by outsiders. (Drawing by Leo Cullum; © 1987 The New Yorker Magazine, Inc.)

& Becker, 1969; Werner, Brown, & Damron, 1981). Such "markers" tell others to stay away, and by and large they are effective.

Those who design facilities for others often ignore the importance of territoriality (Duffy et al., 1986). For example, the residents of nursing homes prefer privacy and the comfort of having their own territories, yet designers tend to stress open arrangements that encourage interaction. The result is emotional discomfort for residents.

Many animals, including birds and fish, behave in a dominant way when they are on their home territory by attacking any intruders (Figler, Wazlavek, & Chaves, 1988; Rajecki et al., 1981). This phenomenon has been termed the **prior residence effect,** and human beings respond in a similar way. In athletics, this tendency is called the *home field advantage*. On one's own turf, performance is better in competitive interactions, and behavior is more dominant (Martindale, 1971; Taylor & Lanni, 1981). The advantage of playing at home has been documented even for professional sports teams (e.g., Hirt & Kimble, 1981).

Because territoriality increases one's feeling of safety, people use various markers to indicate their personal "ownership" of a house, apartment, or room (Normoyle & Lavrakas, 1984; Pollock & Patterson, 1980). Even within a family, territorial behavior affects interactions; sharing a territory brings people together emotionally. For example, Raviv and Palgi (1985) found that if children in an Israeli kibbutz sleep in the primary territory of their parents rather than in a communal room, the family relationships are more cohesive.

Work on environmental psychology, as we have shown in this chapter, provides evidence of the impact that one's physical and interpersonal surroundings have on many aspects of behavior.

Environmental psychology is the field that focuses on the interaction between the physical world and human behavior.

Responding to the Environment Created by People

One reason for the increasing importance of environmental psychology is the continuing growth of the world's population. Even the most optimistic projections indicate that there will be six billion people on this planet by the year 2000, and growth will continue at least until there is a population of 12 billion. As a consequence, cities continue to grow, and some become **mega-cities.** Though large urban areas are assumed to be centers of crime and other types of **psychosocial pathology,** research evidence does not support this simple relationship. Cities do cause *stimulus overload,* which results in defensive noninvolvement that is often characterized by less friendliness and less helpfulness. Even in the largest urban areas, people create their own environments by arranging and furnishing their dwellings and designing outdoor areas to achieve control and privacy.

Behavior That Affects the Environment

Many of the things people do have direct effects on the environment. One of the most serious of these effects is *global warming,* and drastic behavioral changes are required to halt this process. Most people have positive attitudes about the environment but need to be reminded (with *prompts*) about what

to do. For long-term change, the most effective techniques utilize *reinforcement;* in addition, when behavior changes, attitudes shift to restore consistency.

Environmental Effects on Behavior

Because of perceived threats in a world created by people, **environmental stress** is common, and for some this form of stress includes a generalized *technophobia*. Much research has documented the potentially negative emotional and behavioral effects of *noise, heat, atmospheric electricity, air pollution,* as well as fears of *radioactive waste* and of *nuclear accidents* at power plants.

The Effects of People in the Environment

As interpersonal *density* increases, people frequently experience negative reactions attributed to *crowding*. *Social density* has more negative effects than *spatial density*. Long-term exposure to high-density conditions at home, in schools, in dormitories, and in prisons can affect people adversely; however, cultural differences exist in the ability to adapt to such conditions. The size of an individual's **personal space** is affected by sex, age, culture, and situational factors, and violations of one's space by intruders leads to negative feelings, physiological arousal, and escape behavior. People also define specific aspects of the physical world as their turf; such **territorial behavior** allows an individual to control portions of the environment and to achieve privacy.

KEY TERMS

Atmospheric electricity The number of positive and negative ions present in the atmosphere.

Crowding The subjective evaluation of one's surroundings as stressful because of the perception that too many people are occupying a given space.

Density An objective physical measure defined as the number of people occupying a particular space of a given size.

Environmental psychology The field that deals with the interaction between the physical world and human behavior.

Environmental stress A negative emotional reaction to perceived threats in the physical world.

Global warming The gradual increase in the earth's atmospheric temperature caused by human activities.

Greenhouse effect The basis of global warming—gases released into the atmosphere (carbon dioxide, methane, and chlorofluorocarbons) trap the sun's heat, creating a planetary "greenhouse."

Intimate distance The appropriate interpersonal distance for affectionate interactions, contact sports, and aggression.

Mega-city A city having a population of four million or more.

Personal distance The appropriate interpersonal distance for everyday interactions between friends or acquaintances.

Personal space The area around each individual that is treated as part of the self and from which most other people are excluded.

Primary territory Territory occupied and used by an individual or a group for an extended period.

Prior residence effect The "home field advantage" that humans and animals usually have when they are on their home territories. In that location, one's behavior is more dominant, and interactions with others are more effective.

Privacy regulation Behaviors, rules, and physical structures designed to allow individuals to control their social interactions and information about themselves.

Prompt A reminder to encourage a person to engage in behavior about which he or she holds favorable attitudes.

Proxemics The study of the distance people place between and among themselves in various kinds of social interactions.

Psychosocial pathology Personal and interpersonal behavior that is indicative of problems, including alcoholism, suicide, divorce, and crime.

Public distance The appropriate interpersonal distance for formal interactions, such as that between a speaker and his or her audience.

Public territory A territory occupied temporarily, on a first come, first served basis.

Secondary territory A territory that is used regularly for brief periods by multiple individuals.

Social density A type of density that varies as the number of people occupying a given space increases or decreases.

Social distance The appropriate interpersonal distance for impersonal interactions, such as business transactions.

Spatial density A type of density that varies as a given number of people occupy spaces of different sizes.

Stimulus overload When an individual receives too much stimulus information to be able to process it efficiently.

Technophobia Fear of technology and the side effects of technological progress.

Territorial behavior Those actions in which a person engages in order to stake out and identify his or her territory.

Territory An area occupied by an individual or a group that is defended against intrusions by others.

FOR MORE INFORMATION

McKibben, B. (1989). *The end of nature*. New York: Random House.

A well-written overview of the causes and consequences of the greenhouse effect. The author also provides a detailed account of what will happen if nothing is done to change our environment-related behavior. A general point is that the nature humans have always taken for granted will no longer exist.

Nasar, J. L. (Ed.). (1988). *Environmental aesthetics: Theory, research, and applications*. New York: Cambridge University Press.

A detailed description, by a series of authors, of the importance of architectural interiors and exteriors, urban and rural settings, and natural environments.

Stokols, D., & Altman, I. (1986). *Handbook of environmental psychology.* New York: Wiley.

A volume covering the major topics of environmental psychology. The chapters were written by scientists who are actively involved in research, theory, and application in this area.

Taylor, R. B. (1988). *Human territorial functioning: An empirical, evolutionary perspective on individual and small group territorial cognitions, behaviors, and consequences.* New York: Cambridge University Press.

A comprehensive summary of what is known about human territorial behavior. The author summarizes the research to date and provides a theoretical orientation for organizing this material.

Wilson, P. J. (1988). *The domestication of the human species.* New Haven, CT: Yale University Press.

An interesting presentation of the author's theory about what happened some fifteen thousand years ago when people began living in houses, villages, and towns. His proposals deal with the possible effects of moving from life in the natural environment to life in humanly constructed environments.

Applying Social Psychology: Health, Law, and Politics

Health: The Social Psychological Determinants

How Stress Precipitates Illness / Behavioral Factors That Help Prevent Illness / The Anatomy of an Illness Episode: From Recognizing Symptoms to Seeking Professional Help / Once You Know You're Ill: Problems with Medical Care

Social Psychology and the Legal System

External Effects on Courtroom Behavior: The Media / Eyewitness Testimony: How Accurate Is It? / Potential Biases: Police, Attorneys, and the Judge / Defendants and Jurors: They're Only Human, Too

Psychology and Politics: Liking and Leadership

Political Attitudes and Actions: The Media and Personal Involvement / Psychology and Voter Behavior / Choosing a Candidate: Whom Do You Like? / Choosing a Leader: Who Has the Right Stuff?

SPECIAL SECTIONS

ON THE APPLIED SIDE
Stressful Events and Student Health
SOCIAL PSYCHOLOGY: A MULTICULTURAL PERSPECTIVE
Social Support? Husbands in the Delivery Room in Canada and in Israel
FOCUS ON RESEARCH: THE CUTTING EDGE
Winning a Presidential Election: Put On a Happy Face

In his junior year in college, Kevin found himself involved in a political campaign for the first time in his life. Partly as the result of a paper he was assigned to write in a political science class, he learned a lot about the pros and cons of the death penalty. The more background material he read, the more convinced he became that the threat of execution helped deter criminals. Besides, he felt that death was the only appropriate punishment for really vicious criminals. *These slime don't deserve to sit around in prisons at the taxpayers' expense, watching TV and eating free meals,* he thought. And he became even more convinced he was right whenever he argued with his roommate about the topic.

Then, in response to a newspaper story, Kevin became interested in the race for city mayor. One of the candidates—Brad Harrigan—was quoted in the paper as saying that crime was the greatest problem facing all of us and that society had been coddling criminals far too long. Most importantly, the candidate stressed restoring the death penalty to bring a halt to violence in the streets.

Kevin contacted the Harrigan campaign headquarters and volunteered his time. Every afternoon, he worked at folding campaign literature, placing the folded pamphlets in envelopes, and taking the completed stacks to the post office. After several weeks, he was given the assignment of phoning registered voters in the precinct surrounding the campus to help get out the student vote. Once, he actually met Mr. Harrigan and shook his hand when the candidate visited the office where his supporters were hard at work.

When Kevin returned to his room that evening, he excitedly told his roommate about meeting Harrigan. Joel asked why he was spending all of his free time working for this guy. "What is Harrigan going to do that's any different from the mayor we have now?"

Sighing, Kevin replied, "Haven't you been listening? He's going to crack down on crime. He says that the death penalty *has* to be restored."

It was Joel's turn to sigh. "So what? Everybody is against crime except Jack the Ripper. Anyway, a city mayor has nothing to do with executing criminals. Your shining knight should run for the legislature or for governor if that's his big concern."

Kevin was beginning to get angry. "It's his attitude that's important. We need leaders who are concerned about the crime wave and who want to scare these animals."

Joel responded with sarcasm. "Isn't that great! Harrigan is going to sit in City Hall and execute the drug dealers and the serial murderers and the child molesters. Do you even know where he stands on issues that are relevant to the mayor's office? What is he going to do about dishonest political appointees and the third-rate public schools? I write term papers, too. Remember?"

Kevin lost interest in the discussion. "Look, I *care* about the crime problem, and Brad Harrigan does, too. He's also the kind of guy who will do something about it. When he's on TV, I feel really hopeful about the future. He's the kind of leader we need in this country."

Political contests can be interesting, whether in cities or at a higher level. Why does a given voter support a specific political party or one particular candidate? Political preferences are based on a number of factors that should be familiar to you after reading the previous chapters in this book. For example, like Kevin, most people tend to prefer candidates who express attitudes similar to their own and who are perceived to have the appropriate characteristics to take a leadership role. As we will see, the research on attraction (Chapter 6) and on leadership (Chapter 11) is directly relevant to political choices. Equally important, when a candidate is advised to utilize research findings to influence voter responses, the application of basic social psychological principles can help that candidate win—sometimes for the wrong reasons.

As we have suggested throughout this book, social psychology does not begin or end in the laboratory. Many of the ideas for experiments originate in observations of events in the real world, and many of the findings clearly have applied implications. Despite some popular misconceptions, psychological research is not an irrelevant game isolated from everyday concerns, and applied psychology is not confined to clinical psychologists practicing psychotherapy (Altmaier & Meyer, 1985). After reading the previous thirteen chapters, however, you are already aware of that.

By **applied social psychology** we mean the utilization of social psychological principles and research methods in real-world settings in efforts to solve problems involving individual behavior in social situations (Weyant, 1986). We will provide some representative examples of this activity in the present chapter and in the following one.

Basic research in social psychology leads rather naturally to application, often in collaboration with other kinds of psychologists and with professionals in other disciplines. Social psychologists frequently wear two hats—one as a behavioral scientist who constructs theories based on empirical research, continually testing them in controlled experimental and correlational investigations, and the other as a behavioral engineer who uses his or her basic knowledge to solve practical problems outside the laboratory (Carroll, 1982). A sampling of recent applied research indicates how varied these problems can be (see Table 14.1).

The many faces of applied research

TABLE 14.1 Applied psychological research is broadly based and touches on almost every aspect of human behavior, as demonstrated by these examples of recent findings.

Recent Findings in Applied Research	Reference
Psychological factors such as opinions can cause the stock market to go up or down, independent of economic factors.	Hood, 1988
Food aversions and eating problems develop among cancer patients (cancer anorexia) because the nausea following chemotherapy becomes associated with the taste of food recently eaten, through simple conditioning.	Bernstein, 1988
Performance is maximized when athletes focus their thoughts on external events rather than on internal sensations.	Padgett & Hill, 1989
After the showing of *The Day After* on TV, people were less likely to believe they could survive a nuclear war, they had less desire to survive, and their sense of self-efficacy decreased.	Schofield & Pavelchak, 1989

Almost as soon as social psychologists established their field, some became interested in the applied implications of their research. For example, in 1899 William James pointed out ways to improve education based on laboratory findings. In the 1940s, Kurt Lewin was a strong advocate of **action research**— work aimed at understanding and solving social problems. That tradition continues, and many social psychologists devote their primary efforts to application (Kiesler, 1985; Spielberger & Stenmark, 1985).

A concrete indication of the role of application in social psychology is the occupational shift away from academia and into applied settings. Beginning in the 1980s, only about a third of the new Ph.D.'s in this field entered university positions, compared with about half of the new Ph.D.'s in prior years (Stapp & Fulcher, 1984). Social psychologists are now employed in hospitals, government agencies, business organizations, and many other nonacademic institutions.

In this chapter, we first describe *health psychology* and research that extends from preventive medicine to the ways people cope with illness. Next, we turn to the social psychology of the *legal system,* one of the original settings for applied social psychology. Then we turn to the *psychology of politics,* examining the factors that influence voter preferences.

Health: The Social Psychological Determinants

Once, it was possible to consider health and illness as simply physical matters, but today it is widely assumed that behavioral science contributes strongly to an understanding of physical health and illness (Rodin & Salovey, 1989). We define **health psychology** as that field which studies the psychological processes affecting the development, prevention, and treatment of physical illness (Glass, 1989; Taylor, 1985).

Consider just three recent findings that provide evidence of the impact of nonphysical factors on health:

1. Certain illnesses are more likely to occur among individuals with specific personality characteristics (Suls & Rittenhouse, 1987).
2. A patient's recovery depends in part on how the physician interacts with him or her (Krantz, Grunberg, & Baum, 1985).
3. Socioeconomic status obviously affects health, in that many of the required services are expensive, yet there are more subtle effects, too. A study in Great Britain comparing newspapers aimed at the higher socioeconomic classes with those designed for the lower socioeconomic classes revealed a striking difference in the coverage of health issues. Kristiansen and Harding (1988) discovered that the "quality press" prints more information about health than the "popular press." These investigators suggested that such differences in content may be partly responsible for the greater number of illnesses and higher death rates among those lowest on the socioeconomic scale.

In the following section we will describe some of the major applications of social psychological research to health issues.

How Stress Precipitates Illness

Since the 1930s, psychologists have been interested in the effects of **stress.** Selye (1956) defined stress in terms of harmful stimuli, but the concept was soon broadened beyond physical harm to include *psychological stress* (Lazarus,

1966). Whether the danger is physical or psychological, the individual feels threatened and tries to **cope** with the situation; successful coping processes reduce or eliminate the threat (Epstein & Meier, 1989; Taylor, Buunk, & Aspinwall, 1990). Physical health is clearly affected by stress and the way each person copes with it. Hendrix, Steel, and Schultz (1987) report that the most common sources of stress are job related (such as the supervisor's behavior and the work itself) and life related (such as parent-offspring problems and spouse's behavior). The consequences of such stress include an increase in the frequency of colds, flu, and absenteeism.

Life Stress and Illness   Many events occurring in the course of daily life strain our physical and psychological resources, resulting in increased risk for both physical and psychological illnesses (Lazarus & Folkman, 1984). Even such minor everyday hassles as driving in heavy traffic or having to interact with annoying coworkers have negative effects on health (Weinberger, Hiner, & Tierney, 1987). With a more serious disruption—the death of a loved one, for example—the probability of becoming ill increases greatly (Schleifer et al., 1983).

How can *stress* cause physical illness? There are two primary ways. First, during periods of stress and anxiety, people are less likely to engage in preventive health measures, such as eating a balanced diet or exercising (Wiebe & McCallum, 1986).

The second—and most direct—process is a reduced ability to fight off infections. The body's immune system is impaired when the level of stress is high (Kiecolt-Glaser & Glaser, 1987; Stone et al., 1987). Such findings have contributed to the growth of a new interdisciplinary field, **psychoneuro-immunology,** that studies stress, psychological responses, and the immune system simultaneously. One such investigation focused on the body's defense against upper-respiratory infections, a process based on *secretory immunoglobulin A,* present in saliva, which fights these infections. Jemmott and Magloire (1988) sampled the saliva of healthy undergraduates before, during, and after final exams, and the level of immunoglobulin was found to be lowest during the exam period. This finding indicates that the stress of finals interferes with the immune system. As a result, many students develop upper-respiratory infections when taking examinations (Dorian et al., 1982). In a similar way, when stress and anxiety interfere with the immune system, some individuals respond with psoriasis, eczema, or acne (Solomon, 1989).

The college years are a generally stressful time, and the effects on health are widespread. We will examine some of the relevant findings in the following **Applied Side** section.

ON THE APPLIED SIDE

Stressful Events and Student Health

When students enter college for the first time, it is difficult for them to anticipate or even to imagine all the possible sources of stress they will encounter. Most people are stressed by changes in their lives, interpersonal conflicts, the loss of close friends or relatives, failure experiences, and time pressures, and such stresses are all too familiar to college students. As we have suggested, finals week is a busy time at student health centers, but many additional sources of stress compound the problem (see Figure 14.1).

Consider one common difficulty—the transition from high school to college:

> In many cases, students who were in the top of their classes or who were sports heroes in high school, where they were big fish in little ponds, go off to a college with thousands of other top students and hundreds of star athletes and quickly discover they are little fish in big ponds. The psychological adjustment can be difficult, and emerging self-doubts can compromise a student's performance (Brody, 1989, p. B12).

Some kinds of stress are worse than others, and some people are unfortunate enough to encounter more stress than others. Just how much stress is required to produce a negative effect on health? As Table 14.2 indicates, investigators rate stressful events on the basis of their effects, using a scale ranging from 1 (least stressful) to 100 (most stressful). If, over the course of a year, an individual is confronted by stresses that add up to 150 points or more, he or she has a fifty-fifty chance of getting ill. For example, a female student who becomes pregnant, gets a failing grade in an important course, and argues with her boyfriend has a total of 179 points. A male student who is responsible for the unwanted pregnancy during his first semester and who learns that his parents are getting a divorce has 178 points. Even a student with no special problems who transfers from one college to another, changes majors, falls in love, disagrees with an instructor, and changes his or her eating, sleeping, and social patterns accumulates 186 points. For all three students in these examples, the odds for maintaining perfect health are not good.

What can anyone do to avoid these risks—beyond staying home, hiding under the bed? In a useful campus health guide, Otis and Goldingay (1989) recommend such strategies as engaging in aerobic exercise regularly and avoiding big meals just before exams or difficult classes. These authors also point out

College-related stress: Coping is crucial

FIGURE 14.1   Stress is a familiar part of college life, and students who fail to cope with the events and pressures that arise face many health hazards.

Levels of stress on (and off) a college campus

TABLE 14.2 Stressful events differ in their strength and hence in their effects on physical and psychological health. Roughly, a person who experiences stressful events totaling 150 points in a year has about a fifty-fifty chance of developing an illness. The events listed here illustrate common stressful experiences, but note that the two lists are only suggestive, because many of these stresses can occur among either students or nonstudents.

Common Stressful Events among College Students	Common Stressful Events among Nonstudents
High Levels of Stress (71 to 100 points)	
Unwed pregnancy	Death of spouse
Father in unwed pregnancy	Death of parent
	Divorce
Moderate Levels of Stress (31 to 70 points)	
Parents' divorce	Death of close relative
Flunking out	Death of close friend
Loss of financial aid	Jail term
Failing important course	Major injury or illness
Sexual difficulties	Marriage
Argument with romantic partner	Loss of job
On academic probation	Increased work load on job
Change of major	Finding a new love interest
Low Levels of Stress (1 to 30 points)	
Outstanding achievement	Minor violations of the law
Enrolled for first semester	
Conflict with instructor	
Lower grades than expected	
Transfer to a different college	
Change in social activities	
Change in sleeping habits	
Change in eating habits	

Source: Based on data from Brody, 1989.

the importance of learning to deal with interpersonal problems (such as an annoying roommate), reducing test anxiety, and learning to recognize the symptoms of common diseases. And if a student does become ill, it is essential to see a physician without delay.

Though students can't avoid all stress or prevent all illnesses, they can learn to maximize their chances for good health.

Moderating the Effects of Stress   What factors might modify or reduce the effects of stress and thus protect an individual from illness? A familiar recommendation is regular exercise to increase one's *fitness*—endurance, strength, and maintenance of good physical condition. There is also a psychological factor identified as **hardiness,** an element that includes a sense of commitment, the perception of any difficult situation as a challenge and an opportunity, and the belief that one has control over his or her own life (Kobasa, 1979). Knowing how to solve problems and developing a sense of control constitute "learned hopefulness" (Zimmerman, 1990).

Roth and his colleagues (1989) tested the assumption that the negative effects of stress could be reduced by the positive effects of exercise, fitness, and hardiness. Undergraduate males and females were asked to list the stressful experiences in their lives, their illnesses, and their exercise habits and to indicate how fit they were. Each student's attitudes and beliefs were also assessed to determine the individual's degree of hardiness. Analyses revealed how these variables are interrelated, as Figure 14.2 depicts.

The findings are interesting because they indicate just how these factors operate. Stress once again was found to increase the probability of becoming

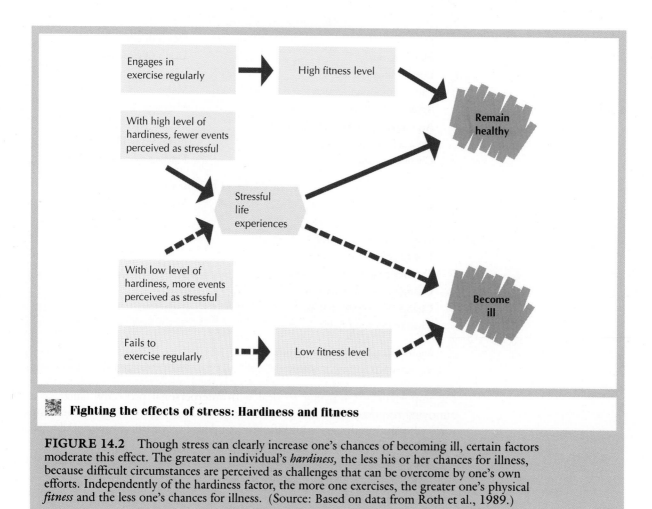

Fighting the effects of stress: Hardiness and fitness

FIGURE 14.2   Though stress can clearly increase one's chances of becoming ill, certain factors moderate this effect. The greater an individual's *hardiness,* the less his or her chances for illness, because difficult circumstances are perceived as challenges that can be overcome by one's own efforts. Independently of the hardiness factor, the more one exercises, the greater one's physical *fitness* and the less one's chances for illness. (Source: Based on data from Roth et al., 1989.)

ill, but the hardiness factor was shown to moderate the negative effects of stressful events by altering how those events are perceived. A person high in hardiness is not overwhelmed by difficult situations; rather, such occurrences spur him or her to find a solution, to do something constructive. The result is a reduction in how much stress is experienced, lower blood pressure (Contrada, 1989), and fewer illnesses.

In a completely independent fashion, the incidence of illness is also reduced if an individual engages in a regular program of exercise and becomes physically fit. One explanation for the role of fitness is provided by other research: Those who are fit experience less cognitive and physiological arousal when confronting stress (McGilley & Holmes, 1988).

It is clear that the health hazards posed by stress can be sharply reduced by hardiness and fitness.

The Role of Personality in the Development of Health Problems Failing grades, romantic difficulties, and other events are upsetting in part because they demonstrate how powerless each of us is. They threaten a person's need to be in control of his or her life. The importance of **perceived control** was highlighted previously, in Chapter 13. When events appear to be uncontrollable, the incidence of physical illness increases (McFarlane et al., 1983), as does that of depression (Brown & Siegel, 1988). The importance of control was also demonstrated in a study of a fictitious illness. When "Haltmar's Disease" was described as uncontrollable, subjects considered it to be much more serious than when it was described as a condition that could be controlled through preventive behaviors (Meyerowitz, Williams, & Gessner, 1987).

Though control is valued by most people, there are times when it is freely given up. Burger, McWard, and LaTorre (1989) point out that *behavioral control* may be surrendered in order to maintain *perceived control* over one's well-being. In an experimental test of that proposition, subjects were presented with a choice of obtaining their own blood sample or letting a competent technician do it. Most preferred to leave the task to the other person. When the technician was described as incompetent, subjects chose to retain control by sampling their own blood. In each instance, they opted for the choice that involved the least pain, thus retaining perceived control of the situation.

In Chapter 12, *locus of control* was described. This concept has frequently been applied to health behavior, using a special measure known as Health Locus of Control (Lau, 1988). Those who strongly believe that internal factors control their health tend to seek more health-related information, remember the information better, and respond more readily to messages encouraging medical examinations than do those who believe in external control (Quadrel & Lau, 1989).

As pointed out in the discussion of hardiness, people differ in interpreting negative events as meaning a lack of control or an opportunity to exert control. If you assume that events are beyond your control and that nothing can be done to improve things in the future, you experience much greater stress and are more likely to become ill. This outlook is pessimistic, and those who view the world in that way report more symptoms of illness after experiencing stressful events (Scheier & Carver, 1987). Pessimistic individuals are even found to die at an earlier age than those who are optimistic (Peterson, Seligman, & Vaillant, 1988). The benefits of optimism were also shown in a study of middle-aged men undergoing bypass surgery. The more optimistic the coronary patient,

The critical role of anger in Type A, coronary-prone behavior

FIGURE 14.3 Though individuals identified as exhibiting the Type A behavior pattern (workaholic, impatient, achievement oriented, time pressured) are found to have an increased risk of developing coronary disease, the key element appears to be anger. The built-up anger suggested in this cartoon is characteristic of those high in the Type A dimension. (Drawing by Chas. Addams; © 1986 The New Yorker Magazine, Inc.)

the better he coped with the surgery (problems were faced and denial was low) and the faster he recovered physically and returned to normal activities (Scheier et al., 1989).

The **Type A** behavior pattern was discussed in Chapter 10 as a personality variable associated with aggression. Interest in Type A behavior originally centered on competitiveness, anger, and the need to achieve as characteristics that increased an individual's chances of developing heart disease. For example, Type A individuals have higher blood pressure than those who are **Type B** (Contrada, 1989), and Type A individuals are twice as likely as Type Bs to suffer from heart disease (Dembroski & Costa, 1987; Engebretson, Matthews, & Scheier, 1989; Weidner, Istvan, & McKnight, 1989). Recent research such as that by Smith and Pope (1990) suggests that the crucial element in coronary problems is the anger component (see Figure 14.3).

Wright (1988) points out that anger and hostility are also involved in some of the other aspects of the overall Type A pattern, such as time urgency. Because Type As are concerned about using their time well, they become angry when others interfere with their work or otherwise slow them down. Striving for achievement does not cause coronary problems; however, for the Type A person, any failure elicits a hostile self-schema, and it is this hostility that is detrimental to good health (Moser & Dyck, 1989).

People also differ along another relevant personality dimension—how much they value good health. Costa, Jessor, and Donovan (1989) found that the more a person values health (being in good shape, energetic, and maintaining proper weight), the more he or she is likely to exercise regularly, use a seat belt, and strive to have a nutritious diet.

Beyond the differing values of individuals, males and females perceive health differently (Kristiansen, 1989). Females conceptualize health as a fundamental issue in their lives. For males, health becomes relevant only after their other needs have been met. Sociobiologists speculate that health may be especially important to women because successful reproduction is more dependent on the mother's long-term good health than on that of the father.

Social Support as a Health Benefit People who interact closely with friends and relatives are better able to avoid illness and, if illness occurs, to recover from it than those who are interpersonally isolated. This cushion of helpful others is termed **social support.**

According to Cohen and Wills (1985), an interpersonal network functions in two ways. First, people who have social support tend to be healthier in general, whether or not stressful events have occurred. Second, when stress is encountered, other people serve as "buffers." For example, if someone has lost a job, friends or relatives can provide a place to stay or food to eat, along with affection and encouragement. Support helps the person get through a bad experience (Pilisuk, Boylan, & Acredolo, 1987).

When a person expresses his or her feelings about stressful events, such as being sexually abused or experiencing the death of a loved one, it is beneficial to have someone who will listen sympathetically. These self-disclosures decrease physiological stress and thus have a positive health effect. Pennebaker, Hughes, and O'Heeron (1987) found that individuals who never confide their traumatic experiences to others have more major and minor health problems than those who do express their feelings to others.

In an interesting experimental test of the effects of expressing emotions, Pennebaker and Beall (1986) asked subjects to write about a personal traumatic event for twenty minutes each day for four days. Compared with subjects who did not engage in this task, those who wrote about their stressful experiences reported fewer health problems over the following months. It seems that confession is good not only for the soul but for the body as well. Other research indicates that the greatest help occurs when the person does not simply express negative feelings but instead concentrates on problem-solving strategies (Costanza, Derlega, & Winstead, 1988).

Stress caused by life events not only leads to illness but also to the increased likelihood of athletic injuries for some individuals. Specifically, adolescents who lack social support and who have poor coping skills are injured most often when they are experiencing stress (Smith, Smoll, & Ptacek, 1990).

A specific form of social support that has been of interest in recent years is that provided by the husband during his wife's pregnancy—attending birthing classes together, acting as part of a two-person team during labor, and being present during delivery. In the **Multicultural Perspective** section that follows, you will find that studies in two nations indicate individual differences in the willingness of males to take on this role and individual differences among females in how much they benefit from such support.

SOCIAL PSYCHOLOGY: A MULTICULTURAL PERSPECTIVE

Social Support? Husbands in the Delivery Room in Canada and in Israel

Although social support is usually assumed to have a positive physical and psychological effect on those facing stress (Cohen & Ashby-Wills, 1985), individual differences are critical. For example, those high in need for affiliation require more interpersonal support than do those low in this need (Hill & Christensen, 1989). In addition, not all individuals are necessarily a good source of support; some people benefit from receiving support, while others do not; and support is more helpful in some situations than in others. We will describe international research indicating how personality variables affect the role of support during childbirth.

Most women find childbirth stressful, in that it is painful and (especially for the first delivery) arouses fear and anxiety. For some, there is also anger, usually directed at the spouse. Only in relatively recent years have husbands been viewed as a potentially helpful part of the childbirth process and permitted to remain in the delivery room with their wives (see Figure 14.4). A question of importance is whether and under what circumstances the wife's negative feelings can be alleviated by the husband's supportive presence when their baby is born.

For the male who is expected to provide social support for his wife, negative attitudes about sexuality (**erotophobia** as discussed in Chapter 12) affect his willingness to participate in the delivery process. Fisher and Gray (1988) proposed that erotophobic males would find childbirth sufficiently aversive that they would not want to join their wives in the delivery room. To test this hypothesis, the investigators first contacted Canadian couples during the wife's pregnancy and assessed their sexual attitudes. They recontacted the spouses after the birth of their babies. Those males who had chosen to participate in the delivery process were found to be less erotophobic than those who had stayed away. A male who avoids the delivery process because of negative sexual atti-

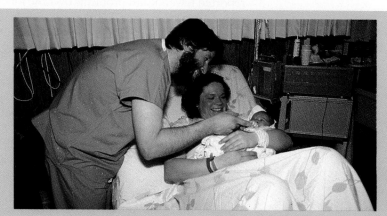

Social support during childbirth: Sometimes helpful, sometimes not

FIGURE 14.4   It is generally thought that a husband can provide *social support* to his wife by being present in the delivery room when she goes through the stress of childbirth. Research has shown, however, that the value of such support is affected by personality factors that play a role in the man's ability to help in this situation and in the woman's need for such support.

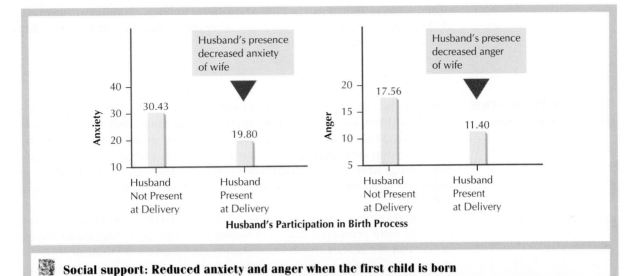

Social support: Reduced anxiety and anger when the first child is born

FIGURE 14.5 The social support provided by the husband's presence in the delivery room was found to be important only when the wife was having her first baby. The new mothers were found to experience more anxiety and more feelings of anger when they had to go through the experience alone rather than with their spouses' support. During subsequent deliveries, no differences were found as a function of the presence or absence of the husband during childbirth. (Source: Based on data from Keinan & Hobfoll, 1989.)

tudes may well be doing the right thing; were he present, he could create additional anxiety, rather than providing comfort and support.

Though the husband's presence or absence in the delivery room is related to his attitudes about sex, the effect of his being there on the wife's reactions is another matter. In Israel, Keinan and Hobfoll (1989) investigated the amount of stress expressed by women giving birth, assessing the amount of anxiety and anger felt by women whose spouses either were or were not present at delivery. The women were categorized into those who were giving birth for the first time and those who had become mothers previously. As Figure 14.5 shows, the first-time mothers expressed much less anxiety and less anger when the husband was present rather than absent. For those who had gone through childbirth previously, anxiety and anger were unrelated to the husband's participation. Presumably, because the experienced mothers knew what to expect, the social support of their mates was less relevant. The wife's *dependency*—that is, her need to let others make decisions and to provide nurturance—was also found to affect a woman's anxiety level. The husband's absence during childbirth caused the greatest anxiety among the women highest in dependency.

These investigations suggest the complex role of social support in reducing stress. In a specific situation like childbirth, support is more likely to be provided by males who have positive rather than negative attitudes about sexuality. Women are helped most by support if this is their first experience with birth, especially if they are high in dependency. Social support is affected by the personalities of those who give and receive it as well as by the past experience of the stressed individual. Summarizing these findings, Hobfoll (1985) concluded that the benefits of social support are determined in part by personality and in part by situational factors.

Behavioral Factors That Help Prevent Illness

Some illnesses cannot be avoided, no matter what we do. Others can be prevented or their risk decreased by preventive measures, and these measures are widely known. For example, most of us are aware that exercise and good nutrition are beneficial and that substances such as cigarettes, alcohol, and illegal drugs have negative health effects. We also know that it is important to brush and floss our teeth, fasten our seat belts, have regular medical checkups, and so on.

Knowing these facts does not necessarily lead to the appropriate behavior, however. Most preventive behaviors require time and the willingness to engage in acts that are at least mildly unpleasant (e.g., getting a flu shot) or to avoid pleasant activities (e.g., passing up fried food that is high in saturated fats). Some of the research in health psychology is directed at understanding why people avoid "doing the right thing" and at developing ways to alter maladaptive patterns of behavior.

Perceived Vulnerability to Illness   One reason that some people avoid preventive behaviors is that they hold unreasonably optimistic beliefs about their health risks (Weinstein, 1987). For example, most people estimate that they are less likely than others to have a heart attack, develop a drinking problem, or be involved in a serious traffic accident. Most of us are also reluctant to make any connection between what we do and the probability of having an illness or accident: If you can convince yourself that you are invulnerable, you will be comforted in the short term, but if this self-confidence leads you to avoid preventive behaviors, the long-term effects can be disastrous.

The **illusion of invulnerability** results in part from the optimistic tendency to view oneself as forever healthy and alive. As you might guess from the research on optimism described in Chapter 12, the happier a person is, the more likely he or she is to feel invulnerable to future negative events (Salovey & Birnbaum, 1989). Those who are depressed are more fearful about illness and more likely to try to prevent it.

Another barrier to healthful behavior is that information about health risks is usually presented in the form of abstract statistics and probabilities. For many, learning that a given activity doubles one's chances of developing a certain health problem over the next twenty years is not especially motivating. As we discussed in Chapter 3, people use *heuristics*—shortcuts and strategies that help make sense of their surroundings. Such simplifying cognitions can sometimes create problems. For example, an individual who employs the *availability heuristic* can easily ignore data based on thousands of research subjects and rely instead on a limited and selective personal experience that is memorable: "I know a man who smoked three packs of cigarettes a day and lived to be ninety-nine" (Rook, 1987). The fact that hundreds of other people smoked that much and died of lung cancer in their forties is more complex and not as easily recalled.

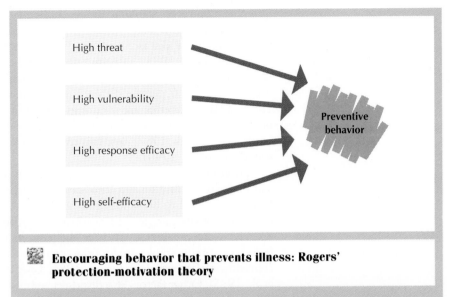

High threat

High vulnerability

High response efficacy

High self-efficacy

Preventive behavior

**Encouraging behavior that prevents illness: Rogers'
protection-motivation theory**

FIGURE 14.6 People can be motivated to engage in behavior that helps
prevent illness if the message contains the four elements indicated here.
The illness must be a threatening one, the individual must be vulnerable to
it, specific behaviors must be perceived as effective in preventing it, and the
individual must believe he or she can effectively engage in those behaviors.
This is the basic outline of Rogers' *protection-motivation theory.*

Motivating Preventive Behavior: The Protection-Motivation Model How can
people be motivated to engage in preventive activities? Although public health
messages on television and in other media are designed for this purpose, they
are often ineffective.

Rogers (1983) developed the **protection-motivation theory** in an attempt to increase the effectiveness of persuasive appeals. To motivate action,
four kinds of information are deemed essential. People need to be informed
that (1) the illness or disease is severe *(high threat),* (2) the individual himself
or herself is *vulnerable* to the threat, (3) the threat can be effectively prevented
by specific behaviors *(high response efficacy),* and (4) it is possible for the person
to perform the necessary preventive behaviors *(high self-efficacy).* These four
elements are summarized in Figure 14.6.

The model's effectiveness was tested in a program designed to increase
participation in regular physical exercise (Wurtele & Maddux, 1987). Subjects
read messages about the severity and potential threat of heart disease and about
the health benefits of physical exercise; they were then given instructions about
how to maintain a exercise program. Perceived vulnerability and feelings of self-
efficacy were found to be especially important in actually increasing the amount
of exercise. Similar results were found in efforts to motivate women to engage
in breast self-examination (Rippetoe & Rogers, 1987). This general model
appears to be useful as a guide to the key factors that result in improved
preventive behavior.

Stopping Cigarette Smoking Before It Begins There is abundant evidence linking cigarette smoking with such life-threatening health problems as lung cancer and heart disease, and most people are well aware that smoking is dangerous (Eiser, 1983). Despite a decline in the proportion of adult Americans who smoke (from about 40 percent to less than 30 percent over the past three decades), 390,000 people die each year as the result of smoking (Whitaker, 1989). Once cigarettes are used regularly, however, the addictive qualities of nicotine make giving up the habit extremely difficult (Abrams et al., 1987; Shiffman & Jarvik, 1987). For this reason, prevention is crucial (Chassin, Presson, & Sherman, 1990).

Health campaigns may encourage children to say no to cigarettes, but the vast majority of children and adolescents nevertheless experiment with smoking. Some then go on to become regular smokers, while some do not. What factors encourage or discourage continued smoking after youngsters first try it? Children who are rebellious, who feel helpless in response to failure, or whose friends or parents smoke are found to be most likely to become regular smokers (Hirschman, Leventhal, & Glynn, 1984; Eiser & van der Pligt, 1984; Collins et al., 1987). Other factors also dispose a youngster to continue using cigarettes. Consistent with the false consensus effect (see Chapter 6), those adolescents who become smokers are found to overestimate the percentage of people who smoke, both among their peers and among adults, as Figure 14.7 shows (Leventhal, Glynn, & Fleming, 1987). Moreover, adolescents who smoke also be-

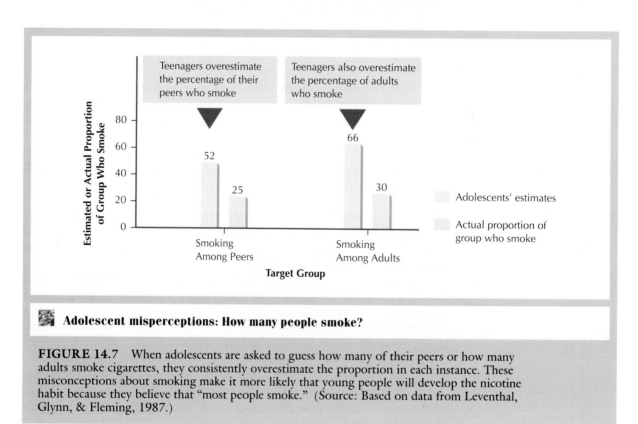

Adolescent misperceptions: How many people smoke?

FIGURE 14.7 When adolescents are asked to guess how many of their peers or how many adults smoke cigarettes, they consistently overestimate the proportion in each instance. These misconceptions about smoking make it more likely that young people will develop the nicotine habit because they believe that "most people smoke." (Source: Based on data from Leventhal, Glynn, & Fleming, 1987.)

lieve, incorrectly, that all it takes to quit is a little willpower. They falsely assume that anyone can "kick the habit" anytime.

In one Canadian study, sixth-graders who were most likely to become smokers were the target of an intervention program (Flay et al., 1985). These young people were at high risk either because of parents or friends who smoked or because they had already developed the habit themselves. An experimental group attended sessions that focused on the negative effects of smoking, the skills required to resist social pressure to smoke, and the importance of making a public no-smoking commitment to their classmates. A control group of high-risk students participated in a health education program that did not involve smoking. Two and a half years later, 75 percent of the experimental group did not smoke, compared with 47 percent of the control group.

Other successful programs aimed at sixth-, seventh-, and eighth-graders have used slides, tapes, and group discussions (Hirschman & Leventhal, 1989). Such results encourage cautious optimism about the possibility of instituting these procedures on a regular basis to prevent youngsters from developing a lifelong cigarette habit. Less encouraging is the finding that a one-shot intervention stressing health risks, social consequences, or both has no effect on smokers (Norman & Tedeschi, 1989).

Even the successful programs may have only short-term effects if they ignore a somewhat surprising variable. Newcomb, McCarthy, and Bentler (1989) studied more than seven hundred male and female adolescents over an eight-year period. This longitudinal approach revealed only a moderate association between teenage smoking and young-adult smoking. The most important set of behaviors and attitudes affecting smoking was termed **academic lifestyle orientation,** a component that included subjects' plans and expectancies to continue their education, plus good school performance—as indicated by grade point average. The researchers found that with positive academic expectations and good grades, the teenagers were less likely to continue smoking as adults, because that orientation is apparently incompatible with smoking. These findings led the investigators to suggest that the best preventive measures may not involve focusing on smoking but, instead, encouraging teenagers to spend more time reading, doing homework, and pursuing some form of academic training. Consistent with these findings is the fact that among adults, amount of education is positively related to success in giving up cigarettes (Kirscht, Janz, & Becker, 1989).

The Anatomy of an Illness Episode: From Recognizing Symptoms to Seeking Professional Help

You might think that once you become ill, only physiological factors are important. We will now describe how psychological factors continue to play a vital role. Figure 14.8 outlines the decisions that must be made in response to symptoms and the behavioral consequences that follow.

Attending to Physical Symptoms   You clearly must have the relevant information to be able to recognize the symptoms of a given medical problem. Beyond information, however, people vary widely in how much attention they pay to internal bodily sensations. Some people are not very introspective, and they are less likely to notice unusual feelings or to conclude that those sensations indicate illness (Mechanic, 1983). The opposite tendency is represented by the "worried well," who regularly overestimate the seriousness of every minor symptom and

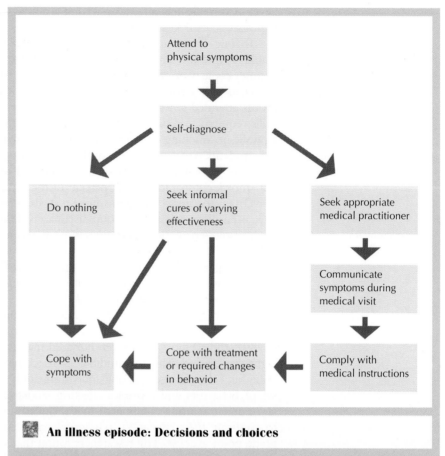

An illness episode: Decisions and choices

FIGURE 14.8 When the symptoms of illness develop, an individual is faced with a series of decisions and choices. It is first necessary to attend to the symptoms and become aware of their presence. Depending on one's self-diagnosis, the response may be to do nothing, to try informal cures (such as nonprescription drugs and folk remedies), or to seek medical help by communicating the symptoms to a practitioner. No matter what action is taken, it is necessary to cope with the outcome—the continued symptoms or the necessary treatment procedures.

seek unneeded medical help (Wagner & Curran, 1984). In its most extreme form, this overattention to symptoms is labeled *hypochondria*.

Noticing symptoms is also a matter of mood. When college students are exposed to a sad or depressing movie, they report more physical symptoms than when they have not seen such a film (Croyle & Uretsky, 1987). When people feel happy, in contrast, minor physical problems are brushed aside.

Diagnosing Your Symptoms After you notice a pain, a lump, a rash, a stiffness, or whatever, you must decide whether or not that symptom indicates illness. If you conclude that it does not, there is no reason to seek help. You may recall the discussion of self-attributions and self-misattributions in Chapter 2. When engaging in self-diagnosis, most people use a commonsense attributional model (Leventhal, Nerenz, & Steele, 1984). For example, your stomach hurts and you begin vomiting; you probably decide that you just have an intestinal virus that will soon go away. But if you actually have appendicitis, your misdiagnosis and the resulting delay in seeking medical help could result in a ruptured appendix—a very serious, even potentially fatal complication.

Examples of this kind of mislabeling are common (Routh & Ernst, 1984). The elderly may attribute their aches and pains to "old age" and thus fail to seek needed medical help (Prohaska et al., 1987). Because high blood pressure (hypertension) has no obvious overt indicators, clients may falsely attribute the lack of symptoms to the disappearance of the disease and thus stop taking medication (Meyer, Leventhal, & Gutman, 1985).

Responding to Symptoms   When a given symptom is noticed and labeled, what does the person do next? He or she can ignore the problem, try to treat himself or herself, or seek professional help.

According to research by Bishop (1987), people tend to classify symptoms along four dimensions. The important considerations are whether the problem (1) is assumed to be caused by a virus, (2) affects the upper or lower body, (3) has a psychological versus a physiological cause, and (4) disrupts their activities. The most common response to a viral infection or a disruptive illness is self-care with nonprescription medicines or home remedies. Professional help is reserved for nonviral physiological problems in the lower part of the body.

Personality factors influence people's responses to some extent. For example, individuals who are most on the alert for threatening information (high monitors) are more likely to visit a physician when they have mild problems than low monitors are (Miller, Brody, & Summerton, 1988).

Once You Know You're Ill: Problems with Medical Care

It is essential to recognize when medical help is needed; however, visiting a physician, undergoing diagnostic procedures, and receiving treatment can each be frightening and sometimes painful.

Interacting with a Doctor   Because of fear, clients frequently forget to mention crucial symptoms or to ask important questions. It helps if the person plans beforehand just what he or she wants to say and ask (Roter, 1984). When prepared in this way, clients say more and obtain more information than when they visit a physician without thinking about what they need to find out.

The communication skills of the doctor are also important. Practitioners who are skilled in sending nonverbal messages and in understanding such messages sent by others have satisfied clients who are most likely to follow the doctor's recommendations (DiMatteo, Hays, & Prince, 1986). By contrast, physicians who are unable to control their own nonverbal communications create problems. Signs of anxiety may be detected by a client, who then assumes the worst: *My condition is so bad that the doctor is afraid to tell me the truth.* Programs for medical personnel can counteract these problems by teaching them better ways to communicate (Hays & DiMatteo, 1984).

Even the phrasing of medical information can be crucial, as you might expect from the discussion of *framing* in Chapter 3. Wilson, Kaplan, and Schneiderman (1987) found that when an individual is told that a pregnancy has a 50 percent chance of producing a normal offspring, the choice of abortion is less likely than if the message states a 50 percent chance of producing an abnormal child. Similarly, people feel that intensive care is less necessary if they are told there is a 90 percent chance of surviving rather than a 10 percent chance of dying.

Coping with the Procedures of Diagnosis and Treatment Many medical procedures consist of interventions that are intrusive, painful, and sometimes dangerous. Undergoing such experiences is stressful, and clients must develop ways to cope with them. What behaviors, feelings, and thoughts are most useful in response to these medical "threats"?

An avoidance strategy can be helpful during treatment; in a dentist's chair, it is adaptive to think about something else or to listen to music, for example. At the self-diagnosis stage, when symptoms of any kind first develop, a person's refusal to think about the problem also serves to reduce any stress caused by the symptoms or by potential medical interventions (Suls & Fletcher, 1985). If, however, the symptoms worsen and the individual continues to ignore them and deny the need to consult a physician, this strategy quickly becomes maladaptive.

As in other stressful situations, coping is enhanced when the patient perceives that he or she has control over the symptoms (Affleck et al., 1987). Active participation in the treatment is helpful, and a client benefits from having information about what is being done and why. Accurate knowledge is much less stressful than ignorance and fear of the unknown (Johnson, 1984; Suls & Wan, 1988). Information provides a cognitive "road map" for the client so that the experience can be interpreted, thus reducing the threat. Even small children can effectively cope with painful procedures if they are well informed beforehand (Jay et al., 1983).

In Chapter 6, we described research in which hospital patients facing surgery preferred having a roommate who had already undergone that same operation rather than a roommate about to undergo surgery. Beyond preferences, having an experienced roommate also hastens the recovery process. Kulik and Mahler (1987) found startling differences between surgical patients who were randomly assigned to rooms with a fellow patient about to have the operation versus those assigned a roommate who had already had it. As Figure 14.9 shows, those with a postoperative roommate walked farther each day following surgery than did those with a preoperative roommate; in addition, they were less unhappy and anxious, needed less medication for pain, and were able to leave the hospital a day earlier than those assigned a preoperative roommate.

Attributions (see Chapter 2) play a role in how people respond to serious illness. Bar-On (1987) interviewed males who had experienced heart attacks and were hospitalized in intensive coronary care units. When asked to explain *why* they'd experienced the coronary problem, some emphasized external, uncontrollable events, such as bad luck, while others pointed to internal, controllable causes, such as being an angry person. In a six-month follow-up, the investigator found that those who made external attributions had returned to work less quickly and avoided resumption of sexual activity for a longer period than had those making internal attributions.

This sampling of research in health psychology provides convincing evidence that psychological factors are involved in every aspect of preventing and responding to illness. Let us next turn to a quite different setting in which social psychology is applied—the courtroom.

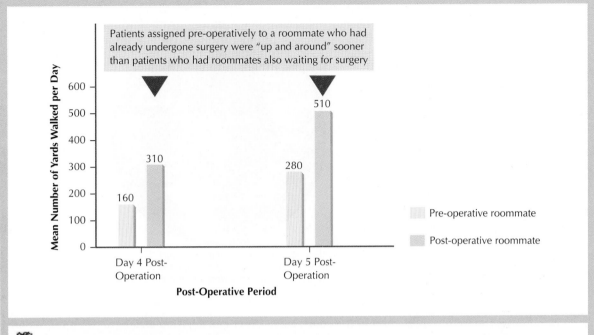

Patients assigned pre-operatively to a roommate who had already undergone surgery were "up and around" sooner than patients who had roommates also waiting for surgery

Pre-operative roommate

Post-operative roommate

The health benefits of a postoperative roommate

FIGURE 14.9 When surgery patients were assigned a roommate who had already undergone the operation, recovery was facilitated, as indicated by how far the patients walked each day in the postoperative period. Patients who had such a roommate were also found to express less anxiety, require less medication, and leave the hospital earlier. (Source: Based on data from Kulik & Mahler, 1987.)

Social Psychology and the Legal System

Ideally, the rule of law provides a way to reach objective, unbiased decisions based on explicit procedures. Despite this ideal, research in **forensic psychology** indicates clearly that human beings may not always function in precisely that way (Davis, 1989). As shown throughout this book, when people interact, their behavior and their judgments are affected by their attitudes, cognitions, and emotions. When the interaction takes place in a courtroom (see Figure 14.10, p. 588), these same factors are equally relevant.

External Effects on Courtroom Behavior: The Media

Newspapers, radio, and television often deal with crime and with criminal cases. Editorial and marketing judgments determine what is emphasized at a particular time. In turn, public opinion can be affected by the resulting news content. For example, though most Americans have had no contact with cocaine or heroin and have never even seen a drug dealer, polls indicate that drugs are perceived as our number one problem by 57 percent of those polled (Barnes, 1989). Presumably, the explanation is the heavy media coverage of drugs and drug-related crimes.

"Yes, Your Honor, we find the court proceedings boring, the company dull, the food terrible and the defendant guilty."

 Bias in the courtroom: Affect and decision making

FIGURE 14.10 Though the ideal of our legal system is to seek the truth through objective procedures, human biases can interfere with this ideal at each step in the process. The affective responses of jurors, for example, can influence their decisions, as illustrated in this cartoon. (Reprinted with special permission of North America Syndicate, Inc.)

Selectivity is necessarily involved in crime coverage. It is simply not possible, even within a single city, to cover *every* violation of the law. Partly in response to public preferences, the emphasis tends to be on crimes that are the most serious, the most violent, or the most bizarre. People are much more interested in learning about a serial murderer who dismembers the victims than about an embezzler who steals money from an employer. As a result, though only 0.2 percent of reported crimes involve murder, 25.0 percent of the crime stories in the news involve murder (Graber, 1980).

One possible consequence of media concentration on only the most serious crimes is a shift in our perceptions of crime and criminals. Because of differences in coverage and because unusual, vivid events are easier to remember (see Chapter 3), sensational stories are most likely to influence our judgments.

Roberts and Edwards (1989) proposed that exposure to descriptions of very serious crimes would lead people to view other offenses more harshly and other offenders more negatively; if so, media emphasis could shift opinions toward harsher punishment for wrongdoers. These hypotheses were tested in an experiment in which subjects read actual newspaper accounts of a crime that was at one of three levels of seriousness: low (petty theft), medium (assault), or high (homicide). Afterward, subjects were exposed to stories of a different crime and different offenders and asked to make several judgments.

As Figure 14.11 indicates, the more serious the crime covered in the newspaper story, the more serious the ratings of the crime and of the offender, and the more severe the recommended sentence. It appears that exposure to stories about major crimes changes how we view other, less dramatic crimes.

Eyewitness Testimony: How Accurate Is It?

When anyone witnesses a crime, an accident, or any event relevant to a legal matter, he or she may later be required to testify about what was seen or heard. A survey of prosecutors indicates that eyewitness testimony is critical in only a minority of their felony cases; nevertheless, they must rely on witnesses as the major source of evidence concerning approximately seventy-seven thousand suspects each year in the United States (Goldstein, Chance, & Schneller, 1989). Further, the testimony of courtroom witnesses clearly has an impact on jurors (Wolf & Bugaj, 1990).

Research on such testimony indicates that eyewitnesses are frequently wrong. Even the most honest and well-meaning citizen may be totally inaccurate when asked to remember the details of a past event or to identify a suspect (Wells & Murray, 1983). Attempts to pick out the guilty individual standing

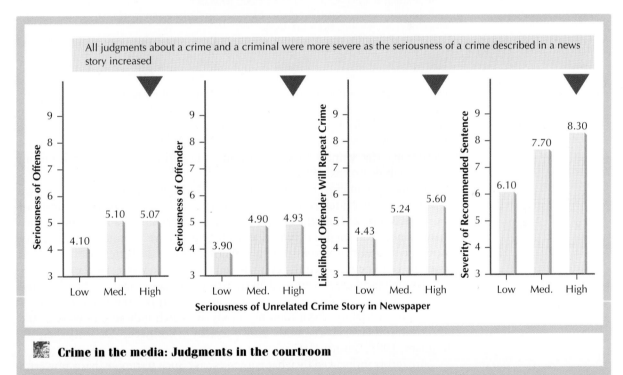

Crime in the media: Judgments in the courtroom

FIGURE 14.11   When subjects read newspaper stories about one crime before making judgments about a second, different crime, their judgments were influenced by the seriousness of the offense described in the newspaper story. The more serious the crime in that story, the more serious subjects rated the second offense and the offender. Further, the more serious the story, the more subjects rated the offender as likely to repeat the offense and the more severe the sentence they assigned. It was suggested that the media emphasis on the most violent and serious crimes exerts a biasing influence on juror perceptions of other crimes. (Source: Based on data from Roberts & Edwards, 1989.)

Identifying the suspect: Many mistakes are made

FIGURE 14.12 Eyewitnesses to a crime are often asked to identify the individual who committed the offense. Research in the laboratory and in field studies consistently indicate that this procedure is not reliable unless a number of modifications are made.

among others in a lineup (see Figure 14.12) very often result in error. Experiments indicate that witness accuracy is decreased if there is a weapon in the suspect's hand (Tooley et al., 1987), if the suspect belongs to a racial or ethnic group different from that of the witness (Platz & Hosch, 1988), and if those questioning the witness make misleading suggestions (Lindsay & Johnson, 1989; Wells & Loftus, 1984).

In one experimental test of eyewitnesses, Buckhout (1980) exposed subjects to a mock crime on television. Given a six-person lineup, only 14.1 percent of the witnesses picked out the correct person as the criminal—a figure no greater than chance. You might assume that such findings are confined to laboratory experiments and that witnesses to a real crime would do better. Sadly enough, accuracy is no better when the event is real (Murray & Wells, 1982).

Though legal experts are well aware that eyewitnesses may be mistaken, the U.S. Supreme Court has ruled that eyewitnesses can be considered credible if they express certainty about their testimony. Research indicates, however, little relationship between certainty and accuracy (Bothwell, Deffenbacher, & Brigham, 1987; Yarmey, 1986).

Are jurors influenced by what witnesses say? Such testimony has a powerful effect, and the impact increases when there are multiple witnesses (Leippe, 1985; Lindsay et al., 1986). Further, eyewitnesses who speak confidently and without hesitation influence the jury even more (Whitley & Greenberg, 1986). The presence of many details in the testimony also makes it more believable and thus has more effect on jurors' decisions (Bell & Loftus, 1988).

Before appearing in a lineup, guilty suspects often try to change their appearance in order to confuse witnesses, and these tactics tend to be successful (Cutler, Penrod, & Martens, 1987). Even worse, an innocent person in the lineup who happens to wear the same kind of clothing worn by the criminal when the crime was committed is likely to be incorrectly identified as the guilty party (Sanders, 1984).

How can the problem of inaccurate witnesses be overcome? It should first be noted that witnesses are better at remembering the details of a crime than at identifying a criminal (Yuille & Cutshall, 1986). Wells (1984) reports that identification can be improved by providing witnesses with practice and informing them how serious it is when errors are made. The procedure is to "train" witnesses by giving them a practice lineup consisting only of innocent volunteers before they participate in the real thing. When they discover that they have incorrectly identified an innocent person as the criminal, their accuracy in the actual lineup increases. This kind of learning experience sharpens the witness's ability to recall crucial details about the suspect and so leads to more reliable testimony.

Another way to improve the performance of witnesses is to "reinstate the context" when the identification is being made. When witnesses are first shown photographs of the victim and the crime setting, they have better recall of the criminal and the accuracy of identification increases (Cutler, Penrod, & Martens, 1987). In addition, Cutler and Penrod found that false identifications are reduced by as much as 50 percent when witnesses see one suspect at a time in the lineup rather than all of them at once (Leary, 1988). Procedural changes also help. Accurate testimony is enhanced when eyewitnesses are simply asked to recall what happened rather than responding to questions containing suggestive implications (Sanders & Chiu, 1988).

With concerted effort, then, the problem of eyewitness inaccuracy can be eliminated or greatly reduced (Wells & Luus, 1990).

Potential Biases: Police, Attorneys, and the Judge

Trials do not occur in a vacuum; they are shaped by what is said and done by the police investigating the case, by the opposing attorneys, and by the judge. The police gather evidence, identify witnesses, and sometimes testify in court. Attorneys decide who will testify, what evidence to present, what questions will be asked, and how to summarize the case to the jury. The judge presides over the interactions, rules on the admissibility of evidence, and explains the case and the law to the jury. Each of these many acts has been found to influence what the jurors decide.

The Police: Questions Seldom Reveal "Just the Facts" One police function is to question those at the scene of a crime. Here, the way questions are worded influences the accuracy of the replies. Loftus (1980) compared the effects of an unbiased question, such as "Did the guy have a gun?" with the effects of a **leading question,** such as "What did the guy's gun look like?" After a leading question, witnesses are more likely to indicate that they remember seeing a gun. In effect, they incorporate false information from the leading questions into their responses.

In a study of police interrogation, Smith and Ellsworth (1987) presented subjects with a videotape of a bank robbery. Afterward, questions were asked about the crime. The confederate who asked the questions was described either as being very *knowledgeable* about what had happened or as being *naive*. In addition, half the subjects with each type of questioner were asked unbiased

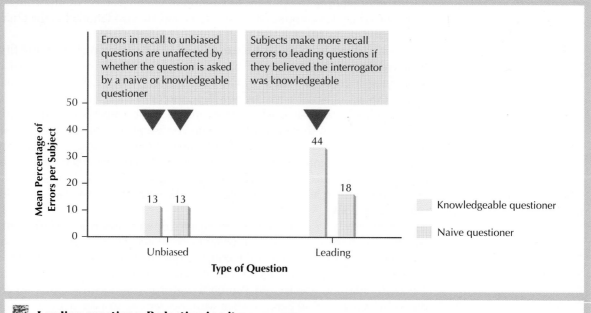

Errors in recall to unbiased questions are unaffected by whether the question is asked by a naive or knowledgeable questioner

Subjects make more recall errors to leading questions if they believed the interrogator was knowledgeable

Mean Percentage of Errors per Subject

Type of Question

Knowledgeable questioner

Naive questioner

Leading questions: Reduction in witness accuracy

FIGURE 14.13 Whether witnesses are asked *leading questions* or *unbiased questions* affects the accuracy of their responses, especially when the questioner is identified as knowledgeable. Leading questions from a knowledgeable interrogator result in a high percentage of errors. (Source: Based on data from Smith & Ellsworth, 1987.)

questions ("Was there a getaway car?"), while half were asked leading questions ("Where was the getaway car parked?"). As Figure 14.13 indicates, the unbiased questions produced the most accurate answers, regardless of who asked them, whereas with the leading questions, accuracy decreased, especially when the questioner was supposed to be knowledgeable. It seems obvious that the truth is best served by training interrogators to ask unbiased questions.

The Attorney as Advocate or as Foe Lawyers play a critical role in the courtroom. For example, they too can ask leading questions and bias the testimony in one direction or the other.

Lawyers' questions influence not only what a witness says but what the jury perceives. When questioning their own witnesses, attorneys tend to request information with unbiased questions, such as "Can you tell me exactly what happened on the afternoon of the murder?" When cross-examining witnesses for the opposing side, however, they ask leading questions, such as "You opened the door to the victim's apartment with your own key, didn't you?" Jurors tend to perceive the witness as more competent and more credible when unbiased questions are asked (McGaughey & Stiles, 1983).

How Impartial Is the Judge? Judges as well as attorneys can behave in ways that influence a trial's outcome. Judges decide what evidence may be used, and this aspect is important because when jurors are exposed to inadmissible evidence, their verdicts are affected (Cox & Tanford, 1989). Judges also react to witnesses and can attack a witness's credibility when explaining the case to the jury. When judges do so, the final verdict is swayed (Cavoukian & Doob, 1980).

Judges also differ in the severity of the punishment they assign to those who are found guilty. People frequently accuse judges of coddling criminals or of favoring the maximum penalties. Carroll et al. (1987) found that judges do in fact tend to fall into one of two categories: Some emphasize the social or economic causes of crime and stress the benefits of rehabilitation, while others emphasize punishment and retribution, believing that the criminal is to blame for the crime. A defendant who is found guilty in a trial is obviously treated more leniently by the former type of judge. Whether you agree with "soft" or "hard" judges probably depends on your own views about the basic causes of crime and the proper role of prisons. Where do such views originate? Studies of college students suggest that those majoring in social science learn to blame society, while business and engineering majors learn to blame the individual for maladaptive behavior (Guimond & Palmer, 1990).

Defendants and Jurors: They're Only Human, Too

In ancient Egypt, to prevent a defendant's appearance from biasing the jury, trials were held in dimly lighted rooms, making it difficult to see. These early legal experts had the right idea. Social psychological research on prejudice, attraction, and attributions indicates that we respond to others on the basis of race, sex, attractiveness, and other characteristics that are (or should be) irrelevant in the courtroom. Such variables affect the outcome of both real and simulated trials.

Are Defendants Treated Equally? A defendant's physical attractiveness is obviously irrelevant to guilt or innocence. Nevertheless, attractive defendants are acquitted more often than unattractive ones (Michelini & Snodgrass, 1980) and, when found guilty, receive lighter sentences (Stewart, 1980). Juries are much more sympathetic to an attractive defendant than to an unattractive one (Kerr, 1978a). Esses and Webster (1988) presented subjects with photographs of adults identified as sex offenders. The least attractive offenders were rated as more dangerous and as more likely to engage in future criminal acts than were average-looking and attractive offenders. Because attorneys are aware of the attractiveness bias, they advise their clients to do everything possible to improve their appearance before entering the courtroom.

The effects of attractiveness can be at least partly overcome if a sufficient amount of factual information is presented to the jury (Baumeister & Darley, 1982) and if the judge reminds the jurors about the basis on which a verdict should be made (Weiten, 1980).

The defendant's sex also affects the verdict. In a mock trial, Cruse and Leigh (1987) presented jurors with the testimony of a trial for second-degree assault in which—during an argument about ending their relationship—the defendant was alleged to have cut the victim with a kitchen knife. Some of the jurors responded to a case in which "Jack Bailey" was accused of cutting "Lucy Hill"; here, fewer than half (43 percent) found Jack guilty. For the other jurors, all the details remained the same, except that the roles were reversed—Lucy Hill was on trial for cutting Jack Bailey; under these conditions, more than two-thirds (69 percent) found Lucy guilty. Thus, in this experiment the sex of the defendant clearly influenced what the jurors decided about guilt versus innocence. The investigators suggested that the female was more likely to be perceived as guilty in this case because attacking another person with a knife is more consistent with traditional views of male behavior than of female behavior. In effect, an aggressive female must be guilty because women "shouldn't act that way."

As you might guess, the defendant's race also affects the verdict. Black defendants in the United States are more likely to be convicted and more likely to receive a prison sentence than white defendants are (Stewart, 1980). Explanations for such findings include the possibility of racist bias, the suggestion that blacks commit more serious crimes, and the argument that economic differences permit white defendants to employ better attorneys.

The victim's race plays a role as well. A study of U.S. trials revealed that 11.1 percent of criminals who kill a white victim receive the death sentence, while only 4.5 percent of those who kill a black victim receive that sentence (Henderson & Taylor, 1985).

Biases on the Jury Jurors and the decisions they make are affected by many factors (Pennington & Hastie, 1990). One such factor is their past judicial experience. Analysis of actual trials has revealed that when a small jury has a large proportion of experienced jurors, this group is more likely to convict the defendant (Werner et al., 1985).

Then too, when a law is unpopular (for example, possession of marijuana), acquittal is more probable, regardless of the evidence. And still another variable influencing decisions is the severity of the punishment—many people seem to believe that harsh laws serve to discourage crime, but as severity increases, jurors become less likely to vote for conviction (Kerr, 1978b).

Certain attitudes, too, are common among jurors, including a bias in favor of the defendant, called **leniency bias** (MacCoun & Kerr, 1988). When jurors differ in their attitudes about issues relevant to a trial, their judgments can be affected accordingly. For this reason, the opposing sides in a case try to determine the attitudes of prospective jurors. For example, many people strongly favor the death penalty, and many strongly oppose it. In those states having the death penalty, jury selection routinely eliminates persons who are opposed to such a punishment. A problem with this particular selection criterion is that those who favor the death penalty are more likely to vote for conviction of a defendant than those who oppose it (Turkington, 1986; Bersoff, 1987). This means that a jury composed of pro-death-penalty individuals is also stacked against the defendant in terms of decisions about guilt or innocence. One way to increase fairness would be to have two juries—a balanced one to judge guilt and (if guilt is determined) a pro-death-penalty jury to address the question of punishment.

Even the procedures used by the jury can affect the verdict. Consider a criminal trial in which the defendant is charged with murder in the first degree. He is accused of having stabbed an acquaintance in a fight outside a bar, resulting in the other man's death. When the jury is ready to begin deliberations, the normal procedure in U.S. criminal cases is for the judge to instruct the jurors to consider whether the defendant is guilty of *first-degree murder*. If they cannot agree, they are next instructed to consider whether he is guilty of *second-degree murder*. If agreement is not reached on this verdict, they consider his guilt for the crime of *involuntary manslaughter*. In other words, they begin with the most serious charge—one carrying the most severe penalty—and afterward

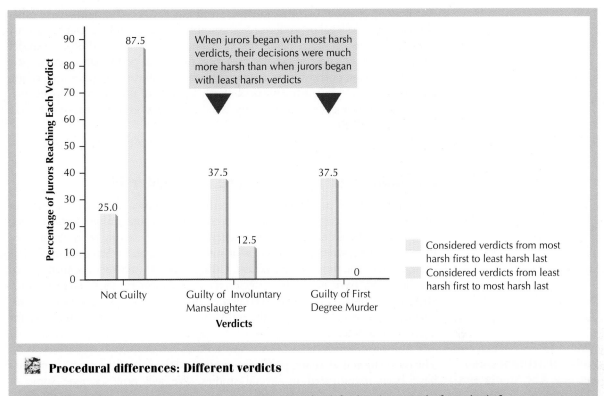

Procedural differences: Different verdicts

FIGURE 14.14 The usual procedure in a trial when the defendant is accused of murder is for the jury members first to consider the most harsh verdict (murder in the first degree). If they do not agree on this verdict, they consider less harsh verdicts (second-degree murder, involuntary manslaughter, not guilty). This procedure results in much harsher decisions than occur when the order is reversed, so the least harsh verdict is considered first. (Source: Based on data from Greenberg, Williams, & O'Brien, 1986.)

proceed to less serious charges with less severe penalties. Could this procedure affect the decisions that are made?

Greenberg, Williams, and O'Brien (1986) proposed that beginning with the most serious charge introduces a bias against the defendant. They had subjects first examine the evidence from a murder trial and then consider possible verdicts in either the usual way or the reverse order—beginning with the least harsh verdict. As expected, the mock jurors in the two conditions reached quite different verdicts (see Figure 14.14). The vast majority found the defendant not guilty in the lenient-to-harsh condition, and 12.5 percent thought he was guilty of involuntary manslaughter. In sharp contrast, only one-fourth of the mock jurors following the usual harsh-to-lenient procedure found the defendant not guilty, and over a third decided he was guilty of first-degree murder. This seemingly minor procedural difference obviously leads to very different judicial decisions.

Research on the legal system provides ample evidence that additional effort is needed to increase judicial fairness and objectivity. The elimination of biases and inaccuracies should be a noncontroversial legal goal.

Beyond issues of bias and attempts to eliminate it, psychologists make other contributions to legal procedures. For example, research findings can be directly relevant to the decisions being made (Monahan & Walker, 1988). Consider such issues as the effect of racial segregation on school performance, the impact of violent media portrayals on aggressive behavior, and the implications of job advancement based on attractiveness. Partly because of their knowledge of such research, psychologists are frequently asked to serve as expert witnesses (Brekke & Borgida, 1988).

Psychology and Politics: Liking and Leadership

The earliest social psychological involvement in political research consisted of surveys. Voters were asked about their choices in an upcoming election. Such polls tend to be accurate predictors when the sample is truly representative of those who vote, when the sample is of sufficient size, and when the sampling is done close to the time of the election. Going beyond voter surveys, many social psychologists have in recent years directed attention to those factors which affect the popularity of specific candidates and hence the outcome of elections. The question is not for whom the individual votes but *why* he or she votes for a given candidate.

Political Attitudes and Actions: The Media and Personal Involvement

The motivation underlying political activism and the role of the media in politics have been investigated in several studies. We will now examine some of this research.

Political Activism   Some citizens, like Kevin in our opening story, become active in campaigns and work hard on behalf of the candidate they prefer. What motivates this kind of participation? Waldron and her colleagues (1988) compared students who campaigned for presidential and congressional candidates in the 1984 Democratic party primaries with students who were not politically active.

One of the leading issues at the time was fear of nuclear war, and—as you might guess—active participants in the campaigns were more fearful of such a catastrophe than nonparticipants. Fear, however, was not enough to motivate political action. In addition, those most involved in campaigns expressed a moral obligation to help prevent nuclear war and placed a higher priority on working for political and social change than on competing activities.

Media Effects   On what basis do people become emotionally involved in such issues as nuclear war, and how do they decide to support a given candidate on such an issue? The most common assumption is that they are influenced by the media. A great many people complain about this influence because they perceive a general bias against their own views (Vallone, Ross, & Lepper, 1985). Actually, analyses of network news shows indicates a generally fair and equal treatment of candidates and of liberal versus conservative issues (Mullen et al., 1987; Robinson, 1985). What the average person wants is apparently not fairness but agreement with his or her attitudes.

Another common perception of the media is termed the **third-person effect** (Davidson, 1983)—the belief that others are influenced by the mass

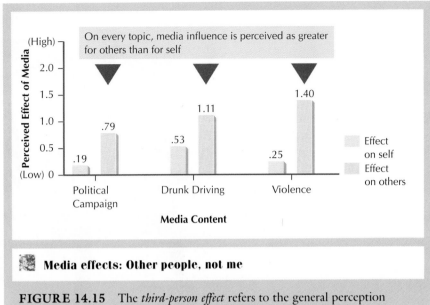

Media effects: Other people, not me

FIGURE 14.15 The *third-person effect* refers to the general perception that other people are influenced by the media but not oneself. When subjects were asked about three different types of media presentations, they consistently perceived more impact on other people than on themselves. (Source: Based on data from Innes & Zeitz, 1988.)

media but not oneself. Such an effect was tested by Innes and Zeitz (1988) in Australia. There, customers at shopping centers were interviewed and asked their opinions about media influences on people in general and on themselves in particular. The specific topics involved a political contest that was then under way, the depiction of violence in the media, and a campaign against drunk driving. The results (see Figure 14.15) clearly supported the third-person effect. Other people are perceived as much more easily influenced than oneself.

Psychology and Voter Behavior

Perhaps the most important decisions made by the citizens of a democracy are reflected in voting. The power to decide who represents you and who is to be placed in a leadership position is one for which people have suffered, immigrated to other lands, and sometimes risked their lives. The secret ballot gives every citizen an equal role in choosing among candidates for political office, and this concept is truly noble.

As social psychologists we are compelled, however, to look closely at how voting decisions are made. Assuming honest elections with an accurate count of the votes (Caro, 1990), one can visualize two extremes. Ideally, informed voters go regularly to the polls to make their wishes known. The most able candidates will be elected, and those who are effective in office will be retained in future elections, while those who do not perform well will be voted out. In contrast, a discouraging view of a modern democracy suggests an ignorant and indifferent electorate being manipulated by cynical and dishonest politicians and their clever advisers (see Figure 14.16, p. 598). According to this view, an election victory is based on who does the best job in deceiving the voters (Young, 1988).

"*Let's run through this once more—and, remember, you choke up at Paragraph Three and brush away the tear at Paragraph Five.*"

 Creating a candidate: The manipulation of voters

FIGURE 14.16 Among the more disheartening aspects of political campaigns is the sophisticated skill of political advisers in manipulating voters' emotions and thus their voting decisions. The scene depicted in this cartoon is not actually a major distortion of what takes place in real life. (Drawing by D. Reilly; © 1988 The New Yorker Magazine, Inc.)

We would like to believe that reality is not as bad as the second characterization suggests. Nevertheless, research on political behavior indicates a number of ways in which decisions *can* be based on irrelevant factors. Television coverage tends to stress pictorial images and brief segments ("sound bites") rather than in-depth political analysis. Between 1968 and 1988, the length of the sound bites involving candidates in election campaigns dropped from an average of 42.3 seconds to 9.8 seconds on network news (Adatto, 1990). Despite the role of irrelevancies, the *intent* of most voters is to select candidates who meet two criteria. They tend to vote for the individual *they like best* (Stengel, 1988) and also for the candidate who seems to be *a good leader* (Adler, 1988). What are the specifics underlying this broad statement?

Choosing a Candidate: Whom Do You Like?

Research on attraction (see Chapter 6) has identified many variables that influence our interpersonal likes and dislikes. Some of these same variables have also been investigated in the political realm, and they are found to affect voting in the same way they affect the formation of friendships.

Repeated Exposure   You may remember that the effect of propinquity on attraction was explained on the basis of *repeated exposure* (Zajonc, 1968). The more times you come into contact with a given person, the more favorably you evaluate him or her. How does this concept apply to a political contest?

Candidates for political office want to appear on television as frequently as possible partly because they want you to see them so often that they become familiar faces with familiar names. Billboards, posters, printed handouts, and buttons serve the same purpose. The resulting "recognition factor" is crucial to a candidate. Political advertising, then, is not always designed to present a substantive message that may only annoy you but rather to utilize repeated exposure to increase your attraction toward the individual running for office. As Grush and McKeogh (1975) found in a study of congressional primaries in the United States, the more such exposure, the more votes. Because this process is costly, the investigators described the outcome as "the finest representation that money can buy."

The crucial role of *affect* is described in the following **Cutting Edge** section. Attraction research leads to the prediction that with other factors being equal, the candidate who successfully arouses positive emotions is the candidate who will win.

FOCUS ON RESEARCH: THE CUTTING EDGE

Winning a Presidential Election: Put On a Happy Face

In the United States as well as in other nations, there is a long tradition of using emotion-arousing cues to please the voters—brass bands and flags, for example. Because these have become standard props, they tend not to differentiate rival candidates. As a result, more importance is placed on what a candidate says and how his or her words make us feel. One goal of a political adviser, then, is to associate positive feelings with a given candidate (patriotism, family values) and negative feelings with the opposing candidate (soft on crime, weak on defense).

This tactic may sound too obvious and simple to have any influence on voters, yet it is highly effective. Consider two candidates running for the presidency. Would you prefer the one who raises doubts about the country's future and promises to raise your taxes or the one who describes a rosy future and vows to cut your taxes? As Walter Mondale discovered in the 1984 presidential race, Ronald Reagan's "feel good" tactics were much more successful. Only in times of extreme danger such as Britain faced in World War II can someone like Winston Churchill offer only "blood, toil, tears and sweat" and still win. Even in that instance, Churchill's message was an optimistic one that predicted victory in the war against Germany.

In peacetime, optimism is an asset for political candidates (Zullow et al., 1988). Zullow and Seligman (1988), in a large-scale project, measured the level of optimism versus pessimism in the speeches given by the major U.S. presidential candidates at the nominating conventions since 1948. In all but one of the ten contests studied, the more optimistic candidate won the general election.

The single exception occurred in 1968, when the ever-optimistic Hubert Humphrey lost to Richard Nixon. The investigators noted that Humphrey carried the burden of being Lyndon Johnson's vice-president during the escalation of the unpopular war in Vietnam; even so, Humphrey only barely lost the election.

Whatever the explanation for Humphrey's loss, the relative optimism of the acceptance speeches predicted the winner 90 percent of the time. An optimistic speech is one in which the candidate characterizes current problems as temporary and solvable; a pessimistic speech is one in which the candidate either takes the blame for problems or describes them as insolvable. Candidates whose speeches are pessimistic also tend to engage in **rumination,** dwelling repeatedly on conditions that are bad for either the candidate personally or the country as a whole.

Excerpts from two such speeches are presented in Figure 14.17, comparing the 1952 acceptance speeches of Dwight Eisenhower and Adlai Stevenson. Eisenhower (who won) gave an optimistic speech with little rumination, while Stevenson's speech was both pessimistic and ruminative. Their styles contrasted dramatically, and the average American concluded "I like Ike" and his smiling optimism, rather than the intellectual Stevenson, who expressed realistic doubts and emphasized unpleasant alternatives.

Excerpts from Speech Accepting Republican Nomination for President
Ladies and gentlemen, you have summoned me on behalf of millions of your fellow Americans to lead a great crusade—for freedom in the world.

I know something of the solemn responsibility of leading a crusade. I have led one.

In this battle to which all of us are now committed, it will be my practice to meet and talk with Americans face to face in every section, every corner, every nook and cranny of this land.

Excerpts from Speech Accepting Democratic Nomination for President
I accept your nomination—and your program.

I should have preferred to hear those words uttered by a stronger, a wiser, a better man than myself.

I have not sought the honor you have done me.

I would not seek your nomination for the presidency because the burdens of that office stagger the imagination. Its potential for good and evil now and in the years of our lives smothers exultation and converts vanity to prayer.

 Winning with optimism, losing with pessimism

FIGURE 14.17 Zullow and Seligman (1988) found that the outcome of U.S. presidential elections can be predicted on the basis of the relative amount of optimism expressed in the candidates' speeches accepting their party's nomination. In nine out of the ten elections since 1948, the candidate with the more optimistic speech won, and the one with the more pessimistic speech lost. Attraction research suggests that the explanation lies in the positive versus negative affect associated with the two candidates; the more positive the affect, the better liked is the candidate. Shown here are portions of the optimistic speech of Dwight Eisenhower (who won the election) and the pessimistic speech of Adlai Stevenson (who lost) in 1952.

In studying the 1988 campaigns for the nomination within each party, these investigators used the same kind of analysis of the early (pre-Iowa-caucuses) speeches of the seven Democrats and six Republicans in the race. Knowing the outcome of those contests, you will not be surprised to learn that Michael Dukakis and George Bush gave the most optimistic speeches within their respective parties. Further, Bush expressed more optimism than Dukakis did, and he went on to win the general election easily. It is also interesting to learn that Gary Hart and Alexander Haig were the most pessimistic of the potential nominees.

An intriguing footnote to this research is provided by a study comparing optimism and pessimism in East and West Berlin (Ottinger, Seligman, & Morawska, 1988). The investigators found more pessimism in the East than in the West, as indicated by newspaper stories covering the Olympics and by the overt behavior of samples of working men as they sat drinking in bars. After that study was completed, dramatic changes occurred in East Germany; travel restrictions to the West were lifted, sections of the Berlin Wall were demolished, and a new government was installed. Once again, there is a strong suggestion of the possible predictive power of optimistic versus pessimistic outlooks in the world of politics.

Physical Appearance: Voting for a Candidate Who Looks Right   Though few people will admit that appearance has anything to do with their voting preferences, research indicates that indeed it does. One example is provided by a study of candidates running for office in a Canadian federal election (Efran & Patterson, 1974). The physically attractive candidates received almost three times as many votes as the unattractive candidates. Moreover, height—a positive asset for males (see Chapter 6)—is also an important aspect of appearance in elections. In a political contest between two males, the taller one most often wins (Feldman, 1975; Gillis, 1982; Kassarjian, 1963).

What's in a Name?   In many elections, voters are reasonably well informed about those leading candidates who have repeatedly presented themselves to the public. Yet with respect to other candidates—including judges, county coroners, and even vice-presidents—the voter may have little information beyond the name that appears on the ballot. Could the name alone affect voter behavior?

Research has shown positive interpersonal effects for socially desirable first names (Busse & Seraydarian, 1979; Seraydarian & Busse, 1981) and for common rather than uncommon names (Titus & Frankel, 1984). In addition, names that indicate a specific ethnic identity have been shown to appeal primarily to voters who belong to the same group, though not to those in other groups (Byrne & Pueschel, 1973; Kamin, 1958).

O'Sullivan et al. (1988) proposed that names would determine votes in the absence of substantive information about a candidate. Here, the investigators borrowed the actual names of two candidates from an Illinois primary, one a "smooth" or "soap opera" name and the other a less familiar ethnic name. Subjects in a different state were given the following information:

> As you know, many candidates appear to be in the running to be the Democratic Party's nominee for Lieutenant Governor. Two of the candidates are Mark Fair-

child and George Sangmeister. If you could vote in a Democratic Party primary today, which of these two candidates would you choose? (O'Sullivan et al., 1988, p. 1097.)

The order of the two names was reversed for half the subjects. In response to this limited information, more than twice as many subjects chose Fairchild as chose Sangmeister. Almost one-third of the subjects abstained, which is a reasonable response in the absence of information.

The experimenters next added information to the names, providing purported candidate opinions about drugs, AIDS screening, and taxes, and then presented the choice to new subjects (each opinion was associated with each name equally often). With such information present, the name effect disappeared, and very few participants abstained (see Figure 14.18). This experiment emphasizes the importance of voters' being informed about candidates, as opposed to their forming unwarranted impressions based on emotional reactions to superficial information (Zajonc, 1980).

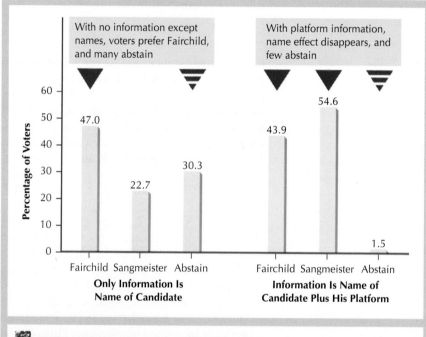

Uninformed voters: Name preferences

FIGURE 14.18   When voters are uninformed about candidates, their decisions are based on reactions to such superficial details as familiarity, social desirability, and ethnicity of the names on the ballot. Responding to candidates on the basis of name but no other information, subjects in this study either abstained or preferred "Fairchild" over "Sangmeister." When subjects received more information, the name effect disappeared and the number of abstentions fell sharply. (Source: Based on data from O'Sullivan et al., 1988.)

Similarity: Voting for Candidates Who Agree with Us It is scarcely surprising that one can predict a person's voting choice on the basis of general political attitudes, such as authoritarianism (Byrne & Przybyla, 1980), or on the basis of specific attitudes about various issues (Byrne, Bond, & Diamond, 1969). In a democracy, a voter is expected to choose a candidate who agrees with his or her own views (Krosnick, 1988). Are there any problems with this practice?

Candidates have a long history of expressing views that match those of their audience. Abraham Lincoln, for example, tended to tell each group to whom he spoke "what they wanted to hear." Today, with instant communication, that technique does not work well. Instead, candidates avoid stating opinions, and they stick to generally popular positions (being for peace and prosperity and against crime and poverty). The candidate who honestly expresses attitudes about any controversial issue is very likely to lose.

Voting for a candidate whose attitudes are similar to yours seems quite reasonable, but voter preference is also based on similarity between the candidate and oneself in age, race, and sex (Piliavin, 1987; Sigelman & Sigelman, 1982). The similarity effect, then, leads to preferences based on ageism, racism, and sexism.

Choosing a Leader: Who Has the Right Stuff?

Liking is not the only consideration in voting; a voter must also believe that the candidate will be a *good leader*. In terms of research on leadership (see Chapter 11), what does this phrase mean? An ideal candidate appears to have specific qualities that suggest he or she is able to help the group reach its goals.

Characteristics of a Leader A leader should be perceived as *intelligent*. When President Gerald Ford stumbled a few times as he walked down an airplane ramp, he quickly (and unfairly) became someone to joke about as a clumsy, not-very-bright ex–football player. Running against Annapolis graduate Jimmy Carter (with an engineering and physics background), Ford was seen as a less acceptable choice.

A leader must also appear to be *self-confident*, to be *achievement oriented*, and to be *dominant*. The candidate who changes his or her mind on issues (as George McGovern did in 1972) is perceived as weak and wishy-washy (Allgeier et al., 1979). Ronald Reagan moved ahead of the other Republican candidates for the nomination in 1980 when he overruled the moderator of a debate by saying, "I paid for this microphone, Mr. Green." The fact that the moderator's name actually was Breen seemed to be irrelevant—it was vital that Reagan had demonstrated the ability to take charge. There is also an almost universal attempt among male candidates to sound tough and manly, leading to what has been labeled "macho-mouth rhetoric" (Kimmel, 1988).

The *self-monitoring* skills of a leader are also an asset (see Chapter 12). A candidate does well if he or she is *sensitive* to the reactions of the audience and is a good *actor*. When a high self-monitor runs against a low self-monitor (Roosevelt versus Hoover, Kennedy versus Nixon, Reagan versus Carter), the higher self-monitor seems to win. Among voters, it is interesting to find that those high in self-monitoring are more inclined to respond to image-based information about candidates, such as appearance, while low self-monitors are more responsive to issues (Young & Osborne, 1989).

Presidential Style

Interpersonal
Gives credit to others for work done
Endears himself to staff through courtesy and consideration
Willing to make compromises
Is not impatient or abrupt in conferences

→ Millard Fillmore
→ George Washington
→ Gerald Ford

Gerald Ford

Charismatic
Enjoys the ceremonial aspects of the office
Has a flair for the dramatic
Uses rhetoric effectively
Is a dynamo of energy and determination
Keeps in contact with the American public and its moods
Rarely shy or awkward in public

→ Franklin Roosevelt
→ Andrew Jackson
→ Lyndon Johnson
→ John Kennedy
→ Theodore Roosevelt
→ Ronald Reagan

Ronald Reagan

Deliberative
Able to visualize alternatives and weigh long-term consequences
Keeps himself thoroughly informed
Cautious and conservative in action
Avoids emotional outbursts

→ Millard Fillmore
→ George Washington
→ James Madison

George Washington

Creative
Initiates new legislation and programs
Innovative in his role as an executive
Rarely a middle-of-the-roader

→ Andrew Jackson
→ Thomas Jefferson
→ Franklin Roosevelt
→ Richard Nixon

Franklin Roosevelt

Neurotic
Places political success over effective policy
Suffers health problems during difficult and critical periods in office
Avoids the direct, uncomplicated approach

→ James Polk
→ Ulysses Grant
→ Martin Van Buren
→ Lyndon Johnson

Lyndon Johnson

 Five leadership styles: Presidential differences

FIGURE 14.19 The thirty-nine U.S. presidents from Washington to Reagan were analyzed to identify presidential styles. Five quite different styles were found. Shown here are the characteristics of the interpersonal, charismatic, deliberative, creative, and neurotic styles and the presidents judged to be highest on each dimension. (Source: Based on data from Simonton, 1988.)

Leadership Styles   Not all leaders are the same, of course, and Simonton (1988) identified five distinct styles among the thirty-nine American presidents from George Washington to Ronald Reagan. Basing his analysis on extensive data from previous research, biographical information, and performance, Simonton identified the presidential styles as *interpersonal, charismatic, deliberative, creative,* and *neurotic.* A description of each style, along with the names of the presidents highest on each dimension, is presented in Figure 14.19.

Simonton pointed out that these styles can be conceptualized as person oriented (interpersonal and charismatic) or task oriented (deliberative and creative). The least successful style is the neurotic one, characterizing a president who is oriented not toward people or tasks but only toward self.

Considering the attention often focused on charisma, should voters select a leader with this quality? Simonton describes the charismatic leader as forceful, able to manipulate others, intellectually skillful, driven to achieve, and innovative. The most charismatic presidents—the two Roosevelts, Andrew Jackson, Lyndon Johnson, John Kennedy, and Ronald Reagan—each had a major impact on this nation.

As you may recall from Chapter 11, three elements distinguish the charismatic leader: (1) A charismatic leader indicates anger about some intolerable aspect of society that must be corrected. For example, Kennedy stressed the nation's drift and military weakness, promising "to get America moving again." (2) A leader with charisma appears emotionally involved in very important goals, and this emotion excites the audience. In addition to the presidents, candidates like Robert Kennedy and Jesse Jackson revealed just such emotional involvement. (3) The charismatic candidate is willing to take risks and try something new. Franklin Roosevelt promised a "New Deal," and Ronald Reagan said he would stimulate the economy by cutting taxes—daring to use unfamiliar economic principles.

When a candidate has charismatic skills, the result is enthusiastic emotional support as well as votes. This development can be good or bad. Whereas a charismatic leader like Roosevelt can lead a nation out of economic despair and mobilize the population to defend itself and win a war, a quite different charismatic leader like Hitler can convince a nation to initiate war and to murder innocent victims in death camps.

Knowledge about the factors affecting voter preferences and about the candidates running for office should provide a basis for making the most intelligent possible electoral choices.

SUMMARY AND REVIEW

Basic research in social psychology has often led to **applied social psychology**—the use of social psychological principles and research methods to solve societal problems involving human behavior.

Health as a Psychological Issue

Health psychology deals with the psychological processes that affect the development, prevention, and treatment of physical illness. Among the topics of investigation are the role of *life stress* in causing illness and ways to moderate stress, *personality dispositions* that lead to the development of health problems, the importance of *social support* as a health benefit, and the *prevention* of illness. Once an illness develops, psychological factors are found to influence the extent to which individuals pay *attention* to symptoms, as well as how they *diagnose* and *respond* to those symptoms. After an illness is diagnosed, health psychology centers on *doctor-client interactions* and on *coping* with medical procedures.

Psychology and the Law

Forensic psychology has made it clear that legal ideals are sometimes unmet because of the way humans are influenced by the *media,* make mistakes in giving *eyewitness testimony,* and express *biases* in functioning as police officers, attorneys, and judges. *Equal treatment for all defendants* is not always achieved, in that *juror bias* is reflected in jurors' responding to irrelevant characteristics of a defendant and in the way jurors' attitudes and procedures affect the judgments they make.

The Psychological Aspects of Political Contests

As important as elections are in a democracy, political behavior often is based on psychological processes. Political choices are in part a matter of *attraction* toward one specific candidate. The critical variables include *repeated exposure* to a candidate's face and name, the manipulation of *affect* so that positive feelings are associated with one of the individuals running for office, the candidate's *physical appearance,* his or her *name,* and *similarity* between voter and candidate. In addition to the element of liking, voters respond on the basis of perceptions of who will be a good *leader.* Five presidential styles have been identified, including the charismatic style.

KEY TERMS

Academic life-style orientation The behaviors and attitudes of an individual involving school, including school performance and any plans and expectations about one's educational future.

Action research Lewin's term for research designed to understand and solve social problems.

Applied social psychology Social psychological research and practice in real-world settings directed toward the understanding of human social behavior and the attempted solution of social problems.

Cope The response to stress, including what a person does, feels, or thinks in order to master, tolerate, or decrease the negative effects of a threatening situation.

Erotophobia An attitudinal disposition composed of relatively negative emotional reactions to many aspects of sexuality.

Forensic psychology The study of the relationship between psychology and the law, including eyewitness reliability and factors involving the media, the police, attorneys, judges, defendants, victims, and jurors.

Hardiness A cluster of characteristics that includes feeling a sense of commitment, responding to each difficulty as representing a challenge and an opportunity, and perceiving that one has control over one's own life.

Health psychology The study and practice of the role of psychological factors that affect the origin, prevention, and treatment of physical illness.

Illusion of invulnerability A person's false belief that risk factors involving health are irrelevant because he or she will never become seriously ill.

Leading questions Those questions asked of witnesses by police investigators or by attorneys which are worded in such a way as to mislead. Such questions provide information that is inconsistent with what the witness actually observed.

Leniency bias A general bias among jurors that leads them to sympathize with and favor the defendant.

Perceived control The extent to which an individual believes he or she is able to affect important aspects of life events.

Protection-motivation theory A formulation suggesting that persuasive appeals can increase preventive health behavior if they convey that (1) the illness is a severe one, (2) the individual is vulnerable to it, (3) certain behaviors are effective in preventing it, and (4) the person is able to perform the necessary behaviors.

Psychoneuroimmunology The study of the way one's responses to external events affect internal physiological states that are crucial to the immune system in defending the body against disease.

Rumination In a pessimistic communication, the tendency to dwell repeatedly on negative events and negative conditions.

Social support The help provided by friends and relatives who give physical and psychological comfort to an individual facing stress. Those having social support tend to be in better physical health and to be better able to resist stress than those lacking such support.

Stress The responses elicited by physical or psychological events perceived by an individual as harmful.

Third-person effect The belief that the mass media influence what others, but not oneself, think and do.

Type A Those individuals who are at the extreme of a personality dimension involving coronary-prone behavior—characterized by a hardworking, aggressive, time-pressured life-style.

Type B Those individuals at the low-risk extreme of the coronary-prone personality dimension. Type Bs are easygoing and relaxed, unconcerned about time pressures, and less likely than Type As to develop cardiovascular disease.

FOR MORE INFORMATION

Kassin, S. M., & Wrightsman, L. S. (1988). *The American jury on trial: Psychological perspectives*. New York: Hemisphere.

A comprehensive book dealing with many of the crucial psychological factors in the legal process, including pretrial bias, the psychology of evidence, decisions about admitting or not admitting testimony, and the dynamics of jury deliberations. Starting with the assumption that juries often fail to reach objective decisions, the authors focus on those factors which influence the decision-making process.

Piven, F. F., & Cloward, R. A. (1988). *Why Americans don't vote*. New York: Pantheon.

A study that traces the declining interest among American voters in participating in the elective process, a decline that began almost a century ago. This lack of interest in voting in the United States differs from the attitudes and behavior of citizens in other democracies and is based in part on social class. Suggestions are made as to how this trend might be changed.

Taylor, S. E. (1985). *Health psychology*. New York: Random House.

A very readable text that describes the application of social psychological methods and research to health, illness, and the medical care system.

Social Psychology in Work Settings: Applications of Its Principles, Methods, and Findings

So you're really going to quit," Angie Lomano says to her friend Brad Thompson. "I can't believe it—you were so up on Consolidated when you went to work there."

"I was, but things have changed," Brad replies. "Let me tell you, it's not the same place anymore."

"What do you mean?" Angie asks.

"I don't know . . . a lot of different things."

"Like what? Be specific."

"Well, the way they handle raises, for instance. When I started there three years ago, the system really seemed fair. Now, it's the pits."

"Why? Don't you have performance reviews and all that stuff?"

"Oh sure, but it's just a farce. The raise you get has practically nothing to do with your work."

"I don't understand," Angie says, puzzled by Brad's remarks. "How can that be?"

"Because raises depend on who you know and how friendly you are with your supervisor. Good work, effort—they count for zilch."

"Whew!" Angie exclaims. "That's pretty bad."

"You bet. And that's not all. The other thing I can't stand is all that tension. Argue, bicker—that's all everyone seems to do. And don't bother asking for help if you need it. No one's going to give it to you. They're all out for themselves, period."

"But why? You're all working together. How can people let each other down like that? In my company, you can really count on help when you need it, especially from your friends."

"Well, you work for a *normal* outfit. I work for a sick one. Profits are down, costs are up, and everyone's scared about their job. They've closed two operations so far this year. Talk about stress; no one knows when *their* number is going to come up."

"I'm surprised. I thought Consolidated was doing well."

"They were, until they decided to get into heavy equipment. They really don't know anything about that market, so they're being murdered by the competition. Even worse, they don't have the sense to cut their losses and get out."

"But that's so stupid!" Angie exclaims. "Why stick with a losing proposition?"

"Don't ask me, I only work there," Brad replies bitterly. "I guess it has to do mainly with politics. The people who pushed so hard for getting into that market in the first place don't want to admit they were wrong. So they just keep throwing more money into it, hoping it'll turn around. But it won't, and in the meantime it's wrecking all our good operations."

"Mmm . . . sounds like they've got real trouble."

"Right, and I want out. I've had it up to here. And I'm not the only one, either. Someone in my department gives notice every few weeks. It's the best people, too. I'd better get out soon or I'll be the last one left!"

"Well, go for it, but don't do anything until you have another job lined up. Remember, it's a pretty tough world out there."

What single activity fills more of most people's time than any other? The answer is simple: *work*. Unless they are fortunate enough to be born with or to acquire vast wealth, most people spend a majority of their waking hours performing some type of job. At first glance, the motivation for such lifelong toil seems straightforward: People work in order to earn a living. While this is certainly true, even a moment's reflection suggests that jobs provide much more than economic benefits. For many individuals, their job or occupation becomes an important part of their self-concept. When asked, "Who are you?" a large

Work: An important part of self-identity

FIGURE 15.1   When asked, "Who are you?" many individuals reply in terms of their occupations or jobs. This illustrates an important fact: The work we do is often central to our self-concept.

proportion reply, "A carpenter," "A dentist," "A secretary," or simply, "A worker" (refer to Figure 15.1). Moreover, because of long-standing beliefs about the necessity and virtue of productive work, a large majority of adults experience guilt if they do not participate in such activities at least part of the time (Riggio, 1990). Finally, we should note that for many persons, work settings are the source of many friendships and pleasant social interactions.

Given the importance of work in our lives, it is not surprising that it has long been the subject of systematic study by psychologists and others (cf. Baron & Greenberg, 1990; Saal & Knight, 1988). The basic goals behind such research have generally been twofold: (1) increasing the efficiency with which individuals can perform various jobs, and (2) making these jobs more interesting and satisfying to the persons who hold them. Does social psychology have anything to contribute to such efforts? We are confident it does. First, work settings are clearly *social settings*—ones in which a great deal of social interaction takes place. It is the rare person who can perform a job entirely on her or his own, without input or assistance from others. Second, many of the key activities occurring in organizations involve processes that have long been the subject of systematic study by social psychologists—leadership, decision making, social influence, and social perception/social cognition, to name just a few (see Figure 15.2, p. 612). The importance of such processes in work settings is suggested by the story on page 609. What's really wrong with the system Brad's company uses for determining raises? Why are so many of his coworkers experiencing interpersonal friction? What accounts for top management's reluctance to pull out of a business venture that threatens to bankrupt the company? As we'll soon see, social psychology offers important insights into these and many other work-related issues.

These comments about the role of social processes in work and work settings probably strike you as obvious. You may be surprised to learn, there-

"You'll go far in this organization, Taylor,
unless I manage to stop you."

The social nature of work and work settings: One illustration

FIGURE 15.2   Work settings are social settings, and behavior in them involves many of the processes studied by social psychologists (e.g., influence and power, social perception). (Drawing by Gahan Wilson; © 1987 The New Yorker Magazine, Inc.)

fore, that it was largely ignored until well into the present century. Only in the Roaring Twenties did widespread recognition of the importance of social factors in work settings begin to develop. And even then, it took the publication of some very puzzling research findings to drive the point home. That research, known as the *Hawthorne studies,* has become a true classic not only in social psychology but in the closely related field of **industrial/organizational psychology**—the branch of psychology that focuses primarily on behavior in work settings. The Hawthorne studies are described in the **Classic Contributions** section on page 613.

Once the social nature of work settings became apparent, the stage was set for an important process: applying the findings and principles of social psychology to the task of understanding many aspects of work-related behavior. Such "information transfer" has continued unabated for several decades, so that in a sense, social psychology serves as one of the major foundations of industrial/ organizational psychology. Recently, however, the pace of this process seems to have accelerated. This is the result of two continuing trends. First, as we noted in Chapter 1, social psychologists themselves have shown growing interest in applying the knowledge of their field to many practical problems, and those occurring in work settings are no exception. Second, increasing numbers of social psychologists have accepted positions in schools of management and in large organizations. In these settings they have turned, quite naturally, to the task of applying their knowledge of social behavior and social thought to many work-related issues.

In this chapter, we will describe several concrete ways in which social psychology has contributed to increased understanding of behavior in work settings. First, we'll indicate how **dissonance theory,** a major framework in social psychology, has shed much light on several forms of complex work-related decisions. Next, we'll turn to ways in which social psychological frameworks dealing with fairness and justice (e.g., *equity theory*) have enhanced understanding of work motivation and related processes. Third, we'll summarize applications of *attribution theory* to such key organizational processes as *performance appraisal* (evaluation of individuals' past work performance) and *conflict.* Finally, we'll indicate how knowledge about the impact of affective states (positive and negative moods) has added much to our current understanding of such work-related processes as job interviews, risk taking, and job satisfaction (cf. Isen, 1987; Isen & Baron, 1990).

SOCIAL PSYCHOLOGY: CLASSIC CONTRIBUTIONS

The Social Nature of Work Settings: Hawthorne Revisited

In the mid-1920s, a series of seemingly straightforward studies was begun at the Hawthorne plant of the Western Electric Company—a plant located just outside Chicago. One purpose of the research was to determine the impact of level of illumination on worker productivity. Several groups of female employees took part. One group worked in a *control room,* where the level of lighting was held constant. Another worked in a *test room,* where the level of lighting was systematically varied. Results were puzzling: Productivity increased in both locations over time. Further, there seemed to be no orderly link between the level of lighting and worker performance. In the test room, output remained high even when illumination was reduced to the level of moonlight—a level so dim that workers could barely see what they were doing.

Puzzled by these findings, Western Electric officials called in a team of experts headed by Elton Mayo. The evidence Mayo and his colleagues uncovered proved crucial in calling attention to the important role of social factors in work and work settings (Roethlisberger & Dickson, 1939). In an initial series of studies, Mayo and his colleagues examined the impact of thirteen different factors on productivity. These elements included length of rest pauses, length of workday and workweek, method of payment, place of work, and even a free midmorning lunch. Subjects were again female employees who worked in a special test room. Once more results were surprising: Productivity increased with almost every change in work conditions. Indeed, even when subjects were returned to the original, standard conditions, productivity continued to increase (see Figure 15.3, p. 614).

To try to clarify these results, the researchers conducted a second series of studies. Here, members of an established work group were carefully observed. No attempts were made to alter their working conditions, but they were interviewed repeatedly during nonwork periods. Results were quite different from those in the earlier studies. Productivity did *not* rise continuously. On the contrary, it soon became apparent that workers in this group were deliberately *restricting* their output. This was indicated both by their actual work behavior

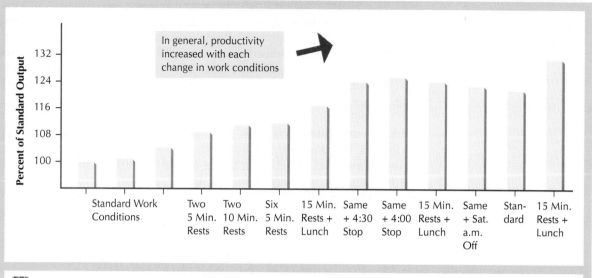

In general, productivity increased with each change in work conditions

The Hawthorne project: Some surprising results

FIGURE 15.3 In one part of the Hawthorne project, female employees were exposed to several changes in their working conditions. Surprisingly, virtually every one of these alterations resulted in increased productivity. These and other findings soon led researchers to conclude that full understanding of work and work settings requires careful attention to many social factors. (Source: Based on data from Roethlisberger & Dickson, 1939.)

(e.g., all men stopped work well before quitting time) and by the interviews (almost all admitted they could easily do more if they wished). Why was this the case? And why did these workers restrict their output when those in the first series of studies did not? Gradually, Mayo and his colleagues reached the following conclusion: The explanation for both sets of results centered around the fact that work settings are actually complex *social systems*. In order to fully comprehend behavior within them, it is necessary to understand worker attitudes, patterns of communication between them, the social norms they have established, plus many other social factors.

Armed with this basic insight, Mayo and his associates were soon able to interpret the puzzling findings of their research. With respect to the first series of studies, productivity rose because subjects reacted favorably to receiving special attention. In short, they knew they were being observed, and because they enjoyed the attention, their motivation—and productivity—rose. In contrast, output in the second series of studies was held low because the men in that work group feared that high productivity would lead to an increase in the amount they were expected to produce each day and might even cost some of them their jobs. The result? These men established informal norms about behavior on the job—norms that tended to reduce overall output.

At this point, we should hasten to note that the Hawthorne studies, important as they proved to be, were seriously flawed. No attempt was made to ensure that participants were representative of all workers in the plant or all manufacturing personnel generally. No efforts were undertaken to ensure that the rooms in which participants were tested were identical to those in other parts of the plant. And different groups of employees were exposed to contrasting conditions or treatments. Because of these and many other problems, it is impossible to determine which factors were most important in generating the obtained results. Yet despite these difficulties, the significance of the Hawthorne project remains. The findings of these studies called attention to the social nature of work settings. As a result, they paved the way for the application of social psychology's findings, theories, and principles to many practical problems in such settings. As the remainder of this chapter will suggest, this has continued to the present time and added much to our understanding of the processes that shape behavior at work. In this sense, certainly, the employees of that long-vanished plant outside Chicago have had a greater and more lasting impact on the world of work than most of them might ever have imagined.

Dissonance and Work-Related Decisions: Job Satisfaction and the Escalation of Commitment

If you recall our discussion of the theory of **cognitive dissonance** (see Chapter 4), you may remember its central assumption: *Human beings dislike inconsistency* (Festinger, 1957). They find inconsistency between various attitudes they hold or between their attitudes and their behavior to be unpleasant. The negative state generated by recognition of such inconsistencies is known as *cognitive dissonance* (or simply *dissonance*), and as we have already noted, it produces strong motivation to reduce it. In other words, persons experiencing dissonance are motivated to engage in actions that will help them eliminate or at least reduce cognitive dissonance.

Unfortunately, dissonance is a common occurrence in everyday life. Each time we make a difficult decision (e.g., choosing between two schools, two automobiles, two lovers), dissonance is produced. After all, the positive features of the choices we decline are inconsistent with our final choice. Similarly, dissonance arises in many situations in which individuals must say one thing even though they think or feel quite another. How can the dissonance generated in such situations be reduced? In general, either by changing one's attitudes or behavior or by acquiring new information that is consistent with (supports) those attitudes or actions. For example, consider an investor who, after buying a stock, learns that the company is in serious trouble and may soon go out of business. This person will experience considerable dissonance; after all, investing one's hard-earned money in a soon-to-be-worthless stock is inconsistent with the value one places on such funds. What can she do to reduce her painful dissonance? Several things. She can reduce her liking for the stock or perhaps sell it, taking a small loss now to avoid a larger one later. Alternatively, she can seek out other opinions suggesting that the company will soon recover and go on to higher profits and a rosy future.

However individuals choose to reduce dissonance, there is little doubt that its occurrence can exert powerful effects on their attitudes, other cognitions, and behavior. But do the principles of dissonance theory have any bearing on behavior in work settings? A growing body of research evidence suggests they do. Dissonance theory has been successfully applied to several aspects of work behavior. Two, though, have received most attention: (1) *job satisfaction* and (2) one aspect of complex decision making known as *escalation of commitment*.

Dissonance and Job Satisfaction: Do People Have to Like Their Jobs?

Do people like their jobs? Many films and television shows paint a negative picture, suggesting that large numbers of people find their jobs boring or dull and would readily change them if they could. Yet contrary to such beliefs, long-term surveys of **job satisfaction**—people's positive or negative attitudes toward their jobs—indicate that most actually express fairly positive views about their jobs. Indeed, between 80 and 90 percent report being relatively satisfied with their current positions (Quinn & Staines, 1979). How can this be so? And how do these reports square with recent trends toward rising absenteeism and turnover in many businesses and toward declining productivity in the United States and several other countries? (See Figure 15.4.) If most persons have positive attitudes about their jobs, what accounts for these trends? One potential answer involves the operation of cognitive dissonance.

Remember that according to dissonance theory, people dislike inconsistency. Thus, they will usually avoid saying or doing things inconsistent with their true beliefs if at all possible. Now, consider what happens when individuals are asked to report their attitudes toward their jobs. Most persons realize that they will have to remain in their current position, or one quite similar to it, for the foreseeable future. Economic conditions and family obligations rarely afford people the luxury of a high degree of job mobility, especially after they enter their thirties. Thus, if they report being dissatisfied with their present work, such persons will experience considerable dissonance. After all, stating that one dislikes one's job is clearly inconsistent with the knowledge that remaining in it is a necessity. To avoid such inconsistency, many persons may choose both to

 Job satisfaction, dissonance, and productivity

FIGURE 15.4 Productivity has declined in the United States and many other nations in recent years. Yet most people report relatively high levels of job satisfaction. *Dissonance theory* helps explain this seeming paradox.

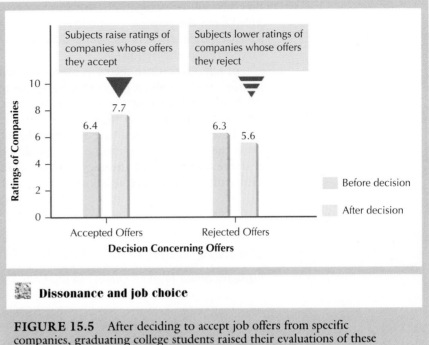

Dissonance and job choice

FIGURE 15.5 After deciding to accept job offers from specific companies, graduating college students raised their evaluations of these firms. In contrast, they lowered their evaluations of companies whose offers they rejected. *Dissonance theory* explains both these results. (Source: Based on data from Lawler et al., 1975.)

report and to perceive their work in relatively favorable terms. In other words, as in other situations involving *forced compliance* (cases in which people are induced to say something they don't believe), once they report that they are satisfied with their jobs, they actually shift in the direction of *being* more satisfied (Baumeister & Tice, 1984).

Evidence consistent with this reasoning has been reported in several studies. For example, consider an ingenious project carried out by Lawler and his colleagues (Lawler et al., 1975). In this investigation, accounting students about to graduate from college were asked to indicate how desirable it would be to work at various firms that had expressed interest in hiring them (i.e., the students reported on their initial predecision attitudes toward these companies). Several months later, after they had actually chosen a specific job, the same students were asked to rate the companies once again. Dissonance theory predicts that they would raise their evaluations of the companies whose offers they accepted, but would lower their evaluations of the companies whose offers they rejected. As shown in Figure 15.5, this is precisely what happened.

These findings agree with the view that once individuals go to work for a particular organization, down-rating their satisfaction with it and with their specific jobs generates dissonance. To avoid this unpleasant state, they come to rate—and to perceive—their jobs in relatively favorable terms. Further support for this line of reasoning is provided by research in which subjects are first asked to imagine they can turn the clock back and start their careers over (Kahn, 1972). They are then asked whether, under these conditions, they would choose the same job or occupation. Not surprisingly, a large proportion answer no. Freed from the constraints of current reality—and from the possibility of dissonance—their answers are quite different from those obtained in standard surveys of job satisfaction.

In sum, dissonance theory provides valuable insights into one of the more puzzling findings about job satisfaction—that reported levels of satisfaction are much higher than might reasonably be expected. The theory suggests that job satisfaction seems so high because, in a psychological sense, people feel they have *no choice:* They have to report liking their current jobs in order to avoid the unpleasant dissonance that would otherwise result. (For additional evidence on the role of attitudes in business and work settings, please see the **Multicultural Perspective** below.)

SOCIAL PSYCHOLOGY: A MULTICULTURAL PERSPECTIVE

Attitudes about Product Quality in the United States and Japan

In recent years, Japanese products have gained increasing popularity in the United States. Most cameras, virtually all video recorders, and a substantial proportion of automobiles sold in the United States are now manufactured either in Japan or in Japanese-owned plants in the United States. While price and product design certainly play a role in these trends (the success of the Mazda Miata provides one example; see Figure 15.6), another factor seems especially important: *quality*. Many consumers believe that Japanese products are much more reliable, more carefully finished, and much less likely to suffer from defects than corresponding products made in the United States. Is this

Japanese products: Are they as good as people believe?

FIGURE 15.6 Why are Japanese products so popular in the United States and elsewhere? While attractive design plays a role, an even more important factor is the widespread belief that these products are very high in *quality*.

Quality in Japanese and U.S. products: Some major differences

TABLE 15.1   Air conditioners manufactured in Japan had fewer defects than air conditioners manufactured in the United States. This was true even when Japanese plants were compared only with the best U.S. plants.

	Number of Assembly-Line Defects per 100 Units	Service Calls per 100 Units
Japanese plants	0.95	0.6
Best U.S. plants	9.00	7.2
Worst U.S. plants	135.00	22.9

Source: Based on data from Garvin, 1986.

really true? And if so, what factors are responsible for such differences? A study by Garvin (1986) conducted in both the United States and Japan provides some intriguing answers.

In this investigation, product quality was studied at nine U.S. and seven Japanese companies that manufactured room air conditioners. The quality of these products was assessed in several ways (through the number of assembly-line defects per one hundred units, the number of service calls per one hundred units during the first year of use, etc.). Together, these measures painted a discouraging picture for the American companies: In all cases, the products made in Japan were clearly superior (refer to Table 15.1).

What was responsible for these differences? To find out, Garvin asked first-line supervisors at all the companies to provide information on the importance of various manufacturing goals within their companies. In other words, the supervisors reported on companywide attitudes toward various goals. Again, results were clear and somewhat disturbing, at least for Americans. Japanese managers reported that their companies placed a great deal of emphasis on producing high-quality, defect-free products. American managers, in contrast, reported that this goal was considerably less important to them. Conversely, while American managers reported that meeting production schedules was very important in their organizations, Japanese managers indicated that this goal was less important and was in fact less important than producing high-quality products (refer to Figure 15.7, p. 620).

In sum, Garvin's (1986) findings suggest that perceived differences in quality between Japanese and U.S. products are indeed real and that the basis for these differences lies at least partly in contrasting attitudes. Japanese managers—and Japanese employees—place greater emphasis on defect-free products as a central organizational goal. And these attitudes, it seems, translate into on-the-job actions that actually produce high-quality results. In view of these results, Garvin suggests that the key to higher quality in American companies lies not in better equipment or more modern plants (though these are certainly impor-

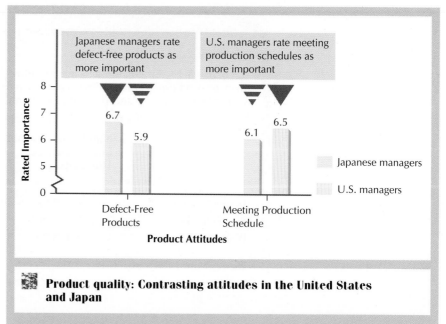

Japanese managers rate defect-free products as more important

U.S. managers rate meeting production schedules as more important

Rated Importance

6.7

5.9

6.1

6.5

Defect-Free
Products

Meeting Production
Schedule

Product Attitudes

Japanese managers

U.S. managers

Product quality: Contrasting attitudes in the United States and Japan

FIGURE 15.7 Japanese managers reported that manufacturing defect-free products was more important to their companies than did U.S. managers. In contrast, U.S. managers reported that meeting production schedules was more important than did Japanese managers. (Source: Based on data from Garvin, 1986.)

tant) but in shifts in key attitudes held by managers and employees alike. As Garvin puts it, "Without a management and workforce dedicated to quality, little is likely to be accomplished" (1986, p. 669). These are chilling words, but they are offset, at least to a degree, by the many practical techniques for changing attitudes suggested by social psychological research (refer to our discussion of this topic in Chapter 4). Altering long-established attitudes is never easy—far from it. Yet such views often *can* be changed. Thus, increased commitment to quality can be developed in American factories. The techniques for doing so already exist; all that's needed is the decision—and the will—to put them to use.

Dissonance and the Escalation of Commitment: One Reason Why People— and Companies—Often Throw Good Money after Bad

Have you ever heard the phrase *throwing good money after bad?* It refers to the fact that in many situations, persons who have made a bad decision tend to stick to it even as the evidence for its failure mounts. Even worse, such persons will often continue to commit time, effort, and resources to failing courses of action once these have been chosen. Examples of this phenomenon—generally known as **escalation of commitment**—abound (e.g., Staw, 1981; Staw & Ross, 1987, 1989). For example, consider the Vietnam War. The United States continued to send more troops and to spend huge sums on this war even as it became increasingly apparent that it could never be won. Less dramatic but equally clear examples of the unsettling tendency to get trapped in bad decisions or in failing courses of action are provided by recent world's fairs and expositions (e.g., the ones held in Knoxville in 1987 and in Vancouver in 1986). In all these cases, it soon became obvious to most persons that the fair or exposition was a losing proposition—that they could never recoup the huge costs of staging it. Yet, despite this fact, once the decision to proceed was made, it was maintained until the end—which, unfortunately, proved to be quite bitter, financially, for the cities involved (see Figure 15.8).

More systematic evidence for the occurrence of escalation of commitment is provided by a large number of laboratory studies (e.g., Staw, 1976). In these experiments, individuals who made initial decisions that turned out to be poor ones demonstrated strong tendencies to stick to these choices, even when doing so was quite costly (Staw, 1981). Moreover, such effects have been observed in a wide range of contexts, ranging from simulated financial business decisions (Staw, 1976; Staw & Ross, 1987) to games involving elements of both luck and skill (Brockner et al., 1986). In short, escalation of commitment appears to be both a real and a general phenomenon. But why does it occur? What factors lead individuals to act in what seems, at least at first, to be a relatively irrational manner (Bowen, 1987)? Once again, dissonance theory offers a potential answer.

Consider the situation faced by persons who learn that a decision they have made is a poor one, and has lead to negative results. Can they readily reverse their initial choice? Doing so is certainly consistent with growing evidence that the decision has failed. On the other hand, reversing their judgment, and admitting that they made a serious mistake, is inconsistent with basic attitudes about their own abilities which, for most persons, are quite favorable. This can lead to considerable dissonance. In addition, if such persons change their minds and act so as to "cut their losses," they are left facing yet another source of dissonance: There is no longer any possibility of justifying the losses already

Escalation of commitment: The costs can be high

FIGURE 15.8   Once plans for fairs such as the one shown here (in Knoxville, Tennessee) are formulated, the cities involved usually go ahead with the projects. That they do so even when it becomes apparent that the events will lose large amounts of money is an example of *escalation of commitment.*

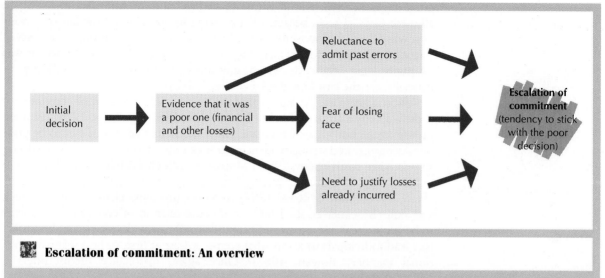

Initial decision → Evidence that it was a poor one (financial and other losses) →

Reluctance to admit past errors

Fear of losing face

Need to justify losses already incurred

→ Escalation of commitment (tendency to stick with the poor decision)

Escalation of commitment: An overview

FIGURE 15.9   Once resources have been committed to a course of action and losses have oc-curred, many people find it difficult to reverse their initial decisions, even though it is clear those decisions were poor ones. As shown here, several factors contribute to such *escalation of commitment.*

incurred. Returning to the Vietnam War as an example of escalation of com-mitment, consider the unhappy situation faced by top military advisers in the United States. Where once they had recommended the commitment of addi-tional troops and resources to the struggle, growing evidence now suggested that the war could not be won. At this point, they could admit their previous error and call for an end to hostilities. But doing so would threaten their own self-images as competent, rational decision makers (Staw & Ross, 1987). Fur-ther, how could they then justify the unsettling costs already experienced in terms of killed or wounded troops and many billions of dollars spent? Faced with this situation, it is little wonder that the advisers—and persons in many other situations involving escalation of commitment—stuck to the failing course they had chosen. Indeed, they saw little choice in the matter. (See Figure 15.9 for a summary of the nature of escalation of commitment.)

Direct evidence for the role of such pressures toward self-justification in the occurrence of escalation effects is provided by several different studies (e.g., Staw, 1981). For example, in one of these experiments (Bazerman, Giuliano, & Appleman, 1984) subjects were asked to play the role of financial officer in a large organization. Their task was to divide $20 million in available Research and Development funds between two of the company's divisions. Before mak-ing this allocation, subjects learned that three years earlier, one of the divisions had received $10 million in development funds. Despite this fact, it had shown a steady drop in earnings ever since. How would subjects now choose to divide the current funds? Dissonance theory suggests that they might well decide to give most of the current $20 million to the division that had previously received such funds, but only if they felt personally responsible for the earlier decision. Under such conditions, subjects would experience strong pressures to justify their previous actions and the resulting losses. If, instead, someone else had made the initial decision, subjects might decide to give more funds to the other division, which, after all, had received nothing before and deserved its chance to develop. To test this prediction, the experimenters asked half the subjects to imagine they had made the previous funding decision (the *high-responsibility* condition) and the remaining half to imagine someone else had made that decision (the *low-responsibility* condition). As expected—and consistent with predictions derived from dissonance theory—only subjects in the high-responsibility condition demonstrated escalation of commitment; they gave most of the current funds to the previously favored, but failing, division. Similar tendencies did not occur among subjects in the low-responsibility group. They did not feel committed to decisions they personally had not made.

Additional and even more intriguing evidence for the role of strong pressures toward self-justification in such situations is provided by a study conducted by Schoorman (1988). He reasoned that the tendency to stick to prior decisions and to attempt to justify them would occur with respect to evaluating employees' performance, as well as in other (e.g., military, financial) contexts. Specifically, Schoorman predicted that managers would evaluate persons whom they personally had hired (or in whose hiring they had been involved) more favorably than persons whom they had recommended not be hired (or in whose hiring they had not been involved). This would be the case because by evaluating persons in the first group positively but those in the second group negatively, the managers could justify their earlier decisions.

To test these predictions, Schoorman asked managers in a large organization to evaluate the performance of clerical workers. Information on whether the managers had been involved in the hiring of each of these persons was also obtained from the organization's records. As you can see from Figure 15.10 (p. 624), results supported both predictions. Managers evaluated employees they had hired or recommended be hired more favorably than ones they recommended not be hired or in whose hiring they had not been involved. Since the clerical workers in both groups were approximately equal in job-related abilities (these were assessed when they were hired), it appears that it was indeed tendencies toward escalation of commitment—not differences between the two groups of employees—that produced this pattern of findings.

In sum, it appears that cognitive dissonance and related processes (e.g., pressures toward self-justification) offer a useful explanation for escalation of commitment. Further, this explanation points to several techniques that may prove helpful in countering such escalation. For example, it may be helpful for managers to assign the development or planning of a project to one group of persons and its actual implementation to another group. In this way, those who put the project into operation will not be subject to the pressures toward self-justification noted above. Then, they should encounter much less difficulty in recommending that it be terminated if early results are disappointing. Similarly, it is probably helpful to provide individuals who wish to reverse a decision that now appears to be a poor one with some means of doing so without damage to either their self-image or their public image. This can be accomplished by establishing norms emphasizing the importance of flexibility and by providing praise and other rewards to persons who admit errors in judgment. Such steps can reduce the magnitude of dissonance generated and so should also lessen decision makers' tendencies to get trapped in escalating spirals from which they see no ready escape.

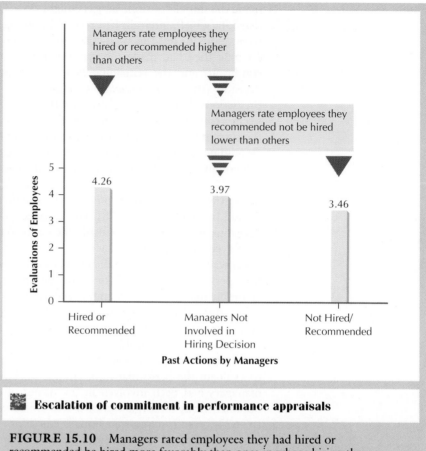

Managers rate employees they hired or recommended higher than others

Managers rate employees they recommended not be hired lower than others

Escalation of commitment in performance appraisals

FIGURE 15.10 Managers rated employees they had hired or recommended be hired more favorably than ones in whose hiring they had not been directly involved. Similarly, they rated employees they recommended *not* be hired less favorably than those in whose hiring they had not been involved. These findings indicate that escalation of commitment can occur even with respect to performance appraisals. (Source: Based on data from Schoorman, 1988.)

Perceived Fairness in Work Settings: Equity Theory, Procedural Justice, and Work Motivation

Suppose that you asked a large number of individuals what was most important to them about their jobs. Certainly, you would receive a wide range of replies. Some individuals would mention pay and various economic benefits; others would focus on the pleasantness of the work itself—on whether or not they enjoyed it. And still others would mention opportunities for advancement or good relations with their supervisor and coworkers. One of the most frequent replies you'd hear, however, would probably go something like this: "Being treated fairly." *Fairness* is a basic value in many cultures, and it is one most people want to see put into practice where they work. In short, they want to be *evaluated* and then *rewarded* fairly (refer to Figure 15.11). If they are not, their morale and motivation may suffer greatly (Greenberg, 1989), with serious consequences for their organizations. But what, precisely, constitutes fairness in work settings? On what grounds do individuals conclude that they are or are not being treated justly? Important insights into this issue are provided by **equity theory,** a framework developed and refined primarily by social psychologists (Adams, 1965; Greenberg, 1988, 1989).

**Equity Theory:
An Overview**

Stated simply, *equity theory* proposes that in determining whether conditions in a work setting (or elsewhere) are fair, individuals compare themselves with others. More specifically, individuals compare the ratio of their own *inputs* and *outcomes* (everything they contribute to their jobs or organization and everything they receive from it) with the same ratio for other persons. Fairness (perceived equity) is assumed to exist when these ratios are approximately equal.

Please note: This does *not* imply that all persons with whom an individual compares herself or himself must receive the same outcomes or offer the same contributions. Rather, what is crucial is that the *ratios* of these factors be roughly equal. For example, consider the case of two employees who work down the hall from each other. Employee A receives an annual salary of $100,000 and has a private secretary, a plush office, and a reserved parking space in the company garage. Employee B receives an annual salary of $35,000, shares a secretary with three other persons, and has a small, simple office and no reserved parking space. Would Employee B perceive his treatment as fair? From just this information, we really can't tell. Remember: what's crucial is the *ratio* of outcomes to inputs. So, to determine whether Employee B will perceive equity or inequity (unfairness) in this situation depends on his views concerning the relative size of his inputs and those of Employee A. If Employee A has many more years' experience, more degrees, and works longer hours than Employee B, this latter person may well conclude that he is being treated fairly. In contrast,

Equity: A crucial issue in most organizations

FIGURE 15.11   As shown here, most persons are highly concerned with comparing their compensation with that of others. (Cathy Copyright 1987, Universal Press Syndicate. Reprinted with permission. All rights reserved.)

if Employee A has only a few more years' experience, no additional degrees, and actually works fewer hours (or less hard), Employee B will perceive that *inequity* exists—he is not being treated fairly (refer to Figure 15.12).

It is important to note that equity (or inequity) is largely in the eye of the beholder. Each individual makes her or his own judgment about the relative size of the outcomes and inputs of each party involved in the comparison. Thus, one person may perceive fairness where another perceives gross inequity. Unfortunately, the *self-serving bias* and other attributional errors (see Chapter 2) often lead individuals to exaggerate their own inputs while underestimating those of others. The result can be considerable friction and conflict. Please note that feelings of inequity can also arise when individuals conclude that they are receiving *more* than they deserve. For example, consider a young woman who believes that her salary is much higher than it should be simply because she belongs to a specific minority group and her company wishes to demonstrate that it treats such persons very well. Under these conditions, strong feelings of inequity may arise and add to the discomfort the woman experiences in this situation. As a result, her motivation and commitment to the company may both be reduced (Chacko, 1982).

According to equity theory, people are motivated to reduce feelings of inequity when they occur, just as they are motivated to reduce dissonance. Indeed, equity theory was originally derived from dissonance theory, and the two are closely related in several respects (Adams, 1965). How do individuals attempt to reduce such feelings? Through a number of techniques that we will review below.

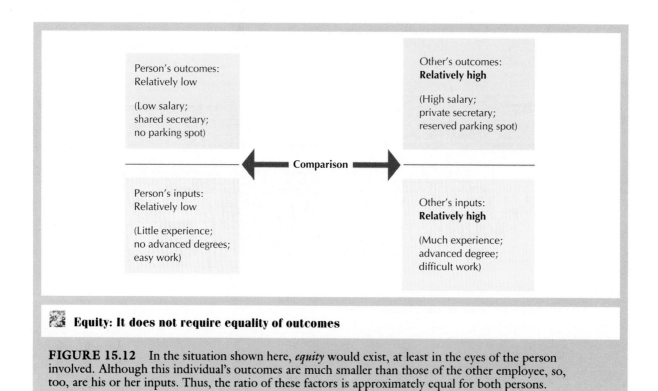

Equity: It does not require equality of outcomes

FIGURE 15.12   In the situation shown here, *equity* would exist, at least in the eyes of the person involved. Although this individual's outcomes are much smaller than those of the other employee, so, too, are his or her inputs. Thus, the ratio of these factors is approximately equal for both persons.

Tactics for Reducing Inequity

When individuals conclude that they are being treated unfairly in some manner, they can take a number of steps to reduce such reactions. First, they can alter their contributions *(inputs)*. Thus, if they feel *undercompensated,* they can reduce their effort or output. Similarly, if they feel *overcompensated,* they can work harder and produce more or can expand the scope of their work activities to ones outside their job description (Brockner, Davy, & Carter, 1986; Organ, 1988).

Second, they can attempt to alter their *outcomes*. If they feel they are getting less than they deserve, they can request a raise, go on strike, or seek a higher-paying job. Conversely, if they believe they are getting more than their fair share, they can offer to reduce their share of available resources. As you can readily guess, this last reaction is rare. Research findings indicate that individuals are much less sensitive to overcompensation than to undercompensation and thus seldom feel much pressure to reduce their own outcomes (Greenberg, 1989). As far as they are concerned, they are simply getting what they deserve!

Third, since equity and inequity are largely in the eye of the beholder, individuals experiencing inequity can engage in various *psychological strategies*. These do not change the actual situation but, rather, alter perceptions of it. For example, individuals who feel underpaid may convince themselves that others' inputs are actually greater than they initially believed. In this way, they may reduce feelings of inequity. Similarly, they may devalue their own contributions and thereby psychologically restore equity.

Effects of Perceived Fairness in Work Settings

Do people really respond to feelings of inequity in the ways just described? Research in actual work settings that has been guided by equity theory indicates that they do (Greenberg, 1989). In what is perhaps the most impressive test of the theory, Pritchard, Dunnette, and Jorgenson (1972) set up a simulated company and actually hired male employees to perform clerical tasks for a two-week period. One group of employees (those who were *overpaid*) were told that the pay they received was higher than that given to others doing the same work. Another group (those who were *underpaid*) were told that the pay was lower than that given to others for doing the same work. Finally, a third group (those who were *equitably paid*) were informed that their pay was equal to that of others doing the same work. In fact, all employees received identical pay. Results agreed with predictions derived from equity theory. Subjects who believed that they were overpaid were more productive than those who thought they were equitably paid. Similarly, subjects who believed they were underpaid were less productive than those who thought they were equitably paid. In addition, those who believed they were equitably paid reported being more satisfied with their jobs than those in the other two groups—even the one that was supposedly receiving higher-than-ordinary pay. This last finding suggests that people value fairness very highly; in fact, in some respects, they react more favorably to fair pay than to excessively high pay.

Additional support for equity theory is provided by reactions to the **two-tier wage systems** adopted recently by many U.S. companies (Martin & Peterson, 1987). Such systems pay newly hired employees much less than those who were hired previously. Even worse, they place lower ceilings on their potential earnings. Equity theory predicts that new employees will react very negatively to such systems; after all, these systems guarantee that such persons will receive much less pay for the same work than more senior employees. Not surprisingly, such reactions have been widely reported. For example, many companies that have instituted such two-tier systems have experienced sharp increases in turnover among employees. In one large supermarket chain, fully two-thirds of the lower-paid employees quit during the first three months on the job—a much higher proportion than in the past, prior to use of the two-tier system (Ross, 1985). Since hiring and training new employees can be quite costly, these findings suggest that two-tier wage systems, because of the intense feelings of inequity they induce, may actually fail to generate substantial savings for the companies that use them. If this is indeed the case, then their continued use is certainly questionable. (In addition to being concerned with fairness in terms of the size of the rewards they receive, most persons are also concerned with fairness in terms of the *procedures* used to determine these rewards. For a discussion of such **procedural justice,** see the **Cutting Edge** section below.)

FOCUS ON RESEARCH: THE CUTTING EDGE

Procedural Justice and Referent Cognitions: Beyond Equity Theory

Imagine that at some point in the future, you fail to get a promotion you hoped to obtain. You are upset but feel that the individual who received it was also a strong candidate. *Those are the breaks,* you tell yourself. *Next time, it will be my turn.* Just as you are about to get over your disappointment, you learn that the process used to assign the promotion was unfair. The committee that made the decision had only incomplete records at its disposal when its members met. If they had had access to all the relevant information, *you,* not the other person, would have received the promotion. How would you react? In all probability, with intense anger. You might be able to live with the outcome—after all, the other person, too, deserved a promotion. But the fact that the *procedures* used to make the selection were unfair is very disturbing.

This incident calls attention to an important point: In deciding whether they are being treated fairly, most individuals pay careful attention to the way in which decisions about the distribution of outcomes are reached, not just to the outcomes themselves. In short, they are concerned about **procedural justice** as well as *distributive justice* (a synonym for equity; Folger, 1987; Greenberg, 1987). What factors enter into the picture in such judgments? According to Folger (1986, 1987), the most important involve individuals' beliefs about whether, had other procedures been used, they would have received better outcomes and whether the decision maker should have used these alternate procedures. Folger (1986) describes such beliefs as *referent cognitions* and has proposed that feelings of unfairness are maximized under conditions where individuals conclude that (1) the decision maker *should* have used other procedures for dividing available rewards and (2) had he or she done so, they would actually have received better outcomes. Clear evidence for the accuracy of these suggestions is provided by a study conducted by Cropanzano and Folger (1989).

In this experiment, female subjects performed two different tasks: a card game known as "Concentration" and a computer game known as "Simon." They were told that if their performance on one of these games met an established criterion, they would receive a bonus (an extra hour of credit for being in the study). Their performance on the other task would not count toward this bonus. Half the subjects were then permitted to choose which task would count as their incentive task; the remainder were merely assigned a task by the experimenter. After performing both tasks, all subjects were told that they had failed to meet the cutoff on their incentive task and would not receive the bonus. Within each condition *(experimenter-choice, subject-choice)*, however, half were told that they *had* met the cutoff on the other task. Thus, if it had been chosen instead, they *would* have earned the bonus. (This was the *high-referent* condition.) In contrast, the remaining subjects were told that they had not met the cutoff on the second task and would not have earned the bonus even if this task had been the one chosen. (This was the *low-referent* condition.) At this point, all subjects rated the extent to which they felt they had been fairly treated and the extent to which they felt understanding or resentful about their treatment.

On the basis of **referent cognitions theory,** Cropanzano and Folger predicted that those subjects whose incentive task had been chosen by the experimenter and who later learned that they would have earned the bonus had the other task been selected *(experimenter-choice, high-referent* group) would react most negatively. In fact, as shown in Figure 15.13, this was the case. Subjects in this condition reported feeling less fairly treated, less understanding, and more resentful than those in any other group.

These findings and those obtained in related research (e.g., Greenberg, 1987) emphasize the fact that in determining whether they are being treated

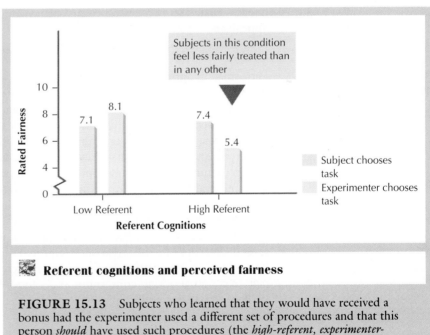

Referent cognitions and perceived fairness

FIGURE 15.13 Subjects who learned that they would have received a bonus had the experimenter used a different set of procedures and that this person *should* have used such procedures (the *high-referent, experimenter-choice* condition) felt less fairly treated and more resentful than subjects in several other conditions. These findings are consistent with predictions from *referent cognitions theory.* (Source: Based on data from Cropanzano & Folger, 1989.)

fairly, individuals are concerned with more than simply what they get—the rewards they receive relative to others. *How* these rewards were determined, too, is important. This seems to be one reason why allowing employees to participate in decisions affecting their jobs often yields beneficial outcomes (e.g., higher job satisfaction or commitment to the organization; Locke, 1990). Such participation may help prevent individuals from assuming that their outcomes would have been much better had different procedures been followed; after all, they themselves participated in the process. In short, permitting employees to participate in key decisions may have positive effects because it prevents them from concluding that "things really would have turned out much better if *I* had been in charge."

Attributions in Work Settings: Performance Appraisal and Conflict

Why do other people behave as they do? What motives, intentions, or characteristics lie behind their words and deeds? As we noted in our discussion of **attribution theory** in Chapter 2, these are questions people ask repeatedly during the course of social interaction (Ross & Fletcher, 1985). Work settings are definitely no exception to this general rule. Individuals who work together frequently attempt to determine one another's motives and to identify one another's traits and characteristics. This occurs in many contexts and with respect to several important processes (e.g., negotiations, organizational politics). Existing evidence suggests, however, that attribution theory is perhaps most directly related to two key aspects of behavior in work settings: **performance appraisals** (Mohrman, Resnick-West, & Lawler, 1989) and **organizational conflict** (Thomas, 1990).

Attributions and Performance Appraisal

Performance appraisal—the process through which employees' past performance is evaluated—is crucial in most organizations. After all, it is on the basis of such assessments that raises, bonuses, promotions, and other available rewards are distributed. For this reason, a great deal of attention has been directed to this topic by industrial/organizational psychologists and experts in human resource management. Such research has focused on the tasks of (1) understanding the nature of the appraisal process—how, specifically, supervisors actually go about evaluating the performance of subordinates—and (2) developing specific procedures to help supervisors be as fair and accurate as possible in this respect (Hedge & Kavanagh, 1988). One of the key findings of such research can be stated as follows: Performance appraisal is a complex process, involving several elements of *social cognition* (e.g., memories about others' past behavior, frameworks for integrating and combining such information) and *social perception* (e.g., attributions concerning the causes behind others' performance). Perhaps a concrete example will help illustrate the practical impact of this conclusion.

Imagine that at some future time, you are a supervisor faced with the task of evaluating the performance of two persons who work under your direction. When you examine their records, you find that both individuals are about equal. But you also know that they have attained these similar levels of performance in different ways. One individual is highly talented but is coasting along, putting little effort into her work. The other is lower in ability but has worked very hard to attain success. To whom would you assign the higher ratings? While it is difficult to say for sure, chances are good that you would rate the hard worker of modest ability somewhat higher, for in many cases we seem to assign greater credit to effort and commitment than to innate talent or ability. Whatever your decision, though, it is likely that you would take into account the causes behind each person's behavior, as well as his or her actual performance. In short, *attributions* would count heavily in your evaluations.

That attributions really do enter into the process of performance appraisal in this manner is suggested by the findings of many recent studies. Together, these projects indicate that attributions can influence (1) supervisors' ratings of their subordinates, (2) the kind of feedback they provide to these persons, (3) supervisors' conclusions regarding the causes behind poor performance, and (4) the specific steps supervisors then take to correct such problems (Greenberger & Strasser, 1986; Martinko & Gardner, 1987; Mitchell, Green, & Wood, 1981). An especially revealing study of such effects has recently been conducted by Dugan (1989).

In this investigation, advanced business students were asked to play the role of either a manager or a subordinate and to participate in a simulated appraisal interview. During this interview, they discussed the subordinate's performance, and managers made decisions concerning her or his future salary. Prior to the interview, all subordinates were given information suggesting that their performance had been relatively poor but that this had been due primarily to difficult task assignments. Managers, too, learned that the subordinates' performance had been poor. However, half received information indicating that this poor performance was due primarily to a lack of effort, while the others received information suggesting it was due mainly to a lack of ability.

The conversations were videotaped, and these tapes were analyzed to determine whether the behavior of the two persons during the simulated interviews was affected by the roles they played (manager, subordinate) and by information concerning the supposed causes for the subordinate's poor performance. In addition, before and after the interviews, both individuals rated the extent to which the subordinate's performance was due to lack of ability, effort, job difficulty, luck, and several other causes.

It was predicted that information concerning the causes behind the subordinate's performance would affect many of these measures, and in fact this was the case. First, as expected, managers assigned smaller raises to the subordinates when their poor performance seemed to stem from lack of effort (a 4.54 percent raise) than when it seemed to stem from lack of ability (a 5.78 percent raise). Thus, managers were more willing to excuse poor performance deriving from a lack of talent than from a lack of effort. Second—and perhaps of even greater interest—the nature of the discussions was strongly affected by the attributional information provided to managers. When managers learned that the subordinate's poor performance stemmed from a lack of ability, they were more likely to take charge of the discussions and direct them. Subordinates, in turn, adopted a relatively deferential, submissive posture. In contrast, when managers learned that the poor performance stemmed from a lack of effort, a more problem-solving pattern of discussion emerged—one in which managers did not assert their higher status and were more willing to listen to what their subordinates had to say. The result was a more effective two-way pattern of communication, with both sides converging toward agreement about the causes behind the subordinate's poor performance. (That is, the attributional ratings of managers and subordinates were more similar after the interviews than before they took place).

In sum, Dugan's (1989) findings suggest that when managers attribute poor performance by a subordinate to lack of effort, they adopt a somewhat mixed but seemingly rational pattern of interacting with such persons. On the one hand, they punish them with smaller raises than they assign to persons whose poor performance stems mainly from factors beyond their control—a lack of ability. They also communicate more effectively with low-effort subordinates during appraisal interviews and work harder toward the goal of helping them improve. Thus, both managers' decisions about their subordinates and their behavior toward these persons are strongly affected by managers' attributions.

Attributional Bias during Performance Appraisals: How Managers Deal with Ingroup and Outgroup Subordinates When we considered attribution theory in Chapter 2, we noted that attribution is *not* an entirely rational process. On the contrary, it is subject to several important forms of bias and error (Fletcher & Ross, 1985). Do such processes also play a role in performance appraisal? Growing evidence suggests that they do (Green & Mitchell, 1979; Martinko & Gardner, 1987). To illustrate the impact of such sources of error, we will consider a study by Heneman, Greenberger, and Anonyuo (1989).

These researchers examined the question of whether managers would demonstrate more favorable attributions toward subordinates they liked (ones in their ingroup) than toward subordinates they disliked (ones in their outgroup). To determine if this was the case, the researchers asked a large group of supervisors to identify the subordinate with whom they had the *best* working relationship and the subordinate with whom they had the *worst* working relationship. Then Heneman and his colleagues asked the supervisors to think about incidents in which each person's behavior exceeded or fell short of appropriate performance standards. Finally, the supervisors rated the extent to which these examples of effective or ineffective performance had stemmed from ability, effort, luck, or task difficulty.

Heneman and his colleagues (1989) predicted that supervisors would favor ingroup subordinates in terms of their attributions for both effective performance and ineffective performance. Thus, the supervisors would be more likely to attribute *effective* performance to internal causes (ability, effort) but less likely to attribute *ineffective* performance to such causes for ingroup than for outgroup members. As you can see from Figure 15.14, results offered support for these predictions. The supervisors did attribute effective performance to internal causes to a greater extent when evaluating ingroup subordinates than when evaluating outgroup subordinates. However, this pattern was reversed for ineffective performance.

In sum, findings reported by many researchers indicate that attributions are central to the process of evaluating employees' performance. This information has in turn been applied to several procedures designed to increase the accuracy and validity of performance appraisals (e.g., Athey & McIntyre, 1987; Hedge & Kavanagh, 1988). In this way, a theoretical framework developed by social

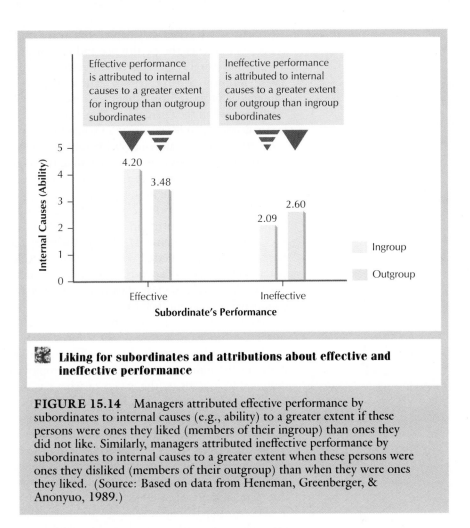

Effective performance is attributed to internal causes to a greater extent for ingroup than outgroup subordinates

Ineffective performance is attributed to internal causes to a greater extent for outgroup than ingroup subordinates

Liking for subordinates and attributions about effective and ineffective performance

FIGURE 15.14   Managers attributed effective performance by subordinates to internal causes (e.g., ability) to a greater extent if these persons were ones they liked (members of their ingroup) than ones they did not like. Similarly, managers attributed ineffective performance by subordinates to internal causes to a greater extent when these persons were ones they disliked (members of their outgroup) than when they were ones they liked. (Source: Based on data from Heneman, Greenberger, & Anonyuo, 1989.)

psychologists has contributed to progress in dealing with a central process in most work settings.

Attributions and Organizational Conflict

Conflict—a process in which individuals or groups take actions that interfere with or block the interests of others—is a serious matter for many organizations. Practicing managers report that they spend almost 20 percent of their time dealing with conflict and its impact (Baron, 1989a; Thomas & Schmidt, 1976). Further, once it develops, conflict tends to exert negative effects on several other aspects of organizational functioning (e.g., coordination, communication). Given these potential costs, it is not surprising that organizational conflict has been studied in detail by investigators from several different fields (cf. Thomas, 1990). The results of such research indicate that conflict in work settings stems from many factors, such as direct competition for scarce resources, struggles over power or influence, long-standing grudges, and occupational stereotypes (Baron & Greenberg, 1990). Do attributions, too, play a role in this regard? A growing body of empirical evidence suggests they do.

First, as we noted in Chapter 10, many studies indicate that attributional processes influence the occurrence and intensity of aggression, a form of behavior that in several respects is closely related to conflict (e.g., Ferguson & Rule, 1983; Johnson & Rule, 1986). These studies indicate that persons who are angered or provoked by others are much more likely to react with anger and retaliation when they perceive such provocations as intentional (stemming from internal, controllable factors) than when they perceive them as accidental (stemming from external, uncontrollable causes). Since organizational conflict often develops in situations in which one individual or group adopts a confrontational stance toward one or more others, it seems possible that similar attributional mechanisms play a role in this process.

Second, direct evidence for the impact of attributions on organizational conflict has been reported in several related studies (e.g., Baron, 1985, 1988b; Bies, Shapiro, & Cummings, 1989). Together, the findings of these investigations indicate that whether conflict actually develops in situations in which the potential for it exists depends to an important degree on the attributions of the persons involved. A clear illustration of this point is provided by research conducted by Baron (1988b).

As is true of much research that seeks to apply the findings of social psychology to work settings, this project involved two separate studies, one conducted under controlled laboratory conditions and the other carried out under field conditions with a sample of employed persons. Both studies were designed to investigate the effects of what has sometimes been termed the *"my hands are tied"* strategy (Rubin et al., 1980). In this strategy, individuals who engage in some anger-provoking, confrontational action attribute it to causes beyond their control. "My hands are tied," they remark. "I had no choice but to do what I did." Presumably, to the extent that recipients believe such statements, their resulting anger and tendencies to retaliate will be reduced (Johnson & Rule, 1986). On the basis of previous findings, Baron (1988b) reasoned that this tactic might well be effective in reducing subsequent conflict if it is accepted as accurate but that if statements are rejected as false, the opposite might be true: The "my hands are tied" tactic might serve to increase rather than reduce later conflict.

To test this possibility, male and female subjects played the roles of executives in a large organization and negotiated with another person (actually an accomplice) over the division of surplus budgetary funds. The accomplice behaved in a uniformly confrontational stance, demanding fully $800,000 of the $1,000,000 available and making only two small concessions during the exchange of offers and counteroffers. Statements by this individual during the negotiations were used to vary the apparent causes behind these actions. In two different conditions *(external attribution—sincere; external attribution—insincere),* the accomplice stated repeatedly that he or she had been instructed to behave in this confrontational fashion by his or her department ("I've got firm instructions to get as much as possible. I really have no choice—I have to do the best I can."). To vary the apparent accuracy (sincerity) of these attributional statements by the accomplice, subjects received information about the instructions the accomplice had actually been given by his or her department. In one group *(external attribution—sincere),* this information indicated that the accomplice was truthful—he or she *had* been told to be tough. In the other *(external attribution—insincere),* this information indicated that he or she was lying; instructions actually urged the accomplice to be conciliatory and to make many concessions.

At the conclusion of the negotiations, subjects answered several questions designed to assess their perceptions of the causes behind the accomplice's behavior. In addition, they indicated their own likelihood of resolving future conflicts with this person in five different ways: *avoidance, competition, accommodation* (giving in to the demands of the accomplice), *compromise,* or *collaboration* (attempting to work out a solution that would maximize the gains of both sides). These have been found to be the basic modes of conflict resolution in work settings (Thomas, 1990).

Results indicated that, as expected, subjects of both sexes reported stronger tendencies to handle future conflicts with the accomplice through avoidance and competition in the external attribution—insincere condition than in the external attribution—sincere condition (refer to Figure 15.15). Thus, as predicted, the "my hands are tied" strategy backfired under conditions in which subjects viewed the accomplice's attributional statements as false.

This pattern of results was replicated in a follow-up field study, conducted with officers of a large urban fire department. These persons, too, reported that they would be "tougher" in dealing with an individual who lied about the causes of his or her own confrontational actions than they would be in dealing

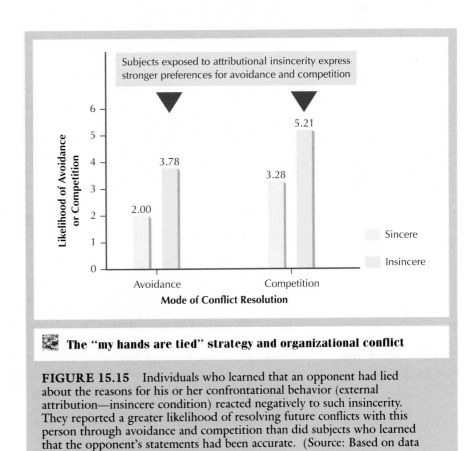

The "my hands are tied" strategy and organizational conflict

FIGURE 15.15   Individuals who learned that an opponent had lied about the reasons for his or her confrontational behavior (external attribution—insincere condition) reacted negatively to such insincerity. They reported a greater likelihood of resolving future conflicts with this person through avoidance and competition than did subjects who learned that the opponent's statements had been accurate. (Source: Based on data from Baron, 1988b.)

with someone who accurately represented these causes. In short, subjects reported that they would react quite negatively to misuse of the "my hands are tied" strategy. The practical message contained in these and related findings (e.g., Bies, Shapiro, & Cummings, 1988) seems clear. Individuals who find it necessary to behave in a confrontational or conflict-provoking manner should carefully consider the attributions others will make about such actions. Often, it appears, these attributions may be more important in shaping subsequent relations than the provocative actions themselves.

Positive Affect: Its Influence in Work Settings

In recent years, social psychologists have directed increasing attention to the impact of **affective states** (positive and negative moods) on behavior and cognition (Isen, 1987). While such research has examined the effects of both positive affect and negative affect, findings regarding the former have generally been much more consistent. For this reason, in this discussion we will focus primarily on the influence of positive affect. Many intriguing results have been obtained in experiments addressing this topic. With respect to interpersonal behavior, it has been found that people are generally more helpful and cooperative and are less aggressive when they are in a positive mood than when they are in a neutral one (e.g., Baron, 1984; Isen, 1987).

Turning to cognition, results indicate that even relatively mild shifts in affect can influence several important processes. First, both positive and negative moods have an impact on memory. In general, information consistent with current moods is recalled more accurately than information inconsistent with such moods (Isen, 1987). Second, persons experiencing positive affect seem to organize information more inclusively than persons not experiencing such feelings (Isen & Daubman, 1984). Thus, they provide more unusual associates to neutral words and perceive unusual instances of various categories as being more representative of those categories than do subjects not experiencing positive affect. (For example, subjects in a good mood rate the word *elevator* as a better example of the category "vehicles" than do subjects in a neutral mood.) Third, persons experiencing positive affect also perform certain tasks—especially ones involving creativity—more effectively than persons not experiencing positive affect (Isen, 1987).

Given the scope and generality of such findings, it seems only reasonable to assume that they might be relevant to several processes occurring in work settings. In fact, this appears to be the case; the way individuals feel *does* influence several important forms of work-related behavior (cf. Isen and Baron, 1990).

Positive Affect and Job Interviews

Imagine you were on a job interview. When you entered the room, you could tell at once that the interviewer was in an especially happy mood. How would you react to this fact? Probably with great pleasure, for you would realize that the interviewer's positive feelings might lead her or him to evaluate you more favorably than would otherwise be the case (refer to Figure 15.16). Conversely, if you found that this person was in a truly rotten mood, you would be dismayed; your ratings might then be much worse than if the interviewer were feeling more cheerful.

Interviewers: Does their current mood really matter?

FIGURE 15.16 Most people believe that an interviewer who is in a good mood will give them higher ratings than one who is in a bad mood. Evidence from systematic research confirms this assumption.

Do such effects actually occur? The findings of several recent studies indicate that they do (Baron, 1987). For example, in one investigation of this topic, Williams, Alliger, and Pulliam (1989) asked interviewers in a leadership training program to rate their own affective states after conducting interviews with prospective candidates. Results indicated that the more positive the interviewers' reported moods, the greater their tendency toward leniency in their ratings—that is, the greater their tendency to assign higher ratings to the applicants than they really deserved.

In related research, Cardy and his colleagues (Cardy, 1987; Cardy & Dobbins, 1986) have found that when individuals are induced to experience a special type of positive affect—liking for another person—they tend to rate him or her more favorably but perhaps less accurately than when such affect is not present. These findings and those of related studies suggest that positive affect—and especially feelings of liking—tends to exert two effects on evaluations of others. First, such reactions raise ratings of others above what they would receive if evaluaters were in a more neutral mood. Second, such feelings also reduce the accuracy of evaluations, perhaps by introducing several forms of error into the process (e.g., halo errors, leniency errors; Tsui & O'Reilly, 1989). Clearly, it is important for interviewers and anyone else who assesses others' qualifications or performance to be aware of such effects. If they are not, the result may be errors in hiring, promotion, and related decisions—errors that can prove costly to both organizations and the individuals involved.

Positive Affect and Negotiations: The Sweet Voice of Reason?

Would you rather bargain with someone who is in a good mood or with someone who is feeling angry and irritable? The answer seems obvious: An opponent who is experiencing positive affect would be a better bet for reaching an amicable agreement. There are several reasons why this should be so. First, as noted above, persons in a positive mood are often more cooperative and less aggressive than those in a neutral or negative mood (e.g., Baron, 1983). Given this fact, they might also be expected to offer more or larger concessions and to be more likely to agree to mutually beneficial compromises. Second, persons in a good mood might be more likely than those in a negative or neutral mood to formulate or recognize creative ways of reaching *integrative solutions*—agreements that maximize the outcomes of both sides (Pruitt, 1983). Third, they may be more willing to trust opponents and may make favorable attributions about the sincerity and reasonableness of their offers. That positive affect actually does facilitate productive negotiations is indicated by the results of several studies (e.g., Baron, 1984; Carnevale & Isen, 1986).

In one of these experiments (Carnevale & Isen, 1986), subjects played the roles of buyer and seller and bargained over the price of several items (television sets, typewriters, vacuum cleaners). Before the start of negotiations, some subjects were exposed to events designed to put them in a good mood (they rated some funny cartoons and received a small gift—a tablet of paper). Others were not exposed to such treatment. Carnevale and Isen predicted that those who had been placed in a positive mood would be more likely to reach agreement, to reach an optimal agreement (one that maximized the joint outcomes of both persons), and to have more favorable evaluations of both the situation and their opponent. In addition, subjects in a positive mood were expected to be less likely to engage in *contentious tactics*—efforts to defeat or intimidate their opponent (e.g., through threats). As shown in Figure 15.17, results confirmed these predictions.

Given the frequency and importance of negotiations in most organizations, these findings have several practical implications. They suggest that steps to put one's opponents in a good mood may well be worth the effort. Indeed, any costs involved may well be more than offset by the gains provided by relatively smooth and speedy progress toward a workable agreement. (We should note, incidentally, that the use of such procedures seems to vary greatly from culture to culture. For example, American negotiators often attempt to get down to the difficult business of bargaining immediately, without any lengthy preliminaries. In contrast, Japanese negotiators spend hours, days, or even longer getting to know their opponents, treating them to dinners and other entertainment, before even mentioning the business at hand [Pfeiffer, 1988]. Given the findings reported by Carnevale and Isen and others, it would seem that this is one instance in which haste may indeed make waste!)

Positive Affect and Risk Taking

Pause for a moment and think about this question: Would you be more willing or less willing to take risks when you are in a good mood as compared with times when you are feeling more neutral? At first glance, the answer seems obvious: People are more willing to take risks when feeling elated than when feeling neutral, aren't they? Perhaps, but the issue turns out to be more complex than this. Isn't it also possible that individuals might be less willing to take risks when in a good mood than when in a bad one? After all, risks involve potential losses, and thinking about these might well tend to reduce or even cancel the positive feelings they are experiencing. So, which pattern actually occurs? In fact, systematic research on this question indicates that both are valid. Each may occur, but only under somewhat different conditions. Specifically, persons experiencing positive affect are more willing to take risks when the potential losses involved are small or trivial. However, they are actually *less* willing to take risks

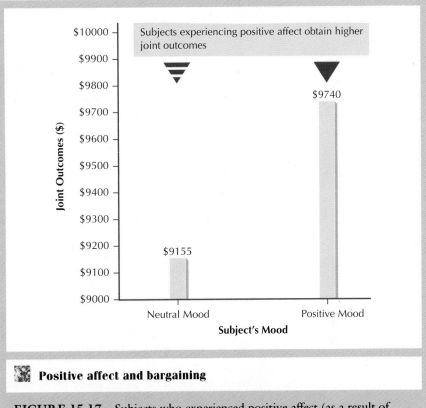

Positive affect and bargaining

FIGURE 15.17 Subjects who experienced positive affect (as a result of receiving a small gift and examining funny cartoons) earned larger joint outcomes during bargaining than subjects in a neutral mood. In addition, subjects in a good mood were less likely to use *contentious tactics* (e.g., threats). (Source: Based on data from Carnevale & Isen, 1986.)

when potential losses are significant and they think about these (e.g., Isen & Geva, 1987; Isen & Means, 1983). Both patterns have recently been demonstrated, and under the expected conditions, by Arkes, Herren, and Isen (1988).

These researchers first placed subjects in a good mood by providing them with a small, unexpected gift and then measured their willingness to take risks under two sets of conditions. In one situation, potential losses were small, and subjects were induced to concentrate on possible gains by indicating how much they would pay for lottery tickets that might enable them to win cash prizes. Here, persons in a good mood were willing to pay more than those in a neutral mood. Moreover, the greater "riskiness" of subjects in a good mood increased as the chances of winning and the size of the prizes available rose. In another situation, potential losses were large, and subjects were induced to concentrate on these by indicating how much they would pay for insurance to protect themselves against the loss of valuable items. Here, persons in a good mood were willing to pay more for the insurance. And again, this tendency to avoid risk increased as the size of the potential losses increased. Together, these findings support the reasoning outlined above: People in a good mood are more

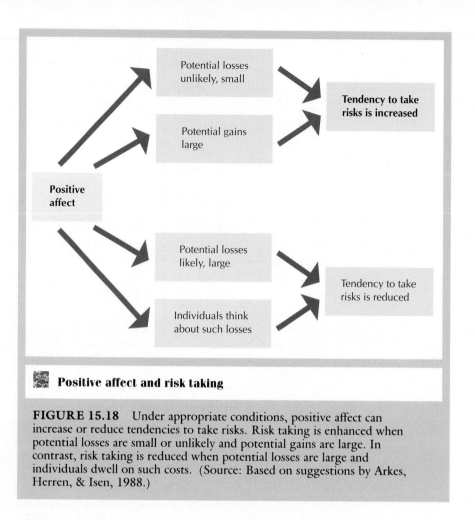

Potential losses unlikely, small

Potential gains large

Positive affect

Tendency to take risks is increased

Potential losses likely, large

Individuals think about such losses

Tendency to take risks is reduced

Positive affect and risk taking

FIGURE 15.18 Under appropriate conditions, positive affect can increase or reduce tendencies to take risks. Risk taking is enhanced when potential losses are small or unlikely and potential gains are large. In contrast, risk taking is reduced when potential losses are large and individuals dwell on such costs. (Source: Based on suggestions by Arkes, Herren, & Isen, 1988.)

willing to take risks, provided that potential losses are unlikely or small in magnitude. However, they actually become less willing to take risks than those in a neutral mood when potential losses are probable or large, and they dwell on these negative outcomes (refer to Figure 15.18).

As you can readily see, this pattern has important implications for persons in work settings who must make decisions involving risk. Individuals whose jobs involve this type of responsibility should avoid making risk-related decisions at times when they are elated. Under such conditions, they may tend to choose courses of action involving relatively high levels of risk, or at least levels that they would find unacceptable at other times. One technique for countering such effects would be to build in safeguards designed to emphasize potential losses. As noted above, attention to losses tends to counter or even reverse tendencies toward risk on the part of persons experiencing positive affect. In any case, it appears that positive affect is one more factor that can serve to distort the judgment of decision makers. (We described several others in our discussion of group decisions in Chapter 11.) Thus, its impact should not be overlooked in situations in which the stakes, for individuals, groups, or organizations, are high.

Additional Effects of Positive Affect: Job Satisfaction and Absence from Work

When we are in a good mood, we have a tendency to view the world through rose-colored glasses—to evaluate many events and experiences more favorably than we would otherwise. This tendency has been confirmed in systematic research, suggesting that people in a good mood do indeed evaluate relatively neutral or ambiguous stimuli more favorably than persons not in a good mood (Isen, 1987). Again, we may ask, are such effects related to important aspects of work behavior? Once more the answer seems to be yes.

First, people in a good mood tend to evaluate their jobs (and specific aspects of them) more favorably than those not in a good mood. In a recent study on such effects, Kraiger, Billings, and Isen (1989) had male and female subjects perform a task in which they coded information about twenty imaginary candidates for teaching associate positions at a large university. Subjects performed this task in two different ways: Either they were simply given the applications and told how to code the information (the *unenriched* version), or they were allowed to select the applications they wished to code and permitted to enter the information in any way they wished (the *enriched* version). In addition, before beginning work, half were exposed to conditions designed to generate positive affect (they saw amusing comedy films); the remaining subjects did not have this experience. After working on the tasks, subjects rated them on several dimensions (e.g., their seeming importance, the extent to which they provided them with variety and autonomy).

Kraiger and his colleagues predicted that subjects would report more favorable reactions to the enriched version of the task than to the unenriched version—this would merely confirm the findings of previous research on job satisfaction (e.g., Hackman & Oldham, 1976; Locke, 1990). In addition, the researchers predicted that subjects experiencing positive affect would also evaluate the tasks more favorably than those in a more neutral mood. Both predictions were confirmed. Further, as shown in Figure 15.19 (p. 642), it appeared that at least for some measures of subjects' reactions, the influence of positive affect was stronger for the enriched than for the unenriched version.

Finally, we should note that other evidence suggests that positive and negative affect may even play a role in absence from work (Graham, 1989). The more positive the feelings individuals report experiencing while at work, the lower their rate of absenteeism. Apparently, when being on the job is associated with positive feelings, people act on this relationship by showing up for work regularly. When, in contrast, they experience mainly negative feelings, they stay away—and so avoid at least one source of such reactions (George, 1989). Of course, many factors besides temporary moods influence individuals' decisions to attend or be absent from work. Economic necessity, health, family obligations, and a host of other variables enter the picture (Hackett & Guion, 1985). Still, it appears that affective reactions to one's job and work environment can exert important effects and should be taken into account in efforts to enhance productivity.

Inducing Positive Affect in Work Settings

Admittedly, this discussion of positive affect has touched on many topics and reviewed a wide range of research findings. Before concluding, it might therefore be helpful to indicate how the beneficial effects described earlier may actually be realized in many work settings. This issue in turn leads to an essential question: How can positive affect be induced among individuals at work?

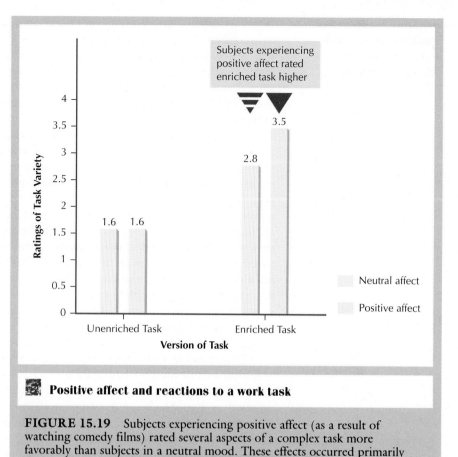

Subjects experiencing positive affect rated enriched task higher

Positive affect and reactions to a work task

FIGURE 15.19 Subjects experiencing positive affect (as a result of watching comedy films) rated several aspects of a complex task more favorably than subjects in a neutral mood. These effects occurred primarily for an *enriched* version of the task (one offering more autonomy and variety) than for a standard (unenriched) version. (Source: Based on data from Kraiger, Billings, & Isen, 1989.)

Several techniques—many of them suggested by the findings of social psychology—appear to be potentially useful.

First, efforts to induce positive affect among working people might focus on enhancing various aspects of the *physical environment*. A large body of research in social psychology suggests that people's moods, social behavior, and task performance are all affected by a number of environmental variables (e.g., temperature, lighting, air quality, noise; Bell, Fisher, & Baum, 1989). Moreover, related findings indicate that such factors also influence reported job satisfaction and motivation (Oldham & Fried, 1987). Improvements in such conditions can be costly; soundproofing, air-conditioning, improved heating—all represent substantial capital costs. Yet given the many benefits that may follow from the positive shifts in affect they produce, such investments may well prove worthwhile. In addition, some evidence indicates that mild increments in positive affect can be obtained through relatively inexpensive means. A recent study by Baron (1990b) suggests that most individuals experience positive affect when they are in the presence of pleasant artificial scents (e.g., commercially available air fresheners). Moreover, this fragrance-generated positive affect is then reflected in increased self-confidence, higher self-set goals, and greater willingness to cooperate with others. Of course, such findings are only preliminary; additional research is needed before the potential usefulness of such interventions can be determined. Still, these results point to one potential cost-effective means for generating mild levels of positive affect among employees.

A second and sharply different approach to inducing positive affect in work settings is suggested by a basic finding of social psychology: In most cases, people strongly prefer to have a degree of control over their outcomes and over important events in their lives (Langer, 1984). This principle suggests that employees will experience higher levels of positive affect (and lower levels of negative affect) when they are permitted to take part in decisions affecting their jobs. Such *participative decision making* has been found to enhance both job satisfaction and output (Crouch & Yetton, 1988; Heilman et al., 1984), and it seems possible that such effects stem at least in part from the positive affect individuals experience when they know that their opinions and preferences are being heeded in an autocratic system in which they otherwise have little or no opportunity to offer input (Crouch & Yetton, 1988; Heilman et al., 1984).

Third, organizations can both enhance positive affect and minimize negative affect among their employees through changes designed to eliminate unnecessary causes of stress, by facilitating communication between employees and management, and by providing adequate and accurate feedback on employees' work (Thayer, 1989). Needless to say, such goals are easier to state than to attain. Still, there is room for optimism. As worldwide competition has grown increasingly intense, top managers in more and more companies have come to realize that people are, after all, their most precious resource. Thus, such managers have shown increasing willingness to heed the advice of social psychologists working in organizations or of other professionals familiar with our field's findings in efforts to enhance motivation and productivity. In this and other ways, social psychology has already contributed much to enhancing human welfare in work settings. Given current trends, we fully expect such contributions to continue—and perhaps to accelerate—in the years ahead.

SUMMARY AND REVIEW

Dissonance and Work-Related Decisions

Dissonance theory, a major theoretical framework in social psychology, contributes to the understanding of several forms of behavior in work settings. First, dissonance theory helps explain why most people report high levels of job satisfaction: By doing so, they avoid the dissonance that would result from rating jobs they cannot leave as unappealing. Dissonance theory also helps explain *escalation of commitment*—the tendency to stick to a decision even in the face of evidence indicating it is a poor one. Dissonance theory suggests that this tendency may stem, at least in part, from the desire to justify losses incurred by the poor decision.

Fairness in Work Settings

Equity theory proposes that individuals will feel fairly compensated in their jobs when the ratio of their contributions to it (inputs) and their benefits from it (outcomes) is roughly equal to the same ratio for other persons. When this is not the case, individuals may take several actions designed to restore feelings of equity (e.g., they may reduce or increase their effort, demand higher pay, or seek another job). In addition, they may psychologically distort their perceptions of the situation, convincing themselves that it is fair when in fact it is not. Judgments of fairness are not determined solely by the relative size of individuals' outcomes. Such judgments are strongly affected by perceptions concerning the *procedures* used to distribute rewards. According to **referent cognitions theory,** individuals experience the strongest feelings of unfairness when they realize that they would have obtained larger rewards if the person responsible for distributing these had followed different rules, and when they conclude that this person *should* have followed such rules.

Attributions in Work Settings

Attributions play an important role in the process of *performance appraisal.* Persons who perform poorly receive more lenient ratings from supervisors if their performance is perceived as deriving from factors beyond their control (e.g., lack of ability) than from factors within their control (e.g., lack of effort). Similarly, persons who perform well receive higher ratings if their performance is viewed as stemming mainly from effort rather than from ability. Managers tend to favor subordinates they like when making attributions about performance. Effective performance by such persons is attributed to internal causes (ability, effort) to a greater extent than similar performance by persons the managers dislike.

Attributions are also relevant to organizational conflict. Individuals who engage in confrontational actions often attribute these actions to external causes beyond their control (the *"my hands are tied"* strategy). This tactic can succeed in reducing subsequent conflict if such statements are accepted as true. If they are perceived as insincere, however, the procedure may backfire and intensify rather than reduce later conflict.

Positive Affect and Work Behavior

Positive affect has been found to influence several forms of social behavior and many aspects of cognition. Such effects also play an important role in work behavior. Persons in a positive mood rate job candidates and others they are asked to evaluate more favorably than persons in a more neutral mood. However, they are also less accurate in such ratings than persons not experiencing positive affect. Individuals experiencing positive affect are more willing to take risks than persons in a more neutral mood, but only when potential losses are small. When such losses are great and individuals are induced to concentrate on them, the opposite is true: Persons in a good mood are less willing to take risks. Positive affect also facilitates negotiations, enhances ratings of specific jobs, and may even reduce the incidence of absences from work.

KEY TERMS

Affective states Relatively mild, subtle, and short-lived feeling states.

Attribution theory A body of knowledge and theoretical frameworks that focus on the processes through which individuals attempt to determine the causes behind others' behavior.

Cognitive dissonance The unpleasant state that occurs when individuals discover that various attitudes they hold or their attitudes and their overt behavior are somehow inconsistent.

Dissonance theory A theory that explains how recognized inconsistencies between individuals' attitudes or between their attitudes and their behavior affect both their overt actions and the attitudes they hold.

Escalation of commitment The tendency to stick with initial decisions, even when growing evidence suggests they were poor ones that led to negative outcomes.

Equity theory A theoretical framework that explains

how individuals determine whether reward allocations in some social exchange are fair or unfair and how individuals react to perceptions of unfairness in this respect.

Job satisfaction Individuals' positive or negative attitudes toward their jobs.

Industrial/organizational psychology The branch of psychology which seeks increased understanding of all facets of behavior in work settings.

Organizational conflict Conflict occurring in organizational settings. Such conflict involves actions by one group or individual that impinge negatively on the interests of another group or individual.

Performance appraisals The process through which employees' performance is assessed in work settings.

Procedural justice The extent to which individuals perceive the procedures used to allocate available rewards as being fair.

Referent cognitions theory A theoretical framework concerned with both procedural and distributive justice (i.e., equity). This theory suggests that individuals are most likely to perceive their outcomes as unfairly low if they believe that such outcomes would have been higher had the reward allocator followed different procedural rules.

Two-tier wage systems Wage systems in which newly hired employees receive lower compensation than those already on the job. Such systems often induce strong feelings of inequity among new employees.

FOR MORE INFORMATION

Baron, R. A., & Greenberg, J. (1990). *Behavior in organizations: Understanding and managing the human side of work* (3rd ed.). Boston: Allyn and Bacon.

This text provides a very broad introduction to the field of organizational psychology. Many of the chapters describe applications of the principles and findings of social psychology to behavior in work settings (e.g., work-related attitudes, work motivation, leadership, influence and politics).

Saal, F. E., & Knight, P. A. (1988). *Industrial/organizational psychology: Science and practice*. Belmont, CA: Wadsworth.

This up-to-date text provides extensive coverage of the field of industrial/organizational psychology. It includes chapters on such important topics as the measurement and evaluation of work performance, training of employees, work motivation, and organizational change. If you'd like to know more about industrial/organizational psychology, this is an excellent source to consult.

REFERENCES

Abelson, R. P. (1982). Three models of attitude behavior consistency. In M. P. Zanna, E. T. Higgins, & C. P. Herman (Eds.), *Consistency in social behavior: The Ontario symposium* (Vol. 2). Hillsdale, NJ: Erlbaum.

Abrams, D. B., Monti, P. M., Pinto, R. P., Elder, J. P., Brown, R. A., & Jacobus, S. I. (1987). Psychological stress and coping in smokers who relapse or quit. *Health Psychology, 6,* 289–304.

Abramson, L. Y., Metalsky, G. I., & Alloy, L. B. (1990). The hopelessness theory of depression: Does the research test the theory? In L. Y. Abramson (Ed.), *Social cognition and clinical psychology: A synthesis.* New York: Guilford Press.

Adams, J. S. (1965). Inequity in social exchange. In L. Berkowitz (Ed.), *Advances in experimental social psychology* (Vol. 2, pp. 267–299). New York: Academic Press.

Adatto, K. (1990). The incredible shrinking sound bite. *New Republic, 202* (22), 20–23.

Adler, V. (1988, November). Heart votes. *Psychology Today,* pp. 61, 64.

Adorno, T. W., Frenkel-Brunswick, E., Levinson, D. J., & Sanford, R. N. (1950). *The authoritarian personality.* New York: Harper & Row.

Affection gets low mention for Soviet matches. (1986, August 16). *Albany Times Union,* p. A2.

Affleck, G., Tennen, H., Pfeiffer, C., & Fifield, J. (1987). Appraisals of control and predictability in adapting to a chronic disease. *Journal of Personality and Social Psychology, 53,* 273–279.

Agostinelli, G., Sherman, S. J., Fazio, R. H., & Hearst, E. S. (1986). Detecting and identifying change: Additions versus deletions. *Journal of Experimental Psychology: Human Perception and Performance, 12,* 445–454.

Aguero, J. E., Bloch, L., & Byrne, D. (1984). The relationships among sexual beliefs, attitudes, experience, and homophobia. *Journal of Homosexuality, 10,* 95–107.

Ajzen, I., & Fishbein, M. (1977). Attitude-behavior relations: A theoretical analysis and review of empirical research. *Psychological Bulletin, 84,* 888–918.

Albert, S., & Dabbs, J. M., Jr. (1970). Physical distance and persuasion. *Journal of Personality and Social Psychology, 15,* 265–270.

Albright, L., Kenny, D. A., & Malloy, T E. (1988). Consensus in personality judgments at zero acquaintance. *Journal of Personality and Social Psychology, 55,* 387–395.

Alicke, M. D., Smith, R. H., & Klotz, M. L. (1986). Judgments of physical attractiveness: The role of faces and bodies. *Personality and Social Psychology Bulletin, 12,* 381–389.

Allen, J. B., Kenrick, D. T., Linder, D. E., & McCall, M. A. (1989). Arousal and attraction: A response-facilitation alternative to

misattribution and negative-reinforcement models. *Journal of Personality and Social Psychology, 57,* 261–270.

Allen, V. L., Levin, J. M. (1971). Social support and conformity: The role of independent assessment of reality. *Journal of Experimental Social Psychology, 4,* 48–58.

Allgeier, A. R., Byrne, D., Brooks, B., & Revnes, D. (1979). The waffle phenomenon: Negative evaluations of those who shift attitudinally. *Journal of Applied Social Psychology, 9,* 170–182.

Alloy, L. B., Abramson, L. Y., & Dykman, B. M. (1990). Depressive realism and nondepressive optimistic illusions: The role of the self. In R. E. Ingram (Ed.), *Contemporary psychological approaches to depression: Treatment, research, and theory.* New York: Plenum.

Allport, F. H. (1924). *Social psychology.* Boston: Houghton Mifflin.

Allport, G. W. (1935). Attitudes. In C. Murchisom (Ed.), *Handbook of social psychology.* Worcester, MA: Clark University Press.

Allport, G. W., & Odbert, H. S. (1936). Trait-names: A psycholexical study. *Psychological Monographs, 47* (211).

Allyn, J., & Festinger, L. (1961). The effectiveness of unanticipated persuasive communications. *Journal of Abnormal and Social Psychology, 62,* 35–40.

Altmaier, E. M., & Meyer, M. E. (Eds.) (1985). *Applied specialities in psychology.* New York: Random House.

Altman, I. (1975). *The environment and social behavior.* Monterey, CA: Brooks/Cole.

Altman, I., & Gauvain, M. (1981). A cross-cultural and dialectic analysis of homes. In L. S. Lieben, A. H. Patterson, & N. Newcombe (Eds.), *Spatial representation and behavior across the life span.* New York: Academic Press.

Altruism in action. (1988). *Psychology Today,* p. 6.

Amabile, T. M. (1983). Brilliant but cruel: Perceptions of negative evaluators. *Journal of Experimental Social Psychology, 19,* 146–156.

Amato, P. R. (1983). Helping behavior in urban and rural environments: Field studies based on a taxonomic organization of helping episodes. *Journal of Personality and Social Psychology, 45,* 571–586.

Amato, P. R., & McInnes, I. R. (1983). Affiliative behavior in diverse environments: A consideration of pleasantness, information rate, and the arousal-eliciting quality of settings. *Basic and Applied Social Psychology, 4,* 109–122.

Anderson, C. A. (1987). Temperature and aggression: Effects on quarterly, yearly, and city rates of violent and nonviolent crime. *Journal of Personality and Social Psychology, 46,* 91–97.

Anderson, C. A. (1989). Temperature and aggression: The ubiquitous effects of heat on the occurrence of human violence. *Psychological Bulletin, 106,* 74–96.

Anderson, C. A., & Anderson, D. C. (1984). Ambient temperature and violent crime: Tests of the linear and curvilinear hypotheses. *Journal of Personality and Social Psychology, 46,* 91–97.

Anderson, J. L. (1989). A methodological critique of the evidence for genetic similarity detection. *Behavioral and Brain Sciences, 12,* 518–519.

Anderson, N. H. (1981). *Foundations of information integration theory.* New York: Academic Press.

Antill, J. K. (1983). Sex role complementarity versus similarity in married couples. *Journal of Personality and Social Psychology, 45,* 145–155.

Appleyard, D., & Lintell, M. (1972). The environmental quality of city streets: The residents' viewpoint. *Journal of the American Institute of Planners, 38,* 84–101.

Archer, R. L. (1984). The farmer and the cowman should be friends: An attempt at reconciliation with Batson, Coke, and Psych. *Journal of Personality and Social Psychology, 46,* 709–711.

Archer, R. L., Diza-Loving, R., Gollwitzer, P. M., Davis, M. H., & Foushee, H. C. (1981). The role of dispositional empathy and social evaluation in the empathetic mediation of helping. *Journal of Personality and Social Psychology, 40,* 786–796.

Argyle, M. (1987). *The psychology of happiness.* London: Methuen.

Arkes, H. R., Herren, L. T., & Isen, A. M. (1988). The role of potential loss in the influence of affect on risk-taking behavior. *Organizational Behavior and Human Decision Processes, 42,* 181–193.

Arkin, R. M., & Baumgardner, A. H. (1985). Self-handicapping. In J. H. Harvey & G. W. Weary (Eds.), *Attribution: Basic issues and applications* (pp. 169–202). Orlando, FL: Academic Press.

Arkin, R. M., Lake, E. A., & Baumgardner, A. B. (1986). Shyness and self-presentation. In W. H. Jones, J. M. Cheek, & S. R. Briggs (Eds.), *Shyness: Perspective on research and treatment* (pp. 189–203). New York: Plenum.

Aron, A., Dutton, D. G., Aron, E. N., & Iverson, A. (1989). Experiences of falling in love. *Journal of Social and Personal Relationships, 6,* 243–257.

Aronson, E. (1990). Applying social psychology to desegregation and energy conservation. *Personality and Social Psychology Bulletin, 16,* 118–132.

Aronson, E., Bridgeman, D. L., & Geffner, R. (1978). Interdependent interactions and prosocial behavior. *Journal of Research and Development in Education, 12,* 16–27.

Aronson, E., & Mills, J. (1959). The effect of severity of initiation on liking for a group. *Journal of Abnormal and Social Psychology, 12,* 16–27.

Arvey, R. D., Bouchard, T. J., Jr., Segal, N. L., & Abraham, L. M. (1989). Job satisfaction: Environmental and genetic components. *Journal of Applied Psychology, 74,* 187–192.

Arvey, R. D., & Campion, J. E. (1982). The employment interview: A summary and review of recent research. *Personnel Psychology, 35,* 281–322.

Asch, S. (1946). Forming impressions of personality. *Journal of Abnormal and Social Psychology, 41,* 258–290.

Asch, S. E. (1951). Effects of group pressure upon the modification and distortion of judgment. In H. Guetzkow (Ed.), *Groups, leadership, and men.* Pittsburgh, PA: Carnegie.

Asch, S. E. (1957). An experimental investigation of group influence. In *Symposium on preventive and social psychiatry* (pp. 15–17). Walter Reed Army Institute of Research. Washington, DC: U.S. Government Printing Office.

Asendorpf, J. B. (1989). Shyness as a final common pathway for two different kinds of inhibition. *Journal of Personality and Social Psychology, 57,* 481–492.

Ashton, N. L., Shaw, M. E., & Worsham, A. P. (1980). Affective reactions to interpersonal distances by friends and strangers. *Bulletin of the Psychonomic Society, 15,* 306–308.

Athey, T. R., & McIntyre, R. M. (1987). Effect of rater training on rater accuracy: Levels-of-processing theory and social facilitation theory perspectives. *Journal of Applied Psychology, 72,* 567–572.

Averill, J. R., & Boothroyd, P. (1977). On falling in love: Conformance with romantic ideal. *Motivation and Emotion, 1,* 235–247.

Avery, C. S. (1989, May). How do you build intimacy in an age of divorce? *Psychology Today, 23* (pp. 27–31).

Axsom, D. (1989). Cognitive dissonance and behavior change in psychotherapy. *Journal of Experimental Social Psychology, 25,* 234–252.

Axsom, D., & Cooper, J. (1985). Cognitive dissonance and psychotherapy: The role of effort justification in inducing weight loss. *Journal of Experimental Social Psychology, 21,* 149–160.

Axsom, D., Yates, S., Chaiken, S. (1987). Audience response to a heuristic cue in persuasion. *Journal of Personality and Social Psychology, 53,* 30–40.

Baba, Y., & Austin, D. M. (1989). Neighborhood environmental satisfaction, victimization, and social participation as determinants of perceived neighborhood safety. *Environment and Behavior, 21,* 763–780.

Baker, R. L., & Mednick, B. R. (1984). *Influences on human development: A longitudinal perspective.* Boston: Kluwer-Nijhoff.

Bakker, F. C. (1988). Personality differences between young dancers and non-dancers. *Personality and Individual Differences, 9,* 121–131.

Baldassare, M. (1981). The effects of household density on subgroups. *American Sociological Review, 46,* 110–118.

Balling, J. D., & Falk, J. H. (1982). Development of visual preference for natural environments. *Environment and Behavior, 14,* 5–28.

Bandura, A. (1973). *Aggression: A social learning analysis.* Englewood Cliffs, NJ: Prentice Hall.

Bandura, A. (1977). *Social learning theory.* Englewood Cliffs, NJ: Prentice Hall.

Bandura, A., Cioffi, D., Taylor, C. B., & Brouillard, M. E. (1988). Perceived self-efficacy in coping with cognitive stressors and opioid activation. *Journal of Personality and Social Psychology, 55,* 479–488.

Bandura, A., Ross, D., & Ross, S. (1963). Imitation of film-mediated aggressive models. *Journal of Abnormal and Social Psychology, 66,* 3–11.

Banner, L. W. (1983). *American beauty.* New York: Knopf.

Banuazizi, A., & Movahedi, S. (1975). Interpersonal dynamics in a simulated prison: A methodological analysis. *American Psychologist, 30,* 152–160.

Barden, R. C., Garber, J., Duncan, S. W., & Masters, J. C. (1981). Cumulative effects of induced affective states in children: Accentuation, inoculation, and remediation. *Journal of Personality and Social Psychology, 43,* 750–760.

Bargh, J. A., & Pietromonaco, P. (1982). Automatic information processing and social perception: The influence of trait information presented outside of conscious awareness on impression formation. *Journal of Personality and Social Psychology, 43,* 437–449.

Barnes, F. (1989). Fearless leader. *New Republic, 201(22),* 11–13.

Bar-On, D. (1987). Causal attributions and the rehabilitation of myocardial infarction victims. *Journal of Social and Clinical Psychology, 5,* 114–122.

Baron, R. A. (1971). Magnitude of victim's pain cues and level of prior anger arousal as determinants of adult aggressive behavior. *Journal of Personality and Social Psychology, 17,* 236–243.

Baron, R. A. (1972). Reducing the influence of an aggressive model: The restraining effects of peer censure. *Journal of Experimental Social Psychology, 8,* 266–275.

Baron, R. A. (1973). The "foot-in-the-door" phenomenon: Mediating effects of size of first request and sex of requester. *Bulletin of the Psychonomic Society, 2,* 113–114.

Baron, R. A. (1974a). Aggression as a function of victim's pain cues, level of prior anger arousal, and exposure to an aggressive model. *Journal of Personality and Social Psychology, 24,* 117–124.

Baron, R. A. (1974b). The aggression-inhibiting influence of heightened sexual arousal. *Journal of Personality and Social Psychology, 30,* 318–332.

Baron, R. A. (1976). The reduction of human aggression: A field study on the influence of incompatible responses. *Journal of Applied Social Psychology, 6,* 95–104.

Baron, R. A. (1977). *Human aggression.* New York: Plenum.

Baron, R. A. (1978). Aggression-inhibiting influence of sexual humor. *Journal of Personality and Social Psychology, 36,* 189–197.

Baron, R. A. (1979). Aggression, empathy, and race: Effects of victim's pain cues, victim's race, and level of instigation on physical aggression. *Journal of Applied Social Psychology, 9,* 103–114.

Baron, R. A. (1981). The "Costs of Deception" revisited: An openly optimistic rejoinder. *IRB: A Review of Human Subjects Research, 3,* 8–10.

Baron, R. A. (1983). The control of human aggression: An optimistic perspective. *Journal of Social and Clinical Psychology, 1,* 97–119.

Baron, R. A. (1984). Reducing organizational conflict: An incompatible response approach. *Journal of Applied Psychology, 69,* 272–279.

Baron, R. A. (1985). Reducing organizational conflict: The role of attributions. *Journal of Applied Psychology, 70,* 434–441.

Baron, R. A. (1986). Self-presentation in job interviews: When there can be "too much of a good thing." *Journal of Applied Social Psychology, 16,* 16–28.

Baron, R. A. (1987a). Effects of negative air ions on interpersonal attraction: Evidence for intensification. *Journal of Personality and Social Psychology, 52,* 547–553.

Baron, R. A. (1987b). Interviewer's moods and reactions to job applicants: The influence of affective states on applied social judgments. *Journal of Applied Social Psychology, 16,* 16–28.

Baron, R. A. (1988a). Attributions and organizational conflict: The mediating role of apparent sincerity. *Organizational Behavior and Human Decision Processes, 41,* 111–127.

Baron, R. A. (1988b). Negative effects of destructive criticism: Impact on conflict, self-efficacy, and task performance. *Journal of Applied Psychology, 73,* 199–207.

Baron, R. A. (1989). Personality and organizational conflict: The Type A behavior pattern and self-monitoring. *Organizational Behavior and Human Decision Processes, 44,* 281–297.

Baron, R. A. (1990a). Attributions and organizational conflict. In S. Graham & V. Folkes (Eds.), *Attribution theory: Applications to achievement, mental health, and interpersonal conflict.* Hillsdale, NJ: Erlbaum.

Baron, R. A. (1990b). *Effects of interviewers' moods and applicant qualifications on ratings of job applicants.* Manuscript submitted for publication.

Baron, R. A. (1990c). Environmentally induced positive affect: Its impact on self-efficacy, task performance, negotiation, and conflict. *Journal of Applied Social Psychology, 20,* 368–384.

Baron, R. A. (1990d). Countering the effects of destructive criticism: The relative efficacy of four interventions. *Journal of Applied Psychology, 75,* 235–245.

Baron, R. A., & Bell, P. A. (1973). Effects of heightened sexual arousal on physical aggression. *Proceedings of the American Psychological Association of the 81st Annual Convention,* 171–172.

Baron, R. A., & Bingley, J. (1989). *Perceived conflict in merging health organizations.* Unpublished manuscript, Rensselaer Polytechnic Institute, Troy, NY.

Baron, R. A., Fortin, S. P., Frei, R. L., Hauver, L. A., & Shack, M. L. (1990). Reducing organizational conflict: The role of socially-induced positive affect. *International Journal of Conflict Management, 1,* 133–152.

Baron, R. A., & Greenberg, J. (1990). *Behavior in organizations: Understanding and managing the human side of work* (3rd ed.). Boston: Allyn & Bacon.

Baron, R. A., & Ransberger, V. M. (1978). Ambient temperature and the occurrence of collective violence: The "long hot summer" revisited. *Journal of Personality and Social Psychology, 36,* 351–360.

Baron, R. A., & Richardson, D. R. (in press). *Human aggression* (2nd ed.). New York: Plenum.

Baron, R. A., Russell, G. W., & Arms, R. L. (1985). Negative ions and behavior: Impact on mood, memory, and aggression among Type A and Type B persons. *Journal of Personality and Social Psychology, 48,* 746–754.

Baron, R. M., Mandel, D. R., Adams, C. A., & Griffen, L. M. (1976). Effects of social density in university residential environments. *Journal of Personality and Social Psychology, 34,* 434–446.

Baron, R. M., & Rodin, J. (1978). Personal control as a mediator of crowding. In A. Baum, J. E. Singer, & S. Valins (Eds.), *Advances in environmental psychology* (Vol. 1). Hillsdale, NJ: Erlbaum.

Baron, R. S. (1986). Distraction-conflict theory: Progress and problems. In L. Berkowitz (Ed.), *Advances in experimental social psychology* (Vol. 20). New York: Academic Press.

Baron, R. S., Moore, D., & Sanders, G. S. (1978). Distraction as a source of drive in social facilitation research. *Journal of Personality and Social Psychology, 36,* 816–824.

Bar-Tal, D., & Bar-Zohar, Y. (1977). The relationship between perception of locus of control and academic achievement. *Contemporary Educational Psychology, 2,* 181–199.

Bass, B. M. (1985). *Leadership and performance beyond expectations.* New York: Free Press.

Batson, C. D., Batson, J. G., Griffitt, C. A., Carrientos, S., Brandt, J. R., Sprengelmeyer, P., & Bayly, M. J. (1989). Negative state relief and the empathy-altruism hypothesis. *Journal of Personality and Social Psychology, 56,* 922–933.

Batson, C. D., Duncan, B. D., Ackerman, P., Buckley, T., & Birch, K. (1981). Is empathetic emotion a source of altruistic motivation? *Journal of Personality and Social Psychology, 40,* 290–302.

Batson, C. D., Oleson, K. C., Weeks, J. L., Healy, S. P., Reeves, P. J., Jennings, P., & Brown, T. (1989). Religious prosocial motivation: Is it altruistic or egoistic? *Journal of Personality and Social Psychology, 57,* 873–884.

Batson, C. D., O'Quin, K., Fultz, J., Vanderplas, M., & Isen, A. M. (1983). Influence of self-reported distress and empathy on egoistic versus altruistic motivation to help. *Journal of Personality and Social Psychology, 45,* 706–718.

Baubion-Broye, A., Megemont, J. L., & Sellinger, M. (1989). Evolutions des sentiments de controle et de la receptivite a l'information au cours du chomage. *Applied Psychology: An International Review, 38,* 265–275.

Baucom, D. H., Sayers, S. L., & Duhe, A. (1989). Attributional style and attributional patterns among married couples. *Journal of Personality and Social Psychology, 56,* 596–607.

Baum, A., & Gatchel, R. J. (1981). Cognitive determinants of response to uncontrollable events: Development of reactance and learned helplessness. *Journal of Personality and Social Psychology, 40,* 1078–1089.

Baum, A., Gatchel, R. J., & Schaeffer, M. A. (1983). Emotional, behavioral, and physiological effects of chronic stress at Three Mile Island. *Journal of Consulting and Clinical Psychology, 51,* 565–572.

Baum, A., & Valins, S. (1977). *Architecture and social behavior: Psychological studies of social density.* Hillsdale, NJ: Erlbaum.

Baum, A., & Valins, S. (1979). Architectural mediation of residential density and control: Crowding and the regulation of social contact. In L. Berkowitz (Ed.), *Advances in experimental social psychology* (Vol. 12). New York: Academic Press.

Baumeister, R. F. (1986). *Identity.* New York: Oxford University Press.

Baumeister, R. F. (1989). The optimal margin of illusion. *Journal of Social and Clinical Psychology, 8,* 176–189.

Baumeister, R. F., Chesner, S. P., Sanders, P. S., & Tice, D. M. (1988). Who's in charge here? Group leaders do lend help in emergencies. *Personality and Social Psychology Bulletin, 14,* 17–22.

Baumeister, R. F., & Covington, M. V. (1985). Self-esteem, persuasion, and retrospective distortion of initial attitudes. *Electronic Social Psychology, 1,* 1–22.

Baumeister, R. F., & Darley, J. M. (1982). Reducing the biasing effect of perpetrator attractiveness in jury simulation. *Personality and Social Psychology Bulletin, 8,* 286–292.

Baumeister, R. F., & Steinhilber, A. (1984). Paradoxical effects of supportive audiences on performance under pressure: The home field disadvantage in sports championships. *Journal of Personality and Social Psychology, 47,* 85–93.

Baumeister, R. F., Stillwell, A., & Wotman, S. R. (1991, in press.). Victim and perpetrator accounts of interpersonal conflict: Autobiographical narratives about anger. *Journal of Personality and Social Psychology.*

Baumeister, R. F., & Tice, D. M. (1984). Role of self-presentation and choice in cognitive dissonance under forced compliance: Necessary or sufficient causes? *Journal of Personality and Social Psychology, 46,* 5–13.

Baumeister, R. F., & Tice, D. M. (1988). Metatraits. *Journal of Personality, 56,* 571–598.

Baumgardner, A. H., Heppner, P. P., & Arkin, R. M. (1986). Role of causal attribution in personal problem solving. *Journal of Personality and Social Psychology, 50,* 636–643.

Baumgardner, A. H., Kaufman, C. M., & Levy, P. E. (1989). Regulating affect interpersonally: When low esteem leads to greater enhancement. *Journal of Personality and Social Psychology, 56,* 907–921.

Baumgardner, A. H., & Levy, P. E. (1988). Role of self-esteem in perceptions of ability and effort: Illogic or insight? *Personality and Social Psychology Bulletin, 14,* 429–438.

Baumrind, D. (1979). The costs of deception. *IRB: A Review of Human Subjects Research, 6,* 1–4.

Baxter, L. A. (1984). Trajectories of relationship disengagement. *Journal of Social and Personal Relationships, 1,* 29–48.

Baxter, L. A. (1990). Dialectical contradictions in relationship development. *Journal of Social and Personal Relationships, 7,* 69–88.

Bazerman, M. H., Guiliano, T., & Appleman, A. (1984). Escalation of commitment in individual and group decision making. *Organizational Behavior and Human Performance, 33,* 141–152.

Beaman, A. L., Cole, M., Preston, M., Klentz, B., & Steblay, N. M. (1983). Fifteen years of the foot-in-the-door research: A meta-analysis. *Personality and Social Psychology Bulletin, 9,* 181–186.

Beck, A. T., Rush, A. J., Shaw, B. F., & Emery, G. (1979). *Cognition therapy of depression.* New York: Guilford Press.

Becker, M. A., & Byrne, D. (1985). Self-regulated exposure to erotica, recall of errors, and subjective reactions as a function of erotophobia and Type A coronary-prone behavior. *Journal of Personality and Social Psychology, 48,* 228–235.

Bell, B. E., & Loftus, E. F. (1988). Degree of detail of eyewitness testimony and mock juror judgments. *Journal of Applied Social Psychology, 18,* 1171–1192.

Bell, P. A., Fisher, J. D., & Baum, A. (1990). *Environmental psychology* (3rd ed.). New York: Holt, Rinehart, & Winston.

Bem, D. J. (1972). Self-perception theory. In L. Berkowitz (Ed.), *Advances in experimental social psychology* (Vol. 6). New York: Academic Press.

Bem, S. L. (1974). The measurement of psychological androgyny. *Journal of Consulting and Clinical Psychology, 42,* 155–162.

Benesch, K. F., & Page, M. M. (1989). Self-construct systems and interpersonal congruence. *Journal of Personality, 57,* 139–173.

Benson, P. L., Karabenick, S. A., & Lerner, R. M. (1976). Pretty pleases: The effects of physical attractiveness, race, and sex on receiving help. *Journal of Experimental Social Psychology, 12,* 409–415.

Bentler, P. M., & Newcomb, M. D. (1978). Longitudinal study of marital success and failure. *Journal of Consulting and Clinical Psychology, 46,* 1053–1070.

Berg, J. H., & McQuinn, R. D. (1989). Loneliness and aspects of social support networks. *Journal of Social and Personal Relationships, 6,* 359–372.

Berg, J. H., & Peplau, L. A. (1982). Loneliness: The relationship of self-disclosure and androgyny. *Personality and Social Psychology Bulletin, 8,* 624–630.

Berk, L. E. (1989). *Child development.* Boston: Allyn & Bacon.

Berkowitz, L. (1962). *Aggression: A social psychological analysis.* New York: McGraw-Hill.

Berkowitz, L. (1968, September). Impulse, aggression, and the gun. *Psychology Today,* pp. 18–22.

Berkowitz, L. (1969). The frustration-aggression hypothesis revisited. In L. Berkowitz (Ed.), *Roots of aggression: A re-examination of the frustration-aggression hypothesis* (pp. 1–28). New York: Atherton Press.

Berkowitz, L. (Ed.). (1969). *Roots of aggression: A re-examination of the frustration-aggression hypothesis.* New York: Atherton Press.

Berkowitz, L. (1972). Social norms, feelings, and other factors affecting helping and altruism. In L. Berkowitz (Ed.), *Advances in experimental social psychology,* vol. 6. New York: Academic Press.

Berkowitz, L. (1982). Aversive conditions as stimuli to aggression. In L. Berkowitz (Ed.), *Advances in experimental social psychology* (pp. 249–288). New York: Academic Press.

Berkowitz, L. (1983). Aversively simulated aggression. *American Psychologist, 38,* 1135–1144.

Berkowitz, L. (1984). Some effects of thought on anti- and pro-social influence of media events: A cognitive-neoassociation analysis. *Psychological Bulletin, 95,* 410–427.

Berkowitz, L. (1987). Mood, self-awareness, and willingness to help. *Journal of Personality and Social Psychology, 52,* 721–724.

Berkowitz, L. (1988). Frustrations, appraisals, and aversively stimulated aggression. *Aggressive Behavior, 14,* 3–11.

Berkowitz, L. (1989). Frustration-aggression hypothesis: Examination and reformulation. *Psychological Bulletin, 106,* 59–73.

Berkowitz, L., & Donnerstein, E. (1982). External validity is more than skin deep: Some answers to criticism of laboratory experiments. *American Psychologist, 37,* 245–257.

Berkowitz, L., & LePage, A. (1967). Weapons as aggression-eliciting stimuli. *Journal of Personality and Social Psychology, 11,* 202–207.

Bernstein, I. L. (1988). *What does learning have to do with weight loss and cancer?* Washington, DC: Federation of Behavioral, Psychological, and Cognitive Sciences.

Bernstein, W. M., Stephenson, B. O., Snyder, M. L., & Wicklund, R. A. (1983). Causal ambiguity and heterosexual affiliation. *Journal of Experimental Social Psychology, 19,* 78–92.

Berry, D. S., & Brownlow, S. (1989). Were the physiognomists right? Personality correlates of facial babyishness. *Personality and Social Psychology Bulletin, 15,* 266–279.

Berry, D. S., & McArthur, L. Z. (1986). Perceiving character in faces: The impact of age-related craniofacial changes on social perception. *Psychological Bulletin, 100,* 3–18.

Berscheid, E. (1985). Interpersonal attraction. In G. Lindzey & E. Aronson (Eds.), *Handbook of social psychology* (Vol. 2, 3rd ed.). New York: Random House.

Berscheid, E., Dion, K., Walster, E., & Walster, G. W. (1971). Physical attractiveness and dating choice: A test of the matching hypothesis. *Journal of Experimental Social Psychology, 7,* 173–189.

Berscheid, E., Snyder, M., & Omoto, A. M. (1989a). Issues in studying close relationships: Conceptualizing and measuring closeness. In C. Hendrick (Ed.), *Review of personality and social psychology* (Vol. 10, pp. 63–91). Newbury Park, CA: Sage.

Berscheid, E., Snyder, M., & Omoto, A. M. (1989b). The Relationship Closeness Inventory: Assessing the closeness of interpersonal relationships. *Journal of Personality and Social Psychology, 57,* 792–807.

Berscheid, E., & Walster, E. (1974). A little bit about love. In T. L. Huston (Ed.), *Foundations of interpersonal attraction.* New York: Academic Press.

Bersoff, D. (1987). Social science data and the Supreme Court: Lockhart as a case in point. *American Psychologist, 42,* 52–58.

Bickman, L. (1972). Social influence and diffusion of responsibility in an ememrgency. *Journal of Experimental Social Psychology, 8,* 438–445.

Bies, R. J., Shapiro, D. L., & Cummings, L. L. (1988.). Causal accounts and managing organizational conflict: Is it enough to say it's not my fault? *Communication Research, 5,* 381–399.

Bisanz, G. L., & Rule, B. G. (1989). Gender and the persuasion schema: A search for cognitive invariants. *Personality and Social Psychology Bulletin, 15,* 4–18.

Bishop, G. D. (1987). Lay conceptions in physical symptoms. *Journal of Applied Social Psychology, 17,* 127–146.

Black, T. E., & Higbee, K. L. (1973). Effects of power, threat, and sex on exploitation. *Journal of Personality and Social Psychology, 27,* 382–388.

Blankenship, V., Hnat, S. M., Hess, T. G., & Brown, D. R. (1984). Reciprocal interaction and similarity of personality attributes. *Journal of Social and Personal Relationships, 1,* 415–432.

Bleda, P. R. (1976). Conditioning and discrimination of affect and attraction. *Journal of Personality and Social Psychology, 34,* 1106–1113.

Bleda, P. R., & Bleda, S. (1978). Effects of sex and smoking on reactions to spatial invasion at a shopping mall. *Journal of Social Psychology, 104,* 311–312.

Blount, R., Jr. (1986, October 13). Buddy can you spare a ten? To give or not to give on the street. *New York,* pp. 80–84.

Bodenhausen, G. V. (1988). Stereotypic biases in social decision making and memory: Testing process models of stereotype use. *Journal of Personality and Social Psychology, 55,* 726–737.

Bodenhausen, G. V., & Lichtenstein, M. (1987). Social stereotypes and information-processing strategies. The impact of task complexity. *Journal of Personality and Social Psychology, 52,* 871–880.

Bohner, G., Bless, H., Schwarz, N., & Strack, H. (1988). What triggers causal attributions? The impact of valence and subjective probability. *European Journal of Social Psychology, 18,* 335–348.

Bonacich, P. (1972). Norms and cohesion as adaptive responses to political conflict: An experimental study. *Sociometry, 35,* 357–375.

Bonacich, P., Shure, G. H., Kahan, J. P., & Meeker, R. J. (1976). Cooperation and group size in the n-person prisoner's dilemma. *Journal of Conflict Resolution, 20,* 687–705.

Bond, C. F. (1982). Social facilitation: A self-presentational view. *Journal of Personality and Social Psychology, 42,* 1042–1050.

Bond, C. F., Jr., & Anderson, E. L. (1987). The reluctance to transmit bad news: Private discomfort of public display? *Journal of Experimental Social Psychology, 23,* 176–187.

Bond, M. H., & King, A. Y. C. (1985). Coping with the threat of Westernization in Hong Kong. *International Journal of Intercultural Relations, 9,* 351–364.

Bond, M. H., & Tak-Sing, C. (1983). College students' spontaneous self-concept: The effect of culture among respondents in Hong Kong, Japan, and the United States. *Journal of Cross-Cultural Psychology, 14,* 153–171.

Bonnes, M., Giuliani, M. V., Amoni, F., & Bernard, Y. (1987). Cross-cultural rules for the optimization of the living room. *Environment and Behavior, 19,* 204–227.

Borkenau, P. (1988). The multiple classification of acts and the big five factors of personality. *Journal of Research in Personality, 22,* 337–352.

Bornstein, G., Rapaport, A., Kerpel, L., & Katz, T. (1989). Within- and between-group communication in intergroup competition for public goods. *Journal of Experimental Social Psychology, 25,* 422–436.

Bornstein, R. F., Leone, D. R., & Galley, D. J. (1987). The generalizability of subliminal mere exposure effects: Influence of stimuli perceived without awareness on social behavior. *Journal of Personality and Social Psychology, 53,* 1070–1079.

Borowski, N. A. (1990, June 3). U.S. birthrate booms again. *Albany Times Union,* E-4.

Bothwell, R. K., Deffenbacher, K. A., & Brigham, J. C. (1987). Correlation of eyewitness accuracy and confidence: Optimality hypothesis revisited. *Journal of Applied Psychology, 72,* 691–695.

Botwin, M. D., & Buss, D. M. (1989). Structure of act-report data: Is the five-factor model of personality recaptured? *Journal of Personality and Social Psychology, 56,* 988–1001.

Bouvier, L. F. (1990). U.S. population in the 21st century: Which scenario is reasonable? *Population and Environment, 11,* 193–202.

Bowen, M. G. (1987). The escalation phenomenon reconsidered: Decision dilemma or decision errors? *Academy of Management Review, 12,* 52–66.

Bower, G. H., & Hilgard, E. R. (1981). *Theories of learning* (5th ed.). Englewood Cliffs, NJ: Prentice Hall.

Braver, S L., & Wilson, L. A. (1986). Choices in social dilemmas: Effects of communication within subgroups. *Journal of Conflict Resolution, 30,* 51–62.

Bray, R. M., Sugarman, R. (1980). Social facilitation among interaction groups: Evidence for the evaluation apprehension hypothesis. *Personality and Social Psychology Bulletin, 6,* 137–142.

Breckler, S. J., & Wiggins, E. C. (1989a). Affect versus evaluation in the structure of attitudes. *Journal of Experimental Social Psychology, 25,* 253–271.

Breckler, S. J., & Wiggins, E. C. (1989b). On defining attitude and attitude theory: Once more with feeling. In A. R. Pratkanis, S. J. Breckler, & A. G. Greenwald (Eds.), *Attitude structure and function.* Hillsdale, NJ: Erlbaum.

Brehm, J. W. (1966). *A theory of psychological reactance.* New York: Academic Press.

Brekke, N., & Borgida, E. (1988). Expert psychological testimony in rape trials: A social-cognitive analysis. *Journal of Personality and Social Psychology, 55,* 372–386.

Brennan, T. (1982). Loneliness at adolescence. In L. A. Peplau & D. Perlman (Eds.), *Loneliness: A sourcebook of current theory, research, and therapy.* New York: Wiley.

Brennan, T., & Auslander, N. (1979). *Adolescent loneliness: An exploratory study of social and psychological predispositions and theory,* vol. 1. Prepared for the National Institute of Mental Health, Juvenile Problems Division, Grant No. R01-MH289 12-01, Behavioral Research Institute.

Brewer, M. B. H., Lee, J., & Miller, M. (1987). Social identity and social distance among Hong Kong school children. *Personality and Social Psychology Bulletin, 13,* 156–165.

Brickman, P., Becker, L. J., & Castle, S. (1979). Making trust easier and harder through two forms of sequential interaction. *Journal of Personality and Social Psychology, 37,* 515–521.

Brickman, P., Coates, D., & Janoff-Bulman, R. (1978). Lottery winners and accident victims: Is happiness relative? *Journal of Personality and Social Psychology, 36,* 917–927.

Brickner, M., Harkings, S., & Ostrom, T. (1986). Personal involvement: Thought-provoking implications for social loafing.

Journal of Personality and Social Psychology, 51, 763–769.

Briggs, S. R., & Cheek, J. M. (1988). On the nature of self-monitoring: Problems with assessment, problems with validity. *Journal of Personality and Social Psychology, 54,* 663–678.

Brigham, J. C. (1980). Limiting conditions of the "physical attractiveness stereotype": Attributions about divorce. *Journal of Research in Personality, 14,* 365–375.

Bringle, R. G., & Boebinger, K. L. G. (1990). Jealousy and the 'third' person in the love triangle. *Journal of Social and Personal Relationships, 7,* 119–133.

Brockner, J., Davy, J., & Carter, C. (1986). Layoffs, self-esteem, and survivor guilt: Motivational, affective, and attitudinal consequences. *Academy of Management Journal, 26,* 642–656.

Brockner, J., & Guare, J. (1983). Improving the performance of low-self-esteem individuals: An attribution approach. *Academy of Management Journal, 26,* 642–656.

Brody, G. H., Neubaum, E., & Forehand, R. (1988). Serial marriage: A heuristic analysis of an emerging family form. *Psychological Bulletin, 103,* 211–222.

Brody, J. E. (1989, August 24). Boning up on possible mental and physical health needs of children who are bound for college. *New York Times,* p. B12.

Broome, B. J. (1983). The attraction paradigm revisited: Response to dissimilar others. *Human Communication Research, 10,* 137–151.

Brown, D., Fulkerson, K. F., Furr, S., Ware, W. B., & Voight, N. L. (1984). Locus of control, sex role orientation, and self-concept in black and white third- and sixth-grade male and female leaders in a rural community. *Developmental Psychology, 20,* 717–721.

Brown, J. D., Collins, R. L., & Schmidt, G. W. (1988). Self-esteem and direct versus indirect forms of self-enhancement. *Journal of Personality and Social Psychology, 55,* 445–453.

Brown, J. D., & McGill, K. L. (1989). The cost of good fortune: When positive life events produce negative health consequences. *Journal of Personality and Social Psychology, 57,* 1103–1110.

Brown, J. D., & Siegel, J. M. (1988). Attributions for negative life events and depression: The role of perceived control. *Journal of Personality and Social Psychology, 54,* 316–322.

Browning, D. L. (1983). Aspects of authoritarian attitudes in ego development. *Journal of Personality and Social Psychology, 45,* 137–144.

Bruch, M. A., Gorsky, J. M., Collins, T. M., & Berger, P. A. (1989). Shyness and sociability reexamined: A multicomponent analysis. *Journal of Personality and Social Psychology, 57,* 904–915.

Bryan, J. H., & Test, M. A. (1967). Models and helping: Naturalistic studies in aiding behavior. *Journal of Personality and Social Psychology, 6,* 400–407.

Bryant, F. B. (1989). A four-factor model of perceived control: Avoiding, coping, obtaining, and savoring. *Journal of Personality, 57,* 773–797.

Buck, R. (1984). *The communication of emotion.* New York: Guilford Press.

Buckhout, R. (1980). Nearly 2000 witnesses can be wrong. *Bulletin of the Psychonomic Society, 16,* 307–310.

Burchill, S. A. L., & Stiles, W. B. (1988). Interactions of depressed college students with their roommates: Not necessarily negative. *Journal of Personality and Social Psychology, 55,* 410–419.

Burger, J. M. (1984). Desire for control, locus of control, and proneness to depression. *Journal of Personality, 52,* 71–89.

Burger, J. M. (1986). Increasing compliance by improving the deal: The that's-not-all technique. *Journal of Personality and Social Psychology, 51,* 277–283.

Burger, J. M. (1987). Desire for control and conformity to a perceived norm. *Journal of Personality and Social Psychology, 53,* 355–360.

Burger, J. M., & Cooper, H. M. (1979). The desirability of control. *Motivation and Emotion, 3,* 381–393.

Burger, J. M., McWard, J., & LaTorre, D. (1989). Boundaries of self-control: Relinquishing control over aversive events. *Journal of Social and Clinical Psychology, 8,* 209–221.

Burgess, J. W. (1981). Development of social spacing in normal and mentally retarded children. *Journal of Nonverbal Behavior, 6,* 89–95.

Buri, J. R., Louiselle, P. A., Misukanis, T. M., & Mueller, R. A. (1988). Effects of parental authoritarianism and authoritativeness on self-esteem. *Personality and Social Psychology Bulletin, 14,* 271–282.

Burns, M. O., & Seligman, M. E. P. (1989). Explanatory style across the life span: Evidence for stability over 52 years. *Journal of Personality and Social Psychology, 56,* 471–477.

Burnstein, E. (1983). Persuasion as argument processing. In M. Brandstatter, J. H. Davis, & G. Stocker-Kreichgauer (Eds.), *Group decision processes.* London: Academic Press.

Burnstein, E., & Schul, Y. (1982). The informational basis of social judgments: Operations in forming an impression of another person. *Journal of Experimental Social Psychology, 18,* 217–234.

Bushman, B. J. (1984). Perceived symbols of authority and their influence on compliance. *Journal of Applied Social Psychology, 14,* 501–508.

Bushman, B. J. (1988). The effects of apparel on compliance: A field experiment with a female authority figure. *Personality and Social Psychology Bulletin, 14,* 459–467.

Buss, A. H. (1961). *The psychology of aggression.* New York: Wiley.

Buss, A. H., Booker, A., & Buss, E. (1972). Firing a weapon and aggression. *Journal of Personality and Social Psychology, 22,* 296–302.

Buss, D. M. (1988). Love acts: The evolutionary biology of love. In R. J. Sternberg & M. L. Barnes (Eds.), *The psychology of love* (pp. 100–118). New Haven, CT: Yale University Press.

Buss, D. M. (1989a). Conflict between the sexes: Strategic interference and the evocation of anger and upset. *Journal of Personality and Social Psychology, 56,* 735–747.

Buss, D. M. (1989b). Sex differences in human mate preferences: Evolutionary hypotheses tested in 37 cultures. *Behavioral and Brain Sciences, 12,* 1–49.

Butler, D., & Geis, F. L. (1990). Nonverbal affect responses to male and female leaders: Implications for leadership evaluations. *Journal of Personality and Social Psychology, 58,* 48–59.

Buunk, B. (1987). Conditions that promote breakups as a consequence of extradyadic involvements. *Journal of Social and Clinical Psychology, 5,* 271–284.

Buunk, B., & Bringle, R. G. (1987). Jealousy in love relationships. In D. Perlman & S. Duck (Eds.), *Intimate relationships. Development, dynamics, and deterioration.* Newbury Park, CA: Sage.

Buunk, B., & Hupka, R. B. (1986). Autonomy in close relationships: A cross-cultural study. *Family Perspectives, 20,* 209–221.

Buunk, B., & Hupka, R. B. (1987). Cross-cultural differences in the elicitation of sexual jealousy. *Journal of Sex Research, 23,* 12–22.

Buzzanga, V. L., Miller, H. R., Perne, S. E., Sander, J. A., & Davis, S. F. (1989). The relationship between death anxiety and level of self-esteem: A reassessment. *Bulletin of the Psychonomic Society, 27,* 570–572.

Byrne, D., Bond, M. H., & Diamond, M. J. (1969). Response to political candidates as a function of attitude similarity-dissimilarity. *Human Relations, 22,* 251–262.

Byrne, D., & Clore, G. L. (1970). A reinforcement-affect model of evaluative responses. *Personality: An International Journal, 1,* 103–128.

Byrne, D., Clore, G. L., & Smeaton, G. (1986). The attraction hypothesis: Do similar attitudes affect anything? *Journal of Personality and Social Psychology, 51,* 1167–1170.

Byrne, D., & Fisher, W. A. (1983). *Adolescents, sex, and contraception.* Hillsdale, NJ: Erlbaum.

Byrne, D., Gouaux, C., Griffitt, W., Lamberth, J., Murakawa, N., Prasad, M. B., Prasad, A., & Ramirez, M., III. (1971). The ubiquitous relationship: Attitude similarity and attraction. A cross-cultural study. *Human Relations, 24,* 201–207.

Bryne, D., & Greendlinger, V. (1989). *Need for affiliation as a predictor of classroom friendships.* Unpublished manuscript, State University of New York at Albany.

Byrne, D., & Kelley, K. (1981). *An introduction to personality* (3rd ed.). Englewood Cliffs, NJ: Prentice Hall.

Byrne, D., & Murnen, S. K. (1988). Maintaining loving relationships. In R. J. Sternberg & M. L. Barnes (Eds.), *The psychology of love* (pp. 293–310). New Haven, CT: Yale University Press.

Byrne, D., & Nelson, D. (1965). Attraction as a linear function of proportion of positive reinforcements. *Journal of Personality and Social Psychology, 1,* 659–663.

Byrne, D., & Przybyla, D. P. J. (1980). Authoritarianism and political preferences in 1980. *Bulletin of the Psychonomic Society, 16,* 471–472.

Byrne, D., & Schulte, L. J. (1990). Personality dimensions as predictors of sexual behavior. In J. Bancroft (Ed.), *Annual review of sexual research* (Vol. 1). Philadelphia: Society for the Scientific Study of Sex.

Byrne, G. C., & Pueschel, J. K. (1973). But who shall I vote for county coroner? *Journal of Politics, 36,* 778–784.

Cacioppo, J. T., & Petty, R. E. (1981). Effects of extent of thought on the pleasantness of P-O-X triads: Evidence for three judgmental tendencies in evaluating social situations. *Journal of Personality and Social Psychology, 40,* 1000–1009.

Cacioppo, J. T., Petty, R. E., Losch, M. E., & Kim, H. S. (1986). Electromyographic specificity during simple physical and attitudinal tasks: Location and topographical features of integrated EMG responses. *Biological Psychology, 18,* 85–121.

Cacioppo, J. T., Martzke, J. S., Petty, R. E., & Tassinary, L. G. (1988). Specific forms of facial EMG response index emotions during an interview: From Darwin to the continuous flow hypothesis of affect-laden information processing. *Journal of Personality and Social Psychology, 54,* 552–604.

Calhoun, J. B. (1962). Population density and social pathology. *Scientific American, 206,* 139–148.

Calhoun, J. B. (1971). Space and the strategy of life. In A. H. Esser (Ed.), *Environment and behavior: The use of space by animals and men.* New York: Plenum.

Calvert, J. D. (1988). Physical attractiveness: A review and reevaluation of its role in social skill research. *Behavioral Assessment, 10,* 29–42.

Campbell, D. T. (1965). Ethnocentric and other altruistic motives. In D. Levine (Ed.), *Nebraska symposium on motivation* (pp. 283–311). Lincoln: University of Nebraska Press.

Campbell, D. T. (1975). On the conflicts between biological and social evolution and between psychology and moral tradition. *American Psychologist, 30,* 1103–1126.

Campbell, J. D. (1986). Similarity and uniqueness: The effects of attribute type, relevance, and individual differences in self-esteem and depression. *Journal of Personality and Social Psychology, 50,* 281–294.

Cann, A., Sherman, S. J., & Elkes, R. (1975). Effects of initial request size and timing of a second request on compliance: The foot-in-the-door and the door-in-the-face. *Journal of Personality and Social Psychology, 32,* 774–782.

Caplow, T., & Forman, R. (1950). Neighborhood interaction in a homogeneous community. *American Sociological Review, 15,* 357–366.

Cardy, R. L. (1987, April). *Liking as a source of level bias in performance ratings.* Paper presented at the meetings of the Society of Industrial and Organizational Psychology, Atlanta, GA.

Cardy, R. L., & Dobbins, G. H. (1986). Affect and appraisal accuracy: Liking as an integral dimension in evaluating performance. *Journal of Applied Psychology, 71,* 672–678.

Carli, L. L. (1989). Gender differences in interaction style and influence. *Journal of Personality and Social Psychology, 56,* 565–576.

Carnevale, P. J. D., & Isen, A. M. (1986). The influence of positive affect and visual access on the discovery of integrative solutions in bilateral negotiation. *Organizational Behavior and Human Decision Processes, 37,* 1–13.

Caro, R. A. (1990). *The years of Lyndon Johnson: Means of ascent.* New York: Knopf.

Carroll, J. L., Volk, K. D., & Hyde, J. S. (1985). Differences between males and females in motives for engaging in sexual intercourse. *Archives of Sexual Behavior, 14,* 131–139.

Carroll, S. J. (1982). What is this thing called "applied social psychology"? *Contemporary Psychology, 27,* 772–773.

Carroll, S. J., Perkowitz, W. T., Lurigio, A. J., & Waver, F. M. (1987). Sentencing goals, causal attributions, ideology, and personality. *Journal of Personality and Social Psychology, 50,* 107–118.

Carrot and stick. (1989, October 9). *Time,* p. 85.

Carver, C. S., & Glass, D. C. (1978). Coronary-prone behavior pattern and interpersonal aggression. *Journal of Personality and Social Psychology, 36,* 361–366.

Carver, C. S., & Scheier, M. F. (1981). *Attention and self-regulation: A control-theory approach to human behavior.* New York: Springer-Verlag.

Cash, T. F., & Derlega, V. J. (1978). The matching hypothesis: Physical attractiveness among same-sexed friends. *Personality and Social Psychology Bulletin, 4,* 240–243.

Cash, T. F., & Duncan, N. C. (1984). Physical attractiveness stereotyping among black American college students. *Journal of Social Psychology, 122*, 71–77.

Cash, T. F., & Kilcullen, R. N. (1985). The aye of the beholder: Susceptibility to sexism and beautyism in the evaluation of managerial applicants. *Journal of Applied Social Psychology, 15*, 591–605.

Cash, T. F., Rissi, J., & Chapman, R. (1985). Not just another pretty face: Sex roles, locus of control, and cosmetics use. *Personality and Social Psychology Bulletin, 11*, 246–257.

Caspi, A., Bem, D. J., & Elder, G. H., Jr. (1989). Continuities and consequences of interactional styles across the life course. *Journal of Personality, 57*, 375–406.

Caspi, A., & Herbener, E. S. (1990). Continuity and change: Assortative marriage and the consistency of personality in adulthood. *Journal of Personality and Social Psychology, 58*, 250–258.

Castaneda, G., Hendrick, S., & Fanary, R. (1986, April 18). *Housework allocation, role conflicts, and coping strategies in dual-career couples.* Paper presented at the meeting of the Southwest Psychological Association, Fort Worth, TX.

Catania, J. A., McDermott, L. J., & Wood, J. A. (1984). Assessment of locus of control: Situational specificity in the sexual context. *Journal of Sex Research, 20*, 310–324.

Cavoukian, A., & Doob, A. N. (1980). The effects of a judge's charge and subsequent recharge of judgments of guilt. *Basic and Applied Social Psychology, 1*, 103–114.

Chacko, T. I. (1982). Women and equal employment opportunity: Some unintended effects. *Journal of Applied Psychology, 67*, 119–123.

Chaiken, S. (1980). Heuristic versus systematic information processing and the use of sources versus message cues in persuasion. *Journal of Personality and Social Psychology, 39*, 752–766.

Chaiken, S. (1987). The heuristic model of persuasion. In M. P. Zanna, J. M. Olson, & C. P. Herman (Eds.), *Social influence: The Ontario symposium* (Vol. 5, pp. 3–39). Hillsdale, NJ: Erlbaum.

Chaiken, S., & Stagnor, C. (1987). Attitudes and attitude change. *Annual Review of Psychology, 38*, 575–630.

Chance, J. E. (1965, April). *Internal control of reinforcements and the school learning process.* Paper presented at the meeting of the Society for Research in Child Development, Minneapolis.

Chassin, L., Presson, C. C., & Sherman, S. J. (1990). Social psychological contributions to the understanding and prevention of adolescent cigarette smoking. *Personality and Social Psychology Bulletin, 16*, 133–151.

Cheney, A. B., & Bleker, E. G. (1982, August). *Internal-external locus of control and repression-sensitization in battered women.* Paper presented at the meeting of the American Psychological Association, Washington, DC.

Chhabra, V. (1990, March 20). Tropical paradise doomed to be "next Atlantis." *Albany Times Union,* pp. C1–C2.

Chidester, T. R. (1986). Problems in the study of interracial aggression: Pseudo-interracial dyad paradigm. *Journal of Personality and Social Psychology, 50*, 74–79.

Christensen, H. T. (1973). Attitudes toward marital infidelity: A nine-culture sampling of university student opinion. *Journal of Comparative Family Studies, 4*, 197–214.

Christopher, F. S., & Cate, R. M. (1985). Premarital sexual pathways and relationship development. *Journal of Social and Personal Relationships, 2*, 271–288.

Christy, P. R., Gelfand, D. M., & Hartmann, D. P. (1971). Effects of competition-induced frustration on two classes of modeled behavior. *Developmental Psychology, 5*, 104–111.

Church, A. T., & Katigbak, M. S. (1989). Internal, external, and self-report structure of personality in a non-Western culture: An investigation of cross-language and cross-cultural generalizability. *Journal of Personality and Social Psychology, 57*, 857–872.

Cialdini, R. B. (1988). *Influence: Science and practice* (2nd ed.). Glenview, IL: Scott, Foresman.

Cialdini, R. B., Baumann, D. J., & Kenrick, D. T. (1981). Insights from sadness: A three-step model of the development of altruism as hedonism. *Developmental Review, 1*, 207–223.

Cialdini, R. B., Darby, B. L., & Vincent, J. E. (1973). Transgression and altruism: A case for hedonism. *Journal of Experimental Social Psychology, 9*, 502–516.

Cialdini, R. B., Kenrick, D. T., & Bauman, D. J. (1982). Effects of

mood on prosocial behavior in children and adults. In N. Eisenberg-Berg (Ed.), *Development of prosocial behavior.* New York: Academic Press.

Cialdini, R. B., & Petty, R. (1979). Anticipatory opinion effects. In R. B. Petty, T. Ostrom, & T. Brock (Eds.), *Cognitive responses in persuasion.* Hillsdale, NJ: Erlbaum.

Cialdini, R. B., Schaller, M., Houlainhan, D., Arps, K., Fultz, J., & Beaman, A. L. (1987). Empathy-based helping: Is it selflessly or selfishly motivated? *Journal of Personality and Social Psychology, 52*, 749–758.

Cialdini, R. B., Vincent, J. E., Lewis, S. K., Catalan, J., Wheeler, D., & Darby, B. L. (1975). Reciprocal concessions procedure for inducing compliance: The door-in-the-face technique. *Journal of Personality and Social Psychology, 31*, 206–215.

Clark, L. A., & Watson, D. (1988). Mood and the mundane: Relations between daily life events and self-reported mood. *Journal of Personality and Social Psychology, 54*, 296–308.

Clark, M. S., Mills, J. R., & Corcoran, D. M. (1989). Keeping track of needs and inputs of friends and strangers. *Personality and Social Psychology Bulletin, 15*, 533–542.

Clark, M. S., Ouellette, R., Powel, M. C., & Milberg, S. (1987). Recipient's mood, relationship type, and helping. *Journal of Personality and Social Psychology, 53*, 94–103.

Clark, M. S., & Reis, H. (1988). Interpersonal processes in close relationships. *Annual Review of Psychology, 39*, 609–672.

Clark, R. D., III, & Word, L. E. (1972). Why don't bystanders help? Because of ambiguity? *Journal of Personality and Social Psychology, 24*, 392–400.

Clark, R. N., Hendee, J. C., & Burgess, R. L. (1972). The experimental control of littering. *Journal of Environmental Education, 4*, 22–28.

Clarke, D. D., & Hoyle, R. (1988). A theoretical solution to the problem of personality-situational interaction. *Personality and Individual Differences, 9*, 133–138.

Clement, U., Schmidt, G., & Kruse, M. (1984). Changes in sex differences in sexual behavior: A replication of a study on West German students (1966–1981). *Archives of Sexual Behavior, 13*, 99–120.

Clore, G. L., & Byrne, D. (1974). A reinforcement-affect model of attraction. In T. L. Huston (Ed.), *Foundations of interpersonal attraction* (pp. 143–170). New York: Academic Press.

Coale, A. J. (1974). The history of human population. *Scientific American, 231(3)*, 40–51.

Coates, B., Pusser, H. E., & Goodman, I. (1976). The influence of "Sesame Street" and "Mister Rogers' Neighborhood" on children's social behavior in the preschool. *Child Development, 47*, 138–144.

Codol, J. P., Jarymowicz, M., Kaminska-Feldman, M., & Szuster-Zbrojewicz, A. (1989). Asymmetry in the estimation of interpersonal distance and identity affirmation. *European Journal of Social Psychology, 19*, 11–22.

Cohen, S. (1978). Environmental load and the allocation of attention. In A. Baum, J. E. Singer, & S. Valins (Eds.), *Advances in environmental psychology* (Vol. 1). Hillsdale, NJ: Erlbaum.

Cohen, S., Evans, G. W., Stokols, D., & Krantz, D. (1986). *Behavior, health and environmental stress.* New York: Plenum.

Cohen, S., Glass, D. C., & Singer, J. E. (1973). Apartment noise, auditory discrimination, and reading ability in children. *Journal of Experimental Social Psychology, 9*, 407–422.

Cohen, S., & Ashby-Wills, T. (1985). Stress, social support, and the buffering hypothesis. *Psychological Bulletin, 98*, 310–357.

Cohn, E. G. (1990). Weather and violent crime: A reply to Perry and Simpson, 1987. *Environment and Behavior, 22*, 280–294.

Coleman, L. M., Jussim, L., & Abraham, J. (1987). Students' reactions to teachers' evaluations: The unique impact of negative feedback. *Journal of Applied Social Psychology, 17*, 1051–1070.

Collins, E. G. C. (1983). Managers and lovers. *Harvard Business Review, 83*, 142–153.

Collins, L. M., Sussman, S., Rauch, J. M., Dent, C. W., Johnson, C. A., Hansen, W. B., & Flay, B. R. (1987). Psychological predictors of young adolescent cigarette smoking: A sixteen-month, three-wave longitudinal study. *Journal of Applied Social Psychology, 17*, 554–573.

Comstock, G., Chafee, S., Katzman, N., McCombs, N., & Roberts, D.

(1978). *Television and human behavior.* New York: Columbia University Press.

Condon, J. W., & Crano, W. D. (1988). Inferred evaluation and the relation between attitude similarity and interpersonal attraction. *Journal of Personality and Social Psychology, 54,* 789–797.

Conger, J. A., & Kanungo, R. N. (1988). *Charismatic leadership: The elusive factor in organizational effectiveness.* San Francisco: Jossey-Bass.

Connell, E. B. (1983). What practical advice can physicians give patients on avoiding genital herpes? *Medical Aspects of Human Sexuality, 17(8),* 157–158, 160, 163–164, 169, 173, 176–177.

Contrada, R. J. (1989). Type A behavior, personality hardiness, and cardiovascular responses to stress. *Journal of Personality and Social Psychology, 57,* 895–903.

Cook, S. W. (1984). Cooperative interaction in multiethnic contexts. In N. Miller & M. Brewer (Eds.), *Groups in contact: The psychology of desegregation* (pp. 155–185). New York: Academic Press.

Cook, S. W. (1985). Experimenting on social issues: The case of school desegregation. *American Psychologist, 40,* 452–460.

Cooley, C. H. (1902/1964). *Human nature and the social order.* New York: Schocken Books.

Coombs, R. H. (1969). Social participation, self-concept and interpersonal valuation. *Sociometry, 32,* 273–286.

Coombs, W. N., & Schroeder, H. E. (1988). Generalized locus of control: An analysis of factor analytic data. *Personality and Individual Differences, 9,* 79–85.

Cooper, J., & Fazio, R. H. (1984). A new look at dissonance theory. In L. Berkowitz (Ed.), *Advances in experimental social psychology* (Vol. 17, pp. 229–266). New York: Academic Press.

Cooper, J., & Scher, S. J. (in press). Actions and attitudes: The role of responsibility and aversive consequences in persuasion. In T. Brock & S. Shavitt (Eds.), *The psychology of persuasion.* San Francisco: Freeman.

Costa, F. M., Jessor, R., & Donovan, J. E. (1989). Value of health and adolescent conventionality: A construct validation of a new measure in problem-behavior theory. *Journal of Applied Social Psychology, 19,* 841–861.

Costa, P. T., Jr., & McCrae, R. R. (1984). Personality as a lifelong determinant of well-being. In C. Malatesta & C. Izard (Eds.), *Affective processes in adult development and aging* (pp. 141–156). Beverly Hills, CA: Sage.

Costa, P. T., Jr., & McCrae, R. R. (1985). *The NEO Personality Inventory manual.* Odessa, FL: Psychological Assessment Resources.

Costa, P. T., Jr., & McCrae, R. R. (1988). Personality in adulthood: A six-year longitudinal study of self-reports and spouse ratings on the NEO Personality Inventory. *Journal of Personality and Social Psychology, 54,* 853–863.

Costantini, E., & Craik, K. H. (1980). Personality and politicians: California party leaders, 1960–1976. *Journal of Personality and Social Psychology, 38,* 641–646.

Costanza, R. S., Derlage, V. J., & Winstead, B. A. (1988). Positive and negative forms of social support: Effects of conversation topics on coping with stress among same-sex friends. *Journal of Experimental Social Psychology, 24,* 182–193.

Costanzo, M., Archer, D., Aronson, E., & Pettigrew, T. (1986). Energy conservation behavior: The difficult path from information to action. *American Psychologist, 41,* 521–528.

Cotton, J. L. (1986). Ambient temperature and violent crime. *Journal of Applied Social Psychology, 16,* 786–801.

Cottrell, N. B., Wack, K. L., Sekerak, G. J., Rittle, R. (1968). Social facilitation of dominant responses by the presence of an audience and the mere presence of others. *Journal of Personality and Social Psychology, 9,* 245–250.

Cousins, S. D. (1989). Culture and self-perception in Japan and the United States. *Journal of Personality and Social Psychology, 56,* 124–131.

Cowen, E. L., Weissberg, R. P., & Lotyczewski, B. S. (1982). Physical contact in helping interaction with young children. *Journal of Consulting and Clinical Psychology, 50,* 219–225.

Cox, M., & Tanford, S. (1989). Effects of evidence and instructions in civil trials: An experimental investigation of rules of admissibility. *Social Behavior, 4,* 31–55.

Cox, V. C., Paulus, P. B., & McCain, G. (1984). Prison crowding research: The relevance for prison housing standards and a

general approach regarding crowding phenomena. *American Psychologist, 39,* 1148–1160.

Cramer, R. E., McMaster, M. R., Bartell, P. A., & Dragna, M. (1988). Subject competence and minimization of the bystander effect. *Journal of Applied Social Psychology, 18,* 1133–1148.

Cramer, R. E., Weiss, R. F., Steigleder, M. K., & Balling, S. S. (1985). *Journal of Personality and Social Psychology, 49,* 1221–1230.

Crandall, C. S. (1988). Social contagion of binge eating. *Journal of Personality and Social Psychology, 55,* 588–598.

Crano, W. D., Gorenflo, D. W., & Schackelford, S. L. (1988). Overjustification, assumed consensus, and attitude change: Further investigation of the incentive-aroused ambivalence hypothesis. *Journal of Personality and Social Psychology, 55,* 12–22.

Crano, W. D., & Sivacek, J. (1984). The influence of incentive-aroused ambivalence of overjustification effects in attitude change. *Journal of Experimental Social Psychology, 20,* 137–158.

Crocker, J., Alloy, L. B., & Kayne, N. T. (1988). Attributional style, depression, and perceptions of consensus for events. *Journal of Personality and Social Psychology, 54,* 840–846.

Crocker, J., & Luhtanen, R. (1990). Collective self-esteem and ingroup bias. *Journal of Personality and Social Psychology, 58,* 60–67.

Cropanzano, R., & Folger, R. (1989). Referent cognitions and task decision autonomy: Beyond equity theory. *Journal of Applied Psychology, 74,* 293–299.

Crouch, A., & Yetton, P. (1987). Manager behavior, leadership style, and subordinate performance: An empirical extension of the Vroom-Yetton conflict rule. *Organizational Behavior and Human Decision Processes, 39,* 384–396.

Crouch, A., & Yetton, P. (1988). Manager-subordinate dyads: Relationships among task and social contact, manager friendliness, and subordinate performance in management groups. *Organizational Behavior and Human Decision Processes, 41,* 65–82.

Crouse, B. B., & Mehrabian, A. (1977). Affiliation of opposite-sexed strangers. *Journal of Research in Personality, 11,* 38–47.

Croyle, R., & Uretsky, M. B. (1987). Effects of mood on self-appraisal of health status. *Health Psychology, 6,* 239–254.

Cruse, D., & Leigh, B. C. (1987). 'Adam's Rib' revisited: Legal and non-legal influences on the processing of trial testimony. *Social Behavior, 2,* 221–230.

Crutchfield, R. A. (1955). Conformity and character. *American Psychologist, 10,* 191–198.

Cummins, R. (1989). Locus of control and social support. Clarifiers of the relationship between job stress and job satisfaction. *Journal of Applied Social Psychology, 19,* 772–788.

Cunningham, M. R. (1979). Weather, mood, and helping behavior: Quasi-experiments with the sunshine Samaritan. *Journal of Personality and Social Psychology, 37,* 1947–1956.

Cunningham, M. R. (1986). Measuring the physical in physical attractiveness: Quasi-experiments on the sociobiology of female facial beauty. *Journal of Personality and Social Psychology, 50,* 925–935.

Cunningham, M. R. (1988). Does happiness mean friendliness? Induced mood and heterosexual self-disclosure. *Personality and Social Psychology Bulletin, 14,* 283–297.

Cunningham, M. R., Shaffer, D. R., Barbee, A. P., Wolff, P. L., & Kelley, D. J. (1990). Separate processes in the relation of elation and depression to helping: Social versus personal concerns. *Journal of Experimental Social Psychology, 26,* 13–33.

Cunningham, M. R., Steinberg, J., & Grev, R. (1980). Wanting to and having to help: Separate motivations for positive mood and guilt-induced helping. *Journal of Personality and Social Psychology, 38,* 181–192.

Curtis, R. C., & Miller, K. (1986). Believing another likes or dislikes you: Behavior making the beliefs come true. *Journal of Personality and Social Psychology, 51,* 284–290.

Cutler, B. L., Penrod, S. D., & Martens, T. K. (1987). Improving the reliability of eyewitness identification: Putting content into context. *Journal of Applied Psychology, 72,* 629–637.

Daly, M. (1989). On distinguishing evolved adaptation from epiphenomena. *Behavioral and Brain Sciences, 12,* 520.

Darley, J. M., & Batson, C. D. (1973). From Jerusalem to Jericho: A study of situational and dispositional variables in helping behavior. *Journal of Personality and Social Psychology, 27,* 100–108.

Darley, J. M., & Cooper, J. (1972). The "clean for Gene" phenomenon:

The effect of students' appearance on political campaigning. *Journal of Applied Social Psychology, 2,* 24–33.

Darley, J. M., & Latané, B. (1968). Bystander intervention in emergencies: Diffusion of responsibility. *Journal of Personality and Social Psychology, 8,* 377–383.

Davids, A., & Lawton, M. J. (1961). Self-concept, mother concept, and food aversion in emotionally disturbed and normal children. *Journal of Abnormal and Social Psychology, 62,* 309–314.

Davidson, L. M., Baum, A., & Collins, D. (1982). Stress and control-related problems at Three Mile Island. *Journal of Applied Social Psychology, 12,* 349–359.

Davidson, W. P. (1983). The third-person effect in communication. *Public Opinion Quarterly, 47,* 1–15.

Davis, J. H. (1989). Psychology and law: The last 15 years. *Journal of Applied Social Psychology, 19,* 119–230.

Davis, J. H., Stasson, M., Ono, K., & Zimmerman, S. (1988). Effects of straw polls on group decision making: Sequential voting pattern, timing, and local majorities. *Journal of Personality and Social Psychology, 55,* 918–926.

Davis, J. H., Tindale, R. S., Nagao, D. H., Hinsz, V. B., & Robertson, B. (1984). Order effects in multiple decisions by groups: A demonstration with mock juries and trial procedures. *Journal of Personality and Social Psychology, 47,* 1003–1012.

Davis, M. H., & Kraus, L. A. (1989). Social contact, loneliness, and mass media use: A test of two hypotheses. *Journal of Applied Social Psychology, 19,* 1100–1124.

Davis, W. L., & Phares, E. J. (1969). Parental antecedents of internal-external control of reinforcement. *Psychological Reports, 24,* 427–436.

Dawes, R. M. (1980). Social dilemmas. In M. Rosenzweig & L. Porter (Eds.), *Annual review of psychology* (Vol. 31, pp. 169–193). Palo Alto, CA: Annual Reviews.

Dawes, R. M. (1989). Statistical criteria for establishing a truly false consensus effect. *Journal of Experimental Social Psychology, 25,* 1–17.

Dawes, R. M., McTavish, J., & Shaklee, H. (1977). Behavior communication and assumptions about other people's behavior in a commons dilemma situation. *Journal of Personality and Social Psychology, 35,* 1–11.

Deaux, K. (1982). *Sex as a social category: Evidence for gender stereotypes.* Invited address, American Psychological Association, Washington, DC.

Deaux, K., & Farris, E. (1977). Attribution causes for one's own performance: The effects of sex, norms and outcomes. *Journal of Research in Personality, 11,* 59–72.

Deaux, K., & Lewis, L. L. (1984). The structure of gender stereotypes: Interrelationships among components and gender label. *Journal of Personality and Social Psychology, 46,* 991–1004.

DeBono, K. G., & Harnish, R. J. (1988). Source expertise, source attractiveness, and the processing of persuasive information: A functional approach. *Journal of Personality and Social Psychology, 55,* 541–546.

DeBono, K. G., & Snyder, M. (1989). Understanding consumer decision-making processes: The role of form and function in product evaluation. *Journal of Applied Social Psychology, 19,* 416–424.

Deci, E. L. (1975). *Intrinsic motivation.* New York: Plenum.

DeFronzo, J. (1984). Climate and crime: Tests of an FBI assumption. *Environment and Behavior, 16,* 185–210.

DeJong, W., & Musilli, L. (1982). External pressure to comply: Handicapped versus nonhandicapped requesters and the foot-in-the-door phenomenon. *Personality and Social Psychology Bulletin, 8,* 522–527.

DeLamater, J. (1981). The social control of sexuality. *Annual Review of Sociology, 7,* 263–290.

Dellinger, R. W. (1979). Jet roar: Health problems take off near airports. *Human Behavior, 8,* 50–51.

Dembroski, T. M., & Costa, P. (1987). Coronary-prone behavior: Components of the Type A pattern and hostility. *Journal of Personality, 55,* 211–236.

Demeny, P. (1974). The populations of underdeveloped countries. *Scientific American, 231(3),* 148–159.

Dengerink, H. A., Schnedler, R. W., & Covey, M. K. (1978). Role of avoidance in aggressive responses to attack and no attack. *Journal of Personality and Social Psychology, 36,* 1044–1053.

Denno, D. J. (1982). *Sex differences in cognition and crime: Early developmental, biological, and social correlates.* Unpublished doctoral dissertation, University of Pennsylvania, University Park.

DePaulo, B. M., & Pfeifer, R. L. (1986). On-the-job experience and skill at detecting deceit. *Journal of Applied Social Psychology, 16,* 249–267.

DePaulo, B. M., Stone, J. L., & Lassiter, G. D. (1985). Deceiving and detecting deceit. In B. R. Schlenker (Ed.), *The self and social life* (pp. 323–370). New York: McGraw-Hill.

Derlega, V. J., & Grzelak, J. (Eds.). (1982). *Cooperation and helping behavior: Theories and research.* New York: Academic Press.

Derlega, V. J., & Winstead, B. A. (Eds.). (1986). *Friendship and social interaction.* New York: Springer-Verlag.

Deutsch, M., & Krauss, R. M. (1960). The effects of threat upon interpersonal bargaining. *Journal of Abnormal and Social Psychology, 61,* 181–189.

Devine, P. G. (1989). Stereotypes and prejudice: Their automatic and controlled components. *Journal of Personality and Social Psychology, 56,* 5–18.

Devins, G. M., Binik, Y. M., Gorman, P., Dattel, M., McCloskey, B., Oscar, G., & Briggs, J. (1982). Perceived self-efficacy, outcome expectancies, and negative mood states in end-stage renal disease. *Journal of Abnormal Psychology, 91,* 241–244.

DeWaal, F. (1989). *Peacemaking among primates.* Cambridge, MA: Harvard University Press.

Diamond, R., Seller, L., & Russo, N. F. (1981). *Sexual harassment action kit.* Washington, DC: Federation of Organizations for Women.

Diener, E., Larsen, R. J., & Emmons, R. A. (1984). Person X Situation interactions: Choice of situations and congruence response models. *Journal of Personality and Social Psychology, 47,* 580–592.

Digman, J. M. (1989). Five robust trait dimensions: Development, stability, and utility. *Journal of Personality, 57,* 195–214.

Digman, J. M. (1990). Personality structure: Emergence of the five-factor model. In M. R. Rosenzweig & L. W. Porter (Eds.), *Annual review of psychology* (Vol. 41, pp. 417–440). Palo Alto, CA: Annual Reviews.

Digman, J. M., & Inouye, J. (1986). Further specification of the five robust factors of personality. *Journal of Personality and Social Psychology, 50,* 116–123.

Dillard, J. P., & Broetzmann, S. M. (1989). Romantic relationships at work: Perceived changes in job-related behaviors as a function of participant's motive, partner's motive, and gender. *Journal of Applied Social Psychology, 19,* 93–110.

DiMatteo, M. R., Hays, R. D., & Prince, L. M. (1986). Relationships of physicians' nonverbal communication skill to patient satisfaction, appointment noncompliance, and physician workload. *Health Psychology, 5,* 581–594.

DiMento, J. F. (1989). Can social science explain organization noncompliance with environmental law? *Journal of Social Issues, 45(1),* 109–132.

Dion, K. K., & Dion, K. L. (1975). Self-esteem and romantic love. *Journal of Personality, 43,* 39–57.

Dion, K. L., & Dion, K. K. (1987). Belief in a just world and physical attractiveness stereotyping. *Journal of Personality and Social Psychology, 52,* 775–780.

Dion, K. L., & Dion, K. K. (1988). Romantic love: Individual and cultural perspectives. In R. J. Sternberg & M. L. Barnes (Eds.), *The psychology of love* (pp. 264–289). New Haven, CT: Yale University Press.

DiVasto, P. V., Pathak, D., & Fishburn, W. R. (1981). The interrelationship of sex guilt, sex behavior, and age in an adult sample. *Archives of Sexual Behavior, 10,* 119–122.

Dixit, N. (1985). *The effect of verbal contact and spatial positioning on job satisfaction, job performance, and interpersonal attraction: An experimental investigation.* Unpublished doctoral dissertation, State University of New York at Albany.

Dodge, K. A., & Coie, J. D. (1987). Social-information-processing factors in reactive and proactive aggression in children's peer groups. *Journal of Personality and Social Psychology, 53,* 1146–1158.

Dodge, K. A., Murphy, R. R., & Buchsbaum, K. (1984). The assessment of intention-cue detection skills in children: Implications for developmental psychopathology. *Child Development, 55,* 163–173.

Doherty, W. J. (1983). Impact of divorce on locus of control orientation in adult women: A longitudinal study. *Journal of Personality and Social Psychology, 44,* 834–840.

Dollard, J., Doob, L., Miller, N., Mowrer, O. H., & Sears, R. R. (1939). *Frustration and aggression.* New Haven, CT: Yale University Press.

Donnerstein, E., & Donnerstein, M. (1976). Research in the control of interracial aggression. In R. G. Green & E. C. O'Neal (Eds.), *Perspectives on aggression.* New York: Academic Press.

Donnerstein, E., & Wilson, D. W. (1976). The effects of noise and perceived control upon ongoing and subsequent aggressive behavior. *Journal of Personality and Social Psychology, 34,* 774–781.

Donnerstein, M., Donnerstein, E., Berkowitz, L., & Linz, D. (1987). In E. Donnerstein, D. Linz, & S. Penrod, *The question of pornography: Research findings and policy implications.* New York: Free Press.

Donovan, J. M., Hill, E., & Jankowiak, W. R. (1989). Gender, sexual orientation, and truth-of-consensus in studies of physical attractiveness. *Journal of Sex Research, 26,* 264–271.

Dorian, B. J., Keystone, E., Garfinkel, P. E., & Brown, J. M. (1982). Aberrations in lymphocyte subpopulations and function during psychological stress. *Clinical and Experimental Immunology, 50,* 132–138.

Dovidio, J. F. (1984). Helping behavior and altruism: An empirical and conceptual overview. In L. Berkowitz (Ed.), *Advances in experimental social psychology* (Vol. 17, pp. 361–427). New York: Academic Press.

Dovidio, J. F., & Gaertner, S. L. (Eds.). (1986). *Prejudice, discrimination, and racism.* Orlando, FL: Academic Press.

Dovidio, J. F., Evans, N., & Tyler, R. B. (1986). Racial stereotypes: The contents of their cognitive representations: *Journal of Experimental Social Psychology, 22,* 22–37.

Drachman, D., DeCarufel, A., & Insko, C. A. (1978). The extra credit effect in interpersonal attraction. *Journal of Experimental Social Psychology, 14,* 458–465.

Driscoll, R., Davis, K. E., & Lipetz, M. E. (1972). Parental interference and romantic love: The Romeo and Juliet effect. *Journal of Personality and Social Psychology, 24,* 1–10.

Duffy, M., Bailey, S., Beck, B., & Barker, D. G. (1986). Preferences in nursing home design: A comparison of residents, administrators, and designers. *Environment and Behavior, 18,* 246–257.

Dugan, K. W. (1989). Ability and effort attributions: Do they affect how managers communicate performance feedback information? *Academy of Management Journal, 32,* 87–114.

Dumanoski, D. (1990, February 13). Population growth seen as major force in our global environmental problems. *Albany Times Union,* pp. C1, C4.

Dunbar, R. I. M. (1989). Genetic similarity theory needs more development. *Behavioral and Brain Sciences, 12,* 520–521.

Durdan, C. A., Reeder, G. D., & Hecht, P. R. (1985). Litter in a university cafeteria: Demographic data and the use of prompts as an intervention strategy. *Environment and Behavior, 17,* 387–404.

Dutton, D. G., & Aron, A. P. (1974). Some evidence for heightened sexual attraction under conditions of high anxiety. *Journal of Personality and Social Psychology, 30,* 510–517.

Dutton, D. G., & Lake, R. A. (1973). Threat of own prejudice and reverse discrimination in interracial situations. *Journal of Personality and Social Psychology, 28,* 94–100.

Dykman, B. M., Abramson, L. Y., Alloy, L. B., & Hartlage, S. (1989). Processing of ambiguous and unambiguous feedback by depressed and nondepressed college students: Schematic biases and their implications for depressive realism. *Journal of Personality and Social Psychology, 56,* 431–445.

Eagly, A. H. (1987). *Sex differences in social behavior: A social-role interpretation.* Hillsdale, NJ: Erlbaum.

Eagly, A. H., & Carli, L. (1981). Sex of researchers and sex-typed communications as determinants of sex differences in influence-ability. A meta-analysis of social influence studies. *Psychological Bulletin, 90,* 1–20.

Eagly, A. H., & Chaiken, S. (1984). Cognitive theories of persuasion. In L. Berkowitz (Ed.), *Advances in experimental social psychology* (Vol. 17, pp. 267–359). New York: Academic Press.

Eagly, A. H., & Johnson, B. T. (in press). Gender and leadership style: A meta-analysis. *Psychological Bulletin.*

Eagly, A. H., & Steffen, V. J. (1986). Gender and aggressive behavior: A meta-analytic review of the social psychological literature. *Psychological Bulletin, 100,* 309–330.

Eagly, A. H., & Wood, W. (1982). Inferred sex differences in status as a determinant of gender stereotypes about social influence. *Journal of Personality and Social Psychology, 43,* 915–928.

Ebbesen, E. B., Kjos, G. L., & Konecni, V. J. (1976). Spatial ecology: Its effects on the choice of friends and enemies. *Journal of Experimental Social Psychology, 12,* 505–518.

Eccles, J. S., Wigfield, A., Flanagan, C. A., Miller, C., Reuman, D. A., & Yee, D. (1989). Self-concepts, domain values, and self-esteem: Relations and changes at early adolescence. *Journal of Personality, 57,* 283–310.

Edney, J. J. (1979a, August). Free riders en route to disaster. *Psychology Today, 102,* pp. 80–87.

Edney, J. J. (1979b). The nuts game: A concise commons dilemma analog. *Environmental Psychology and Nonverbal Behavior, 3,* 252–254.

Edney, J. J., & Harper, C. S. (1978). The effects of information in a resource management problem: A social trap analog. *Human ecology, 6,* 387–395.

Efran, M. G., & Patterson, E. W. J. (1974). Voters vote beautiful: The effect of physical appearance on a national election. *Canadian Journal of Behavioral Science, 6,* 352–356.

Ehrlich, P. R., & Ehrlich, A. H. (1971). The population crisis. *Britannica book of the year.* Chicago: William Benton.

Einhorn, H. J., & Hogarth, R. M. (1986). Judging probable cause. *Psychological Bulletin, 99,* 3–19.

Eisenberg, N. (1983). The relation between empathy and altruism: Conceptual and methodological issues. *Academic Psychology Bulletin, 5,* 195–208.

Eisenberg, N., Cialdini, R. B., McCreath, H., & Shell, R. (1987). Consistency-based compliance: When and why do children become vulnerable? *Journal of Personality and Social Psychology, 52,* 1174–1181.

Eisenberg, N., Roth, K., Bryniasrski, K. A., & Murray, E. (1984). Sex differences in the relationship of height of children's actual and attributed social and cognitive competencies. *Sex Roles, 11,* 719–734.

Eisenman, R. (1985). Marijuana use and attraction: Support for Byrne's similarity-attraction concept. *Perceptual and Motor Skills, 61,* 582.

Eiser, J. R. (1983). Smoking, addiction, and decision-making. *Journal of Applied Social Psychology, 32,* 11–28.

Eiser, J. R., & van der Pligt, J. (1984). Attitudinal and social factors in adolescent smoking: In search of peer group influence. *Journal of Applied Social Psychology, 14,* 348–363.

Ekman, P., Davidson, R. J., & Friesen, W. V. (1990). The Duchenne smile: Emotional expression and brain physiology II. *Journal of Personality and Social Psychology, 58,* 342–353.

Ekman, P. Friesen, W., O'Sullivan, C. A., Diacoyanni-Tariatzis, H. K., Heider, K., Krause, R., LeCompte, W., Pitcarin, T., Ricci-Biti, P. E., Schener, K., Tomita, M., & Tzavaras, A. (1987). Universals and cultural differences in the judgments of facial expressions of emotion. *Journal of Personality and Social Psychology, 53,* 712–717.

Ekman, P., & Friesen, W. V. (1975). *Unmasking the face.* Englewood Cliffs, NJ: Prentice Hall.

Electric lines linked to cancer. (1989, November 30). *Albany Times Union,* p. A8.

Ellis, R. J. (1988). Self-monitoring and leadership emergence in groups. *Personality and Social Psychology Bulletin, 14,* 681–693.

Ellis, S., Rogoff, B., & Cramer, C. C. (1981). Age segregation in children's social interactions. *Developmental Psychology, 17,* 399–407.

Ellsworth, P. C., & Carlsmith, J. M. (1973). Eye contact and gaze aversion in aggressive encounter. *Journal of Personality and Social Psychology, 33,* 117–122.

Elms, A. C., & Milgram, S. (1966). Personality characteristics associated with obedience and defiance toward authoritative command. *Journal of Experimental Research in Personality, 1,* 282–289.

Engebretson, T. O., Matthews, K. A., & Scheier, M. F. (1989). Relations between anger expression and cardiovascular reactivity:

Reconciling inconsistent findings through a matching hypothesis. *Journal of Personality and Social Psychology, 57,* 513–521.

Environmental Task Force. (1984). *National environmental survey.* Washington, DC: U.S. Government Printing Office.

Enzel, M. E., Hanson, R. D., & Lowe, C. A. (1975). Causal attribution in the mixed-motive game: Effects of facilitory and inhibitory environmental forces. *Journal of Personality and Social Psychology, 31,* 50–54.

Epstein, S., & Meier, P. (1989). Constructive thinking: A broad coping variable with specific components. *Journal of Personality and Social Psychology, 57,* 332–350.

Erber, R., & Fiske, S. T. (1984). Outcome dependency and attention to inconsistent information. *Journal of Personality and Social Psychology, 47,* 709–726.

Erdley, C. A., & D'Agostine, P. R. (1989). Cognitive and affective components of automatic priming effects. *Journal of Personality and Social Psychology, 54,* 741–747.

Eron, L. D. (1982). Parent-child interaction, television violence, and aggression of children. *American Psychologist, 37,* 197–211.

Esser, J. K. (1989). Agreement pressure and opponent strategies in oligopoly bargaining. *Personality and Social Psychology Bulletin, 15,* 596–603.

Esses, V. M. (1989). Mood as a moderator of acceptance of interpersonal feedback. *Journal of Personality and Social Psychology, 57,* 769–781.

Esses, V. M., & Wester, C. D. (1988). Physical attractiveness, dangerousness, and the Canadian criminal code. *Journal of Applied Social Psychology, 18,* 1017–1031.

Evans, G. W., Jacobs, S. V., & Frager, N. B. (1982). Behavioral responses to air pollution. In A. Baum & J. E. Singer (Eds.), *Advances in environmental psychology* (Vol. 4). Hillsdale, NJ: Erlbaum.

Evans, G. W., Palsane, M. N., Lepore, S. J., & Martin, J. (1989). Residential density and psychological health: The mediating effects of social support. *Journal of Personality and Social Psychology, 57,* 994–999.

Evans, G. W., Palsane, M. N., & Carrere, S. (1987). Type A behavior and occupational stress: A cross-cultural study of blue-collar workers. *Journal of Personality and Social Psychology, 52,* 1002–1007.

Eysenck, H. J. (1986). Can personality study ever be scientific? *Journal of Social Behavior and Personality, 1,* 3–19.

Fajardo, D. M. (1985). Author race, essay quality, and reverse discrimination. *Journal of Applied Social Psychology, 15,* 255–268.

Farb, B. (1978). *Humankind.* Boston: Houghton Mifflin.

Fazio, R. H. (1989). In M. P. Zanna (Ed.), *Advances in experimental social psychology.* New York: Academic Press.

Fazio, R. H., Chen, J., McDonel, E. C., & Sherman, S. J. (1982). Attitude accessibility, and the strength of the object-evaluation association. *Journal of Experimental Social Psychology, 18,* 339–357.

Fazio, R. H., & Williams, C. J. (1986). Attitude-accessibility as a moderator of the attitude-perception and attitude-behavior relations: An investigation of the 1984 presidential election. *Journal of Personality and Social Psychology, 51,* 505–514.

Fazio, R. H., & Zanna, M. P. (1978). Attitudinal qualities relating to the strength of the attitude-behavior relationship. *Journal of Experimental Social Psychology, 14,* 398–408.

Fazio, R. H., & Zanna, M. P. (1981). Direct experience and attitude-behavior consistency. In L. Berkowitz (Ed.), *Advances in experimental social psychology* (Vol. 14, pp. 161–202). New York: Academic Press.

Feather, N. T., & Volkmer, R. E. (1988). Preference for situations involving effort, time pressure, and feedback in relation to Type A behavior, locus of control, and test anxiety. *Journal of Personality and Social Psycholoqy, 55,* 266–271.

Feeney, J. A., & Noller, P. (1990). Attachment style as a predictor of adult romantic relationships. *Journal of Personality and Social Psychology, 58,* 281–291.

Feingold, A. (1988). Matching for attractiveness in romantic partners and same-sex friends: A meta-analysis and theoretical critique. *Psychological Bulletin, 104,* 226–235.

Feingold, A. (1989). *Gender differences in effects of attractiveness and similarity on opposite-sex attraction: Integration of self-report and experimental findings.* Unpublished manuscript, Yale University, New Haven, CT.

Feingold, A. (1990a, in press). Gender differences in effects of physical attractiveness on romantic attraction: A comparison across five research paradigms. *Journal of Personality and Social Psychology.*

Feingold, A. (1990b). *Good-looking people are not what we think: An integration of the experimental literature on physical attractiveness stereotyping with the literature on correlates of physical attractiveness.* Unpublished manuscript, Yale University, New Haven, CT.

Feldman, S. D. (1975). The presentation of shortness in everyday life—Height and heightism in American society: Toward a sociology of stature. In S. D. Feldman & G. W. Thielbar (Eds.), *Life styles: Diversity in American society.* Boston: Little, Brown.

Felson, R. B. (1989). Parents and the reflected appraisal process: A longitudinal analysis. *Journal of Personality and Social Psychology, 56,* 965–971.

Feltz, D. L. (1982). Path analysis of the causal elements in Bandura's theory of self-efficacy and an anxiety-based model of avoidance behavior. *Journal of Personality and Social Psychology, 42,* 764–781.

Fenigstein, A. (1987). On the nature of public and private self-consciousness. *Journal of Personality, 55,* 543–554.

Fenigstein, A., Scheier, M. F., & Buss, A. H. (1975). Public and private self-consciousness: Assessment and theory. *Journal of Consulting and Clinical Psychology, 43,* 522–527.

Ferguson, T. J., & Rule, B. G. (1983). An attributional perspective on anger and aggression. In R. G. Geen & E. I. Donnerstein (Eds.), *Aggression: Theoretical and empirical reviews: Vol. 1. Theoretical and methodological issues* (pp. 41–74). New York: Academic Press.

Ferrari, J. R., Baldwin, C. H. (1989). Promoting safety belt use in shopping carts: "Buckle-up your baby." *Environment and Behavior, 21,* 603–619.

Feshbach, S. (1984a). The catharsis hypothesis, aggressive drive, and the reduction of aggression. *Aggressive Behavior, 10,* 91–101.

Feshbach, S. (1984b). The "personality" of personality theory and research. *Personality and Social Psychology Bulletin, 10,* 446–456.

Festinger, L. (1954). A theory of social comparison processes. *Human Relations, 7,* 117–140.

Festinger, L. (1957). *A theory of cognitive dissonance.* Evanston, IL: Row, Peterson.

Festinger, L., & Carlsmith, J. M. (1959). Cognitive consequences of forced compliance. *Journal of Abnormal and Social Psychology, 58,* 203–210.

Festinger, L., Schachter, S., & Back, K. (1950). *Social pressures in informal groups: A study of a housing community.* New York: Harper.

Fichten, C. S., & Amsel, R. (1986). Trait attributions about college students with a physical disability: Circumplex analyses and methodological issues. *Journal of Applied Social Psychology, 16,* 410–427.

Fiedler, F. E. (1978). Contingency model and the leadership process. In L. Berkowitz (Ed.), *Advances in experimental social psychology* (Vol. 11). New York: Academic Press.

Fiedler, F. E., & Garcia, J. E. (1987). *Leadership: Cognitive resources and performance.* New York: Wiley.

Fiedler, K., & Forgas, J. P. (Eds.). (1988). *Affect, cognition, and social behavior.* Toronto: Hogrefe.

Figler, M. H., Wazlavek, B. E., & Chaves, L. M. (1988). Territorial prior advantage in convict cichlids (Cichlasoma nigrofasciaturm Gunther). *Bulletin of the Psychonomic Society, 26,* 469–470.

Finch, J. F., & Cialdini, R. B. (1989). Another indirect tactic of (self-) image management: Boosting. *Personality and Social Psychology Bulletin, 15,* 222–232.

Finchilescu, G. (1988). Interracial contact in South Africa within the nursing context. *Journal of Applied Social Psychology, 18,* 1207–1221.

Findley, M. J., & Cooper, H. M. (1983). Locus of control and academic achievement: A literature review. *Journal of Personality and Social Psychology, 44,* 419–427.

Fischer, G. (1989). Atmospheric lifetime of carbon dioxide. *Population and Environment, 10,* 177–181.

Fischman, J. (1986, January). Women and divorce: Ten years after. *Psychology Today, 18,* p. 15.

Fisher, W. A. (1980). *Erotophobia-erotophilia and performance in a human sexuality course.* Unpublished manuscript, University of Western Ontario, London, Canada.

Fisher, W. A. (1984). Predicting contraceptive behavior among university men: The roles of emotions and behavioral intentions. *Journal of Applied Social Psychology, 14,* 104–123.

Fisher, W. A. (1989). Understanding and preventing adolescent pregnancy and sexually transmissible disease–AIDS. In J. Edwards et al. (Eds.), *Applying social influence processes in preventing social problems.* Beverly Hills, CA: Plenum.

Fisher, W. A., Byrne, D., & White, L. A. (1983). Emotional barriers to contraception. In D. Byrne & W. A. Fisher (Eds.), *Adolescents, sex, and contraception* (pp. 207–239). Hillsdale, NJ: Erlbaum.

Fisher, W. A., Byrne, D., White, L. A., & Kelley, K. (1988). Erotophobia-erotophilia as a dimension of personality. *Journal of Sex Research, 25,* 123–151.

Fisher, W. A., & Gray, J. (1988). Erotophobia-erotophilia and sexual behavior during pregnancy and postpartum. *Journal of Sex Research, 25,* 379–396.

Fisher, W. A., Grenier, G., Watters, W. W., Lamont, J., Cohen, M., & Askwith, J. (1988). Students' sexual knowledge, attitudes toward sex, and willingness to treat sexual concerns. *Journal of Medical Education, 63,* 379–385.

Fiske, S. T. (1989). *Interdependence and stereotyping: From the laboratory to the Supreme Court (and back).* Invited address, American Psychological Association, New Orleans.

Fiske, S. T., & Neuberg, S. L. (1990). A continuum model of impression formation, from category-based to individuating processes: Influence of information and motivation on attention and interpretation. In M. P. Zanna (Ed.), *Advances in experimental social psychology* (Vol. 23). New York: Academic Press.

Fiske, S. T., & Taylor, S. E. (1984). *Social cognition.* Reading, MA: Addison-Wesley.

Fitch, G. (1970). Effects of self-esteem, perceived performance, and choice on causal attributions. *Journal of Personality and Social Psychology, 16,* 311–315.

Flay, B. R., Ryan, K. B., Best, J. A., Brown, K. S., Kersell, M. W., d'Avernas, J., & Zanna, M. P. (1985). Are social psychological smoking prevention programs effective? *Journal of Behavioral Medicine, 8,* 37–60.

Flippo, J. R., & Lewinson, P. M. (1971). Effects of failure on the self-esteem of depressed and nondepressed subjects. *Journal of Consulting and Clinical Psychology, 36,* 151.

Folger, R. (1986). Rethinking equity theory: A referent cognitions model. In W. Bierhoff, R. L. Cohen, and J. Greenberg (Eds.), *Justice in social relations* (pp. 145–162). New York: Plenum.

Folger, R. (1987). Reformulation of the preconditions of resentment: A referent cognitions model. In J. C. Masters and W. P. Smith (Eds.), *Social comparison, justice, and relative deprivation: Theoretical, empirical, and policy perspectives* (pp. 183–215). Hillsdale, NJ: Erlbaum.

Folkes, V. S. (1982). Forming relationships and the matching hypothesis. *Journal of Personality and Social Psychology, 8,* 631–636.

Forest, D., Clark, M. S., Mills, J., & Isen, A. M. (1980). Helping as a function of feeling state and nature of the helping behavior. *Motivation and Emotion, 3,* 161–170.

Forgas, J. P., & Bower, G. H. (1987). Mood effects on person-perception judgments. *Journal of Personality and Social Psychology, 53,* 53–60.

Forgas, J. P., & Bower, G. H. (1988). Affect in social and personal judgments. In K. Fiedler & J. P. Forgas (Eds.), *Affect, cognition, and social behavior.* Toronto: Hogrefe.

Forgas, J. P., Burnham, D. K., & Trimboli, C. (1988). Mood, memory, and social judgments in children. *Journal of Personality and Social Psychology, 54,* 697–703.

Forgas, J. P., & Moylan, S. (1987). After the movies: Transient mood and social judgments. *Personality and Social Psychology Bulletin, 13,* 467–477.

Forge, K. L., & Phemister, S. (1987). The effect of prosocial cartoons on preschool children. *Child Study Journal, 17,* 83–88.

Forsyth, D. R. (1983). *An introduction to group dynamics.* Monterey, CA: Brooks/Cole.

Frank, D. I., & Maass, A. (1985). Relationship factors as predictors of causal attribution about sexual experiences. *Sex Roles, 12,* 697–711.

Frank, M. G., & Gilovich, T. (1988). The dark side of the self and social perception: Black uniforms and aggression in professional sports. *Journal of Personality and Social Psychology, 54,* 74–85.

Frank, M. G., & Gilovich, T. (1989). Effect of memory perspective on retrospective causal attributions. *Journal of Personality and Social Psychology, 57,* 399–403.

Franzoi, S. L., & Herzog, M. E. (1987). Judging physical attractiveness: What body aspects do we use? *Personality and Social Psychology Bulletin, 13,* 19–33.

Freedman, J. L. (1984). Effects of television violence on aggressiveness. *Psychological Bulletin, 96,* 227–246.

Freedman, J. L., & Fraser, S. C. (1966). Compliance without pressure: The foot-in-the-door technique. *Journal of Personality and Social Psychology, 4,* 195–202.

Freud, S. (1933). *New introductory lectures on psycho-analysis.* New York: Norton.

Fridlund, A. J. (1990). Evolution and facial action in reflex emotion, and paralanguage. In P. K. Ackles, J. R. Jennings, & M. G. H. Coles (Eds.), *Advances in psychophysiology.* Greenwich, CT: JAI Press.

Fried, R., & Berkowitz, L. (1979). Music hath charms . . . and can influence helpfulness. *Journal of Applied Social Psychology, 9,* 199–208.

Friedman, H. W., Riggio, R. E., & Casella, D. F. (1988). Nonverbal skill, personal charisma, and initial attraction. *Personality and Social Psychology Bulletin, 14,* 203–211.

Friedman, J. (1986, October). *Reported shopping cart accidents: Data from 1979 to 1986.* Washington, DC: U.S. Consumer Product Safety Commission.

Friedrich, L. K., & Stein, A. H. (1973). Aggressive and prosocial television programs and the natural behavior of preschool children. *Monographs of the Society for Research in Child Development, 38* (4, Whole No. 151).

Friedrich, L. K., & Stein, A. H. (1975). Prosocial television and young children: The effects of verbal labeling and role-playing on learning and behavior. *Child Development, 46,* 27–38.

Frieze, I. H., Whitley, B. E., Hanusa, B. H., & McHugh, M. C. (1982). Assessing the theoretical models for sex differences in causal attributions for success and failure. *Sex Roles, 8,* 333–343.

Fultz, J., Batson, C. D., Fortenbach, V. A., McCarthy, P. M., & Varney, L. L. (1986). Social evaluation and the empathy-altruism hypothesis. *Journal of Personality and Social Psychology, 50,* 761–769.

Fultz, J., Shaller, M., & Cialdini, R. B. (1988). Empathy, sadness, and distress: Three related but distinct vicarious affective responses to another's suffering. *Personality and Social Psychology Bulletin, 14,* 312–325.

Funder, D. C., & Colvin, C. R. (1988). Friends and strangers: Acquaintanceship, agreement, and the accuracy of personality judgment. *Journal of Personality and Social Psychology, 55,* 149–158.

Funder, C. C., & Ozer, D. J. (1983). Behavior as a function of the situation. *Journal of Personality and Social Psychology, 44,* 107–112.

Fussell, S. R., & Krauss, R. M. (1989). Understanding friends and strangers: The effects of audience design on message comprehension. *European Journal of Social Psychology, 19,* 509–525.

Gadenne, V., & Oswald, M. (1986). Enstehung und Veranderung von Bestatigungstendenzen beim Testen von Hypothesen [Formation and alteration of confirmatory tendencies during the testing of hypotheses]. *Zeitschrift für Experimentelle und Angewändte Psychologie, 33,* 360–374.

Gaertner, S. L., & Dovidio, J. F. (1986). The aversive form of racism. In J. F. Dovidio & S. L. Gaertner (Eds.), *Prejudice, discrimination, and racism* (pp. 61–89). New York: Academic Press.

Gaertner, S. L., Mann, J., Murrell, A., & Dovidio, J. F. (1989). Reducing intergroup bias: The benefits of recategorization. *Journal of Personality and Social Psychology, 57,* 239–249.

Gaily, P. (1982, January 15). Four rescuers praised: Courage of fourth is known, but not the name. *New York Times,* p. D14.

Gangestad, S., & Snyder, M. (1985). On the nature of self-monitoring: An examination of latent causal structure. In P. Shaver (Ed.), *Review of personality and social psychology* (Vol. 6, pp. 65–85). Beverly Hills, CA: Sage.

Gangestad, S. W. (1989). Uncompelling theory, uncompelling data. *Behavioral and Brain Sciences, 12,* 525–526.

Garland, H., Weinberg, R., Bruya, L., Jackson, A. (1988). Self-efficacy and endurance performance: A longitudinal field test of cognitive mediation theory. *Applied Psychology: An International Review, 37,* 381–394.

Garvin, D. A. (1986). Quality problems, policies, and attitudes in the United States and Japan: An explorative study. *Academy of Management Journal, 29,* 653–673.

Geen, R. G. (1978). Some effects of observing violence upon the behavior of the observer. In B. A. Maher (Ed.) *Progress in experimental personality research* (Vol. 8). New York: Academic Press.

Geen, R. G. (1981). Behavioral and physiological reactions to observed violence: Effects of prior exposure to aggressive stimuli. *Journal of Personality and Social Psychology, 40,* 868–875.

Geen, R. G., & Gange, J. J. (1977). Drive theory of social facilitation: Twelve years of theory and research. *Psychological Bulletin, 84,* 1267–1288.

Geier, J. G. (1969). A trait approach to the study of leadership in small groups. *Journal of Communication, 17,* 316–323.

Geiselman, R. E., Haight, N. A., & Kimata, L. G. (1984). Context effects on the perceived physical attractiveness of faces. *Journal of Experimental Social Psychology, 20,* 409–424.

Geller, E. S. (1989). Applied behavioral analysis and social marketing: An integration for environmental preservation. *Journal of Social Issues, 45(1),* 17–36.

George, J. M. (1989). Mood and absence. *Journal of Applied Psychology, 74,* 287–324.

Gerard, H. B., & Mathewson, G. C. (1966). The effects of severity of initiation on liking for a group: A replication. *Journal of Experimental Social Psychology, 2,* 278–287.

Gerard, H. B., Wilhelmy, R. A., & Conolley, E. S. (1968). Conformity and group size. *Journal of Personality and Social Psychology, 8,* 79–82.

Gergen, K. J., Hepburn, A., & Fisher, D. C. (1986). Hermeneutics of personality description. *Journal of Personality and Social Psychology, 50,* 1261–1270.

Gergen, M. (1991, in press). Beyond the evil empire: Horseplay and aggression. *Aggressive Behavior.*

Gerrard, M. (1980). Sex guilt and attitudes toward sex in sexually active and inactive female college students. *Journal of Personality Assessment, 44,* 258–261.

Gerrard, M. (1986). Are men and women really different? In K. Kelley (Ed.), *Females, males, and sexuality.* Albany, NY: SUNY Press.

Gerrard, M. (1987). Sex, sex guilt, and contraceptive use revisited: The 1980s. *Journal of Personality and Social Psychology, 52,* 975–980.

Gerrard, M., & Gibbons, F. X. (1982). Sexual experience, sex guilt, and sexual moral reasoning. *Journal of Personality, 50,* 345–359.

Gerrard, M., Kurylo, M., & Reis, T. (1990). *Self-esteem, erotophobia, and retention of contraceptive and AIDS information in the classroom.* Manuscript submitted for publication.

Gerrard, M., McCann, L., & Geis, B. (1982). The antecedents and prevention of unwanted pregnancy. In A. Rickel, M. Gerrard, & I. Iscoe (Eds.), *Social and psychological problems of women: Prevention and crisis intervention.* New York: McGraw-Hill.

Gerstein, L. W., White, J. J., & Barke, C. R. (1988). A well-kept secret: What counseling psychology can offer social psychology. *Journal of Applied Social Psychology, 18,* 1193–1206.

Gesensway, D. (1989, December 11). Risk in radiation still controversial. *Albany Times Union,* pp. A1, A9.

Gilbert, D., & Jones, E. E. (1986). Perceiver-induced constraint: Interpretations of self-generated reality. *Journal of Personality and Social Psychology, 50,* 269–280.

Gillen, B. (1981). Physical attractiveness: A determinant of two types of goodness. *Personality and Social Psychology Bulletin, 7,* 277–281.

Gillig, P. M., & Greenwald, A. G. (1974). Is it time to lay the sleeper effect to rest? *Journal of Personality and Social Psychology, 29,* 132–139.

Gillis, A. R., Richard, M. A., & Hagan, J. (1986). Ethnic susceptibility to crowding: An empirical analysis. *Environment and Behavior, 18,* 683–706.

Gillis, J. S. (1982). *Too small, too tall.* Champaign, IL: Institute for Personality and Ability Testing.

Gillis, J. S., & Avis, W. E. (1980). The male-taller norm in mate selection. *Personality and Social Psychology Bulletin, 6,* 396–401.

Giuliani, M. V. (1987). Naming the rooms: Implications of a change in the home model. *Environment and Behavior, 19,* 180–203.

Glaberson, W. (1990, February 19). Mean streets teach New Yorkers to just walk on by. *New York Times,* pp. B1–B2.

Glaser, R. D., & Thorpe, J. S. (1986). Unethical intimacy: A survey of sexual contact and advances between psychology educators and female graduate students. *American Psychologist, 41,* 43–51.

Glass, D. C. (1977). *Behavior patterns, stress, and coronary disease.* Hillsdale, NJ: Erlbaum.

Glass, D. C. (1989). Psychology and health: Obstacles and opportunities. *Journal of Applied Social Psychology, 19,* 1145–1163.

Glass, D. C., Singer, J. E., & Friedman, L. N. (1969). Psychic cost of adaptation to an environmental stressor. *Journal of Personality and Social Psychology, 12,* 200–210.

Glenn, N. D., & Weaver, C. N. (1988). The changing relationship of marital status to reported happiness. *Journal of Marriage and the Family, 50,* 317–324.

Glick, P. (1985). Orientations toward relationships: Choosing a situation in which to begin a relationship. *Journal of Experimental Social Psychology, 21,* 544–562.

Glick, P., DeMorest, J. A., & Hotze, C. A. (1988). Self-monitoring and beliefs about partner compatibility in romantic relationships. *Personality and Social Psychology Bulletin, 14,* 485–494.

Glick, P., Zion, C., & Nelson, C. (1988). What mediates sex discrimination in hiring decisions? *Journal of Personality and Social Psychology, 55,* 178–186.

Glick, P. C. (1983). Seventh-year itch. *Medical Aspects of Human Sexuality, 17(5),* 103.

Godfrey, D. K., Jones, E. E., & Lord, C. G. (1986). Self-promotion is not ingratiating. *Journal of Personality and Social Psychology, 50,* 106–115.

Goethals, G. R. (1986a). Fabricating and ignoring social reality: Self-serving estimates of consensus. In J. Olson, C. P. Herman, & M. P. Zanna (Eds.), *Relative deprivation and social comparison: The Ontario symposium on social cognition IV.* Hillsdale, NJ: Erlbaum.

Goethals, G. R. (1986b). Social comparison theory: Psychology from the lost and found. *Personality and Social Psychology Bulletin, 12,* 261–278.

Goethals, G. R., Cooper, J., & Naficy, A. (1979). Role of foreseen, foreseeable, and unforeseeable behavioral consequences in the arousal of cognitive dissonance. *Journal of Personality and Social Psychology, 37,* 1179–1185.

Goethals, G. R., & Zanna, M. P. (1979). The role of social comparison in choice of shifts. *Journal of Personality and Social Psychology, 37,* 1469–1476.

Goktepe, J. R., & Schneier, C. E. (1989). Role of sex, gender roles, and attraction in predicting emergent leaders. *Journal of Applied Psychology, 74,* 165–167.

Gold, J. A., Ryckman, R. M., & Mosley, N. R. (1984). Romantic mood induction and attraction to a dissimilar other: Is love blind? *Personality and Social Psychology Bulletin, 10,* 358–368.

Goldberg, L. (1985, September 11). Helping married couples rekindle love. *Albany Times Union,* pp. C1, C3.

Goldfarb, L., Gerrard, M., Gibbons, F. X., & Plante, T. (1988). Attitudes toward sex, arousal, and the retention of contraceptive information. *Journal of Personality and Social Psychology, 55,* 634–641.

Goldstein, A. G., Chance, J. E., & Schneller, G. R. (1989). Frequency of eyewitness identification in criminal cases: A survey of prosecutors. *Bulletin of the Psychonomic Society, 27,* 71–74.

Goleman, D. (1986, April 8). Studies point to power of nonverbal signals. *New York Times,* pp. C1, C6.

Goleman, D. (1989, June 13). Study defines major sources of conflict between sexes. *New York Times,* pp. C1, C14.

Gonzales, M., Hope, D. J. M., Loney, G. L., Lukens, C. K., & Junghans, C. M. (1983). Interactional approach to interpersonal attraction. *Journal of Personality and Social Psychology, 44,* 1192–1197.

Goode, E. (1981). Remarriage rates. *Medical Aspects of Human Sexuality, 15(12),* 81, 84.

Goranson, R. E., & Berkowitz, L. (1966). Reciprocity and responsibility reactions to prior help. *Journal of Personality and Social Psychology, 3,* 227–232.

Gore, P. M., & Rotter, J. B. (1963). A personality correlated of social action. *Journal of Personality, 31,* 58–64.

Gormley, F. F., & Aiello, J. R. (1982). Social density, interpersonal relationships, and residential crowding stress. *Journal of Applied Social Psychology, 12,* 22–36.

Gormly, J. P. (1983). Predicting behavior from personality trait scores. *Personality and Social Psychology Bulletin, 9,* 267–270.

Gottlieb, J., & Carver, C. S. (1980). Anticipation of future interaction and the bystander effect. *Journal of Experimental Social Psychology, 16,* 253–260.

Gouaux, C. (1971). Induced affective states and interpersonal attraction. *Journal of Personality and Social Psychology, 20,* 37–43.

Gouldner, A. W. (1960). The norm of reciprocity: A preliminary statement. *American Sociological Review, 25,* 161–178.

Gove, W., & Hughes, M. (1983). *Overcrowding in the household: An analysis of determinants and effects.* New York: Academic Press.

Graber, D. A. (1980). *Crime news and the public.* New York: Praeger.

Grace, J. S., & Harris, J. (1990). Conflict resolution styles and their relation to conflict type, individual differences, and formative influences. *Bulletin of the Psychonomic Society, 28,* 144–146.

Grams, R., & Schwab, D. P. (1985). An investigation of systematic gender-related error in job evaluation. *Academy of Management Journal, 28,* 279–290.

Graves, L. M., & Powell, L. M. (1988). An investigation of sex discrimination in recruiters' evaluations of actual applicants. *Journal of Applied Psychology, 73,* 20–29.

Graziano, W., Brothen, T., & Berscheid, E. (1978). Height and attraction: Do men and women see eye-to-eye? *Journal of Personality, 46,* 128–145.

Green, S. E., & Mosher, D. L. (1985). A causal model of sexual arousal to erotic fantasies. *Journal of Sex Research, 21,* 1–23.

Green, S. G., & Mitchell, T. R. (1979). Attributional processes of leader-member interactions. *Organizational Behavior and Human Decision Processes, 23,* 429–458.

Green, S. K., Buchanan, D. R., & Heuer, S. K. (1984). Winners, losers, and choosers: A field investigation of dating initiation. *Personality and Social Psychology Bulletin, 10,* 502–511.

Greenbaum, P., & Rosenfield, H. W. (1978). Patterns of avoidance in responses to interpersonal staring and proximity: Effects of bystanders on drivers at a traffic intersection. *Journal of Personality and Social Psychology, 36,* 575–587.

Greenberg, J. (1986). Organizational performance evaluations: What makes them fair? In R. J. Lewicki, B. Sheppard, & M. Bazerman (Eds.), *Negotiation in organizations* (pp. 25–41). Greenwich, CT: JAI Press.

Greenberg, J. (1987). A taxonomy of organizational justice theories. *Academy of Management Review, 12,* 9–22.

Greenberg, J. (1988a). Equity and workplace status: A field experiment. *Journal of Applied Psychology, 73,* 606–613.

Greenberg, J. (1988b). Using social accounts to manage impressions of performance appraisal fairness. In J. Greenberg & R. J. Bies (Co-chairs), *Communicating fairness in organizations.* Symposium presented at the meetings of the Academy of Management, Anaheim, CA.

Greenberg, J. (1989). Cognitive re-evaluation of outcomes in response to underpayment inequity. *Academy of Management Journal, 32,* 174–184.

Greenberg, J. (1990). Looking fair vs. being fair: Managing impressions of organization justice. In B. M. Staw & L. L. Cummings (Eds.), *Research in organizational behavior* (Vol. 12). Greenwich, CT: JAI Press.

Greenberg, J. & Cohen, R. L. (Eds.). (1982). *Equity and justice in social behavior.* New York: Academic Press.

Greenberg, J., & Pyszczynski, T. (1985). The effect of an overheard slur on evaluations of the target: How to spread a social disease. *Journal of Experimental Social Psychology, 21,* 61–72.

Greenberg, J., Pyszczynski, T., & Solomon, S. (1982). The self-serving attributional bias: Beyond self-presentation. *Journal of Experimental Social Psychology, 18,* 56–67.

Greenberg, J., Solomon, S., Pyszczynski, T., & Steinberg, L. (1988). A reaction to Greenwald, Atkanis, Eippe, and Baumgardner (1986): Under what conditions does research obstruct theory progress? *Psychological Review, 95,* 566–571.

Greenberg, J., Williams, K. D., & O'Brien, M. K. (1986). Considering the harshest verdict first: Biasing effects on mock juror verdicts. *Personality and Social Psychology Bulletin, 12,* 41–50.

Greenberger, D. B., & Strasser, S. (1986). Development and application of a model of personal control in organizations. *Academy of Management Review, 11,* 164–177.

Greenwald, A. G. (1989). Why are attitudes important? In A. R. Partkanis, S. J. Breckler, & A. G. Greenwald (Eds.), *Attitude structure and function.* Hillsdale, NJ: Erlbaum.

Greenwald, A. G., & Pratkanis, A. R. (1984). The self. In R. S. Wyer & T. K. Srull (Eds.), *Handbook of social cognition* (pp. 129–178). Hillsdale, NJ: Erlbaum.

Greenwald, A. G., & Pratkanis, A. R. (1988). On the use of "theory" and the usefulness of theory. *Psychological Review, 95,* 575–579.

Greenwald, A. G., Pratkanis, A. R., Leippe, M. R., & Baumgardner, M. H. (1986). Under what conditions does theory obstruct research progress? *Psychological Review, 93,* 216–229.

Grieshop, J. I., & Stiles, M. C. (1989). Risk and home pesticide users. *Environment and Behavior, 21,* 699–716.

Griffin, E., & Sparks, G. G. (1990). Friends forever: A longitudinal exploration of intimacy in same-sex friends and platonic pairs. *Journal of Social and Personal Relationships, 7,* 29–46.

Griffitt, W. (1970). Environmental effects on interpersonal affective behavior: Ambient effective temperature and attraction. *Journal of Personality and Social Psychology, 15,* 240–244.

Griffitt, W., & Kaiser, D. L. (1978). Affect, sex guilt, gender, and the rewarding-punishing effects of erotic stimuli. *Journal of Personality and Social Psychology, 36,* 850–858.

Grigg, F., Fletcher, G. J. O., & Fitness, J. (1989). Spontaneous attributions in happy and unhappy dating relationships. *Journal of Social and Personal Relationships, 6,* 61–68.

Groff, D. B., Baron, R. S., & Moore, D. L. (1983). Distraction, attentional conflict, and drive-like behavior. *Journal of Experimental Social Psychology, 19,* 353–380.

Grondahl, P. (1989, December 5). Trees of life: Reforestation begins in the backyard. *Albany Times Union,* pp. C1, C12.

Gross, A. E., & Fleming, I. (1982). Twenty years of deception in social psychology. *Personality and Social Psychology Bulletin, 8,* 402–408.

Gruder, C. L., Cook, T. D., Hennigan, K. M., Flay, B. R., Alessis, C., & Halamaj, L. (1978). Empirical tests of the absolute sleeper effect predicted from the discounting cue hypothesis. *Journal of Personality and Social Psychology, 36,* 1061–1074.

Grush, J. E., & McKeogh, K. L. (1975, May). *The finest representation that money can buy: Exposure effects in the 1972 congressional primaries.* Paper presented at the meeting of the Midwestern Psychological Association, Chicago.

Guerry, A. M. (1833). Essai sur la statistique moral de la France. Quoted in Bochme, M. (1971), *Die moral statistic.* Cologne: Bohlanverlag.

Guidubaldi, J., Perry, J. D., & Nastasi, B. K. (1987). Growing up in a divorced family: Initial and long-term perspectives on children's adjustment. In S. Oskamp (Ed.), *Family processes and problems: Social psychological aspects* (pp. 202–237). Beverly Hills, CA: Sage.

Guimond, S., & Palmer, D. L. (1990). Type of academic training and causal attributions for social problems. *European Journal of Social Psychology, 20,* 61–75.

Gully, K. J., & Dengerink, H. A. (1983). The dyadic interaction of persons with violent and nonviolent histories. *Aggressive Behavior, 7,* 13–20.

Gustafson, R. (1989). Frustration and successful vs. unsuccessful aggression: A test of Berkowitz' completion hypothesis. *Aggressive Behavior, 15,* 5–12.

Gutek, B. A. (1985). *Sex and the workplace.* San Francisco: Jossey-Bass.

Hacker, A. (Ed.). (1983). *US: A statistical portrait of the American people.* New York: Penguin Books.

Hackett, R. D., & Guion, R. M. (1985). A reevaluation of the absenteeism–job satisfaction relationship. *Organizational Behavior and Human Decision Processes, 35,* 340–381.

Hackman, J. R., & Oldham, G. R. (1976). Motivation through the design of work: Test of a theory. *Organizational Behavior and Human Performance, 16,* 250–279.

Haley, W. E., & Strickland, B. R. (1986). Interpersonal betrayal and cooperation: Effects on self-evaluation in depression. *Journal of Personality and Social Psychology, 50,* 386–391.

Hall, E. T. (1966). *The hidden dimension.* New York: Doubleday.

Hamill, P. (1986, October 13). Had it with pride, covetousness, lust, anger, gluttony, envy, and sloth? It's time to start doing good. *New York,* pp. 35–47.

Hamilton, D. L., & Gifford, R. K. (1976). Illusory correlation in interpersonal perception: A cognitive basis of stereotypic judgments. *Journal of Experimental Social Psychology, 12,* 392–407.

Hamilton, D. L., Swap, W. C., & Rubin, J. Z. (1981). Predicting the effects of anticipated third party intervention: A template-matching approach. *Journal of Personality and Social Psychology, 41,* 1141–1152.

Hamilton, D. L., & Trolier, T. K. (1986). Stereotypes and stereotyping: An overview of the cognitive approach. In J. F. Dovidio & S. L. Gaertner (Eds.), *Prejudice, discrimination, and racism* (pp. 127–163). Orlando, FL: Academic Press.

Hamilton, L. C. (1985). Self-reported and actual savings in a water conservation campaign. *Environment and Behavior, 17,* 315–326.

Hampson, S. E. (1983). Trait ascription and depth of acquaintance: The preference for traits in personality descriptions and its relation to target familiarity. *Journal of Research in Personality, 17,* 398–411.

Haney, C. Banks, W., & Zimbardo, P. (1983). Interpersonal dynamics in a simulated prison. *International Journal of Criminology, 1,* 69–97.

Hansen, C. H., & Hansen, R. D. (1988). Finding the face in the crowd: An anger superiority effect. *Journal of Personality and Social Psychology, 54,* 917–924.

Hansen, R. D. (1980). Common sense attribution. *Journal of Personality and Social Psychology, 17,* 398–411.

Hansen, R. D., & O'Leary, V. E. (1985). Sex-determined attributions. In V. E. O'Leary, R. B. Kesler-Unger, & B. Strudler-Wallston (Eds.), *Women, gender, and social psychology* (pp. 67–99). Hillsdale, NJ: Erlbaum.

Hardin, G. R. (1968). The tragedy of the commons. *Science, 162,* 1243–1248.

Harkins, S. (1987). Social loafing and social facilitation. *Journal of Experimental Social Psychology, 23,* 1–18.

Harkins, S., & Petty, R. (1982). Effects of task difficulty and task uniqueness on social loafing. *Journal of Personality and Social Psychology, 43,* 1214–1229.

Harkins, S., & Szymanski, K. (1988). Social loafing and self-evaluation with an objective standard. *Journal of Experimental Social Psychology, 24,* 354–365.

Harkins, S., & Szymanski, K. (1989). Social loafing and group evaluation. *Journal of Personality and Social Psychology, 56,* 934–941.

Harper, C. S. (1977). Competition and cooperation in a resource management task: A social trap analog. In S. Weidman & J. R. Anderson (Eds.), *Priorities for environmental design research* (pp. 305–312). Washington, DC: Environmental Resources Association.

Harries, K. D., & Stadler, S. J. (1988). Heat and violence: New findings from Dallas field data, 1980–1981. *Journal of Applied Social Psychology, 18,* 129–138.

Harris, M. B., Harris, R. J., & Bochner, S. (1982). Fat, four-eyed, and female: Stereotypes of obesity, glasses, and gender. *Journal of Applied Social Psychology, 12,* 503–516.

Harris, P. R., & Wilshire, P. (1988). Estimating the prevalence of shyness in the "global village": Pluralistic ignorance or false consensus? *Journal of Personality, 56,* 405–415.

Harris, R. N., Snyder, R. L., Higgins, R. L., & Schrag, J. L. (1986). Enhancing the prediction of self-handicapping. *Journal of Personality and Social Psychology, 51,* 451–458.

Harvey, J. H. (1987). Attributions in close relationships: Research and theoretical developments. *Journal of Social and Clinical Psychology, 5,* 420–434.

Harvey, J. H., & Weary, G. (Eds.). (1989). *Attribution: Basic issues and applications.* New York: Academic Press.

Harvey, J. M. (1971). Locus of control shift in administrators. *Perceptual and Motor Skills, 33,* 980–982.

Hassebrauck, M. (1988). Beauty is more than "name" deep: The effect of women's first names on ratings of physical attractiveness and personality attributes. *Journal of Applied Social Psychology, 18,* 721–726.

Hastie, R., & Kumar, P. A. (1979). Person memory: Personality traits as organizing principles in memory for behavior. *Journal of Personality and Social Psychology, 37,* 25–38.

Hatfield, E. (1983). What do women and men want from love and sex? In E. R. Allgeier & N. B. McCormick (Eds.), *Changing boundaries: Gender roles and sexual behavior.* Palo Alto, CA: Mayfield.

Hatfield, E. (1988). Passionate and companionate love. In R. J. Sternberg & M. L. Barnes (Eds.), *The psychology of love* (pp. 191–217). New Haven, CT: Yale University Press.

Hatfield, E., & Rapson, R. L. (1987). Passionate love/sexual desire: Can the same paradigm explain both? *Archives of Sexual Behavior, 16,* 259–278.

Hatfield, E., & Sprecher, S. (1986a). Measuring passionate love in intimate relations. *Journal of Adolescence, 9,* 383–410.

Hatfield, E., & Sprecher, S. (1986b). *Mirror, mirror . . . The importance of looks in everyday life.* Albany, NY: SUNY Press.

Hatfield, E., Sprecher, S. Pillemer, J. T., Greenberger, D., & Wexler, P. (1989). Gender differences in what is desired in the sexual relationship. *Journal of Psychology and Human Sexuality, 1,* 39–52.

Hatfield, E., & Walster, G. W. (1981). *A new look at love.* Reading, MA: Addison-Wesley.

Hathaway, S. R., & McKinley, J. C. (1940). A multiphasic personality schedule (Minnesota): I. Construction of the schedule. *Journal of Personality, 10,* 249–254.

Hayes, S. C., Johnson, S. V., & Cone, J. D. (1975). *The marked item technique: A practical procedure for litter control.* Unpublished manuscript, West Virginia University, Morgantown.

Hays, R. B. (1984). The development and maintenance of friendship. *Journal of Social and Personal Relationships, 1,* 75–98.

Hays, R. B. (1989). The day-to-day functioning of close versus casual friendships. *Journal of Social and Personal Relationships, 6,* 21–37.

Hays, R. B., & DiMatteo, M. R. (1984). Toward a more therapeutic physician-patient relationship. In S. Duck (Ed.), *Personal relationships: Vol. 5. Repairing personal relationships* (pp. 1–20). New York: Academic Press.

Hazan, C., & Shaver, P. (1987). Romantic love conceptualized as an attachment process. *Journal of Personality and Social Psychology, 52,* 511–524.

Headey, B., Holmstrom, E. L., & Wearing, A. J. (1985). Models of well-being and ill-being. *Social Indicators Research, 17,* 211–234.

Headey, B., & Wearing, A. (1989). Personality, life events, and subjective well-being: Toward a dynamic equilibrium model. *Journal of Personality and Social Psychology, 57,* 731–739.

Heaven, P. C. L. (1988). Locus of control and attitudes to authority among adolescents. *Personality and Individual Differences, 1,* 181–183.

Hedge, J. W., & Kavanagh, M. J. (1988). Improving the accuracy of performance evaluations: Comparison of three methods of performance appraiser training. *Journal of Applied Psychology, 73,* 68–73.

Heider, F. (1985). *The psychology of interpersonal relations.* New York: Wiley.

Heilbroner, R. L. (1974). *An inquiry into the human prospect.* New York: Norton.

Heilman, M. E., Hornstein, H. A., Cage, J. H., & Herschlag, J. K. (1984). Reactions to prescribed leader behavior as a function of role perspective: The case of the Vroom-Yetton model. *Journal of Applied Psychology, 69,* 50–60.

Heilman, M. E., & Martell, R. F. (1986). Exposure to successful women: Antidote to sex discrimination in applicant screening decisions? *Organizational Behavior and Human Decision Processes, 37,* 376–390.

Heilman, M. E., Martell, R. F., & Simon, M. C. (1988). The vagaries of sex bias: Conditions regulating the undervaluation, equivaluation, and overvaluation of female job applicants. *Organizational Behavior and Human Decision Processes, 41,* 98–110.

Henderson, A. S., Byrne, D. G., & Duncan-Jones, P. (1981). *Neurosis and the social environment.* New York: Academic Press.

Henderson, J., & Taylor, J. (1985, November 17). Study finds bias in death sentences: Killers of whites risk execution. *Albany Times Union,* p. A19.

Hendrick, C., & Hendrick, S. (1986). A theory and method of love. *Journal of Personality and Social Psychology, 50,* 392–402.

Hendrick, C., Hendrick, S., Foote, F. H., & Slapion-Foote, M. J. (1984). Do men and women love differently? *Journal of Social and Personal Relationships, 1,* 177–195.

Hendrick, S. S., Hendrick, C., & Adler, N. L. (1988). Romantic relationships: Love, satisfaction, and staying together. *Journal of Personality and Social Psychology, 54,* 980–988.

Hendrix, W. H., Steel, R. P., & Schultz, S. A. (1987). Job stress and life stress: Their causes and consequences. *Journal of Social Behavior and Personality, 2,* 291–302.

Heneman, R. L., Greenberger, D. B., & Anonyuo, C. (1989). Attributions and exchanges: The effects of interpersonal factors on the diagnosis of employee performance. *Academy of Management Journal, 32,* 466–476.

Hepworth, J. T., & West, S. G. (1988). Lynchings and the economy: A time-series reanalysis of Hovland and Sears (1940). *Journal of Personality and Social Psychology, 55,* 239–247.

Heshka, S., & Nelson, Y. (1972). Interpersonal speaking distance as a function of age, sex, and relationship. *Sociometry, 35,* 491–498.

Higgins, E. T. (1987). Self-discrepancy: A theory relating self and affect. *Psychological Review, 94,* 319–340.

Higgins, E. T., & Bargh, J. A. (1987). Social cognition and social perception. *Annual Review of Psychology, 38,* 369–425.

Higgins, E. T., & King, G. (1981). Accessibility of social constructs: Information processing consequences of individual and contextual variability. In N. Cantor & J. Kihlstrom (Eds.), *Personality, cognition, and social interaction* (pp. 69–121). Hillsdale, NJ: Erlbaum.

Higgins, E. T., Rohles, W. S., & Jones, C. R. (1977). Category accessibility and impression formation. *Journal of Experimental Social Psychology, 13,* 141–154.

Hill, C. A. (1987). Affiliation motivation: People who need people but in different ways. *Journal of Personality and Social Psychology, 52,* 1008–1018.

Hill, C. A., & Christensen, A. J. (1989). Affiliative need, different types of social support, and physical symptoms. *Journal of Applied Social Psychology, 19,* 1351–1370.

Hill, C. T., Rubin, Z., & Peplau, L. A. (1976). Breakups before marriage: The end of 103 affairs. *Journal of Social Issues, 32,* 147–168.

Hill, G. J. (1989). An unwillingness to act: Behavioral appropriateness, situational constraint, and self-efficacy in shyness. *Journal of Personality, 57,* 871–890.

Hill, T., Smith, N. D., & Lewicki, P. (1989). The development of self-image bias: A real-world demonstration. *Personality and Social Psychology Bulletin, 15,* 205–211.

Hilton, D. J., & Slugoski, B. R. (1986). Knowledge-based causal attribution: The abnormal conditions focus model. *Psychological Review, 93,* 75–88.

Hiltrop, J. M., & Rubin, J. Z. (1981). Effects of intervention mode and conflict of interest on dispute resolution. *Journal of Personality and Social Psychology, 42,* 665–672.

Hirschman, R. S., & Leventhal, H. (1989). Preventing smoking behavior in school children: An initial test of a cognitive-development program. *Journal of Applied Social Psychology, 19,* 559–583.

Hirschman, R. S., Leventhal, H., & Glynn, K. (1984). The development of smoking behavior: Conceptualization and supportive cross-sectional survey data. *Journal of Applied Social Psychology, 14,* 184–206.

Hirt, E., & Kimble, C. E. (1981, May). *The home-field advantage in sports: Differences and correlates.* Paper presented at the meeting of the Midwestern Psychological Association, Detroit.

Hobfoll, S. E. (1985). The limitations of social support in the stress process. In I. G. Sarason & B. R. Sarason (Eds.), *Social support, theory, research, and applications.* The Hague, Amsterdam: Martinus, Nijhof.

Hoffman, M. L. (1981). Is altruism part of human nature? *Journal of Personality and Social Psychology, 40,* 121–137.

Hogg, M. A., & Abrams, D. (1988). *Social identifications: A social psychology of intergroup relations and group processes.* London: Routledge & Kegan Paul.

Hojat, M., & Crandall, R. (Eds.). (1987). *Loneliness: Theory, research, and applications.* Newbury Park, CA: Sage.

Hokanson, J. E., Burgess, M., & Cohen, M. E. (1963). Effects of displaced aggression on systolic blood pressure. *Journal of Abnormal and Social Psychology, 67,* 214–218.

Holahan, C. J. (1986). Environmental psychology. In M. R. Rosenzweig & L. W. Porter (Eds.), *Annual review of psychology* (Vol. 37, pp. 381–407). Palo Alto, CA: Annual Reviews.

Hollander, E. P. (1985). Leadership and power. In G. Lindzey & E. Aronson (Eds.), *The handbook of social psychology* (Vol. 2, 3rd ed., pp. 485–537). New York: Random House.

Holloway, J. B., Beuter, A., & Duda, J. L. (1988). Self-efficacy and training for strength in adolescent girls. *Journal of Applied Social Psychology, 18,* 699–719.

Holmes, J. G., & Boon, S. D. (1990). Developments in the field of close relationships: Creating foundations for intervention strategies. *Personality and Social Psychology Bulletin, 16,* 23–41.

Holtgraves, T., & Srull, T. K. (1989). The effect of positive self-descriptions on impressions: General principles and individual differences. *Personality and Social Psychology Bulletin, 15,* 452–462.

Holtzworth-Munroe, A., & Jacobson, N. S. (1985). Causal attributions of married couples: When do they search for causes? What do they conclude when they do? *Journal of Personality and Social Psychology, 48,* 1398–1412.

Hood, D. C. (1988). *Toward understanding stock market movements: A marriage of psychology and economics.* Washington, DC: Federation of Behavioral, Psychological, and Cognitive Sciences.

Horney, K. (1945). *Our inner conflicts.* New York: Norton.

Houston, B. K., & Kelly, K. E. (1989). Hostility in employed women: Relation to work and marital experiences, social support, stress, and anger expression. *Personality and Social Psychology Bulletin, 15,* 175–182.

Hovland, C. I., Janis, I. L., & Kelley, H. H. (1953). *Communication and persuasion: Psychological studies of opinion changes.* New Haven, CT: Yale University Press.

Hovland, C. I., Lumsdaine, A. A., & Sheffield, F. D. (1949). *Experiments on mass communications.* Princeton, NJ: Princeton University Press.

Hovland, C. I., & Sears, R. R. (1940). Minor studies in aggression: VI. Correlation of lynchings with economic indices. *Journal of Psychology, 9,* 301–310.

Hovland, C. I., & Weiss, W. (1951). The influence of source credibility on communication effectiveness. *Public Opinion Quarterly, 15,* 635–650.

Howard, G. S. (1985). The role of values in the science of psychology. *American Psychologist, 40,* 255–265.

Howell, J. M., & Frost, P. J. (1989). A laboratory study of charismatic leadership. *Organizational Behavior and Human Decision Processes, 43,* 243–269.

Hudson, J. W. (1980). College men's attitudes regarding female chastity. *Medical Aspects of Human Sexuality, 14(1),* 137.

Huesmann, L. R. (1982). Television violence and aggressive behavior. In D. Pearly, L. Bouthilet, & J. Lazar (Eds.), *Television and behavior: Vol. 2. Technical reviews* (pp. 220–256). Washington, DC: National Institute of Mental Health.

Huesmann, L. R. (1988). An information processing model for the development of aggression. *Aggressive Behavior, 14,* 13–24.

Hull, R. B., IV. (1989). Explaining the emotion people experience in suburban parks. *Environment and Behavior, 21,* 323–345.

Hummert, M. L., Crockett, W. H., & Kemper, S. (1990). Processing mechanisms underlying use of the balance schema. *Journal of Personality and Social Psychology, 58,* 5–21.

Humphriss, N. (1989, November 20). Letters. *Time,* p. 12.

Hupka, R. B. (1981). Cultural determinants of jealousy. *Alternative Lifestyles, 4,* 310–356.

Hupka, R. B., Jung, J., & Silverthorn, K. (1987). Perceived acceptability of apologies, excuses, and justifications in jealousy predicaments. *Journal of Social Behavior and Personality, 2,* 303–313.

Ickes, W., Reidhead, S., & Patterson, M. (1986). Machiavellianism and self-monitoring: As different as "me" and "you." *Social Cognition, 4,* 58–74.

Ickes, W., & Turner, M. (1983). On the social advantages of having an older, opposite-sex sibling: Birth order influences in mixed-sex dyads. *Journal of Personality and Social Psychology, 45,* 210–222.

Identifying crime suspects. (1988, May 10). *New York Times,* p. C9.

Ilgen, D. R., Fisher, C., & Taylor, S. (1979). Consequences of individual feedback on behavior in organizations. *Journal of Applied Psychology, 64,* 349–371.

Ilgen, D. R., Mitchel, T. R., & Fredrickson, J. W. (1981). Poor performers: Supervisors' and subordinates' responses. *Organizational Behavior and Human Performance, 27,* 386–410.

Ingram, R. E., Cruet, D., Johnson, B. R., & Wisnicki, K. S. (1988).

Self-focused attention, gender, gender role, and vulnerability to negative affect. *Journal of Personality and Social Psychology, 55,* 967–978.

Innes, J. M., & Zeitz, H. (1988). The public's view of the impact of the mass media: A test of the "third person" effect. *European Journal of Social Psychology, 18,* 457–463.

Insko, C. A. (1985). Balance theory, the Jordan paradigm, and the West tetrahedron. In L. Berkowitz (Ed.), *Advances in experimental social psychology.* New York: Academic Press.

Insko, C. A., Hoytle, R. H., Pinkely, R. L., Hong, G. Y., Slim, R. M., Dalton, B., Lin, Y. H. W., Ruffin, P. P., Dardis, G. J., Brenthal, P. R., & Schopler, J. (1988). Individual-group discontinuity: The role of a consensus rule. *Journal of Experimental Social Psychology, 24,* 505–519.

Insko, C. A., Sedlak, A. J., & Lipsitz, A. (1982). A two-valued logic or two-valued balance resolution of the challenge of agreement and attraction effects in p-o-x triads, and a theoretical perspective on conformity and hedonism. *European Journal of Social Psychology, 12,* 143–167.

Isac, R. M., & Walker, J. M. (1986). *Group size effects in public good provision: The voluntary contribution mechanism.* Unpublished manuscript.

Isen, A. M. (1970). Success, failure, attention, and reaction to others: The warm glow of success. *Journal of Personality and Social Psychology, 15,* 294–301.

Isen, A. M. (1984). Toward understanding the role of affect in cognition. In R. S. Wyer & T. K. Srull (Eds.), *Handbook of social cognition* (Vol. 3, pp. 179–236). Hillsdale, NJ: Erlbaum.

Isen, A. M. (1987). Positive affect, cognitive processes, and social behavior. In L. Berkowitz (Ed.), *Advances in experimental social psychology* (Vol. 20, pp. 203–253).

Isen, A. M., & Baron, R. A. (1990). Positive affect and organizational behavior. In B. M. Staw & L. L. Cummings (Eds.), *Research in organizational behavior* (Vol. 12). Greenwich, CT: JAI Press.

Isen, A. M., & Daubman, K. A. (1984). The influence of affect on categorization. *Journal of Personality and Social Psychology, 47,* 1206–1217.

Isen, A. M., Daubman, K. A., & Nowicki, G. P. (1987). Positive affect facilitates creative problem solving. *Journal of Personality and Social Psychology, 52,* 1122–1131.

Isen, A. M., Johnson, M. M. S., Merz, E., & Robinson, G. (1985). The influence of positive affect on the unusualness of work association. *Journal of Personality and Social Psychology, 48,* 1413–1426.

Isen, A. M., & Levin, P. A. (1972). Effect of feeling good on helping: Cookies and kindness. *Journal of Personality and Social Psychology, 21,* 384–388.

Isen, A. M., & Means, B. (1983). The influence of positive affect on decision-making strategy. *Social Cognition, 2,* 18–31.

Isen, A. M., & Shalker, T. E. (1982). Do you "accentuate the positive, eliminate the negative" when you are in a good mood? *Social Psychology Quarterly, 41,* 345–349.

Isen, A. M., & Simmonds, S. F. (1978). The effect of feeling good on a helping task that is incompatible with good mood. *Social Psychology, 41,* 346–349.

Isleib, R. A., Vuchinich, R. E., & Tucker, J. A. (1988). Performance attributions and changes in self-esteem following self-handicapping with alcohol consumption. *Journal of Social and Clinical Psychology, 6,* 88–103.

Istvan, J., & Griffitt, W. (1980). Effects of sexual experience on dating desirability and marriage desirability. *Journal of Marriage and the Family, 42,* 377–385.

Istvan, J., Griffitt, W., & Weidner, G. (1983). Sexual arousal and the polarization of perceived sexual attractiveness. *Basic and Applied Social Psychology, 4,* 307–318.

Izard, C. (1977). *Human emotions.* New York: Plenum.

Izraeli, D. N., Izraeli, D., & Eden, D. (1985). Giving credit where credit is due: A case of no sex bias in attribution. *Journal of Applied Social Psychology, 15,* 516–530.

Jackson, L. A., & Grabski, S. V. (1988). Perceptions of fair play and the gender wage gap. *Journal of Applied Social Psychology, 18,* 606–625.

Jaffe, Y., Malamuth, N., Feingold, J., & Feshback, S. (1974). Sexual arousal and behavioral aggression. *Journal of Personality and Social Psychology, 30,* 759–764.

James, W. (1899). *Talks to teachers on psychology.* New York: Holt.

James, W. (1890). *The principles of psychology.* New York: Holt.

Jamieson, D. W., Lydon, J. E., & Zanna, M. P. (1987). Attitude and activity preference similarly: Differential bases of interpersonal attraction for low and high self-monitors. *Journal of Personality and Social Psychology, 53,* 1052–1060.

Janis, I. L. (1954). Personality correlates of susceptibility to persuasion. *Journal of Personality, 22,* 504–518.

Janis, I. L. (1982). *Groupthink: Psychological studies of policy decisions and fiascoes* (2nd ed.). Boston: Houghton Mifflin.

Janoff-Bulman, R. (1989). The benefits of illusions, the threat of disillusionment, and the limitations of inaccuracy. *Journal of Social and Clinical Psychology, 8,* 158–175.

Jaspars, J. (1983). The process of attribution. In M. R. C. Hewstone (Ed.), *Attribution theory: Social and functional extensions* (pp. 28–44). Oxford, England: Blackwell.

Jay, S. M., Ozolins, M., Elliott, C. H., & Caldwell, S. (1983). Assessment of children's distress during painful medical procedures. *Health Psychology, 2,* 133–147.

Jeavons, C. M., & Taylor, S. P. (1985). The control of alcohol-related aggression: Redirecting the inebriate's attention to socially appropriate conduct. *Aggressive Behavior, 11,* 93–101.

Jemmott, J. B., III, Ashby, K. L., & Lindenfeld, K. (1989). Romantic commitment and the perceived availability of opposite-sex persons: On loving the one you're with. *Journal of Applied Social Psychology, 19,* 1198–1211.

Jemmott, J. B., III, & Magloire, K. (1988). Academic stress, social support, and secretory immunoglobulin. *Journal of Personality and Social Psychology, 55,* 803–810.

Joardar, S. D. (1989). Use and image of neighborhood parks: A case of limited resources. *Environment and Behavior, 21,* 734–762.

Johnson, B. L., & Kilmann, P. R. (1975). The relationship between recalled parental attitudes and internal-external control. *Journal of Clinical Psychology, 31,* 40–42.

Johnson, B. T., & Eagly, A. H. (1989). Effects of involvement on persuasion: A meta-analysis. *Psychological Bulletin, 106,* 290–314.

Johnson, D. F., & Pittenger, J. B. (1984). Attribution, the attractiveness stereotype, and the elderly. *Developmental Psychology, 20,* 1168–1172.

Johnson, D. J., & Rusbult, C. E. (1989). Resisting temptation: Devaluation of alternative partners as a means of maintaining commitment in close relationships. *Journal of Personality and Social Psychology, 57,* 967–980.

Johnson, J. E. (1984). Psychological interventions and coping with surgery. In A. Baum, S. E. Taylor, & J. E. Singer (Eds.), *Handbook of psychology and health* (Vol. 4, pp. 167–187). Hillsdale, NJ: Erlbaum.

Johnson, R. D., & Downing, L. L. (1979). Deindividuation and valence of cues: Effects on prosocial and antisocial behavior. *Journal of Personality and Social Psychology, 37,* 1532–1538.

Johnson, T. E., & Rule, B. G. (1986). Mitigating circumstance information, censure, and aggression. *Journal of Personality and Social Psychology, 50,* 537–542.

Jones, E. E. (1964). *Ingratiation: A social psychological analysis.* New York: Appleton-Century-Crofts.

Jones, E. E. (1990). *Interpersonal perception.* New York: W. H. Freeman.

Jones, E. E., & Berglas, S. (1978). Control of attributions about the self through self-handicapping strategies: The appeal of alcohol and the role of underachievement. *Personality and Social Psychology Bulletin, 4,* 200–206.

Jones, E. E., Brenner, K. J., & Knight, J. G. (1990). When failure elevates self-esteem. *Personality and Social Psychology Bulletin, 16,* 200–209.

Jones, E. E., & Davis, K. E. (1965). From acts to disposition: The attribution process in person perception. In L. Berkowitz (Ed.), *Advances in experimental social psychology* (Vol. 2, pp. 219–266). New York: Academic Press.

Jones, E. E., & McGillis, D. (1976). Corresponding inferences and the attribution cube: A comparative reappraisal. In J. H. Harvey, W. J. Ickes, & R. F. Kidd (Eds.), *New directions in attribution research* (Vol. 1). Morristown, NJ: Erlbaum.

Jones, E. E., & Nisbett, R. E. (1971). *The actor and the observer: Divergent perceptions of the causes of behavior.* Morristown, NJ: Erlbaum.

Jones, M. E., & Stanton, A. L. (1988). Dysfunctional beliefs, belief similarity, and marital distress: A comparison of models. *Journal of Social and Clinical Psychology, 7,* 1–14.

Jones, W. H., Hansson, R., & Smith, T. G. (1980). *Loneliness and love: Implications for psychological and interpersonal functioning.* Unpublished manuscript, University of Tulsa, Oklahoma.

Jones, W. H., Hobbs, S. A., & Hockenbury, D. (1982). Loneliness and social skill deficits. *Journal of Personality and Social Psychology, 42,* 682–689.

Jones, W. H., Freeman, J. A., & Goswick, R. A. (1981). The persistence of loneliness: Self and other determinants. *Journal of Personality, 49,* 27–48.

Josephson, W. D. (1987) Television violence and children's aggression: Testing the priming, social script, and disinhibition prediction. *Journal of Personality and Social Psychology, 53,* 882–890.

Judson, F. N. (1980). Coexisting sexually transmitted diseases. *Medical Aspects of Human Sexuality, 14(6),* 138.

Kahle, L. R., & Beatty, S. E. (1987). Cognitive consequences of legislating post-purchase behavior: Growing up with the bottle bill. *Journal of Applied Social Psychology, 17,* 828–843.

Kahn, A., & Tice, T. (1973). Returning a favor and retaliating harm: The effects of stated intentions and actual behavior. *Journal of Experimental Social Psychology, 9,* 43–56.

Kahn, R. L. (1972). The meaning of work: Interpretations and proposals for measurement. In A. A. Campbell & P. E. Converseg (Eds.), *The human meaning of social change.* New York: Basic Books.

Kahneman, D., & Miller, D. T. (1986). Norm theory: Comparing reality to its alternatives. *Psychological Review, 93,* 136–153.

Kahneman, D., Slovic, P., & Tversky, A. (Eds.). (1982). *Judgment under uncertainty: Heuristics and biases.* Cambridge, England: Cambridge University Press.

Kahneman, D., & Tversky, A. (1982). The simulation heuristic. In D. Kahneman, P. Slovic, & A. Tversky (Eds.), *Judgment under uncertainty: Heuristics and biases* (pp. 201–208). Cambridge, England: Cambridge University Press.

Kalick, S. M. (1988). Physical attractiveness as a status cue. *Journal of Experimental Social Psychology, 24,* 469–489.

Kalick, S. M., & Hamilton, T. E. (1986). The matching hypothesis reexamined. *Journal of Personality and Social Psychology, 51,* 673–682.

Kamin, L. J. (1958). Ethnic and party affiliations of candidates as determinants of voting. *Canadian Journal of Psychology, 12,* 205–212.

Kandel, D. B. (1978). Similarity in real-life adolescent friendship pairs. *Journal of Personality and Social Psychology, 36,* 306–312.

Kanekar, S., Kolsawalla, M. B., & Nazareth, T. (1988). Occupational prestige as a function of occupant's gender. *Journal of Applied Social Psychology, 19,* 681–688.

Kaplan, H. B. (1970). Self-derogation and adjustment to recent life experience. *Archives of General Psychiatry, 22,* 324–331.

Kaplan, H. B., & Pokorny, A. D. (1970). Age-related correlates of self-derogation: Report of childhood experiences. *British Journal of Psychiatry, 117,* 533–534.

Kaplan, H. B., & Pokorny, A. D. (1971). Self-derogation and childhood broken home. *Journal of Marriage and the Family, 33,* 328–337.

Kaplan, M. F. (1981). State dispositions in social judgment. *Bulletin of the Psychonomic Society, 18,* 27–29.

Kaplan, M. F., & Miller, C. E. (1987). Group decision making and normative versus informational influence: Effects of type of issue and assigned decision rule. *Journal of Personality and Social Psychology, 53,* 306–313.

Kaplan, S. (1987). Aesthetics, affect, and cognition: Environmental preference from an evolutionary perspective. *Environment and Behavior, 19,* 3–32.

Karlin, R. A., Rosen, L., & Epstein, Y. (1979). Three into two doesn't go: A follow-up of the effects of overcrowded dormitory rooms. *Personality and Social Psychology Bulletin, 5,* 391–395.

Karraker, K. H., Vogel, D. A., & Evans, S. (1987, August). *Responses of students and pregnant women to newborn physical attractiveness.* Paper presented at the meeting of the American Psychological Association, New York.

Kassarjian, H. (1963). Voting intention and political perception. *Journal of Psychology, 56,* 85–88.

Katkovsky, W., Crandall, V. C., & Good, S. (1967). Parental antecedents of children's beliefs in internal-external control of reinforcement in intellectual achievement situations. *Child Development, 28,* 765–776.

Kaufman, M. T. (1980, November 16). Love upsetting Bombay's view of path to altar. *New York Times,* p. 12.

Keinan, G., & Hobfoll, S. E. (1989). Stress, dependency, and social support: Who benefits from husband's presence in delivery? *Journal of Social and Clinical Psychology, 8,* 32–44.

Kellerman, J., Lewis, J., & Laird, J. D. (1989). Looking and loving: The effects of mutual gaze on feelings of romantic love. *Journal of Research in Personality, 23,* 145–161.

Kelley, H. H. (1972). Attribution in social interaction. In E. E. Jones et al. (Eds.), *Attribution: Perceiving the causes of behavior.* Morristown, NJ: General Learning Press.

Kelley, H. H., Berscheid, E., Christensen, A., Harvey, J. H., Huston, T. L., Levenger, G., McClintock, E., Peplau, L. A., & Peterson, D. R. (1983). *Close relationships.* New York: Freeman.

Kelley, H. H., & Michela, J. L. (1980). Attribution theory and research. *Annual Review of Psychology, 31,* 457–501.

Kelley, K. (1985a). Nine social indices as functions of population size or density. *Bulletin of the Psychonomic Society, 23,* 124–126.

Kelley, K. (1985b). Sex, sex guilt, and authoritarianism: Differences in responses to explicit heterosexual and masturbatory slides. *Journal of Sex Research, 21,* 68–85.

Kelley, K. (1985c). Sexual attitudes as determinants of the motivational properties of exposure to erotica. *Personality and Individual Differences, 6,* 391–393.

Kelley, K. (1985d). Sexual fantasy and attitudes as functions of sex of subject and content of erotica. *Imagination, Cognition, and Personality, 4,* 339–347.

Kelley, K., Cheung, F., Rodriguez-Carrillo, P., Singh, R., Wan, C. K., & Becker, M. A. (1986). Chronic self-destructiveness and locus of control in cross-cultural perspective. *Journal of Social Psychology, 126,* 573–577.

Kelley, K., Smeaton, G., Byrne, D., Przybyla, D. P. J., & Fisher, W. A. (1987). Sexual attitudes and contraception among females across five college samples. *Human Relations, 40,* 237–254.

Kelman, H. C. (1967). Human use of human subjects: The problems of deception in social psychological experiments. *Psychological Bulletin, 67,* 1–11.

Kelman, H. C., & Hovland, C. I. (1953). "Reinstatement" of the communicator in delayed measurement of opinion change. *Journal of Abnormal and Social Psychology, 48,* 327–335.

Kenrick, D. T. (1986). How strong is the case against contemporary social and personality psychology? A response to Carlson. *Journal of Personality and Social Psychology, 50,* 839–844.

Kenrick, D. T., & Funder, D. C. (1988). Profiting from controversy: Lessons from the person-situation debate. *American Psychologist, 43,* 23–34.

Kenrick, D. T., & Johnson, G. A. (1979). Interpersonal attraction in aversive environments: A problem for the classical conditioning paradigm. *Journal of Personality and Social Psychology, 37,* 572–579.

Kenrick, D. T., & Keefe, R. C. (1990). *Age preferences in mates reflect sex differences in reproductive strategies.* Manuscript submitted for publication.

Kenrick, D. T., & MacFarlane, S. W. (1986). Ambient temperature and horn honking: A field study of the heat/aggression relationship. *Environment and Behavior, 18,* 179–191.

Kenrick, D. T., & Stringfield, D. O. (1980). Personality traits and the eye of the beholder: Crossing some traditional philosophical boundaries in the search for consistency in all the people. *Psychological Review, 87,* 88–104.

Kent, D. (1990). A conversation with Claude Steele. *APS Observer, 3(3),* 11–15, 17.

Kent, G. G., Davis, J. D., & Shapiro, D. A. (1981). Effect of mutual acquaintance on the construction of conversation. *Journal of Experimental Social Psychology, 17,* 197–209.

Kernis, M. H., Brockner, J., & Frankel, B. S. (1989). Self-esteem and relations to failure: The mediating role of overgeneralization. *Journal of Personality and Social Psychology, 57,* 707–714.

Kernis, M. H., Grannemann, B. D., & Barclay, L. C. (1989). Stability and level of self-esteem as predictors of anger arousal and hostility. *Journal of Personality and Social Psychology, 56,* 1013–1022.

Kerr, N. L. (1978a). Beautiful and blameless: Effects of victim awareness and responsibility on mock juror verdicts. *Personality and Social Psychology Bulletin, 4,* 479–482.

Kerr, N. L. (1978b). Severity of prescribed penalty and mock juror's verdicts. *Journal of Personality and Social Psychology, 36,* 1431–1442.

Kerr, N. L. (1989). Illusions of efficacy: The effects of group size on perceived efficacy in social dilemmas. *Journal of Experimental Social Psychology, 25,* 287–313.

Kerr, N. L., & McCoun, R. J. (1985). Role of expectations in social dilemmas: Sex roles and task motivation in groups. *Journal of Personality and Social Psychology, 49,* 1547–1556.

Kiecolt-Glaser, J. K., & Glaser, R. (1987). Psychosocial moderators of immune function. *Annals of Behavioral Medicine, 9,* 16–20.

Kiesler, C. A. (1985). Psychology and public policy. In E. M. Altmaier & M. E. Meyer (Eds.), *Applied specialties in psychology* (pp. 375–390). New York: Random House.

Kiesler, C. A., & Kiesler, S. B. (1969). *Conformity.* Reading, MA: Addison-Wesley.

Kihlstrom, J. F., Cantor, N., Albright, J. S., Chew, B. R., Klein, S. B., & Niedenthal, P. M. (1988). Information processing and the study of the self. In L. Berkowitz (Ed.), *Advances in experimental social psychology* (Vol. 21, pp. 145–177). New York: Academic Press.

Kilham, W., & Mann, L. (1974). Level of destructive obedience as a function of transmitter and executant roles in the Milgram obedience paradigm. *Journal of Personality and Social Psychology, 29,* 696–702.

Kimmell, M. S. (1988, October). Macho mouth on the campaign trail. The winning strategy in '88: Talk like a man. *Psychology Today,* p. 27.

Kirchler, E., & Davis, J. H. (1986). The influence of member status differences and task type on group consensus and member position change. *Journal of Personality and Social Psychology, 51,* 83–91.

Kirscht, J. P., Janz, N. K., & Becker, M. H. (1989). Psychosocial predictors of change in cigarette smoking. *Journal of Applied Social Psychology, 19,* 298–308.

Klein, S. B., & Loftus, J. (1988). The nature of self-referent encoding: The contributions of elaborative and organizational processes. *Journal of Personality and Social Psychology, 55,* 5–11.

Klein, S. B., Loftus, J., & Burton, H. A. (1989). Two self-reference effects: The importance of distinguishing between self-descriptiveness judgments and autobiographical retrieval in self-referent encoding. *Journal of Personality and Social Psychology, 56,* 853–865.

Kleinke, C. L. (1986). Gaze and eye contact: A research review. *Psychological Review, 100,* 78–100.

Kleinke, C. L., Meeker, F. B., & Staneski, R. A. (1986). Preference for opening lines: Comparing ratings by men and women. *Sex Roles, 15,* 585–600.

Kleinke, C. L., & Staneski, R. A. (1980). First impressions of female bust size. *Journal of Social Psychology, 110,* 123–134.

Knapp, M. L. (1978). *Nonverbal communication in human interaction.* New York: Holt, Rinehart, & Winston.

Knight, G. P. (1980). Behavioral similarity, confederate strategy, and sex composition of dyad as determinants of interpersonal judgments and behavior in the prisoner's dilemma game. *Journal of Research in Personality, 14,* 91–103.

Knight, G. P., & Dubro, A. F. (1984). Cooperative, competitive, and individualistic social values: An individualized regression and clustering approach. *Journal of Personality and Social Psychology, 46,* 98–105.

Knox, R. E., & Safford, R. K. (1976). Group causation at the racetrack. *Journal of Experimental Social Psychology, 12,* 317–324.

Kobasa, S. C. (1979). Stressful life events, personality, and health: An inquiry into hardiness. *Journal of Personality and Social Psychology, 37,* 1–11.

Koestner, R., Bernieri, F., & Zuckerman, M. (1989). Trait-specific versus person-specific moderators of cross-situational consistency. *Journal of Personality, 57,* 1–16.

Kolditz, T. A., & Arkin, R. M. (1982). An impression management interpretation of the self-handicapping strategy. *Journal of Personality and Social Psychology, 43,* 492–502.

Konecni, V. J., Libuser, L., Morton, H., & Ebbesen, E. G. (1975).

Effects of a violation of personal space on escape and helping responses. *Journal of Experimental Social Psychology, 11,* 288–299.

Koocher, G. P. (1971). Swimming, competence, and personality change. *Journal of Personality and Social Psychology, 18,* 275–278.

Korda, M. (1987, July 11–12). *International Herald Tribune,* p. 5.

Korte, C. (1980). Urban-nonurban differences in social behavior and social psychological models of urban impact. *Journal of Social Issues, 36,* 29–51.

Korte, C. (1981). Constraints on helping in an urban environment. In J. P. Rushton & R. M. Sorrentino (Eds.), *Altruism and helping behavior.* Hillsdale, NJ: Erlbaum.

Kraiger, K., Billings, R. S., & Isen, A. M. (1989). The influence of positive affective states on task perceptions and satisfaction. *Organizational Behavior and Human Decision Processes, 44,* 12–25.

Kramer, R. M., & Brewer, M. B. (1984). Effects of group identity on source use in a simulated commons dilemma. *Journal of Personality and Social Psychology, 46,* 1044–1057.

Krantz, D. S., Grunberg, N. E., & Baum, A. (1985). Health psychology. In M. R. Rosenzweig & L. W. Proter (Eds.), *Annual review of psychology* (Vol. 36). Palo Alto, CA: Annual Reviews.

Kremer, J. F., & Stephens, L. (1983). Attributions and arousal as mediators of mitigation's effects on retaliation. *Journal of Personality and Social Psychology, 45,* 335–343.

Kristiansen, C. M. (1989). Gender differences in the meaning of "health." *Social Behavior, 4,* 185–188.

Kristiansen, C. M., & Harding, C. M. (1988). A comparison of the coverage of health issues by Britain's quality and popular press. *Social Behavior, 3,* 25–32.

Krosnick, J. A. (1988). The role of attitude importance in social evaluation: A study of political preferences, presidential candidate evaluations, and voting behavior. *Journal of Personality and Social Psychology, 55,* 196–210.

Krosnick, J. A. (1989). Attitude importance and attitude accessibility. *Personality and Social Psychology Bulletin, 15,* 297–308.

Krosnick, J. A., & Alwin, D. F. (1989). Aging and susceptibility to attitude change. *Journal of Personality and Social Psychology, 57,* 416–425.

Kruglanski, A. E., & Mayseless, O. (1987). Motivational effects in the social comparison of opinions. *Journal of Personality and Social Psychology, 53,* 834–842.

Krupat, E. (1975). *Psychology is social.* Glenview, IL: Scott, Foresman.

Krupat, E., & Guild, W. (1980). Defining the city: The use of objective and subjective measures of community description. *Journal of Social Issues, 36,* 9–28.

Kulik, J. A., & Mahler, H. I. M. (1987). Effects of preoperative roommate assignment on preoperative anxiety and recovery from coronary-bypass surgery. *Health Psychology, 6,* 525–544.

Kulik, J. A., & Mahler, H. I. M. (1989). Stress and affiliation in a hospital setting: Preoperative roommate preferences. *Personality and Social Psychology Bulletin, 15,* 183–193.

Kulman, I. R., & Akamatsu, T. J. (1988). The effects of television on large-scale attitude change: Viewing "The Day After." *Journal of Applied Social Psychology, 18,* 1121–1132.

Kunda, Z., & Nisbett, R. E. (1986). The psychometrics of everyday life. *Cognitive Psychology, 18,* 195–224.

Kurdek, L. A., Blisk, D., & Siesky, A. E., Jr. (1981). Correlates of children's long-term adjustment to their parents' divorce. *Developmental Psychology, 17,* 565–579.

Kushler, M. G. (1989). Use of evaluation to improve energy conservation programs: A review and case study. *Journal of Social Issues, 45,* 153–168.

Lamm, H., & Myers, D. G. (1978). Group-induced polarization of attitudes and behavior. In L. Berkowitz (Ed.), *Advances in experimental social psychology.* New York: Academic Press.

Landers, A. (1977, March 28). "Like spouse?" Poll startles Field Enterprises.

Langer, E. J. (1984). *The psychology of control.* Beverly Hills, CA: Sage.

Langston, C. A., & Cantor, N. (1989). Social anxiety and social constraint: When making friends is hard. *Journal of Personality and Social Psychology, 56,* 649–661.

LaPiere, R. T. (1934). Attitudes and actions. *Social Forces, 13,* 230–237.

Larson, J. H., & Bell, N. J. (1988). Need for privacy and its effect upon interpersonal attraction and interaction. *Journal of Social and Clinical Psychology, 6,* 1–10.

Lasswell, M. E., & Lobsenz, N. M. (1980). *Styles of loving*. New York: Ballantine.

Latané, B., & Darley, J. M. (1968). Group inhibition of bystander intervention in emergencies. *Journal of Personality and Social Psychology, 10*, 215–221.

Latané, B., & Darley, J. M. (1970). *The unresponsive bystander: Why doesn't he help?* New York: Appleton-Century-Crofts.

Latané, B., & Rodin, J. (1969). A lady in distress: Inhibiting effects of friends and strangers on bystander intervention. *Journal of Experimental Social Psychology, 5*, 189–202.

Latané, B., Williams, K., & Harkins, S. (1979). Many hands make light the work: The causes and consequents of social loafing. *Journal of Personality and Social Psychology, 37*, 822–832.

Lau, R. R. (1988). Beliefs about control and health behavior. In D. Gochman (Ed.), *Health behavior: Emerging research perspectives* (pp. 43–63). New York: Plenum.

Lauer, J., & Lauer, R. (1985, June). Marriages made to last. *Psychology Today*, pp. 22–26.

Lavrakas, P. J. (1975). Female preferences for male physiques. *Journal of Research in Personality, 9*, 324–334.

Lawler, E. E., III, Kuleck, W. J., Jr., Rhode, J. G., & Sorensen, J. E. (1975). Job choice and post-decision dissonance. *Organizational Behavior and Human Performance, 13*, 133–145.

Lawler, E. J., & MacMurray, B. K. (1980). Bargaining toughness: A qualification of level-of-aspiration and reciprocity hypotheses. *Journal of Applied Social Psychology, 34*, 885–894.

Lawson, A. (1988). *Adultery: An analysis of love and betrayal*. New York: Basic Books.

Lazarus, R. S. (1966). *Psychological stress and the coping process*. New York: McGraw-Hill.

Lazarus, R. S., & Folkman, S. (1984). *Stress, appraisal, and coping*. New York: Springer-Verlag.

Lea, M. (1989). Factors underlying friendship: An analysis of responses on the Acquaintance Description Form in relation to Wright's friendship model. *Journal of Social and Personal Relationships, 6*, 275–292.

Leary, W. E. (1988, November 15). Novel methods unlock witnesses' memories. *New York Times*, pp. C1, C15.

Lebo, C. P., & Oliphant, K. P. (1968). Music as a source of acoustical trauma. *Laryngoscope, 78*, 1211–1218.

Lee, J. A. (1988). Love-styles. In R. J. Sternberg & M. L. Barnes (Eds.), *The psychology of love* (pp. 38–67). New Haven, CT: Yale University Press.

Lee, J. A. (1973). *Colors of love*. Toronto: New Press.

Lee, L. (1984). Sequences in separation: A framework for investigating endings of the personal (romantic) relationships. *Journal of Social and Personal Relationships, 1*, 49–73.

Lefcourt, H. M. (1982). *Locus of control: Current trends in theory and research* (3rd ed.). Hillsdale, NJ: Erlbaum.

Leippe, M. R. (1985). The influence of eyewitness nonidentifications on mock-jurors' judgments of a court case. *Journal of Applied Social Psychology, 15*, 656–672.

Lemery, C. R. (1983). *Children's sexual knowledge as a function of parents' affective orientation to sexuality and parent-child communication about sex: A causal analysis*. Unpublished master's thesis, University of Western Ontario, London, Canada.

Lennox, R. D., & Wolfe, R. N. (1984). Revision of the Self-Monitoring Scale. *Journal of Personality and Social Psychology, 46*, 1349–1364.

Leo, J. (1985). Battling the green-eyed monster. *Time*, p. 126.

Lepper, M., & Greene, D. (Eds.). (1978). *The hidden costs of reward*. Hillsdale, NJ: Erlbaum.

Lesnik-Oberstein, M., & Coihen, L. (1984). Cognitive style, sensation-seeking, and assortative mating. *Journal of Personality and Social Psychology, 46*, 112–117.

Leung, K., & Bond, M. H. (1984). The impact of cultural collectivism on reward allocation. *Journal of Personality and Social Psychology, 47*, 793–804.

Leventhal, A., Nerenz, D. R., & Steele, D. J. (1984). Illness representations and coping with health threats. In A. Baum & J. Singer (Eds.), *Handbook of psychology and health* (pp. 219–252). Hillsdale, NJ: Erlbaum.

Leventhal, G. S. (1980). What should be done with equity theory? In K. J. Gergen, M. S. Greenberg, & R. H. Willis (Eds.), *Social exchange: Advances in theory and research* (pp. 27–55). New York: Plenum.

Leventhal, H., Glynn, K., & Fleming, R. (1987). Is the smoking decision an "informed choice"? Effect of smoking risk factors on smoking. *Journal of the American Medical Association, 257*, 3373–3376.

Leventhal, H., Singer, R., & Jones, S. (1965). The effects of fear and specificity on recommendation upon attitudes and behavior. *Journal of Personality and Social Psychology, 2*, 20–29.

Levin, I. P. (1987). Associative effects of information framing. *Bulletin of the Psychonomic Society, 25*, 85–86.

Levin, I. P., Schnittjer, S. K., & Thee, S. L. (1988). Information framing effects in social and personal decisions. *Journal of Experimental Social Psychology, 24*, 520–529.

Levine, R. V., Miyake, K., & Lee, M. (1989). Places rated revisited: Psychosocial pathology in metropolitan areas. *Environment and Behavior, 21*, 531–553.

Levinger, G. (1988). Can we picture "love"? In R. J. Sternberg & M. L. Barnes (Eds.), *The psychology of love* (pp. 139–158). New Haven: Yale University Press.

Levinger, G. (1980). Toward the analysis of close relationships. *Journal of Experimental Social Psychology, 16*, 510–544.

Levitt, M. J. (1980). Contingent feedback, familiarization, and infant affect: How a stranger becomes a friend. *Developmental Psychology, 16*, 425–432.

Levy, S. (1979). Authoritarianism and information processing. *Bulletin of the Psychonomic Society, 13*, 240–242.

Lewicki, R. J., & Litterer, J. A. (1985). *Negotiation*. Homewood, IL: Richard D. Irwin.

Lewin, K., Lippitt, R., & White, R. K. (1939). Patterns of aggressive behavior in experimentally created "social climates." *Journal of Social Psychology, 10*, 271–299.

Lewis, D. A., & Salem, G. (1981). Community crime prevention: An analysis of a development strategy. *Crime and Delinquency, 27*, 405–421.

Leyens, J. P., Camino, L., Parke, R. D., & Berkowitz, L. (1975). Effects of movie violence on aggression in a field setting as a function of group dominance and cohesion. *Journal of Personality and Social Psychology, 32*, 340–346.

Liden, R. C., & Mitchel, T. R. (1985). Reactions to feedback: The role of attributions. *Academy of Management Journal, 28*, 291–308.

Liden, R. C., & Mitchell, T. R. (1988). Ingratiatory behaviors in organizational settings. *Academy of Management Review, 13*, 572–587.

Liebert, R. M., & Baron, R. A. (1972). Some immediate effects of televised violence on children's behavior. *Developmental Psychology, 6*, 469–475.

Liebert, R. M., Sprafkin, J. N., & Davidson, E. S. (1989). *The early window: Effects of television on children and youth* (3rd ed.). New York: Pergamon.

Lim, R. G., & Carnevale, P. J. D. (1990). Contingencies in the mediation of disputes. *Journal of Personality and Social Psychology, 58*, 259–272.

Lindley, D. (1989, January 10). Wait a bit. *Albany Times Union*, pp. C1–C2.

Lindsay, D. S., & Johnson, M. K. (1989). The reversed eyewitness suggestibility effect. *Bulletin of the Psychonomic Society, 27*, 111–113.

Lindsay, R. C. L., Lim, R., Marando, L., & Culley, D. (1986). Mock-juror evaluations of eyewitness testimony: A test of metamemory hypotheses. *Journal of Applied Social Psychology, 16*, 447–459.

Linn, R. T., & Hodge, G. K. (1982). Locus of control in childhood hyperactivity. *Journal of Consulting and Clinical Psychology, 50*, 592–593.

Linsky, A., & Straus, M. (1986). *Social stress in the United States: Links to regional patterns in crime and illness*. Dover, MA: Auburn House.

Linville, P. W. (1982). The complexity-extremity effect and age-based stereotyping. *Journal of Personality and Social Psychology, 42*, 193–211.

Linville, P. W., Fischer, G. W., & Salovey, P. (1989). Perceived distributions of the characteristics of in-group and out-group members: Empirical evidence and a computer simulation. *Journal of Personality and Social Psychology, 57*, 165–188.

Linville, P. W., Salovey, P., & Fischer, G. W. (1986). Stereotyping and perceived distribution of social characteristics: An application to ingroup-outgroup perception. In J. Dovidio & S. L. Gaertner

(Eds.), *Prejudice, discrimination, and racism* (pp. 165–208). New York: Academic Press.

Linz, D., Donnerstein, E., & Penrod, S. (1984). The effects of multiple exposure to filmed violence against women. *Journal of Communication, 34,* 130–137.

Linz, D., Donnerstein, E., & Penrod, S. (1988). Effects of long-term exposure to violent and sexually degrading depictions of women. *Journal of Personality and Social Psychology, 55,* 758–768.

Litt, M. D. (1988). Self-efficacy and perceived control: Cognitive mediators of pain tolerance. *Journal of Personality and Social Psychology, 54,* 149–160.

Locke, E. A. (1990). The nature and causes of job satisfaction. In M. Dunnette (Ed.), *Handbook of industrial and organizational psychology* (2nd ed.). Chicago: Rand McNally.

Loden, M. (1985). *Feminine leadership of how to succeed in business without being one of the boys.* New York: Times Books.

Loftus, E. F. (1980). *Eyewitness testimony.* Cambridge, MA: Harvard University Press.

Logan, J., & Molotch, H. (1986). *Urban fortunes.* Berkeley: University of California Press.

Lord, R. G., De Vader, C. L., & Alliger, G. M. (1986). A meta-analysis of the relationship between personality traits and leadership perceptions: An application of validity generalization procedures. *Journal of Applied Psychology, 71,* 401–410.

Lorenz, K. (1966). *On aggression.* New York: Harcourt, Brace, & World.

Lorenz, K. (1974). *Civilized man's eight deadly sins.* New York: Harcourt Brace Jovanovich.

Luks, A. (1988, October). Helper's high. *Psychology Today,* pp. 39–40.

Lumpkin, J. R. (1986). The relationship between locus of control and age: New evidence. *Journal of Social Behavior and Personality, 1,* 245–252.

Lupfer, M. B., Clark, L. F., & Hutcherson, H. W. (1990). Impact of context on spontaneous trait and situational attributions. *Journal of Personality and Social Psychology, 58,* 239–249.

Luyben, P. D. (1982). Prompting thermostat setting behavior: Public response to a presidential appeal for conservation. *Environment and Behavior, 14,* 113–128.

Lynch, M. D., Norem-Hebeisen, & Gergen, K. H. (1981). *Self-concept: Advances in theory and research.* Cambridge, MA: Ballinger.

Lynn, M., & Shurgot, B. A. (1984). Responses to lonely hearts advertisements: Effects of reported physical attractiveness, physique, and coloration. *Personality and Social Psychology Bulletin, 10,* 349–357.

Lysak, H., Rule, B. G., & Dobbs, A. R. (1989). Conceptions of aggression: Prototypes or defining features? *Personality and Social Psychology Bulletin, 15,* 233–243.

Maas, A., Clark, R. D., III. (1984). Hidden impact of minorities: Fifteen years of minority influence research. *Psychological Bulletin, 95,* 428–450.

Maass, A., & Volpato, C. (1989). Gender differences in self-serving attributions about sexual experiences. *Journal of Applied Social Psychology, 19,* 517–542.

Macaulay, J. (1970). A shill for charity. In J. Macaulay & L. Berkowitz (Eds.), *Altruism and helping behavior* (pp. 43–59). New York: Academic Press.

MacCoun, R. J., & Kerr, N. L. (1988). Asymmetric influence in mock jury deliberation: Jurors' bias for leniency. *Journal of Personality and Social Psychology, 54,* 21–33.

Mackie, D. M. (1986). Social identification effects in group polarization. *Journal of Personality and Social Psychology, 40,* 720–728.

Mackie, D. M., & Worth, L. T. (1989). Processing deficits and the mediation of positive affect in persuasion. *Journal of Personality and Social Psychology, 57,* 27–40.

Madden, M. E. (1987). Perceived control and power in marriage: A study of marital decision making and task performance. *Personality and Social Psychology Bulletin, 13,* 73–82.

Major, B., Carrington, P. I., & Carnevale, P. J. D. (1984). Physical attractiveness and self-esteem: Attributions for praise from an other-sex evaluator. *Personality and Social Psychology Bulletin, 10,* 43–50.

Major, B., & Konar, E. (1984). An investigation of sex differences in pay expectations and their possible causes. *Academy of Management Journal, 27,* 777–792.

Malamuth, N. M., Check, J., & Briere, J. (1986). Sexual arousal in response to aggression: Ideological, aggressive, and sexual correlates. *Journal of Personality and Social Psychology, 50,* 330–350.

Mallick, S. K., & McCandless, B. R. (1966). A study of catharsis of aggression. *Journal of Personality and Social Psychology, 4,* 591–596.

Malloy, T. E., & Kenny, D. A. (1986). The social relations model: An integrative method for personality research. *Journal of Personality, 54,* 199–225.

Manzo, L. C., & Weinstein, N. D. (1987). Behavioral commitment to environmental protection: A study of active and nonactive members of the Sierra Club. *Environment and Behavior, 19,* 673–694.

Marangoni, C., & Ickes, W. (1989). Loneliness: A theoretical review with implications for measurement. *Journal of Social and Personal Relationships, 6,* 93–128.

Margolin, G., John, R. S., & O'Brien, M. (1989). Sequential affective patterns as a function of marital conflict style. *Journal of Social and Clinical Psychology, 8,* 45–61.

Markman, H. J. (1981). Prediction of marital distress: A 5-year follow-up. *Journal of Consulting and Clinical Psychology, 49,* 760–762.

Marks, G., & Miller, N. (1982). Target attractiveness as a mediator of assumed attitude similarity. *Personality and Social Psychology Bulletin, 8,* 728–735.

Marks, M. L., & Miller, N. (1987). Ten years of research on the false-consensus effect: An empirical and theoretical review. *Psychological Bulletin, 8,* 728–735.

Markus, H. (1977). Self-schemata and processing information about the self. *Journal of Personality and Social Psychology, 35,* 63–78.

Markus, H. (1978). The effects of mere presence on social facilitation: An unobtrusive test. *Journal of Experimental Social Psychology, 14,* 389–397.

Markus, H., & Nurius, P. (1986). Possible selves. *American Psychologist, 41,* 954–969.

Markus, H., & Wurf, E. (1987). The dynamic self-concept: A social psychological perspective. *Annual Review of Psychology, 38,* 299–377.

Markus, H., & Zajonc, R. B. (1985). The cognitive perspective in social psychology. In G. Lindzey and E. Aronson (Eds.), *Handbook of social psychology.* New York: Random House.

Marsh, H. W., Richards, G. E., & Barnes, J. (1986a). Multidimensional self-concepts: A long-term follow-up of the effect of participation in an Outward Bound program. *Personality and Social Psychology Bulletin, 12,* 475–492.

Marsh, H. W., Richard, G. E., & Barnes, J. (1986b). Multidimensional self-concepts: The effects of participation in an Outward Bound program. *Journal of Personality and Social Psychology, 50,* 195–204.

Marsh, K. L., & Weary, G. (1989). Depression and attributional complexity. *Personality and Social Psychology Bulletin, 15,* 325–336.

Marshall, G. D., & Zimbardo, P. G. (1979). Affective consequence of inadequately explained physiological arousal. *Journal of Personality and Social Psychology, 37,* 970–988.

Martin, J. E., & Peterson, M. M. (1987). Two-tier wage structures: Implications for equity theory. *Academy of Management Journal, 30,* 297–315.

Martin, N. G., Eaves, L. J., Heath, A. C., Jardine, R., Feingold, L. M., & Eysenck, H. J. (1986). The transmission of social attitudes. *Proceedings of the National Academy of Sciences of the United States of America, 83,* 4365–4368.

Martindale, D. A. (1971). Territorial dominance behavior in dyadic verbal interactions. *Proceedings of the American Psychological Association, 6,* 305–306.

Martinko, M. J., & Gardner, W. L. (1987). The leader/member attribution process. *Academy of Management Review, 12,* 235–249.

Maruyama, G., & Miller, N. (1981). Physical attractiveness and personality. In B. Maher (Ed.), *Advances in experimental research in personality* (Vol. 10). New York: Academic Press.

Marwell, G., & Schmidt, D. R. (1972). *Journal of Personality and Social Psychology, 19,* 353–362.

Maslach, C., Santee, R. T., & Wade, C. (1987). Individuation, gender role, and dissent: Personality mediators of situational forces. *Journal of Personality and Social Psychology, 53,* 1088–1094.

Massey, A., & Vanderbergh, J. G. (1980). Puberty delay by a urinary cue from female house mice in feral populations. *Science, 209,* 821–822.

Mathes, E. W., Adams, H. E., & Davies, R. M. (1985). Jealousy: Loss of relationship rewards, loss of self-esteem, depression, anxiety, and anger. *Journal of Personality and Social Psychology, 48,* 1552–1561.

Mathews, K. E., & Cannon, L. K. (1975). Environmental noise level as a determinant of helping behavior. *Journal of Personality and Social Psychology, 32,* 571–577.

Matlin, M. W., & Zajonc, R. B. (1968). Social facilitation of work associations. *Journal of Personality and Social Psychology, 10,* 455–460.

Matsumoto, D. (1987). The role of facial response in the experience of emotion: More methodological problems and a meta-analysis. *Journal of Personality and Social Psychology, 52,* 769–774.

Maugh, T. H., II. (1990, February 19). Love, American style: Surveys say risks overstated. *Los Angeles Times.*

May, J. L., & Hamilton, P. A. (1980). Effects of musically evoked affect on women's interpersonal attraction and perceptual judgments of physical attractiveness of men. *Motivation and Emotion, 4,* 217–228.

McAdams, D. P., & Losoff, M. (1984). Friendship motivation in fourth and sixth graders: A thematic analysis. *Journal of Social and Personal Relationships, 1,* 11–27.

McAllister, H. A., & Bergman, N. J. (1983). Self-disclosure and liking: An integration theory approach. *Journal of Personality, 51,* 202–212.

McArthur, L. Z., & Baron, R. M. (1983). Toward an ecological theory of social perception. *Psychological Review, 90,* 215–238.

McArthur, L. Z., & Berry, D. S. (1987). Cross-cultural agreement in perceptions of babyfaced adults. *Journal of Cross-Cultural Psychology, 18,* 156–174.

McCabe, M. P. (1987). Desired and experienced levels of premarital affection and sexual intercourse during dating. *Journal of Sex Research, 23,* 23–33.

McCain, G., Cox, V. C., Paulus, P. B., Luke, A., & Abaczi, H. (1985). Some effects of reduction of extra-classroom crowding in a school environment. *Journal of Applied Social Psychology, 15,* 503–515.

McCanne, T. R., & Anderson, J. A. (1987). Emotional responding following experimental manipulation of facial electromyographic activity. *Journal of Personality and Social Psychology, 52,* 759–768.

McCarty, P. A. (1986). Effects of feedback on the self-confidence of men and women. *Academy of Management Journal, 29,* 840–847.

McCauley, C. (1989). The nature of social influence in groupthink: Compliance and internalization. *Journal of Personality and Social Psychology, 57,* 250–260.

McCauley, C., Coleman, G., & DeFusco, P. (1977). Commuters' eye contact with strangers in city and suburban train stations: Evidence of short-term adaptation to interpersonal overload in the city. *Environmental Psychology and Nonverbal Behavior, 2,* 215–225.

McClelland, D. C., & Boyatzis, R. E. (1982). Leadership motive pattern and long-term success in management. *Journal of Applied Psychology, 674,* 737–743.

McClintock, C. G., & Allison, S. T. (1989). Social value orientation and helping behavior. *Journal of Applied Social Psychology, 19,* 353–362.

McCormack, P. (1980, January 4). Sex creates stress on college campuses. *Albany Knickerbocker News,* p. 1B.

McCrae, R. R. (1989). Why I advocate the five-factor model: Joint factor analyses of the NEO-PI with other instruments. In D. M. Buss & N. Cantor (Eds.), *Personality psychology: Recent trends and emerging directions* (pp. 237–345). New York: Springer-Verlag.

McDougall, W. (1908). *Introduction to social psychology.* London: Methuen.

McFarland, C., & Ross, M. (1987). The relation between current impressions and memories of self and dating partners. *Personality and Social Psychology Bulletin, 13,* 228–238.

McFarland, C., Ross, M., & DeCourville, N. (1989). Women's theories of menstruation and biases in recall of menstrual symptoms. *Journal of Personality and Social Psychology, 57,* 522–531.

McFarlane, A. H., Norman, G. R., Streiner, D. L., & Roy, R. G. (1983). The process of social stress: Stable, reciprocal, and mediating relationships. *Journal of Health and Social Behavior, 24,* 160–173.

McGaughey, K. J., & Stiles, W. B. (1983). Courtroom interrogation of rape victims: Verbal response mode used by attorneys and witnesses during direct examination vs. cross-examination. *Journal of Applied Social Psychology, 13,* 78–87.

McGill, A. L. (1989). Context effects in judgments of causation. *Journal of Personality and Social Psychology, 57,* 189–200.

McGilley, B. M., & Holmes, D. S. (1988). Aerobic fitness and response to psychological stress. *Journal of Research in Personality, 22,* 129–139.

McKibben, B. (1989). *The end of nature.* New York: Random House.

McKillip, J., & Reidel, S. L. (1983). External validity of matching on physical attractiveness for same and opposite sex couples. *Journal of Applied Social Psychology, 13,* 328–337.

McLaughlin, M. L., Cody, M. J., & Rosenstein, M. E. (1983). Account sequences in conversations between strangers. *Communication Monographs, 50,* 102–125.

McQuay, D. (1985, December 1). It's hard to identify winners of the sexual revolution. *Albany Times Union,* pp. D1, D10.

Mead, M. (1977). Jealousy: Primitive and civilized. In G. Clanton & L. G. Smith (Eds.), *Jealousy* (pp. 115–127). Englewood Cliffs, NJ: Prentice Hall.

Mechanic, D. (1983). Adolescent health and illness behavior: Hypotheses for the study of distress in youth. *Journal of Human Stress, 9,* 4–13.

Mednick, S. A., Brennan, P., & Kandel, E. (1988). Predispositions to violence. *Aggressive Behavior, 14,* 25–33.

Meecham, W. C., & Smith, H. G. (1977, June). [British Journal of Audiology.] Quoted in N. Napp, Noise drives you crazy—jets and mental hospitals. *Psychology Today,* p. 33.

Meer, J. (1986, May). The strife of bath. *Psychology Today,* p. 6.

Mega-cities: New 3rd world phenomenon. (1986, April). *Popline,* p. 4.

Meindl, J. R., & Lerner, M. J. (1985). Exacerbation of extreme responses to an out-group. *Journal of Personality and Social Psychology, 47,* 71–84.

Meoli, J., & Feinberg, R. A. (1989, May). *Stores as stimulus reinforcement: A learning theory approach to retail mall assessment.* Paper presented at the Symposium on Patronage Behavior and Retail Strategy, Baton Rouge, LA.

Messe, L. A., & Sivacke, J. M. (1979). Predictions of others' responses in a mixed-motive game: Self-justification or false consensus? *Journal of Personality and Social Psychology, 37,* 602–607.

Messick, D. M., & Brewer, M. B. (1983). Solving social dilemmas: A review. In L. Wheeler (Ed.), *Review of personality and social psychology* (Vol. 4, pp. 11–49). Beverly Hills, CA: Sage.

Metts, S., Cupach, W. R., & Bejlovec, R. A. (1989). "I love you too much to ever start liking you": Redefining romantic relationships. *Journal of Social and Personal Relationships, 6,* 259–274.

Meyer, D., Leventhal, H., & Gutman, M. (1985). Common-sense models of illness: The example of hypertension. *Health Psychology, 4,* 115–135.

Meyer, J. P., & Mulherin, A. (1980). From attribution to helping: An analysis of the mediating effects of affect and expectancy. *Journal of Personality and Social Psychology, 39,* 201–210.

Meyerowitz, B. E., Williams, J. G., & Gessner, J. (1987). Perceptions of controllability and attitudes toward cancer and cancer patients. *Journal of Applied Social Psychology, 17,* 471–492.

Michelini, R. L., & Snodgrass, S. S. (1980). Defendant characteristics and juridic decisions. *Journal of Research in Personality, 14,* 340–350.

Middlemist, R. D., Knowles, E. S., & Matter, C. F. (1976). Personal space invasions in the lavatory: Suggestive evidence for arousal. *Journal of Personality and Social Psychology, 33,* 541–546.

Midlarsky, E. (1968). Aiding responses: An analysis and review. *Merrill-Palmer Quarterly, 14,* 229–260.

Milardo, R. M., Johnson, M. P., & Huston, T. L. (1983). Developing close relationships: Changing patterns of interaction between pair members and social networks. *Journal of Personality and Social Psychology, 44,* 964–976.

Milestones. (1989, September 18). *Time,* p. 75.

Milgram, S. (1963). Behavior study of obedience. *Journal of Abnormal and Social Psychology, 67,* 371–378.

Milgram, S. (1965a). Liberating effects of group pressure. *Journal of Personality and Social Psychology, 1,* 127–134.

Milgram, S. (1965b). Some conditions of obedience and disobedience to authority. *Human Relations, 18,* 57–76.

Milgram, S. (1970). The experience of living cities. *Science, 167,* 1461–1468.

Milgram, S. (1974). *Obedience to authority.* New York: Harper.

Milgram, S. (1977). *The individual in a social world.* Reading, MA: Addison-Wesley.

Millar, M. G., & Tesser, A. (1989). The effects of affective-cognitive consistency and thought on the attitude-behavior relation. *Journal of Experimental Social Psychology, 25,* 189–202.

Miller, D. T., & McFarland, C. (1986). Counterfactual thinking and victim compensation: A test of norm theory. *Personality and Social Psychology Bulletin, 12,* 513–519.

Miller, D. T., & Ross, M. (1975). Self-serving biases in the attribution of causality: Fact or fiction? *Psychological Bulletin, 82,* 313–325.

Miller, D. T., Turnbull, W., & McFarland, C. (1989). When a coincidence is suspicious: The role of mental simulation. *Journal of Personality and Social Psychology, 57,* 581–589.

Miller, D. T., Turnbull, W., & McFarland, C. (1990). Counterfactual thinking and social perception: Thinking about what might have been. In M. P. Zanna (Ed.), *Advances in experimental social psychology* (Vol. 23). Orlando, FL: Academic Press.

Miller, M. L., & Thayer, J. F. (1988). On the nature of self-monitoring: Relationships with adjustment and identity. *Personality and Social Psychology Bulletin, 14,* 544–553.

Miller, M. L., & Thayer, J. F. (1989). On the existence of discrete classes in personality: Is self-monitoring the correct joint to carve? *Journal of Personality and Social Psychology, 57,* 143–155.

Miller, N., Maruyama, G., Beaber, R. J., & Valone, K. (1976). Speed of speech and persuasion. *Journal of Personality and Social Psychology, 34,* 615–624.

Miller, S. N., Brody, D. S., & Summerton, J. (1988). Styles of coping with threat: Implications for health. *Journal of Personality and Social Psychology, 54,* 142–148.

Mischel, W. (1968). *Personality and assessment.* New York: Wiley.

Mischel, W. (1977). On the future of personality measurement. *American Psychologist, 32,* 246–254.

Mischel, W. (1985, August 25). *Personality: Lost or found? Identifying when individual differences make a difference.* Paper presented at the meeting of the American Psychological Association, Los Angeles.

Mitchell, T. R., Green, S. G., & Wood, R. R. (1981). An attributional model of leadership and the poor performing subordinate: Development and validation. In L. L. Cummings & B. M. Staw (Eds.), *Research in Organizational Behavior* (Vol. 3, pp. 197–234). Greenwich, CT: JAI Press.

Mohrman, A. M., Jr., Resnick-West, S. M., & Lawler, E. E., III. (1989). *Designing performance appraisal systems: Aligning appraisals and organizational realities.* San Francisco: Jossey-Bass.

Monahan, J., & Walker, L. (1988). Social science research in law: A new paradigm. *American Psychologist, 43,* 465–472.

Monson, T. C., Hesley, J. W., & Chernick, L. (1982). Specifying when personality traits can and cannot predict behavior: An alternative to abandoning the attempt to predict single-act criteria. *Journal of Personality and Social Psychology, 43,* 385–399.

Montag, I., & Levin, J. (1990). The location of the Self-Monitoring Scale in the factor space of the EPQ and the IGPF. *Journal of Research in Personality, 24,* 45–56.

Montepare, J. M., & Zebrowitz-McArthur, L. (1987). Perceptions of adults with childlike voices in two cultures. *Journal of Experimental Social Psychology, 23,* 331–349.

Montepare, J. M., & Zebrowitz-McArthur, L. (1988). Impressions of people created by age-related qualities of their gaits. *Journal of Personality and Social Psychology, 54,* 547–556.

Moore, J. S., Graziano, W. G., & Millar, M. G. (1987). Physical attractiveness, sex role orientation, and the evaluation of adults and children. *Personality and Social Psychology Bulletin, 13,* 95–102.

Moreland, R. L., & Zajonc, R. B. (1982). Exposure effects in person perception: Familiarity, similarity, and attraction. *Journal of Experimental Social Psychology, 18,* 395–415.

Morell, M. A., Twillman, R. K., & Sullaway, M. E. (1989). Would a Type A date another Type A?: Influence of behavior type and personal attributes in the selection of dating partners. *Journal of Applied Social Psychology, 19,* 918–931.

Moretti, M. M., & Higgins, E. T. (1990). Relating self-discrepancy to self-esteem: The contribution of discrepancy beyond actual-self ratings. *Journal of Experimental Social Psychology, 26,* 108–123.

Morgan, C. D., & Murray, H. A. (1938). Thematic Apperception Test. In H. A. Murray, *Explorations in personality.* New York: Science Editions.

Morris, W. N., & Miller, R. S. (1975). The effects of consensus-breaking and consensus-preempting partners on reduction of conformity. *Journal of Personality and Social Psychology, 11,* 215–223.

Morris, W. N., Miller, R. S., & Spangenberg, S. (1977). The effects of dissenter position and task difficulty on conformity and response to conflict. *Journal of Personality, 45,* 251–266.

Morris, W. N., Worchel, S., Bois, J. L., Pearon, J. A., Rountree, C. A., Samaha, G. M., Wachtler, J., & Wright, S. L. (1976). Collective coping with stress: Group reactions to fear, anxiety, and ambiguity. *Journal of Personality and Social Psychology, 33,* 674–679.

Moscovici, S. (1985). Social influence and conformity. In G. Lindzey & E. Aronson (Eds.), *Handbook of social psychology* (3rd ed.). New York: Random House.

Moser, C. G., & Dyck, D. G. (1989). Type A behavior, uncontrollability, and the activation of hostile self-schema responding. *Journal of Research in Personality, 23,* 248–267.

Moser, K., Gadenne, V., & Schroder, J. (1988). Under what conditions does confirmation seeking obstruct scientific progress? *Psychological Review, 95,* 572–574.

Mosher, D. L. (1968). Measurement of guilt in females by self-report inventories. *Journal of Consulting and Clinical Psychology, 32,* 690–695.

Mosher, D. L., & O'Grady, K. E. (1979). Sex guilt, trait anxiety, and females' subjective sexual arousal to erotica. *Motivation and Emotion, 3,* 235–249.

Mosher, D. L., & Sirkin, M. (1984). Measuring a macho personality constellation. *Journal of Research in Personality, 18,* 150–163.

Muecher, H., & Ungeheuer, H. (1961). Meteorological influence on reaction time, flicker-fusion frequency, job accidents, and medical treatment. *Perceptual and Motor Skills, 12,* 163–168.

Mueller, P., & Major, B. (1989). Self-blame, self-efficacy, and adjustment to abortion. *Journal of Personality and Social Psychology, 57,* 1059–1068.

Mugny, G. (1975). Negotiations, image of the other, and the process of minority influence. *European Journal of Social Psychology, 5,* 209–229.

Mullen, B., Atkins, J. L., Champion, D. S., Edwards, C., Hardy, D., Story, J. E., & Vanderklok, M. (1985). The false consensus effect: A meta-analysis of 115 hypothesis tests. *Journal of Experimental Social Psychology, 21,* 262–283.

Mullen, B., Futrell, D., Stairs, D., Tice, D., Baumeister, R., Dawson, K., Riordan, C., Radloff, C., Kennedy, J., & Rosenfield, P. (1986). Newscasters' facial expressions and voting behavior of viewers: Can a smile elect a president? *Journal of Personality and Social Psychology, 51,* 291–295.

Murnen, S. K., & Byrne, D. (1988). *Development of a scale to measure hyperfemininity.* Unpublished manuscript, State University of New York at Albany.

Murray, D. M., & Wells, G. L. (1982). Does knowledge that a crime was staged affect eyewitness performance? *Journal of Applied Social Psychology, 12,* 42–53.

Murray, H. A. (1962). *Explorations in personality.* New York: Science Editions. (Original work published 1938)

Murstein, B. I. (1972). Physical attractiveness and marital choice. *Journal of Personality and Social Psychology, 22,* 8–12.

Murstein, B. I. (1980). Love at first sight: A myth. *Medical Aspects of Human Sexuality, 14,* 39–41.

Nagar, D., & Pandey, J. (1987). Affect and performance on cognitive task as a function of crowding and noise. *Journal of Applied Social Psychology, 17,* 147–157.

Nagar, D., Pandey, J., & Paulus, P. B. (1988). The effects of residential crowding experience on reactivity to laboratory crowding and noise. *Journal of Applied Social Psychology, 18,* 1423–1442.

Nahemow, L., & Lawton, M. P. (1975). Similarity and propinquity in friendship formation. *Journal of Personality and Social Psychology, 32,* 205–213.

Nasar, J. L. (Ed.). (1988). *Environmental aesthetics: Theory, research, and applications.* New York: Cambridge University Press.

Neale, M. A., & Bazerman, M. H. (1985). The effects of framing and negotiator overconfidence on bargaining behaviors and outcomes. *Academy of Management Journal, 28,* 34–49.

Neimeyer, G. J. (1984). Cognitive complexity and marital satisfaction. *Journal of Social and Clinical Psychology, 2,* 258–263.

Nemeth, C. J. (1986). Differential contributions of majority and minority influence. *Psychological Review, 93,* 23–32.

Neuberg, S. L. (1989). The goal of forming accurate impressions during social interactions: Attenuating the impact of negative expectancies. *Journal of Personality and Social Psychology, 56,* 374–386.

Newbit, P., & Steven, G. (1974). Personal space and stimulus intensity at a Southern California amusement park. *Sociometry, 37,* 105–115.

Newcomb, M. D., McCarthy, W. J., & Bentler, P. M. (1989). Cigarette smoking, academic lifestyle, and social impact efficacy: An eight-year study from early adolescence to young adulthood. *Journal of Applied Social Psychology, 19,* 251–281.

Newcomb, P. R. (1979). Cohabitation in America: An assessment of consequences. *Journal of Marriage and the Family, 41,* 597–603.

Newcomb, T. M. (1961). *The acquaintance process.* New York: Holt, Rinehart, & Winston.

Newman, O. (1972). *Defensible space.* New York: Macmillan.

Newman, P. J., & Cochrane, R. (1987). Wives' employment and husbands' depression. *Social Behavior, 2,* 211–219.

Nicola, J. A. S., & Hawkes, G. R. (1986). Marital satisfaction of dual-career couples: Does sharing increase happiness? *Journal of Social Behavior and Personality, 1,* 47–60.

Nieva, V. F., & Gutek, B. A. (1981). *Women and work: A psychological perspective.* New York: Praeger.

Nisbett, R. E., & Kunda, Z. (1985). Perception of social distributions. *Journal of Personality and Social Psychology, 48,* 297–311.

Nisbett, R. E., & Ross, L. (1980). *Human inference: Strategies and shortcomings of social judgment.* Englewood Cliffs, NJ: Prentice Hall.

No home for hot trash. (1989, December 11). *Time,* p. 81.

Norman, N. M. & Tedeschi, J. T. (1989). Self-presentation, reasoned action, and adolescents' decisions to smoke cigarettes. *Journal of Applied Social Psychology, 19,* 543–558.

Normoyle, J., & Lavrakas, P. J. (1984). Fear of crime in elderly women: Perceptions of control, predictability, and territoriality. *Personality and Social Psychology Bulletin, 10,* 191–202.

Northcraft, G. B., & Neale, M. A. (1987). Experts, amateurs, and real estate: An anchoring-and-adjustment perspective on property pricing decisions. *Organizational Behavior and Human Decision Processes, 39,* 84–97.

Nowicki, S., Jr. (1982). Competition-cooperation as a mediator of locus of control and achievement. *Journal of Research in Personality, 16,* 157–164.

Oettingen, G., Seligman, M. E. P., & Morawska, E. (1988). *Pessimism across cultures: Russian Judaism versus Orthodox Christianity and East versus West Berlin.* Manuscript submitted for publication.

O'Grady, K. E. (1982). "Affect, sex guilt, gender, and the rewarding-punishing effects of erotic stimuli": A reanalysis and reinterpretation. *Journal of Personality and Social Psychology, 43,* 618–622.

O'Grady, K. E. (1989). Physical attractiveness, need for approval, social self-esteem, and maladjustment. *Journal of Social and Clinical Psychology, 8,* 62–69.

Ohbuchi, K., & Kambara, T. (1985). Attacker's intent and awareness of outcome, impression management, and retaliation. *Journal of Experimental Social Psychology, 21,* 321–330.

Ohbuchi, K., Kamdea, M., & Agarie, N. (1989). Apology as aggression control: Its role in mediating appraisal of and response to harm. *Journal of Personality and Social Psychology, 56,* 219–227.

Ohbuchi, K. I., & Ogura, S. (1984). The experience of anger (1): The survey for adults and university students with Averill's questionnaire (Japanese). *Japanese Journal of Criminal Psychology, 22,* 15–35.

Olbrisch, M. E., Weiss, S. M., Stone, G. C., & Schwartz, G. E. (1985). Report of the National Working Conference on Education and Training in Health Psychology. *American Psychologist, 40,* 1038–1041.

Oldham, G. R., & Fried, Y. (1987). Employee reactions to work space characteristics. *Journal of Applied Psychology, 72,* 75–80.

Olson, J. M. (1988). Misattribution, preparatory information, and speech anxiety. *Journal of Personality and Social Psychology, 54,* 758–767.

Olson, J. M., & Ross, M. (1988). False feedback about placebo effectiveness: Consequences for the misattribution of speech anxiety. *Journal of Experimental Social Psychology, 24,* 275–291.

O'Malley, M. N., & Becker, L. A. (1984). Removing the egocentric bias: The relevance of distress cues to evaluation of fairness. *Personality and Social Psychology Bulletin, 10,* 235–242.

O'Malley, P. M., & Bachman, J. G. (1983). Self-esteem: Change and stability between ages 13 and 23. *Developmental Psychology, 19,* 257–268.

O'Neill, P., Duffy, C., Enman, M., Blackmer, E., & Goodwin, J. (1988). Cognition and citizen participation in social action. *Journal of Applied Social Psychology, 18,* 1067–1083.

Orbell, J. M., Van-de-Kargt, A. J., & Dawes, R. M. (1988). Explaining discussion-induced cooperation. *Journal of Personality and Social Psychology, 54,* 811–819.

Organ, D. W. (1988). *Organizational citizenship behavior: The good soldier syndrome.* Lexington, MA: Lexington Books.

Orive, R. (1988). Social projective and social comparison of opinions. *Journal of Personality and Social Psychology, 54,* 953–964.

Osborn, D. R. (1988). Personality traits expressed: Interior design as a behavior-setting plan. *Personality and Social Psychology Bulletin, 14,* 368–373.

O'Sullivan, C. S., Chen, A., Mohapatra, S., Sigelman, L., & Lewis, E. (1988). Voting in ignorance: The politics of smooth-sounding names. *Journal of Applied Social Psychology, 18,* 1094–1106.

O'Sullivan, C. S., & Durso, F. T. (1984). Effects of schema-incongruent information on memory for stereotypical attributes. *Journal of Personality and Social Psychology, 47,* 55–70.

Otis, C. L., & Goldingay, R. (1989). *Campus health guide.* New York: College Board.

Otten, M. W. (1977). Inventory and expressive measures of locus of control and academic performance: A five-year outcome study. *Journal of Personality Assessment, 41,* 644–649.

Ozer, D. J. (1989). Construct validity in personality assessment. In D. M. Buss & N. Cantor (Eds.), *Personality psychology: Recent trends and emerging directions* (pp. 224–234). New York: Springer-Verlag.

Ozer, D. J., & Gjerde, P. F. (1989). Patterns of personality consistency and change from childhood through adolescence. *Journal of Personality, 57,* 483–507.

Padgett, V. R., & Hill, A. K. (1989). Maximizing athletic performance in endurance events: A comparison of cognitive strategies. *Journal of Applied Social Psychology, 19,* 331–340.

Pagan, G., & Aiello, J. R. (1982). Development of personal space among Puerto Ricans. *Journal of Nonverbal Behavior, 7,* 59–68.

Page, R. R. (1978, May). *Environmental influences on prosocial behavior: The effect of temperature.* Paper presented at the meeting of the Midwestern Psychological Association, Chicago.

Paloutzian, R. F., & Ellison, C. W. (1979, May). *Emotional, behavioral, and physical correlates of loneliness.* Paper presented at the UCLA Research Conference on Loneliness, Los Angeles.

Park, B., & Flink, C. (1989). A social relations analysis of agreement in liking judgments. *Journal of Personality and Social Psychology, 56,* 506–518.

Park, K. S. (1980). *The effects of attitude similarity and dissimilarity on interpersonal attraction.* Unpublished manuscript, Jeobuk National University, Jeonju, Korea.

Parke, R. D., Berkowitz, L., Leyes, J. P., West, S. G., & Sebastian, R. J. (1977). Some effects of violent and nonviolent movies on the behavior of juvenile delinquents. In L. Berkowitz (Ed.), *Advances in experimental social psychology* (Vol. 10). New York: Academic Press.

Patch, M. E. (1986). The role of source legitimacy in sequential request strategies of compliance. *Personality and Social Psychology Bulletin, 12,* 199–205.

Patterson, M. L. (1976). An arousal model of interpersonal intimacy. *Psychological Review, 83,* 235–245.

Paulus, P. B. (1980). Crowding. In P. B. Paulus (Ed.), *Psychology of group influence.* Hillsdale, NJ: Erlbaum.

Paulus, P. B. (Ed.). (1989). *Psychology of group influence* (2nd ed.). Hillsdale, NJ: Erlbaum.

Paulus, P. B., Aunis, A. B., Seta, J. J., Schkade, J. K., & Matthews, R. W. (1976). Crowding does affect task performance. *Journal of Personality and Social Psychology, 34,* 248–253.

Paulus, P. B., & McCain, G. (1983). Crowding in jails. *Basic and Applied Social Psychology, 4,* 89–107.

Paunonen, S. V. (1988). Trait relevance and the differential predictability of behavior. *Journal of Personality, 56,* 599–619.

Peabody, D., & Goldberg, L. R. (1989). Some determinants of factor structures from personality-trait descriptors. *Journal of Personality and Social Psychology, 57*, 552–567.

Pelham, B. W., & Swann, W. B., Jr. (1989). From self-conceptions to self-worth: On the sources and structure of global self-esteem. *Journal of Personality and Social Psychology, 57*, 672–680.

Pendleton, M. G., & Batson, C. D. (1979). Self-presentation and the door-in-the-face technique for inducing compliance. *Personality and Social Psychology Bulletin, 5*, 77–81.

Penk, W. (1969). Age changes and correlates of internal-external locus of control scales. *Psychological Reports, 25*, 856.

Pennebaker, J. W., & Beall, S. (1986). Confronting a traumatic event: Toward an understanding of inhibition and disease. *Journal of Abnormal Psychology, 95*, 274–281.

Pennebaker, J. W., Hughes, C. F., & O'Heron, R. C. (1987). The psychophysiology of confession: Linking inhibitory and psychosomatic processes. *Journal of Personality and Social Psychology, 52*, 781–793.

Pennington, N., & Hastie, R. (1990). Practical implications of psychological research on juror and jury decision making. *Personality and Social Psychology Bulletin, 16*, 90–105.

People say love still important. (1987, February 14). *Albany Times Union*, p. A2.

Peplau, L. A., & Perlman, D. (1982). Perspectives on loneliness. In L. A. Peplau & D. Perlman (Eds.), *Loneliness: A sourcebook of current theory, research, and therapy*. New York: Wiley.

Perdue, C. W., & Gurtman, M. B. (1990). Evidence for the automaticity of ageism. *Journal of Experimental Social Psychology, 26*, 199–216.

Perry, J. D., & Simpson, M. E. (1987). Violent crimes in a city: Environmental determinants. *Environment and Behavior, 19*, 77–90.

Peters, L. H., Hartke, D. D., & Pohlmann, J. T. (1985). Fiedler's contingency theory of leadership: An application of the meta-analysis procedures of Schmidt and Hunter. *Psychological Bulletin, 97*, 274–285.

Peters, L. H., O'Connor, E. J., Weekley, J., Pooyan, A., Frank, B., & Erenkrantz, B. (1984). Sex bias and managerial evaluations: A replication and extension. *Journal of Applied Psychology, 69*, 349–352.

Peterson, C. (1980). Memory and the "dispositional shift." *Social Psychology Quarterly, 43*, 372–380.

Peterson, C., Seligman, M. E. P., & Vaillant, G. (1988). Pessimistic explanatory style is a risk factor for physical illness: A thirty-five-year longitudinal study. *Journal of Personality and Social Psychology, 55*, 23–27.

Peterson, E. A., Augenstein, J. S., Tanis, D. C., & Augenstein, A. G. (1981). Noise raises blood pressure without impairing auditory sensitivity. *Science, 211*, 1450–1452.

Peterson, R. C., & Thurstone, L. (1933). *The effect of motion pictures on the social attitudes of high school children*. Chicago: University of Chicago Press.

Pettigrew, T. F. (1959). Regional differences in anti-Negro prejudice. *Journal of Abnormal and Social Psychology, 59*, 28–36.

Pettigrew, T. F. (1981). Extending the stereotype concept. In D. L. Hamilton (Ed.), *Cognitive processes in stereotyping and intergroup behavior* (pp. 303–331). Hillsdale, NJ: Erlbaum.

Petty, R. E., & Cacioppo, J. T. (1981). *Attitudes and persuasion: Classic and contemporary approaches*. Dubuque, IA: Brown.

Petty, R. E., & Cacioppo, J. T. (1985). *Communication and persuasion: Central and peripheral routes to attitude change*. New York: Springer-Verlag.

Petty, R. E., & Cacioppo, J. T. (1986). The elaboration likelihood model of persuasion. In L. Berkowitz (Ed.), *Advances in experimental social psychology* (Vol. 19, pp. 123–205). New York: Academic Press.

Petty, R. E., Ostrom, T. M., & Brock, T. C. (Eds.). (1981). *Cognitive responses in persuasion*. Hillsdale, NJ: Erlbaum.

Petty, R. E., Wells, G. L., & Brock, T. C. (1976). Distraction can enhance or reduce yielding to propaganda: Thought disruption versus effort justification. *Journal of Personality and Social Psychology, 34*, 874–884.

Pfeiffer, J. (1988). How not to lose the trade wars by cultural gaffs. *Smithsonian, 18*, 145–156.

Piliavin, J. A. (1987). Age, race, and sex similarity to candidates and voting preference. *Journal of Applied Social Psychology, 17*, 351–368.

Piliavin, J. A., Dovidio, J. F., Gaertner, S. S., & Clark, R. D., III. (1981). *Emergency intervention*. New York: Academic Press.

Pilisuk, M., & Acredolo, C. (1988). Fear of technological hazards: One concern or many? *Social Behavior, 3*, 17–24.

Pilisuk, M., Boylan, R., & Acredolo, C. (1987). Social support, life stress, and subsequent medical care utilization. *Health Psychology, 6*, 273–288.

Pines, A., & Aronson, E. (1983). Antecedents, correlates, and consequences of sexual jealousy. *Journal of Personality, 51*, 108–136.

Pinto, R. P., & Hollandsworth, J. G., Jr. (1984). A measure of possessiveness in intimate relationships. *Journal of Social and Clinical Psychology, 2*, 273–279.

Pittenger, J. B., Mark, L. S., & Johnson, D. F. (1989). Longitudinal stability of facial attractiveness. *Bulletin of the Psychonomic Society, 27*, 171–174.

Platz, S. G., & Hosch, H. M. (1988). Cross-racial/ethnic eyewitness identification: A field study. *Journal of Applied Social Psychology, 18*, 972–984.

Pliner, P., & Chaiken, S. (1990). Eating, social motives, and self-presentation in women and men. *Journal of Experimental Social Psychology, 26*, 240–254.

Pliner, P., Hart, H., Kohl, J., & Saari, D. (1974). Compliance without pressure: Some further data on the foot-in-the-door technique. *Journal of Experimental Social Psychology, 10*, 17–22.

Plous, S. (1989). Thinking the unthinkable: The effects of anchoring on likelihood estimates of nuclear war. *Journal of Applied Social Psychology, 19*, 67–91.

Pollock, L. M., & Patterson, A. H. (1980). Territoriality and fear of crime in elderly and nonelderly home owners. *Journal of Social Psychology, 111*, 119–129.

Popper, K. (1959). *The logic of scientific discovery*. London: Hutchinson.

Porter, C., Markus, H., & Nurius, P. S. (1984). *Conceptions of possibility among people in crisis*. Unpublished manuscript, University of Michigan, Ann Arbor.

Powers, P. C., & Geen, R. G. (1972). Effects of the behavior and perceived arousal of a model on instrumental aggression. *Journal of Personality and Social Psychology, 23*, 175–184.

Pratkanis, A. R., Breckler, S. J., & Greenwald, A. G. (Eds.). (1989). *Attitude structure and function*. Hillsdale, NJ: Erlbaum.

Pratkanis, A. R., Greenwald, A. G., Leippe, M. R., & Baumgardner, M. H. (1988). In search of reliable persuasion effects: III. The sleeper effect is dead. Long live the sleeper effect. *Journal of Personality and Social Psychology, 54*, 203–218.

Pretty, G. H., & Seligman, C. (1984). Affect and the overjustification effect. *Journal of Personality and Social Psychology, 46*, 1241–1253.

Price, K. H., & Vandenberg, S. G. (1979). Matching for physical attractiveness in married couples. *Personality and Social Psychology Bulletin, 5*, 398–400.

Prince-Embury, S., & Rooney, J. F. (1989). A comparison of residents who moved versus those who remained prior to restart of Three Mile Island. *Journal of Applied Social Psychology, 19*, 959–975.

Pritchard, R. D., Dunnette, M. D., & Jorgenson, D. O. (1972). Effects of perceptions of equity and inequity on worker performance and satisfaction. *Journal of Applied Psychology, 56*, 75–94.

Prohaska, T. R., Keller, M. L., Leventhal, E. A., & Leventhal, H. (1987). Impact of symptoms and aging attribution on emotions and coping. *Health Psychology, 6*, 495–514.

Pruitt, D. G. (1983). Integrative agreements: Nature and antecedents. In M. H. Bazerman & R. J. Lewicki (Eds.), *Negotiation in organizations*. Beverly Hills, CA: Sage.

Pruitt, D. G., & Rubin, J. Z. (1986). *Social conflict: Escalation, stalemate, and settlement*. New York: Random House.

Pryor, J. B., Biggons, F. X., Wicklund, R. A., Fazio, R. H., & Hood, R. (1977). Self-focus attention and self-report validity. *Journal of Personality, 45*, 514–527.

Przybyla, D. P. J., Byrne, D., & Allegeier, E. R. (1988). Sexual attitudes as correlates of sexual details in human figure drawing. *Archives of Sexual Behavior, 17*, 99–105.

Przybyla, D. P. J., Murnen, S., & Byrne, D. (1985). *Arousal and attraction: Anxiety reduction, misattribution or response strength?* Unpublished manuscript, State University of New York at Albany.

Pursell, S. A., & Banikiotes, P. G. (1978). Androgyny and initial interpersonal attraction. *Personality and Social Psychology Bulletin, 4,* 235–243.

Putallaz, M. & Gottman, J. M. (1981). Social skills and group acceptance. In S. R. Asher & J. M. Gottman (Eds.), *The development of children's friendships.* New York: Cambridge University Press.

Quadrel, M. J., & Lau, R. R. (1989). Health promotion, health locus of control, and health behavior: Two field experiments. *Journal of Applied Social Psychology, 19,* 1497–1521.

Quattrone, G. A. (1986). On the perception of a group's variability. In S. Worchel & W. Ausin (Eds.), *The psychology of intergroup relations* (Vol. 2, pp. 25–48). Chicago: Nelson-Hall.

Quinn, R. E. (1977). Coping with Cupid: The formation, impact, and management of romantic relationships in organizations. *Administrative Science Quarterly, 22,* 30–45.

Quinn, R. P., & Staines, G. L. (1979). *The 1977 quality of employment survey.* Ann Arbor, MI: Institute for Social Research.

Raeburn, P. (1989, September 19). One in 24 inmates infected with AIDS. *Albany Times Union,* pp. A1, A8.

Raelin, J. A. (1984). An examination of deviant-adaptive behavior in the organizational careers of professionals. *Academy of Management Review, 9,* 413–427.

Raine, A., Roger, D. B., & Venables, P. H. (1982). Locus of control and socialization. *Journal of Research in Personality, 16,* 147–156.

Rainwater, L. (1966). Fear and the house-as-haven in the lower class. *Journal of the American Institute of Planners, 32,* 23–31.

Rajecki, D. J. (1989). *Attitudes* (2nd ed.). Sunderland, MA: Sinauer Associates.

Rajecki, D. W., Kidd, R. F., & Ivins, B. (1976). Social facilitation in chickens: A different level of analysis. *Journal of Experimental Social Psychology, 12,* 233–246.

Rajecki, D. W., Nerenz, D. R., Freedenberg, T. G., & McCarthy, P. J. (1981). Components of aggression in chickens and conceptualizations of aggression in general. *Journal of Personality and Social Psychology, 37,* 1902–1914.

Ramirez, J., Byrant, J., & Zillmann, D. (1983). Effects of erotica on retaliatory behavior as a function of level of prior provocation. *Journal of Personality and Social Psychology, 43,* 971–978.

Rapaport, A. (1973). *Experimental games and their uses in psychology.* Morristown, NJ: General Learning Press.

Rapaport, A. (1980). *Fights, games, and debates.* Ann Arbor: University of Michigan Press.

Rapaport, A., & Bornstein, G. (1987). Intergroup competition for the provision of binary public goods. *Psychological Review, 94,* 291–299.

Rapaport, A., & Bornstein, G. (1989). Solving public good problems in competition between equal and unequal size groups. *Journal of Conflict Resolution, 33,* 460–479.

Rapaport, A., Bornstein, G., & Erev, I. (1989). Intergroup competition for public goods: Effects of unequal resources and relative group size. *Journal of Personality and Social Psychology, 56,* 748–756.

Rasmussen, K. G., Jr. (1984). Nonverbal behavior, verbal behavior, résumé credentials, and selection interview outcomes. *Journal of Applied Psychology, 69,* 551–556.

Raven, B. H., & Kruglanski, A. (1970). Conflict and power. In P. Swingle (Ed.), *The structure of conflict.* New York: Academic Press.

Raviv, A., & Palgi, Y. (1985). The perception of social-environmental characteristics in Kibbutz families with family-based and communal sleeping arrangements. *Journal of Personality and Social Psychology, 49,* 376–385.

Reed, D., & Weinberg, M. S. (1984). Premarital coitus: Developing and establishing sexual scripts. *Social Psychology Quarterly, 47,* 129–138.

Reeder, G. D., Fletcher, G. J. O., & Furman, K. (1989). The role of observers' expectations in attitude attribution. *Journal of Experimental Social Psychology, 25,* 168–188.

Reimanis, G. (1971). *Effects of experimental IE modification techniques and home environment variables on IE.* Paper presented at the meeting of the American Psychological Association, Washington, DC.

Reis, H. T., Nezlek, J., & Wheeler, L. (1980). Physical attractiveness in social interaction. *Journal of Personality and Social Psychology, 38,* 604–617.

Reisenzein, R. (1983). The Schachter theory of emotion: Two decades later. *Psychological Bulletin, 94,* 239–264.

Reisenzein, R. (1986). A structural equation analysis of Weiner's attribution-affect model of helping behavior. *Journal of Personality and Social Psychology, 50,* 1123–1133.

Reisman, J. M. (1984). Friendliness and its correlates. *Journal of Social and Clinical Psychology, 2,* 143–155.

Renshaw, D. C. (1982). Divorce and loneliness. *Medical Aspects of Human Sexuality, 16(7),* 23–25, 29–32.

Repetti, R. L. (1989). Effects of daily workload on subsequent behavior during marital interaction: The roles of social withdrawal and spouse support. *Journal of Personality and Social Psychology, 57,* 651–659.

Research and Forecasts, Inc. (1981). *The Connecticut Mutual Life report on American values in the '80s: The impact of belief.* Hartford: Connecticut Mutual Life Insurance.

Revenson, T. A. (1981). Coping with loneliness: The impact of causal attributions. *Personality and Social Psychology Bulletin, 7,* 565–571.

Reychler, L. (1979). The effectiveness of a pacifist strategy in conflict resolution. *Journal of Conflict Resolution, 23,* 228–260.

Reynolds, V., Falger, V. S. E., & Vine, I. (Eds.). (1987). *The sociobiology of ethnocentrism: Evolutionary dimensions of xenophobia, discrimination, racism, and nationalism.* Athens: University of Georgia Press.

Rhodewalt, R., & Davison, J., Jr. (1983). Reactance and the coronary-prone behavior pattern: The role of self-attribution in response to reduced behavioral freedom. *Journal of Personality and Social Psychology, 44,* 220–228.

Richardson, B., Sorensen, J., & Sonderstrom, E. J. (1987). Explaining the social and psychological impacts of a nuclear power plant accident. *Journal of Applied Social Psychology, 17,* 16–36.

Ridley, M., & Dawkins, R. (1981). The natural selection of altruism. In J. P. Rushton & R. M. Sorrentino (Eds.), *Altruism and helping behavior.* Hillsdale, NJ: Erlbaum.

Riess, M., & Schlenker, B. R. (1977). Attitude change and responsibility avoidance as modes of dilemma resolution in forced-compliance situations. *Journal of Personality and Social Psychology, 35,* 21–30.

Rigby, K. (1988). Sexist attitudes and authoritarian personality characteristics among Australian adolescents. *Journal of Research in Personality, 22,* 465–473.

Riggio, R. E. (1986). Assessment of basic social skills. *Journal of Personality and Social Psychology, 51,* 649–660.

Riggio, R. E. (1990). *Industrial and organizational psychology.* New York: Harcourt Brace Jovanovich.

Riggio, R. E., & Friedman, H. S. (1986). Impression formation: The role of expressive behavior. *Journal of Personality and Social Psychology, 50,* 421–427.

Riordan, C. A. (1978). Equal-status interracial contact: A review and revision of a concept. *International Journal of Intercultural Relations, 2,* 161–185.

Riordan, C. A., & Tedeschi, J. T. (1983). Attraction in aversive environments: Some evidence for classical conditioning and negative reinforcement. *Journal of Personality and Social Psychology, 44,* 684–692.

Rippetoe, P. A., & Rogers, R. W. (1987). Effects of components of protection-motivation theory on adaptive and maladaptive coping with a health threat. *Journal of Personality and Social Psychology, 52,* 596–604.

Riskind, J. H., & Wilson, D. W. (1982). Interpersonal attraction for the competent person: Unscrambling the competition paradox. *Journal of Applied Social Psychology, 12,* 444–452.

Rittle, R. H. (1981). Changes in helping behavior: Self- versus situation perception as mediators of the foot-in-the-door effect. *Personality and Social Psychology Bulletin, 7,* 431–437.

Robberson, M. R., & Rogers, R. W. (1988). Beyond fear appeals: Negative and positive persuasive appeals to health and self-esteem. *Journal of Applied Social Psychology, 18,* 277–287.

Robbins, S. P. (1989). *Organizational behavior: Concepts, controversies, and applications* (4th ed.). Englewood Cliffs, NJ: Prentice Hall.

Roberts, J. V., & Edwards, D. (1989). Contextual effects in judgments of crimes, criminals, and the purposes of sentencing. *Journal of Applied Social Psychology, 19,* 902–917.

Robinson, M. (1985). Jesse Helms, take stock: Study shows Rather bears no liberal bias. *Washington Journalism Review, 7,* 14–17.

Rodgers, J. L., Billy, J. O. B., & Udry, J. R. (1984). A model of friendship similarity in mildly deviant behaviors. *Journal of Applied Social Psychology, 14,* 413–425.

Rodin, J., & Salovey, P. (1989). Health psychology. In M. R. Rosenzweig & L. W. Porter (Eds.), *Annual review of psychology* (Vol. 40, pp. 533–579). Palo Alto, CA: Annual Reviews.

Rodin, M. J. (1987). Who is memorable to whom: A study of cognitive disregard. *Social Cognition, 5,* 144–165.

Roethlisberger, F. G., & Dickson, W. J. (1939). *Management and the worker.* Cambridge, MA: Harvard University Press.

Rofe, Y. (1984). Stress and affiliation: A utility theory. *Psychological Review, 91,* 235–250.

Rofe, Y., Lewin, I., & Hoffman, M. (1987). Affiliation patterns among cancer patients. *Psychological Medicine, 17,* 419–424.

Rogers, R. W. (1980). *Subjects' reactions to experimental deception.* Unpublished manuscript, University of Alabama, Tuscaloosa.

Rogers, R. W. (1983). Cognitive and physiological processes in fear appeals and attitude change: A revised theory of protection motivation. In J. R. Cacioppo & R. E. Petty (Eds.), *Social psychophysiology: A sourcebook* (pp. 153–176). New York: Guilford Press.

Rogers, R. W., & Ketcher, C. M. (1979). Effects of anonymity and arousal on aggression. *Journal of Psychology, 102,* 1–13.

Rook, K. S. (1987). Effect of case history versus abstract information on health attitudes and behavior. *Journal of Applied Social Psychology, 17,* 533–554.

Rook, K. S., & Peplau, L. A. (1982). Perspectives on helping the lonely. In L. A. Peplau & D. Perlman (Eds.), *Loneliness: A sourcebook of current theory, research, and therapy.* New York: Wiley.

Rorschach, H. (1921). *Psychodiagnostics.* Berne: Hans Huber.

Rose, S. M. (1984). How friendships end: Patterns among young adults. *Journal of Social and Personal Relationships, 1,* 267–277.

Rosenbaum, M. E. (1980). Cooperation and competition. In P. B. Paulus (Ed.), *The psychology of group influence.* Hillsdale, NJ: Erlbaum.

Rosenbaum, M. E. (1986). The repulsion hypothesis: On the nondevelopment of relationships. *Journal of Personality and Social Psychology, 51,* 1156–1166.

Rosenblatt, A., & Greenberg, J. (1988). Depression and interpersonal attraction: The role of perceived similarity. *Journal of Personality and Social Psychology, 54,* 112–119.

Rosenfield, D., Folger, R., & Adelmann, H. F. (1980). When rewards reflect competence: A qualification of the overjustification effect. *Journal of Personality and Social Psychology, 39,* 368–376.

Rosenfield, D., Greenberg, J., Folger, R., & Borys, R. (1982). Effect of an encounter with a black panhandler on subsequent helping for blacks: Tokenism or conforming to a negative stereotype? *Personality and Social Psychology Bulletin, 8,* 664–671.

Rosenhan, D. L., Salovey, P., & Hargis, K. (1981). The joys of helping: Focus of attention mediates the impact of positive affect on altruism. *Journal of Personality and Social Psychology, 40,* 899–905.

Rosenhan, D. L., Underwood, B., & Moore, B. (1974). Affect moderates self-gratification and altruism. *Journal of Personality and Social Psychology, 30,* 546–552.

Rosenthal, A. M. (1964). *Thirty-eight witnesses.* New York: McGraw-Hill.

Rosenthal, R., Hall, J. A., DiMatteo, M. R., Rogers, P. L., & Archer, D. (1979). *Sensitivity to nonverbal communication: The PONS test.* Baltimore, MD: John Hopkins University Press.

Ross, I. (1985, April 29). Employers win big on the move to two-tier contracts. *Fortune,* pp. 82–92.

Ross, M. (1989). Relation of implicit theories to the construction of personal histories. *Psychological Review, 96,* 341–357.

Ross, M., & Fletcher, G. J. O. (1985). Attribution and social perception. In G. Lindzey & E. Aronson (Eds.), *Handbook of social psychology.* New York: Random House.

Ross, M., Layton, B., Erickson, B., & Schopler, J. (1973). Affect, facial regard, and reactions to crowding. *Journal of Personality and Social Psychology, 28,* 69–76.

Ross, M., & Olson, J. M. (1981). An expectancy-attribution model of the effects of placebos. *Psychological Review, 88,* 418–437.

Roter, D. L. (1984). Patient question asking in physician-patient interaction. *Health Psychology, 3,* 395–409.

Roth, D. L., Wiebe, D. J., Fillingim, R. B., & Shay, K. A. (1989). Life events, fitness, hardiness, and health: A simultaneous analysis of

proposed stress-resistance effects. *Journal of Personality and Social Psychology, 57,* 136–142.

Rothbart, M., & Hallmark, W. (1988). In-group–out-group differences in the perceived efficacy of coercion and conciliation in resolving social conflict. *Journal of Personality and Social Psychology, 55,* 248–257.

Rotter, J. B. (1954). *Social learning and clinical psychology.* Englewood Cliffs, NJ: Prentice Hall.

Rotter, J. B. (1966). Generalized expectancies for internal versus external control of reinforcement. *Psychological Monographs, 80* (Whole No. 609).

Rotton, J., & Frey, J. (1985a). Air pollution, weather, and violent crimes: Concomitant time-series analysis of archival date. *Journal of Personality and Social Psychology, 49,* 1207–1220.

Rotton, J., & Frey, J. (1985b). Psychological costs of air pollution: Atmospheric conditions, seasonal trends, and psychiatric emergencies. *Population and Environment, 7,* 3–16.

Rotton, J., Frey, J., Barry, T., Milligan, M., & Fitzpatrick, M. (1979). The air pollution experience and physical aggression. *Journal of Applied Social Psychology, 9,* 397–412.

Rotton, J., & Kelley, I. W. (1985). Much ado about the full moon: A meta-analysis of lunar-lunacy research. *Psychological Bulletin, 97,* 286–306.

Routh, D. K., & Ernst, A. R. (1984). Somatization disorder in relatives of children and adolescents with functional abdominal pain. *Journal of Pediatric Psychology, 50,* 427–437.

Rozin, P., Millman, L., & Nemeroff, C. (1986). Operation of the laws of sympathetic magic in disgust and other domains. *Journal of Personality and Social Psychology, 50,* 703–712.

Ruback, R. B., Carr, T. S., & Hopper, C. H. (1986). Perceived control in prison: Its relation to reported crowding stress, and symptoms. *Journal of Applied Social Psychology, 16,* 375–386.

Rubin, J. Z. (1985). Deceiving ourselves about deception: Comment on Smith and Richardson's "Amelioration of deception and harm in psychological research." *Journal of Personality and Social Psychology, 48,* 252–253.

Rubin, J. Z., Brockner, J., Eckenrode, J., Enright, M. A., & Johnson-George, C. (1980). Weakness as strength: Test of a "my hands are tied" ploy in bargaining. *Personality and Social Psychology Bulletin, 6,* 216–221.

Rubin, Z. (1973). *Liking and loving: An invitation to social psychology.* New York: Holt, Rinehart, & Winston.

Rubin, Z. (1974). From liking to loving: Patterns of attraction in dating relationships. In T. L. Huston (Ed.), *Foundations of interpersonal attraction.* New York: Academic Press.

Rubin, Z. (1982). Children without friends. In L. A. Peplau & D. Perlman (Eds.), *Loneliness: A sourcebook of current theory, research, and therapy.* New York: Wiley.

Rubin, Z., Peplau, L. A., & Hill, C. T. (1981). Loving and leaving: Sex differences in romantic attachments. *Sex Roles, 7,* 821–835.

Rule, B. G., Bisanz, G. L., & Kohn, M. (1985). Anatomy of a persuasion schema: Targets, goals, and strategies. *Journal of Personality and Social Psychology, 48,* 1127–1140.

Rule, B. G., Taylor, B. R., & Dobbs, A. R. (1987). Priming effects of heat on aggressive thoughts. *Social Cognition, 5,* 131–143.

Rusbult, C. E. (1980). Commitment and satisfaction in romantic associations: A test of the investment model. *Journal of Experimental Social Psychology, 16,* 172–186.

Rusbult, C. E. (1983). A longitudinal test of the investment model: The development (and deterioration) of satisfaction and commitment in heterosexual involvements. *Journal of Personality and Social Psychology, 45,* 101–117.

Rusbult, C. E., Johnson, D. J., & Morrow, G. D. (1986). Impact of couple patterns of problem solving on distress and nondistress in dating relationships. *Journal of Personality and Social Psychology, 50,* 744–753.

Rusbult, C. E., Morrow, G. D., & Johnson, D. J. (1990). Self-esteem and problem-solving behavior in close relationships. *British Journal of Social Psychology.*

Rusbult, C. E., Musante, L., & Solomon, M. (1982). The effects of clarity of decision rule and favorability of verdict on satisfaction with resolution of conflicts. *Journal of Applied Social Psychology, 12,* 304–317.

Rusbult, C. E., & Zembrodt, I. M. (1983). Responses to dissatisfaction in romantic involvements: A multidimensional scaling analysis. *Journal of Experimental Social Psychology, 19,* 274–293.

Rushton, J. P. (1988a). Epigenetic rules in moral development: Distal-proximal approaches to altruism and aggression. *Aggressive Behavior, 14,* 35–50.

Rushton, J. P. (1988b). Genetic similarity, mate choice, and fecundity in humans. *Ethology and Sociobiology, 9,* 329–333.

Rushton, J. P. (1989a). Genetic similarity, human altruism, and group selection. *Behavioral and Brain Sciences, 12,* 503–559.

Rushton, J. P. (1989b). Genetic similarity in male friendships. *Ethology and Sociobiology, 10,* 361–373.

Rushton, J. P., & Nicholson, I. R. (1988). Genetic similarity theory, intelligence, and human mate choice. *Ethology and Sociobiology, 9,* 45–57.

Rushton, J. P., Russell, R. J. H., & Wells, P. A. (1984). Genetic similarity theory: Beyond kin selection. *Behavior Genetics, 14,* 179–193.

Russell, D., Peplau, L. A., & Cutrona, C. E. (1980). The revised UCLA Loneliness Scale: Concurrent and discriminant validity evidence. *Journal of Personality and Social Psychology, 39,* 472–480.

Russell, J. A., Ward, L. M., & Pratt, G. (1981). Affective quality attributed to environments: A factor analytic study. *Environment and Behavior, 13,* 259–288.

Rustemli, A. (1986). Male and female personal space needs and escape reactions under intrusion: A Turkish sample. *International Journal of Psychology, 21,* 503–512.

Rutkowski, G. K., Gruder, C. L., & Romer, D. (1983). Group cohesiveness, social norms, and bystander intervention. *Journal of Personality and Social Psychology, 44,* 545–552.

Rutledge, L. L., & Hupka, R. B. (1985). The facial feedback hypothesis: Methodological concerns and new supporting evidence. *Motivation and Emotion, 9,* 219–240.

Ryckman, R. M., Robbins, M. A., Kaczor, L. M., & Gold, J. A. (1989). Male and female raters' stereotyping of male and female physiques. *Personality and Social Psychology Bulletin, 15,* 244–251.

Saal, F. E., & Knight, P. A. (1988). *Industrial/organizational psychology: Science and practice.* Belmont, CA: Wadsworth.

Sadalla, E. K., Kenrick, D. T., & Vershure, B. (1987). Dominance and heterosexual attraction. *Journal of Personality and Social Psychology, 52,* 730–738.

Sadalla, E. K., Sheets, V., & McCreath, H. (1990). The cognition of urban tempo. *Environment and Behavior, 22,* 230–254.

Saegert, S. (1985). The role of housing in the experience of dwelling. In I. Altman & C. Werner (Eds.), *Home environments: Human behavior and environment* (Vol. 8, pp. 287–309). New York: Plenum.

Sagan, C. (1989, February 5). The secret of the Persian chessboard. *Parade,* pp. 14–15.

Salovey, P., & Birnbaum, D. (1989). Influence of mood on health-relevant cognitions. *Journal of Personality and Social Psychology, 57,* 539–551.

Salovey, P., & Rodin, J. (1986). The differentiation of social-comparison jealousy and romantic jealousy. *Journal of Personality and Social Psychology, 50,* 1100–1112.

Samdahl, D. M., & Robertson, R. (1989). Social determinants of environmental concern: Specification and test of the model. *Environment and Behavior, 21,* 57–81.

Sanchez, E., & Wiesenfeld, E. (1987). Environmental psychology: A new field of application in psychology and a new professional role for the psychologist. *Interamerican Journal of Psychology, 21,* 90–100.

Sande, G. N., Goethals, G. R., & Radloff, C. E. (1988). Perceiving one's own traits and others': The multifaceted self. *Journal of Personality and Social Psychology, 54,* 13–20.

Sanders, G. S. (1983). An attentional process model of social facilitation. In A. Hare, H. Bumberg, V. Kent, & M. Davies (Eds.), *Small groups.* London: Wiley.

Sanders, G. S. (1984). Effects of context cues on eyewitness identification responses. *Journal of Applied Social Psychology, 14,* 386–397.

Sanders, G. S., & Chiu, W. (1988). Eyewitness errors in the free recall of actions. *Journal of Applied Social Psychology, 18,* 1241–1259.

Sanna, L. J., & Shotland, R. L. (1990). Valence of anticipated evaluation and social facilitation. *Journal of Experimental Social Psychology, 26,* 82–92.

Sato, K. (1987). Distribution of the cost of maintaining common resources. *Journal of Experimental Social Psychology, 23,* 19–31.

Schachter, S. (1951). Deviation, rejection, and communication. *Journal of Abnormal and Social Psychology, 46,* 190–207.

Schachter, S. (1959). *The psychology of affiliation.* Stanford, CA: Stanford University Press.

Schachter, S. (1964). The interaction of cognitive and physiological determinants of emotional state. In L. Berkowitz (Ed.), *Advances in experimental social psychology* (Vol. 1, pp. 48–81). New York: Academic Press.

Schachter, S., & Singer, J. E. (1962). Cognitive, social, and physiological determinants of emotional states. *Psychological Review, 69,* 379–399.

Schaeffer, M. A., Baum, A., Paulus, P. B., & Gaes, G. G. (1988). Architecturally mediated effects of social density in prison. *Environment and Behavior, 20,* 3–19.

Schaeffer, M. H., Street, S. W., Singer, J. E., & Baum, A. (1988). Effects of control on the stress reactions of commuters. *Journal of Applied Social Psychology, 18,* 944–957.

Schaller, M., & Cialdini, R. B. (1988). The economics of empathetic helping: Support for a mood management motive. *Journal of Experimental Social Psychology, 24,* 163–181.

Schaller, M., & Maas, A. (1989). Illusory correlation and social categorization: Toward an integration of motivational and cognitive factors in stereotype formation. *Journal of Personality and Social Psychology. 56,* 709–721.

Scheier, M. F., & Carver, C. S. (1987). Dispositional optimism and physical well-being: The influence of generalized outcome expectancies in health. *Journal of Personality, 55,* 169–210.

Scheier, M. F., Matthews, K. A., Owens, J. F., Magovern, G. J., Sr., Lefebvre, R. C., Abbott, R. A., & Carver, C. S. (1989). Dispositional optimism and recovery from coronary artery bypass surgery: The beneficial effects on physical and psychological well-being. *Journal of Personality and Social Psychology, 57,* 1024–1040.

Scher, S. J., & Cooper, J. (1989). Motivational basis of dissonance: The singular role of behavioral consequences. *Journal of Personality and Social Psychology, 56,* 899–906.

Schleifer, S. J., Keller, S. E., Camerino, M., Thornton, J. C., & Stein, M. (1983). Suppression of lymphocyte function following bereavement. *Journal of American Medical Association, 250,* 374–377.

Schlenker, B. R. (1980). *Impression management: The self-concept, social identity, and interpersonal relations.* Belmont, CA: Brooks/Cole.

Schlenker, B. R. (1982). Self-contemplations. *Contemporary Psychology, 27,* 615–616.

Schmidt, G., & Weiner, B. (1988). An attributional-affect-action theory of behavior: Replications of judgments of helping. *Personality and Social Psychology Bulletin, 14,* 610–621.

Schmitt, B. H. (1988). Social comparison in romantic jealousy. *Personality and Social Psychology Bulletin, 14,* 374–387.

Schmitt, B., Gilvoch, T. K., Goore, N., & Joseph, L. (1986). Mere presence and social facilitation: One more time. *Journal of Experimental Social Psychology, 22,* 242–248.

Schneider, B. E. (1982). Consciousness about sexual harassment among heterosexual and lesbian women workers. *Journal of Social Issues, 38(4),* 75–98.

Schneider, S. H. (1989). *Global warming.* San Francisco: Sierra Club.

Schoenrade, P. A., Batson, C. D., Brandt, J. R., & Loud, R. E. (1986). Attachment, accountability, and motivation to benefit another not in distress. *Journal of Personality and Social Psychology, 51,* 557–563.

Schofield, J. W., & Pavelchak, M. A. (1989). Fallout from "The Day After": The impact of a TV film on attitudes related to nuclear war. *Journal of Applied Social Psychology, 19,* 433–448.

Schoorman, F. D. (1988). Escalation bias in performance appraisals: An unintended consequence of supervisor participation in hiring decisions. *Journal of Applied Psychology, 73,* 58–62.

Schopler, J., & Stockdale, J. (1977). An interference analysis of crowding. *Environmental Psychology and Nonverbal Behavior, 1,* 81–88.

Schrank, R. (1984). [Letter to the editor]. *Harvard Business Review, 1,* 150.

Schroeder, D. A., Dovidio, J. R., Sibicky, M. E., Matthews, L. L., & Allen, J. L. (1988). Empathy concern and helping behavior: Egoism or altruism? *Journal of Experimental Social Psychology, 24,* 333–353.

Schullo, S. A., & Alperson, B. L. (1984). Interpersonal phenomenology as a function of sexual orientation, sex, sentiment, and trait categories in long-term dyadic relationships. *Journal of Personality and Social Psychology, 47,* 983–1002.

Schutte, N. S., Malouff, J. M., Post-Gorden, J. C., & Rodasts, A. L. (1988). Effect of playing videogames on children's aggressive and other behavior. *Journal of Applied Social Psychology, 18,* 454–460.

Schwartz, S. H., & Gotleib, A. (1980). Bystander anonymity and reaction to emergencies. *Journal of Personality and Social Psychology, 39,* 418–430.

Schwartz, S. H., & Howard, J. A. (1982). Helping and cooperation: A self-based motivational model. In V. J. Derlega & J. Grzelak (Eds.), *Cooperation and helping behavior: Theories and research* (pp. 327–353). New York: Academic Press.

Scott, J. A. (1984). Comfort and seating distance in living rooms: The relationship of interactants and topic of conversation. *Environment and Behavior, 16,* 35–54.

Scott, N. (1979, December 29). What qualities make wife ideal? Here's what men say. *Albany Times Union,* p. 5.

Sebba, R., & Churchman, A. (1983). Territories and territoriality in the home. *Environment and Behavior, 15,* 191–210.

Segal, M. W. (1974). Alphabet and attraction: An unobtrusive measure of the effect of propinquity in a field setting. *Journal of Personality and Social Psychology, 30,* 654–657.

Seligman, M. E. P., & Schulman, P. (1986). Explanatory style as a predictor of productivity and quitting among life insurance sales agents. *Journal of Personality and Social Psychology, 50,* 832–838.

Selye, H. (1956). *The stress of life.* New York: McGraw-Hill.

Seraydarian, L., & Busse, T. V. (1981). First-name stereotypes and essay grading. *Journal of Psychology, 108,* 253–257.

Shaffer, D. R., & Graziano, W. G. (1983). Effects of positive and negative moods on helping tasks having pleasant or unpleasant consequences. *Motivation and Emotion, 7,* 269–278.

Shaffer, D. R., Plummer, D., & Hammock, G. (1986). Hath he suffered enough? Effects of jury dogmatism, defendant similarity, and defendant's pretrial suffering on juridic decisions. *Journal of Personality and Social Psychology, 50,* 1059–1067.

Shaffer, D. R., Smith, J. E., & Tomarelli, M. (1982). Self-monitoring as a determinant of self-disclosure reciprocity during the acquaintance process. *Journal of Personality and Social Psychology, 43,* 163–175.

Shanab, M. E., & Yahya, K. A. (1977). A behavioral study of obedience in children. *Journal of Personality and Social Psychology, 35,* 530–536.

Shapiro, J. P. (1988). Relationships between dimensions of depressive experience and evaluative beliefs about people in general. *Personality and Social Psychology Bulletin, 14,* 388–400.

Shaver, P., & Hendrick, C. (Eds.). (1987). *Sex and gender.* Newbury Park, CA: Sage.

Shavitt, S. (1990). The role of attitude objects in attitude functions. *Journal of Experimental Social Psychology, 26,* 124–148.

Shea, J. D. C. (1981). Changes in interpersonal distances and categories of play behavior in the early weeks of preschool. *Developmental Psychology, 17,* 417–425.

Sheldon, W. H., Stevens, S. S., & Tucker, W. B. (1940). *The varieties of human physique.* New York: Harper.

Shelom, K. J., Walker, J. L., Esser, J. K. (1985). A choice of alternative strategies in oligopoly bargaining. *Journal of Applied Social Psychology, 15,* 345–353.

Shelton, M. L., & Rogers, R. W. (1981). Fear-arousing and empathy-arousing appeals to help: The pathos of persuasion. *Journal of Applied Social Psychology, 11,* 366–378.

Sheppard, B. H. (1984). Third-party conflict intervention: A procedural framework. In B. M. Staw & L. L. Cummings (Eds.), *Research in organizational behavior* (Vol. 6, pp. 141–190). Greenwich, CT: JAI Press.

Sheppard, J. A., & Arkin, R. M. (1989a). Determinants of self-handicapping: Task importance and the effects of preexisting handicaps on selfgenerated handicaps. *Personality and Social Psychology Bulletin, 15,* 101–112.

Sheppard, J. A., & Arkin, R. M. (1989b). Self-handicapping: The moderating role of public self-consciousness and task importance. *Personality and Social Psychology Bulletin, 15,* 252–265.

Sheppard, J. A., & Strathman, A. J. (1989). Attractiveness and height: The role of stature in dating preference, frequency of dating, and perceptions of attractiveness. *Personality and Social Psychology Bulletin, 15,* 617–627.

Sherif, M. (1935). A study of some social factors in perception. *Archives of Psychology,* No. 187.

Sherif, M. (1966). *In common predicament: Social psychology of intergroup conflict and cooperation.* Boston: Houghton Mifflin.

Sherif, M., Harvey, O. J., White, B. J., Hood, W. E., & Sherif, C. W. (1961). *Intergroup conflict and cooperation: The Robbers cave experiment.* Norman, OK: Institute of Group Relations.

Sherman, S. J., Presson, C. C., & Chassin, L. (1984). Mechanisms underlying the false consensus effect: The special role of threats to the self. *Personality and Social Psychology Bulletin, 10,* 127–138.

Sherman, S. S. (1980). On the self-erasing nature of errors of prediction. *Journal of Personality and Social Psychology, 16,* 388–403.

Shiffman, S., & Jarvik, M. E. (1987). Situational determinants of coping in smoking relapse crises. *Journal of Applied Social Psychology, 17,* 3–15.

Shotland, R. L., & Mark, M. M. (1985). *Social science and social policy.* London: Sage.

Shotland, R. L., & Strau, M. K. (1976). Bystander response to an assault: When a man attacks a woman. *Journal of Personality and Social Psychology, 34,* 990–999.

Shrauger, J. S., & Rosenberg, S. E. (1970). Self-esteem and the effect of success and failure feedback on performance. *Journal of Personality, 38,* 404–417.

Shupe, L. M. (1954). Alcohol and crimes: A study of the urine alcohol concentration found in 882 persons arrested during or immediately after the commission of a felony. *Journal of Criminal Law and Criminology, 33,* 661–665.

Shure, G. H., Meeker, R. J., & Hansford, E. A. (1965). The effectiveness of pacifist strategies in bargaining games. *Journal of Conflict Resolution, 9,* 106–117.

Shute, G. E., Howard, M. M., & Steyartt, J. P. (1984). The relationships among cognitive development, locus of control, and gender. *Journal of Research in Personality, 18,* 335–341.

Siegman, A. W., & Feldstein, S. (Eds.). (1987). *Nonverbal behavior and communication.* Hillsdale, NJ: Erlbaum.

Sigelman, C. K., Thomas, D. B., Sigelman, L., & Robich, F. D. (1986). Gender, physical attractiveness, and electability: An experimental investigation of voter biases. *Journal of Applied Social Psychology, 16,* 229–248.

Sigelman, L., & Sigelman, C. K. (1982). Sexism, racism, and ageism in voting behavior: An experimental analysis. *Social Psychology Quarterly, 45,* 263–269.

Silverstein, A. (1988). An Aristotelian resolution of the idiographic versus nomothetic tension. *American Psychologist, 43,* 425–430.

Simonton, D. K. (1985). Intelligence and personal influence in groups: Four nonlinear models. *Psychological Review, 92,* 532–547.

Simonton, D. K. (1988). Presidential style: Personality, biography, and performance. *Journal of Personality and Social Psychology, 55,* 928–936.

Simpson, J. A. (1987). The dissolution of romantic relationships: Factors involved in relationship stability and emotional stress. *Journal of Personality and Social Psychology, 53,* 683–692.

Simpson, M., & Perry, J. D. (1990). Crime and climate: A reconsideration. *Environment and Behavior, 22,* 295–300.

Singer, J. E., Lundberg, U., & Frankenhaeuser, M. (1978). Stress on the train: A study of urban commuting. In A. Baum, J. E. Singer, & S. Valines (Eds.), *Advances in environmental psychology* (Vol. 1). Hillsdale, NJ: Erlbaum.

Singh, R. (1974). Reinforcement and attraction: Specifying the effects of affective states. *Journal of Research in Personality, 8,* 294–305.

Sistrunk, F., & McDavid, J. W. (1971). Sex variable in conforming behavior. *Journal of Personality and Social Psychology, 17,* 200–207.

Sivacek, J., & Crano, W. D. (1982). Vested interest as a moderator of attitude-behavior consistency. *Journal of Personality and Social Psychology, 43,* 210–221.

Skaalvik, E. M., & Hagtvet, K. A. (1990). Academic achievement and self-concept: An analysis of causal predominance in a developmental perspective. *Journal of Personality and Social Psychology, 58,* 292–307.

Skinner, B. F. (1986). What is wrong with daily life in the Western world? *American Psychologist, 41,* 568–574.

Slater, E. J., & Calhoun, K. S. (1988). Familial conflict and marital dissolution: Effects on the social functioning of college students. *Journal of Social and Clinical Psychology, 65,* 118–126.

Slater, E. J., & Haber, J. D. (1984). Adolescent adjustment following divorce as a function of familial conflict. *Journal of Consulting and Clinical Psychology, 52,* 920–921.

Smeaton, G. (1990). Personal communication.

Smeaton, G., Byrne, D., & Murnen, S. K. (1989). The revulsion hypothesis revisited: Similarity irrelevance or dissimilarity bias? *Journal of Personality and Social Psychology, 56,* 54–59.

Smith, B. D., & Teevan, R. C. (1971). Relationships among self-ideal congruence, adjustment, and fear-of-failure motivation. *Journal of Personality, 39,* 44–56.

Smith, E. R. (1989). *Interpersonal attraction as a function of similarity and assumed similarity in traditional gender role adherence.* Unpublished doctoral dissertation, State University of New York at Albany.

Smith, E. R., Becker, M. A., Byrne, D., & Przybyla, D. P. J. (1990). *Sexual attitudes of males and females as predictors of interpersonal attraction and marital compatibility.* Manuscript submitted for publication.

Smith, K. D., Keating, J. P., & Stotland, E. (1989). Altruism reconsidered: The effect of denying feedback on a victim's status to empathetic witnesses. *Journal of Personality and Social Psychology, 57,* 641–650.

Smith, R. E., Smoll, F. L., & Ptacek, J. T. (1990). Conjunctive moderator variables in vulnerability and resiliency research: Life stress, social support and coping skills, and adolescent sport injuries. *Journal of Personality and Social Psychology, 58,* 360–370.

Smith, R. H., Kim, S. H., & Parrott, W. G. (1988). Envy and jealousy: Semantic problems and experiential distinctions. *Personality and Social Psychology Bulletin, 14,* 401–409.

Smith, R. J., & Knowles, E. S. (1979). Attributional consequences of personal space invasions. *Personality and Social Psychology Bulletin, 4,* 429–433.

Smith, S. S., & Richardson, D. (1983). Amelioration of deception and harm in psychology research: The important role of debriefing. *Journal of Personality and Social Psychology, 45,* 1075–1082.

Smith, S. S., & Richardson, D. (1985). On deceiving ourselves about deception: Reply to Rubin. *Journal of Personality and Social Psychology, 48,* 254–255.

Smith, T. W., & Pope, M. K. (1990). Cynical hostility as a health risk: Current status and future directions. *Journal of Social Behavior and Personality, 5,* 77–88.

Smith, V. I., & Ellsworth, P. C. (1987). The social psychology of eyewitness accuracy: Misleading questions and communicator expertise. *Journal of Applied Psychology, 72,* 294–300.

Snyder, C. R. (1989). Reality negotiation: From excuses to hope and beyond. *Journal of Social and Clinical Psychology, 8,* 130–157.

Snyder, C. R., & Fromkin, H. L. (1980). *Uniqueness: The human pursuit of difference.* New York: Plenum.

Snyder, M. (1974). Self-monitoring of expressive behavior. *Journal of Personality and Social Psychology, 30,* 526–537.

Snyder, M., Berscheid, E., & Glick, P. (1985). Focusing on the exterior and the interior: Two investigations of the initiation of personal relationships. *Journal of Personality and Social Psychology, 48,* 1427–1439.

Snyder, M., & DeBono, K. G. (1989). Understanding the functions of attitudes: Lessons from personality and social behavior. In A. R. Pratkanis, S. J. Breckler, & A. G. Greenwald (Eds.), *Attitude structure and function.* Hillsdale, NJ: Erlbaum.

Snyder, M., & Gangestad, S. (1986). On the nature of self-monitoring: Matters of assessment, matters of validity. *Journal of Personality and Social Psychology, 51,* 125–139.

Snyder, M., Gangestad, S., & Simpson, J. A. (1983). Choosing friends as activity partners: The role of self-monitoring. *Journal of Personality and Social Psychology, 45,* 1061–1072.

Snyder, M., & Ickes, W. (1985). Personality and social behavior. In G. Lindzey & E. Aronson (Eds.), *The handbook of social psychology* (Vol. 1, 3rd ed., pp. 883–947). New York: Random House.

Snyder, M., & Simpson, J. A. (1984). Self-monitoring and dating relationships. *Journal of Personality and Social Psychology, 47,* 1281–1291.

Sogin, S. R., & Pallak, M. S. (1976). Bad decisions, responsibility, and attitude change: Effects of volition, foreseeability, and locus of causality of negative consequences. *Journal of Personality and Social Psychology, 33,* 300–306.

Sohn, D. (1982). Sex differences in achievement self-attributions: An effect-size analysis. *Sex Roles, 8,* 345–358.

Solano, C. H., Batten, P. G., & Parish, E. A. (1982). Loneliness and patterns of self-disclosure. *Journal of Personality and Social Psychology, 43,* 524–531.

Solomon, R. C. (1981, October). The love lost in clichés. *Psychology Today,* pp. 83–85, 87–88.

Solomon, W. (1989, Nov. 21). Skin troubles may be tied to anxiety. *New York Times,* C6.

Sommer, R. (1980). Environmental psychology—A blueprint for the future. *APA Monitor, 11,* 47.

Sommer, R., & Becker, F. D. (1969). Territorial defense and the good neighbor. *Journal of Personality and Social Psychology, 11,* 85–92.

Sorrentino, R. M., Bobocel, D. R., Gitta, M. Z., Olson, J. M., & Hewitt, E. C. (1988). Uncertainty orientation and persuasion: Individual differences in the effects of personal relevance on social judgments. *Journal of Personality and Social Psychology, 55,* 371–375.

Spacapan, S., & Oskamp, S. (Eds.). (1988). *The social psychology of health.* Newbury Park, CA: Sage.

Spielberger, C. D., & Stenmark, D. E. (1985). Community psychology. In E. M. Altmaier & E. Meyer (Eds.), *Applied specialties in psychology* (pp. 75–97). New York: Random House.

Sprafkin, J. N., Liebert, R. M., & Poulous, R. W. (1975). Effects of a prosocial televised example on children's helping. *Journal of Personality and Social Psychology, 48,* 35–46.

Srull, T. K., & Wyer, R. S. (1988). *Advances in social cognition: A dual model of impression formation.* Hillsdale, NJ: Erlbaum.

Staats, A. W., & Burns, G. L. (1982). Emotional personality repertoire as a cause of behavior: Specification of personality and interaction principles. *Journal of Personality and Social Psychology, 43,* 873–881.

Standing, L., Lynn, D., & Moxness, K. (1990). Effects of noise upon introverts and extraverts. *Bulletin of the Psychonomic Society, 28,* 138–140.

Stangor, C., & Ruble, D. N. (1989). Strength of expectancies and memory for social information: What we remember depends on how much we know. *Journal of Experimental Social Psychology, 25,* 18–35.

Stapp, J., & Fulcher, R. (1984). The employment of 1981 and 1982 doctorate recipients in psychology. *American Psychologist, 39,* 1408–1423.

Stasser, G., & Davis, J. H. (1981). Group decision making and social influence: A social interaction sequence model. *Psychological Review, 88,* 523–551.

Stasser, G., Kerr, N. L., & Davis, J. H. (1989). Influence processes and consensus models in decision making groups. In P. B. Paulus (Ed.), *Psychology of group influence* (2nd ed.). Hillsdale, NJ: Erlbaum.

Stasser, G., Taylor, L. A., & Hanna, C. (1989). Information sampling in structured and unstructured discussion of three- and six-person groups. *Journal of Personality and Social Psychology, 57,* 67–78.

Stasser, G., & Titus, W. (1985). Pooling of unshared information in group decision making: Biased information sampling during discussion. *Journal of Personality and Social Psychology, 48,* 1467–1478.

Stasser, G., & Titus, W. (1987). Effects of information load and percentage of shared information on the dissemination of unshared information during group discussion. *Journal of Personality and Social Psychology, 53,* 81–93.

Staw, B. M. (1976). Knee-deep in the big muddy: A study of escalating commitment to a course of action. *Organizational Behavior and Human Performance, 16,* 27–44.

Staw, B. M. (1981). The escalation of commitment to a course of action. *Academy of Management Review, 6,* 577–587.

Staw, B. M., & Ross, J. (1987). Behavior in escalation situations: Antecedents, prototypes, and solutions. In L. L. Cummings & B. M. Staw (Eds.), *Research in organizational behavior* (Vol. 9, pp. 39–78). Greenwich, CT: JAI Press.

Staw, B. M., & Ross, J. (1989). Understanding behavior in escalation situations. *Science, 246,* 216–220.

Steck, L., Levitan, D., McLane, D., & Kelley, H. H. (1982). Care, need, and conceptions of love. *Journal of Personality and Social Psychology, 43,* 481–491.

Steele, C. M., Critchlow, B., & Liu, T. J. (1985). Alcohol and social behavior: The helpful drunkard. *Journal of Personality and Social Psychology, 48,* 35–46.

Stefanko, M., & Horowitz, J. (1989). Attitudinal effects associated with an environmental hazard. *Population and Environment, 11,* 43–57.

Steffen, V. J., & Eagly, A. H. (1985). Implicit theories about influence style: The effects of status and sex. *Personality and Social Psychology Bulletin, 11,* 191–205.

Stein, A. K., & Friedrich, L. K. (1972). Television content and young children's behavior. In J. P. Murray, E. A. Rubenstein, & C. A. Comstock (Eds.), *Television and social learning.* Washington, DC: U.S. Government Printing Office.

Steinberg, R., & Shapiro, S. (1982). Sex differences in personality traits of female and male master of business administration students. *Journal of Applied Psychology, 67,* 306–310.

Steiner, I. D. (1972). *Group process and productivity.* New York: Academic Press.

Steiner, I. D. (1976). Task-performing groups. In J. W. Thibaut, J. T. Spence, & R. C. Cardon (Eds.), *Contemporary topics in social psychology.* Morristown, NJ: General Learning Press.

Stengel, R. (1988, October 24). The likability sweepstakes. *Time,* p. 20.

Stephan, W. G. (1985). Intergroup relations. In G. Lindzey & E. Aronson (Eds.), *Handbook of social psychology* (Vol. 3, pp. 599–658). Reading, MA: Addison-Wesley.

Stephan, W. G., & Stephan, C. W. (1988). Emotional reactions to interracial achievement outcomes. *Journal of Applied Social Psychology, 19,* 608–621.

Sternberg, R. J. (1986). A triangular theory of love. *Psychological Review, 93,* 119–135.

Sternberg, R. J. (1988). Triangulating love. In R. J. Sternberg & M. J. Barnes (Eds.), *The psychology of love* (pp. 119–138). New Haven, CT: Yale University Press.

Stevens, W. K. (1989a, November 21). Methane from guts of livestock is now focus in global warming. *New York Times,* p. C4.

Stevens, W. K. (1989b, December 13). Skeptics are challenging dire "greenhouse" view. *New York Times,* pp. A1, B12.

Stewart, J. E., II. (1980). Defendant's attractiveness as a factor in the outcome of criminal trials: An observational study. *Journal of Applied Social Psychology, 10,* 348–361.

Stiff, J. B., Miller, G. R., Sleight, C., Mongeau, P. L., Garlick, R., & Rogan, R. (1989). Explanations for visual cue primacy in judgments of honesty and deceit. *Journal of Personality and Social Psychology, 56,* 555–564.

Stockard, J., Van-de-Dragt, A. J., Dodge, P. J. (1988). Gender roles and behavior in social dilemmas: Are there sex differences in cooperation and its justification? *Social Psychology Quarterly, 51,* 154–163.

Stokols, D. (1972). On the distinction between density and crowding: Some implications for future research. *Psychological Review, 79,* 275–277.

Stokols, D., & Altman, I. (1986). *Handbook of environmental psychology.* New York: Wiley.

Stone, A. A., Cox, D. S., Valdimarsdotti, H., Jandorf, L., Neale, J. M. (1987). Evidence that secretory IgA antibody is associated with daily mood. *Journal of Personality and Social Psychology, 52,* 988–993.

Stone, A. A., & Neale, J. M. (1984). Effects of severe daily events on mood. *Journal of Personality and Social Psychology, 46,* 137–144.

Stone, L. (1977). *The family, sex, and marriage in England: 1500–1800.* New York: Harper.

Stoner, J. A. F. (1961). *A comparison of individual and group decisions involving risk.* Unpublished master's thesis, School of Industrial Management, MIT, Cambridge, MA.

Storms, M., & Thomas, G. C. (1977). Reactions to physical closeness. *Journal of Personality and Social Psychology, 35,* 412–418.

Strack, F., Martin, L. L., & Stepper, S. (1988). Inhibiting and facilitating conditions of facial expressions: A non-obtrusive test of the facial feedback hypothesis. *Journal of Personality and Social Psychology, 54,* 768–777.

Strauman, T. J., & Higgins, E. T. (1988). Self-discrepancies as predictors of vulnerability to distinct syndromes of chronic emotional distress. *Journal of Personality, 56,* 685–707.

Strickland, B. R. (1984). This week's Citation Classic. *Current Contents, Social and Behavioral Sciences, 16(5),* 20.

Strickland, B. R. (1989). Internal-external control expectancies: From contingency to creativity. *American Psychologist, 44,* 1–12.

Strom, J. C., & Buck, R. W. (1979). Staring and participants' sex: Physiological and subjective reactions. *Personality and Social Psychology Bulletin, 5,* 114–117.

Strube, M. J. (1989). Evidence for the type in Type A behavior: A taxonometric analysis. *Journal of Personality and Social Psychology, 56,* 972–987.

Strube, M. J., & Garcia, J. E. (1981). A meta-analytic investigation of Fiedler's contingency model of leadership effectiveness. *Psychological Bulletin, 90,* 307–321.

Strube, M., Turner, C. W., Cerro, D., Stevens, J., & Hinchey, F. (1984). Interpersonal aggression and the Type A coronary-prone behavior pattern: A theoretical distinction and practical implications. *Journal of Personality and Social Psychology, 47,* 839–847.

Sulman, F. G., Levy, D., Levy, A., Pfeifer, Y., Saperstein, E., & Tal, E. (1974). Ionometry of hot, dry desert winds (*sharav*) and application of ionizing treatment to weather-sensitive patients. *International Journal of Biometeorology, 18,* 393.

Suls, J., & Fletcher, B. (1983). Social comparison in the social and physical sciences: An archival study. *Journal of Personality and Social Psychology, 44,* 575–580.

Suls, J., & Fletcher, B. (1985). The relative efficacy of avoidant and nonavoidant coping strategies: A meta-analysis. *Health Psychology, 4,* 249–288.

Suls, J., & Greenwald, A. G. (Eds.). (1986). *Psychological perspectives on the self* (Vol. 3). Hillsdale, NJ: Erlbaum.

Suls, J., & Rittenhouse, J. D. (1987). Personality and physical health. *Journal of Personality, 55,* 155–168.

Suls, J., & Rosnow, J. (1988). Concerns about artifacts in behavioral research. In M. Morawski (Ed.), *The rise of experimentation in American psychology* (pp. 163–187). New Haven, CT: Yale University Press.

Suls, J., & Wan, C. K. (1987). In search of the false uniqueness phenomenon: Fear and estimates of social consensus. *Journal of Personality and Social Psychology, 52,* 211–217.

Suls, J., & Wan, C. K. (1989). The effects of sensory and procedural information on coping with stressful medical procedures and pain: A meta-analysis. *Journal of Consulting and Clinical Psychology, 57,* 372–379.

Suls, J., Wan, C. K., & Sanders, G. S. (1988). False consensus and false uniqueness in estimating the prevalence of health-protective behaviors. *Journal of Applied Social Psychology, 18,* 66–79.

Sunnafrank, M. J., & Miller, G. R. (1981). The role of initial conversations in determining attraction to similar and dissimilar strangers. *Human Communication Research, 8,* 16–25.

Swallow, S. R., & Kuiper, N. A. (1987). The effects of depression and cognitive vulnerability to depression on judgments of similarity between self and other. *Motivation and Emotion, 11,* 157–167.

Swann, W. B., Jr., & Ely, R. J. (1984). A battle of wills: Self-verification versus behavioral confirmation. *Journal of Personality and Social Psychology, 46,* 1287–1302.

Swann, W. B., Jr., Griffin, J. J., Jr., Predmore, S. C., & Gaines, B. (1987). Cognitive-affective crossfire: When self-consistency meets self-enhancement. *Journal of Personality and Social Psychology, 52,* 881–889.

Swann, W. B., Jr., Pelham, B., & Chidester, T. (1988). Change through paradox: Using self-verification to alter beliefs. *Journal of Personality and Social Psychology, 54,* 268–273.

Swap, W. C. (1977). Interpersonal attraction and repeated exposure to rewarders and punishers. *Personality and Social Psychology Bulletin, 3,* 248–251.

Sweeney, P. D., Anderson, A., & Bailey, S. (1986). Attributional style in depression: A meta-analytic view. *Journal of Personality and Social Psychology, 50,* 974–991.

Szymanski, K., & Harkins, S. (1987). Social loafing and self-evaluation with a social standard. *Journal of Personality and Social Psychology, 53,* 891–897.

Tajfel, H. (1982). *Social identity and intergroup relations.* Cambridge, England: Cambridge University Press.

Tanford, S., & Penrod, S. (1984). Social influence model: A formal integration of research on majority and minority influence processes. *Psychological Bulletin, 95,* 189–225.

Taylor, D. E. (1989). Blacks and the environment: Toward an explanation of the concern and action gap between blacks and whites. *Environment and Behavior, 21,* 175–205.

Taylor, M. S., Locke, E. A., Lee, C., & Gist, M. E. (1984). Type A behavior and faculty research productivity: What are the mechanisms? *Organizational Behavior and Human Performance, 34*, 402–418.

Taylor, R. B. (1988). *Human territorial functioning: An empirical, evolutionary perspective on individual and small group territorial cognitions, behaviors, and consequences.* New York: Cambridge University Press.

Taylor, R. B., & Lanni, J. C. (1981). Territorial dominance: The influence of the resident advantage in triadic decision making. *Journal of Personality and Social Psychology, 41*, 909–915.

Taylor, R. B., & Stough, R. R. (1978). Territorial cognition: Assessing Altman's typology. *Journal of Personality and Social Psychology, 36*, 418–423.

Taylor, S. E. (1985). *Health psychology.* New York: Random House.

Taylor, S. E., Buunk, B. P., & Aspinwall, L. G. (1990). Social comparison, stress, and coping. *Personality and Social Psychology Bulletin, 16*, 74–89.

Taylor, S. E., Collins, R. L., Skokan, L. A., & Aspinwall, L. G. (1989). Maintaining positive illusions in the face of negative information: Getting the facts without letting them get to you. *Journal of Social and Clinical Psychology, 8*, 114–129.

Taylor, S. P., & Leonard, K. E. (1983). Alcohol and human physical aggression. In R. Geen & E. Donnerstein (Eds.), *Aggression: Theoretical and empirical reviews.* New York: Academic Press.

Taylor, S. P., & Sears, J. D. (1988). The effects of alcohol and persuasive social pressure on human physical aggression. *Aggressive Behavior, 14*, 237–243.

Tedeschi, J. T., & Melburg, V. (1984). Impression management and influence in organizations. In S. B. Bacharach & E. J. Lawler (Eds.), *Research in the sociology of organizations* (Vol. 3, pp. 31–58). Greenwich, CT: JAI Press.

Teenage pregnancy: The problem that hasn't gone away. (1981). New York: Alan Guttmacher Institute.

Tellegen, A. (1988). The analysis of consistency in personality assessment. *Journal of Personality, 56*, 521–663.

Tesser, A., Campbell, J., & Smith, M. (1984). Friendship choice and performance: Self-evaluation maintenance in children. *Journal of Personality and Social Psychology, 46*, 561–574.

Tetlock, P. E., & Boettger, R. (1989). Accountability: A social magnifier of the dilution effect. *Journal of Personality and Social Psychology, 57*, 388–398.

Thayer, L. (Ed.). (1989). *Organizational communication: Emerging perspectives II.* Norwood, NJ: Ablex.

Thayer, S., & Saarni, C. (1975). Demand characteristics are everywhere (anyway): A comment on the Stanford prison experiment. *American Psychologist, 30*, 1015–1016.

Thomas, K. W. (1989). Conflict and negotiation. In M. D. Dunnette (Ed.), *Handbook of industrial and organizational psychology* (2nd ed.). Chicago: Rand McNally.

Thomas, K. W. (1990). Conflict and negotiation processes. In M. D. Dunnette (Ed.), *Handbook of industrial and organizational psychology* (2nd ed.). Chicago: Rand McNally.

Thomas, K. W., & Schmidt, W. H. (1976). A survey of managerial interests with respect to conflict. *Academy of Management Journal, 19*, 315–318.

Thompson, W. C., Cowan, C. L., & Rosenhan, D. L. (1980). Focus of attention mediates the impact of negative affect on altruism. *Journal of Personality and Social Psychology, 38*, 291–300.

Thorne, A. (1987). The press of personality: A study of conversations between introverts and extraverts. *Journal of Personality and Social Psychology, 53*, 718–726.

Thornton, A., & Freedman, D. (1982). Changing attitudes toward married and single life. *Family Planning Perspectives, 14(6)*, 297–303.

Tice, D. M. (1989). Metatraits: Interitem variance as personality assessment. In D. M. Buss & N. Cantor (Eds.), *Personality psychology: Recent trends and emerging directions* (pp. 194–200). New York: Springer-Verlag.

Tindale, R. S., Davis, J. H., Vollrath, D. A., & Nagao, D. H. (1990). Asymmetrical social influence in freely interacting groups: A test of three models. *Journal of Personality and Social Psychology, 58*, 438–449.

Titus, J., & Frankel, A. (1984, April). *What's in a name: Maybe a face?* Paper presented at the meeting of the Eastern Psychological Association, Baltimore, MD.

Toch, H. (1980a). The catalytic situation in the violence equation. *Journal of Applied Social Psychology, 15*, 105–123.

Toch, H. (1980b). *Violent men* (rev. ed.). Cambridge, MA: Schenkman.

Toi, M., & Batson, C. D. (1982). More evidence that empathy is a source of altruistic motivation. *Journal of Personality and Social Psychology, 43*, 281–292.

Tooley, V., Brigham, J. C., Maass, A., & Bothwell, R. K. (1987). Facial recognition: Weapon effect and attentional focus. *Journal of Applied Social Psychology, 17*, 845–859.

Topf, M. (1989). Sensitivity to noise, personality hardiness, and noise-induced stress in critical care nurses. *Environment and Behavior, 21*, 717–733.

Toufexis, A. (1989, July 17). Panic over power lines. *Time*, p. 71.

Triandis, H. T. (1989). The self and social behavior in differing cultural contexts. *Psychological Review, 96*, 506–520.

Triplett, N. (1898). The dynamogenic factors in pace making and competition. *American Journal of Psychology, 9*, 507–533.

Trope, Y. (1986). Identification and inferential processes in dispositional attribution. *Psychological Review, 93*, 239–257.

Trope, Y., Cohen, O., & Maoz, Y. (1988). Perceptual and inferential effects of situational inducements on dispositional attribution. *Journal of Personality and Social Psychology, 55*, 165–177.

Tsui, A. S., & O'Reilly, C. A., III. (1989). Beyond simple demographic effects: The importance of relational demography in superior-subordinate dyads. *Academy of Management Journal, 32*, 402–423.

Tuckman, B. W., & Jensen, M. A. (1977). Stages of small group development revisited. *Group and Organizational Studies, 2*, 419–427.

Turkington, C. (1986, February). High court weighs value of research by social scientists. *APA Monitor, 17*, 1–30.

Turner, C. W., & Simmons, L. S. (1974). Effects of subject sophistication and evaluation apprehension on aggressive responses to weapons. *Journal of Personality and Social Psychology, 30*, 341–348.

Turner, J. C., Hogg, M. A., Oakes, P. J., Reicher, S. D., & Wetherell, M. S. (1987). *Rediscovering the social group: A self-categorization theory.* Oxford, England: Blackwell.

Tversky, A., & Kahneman, D. (1973). Availability: A heuristic for judging frequency and probability. *Cognitive Psychology, 5*, 207–232.

Tversky, A., & Kahneman, D. (1982). Judgment under uncertainty: Heuristics and biases. In D. Kahneman, P. Slovic, & A. Tversky (Eds.), *Judgment under uncertainty* (pp. 3–20). New York: Cambridge University Press.

Tyler, F. B., Labarta, M. M., & Otero, R. F. (1986). Attributions of locus of control in a Puerto Rican sample. *Interamerican Journal of Psychology, 20*, 20–40.

Umberson, D., & Hughes, M. (1984, August). *The impact of physical attractiveness on achievement and psychological well-being.* Paper presented at the meeting of the American Sociological Association, San Antonio, TX.

Umpleby, S. A. (1990). The scientific revolution in demography. *Population and Environment, 11*, 159–174.

Underwood, B., Berenson, J. F., Berenson, R. J., Cheng, K. K., Wilson, D., Kulik, J., Moore, B. S., & Wenze, G. (1977). Attention, negative affect, and altruism: An ecological validation. *Personality and Social Psychology Bulletin, 3*, 51–53.

U.S. Bureau of the Census (1984). *Statistical abstract of the United States, 1982–1983* (103rd ed.). Washington, DC: U.S. Government Printing Office.

Vallacher, R. R., & Wegner, D. M. (1987). What do people think they're doing? Action identification and human behavior. *Psychological Review, 94*, 3–15.

Vallone, R., Ross, L., & Lepper, M. R. (1985). The hostile media phenomenon: Biased perception and perceptions of media bias in coverage of the Beirut massacre. *Journal of Personality and Social Psychology, 49*, 577–585.

Vanbeselaere, N. (1987). The effects of dichotomous and crossed social categorization upon intergroup discrimination. *European Journal of Social Psychology, 17*, 143–156.

Van de Vliert, E. (1984). Conflict: Prevention and escalation. In P. J. Drenth, H. Thierry, P. J. Willems, & C. J. de Wolff (Eds.), *Handbook of work and organizational psychology.* New York: Wiley.

Van de Vliert, E. (1990). Escalative intervention in small-group conflicts. *Journal of Applied Behavioral Sciences.*

Van der Pligt, J., Eiser, J. R., & Spears, R. (1987). Nuclear waste: Facts, fears, and attitudes. *Journal of Applied Social Psychology, 17,* 453–470.

Van Hook, E., & Higgins, E. T. (1988). Self-related problems beyond the self-concept: Motivational consequences of discrepant self-guides. *Journal of Personality and Social Psychology, 55,* 625–633.

Van Lange, P. A. M., Liebrand, W. B. G., & Kuhlman, D. M. (1990). Causal attribution of choice behavior in three n-person prisoner's dilemmas. *Journal of Experimental Social Psychology, 26,* 34–48.

Vecchio, R. P. (1987). Situational leadership theory: An examination of a prescriptive theory. *Journal of Applied Psychology, 72,* 444–451.

Veitch, R., DeWood, R., & Bosko, K. (1977). Radio news broadcasts: Their effects on interpersonal helping. *Sociometry, 40,* 383–386.

Veitch, R., & Griffitt, W. (1976). Good news, bad news: Affective and interpersonal effects. *Journal of Applied Social Psychology, 6,* 69–75.

Verplanken, B. (1989). Beliefs, attitudes, and intentions toward nuclear energy before and after Chernobyl in a longitudinal within-subjects design. *Environment and Behavior, 21,* 371–392.

Videbeck, R. (1960). Self-conception and the reactions of others. *Sociometry, 23,* 351–359.

Vig, P. S. (1985). Respiration, nasal airway, and orthodontics; A review of current clinical concepts and research. In L. E. Johnston (Ed.), *New vistas in orthodontics* (pp. 76–102). Philadelphia: Lea & Febiger.

Vinokur, A., & Burnstein, E. (1974). Effects of partially shared persuasive arguments on group-induced shifts: A problem-solving approach. *Journal of Personality and Social Psychology, 29,* 305–315.

Vinsel, A., Brown, B. B., Altman, I., & Foss, C. (1980). Privacy regulation, territorial displays, and effectiveness of individual functioning. *Journal of Personality and Social Psychology, 39,* 1104–1115.

Vroom, V. H., & Jago, A. G. (1978). On the validity of the Vroom-Yetton model. *Journal of Applied Psychology, 63,* 151–162.

Vroom, V. H., & Yetton, P. W. (1973). *Leadership and decision-making.* Pittsburgh: University of Pittsburgh Press.

Wagner, J. (1986). *The search for signs of intelligent life in the universe.* New York: Harper & Row.

Wagner, P. J., & Curran, P. (1984). Health beliefs and physician identified "worried well." *Health Psychology, 3,* 459–474.

Waldron, I., Baron, J., Frese, M., & Sabini, J. (1988). Activism against nuclear weapons build-up: Student participation in the 1984 primary campaigns. *Journal of Applied Social Psychology, 18,* 826–836.

Walker, J. (1983). *Sexual activities and fantasies of university students as a function of sex role orientation.* Unpublished honors thesis, University of Western Ontario, London, Canada.

Wall, G. (1973). Public response to air pollution in South Yorkshire, England. *Environment and Behavior, 5,* 219–248.

Walmsley, D. J., & Lewis, G. J. (1989). The pace of pedestrian flows in cities. *Environment and Behavior, 21,* 123–150.

Walster, E., & Festinger, L. (1962). The effectiveness of "overheard" persuasive communication. *Journal of Abnormal and Social Psychology, 65,* 395–402.

Walter, D. A., & Ziegler, C. A. (1980). The effects of birth order on locus of control. *Bulletin of the Psychonomic Society, 15,* 293–294.

Walton, R. E., & McKersie, R. B. (1965). *A behavioral theory of labor negotiations: An analysis of a social interaction system.* New York: McGraw-Hill.

Warner, R. M., & Sugarman, D. B. (1986). Attributions of personality based on physical appearance, speech, and handwriting. *Journal of Personality and Social Psychology, 50,* 792–799.

Watts, B. L. (1982). Individual differences in circadian activity rhythms and their effects on roommate relationships. *Journal of Personality, 50,* 374–384.

Waynbaum, I. (1907). *La physionomie humaine: Son mecanisme et son role social* [The human face: Its mechanism and social function]. Paris: Alcan.

Weary, G., Elbin, S., & Hill, M. G. (1987). Attributional and social comparison processes in depression. *Journal of Personality and Social Psychology, 52,* 605–610.

Webb, B., Worchel, S., Riechers, L., & Wayne, W. (1987). The influence of categorization on perceptions of crowding. *Personality and Social Psychology Bulletin, 12,* 539–546.

Wedell, D. H., Parducci, A., & Geiselman, R. E. (1987). A formal analysis of ratings of physicalattractiveness: Successive contrast and simultaneous assimilation. *Journal of Experimental Social Psychology, 23,* 230–249.

Weeks, M. O., & Gage, B. A. (1984). A comparison of the marriage-role expectations of college women enrolled in a functional marriage course. *Sex Roles, 11,* 377–388.

Wegner, D. M., & Schaefer, D. (1978). The concentration of responsibility: An objective self-awareness analysis of group size effects in helping situations. *Journal of Personality and Social Psychology, 36,* 147–155.

Wegner, D. M., Shortt, J. W., Blake, A. W., & Page, M. S. (1990). The suppression of exciting thoughts. *Journal of Personality and Social Psychology, 58,* 409–418.

Wegner, D. M., & Vallacher, R. R. (1986). Action identification. In R. M. Sorrentino & E. T. Higgins (Eds.), *Handbook of motivation and cognition: Foundations of social behavior* (pp. 550–582). New York: Guilford Press.

Wegner, D. M., Vallacher, R. R., & Dizadji, D. (1989). Do alcoholics know what they're doing? Identifications of the act of drinking. *Basic and Applied Social Psychology, 10,* 197–210.

Weidner, G., Istvan, J., & McKnight, J. D. (1989). Clusters of behavioral coronary risk factors in employed women and men. *Journal of Applied Social Psychology, 19,* 468–480.

Weinberger, M., Hiner, S. L., & Tierney, W. M. (1987). In support of hassles as a measure of stress in predicting health outcomes. *Journal of Behavioral Medicine, 10,* 19–32.

Weiner, B. (1980). A cognitive (attribution) emotion-action model of motivated behavior: An analysis of judgments of helpgiving. *Journal of Personality and Social Psychology, 39,* 186–200.

Weiner, B., Amirkhan, J., Folkes, V. S., & Verette, J. A. (1987). An attributional analysis of excuse giving: Studies of a native theory of emotion. *Journal of Personality and Social Psychology, 52,* 316–324.

Weinstein, N. D. (1987). Unrealistic optimism about susceptibility to health problems: Conclusions from a community-wide sample. *Journal of Behavioral Medicine, 10,* 481–500.

Weir, R. M., & Okon, M. A. (1989). Social support, positive college events, and college satisfaction: Evidence for boosting effects. *Journal of Applied Social Psychology, 19,* 758–771.

Weis, D. L. (1983). Affective reactions of women to their initial experience of coitus. *Journal of Sex Research, 19,* 209–237.

Weiten, W. (1980). The attraction-leniency effect in jury research: An examination of external validity. *Journal of Applied Social Psychology, 10,* 340–347.

Weitzman, L. (1985). *The divorce revolution.* New York: Free Press.

Weldon, E., & Gargano, G. M. (1988). Cognitive loafing: The effects of accountability and shared responsibility on cognitive effort. *Personality and Social Psychology Bulletin, 14,* 159–171.

Weldon, E., & Mustari, L. (1988). Felt dispensability in groups of coactors: The effects of shared responsibility and explicit anonymity on cognitive effort. *Organizational Behavior and Human Decision Processes, 41,* 330–351.

Wells, G. L. (1984). The psychology of lineup identification. *Journal of Applied Social Psychology, 14,* 89–103.

Wells, G. L., & Bavanski, I. (1989). Mental simulation of causality. *Journal of Personality and Social Psychology, 56,* 161–169.

Wells, G. L., & Loftus, E. F. (Eds.). (1984). *Eyewitness testimony: Psychological perspectives.* New York: Cambridge University Press.

Wells, G. L., & Luus, C. A. E. (1990). Police lineups as experiments: Social methodology as a framework for properly conducted lineups. *Personality and Social Psychology Bulletin, 16,* 106–117.

Wells, G. L., & Murray, D. M. (1983). What can psychology say about the "Neil v. Biggers" criteria for judging eye-witness accuracy? *Journal of Applied Psychology, 68,* 347–362.

Werner, C. M., Brown, B. B., & Damron, G. (1981). Territorial marking in a game arcade. *Journal of Personality and Social Psychology, 41,* 1094–1104.

Werner, C. M., Strube, M. J., Cole, A. M., & Kagehiro, D. K. (1985). The impact of case characteristics and prior jury experience on jury verdicts. *Journal of Applied Social Psychology, 15,* 409–427.

Weyant, J. M. (1986). *Applied social psychology.* New York: Oxford University Press.

Wheeler, L. (1988). My year in Hong Kong: Some observations about social behavior. *Personality and Social Psychology Bulletin, 14,* 410–420.

Whitaker, R. (1989, Dec. 24). New law snuffs out workplace smoke. *Albany Times Union*, D-1.

White, G. L. (1980). Inducing jealousy: A power perspective. *Personality and Social Psychology Bulletin, 6*, 222–227.

White, G. L. (1981). Some correlates of romantic jealousy. *Journal of Personality, 49*, 129–146.

White, G. L., Fishbein, S., & Rutstein, J. (1981). Passionate love and misattribution of arousal. *Journal of Personality and Social Psychology, 41*, 56–62.

White, G. L., & Mullen, P. E. (1990). *Jealousy: Theory, research, and clinical strategies*. New York: Guilford Press.

White, G. L., & Shapiro, D. (1987). Don't I know you? Antecedents and social consequences of perceived familiarity. *Journal of Experimental Social Psychology, 23*, 75–92.

White, R. K. (1977). Misperception in the Arab-Israeli conflict. *Journal of Social Issues, 33*, 190–221.

Whitley, B. E., & Greenberg, M. S. (1986). The role of eyewitness confidence in juror perceptions of credibility. *Journal of Applied Social Psychology, 16*, 387–409.

Whyte, W. H. (1989). *City: Rediscovering the center*. New York: Doubleday.

Wicker, A. W. (1969). Attitudes versus actions: The relationship of verbal and overt behavioral responses to attitude objects. *Journal of Social Issues, 25*, 41–78.

Wicklund, R. A., & Gollwitzer, P. M. (1987). The fallacy of the private-public self-focus distinction. *Journal of Personality, 55*, 491–523.

Wiebe, D. J., & McCallum, D. M. (1986). Health practices and hardiness as mediators in the stress-illness relationship. *Health Psychology, 5*, 425–438.

Wilder, D. A. (1977). Perception of groups, size of opposition, and social influence. *Journal of Experimental Social Psychology, 13*, 253–268.

Wilder, D. A. (1984). Intergroup contact: The typical member and the exception to the rule. *Journal of Experimental Social Psychology, 20*, 177–194.

Wilder, D. A. (1986). Social categorization: Implications for creation and reduction of intergroup bias. In L. Berkowitz (Ed.), *Advances in experimental social psychology* (pp. 291–355). Orlando, FL: Academic Press.

Williams, J. G., & Solano, C. H. (1983). The social reality of feeling lonely: Friendship and reciprocation. *Personality and Social Psychology Bulletin, 9*, 237–242.

Williams, K., Harkins, S., & Latané, B. (1981). Identifiability as a deterrent to social loafing: Two cheering experiments. *Journal of Personality and Social Psychology, 43*, 303–311.

Williams, K. J., Alliger, G. M., & Pulliam, R. (1989). *Interviewer affect and ratings: Evidence for the moderating effects of perceived competence*. Manuscript submitted for publication, State University of New York at Albany.

Willis, F. N., Jr., & Hamm, H. K. (1980). The use of interpersonal touch in securing compliance. *Journal of Nonverbal Behavior, 5*, 49–55.

Wilson, D. K., Kaplan, R. M., & Schneiderman, L. J. (1987). Framing of decisions and selections of alternatives in health care. *Social Behavior, 2*, 51–59.

Wilson, D. W. (1981). Is helping a laughing matter? *Psychology, 18*, 6–9.

Wilson, E. O. (1975). *Sociobiology: The new synthesis*. Cambridge, MA: Harvard University Press.

Wilson, J. P., & Petruska, R. (1984). Motivation, model attributes, and prosocial behavior. *Journal of Personality and Social Psychology, 46*, 458–468.

Wilson, P. J. (1988). *The domestication of the human species*. New Haven, CT: Yale University Press.

Wilson, T. D., & Linville, P. W. (1982). Improving the academic performance of college freshmen: Attributional therapy revisited. *Journal of Personality and Social Psychology, 42*, 367–376.

Wilson, T. D., Lisle, D. J., Kraft, D., & Wetzel, C. G. (1989). Preferences as expectation-driven inferences: Effects of affective expectations on affective experience. *Journal of Personality and Social Psychology, 56*, 519–530.

Winchie, D. B., & Carment, D. W. (1988). Intention to migrate: A psychological analysis. *Journal of Applied Social Psychology, 18*, 727–736.

Winer, D. L., Bonner, T. O., Jr., Blaney, P. H., & Murray, E. J. (1981). Depression and social attraction. *Motivation and Emotion, 5*, 153–166.

Winkel, F. W., Koppelaar, L., & Vrij, A. (1988). Creating suspects in police-citizen encounters: Two studies on personal space and being suspect. *Social Behavior, 3*, 307–318.

Wolf, S., & Bugaj, A. M. (1990). The social impact of courtroom witnesses. *Social Behaviour, 5*, 1–13.

Wolfe, B. M., & Baron, R. A. (1971). Laboratory aggression related to aggression in naturalistic social situations: Effects of an aggressive model on the behavior of college student and prisoner observers. *Psychonomic Science, 24*, 193–194.

Wolfe, S. (1985). Manifest and latent influence of majorities and minorities. *Journal of Personality and Social Psychology, 48*, 899–908.

Wolfle, L. M., & Robertshaw, D. (1982). Effects of college attendance on locus of control. *Journal of Personality and Social Psychology, 43*, 802–810.

Wood, W. (1982). Retrieval of attitude-relevant information from memory: Effects on susceptibility to persuasion on intrinsic motivation. *Journal of Personality and Social Psychology, 42*, 798–810.

Worchel, P. (1958). Personality factors in the readiness to express aggression. *Journal of Clinical Psychology, 14*, 355–359.

Worchel, S., & Brown, E. H. (1984). The role of plausibility in influencing environmental attributions. *Journal of Experimental Social Psychology, 20*, 86–96.

Worchel, S., & Teddle, C. (1976). The experience of crowding: A two-factor theory. *Journal of Personality and Social Psychology, 34*, 36–40.

Wortman, C. B., & Linsenmeier, J. A. W. (1977). Interpersonal attraction and techniques of ingratiation in organizational settings. In B. M. Staw & G. R. Salancik (Eds.), *New directions in organizational behavior* (pp. 133–178). Chicago: St. Clair Press.

Wright, J. C., & Mischel, W. (1988). Conditional hedges and the intuitive psychology of traits. *Journal of Personality and Social Psychology, 55*, 454–469.

Wright, L. (1988). The Type A behavior pattern and coronary artery disease: Quest for the active ingredients and the elusive mechanism. *American Psychologist, 43*, 2–14.

Wright, P. H. (1984). Self-referent motivation and the intrinsic quality of friendship. *Journal of Social and Personal Relationships, 1*, 115–130.

Wu, C., & Shaffer, D. R. (1987). Susceptibility to persuasive appeals as a function of source credibility and prior experience with the attitude object. *Journal of Personality and Social Psychology, 52*, 677–688.

Wurtele, S. K., & Maddux, J. E. (1987). Relative contributions of protection motivation theory components in predicting exercise intentions and behavior. *Health Psychology, 6*, 453–466.

Wyer, R. S., Jr. (1988). Social memory and social judgment. In P. R. Solomon, G. R. Goethals, C. M. Kelley, & B. R. Stephens (Eds.), *Perspectives on memory research*. New York: Springer-Verlag.

Wyer, R. S., Jr. (1965). Self-acceptance, discrepancy between parents' perceptions of their children, and goal-seeking effectiveness. *Journal of Personality and Social Psychology, 2*, 311–316.

Wyer, R. S., Jr., & Srull, T. K. (1986). Human cognition in its social context. *Psychological Review, 93*, 322–359.

Wyer, R. W., & Srull, T. K. (1980). Category accessibility and social perception: Some implications for the study of person memory and interpersonal judgments. *Journal of Personality and Social Psychology, 28*, 841–856.

Yamagishi, T. (1988). Exit from the group as an individualistic solution to free rider problem in the United States and Japan. *Journal of Experimental Social Psychology, 24*, 530–542.

Yarber, W. L., & Fisher, W. A. (1983). Affective orientation to sexuality and venereal disease preventive behaviors. *Health Values, 7*, 19–23.

Yarber, W. L., & McCabe, G. P. (1984). Importance of sex education topics: Correlates with teacher characteristics and inclusion of topics of instruction. *Health Education, 15*, 119–126.

Yarber, W. L., & Whitehill, L. L. (1981). The relationship between parental affective orientation toward sexuality and responses to sex-related situations of pre-school-age children. *Journal of Sex Education and Therapy, 7*, 36–39.

Yarmey, D. A. (1986). Verbal, visual, and voice identification of a rape suspect under different levels of illumination. *Journal of Applied Psychology, 71*, 363–370.

Yinon, Y., & Dovrat, M. (1987). The reciprocity-arousing potential of the requester's occupation, its status, and the cost and urgency of the request as determinants of helping behavior. *Journal of Applied Social Psychology, 17*, 429–435.

Yinon, Y., Dovrat, M., & Avni, A. (1981). The reciprocity-arousing potential of the requester's occupation and helping behavior. *Journal of Applied Social Psychology, 11*, 252–258.

Young, J., & Osborne, R. (1989, June). *"Wimp vs. shrimp": Individual differences in the use of political issues and images.* Paper presented at the meeting of the American Psychological Society, Alexandria, VA.

Young, J. E. (1982). Loneliness, depression, and cognitive therapy: Theory and application. In L. A. Peplau & D. Perlman (Eds.), *Loneliness: A sourcebook of current theory, research, and therapy.* New York: Wiley.

Young, P. (1988, March). Presidential peccadillos. *Psychology Today,* pp. 26–27.

Youngs, G. A., Jr. (1986). Patterns of threat and punishment reciprocity in a conflict setting. *Journal of Personality and Social Psychology, 51*, 541–546.

Yuille, J. C., & Cutshall, J. L. (1986). A case study of eyewitness memory of a crime. *Journal of Applied Psychology, 71*, 291–301.

Yukl, G. (1974). Effects of the opponent's initial offer, concession magnitude, and concession frequency on bargaining behavior. *Journal of Personality and Social Psychology, 30*, 323–335.

Yukl, G. (1981). *Leadership in organizations.* Englewood Cliffs, NJ: Prentice Hall.

Zaccaro, S. J. (1984). Social loafing: The role of task attractiveness. *Personality and Social Psychology Bulletin, 10*, 99–106.

Zajonc, R. B. (1965). Social facilitation. *Science, 149*, 269–274.

Zajonc, R. B. (1968). Attitudinal effects of mere exposure. *Journal of Personality and Social Psychology, Monographs Supplement, 9*, 1–27.

Zajonc, R. B. (1980). Feeling and thinking: Preferences need no inferences. *American Psychologist, 35*, 151–175.

Zajonc, R. B. (1985). Emotion and facial difference: A theory reclaimed. *Science, 228*, 15–21.

Zajonc, R. B., Adelmann, P. K., Murphy, S. T., & Niedenthal, P. M. (1987). Convergence in the physical appearance of spouses. *Motivation and Emotion, 11*, 335–346.

Zajonc, R. B., Heingartner, A., & Herman, E. M. (1969). Social enhancement and impairment of performance in the cockroach. *Journal of Personality and Social Psychology, 13*, 83–92.

Zajonc, R. B., Murphy, S. T., & Inglehart, M. (1989). Feeling and facial efference: Implications of the vascular theory of emotion. *Psychological Review, 96*, 395–416.

Zajonc, R. B., & Sales, S. M. (1966). Social facilitation of dominant and subordinate responses. *Journal of Experimental Social Psychology, 2*, 160–168.

Zanna, M. P., & Olson, J. M. (1982). Individual differences in attitudinal relations. In M. P. Zanna, E. T. Higgins, & C. P. Herman (Eds.), *Consistency in social behavior: The Ontario symposium* (Vol. 2). Hillsdale, NJ: Erlbaum.

Zeichner, A., & Phil, R. O. (1980). Effects of alcohol and instigator intent on human aggression. *Journal of Studies on Alcohol, 41*, 265–276.

Zillmann, D. (1979). *Hostility and aggression.* Hillsdale, NJ: Erlbaum.

Zillmann, D. (1983). Transfer of excitation in emotional behavior. In T. Cacioppo & R. E. Petty (Eds.) *Social psychophysiology: A source book* (pp. 215–240). New York: Guilford Press.

Zillmann, D. (1984). *Connections between sex and aggression.* Hillsdale, NJ: Erlbaum.

Zillmann, D. (1988). Cognition-excitation interdependencies in aggressive behavior. *Aggressive Behavior, 14*, 51–64.

Zillmann, D., Baron, R. A., & Tamborini, R. (1981). Social costs of smoking: Effects of tobacco smoke on hostile behavior. *Journal of Applied Social Psychology, 11*, 548–561.

Zillmann, D., & Bryant, J. (1984). Effects of massive exposure to pornography. In N. M. Malamuth & E. Donnerstein (Eds.), *Pornography and sexual aggression.* New York: Academic Press.

Zillmann, D., & Bryant, J. (1988). Pornography's impact on sexual satisfaction. *Journal of Applied Social Psychology, 18*, 438–453.

Zillmann, D., & Cantor, J. R. (1976). Effects of timing of information about mitigating circumstances on emotional responses to provocation and retaliatory behavior. *Journal of Experimental Social Psychology, 12*, 38–55.

Zimbardo, P. G. (1977). *Shyness: What is it and what you can do about it.* Reading, MA: Addison-Wesley.

Zimbardo, P. G., Haney, C., Banks, W. C., & Jaffe, D. (1973, April 8). A Pirandellian prison: The mind is a formidable jailer. *New York Times Magazine,* pp. 38–60.

Zimmerman, M. A. (1990). Toward a theory of learned hopefulness: A structural model and analysis of participation and empowerment. *Journal of Research in Personality, 24*, 71–86.

Zirkel, S., & Cantor, N. (1990). Personal construal of life tasks: Those who struggle for independence. *Journal of Personality and Social Psychology, 58*, 172–185.

Zuckerman, M., Bernieri, F., Koestner, R., & Rosenthal, R. (1989). To predict some of the people some of the time: In search of moderators. *Journal of Personality and Social Psychology, 57*, 279–293.

Zuckerman, M., DePaulo, B. M., & Rosenthal, R. (1981). Verbal and nonverbal communication of deception. In L. Berkowitz (Ed.), *Advances in experimental social psychology* (Vol. 14, pp. 1–59). New York: Academic Press.

Zuckerman, M., Gioioso, C., & Tellini, S. (1988). Control orientation, self-monitoring, and preference for image versus quality approach to advertising. *Journal of Research in Personality, 22*, 89–100.

Zuckerman, M., Kuhlman, D. M., & Camac, C. (1988). What lies beyond E and N? Factor analyses of scales believed to measure basic dimensions of personality. *Journal of Personality and Social Psychology, 54*, 96–107.

Zuckerman, M., Schmitz, M., & Yosha, A. (1977). Effects of crowding in a student environment. *Journal of Applied Social Psychology, 7*, 67–72.

Zullow, H. M., Oettingen, G., Peterson, C., & Seligman, M. E. P. (1988). Pessimistic explanatory style in the historical record: CAVing LBJ, presidential candidates, and East versus West Berlin, *American Psychologist, 43*, 673–682.

Zullow, H. M., & Seligman, M. E. P. (1988). *Pessimistic rumination predicts electoral defeat of presidential candidates: 1948–84.* Manuscript submitted for publication.

(Photo credits, continued from p. iv.)

London. Page 65 L,R: D. Dempster/Allyn & Bacon. *Chapter Three*   Page 86: "Mystery Woman with Mirror," by Fritz Scholder. 1987, acrylic on canvas. Page 89L: J. Curtis/Offshoot Stock. Page 89R: Robert Harding Picture Library/London. Page 92L: J. Brown/Offshoot Stock. Page 92R: D. Mason/The Stock Market. Page 126: J. Blaustein/Woodfin Camp & Associates. *Chapter Four*   Page 134: "The Scale," by Brigitte Rutenberg. 1989, mixed media collage. Page 145: R. Crandall/The Picture Group. Page 147: P. Brou/The Picture Group. Page 148: Bond/Shooting Star. Page 150: Courtesy of Pepsico Inc. & BBDO Worldwide. *Chapter Five*   Page 180: "Ball Players on Beach," by David Park/Photo courtesy Maxwell Galleries Ltd., Ca. Page 184L: B. Bisson/Sygma. Page 184R: Wide World Photos. Page 196L: J. Chenet/Woodfin Camp & Associates. Page 196R: L. Wongo/The Picture Group. Page 203: Carousel Collections, "Townsend Harris meeting with representatives of the Tokugawa Shogunate," artist unknown. Page 204: TSW/Click, Chicago. Page 205L: G. Ludwig/Woodfin Camp & Associates. Page 205R: K. Faulkner/ Offshoot Stock. Page 212L: A. Hernandez/The Picture Group. Page 212R: Grieves/Robert Harding Picture Library/London. *Chapter Six* Page 222: "Trio," Alex Katz, 1984. Photo courtesy Marlborough Gallery, NY/VAGA, NY 1990. Page 228: D. Dempster/Allyn & Bacon. Page 234: L. Sintay/The Picture Group. Page 245 L,R: Focus On Sports. Page 247L,R: Robert Harding Picture Library/London. Page 250: Shooting Star. *Chapter Seven*   Page 264: "Brad & Carolyn," by Alex Katz. Photo courtesy Marlborough Gallery, NY/VAGA, NY 1990. Page 276: A. Smith/Woodfin Camp & Associates. Page 282: R. Schleipman/Offshoot Stock. Page 285: TSW/Click, Chicago. Page 288: D. Burnett/Woodfin Camp & Associates. Page 290L: F. LaBua/Envision. Page 290R: D. Defays/TSW-Click, Chicago. *Chapter Eight*   Page 308: "A, B, C, D, E, F, G and Hi," by Marisol/Photo courtesy Sydney Janis Gallery/VAGA, NY 1990. Page 313L: TSW/Click, Chicago. Page 313R: F. Siteman/Stock, Boston. Page 327L: J. Sohm/Stock, Boston. Page 327R: Maillac/The Picture Group. Page 329L: E. Eastap/The Stock Market. Page 329R: J. Curtis/Offshoot Stock. Page 331: TSW/Click, Chicago. Page 342: J. P. Laffont/Sygma. Page 344: T. Stoddart/ Woodfin Camp & Associates. *Chapter Nine*   Page 348: "The Checker Players," by Milton Avery, 1938. Terra Museum of American Art, Chicago. Page 351: MacDonald/Envision. Page 356: M. Ruiz/ The Picture Group. Page 359: R. Schleipman/ Offshoot Stock. Page 361: Wilson-Hermeson/Envision. Page 362: Courtesy of Childrens' TV Workshop/Shooting Star. Page 372L,R: D. Dempster/Allyn & Bacon. Page 373: C. Blouin/Offshoot Stock. Page 382: R. Bell/The Picture Group. *Chapter Ten*   Page 392: "Fast Break," by Red Grooms, 1983. Courtesy of Jeffrey H. Loria, N.Y. Page 395L,R: Sygma. Page 406: D. Dempster/Allyn & Bacon. Page 419: Movie Stills Archives. Page 426L: B. Daemmrich/Stock, Boston. Page 426R: D. Woo/Stock, Boston. *Chapter Eleven*   Page 434: "Commuters," by Giancarlo Impiglia, 1989. Photo courtesy of Giancarlo Impiglia Studio, Inco. Page 437TL: D. Dempster/Offshoot Stock. Page 437TR: MacDonald/Envision. Page 437B: T. Gibson/Envision. Page 442L: G. Palmer/The Stock Market. Page 442R: J. Feingersh/The Stock Market. Page 451L: B. Harris/The Stock Market. Page 451R: G. Palmer/The Stock Market. Page 468L: Reflex/The Picture Group. Page 468R: Novosti-Lehtikuva/Woodfin Camp & Associates. Page 472L: C. Gupton/TSW-Click, Chicago. Page 472R: Garfield/The Stock Market. *Chapter Twelve*   Page 480: "La Musique," by Henri Matisse, 1939. Albright-Knox Art Gallery, Buffalo, N.Y. Page 487L,R: D. Dempster/Allyn & Bacon. Page 495L,R: The Bettmann Newsphotos. Page 501L: G. Palmer/The Stock Market. Page 501R: J. Pickerell/TSW-Click, Chicago. Page 514L: W. Moriarty/Envision. Page 514R: J. Japho/The Picture Group. *Chapter Thirteen*   Page 524: "House in Cotton Field," by Romare Bearden/Photo courtesy of ACA Galleries, N.Y. Page 528: J. Holland/Stock, Boston. Page 532: F. Yi/Envision. Page 537L: Robert Harding Picture Library/London. Page 537R: K. Faulkner/Offshoot Stock. Page 545: S. Elmore/The Stock Market. Page 549: A. Heimann/The Stock Market. Page 555: The Picture Group. Page 556L: G. Palmer/The Stock Market. Page 556R: S. Osolinski/The Stock Market. Page 558L: C. Ehle/TSW-Click, Chicago. Page 558R: Envision. *Chapter Fourteen*   Page 566: "City Harbor," by Hilaire Hiler. Page 572: B. Daemmrich/TSW-Click, Chicago. Page 578: J. Brown/The Stock Market. Page 590: D. Dempster/Allyn & Bacon. Page 600L,R: The Bettmann Archives. Page 604 T-B: W. McNamee/Woodfin Camp & Associates; L. Downing/Woodfin Camp & Associates; Culver Pictures; Culver Pictures; Wide World Photos. *Chapter Fifteen*   Page 610: "A Man," by Jean Michel Folon. Page 611L: J. Rowan/TSW-Click, Chicago. Page 611R: D. Dempster/ Offshoot. Page 616: R. Schleipman/Offshoot Stock. Page 618: Courtesy of Mazda Motors Inc. Page 621: W. McNamee/Woodfin Camp & Associates. Page 637: M. Kois/The Stock Market.

ENDSHEETS: Photos of Allport, Lewin, Thurstone, and Hovland courtesy of Profiles West. Triplett courtesy of Emporia State University. Sherif courtesy of the Penn State University Archives. Singer courtesy of Uniformed Services University of the Health Sciences.

NAME INDEX

SUBJECT INDEX

Absenteeism, positive affect and, 643
Academic life-style orientation, 606
Acceptance, private, 315
Achievement, male and female, attributions about, 216–217
Acquaintanceship, development of, 233–250, 261
Acquired immune deficiency syndrome (AIDS), 287–288, 306
Action identification, 129–130
Action research, 570, 606
Actor-observer effect, 67, 84
Adapters, detection of deception and, 54
Additive tasks, 449, 478
Adjourning, in group development, 441
Affect, 132, 261, 646. *See also* Negative affect; Positive affect
  cognition and, 90, 109–118, 131
  expectations and, 119–121
  interpersonal relationships and, 230–233, 261
  marriage and, 302–303
  negative, 131
  positive, 131
  possible selves and, 126
Affiliation
  external events and, 239–240
  interpersonal attraction and, 225
  marriage and, 303
  need for, 233–235, 261, 262
  physical attractiveness and, 241–243
  research applications, opening lines, 237–239
  social skills and, 235–237
Age
  mate preference and, 273
  personal space and, 560
  susceptibility to persuasion and, 164–166
Aggression, 394–400, 431, 432
  alcohol and, 418–420, 431
  apologies and, 428–429, 432
  atmospheric electricity and, 551
  black clothing and, 245–246
  catharsis and, 427–428, 431
  cognitive interventions, 428–429

direct provocation and, 404–406, 431
drive theories of, 397, 431, 432
frustration and, 403–404, 431
gender differences in, 425
heightened arousal and, 412–415, 431
hostile, 421–422, 432
hostile attributional bias and, 423–425, 431
instinct theories of, 396–397, 431, 432
instrumental, 421, 432
in laboratory, 401–402
as learned social behavior, 399–400
media violence and, 406–409, 411, 431
multicultural perspectives, 422–423
negative affect and, 397–399
nonaggressive models and, 430
personal causes of, 420–425, 431
personality and, 421–423, 431
positive affect and, 430–431
prejudice-driven, 186
prevention and control of, 426–430, 431–432
provocative actions by others and, 117–118
punishment and, 426–427, 431
sexual arousal and, 415–416
social determinants of, 400–420, 431
social skills training and, 430
temperature and, 550–551
video games and, 408
violent pornography and, 416–418
Aggression cues, 433, 409–411
Aggression machine, 401–402, 433
Agreeableness, 485
AIDS (acquired immune deficiency syndrome), 287–288, 306
Air fresheners, behavior and, 553
Air pollution, behavior and, 552–553
Alcohol, aggression and, 418–420
Allies, conformity and, 318–320
Altruism, 352, 390
Anchoring, 99–101, 131, 132
Anger, health problems and, 576
Anticipatory change, 176
Apartheid, 186, 207
Apologies, aggression and, 428–429, 432
Applied social psychology, 569, 605, 606

Arbitration, 388, 390
Arousal
  aggression and, 412–415, 431
  attributing to love, 273–275
  social facilitation and, 445–447
Atmospheric electricity, 551, 563
Attitude accessibility, 146–147, 177, 178
Attitude certainty, attitude change and, 172–173
Attitude change, 138–139
  attitude uncertainty and, 172–173
  cognitive dissonance and, 166–172, 177
  delayed (sleeper effect), 153–155
  factors affecting, 177
  forced compliance and, 167–168
  leading questions and, 172–173
  legislating, 544–546
  persuasion and, 149–164
Attitudes, 137–138, 178
  acquiring, 139–141
  attraction and, 250–252
  behavior and, 142–147, 177
  components of, 143–144
  environmentally responsible behavior and, 541–543
  formation of, 177
  general vs. specific, 142–143
  impressionable years and, 164–166
  individual differences in, 510–520
  nature of, 177
  prejudice as, 184
  sexual, 516–520
  strength of, 145–146
  television and, 147–149
Attitude similarity, 261
  effects of, 254–255
  friendships and, 250–252, 261
Attitude specificity, 142–143
Attorneys, bias of, 591, 592
Attraction to opposite sex, hypertraditionality and, 256–258
Attribute-driven processing, 211
Attribution, 16, 55–82, 84, 615, 646
  augmenting principle, 61–64
  causal attribution theory, 57–64

Persuasive arguments view, group polarization and, 462
Pessimism
  health problems and, 575
  political candidates and, 600–601
  possible selves and, 127
Physical appearance, voting behavior and, 601
Physical attractiveness, 262
  acquaintanceships and, 261
  affiliation and, 241–243
  of defendants, 591
  effects of, 246–248
  judging, 248–249
  love and, 271
  marriage and, 303
  social influence and, 310–311
Physical characteristics
  affiliation and, multicultural perspectives, 243
  behavior and, 244–246
  helping behavior and, 364–365
  making judgments according to, 241–243
Physical environment, influence on behavior of, 10, 11
Physical proximity. *See also* Propinquity
  interpersonal attraction and, 225–230
Physical symptoms, 583–585
Physicians, interacting with, 585–586
Pluralistic ignorance, 358
Polarization, group, 461–462
Police, bias of, 591–592
Political activism, 596
Political candidates
  optimism and, 600–601
  pessimism and, 600–601
  physical appearance of, 601
  repeated exposure and, 599
  similarity effect and, 603
Politics, psychology and, 596–605, 606
Population growth, environmental resources and, 528–530
Pornography, violent, aggression and, 416–418
Positive affect, 114–116, 131
  absenteeism and, 643
  aggression and, 430–431
  inducing, in work settings, 643–645
  job interviews and, 638–639
  job satisfaction and, 643
  negotiations and, 639–640
  risk-taking and, 640–642
  in work settings, 638–645, 646
Positive evaluations, replacing with negative ones, 297–298
Positive feedback, importance of, for females, 215–216
Positive frame, bargaining and, 387, 390
Possessive love, 278
Possible selves, 90, 125–127, 133
  affective state and, 126
  as incentives, 126
  as optimistic or pessimistic, 127
Pregnancies
  teenage, prevention of, 519–520
  unplanned, 287
Prejudice, 183–184, 207, 221. *See also* Discrimination
  aggression and, 186
  attitude formation and, 139
  as attitudes, 184
  biological basis for, 202–203
  causes of, 219–220
  children's acquisition of, 204–205
  combatting, 203–212

competition as source of, 191–194
discrimination and, 183–184
gender-based, 212–219, 220
illusionary correlation and, 199
intergroup contact and, 205–207
interracial contact and, 207
multicultural perspectives, 207
nature, of, 219
outgroup homogeneity and, 200
recategorization and, 208–211
reducing, 204–211, 220
roots of, 190–203
schemas and, 184
self-esteem and, 195
social categorization as source of, 194–196
social cognition and, 197–199
social learning and, 196
stereotypes and, 197–199
us-versus-them effect and, 194–196
violence and, 186
Premarital sex, 284–289
Prescriptive norms, 443
Primacy effects, first impressions and, 65
Primary territory, 561
Priming, 94–97, 132, 133
Prior residence effect, 562, 564
Prisoners' dilemma, 377–379, 390
Prisons, crowding in, 559
Privacy, 262
  need for, 229
  personal space and, 560
  propinquity and, 229, 262
Privacy regulation, 536–537, 564
Private acceptance, 315
Procedural processes, in groups, 459–460
Procedural justice, in work settings, 630–632, 647
Product quality, multicultural perspectives on, 620–622
Prompts, 542, 563, 564
Propinquity, 260, 262. *See also* Physical proximity
  interpersonal relationships and, 227–230
  marriage and, 302–303
  negative effects of, 229–230
  privacy and, 229, 262
Proportion of similar attitudes, 251–252, 262
Proscriptive norms, 443
Prosocial behavior, 351–372, 389, 390–391. *See also* Egoism
  bystander effect, 352–354
  genetic similarity and, 371–372
  helping role models, 361–366
  motivations for, 366–372
  responding to emergencies, 354–361
Protection-motivation theory, 581, 607
Provocation, aggression and, 404–406, 431
Provocative actions, aggression and, 117–118
Proxemics, 560, 564
Pruitt-Igoe public housing project, 536
Psychological stress, 570–571
Psychoneuroimmunology, 571, 607
Psychosocial pathology, 564, 533–534
Public compliance, 315
Public distance, 560, 564
Public self-consciousness, self-handicapping and, 82
Public territory, 561, 564
Punishment, aggression and, 426–427, 431, 432

Quality, in workplace, 620–622

Race, of defendants, biases about, 593–594
Radioactive waste, 553, 554

Random assignment of subjects, to groups, 25–26, 38–39
Reactance, 162–163, 177, 178
Realistic conflict theory, 221
  prejudice and, 191–192, 219
Recategorization, prejudice and, 208–211, 221
Reciprocal concessions, compliance and, 334
Reciprocal positive evaluations, 261
Reciprocity, 338
  cooperation and, 379
  friendship and, 256–258
  helping behavior and, 365
  marriage and, 304
Reference points, 99
Referent cognitions theory, 630–632, 646, 647
Regression analysis, 28
Reinforcement-affect model, 233, 262
Reinforcement model, arousal and, 273–274
Rejection-then-retreat tactic, 334
Relationship Closeness Inventory, 268, 307
Relationships
  absence of, 281–284
  close, 266–267, 268, 268–284
  danger signs in, 298–300
  deterioration of, 298–305, 306
  ending, 300–301, 268
  establishing, 267
  interdependent, 268–284
  male-female conflicts in, 294–295
  possible stages of, 298, 299
  responding to problems in, 300–301
  troubled, 267, 294–305
Reliability, of personality tests, 496–498, 522
Repeated exposure, 228–229, 261, 262
  political candidates and, 599
Representativeness, heuristic, 91–93, 133
Reproduction, mate preference and, 272–273
Research methods, 23–36, 37–38
  correlational, 26–29
  debriefing and, 36
  ethics and, 35–36
  experimentation as, 23–26
  informed consent and, 36
Research methods, deception in, 34–36
Resource acquisition, mate preference and, 273
Response-facilitation model, arousal and, 274–275
Responsibility
  assumption of, in emergencies, 358–359
  diffusion of, 353, 390
Resemblance, judging by, 91–93
Revenge, conflict and, 385
Reverse discrimination, 189–190, 221
Risk-taking, positive affect and, 640–642
Risky shifts, 461, 479
Role ambiguity, 442
Role conflict, 442
Roles, in groups, 441–442, 479
Romantic love, 279
Rumination, 607

Schemas, 133, 221
  prejudice and, 184, 219
  self-concept and, 122, 131
Science, defined, 8
Scientific methods, 8–9
Secondary territory, 561, 564
Second-chance meetings, 464
Selective avoidance, of persuasion, 164, 177, 178
Self, 133

Self-awareness, attitude strength and, 145–146
Self-concept, 90, 131–132, 133
   defining, 121–122
   multicultural perspectives on, 127–129
   possible selves and, 125–127
   as a set of traits, 521
   social cognition and, 121–127
   social input and, 122–123
   work and, 612–613
Self-concept as a central disposition, 499–510
Self-confidence
   of females vs. males, 215–216
   low, attribution and, 73
Self-defeating attributions, 73–75
Self-deprecation, for compliance, 329–330
Self-diagnosis, of physical symptoms, 584–585
Self-disclosure, for compliance, 330
Self-efficacy, 505–507, 521, 522
Self-esteem, 522
   attribution to external factors and, 81
   low, attribution and, 73
   maintaining, 503–505
   personality and, 499–505
   prejudice and, 195
   self-serving bias and, 68–69
   situational effects on, 501–503
Self-handicapping, 81–82, 84, 85
Self-justification, escalation of commitment and, 624–625
Self-knowledge. See Self-perception
Selfless love, 277, 278
Self-monitoring, 507–510, 521, 522
   leadership and, 468–469, 603
   persuasion and, 162, 178
Self-Monitoring Scale, 507–508, 522
Self-perception, 43–44, 84, 85
   behavior as source of, 78–81
   Bem's theory of, 78–81
   compliance and, 332–334
   external factors and, 75–78
   intrinsic motivation and, 78–81
   self-handicapping and, 81–82
Self-presentation
   compliance and, 329, 334
   group performance and, 446
   nonverbal cues and, 52–53
Self-reference effect, 123–125, 131–132, 133
Self-schemas, 122, 133, 522
   personality and, 499
   self-esteem and, 521
Self-serving bias, 67–69, 84, 85
   equity theory and, 628
   gender differences in, 69–71
Sentence repairs, detection of deception and, 54
Sex differences, 16
Sex discrimination, 16
Sex Guilt Scale, 516, 522–523
Sexism, 183, 212–219, 220, 221
   in work settings, 218–219
Sex-related behaviors, erotophobia, 516–517
Sexual attitudes
   effects of, 517–519
   locus of control and, 521
   measuring, 516
Sexual attraction, love and, 273–275
Sexual desire, vs. passionate love, 271
Sexual harassment, 274–275, 306, 307
Sexual intimacy
   before marriage, 284–289
   boredom in, 297
   changes in attitudes about, 285–289, 306

male-female differences in feelings about, 285–286
   outside of marriage, multicultural perspectives on, 293–294
   postrevolution sexuality, 287–289
Sexuality, generalized attitudes about, 516–520
Sexually transmitted disease (STD), 287–288, 307
Sexual Opinion Survey, 516, 523
Sexual revolution, 285–287
   postrevolution sexuality, 287–289
Sexual arousal, aggression and, 415–416
Shyness, loneliness and, 283
Similarity
   attitude, 252–255
   friendships and, 250–256
   marriage and, 304
   personality, 255–256
Situational causes, of behavior, underestimating role of, 66–69
Situational determinants, 523
   personality and, 483
   of self-esteem, 501–503
Sleeper effect, 153–155, 177, 178
Social activism, 513–515
Social behavior
   culture-specific, 19–20
   external factors affecting, 56, 58
   individual as basis of, 9–10
   influences on, 5–7, 10–12
   internal causes of, 58
   multicultural, 20
   study of, 10–12
   temporary factors and, 44
Social categorization, 187, 194–196, 220, 221
Social cognition, 89, 131, 133
   prejudice and, 184, 197–199, 220
Social comparison, 235, 239, 262
   group polarization and, 462
Social competition, prejudice and, 195
Social decision schemes, 459, 478, 479
Social density, 557, 564
Social desirability, of actions, 56
Social dilemmas, 374–377, 391
   prisoners' dilemmas and, 378–379
Social distance, 560, 564
Social facilitation, 437, 444–447, 477, 479
Social groups. See Groups
Social identity, group membership and, 440
Social influence, 347
   cultural factors and, 311
   forms of, 311
   physical attractiveness and, 310–311
Social Influence Model (SIM), 318, 347
Social input, self-concept and, 122–123
Social interactions, cultural differences in, 21–22
Social knowledge, development of, 16–17
Social learning
   acquiring attitudes through, 139–141
   of attitudes, 177
   defined, 179
   prejudice and, 196, 221
Social learning view, of aggression, 399–400, 431, 432
Social loafing, 452–457, 477, 479
Social norms, 311, 347
   as basis for social behavior, 13
   conformity and, 312, 345
   prejudice and, 196
   in workplace, 616–617
Social perception, 41–85

Social psychology, 8–12, 37, 39, 523
   development of, 7, 13, 37
   as exporter of knowledge, 22
   future of, 19–20
   history of, 8, 13–17
   information provided through, 6–7, 22
   multicultural perspectives in, 19–22
   personality and, 483
   personality psychology and, 488–489, 521
   research methods in, 8, 17–20, 23–36, 37–38
   role of theory in, 29–36
   scientific nature of, 8–9
   as study of individual behavior, 9–10
   as study of social behavior, 10–12
Social settings, work as, 613
Social skills
   affiliation and, 235–237
   loneliness and, 282
   training in, aggression and, 430
Social skills training, 307
   for overcoming loneliness, 284
Social support, 607
   conformity and, 345
   as a health benefit, 577
   of husbands during delivery, 577–580
Sociobiology, 202, 432
Spatial density, 557, 564
Speech patterns, detection of deception and, 54
Stanford Prison Experiment, 324–325
Staring, 50, 85
Status, in groups, 442–443
Stereotypes, 117, 221
   countering the effects of, 211–212
   gender-based, 213–214, 220
   prejudice and, 197–199
Stimulus overload, 534, 563, 564
Storming, in group development, 441
Straw polls, 459–460, 479
Stress, 607
   in childbirth, 578–579
   illness and, 570–580
   moderating effects of, 574–575
   student health and, 571–573
Stressful events, ratings of, 572–573
Structuring leaders, 470–471
Subgroups, 464
Subjective well-being, 489–492, 523
Subliminal priming, 96–97
Subtraction rule. See also Discounting principle
Suffering-leads-to-liking effect, 174–176, 177, 179
Superordinate goals, 388–389, 391

Take-some game, 374–376, 391
Target-directed tactics, for compliance, 329
Task performance, 436–437
   groups and, 444–457, 477–478
   self-efficacy and, 505–507
Tasks
   additive, 449, 478
   compensatory, 452, 478
   conjunctive, 449, 478
   disjunctive, 449–450, 478
Technophobia, 547–548, 564
Teenage pregnancies, prevention of, 519–520
Television, attitude formation and, 147–149
Temperature
   affect and, 131
   behavior and, 550–551
   emotions and, 112–114
Territorial behavior, 561–562, 563, 564

Territory, 561, 564
"That's not all" (TNA) technique, 337–338, 346, 347
Theories, 39
    components of, 30
    confirmation bias and, 32
    development of, 30
    peer review of, 33–34, 38
    potential disadvantages to, 32–34
    role of, 29–36, 37–38
Third-person effect, 596–597, 607
Threats, 381, 391
Tokenism, 188–189, 221
Tragedy of the commons, 377
Traits
    behavior prediction and, 492–493
    consistency of, 486–487, 492
    personality research and, 484–487
    self-esteem as, 500–501
Trait theory, of leadership, 467
Triangular model of love, 277–279, 306, 307
Two-factor theory, of emotion, 110, 131, 133
Two-tier wage systems, 629–630, 647
Type A behavior, 421–423, 432, 607
    aggression and, 431
    health problems and, 576
Type B behavior, 421–423, 432, 607

UCLA Loneliness Scale, 281, 307

Urban environment
    crowding in, 555–559
    effects of, 530–536
    friendliness in, 534–535
    helping behavior in, 534
    overstimulation of, 534–536
    as pathological, 532–534
Us-versus-them effect, prejudice and, 194–196

Validity, of personality tests, 496–498, 523
Variable game, 377, 391
Variables
    confounded, 26, 38
    dependent, 23, 38
    independent, 23, 38
    interactions among, 24–25
Vascular theory of emotion, 112–114, 131, 133
Vested interest
    attitude strength and, 145
    behavior and, 177, 179
Video games, aggression and, 408
Violence, prejudice-driven, 186. *See also* Aggression
Violent pornography, aggression and, 416–418
Voter behavior, 597–598

Weapons effect, 409–411

Will to achieve, 485
Work
    absence from, 643
    job satisfaction and, 618–622
    product quality and, 620–622
    self-concept and, 612–613
    as social setting, 613, 616–617
Worker productivity, Hawthorne studies and, 615–617
Workplace, love and sexual harassment in, 274–275
Work-related decisions, cognitive dissonance and, 617–625
Work settings
    attributions in, 632–638, 646
    equity theory and, 17–19, 627–630
    organizational conflict in, 635–638
    perceived fairness in, 626–632
    performance appraisals in, 632–638, 646
    physical environment of, 644–645
    positive affect in, 638–645
    sexism in, 218–219
    social knowledge research into, 16

Yale approach, to understanding persuasion, 155

Zero-sum games, 384, 391

CLASSICS OF SOCIAL PSYCHOLOGY

1957

Cognitive Dissonance

Reasoning from the basic idea that people strongly dislike inconsistency between their attitudes, or between their attitudes and their behavior, Leon Festinger developed—and tested—one of the most influential theories in the history of social psychology.

1958

Person Perception and Interpersonal Relations

Fritz Heider published a book which offered many insights into the ways in which we perceive and understand others. Many aspects of modern attribution theory can be traced to this text.

1963

Destructive Obedience

Stanley Milgram published research illustrating the powerful tendency of most persons to obey commands from a source of authority, even if doing so causes them to violate some of their most basic values.

1965

Social Facilitation

Robert Zajonc proposed a theory of social facilitation that, in a single stroke, seemed to clarify more than sixty years of research on the effects of audiences or coactors on behavior.